Sustainable Development

To the loving memory of my father

Kathleen Balutansky
Global Studies
2001

Sustainable Development

Economics and Policy

P. K. RAO

Center for Development Research Princeton, NJ

BLACKWELL
Publishers

First published 2000

Reprinted 2000

Blackwell Publishers Inc.
350 Main Street
Malden, Massachusetts 02148
USA

Blackwell Publishers Ltd
108 Cowley Road
Oxford OX4 1JF
UK

Library of Congress Cataloging-in-Publication Data

Rao, P. K.
    Sustainable development : economics and policy / P.K. Rao.
    p.   cm.
  Includes bibliographical references and index.
  ISBN 0–631–20993–X (hbk. : alk. paper)
  ISBN 0–631–20994–8 (pbk. : alk. paper)
  1. Sustainable development. 2. Environmental policy. I. Title.
  HC79.E5R357 1999
  338.9—dc21   99–22432
                                          CIP

British Library Cataloguing in Publication Data

A CIP catalogue record for this book is available from the British Library.

Typeset in 10 on 12pt Meridien
by Graphicraft Limited, Hong Kong
Printed in Great Britain by TJ International, Padstow, Cornwall

This book is printed on acid-free paper.

Contents

Boxes

Figures

Tables

Preface

A comet may not strike the planet Earth during the next 500,000 years but a doubling of the emissions of greenhouse gases could occur in about 50 years. So what? Anyone who entertains this question may not necessarily be in the class of anti-environmentalists. It is the humble duty of those who may have some answers to enunciate the same. Besides, the issues of sustainable development are not simply those of the environment and society; an integrated set of elements deserves serious consideration in the development of relevant methods and policies. This book is an effort in that direction; it is aimed at educating those who have never heard of the "green life" beyond perhaps green tea or the green color of the monetary instruments in some countries.

Policymakers, researchers, students in graduate and senior undergraduate education will find this book useful for formal and applied analyses relevant in the short run as well as in the longer horizon. Chapters 3 to 5 could pose a few technical or analytical hurdles for those readers who do not enjoy calculus for any reason (or even no reason!). Some of the appendices and boxed material are geared to smooth the consumption of the contents of the book. If some of the review exercises are very demanding, and should not be underestimated; some of these exercises enhance the possibilities of exploring additional avenues of learning for all of us. They also serve as reminders that advancement of knowledge is a strong prerequisite for sustainable development.

A number of permissions were granted generously. In particular, I wish to acknowledge Elsevier Science (for materials cited from the journals *Global Environmental Change* and *Ecological Economics*, and for the material in Box 4.2 and Table 5.3); the American Geophysical Union (for citing material from the journal *Global Biochemical Cycles*); Oxford University Press (for permission to include Table 2.4); Macmillan Magazines Ltd (for the material in Box 4.1); as well as The United Nations Development Program, The Intergovernmental Panel on Climate Change, Carbon Dioxiode Information Analysis Center of the Oakridge National Laboratories, Darrel Posey of The University of Oxford, *Nature* periodical of Macmillan Publishers, and The World Bank.

My list of individual acknowledgments is rather small, but my appreciation to these in this select list is significant. From Blackwell Publishers, Executive Editor Al Bruckner and Development Editor Katie Byrne have demonstrated a keen interest and enthusiastic professional support which led to this finished product. The editorial services and production staff at Blackwell – as well as Jenny Lawson and her editorial associates at First Class Publishing, and a select set of reviewers – all played a valuable role in enhancing the quality of the project. I freely took advantage of some of the remarks of the reviewers – R. Quentin Grafton (University of Ottawa), Francis E. Raymond (Northeastern University), William C. Merrill (Iowa State University), Thomas R. DeGregori (University of Houston), Paul G. Burkett (Indiana State University), Stephen C. Smith (George Washington University), and Stephanie Seguino (University of Vermont) – and wish to thank them for their helpful comments. Last, but most important, the positive contributions of my family in this project remain paramount. My daughters Uma and Usha, and my wife Prema, assisted in several of the tasks, in addition to their understanding of my commitments with this publishing project.

Pinninti Krishna Rao
Center for Development Research
Princeton, NJ, USA
pkrao@att.net

Abbreviations

ADB	Asian Development Bank
AfDB	African Development Bank
ALTY	average long-term yield
BAU	business as usual
BCSD	Business Charter for Sustainable Development
BOD	biochemical oxygen demand
BOP	balance of payments
BSI	British Standards Institute
CARE	Center for American Relief Everywhere
CBA	cost–benefit analysis
CC	carrying capacity
CDM	clean development methods
CE	carbon equivalent
CEMP	Code of Environmental Principles
CEPA	classification of environmental protection activities
CERES	Center for Environmentally Responsible Economics
CFCs	chlorofluorocarbons
CGAP	consultative group to assist the poorest
CSCE	Convention on security cooperation in Europe
CTE	Committee on Trade and Environment
CV	contingent valuation
DALY	disability-adjusted life years
DDT	dichlorodiphenyltrichloroethane
DEC	depreciation of environmental capital
DFE	design for environment
DICE	dynamic intergrated model of climate and the economy
DNA	deoxyribonucleic acid
DNC	depreciation of natural capital
DNS	debt-for-nature swaps
DPC	depreciation of productive capital

DSR	driving-force-state-response
EAI	Enterprise for the Americas Initiative
EBRD	European Bank for Reconstruction and Development
EDE	environmentally defensive expenditures
EDF	Environmental Defense Fund
EDP	environmentally adjusted net domestic product
EKC	environmental Kuznets curve
EMAS	Eco-management and audit scheme
EMS	environmental management system
ESPF	Earth Summit Plus Five
EV	existence value
FAO	Food and Agriculture Organization
FDI	foreign direct investment
FFB	fresh fruit bunches
G3OSs	GCOS, GOOS, and GTOS
GATT	General Agreement on Tariffs and Trade
GCI	Global Carbon Initiative
GCMs	global circulation models
GCOS	Global Climate Observing System
GDP	gross domestic product
GE	greenhouse effect
GEF	Global Environmental Facility
GHG	greenhouse gas
GNP	gross national product
GOOS	Global Ocean Observing System
GPP	gross primary production
GREEN	general equilibrium environmental
GTOS	Global Terrestrial Observing System
GWP	global warming potential
HCFCs	hydrochlorofluorocarbons
HFCs	hydrofluorocarbons
HIPC	heavily indebted poor countries
IBRD	International Bank for Reconstruction and Development
ICBG	International Cooperative Biodiversity Groups
ICJ	International Court of Justice
ICPD	International Conference on Population and Development
ICREA	International Commodity-related Environmental Agreement
ICSU	International Council of Science Unions
IDA	International Development Association
IDRF	IDA Debt Reduction Facility
IEEA	integrated economic and environmental accounting
IFAD	International Fund for Agriculture and Development
IFC	International Finance Corporation
ILO	International Labour Office
IMF	International Monetary Fund
IMO	International Maritime Organization

INCD	International Convention to Combat Desertification
IOC	Intergovernmental Oceanographic Commission
IPCC	Intergovernmental Panel on Climate Change
IPF	Intergovernmental Panel on Forests
IPR	intellectual property rights
ISEW	index of sustainable economic welfare
ISO	International Standards Organization
IUCN	The World Conservation Union
IUR	inverted U relationship
LCA	life-cycle analysis
LESS	low CO_2 – emitting energy supply systems
LPG	liquefied petroleum gas
LSMS	living standards measurement survey
MCPF	marginal cost of public funds
MEA	multilateral environmental agreement
MED	marginal environmental damages
MEW	measure of economic welfare
MFMP	Multilateral Fund for the Montreal Protocol
MIGA	Multilateral Investment Guarantee Agency
MSY	maximum sustainable yield
NDP	net domestic product
NEAP	national environment action plan
NGO	non-governmental organization
NIH	National Institutes of Health
NNP	net national product
NPP	net primary productivity
NPV	net present value
NRDC	Natural Resources Defense Council
NSF	National Science Foundation
NSW	net social welfare
ODA	Official Development Assistance
OECD	Organization for Economic Cooperation and Development
OLG	overlapping generations
ONUV	other nonuse value
OPEC	Oil Producing and Exporting Countries
OPIC	Overseas Private Investment Corporation
OV	option value
PCR	polymerase chain reaction
PDIV	potential direct instrument value
PFCs	perflourocarbons
3P	polluter pays principle
PP	precautionary principle
ppb	parts per billion
ppm	parts per million
PPP	purchasing power parity
ppt	parts per trillion

PR	producer rate of interest
PSA	positive social amenities
QA	quality assurance
QUELRO	quantified carbon emission limitation and reduction commitment
R&D	research and development
RNNP	revised net national product
SAL	structural adjustment lending
SAP	structural adjustment program
SCBA	social cost–benefit analysis
SD	sustainable development
SDA	social disamenities
SDR	social discount rate
SEEA	system of integrated environmental and economic accounting
SMS	safe minimum standard
SNA	system of national accounts
SRTP	social rate of time preference
SSD	strong sustainable development
SSNNP	sustainable social net national product
TEP	tradable emission permit
TEV	total economic value
TQM	total quality management
TRIPS	trade-related intellectual property rights
UN	United Nations
UNCBD	UN Convention on Biological Diversity
UNCED	UN Conference on Environment and Development
UNCSD	UN Commission on Sustainable Development
UNCTAD	UN Conference on Trade and Development
UNDP	UN Development Programme
UNDPCSD	UN Department for policy coordination and sustainable development
UNEP	UN Environment Programme
UNESCO	UN Educational Scientific and Cultural Organization
UNFCCC	UN Framework Convention on Climate Change
UNFPA	UN Fund for Population Activities
UNICEF	UN Children's Fund
UNIDO	UN Industrial Development Organization
UNIFEM	UN Development Fund for Women
USAID	US Agency for International Aid
USEPA	US Environmental Protection Agency
USGS	US Geological Service
UV	ultra violet
UV	use value
UV-B	ultra violet B
VOC	volatile organic compound
WCED	World Commission on Environment and Development
WFP	World Food Programme

WHO	World Health Organization
WMO	World Meteorological Organization
WTO	World Trade Organization
WTP	willingness-to-pay
WWF	World Wide Fund For Nature (formerly known as World Wildlife Fund)

Chemical Symbols

CFCs	chlorofluorocarbons
CH_4	methane
Cl_2	molecular chlorine
CO	carbon monoxide
CO_2	carbon dioxide
H_2	molecular hydrogen
HCFCs	hydrochlorofluorocarbons
H_2O	water
N_2	molecular (ordinary) nitrogen
N_2O	nitrous oxide
NO	nitric oxide
NO_2	nitrogen dioxide
NO_x	nitrogen oxide
O	oxygen
O_2	molecular (ordinary) oxygen
O_3	ozone
OH	hydroxyl radical
SO_2	sulfur dioxide
SO_x	sulfur oxide

chapter outline

● CHAPTER 1 ●

A Brief History

● CHAPTER 1 ●

A Brief History

There is enough in the world for everyone's need,
but not for everyone's greed.
Frank Buchman

● 1.1 INTRODUCTION ●

An appreciation of the relevant socioeconomic history and the lessons that society can draw from this experience are important. This understanding is necessary, whether society continues to follow the same footprints of the past or lead to some others. An assessment of the relative roles of the various salient features that affect the current and future prosperity of a society is useful for any civilization looking to develop appropriate perspectives. The history of human civilization has been strongly interwoven with the history of climate and environment – here, we include all natural resources and other environmental factors in the category "environment." Until recently, the climate and environment were seen as major determinants of the growth and stability of civilizations, and this was perceived as a one-way effect. However, the impact of civilization or human influences on the climate and the environment is now seen to constitute a serious problem. This is because, in the emerging new scenarios, two-way interactions seem to exist between climate–environment, and human activities. We are entering the twenty-first century amid such potential for combined interactive effects. There is a significant need for an analysis of the underlying factors and their potential mitigatory alternatives. This analysis could lead to improved and pragmatic policy framework; hence the necessity. We start with a brief look at historical perspectives, and go on to examine current and future perspectives. Efforts are made to integrate the discussion and analysis with interdisciplinary insights; however, the primary focus involves the application of various approaches of the economic sciences.

Deep into History

Historically, the rise and fall of civilizations was inextricably linked to the vagaries of climate changes and variations in the judicious use of natural resources. These disturbances led to the uprooting of populations, the elimination of segments of populations when severe hunger and famine afflicted the habitats, and they affected geopolitics. To begin with, human settlements were usually influenced by the existence of natural resources, especially water – it was no coincidence that settlements were located mostly along river banks. Most civilizations flourished as "water civilizations," including those which began in Egypt along the Nile River and in southwest Asia along the Indus River system. These were known to have thrived before and around BC 5000. Parts of these regions were later abandoned when, over a period of time, the territory became a desert.

The Mayan civilization in the Western hemisphere began to flourish around the third and the fourth centuries AD; the civilization collapsed rather suddenly during the tenth century, a period which also coincided with temperature rise and climate change in the region. Similarly, the collapse of the Mali civilization in Africa in the fourteenth century was attributed to severe changes in climatic factors; see, for example, Al Gore (1991) for a discussion on the historical highlights of possible connections between climate and civilization. Both the climate change and environmental mismanagement contributed to these disasters.

There is no major evidence to suggest that climate change was due to human influences prior to the twentieth century. Environmental disregard, especially with respect to natural resources, was considered the prime cause of major problems in the erstwhile flourishing regions. Thus, the prosperity and relative stability of the above civilizations were not sustained. The destabilization problems that affected the water civilization societies can be traced to the management of water and soil: lack of appropriate conjunctive use of ground and surface waters led to soil salinity and desertification; water shortages and consequential disputes abound in history. See Maass and Anderson (1978) for an excellent account of the episodes; and Rao (1988) about the rise and fall of a Native American civilization, recognized as Hohokam Indians, in the present-day Arizonian desert area in the USA.

The lessons of economic history indicate that mismanagement of natural resources and the environment led to the disasters cited above. In comparison, the current period is faced with human-induced climatic changes, as well as the problems of environmental degradation. These combined problems, which are discussed in the subsequent chapters, tend to lead to much more complex and potentially disastrous situations than ever felt before in human history. This is not to be alarmist; however, a scientific and objective view suggests the need for rather urgent attention to mitigate the potentially adverse consequences. If inertia and inaction tended to be inconsistent with biological survival, a somewhat similar reasoning suggests that, now, lack of intervention might pose problems for sustained human prosperity and human survival.

These salient characteristics dominate the descriptions of the problems narrated above:

- Irreversibility of losses – whether related to the natural resource, climate, or civilization.
- Relative suddenness of disruptions, which also indicate the phenomena of nonlinear interactions and discontinuities of relationships among environmental features, as explained in chapter 3.
- Severity of the impacts of the environment on the survival and sustainability of civilizations or their prosperity.

Sustainable development (SD) – for its formal definitions, see chapter 3 – has, for several hundreds of years, been an area of concern for different sections of society. Usually, these concerns have been confined to specific components of the ecosystem. Some were built into the traditions of some civilizations, and into faiths and religions of a few others. One of these has been the worship of nature. Some religions advocated unity and harmony of nature in relation to human activities. However, very few traditions were translated formally into laws or legal systems. Historically, social customs and norms were considered cost-effective methods for implementing socially desirable activities. The viewpoint that other species might be entitled to their own existence on this planet was also recognized in certain beliefs, religious or other; see Gottlieb (1996) for details. These viewpoints were also supported by scientists like Henry David Thoreau and George Perkins Marsh in the nineteenth century. Marsh's 1864 contribution analyzed the fall of past civilizations and found that most of these possessed a single common feature: The civilization collapsed when its demands on natural resources exceeded the land's ability to supply the same. There have been experiences of deforestation leading to desertification and the collapse of human life in specific regions. Marsh's book made a very significant impact on the views of people, and Marsh was one of the earliest environmentalists; see also de Steiguer (1997) for historical perspectives. In terms of the current terminology, these concerns favored a form of sustainability; see chapter 3. Some of the modern environmental movements owe their foundations to these concerns.

Thomas Malthus (1766–1834) was perhaps the first to warn of the possibility of severe resource shortages (specifically, food shortages) as populations tend to increase exponentially. His predictions (Malthus, 1798) were primarily based on the assumptions of humans seeking to expand the population with unrestrained additions to the family size (constrained only by the availability of incomes to support themselves), and the lack of any contribution from technical efficiency improvements (including the role of human capital) in the food and other production systems. Fortunately, Malthus has been proved wrong during the past two centuries. Malthusian argument went to the extent of suggesting that paying more than subsistence wages for labor would lead to more children and more strain on food resources. This line of reasoning supported the idea that it may not be desirable to grant relief to the poor; and this earned for economics the name "the dismal science"; see also Johnston (1998) for more details.

Era of Industrial Revolution

The industrial developments, which started around the middle of the nineteenth century, entailed resource depletion and environmental problems. Industrial activities created pollution problems of local, regional and interregional magnitudes. Some legislative efforts were also initiated. The most important ruling regime of the world during the nineteenth century, Britain, passed the Alkali Act of 1863. Subsequently, the government assumed its role for pollution control. During the period 1860–80, the British Parliament enacted several laws to protect various birds and animals; for detailed accounts of these historical milestones, see Shabecoff (1996) and McCormick (1991). In the international arena, one of the earliest environmental agreements was the Boundary Waters Treaty of 1909 between the USA and the UK. The treaty stipulated control of water pollution, and sought to safeguard against adverse environmental effects on either side of the borders of the USA and Canada. The North American Conservation Congress was organized by President Theodore Roosevelt in 1909, and this led to the proposals for organizing global deliberations on related issues.

The industrial era also marked a phase in which several significant economic and environmental philosophers came to the fore. Some economic concerns were expressed by noted economists including John Stuart Mill (1806–73), Karl Marx (1818–83), and Alfred Marshall (1842–1924). The significance of natural resource limitations and their depletion was noted by each of these scholars, although their perspectives differ. Mill (1848) advocated the concept of Homo economicus – which assumes the behavior of humans as rational self-interested wealth maximizers. It was also noted that "unlimited increase of wealth and population" could deprive the earth of its "pleasantness." Marx viewed the problem of unsustainable development as a result of the class structure of the society. The sustainability of food supplies and the loss of soil fertility and land holdings were viewed as the limiting constraints on the food supplies. Marx considered that the capitalist mode of production would not allow sustained soil fertility. Unlike Marx, Marshall believed that people tend to pay attention to sustained land and soil productivity. The relative scarcity of quality air and other environmental public goods was noted when Marshall (1925) argued that, for the sake of a little material wealth, we may be wasting some of the factors of production. Marshall stated: "We are sacrificing those ends towards which material wealth is only a means." The well-known co-founder of "game theory" (now a respected branch of economics and decision sciences), John von Neumann (1955), was concerned with large-scale human interventions. He made two observations:

1 The result of human interventions, like the emissions of carbon dioxide, adversely affect the natural environment.
2 The result will be to "merge each nation's affairs with those of every other, more thoroughly than the threat of nuclear war or any other war may already have done."

This is precisely what we see at the end of the twentieth century.

During the industrial era, a significant influential contribution was made by Gifford Pinchot (1910). Pinchot rightly argued that:

● "the first great fact about conservation is that it stands for development" (p. 42); and
● conservationism is the "use of natural resources for the greatest good to the greatest number for the longest time" (p. 322).

It is rather ironic that, for most of North American history, the most important resource management problem was how to exploit mineral and other natural resources as quickly as possible; for a detailed account of the evolution of policies governing US natural resources, see Nester (1997). The interdependencies of the planet Earth's resources and their finiteness were foreseen by many thinkers. Nations and empires rise and fall on the tides of climate change, argued Wheeler (1946). Soon after World War II, Aldo Leopold (1949) was an early proponent of the ecosystem approach, emphasizing the links between people and the ecological systems.

The extent and intensity of human exploitation of the Earth's resources during the twentieth century resulted in significant effects on major components of the biosphere, namely the atmosphere, land cover, and biodiversity. This was largely due to rapid industrialization, deforestation, and urbanization. The race for resource exploitation and economic growth heated up, especially after World War II. No doubt, at that time, there were dire needs to rebuild societies and economic systems. However, some indiscriminate and desperate methods of tampering with the ecosystem led to current concerns about the potential dangers to the survival of the human race and that of other species.

Rachel Carson's (1962) contribution, *Silent Spring*, is generally credited with laying the foundation for the modern era of environmental awareness and social concern in developed countries. Her book was mainly about the significant risks posed by some categories of pesticides, especially dichlorodiphenyltrichloroethane (DDT), and brought to light the need for environmental alertness to safeguard human health. She examined life in every form on this planet and sought "accommodation between humans and nature." Later, an influential paper by the biologist Garrett Hardin (1968) provided a warning about the imminent dangers of excessive resource exploitation and environmental mismanagement. In the medieval "commons" – defined as open pasture land on which livestock grazing was carried out, for free, by individual herders – as many additional cattle as possible were introduced so as to maximize the herder's use of the commons. This apparent self-interest led to overgrazing and starvation of the herds. In this scenario, the short-term benefits of additional grazing accrued to the herders; however, the ultimate resource loss and costs were incurred by the society as a whole. To quote Hardin (1968): "Ruin is in the destination toward which all men rush, pursuing their own best interest in a society that believes in the freedom of the commons. Freedom in the commons brings ruin to all." This statement is relevant in the management of resources with a free access. Generally, the efficiency of management of commons is affected by the features: traditions, property rights and their enforcement, the relative costs of access to the property, the preferences (individual and societal) for the present enjoyments relative to future interests, and the interplay of these factors.

The alarm raised by Malthus at the end of the eighteenth century was echoed again in the early 1970s, with the release of the influential "Limits to Growth" report. This Club of Rome report (Meadows et al., 1972) constructed a computer model of five variables to study whether there exist limits to the growth of Earth's resource use: Population, food, industrialization, non-renewable resources, and pollution. In all the scenarios considered for future projections, population and industrialization surged high and fell sharply, depicting an "overshoot and collapse" pattern. This was a neo-Malthusian analysis, with little recognition of the role of technical progress. A number of professional investigations into the issues were triggered by these doomsday predictions. For example, some reputed journals, like the *Review of Economic Studies*, devoted a special issue to the theme of resource economics and management. An important contribution by Talbot Page (1977) addressed the sustainability issues and the role of the market institutions, including their failure to affect the long-term efficiency of resources management. Page (1997) also deliberated a few important issues; these are discussed in chapter 3.

Despite its lack of predictive ability, the structural configuration and analysis of the Club of Rome report served one purpose: It alerted the world to the potential dangers of inefficient resource utilization. A decade after the report, Meadows et al. (1982) revised their assessments and made these suggestions:

- There are no known physical scarcities nor technical reasons why the basic needs of all the people of the world cannot be met in the foreseeable future.
- There is relatively partial information about the environmental resources, and this is amenable to widely varying interpretations.

Later, Meadows et al. (1992) shifted the stand to suggest that there is a need for significant reductions in material and energy flows, and it was argued that failure to do so might imply a decline in per capita production of food and industrial goods, with constraints on energy supplies.

Institutional Interventions

The debate on environmental resource management at the global level was formally founded with the 1972 Conference on the Human Environment in Stockholm. Several regional and international activities, geared toward the phenomena of SD, have engaged attention ever since. Free market systems were not seen as self-correcting institutions for the purpose of environmental management, in the absence of regulations or other catalytic interventions. The twentieth century witnessed considerable intervention mechanisms from governments and also from civic action groups, at national and international levels. Environmental law became another method of controlling unregulated and/or uncompensated harm-inducing activities in the industrial countries; these are also described as externalities; details can be seen in chapter 4. After a fair recognition of the interdependencies of the environmental features cutting across national boundaries, several important international agreements were formulated. These laid the foundations for some of the global environmental actions.

At the global level, the Swedish initiative, supported by the USA, led to the first global environmental conference: The United Nations Conference on the Human Environment at Stockholm in 1972. The launching of the institution, the United Nations Environment Programme (UNEP) followed as a by-product. The conference led to the Stockholm Declaration with 29 Principles, and provided a permanent basis for international environmental coordination and diplomacy. It is interesting to note that the Stockholm conference did not maintain a focus on what has become, in the following two decades, the dominant social paradigm: Addressing global warming and related issues. The dominant social paradigm is defined as a set of beliefs, ideas and values from which public policies or systems of behavior flow rather logically; see Harman (1979).

A few illustrative milestones in US policy legislation and initiatives are noteworthy. The US Soil Conservation Service was created as a product of the Soil Conservation and Domestic Allotment Act (1936). The Federal Insecticide, Fungicide, and Rodenticide Act was enacted in 1947. A number of major legislative policy measures were enacted in the USA, beginning in the 1960s. The Clean Air Act (1963), followed by a few amendments from time to time, the Resource Conservation and Recovery Act (1976), the Toxic Substances Control Act (1976), the Clean Water Act (1977) – also with subsequent improvements – are some of the main examples. The National Forest Management Act (1976) and the Federal Land Policy Management Act called for "a combination of balanced and diverse resource uses that takes into account the long-term needs of future generations for renewable and non-renewable resources . . ."

Perhaps in the initial phase, SD entered published literature of the International Union for the Conservation of Nature and Natural Resources (IUCN) around 1980. The vigorous approach, if not a rigorous one, to the concept of SD was provided in the report of the World Commission on Environment and Development (WCED) – popularly known as the Brundtland Report, with Gro Harlem Brundtland as the Chairperson – in 1987. The details of the concept, interpretations and implications are given in chapter 3. This report marked an important milestone in the evolution of thinking on related issues, primarily addressed to intergenerational equity and justice. These features are also known to be dependent on contemporary intragenerational and distributive justice issues.

Several developments followed the publication of the Brundtland report. The UN General Assembly adopted a resolution in December 1988 regarding global climate protection. Soon after, the Hague Declaration on Environment was signed by 24 governments. This Declaration sought to create a new international authority "for combating any further global warming of the atmosphere." This was followed by the Ministerial Declaration of the Second World Climate Conference at Geneva in November 1990. This Declaration was based on deliberations from the representatives of 137 countries including those from the European

Community. The Declaration included a global strategy, policy considerations for action and a suggested framework convention. Here are two statements from the Declaration:

1 "[W]hile climate has varied in the past and there is still a large degree of scientific uncertainty, the rate of climate change predicted by the Intergovernmental Panel on Climate Change (IPCC) to occur over the next century is unprecedented. This is due mainly to the continuing accumulation of greenhouse gas [GHG], resulting from a host of human activities since the Industrial Revolution, hitherto particularly in developed countries. The potential impact of such climate change could pose an environmental threat of an up-to-now unknown magnitude and could jeopardize the social and economic development of some areas. It could even threaten survival in some small island states and in low-lying coastal, arid and semi-arid areas . . ."

2 "[T]o enable developing countries to meet incremental costs required to take the necessary measures to address climate change and sea-level rise, consistent with their development needs, we recommend that adequate additional financial resources should be mobilized and best available environmentally sound technologies transferred expeditiously on a fair and most favorable basis . . ."

● 1.2 THE EARTH SUMMIT ●

A resolution of the UN General Assembly in 1989 lead to the unprecedented UN Conference on Environment and Development (UNCED) – popularly known as the Earth Summit – which was held at Rio de Janeiro in June 1992. The summit succeeded in attracting the largest number of heads of government: 118. This was a clear sign of the times: Societies all over the planet perceived significant changes and problems in resources and environment, and pragmatic (rather than drastic) solutions – especially a few politically feasible ones – were in great demand. The results of the summit were perhaps best stated by the Prime Minister of Norway, Gro Harlem Brundtland: "Progress in many fields, too little progress in most fields, and no progress at all in some fields." The summit's agenda contained a "Rio Declaration" setting forth 27 Principles for SD and an action plan known as "Agenda 21." Box 1.1 lists these Principles.

The Declaration

Agenda 21 was the main document signed at the UNCED. The document was a detailed volume of 40 chapters in about 800 pages. Significant gaps between proposed goals and proposed actions for implementation persisted, however. It was not a legally binding document, but was envisaged as a "work plan," with chapters that dealt with the following, among others: Accelerating SD in developing countries; controlling poverty; demographic dynamics; human health; sustainable health settlements; integrating environment and development in

BOX 1.1   Main Principles of Agenda 21

The Earth Summit Declaration (also called the Rio Declaration) contained principles on environment and development as quoted below. These are classified under the following categories (not necessarily mutually exclusive): environmental, economic, social, and peace.

A. Environmental Principles

1   Human beings are at the center of concerns for sustainable development. They are entitled to a healthy and productive life in harmony with nature.

2   States have, in accordance with the charter of the United Nations and the principles of international law, the sovereign right to exploit their own resources pursuant to their own environmental and developmental policies, and the responsibility to ensure that the activities within their jurisdiction or control do not cause damage to the environment of other States or of areas beyond the limits of national jurisdiction.

4   In order to achieve sustainable development, environmental protection shall constitute an integral part of the development process and cannot be considered in isolation from it.

10   Environmental issues are best handled with the participation of all concerned citizens, at the relevant level. At the national level, each individual shall have appropriate access to information concerning the environment that is held by public authorities, including information on hazardous materials and activities in their communities, and the opportunity to participate in the decision-making processes. States shall facilitate and encourage public awareness and participation by making information widely available. Effective access to judicial and administrative proceedings, including redress and remedy, shall be provided.

11   States shall enact effective environmental legislation. Environmental standards, management objectives and priorities should reflect the environmental and developmental context to which they apply. Standards applied by some countries may be inappropriate and of unwarranted economic and social cost to other countries, in particular, developing countries.

13   States shall develop national laws regarding liability and compensation for the victims of pollution and other environmental damage. States shall also cooperate in an expeditious and more determined manner to develop further international laws regarding liability and compensation for adverse effects of environmental damage caused by activities within their jurisdiction or control to areas beyond their jurisdiction.

14   States should effectively cooperate to discourage or prevent the relocation and transfer of any activities and substances that may cause severe environmental degradation or are found to be harmful to human health.

15   In order to protect the environment, the precautionary approach shall be widely applied by States according to their capabilities. Where there are

threats of serious or irreversible damage, lack of full scientific certainty shall not be used as a reason for postponing cost-effective measures to prevent environmental degradation.

17   Environmental impact assessment, as a national instrument, shall be undertaken for proposed activities that are likely to have a significant adverse impact on the environment and are subject to a decision of competent national authority.

18   States shall immediately notify other States of any natural disasters or other emergencies that are likely to produce sudden harmful effects on the environment of those States. Every effort shall be made by the international community to help States so afflicted.

19   States shall provide prior and timely notification and relevant information to potentially affected States on activities that may have a significant adverse transboundary environmental effect and shall consult with those States at an early stage and in good faith.

23   The environment and natural resources of people under oppression, domination and occupation shall be protected.

B. Economic Principles

3   The right to development must be fulfilled so as to equitably meet developmental and environmental needs of present and future generations.

5   All states and all people shall cooperate in the essential task of eradicating poverty as an indispensable requirement for sustainable development, in order to decrease the disparities in standards of living and better meet the needs of the majority of the people of the world.

6   The special situation and needs of developing countries, particularly the least developed and the most environmentally vulnerable, shall be given special priority. International actions in the field of environment and development should also address the interests and needs of all countries.

7   States shall cooperate in a spirit of global partnership to conserve, protect and restore the health and integrity of the Earth's ecosystem. In view of the different contributions to global environmental degradation, States have common but differentiated responsibilities. The developed countries acknowledge the responsibility that they bear in the international pursuit of sustainable development in view of the pressures their societies place on the global environment and of the technologies and financial resources they command.

8   To achieve sustainable development and a higher quality of life for all people, States should reduce and eliminate unsustainable patterns of production and consumption and promote appropriate demographic policies.

9   States should cooperate to strengthen endogenous capacity-building for sustainable development by improving scientific understanding through exchanges of scientific and technological knowledge, and by enhancing the development adaptation, diffusion and transfer of technologies, including new and innovative technologies.

12 States should cooperate to promote a supportive and open international economic system that would lead to economic growth and sustainable development in all countries, to better address the problems of environmental degradation. Trade policy measures for environmental purposes should not constitute a means of arbitrary and unjustifiable discrimination or a disguised restriction on international trade. Unilateral actions to deal with environmental challenges outside the jurisdiction of the importing country should be avoided. Environmental measures addressing the transboundary or global environmental problems should, as far as possible, be based on international consensus.

16 National authorities should endeavor to promote internationalization of environmental costs and the use of economic instruments, taking into account the approach that the polluter should, in principle, bear the cost of pollution, with due regard to the public interest and without distorting international trade and investment.

C. Social Principles

20 Women have a vital role in environmental management and development. Their full participation is therefore essential to achieve sustainable development.

21 The creativity, ideals and courage of the youth of the world should be mobilized to forge a global partnership in order to achieve sustainable development and ensure a better future for all.

22 Indigenous people and their communities, and other local communities, have a vital role in environmental management and development because of their knowledge and traditional practices. States should recognize and duly support their identity, culture and interest and enable their effective participation in the achievement of sustainable development.

D. Peace Principles

24 Warfare is inherently destructive of sustainable development. States shall therefore respect international law providing protection for the environment in times of armed conflict and cooperate in its further development, as necessary.

25 Peace, development and environmental protection are interdependent and indivisible.

26 States shall resolve all their environmental disputes peacefully and by appropriate means in accordance with the Charter of the United Nations.

27 States and people shall cooperate in good faith and in spirit of partnership in the fulfillment of the principles embodied in this Declaration and in the further development of international law in the field of sustainable development.

Note: The numbers refer to the 27 Principles listed at the Earth Summit meeting at Rio de Janeiro, 1992.

decision making; atmosphere; integrated planning and management of land resources; combating deforestation; combating desertification and drought; promoting sustainable agriculture and rural development; conservation of biological diversity; environmentally sound management of biotechnology; oceans and their living resources; freshwater resources; toxic chemicals; hazardous wastes; solid wastes and sewage; and radioactive wastes. About ten chapters dealt with strengthening the role of major groups – women, children and youth, indigenous peoples, nongovernmental organizations (NGOs), local authorities, trade unions, business and industry, science and technology, and farmers. The remaining chapters were devoted to issues like: The transfer of environmentally sound technology; science for SD; education, public awareness and training; cooperation for capacity building in developing countries; international institutional arrangements; international legal instruments and mechanisms; and information for decision making.

The agenda and coverage of issues at the Earth Summit remained sufficiently general to accommodate rather non-convergent viewpoints of participating nations. This is not an unusual feature at such a forum, but the lack of concreteness and direction on some of the important issues remains a problem. For example, in the areas of international trade and environmental protection, the problems are far from resolved. A new institution, the World Trade Organization (WTO) is entrusted with the responsibility of handling these issues. Some of the agreements reached in Rio represented "lowest common denominator results. They undervalued the importance of benefit sharing, focusing more on short-term economic costs than on long-term environment gains for future generation" (Susskind, 1994, pp. 41–2). These observations seem to be equally relevant in many other similar agreements as well. Nonetheless, the continued effects of the Earth Summit are felt over the years. The summit did provide a rather ambitious link in international efforts between environment and development, although the environment–population–development, or international trade–debt–environment linkages were poorly addressed. The UNCED could not spell out the mechanisms to resolve potential conflicts between the objectives of trade and environmental policies. Realistically, it is not entirely possible to resolve all human activities that have a bearing on the environment and development at a single forum, and a number of declarations are essentially compromises between opposing national interests of the current and future time periods. Nonetheless, the effort constituted a turning point in international development policy formulation, as discussed below.

At the summit, the negotiations for climate protection took place as part of a two-stage process of initial framework building, to be followed by specific policy measures contained in different "protocols." Two important conventions owed their origins to this summit:

- The Convention on Biological Diversity, signed by 165 nations and the European Community, took effect on December 29, 1993.
- The Framework Convention on Climate Change led to a treaty signed by over 150 nations and became effective on March 21, 1994.

The SD approach emerged from the summit with a large following in the international public policy-making community. The summit led to the establishment of a UN Commission on Sustainable Development (UNCSD) to provide a new co-ordination mechanism for the implementation of Agenda 21. The commission was established in February 1993, and comprised representatives from 53 nations. The effectiveness and contribution of this institution remains rather feeble thus far.

● 1.3 MORE RECENT EVENTS ●

During the post-Earth Summit period, several actions were effected at the individual country levels, including the formulation of national environmental policies and action programs. Besides, many regional and international agreements and activities affecting the environment and development have been worked out. A few of the important ones are briefly stated below; several more are listed in the Chronology given in the Appendix to this chapter.

The 1994 International Conference on Population and Development (ICPD) was held in Cairo. Representatives from 183 nations broadly agreed to an action plan to stabilize the human population by the year 2020, and to provide greater equality for women along with improved reproductive health care. The ICPD, like the Earth Summit, largely failed to integrate demographic, environmental, and economic development issues in an operationally meaningful framework. This observation need not be viewed as an indictment of the organizing institutions. Rather, in the absence of a realistic complementary sets of activities or enabling instruments, the grand-scale summits themselves can only highlight the issues. Concerted and coordinated efforts of governmental and NGOs are required for greater effectiveness of directions and agreements evolved at the forum.

The World Conference (Fourth) on Women was held in Beijing in September 1995. This adopted a Bill of Rights for women, and was ratified by about 160 countries by 1997; more details of this conference are discussed in chapter 7.

The Berlin Climate Summit was held in March 1995, the objective being to strengthen the Framework Convention on Climate Change signed at the Earth Summit. In a decision called the "Berlin Mandate," the summit agreed that existing commitments to curb GHG emissions in developed countries were inadequate to meet the Convention's goals and sought a protocol to strengthen the commitments. The member countries of the Berlin Mandate sought to create the Global Environmental Facility (GEF), a funding body to help to finance key global environmental projects. This was particularly relevant for non-ozone depleting GHGs, as these are not covered under the Montreal Protocol. This Protocol covered the ban on the production of ozone-depleting chemicals; more details are provided in chapters 5 and 10.

The World Food Summit was held in Rome in November 1996. This highlighted eight commitments (but not eight commandments!) creating conditions for economic and social progress conducive to food security, poverty eradication and access to adequate food, sustainable increases in food production, complementarity of trade to food security, preparedness for food emergencies, human resource development, sustainable production and rural development, global cooperation in implementation and follow-up actions.

The 1997 five-year review of the Rio Summit, called the Earth Summit Plus Five (ESPF) was expected to mark another milestone for assessing the impact of the Earth Summit. However, the results and the proceedings of this summit were rather unimpressive, and it was much less eventful than the original summit in 1992. This can be inferred from the fact that only about a third of the number of the heads of governments participated, compared to the attendance in 1992: about 42 compared to about 118 at the Rio Summit (out of the 185 UN member countries in 1997). The end product was a resolution to take steps for the implementation of Agenda 21 as well as some of the subsequent declarations in related areas like the Copenhagen Declaration on Social Development (emphasizing combating poverty), the International Conference on Population and Development, the Beijing Platform Actions (regarding women participation), the UN Conference on Human Settlements' (Habitat II) recommendations on sustainable human settlements, and the Report of the Ad Hoc Intergovernmental Panel on Forests (IPF). There was only a one-page agreement that concluded the deliberations at the summit. The progress is proposed to be reviewed again at another summit in 2002.

Part of the reason for this relatively tame incident was the awaiting for the Kyoto round (the third conference of parties) of the UN Framework Convention on Climate Change (UNFCCC), the event of December 1997. This event was taken seriously by the respective governments as well as private industry and NGOs. It was also heavily lobbied and advertised by interest groups with their own agendas. Some businesses sought to ensure that they are not significantly affected because of any "unrealistic" fixing of target levels of GHG, or binding commitments by the participating countries. More details of the protocol are given in the next section.

● 1.4 EFFECTIVENESS OF POLICIES ●

Global environmental efforts have increased in the 1990s. These were undertaken by both formal institutions (like national government agencies and international institutions) and other institutions (like NGOs, and civic forums). Consumer awareness, especially in the Organization for Economic Cooperation and Development (OECD) countries, and environmental movements are on a much firmer footing than ever in the past. January 1, 1996 marked an important milestone in protecting the global environment: Under the provisions of the Montreal Protocol of the Vienna Framework Convention on Ozone-degrading Substances, the production of chlorofluorocarbons (CFCs) ceased in the developed countries. The developing countries were given an additional ten years to phase them out.

The Montreal Protocol is considered an historic event for these reasons (see chapter 2 for more details and also Lang, 1995):

- It was the first global treaty stipulating quantified emission reductions following a relatively rigid time frame.
- It was the first treaty to follow the PP (Precautionary Principle) (see chapter 3), suggesting that governments adopt significant measures for environmental protection well before full scientific knowledge about the threat has been ascertained.
- It was the first environmental treaty under which the participating countries approved a formal noncompliance procedure.
- It was among the rare Treaties which provided a meaningful framework, enabling accelerated fulfillment of targets and advancement of time targets (as carried out under modifications at later Conventions and protocols).

The Montreal Protocol served as a model for similar multilateral undertakings in related areas, possibly including sulfur emissions and climate change. If the potential beneficial impact of such compliance mechanisms in the protocol could be recognized and widely disseminated, the international community could be enthusiastic in the direction of progress. The Montreal Protocol Multilateral Fund, contributed to by the developed world, remains a good example of international environmental concern. This fund was recently replenished and the possibility of phasing out ozone-depleting substances, including methyl bromide, is greater than ever.

The worldwide production of CFCs has declined by over 60 percent since 1988, according to the Worldwatch Institute. The UNEP stated that the production and consumption of halons ended by 1994 in the developed countries, and that of CFCs by 1996. The ozone layer, however, will be damaged for another 50 years or more because of the ozone hole that already exists, and because atmospheric chemical interaction of restoration is a slow process. In addition, the developing countries can continue to add to harmful substance accumulation for another ten years, although on a declining scale. More details of issues governing ozone depletion are presented in chapter 2.

The ESPF of June 1997 noted that the global environment has continued to deteriorate and that "significant environmental problems remain deeply embedded in the socioeconomic fabric of countries in all regions." Since the latter feature is a relatively long-term evolution process, the impediments are not expected to vanish in the near future. The resolutions of this summit noted that the ozone layer continues to be severely depleted and that the Montreal Protocol needs to be strengthened. The ESPF did not lead to any new commitments of resource aid to the poor at the international or intranational levels and, primarily, stressed the need to adhere to the implementation of Agenda 21. The Kyoto Agreement followed in December 1997.

The agreement at Kyoto led to the "Kyoto Protocol," which seeks to reduce GHG emissions. The villain gases considered for this reduction are: carbon dioxide, methane, nitrogen oxide, and three halocarbons used as substitutes for ozone-depleting CFCs. These gases and their role is discussed in chapters 2 and 5. The magnitudes of reductions desired, relative to the corresponding emissions of 1990 levels, are as follows:

- By at least 5 percent during the period 2008–12 for all the industrial countries aggregated;
- EU by 8 percent;
- USA by 7 percent; and
- Japan by 6 percent.

Developing countries with large populations and economies like China and India have been asked to set voluntary targets for reduction, for the present. Also, these targets are yet to be ratified in respect of major countries like the USA, where there has to be considerable internal deliberations and possible agreement. The targets are not as modest as they might appear: for the USA the reduction is of the order of 18 percent relative to the emissions of 1998. The imperatives of the protocol remain nonbinding at this stage, waiting for at least 55 countries to ratify the provisions. The details of various implementation mechanisms have differed for the November 1998 agreement at Buenos Aires. However, this agreement simply emphasized the need to implement the provision of the Kyoto Protocol, and left the details of the implementation mechanism to a later forum.

The roles of international environmental agreements, financial mechanisms, and aid institutions remain critical for the effectiveness of the implementation of global and national environmental policies in the developing countries. The effectiveness of international development aid, directly or indirectly affecting the environmental dimensions, is rather mixed in its results. The history of development assistance reveals coordination failures and organizational inertia. Modern economics refers to these in terms of two major problems:

1   Asymmetric information between the donor and the donee, as well as between the principal and the agent in an organization.
2   Incentive compatibility – the factors affecting motivations of the donors relative to the needs of the recipients, and of the personnel working for the implementing agencies – both in the donor and recipient countries.

These two factors contribute to the aggregate ineffectiveness in environmental aid. The unwillingness or inability of the donor groups and international institutions to coordinate approaches or tailor policy interventions to suit the new problems can have a number of negative effects. In eastern Europe, donor institutions' reliance on their favorite solutions and financial mechanisms has contributed to the widespread neglect of local air-pollution problems, one of the most important priorities in the region from the standpoint of human health; for details, see Connolly and Keohane (1996). Limitations of organizational learning and effectiveness of aid coordination remain some of the impediments in the international transfer of resources and their efficient utilization. Details of the environmental contributions of institutions like the World Bank and the International Monetary Fund (IMF) are provided in chapter 10; also, the interplay of features of debt, trade and the environment are detailed in chapter 8.

● 1.5 MOVING AHEAD ●

So far, the discussion has centered around global issues, international environmental governance and historical developments. Even if all the identified problems of the global commons (defined here summarily as transboundary pollution and biogeochemical features of the ecosystem and the stratosphere) are somehow fully resolved, the sustenance of human prosperity is conditional upon some of the problems that have either been ignored or have not yet been identified. The nature of evolution of the biogeosphere itself brings about problems of gigantic proportions from time to time, whether they are created by humans, or whether they originate from unknown sources, or a combination of both.

If the famous Stockholm Conference of 1972 did not take global warming, ozone depletion or related issues seriously, how have these problems come to the forefront of attention by the time of the Earth Summit only two decades later? Does the difficulty lie with "ignorance" or "ignore-ance"? (Myers, 1995). If the emergence of the theory of probability (which we widely use in all the statistical methods and their applications) had a lot to do with the "needs" and patronage of the early modern age in Europe to enhance the gambling strengths of the rulers in some of the provinces, what does it take to fulfill the needs of humanity as ascertained from time to time by the people themselves? Who would be the patrons of new knowledge for improved understanding of the scientific, technological and socioeconomic factors affecting the features of SD?

Scientifically, an important category of impending problems for environmental processes comprise discontinuities. A discontinuity occurs, for example, when liquid water suddenly changes to ice or steam. Forest ecosystems undergo degradation through acid rain or chronic disturbance of the exploitation of forest products; they manifest slow decline and suddenly display severe deterioration. This has been observed in many areas; see, for example, Singh et al. (1997) regarding the forest features in the Himalayan region. "Environmental discontinuities occur when ecosystems absorb stresses over long periods without much outward sign of injury, then reach a disruption threshold at which the cumulative consequences finally reveal themselves" (Myers, 1995).

The Earth's system does not respond gradually and evenly to change; lags, nonlinearities, thresholds, and (unknown) interactions can be anticipated even when the human-caused activities are gradual and continuous. The best current example of a nonlinear response to change is the Antarctic ozone hole (Vitousek and Lubchenco, 1995): The effect of CFCs on ozone depletion had been identified, but no one predicted the rapid development of the ozone hole, discovered almost by accident (Farman et al., 1985; Rowland, 1989).

The above illustration points to problems of irreversibility and the role of the PP (explained in chapter 3) in environmental decision making at local, regional or global levels. In contrast to the phenomena of discontinuities and irreversibility (also explained in chapter 3), the process of synergism works to the advantage of SD. These synergisms arise when two or more environmental or ecological processes interact in such a way that the outcome is not additive but multiplicative (Ehrlich and Roughgarden, 1987). Large-scale tree planting in the humid and sub-humid tropics could generate a sink for atmospheric carbon dioxide to counter global warming; this process could also supply many spin-off benefits through, for instance, commercial forestry plantations that relieve excessive logging pressure on the remaining natural forests. This could help to safeguard birds and other species as well as genetic resources in tropical forests; some-times there can be large agricultural benefits as, for example, when the disease resistance of a wild rice in India's forests saved much of the Asian rice crop from a pandemic blight; see also Myers (1995).

Usually, the synergistic phenomena are not fully visualized or exploited. An institutional explanation for this comes from regimentations in administrative sys-tems of national and international governmental forms of administration. Two of the key ingredients in organizational (in)efficiency stem from the existence of "agency maximands" (which seek to promote the interests of the organization rather than the broader system which was to be served by the organization) and "internalities" (private goals for the benefit of the personnel or their interests) which tend to promote self-interests at the agency level and/or individual level. The real "bargain," in the sense of cost-effectiveness and innovation, arises in a greater understanding and exploitation of synergistic interlinkages. This should be the spirit behind any interpretation of SD. The goals of the latter cannot be easily sustained in the absence of such a spirit.

The above discussion also suggests the usefulness of a highly interdisciplin-ary approach to the issues, rather than narrow confines of traditional disciplines (which sometimes are governed by simplistic and implicit assumptions). Eco-logical economics (still in the process of perfection), for example, could offer a better basis of analysis than conventional microeconomics or environmental economics alone. A biogeospheric concept promises a useful approach to sus-tainability, but that is unlikely to lead automatically to SD. The latter necessar-ily requires one or the other form of an economic approach; this could involve growth in net national income and also per capita consumption. These issues are detailed in chapter 3.

The impediments to SD are not necessarily only in terms of global factors. A number of regional and local/sectoral interrelationships between various object-ives, goals, means and instruments need to be articulated. These are relevant both for improved understanding of the issues and for non-monolithic intervention and implementation to achieve desired objectives. It is also necessary to recog-nize that societies do not all agree to the same objectives of development nor instruments to attain the stated objectives. This may be attributable to a mix of factors: The role and content of informed decision making, priorities of felt needs, and institutional arrangements governing the specific societal groups or decision-making apparatus.

It is not accurate to state that individuals act in either self-interest or common interest; for most people, the reality lies somewhere between the two. Policies and programs for SD cannot be independent of behavioral dimensions. These aspects are also reflected in inequalities in asset holdings and the prevalence of widespread poverty in different parts of the world. When about a fifth of global population lives on one dollar a day, it is unlikely that these sections of societies can afford to observe the principles of SD, except possibly by coincidence, such as when they recycle certain products for their own use. Their individual human sustenance is the only rightful concern for them. Will subsistence and drudgery of work enhance environmental quality or the potential for SD? It is extremely unlikely. Socially responsible and humanistic civilizations cannot be indifferent to the problems of abject poverty.

It would be extremely simplistic to imagine that a global institution like the UN could ever be equal to the task, much less a quasi-commercial organization like the World Bank. The emergence of multitudes of institutions, peoples' institutions, including green movements, and improving information systems for formal and informal coordination of policies and programs that offer potential for SD, greater awareness of the issues at various levels in the private sector, and improved approaches toward the environment at multilateral institutions (like the World Bank and the UN system of institutions) do provide greater hope than in the past.

Individual nations, the main actors in environmental governance, evolve policies and programs conditioned by interests of the net effects of various segments in the society. There may not always exist a well-documented "white paper" or "Blueprint" for possible action. Even if one exists, it may be sufficiently vague in directing policies and programs. The World Bank, as well as the UN, tends to extract country policy documents from member countries in the developing world either when capital and technical support is proposed or offered, or in the mechanisms of institutional oversight and review. However, the information contained in these documents remains inadequate in its coverage and quality, if any realistic formulations are to be based on these. Further efforts are required to enhance the information bases for decision making at various levels or economic entities.

For the industrial countries, at the multilateral level, the OECD plays an important role in the collection and analysis of relevant information. In the process of formulation of public policies in the USA, the US President's Council on Sustainable Development (1996), representing a cross-section of interests and expertise, led to a document called *Sustainable America – A New Consensus*. It is useful to highlight the specified goals, stated in the chapter on "National Goals Toward Sustainable Development" in order:

1   Health and the environment.
2   Economic prosperity (including the positive role of natural resources and environmental accounting).
3   Equity (intragenerational and long term).
4   Conservation of nature (including ecosystems and habitat loss).
5   Stewardship.
6   Sustainable communities.
7   Civic engagement.
8   Population (stabilization and immigration control).

9   International responsibility (including international leadership).
10   Education (dissemination of information and learning processes).

It may be observed that this report has been based on a functional or utilitarian view. The role of the environmental factors has been viewed largely in terms of what those factors could lead to from the human welfare perspective, rather than emphasizing environmental features for their own sake. Also, the "goals" are liberally intertwined with the means of attaining some of the goals. The theme of civic engagement and education is one such example.

The Clinton administration released its Climate Change Action Plan in October 1993. This included a proposal of 44 recommendations designed to reduce carbon emissions and to combat global warming. The plan was considered cost-effective: While investing over $60 billion in GHG emission reductions between 1994 and 2000, individuals and firms realize over $60 billion in energy savings between 1994 and 2000, and realize continued returns in the form of an additional $207 billion in energy savings between 2001 and 2010. The action plan establishes public–private partnerships in various sectors of the economy, and remains an important milestone in steps toward sustainable environmental development. The White House organized an Interagency Ecosystem Management Task Force. In its 1995 Report (US Task Force, 1995), it was suggested that ecosystem management be based on the "best science," and stated that the goal of the approach was "to restore and sustain the health, productivity, and biological diversity of ecosystems and overall quality of life . . . fully integrated with social and economic goals." Later, preceding the December 1997 Kyoto Negotiations on Climate Change, the US President announced incentives to the extent of about $6 billion for the industry to enhance energy-efficiency and conservation. Similar initiatives by the US Government in the 1970s paid rich dividends in the face of the oil crisis; it more than paid for itself when it led to increased energy efficiencies, especially fuel-use efficiency in the automobile sector.

Among the most comprehensive studies on various scientific and socioeconomic dimensions of climate change are those being brought out by the IPCC constituted by the UN. After its initial reports, the Second Assessment Report of 1995 (published in 1996) deals with a wide variety of issues, and the studies have been conducted by a variety of experts from all over the world. Some of the salient features of these reports are examined in subsequent chapters.

The role of economic growth in promoting or impeding SD, the aspirations and needs of the developing countries in augmenting income levels, the issues of contemporary as well as long-term equity of resource ownership and income distribution within and across different countries are but a few of the ingredients of environmental policy at the national and global levels. The linkages between the economic and environmental forces underlie these issues; the relative roles of the ingredients must be distinguished in relation to the socioeconomic systems considered for analyzing various policies. Although the ultimate objectives of development and environmental coordination remain almost the same, many of the policy prescriptions tend to differ significantly between developing and developed countries. Also, we are entering an era of increasing concern for environmental health problems, applicable to all groups of countries and locations. The health effects of local and global environmental problems remain a major concern for any policy toward SD. The role of global warming and climate change remains very important in this context, in addition to environmental pollution problems. Some of these aspects are deliberated in the next few chapters.

A number of major issues, vital for policies and practices of SD, are proposed for discussion and analysis in the course of the next ten chapters:

- An assessment of the current features governing natural resources (especially water, forests, and biodiversity) and the environment (with reference to GHGs, ozone depletion, and desertification).
- Alternative bases (and their implications) of the concepts for sustainability and SD.
- The relationships between economic growth and environment.
- Foundations for the economic valuation of present and future resources.
- The role of progress in technical innovations and of changing preferences of the society.
- Issues in the management of global commons.
- Improved methods of environmental accounting and of the national income.
- Poverty–environment nexus.
- The environmental dimensions of international debt and trade, reflecting environmental costs in traded goods.
- Enhancing positive roles of the private sector in environmental enhancement.
- Analysis of the roles of international institutions.
- A multilevel policy framework for improved management of inputs and outputs for SD.

Appendix: Chronology of International Events

The following events form major developments, facilitated by international institutional actions in the global context. Clearly, the participating countries and institutions vary from one event to the other. This listing depicts the evolution of policy in varying areas of environmental policy and SD during the post-World War II era. This listing is based on many sources, and is largely self-explanatory in the themes; some of the themes are fairly specific. Some of these developments are reviewed in subsequent chapters.

1946: The International Convention for the Regulation of Whaling signed (Washington Convention)
1950: Paris Convention for the Protection of Birds held
1954: The International Convention for the Prevention of Pollution of the Sea by Oil signed (London Convention)
1958: Geneva Convention on Fishing and Conservation of the Living Resources of the High Seas held
1963: Vienna Convention on Civil Liability for Nuclear Damage held

1969: Brussels International Convention on Civil Liability for Oil Pollution Damage held

1972: The UN Conference on the Human Environment is convened in Stockholm; the term SD was originated here

UNEP created

The World Heritage Convention held in Paris, concerning the Protection of the World Cultural and Natural Heritage; entered into force in 1975

The Convention on the Prevention of Marine Pollution by Dumping of Wastes and other matter (or London Dumping Convention) held

1973: The International Convention for the Prevention of Pollution from Ships (MARPOL) signed in London

The Convention on International Trade in Endangered Species of Wild Fauna and Flora (CITES) held

1974: Convention on the Protection of Marine Environment of the Baltic Sea Areas (Helsinki Convention) held

Paris Convention for the Prevention of Marine Pollution from Land-based Sources held

1975: Convention on Wetlands of International Importance held

1977: The UN Conference on Desertification held at Nairobi (UNCOD)

Geneva Convention Concerning Protection of Workers against Occupational Hazards in the Working Environment Due to Air Pollution, Noise and Vibration held

1979: Bonn Convention on Conservation of Migratory Species of Animals held; entered into force in 1983

First World Climate Conference in Geneva held; warns of danger of global warming

The Convention on Long-range Transboundary Air Pollution (LRTAP) signed at Geneva

1980: The World Conservation Strategy published by UNEP, World Wide Fund for Nature and the IUCN; also formed a major milestone in the popularization of the concept of SD

1982: The UN Convention on the Law of the Sea held

1983: UN-FAO International Undertaking on Plant Genetic Resources adopted in Rome and entered into force in 1984

1984: International Tropical Timber Agreement signed in Geneva; entered into force in 1985

1985: The Helsinki Protocol to the LRTAP signed, and committed the signatories to reduce SO_2 emissions

The Vienna Convention for the Protection of Ozone Layer signed

The Rome International Code of Conduct on the Distribution and Use of Pesticides devised

1986: Geneva Convention Concerning Safety in the Use of Asbestos held

1987: The Montreal Protocol on Substances that Deplete the Ozone Layer signed, based on the 1985 Vienna Convention

The Brundtland Report of the WCED published as *Our Common Future*

1988: The IPCC established by the World Meteorological Organization (WMO) and UNEP

Sofia Protocol concerning the Control of Emissions of Nitrogen Oxides or their Transboundary Fluxes signed

Convention on the Regulation on Antarctic Mineral Resources held

1989: The Basel Convention on the Control of Transboundary Movements of Hazardous Wastes and Their Disposal signed

The UN General Assembly passed a resolution for holding the UNCED in Brazil in June 1992

1990: The GEF became operational

The first report of the IPCC published

1991: Geneva Protocol concerning the Control of Emissions of Volatile Organic Compounds for Their Transboundary Fluxes signed

1992: The Rio de Janeiro Conference (UNCED), also called The Earth Summit; Agenda 21 – a declaration of broad ecological, economic, and environmental principles adopted by more than 178 countries

The UNFCCC held

1993: London Dumping Convention to Ban Nuclear Waste Disposal in Oceans

UN CSD formed

The Convention on Biological Diversity took effect on December 29

1994: The UNFCCC became effective on March 21

The ICPD held in Cairo

Global Conference on the Sustainable Development of Small Island Developing States held in Bridgetown, Barbados

UN Convention on Desertification held (entered into force December 26, 1996)

1995: UNIPF set up

The Berlin Climate Summit (also called the First Conference of the Parties (COP) to the Rio Convention) held

World Summit for Social Development held in Copenhagen

Fourth World Conference on Women held in Beijing

The Second Assessment Report of the IPCC released, and concluded the existence of "discernible human influence on global climate"

1996: World Food Summit held in Rome

The Geneva Climate Summit (also called the Second Conference of the Parties to the Rio Convention) held

1997: Five years after Rio de Janeiro Review, ESPF held at the Special Session of the UN General Assembly to review and appraise the Implementation of Agenda 21

Kyoto Protocol on GHG emissions worked out

1998: Buenos Aires Agreement on GHG regimes reached.

Major International Environmental Agreements

The following agreements were made during 1972–98 (in addition to the Agenda 21 of the Earth Summit of 1992 and the Kyoto Protocol of 1997).

Water Pollution

- Convention on the Prevention of Marine Pollution by Dumping of Wastes and Other Matter (the London Convention), December 29, 1972 (amended 1993); entered into force September 30, 1975.
- IMO International Convention for the Prevention of Pollution from Ships (the MARPOL Convention), November 2, 1973; entered into force October 2, 1983.
- Montreal Guidelines for the Protection of the Marine Environment against Pollution from Land-Based Sources, April 19, 1985.
- International Convention on Oil Pollution Preparedness, Response and Co-operation, November 29, 1990 (not yet in force).

Air Pollution

- Convention on Long-range Transboundary Air Pollution, November 13, 1979; entered into force March 16, 1983, supplemented by a protocol on sulfur emissions (July 8, 1985), one on emissions of nitrogen oxides (October 31, 1988) and one on the control of emissions of volatile organic compounds or their transboundary fluxes (November 18, 1991).
- Vienna Convention for the Protection of the Ozone Layer, March 22, 1985; entered into force September 22, 1988.
- Framework Convention on Climate Change (UNFCCC), May 9, 1992; entered into force, March 21, 1994.

Health and Safety, Chemicals

- ILO Convention Concerning Prevention and Control of Occupational Hazards in the Working Environment Due to Air Pollution, Noise and Vibration, June 20, 1977; entered into force July 11, 1979.
- ILO Convention Concerning Occupational Safety and Health and the Working Environment, June 22, 1981; entered into force August 11, 1983.
- Convention on Transboundary Impacts of Industrial Accidents, March 6, 1992.
- FAO International Code of Conduct on the Distribution and Use of Pesticides; adopted by the 23rd FAO Conference on 19 November 1985 (amended 1989).
- UNEP London Guidelines for the Exchange of Information on Chemicals in International Trade; adopted by UNEP Governing Council Decision on June 17, 1987 (amended 1989).
- ILO Convention Concerning Safety in the Use of Chemicals at Work, June 25, 1990; entered into force November 4, 1994.
- UN Chemical Safety Treaty came into force in May 97.
- Rotterdam Convention on Hazardous Chemicals Trade held in 1998.

Hazardous Waste Management

- UNEP Cairo Guidelines and Principles for the Environmentally Sound Management of Hazardous Wastes, June 17, 1987.

- Basel Convention on the Control of Transboundary Movements of Hazardous Wastes and their Disposal, March 22, 1989 (effective May 5, 1992).
- Bamako Convention on the Ban of the Import into Africa and the Control of Transboundary Movements and Management of Hazardous Wastes within Africa, January 30, 1991 (not yet in force).

For sources, see especially Bryner (1997), Kimball (1992), Caldwell (1990), Fridtjof Nansen Institute (1996), Hempel (1996), UNEP (1995), and the web site www.un.org/Depts/Treaty.

Review Exercises

1 Discuss the set of social principles in terms of their possible impact on economic principles, as set out in Agenda 21.
2 Interpret the equitable fulfillment of "the right to development" (Principle 3 of Agenda 21), viewed from the perspectives of: (a) nations; (b) regions within nations; and (c) sections of the society categorized in terms of poor and other individuals. Is this right to be seen only in terms of the needs of present and future generations? Which of the other elements (if any) of the economic principles provide an additional insight into this issue?
3 Discuss the role and limitations of the "tragedy of commons" in the context of environmental resource management.
4 From the chronology given in the Appendix to this chapter, list the events and agreements which aim to protect biological species other than humans. Are these simply altruistic and ethical issues, or is there an economic issue involved? (This may be assessed in conjunction with the contents of chapter 2, but this issue is posed here to start the process of reflecting on some of the relevant dimensions of environmental management and development.)
5 Examine the significance of the arguments of Malthus, Marx, and Marshall in their expressed concern for one form or other of sustained economic development, and their identification of the limiting factors. Also, examine the explicit and implicit roles of their value preferences and the underlying institutional assumptions.

References

Bryner, G. C. (1997) *From Promise to Performance – Achieving Global Environmental Goals.* New York: W. W. Norton, 20–2.
Caldwell, L. K. (1990) *International Environmental Policy – Emergence and Dimensions.* Durham, NC: Duke University Press, 349–51.
Carson, R. (1962) *Silent Spring.* Boston: Houghton Mifflin Co.
Connolly, B. and Keohane, R. O. (1996) Institutions for environmental aid-politics, lessons and opportunities. *Environment*, 38(5), 41.
de Steiguer, J. E. (1997) *The Age of Environmentalism.* New York: McGraw-Hill.
Ehrlich, P. R. and Roughgarden, J. (1987) *The Science of Ecology.* New York: Macmillan.
Farman, J. C., Gardner, B. G., and Shanklin, J. D. (1985) Large losses of total ozone in Antarctica reveal seasonal C10x/NOx interaction. *Nature*, 315, 207–10.

Fridtjof Nansen Institute (1996) *Green Globe Yearbook of International Cooperation on Environment and Development*. New York: Oxford University Press.

Gore, A. (1991) *Earth in the Balance*. Boston: Houghton Mifflin Co.

Gottlieb, R. S. (ed.) (1996) *This Sacred Earth – Religion, Nature, Environment*. New York: Routledge.

Hardin, G. (1968) The tragedy of the commons. *Science*, 162, 1243–8.

Harman, W. (1979) *An Incomplete Guide to the Future*. New York: Norton & Co.

Hempel, L. (1996) *Environmental Governance – The Global Challenge*. Washington, DC: Island Press, 170–2.

Johnston, C. (1998) *The Wealth or Health of Nations*. Cleveland, OH: The Pilgrim Press.

Kimball, L. A. (1992) *Forging International Agreements*. Washington, DC: World Resources Institute, 75–6.

Lang, H. (1995) Compliance-control in respect of the Montreal protocol. In *Structures of World Order, Proceedings of the 89th Annual Meeting of the American Society of International Law, New York, April 1995*, 206–24.

Leopold, A. (1949) *Sand County Almanac*. New York: Oxford University Press.

Maass, A. and Anderson, R. (1978) *And the Desert Shall Rejoice – Conflict, Growth, and Justice in Arid Environments*. Cambridge, Mass.: MIT Press.

Malthus, T. R. (1798) *An Essay on the Principle of Population*. New York: Modern Library. Published in 1960.

Marsh, G. P. (1864) *Man and Nature – or Physical Geography as Modified by Human Action*. New York: Charles Scribner.

Marshall, A. (1925) *Principles of Economics*. London: Macmillan.

McCormick, J. (1991) *Reclaiming Paradise – The Global Environmental Movement*. Bloomington: Indiana University Press.

Meadows, D. H., Meadows, D. L., and Randers, J. (1992) *Beyond the Limits – Global Collapse or a Sustainable Future*. London: Earthscan Publications.

Meadows, D. H., Richardson, J., and Bruckmann, G. (1982) *Groping in the Dark – The First Decade of Global Modeling*. New York: John Wiley.

Meadows, D. H., Meadows, D. L., Randers, J., and Behrens, W. (1972) *The Limits to Growth – A Report to the Club of Rome*. New York: Universe Books.

Mill, J. S. (1848) *Principles of Political Economy*. Clifton, NJ: A. M. Kelley. Published in 1973; edited by W. Ashley.

Myers, N. (1995) Environmental Unknowns. *Science*, 269, 358–60.

Nester, W. R. (1997) *The War for America's Natural Resources*. New York: St. Martin's Press.

Page, T. (1997) On the problem of achieving efficiency and equity – intergenerationally. *Land Economics*, 73(4), 580–96.

Pinchot, G. (1910) *The Fight for Conservation*. New York: Harcourt Brace.

Rao, P. K. (1988) Planning and financing water resource development in the US. *American Journal of Economics and Sociology*, 43(1), 81–96.

Rowland, F. S. (1989) Chlorofluorocarbons and the depletion of stratospheric ozone. *American Science*, 77, 42–4.

Shabecoff, P. (1996) *A New Name for Peace – International Environmentalism, Sustainable Development, and Democracy*. Hanover: University Press of New England.

Singh, S. P., Rawat, Y. S. and Garkoti, S. C. (1997) Failure of brown oak (*quercus semecarpifolia*) to regenerate in Central Himalaya – a case for environmental semisurprise. *Current Science*, 73, 371–4.

Susskind, L. E. (1994) *Environmental Diplomacy*. New York: Oxford University Press.

UN (1997) *UN Information*. April 1997.

UNEP (1995) Major international environmental agreements relevant to industry 1972–1995. *Industry and Environment*, 18(4), December 1995.

US President's Council on Sustainable Development (1996) *Sustainable America – A New Consensus*. Washington, DC: US Government Printing Office.

US Task Force (1995) *The Ecosystem Approach – Healthy Ecosystems and Sustainable Economies*, vol. 1. Washington, DC: Interagency Task Force.

Vitousek, P. M. and Lubchenco, J. (1995) Limits to sustainable use of resources – from local effects to global change. In M. Munasinghe and S. Shearer (eds), *Defining and Measuring Sustainability*. Washington, DC: UN University and the World Bank, 57–64.

von Neumann, J. (1955) Can we survive technology? *Fortune* (June). Reprinted in Sprout and Sprout (eds) (1962) *Foundations of International Politics*. New York: Van Nostrand Reinhold, 248.

Wheeler, R. H. (1946) Climate and human behavior. In *The Encyclopedia of Psychology*. New York Philosophical Library Inc. Reprinted in Sprout and Sprout (eds) (1962), *Foundations of International Politics*. New York: Van Nostrand Reinhold, 347–9.

chapter outline

● CHAPTER 2 ●

Resources and the Environment

Resources and the Environment

Respect for life and for the dignity of the human
person extends also to the rest of creation, which
is called to join man in praising God.
Pope John Paul II

● 2.1 INTRODUCTION ●

The dynamics of changes in the availability of resources (renewable or non-renewable) affect economic and environmental sustainability. Besides, the production and consumption processes lead to most of the environmental problems, and usually, these problems and their effects are not confined to their sources of origin alone. In addition, some problems, like the emissions and concentrations of the greenhouse gases (GHGs), tend to affect the resilience of the ecological systems. These, in turn, adversely affect the resilience of the economic systems as well. The potential loss of resilience of the ecological systems is of paramount importance in the study of sustainable development (SD). Formal explanations of these features are discussed in chapter 3. The key factors with visible signs are the destabilization of sources of supply of natural capital, including the alteration of productive capacities of sources and sinks which affect the provision of nature's services. This chapter deals with a set of priority issues in this context, including constraints on sources and sinks in their continued potential to provide undiminished services with "efficient" functioning of the ecosystems, the role of rising human population on the stresses affecting the equilibrium of ecosystems, and emerging trends in the natural resource and critical environmental features.

An overview of relatively recent changes in features governing planet Earth's resources, including environmental goods and "ills" (the latter to comprise pollution and waste as well as all other environmental disamenities) is useful. This chapter summarizes significant changes over time:

- The natural resource availability and features of sources of life, namely water, land, forest and biological resources.
- Carrying capacity (CC) – explained below – of the planet.
- Changes affecting sink capacity, namely ozone depletion (GHGs) and pollutant features.

Anthropogenic contributions to these changes are of major interest in these descriptions. Changes and deterioration in forest resources, extinction of biological species, changes in land use, loss of land quality including desertification, and perspectives on water resource availability (quantity and quality) are some of the major areas of concern. Most of these form the sources for sustenance of life. Similarly, the dynamics of ozone-depleting substances like the chlorofluoro-carbons (CFCs), and the role of institutional policies affecting these, are relevant. The role of the human population factor in the process of SD is also very important, and this aspect is deliberated later in this chapter.

A number of policy initiatives have been launched during the past decade at national and international levels to address some of the problems of resource depletion and environmental deterioration. The UN Convention to Combat Desertification, the UN Convention on Biological Diversity, and the Montreal Protocol on Ozone Depletion are among the most significant international initiatives addressing some of the concerns of the unwelcome changes in environmental resources. Most of the mitigating measures, the economics of the problems, and their potential solutions are detailed in subsequent chapters. The discussions in this chapter are expected to furnish the relevant background regarding the underlying environmental features for further analysis.

● 2.2 SOURCE AND SINK PROBLEMS ●

Planet Earth's capacity to supply various resources tends to be fixed in physical terms, as in the case of non-renewable resources, and we should also note that the planet has a finite mass. In addition, the availability of resources is effectively fixed due to relative enhanced costs of resource appropriation, as in some mining of metals, or even groundwater, if proper conjunctive use or rainfall do not apply. There are several areas of concern for the possible diminution in the effective supply of sources for the support of life on Earth; some of these are deliberated later in this chapter. Similarly, the sinks – which provide the function of assimilation of wastes and the renewal of environmental assets for uninterrupted supply of nature's services – tend to be choked to such an extent that the accumulation of environmental "ills" leads to other major biogeophysical effects. These are discussed later in this chapter, as well as in chapters 3 and 5.

The complexity of source and sink problems as impediments to ecological sustainability can be better appreciated if we recognize that these impose limitations on the planet's CC. This CC is defined as the maximum potential to support life for ever on this planet without jeopardizing any major facets. The CC is a dynamic function of various resources, transformation methods, and outputs. The roles of human and other disturbances, adaptation and evolutionary mechanisms, and technical innovations remain contributory factors in the changing levels of the CC. Clearly, CC is affected by the quality of nature and its assets. The latter affect nature's ability to provide life-supporting services, including the supply of the environmental resources, as well as assimilation of wastes and pollution. Most of the proposed definitions of the CC have been advanced by ecologists and these do not explicitly refer to the time horizon under reference.

The CC tends to be adversely affected by the impact of cumulative environmental effects (Rees, 1995): the additions of cumulative environmental effects of a persistent causal agent over time, or by several similar agents or activities at a given time juncture. Here, it must be observed that the additivity does not imply the absence of nonlinear interactive effects that accentuate the adverse environmental effects; some of these, in the case of the greenhouse effect (GE), are illustrated below. The capacity of global sinks to assimilate environmental ills is also a form of natural capital which should be protected and "development that would add to the aggregate pollution load imposed on the ecologically critical sinks may well be uneconomic in a total social cost framework" (Rees, 1995). Thus, in essence, CC is integrally linked to SD and is a dynamic concept – as in the case of the flux of nature. The dynamics of anthropogenic influences (including endogenous tastes discussed in chapter 3) play a major role in affecting the CC. A formal analytical definition of the CC would seek explicitly to recognize the objective function (maximal sustainable size of population) subject to the dynamics of economy–ecology, and to specify the time horizon (whether infinity, i.e. for ever, or a foreseeable time period like a thousand years), as well as specify meaningful constraints or stipulations (like perceived levels of the planet's sink capacities for the GHGs) sought to be maintained. The sensitivity of the CC with respect to each of these is very significant. For instance, in respect of the last feature, if certain food habits of humans are amenable for major change (say reducing the consumption of meat-based products), the CC could be much higher.

The role of sources and sinks is perhaps the single most important fundamental characteristic underlying the dynamics of nature, its resilience, and the CC of the planet. Let us recall that ecosystem resilience may be broadly expressed in terms of its ability to return to a normal equilibrium configuration after any small disturbance. When this does not happen, i.e. when the self-renewing and absorptive capacities are severely constrained, the loss of resilience could pose serious problems including discontinuities with catastrophic consequences. This is the context in which the source and sink features directly face the potential problems of loss of system resilience and hence of SD. Any discontinuous change in ecosystem functions leads the system to flip from one equilibrium to another, and to a possible sudden loss of biological productivity. This diminishes the potential CC, and it may also imply an irreversible change in the set of options open to both present and future generations. Examples include soil erosion, depletion of groundwater reservoirs, desertification, and loss of biodiversity; see also Arrow et al. (1995).

Much of the debate on environmental management and SD tends to deal with issues of environmental degradation and natural resource depletion. The scarcity values of environment and resources are better understood in terms of apparent finiteness and increasing scarcity of many of the individual components of the systems. It is also important to realize that many of the current problems affecting environment and development are critically linked to the self-renewing or regenerative and absorptive capacities of the biosphere, geosphere and ecological system. Thus, the problems of atmospheric and biogeophysical regenerativeness are adversely affected by the recyclability of various ingredients of environmental ills like atmospheric pollution, GHGs, water pollution and solid wastes. These continued problems could pose a major obstacle for continued survival of humanity, even if there are sufficient quantities of non-renewable natural resources to sustain the ever-increasing demand for these resources.

The ecosystem discontinuities and irreversibilities of changes (as explained in chapter 3) affect the source and sink problems of the planet adversely and significantly. The costs cannot be easily estimated. The criticality of the limits affecting these phenomena need to be viewed in terms of the symptomatic evidence diagnosed so far. Clearly, there are several unclear and undiagnosed processes which require identification via additional research investigations.

The focus on constraints affecting SD has shifted from "source" limits to "sink" limits since the 1970s. Some limits are more amenable to substitution and more localized than others, as in case of alternate sources of energy in some regions. Some features are tractable and are being tackled, such as phasing out the CFCs under the Montreal Convention and its follow-up actions; see details in later sections. The key limit, however, is expected to be the sink constraint based on fossil-energy use and loss of carbon sequestration potential due to increasing deforestation. The sink capacity utilization features have much to do with the free rider nature of open access to the common pool. Behaviorally, lack of any semblance of property rights by any segment of the society or institutions in this setting allows open access and the adverse consequences.

There are finite limits in human biomass appropriation. An important finding in this direction was provided by Vitousek et al. (1986): the human enterprise uses, directly or indirectly, about 40 percent of the net primary product (NPP) – see chapter 3 – of terrestrial photosynthesis, although this figure drops to 25 percent if the oceans and other aquatic ecosystems are included. This implies that a doubling of the world's population (which may occur around the end of the twenty-first century) will use about 80 percent of the NPP. However, it must be noted that low energy-use scenarios, like less reliance on meats, could reduce the pressures on the demand for resources in the food chain. Such mechanisms could offset the rise in the pressures of population, but some societies consider that a major cost to forbear.

Broadly stated, some of the features of environmental unsustainability include the trends in global warming (see chapter 5), ozone depletion, deforestation, desertification, and extinction of biological species. Some of the environmental ills include the emissions and concentrations of the GHGs, mainly carbon dioxide (CO_2), nitrous oxide (N_2O), methane (CH_4), CFCs, hydrofluorocarbons (HFCs), and ozone (O_3); ozone depletion; acidification and toxic pollutions primarily resulting from the emissions of sulfur dioxide (SO_2), nitrogen oxide (NO_x), O_3, and particulate metals like lead. Let us note that an unsustainable system is one which possesses features which could not be maintained forever in the absence of significant interventions – whether by nature, or humans, or both.

The GHGs have very diverse sources, sinks, and chemical renewal cycles through the atmosphere, oceans, and the biosphere. Table 2.1 offers a summary of sources and sinks for the main GHGs. The sources of these gases include the combustion of fossil fuel, the burning of global biomass – trees, vegetation, and grasslands – and biogenic production like nitrification and industrial activities. The sinks of these gases include forests and vegetation, physical absorption in the oceans, and chemical decay and transformation within the atmosphere. The World Meteorological Organization (WMO) and the United Nations Environment Programme (UNEP) constituted the Intergovernmental Panel on Climate Change (IPCC). In one of its first reports, the IPCC in 1990 stated that the emissions resulting from human activities are substantially increasing the atmospheric concentrations of the GHGs (IPCC, 1990): CO_2, CH_4, CFCs, and N_2O. It was believed that these increases will enhance the GE, resulting in an additional warming of the Earth's surface and that water vapor will increase in response to global warming and further enhance it. It was estimated that CO_2 has been responsible for

Table 2.1 Sources and sinks for GHGs

	Sources	Sinks
CO_2	Fossil fuel combustion*	Ocean vegetations
	Biomass combustion*	Soil
	Soil tillage*	Forests**
	Industrial production*	
	Logging and deforestation*	Vegetation**
	Volcanoes	
Methane	Rice paddies*	Oxidation in atmosphere and soil
	Ruminant animals*	
	Fossil fuel production*	
	Landfills*	
	Land-use changes*	
	Wetlands	
Nitrous oxide	Fossil fuel combustion*	Conversion to molecular nitrogen
	Biomass combustion*	
	Agriculture and fertilizer use*	
	Soil bacteria	

Notes: * A source wholly or partially anthropogenic
        ** Human behavior affects this sink, especially forestry
Source: Adapted and modified from Watson et al. (1992), and Houghton et al. (1990)

over half the enhanced GE and is likely to remain so in the future, and that the atmospheric concentrations of the long-lived gases (CO_2, NO_x, and the CFCs) adjust only slowly to changes in emissions.

The IPCC report also stated that, given the current status of knowledge, there are many uncertainties in the predictions regarding the timing, magnitude, and regional patterns of climate change. In fact, the possibility of global warming was predicted more than a century ago by Svante Arrhenius (1896), but this was largely ignored until about the 1990s. The IPCC released its First Assessment Report in 1992, and the Second Assessment Report in 1996. The latter report reaffirms IPCC's original estimate of sensitivity of the global atmosphere to increasing GHG levels. It predicts that global temperatures will rise between 1.5°C and 4.0°C if the atmospheric concentration of CO_2 doubles from its present level (of 280 parts per million by volume). The IPCC took a much firmer stand than in the past regarding the positive link between human activities and global warming. The Panel concluded that it is unlikely that the observed temperature changes over the past century (an increase in the global mean surface temperatures of between 0.3°C and 0.6°C) are entirely due to natural causes. Human-induced influence was considered a significant source of changes.

Anthropogenic increases in the concentrations of chemically reactive gases have lead to decreased tropospheric concentrations of hydroxylradical, the major oxidizing agent in the atmosphere (Thompson, 1992). The resulting decrease in the ability of the atmosphere to cleanse itself leads to an increased atmospheric residence lifetime (see chapter 5) and hence in an increased concentration of harmful methane; see also Vitousek and Lubchenco (1995).

Recent assessments of the ozone shield rupture (caused by the CFCs), global warming (contributed by several factors explained later in this chapter), and reduction in biodiversity are some of the features that point to the finite capacity of the terrestrial ecosystem as a sink. This reminds one of the resource limitations indicated several years ago by Kenneth Boulding (1964), commenting on spaceship earth. The major limitations of this spaceship do include those relating to rapid expansion of population. These issues are addressed in the next section.

● 2.3 THE POPULATION PROBLEM ●

One of the major historical contributions to the debate on population was that of Thomas Malthus in his 1798 *Essay on the Principle of Population*. It was argued that population, when unchecked, increases in a geometrical ratio whereas subsistence increases only in an arithmetical ratio and that "misery is an absolute consequence of it." In Malthusian days, subsistence was equated to food availability. This was because of widespread food shortages and famines from time to time in different parts of the world. Potential contributions of technical progress, human responsiveness to expanding populations, and other forms of adaptation were not visualized in this thesis. The world did succeed in avoiding the problems of doomsday suggested by Malthus. Evidences including declining growth rates of population contradict the predictions; the counterevidence is strong enough to reject the premise altogether. In other words, size of the population itself is unlikely to be a threat to the biogeophysical sustainability of planet Earth. It is the combination of patterns of consumption, technology and other human influences with an expanding population that concerns the economic and environmental sustainability.

Ever since the doomsday predictions of Thomas Malthus about two centuries ago, there have been strong arguments in favor of and against population control measures. One thing was surely achieved: the population factor became a standard scapegoat for leadership in many countries for their own lacuna in the uplift of the development processes, or other leadership failures. This was based on a statement of Malthus (1800) who wrote: "the real cause of the continued depression and poverty of the lower classes was the growth of population." Poverty leads to high birth rates, partly because of high infant mortality and usage of children as economic resource augmentation at the household level. The above argument is, at best, simplistic. If the objective was to draw attention to the issue, it succeeded.

Several writings suggest the interdependencies of poverty and population growth. Often, the cause and effect relationship is rather blurred. As a result, the policy prescriptions also tend to be founded on relatively limited scientific or equitable social values. In a rather recent exposition, Dasgupta (1995) concluded that "neither evidence nor analysis has yet disproved the notion that the poor . . . know . . . what is in their self-interest." He also pointed to the significant roles of factors like perceived securities of resources and incomes (including those of morbidity and mortality), civil liberties, education, and religious faiths.

Even when the natural resource availability on the planet is unaffected, per capita availability declines if the resources are not augmented. This occurs because of continual increases in the global population. Thus, on account of population growth alone, the trends in resource availability could be declining and are usually unfavorable to the existing stock of humans. The role of growth and changes in consumption, realized by population growth, improved incomes for some sections of the society and technological changes, is a major force in the state of the utilization of natural and environmental resources. If population peaks and stabilizes by the middle of the twenty-second century, as projected in some of the studies – see, for example UN (1998) – the Earth's CC will be more a function of affluence and technology, or consumption and resource-use efficiencies. In a stabilized population case, the $I = PAT$ equation (see chapter 3) governing the environmental impact reduces to $I = cAT$, where c is a constant based on a stable population (and its demographic features), A represents the economic factors including the levels of affluence, and T denotes the technological configurations of the economic systems.

Current annual growth rate of population at the end of the twentieth century is about 1.48, compared to about 2.7 in 1985 and 3.7 in 1950. In absolute numbers of increases, the annual increment of population rose steadily from 47 million in 1950 to about 81 million in 1995. Compared to a population size of about 2.5 billion in 1950, the estimate rose to about 6 billion by the year 2000. The population stabilization (i.e. net increment levels at zero, or, births equal deaths) was expected to be achieved around the level of 11 billion by the year 2050, according to a previous UN (1996) report. However, recent declining trends in fertility rates during the 1990s are considered hopeful signs of a stabilizing population. The UN (1998) report estimates that, as a result of this fertility decline, the world population is most likely (in the medium-fertility scenario) to grow from 5.7 billion in 1995 to 9.4 billion in 2050, to 10.4 billion in 2100 and to 10.8 billion by 2150. The proportion of persons aged over 60 years is projected to increase from 10 percent to 31 percent during the period 1995–2150. Needless to say, the expanding population continues to exert added stress on the ecological and economic resources.

A simple rule of thumb to assess the time horizon for doubling of population is

$$\text{doubling time (in years)} = \frac{69.3}{R}$$

where R is the annual growth of population; see Cohen (1996) for details.

Thus, it takes 27.7 years to double a given size of population when the annual growth rate is 2.5 percent; it takes 46.2 years at the corresponding growth of 1.5.

How many people can planet Earth support? Cohen (1996) sought to find a set of answers, depending on the assumptions about the CC and anthropogenic influences affecting the planet. The most likely range is estimated to stay between 20 and 40 billion. It does not appear there is any need for alarm if the current trends in population rise are any indication of the future, since the potential stable population will be much less than this range. The important question for SD is: within such a tolerable range, what will a given size of population do with the sources and sinks of the planet and its resilience? Explanations of this will provide informative answers to the main issue. Population size by itself is not a desirable end, although limiting rapid expansion is desirable for a host of reasons. The latter needs to be viewed as a by-product of humane development processes, rather than a mechanistic target-based attainment. For example, measures which reduce infant mortality contribute to reduction in crude birth rate in addition to enhancement of human welfare. Similarly, measures which enhance the status of women and their education lead to reduced birth rates and stabilization of population. The aim should be to influence the changes in the options men and women exercise in their "reasoned choices" to lower their fertility rates; see also Dasgupta (1998). It is also important to note that sudden deceleration in the growth rate of population can only adversely affect the age demographics, and affect the productivity and equity aspects when a small section of population may have to support the majority in the senior age groups (not necessarily in the working age). In essence, human capital and ecological capital are the critical determinants of sustained economic progress and SD.

To summarize, expanding population remains an area of concern in the context of SD. However, a narrow perspective on population control is neither desirable nor feasible. In the medium term and the long term, reduction of poverty and socioeconomic inequalities, enhancement of human capital (education and health), and enhanced empowerment of women in their fertility choices and other rights will pave the way for appropriate stabilization of human population. Some of these issues are addressed in chapter 7. The emerging features affecting natural resources and environmental systems are given in the next two sections.

● 2.4 NATURAL RESOURCES ●

Both renewable and non-renewable resources constitute natural resources. Resource exploitation governed by market and nonmarket factors needs to ensure that these resources are sustainably exploited, and that these are productively and equitably deployed. An environmental dimension of utilization of coal and other fossil fuels should also address the impact of such resource production and consumption on the economy and sustainability of the environment.

The energy sector tends to be a critical ingredient in problems like GHGs and the consequential global warming, as detailed in chapter 5. This sector derives its strength from mineral resources like coal, oil and other fossil fuels – the principal agents of emissions of pollutants like carbon monoxide (CO) and CO_2. Thus, the input–output processes of the technologies and economies involved directly affect the features governing the sources and sinks of resources of the planet. The relative shares of major countries in these phenomena are detailed in chapter 5 and relevant sections of other chapters. Changes in land resources, deforestation, and soil degradation combine to affect the planet's resource base and sink capacity in several ways. In terms of human health and well-being, there are no two more important elements than air and water. The trends in changes of air quality are largely localized in nature, like urban smog and air pollution in several locations including big cities like Bangkok, Mexico City, and New Delhi. Air includes the quality of air in the lower atmosphere as well as the mix with other GHGs; see chapters 5, 7 and 11. The issues involving water resources are summarized below, followed by a description of the salient features on forestry, fisheries and biodiversity. A technical analysis of the interdependencies of 14 prominent physical indicators of the environment led to the conclusion that the four most important ones are water, biodiversity, air, and land; see Yu et al. (1998). The remainder of this chapter addresses these features, except air (which is discussed later).

Water Resources

Historically, the rise and fall of civilizations and their economic prosperity has been very strongly linked to access to water and its utilization. Most known civilizations flourished initially along rivers like the Nile and the Indus. Also, several areas have lost their economic base as a result of excessive exploitation, leading to soil degradation and desertification (Rao, 1988). This phenomenon is standing evidence of irreversible environmental damage caused by unsustainable use of natural resources. It may also be interpreted as a direct consequence of exceeding the sink capacity in a relatively local sense. Water use is not conjunctively and judiciously managed, groundwater and soil quality are degraded, and there is persistent abuse of land and water resources exacerbating congestion of the local sink, i.e. soil rejuvenation capacity and groundwater recharge capacity are exceeded continually over time.

Nature may not have a way of allocating more in proportion to growing populations. Thus, the dynamics of aggregate water availability in different regions of the world indicate systematic decline in per capita terms. Shiklomanov (1993) estimated the following quantities of past and future availability (in 1,000 cubic meters per year per capita):

- Africa – the decline will be from 20.6 in 1950 to 5.1 in 2000.
- Asia – from 9.6 to 3.3.
- Australia and Oceania – from 112 to 50.
- Europe – from 5.9 to 4.1.
- North America – from 37.2 to 17.5.
- South America – from 105 to 28.3.

These estimates suggest greater declines in Asia, Africa, and South America where not only the quantity but also the quality problem of drinking water and sanitation is very significant. Access to safe drinking water remains an area of major concern, especially in these regions where the problem is one of basic survival and a major health concern due to high incidence of water-borne diseases.

About 45 countries are expected to face severe water stress in the years ahead; others tend to have better aggregate availability of quantities of water, but not necessarily the desired quality, nor in every location of the country. The set of countries with projected annual renewable water availability of less than 1,000 cubic meters per capita per year, by the year 2050, are: Afghanistan, Algeria, Bahrain, Barbados, Burkina Faso, Burundi, Cape Verde, Comoros, Cyprus, Djibouti, Egypt, Ethiopia, Ghana, Haiti, Iran, Israel, Jordan, Kenya, Kuwait, Lebanon, Lesotho, Libya, Madagascar, Malawi, Malta, Morocco, Mozambique, Nigeria, Oman, Peru, Qatar, Republic of Korea, Rwanda, Saudi Arabia, Singapore, Somalia, South Africa, Syria, Tanzania, Togo, Tunisia, Uganda, United Arab Emirates, Yemen, and Zimbabwe (Engleman and LeRoy, 1995).

In many developing countries, water supplies are dependent on the ability to control contaminations of river water and groundwater caused by industrial emissions and agricultural, as well as urban, run-off. Future access to usable water resources is partly linked to preventive and curative aspects of water quality control. The demand for water resources increases due to demographic as well as economic factors. Increased industrialization in the developing world enhances the demand for industrial water, as does the expansion of agricultural use of land for enhanced irrigation. The consumptive use of water, defined as the net withdrawal after adjusting for quality and quantity in the return flow after use, is expected to depict increasing trends in aggregative and per capita terms over the years. Thus, the conflicting demands on water are expected to be greater in most regions over the years. Any effects of global warming can only adversely affect these features, especially in the water stress areas and countries.

According to the UN (1997b) report, water use has been growing at more than twice the rate of the population increase during the twentieth century; by 2025, as much as two-thirds of the world population will be under water stress conditions, relative to about one-third in the mid-1990s. During the same period, the world population is expected to grow from 5.7 billion to over 8 billion. Relative to other regions, more rapid growth of population is expected in urban areas (thanks to inadequate attention to regional planning and land-use methods) which already are under water stress; and industrial water demand is expected to more than double. Combined with increased water quality problems, these features suggest an unsustainable trend in the water balances for most areas of the world.

Forest Resources

Forest resources are the most critical for the sustainability of life on the planet. These resources offer natural habitats for other biological resources – animal and plant life. Human life is unlikely to remain sustainable without these, because of the ecological, meteorological (including flood control and watershed functions) and environmental interdependence (including the mechanism of carbon sequestration, important to regulate GEs), health-related values (including the function as a "genetic library") as well as economic linkages with the forest resources; additional details are described in Myers (1997). Despite such paramount significance, one of the most serious depletion of resources occurring on a continuing unsustainable pace on the planet is the devastation of forest resources. An economic view would suggest the role of missing markets and institutions, in addition to the failure of the existing markets to ensure efficient exploitation of natural resources in this context.

The Food and Agriculture Organization's *State of the World's Forests* (FAO, 1997a) presents detailed information on the emerging features of the forests and related features. It was estimated that the area of the world's forests (including natural forests and plantations) was about 3.454 billion hectares in 1995. About half of this area was located in the developing countries. It was also estimated that between 1990 and 1995, the net loss of forests in area was about 56.3 million hectares. It was assessed that the annual loss of natural forests during this period was lower compared to that during the decade 1980–90, and that the global consumption of wood had increased by 36 percent during the period 1970–94.

Woodfuels account for about 7 percent of the world's total energy supply during the mid-1990s, but the dependency of the developing countries on this source is significant. These countries consume about 77 percent of the total woodfuel supplies of the forests. The following assessment of wood share of total energy in select countries in the 1980s (noted here as a relatively early base-time reference) is indicative of the role of forests in energy provision, and also of likely unsustainability (Postel and Heise, 1988):

- Burkina Faso – 96 percent.
- Nepal – 94 percent.
- Malawi – 93 percent.
- Tanzania – 92 percent.
- Nigeria – 82 percent.
- Sudan – 74 percent.
- Kenya – 71 percent.
- Paraguay – 64 percent.
- Indonesia – 50 percent.

These estimates do not necessarily provide insights into the extent and intensity of resource depletion; we need also afforestation features and magnitudes of energy use in proportion to which these numbers can be understood. Estimates of net carbon emissions from forests, resulting from afforestation and deforestation, are derived from Houghton et al. (1987) and Postel and Heise (1988) for select countries in the 1980s. If the total net carbon emissions from forest operations (mainly deforestation) of about 1,659 million tons are apportioned to country-specific contributions, the break up gives the following percentages (4 or above) to specific countries:

- Brazil – 20 percent.
- Indonesia – 12 percent.
- Colombia – 7 percent.
- Ivory Coast – 6 percent.
- Thailand – 6 percent.
- Laos – 5 percent.
- Nigeria – 4 percent.

Relative to the baseline of 1980, the notable countries which possess more wooded area in 1993 than in 1980 per inhabitant are (UNDP, 1997b) Ireland, Hungary, Portugal, and Italy; the countries with no decline are the Netherlands, Belgium, UK, Luxembourg, and Germany.

Land use and deforestation features since the 1980s suggest the following (World Bank, 1997):

- The percentage crop land of land area changed during the period 1980–1994 with increases in Belarus, Cambodia, Malaysia, Rwanda, Thailand, and Uganda.
- The relative declines in the percentages were noted in Azerbaijan, Croatia, Denmark, Italy, and the Slovak Republic.

During the period 1980–90, the countries that featured the largest magnitudes of deforestation are (area in thousand km²): Brazil (36.7), Indonesia (12.1), Russian Federation (15.5), China (8.8), Bolivia (6.3), Colombia (3.7), India (3.4), Mexico (6.8), Myanmar (4.0), Paraguay (4.0), Philippines (3.2), Tanzania (4.4), USA (3.2), Zaire (7.3), and Zambia (3.6). In percentage terms, the countries with the larger magnitudes of deforestation, stated in declining magnitudes are Thailand (3.5), Philippines (3.5), Paraguay (2.8), Mexico (1.3), Myanmar (1.3), Bolivia (1.2), Tanzania (1.2), Indonesia (1.1), and Zambia (1.1). Canada was the only country that is reported to have made a net addition to forest resources.

It is useful to recognize that deforestation leads to several other major consequences: forest fragmentation and loss of habitat for the biological species – usually disproportionate to the area removed from the forest cover. Forest fragmentation leads, over time, to a variety of effects, both physical and biotic (Terborgh, 1992): species population sizes and gene pools are reduced, tree mortality worsens, and unforeseen disequilibrium features could arise. Humans are exposed to strange sets of bacteria and diseases causing problems of epidemic proportions. Ebola is considered one of such outcomes. These are some more concerns that suggest the need to preserve forests.

There are some approaches to harvesting forest products – not equal to deforestation, however, under the doctrine of "use it or lose it." The reasoning behind this proposition is that forests and related habitats can be maintained if they can be shown to provide direct value to people, especially local populations. The FAO (1997a) estimate of the trade in non-wood forest products was about $11 billion in the mid-1990s. Panayotou and Ashton (1992), among others, argued that the harvest of non-timber products from forests (including harvest of medicinal plants) could generate more revenues (Balick and Mendelsohn, 1992) than other forms of forest land use (like logging or forest conversion for agricultural or other uses of land) which are destructive of the forest resources. However, the critical issue is determining the degree of harvesting or the maximum sustainable intervention that does not lead to ecological disequilibrium. A number of scientific and socioeconomic factors need to be examined for this purpose. Some of these are discussed later.

Continued agricultural growth, which is desirable to meet the growing food requirements and to cater for the market demand, is expected to place heavy demands on land and water resources. According to an FAO study (Alexandratos, 1995), about half of the 90 million hectares that could be converted to crop land by 2010, in developing countries (excluding China) currently comprise forests. The continued demand for firewood and energy supplies, slash-and-burn methods of shift cultivation practices in parts of Southeast Asia and Latin America, wood logging and human settlements are among the factors that are expected to lead to continued deforestation; the impact could be severe, in carbon sequestration and GE (see chapter 5), and extinction of biological species and other services of nature (discussed below).

Biodiversity

Edward Wilson (1993) rightly argued that "biodiversity is the key to the maintenance of the world as we know it." It takes several hundred thousands of years to build rich ecosystems and their biodiversity. The term biodiversity did not seem to formally exist until the 1986 National Forum on Bio Diversity under the auspices of the US National Academy of Sciences and the Smithsonian Institution. Biodiversity is defined as "the genetic, taxonomic, and ecological variability among living organisms; this includes the variety and variability within species, between species, and of biotic components of ecosystems" (UNEP, 1992). It is the high diversity that ensures continuity and functioning of the ecosystem, food web and human survival (Patrick, 1997). The interdependencies of the components of the ecological system necessitate due care in maintaining biodiversity.

Biodiversity is but one major segment of ecosystem services. These services include: The conditions and processes through which natural ecosystems, and the species that make them up, sustain and fulfill human life; see Daily (1997) for details. New discoveries of medicine and of life sciences are among the most important factors relevant in the appreciation of contribution of biodiversity to human society. Let us draw upon an illustration (Lovejoy, 1997): Polymerase chain reaction (PCR) was discovered by Kary Mullis who won the 1993 Nobel Prize for Chemistry. The PCR discovery remains an important part of biotechnology and molecular biology. The phenomenon was discovered to be based on an enzyme found in a bacterium located in the hot springs of Yellowstone Park. This park area was set aside in 1872 as the world's first national park for its scenic beauty. Another example of the importance of plant life for human life can be given in the recent finding about the popular medicine Prozac and its class (Andrews, 1997). This product has a market potential in billions of dollars. Its main rival is the medicinal plant known as St John's Wort (Johanniskraut in German), which is also known by its botanical name, *hypericum perforatum*. A number of studies have tried to estimate the monetary values of medicinal plants, and to use biodiversity for pharmaceutical and medical use; see, for example, Balick et al. (1996) and Simpson et al. (1996). These estimates vary but the order of magnitude is in several billion dollars, without accounting for other uses or values of biodiversity.

Biodiversity is perhaps the most important segment of what is generally referred to as ecosystem and its management. This management integrates ecological, economic, and social factors of human and other forms of life on this planet: This is a strongly interconnected system of Earthlings, including humans. A general goal of ecosystem management is defined in the US Interagency Ecosystem Management Task Force (1995): "To restore and sustain the health, productivity, and biological diversity of ecosystems and overall quality of life through a natural resource management approach that is fully integrated with social and economic goals."

The continued productivity of food and agriculture depends vitally on the preservation of biodiversity. Cross-pollination and insect pollination is essential for the productivity of most crops. The pest control role of natural insect predators is also very significant. According to the 1995 Global Biodiversity Assessment of the UNEP:

● About 112 birds and mammal species became extinct during 1810–1995.
● During the early to mid-1980s, humid tropical rain forests were losing nearly 25 million acres (10 million hectares).

The tropical rain forests cover only 7 percent of the Earth's surface but provide about 50–80 percent of the planet's species. Estimated rates of extinction of biological species vary between sources – see, for example Mawdsley and Stork (1995) and Myers (1988) – but most converge to about 7 percent global losses per decade during the period 1980–2000. The International Council for Bird Preservation estimated that about 11 percent, amounting to 1,029, of the surviving species was endangered in the early 1990s. The destruction of physical habitats remains the major factor contributing to the decline and extinction of various species. An analytical approximation between loss of habitat and species (local) loss is explained in box 2.1.

BOX 2.1 Endemic species and habitat area

Edward Wilson (1993) posited that the increase in the number of species is governed by the area–species nonlinear equation

$$S = CA^z$$

where A is the geographic area, S is the number of species, C is a constant, and z is another biologically sensitive constant parameter (with a predicted range of 0.15–0.35) which depends on the group of organisms, and their proximity to the source of areas of the habitat. When the habitat area is reduced, the species extinction rate rises and the extinction continues until the number of species has dropped to a new lower equilibrium scenario. It was projected that if the destruction of the rain forest continues at the present rate to the year 2022, about half of the remaining rain forest could vanish, and the species loss will be in the range of 10–22 percent. These predictions are essentially those of local and not global extinction of species; see also Pimm and Askins (1995). To assess the latter, several additional items of information are required like bird migration, adaptation, and connectivity of different habitats and territories. The above formula remains a relevant method for local extinction analyses, and thus overstates the potential losses of species if used on a global scale. The most important features to note here are the nonlinear nature of losses in relation to drop in the habitat areas and the implications for forest fragmentation and the exponential nature of the relation between deforestation and loss of species.

The World Bank publication, *World Development Indicators 1998*, gives details of the number of species and threatened species, country-wise, with a break up for birds, mammals, and plants. These data are drawn mainly from the World Conservation Monitoring Center – a joint venture of the UNEP, World Wide Fund for Nature (WWF), and World Conservation Union (IUCN). Among the countries which have the largest number of threatened species of birds and mammals (with affected number given in parentheses) are: Australia (94), Brazil (148), China (277), Colombia (86), India (111), Indonesia (161), Peru (89), and Philippines (108).

Concerned with the state of declining biodiversity and the increasing dependence of life on and economic significance of biological resources, the international community launched some policy initiatives. The UN Convention on Biological Diversity became legally binding on December 29, 1993 and at the beginning of December 1996, 165 countries (including the EU) had ratified the convention. This convention was developed to conserve biological species, genetic resources, habitats and ecosystems; to ensure sustainable use of biological resources; and to provide for fair and equitable sharing of benefits of genetic resources globally, and between sources and developers of any commercial products.

Marine Fisheries

Many marine resources continue to decline at rates that are clearly unsustainable. Coral reefs are under constant threat of destruction in most locations of the world. It was estimated that about 58 percent of the reefs are at risk due to human interference. This is especially acute in the species-diverse ecosystems in the Southeast Asia region. These are in addition to serious problems of loss of fisheries resources in most of the oceanic regions, and despite the fact that overfishing was recognized as a problem of management of fishery resources even at the beginning of the twentieth century. The identified problems were originally confined to the North Atlantic and North Pacific regions. Overfishing progressed since the 1950s and the harvest already peaked out in most of the areas, especially in the Northwest Atlantic and Southeast Atlantic. Based on information since the 1970s, FAO (1997b) found that the annual growth rate in the harvest was about 7 percent, and this is no longer sustainable. The highest harvest observed in "mature fishery" represents a multi-species composite average long-term yield (ALTY) which differs from the simple sum of the maximum sustainable yields (MSYs) for the individual species. The top 200 species account for about 77 percent of the world's fish production. During the mid-1990s, about a third of these were showing declining yields, and more were still developing. This suggests that a reduction of at least 30 percent of the fishing effort was required to rebuild the resources (FAO, 1997b).

Marine fisheries constitute an important segment of the economy in several countries like Canada, Norway, and Iceland. Estimates of world marine production, based on total harvest, was about 82 million tonnes in the 1990s. It is important to note that another 27 million tonnes are discarded every year. The benefits from a reduction of these losses would, first, enhance the survival volume of juvenile fish, and, second, contribute toward sustainable harvesting of some of the species. The rising demand for fish due to an expanding human population, and the increasing shortfall in the supply depicts expected market features: rising fish prices, and thus rationing out the poorer sections of the society from their consumption baskets. This is far from conducive to equity in food consumption, considering the assessments that fish remains among the most desirable food item for nutrition and health values, and any effective denial of the poor can aggravate their malnutrition problems and the consequences.

The FAO (1997b) study suggested that sustainable harvesting is feasible if the following measures are taken:

- Rehabilitate the over-harvested and degraded regions.
- Underdeveloped areas of fishing are exploited further at an enhanced but sustainable rate.
- Discarding and wastage are significantly reduced.

Some of these cannot be effected simply by the market factors themselves, and require interventions like improved technology for collection and storage of fish. Fishermen cooperatives or similar associations might require external assistance to upgrade the technologies.

The International Conference on the Sustainable Contribution of Fisheries to Food Security, held in 1995 at Kyoto, was represented by 95 countries. These were some of the decisions made:

- Implementation of the Provisions of the UN Convention on the Law of the Sea of 1982 relating to the Conservation and Management of Straddling Fish Stocks and Highly Migratory Fish Stocks.
- Development and use of selective, environmentally safe and cost-effective fishing apparatus and techniques.
- Allocation of resources for ensuring the effectiveness of multi-species management of the commercial fishery sector.

The need to manage the oceans as common property resources with global cooperation was emphasized in the report of the Independent World Commission on the Oceans (1998), *The Ocean Our Future*, in which the threats to oceans and marine life were reassessed, and a set of major sources of pollution were included. It was estimated that, in addition to other pollutants like discarded nuclear submarines, petroleum hydrocarbons released into the oceans each year amount to about 2.5 million tons, and that this trend shows no sign of slowing, thus adversely affecting the sink's assimilative capacity. Concerted global action is thus a prerequisite for environmental sustainability of the oceans.

● 2.5 ENVIRONMENTAL FEATURES ●

A number of features in the changing environment affect human welfare directly and indirectly. The problems of sustainability and SD tend to be relatively medium-term and long-term issues of concern. This does not mean that there do not exist major problems of degradation in the environmental quality and immediate problems of human welfare. The most direct effect can be seen in terms of the problems of health in relation to environmental features. Some of the direct links between relevant ingredients of the two streams are illustrated in table 2.2, which is partly based on USEPA (1987). Various other significant environmental problems are detailed in the next subsections.

Table 2.2 Environment and health

Environmental feature	Source	Health effect
Ozone	Chemical reaction of pollutants; volatile organic compounds (VOCs) and NO_x	Breathing problems, reduced lung function, asthma, reduced resistance to infections, stress on lung tissues
Volatile organic compounds (VOCs)	Releases from burning fuel, solvents, paints, glues and other products	In addition to ozone effects, many VOCs can cause serious health problems such as cancer
Nitrogen oxide	Burning of gasoline, natural gas, coal, oil, etc.	Lung damage, illnesses of breathing passages and lungs
Carbon monoxide (CO)	Burning of gasoline, natural gas, coal, oil	Reduces ability of blood to bring oxygen to body cells and tissues; cells and tissues need oxygen to work; hazardous to people with heart or circulatory problems
Sulfur dioxide	Burning of coal and oil, especially high-sulfur coal from the eastern USA; industrial processes (paper, metals and others)	Breathing problems, damage to lungs
Lead	Leaded gasoline; paint; smelters; manufacture of lead storage batteries	Brain and other nervous system damage; children are at special risk with irreversible consequences; some lead-containing chemicals cause cancer in animals; lead causes digestive and other heath problems

Source: Partly based on USEPA (1987)

GHGs and Pollution

The most significant environmental problems involve emissions and concentrations of GHGs which are assessed to contribute to the GE and global warming (IPCC, 1996). The main component of these is CO_2 and the primary activities contributing to these emissions involve the energy sector, especially fossil fuel consumption. The *Global Environmental Outlook* series being published by the UNEP suggests these and other related trends. Figure 2.1 narrates some of the most significant linkages of economic and other factors (not necessarily mutually exclusive). In 1992, global emissions of CO_2 amounted to 26.4 billion metric tons for the year, of which 84 percent was from industrial activity (World Resources Institute, 1996). It was also estimated that emissions from the industrial activity increased 38 percent during 1972 to 1992, with the US contributing about

Figure 2.1 The greenhouse effect enhancement

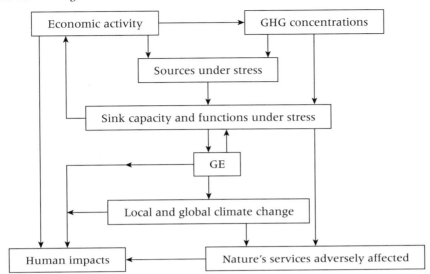

22 percent of global emissions, and a similar amount contributed by the Organization for Economic Cooperation and Development (OECD) countries. The top ten countries with the highest quantities of industrial emissions of CO_2 in 1992 were the USA, China, Russian Federation, Japan, Germany, India, Ukraine, UK, Canada, and Italy. (Table 2.4 lists the top countries and their emissions in this category.) By 2010, China and India are expected to contribute to about 50 percent of the CO_2 emissions due to industrial activities. The top ten countries with the highest per capita CO_2 emissions in 1995 were (in descending order, based on World Resources 1998–9): United Arab Emirates, Kuwait, USA, Norway, Singapore, Australia, Canada, Saudi Arabia, Russian Federation, and Kazakhstan. The top ten countries that contributed to the highest CO_2 emissions in 1995 were (emissions given in million metric tons): USA (5469), China (3192), Russian Federation (1818), Japan (1127), India (909) Germany (835), UK (542), Ukraine (438), Canada (436), and Italy (410).

A comparative indicator of gross domestic product (GDP) per unit of energy uses ($ per kg of oil equivalent) for the years 1980 and 1994 for each of the countries is given by the recent publication of the World Bank's *World Development Indicators 1998*. This source also provides comparisons of CO_2 emissions in total and per capita magnitudes for the chosen years for each of the countries. Using data from Carbon Dioxide Information Analysis Center, the World Resources 1998–9 report furnished a time-series of total global CO_2 emissions from fossil fuel consumption and cement manufacture for the period 1950 to 1995, with an analysis of attributable sources of origin: gas fuels, liquid fuels, solid fuels, cement manufacture, and gas flaring. These indicate a secular trend: these total magnitudes went up from about 6 billion metric tons in 1950 to about

23.8 billion in 1995, and have continued to rise since. The details of time trend in CO_2 emissions from fossil fuel consumption and cement manufacturing are given in table 2.3. Total CO_2 emissions, the share of each country in the world total, and hazardous waste production and waste recycling percentages for paper and glass in the early 1990s for select countries, based on the OECD sources of data, are summarized (UNDP, 1998) in table 2.4.

Table 2.3   Time trend of CO_2 emissions

Year	CO_2 emissions (million metric tons)	Cumulative total (million metric tons)
1755	11	55
1805	33	953
1855	260	5,928
1905	2,433	56,217
1930	3,935	140,111
1955	7,471	277,398
1965	11,457	372,574
1975	16,902	521,395
1985	19,800	709,959
1986	20,504	730,462
1987	20,969	751,431
1988	21,790	773,221
1989	22,178	795,399
1990	22,383	817,783
1991	22,636	840,419
1992	22,292	862,711
1993	22,178	884,889
1994	23,054	907,943
1995	23,838	931,781

Source: Carbon Dioxide Information Analysis Center

Ozone Depletion

The ozone shield stretches 10–25 miles over the Earth's surface and absorbs much of the earth's short-wave ultraviolet (UV) radiation. Any holes or thinning down of this biospheric shield is the most significant source of radiation-induced skin cancers for humans and also harm all living systems on the planet, including the mutation of deoxyribonucleic acid (DNA). Ozone is not only present in the stratosphere but also in the troposphere which is closer to Earth.

Scientists found that ozone is dynamically created with the interactions of solar radiation and atmospheric oxygen; catalytic processes involving CFCs and other gases partly counteract the creation however. Photo decomposition of the CFCs in the stratosphere produces catalysts for the destruction of ozone. The most important CFCs are CFC-11 and CFC-12. Because of the slow process of diffusion

Table 2.4 Environmental pollution – 20 industrial countries

Country	Per capita CO_2 emissions 1000 mt in 1995	Hazardous waste prod'n 1000 mt 1991–4	Percentage of population recycling paper and cardboard
Canada	14.8	5,896	33
France	5.9	7,000	38
Norway	16.7	500	41
USA	20.5	213,620	35
Iceland	6.7	6	30
Finland	10	559	57
Netherlands	8.8	1,520	77
Japan	9		51
New Zealand	7.7	110	
Sweden	5.1		54
Spain	5.8	1,708	52
Belgium	10.3	776	12
Austria	7.4	550	65
UK	9.3	1,844	35
Australia	16.2	426	50
Switzerland	5.4	854	61
Ireland	9.1	248	12
Denmark	10.5	250	44
Germany	10.2	9,100	67
Greece	7.3	450	19
Italy	7.2	2,708	29

Source: Reprinted from UNDP (1998, p. 203) with permission from Oxford University Press

into the stratosphere, the residence lifetime of the CFCs for environmental effects is of the order of about a century or more. For greater details, the collection of papers (based largely on findings in chemical sciences) in Dunnette and O'Brien (1992) constitutes a very useful reference. Less ozone in the stratosphere tends to counteract the GE, but the net effect of the opposing forces of ozone-depleting substances and UV radiation is not clear. However, what is clear is that the increase in ultraviolet B (UV-B) radiation that follows ozone depletion worsens air quality and leads to an increased number of deaths from asthma and chronic respiratory disease as well as damaging plant life; see also Nilsson (1996).

The US Environmental Protection Agency (USEPA) estimated that a 50 percent cutback in CFC emissions from 1986 levels could significantly affect the US economy: $6.4 trillion by 2075 in reduced costs associated with skin cancers alone (USEPA, 1987). Every 1 percent loss in ozone is estimated to lead to a 2 percent increase in harmful UV radiation exposure (de Gruijl, 1995).

The role and function of the stratospheric ozone layer as a cosmic protector against the UV-B radiation (which has wavelengths of sunlight rays in the range 315–280 nanometers) has been crippled due to anthropogenic contributions of concentrations of CFCs and other ozone-depleting substances like methyl chloroform, halons (used in fire extinguishers), and methyl bromide (which are generally used in chlorinated pesticides). The 1995 Nobel Prize in Chemistry was awarded to the three scientists who discovered the relevant mechanisms affecting the ozone layer. Paul Crutzen worked out the role of nitrogen oxides in the natural creation and destruction of ozone; Mario Molina and Sherwood Rowland examined the role of chlorine from CFCs in these interactions.

The CFCs are generally used as refrigerants (propane and butane), foam insulation, aerosol propellants (in air-powered spray devices), electronic goods, and degreasing solvents for cleaning. A number of major initiatives, especially the Montreal Protocol and its follow-up actions are expected to ameliorate the crisis but the possible continuity of damages to human and biotic health are not expected to disappear for another five or more decades. Various CFCs are being replaced by the substitutes hydrochlorofluorocarbons (HCFCs), HFCs, and per-fluorocarbons (PFCs). The phasing out of CFCs applies to HCFCs also, but these are allowed as interim substitutes, as agreed in the 1990 London meeting of the parties of the Montreal Protocol. Like the CFCs themselves, HCFCs and HFCs are both potent gases; during a span of one hundred years after these are injected into the atmosphere, a ton of CFC-11 tends to have about 4,000 times the global warming potential relative to one ton of CO_2, and a ton of HCFC-22 will have the effect of about 1,700 times of a ton of CO_2 (Worldwatch Institute, 1997).

According to the CDIAC (Carbon Dioxide Information Analysis Center) (quoted in World Resources 1998–9), trends in the atmospheric concentrations of CO_2 indicate an increase from 325.5 parts per million (ppm) in 1970 to 362.6 ppm in 1996. Levels of emissions and concentrations of other gases which have ozone-depleting properties have also changed for the worse. Based on the data from late 1970s, the trends indicate the following: concentrations of carbon tetra-chloride (CC14) in the atmosphere went up from 88 parts per trillion (ppt) in 1978 to 99 ppt in 1996; methyl chloroform (CH3CC13) rose from 58 ppt to 89 ppt, CFC-11 from 139 ppt to 261 ppt, CFC-12 from 257 ppt to 522 ppt, total gaseous chlorine from 1,457 ppt to 2,731 ppt, and N_2O from 298 parts per billion (ppb) to 310 ppb during this period. In case of CFC-113, the increase was from 26 ppt to 82 ppt during 1982–96, and in case of CH_4, the increase was from 1,600 ppb in 1986 to 1,670 ppb in 1996.

In terms of major international policy initiatives launched during the recent decades, it is relevant to note that the Convention for the Protection of the Ozone Layer in Vienna, which was held in March 1985, mandated the ratifiers of the convention to study the harmful effects of CFC emissions on the ozone layer, and to conduct scientific research to find substitutes. The Montreal Protocol extended the Vienna Convention provisions by setting targets and limits on the emissions of CFC-11 and CFC-12, with the provision that the other villains of the ozone-depletion process like methyl chloroform and carbon tetrachloride could be included for similar regulations later. The Montreal Protocol came into force on January 1, 1989 with the following features: the ratifiers must reduce their annual consumption and production of CFCs to their 1986 levels by July 1993; from July 1993 to June 1994 and during each year until July 1998, ratifiers' annual production and consumption of CFCs should stay below the limit of 80 percent of their 1986 levels; from July 1998 and after, the corresponding production should be limited to 50 percent of the 1986 levels. By the end of 1995, 149 countries had ratified the Protocol.

The Ozone Factor

The WMO (1986) and the UNEP (1987) reports observed that accumulations of CFC-11 and CFC-12 in the atmosphere had nearly doubled during 1975–85. The WMO/UNEP assessment predicted that continued emissions of these at the 1980 rate could reduce the ozone layer by about 9 percent on a global average by 2050. The possibility was that higher levels of harmful UV-B radiation could reach heavily populated regions of the northern hemisphere. It was also assessed that high atmospheric concentrations of chlorine could result in a potentially significant redistribution of ozone, with depletion in the upper stratosphere partially offset by increases in ozone at lower altitudes. It was also asserted that the CFCs themselves were hundreds of times more powerful than CO_2 in their capability to enhance the GE, and that these could significantly aggravate the global warming effect.

The roles of the related CFCs 113, 114 and 115 and two bromide compounds, halons 1211 and 1301, were also considered significant. All these chemicals possess long atmospheric lifetimes and high efficiency in triggering the catalytic reactions that destroy ozone. The halons had a substantially higher potency than CFCs for the destruction of the ozone layer. More may be seen in a detailed study by Benedick (1998).

The Protocol was strengthened with the 1990 London Amendments, which also expanded the list of ozone-depleting chemicals: for 1997 and the following years the levels could not exceed 15 percent of the base levels of 1986, and a complete phasing out by the year 2000 was mandated. Further enhancement of actions in this direction was sought at the Copenhagen Amendments in November 1992: the initial provision of interim substitutes for CFCs, namely HCFCs were also sought to be eliminated along with carbon tetrachloride and methyl chloroform by 1996. The most significant background for effective international collective action came from the scientific evidence in 1985 about the existence of a significant ozone hole and the analysis of factors behind it. The existence of illicit trade for some CFCs in a few countries remains an area of concern. Analytical and institutional dimensions of the Montreal protocol as a collective public goods issue were examined in Murdoch and Sandler (1997) and details on these issues are given in chapter 5.

Land Degradation and Desertification

Civilizations have drawn great strength from productive land resources. Loss of productivity through mismanagement ushered once-flourishing societies to their ruin. Soil quality deterioration and consequential loss in productivity remains very important, especially for poorer countries in their prospects for development.

One of the most pressing environmental issues in the world is desertification, given the irreversibility of damages to significant geographic areas for very long or infinite periods of time to come. Yet it appears to have received much less attention than it deserves, based on the gravity of the problem. According to UN data, desertification affects about one-third of the world's land area, and seems to obey the phenomenon of "discontinuity" described earlier. There appear serious links between climate change and desertification. The international community seems to have paid very little heed to the causes, effects and adverse roles of international credit-lending institutions in this colossal phenomenon.

Land degradation may be viewed as the process by which land loses some of its natural productivity as a result of excessive grazing, crop production activities, deforestation, waterlogging (which is usually the result of faulty irrigation practices), lack of conjunctive use of ground and surface waters, and inadequate drainage of irrigation water. Soil loss and land-quality degradation are attributable to many factors, but among the most important is water management: waterlogging and salination of soils caused by poor irrigation practices. Although the irrigation and water civilization history of the past 5000 years seems to clarify these interdependencies, the world seems to have learnt surprisingly little in this regard. Even the global institutions like the World Bank in the post-World War II era came to realize a few of these problems only after damages were inflicted in some of the developing countries (Rao, 1997). Irrigation has accounted for more than half of the increase in global food production since the mid-1960s, but about 20 percent of the irrigated land is adversely affected by continued soil degradation caused by faulty irrigation and water management (UN, 1997a, b). It is estimated that land degradation is taking place at record rates: about 6–7 million hectares are being lost annually due to soil erosion, and up to about 20 million hectares of irrigated land are affected by salinity (UNDP, 1997a). The UNEP (1997) Global Environmental Outlook estimated that about 10 percent (i.e. about 1.2 billion hectares) of the current agricultural land area is prone to soil degradation, and that water and wind erosion account for over a billion hectares of the total area degraded. These problems must also be viewed in terms of their implication on the sustainability of productivity of land, considering the projection that the global food demand is expected to increase by about 110 percent by 2050, but the agricultural area is expected to increase only by 42 percent during that period (UNEP, 1997).

Definitions

The international community seems to have had some difficulty in reaching a meaningful definition of the "desertification" phenomenon, if various attempts under the august UN bodies is any frame of reference for this purpose. The UN Conference on Desertification held at Nairobi in 1977 characterized desertification as: "The diminution or destruction of the biological potential of the land that can lead ultimately to desert-like conditions. It is an aspect of the widespread deterioration of ecosystems and has diminished or destroyed the biological potential, i.e. the plant and animal production, for multiple use purposes at a time when increased productivity is needed to support growing populations in quest of development." Later, FAO/UNEP (1984) defined desertification as:

A comprehensive expression of economic and social processes as well as those natural and induced ones which destroy the equilibrium of soil, vegetation, air and water, in the areas subject to edaphic and/or climatic aridity. Continued deterioration leads to a decrease in, or destruction of the biological potential of the land, deterioration of living conditions and an increase of desert landscape.

Subsequently, UNEP (1990) defined "desertification/land degradation" as: land degradation in arid, semi-arid and dry sub-humid areas resulting mainly from adverse human impact. However, that is not enough, and it was defined for the purposes of implementation of the 1994 UN Convention on Desertification held in Paris:

- "Desertification" means land degradation in arid, semi-arid and sub-humid areas resulting from various factors, including climatic variations and human activities.
- "Land degradation" means reduction or loss, in arid, semi-arid and dry sub-humid areas, of the biological or economic productivity and complexity of rainfed crop land, irrigated crop land, or range, pasture, forest and woodlands resulting from land uses or from a process or combination of processes, including processes arising from human activities and habitation patterns such as soil erosion caused by wind and/or water, deterioration of the physical, chemical and biological or economic properties of soil, and long-term loss of natural vegetation.

Causal Factors

The definitions of desertification adopted by the UNEP and the Earth Summit of 1992 both imply linkage between climate change and the extent of desertification. Although finding a strong relationship between climate change and desertification is a complex task, there are a few detailed studies that suggest a valid relationship between the two. Hulme and Kelly (1993) examined data provided by Tucker et al. (1991), who used a satellite index of active vegetative cover to determine the extent of the Sahara Desert, and combined the information with the climate data from the Climate Research Unit in Norwich, England. It was observed that there exists an increasing trend in the area under the desert, not explained by rainfall variations alone; deterioration of vegetative cover caused by human activity was offered as a possible influencing factor. Worldwide estimates (World Resources Institute, 1997) indicated that faulty agricultural practices account for 28 percent of the degraded soils; causes include shortening of the fallow period during shift cultivation, cultivating sloped topographic territories with inadequate soil quality control measures, overgrazing, and insufficient drainage of irrigation water.

The causes of desertification include: overgrazing, over-cultivation, misuse of irrigation water, deforestation, and the impact of urban and industrial activities.

More than 100 countries (mostly in the developing world) suffer the consequences of desertification or some form of severe land degradation. These features were estimated to result in an annual loss of productivity in about 21 million hectares, even to the point at which their use becomes totally unfeasible from an economic point of view (Rozanov, 1990). The Earth Summit of 1992 agreed (chapter 12 of Agenda 21) that projects to mitigate the phenomenon will qualify for allocation from the Global Environmental Facility (GEF), but only to the extent that the projects fulfill the goals of GEF by reducing GHG emissions, preserving biodiversity, and protecting transnational waters.

Surface air temperature has increased significantly in desertified regions owing to changes in land cover and this has substantially affected the global mean temperature. The cyclical and cumulative effects of the desertification-climate change phenomena tend to alternate when we consider the decreasing sink capacity for carbon sequestration. Balling (1991) argued that, during the twentieth century, desertified areas have warmed more than other areas; these regional segments of variations in mean-surface temperature significantly "contaminate" the global mean temperature record and complicate the search for the villains behind global warming.

In an important contribution, Daily (1995) estimated that about 43 percent of Earth's terrestrial vegetated surface has a diminished capacity to supply benefits to humanity because of recent, direct impacts of land use; this represents about a 10 percent reduction in "potential direct instrument value" (PDIV), defined as the potential to yield direct benefits such as agricultural, forestry, industrial, and medicinal products. It was also estimated that, if the current trends continue, the global loss of PDIV could double by 2020. Daily concluded that capitalizing on natural recovery mechanisms is urgently needed to prevent any further irreversible degradation and to retain the multiple perennial values of productive land. Daily's estimate of affected area adding to about 5 billion hectares is the sum of three components:

1   Areas affected by soil degradation (about 2 billion ha).
2   Drylands with vegetation degradation but no soil degradation (about 2.6 billion ha).
3   Degraded tropical moist forest lands (about 427 million ha).

Anthropogenic influences and direct effects of land-use changes are the most consequential components of global change. Change in land use alters local ecosystems substantially enough to contribute directly to increased concentrations of GHGs. These, in turn, affect local/regional climate and atmospheric chemistry. Desertification/land degradation seems to affect most the areas that can afford it the least, mostly the poorer regions, and marginalizes many societies (where the average daily per capita income is around one dollar or less). Considering the biogeophysical and socioeconomic importance of desertification problems, it is still a puzzle how the global community is negligent in this regard. It is likely that the FAO and UNEP did not succeed in convincing other institutions, and the World Bank could not find "bankable" projects for lending loans. If anything, the Bank was perhaps an indirect factor behind some of the problems; see chapter 10.

The phenomena of land degradation and desertification should be of grave concern to the national and international communities for a number of important reasons (Daily, 1995):

- Increasing crop yields and production are crucial to meeting the needs of the growing population for food, fiber, and biomass energy.
- Anthropogenic changes in land use affect biogeochemical cycles that regulate greenhouse fluxes.
- Preservation of biodiversity and the ecosystem depends on appropriate combinations of land quality and use patterns.
- Land is a limiting factor of economic output, and its degradation threatens to undermine economic development in less-developed nations and global social stability. Besides, there are no substitutes for land!

Impacts

Desertification is estimated to threaten the well-being of about 850 million people, embraces an area of about 3.5 billion ha, of which 3.1 billion ha are pasture lands, 335 million ha are rainfed croplands, and 40 million ha are irrigated agricultural lands; desertification causes about 21 million ha annually to lose their productivity, even to the point at which their use becomes totally unfeasible from an economic point of view (Rozanov, 1990).

Soil erosion constitutes an important threat to sustainable agricultural production. Viewed from another angle, it also constitutes a potential opportunity to devise and implement more integrated approaches which can cater for preventive measures and also meet other demands:

- Development of watershed management and raising vegetation to provide natural nutrients to the soil.
- Reducing deployment of excessive fertilizers, leading to nitrification of agricultural lands.
- Reducing harmful pesticide use leading to on-farm and off-farm damages and agricultural water pollution.
- Contributing toward less concentrated regional and sectoral development patterns with a sustained dispersal of productive lands.

Oldeman et al. (1990), using data from the UN FAO calculated that, globally, about 1,965 million ha (constituting 22 percent of the total of 8,735 million ha under crops and permanent pasture or maintained as forest and woodland) were degraded in varying degrees: wind and water erosion accounted for 85 percent of the degradation, and loss of soil nutrients, salinization, and physical neglect of the top soil accounted for the remaining 15 percent. Crosson (1997) estimated that the average annual rate of the loss of 0.1 percent of agricultural production is attributable to erosion problems.

According to one estimate (Pimentel et al., 1995), the direct costs of soil erosion, as measured by the cost of replacing lost water and nutrients on agricultural land, amount to an estimated $250 billion per year globally. An additional cost of about $150 billion per annum is incurred in the form of off-site damages to recreation, health, property, water storage, and conveyance, etc. In the USA alone, these on-site and off-site costs amount to $44 billion per year, whereas the control measures would cost only $8.4 billion per year for crop rotation, terracing and contour planting, etc. The UNEP (1991) study estimated the total direct on-site income foregone as a result of desertification in arid regions at $42.3 billion per year, and the direct cost of all preventive and rehabilitational measures could be $10–$22.4 billion per year. Despite several shortcomings in the estimation methods, these tend to offer some approximations of the magnitudes of damages involved.

One of the early estimates of the annual loss due to desertification was $26 billion (UNEP, 1980), of which about half was estimated to pertain to the developing countries. Although these estimates were rather primitive and possibly overestimated economic loss as a result of lost soil productivity (Bojo, 1991), they tend to suggest the magnitude of one component of the problem set. UNDP (1997a) suggested bioenergy production as a response to land degradation: suitably grown biomass fuels are CO_2 neutral and low in sulfur; growing trees to sequester carbon is an alternate strategy for using degraded lands to cope with climate change (Hall et al., 1991a, b).

A brief summary on the courses of international action in regard to the desertification issues is in order (based on UN, 1997c). Within a year of the United Nations Conference on Environment and Development (UNCED), the first meeting of the Intergovernmental Negotiating Committee for the Elaboration of an International Convention to Combat Desertification (INCD) was held in Nairobi. A series of negotiating sessions in various cities were held. The negotiations were completed within two years of UNCED. There followed a signing ceremony in Paris, in October 1994, at which a number of countries and the EU signed the convention, with the total of 115 signatures by mid-December 1996. The convention recognized the critical role of national and local actions, in addition to international cooperation and partnership in combating desertification and mitigating the effects of drought; it also stressed the important role played by women in regions affected by desertification and/or drought, particularly in rural areas of developing countries. Having received the required 50 ratifications in September 1996, the convention came into force on December 26 1996. The first conference of the parties to the convention took place from September 29 to October 10 1997 in Rome. Even before the convention, efforts were made to encourage rapid action on desertification. A resolution was also drafted on urgent action for Africa, which was adopted by the UN General Assembly in December 1994. The resolution called for immediate steps to be taken in Africa, which is especially affected by desertification, and for interim action in other regions.

Later, the UN Convention to Combat Desertification in Those Countries Experiencing Serious Drought and/or Desertification, particularly in Africa (simply referred to as the UN Convention on Desertification) was held in 1994 and came into force in 1997. This convention defined desertification to imply land degradation resulting from factors including climatic variations and human activities. It was also defined that land degradation means loss or reduction of the "biological or economic productivity and complexity . . . resulting from land uses or from . . . processes . . . arising from human activities and habitation patterns . . ." The operative agreement of the convention includes a number of general and specific provisions applicable to most member countries. The general obligations of the countries include adoption of integrated approaches to affect the processes of desertification and drought, and integration of strategies for poverty reduction with these efforts. The role of environmental conservation and that of optimal management of land and water resources was also emphasized. Concerted efforts in implementing these are still awaited in most countries.

Lack of adequate support and of practical indicators of land degradation has long restricted the availability of good scientific data, which has prevented recognition of the full extent of the scourge of desertification and its human impact (UN, 1997c). This, in its turn, has inhibited the availability of funding for science or for action in the field. The issue of the impact of debt servicing on the implementation of programs should also be considered. For the Africa region, debt servicing is a major impediment to the successful implementation of the programs, but it is increasingly recognized as fundamental to improved development, particularly in Africa.

In summary, Daily's (1995) observations are very relevant:

- The utter dependence of human well-being on productive land makes its continued degradation for short-term gain an unwise course; also, the costs of off-site degradation may be substantial.
- Failure to realize the potential for recovery can result in rapid, essentially irreversible deterioration; historically, land degradation has been implicated in the fall of great civilizations and warrants serious attention by this one.

● 2.6 CONCLUSIONS ●

Trends in resource availability and the planet's sink capacity – the most significant environmental facet – both suggest significant declines. Natural resources reviewed here included water, forests, and biological resources. Water tends to show stress conditions for more areas and more people in areas which have not faced significant stress so far; more efficient uses, improved planning and management and pollution control are required for greater availability at affordable prices. Forest areas continue to be depleted in many parts of the world, adversely affecting biodiversity and habitats, reducing the potential for carbon sequestration and hence contributing to global warming, and diminishing watershed functions as well as other ecological services. Continued phenomena of extinction of biological species poses serious problems for access to medicinal and aesthetic benefits, and also adversely affect various other ecosystem functions.

GHG emissions depict significant increasing trends, especially in developing countries. These are contributed mainly from various applications of fossil fuel and biomass energy use. Economic growth and these emissions are highly correlated in these countries. Energy conservation and greater technological innovations are required to mitigate the effects. Important possibilities in this direction include a drastic reduction in deforestation, and steps to ensure effective carbon sequestration with significant afforestation operations. Regarding the ozone depletion problem, the implementation of the Montreal Protocol promises good solutions, but continued efforts are needed on the part of every country to ensure a complete ban of the CFCs.

Soil erosion, land degradation and desertification are among the most significant and partly irreversible problems being faced by many countries. Lack of sufficient attention to a balanced management of ground and surface waters, deforestation and afforestation, and soil conservation are among the most important initiative required in this context. An integrated ecological systems approach could provide a useful framework, rather than a piecemeal approach which is currently in use in many regions. Both national governments and the international community need to pay attention, more than ever in the past, to combat these colossal problems. Transboundary environmental problems are discussed in chapter 3.

Review Exercises

1 (a) What are the main ingredients of the carrying capacity (CC) of the planet in relation to the human population?

   (b) What are the limitations of the Malthusian hypothesis on population?

2 If the global environmental sink capacity for CO_2 is declining, enumerate the set of physical, biological, and economic activities which are leading to this outcome.

3 Examine the soil erosion and land-degradation problems in terms of their physical, economic, and institutional factors contributing to these phenomena.

4 If we use an annual discount rate of 10 percent, the net benefits of productive land at the end of 2099 becomes zero per year at that time. Does this imply a project proposal (like soil conservation or conjunctive use of ground and surface waters in the relevant region) which ignores the potential benefits effective in 2100 is likely to be a meaningful one? If not, why not?

5 What are the short-term and long-term economic parameters of the preservation of biodiversity?

6 Examine the scope for refinement of the evolving definitions of "desertification."

7 What improvements might be possible in the area–species relationship (box 2.1) when there are possibly known migration patterns for birds in adjacent regions?

References

Alexandratos, N. (ed.) (1995) *World Agriculture Towards 2010 – An FAO Study*. Chichester, UK: John Wiley; Rome: FAO.

Andrews, E. L. (1997) In Germany, humble herb is a rival to Prozac. *The New York Times*, September 9, C1 and C7.

Arrhenius, S. (1896) On the influence of carbonic acid in the air upon the temperature on the ground. *The London, Edinburgh, and Dublin Philosophical Magazine and Journal of Science* (April 1896 issue), 237–76.

Arrow, K. J., Bolin, B., Costanza, R., Dasgupta, P., Folke, C., Holling, C. S., Jansson, B. O., Levin, S., Mater, K. G., Perrings, C. and Pimental, D. (1995) Economic growth, carrying capacity, and the environment. *Science*, 268, 520–21.

Balick, M. J. and Mendelsohn, R. (1992) Assessing the economic value of traditional medicines from tropical rainforests. *Conservative Biology*, 6, 128–30.

Balick, M. J., Elisabetsky, E. and Laird, S. A. (eds) (1996) *Medicinal Resources of the Tropical Forest – Biodiversity and its Importance to Human Health*. New York: Columbia University Press.

Balling, Jr, R. C. (1991) Impact of desertification on regional and global warming. *Bulletin of the American Meteorological Society*, 72, 232–4.

Benedick, R. E. (1998) *Ozone Diplomacy*. Cambridge, Mass.: Harvard University Press.

Bojo, J. P. (1991) Economics and land degradation. *Ambio*, 20, 75–9.

Boulding, K. (1964) *The Meaning of the Twentieth Century*. New York: Harper & Row.

Cohen, J. E. (1996) *How Many People Can the Earth Support?* New York: Norton.

Crosson, P. (1997) Will erosion threaten agricultural productivity? *Environment*, 39(8), 6–9.

Daily, G. (1995) Restoring value to the world's degraded lands. *Science*, 269, 350–54.

Daily, G. (ed.) (1997) *Nature's Services*. Washington, DC: Island Press.

Dasgupta, P. (1995) The population problem – theory and evidence. *Journal of Economic Literature*, 33, 1879–902.

Dasgupta, P. (1998) The Economics of Poverty in Poor Countries. *Scandinavian Journal of Economics*, 100(1), 41–68.

de Gruijl, F. R. (1995) Impacts of a projected depletion in the ozone layer. *Consequences*, 1, 13–21.

Dunnette, D. A. and O'Brien, R. J. (1992) *The Science of Global Change*. Washington, DC: American Chemical Society.

Engelman, R. and LeRoy, P. (1995) *Sustaining Water-An Update*. Washington, DC: Population Action International.

FAO (1997a) *The State of the World's Forests 1997*. Rome: FAO.

FAO (1997b) *Review of the State of World Fisheries Resources – Marine Fisheries, Fisheries Circular No.920FIRM/C920*. Rome: FAO Fisheries Department.

FAO/UNEP (1984) *Provisional Methodology for Assessment and Mapping of Desertification*. Rome: FAO.

Hall, D. O., Mynick, H. E. and Williams, R. H. (1991a) Cooling the greenhouse with biomass energy. *Nature*, 353, 11–12.

Hall, D. O., Mynick, H. E. and Williams, R. H. (1991b) Alternative roles for biomass in coping with greenhouse warming. *Science and Global Security*, 2, 1–39.

Houghton, J. T., Jenkins, G. J. and Ephramus, J. J. (1990) *Climate Change – the IPCC Scientific Assessment*. New York: Cambridge University Press, for IPCC.

Houghton, J. T., Boone, R. D., Fruci, J. R., Hobbie, J. E., Melillo, J. M., Palm, D. A., Peterson, B. J., Shaver, G. R., Woodwell, G. M., Moore, B., Skole, D. L. and Myers, N. (1987)

The flux of carbon from terrestrial ecosystems to the atmosphere in 1980s due to change in land use. *Tellus*, Feb–April 1987.

Hulme, M. and Kelly, M. (1993) Exploring the links between desertification and climate change. *Environment*, 35(6), 4–11; 39–43.

Independent World Commission on the Oceans (1998) *Report on "The Ocean Our Future."* Cambridge: Cambridge University Press.

IPCC (1990) *Climate Change – The Scientific Assessment*. New York: Cambridge University Press.

IPCC (1996) *IPCC Second Assessment-Synthesis of Scientific–Technical Information Relevant to Interpreting Article 2 of the UN Framework Convention on Climate Change 1995, January 1996 Draft*. Geneva: WHO/UNEP, 4, 14.

Lovejoy, T. E. (1997) Biodiversity – What is it? In M. L. Reaka-Kudla, D. E. Wilson and Ł. O. Wilson (eds), *Biodiversity II*. Washington, DC: Joseph Henry Press, 7–14.

Malthus, T. (1798) *Essay on the Principle of Population*. New York: Modern Library. Published in 1960.

Malthus, T. (1800) The present high price of provision. In *The Pamphlets of Thomas Malthus*. New York: Kelly. Published in 1961.

Mawdsley, E. O. and Stork, N. E. (1995) Species extinctions in insects-ecological and bio-geophysical considerations. In R. Harrington and N. E. Stock (eds), *Insects in a Changing Environment*. London: Academic Press, 322–69.

Murdoch, J. C. and Sandler, T. (1997) The voluntary provision of pure public good – the case of reduced CFC emissions and the Montreal Protocol. *Journal of Public Economics*, 63, 331–49.

Myers, N. (1988) Threatened biotas: "hotspots" in tropical forests. *Environmentalist*, 8, 1–20.

Myers, N. (1997) The world's forests and their ecosystem services. In G. Daily (1997, 215–35).

Nilsson, A. (1996) *Ultraviolet Reflections – Life Under Thinning Ozone Layer*. New York: John Wiley.

Oldeman, R., Hakkeling, R. and Sombroeck, W. (1990) *World Map of the Status of Human-Induced Soil Degradation*. Waginingen: International Soil Information and Reference Center, and Nairobi: UNEP.

Panayotou, T. and Ashton, P. S. (1992) *Not by Timber Alone*. Washington, DC: Island Press.

Patrick, R. (1997) Biodiversity – Why is it important? In M. L. Reaka-Kudla, D. E. Wilson and Ł. O. Wilson (eds), *Biodiversity II*. Washington, DC: Joseph Henry Press, 15–24.

Pimentel, D., Harvey, C., Resosudarmo, P., Sinclair, K., Kurz, D., McNair, M., Christ, S., Shpritz, L., Fitton, L., Saffouri, R. and Balir, R. (1995) Environmental and economic costs of soil erosion and conservation benefits. *Science*, 267, 1117–23.

Pimm, S. L. and Askins, R. (1995) Forest losses predict bird extinctions in eastern North America. *Proc. of the National Academy of Sciences*, 92(9), 343–7.

Postel, S. and Heise, L. (1988) *Reforesting the Earth, in State of the World 1988*. Washington, DC: Worldwatch Institute.

Rao, P. K. (1988) Planning and financing water resource development in the US – A review and policy perspective. *American Journal of Economics and Sociology*, 43(1), 81–96.

Rao, P. K. (1997) The World Bank role critical for sustained growth. *The Earth Times*, September 9.

Rees, W. E. (1995) Cumulative environmental assessment and global change. *Environmental Impact Assessment Review*, 15(4), 295–310.

Rozanov, B. G. (1990) Global assessment of desertification – status and methodologies. In *Desertification Revisited*. Nairobi: UNEP – DC/PAC, 45–122.

Shiklomanov, I. (1993) World fresh water resource. In P. Glick (ed.), *Water in Crisis*. New York: Oxford University Press.

Simpson, R. D., Sedjo, R. A. and Reid, J. W. (1996) Valuing biodiversity for use in pharmaceutical research. *Journal of Political Economy*, 104(1), 163–85.

Terborgh, J. (1992) Maintenance of diversity in tropical forests. *Biotropica*, 24(2), 283–92.

Thompson, A. M. (1992) The oxidizing capacity of the Earth's atmosphere – probable past and future changes. *Science*, 256, 1157–64.

Tucker, C. J., Dregne, H. E. and Newcomb, W. W. (1991) Expansion and contraction of the Sahara Desert from 1980 to 1990. *Science*, 253, 299–301.

UN (1996) *Population Projections 1996*. New York: UN Population Division.

UN (1997a) *Global Change and Sustainable Development – Critical Trends, Report of the Secretary General, Commission on Sustainable Development*. New York: UN.

UN (1997b) *Comprehensive Assessment of the Freshwater Resources of the World, Report of the Secretary General, Commission on Sustainable Development*. New York: UN.

UN (1997c) *Managing Fragile Ecosystems – Combating Desertifications and Drought, Report E/CN, 17/1997/2/add.11*. New York: UN.

UN (1998) *World Population Projections to 2150*. New York: UN Population Division, UN Secretariat.

UNDP (1997a) *Energy After Rio-Prospects and Challenges*. New York: UNDP.

UNDP (1997b) *Human Development Report 1997*. New York: Oxford University Press.

UNDP (1998) *Human Development Report 1998*. New York: Oxford University Press.

UNEP (1980) *Study on Financing the UN plan of action to Combat Desertification, Report A/35/396*. Nairobi: UNEP.

UNEP (1987) *The Ozone Layer*. Nairobi: UNEP Secretariat.

UNEP (1990) Global assessment of land degradation/desertification, GAP11. *Desertification Control Bulletin*, 18, 24–5.

UNEP (1991) *States of Desertification and Implementation of the UN plan of Action to Combat Desertification*. Nairobi: UNEP.

UNEP (1992) *Intergovernmental Negotiating Committee for a Convention on Biological Diversity*. Nairobi: UNEP Secretariat.

UNEP (1997) *Global Environmental Outlook*. New York: Oxford University Press.

US Interagency Ecosystem Management Task Force (1995) *The Ecosystem Approach – Healthy Ecosystems and Sustainable Economies*, vol. 1. Washington, DC: US Government.

USEPA (1987) *Assessing the Risks of Trace Gases that can Modify the Stratosphere*. Washington, DC: USEPA.

Vitousek, P. M. and Lubchenco, J. (1995) Limits to sustainable use of resources – from local effects to global change. In M. Munasinghe and W. Shearer (eds), *Defining and Measuring Sustainability – The Biological Foundation*. UN University/World Bank, 57–64.

Vitousek, P. M., Ehrlich, P. R., Ehrlich, A. H. and Matson, P. A. (1986) Human appropriation of the products of photosynthesis. *Bioscience*, 34, 368–73.

Watson, R., Meira Filho, L. G., Sanhueza, E. and Janetos, A. (1992) Greenhouse gases – sources and sinks, 29–43. In J. T. Houghton, B. A. Collander and S. K. Yarney (eds), *Climate Change 1992 – The Supplementary Report to the IPCC Scientific Assessment*. New York: Cambridge University Press.

Wilson, E. O. (1993) *The Diversity of Life*. Cambridge, Mass.: Belknap/Harvard University Press.

WMO (1986) *Atmospheric Ozone 1985 – Assessment of our Understanding of the Processes Controlling Its Present Distribution and Change*. Geneva: WMO Secretariat.

World Bank (1997) *World Development Indicators 1998*. Washington, DC: World Bank.

World Resources Institute (1993) *World Resources 1992–93*. Washington, DC: WRI.

World Resources Institute (1997) *World Resources 1996–97*. New York: Oxford University Press.

Worldwatch Institute (1997) *State of the World 1997*. Washington, DC: Worldwatch Institute.

Yu, C., Quinn, J. T., Dafournaud, C. M., Harrington, J. J., Rogers, P. P. and Lohani, N. (1998) Effective dimensionality of environmental indicators – a principal component analysis with bootstrap confidence intervals. *Journal of Environmental Management*, 53(1), 101–19.

chapter outline

● CHAPTER 3 ●

Sustainable Development: Interpretations

Sustainable Development: Interpretations

The universe will be incomplete without man; but
it would also be incomplete without the smallest
transmicroscopic creature that dwells beyond our
conceitful eyes and knowledge.
John Muir

● 3.1 INTRODUCTION ●

The concept of sustainable development (SD) is essentially an interdisciplinary one. Part of the terminology of SD did not arise out of the principles of economic theory, although the important issue of intergenerational equity was addressed by Robert Solow (1974, 1986). Rigorous theories have been advanced relatively recently, in response to a growing trend in public policy in economic and environmental development. Economic science recognized the critical role of environment and ecology in the managing of economic systems. The concept did have different implications for several sections of society, professions and practitioners in different fields of human endeavor and survival. It is hard to ascertain if there is any unanimity in the theory and application even after about a dozen years of intense debate on these issues. This chapter proposes to explore some of the important ingredients, and attempts to integrate the different viewpoints arising out of professional concerns to the issue of ultimate human survival.

Let us begin with an assessment traced back to Aristotle: human well-being is realized only partly by satisfying whatever people's preferences happen to be at a particular time; it is also necessary for successive generations to leave behind sufficient resources so that future generations are not constrained in their preferences. Thus, the future set of meaningful choices should be at least as good as the set available to the current generation. Since the choices include those of economic and non-economic factors, possibly with limited interdependencies between these, this narration is not amenable entirely to economic interpretations alone. The debate on sustainability and SD – often without a clear distinction between the two – continues to engage attention at various levels of society. Special issues of journals continue to report on the theme, or even try to define the theme; see for example, the November 1997 issue of *Land Economics* on "Defining Sustainability." It may not be possible to define with great precision as well as consensus, but refinements go on.

A few preliminaries in the foundations of alternate approaches may be clarified here. Most alternative objectives and means of achieving these originate either explicitly or implicitly in the fundamental approaches of ecocentrism, and anthropocentrism. Ecocentrism is an environmental philosophy which views human activities in terms of their implications for the ecological ingredients, their relative effects, and balances. Anthropocentrism is based on the view that any and all human activities must be in the primary interests of the humans for achieving the desired objectives and goals of the society, whether or not some of the features of the environment and ecology are kept intact or disturbed. However, every analysis, scientific or other, need not be viewed in terms of the dichotomy of the approaches. This is because of the imperative that a totally anthropocentric approach will, sooner or later, reach a critical stage. At that stage, the ecological and biogeophysical limitations in the functioning of the systems form impediments to the continuity of human survival and stability itself. Perhaps there is enough room on this Earth to accommodate a reasonable balance of both the anthropocentric and ecocentric approaches. The issue is about finding the right balance, the means of achieving it and maintaining it for ever. Some of these issues can be addressed with an interdisciplinary perspective, the main focus of this chapter.

This chapter deals with biological, ecological and economic perspectives on the integrally related themes of sustainability and SD. The economic approaches alone are not comprehensive in the absence of an appreciation of the behavior of the ecosystem and biogeophysical systems. For this reason, the important structural phenomena of resilience, nonlinearities and irreversibilities are examined. These emphasize the point that many situations warrant appropriateness of decisions in their timing as well. The loss of system resilience forms the most significant aspect of unsustainability, with considerable potential for catastrophes and irreversibilities. Any definition of sustainability or SD should recognize this feature. These issues are discussed in the subsequent sections. Also, the Precautionary Principle (PP) is important in environmental governance, so this is deliberated in a later section. Some of the main issues discussed in this chapter include: the ecological and biogeophysical interpretations of sustainability, linkages between economic growth and environmental sustainability, and the distinctions between sustainability and SD. An improved set of definitions governing the concepts of SD are provided.

A wide variety of alternative perspectives on these issues are presented. The deliberations in this chapter are expected to lay the framework for several elements of analysis to follow in the rest of the book. The differences in these perspectives arise largely from their professional origins and/or orientation toward ecocentrism, or anthropocentrism, or a mix of the same. Some of the economic models which integrate environment and economic parameters are discussed in the Appendix to this chapter. Needless to say, the pursuit of knowledge and its translation into real-life activities constitutes the best way to enhance SD, whichever way it is defined.

● 3.2 RESILIENCE, NONLINEARITY, AND IRREVERSIBILITY ●

We need to utilize a set of concepts to elucidate the crucial roles of system resilience, the implications of nonlinear behavioral relationships and the irreversible consequences of these two aspects. Some of the basic concepts relevant for this and also in the subsequent sections are given in box 3.1. In addition, we need to elucidate the role of nonlinearity.

BOX 3.1 Important concepts – biogeophysics and ecology

Biogeophysical feedback: when the anthropogenic and natural processes on biota (defined below) and natural resources interact, these in turn, affect the climate upon which biota depend and this constitutes the biogeophysical feedback

Biogeophysical system: the biological and physical system with reference to one or more geological regions

Biophilia: genetically based inherent human need to affiliate deeply and closely with the natural environment, especially its living organisms – this was seen as a part of human mental and emotional apparatus; many interesting details can be seen in Edward Wilson (1992)

Biosphere: the segments of the Earth and its atmospheric surroundings that can support life, in principle: the region on land, in the oceans, and in the atmosphere inhabited by living organisms

Biota: the collection of all living things, including plants and animals

Carrying capacity (CC): the maximum size of a specific population of species that a given habitat can support for a specified period of time, without disrupting the equilibrium in the long run – a dynamic concept, expressible in terms of relevant parameters

Community: an assemblage of populations living in a specific area or a habitat with individual and population-specific characteristics

Cycles: the circulation of biochemical or other elements in the geosphere from the environment to the biological organisms and back to the environment (biogeochemical cycles include the nitrogen cycle, sulfur cycle, and carbon cycle) representing the interaction of life, air, oceans, land, and various chemicals – the vigor of atmospheric circulation affects the features governing various phase descriptions of these cycles; for a lucid description of related issues, see Stephen Schneider (1997)

Ecosystem: the set of all life forms and their physical environment, including the entire set of interacting entities between them – products of the interactions of all living and nonliving factors of the environment and the biosphere; the functioning of an ecosystem results in several interactions, and these lead to what is known as the "balance of nature" at any given time

Ecosystem services: these include (a) maintaining biodiversity and production of ecosystem goods, like food, fiber, biomass fuels, pharmaceuticals, industrial products, and their precursors; (b) life-support functions like environmental cleansing, recycling, and renewal; and (c) provision of intangible aesthetic and cultural benefits – for a detailed description of the ecosystem, its functions, services and potential approaches to their evaluation, see Gretchen Daily (1997)

Stress: this is the result of an environmental change that reduces the survival fitness of an organism; usually governed by a nonlinear relationship between the influence and the fitness of the organism

Threshold limits: the limits of factors beyond which growth and equilibrium/ stability of populations, or other survival features of life forms and organisms, are likely to be adversely affected – these limits constitute critical levels for survival

Nonlinearity

Most phenomena on this planet obey nonlinear behavior, whether it is the growth in the evolution of the size of a population, or compound interest accumulation on a principal amount of capital. In general, ecological change is neither gradual nor continuous. In several cases, biological growth may depict a continuing growth relationship over time, but the same tend to be rather abrupt when it comes to their decay. These phenomena obey nonlinear behavior rather than a simple linear behavior which forms a special case of the former. Let us illustrate with two examples of nonlinearity in biological behavior. The first relates to the behavioral relationship in a wide variety of animals (and other Earthlings): a nonlinear relationship between the intake of toxic inputs and the physical fitness; see, for example, Hoffmann and Parsons (1997). The typical relationship is depicted in figure 3.1.

Another example of nonlinearity in biology may be given. When environments fluctuate, the mean fitness of a genotype W is usually represented by its geometric mean fitness rather than its arithmetic mean fitness; see, for example, Gillespie (1973).

Figure 3.1 Relationship between fitness of an organism and chemical concentrations

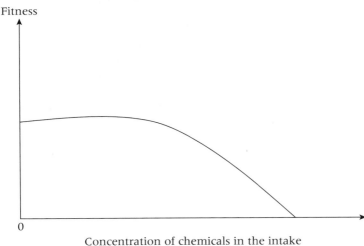

$$W = \sqrt[N]{\prod_{i=1}^{N} X_i} \qquad i = 1, \ldots, N$$

where X_i are fitness levels in each of the N environments.

We need to appreciate the implications of nonlinear behavior in ecosystems so as to assess the relative merits and demerits of various policies affecting these systems. The nonlinearity in ecosystems leads to unpredictable behavior because of two features:

1 Periodic and random small changes can propagate the disturbances dramatically and flip the system into another path of its evolution (as in "chaos theory").
2 Regions of stable relationships collapse as slow processes/influences accumulate and move the system from one set of controlling mechanisms and processes to another (as in "catastrophe theory"); see Holling et al. (1998).

Both these features draw upon the mechanisms of biogeophysical feedback.

Nonlinearities, typically disproportionateness and nonuniform responses in varying ranges of parameters, lead to discontinuities after certain critical ranges. In the area of medical science, an example arises in the phenomenon of heart attacks: discontinuous or nonlinear functions between time units and the quantity of blood pumped into the heart. When forest ecosystems undergo creeping degradation through acid rain, the forests manifest slow but steady decline; chronic stress finally and suddenly exhibits its severe features. Similarly, the increase in fossil fuel consumption can be somewhat linear but the atmospheric pollution's response often is not. Thus, the pollution-absorbing capacity of the atmosphere possesses properties of nonlinearity as well as significant irreversibility.

The phenomena of nonlinearity and irreversibility compound the problems whenever these features are given a chance to play their roles. Some other examples of nonlinearity include environmental costs that rise disproportionately with incremental or cumulative changes in global climate, with the rise of increases in CO_2 emissions. In terms of the economic implications of nonlinearities and uncertainties, Peck and Teisberg (1993) explored the implications of damage function nonlinearity for the value of information about the equilibrium temperature increase per CO_2 doubling. Sensitivity of cost estimates increases dramatically due to nonlinearities in the damage function, with the corresponding implications for controlling costs at less precarious ranges of system characteristics. Peck and Teisberg found that optimal policy is substantially more sensitive to the degree of nonlinearity in damages than to the level of damages at a specified temperature increase. This suggests that there is a problem of a compounding nature when the damages are assessed at any potentially higher temperature ranges.

Resilience

An important concept which is closely related to nonlinearity is that of ecosystem resilience. It is the buffer capacity or the ability of a system to absorb disturbances, i.e. the magnitude of disturbance that can be absorbed before a system changes its structure – its influences and processes that control behavior; see also Holling (1995b). In a much simpler framework (the one conventionally discussed), this may be interpreted as the ability of systems or species and organisms to respond to various disturbances (internal and/or external influences) to their environment, and to restore *status quo ante* features. Usually, resilience is lost when the ranges of tolerance for variations in the environmental factors are crossed by the disturbances or external influences. It is relevant to note that the ranges of tolerance differ significantly across different species and organisms, and a common factor may not be applied to the entire biophilia. The tolerance level of a system for any environmental or ecological stress tends to be reduced when there are other stresses (even remotely related ones). This exacerbates the vulnerability of the system to multiple or cumulative disturbances, and the linkages obey nonlinear relationships; for details, see Myers (1993). Loss of resilience tends to shift a system toward its thresholds, and eventually leads to its flip from one equilibrium state to another. The Great Lakes in the USA are considered an example of an ecosystem which suffered loss of resilience and led to an irreversible loss of some of the biological stocks of species.

Some of the biogeophysical systems may not possess the same level of adaptability to changes as do some other subsystems of the ecological systems. Thus the former are likely to suffer irreversible consequences when their resilience features are lost. This was seen, for example, in almost all the groundwater systems when water withdrawal exceeded their critical limits without appropriate attention to the recharging of the water table. When the limit was exceeded, the system went dry – never to return back to the original configuration. Some historical civilizations underwent these experiences, as stated briefly in chapter 1. As if these were not enough signals to warn against impending problems, some of the current systems (as, for example, in several developing countries) are going through the same set of cycles again. This is observable in a number of fast-growing urban regions with inadequate urban water supply. Many of these exceeded their limits of water withdrawal from the groundwater table with little attention to the recharge requirements.

Ecosystem resilience is a useful index of sustainability. The characteristics of resilience include some components of adaptivity of the system. As argued by Arrow et al. (1995), if human activities are to be sustainable, ecological systems must remain resilient, and any loss of the ecosystem resilience (as, for example, in the cases of desertification process) could imply an irreversible change in the set of options open to present and future generations, and exacerbate adverse environmental consequences of economic activities.

Figure 3.2 provides a system link of influences and responses regarding the phenomenon of loss of resilience.

Figure 3.2 Interdependencies of resilience and human welfare

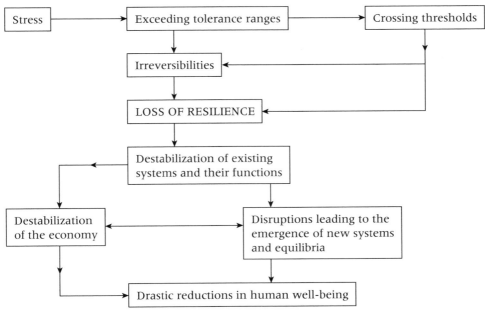

Irreversibilities

The cumulative effects of various activities influencing the erstwhile equilibria of various ecosystems lead to nonlinearities and also to irreversibilities. Some examples of these include bioaccumulation of toxins, desertification, and loss of biodiversity. All of these warrant safe margins of protection of the environmental assets. This is required even before relevant information can be ascertained. If the symptoms of a problem or a certain disaster is the only way to generate relevant information, it would be either too late or very expensive for any corrective restoration. This is an illustration of the well-known Arrow's paradox of information. The original formulation of Kenneth Arrow (1972) was given in the context of the economics of information: the value of information may not be known until we obtained the information, but one may not be willing to pay for such information since the value is not known *a priori*.

The biological extinction of any species is one of the several examples of irreversibility of environmental damage; so are some of the concentrations of the greenhouse gases (GHGs) possessing very long life spans. Even if these GHGs are technically reversible over a period of time, the irreversible damage to the system would have resulted much before the concentration of these GHGs is diffused. These features are largely dependent on the cumulative effects over a period of time and over different ranges at a given point of time: the consequences of multiple sources of environmental disturbance that impinge on the same valued environmental component. The characteristic "multiple" nature of the sources of cumulative impacts may arise in three ways:

1   The same kind of source recurs sufficiently frequently through time.
2   The same kind of source recurs sufficiently densely through space.
3   Different kinds of sources impose similar consequences on a valued environmental component (Clark, 1986).

In a related assertion, Holling (1995a) summarized that a new class of problems is challenging the ability to achieve SD:

● Problems caused by slowly, cumulatively formed human influences on air, land, and oceans that trigger sudden changes affecting the vitality of societies.
● Intensification of the spatial span of biogeophysical interaction.
● Both the ecological and social components of these features possessing an evolutionary character.

These issues warrant greater attention in any of the approaches to sustainability.

Analysis of natural thresholds of resource use that could trigger various discontinuities and nonlinearities remains an area of research interest. An understanding of various nonlinear responses remains a complex task, mainly due to the paucity of data for statistically robust identification of the underlying relationships. The availability of such information could influence social choices affecting the planet Earth and prepare society for a smoother transition into changing scenarios. This can also be stated in terms of the potential value of such information to minimize the adjustment costs in such a transition.

● 3.3 Biogeophysical and Ecological Aspects ●

The adverse consequence of ecological neglect can be felt in a span of a few years rather than very long time intervals like hundreds of years. The impacts surface within decades of ill-treatment of the planet and its sources and sinks. For ready reference, a source is defined as any component of the biogeophysical and atmospheric system in and around planet Earth which is capable or potentially capable of providing resources of current or future significance for any form of life. A sink is defined as a reservoir of any medium (air, water, or solid) which serves to assimilate or absorb pollutants from one or more of the atmospheric cycles of the Earth.

Ecology and Ecosystem

Ecology, the study of structure and its functions of natural environment, has assumed greater importance in recent years. This was natural as human-kinds' survivability is being expressed increasingly in terms of that of most other forms of life on this planet; for an easy reading of the principles of ecology, see Buchholz (1998). The ecological capital, an all-encompassing concept of natural capital, is a function of the stock of biological well-being of all forms of life on the planet. At least four categories of functions can be stated of the ecological capital:

1   Provision of resources for production and the raw materials.
2   Absorption of wastes from production processes as well as consumption processes.
3   Basic survival infrastructural services like climate, radiation effects, and ozone shield.
4   Recreational resources and goods.

Any major disturbance to the ecosystem has direct and rather near future adverse implications for the life-support systems sustaining the economy. This is particularly valid when the limits of the carrying capacity (CC) are being approached or already reached. The trade-off between foregoing one or the other beyond certain critical ranges, like appropriately defined CCs, seems an inevitable prerequisite for the sustained survival of all forms of life.

One of the definitions of the CC states that it is "the maximal sustainable load that humankind can impose on the environment before it loses its capacity to support human activity" (ICPQL, 1996, p. 97). It is evident that when the CC is exceeded, there could be irreversible consequences. Some of the potential benefits and losses (not always in monetary terms) of ecological disturbances and consequences of unsustainable paths of development can be viewed from these perspectives. Biologists apply the concept of CC to examine the maximum limit on the population size of any species or a combination of different species which can be sustained by a habitat indefinitely. At the planet level for all

Earthlings, the limit is expressed in terms of "net primary product" (NPP). This is defined as the total amount of solar energy converted into biochemical energy through plant photosynthesis, called gross primary production (GPP), minus the energy those plants use for their own life processes, also called the energy expenditure of respiration, R. Briefly stated

$$NPP = GPP - R$$

Thus, NPP is the main determinant of food for all life on Earth. The role and value of biodiversity and ecological systems can be understood in this context: person-made capital (manufactured capital) is not independent of the state of nature and the ecological capital.

Regional Dimensions of Sustainability: Two Examples

The problems of examining system features at varying levels of aggregation could possibly mask the realities of the system malfunctions. This is true, for example, when one tries to estimate a relationship between the total area under forests and the extinction of biological species. This is because the fragmented forest with "edges" allows for certain ecological disturbances whereas the unfragmented forest would not depict the same. Similarly, if we seek to maintain desired characteristics only at the average levels, we could be missing the underlying and emerging problems.

A brief narration of the environmental problems of the Chesapeake Bay in the USA is given in box 3.2. The emerging problems, their institutional management aspects, and the role of human influences on the Bay system can be noted. The main lesson here is the need for local actions, first to identify the problems, then to diagnose the solutions, and finally, to adopt measures to remedy the problems. The second illustration is one of biogeophysical complexity compounded by excessive (needs-based?) exploitation of the system resources, leading to a possible stress and unsustainability. This is the case of intensive agricultural development in Bangladesh (box 3.3). Intensive pressures of population and scarcity of land for farming are the obvious contributing factors, but the farm input management issues seem to have taken little note of the need to preserve soil fertility on a sustainable basis.

A number of alternative formulations of sustainability were attempted in scientific literature, from different disciplinary perspectives. The ultimate binding constraints, arising out of biogeophysical and of ecological considerations, tend to remain closer to the laws of nature. However, not all the laws are understood yet. If the physical survival or survivability tends to remain increasingly or constantly at stake as a result of human actions (and inactions), these (in)actions deserve significant attention to avert potential problems or crises. In using the various sources of information, the main differences arise when specific objectives and goals are sought to be formulated. Reasonable pragmatism is required to arrive at any operationally meaningful approaches to the perceived problems and their solutions.

BOX 3.2 Chesapeake Bay and sustainability

The Chesapeake Bay in the USA covers an area of about 16,000 square kilometers. During its history of about two centuries, the Bay underwent several changes which were mostly unplanned. Before World War II, the fisheries and other related resources in the estuary operated at rather high yield levels, but when the measurements were taken in the 1970s, the effects of several influences were clearly visible. The quality of water and its nutrient contents posed problems with quality deterioration. The US congress directed the USEPA to initiate relevant investigations, and the Chesapeake Bay Program was established with the involvement of the governors of the states of Maryland, Pennsylvania, Virginia, the Mayor of Washington D.C., and the Administrator of the USEPA. By 1980, the changes in the Bay region were found to be very significant. The disappearance of benthic vascular plants was generally attributed to the effects of nutrient loadings derived from effluent and runoff. It was also found that most phosphorous pollution came from point sources with its span rather uniformly distributed through the year, and nitrogen pollution arose from non-point sources during the high-flow period of spring. Early plans of the Bay Commission in the mid-1980s were aimed at controlling the point source pollutions, especially the phosphorous additions. In 1987, the management established a goal of a 40 percent reduction in the inputs of both nitrogen and phosphorous to the bay, "a decision based as much on instincts as on early results of a complex mathematical model." The USEPA estimates of the early 1990s indicated that more than 80 percent of the nutrient inputs were tracked down to anthropogenic origins, including a rapid rise in the human population residing in the area. The "issue of sustainability is thus related primarily to managing local impacts of humans rather than global impacts of natural events." The most important of the anthropogenic influences is changes in land use to support agriculture and urban development. Besides, the nitrogen inputs from air pollution enhance the problems.

Source: Summary based on D'Elia (1995) and Thompson (1996)

Let us examine, as an example, a criterion suggested in part of the literature as a useful method in this effort. The safe minimum standard (SMS) of conservation – originally proposed by Ciriacy-Wantrup (1952) – is a criterion suggested to bring about an element of sustainability in physical terms. The SMS rule places biodiversity beyond the reach of routine trade-offs; it takes significant costs to justify a relaxation of the SMS. Since the SMS depends on the current information and judgment as to what constitutes intolerable costs, an overly stringent application could make both the current as well as future generations worse off. In the theory of decision making, this SMS approach is similar to the criterion of "minmax." The latter requires the seeking of decisions or policy choices which tend to minimize the maximum imaginable damage, a principle similar

BOX 3.3   Conflicts in survival and the environment – Bangladesh

Bangladesh has one of the most dense populations in the world, and has a low per capita income. Land is a very scarce resource. Besides, the low-lying areas of the country are likely to be among the adversely affected parts of the world owing to any effects of global warming and sea-level rise. Any such disturbance does mean displacing the habitats of millions of people. The scarce land resources are undergoing serious stress problems, with the possibility of loss of soil productivity, and this poses serious problems in their biogeophysical sustainability.

Intensified agricultural practices and the increased use of fertilizers are considered basic necessities for expanding food production and meeting the food demand for a growing population. The country has achieved self-sufficiency in foodgrains. However, the recent trends in the yield of major crops indicate a decline in their productivity. Long-term trials conducted by the Bangladesh Rice Research Institute suggested that intensive cultivation of rice, the staple food crop, may be declining even with sound management of plant nutrients. This is a clear indication of the degradation in land quality and its productivity. Some suggested that this problem is due to nutrient imbalances. Multiple cropping, felt to be a necessity for food requirements of the local population, is considered a contributory factor in this issue of soil management. The use of farmyard manure for farm fertilizer was dropped and replaced by the increased use of chemical fertilizers; the manure is used for domestic fuel.

Sources: World Bank (1995) and Pagiola (1995)

to the Rawlsian justice (Rawls, 1971). As a result of this attitude in decision making, the approach entails costs of strong risk aversion, namely foregoing certain opportunities for deriving current benefits so as to ensure flexibility in the set of decision alternatives for the future. On the other hand, the implications of relaxing these stringencies could be such as to incur the loss of some biological species. This results in the loss of benefits (directly and indirectly) which could be extremely significant. Besides, some of the biological consequences are irreversible.

Much of the concern in the debate on the biogeophysical and ecological dimensions of SD is simply confined to the sustainability of the planet Earth's resources, with no weightage for the requisite development that concerns humanity. An example is the SMS criterion. It is not unusual for those concerned with issues of sustainability alone to presume that once sustainability is assured, the issue of SD could be handled as a corollary. This becomes an infeasible proposition, without appropriate ecosystem sustainability, but this may never be achieved if we do not accord appropriate priorities for resource exploitation, and the mitigation of corresponding and other problems, with proper phasing of the activities over time and space. Sometimes, the SMS criterion could be deemed a proxy for the adoption of the strong sustainability principle (discussed later in this chapter); see also Farmer and Randall (1998). An appreciation of sustainability in the development sense provides a useful background for the relevant policies and programs. This may be accomplished, in principle, with calculated cost (or risk) to other biological, physical, and terrestrial entities. The complex basis of socioeconomic development in terms of the availability of life-supporting features on the planet is typically the concern of what is becoming a significant addition to the knowledge in the interdisciplinary (and not simply multidisciplinary) approach of ecological economics. Some of the relevant approaches in these directions of analysis are utilized on a select few occasions in this book. An effective integration of ecology and economics could be of greater help in the future.

Symptoms of Unsustainability

Sustainability may be relatively harder to define than indicating features of unsustainability; in fact, the origins of the debate stem from the observations of disturbing trends of possible unsustainability of life on this planet under current trends, with humanity playing a major role against nature. Some of the major impediments were discussed in chapter 2. Based on the current knowledge, some of the important symptoms include these not usually mutually exclusive or independent symptoms:

- Greenhouse effect (GE) and climate change;
- Ozone depletion;
- Atmospheric acidification;
- Toxic pollution;
- Biological species extinction;
- Deforestation;
- Land degradation and desertification;
- Depletion of non-renewable resources like fossil fuels and minerals; and
- Urban air pollution and solid wastes.

Now, can sustainability be defined as a process under which these undesirable features are brought to tolerable levels? This is unlikely, because not only these features but a number of underlying fundamentals of survival need to be addressed systematically for the purpose of sustainability. A number of alternative definitions of biogeophysical and ecological sustainability have been attempted in the literature that provide initial bases to generate the debate and possibly lead to improvements in the clarity of concept policy framework.

Sustainability Concepts

For the purpose of discussion and the clarification of issues, let us take an example. A proposal for a "working definition" of biophysical sustainability was given by Keiichiro Fuwa (1995). It seeks to maintain or improve

ideal definition

the integrity of the life support system of Earth. Sustaining the biosphere with adequate provisions for maximizing future options includes enabling current and future generations to achieve economic and social improvement within a framework of cultural diversity while maintaining (a) biological diversity, and (b) the biogeochemical integrity of the biosphere by means of conservation and proper use of air, water, and land resources . . . Biophysical sustainability must, therefore, mean the sustainability of the biosphere minus humanity . . . Likewise, sustainable development should mean both sustainability of the biophysical medium or environment and sustainability of human development, with the latter sustaining the former.

It is doubtful if concrete guidelines could be derived from these requirements, but advocating a set of concerns relevant for further consideration seems to have been the purpose of evolving such a definition.

Another relatively strong assertion tends to assume the following form, spelled out by Harremoes (1996):

Mankind has the potential ultimately to reach a solution: a sustainable society, that can continue for generations. Current development is, however, not even close to anything like sustainability; in fact, development is rapidly decreasing the prospects for sustainability. This applies to both the industrial and developing countries. A sustainable society cannot be achieved without fundamental changes in our basic thinking, ethical values, moral concepts and religious beliefs.

Although relevant, the prescription seems like a tall order. Very little is known about the set of activities or potential interventions needed to effect these desirable objectives and goals.

A closer approximation to a workable definition or approach can be attempted in several directions. According to Vellinga et al. (1995):

realistic defini- tion

The concept of sustainable development can be defined as maintenance and sustainable utilization of the functions (goods and services) provided by natural ecosystems and biospheric processes. Conversely, in a situation of unsustainability, where the limits of the biosphere's carrying capacity are exceeded, not all of the environmental functions can be fully fulfilled anymore.

There does not, however, exist any consensus on the CC limits and fulfillment of various functions at "full" levels. The concept of CC, defined earlier, needs a reasonable agreement on the specifications of the maximal load that supports a pre-defined (possibly fixed, or changing, but unknown) level of human activity. What is really of operational significance is to discern the biogeophysical and ecological stresses. An assessment of the types and magnitudes of the disturbances attributable to human activity will be most relevant.

Many definitions can be seen in the literature. Each of these focus around the disciplinary area that is primarily seeking to define the concept. Besides, several of these mix up the objectives with the means of achieving an implicit sustainability or SD goal. A few illustrations may be given.

The Civil Engineering Research Foundation (1996), for example, stated that SD is "the challenge of meeting growing human needs for natural resources, industrial products, energy, food, transportation, shelter, and effective waste management while conserving and protecting environmental quality and the natural resource base essential for future development," and that it represents "a new way of thinking in planning, designing, building, operating, maintaining, and disposing of infrastructure facilities, such as roads, buildings and bridges." It is reasonable to view these formulations or approaches as very relevant, even in the absence of an accurately defined concept of SD.

Let us recall some of the concepts and definitions of SD which integrate ecological and economic regimentations. These concepts suggest that SD is:

- to maximize the biological system goals (genetic diversity, resilience, biological productivity), economic system goals (meeting basic minimum needs, equity etc.), and social system goals (social justice, people's participation, etc.) simultaneously (Barbier, 1987);
- improving the quality of human life while living within the CC of supporting ecosystems (The World Conservation Union (IUCN), UNEP & Worldwide Fund for Nature, 1991).

A broadly accepted ecological economics definition states that sustainability is a relationship between dynamic economic systems and larger dynamic, but normally slower-changing ecological systems, in which

- human life can continue indefinitely;
- human individuals can flourish; and
- human cultures can develop, but in which effects of human activities remain within bounds, so as not to destroy the diversity, complexity, and function of the ecological life-support system (Costanza et al., 1991).

This definition comes close to a reasonable definition of SD, and not simply of sustainability. This could possibly offer useful directions for further improvements of the concept. Most of these concerns are discussed in the next two sections of this chapter. We conclude with an assertion: an application of the biogeophysical definition of sustainability would normally require the creation and preservation of physical and biological resources that possess the potential to maintain undiminished human well-being as well as balance the coexistence of other species for the entire future time horizon.

Alternative Perspectives

A broad range of theoretical perspectives on sustainability are briefly summarized in box 3.4. Most of the perspectives are concerned with resource and environmental and, hence, human sustainability rather than SD. The latter would call for a whole range of balances and the exercise of value judgments:

BOX 3.4 Perspectives on sustainability

Some of the major theoretical perspectives and their salient features – partly adapted from van den Bergh (1996) – are given below:

Neoclassical economic equilibrium: non-declining human welfare or quality of human life; sustainable growth based on technical progress and substitution possibilities; optimizing environmental externalities; maintaining aggregate or sub-group-specific stocks of natural and economic capital with substantial reliance on market factors (possibly with specifications of legal and other institutional regulations); predominant role of individual enterprises and individuals in decisions affecting income generation, consumption, and environmental implications

Evolutionary ecology: maintaining resilience of natural systems; allowing for variations and biological cycles; learning from uncertainty in natural processes; humans forming only a component of the list of biological species with no presumed dominant role; fostering genetic/biotic/ecosystem diversity

Physico-economic: quantitative restrictions on materials usable in the input–output systems of the economy; industrial metabolism based on materials – product chain policy, integrated waste treatment, pollution abatement, recycling, and product development

Socio-cultural: maintaining cultural and social system of interactions with ecosystems; respect for nature integrated in culture and daily life; survival of life

Human ecology: remaining within the CC with limitations on scales of material throughput for economic activities including human consumption; considering multiple effects of human actions over regional and temporal dimensions and in relation to the ecological features

trade-off between growth, social justice, and intragenerational as well as intergenerational equity of living standards or quality of life. These details are offered in the next section. A few of the applications and improvements of the neoclassical economic approaches are provided later in this chapter and in chapter 4.

● 3.4 ECONOMIC APPROACHES ●

A number of broad policy measures were sought to be prescribed under the Rio Declaration of the Earth Summit of 1992. These included eight "Economic Principles," including these three:

1   The right to development must be fulfilled so as to equitably meet developmental and environmental needs of present and future generations (Principle 3).

2   All States and all people shall cooperate in the essential task of eradicating poverty as an indispensable requirement for SD, in order to decrease the disparities in standards of living and better meet the needs of the majority of the people of the world (Principle 5).

3   To achieve SD and a higher quality of life for all people, States should reduce and eliminate unsustainable patterns of production and consumption and promote appropriate demographic policies (Principle 8).

All these principles emphasize economic development in addition to sustainability. The concept of sustainability admits varying notions and definitions. Development is fundamentally a broad-based specification of economic progress. The resulting concept of SD is thus fraught with a multitude of potentially conflicting requirements. The concept of "sustainability" in one of its definitions could lead simply to some kind of SMS in resource use, including preservation of environmental quality and its assets.

The central criterion, in a real long-term sense, focuses on the sustainability of life on this planet in relation to ecosystems and biodiversity. If we reduce the time-horizon of concern to hundreds of years rather than thousands of years, we tend to come closer to appreciating the role of environmental and bioeconomic constraints in the process of economic development. In such a context, the roles of economic growth, development, and environment affecting a range of SD alternatives need to be explored; these alternatives make sense only if they can be viewed as consistent with specified time-horizons, social time preferences, and relative importance is attached to interests of future generations, quality of environment and its complementarity with accelerated economic growth, and with demographic features. If the concept of SD is itself to be "sustained" as a development paradigm, a few ingredients might be required (Lele, 1991): reasonable precision of the concept built on meaningful, flexible, and diverse approaches, and harmonization of society with changes in environmental issues and development. Is this any precise direction of inquiry? Very unlikely. The suggested refinements are unsustainable because of missing specifications of crucial ingredients. The discussion below is an attempt to arrive at an improved level of precision and objectivity.

A Broad Definition

The Brundtland Report (WCED, 1987, p. 43) contributed to much of the ongoing concern for SD:

> Sustainable development is development that meets the needs of the present without compromising the ability of future generations to meet their own needs. It contains within it two key concepts: the concept of "needs," in particular the essential needs of the world's poor, to which overriding priority should be given; and the idea of limitations imposed by the state of technology and social organization on the environment's ability to meet present and future needs.

This seems to hold good as a definition, at a general level. Clearly, this approach does address the issue of intragenerational resource distribution, with expressed concern for the poor. However, it is most common that the debate on the issue during the last ten years is very substantially centered only around the intergenerational dimension. Most reports on the theme quote the first sentence, and make no mention of the attendant vital explanation and interpretation. Thus, those writings are possibly less than fair to the spirit of the original contributors. It is rather surprising that the poverty dimension is not well-examined in the literature even to the extent that it adversely contributes to quality of environment and to any measure of quality of life – present as well as future. Some of these issues are discussed in chapter 7. No doubt, the needs of future generations have to be understood based on information available at this time. Assumptions about future preferences and tastes of future generations remain crucial in this understanding. Analytical details of these issues are explained in chapter 4.

Many economists transformed the above concept and suggested that nondeclining per capita consumption measure would be a suitable indicator of sustainability. This was not suggested as an indicator of SD, however. This narrow specification could allow for "business as usual" scenarios governing socioeconomic inequities, unjust resource ownership and income distribution systems, or other structural and institutional impediments to judicious resource management. Also, it is doubtful if the concern in the second part of the Brundtland Report's definition above is properly (or even marginally) recognized. Among the notable exceptions is an assertion of Solow, quoted in the UN Development Programme's (UNDP) Human Development Report (UNDP, 1996, p. 16): the case for reducing contemporary inequality is as strong as for worrying about the uncertain status of future generations. So far it appears that most analysts have neglected an integral part of the above definition while accepting possibly a more "convenient" part of the same definition. This poses a potential inconsistency in the operational approaches, which continue to claim their origins to the directions of the Brundtland Report. In fact, as Solow argued (UNDP, 1996, p. 16): "those who are so urgent about not inflicting poverty on the future have to explain why they do not attach even higher priority to reducing poverty today."

It is rather naive to believe that SD can be viewed as a meaningful approach when it is formulated totally independent of income distribution policies. This feature is also relevant in the processes governing initial allocation of resources or their endowments. Ownership of resources and the processes of accumulation of resources under varying ownership regimes, or more generally property rights and legal entitlement regimes are critical in this phenomenon. These play an important role in the consumption and production decisions with direct implications for the SD. Since any redirection of existing resource and income distribution patterns cannot be achieved within a reasonable time frame and without enormous socioeconomic costs, a softer approach is usually taken to devise what may be considered pragmatic. This takes note of the existing legal entitlements and property rights regimes. Fiscal and monetary policies constitute examples of potentially flexible, income redistribution favoring and environment-enhancing policy packages within this context. Most economic democracies in the world tend to fit into this configuration. Some of the neoclassical economic models depicting how resource ownership affects resource consumption, conservation, and sustainability can be seen in Howarth and Norgaard (1992).

Issues concerning resource control and management need to be related to principles of ethical fairness and economic justice. Two aspects are relevant here. First, a just society cannot be indifferent to the background conditions against which markets function. Second, existing distributions and preferences need not be taken as the fairest or inevitable; see Sunstein (1997, p. 385) for a useful description of related socioeconomic issues. While these are very important normative and ethical issues, it is not easy to foresee how these might be effected. However, the least one could do is to take note of these when issues of resource valuation and income distribution are considered. In the extreme, abject poverty degrades human dignity and adversely affects the potential for SD. Some of the details can be seen in chapter 7.

The Brundtland definition needs to be followed up in several more directions to enable greater precision and applicability. This is done with several explorations into different postulates and their implications for one form of sustainability or another. Since the role of capital remains very important in the development processes, it is useful to examine the ingredients of various forms of capital, its stocks and flows. It is possible to carry out a disaggregation of resources in terms of various components of capital relevant for development. Broadly, four types of capital may be classified (see also Seralgeldin, 1996a):

- Person-made capital, based on manufacturing or related economic activities.
- Natural capital, consisting of non-renewable and renewable resources including the atmosphere, sources and sinks of the planet, and several other ecological resources.
- Human capital; knowledge, technical know-how, and health.
- Social capital; culture, people's institutions, efficacy and quality of various institutions, cooperative behavior, trust, social norms, and people's participation in decision making.

Clearly, these forms of capital components are partly complementary, and are not mutually exclusive in most feasible ranges. The comprehensive valuation and assessment of these features could form a beginning in the interpretation of sustainability. In this context, any valuation of the social capital continues to remain a complex issue.

Economic Definitions

Some authors suggest that a free market oriented economic approach to sustainability could incorporate the importance of the environment. They argue that if the features of the environment (in terms of their economic significance of the source and sink characteristics) reflect adversely on the health of the economy and other systems, the economy will receive the feedbacks to adjust itself. This presumes the existence of policy and institutional mechanisms (especially efficient functioning of markets) for such corrections. Even if this position is accepted, the time frame over which the self-correction feedbacks might happen is not expected to be synonymous with that relevant to preserve the ecosystem resilience. The attainment of such a pseudo-sustainability could be consistent with massive environmental degradation. The narrow economic approach to sustainability usually yields a precise definition but one that is not useful enough to meet the objective from an earthly problem-solving approach. Let us note that even the economic resilience of a system is bound to be threatened in a framework that does not recognize the considerations discussed in the previous section.

In most studies, the debate on SD was interpreted simply in terms of sustainability. The interactions of features of sustainability with those of desirable development patterns were accorded less priority. Within such a framework, the alternatives of sustainability are classified in terms of weak sustainability and strong sustainability, and something in-between (like so-called sensible sustainability and other variants); see Serageldin (1996b). Weak sustainability refers to maintaining total capital intact without regard to the composition of that capital among different kinds of capital; this implies that alternative ingredients of the vector of components of capital are substitutes (within foreseeable ranges of the individual components). Strong sustainability refers to maintaining every component of the capital vector intact; this assumes that natural and person-made capital are not necessarily substitutes, but are likely complements in the production process.

Weak sustainability is also interpreted as the requirement that the aggregate capital be kept intact over time, without any decline in the welfare of consumption; strong sustainability is the requirement that natural capital be kept intact over time; see Serageldin (1996b) for a detailed discussion on the interpretation. The second version seeks to maintain a critical minimum level of natural capital stocks, specified in physical terms. Weak sustainability permits a large degree of substitutability consistent with the requirements of overall welfare maximization at any given time instant. The substitution is assumed to be such as not to cause an irreversible impediment to the growth processes. It also believes that some of the problems of environmental and ecological degradation may be worth incurring if the benefits of such exploitation render more income for society than the apparent costs. Thus, the nonmonetary losses are sought to be bought off with some monetary levels of potential compensation.

The weak sustainability approaches raise a number of serious objections from environmentalists and ecologists, among others. Implicit in the assumption of a high degree of substitution is to treat manufactured capital and ecological capital as close substitutes. Here is what is called the commensurability problem: how to trade the spotted owl, if need be, with more newsprint? Although this appears a formidable problem, it can be handled with some potential alternatives for decision making. There are several issues requiring clarification: Can we delineate a meaningful region over which this issue needs to be examined? What are the local and regional dimensions of the ecological and economic dependencies? What is a meaningful time frame to resolve the conflict in a cost-effective manner? What are the corresponding implications on the stresses and resilience required of the systems and their specific components? Who are the current and future winners and gainers?

Many of the differences among environmentalists – and others who might or might not be as concerned about the environment – arise from their adoption of one form or the other of alternative configurations of sustainability. Whether the spotted owl, for example, is an item that can be aggregated into the sum total valuation of biological resources and allowed to be substituted by some other owl or some other bird, seems to form a premise for those who advocate weak sustainability. This interpretation may not be entirely valid, since even those who advocate this approach admit that there may be certain forms of life or other resource that are irreplaceable and should not be compromised in any aggregation of resources. However, if an aggregation could be allowed, this approach forms an intermediary compromise between the two forms of sustainability spanning the continuum of combinations of the two polar or somewhat extreme positions. This is sometimes called the "sensible sustainability" approach.

A number of economic definitions are offered in the literature that define economic approaches to the theme of SD. A select few are elucidated here. These are not necessarily the most acceptable ones but are given here to motivate the issues and examine the scope for improvements.

First, to make development sustainable at the level of countries – or at the global level – requires that societies, in seeking to achieve development objectives, also seek to maintain a constant stock of environmental assets for use by future generations and to avoid irreversible damage to any single asset (Mitlin and Satterthwaite, 1990). This approach suggests an attempt to balance ecological and economic considerations. However, the specification of avoiding an irreversible damage may not be good enough when we recognize the interdependencies of ecological features when thresholds are crossed. It is desirable to focus on the latter, in addition to the economic criteria.

Second, SD may be described as "a pattern of social and structural transformation which optimizes the economic and other social benefits available in the present without jeopardizing the likely potential for similar benefits in the future" (Gilbert and Braat, 1991, p. 261). This approach follows the footsteps of the Brundtland Report, but falls short of providing requisite precision. The real problem is centered around two features:

- Perceived and interpreted potential for future benefits.
- Specifications for optimization of resource use and of corresponding benefits.

The recognition of these two features helps to improve the formulation of SD models.

Third, an all-inclusive set of social, economic, and institutional aspects are sought to be incorporated in the concept of SD in the approach advocated by Gladwin et al. (1995) who defined the concept as "a process of achieving human development . . . in an inclusive, connected, equitable, prudent, and secure manner." Here, the inclusiveness implies human development over time and space; connectivity entails an embrace of ecological, social, and economic interdependence; equity refers to both intergenerational and intragenerational, and also to interspecies fairness. Prudence concerns care and prevention – technologically, scientifically, and politically; security demands safety from chronic threats and protection from harmful disruptions. This definition appears important, but rather utopian in its specifications.

New Definitions

Originally, the concept of sensible sustainability was intended only to allow limited substitutability within allowable limits, between different forms of capital. We require that for any sustainability, each component of the ecological capital vector be equipped with certain critical threshold levels, dictated by the considerations of avoiding stresses and maintaining system resilience. A number of components of natural capital and other forms of capital are allowed substitution, subject to preserving these critical levels. We refer to this process as sustainability, distinguishable from the two extremes of weak sustainability and strong sustainability, and also from sensible sustainability.

Much of the above discussion is largely centered around sustainability, and not SD. Hence, there is a need for a meaningful concept, built on sustainability approaches but also stipulating development aspects. It is proposed to define two important concepts; these will form relevant foundations for the analysis and discussion in the rest of the book.

Before we provide a new set of definitions which integrate biogeophysical, ecological and economic considerations, it is necessary to introduce another concept, applied in greater detail in chapter 4: "shadow prices." These are estimated to measure the "true" worth of a resource, and this assessment usually deviates from market prices. These can be computed only with reference to the relative levels of operation of each of the variables (and their constraint levels), formulation of objective functions (summation of net benefits or valuation, or broader welfare function), time horizons of evaluation and planning, and the time-dependency or endogeneity of discount functions applied to obtain the valuation of time profiles of the objective function; see the appendix of this chapter for a formal representation in the context of the economic models. Considerable additional information and clarity of assumptions is required – a price to be paid in search of precision.

The shadow prices are related to the specification of objectives, derived from a general socioeconomic philosophy. The relevant foundations for arriving at shadow prices are seen in chapter 4. For the present, it is useful to note that these prices are designed to reflect the opportunity costs and, thus, the real worth of a resource. It is easier stated than done: usually there are a range of values assignable as shadow prices. This is because these are sensitive to the explicit and implicit assumptions governing the specifications of the objectives and constraints. Do we value a dollar income for the poor at the same level as for the rich? Is the CO_2 assimilating capacity of a forest in Nepal a free good for the world and thus worth zero, or do we assign this function a value based on the opportunity cost of controlling CO_2 emissions by alternative means? Whose costs are valued or for whom are the benefits worth? Many similar questions need to be addressed in the context of assessing the shadow prices. Even though this may seem like raising more questions than answering them, the direction of analysis enables greater clarity regarding the evaluation framework and a conscious approach to evolve directions of progress.

The ecological definition of sustainability advanced at the end of the previous section can be narrowed down to the implications for the economic arena. This approach suggests that we can draw upon the economic and ecological resources to such an extent that the generalized economic capacity (the productive capacity which includes all forms of ecological capital) to produce material well-being of the human population is retained intact for ever (Rao, 1999). This concept has an important feature, explained below. The "rental" or "return" on this generalized capacity, when partitioned into relevant time periods (typically on a yearly basis) and applied to individual national economic systems, leads to an approximation of an adjusted Net National Product (NNP). This is based on a specific set of assumptions, and the related analytical details are provided in chapter 4. Using these considerations, we propose the new schematic representation depicted in figure 3.3 below, which is relevant for the rest of this text:

Figure 3.3 Schematic representation of SD

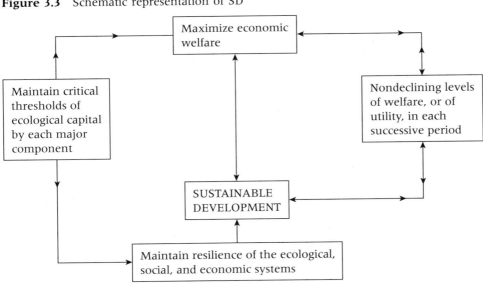

SD is the process of socioeconomic development which is built on the sustainability approach (defined above), with an additional requirement that the worth of the capital stocks vector (valued at applicable shadow prices) is maintained constant, or undiminished, at each time interval, for ever.

In contrast, a stronger version can be proposed, but this does not arise out of the economic efficiency considerations integrated in the above. Strong sustainable development (SSD) may be defined as the process of socioeconomic development which is built on the strong sustainability approach with the additional requirement that each individual component of the ecological capital stocks vector is preserved at constant or undiminished levels at each time interval for ever.

A number of pre-specified items are sought to be preserved without any reference to valuations of any type, in either of these two approaches: SD and SSD. This is the feature that bridges the gaps between the traditionally touted concepts of weak sustainability and strong sustainability. This also possesses requisite features to bridge some of the gaps between ecological and economic concepts of sustainability. SD becomes feasible with the provision of measures to protect certain assets purely based on societal and individual preferences unrelated to any calculations regarding gains and losses: ethical and other values do have a place here.

The well-known concept of sustainability advanced by Robert Solow (1994) stands closer to the SD approach, when it states that a society that invests aggregate resource rents in reproducible capital is preserving its capacity to sustain a constant level of consumption. Solow argued that a concept of sustainability implies a bias toward investment with a general interpretation: just enough investment to maintain the broad stock of capital intact. It does not mean maintaining the stock of every single thing intact. Substitution of resources is essential for continued economic progress. This statement does imply the need for continued technical progress, and continued improvements in the resource-use efficiencies. It is useful to note that Solow's insight comes very close to some of the philosophical observations of Rawls (1973), who argued that if savings processes continue for each successive generation, there will eventually be a point beyond which the rate of saving may stagnate and "it is sufficient that improvements in productive techniques be introduced only to the extent covered by depreciation." Solow's approach is very pragmatic, but is largely confined to generalized economic capacity to enable capital reproducibility and maintaining constancy of consumption. The role of the physical CC or of the environmental protection is reflected only through the effects on the economic potential and its realization in different intervals of time. The pragmatism of the approach arises when pre-specified unique features of the nature and environmental amenities like the Yellowstone Park, for example, are sought to be preserved without any reference to the aggregate resource valuation approach. Such an approach was part of Solow's approach: something unique and irreplaceable should be preserved for its own sake, but most natural resources are desirable for what they do, and not for what they are.

Is the above SD approach good enough for all countries, developed and less developed? Sustainability may not be an adequate goal in less-developed countries where addressing poverty remains the most important concern. Solow suggested that the less-developed countries may be able to exercise a set of options ranging from allowing a calculated degree of environmental degradation or acquiescing in their own poverty. It was indicated that temporary localized negligence may be paid for if these societies do care to set aside a part of gains to income to restore or build up the environmental infrastructure. The pre-requisites for this are to ensure that the resilience features are not lost in this process. If the episode given in figure 3.3 is any indication of the types of problems the less-developed countries might encounter, it is perhaps risky to adopt this approach. Hence the relevance of the SD approach here as well.

Sustainability and National Income

The implication of sustainability on national income or an approximation to this income is a relevant macroeconomic issue. When we deal with developed or largely monetized/marketized economies, we tend to apply the concepts of income, interest, and monetized values of national product and related economic parameters. Building upon such a background, several attempts to incorporate environmental accounting and valuation can be advanced, as was done during the 1990s. A good collection of papers can be seen, for example, in Lutz (1993). Several recent developments and perspectives are discussed in chapter 6. For the present, we need to examine the concepts of economic sustainability and their interpretation for national income.

The Hicksian concept of income remains one of the most important starting points for the debate. John Hicks (1946) stated: "We ask, not how much a person actually does receive in the current week, but how much he would be receiving if he were getting a standard stream of the same present value as his actual expected receipts. That amount is his income." It was also clarified that the purpose of such a concept of income was to give people an estimate of the amount which they "can consume without impoverishing themselves."

The above definition can be seen as an annuity-like measure, and is thus a dynamical one rather than a single time period measurement. Herein lies its strength. The Hicksian concept of income has been applied to national income concepts in several studies. Using rigorous analysis, Weitzman (1976) demonstrated that, under optimal growth with certain assumptions (discussed in chapter 4), the NNP (this being the consumption-adjusted gross national income) should be seen as income in the Hicksian sense. This forms a useful beginning in interpreting economic sustainability. Under the assumptions, the reasoning leads to the expression

$$NNP(t) = rW(t)$$

where r represents the rate of return on national wealth W, for each time instant (usually year, t). The NNP is thus the return on the magnitude of (possibly generalized) wealth, without diminishing the wealth and its productive capacity. It is thus an indicator of sustainability: NNP measures the maximum current level of satisfaction of human consumption that can be sustained for ever.

The above interpretations are not universally valid, for example, in the presence of continually or occasionally changing preferences reflected in the interest rates, unforeseen technological innovations, and other uncertainties. Under such configurations, NNP is not an indicator of sustainability. More details on these issues can be seen in chapters 4 and 6, using some of the optimizing models. A significant set of insights into economic approaches is advocated using the well-developed theories of "optimal development," which are founded on neo-classical economic growth theories, development economics, and institutional economics.

Readers familiar with optimization models recognize that the definition allows analytical formulations more in the style of "optimal development models." The concept of optimization and a simple model are provided in the appendix to this chapter. SD could be viewed as an application of the theory of optimal development; in the absence of such an approach, the ideas could be less useful for quantitative analysis. Dasgupta (1994) made two observations:

- The sharpest formulation of the idea suffers from the drawback that it is totally anchored to the present: no net accumulation of the overall capital base is recommended.
- Today's resource-poor economy is condemned to poverty in perpetuity.

Note that Solow's approach allows us to incorporate these aspects; he suggested the need for a greater role of capital accumulation in the near future for less-developed economic systems. Besides, most of the analytical tools used in Solow's reasoning are essentially based on the logic of optimal development. These considerations weigh heavily in our further treatment of various issues and models for policy analysis, discussed later in this book.

An important aspect of SD involves the production of knowledge. It is reasonable to assume that the growth of the stock of knowledge is itself a function of the deployment of relevant resources in a production sense. It is in the context of creation of knowledge that enhanced efficiency and improved use of resources with environmental upgradation is facilitated. This is the most powerful counterargument to the "entropy law" advocated in Georgesue-Rogen (1971). Without the creation of new knowledge, economic growth could lead to negative net returns to the society when all the inputs are properly accounted.

● 3.5 ECONOMIC GROWTH AND SUSTAINABILITY ●

Economic growth is conventionally measured in terms of increases in income. We are interested in the dynamics of sustainable economic growth with the requirement that desirable environmental features (specified type and degree) are sustainable. This formulation incorporates the inevitable link between economy and environment. Some of the analytical models are summarized in the appendix to this chapter. Some models treat economic growth as endogenous, relative to stock and flow of environment (and in some cases, to technical progress, or more generally, knowledge). The social utility function is most commonly formulated in terms of the utility of consumption, but this need not be the main approach. The utility function would be better served to recognize that humans do care for the benefits of environmental quality (directly and indirectly).

Empirical Studies

The empirical linkages between economic growth and impact on the environment and its sustainability have been explored by several authors in the 1990s. However, most of these investigations suffer from serious limitations imposed by the quality and availability of relevant data, weak theoretical and statistical foundations of the analyses, and the formulation of simplistic hypotheses for testing. It is, therefore, not surprising that there are no definitive or robust conclusions to the broadly posed question about relevant linkages. However, there are a few partial answers to related questions. Some of these are discussed below.

An "all-important equation" expressing the relationship between environmental impact and human activity was suggested as the IPAT model by Holdren and Ehrlich (1974). Although several improvements on the original framework exist, it is useful to discuss the early formulation as a starting point. The relationship is expressed as

$$I = PAT$$

where I is the environmental impact, P is population, A is affluence or economic activity per person (in other variations, this A could be per capita consumption), and T, the environmental impact per unit of economic activity, is a function of the technology used for the production of goods and services and by the institutional, social organization that influences deployment of technology.

If the population approximately doubles by the year 2150, as estimated in some studies, the resultant effect on I is not doubling, but it is affected by a multiplier factor. This factor is the product of effects of consumption (which is also influenced by any changes in income inequalities) and of technology (which is subject to changes with improved technical efficiency in production and in the treatment of industrial or other pollution). Thus, if the above formulation can be generalized to account for at least two more multipliers, each corresponding to changes in consumption and technology the outcome will be different. An attempt in this direction is seen in the study discussed below.

One of the recent and significant studies in this direction of inquiry is due to Dietz and Rosa (1997). The above formulation is converted to its stochastic version to account for potential discrepancies and uncertainties in the relationship or in data observations (or both) and applied to the specific environmental component: CO_2 emissions.

The model is specified as

$$I = aP_i A_i^b e_i^c$$

where the subscript i refers to the observation item; the coefficients a, b, c, e are to be obtained as statistical parameters using the data. The coefficients b and c determine the net effect of population and affluence on impact, and a is a constant that scales the model; technology (and other social, institutional, and cultural factors) is modeled as a residual term e. This version allows for identification of diminishing or increasing impacts due to increases in population or in affluence and, thereby, captures a relevant feature of the original framework. The empirical results, using data for 1989 for 111 countries, suggested that the effects of affluence on CO_2 emissions reach a maximum at about $10,000 in per capita gross domestic product and that these decline thereafter (75 percent of the 111 countries in the study possess per capita income at less than $5,000). This finding has a clear policy message: in the absence of active measures to reduce CO_2 emissions, the problem will continue to be exacerbated during the next several years due to economic growth in most parts of the world.

In both the above formulations, one robust formulation that remains generally intact is the postulate of some proportionality between I and P, A, and T or e; the constants or the non-constants of proportionality and the degree of proportionality varies over regions and time intervals. Technically, a nonlinear statistical estimation methodology is required to identify the parameters involved. It is useful to note that, even when some of the above formulations identify relative roles of contributing factors, this analysis is carried out at a very high level of aggregation and may not suggest substantive policy guidelines. Reducing population, consumption, and improving technology could be a solution, but it constitutes a rather trivial prescription. The planet did have less of the first two for a very long time but the quality of life, as we understand today, was not apparently great: let us consider the major ingredient of the quality of life, namely the life expectancy or its component, infant mortality rate, which was substantially less during the last century than in the current period in almost every region of the world. The question that still remains important is: Even after such advancements in the quality of life, if life itself is unsustainable on this planet, what good are those lifespan other achievements? We continue to answer these questions in various subsequent sections of this book. Let us note that human capital and its infrastructure (including knowledge, education, morbidity and mortality) are not fully reflected in the above framework. To illustrate the importance of these factors, let us pose the question: Is it implausible that we could have increasing population, greater affluence (especially in less-developed regions) and yet be innovative enough to accomplish goals of sustainability in terms of taking due care of source and sink problems of the planet? The challenge for the present generation is to find those feasible policies and programs.

Environmental Kuznets Curve

It was found that economic growth leads to enhanced environmental pollution and other problems in the quality of the environment. There are several studies which seek to establish possible links between the rise in national incomes and changes in environmental pollution. These are sometimes referred to as studies on the environmental Kuznets curve. Their role, merits and demerits are examined in this subsection.

One of the approximate estimates of per capita elasticity (global average) of CO_2 with respect to per capita gross national product (GNP) is 1.2; for details of estimation, see Parikh (1996). This implies that an increase of 1 percent in per capita GNP leads to an increase of 1.2 percent in CO_2 emissions. This is not to suggest that such an estimate holds in all countries and at every level of per capita income. It is also not proper to interpret the estimate for universal policy prescriptions. We need to establish if there is any direct relationship between rises in per capita incomes and the changes in per capita emissions of pollutants. An important aspect of investigations that sought to link up economic growth and the quality of the environment is the formulation testing the existence of an inverted U-shaped curve, e.g. $GNP per capita influencing CO_2 per capita. This is unfairly called the Environmental Kuznets Curve (EKC) in a part of the literature, simply because it is sought to be projected as an environmental counterpart to the original Kuznets curve (Kuznets, 1955): an inverted U relationship (IUR) between a measure of inequality in the distribution of income and economic growth. Since Simon Kuznets was not involved in any of the EKC hypotheses and since these seem too often to be misused, we refer to these relationships, as did Arrow et al. (1995), as an IUR rather than as an EKC. See figure 3.4 for the hypothesized but questionable relationship.

In a few economies, it has been observed that the positive link between economic growth and the quality of the environment changes its direction after a peak level in the case of some of the pollutants like SO_2; see, for example, Selden and Song (1994), and Grossman and Krueger (1995). This peak is expressed in terms of the incremental ratio of increase in environmental pollution per unit

Figure 3.4 Environmental Kuznets curve

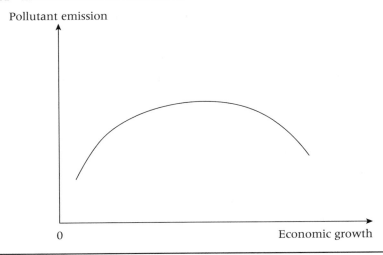

rise in income. It is useful to recognize that the relationship, wherever it can be established logically and empirically, applies only to a select set of environmental pollutants, and not to environmental quality generally (Arrow et al., 1995). Most empirical studies have not been successful in establishing the relevant relationships, and they did not provide a meaningful analytical basis on which the relationships were sought to be identified. In general, it is useful to note that all pollutants do not depict the same patterns of their accumulation. Hettige et al. (1997) found that the IUR tends to hold in respect of share of pollution from manufacturing activities, but not in the cases of the intensity (per unit of output) of industrial pollution at the emission/production level. Local air pollution (intensity per usage, but not the total pollution) in a few cases obeyed the IUR; see, for example, Hilton and Levinson (1998). However, the GHGs and municipal wastes usually increase with economic growth. It is important to recognize that the concept of the IUR is based on a model of the economy in which there is no feedback from the state of the environment to economic growth. Rising levels of deforestation and pollution are seen as having harmful effects on the quality of life but not in production possibilities. In the absence of any such feedback to production, if the EKC hypothesis were confirmed, this could imply that growth maximization is the solution to the pollution problems in less developed countries. Based on a critical review of several studies in circulation, Stern et al. (1996) made these suggestions:

- Given the skewness in income distributions in most societies, the existence of the IUR between the median income levels rather than the average per capita and the indicators of the environment may be a little more logical.
- The relationship offers very little in the way of guidance on real policy choices concerning SD.
- Even if the relationship holds in some cases, any structural relationship based on past technologies and institutions is no indicator of the future relationship.

In summary, economic growth does not automatically lead to a turning point after which economic growth leads to enhanced environmental quality. Similarly, a stationary zero level of economic growth is neither a necessary nor sufficient condition for SD. Further, even a zero growth in the "throughput" (deployment of physical resources in the systems that humans tend to affect directly) is also neither necessary nor sufficient to ensure SD. The fallacy of any such suggested requirements lies in ignoring the role of technical progress, and recognizing the feature that several scenarios of loss of resilience of the systems are compatible with an aggregate zero growth rate in the net throughput. Clearly, it is not suggested here that the latter will automatically bring about SD.

It is useful to recall some of the observations of Arrow et al. (1995):

- The IUR evidence neither guarantees that it will happen in all regions nor that it will occur in time to avert the important and irreversible global consequences.

- Economic growth is not a panacea for environmental quality. The composition of inputs (including environmental resources) and outputs (including waste products) in the growth process is of significance.
- The need to sustain ecological systems and their productive capacity is of importance to all countries, less-developed or developed.

Let us also recognize that the conventional methods of income accounting, and thus deriving estimates of economic growth, are founded on rather fallacious assumptions such as the irrelevance of the quality of environment in determining the economic efficiency. In the revised approach, involving appropriate environmental accounting and resource valuation, the economic growth (based on the concept of NNP, explained in chapters 4 and 6) tends to be smaller than that claimed in many countries. The significance of the IUR debate diminishes when the estimates of economic growth are properly revised to reflect these factors.

The operational issues implied by the relative priorities and time-discounting processes at work in different regions, societies, and institutions make a tremendous difference in the varying interpretations and application of the principles of SD. A less-developed country, for example, may maintain the stand that carbon sequestration via conservation of forest resources contributes to mitigating GHGs and hence to global commons problems but may enjoy greater immediate benefit in harvesting the forest resources in the process of economic growth and capital formation. Such regimes may be discounting the future more than developed countries do, and may be estimating that the divisible benefits of resource use are far greater than indivisible benefits of global commons and their preservation. A country like Bhutan, for instance, cannot be expected to retain its 75 percent of land covered under forest without realizing much current income because preservation does good to global commons, while the per capita income of the population continues to remain among the lowest in the world. These are areas of global concern in the design of international environmental policy and will be discussed in chapter 10. In this context, an important argument of Page (1997) warrants further consideration: an interactive approach to the intertemporal efficiency and equity of resource utilization. Such an effort is likely to be useful at national and international levels.

We conclude these arguments with these observations:

- Various methods used in the estimation of the interrelationship between economic growth and environmental quality remain largely too weak in the information base and analysis to be able to offer any significant policy guidance.
- To the extent that the results can be viewed as robust, the analysis so far suggests that the possibility of economic growth itself taking care of environmental sustainability is extremely remote.
- This does not imply that economic growth is not a necessary prerequisite for improved quality of life in less-developed regions.

- A realistic intervention policy in terms of incentives and disincentives for SD remains an important contributor to achieve desired goals, at global, national, and local levels.

● 3.6 THE PRECAUTIONARY PRINCIPLE (PP) ●

Environmental unknowns and surprises constitute a part of "ignorance" and a part of "ignore-ance" (Myers, 1995). At the time of the first major international conference on the environment in Stockholm in 1972, there was little mention of the currently recognized problems of global warming, acid rain, and deforestation. This was the case, despite the fact that the problem of global warming was argued in early 1896 by the Swedish scientist Svante Arrenius. SD cannot afford to ignore development policies that are based on incomplete and uncertain information. In addition to these features, system uncertainties or stochastic features of the biogeophysical (not necessarily to include socioeconomic) combined with nonlinear and irreversible phenomena do call for a cautious approach, largely expressed in terms of the PP.

The PP is based on the idea that any uncertainty should be interpreted toward a measure of safeguard. The PP is equivalent in a sense to a "better safe than sorry" principle, or "no regrets" policy. The Ministerial Declaration concluding the Second World Climate Conference in 1990 in Geneva stated that "where there are threats of serious or irreversible damage, lack of full scientific certainty should not be used as [a] reason for postponing cost-effective measures to prevent such environmental degradation." An urgent concern and application of the PP should be in the area of loss of biodiversity, which has biological, ecological, genetic, economic and other dimensions to the phenomenon.

The Rio Declaration of the Earth Summit 1992, Agenda 21, Principle 15 states: "In order to protect the environment, the precautionary approach shall be widely applied by States according to their capabilities . . ." The first international formulation of the principle was at the First International Conference on the Protection of the North Sea in 1984 when the focus was on emissions into the marine environment. The PP played an increasingly significant role since its endorsement by the Second International Conference of the North Sea in 1987.

Historically, the PP has been most frequently advocated in governing marine resources and pollution. Since many environmental problems are fraught with system uncertainties and incomplete information about the system characteristics, the principle tends to be equally applicable, especially in problems like GE. The increasing role of PP suggests that it is ripening into a norm of international law; some of the key elements of a legal definition rely on:

- a threshold of perceived threat against which advance action would be deemed justifiable; and
- a burden of proof on the activity contributor or entrepreneur to show that a proposed action will not cause actual harm; see also Cameron and Abouchar (1991).

The PP implies a current commitment of resources to safeguard against the likelihood of future occurrence of adverse outcomes of certain activities. This approach is implicitly seeking trade-offs in the interests of the present with those of the future, and thus depends on implicitly assumed time-discounting and future resource valuation. These factors are usually not examined in the current practices in the application of the principle. This is because the role of the PP is largely confined so far to providing guidance to policy judgment and providing the benefit of the doubt in favor of the environmental resources.

In the parlance of decision sciences, the PP is equivalent to "risk-averse" behavior in cases that involve irreversibilities or extremely high costs in socioeconomic or biogeophysical or other terms. When sought to be applied in general situations not necessarily involving these features, the PP could lead to a caution that may be attained at the expense of substantial potential gains. It would be similar to imposing a ban on any driving of an automobile since there is a positive probability of an accident in that activity. However, the risk-averse nature of the principle is relevant if scientific knowledge is too limited to quantify uncertainty and thus cannot establish probability distributions of potential outcomes; see also Bodansky (1991).

Although a useful approach, the PP cannot offer specific directions of policy since the role is primarily to set the direction of activities rather than the corresponding magnitudes. It is therefore important to view this important principle in conjunction with additional exercises in resource optimization for evolving an operationally specified program. This could also be accomplished with the use of select models and methods similar to those discussed in chapters 4 and 6. In the absence of such efforts, there is hardly any guarantee that simple adoption of the principle would prevent serious environmental and other damages. Nonetheless, the application of the PP may be viewed as a form of down payment for obtaining some environmental insurance. It is also important to ensure that the application of the PP involves both sides of the equation. For example, some of the pesticides can be avoided if there are organic substitutes or other less harmful alternatives; but a total ban on the former may not do much good if it leads to significant crop losses and food shortages. One may seek to apply the PP in protecting people and the environment against adverse effects of the use of such chemicals, but may be ignoring the relevance of application of the same principle in saving people's lives with the provision of uninterrupted food supplies. Thus, a risk-based cost–benefit analysis (see chapter 4) is an added requirement in the application of the PP.

The judicious use of the PP for SD requires identification of the areas of applicability, as in the case of atmospheric concentration of GHGs, loss of biodiversity, and soil degradation and desertification. This is not to suggest that the principle is any less relevant in apparently "non-environmental" sectors. Problems like those in child nutrition, health, and mortality issues, i.e. those that involve irreversibilities, also require application of one form or another of the PP. Let us note that some of these features, when neglected in their timely intervention, result in adverse consequences of low human capital levels on environment and SD. In all such cases, "help cannot wait" and adequate safeguards are essential against misery, low quality of life or lack of sustainability of divisible life at individual levels, household levels, and regional or other aggregative levels. Prevalence of such conditions poses major challenges for SD. It was estimated that the economic costs, including resources lost, due to high infant mortality rates in less-developed countries constitute about 2 percent of corresponding gross domestic products (GDPs) of each of these countries (Rao, 1982). A stinted population cannot enhance sustainability or SD. Clearly, this feature can only form a component of indicators of SD. The role of the PP in all such situations is to enable advance preventive measures, possibly with improved resource distribution mechanisms (including the role of education and human capital).

● 3.7 CONCLUSIONS ●

The important distinction between sustainability and SD allows one to examine more real-life solutions to identified and potential problems that affect the welfare of the human society. Some advocate assigning equal importance to all species on this planet. It is suggested here to accept the premise that humans continue to remain the dominant species but will need greater realization and action to ensure that other constituents of the ecosystems need to be preserved if the life-supporting nature of those systems is not disturbed to the detriment of the human population. Thus, SD continues to play a dominant role over sustainability, and the latter is deemed as a binding constraint on the socioeconomic development processes. Even after accepting such a premise, a number of factors – like the valuation of future and resources, perceptions and the role of uncertainty – contribute to alternative interpretations and policy guidelines.

Within the above framework, the concept of sustainability improvised with additional considerations of unique and irreplaceable assets (biological or other) tends to offer guidance to policies for pragmatic SD. This approach, strengthened with the use of comprehensive methods of optimal development, promises proper directions of economic inquiry applicable in a wide variety of socioeconomic systems. This is attainable with the application of select approaches for SD.

Environmental irreversibilities, cumulative effects and nonlinearities in environmental response to resource use pose major potential problems. These require extensive application of the PP and related decision-making mechanisms for environmental governance. All these salient features of life on planet Earth should form ingredients of comprehensive approaches to SD.

Economic growth remains a necessary requirement for the above development, but is not sufficient. A noninterventionist approach to the process is unlikely to mitigate the problems of environmental degradation and features of unsustainability in the economic sphere and ecosystems. Environmental improvement does not automatically follow economic growth. Active policies and implementation mechanisms are needed to achieve desirable environmental quality and sustainable standards of living.

Based on the different dimensions of the problems of sustainability, it is reasonable to summarize the following. The concern should not be any one of the following by itself: the rise of global mean temperatures, deforestation, the ozone depletion, the emissions of GHGs, the expanded scale of operations influenced by the growing population and consumption, or the general environmental pollution. Rather, it is the combined interdependent effects of these phenomena which are simultaneously at work, to an extent never experienced on Earth. This is precisely the problem of losing ecosystem resilience. The synergism here is of a strongly interwoven nonlinear relationship. The resultant outcome can be a set of unprecedented catastrophic problems cutting across all aspects of life and its potential for sustainability. Humanity is not prepared to face such large-scale adverse phenomena. If there is one area for application of the problem of "the fear of the unknown," perhaps this is it.

Appendix: Optimal Sustainable Development Models

Systems models are relevant for exploring the linkages between the environment/ecology and the economy. Some can lead to greater insights into the complex relationships and optimal interventions, if properly formulated. The brief presentation below is purely introductory, and a more complex formulation is required to represent realistic settings for their analysis. Models using different methods of optimization are useful when there is substantial clarity about various ingredients for their further formulation and processing. It is necessary to obtain a quantified assessment of options as well as their sensitivity to known influences or changes in the parameters identified, called structural equations and dynamics.

The following is an illustrative set of economic models which incorporate the role of environment/ecology as providers of infrastructural services, enabling the creation of conventional (manufactured or person-made) capital. A typical model is expected to specify:

- the set of policy instruments;
- their response variables or state variables;
- any applicable upper and lower limits or regions of operation of these, i.e. define the relevant ranges, including threshold levels;
- the time horizons – in the sustainability cases, these are usually infinite;
- objective function, like social welfare, social utility, or per capita utility of consumption or other meaningful specification;
- the dynamics of the interrelationships of the state variables and policy instruments via appropriate production functions (which incorporate the technological parameters in the production processes); and
- applicable balancing equations to "close the model."

These models can generate results like optimal levels of environmental abatement, pollution, and economic growth consistent with the maximization of the objective function over an infinite time period, subject to various specifications of constraints and a time-discount rate.

A few definitions are relevant here.

Policy instruments are the choice variables which are used to affect the system in a desired fashion. Some of the examples, depending on the context and structure of the model, include quantities and timing of resource extraction, environmental improvement expenditure, ecotaxes, farm input levels, and consumption in a specified sense.

The parameters affected by each of the policy instruments are termed *responses*, and the interrelationships between the two categories are required for any further formulations in the model.

Constraints could deal with availability of capital in a specified period, or limiting the emission of pollution within a specified limit in a given period, or other related features. If only a certain subsistence level of a commodity or resource is allowed, the same is reflected as an inequality constraint.

An *objective function* is usually one of the expressions for social welfare maximization, sometimes expressed as the maximization of utility of aggregate consumption.

$$J = \int_0^\infty U(C(t), E(t)) \, e^{-rt} \, dt \tag{3.1}$$

where $U(\cdot,\cdot)$ is the utility function, r the time-discount rate, $C(t)$ the consumption at time t, and $E(t)$ the corresponding magnitude of environmental quality.

Structural dynamics relate to the time-dependent evolution of various response variables. One of these is usually governing the dynamics of capital

$$\dot{K} = F(\cdot) - C - a \tag{3.2}$$

with $K(0) = c$, where F is the production function governing person-made capital, and a is the environmental improvement expenditure.

The dynamics of the stock of a pollutant can be described by

$$\dot{E} = -\bar{d}E + A \tag{3.3}$$

with $E(0) = q$, where $\bar{d}$ is the coefficient of natural dissipation of the pollutant, and A is the added flow of the pollutant during the period of concern.

Very few models treat environment explicitly as a stock and flow relationship, partly because of the problem of quantifying the dynamics except when dealing with resources, renewable or non-renewable.

Time horizon, T, is usually governed by the time horizon of concern, and is infinite in several types of SD models.

Discount rate, r, is perhaps the most critical parameter in the process of lumping the discounted sum of utilities or other benefits over the entire time horizon. Chapter 4 provides several insights into the issues involved in the selection of this factor.

One of the basic requirements of SD is to ensure that the set of feasible consumption paths potentially available to each successive generation is at least as comprehensive as the set available for the current generation. A feasible consumption path is a candidate in the set of consumption paths which obey all the constraints and other specifications of the model but may or may not satisfy the maximization criterion using the objective function.

What is an optimal SD model? The optimal economic growth model integrating environmental factors above should be rich enough to incorporate the dynamics and constraints of the ecological capital, in addition to the relevant threshold limits expressed as constraints. The requirements like nondeclining utility of consumption are also specified as additional constraints. The economy/ecology linkages thus are integrated.

In addition to (3.1) to (3.3), the system dynamics and specifications relevant for the optimal SD model are:

$$\dot{G}_i = L(G_i, E, K, V, t) \quad G_i(0) = g_i(0) \tag{3.4}$$

$$G_i(t) > g_i(t) \tag{3.5}$$

where G are the various components of the ecological capital, L is the generalized production function involving its conventional inputs K and V, and the conventionally recognized features of the environment E, and G the ecological inputs (such as any withdrawal of the carbon sink capacity, or assimilative and renewal or other features). In these specifications, (3.4) deals with the system dynamics and (3.5) specifies the critical threshold levels which are stipulated to be preserved to ensure system resilience. Clearly, the model described by (3.1)–(3.5) is preliminary and is provided to illustrate the definitions and the applicable models. More complex modeling exercises are expected to provide greater insights – not yet found in the literature.

This setting enables relevant shadow prices to be established for all the resources and inputs involved in the model. This is done by formulating a Lagrangean-type expression (called a Hamiltonian in dynamic models). This is essentially a weighted lumping of the objective function and the system dynamics as well as constraints. These weights, or auxiliary parameters (which are also time-dependent) are precisely the shadow prices. These are always sensitive to the specifications of the objective function and other ingredients of the model. A detailed application will emerge during the analysis in chapter 4, where alternative, simpler methods of inputing opportunity costs are also discussed.

Is sustainable growth optimal? We need some clarifications and more information to seek an answer. What constitutes sustainable growth and with respect to what objective function (and constraints) is it sought to be optimal? Sustainable growth is defined as the economic growth on a perennial path which does not incur any environmental risk and which allows nondecreasing consumption. The objective function for optimization is taken simply as a function of utility of consumption. The answer is conditional: it is not always true that there are optimal growth paths; for example, such an existence may be possible when there is time discounting above a certain technical minimum. Also, the stated formulation suggests that sustainable growth may, ultimately, have to do with a cardinalization problem of the social utility of consumption. It may be possible that the formulation can be enriched with the utility function directly incorporating stock of environment or, perhaps, some assessment of its quality could provide better insight.

Review Exercises

1   What inference, if any, can be drawn regarding long-term sustainability when an economy possesses the following features:
    (a)   positive but fluctuating growth rate; and
    (b)   systematically declining forest resources, with the decline in the growth rate at an average level below the average under (a)?
2   Based on the experience in Bangladesh (Box 3.3), (a) examine the short-term and long-term alternatives (from a multidisciplinary perspective) for the biogeophysical sustainability; (b) comment upon the system resilience aspects; and (c) examine if there is any relevance in the application of the concept of carrying capacity.
3   What could be potential costs to various sections of the society if we endorse strong sustainable development criteria? And, what are the likely benefits of this approach in the short run and in the long run? (Use a dividing line of one century for the two time horizons.)
4   Why is desertification an irreversible phenomenon? Is there any evidence historically, or scientifically, to support this conclusion?
5   What could be the likely costs of excessive deployment of the Precautionary Principle in economic and environmental decision making? What constitute the necessary prerequisites for a just application of the principle?
6   If the creation of applicable knowledge obeys the law of increasing returns to scale in the production functions, what are the implications of this process for environmental sustainability? Explain why it may not be sufficient (for sustainable development) to allocate most resources simply on knowledge and discovery processes, even if the human capital and financial resources allow such a deployment.
7   Examine the relationships between the criteria of safe minimum standards and of strong sustainability. Which of the two criteria is likely to be applicable in the preservation of endangered species, and why?
8   If the planet's sink capacity is to be treated as a part of the ecological wealth, how do we reflect the ecological capital in any of the economic growth and environment models?
9   How are the relative roles of stocks and flows of ecological capital linked to the stocks and flows of environmental and manufactured capital?
10   What are the underlying relationships between resilience, tolerance limits, thresholds, and stress? Examine these with a single period and multi-period time perspectives to gain relevant insights.

References

Arrow, K. J. (1972) *The Limits of Organization.* New York: W. W. Norton.

Arrow, K. J., Bolin, B., Costanza, R., Dasgupta, P., Folke, C., Holling, C. S., Jansson, B. O., Levin, S., Mahler, K. G., Perrings, C. and Pimental, D. (1995) Economic growth, carrying capacity, and the environment. *Science,* 26(8), 520–2.

Barbier, E. (1987) The Concept of Sustainable Economic Development. *Environmental Conservation,* 14(2), 101–10.

Bodansky, E. (1991) Scientific uncertainty and the precautionary principle. *Environment,* 33(7), 4–7.

Buchholz, R. A. (1998) *Principles of Environmental Management.* Upper Saddle River NJ: Prentice-Hall.

Cameron, J. and Abouchar, J. (1991) The precautionary principle – a fundamental principle of law and policy for the protection of the global environment. *Boston College International and Comparative Law Review,* 14, 1–27.

Ciriacy-Wantrup, S. V. (1952) *Resource Conservation – Economics and Policies.* Berkeley: University of California Press.

Civil Engineering Research Foundation (1996) *Symposium on Engineering and Construction for Sustainable Development in the 21st Century, CERF Report #96 – 5016A.* Washington, DC: CERF.

Clark, W. C. (1986) The cumulative impacts of human activities on the atmosphere. In *Cumulative Environmental Effects – A Binational Perspective, Proceedings of Workshop.* Ottawa: Canadian Environmental Assessment Research Council & National Research Council of Canada.

Costanza, R., Daly, H. E. and Bartholomew, J. A. (1991) Goals, agenda, and policy recommendations for ecological economics. In R. Costanza (ed.), *Ecological Economics – The Science and Management of Sustainability.* New York: Columbia University Press, 1–20.

Daily, G. (ed.) (1997) *Nature's Services – Societal Dependence on Natural Ecosystems.* Washington, DC: Island Press.

Dasgupta, P. (1994) Optimal versus sustainable development. In I. Serageldin and A. Steer (eds), *Valuing the Environment.* Washington, DC: The World Bank, 35–46.

D'Elia, C. F. (1995) Sustainable development and the Chesapeake Bay – a case study. In Munasinghe and Shearer (1995, 161–76).

Dietz, T. and Rosa E. (1997) Effects of Population and Affluence on CO Emissions. *Proc. National Academy of Sciences,* 94, 175–9.

Farmer, M. C. and Randall, A. (1998) The rationality of a safe minimum standard. *Land Economics,* 74(3), 287–302.

Fuwa, K. (1995) Definition and measurement of sustainable development – the biogeophysical foundations. In Munasinghe and Shearer (1995, 7).

Georgesue-Rogen, N. (1971) *The Entropy Law and the Economic Process.* Cambridge, Mass.: Harvard University Press.

Gilbert, A. J. and Braat, I. C. (1991) *Modeling for Population and Sustainable Development.* London: Routledge Publication.

Gillespie, J. (1973) Polymorphism in random environments. *Theoretical Population Biology,* 4, 193–5.

Gladwin, T. N., Kennelly, J. J. and Krause, T. (1995) Shifting paradigms for sustainable development – implications for management theory and research. *Academy of Management Review,* 20(4), 874–907.

Grossman, G. M. and Krueger, A. B. (1995) Economic growth and environment. *Quarterly Journal of Economics*, 112, 353–78.

Harremoes, P. (1996) Dilemmas in ethics – towards a sustainable society. *Ambio*, 25(6), 390–4.

Hettige, H., Manic, M. and Wheeler, D. (1997) *Industrial Pollution in Economic Development – Kuznets Revisited, World Bank PRD Working Paper #1876*. Washington, DC: World Bank.

Hicks, J. R. (1946) *Value and Capital*. Oxford: Clarendon Press.

Hilton, F. and Levinson, A. (1998) Factoring the environmental Kuznets curve – evidence from automotive lead emissions. *Journal of Environmental Economics and Management*, 35, 126–41.

Hoffmann, A. A. and Parsons, P. A. (1997) *Extreme Environmental Change and Evolution*. Cambridge: Cambridge University Press.

Holdren, J. and Ehrlich, P. (1974) Human Population and the Global Environment. *American Scientist*, 62, 282–92.

Holling, C. S. (1995a) Sustainability – the Cross-scale dimension. In Munasinghe and Shearer (1995, 65–76).

Holling, C. S. (1995b) Biodiversity in the functioning of ecosystem – an ecological synthesis. In C. Perrings, K. G. Maler, C. Folke, C. S. Holling, and B. Jansson (eds), *Biodiversity Loss – Economic and Ecological Issues*. Cambridge: Cambridge University Press.

Holling, C. S., Berkes, F. and Folke, C. (1998) Science, sustainability, and resource management. In F. Berkes, C. Folke, and J. Colding (eds), *Linking Social and Ecological Systems*. Cambridge: Cambridge University Press, 342–62.

Howarth, R. B. and Norgaard, R. B. (1992) Environmental valuation under sustainable development. *American Economic Review*, 82, 473–7.

ICPQL (The Independent Commission on Population and Quality of Life) (1996) *Caring for the Future*. New York: Oxford University Press.

Kuznets, S. (1955) Economic growth and income inequality. *American Economic Review*, 45(1), 1–24.

Lele, S. M. (1991) Sustainable development – a critical view. *World Development*, 19(6), 607–21.

Lutz, E. (ed.) (1993) *Toward Improved Accounting for the Environment*. Washington, DC: The World Bank.

Mitlin, D. and Satterthwaite, D. (1990) *Human Settlements and Sustainable Development*. Nairobi: UN Center for Human Settlements (Habitat).

Munasinghe, M. and W. Shearer (eds) (1995) *Defining and Measuring Sustainability – The Biogeophysical Foundations*. Washington, DC: The World Bank/UN University.

Myers, N. (1993) *Ultimate Security – The Environmental Basis of Political Stability*. New York: W. W. Norton.

Myers, N. (1995) Environmental unknowns. *Science*, 269, 358–60.

Page, T. (1997) On the problem of achieving efficiency and equity – intergenerationally. *Land Economics*, 73(4), 580–96.

Pagiola, S. (1995) *Environmental and Natural Resource Degradation in Intensive Agriculture in Bangladesh, World Bank Environment Department Environmental Economics Series Paper 15*. Washington, DC: The World Bank.

Parikh, J. (1996) Consumption patterns – the driving force of environmental stress. In P. H. May and R. S. da Motta (eds), *Pricing the Planet*. New York: Columbia University Press.

Peck, S. C. and Teisberg, T. J. (1993) The importance of nonlinearities in global warming damage costs. In J. Darmstadter and M. Toman, *Assessing Surprises and Nonlinearities in Greenhouse Warming*. Washington, DC: Resources for the Future, 90–105.

Rao, P. K. (1982) *Child Nutrition, Infant Mortality, and GNP*. Mimeo, Hyderabad, India: Centre for Development Research.

Rao, P. K. (1999) *Is Net National Product an Indicator of Sustainability?* (in press).

Rawls, J. (1971) *A Theory of Justice*. Cambridge, Mass.: Harvard University Press.

Rawls, J. (1973) Distributive justice. In E. S. Phelps (ed.), *Economic Justice*. Baltimore: Penguin Books, 319–62.

Schneider, S. H. (1997) *Laboratory Earth*. New York: Basic Books.

Selden, T. M. and Song, D. (1994) Environmental quality and development – Is there a Kuznets Curve for air pollution emissions? *Journal of Environmental Economics and Management*, 27, 147–62.

Serageldin, I. (1996a) Sustainability as opportunity and the problem of social capital. *Brown Journal of World Affairs*, 3(2), 187–203.

Serageldin, I. (1996b) *Sustainability and the Wealth of Nations – First Steps in an Ongoing Journey*. Washington, DC: The World Bank.

Solow, R. M. (1974) Intergenerational equity and exhaustible resources. *Review of Economic Studies*, 41, 29–45.

Solow, R. M. (1986) On the Intergenerational Allocation of Natural Resources. *Scandinavian Journal of Economics*, 88(1), 141–9.

Solow, R. M. (1994) An almost practical step towards sustainability. In *Assigning Economic Values to Natural Resources*. Washington, DC: National Academy Press.

Stern, D. I., Common, M. S. and Barbier, E. B. (1996) Economic growth and environmental degradation – the environmental Kuznets curve and sustainable development. *World Development*, 24(7), 1151–60.

Sunstein, C. (1997) *Free Markets and Social Justice*. New York: Oxford University Press.

Thompson, Q. (1996) Agricultural fertilizers as a source of pollution. In I. L. Pepper, C. P. Gerba and M. L. Brusseau (eds), *Pollution Science*. New York: Academic Press, 211–23.

UNDP (1996) *Human Development Report 1996*. New York: Oxford University Press.

van den Bergh, J. C. (1996) *Ecological Economics and Sustainable Development*. Brookfield: Edward Elgar.

Vellinga, P. et al. (1995) An ecologically sustainable biosphere. In DCLTEP (Dutch Committee for Long-Term Environmental Policy) (1994) *The Environment – Towards a Sustainable Future*. Boston: Kluwer Academic Publishers, 317–46.

WCED (World Commission on Environment and Development) (1987) (Brundtland Report) *Our Common Future*. Oxford: Oxford University Press.

Weitzman, M. L. (1976) On the welfare significance of national product in a dynamic economy. *Quarterly Journal of Economics*, 90, 156–62.

Wilson, E. O. (1992) *The Diversity of Life*. Cambridge, Mass.: Belknap/Harvard University Press.

World Bank (1995) *Mainstreaming the Environment – Fiscal 1995*. Washington, DC: The World Bank.

The World Conservation Union (IUCN), UNEP & Worldwide Fund for Nature (1991) *Caring for the Earth – A Strategy for Sustainable Living*. Gland, Switzerland: IUCN.

chapter outline

● CHAPTER 4 ●

Valuing Resources and the Future

● CHAPTER 4 ●

Valuing Resources and the Future

Do not do unto others as you would that they
should do unto you. Their tastes may not
be the same.
George Bernard Shaw

● 4.1 INTRODUCTION ●

The concept of sustainable development (SD) needs to be translated into meaningful policies and programs. This requires an understanding of different methods of evaluating relevant alternatives. These methods are also required for reconciling any conflicts in resource use and attainment of development objectives. Critical in these approaches are the valuation of resources for the current period and for various time intervals in the future. Conventional methods of analysis like cost–benefit analysis (CBA) form only some initial bases to improve upon. This is because these traditional methods did not consider some of the possibilities of disturbing the structure of the economic system and the locus of its equilibrium. These disturbances could be exogenous or they could be the result of adoption of policies based on such valuations. What good is it, for example, to assess the value of a resource based on the information available at one point of time and then to use that yardstick for several hundreds of years to come? Much worse would be the case when one adopts these yardsticks on a system which is to be modified when the yardstick itself is a product of the troubled system. These issues can also be stated in terms of the limitations of inferences based on *ex-ante* system features for their use in *ex-post* scenarios. Some of these issues can be viewed in terms of changes in different ecological and physical equilibria, as explained in the following section.

We need to reach beyond conventional environmental economics to derive relevant insights. Whether this is to be called ecological economics or modern environmental economics is a matter of interpretation. Environmental economics was, for several years, considered an area of economics which examines environmental externalities so as to analyze pollution taxes, incentives for minimizing such externalities and the valuation of natural environmental resources. These tasks remain relevant but, increasingly, concern is in terms of relatively macro issues like realization and valuation of nonmarket factors in the biosphere, sustainability of net national income and its possible role as an indicator of sustainability, economics of time discounting, and valuations of resources in an infinite horizon framework relevant for SD.

Why are a number of differences in the concept and implementation of SD as seen by ecologists, environmentalists, and economists differentiated again in terms of their areas of specialization? Part of the explanation lies in their implicit valuation of present and future resources, their varying levels of appreciation of the critical roles of different factors to ensure resilience of the systems, and the rules of trade-off involved in various benefits weighed against costs. When some economists emphasize the role of economic growth more than environmental preservation, the trade-offs are rather direct in a qualitative sense only; the amount of sacrifice involved in environmental resources to ensure desired economic growth is not usually quantified. Some of the methods of valuation discussed in this chapter are expected to play a useful role in any such attempts. It is not implied here that there are easily computable ready reckoners for this purpose. On the other hand, anyone professing the existence and applicability of such aids is simply ignoring the complexity of the problem. This, unfortunately, seems to apply to a number of "practical" CBA suggested in the literature.

Of interest in this chapter are approaches and methods of resource valuation in a static and dynamic context. These include the economics of exhaustible resources, the role of CBA, methods of discounting future values at current terms, the role and limitations of net national product (NNP) as an indicator of sustainability, and implications of changes in technical progress and preferences for most of the above. An element of technicality remains in some parts of the text, but it is possible to assess the main ingredients of the arguments even if some readers are not familiar with some of the analytical methods. The appendix to this chapter details the use of optimization techniques to study the implications of changes in technical progress and consumer preferences in interpreting NNP. Policy implications of the technical results continue to merit attention and these are explored at different levels of analysis.

● 4.2 GENERAL METHODS OF VALUATION ●

The logic of interdependencies in general systems is applicable for economic and ecological systems. The global environmental and climate change problems tend to alter these system characteristics in such an unprecedented manner that the definitions of the new equilibria differ from those of the undisturbed old system. A relatively closed system then becomes an open one and the interrelationships of the previous system do not hold any more. The concept of "balance of nature" in natural sciences is a static one, and valuations of resources cannot be based simply on such a framework. The "flux of nature" is a dynamic equilibrium concept which allows a number of changes to interact and evolve in the system. With issues like global climate change, we need to bear the valuation problems in close relation to the flux of nature rather than to the balance of nature. This is the required integration of an economic system with the functioning of the ecosystem and vice versa. The features of the ecosystem resilience as discussed in chapter 3 become very pertinent here.

The flux of nature is an influence which may lead to loss of system resilience if certain thresholds are not maintained. These thresholds are the physiological limits under which organisms can continue to survive and function without stress. Within such limits, the biological processes do permit some degree of adaptation in response to marginal random disturbances, induced anthropologically or otherwise. The time required for such adaptation responses is critical: if a naturally (literally) determined time-lag is not allowed, the outcome is an unsustainable continued perturbation of the ecosystem leading to nonlinearities, irreversibilities and consequent surprises. These are the fundamental considerations which mandate a more careful approach toward the assessment of resource values and prescription of policies on these bases. Figure 4.1 provides the linkages between static equilibria (balance of nature), dynamic equilibria (flux of nature), and resilience.

The classical paradigm in ecology emphasized the phenomena of balance of nature, but recent trends support the approach of the flux of nature as a relevant direction of the study of the dynamics of ecosystems. This is largely due to the relatively recent realization that stable equilibria are usually non-existent. The emphasis in the new paradigm, with its focus on the flux of nature, is on the impact of continued disturbances to the ecosystem. Many biotic interactions

Figure 4.1 Equilibria and resilience

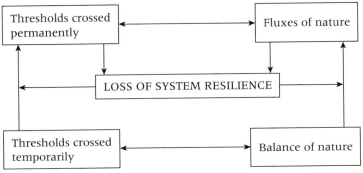

tend to have the same type of impact as physical disturbances. For example, deforestation and loss of biodiversity are attributable to anthropogenic influences or disturbances; and these contribute to changes in biotic interactions and aggravate the influences with positive feedback, and possibly lead to loss of resilience with implications for SD. Proper offsets of such effects and related management of fluxes of nature remain areas of concern in the arena of SD. Relevant principles of management draw on a group of interdisciplinary approaches, especially in the ecological economic sense. An important component of this is the valuation of various resources, market-based and other. Usually, there may not be any explicit markets to assist in this attempt, and hence there is a need for a comprehensive assessment in the valuation mechanisms.

Valuation of natural capital, environmental and ecological resources, and their assessment over a period of time (usually a long or very long horizon into the future) remains a complex issue. Acceptance that human systems operate within the global ecological system, and that the resources of the latter are finite, leads us to the realization of the relative scarcity value of exploited capacities of the sources and sinks of the planet in their performance of ecosystem services, the fundamental ingredients of life and economy. This should facilitate a better understanding of the opportunity costs or true worth values of various factors for their valuation in the context of SD. An evaluation of economy–environment policies at the national level does require a framework of optimizing social well-being, subject to preservation of environmental capital and potentially changing preferences and production. These considerations include the effect of valuation over time via time discounting, intergenerational interests, and technological changes.

The single most important factor to be reflected in any valuation of the resources is that their availability is limited; these are relatively scarce in some of the regions and time periods, and thus the economic institutions must be sensitive to the natural constraints. The failure to formulate these constraints in economic models is a limitation of the state of economic science. This can be resolved with an interdisciplinary approach and integrated ecology–economy models. The role of the biophilia adds an additional dimension to these issues, especially in the dynamics of the systems.

The ability of the ecosystem to retain its resilience is unlikely to be reflected by linking the system with consumer-oriented economic systems. This assertion holds, in particular, when the present structure of individual preferences is utilized in analyses seeking to prescribe policies for the overall system. The preferences are usually endogenous to existing mechanisms of resource allocation, institutions and legal entitlements governing the same; also, expressed preferences are rarely acontextual. See Sunstein (1997) for the effects of legal provisions on the endogenous preference structures. It does not offer much help to prescribe policies for SD when such an endogeneity of preferences prevails.

We return to the approaches of anthropocentrism and ecocentrism briefly. As clarified in chapter 3, these are not necessarily mutually exclusive, except in a small region of levels of use of resources before losing the resilience of the ecological systems. However, the real issue is, before losing the resilience, are we likely to consider the ecocentric views in addition to the anthropocentric approaches? Or, even worse, are we going to adopt the conventional economic evaluation of resources where some of the resources of the planet are not usually considered finite or scarce? We believe that a pragmatic approach would call for a balance of these alternate premises simultaneously considered. The last ingredient first: the conventional economic analysis has an important place, provided it is confined to its meaningful limits. A whole new economics is unlikely to emerge before the current pressing problems of the planet are resolved. We need to improvise relevant new approaches with awareness about the roles and limitations of each approach.

Reverting to anthropocentrism, do people care about other species in a sense not necessarily utilitarian? A partial answer may be given with an illustration. A survey in the New England region of the USA reported that 79 percent of respondents supported the position that "all species of wildlife have a right to live independent of any benefit or harm to people"; see Stevens et al. (1991). This may not automatically imply that public policies and public expenditure programs attach enough significance to these aspects to ensure the sustainability features: the same coastal region underwent serious problems with depleting fish stocks due to excessive fishing activity. For a utilitarian framework, the survey reveals that there is an "existence value" (see below) of species. This does not imply that a utilitarian framework is sufficient to safeguard the interests of SD unless the constraints on the functioning of the system are explicitly reflected in every decision.

In the approach of utilitarianism, things have value to the extent that they confer satisfaction to humans; however, this does not necessarily imply abuse of the planet's resources or lack of any interest, say, in the rights of animals or regard for various segments of nature. It asserts that we can assign value only insofar as we humans take satisfaction from doing so. This line of valuation, though, can only go this far: it may not be consistent with a biogeophysical or ecological approach required for SD. Hence there is a role for normative scientific considerations which ensure resilience of the ecosystems. In other words, any features of potential loss of resilience are unlikely to be reflected in market signals like scarcity prices, until it is too late to rectify the problems. We may, therefore, summarize this predicament with the suggestion that utilitarianism has its place if this premise can be broadened to include concerns for system-wide implications of alternative choices and anthropogenic influences on resilience features.

Valuation of Natural Resources

We need to clarify the distinctions between the main categories of natural resources: renewable, non-renewable, and exhaustible resources. There are physical, technical, and economic definitions relevant here. We shall approach these primarily from an economic viewpoint. Renewable ones, like water or marine fish, have their thresholds. When these are crossed, their renewal characteristics are physically diminished (with excessive mining of groundwater or overfishing).

The consequences of such reductions tend to be reflected in their market prices (although not universally). A non-renewable resource differs from the exhaustible resource insofar as the former asserts only its depletive feature without reference to the possible exhaustiveness itself. An exhaustible resource is a non-renewable resource, but the converse need not be true. This is because of the potential for technical and economic barriers to exhaust the resource.

Valuations are usually linked directly or indirectly to some market mechanisms. Markets constitute a part of the mechanisms affecting resource prices, and it is only rarely that the prices approximate to the "real value" of any resource. This is because the constellation of market and nonmarket institutions and their functioning efficiencies affect any observed market prices. Do declining prices over the years of commodities suggest their relative abundance? A study by Barnett and Morse (1963) indicated that the cost of deriving many of the resources from their natural sources had declined rather systematically for about a century. There are evidences in both renewable and non-renewable categories of resources which indicate that their real costs of extraction are on the rise (as is the case with depleting water supplies in some regions of the world). However, a few studies attempted to use the Barnett and Morse study to suggest the role of technical progress and underplay the problems of resource management. These interpret the declining trends in some of the commodity prices as an indication that there is no problem of exhaustible resources to worry about. Two reasons are given:

1   What was once thought of as a fairly limited quantity of availability of certain natural resource stock happens, from time to time, to exceed the limits of such expectations because of new discoveries in the natural stock deposits.
2   Continued technical progress leads to efficiency improvements in resource use and the utilization of alternative inputs (either in the form of substitutes or choice of new inputs as a result of new technologies).

An illustrative example to this position is the price of crude oil in the international (and several domestic) markets during the late 1990s: in some parts of the world the price is less than that of filtered water. Does this mean oil is now a cheaper "renewable resource" (like water), or that there is a glut in the stocks of oil reserves and their discoveries, or are there some other reasons of international trade and political economy affecting the prices of oil? The last point constitutes a relatively temporary phenomenon. Here, the traditional concept of prices reflecting scarcity is relevant when appropriate information about demand and supply factors is fully transmitted and assimilated by all economic agents in the marketplace, assuming that the markets function efficiently and that there is no exogenous role of various institutions affecting the price mechanism. In the presence of institutionally transmitted transaction costs – as in the case of international political economy with oil, in spite of the forum of the oil-producing and exporting countries (OPEC) – the price mechanisms are not usually reflective of resource scarcities or their abundance.

Conservation of Mass

The following proposition, due to Perrings (1997), is a fundamental statement with its implications for time-dependent valuation of resources, and for the validation of a positive value under all transformations and conditions for the source as well as sink features (see chapter 2 for details) of the planet Earth:

Proposition 1 (Perrings, 1997)
(a) Given the conservation of mass, any system generating non-zero residuals will be time varying in its coefficients of production.
(b) A subsystem within the global economy–environment system may become technologically stationary at equilibrium with the existence of residuals if, and only if, these have no effect on the usable technology.

The proof of these results was based on a systems model with an input–output approach and properties of long-run equilibrium; it does not involve very restrictive assumptions to arrive at these results. Given the relative robustness of these assertions, it is prudent to account for these aspects in the framework for valuation of resources, at the source or sink, or other levels. Also, the interpretations of this proposition tend to coincide with those resulting from the application of the ecological paradigm suggesting the relevance of the phenomena of flux of nature.

It is important to view the significance of global ecological and environmental resources in terms of the service function in converting flows of services into the consumption sector with or without depleting their stocks and interrelationships with the value of their services. The least that can be done is to assign a positive value to any flow of services which has some relation to one or more of the stocks of environmental and ecological capital, whether or not these stocks are quantified in monetary terms. In a bold and rather crude approximation of values of nature's services, Costanza et al. (1997) observed that, for the entire biosphere, the value of nature's services annually added to no less than about $16 trillion (1994 prices) and could be in the range of $54 trillion, compared to the global gross national product (GNP) of about $18 trillion a year in the mid-1990s; see box 4.1 for details. So much for nature's generosity! It is also useful to note that nature's services can be transformed to a set of higher levels values (without necessarily relying on market mechanisms) with improved management of the current systems of withdrawal of natural resources and restoration of their regenerative capacities.

The utilitarianism approach allows the valuation of resources: it embraces both direct use values and indirect use values, for consumptive and nonconsumptive uses. It also includes nonuse values (values that do not involve any actual direct or indirect physical involvement with the natural thing in question) and these could be the greatest of all values. It is the wealth of this sink or source which generates relevant flows of ecosystem services supporting the functioning of

BOX 4.1   Estimates of Nature's services

The Costanza et al. (1997) study was considered the first approximation of valuation efforts. The estimates of the values of the ecosystem services are based on a biogeophysical approach: the services by each type are estimated per unit area by biome and then multiplied by the area of each biome, leading to the sum.

The 17 ecosystem services included in the study are: GHG regulation, climate regulation, environmental disaster regulation, regulation of hydrological cycles, water resource supply, soil erosion control and sedimentation retention, soil formation, nutrient cycling, waste treatment and assimilation, botanical pollination, biological control and regulation, refugia applicable to various species, food production, raw materials, genetic resources, recreation, and cultural opportunities. One of the most significant shortcomings, as stated in the study, is of intercountry comparisons in valuation and relating to purchasing power. Despite several crude approximations, the point is made: the quantum of Nature's subsidies is significantly greater than conventional production in each year, and this production itself is critically dependent on the continued provision of services by nature.

Several methods were deployed to estimate the values of various services involved, including the use of secondary sources of information. The public goods nature of the services requires using a variety of methods to assess the values. Most of the estimates were derived from the valuation of nonmarket factors and were based, directly or indirectly, on many estimates of consumer willingness to pay (WTP) and other survey methods. Given the incomplete public understanding of the significance of some of Nature's ingredients, any of these are expected to lead to relative underestimates. Thus the estimates given in the study are minimal levels only.

The study estimated that the average value of the ecosystem services at current margins of their levels of operation or flow of services is of the order of $33 trillion annually, which is 1.8 times the current global GNP. The major part of the services valued stand outside the existing systems of markets of traded items. Some of these annual values include: GHG regulation valued at $1.3 trillion, waste treatment at $2.3 trillion, and nutrient cycling at $17 trillion. In terms of biogeophysical classifications, the major part of the contributions comes from the marine systems; the forests contribute about $4.7 trillion and wetlands also about a similar amount.

The authors concluded that, if the ecosystem services were paid for, the global price system would be very different from what it currently is.

Source: Summary based on Costanza et al. (1997)
Reprinted by permission from *Nature*. Copyright © 1997 Macmillan Magazines Ltd.

economic systems. It is thus a misnomer to dub much of the worth of the eco-system as a "nonuse value."

The array of services provided by ecosystems spans all of these category values. The pest-control and flood-control services offered have a direct use value for nearby agricultural produces. The provision of habitats for migratory birds implies an indirect use value to people who enjoy bird-watching or bird songs and, depending on whether such birds are watched or heard or hunted, the indirect value to the consumer may be consumptive or nonconsumptive. There are two forms of utilitarianism; see, for example, Goulder and Kennedy (1997). The first is called the weak form of utilitarianism; this asserts that the value of a given species or form of nature to an individual is entirely based on its ability to yield satisfaction to the person (directly or indirectly). The second is called the strong form of utilitarianism which makes an assertion about the value of a species (or other natural thing) to society, inherent in the CBA methods.

Traditionally, total economic value (TEV) has been a useful concept; see figure 4.2. TEV is defined as the sum of use value (UV) (direct plus indirect), option value (OV), existence value (EV), and other nonuse value (ONUV):

$$TEV = UV + OV + EV + ONUV$$

The EV is not the same as the preservation value: the latter corresponds to the continued existence of an entity for reasons other than any expected benefit for the valuing people. It is thus meaningful to expect the preservation value to be reflected in the ONUV. Nonuse values comprise two components: EV and OV. The EV is the value that derives from the sheer contemplation of the existence – apart from any direct or indirect uses of goods and services; survey approaches such as ontingent valuation assessments are considered relevant. The OV can be interpreted in two ways. In the first, this refers to a premium that people are willing to pay to preserve an environmental amenity, over and above the mean

Figure 4.2   Ingredients of TEV

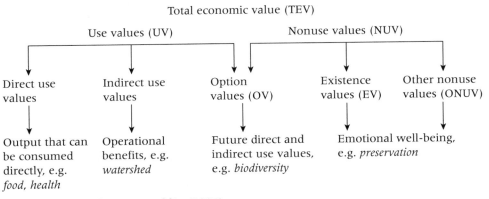

Total economic value (TEV)

Use values (UV)   Nonuse values (NUV)

| Direct use values | Indirect use values | Option values (OV) | Existence values (EV) | Other nonuse values (ONUV) |

| Output that can be consumed directly, e.g. *food, health* | Operational benefits, e.g. *watershed* | Future direct and indirect use values, e.g. *biodiversity* | Emotional well-being, e.g. *preservation* | |

Source: Modified from Serageldin (1995)

value (or expected value) of the use values anticipated from the amenity. This premium reflects individual risk-aversion; in the absence of the latter, people's WTP would equal the mean use value, and OV equals zero. In the second approach, the future value is not necessarily assessed by individual members of the society but the system realizes the benefits – as in for example, the medicinal value of a plant variety which might be commercially exploited at some time point.

The question as to whether these different components should be brought to the same units of numéraire is debatable; any simple computations warrants such approximations, however crude. This may be tolerable as long as we recognize the existence of this feature. The UVs include direct UVs – which are primarily outputs that can be measured directly – and indirect UVs, including functional benefits like flood control as a result of afforestation. The nonuse values comprise OVs, EVs and ONUVs hedging like genetic diversity and hedging.

Another related concept for valuation is that of WTP. This is regarded as the measure of satisfaction, and is usually estimated from information generated from surveys administered on relevant samples of population. However, heavy reliance on an assessment of WTP can be misleading sometimes for policy assessment or valuation of a resource for the following reasons:

- Individuals are not necessarily fully informed of some structural linkages and the worth in a long-term sense.
- Depending on the specific society and sample of people involved, their degree of self-interest can be highly significant and subject to large variations.
- This approach tries to convert a public goods issue into a consumer sovereignty problem and thus misplaces the whole focus.

Let us consider an illustration of the last component: if a society prefers to discount the future at an extremely high rate, is that a beneficial method of assessing the parameters for any further use? The high discount rate is an indicator of relative impatience for consumption possibly due to dire present needs or other reasons. The estimate of such a potentially counterproductive time preference requires a balanced approach to resolve present versus future consumption profiles. A detailed discussion of the implications of choice of discount rates appears later in this chapter.

Contingent Valuation (CV) Method

When some of the ecological goods and services are not transacted in the marketplace or when there are serious deficiencies in the competitiveness of markets or in the governmental institutions affecting the same, we need a set of assessments about perceived values of the goods and services for any trade-off at the margin between different scarce resources. The CV method is one aid in this process of assessment. By means of the questionnaires or gaming situations, people are asked to indicate the amount of money they are willing to pay to maintain or improve specific natural environmental features. The CV approach posits a virtual or hypothetical market for an unpriced good or service, and elicits information from individuals to assess the monetary value they place on a specific entity; see, for example, Portney (1994) and Cummings et al. (1986) for a detailed discussion.

Although the CV method is under increasing attack from environmentalists and a few others, it is interesting to note that its early origins had a lot to do with concerns about environmental issues. The first reference is to Ciriacy-Wantrup (1947), who explored the use in devising means to prevent soil erosion and siltation of water streams. Since the latter belonged to the arena of public goods, he suggested it would be useful to elicit information on the demand for these goods by asking individuals how much they were prepared to pay for the preservation and improvement of such assets.

Environmental resources are usually complex and are valued across several diverse dimensions, not all of which are commensurable on the same scale of measure. This calls for a multi-attribute evaluation approach. An approach to CV methods wherein the multi-attribute nature of the individual utility function is recognized is detailed in Gregory et al. (1993). It is useful to note that preferences or individual valuation of environmental resources can be endogenous to the setting in which these are expressed: private preferences for environmental goods may be adaptive to existing perceptions of environmental options; preferences are also endogenous to existing legal policy, including the setting of the legal entitlement (Sunstein, 1997).

A high-powered expert report (Arrow et al., 1993, hereafter referred to as the Arrow Panel Report) for the US National Oceanic and Atmospheric Administration advocated that when the CV method is used to elicit values for nonmarketed environmental goods and services, WTP questions should be administered using a discrete choice framework: individuals tend to make reliable responses if asked to choose from a set of distinct alternatives relating to their WTP for the goods and service, rather than having to assess a maximum sum which they might be willing to pay (as sought in some administered surveys).

One survey in a developing country attempted to utilize the Arrow Panel Report to gauge the public WTP for recreational facilities in an urban region. This study, due to Hadker et al. (1997), is summarized in box 4.2. It does reveal a few important features – the significance people attach to other forms of life, and the need to provide for such facilities in developing countries with a substantial element of potential self-financing of operations (given the WTP features) just as in the developed world. The example in box 4.2 also lends support to some endogenous characteristics, like some people expecting the government to take care of the expenses for maintaining the park. This is due to the general belief in the omnipotent government.

In the US systems, the practical significance of CV methods was enhanced after the interpretation of the US Comprehensive Environmental Response, Compensation, and Liability Act (CERCLA) of 1986, by the District of Columbia Circuit Court of Appeals (in Ohio v. US Department of Interior). This verdict granted equal standing to expressed and revealed preference evaluation techniques,

BOX 4.2   Borivili National Park – Bombay (Mumbai) case study

Following part of the framework given in the Arrow Panel Report, this study conducted a survey and analysis of the Bombay city area. The main objective was to elicit WTP from the residents for the maintenance and preservation of the Borivili National Park (BNP), using the CV method. BNP is the largest reserve in the Bombay metropolitan region, with a total land area of around 103 square kilometers. BNP is the home for several endangered species. On an annual basis, about 2.5 million people (the highest for any Park in India) are estimated to visit the Park.

The survey for this study was canvassed physically, not by mail or phone methods. Information brochures about the Park were given to the respondents since it was felt that the survey would not elicit the right valuation in the absence of such information at the respondent level. The final sample consisted of 494 respondents. The average household comprised of 4.35 members, who had lived in the area for about 28 years, and the monthly per capita income averaged to Rs. 2,113 (about $65 at 1996 prices). The sample did include about 22 percent respondents who never visited the Park. The summary highlights of the study are given below.

About 32 percent of respondents stated that they would contribute to the upkeep of the natural asset even if they did not visit it; 91 percent responded that animals had a right to exist even if they may be of no use to humans, and 25 percent stated the government should pay for environmental preservation. The main assessment of the WTP led to the estimate of Rs. 7.5 per month per household at least for the next five years. This was discounted over time and aggregated for the Bombay city region to about one billion Rupees, i.e. about $27 million.

Source: Reprinted from Hadker et al. (1997) with permission from Elsevier Science

and accepted nonuse values as a legitimate component of total resource value (Gregory et al., 1993). Although the CV methods admit potential variations in the estimates, properly conducted studies can be meaningful within a given market and institutional configuration. The next section addresses the market-based methods of studying the economics of exhaustible resources, useful for economic behavioral interpretations.

● 4.3 ECONOMICS OF EXHAUSTIBLE RESOURCES ●

What constitutes an exhaustible resource? Any resource need not be physically exhaustible at some time point, or in some geographic region, to deserve this distinction. Much of the analysis in traditional economic literature refers to non-renewable resources when it refers to exhaustible resources. Resource use leads to an increase in the relative scarcity value of the corresponding resource and tends to reflect this (in the absence of other institutional influences or transaction costs) in increasing market prices if the resource or its products are channeled into the marketplace via the market institutions. In the nonmarket scenarios, the valuation is subject to some of the nonmarket valuation methods which also depict similar trends. The finiteness of most mineral stocks (physical stocks or reserves) brings them directly into the list of commodities under this category, whether or not there exists a consistent increasing trend in their relative prices. The feature of non-renewableness is more significant than exhaustibleness in most resources. For all practical purposes, the existence of an inaccessible (technically or cost-prohibiting) quantity of a non-renewable resource is just as bad as an exhaustible one. No doubt, technical progress in devising substitutes and modes of production plays a key role in the utilization of the original resource and its price movements. In fact, there are several configurations in the real world when relative price declines were noticed and these symptoms are sought to be used by some analysts to interpret that there is little problem of sustainability in these resources. The relative decline of relative prices is partly due to new discoveries, which create a temporary sense of euphoria; markets may not be capable of optimizing infinite horizon decision models. One of the fundamental considerations in the economics of exhaustible resources is the economics of infinite time horizons: if we cannot improvise constraints relevant in the long run, we may not be able to find a rational solution for current policies and practices. Although, in the long run we are all dead, there will be our descendants (assuming we adopt SD patterns of consumption and production), whose interests should not be usurped by us.

One of the earliest and most significant methodological contributions is due to Harold Hotelling (1931) in the context of the economics of exhaustible mineral resource extraction. The Hotelling rule went almost unnoticed for a few decades and became a widely debated method only since the 1970s. It is interesting to recall an observation of Hotelling, in the wake of a growing trend of environmental conservationism. Hotelling stated that the conservation movement, insofar as it seeks an absolute ban on certain production activities rather than a desire for relevant taxation or regulation policies "in the interests of efficiency, may be accused of playing into the hands of those who are interested in maintaining high prices for the sake of their own pockets rather than of posterity."

The Hotelling rule for optimal resource extraction states that, in a certainty-governed world, an additional unit of resource will be conserved only if the resource price (net of costs) rises at a rate faster than the market rate of interest. Some of the economic concepts relevant for the analysis in the discussion to follow are given in box 4.3.

Theorem 1 (Hotelling, 1931)
In the context of a competitive resource extraction industry, the rule states that the optimal extraction policies obey the condition:

BOX 4.3   Concepts and definitions – resource economics

Certainty equivalent: the comparison of an uncertain quantity X in relation to the probability of its attainment of different values and then comparing the resultant with its certainty c, i.e. if the expected value is $E(X) = c$ then X is considered the certainty equivalent of c; in the discrete version case, the expected value is given by the sum

$$\sum_{i=1}^{n} p_i x_i$$

where p_i are the probabilities of realization of values x_i in all the n states which cover the possible alternatives

Consumer surplus: the additional utility that might be available to a consumer as a result of a change in price or non-price intervention relative to the scenario without such a change

Endogenous: the dependent entity which responds to an evolving or changing feature or structural relation in the system affected by the factor or the entity under consideration

Exogenous: any variable or influence which is prescribed without any direct influence of the system under its influence

Expected value: the sum of the products of quantities with their corresponding probabilities of occurrence or realization

Non-additive utility: the utility levels which do not simply add from one period to another without their inter-period dependency

Recursive utility: the emergence of successive periods of utility in terms of the preceding ones

Risk-averse behavior: the decision-making approach where the certainty equivalence is not enough to offset the involved uncertainties, and the decision situation warrants greater risk premium g to compensate for the uncertainties, i.e.

$$E(X) + g = c$$

Risk-taking behavior is the converse of the above. Here

$$E(X) - g = c$$

These definitions are based on the approach of "expected values" for decision making, sometimes called first-order risk-aversion criteria. There are other alternative criteria for decision making, and those lead to a different set of estimates for the risk premia.

Risk-neutral behavior: the acceptance of certainty equivalence as a relevant decision criterion, i.e. being indifferent between the certainty equivalent quantity and the corresponding level of quantity with certainty

Time-consistency: in a multi-period decision-making process, sticking to the multi-period decision at the end of each successive period as if the original decision still holds for the remaining periods even with new information or other changes; consistency of preferences over time was also defined by Gary Becker (1998) as the choices an individual would like to make in the future, if he/she knew at current time what would happen in the interim, are exactly the same as the choices he/she will actually make then

$$\frac{\dot{P}}{P} = \rho$$

where P is the net price (i.e. net of extraction costs) of the resource and ρ is the constant rate of return on a risk-free alternative asset (like a bond). The left-hand side of the above equation represents the rate of increase in the net price – a constant (since the right-hand side is a constant).

A number of studies have tried to test the theory empirically for some mineral commodities. The empirical support to the rule has been extremely meager – see, for example, Halvorsen and Smith (1991) – due to the role of risks in investments and returns. Some of the recent investigations for generalization of the theory incorporated the role of risk and uncertainty in the resource extraction policies. Theorem 2 is a relevant conclusion from these.

Theorem 2 (Malliaris and Stefani, 1991)
In a competitive market situation, the expected rate of return on an exhaustible resource will differ from the expected rate of return on alternative assets by the magnitude of the risk premium δ (i.e. the excess return required, relative to risk-free return on investments like the US Treasury Bills, to compensate for the specific risk) associated with the resource asset; see, for example, Malliaris and Stefani (1991). In this case, the Hotelling rule is modified as follows:

$$\frac{\dot{P}}{P} = \delta + \rho$$

Another useful result incorporates the role of heterogeneous discount rates (valuation of future costs and benefits at different time points) by different firms in the competitive market.

Theorem 3 (Malliaris and Stefani, 1991)
At constant extraction costs, firms with discount rates higher than the market price growth rate will all extract resources at maximum capacity, possibly till the total exhaustion of the resource.

The proof for each of the theorems is based on a series of optimizing models and the details are not proposed here. For a detailed discussion on the meaning and interpretations of discount rates, see section 4.6. A further improvement of the models and the possibility of non-constant extraction costs leads to the following stochastic version of the Hotelling rule.

Theorem 4 (Slade and Thille, 1997)
The expected average rate of change of the shadow price of the resource reserves should equal the (risk-neutral) rate of return for the resource asset.

This is the relevant rule for the risk-neutral entrepreneur.

The prescriptions arising from this theorem seem rather robust. The assessment of relevant shadow prices, however, is sensitive to the specifications of the relevant objective functions. Also, when the risk-neutral attitude is not tenable or unwise, the prescriptions differ; these aspects are discussed later in this chapter. A number of limitations of the original formulation indicate that the rule may be relevant for the debate on SD only with substantial improvements, not yet seen in the literature. As pointed out by Hotelling, the features of the assumed competitive equilibrium market leads to maximization of the sum of consumer surplus and producer surplus arising from the natural resource production activity, only when the society wishes to discount future consumer surpluses at the same rate as the mine owners choose to discount their own future profits; see also Solow (1974a).

In related investigations, Krautkraemer (1985) made a significant contribution which examined the link between preservation of natural environment and the opportunity cost of resource extraction in the presence of technological progress. Sinclair (1994) formulated the link between resource exhaustion and pollution stock externalities for evolving an optimal environmental tax profile; but the depreciation in the pollution stock like CO_2 concentration was not properly accounted in this study. In a useful further development, Babu et al. (1997) took into account accumulation (subject to constant depreciation) of pollution with resource use and established two things:

1   If the pollution stock externality does not affect social utility function, intergenerationally efficient taxation may not be entirely feasible.
2   The equilibrium price of a resource rises more slowly than the rate of interest so as to account for the damages due to the stock of pollution generated by the resource use.

Most of these studies remain largely analytical; more work is needed for their empirical validity. The economics of exhaustible resources continue to attract attention in the directions of optimal resource extraction and taxation with technological progress, incomplete information, changing discount rates, and environmental stock and flow externalities.

● 4.4 COST–BENEFIT ANALYSIS (CBA) ●

The standard financial methods of cost–benefit calculations draw upon the calculation of the discounted stream of cash flows, both the sequences of costs C_t and of benefits B_t, for the period of concern T for a project or component of economic activity. The discounted lumped sum is called the net present value (NPV) and depends on the choice of the discount rate r. This is given by the expression:

$$NPV = \sum_{t=1}^{T} (1 + r)^{-t} [B_t - C_t]$$

If inflation needs to be taken into account, r is replaced by $r - i$, where i is the rate of annual inflation. The new measure, $r - i$, corresponds to the real rate of interest wherever the formulation is carried out only in financial terms.

This description holds for cash-flow-based CBA. In general, the true worth of resources is hardly reflected in the above estimates of benefits and costs. At the minimum, one needs to assess the shadow prices for each of the inputs and outputs involved in the flows of benefits and costs. This has, so far, nothing to do with environment and SD issues. It still remains a standard version of social cost–benefit analysis (SCBA) when the main objective or frame of reference for the analysis is that of maximizing social welfare or an equivalent social objective. As indicated in the optimizing model in the appendix to chapter 3, the shadow prices corresponding to such an objective function are reflected in the costate variables. It is not always possible to construct and solve complex optimizing models to generate these shadow prices. Instead, approximations are often made to assess these "true values" of resources with an intuitive approach. Usually, this requires an assessment of opportunity costs (benefits), albeit in a partial equilibrium sense, of each of the inputs involved in the SCBA. If, for example, groundwater is supplied at a government-fixed price P, this is transformed into $G(P)$ where G is reflective of the costs of providing unit supply of the resource, and $G(P)$ may be more or less than P depending on:

● the existence of subsidy or other distortion to the real costs of provision of the resource; and
● the set of elements (direct and indirect costs and their apportionment methods) constituting the cost function.

Similarly, the benefit of this input is its total social contribution in the consumption and/or production function, including the linkages of this input to the rest of the relevant system. Also, since many inputs/resources in the context of environment and SD are not in the market, or even directly connected to the market characteristics, a series of nonmarket valuations like the TEV approach or others discussed above become relevant. The formula for computing the benefits net of costs with "appropriate" discounting over time (see later sections of this chapter for details) remains very much similar to the cash-flow-based formula given above.

CBA has assumed an important role in various aspects of public and private decision making. In the context of environmental issues, especially management of global commons and related policies which arise largely in the public arena, the methods require considerable further strengthening because of these factors:

- The time-scale involved is usually hundreds of years or longer.
- There is no unitary decision-making mechanism.
- Most factors to be considered are largely outside market parameters – as they are not necessarily affecting the market signals at the present time instant.
- There are unusually predominant unknowns and uncertainties in the cost and benefit configurations.
- Assigning numerical values to bring the multiple factors to a common numéraire and scale is extremely complex and possibly founded on many arbitrary assumptions.

Much economics literature suggests that society can generally be risk-neutral relative to individuals when considering future costs and benefits of project investments and various policies and programs. This was suggested because, in a society, a large number of people tend to share the burden of costs and provide some kind of risk pooling; some activities can be very productive while others "drag" on the system. However, these arguments do not help to analyze some of the components of global climate change or such other problems of global commons where collective doom is a real possibility of inaction or wrong actions.

Commensurability

Much of the application of CBA presumes some type of "commensurability." This tends to carry sense in a pure corporate private sector context with profit maximization as the underlying objective and driving force, but not in general. Strong commensurability assumes the existence of a common numéraire which enables the assigning of numerical values to each factor and function involved in the decision-making context, models, and policies. The preferences are usually based on the magnitudes of the numerical values assessed. The numbers also assist in arriving at trade-offs, wherever necessary, in compromising otherwise conflicting objectives. This approach could directly contrast some of the requirements of SD, unless this is used only in relatively well-defined monetized sections of the system, with the sustainability criteria serving as the binding constraints.

A "weak commensurability" approach relies only on ordinal ranking of preferences among alternatives, and does not require the assigning of numerical values to all the parameters involved, but this may not be enough to suggest relevant policies and the scale of operations or interventions in the environmental governance. None of the approaches can make sense devoid of the institutional implications, constraints and effectiveness. The market and the state institutions form the relevant background, but their effectiveness makes the difference as to how far they can operate in an ecologically rational manner.

CBA must take into account sustainability requirements at different stages of valuation, and one of the key elements in this process is to choose an appropriate discount function. The relevant details of this critical issue are given in subsequent sections in this chapter. It is also important that the valuation of environmental and other resources must first be done within a framework of sustainability and then converted into appropriate equivalents using a common numéraire like consumption. This broader approach is usually ignored when tried by some of the conventional but controversial methods like CV and surveys of WTP. Some of the valuations for various resources that generated numerical values, seen in part of the literature claiming to deal with sustainability issues, are usually carried out in a very narrow context. These ignore any sensitivity of values with respect to the market and nonmarket institutional settings where these numbers or methods of valuation might have relevance and may not therefore be applicable in a wide variety of settings all over the world without major modifications. Besides, the valuations are usually sought to be made based on existing unsustainable conditions and then sought to be applied for obtaining some kind of sustainability. These tend to be methods where one can be precise up to the fifth or higher decimal but basically wrong on the premise: this is one scenario where one could be precisely right if only one is right at all! It serves no useful purpose to generate such numbers and use them for project valuation and CBA. The critical ingredients required to be clarified are in terms of the analytical or logical decision model or structure (with or without extensive mathematical methods) which clarify the objectives, constraints, factors and institutions, in addition to the choice of appropriate discount rate. Both efficiency and equity issues must be taken into account together; see also Page (1997). Only such a framework can lead to consistent valuations (shadow prices) relevant for SD. Some of the details given in this chapter are expected to set forth relevant foundations for further development.

Transient Costs and Equilibrium Costs

Any assessment of costs and benefits is based on a pattern of equilibrium which enables such assessment. However, in a relatively medium- or long-term (ten or more years) framework, it is important to recognize that the equilibrium is not expected to remain invariant to the continued disturbances to the systems involved and the significant possibilities of mechanisms of adaptation. In other words, it is not only the common forms of uncertainty that alter the equilibria, but also the systematic feedback mechanisms and adaptation responses of the components of the system which lead to transient equilibria. The effects of such changes on relevant costs and benefits are sometimes viewed in terms of substitution or other effects, but these cover a partial set of adaptations involved. The mechanisms of interlinks between equilibria and influences are shown in figure 4.3.

Figure 4.3   Alternative concepts of equilibria

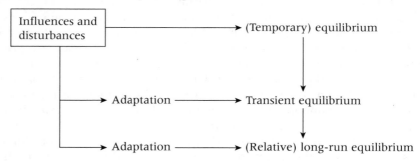

With reference to the general usefulness of CBA or SCBA, some of the arguments of Arrow et al. (1996) are relevant:

- SCBA can play an important role in legislative and regulatory policy debates on protecting and improving health, safety and the natural environment.
- Although it is neither necessary nor sufficient for designing sensible policy, it can provide an "exceptionally useful framework" for consistently organizing information.
- It can improve the process and outcome of policy analysis.

It was also suggested that if "properly done," SCBA can be of great help to agencies participating in the development of environmental, health and safety regulations and can be useful in evaluation agency decision making and rule making. There are concerns that SCBA is an economist's paradise (if at all!) and is very restrictive in its applications, but an interdisciplinary approach could enrich the considerations involved in the evaluation and a robust validity rather than a false sense of precision could definitely enhance its standing as a relevant tool. One of the key concerns in the application of the SCBA pertains to problems involving intergenerational efficiency issues which are significant in the arena of environment and SD. These are deliberated below.

Intergenerational Efficiency and SCBA

Can we rely on markets and related institutions to lead to intergenerational efficiency? The most significant bottlenecks in this regard are the absence of informational and institutional settings, especially missing markets. Markets are missing in the sense that there is no willful interaction and exchange for mutual gain taking place between present and future generations; see Bromley (1991) for details. Missing markets, like other missing institutions, make it impossible to realize intergenerational efficiency. This is besides the well-known problems of "market failures" in terms of their inability to correct for "externalities" like pollution in the industrial processes. This is particularly valid if proper regulatory mechanisms and secondary markets (with legal standing) for these undesirable by-products are not in place. Problems of excessive environmental misuse can also be viewed in terms of the failure of intergenerational product and environmental markets. It may be the absence of relevant markets: these do not exist, and the question of their failure may be secondary. This is further enhanced with the limitations of CBA (except with near zero discounting of future time or of streams of costs and benefits in the future). The possibility that the current generation could use conventional or relatively narrow interpretations of the SCBA methods to reallocate part of the endowment back to itself is not too remote if the methods do not properly incorporate valuation issues.

The formulations involving "overlapping generations" (OLG) models – where the interests of different generations are simultaneously considered with forward and backward linkages relative to the dominant generation – are, in principle, capable of examining potential implications of the existence of relevant markets. An attempt toward relevant formalization of the OLG models for environmental analysis can be seen in Marini and Scaramozzino (1995). However, some of the results need further analysis before operationally significant interpretations can be made for policy purposes.

One of the major impediments to some formal models is to ensure what is known as "time-consistency": in an intergenerational setting, how to ensure that future decision-making systems will, in fact, respect the continuity and ensure the furtherance of future interests at every point of time or point of start of new decision horizons?

In the project evaluation methods for exhaustible resources, the original classical formulation of Hotelling (1931) has been a good start and was considered useful for a long time. This approach draws on discounted utility maximization subject to appropriate constraints on the finiteness of resources of concern. Obviously, the framework of sink capacity or nature's assimilative constraints have not been part of the concern in these conventional formulations. Minor modifications such as incorporating more arguments in the utility function, like the quality of environment, are relatively straightforward. It can be seen (using arguments set forth in the rest of this chapter) that a major effect of improvising the sustainability constraints relating to source and capacities is to raise the shadow price of exhaustible resources as well as of other environmental resources. The same effect can be seen in lowering the discount rate. These issues and the role of changing preferences are addressed below.

● 4.5 ENDOGENOUS PREFERENCES ●

The role of endogenous preference tends to be particularly important in analyses involving long horizons. This is due to people's responses to changes in knowledge, institutions, and economic or other factors. In much of the economic literature, the preferences are largely sought to be reflected in the time-discounting methods, but this is hardly a satisfactory accounting of changes that occur in the preference structures over a period of time. The assumption of a constant exo-genously prescribed rate of social time preference or stationarity of preferences over the entire horizon of relevance has been a feature of technical convenience rather than of realism in many economic studies.

An economic model concerned with long-term issues like SD or global warm-ing, can hardly justify its existence if it is built on such a foundation. Because the benefits of reducing emissions today would be realized primarily in a half-century or more, even small differences in the discount rate used can lead to large variations in the results. At a 4 percent discount rate per year for the future values, an amount of $7.106 billion in the year 2050 is worth $1 billion in the year 2000, whereas with a 7 percent discount rate an amount of $29.457 billion is required in 2050 to be worth investing or foregoing a benefit of $1 billion in 2000. In this example, a mere 3 percentage points lead to over a fourfold dif-ference in a span of only 50 years. Longer time horizons amplify very small differences to huge deviations. Also, it is useful to note that application of con-stant discount rate implies the discount factor at any time instant is independent of the underlying consumption path, which is not a realistic feature in long-horizon analysis.

It is useful to recognize that time preferences are not simply current versus future consumption preferences. In general, these preferences comprise two components:

1   Relative weightage is placed by the consumer or the decision maker on pre-sent versus future consumption, depending on the relative consumption levels – called consumption impatience.
2   For a given consumption path or a constant consumption path, the present and future consumption are distinguished by the element of time impatience.

A similar argument was advanced by Becker and Mulligan (1997) without an accompanying dynamic endogenous model to isolate the two effects. The models in Rao (1999a, 1999b) provide these insights for assessing the two effects. A brief summary of these appear later in this chapter.

Time-inconsistency problems arise in many economic approaches and these require solutions in terms of recognition of the changes in preference patterns. The preferences here are those of decision makers, whether typical consumers or aggregative planning agencies. These are highly desirable when the planning horizon is very long term or infinite, as is the case with SD policy issues. Origin-ally, Strotz (1956) posed the problem of time inconsistency in dynamic utility maximization and sought to remedy the problem with the incorporation of a dis-counting function in the additive utility model via an exponential form. Strotz's finding was that if the discount at time t of future consumption at time τ depends only on the time difference $\tau - t$, then preferences are time-consistent when and only when there is an exponential discounting. This implies a consumption weight of

$$\exp[-\delta(\tau - t)]$$

for some δ. The selection of an exponential class is not necessarily questionable, but the specification of the function in terms of the decision-maker's true discount function at the initial time of the decision horizon was not considered appropriate (Pollak, 1968). This is because such an attempt implied the gross simplification that the only relevant characteristic of the true discount function is the rate at which it changes at the present moment.

Viewed from a different angle, the conventional time-separable of additive utility functions imply that the marginal rates of substitution between two time instants depend on the corresponding levels of consumption at those two instants only. In fact, the relevance of nonseparable utility formation was pointed out by Irving Fisher (1930). In recent years, recursive utility functions were sought to recognize Fisher's notion of "impatience" with the desired properties which:

- account for partial complementarity in inter-temporal consumption; and
- allow a flexible rate of time preference endogenously evolved according to the underlying consumption stream.

Recursive utility formulation achieves a separation between risk aversion (behavior towards risk) and the degree of inter-temporal substitution (ranking of deterministic consumption programs) if there is non-indifference to the temporal resolution of uncertainty (Joshi, 1995).

Much of the economic debate in the fields of environmental and resource economics was concerned with a preset question: Is it desirable to discount (if at all) the future when evaluating various streams of costs and benefits of project activities, at a "low rate" or "high rate" (both these rates were presumed constant!) in relation to private market rate of return? A number of authors were concerned about the complexities of handling variable discount rates, especially if they were sought to be endogenized with respect to relevant functions of consumption, capital growth or variable interest rates at different points of time. Even though a select few contributions offered an analytical framework to deal with the problem, they fell short of providing a computable formulae of methods enabling application in realistic economic systems. Becker and Mulligan (1997) concluded that by endogenizing discount rates, it may be possible, with an underlying optimizing model, to explain some of the assertions in the literature about so-called irrational behavior.

Model Formulation

Let us, at the outset, note that the model formulation is one of the analytical aids to derive a few additional insights or to establish some results in rather simplified settings. There is no single comprehensive model capable of handling all the interrelated and conflicting objectives and constraints with an infinite horizon perspective. Endogeneization is an acceptance of such formidable problems, or rather the logical impossibility of the existence of such a super model, and resorting to conscious approximations and revisions as one learns more information.

New results with the application of Pontryagin's Maximum Principle (Pontryagin et al., 1968; Clark, 1990) to the sustainable economy model are given in Rao (1999a, b). The optimality conditions provide new insights into the dynamics of a sustainable economy with endogenous preferences. A number of alternative mathematical formulations will be eligible for modeling various relevant definitions of SD. These definitions are centered around intergenerational equity and contemporary socioeconomic efficiency requirements which ensure that the equality of environment is not depreciated any further relative to its current status (which need not be optimal in any pre-specified sense). If one of the relevant definitions of SD requires an infinite-horizon formulation – for most practical purposes thousands of years can be treated as if the time horizon is near infinity – any exogenously prescribed constant time-discounting or social time preference will have less appeal to realistic requirements. This is because constant discounting ignores changing levels of marginal utility and social welfare. The following result, using a constant discount rate model and a number of other simplifying assumptions, was a considered a rule of thumb for developed economies in their path toward economic sustainability.

Theorem 5 (Hartwick, 1977)
Sustainability requires setting investment equal to resource rent from contemporary time onwards.

It was suggested that only by measuring resource rents based on shadow prices which reflect the sustainability constraint could the Hartwick's rule provide a correct guide to sustainability. Let us note that this does not come any closer to the SD specifications, except possibly in very special configurations. Let us begin with a qualifying assertion about the validity of the Hartwick rule for prescribing sustainability conditions.

Theorem 6 (Asheim, 1994)
The Hartwick's rule is a necessary but not sufficient condition for sustainability.

Asheim (1994) showed that an economy in which current investment exceeds the level of resource rent is not necessarily able to sustain its current level of utility by following Hartwick's rule. The flaw in the Hartwick rule arises in using prices estimated under unsustainable conditions: only by measuring resource rents using shadow prices which reflect the sustainability constraint will the rule provide a current guide to sustainability. Asheim (1994) offered a counterexample to show that the Hartwick rule was obeyed but that the path did not lead to sustainability. The problem lies in using resource prices under unsustainable conditions. When the recursive preference structure is not recognized in the model formulation, the corresponding shadow prices (even with the sustainability constraint) will differ substantially from true shadow prices governing the evolution of the system dynamics. The detailed nature of these deviations becomes apparent in the following discussions. A number of significant contributions in economic models chose not to recognize recursive preferences in formulating their utility functions. In the case of a constant discount rate, corresponding to the additive preferences, this is possible only when a steady state is reached, i.e. when no long-run growth occurs. Besides, any "change of taste" at consumption level is not allowed for the entire horizon.

A typical endogenous discount function at time t assumes the form, with $v(c)$ as the time-dependent consumption:

$$D(t) = \exp\left\{-\int_0^t v(c_s)\,ds\right\}$$

where $[0, t]$ is a sub-interval of the relevant horizon, and the integrand is the corresponding discount factor affected by the consumption level at each time instant.

More general forms of endogenous discount functions can be formulated to allow the integrand (the discount factor) to depend on the state variables, the control variables and time; these recognize the role of changes in consumption "tastes" and in "habits."

Various general forms of discount factors, and hence discount functions, can be accommodated in the present approach; these functions are endogenous with respect to control variables, state variables and time (explicitly). The method that allows amenability of these features within the framework of standard optimal control models augments the structure of the model with an additional state variable. If the discount function is of the form

$$\exp\left\{-\int_0^t g(x, u, \tau)\,d\tau\right\}$$

a new state variable z_2 is introduced and given by

$$\dot{z}_2 = -g(x, u, \tau)$$

Using these discount functions and an optimizing model, some of the results established in Rao (1999b) lead to the next theorem.

Theorem 7 (Rao, 1999b)
(a) An optimality requirement of SD is that the marginal productivity of resources deployed for environmental improvement should equal the ratio of the shadow prices of capital and environment. In other words, any rise in the shadow price of capital imposes a greater level of required productivity of resources deployed for environmental improvement.
(b) In each period, the marginal opportunity cost of environmental improvement equals the shadow price of the environment.

The first part of the theorem is a new prescription for optimal SD, not seen in the literature. Part (b) of the theorem points to a result which mimics some of the familiar first-order optimality conditions which are usually seen in most of the environmental economics literature. However, the formulae underlying the shadow prices (not presented here because of their mathematical complexities) are significantly different.

Theorem 8 (Rao, 1999b)
The discounted marginal utility at each time point equals the shadow price of capital less a factor which is affected by "marginal impatience" with respect to time and consumption.

The reducing effect of the factor referred to in the theorem is not seen in most of the conventional discounting forms. Theorem 8 constitutes an advancement over Gary Becker's (1998) contributions in that the result isolates and provides formulae for the two effects of time impatience and consumption impatience.

The role of discount functions remains critical in all valuations, as already seen in some of the results discussed above. The logic and foundations of discounting as well as relevant methods are given in the next section.

● 4.6 CHOICE OF DISCOUNT RATES ●

It was with a strong reason that Robert Solow (1974b) devoted significant part of his seminal address "The economics of resources or the resources of economics" to the criticality of the role of discounting the future or the valuation of resources and benefits accruing in the future. He stated that when there is a concern for the exhaustible resources, "the balance between present and future is more delicate than we are accustomed to think; and then the choice of a discount rate can be pretty important and one ought not to be too casual about it." Twenty years later, William Nordhaus (1994), who used a set of powerful models for the economic analysis of global climate change, asserted that no issue has raised "more concern and confusion than the question of the appropriate discounting of the future." We will not be able to resolve all the issues here, but a set of new approaches and insights are given in this section.

The 1789 contribution of Bentham in his treatise on the *Principles of Morals and Legislation* stated that "the value of a pain or pleasure . . . will be greater or less, according to . . . its certainty or uncertainty" of incidence, among other factors. It was also stated in terms of "the nearness or remoteness of the time at which it is to come into possession." Many philosophers and economists of later periods also opined similarly; see, for example, Sidgwick (1907), Pigou (1932), and Rawls (1972). However, if the application of discounting over time is partly due to prevalent uncertainties in the future, it is not very reasonable to regard certain basic essentials of life on the planet as anything but essential at any point of time, and the discounting has to be properly handled in respect of any surrogate valuation involving these factors.

Economists have been taking conflicting positions on whether there should be any discounting of the future at all and, if there has to be some discounting, whether it should be "relatively" low or high. The global environmental issues brought the theme of discounted valuation to the forefront of debate in the 1990s much more than ever in the past several decades. It is not only the complexity of uncertainty and incomplete information that is bothering the analysts but also the need to deal with infinite or extremely long time horizons for valuation. This horizon issue alone discourages any positive discounting since after a few decades anything is ignored to null valuation by the "tyranny of discounting." A project using a discount rate of 5 percent per annum can lead to a high magnitude of profits in 20 years, but the same with 10 percent can lead to high losses by the end of 20 years – so much for the sensitivity of the profitability with respect to the discount rates. There are a number of economic efficiency and intergenerational ethical issues involved in this context. The existing literature falls short of requirements to prescribe a meaningful policy. The next sections deal with the approach of endogenized discounting as a possible improvement.

Discounting Discounting?

There are several who argue against any type of discounting future at all, but most then suggest by implication that the discount rate should be zero. This is devoid of sound logic, because zero then becomes the chosen rate of discounting the future and this rate is required to remain a constant forever, irrespective of any changes in the tastes or well-being of the future generations. We summarize two of the illustrative and detailed contributions in this direction.

The first major set of arguments are due to Goodin (1982) who suggested that discounting methods are possibly devoid of sound logic. Contrary to the notion of Goodin that discounting amounts to ignoring the future generations, productive utilization of resources at current and foreseeable future periods gives scope for accommodating the interests of the present and future if only the resources are properly utilized and due attention is paid to the future generations. An enlightened and/or egalitarian society can do better than others. Let us also note that a society which does not discount the future at all but is capable of efficiently utilizing its resources is unlikely to protect the interests of the current as well as future generations. It was stated by Goodin (1982, p. 56) that "a constant discount rate across all periods and all goods . . . seems without psychological warrant, just as psychological discounting is itself without moral warrant." There should be little disagreement that the discount rate should be the same in each future period.

It must be noted that any proposal to recommend the use of discounting future valuations mainly to reflect future uncertainties and risks does not necessarily take into account another important requirement under such conditions: probability-weighted evaluation of outcomes. Goodin (1982) stated that "outcomes that are equidistant in time would have to be discounted equally" (p. 57). There is neither an observed behavioral justification for such behavior nor an economic rationale for maintaining such a position. This issue is better resolved below in the discussion on hyperbolic discounting. Goodin could be correct in suggesting that "in a declining economy, the logic of diminishing marginal utility leads to weighting future payoffs more heavily than present ones." This might, unfortunately, be the case if the requirements of SD are ignored. Besides, nothing in the general theory of discounting rules out negative discounting. According to Goodin, discounting may be applied only to "interest-bearing" resources. This position presumes that the resources are readily monetized in the valuation process. It was also suggested that the rate and structure of discounting applied to nontradable goods should match the corresponding features of investments in those goods. This position presumes the existence of investments in the nontraded goods, an unlikely or unusual scenario in environmental features like the GHGs.

The second illustration is due to Broome (1992), who argued that the process of discounting the future is the same as discounting future well-being. It is known that the consumer interest rate is not necessarily good since it does not take into account the effects of the preferences of future generations. Similarly, the producer rate of interest is not considered useful because the production of goods and services is involved with environmental damages affecting sources and sinks, especially emissions of the GHGs – and thus does not reflect the true opportunity cost of products and services. Broome's solution was to adopt a zero discount rate. However, this is itself without a rationale when considered for different generations facing a nonmonotonic trend in the availability of resources.

It is doubtful if Frank Ramsey (1928) – an important contributor to the development of the modern neoclassical growth theory – was very accurate in asserting that pure time preference is a "practice which is ethically indefensible and arises merely from the weakness of the imagination." Attempts are needed to imagine a distant future even with several unknowns and uncertainties and to try to grapple with such limited information basis so that the direction of progress is at least approximately right; a possible alternative is to neglect the due recognition of the future on the presumption of an inability to handle the complexities.

Changing Preferences and Discounting

The basic premise of keeping generalized wealth intact and realizing its rent as annual income seems an appealing notion of sustainability, subject to ensuring the requisite ecological and resource balances. There could be a continuum of alternate growth paths and policies and these require a rational ordering for the possible ranking of alternatives. This ranking need not be entirely dependent on the content of currently available information.

Fisher (1930) argued that the pure rate of time preference should not be independent of the size and shape of the consumption profile. However, in the conventional intertemporal utility maximization approach, the independence arises from the strong separability property of utility: marginal rates of substitution for consumption at any two time instants are independent of the rest of the consumption profile. A constant time discounting does imply that the discount factor at any instant is independent of the underlying consumption path.

Another related viewpoint on recognizing changes in consumption and tastes suggests that it is the satisfaction of wants as they arise that matters: tomorrow's satisfaction matters, not simply today's assessment of tomorrow's satisfaction; see also Goodin (1986).

An ingredient in the definition of sustainability is a possible change relative to the present in preferences of future generations about consumption and environmental assets (Solow, 1992). These observations suggest the need for specifying discount factors that are endogenized with respect to consumption and resource stock levels at different future time instants. The discount rate must reflect the rate of return on alternative sustainable uses, and not just any uses, of capital if we are to have a policy consistent with SD. If an industrial project is estimated to yield a return on capital at 12 percent a year, and an alternative project like forest plantations gives a corresponding return of 7 percent, the basic question remains: do we accept the 12 percent case as preferable even though a multitude of such projects can only lead to time-bound environmental unsustainability and hence a lack of SD? This issue cannot be resolved without clarifying who are the owners of the projects or the investors. Assuming both are in the public sector, the issue then becomes one of greater comprehension of costs of the project and accounting for all the elements of costs and benefits over a long period of time like infinity. One premise is clear, however: the efficiency allocation rule of maximizing present value can subvert the goal of SD by application of an unsustainable discount rate, i.e. a discount rate based on alternate uses of capital that are unsustainable (Daly, 1991, p. 255).

In an interesting contribution to the modeling and analysis of global commons, Nordhaus (1994) believed that his dynamic integrated model of climate and the economy (DICE) model used in the investigations could not accommodate gradual change in tastes and also stated that "no issue has raised more concern and confusion than the question of the appropriate discounting of the future" (p. 122). The DICE model of Nordhaus (1993) uses a 3 percent discount rate. If the discount rate were zero percent, the optimal abatement path cuts emissions by 50 percent from the baseline by the year 2100, compared with 10 percent reduction at the 3 percent discount rate (Plambeck et al., 1997).

Much of the conventional literature on the methods of project appraisal and CBA were content with two concepts toward discount rates. These were the consumption rate of interest (also called the pure time preference in some writings), and the opportunity cost of capital which is based on the marginal productivity of capital. Neither is appealing for the purpose of their relevance for SD for the simple reason that they do not carry with them required informational ingredients to put a value on time discounting. The conventional criteria were of some use in capital investment decisions and appraisal of small projects.

What constitutes a discount rate? This may be defined as the rate of fall in the value of the numéraire against which goods are valued each time instant; this could also be each year, for example. The numéraire and the discount rate need to be considered together. Dreze and Stern (1987) provide a rigorous analysis of the theoretical issues in this framework. The shadow discount factor in their analysis is the valuation of the discount factor in accordance with the underlying objective function or net benefit computing formulation. It can be seen as the marginal social value of a unit of numéraire accruing in year t. The shadow's own rate of return on the numéraire is generally known as the social discount rate (SDR).

The social value of a project or activity is a discounted stream of social benefits expressed in terms of a common numeraire. The shadow discount rate is a scalar defined as the rate of fall of the discount factor $D(\cdot)$ which is an implicit function of time, given by the expression:

$$\rho = -\left(\frac{d}{dt}\right) \log D(\cdot)$$

This also depicts the rate of fall in the marginal social value of the numéraire.

The shadow discount rate is defined as the rate of decline in the discount factor

$$\rho_\tau = \frac{\alpha_\tau - \alpha_{\tau+1}}{\alpha_{\tau+1}}$$

From this, it follows that, if $\alpha_0 = 1$

$$\alpha_{\tau+1} = (1 + \rho_\tau)(1 + \rho_{\tau-1})\cdots(1 + \rho_0)$$

It can be seen that when the shadow discount rate is a constant, the discounting formulation reduces to the conventional inversion of the compounding formula for n periods, as in $(1 + r)^{-n}$.

In general, there is no reason to expect that the shadow discount rate in the private sector equals the social rate of return. If private producers are unconstrained and relative producer prices are equal or proportional to relative shadow prices, the marginal rates of the shadow discount rate is the same as the private rate of return, i.e. the rate of return in terms of market prices. Also, for a given numéraire, the shadow discount rate is equal to the producer rate of interest if, and only if, the ratio of shadow price to producer price for this numéraire remains constant over time. The consumer rate of interest is analogous to the producer rate of interest, and each is conditioned by the choice of the numéraire: in the latter, it represents the amount that, by giving up or selling one specified unit in this year, the producer can obtain or buy 1 + PR units next year, where PR is the producer rate of interest.

The application of SDRs requires that all relevant effects of an activity or project are transformed into their equivalents in a common numéraire, usually consumption. This implies that it may be difficult to avail this ingredient as such in a situation like the global climate change where the conversion of every thing or entity into its consumption equivalent may not be feasible. SDRs are to be viewed as percentage rates of change of intertemporal relative shadow prices of the consumption bundle. There are few proxies for SDR:

(a)   The application of the concept of social rate of time preference (SRTP), explained below;

(b) Comparable market rates of return (even though these are, typically, unsustainable);
(c) Real rates of risk-free interest; and
(d) Variable endogenous discount functions which reflect changing preferences and consumption levels, and possibly additional factors.

Among these, (b) and (c) are not usually equated with SDRs due to the nature of pure capital appraisal in perfectly competitive markets that should form the relevant arena for its application, and not socioeconomic and environmental concerns of the long term.

In the conventional approach, the SRTP can be estimated using a utility-based discount rate. In this framework, the SRTP (observed from the consumption rate of interest) and the opportunity cost of private capital (observed from the marginal rate of return on private investment) are the same and they equal the market rate of interest in a perfectly competitive ideal non-distortionary economy. This follows the Solow (1970) derivation, explained below.

The optimality criterion is to maximize the discounted social value of all future utility streams of consumption:

$$W = \int_0^\infty \exp[-(\rho - n)t]\, U[c(t)]\, dt$$

where W is the social value of consumption stream, ρ the pure time preference factor, n the rate of growth of population, and c is per capita consumption.

The first-order necessary condition for optimality yields the expression

$$\frac{\frac{d}{dt}[U']}{U'} = -(r^*(t) - \rho)$$

which, upon differentiation, leads to

$$\frac{U''(c^*) \cdot \frac{d}{dt}(c^*)}{U'(c^*)} = -\{r^* - \rho\}$$

This is summarized as

$$r(t) = \alpha g + \rho$$

where α is the absolute value of the elasticity of the social marginal utility of per capita consumption, and g is the growth rate of consumption.

The above expression makes it clear that the discount function r is a composite effect of three ingredients:

- The pure time preference or time-impatience.
- The consumption-impatience represented through the elasticity parameter.
- The growth effect.

Thus, r is not simply a time-discounting factor as sometimes referred to in the literature, but a measure of discounting of goods. This is the one that should be used in the CBAs. If one suggests that the welfare of future generations should not be heavily discounted, the suggestion is simply that ρ, the pure time-impatience factor, should be low, and not that r should be low for that reason. Robert Solow (1996) emphasized that along any optimal path, the appropriate discount rate to apply to goods has two components:

- The pure rate of time preference.
- The factor which depends on the marginal product of capital (thus allowing transformation of goods into greater quantities of goods over time).

The second component usually dominates the first, except in very inefficient economies. These features provide a fundamental explanation to the suggested phenomenon in Gary Becker (1998): preferences and rates of economic growth are correlated partly because tastes like a lower rate of preference for present utilities are more conducive to rapid economic growth.

From the above expression for $r(t)$, it is readily observed that even when the utility rate of discount is set equal to zero, the SRTP will be positive as long as consumption is growing over time. The consumption rate of discount need not equal the utility rate of discount. Thus, discounting benefits and costs at a positive rate does not necessarily entail lesser weightage to the welfare (as measured by utility) of the future generations or future itself. There is no contradiction between those who claim that the "well-being" of future generations should not be discounted and those who argue that future incomes should not be discounted at a positive rate. However, this reasoning may not entirely hold good in economies where future prospects of higher consumption levels are bleak. There is a technical imperative, based on the convergence of an infinite sum of felicity in an optimal depletion of resources problem for infinite time horizon: positive discounting is a necessary requirement if the model is to yield any rational optimizing solutions under plausible conditions and properties of the class of utility functions; details are given in Heal (1985).

The growth component, g, in the expression for the discount rate allows several alternative decompositions and interpretations. These have implications for the choice of discount rates in relation to the underlying factors affecting growth. Such an assessment also clarifies the need for a variable rather than fixed discount rate. Let g be expressed, by definition, as

$$g(t) = \frac{\dfrac{d}{dt}\dfrac{C(t)}{P(t)}}{\dfrac{C(t)}{P(t)}}$$

where $C(t)$ is the total consumption and $P(t)$ is the population at time t. Country-specific profiles of consumption and population in different time-intervals do make it rather essential to define the discount rate in terms of these variable factors. Even the size of the population can be indexed to a common numéraire to enable adjustments to changes in the age–demography features in terms of the common units of consumption, like the number of adult-equivalent units.

The above expression for $g(t)$ can also be stated in terms of the growth rates of consumption and population:

$$g(t) = \frac{\dot{C}}{C} - \frac{\dot{P}}{P}$$

This clarifies the possibilities of negative values of g in some cases. As already discussed, the discount rate follows as the combined effect of the three ingredients. Clearly, when consumption growth rate is near zero and the population growth is significant, there will be little incentive or capacity to save for future generations.

In general, time preferences comprise at least two effects:

- Relative value attached to present consumption (in relation to the level of consumption) and its comparative valuation of a future specified level of consumption at a specified time point.
- Impatience as defined by pure time preference (for a given level of consumption, held constant, but occurring at two different time instants).

The optimization and decision framework should be capable of responding to new information and should take into account the option value of alternate courses of action from time to time. In principle, this can be carried out with an endogenized discount function and recursive utility framework.

Discount Factors and Discount Rates

Conventional constant rate of discounting brings the valuation very rapidly to zero level, even with rather modest rates of discount, after a period of about 50 years. A class of functions, called hyperbolic discount functions, is found to have some merits in overcoming these artificial structures of discounting; they are also based on a description of the behavior of humans over long time horizons. These functions are explained in box 4.4. Many of these are advanced by analytical psychologists and behavioral economists, among others. The use of these functions is to depict valuation of resources over time in such a manner as to enable non-zero finiteness at a distant future.

The use of discount rates is closely tied to the implicit and explicit framework governing the configuration of CBA. It is important to note that a constant rate of time discounting does imply the independence of the discount factor at any time point of the underlying consumption path (and hence, also of the

BOX 4.4 Hyperbolic discount functions

Hyperbolic discount functions were found to be relevant in the psychological studies of humans and animals (Ainslie, 1992). Hyperbolic discount functions imply discount rates which decline as the discounted event is moved further away in time (Lowenstein and Prelec, 1992). Prelec (1989) suggested a hyperbolic form of discounting function

$$D(t) = (1 + \alpha t)^{-\frac{\beta}{\alpha}} \qquad \alpha, \beta > 0$$

These are characterized by a relatively high discount rate over shorter horizons and lower discount rates over longer horizons.

Within the class of hyperbolic functions, Laibson (1997) suggested the discount rate function which falls with increasing time t:

$$D(t) = \frac{\beta}{1 + \alpha t}$$

Harvey (1995) gives a number of alternative formulations of non-constant discounting functions, including "slow discount functions." These have a main characteristic of changing preferences, and these preferences are also classified into different main categories: relative timing constant, slow timing averse, and decreasing timing averse. Although these are interesting and possess desirable properties like declining over time and not exponentially declining to zero at fast speed (as in regular exponential discounting functions), the models based on these may not always possess meaningful or rational optimal solutions. However, more analyses into some of these directions and improvements are expected to yield rich dividends in choosing the right discounting approaches, both prescriptive and positive (in the sense of accounting for real-life descriptive behavior of societies and individuals).

The discount functions of the type given below are special cases of the above hyperbolic class and were suggested in the class of proportional discounting or "relative timing preference" (Harvey, 1986), and depict inverse proportionality with the distance of time element from the present time:

$$a(t) = \left(\frac{b}{b + t}\right)^r \qquad t \geq 0, \, b > 0, \, -\infty < r < \infty$$

Measuring time by equal proportional increments, rather than equal absolute values, is sometimes referred to as "logarithmic discounting." This discounting function attaches greater weight to time and valuation of resources at distant time points, unlike the case of conventional exponential discounting.

Also, a few other important features of hyperbolic discounting must be noted: hyperbolic discount functions induce dynamically inconsistent preferences, with the implication that they offer a motive for individuals to constrain their own future choices. As seen by Strotz (1956), commitment will be chosen only by decision makers whose preferences are dynamically inconsistent, or equivalently, when the discount functions of time do not belong to the exponential class of functions.

corresponding changes in other related factors). Significant income distributional effects of policies and compensation adjustments are not automatically attainable with the deployment of other policy instruments. This suggests that simple aggregation of gains and losses, in grand-scale programs like control of GEs, is unlikely to provide a convincing basis for action or a predictor of policy in the global or national economy. The implications of a very high discount rate are that too little value is placed on future possibilities like global warming; conversely, a very low discount rate could lead to too much investment in the control of potential global warming problems and thus drive out possibly more efficient or better uses of resources. A study by the US National Academy of Sciences (Stern et al., 1992) reached these conclusions:

- If current economic activity tends to destroy the fundamental life-support systems on which human survival depends, no amount of investment at compound interest could ever recoup this cost.
- Market-based discount rates, like interest rates, do not usually correspond to social valuation of the long run relevant in global climate change issues, even if these might reflect the current period factors for social time preferences.

We briefly review some of the applied studies which dealt with the approaches and methods of choosing discount rates. Toth (1995) reviewed a number of studies which tried to deal with the issue of discount rates, in a rather integrative framework for environmental modeling and analysis. It was concluded that the selection of the technique of discounting makes a difference in the outcome of integrated assessments, and that the discount rate is a sensitive parameter in these models; the recommendation for future studies is to carry out sensitivity analyses with respect to changes in the discount factor so as to assess the robustness – or lack of it – in the results.

One view was that the SRTP as determined by the consumption rate of interest is the SDR (Lind, 1982). In the long-term project economics context, the resource allocations should be based on considerations involving intergenerational equity. A proxy for these was suggested as the government's long-term borrowing rate (Lind, 1990). Using the standard methods for assessing costs and benefits or project appraisal requires finding the relevant "shadow price on capital" and translating all capital investment effects into "consumption equivalents," and discount consumption at the SRTP for consumption; this is known as the Arrow–Bradford–Feldstein–Kurz method due to the authors' several contributions to this. It is useful to note that this method is particularly relevant when there is no concern of SD. This may not be optimal for SD issues, however. Relevant modifications include comprehensive valuation of goods and services to reflect their environmental implications or their drag on the environmental assets, and also recognition of an environmentally meaningful or sustainable discount rate, i.e. the rate from the standard derivations of the literature, adjusted for ensuring SD. Corrections are required because the estimates of shadow prices and consumption equivalents do not address these implications and are inherently based on parameters within an unsustainable development configuration.

Using one of the versions of an OLG model for optimal economic growth linked to population and environmental parameters, Marini and Scaramozzino (1995) suggested an intuitively appealing proposition: the appropriate discount rate on environmental valuation is the growth-corrected social rate of time preference, augmented by the rate at which the natural environment is able to assimilate pollution.

Uncertainty and Discount Rates

There has been considerable debate and disagreement regarding the choice of discount rates for environmental projects, especially those affecting global commons associated with global warming. There are several unknowns and uncertainties. Besides, ecological and environmental changes occur relatively exogenously; see, for example, Myers (1995). All these unknowns, information and event uncertainties, imperfect perceptions and analyses suggest a cautious approach in the design and implementation of policies and programs aimed at the control of the phenomena and their adverse consequences.

From the viewpoint of socioeconomic decision making and appraisal of various actions and inactions, the analysis relies very heavily on the explicit and implicit time-valuation of associated benefits and costs over a long time horizon. The intergenerational preferences and trade-offs are directly relevant. The critical parameter that affects choice of policies in this set-up is the discount rate over time. A number of authors argued in favor of a choice of low (but constant) discount rates so that the distant future may not be ignored. There are others who argue the opposite so as to enhance the current efficiency levels of resource use and possibly reap the benefits for the future. Neither address the implications of the uncertainty and risk-averse decision making. This is not an accurate way of resolving or even addressing the issue.

The standard economics under uncertainty and risk gives the result that the expected value of marginal utility is greater than the marginal utility of expected income. On this basis, the Intergovernmental Panel on Climate Change (IPCC, 1996) recommended that there would be grounds for reducing the growth-based component of the SRTP under circumstances of risk, and that this consideration is particularly relevant for problems of global warming. This is because the risk in predicting per capita growth on a centuries scale horizon is high.

Under uncertainty, the simplistic view of treating costs as negative benefits does not hold any more. If there is any risk-averse attitude, the benefit stream should be discounted at a higher rate than in the certainty case or the certainty-equivalent case. For a risk-averse decision maker, the expected utility of initial wealth plus the random increment is less than the utility of the expected value of the initial wealth plus the random increment. This follows from the well-known inequalities applicable when the utility function U possesses the properties of a strictly concave function:

$$E[U(W_t + W_{t+1})] < U[E(W_t + W_{t+1})] = U[W_t + E(W_{t+1})]$$

The above inequality (Thompson, 1997) shows that the certainty-equivalent of the random wealth W_t is less than the expected value of W_t. Enhancement in the certainty-equivalent is possible with an increased discount rate. Similarly, in risk-averse decision making, if the costs are ranked under uncertainty, the converse holds: lower the discount rate for valuing costs over time. A rigorous technical support for these assertions in the risk-averse cases is given by Prelec (1998).

In a general optimizing approach, it may be noted that the following well-known inequality for the strict concave utility function U leads to a similar interpretation:

$$\max(U(E(b), X)) < \max(E(U(b, X))) < E(\max(U(b, X)))$$

where b is the stochastic net benefit coefficient in the utility function and X represents the activity vector.

An application of the Precautionary Principle (PP) or risk-averse decision-making approach leads to a lower discount rate in assessing costs under uncertainty relative to the certainty case or the certainty-equivalent case. Rao (1999b) gives a rigorous derivation of this assertion, with an endogenized variable discount function; the discount rates are revised with a changing consumption level, environment–production linkages, and social time preferences. The role of time-varying discount functions, or more generally, of endogenous discount functions in the methods of valuation of NNP and its role as an indicator of economic sustainability is examined in the next section.

● 4.7 NET NATIONAL PRODUCT (NNP) ●

A biogeophysical definition of sustainability would normally require the creation and preservation of physical and biological resources that possess the potential to maintain undiminished human well-being as well as balance the coexistence of other species, for the entire future time horizon. If we narrow down the implication to the economic arena, this requires (though is not necessarily implied by) drawing upon the economic (including natural and environmental) resources to such an extent that the generalized economic capacity to produce material well-being of the human population is retained intact for ever. This concept, when conditioned by time partition in terms of years, and applied to individual national economic systems, leads to an approximation of adjusted NNP under certain assumptions – but not in general. The details are deliberated below.

The usefulness of a "wealth-like magnitude," such as the present discounted value of future consumption, if it bears a meaningful relationship with economic welfare in a dynamic economy was indicated by Paul Samuelson (1961). This concept was explored in detail by Martin Weitzman (1976) who argued that the welfare justification of the NNP is "just the idea that in theory it is a proxy for the present discounted value of future consumption." This reasoning was based on a few assumptions:

- All sources of economic growth have been identified and attributed to one or other form of capital.
- Future felicity can be discounted at a constant rate forever, based on current content of information.
- There are no influences that are not reflected in the consumption-capital stock relationships.

Weitzman's (1976) methodology relied on the current value Hamiltonian interpretation of NNP, based on an optimal control-theoretic modeling of the economy.

The approach was extended by Dasgupta and Heal (1979, pp. 244–6) and Solow (1986) to include natural and exhaustible resources that generate income and/or deplete in various time intervals. Solow's extension was partly based on the validity of the Hartwick's rule (Hartwick, 1977) for exhaustible resources: a society that invests aggregate resource rents in reproducible capital is preserving its capacity to sustain a constant level of consumption (forever). It is useful to note that Hartwick derived this proposition using a simplified growth model with Cobb-Douglas technology, using constant rates of substitution and time preferences, for a closed economy. Solow (1986) proved that – under assumptions as in Weitzman (1976) – along an efficient growth path, the NNP in a year is representable as interest on the accumulation of capital value (from the beginning of the year) in an inclusive sense that records the decumulation of the stock of exhaustible resources. More recent results led to propositions.

Proposition 2 (Solow, 1994)
NNP measures the maximum current level of consumer satisfaction that can be sustained forever; it is, therefore, a measure of sustainable income given the state of the economy at that very instant.

Proposition 3 (Solow, 1994)
Investment and depletion decisions determine the real wealth of the economy, and each year's NNP appears as the return to society on the wealth it has accumulated in all forms.

These two propositions are built on the assumption of perfect foresightedness and on the availability of time profiles of relevant accounting prices of resources. The restrictions that apply to the validity of the Hartwick rule apply here as well. Nonetheless, the following argument advanced by Solow is valid: the very same calculation that is required to construct an adjusted NNP for current economic evaluation of economic benefit is also essential for the construction of a strategy aimed at sustainability. Relevant adjustments to this adjusted NNP are needed, however.

These assertions assume a high degree of substitutability of various forms of capital and hence are relevant under the "weak sustainability" criterion that allows the aggregation of capital vector components with weighted valuations of each of the components. These rely on competitive market prices for valuation and expect markets to govern the factors involved, including an exogenous discounting factor of the future values of resources. The moment any of these assumptions are relaxed, we arrive at a wealth-like magnitude alright, but the NNP inter-pretation is then subject to several modifications.

The NNP measure advocated by Weitzman (1976) as "the stationary equival-ent of future consumption (or utility), and this is its primary welfare interpreta-tion" is valid when the economy is described by constant time discounting. The corresponding results for the variable time-discounting case were obtained by Sefton and Weale (1996). However, this improvement is inadequate for taking into account endogenous preferences and relevant externalities. If the pure effect of time alone is due solely to identified exogenous factors (expressed in terms of a fraction of income) – like new resource discoveries, changes in technology, consumer tastes, or population growth – the expression for the NNP admits a straightforward generalization, suggested by Sefton and Weale (1996). If any of these are treated endogenously, we need further investigations. Since the relat-ive price of manmade capital in terms of natural capital depends on the entire future equilibrium path, the concept of NNP as an indicator of sustainability may not be tenable in the conventional form, as argued by Asheim (1994). Asheim sought to deploy time-varying discount factors, but these cannot account for endogenous factors like non-constant substitution among multiple capital goods and contemporaneous consumption levels affecting discount factors.

Explicit Time Factor

Is explicit time-dependence important? The answer is "Yes," for several reasons. Separate time argument leads to non-autonomous Hamiltonian formulation of the NNP. This representation arises naturally whenever positive or negative ex-ternalities exist. In such a world (i.e. the real world), there is no static equival-ent of the expression for wealth; see also Lofgren (1992). The usual Hamiltonian representation of the economic welfare measure requires substantial modifica-tions for any realistic setting. When the economic system is fundamentally non-autonomous, as a consequence of externalities and/or technical progress not reflected in the production functions or other constraints, the shadow prices in the framework of Weitzman and Hartman do not reflect the true accounting prices for the purpose of CBA (Aronsson and Lofgren, 1995). This is because the lat-ter are to be corrected for future information reflected in the non-autonomous parameters.

It is rather surprising that several significant contributions in the area of economics of SD ignored the existence of an explicit time factor in the objective function, discount factor, or the constraint set (or a combination of these). This led to autonomous optimal control structures where the Hamiltonian is constant along an optimal path.

Theorem 9 (Rao, 1999a)
Hartwick's rule and Weitzman's interpretation of the expression for the NNP do not apply when we deal with non-autonomous systems which arise with factors like changes in technical progress, in tastes and preferences, and in externalities.

(For the proof, see the appendix to this chapter.)

It is important to note that the following assertion, due to Dasgupta and Maler (1994), holds only when the Hamiltonian is autonomous (sometimes called time-homogeneous), and not in general.

If the intergenerational measure of well-being is stationary, then along the optimal program the Hamiltonian remains constant through time, and this provides the necessary connection between the current-value Hamiltonian and NNP.

The Hartwick rule was modified by Lozada (1995) using non-constant discounting. This led to the rule: invest the depreciation so as to maintain constant income. This modification did not deal with endogenized discount functions. The Hamiltonian measure of income ceases to function as a measure of return on wealth (even with any variations in terms of "generalized wealth") whenever economic growth cannot be directly attributed to capital formation, and is only partially valid when the Hamiltonian is autonomous. It is necessary to formulate the optimizing problem as a non-autonomous problem and interpret the Hamiltonian in terms of relevant contributing factors and parameters. A detailed investigation into these features is given in the appendix to this chapter.

Finally, let us conclude this section with the following observations. An increase in uncertainty diminishes the expected national income – see, for example, Rothenberg and Smith (1971) – but an increase in technological progress enhances the same (Weitzman, 1997); the resulting effect determines whether NNP underestimates or overestimates a measure of sustainable consumption. The role of time factor, human capital, changes in externalities, and in tastes/preferences can similarly be assessed: the effects could be positive or negative depending on the specific contents of these changes. It is important, here, to ensure that these effects are taken into account in any measure of sustainability.

● 4.8 CONCLUSIONS ●

Environmental resource valuation with long time horizons continues to remain a very complex subject. More emphasis is required in devising robust sets of assumptions and methods of assessment, in addition to increased sophistication in the decision models. The latter is needed in the sense of comprehensive consideration of the dynamics of the relevant stocks and flows of environmental resources. This is dependent on an appreciation of the effects of the flux of nature and features affecting the dynamics of ecological evolution. Once the economic system is integrated as a component of the larger ecosystem, it is easier to understand the linkages. Many economic analyses tend to view these in the reverse order or worse, imply zero values for ecological resources. Such an approach is unrealistic when unprecedented impacts of anthropogenic activities are experienced with discernible adverse impacts, as detailed in chapters 3 and 5.

Environmental externalities, technological externalities, and changing prefer-ences, as well as non-constant discount rates in an infinite horizon decision frame-work, cast serious doubts on the standard methods which advocate the NNP as an indicator of sustainability. The suggested role of the NNP in the traditional literature is founded on some major assumptions. In general, it is not an indic-ator of economic sustainability. This measure, when adjusted for technological progress in future, and taste premium or discount, could be a better indicator of sustainability; this relies on continuous revision of the indicator and has implica-tions for paths of SD in that these should be more flexible to adopting changes. Irreversible decisions are not necessarily the prescription in many cases. These considerations tend to bring greater flexibility and pragmatism to policies dic-tated by the requirements of SD, than conventionally viewed.

The choice of discount rates or time-discounting of the future is a very critical area of valuation of resources and the future. The least that needs to be done at this juncture seems to be to do away with assumptions of constant discount rate. This is especially important when the rate or trade-off involved in current and future time periods is based on unsustainable features, i.e. based on current information or historical considerations. A few important conclusions emerged during the discussions and analyses:

- With risk-averse behavior, uncertain cost streams should be discounted lower than their certainty-equivalent case, and benefit streams should be higher than the certainty-equivalent case.
- Non-constant and endogenous discounting is the only relevant form of dis-counting for environmental decision making.
- The sustainability requirements following these foundations of valuation of future are significantly different from those using the conventional methods of constant rate of time discounting.

Technically, non-autonomous Hamiltonians do not allow the classical Weitzman interpretation of the Hamiltonian as the maximum attainable consumption in a model involving the maximization of utility of consumption of economic sus-tainability. As a result, some of the conclusions of Hartwick and Solow hold only under special cases, but not in general. Besides, these analyses do not address issues of ecological resilience and SD explicitly. The salient features of the state of the environment, and of the source and sink constraints are given in chapter 2.

Appendix: NNP and Sustainability

A detailed discussion on endogenous discount functions is given by Rao (1999b), who provides the basis for the model examined further in this section. In what follows, capital simply means the conventional capital, i.e. person-made or man-ufactured/reproducible.

The following analysis draws upon the application of the concepts of Poisson brackets and their properties, widely used in the study of quantum mechanics. These are not known to have been used in the study of economic systems so far.

Dynamics of Conservation

A basis of investigations into conserving wealth begins with two conservation laws offered by Samuelson (1990), assuming autonomous Hamiltonian, constant return to scale in the production function, and time-additive preferences.

1   The value of net output (NNP), expressed in terms of any selected good as numéraire, accumulates through time as the (numéraire-good's own) rate of interest just as the value of capital does.
2   Along any optimal path, the ratio between the value of income and the value of capital wealth is a constant.

These two laws lend support to Weitzman's (1976) NNP interpretation, but these require extensions to include time-varying and endogenized discounts as well as preferences. It is useful to note here that the equivalence of the Hamiltonian with total "energy" – argued by Samuelson (1990) – i.e. kinetic energy plus potential energy, is a sufficient but not necessary condition for the law of conservation of energy; see, for example, Marion and Thornton (1995, p. 266).

When the utility function is subject to changes in taste and in technical progress, the modified conservation law under constant time discounting states that (Sato, 1990):

Income (NNP) + current worth of taste/technical change
= discount rate × wealth

This result suggests that there is a "cost" or "penalty" or gain associated with taste and technical factors. However, the valuation of these factors is rather simplistic. This is because the valuation was only a result of the effect of change in utility (with time) for the entire remaining time horizon, using a constant discount rate.

We derive a new set of results that are facilitated with the application of Poisson brackets. When these are applied to Hamiltonian mechanics relevant for the SD models, the optimality properties can be interpreted. These include the sensitivity of desired trajectories in terms of other parameters. Endogeneized discount factors are handled in an elegantly simple manner. The sustainability requirement of constancy of consumption or of the discounted utility is viewed in terms of the property of the corresponding function that forms an "integral of motion." It is not proposed to elucidate the details of the methodology; these can be seen in many books on classical mechanics and quantum mechanics; see, for example, Marion and Thornton (1995).

It is useful to note that the Hamiltonian H is considered as a function on (p_k, q_k, t) space whereas the Lagrangian is formulated as a function on $(p_k, \dot{p}_k, t)$ space $(k = 1, 2, \ldots, n)$, where ps are the state variables and qs are the costate variables.

For F defined on the Hamiltonian phase space, the following holds:

$$\frac{dF}{dt} = \frac{\partial F}{\partial t} + \sum_{i=1}^{n}\left(\frac{\partial F}{\partial q_i}\dot{q}_i + \frac{\partial F}{\partial p_i}\dot{p}_i\right)$$

$$= \frac{\partial F}{\partial t} + \sum_{i=1}^{n}\left(-\frac{\partial F}{\partial q_i}\cdot\frac{\partial H}{\partial p_i} + \frac{\partial F}{\partial p_i}\cdot\frac{\partial H}{\partial q_i}\right)$$

$$= \frac{\partial F}{\partial t} + [F, H]$$

where $[F, H]$ is the Poisson bracket of F and H.

When $[F, H] = 0$, the Hamiltonian is stationary and so is the entity represented by F (called an integral of motion) and F is constant. Let us note that the Envelope theorem can be derived using the above approach, providing its simplest proof ever! This can be seen from the result:

$$\frac{dF}{dt} = \frac{\partial F}{\partial t}$$

For a relevant application of the results above, let us consider a utility function

$$U = U(C, K, E)$$

where the arguments of U are time-dependent differentiable functions representing consumption, capital (person-made), and environmental asset stock, respectively.

Let the environmental production function be

$$F = f(C, E)$$

with f differentiable. The endogenized discount function, D, is given by

$$\dot{D} = -D(C, K, t) \qquad t \in [0, \infty) \tag{4.1}$$

The state equations of the system are given by

$$\dot{K} = g(K, E, C) \qquad K(0) = K_0 \tag{4.2}$$

$$\dot{E} = h(K, E, C) \qquad E(0) = E_0 \tag{4.3}$$

The relevant problem is to maximize

$$J = \int_0^\infty D(c, k, t)\, U(c, k, E)\, dt \tag{4.4}$$

subject to (4.2) and (4.3).

When $D = \exp(-st)$ for some fixed s, and E is dropped, the formulation corresponds to that of Weitzman (1976).

The Hamiltonian function arising out of (4.1)–(4.4) is

$$H = DU + q_1 g + q_2 h + q_3(-D)$$

where q_i ($i = 1, 2, 3$) are costate variables which represent corresponding shadow prices of the multiplying factors. Let us, for the convenience of notation, use p_i as state variables K, E, D.

The Poisson bracket governing H and DU is given by

$$[H, DU] = \sum_{i=1}^{3} \left(\frac{\partial(DU)}{\partial q_i} \cdot \frac{\partial H}{\partial p_i} - \frac{\partial(DU)}{\partial p_i} \cdot \frac{\partial H}{\partial q_i} \right)$$

$$= \sum_{i=1}^{3} \left(U \frac{\partial H}{\partial q_i} \cdot \frac{\partial D}{\partial p_i} - D \frac{\partial H}{\partial q_i} \cdot \frac{\partial U}{\partial p_i} \right)$$

We would like to examine the implication of the requirement that the discounted utility be constant for ever. This states $[H, DU] = 0$, which gives

$$U \sum_{i=1}^{3} \left(\frac{\partial D}{\partial p_i} \cdot \frac{\partial H}{\partial q_i} \right) = D \sum_{i=1}^{3} \left(\frac{\partial U}{\partial p_i} \cdot \frac{\partial H}{\partial q_i} \right) \tag{4.5}$$

Let us formulate a new Hamiltonian that typically augments the usual NNP expression H with the valuation of environmental factors. This is given by

$$H_2 = H_1 + MG$$

If we wish to examine the implication of treating the stationarity and constancy of H_2, we require $[H_1, H_2] = 0$, i.e.

$$\sum_i \left(\frac{\partial H_2}{\partial q_i} \cdot \frac{\partial H_1}{\partial p_i} - \frac{\partial H_2}{\partial p_i} \cdot \frac{\partial H_1}{\partial q_i} \right) = 0$$

$$\Rightarrow \frac{\partial H_1}{\partial q_1} \left(-\frac{\partial H_2}{\partial k} \right) + \frac{\partial H_1}{\partial k} \left(\frac{\partial H_2}{\partial q_1} \right) = 0$$

$$\Rightarrow \frac{\partial H_2}{\partial k} = \Delta \frac{\partial H_1}{\partial k}$$

where

$$\Delta = \left(\frac{\partial H_2}{\partial q_1} \right) \left(\frac{\partial H_1}{\partial q_1} \right)^{-1}$$

The above relations establish that the marginal productivity of capital (person-made) in the environmentally augmented Hamiltonian H_2 is proportional to that in the usual NNP-related Hamiltonian H_1; the proportionality factor Δ is the ratio of the effect of a change in the shadow price of capital (value of capital) on H_2 and of similar quantity on H_1. The interrelationship between capital (person-made) and the environmental assets determines the magnitude of Δ, i.e. on the specific features of the underlying production function.

As a simple illustration, let the conventional reproducible capital growth be given by

$$\dot{K} = f(K) - C - a$$

where C is the consumption, a the expenditure on environmental improvement, and K the capital. Clearly K, C, and a are functions of time.

Let the environmental asset stock be governed by

$$\dot{E} = m(a) - zf(K)$$

where z represents the emission coefficient per unit output, and m the environmental improvement coefficient.

Some of the findings of these investigations are: In the optimal set up, the marginal productivity of conventional (manufactured) capital in the endogeneized model is proportional to the one in the conventional models (which use exogenous discount functions), and the proportional factor is the ratio of the effect of a change in the shadow price of capital (value of capital) on the new Hamiltonian and of similar quantity under the conventional Hamiltonian. The interrelationship between conventional capital and the environmental assets determines the magnitude of this ratio, which include the specific characteristics of the production function.

Review Exercises

1   What are the implications of the application of the Precautionary Principle (PP) for the extraction and management of exhaustible resources when there is an expected continued technical progress? How do these implications differ from those arising from an application of the classic Hotelling rule?
2   If discount functions lead to discount factors, what are the required parameters to translate the latter into numerical values? What is the meaning of robustness in this context?
3   (a)   Why is the NNP unacceptable as an indicator of sustainability?
    (b)   What is the role and limitation of the NNP in a world with changing tastes?

4   If one of the interpretations of intergenerational justice does not allow any discounting of the future accrual values, what justifies a positive discount rate? And, how positive can this be? How does uncertainty affect this choice of discount rate?

5   What considerations are relevant in choosing the discount rates in country-specific systems?

6   In the total economic value (TEV) concept, what is the role of uncertainty and how can this be reflected in the valuation?

7   Examine the role and limitations of the contingent valuation method in obtaining nonmarket valuation of the problem of concentrations of carbon dioxide from industrial emissions. Who are the target respondents and what role is expected of that group if the valuation is given to the group?

8   In addition to the proper valuation of resources and application of the Hotelling rule, what stipulations can lead to sustainable development (as defined in chapter 3)?

9   Why is the suggested discount rate for benefits under uncertainty less than that for costs under uncertainty in the case of risk-averse decision making?

10 In the Costanza et al. study (box 4.1), what specific features could lead to an enhanced assessment of nature's services?

References

Ainslie, G. W. (1992) *Picoeconomics*. Cambridge: Cambridge University Press.

Aronsson, T. and Lofgren, K. G. (1995) National product related welfare measures in the presence of technological change. *Environmental and Resource Economics*, 5, 321–32.

Arrow, K. J., Solow, R., Portney, P. R., Leamer, E. E., Radner, R. and Schuman, H. (1993) Report of the NOAA Panel on Contingent Valuation. *Federal Register (US)*, 58, 4601–14.

Arrow, K. J., Cropper, M. L., Eads, G. C., Helin, R. W., Lave, L. B., Noll, R. G., Portney, P. R., Russell, M., Schmalensee, R., Smith, V. K. and Stavins, R. N. (1996) Is there a role for benefit–cost analysis in environmental, health and safety regulation? *Science*, 272, 221–2.

Asheim, G. B. (1994) Net national product as an indicator of sustainability. *Scandinavian Journal of Economics*, 96, 257–65.

Babu, P. G., Kumar, K. K. and Murthy, N. S. (1997) An overlapping generations model with exhaustible resources and stock pollution. *Ecological Economics*, 21, 35–43.

Barnett, H. and Morse, C. (1963) *Scarcity and Growth – The Economics of Natural Resource Availability*. Baltimore: Johns Hopkins University Press.

Becker, G. (1998) *Accounting for Tastes*. Cambridge, Mass.: Harvard University Press.

Becker, G. and Mulligan, C. (1997) The endogenous determination of time preferences. *Quarterly Journal of Economics*, 112(3), 729–58.

Bromley, D. (1991) The commons, common property, and environmental policy. *Environmental and Resource Economics*, 1.

Broome, J. (1992) *Counting the Cost of Global Warming*. London: White Horse Press.

Ciriacy-Wantrup, S. V. (1947) Capital returns for soil conservation practices. *Journal of Farm Economics*, 29, 1181–96.

Clark, C. (1990) *Mathematical Bioeconomics* (2nd edn). New York: Wiley Interscience.

Costanza, R., d'Arge, R., deGroot, R., Farber, S., Grasso, M., Hannon, B., Limburg, K., Naeem, S., O'Neill, R. V., Paruelo, J., Raskin, R. G., Sutton, P. and van den Belt, M.

(1997) The value of the world's ecosystem services and natural capital. *Nature*, 387 (May 15), 253–60.

Cummings, R. G., Brookshire, D. and Schultze, W. (1986) *Valuing Environmental Goods – Assessment of the Contingent Valuation Method*. Totowa, NJ: Rowman and Allanheld.

Daly, H. E. (1991) *Steady-State Economics*. Washington, DC: Island Press.

Dasgupta, P. and Heal, G. (1979) *Economic Theory and Exhaustible Resources*. Cambridge: Cambridge University Press.

Dasgupta, P. and Maler, K. G. (1994) The environment and emerging development issues. In R. Layard and S. Glaister (eds), *Cost–Benefit Analysis*, Cambridge: Cambridge University Press, 319–48.

Dreze, J. and Stern, N. (1987) The theory of cost–benefit analysis. In A. J. Auerbach and M. Feldstein (eds), *Handbook of Public Economics*, vol. II. New York: North-Holland, 909–89.

Fisher, I. (1930) *The Theory of Interest*. New York: Macmillan.

Goodin, R. (1982) Discounting discounting. *Journal of Public Policy*, 2(1), 53–72.

Goodin, R. (1986) *Protecting the Vulnerable*. Chicago: University of Chicago Press.

Goulder, L. H. and Kennedy, D. (1997) Valuing ecosystem services – philosophical bases and empirical methods. In G. Daily (ed.), *Nature's Services*. Washington, DC: Island Press, 23–47.

Gregory, R., Lichenstein, S. and Slovic, P. (1993) Valuing environmental resources – a constructive approach. *Journal of Risk and Uncertainty*, 7, 177–97.

Hadker, N., Sharma, S., David, A. and Muraleedharan, T. R. (1997) Willingness-to-pay for Borivli National Park – evidence from a contingent valuation. *Ecological Economics*, 21, 105–22.

Halvorsen, R. and Smith, T. (1991) A test of the theory of exhaustible resources. *Quarterly Journal of Economics*, 106, 123–40.

Hartwick, J. (1977) Intergenerational equity and the investing of rents from exhaustible resources. *American Economic Review*, 67, 972–4.

Harvey, C. M. (1986) Value functions for infinite-period planning. *Management Science*, 32, 1123–39.

Harvey, C. M. (1995) Proportional discounting of future costs and benefits. *Mathematics of Operations Research*, 20(2), 381–99.

Heal, G. M. (1985) Depletion and discounting – a classical issue in the economics of exhaustible resources. In *Environmental and Natural Resource Mathematics*. Providence, RI: American Mathematical Society, 33–43.

Hotelling, H. (1931) The economics of exhaustible resources. *Journal of Political Economy*, 39, 137–75.

IPCC (1996) *Climate Change 1995 – Economic and Social Dimensions of Climate Change*. Cambridge: Cambridge University Press.

Joshi, S. (1995) Recursive utility and optimal growth under uncertainty. *Journal of Mathematical Economics*, 24, 601–17.

Krautkraemer, J. A. (1985) Optimal growth, resource amenities, and the preservation of natural environments. *Review of Economic Studies*, 52, 153–70.

Laibson, D. (1997) Golden eggs and hyperbolic discounting. *Quarterly Journal of Economics*, 62(2), 443–77.

Lind, R. C. (1982) A premier on the major issues relating to the discount rate for evaluating national energy options. In R. C. Lind et al. (eds), *Discounting for Time and Risk in Energy Policy*. Baltimore: Johns Hopkins University Press.

Lind, R. C. (1990) Reassessing the government's discount rate policy in light of new theory and data in a world economy with a high degree of capital mobility. *Journal of Environmental Economics and Management*, 18(2), S8–S28.

Lofgren, K. G. (1992) Comment on C. R. Hulten, "Accounting for the wealth of nations – the net versus gross output controversy and its ramifications." *Scandinavian Journal of Economics*, 94, S25–S28.

Lowenstein, G. and Prelec, D. (1992) Anomalies in intertemporal choice – evidence and an interpretation. *Quarterly Journal of Economics*, 57, 573–98.

Lozada, G. A. (1995) Resource depletion, national income accounting and the value of optimal dynamic programs. *Resource and Energy Economics*, 17, 137–54.

Malliaris, A. G. and Stefani, S. (1991) Heterogeneous discount rates – a generalization of Hotelling's rule. In R. P. Hamalainen and H. K. Ehtamo (eds), *Dynamic Games in Economic Analysis*. New York: Springer-Verlag.

Marini, G. and Scaramozzino, P. (1995) Overlapping generations and environmental control. *Journal of Environmental Economics and Management*, 29(1), 64–77.

Marion, J. B. and Thornton, S. T. (1995) *Classical Dynamics of Particles and Systems*. New York: Harcourt Bruce.

Myers, N. (1995) Environmental unknowns. *Science*, 269, 358–60.

Nordhaus, W. D. (1993) Rolling the DICE – an optimal transition path for controlling greenhouse gases. *Resource and Energy Economics*, 15, 27–50.

Nordhaus, W. D. (1994) *Managing Global Commons – The Economics of Climate Change*. Cambridge, Mass.: MIT Press.

Page, T. (1997) On the problem of achieving efficiency and equity – intergenerationally. *Land Economics*, 73(4), 580–96.

Perrings, C. (1997) *Economics of Ecological Resources*. Cheltenham: Edward Elgar.

Pigou, A. C. (1932) *The Economics of Welfare*. London: Macmillan.

Plambeck, E. L., Hope, C. and Anderson, J. (1997) The "Page 95" model – integrating the science and economics of global warming. *Energy Economics*, 19(1), 77–101.

Pollak, R. A. (1968) Consistent planning. *Review of Economic Studies*, 35(2), 201–8.

Pontryagin, L. S., Boltyanskii, V. G., Gamkrelidze, R. V. and Mishchenko, E. F. (1968) *The Theory of Optimal Processes*. New York: Wiley Interscience.

Portney, P. (1994) The contingent valuation debate – why economists should care. *Journal of Economic Perspectives*, 8(4), 3–17.

Prelec, D. (1989) *Decreasing Impatience – Definition and Consequences*. New York: Russell Sage Foundation Working Paper.

Prelec, D. (1998) The probability weighting function. *Econometrica*, 66(3), 497–527.

Ramsey, F. P. (1928) A mathematical theory of savings. *Economic Journal*, 38, 543–59.

Rao, P. K. (1999a) *Is Net National Product an Indicator of Sustainability?* (in press).

Rao, P. K. (1999b) *Sustainable Development with Endogenous Preferences* (under review).

Rawls, J. (1972) *A Theory of Justice*. Oxford: Clarendon Press.

Rothenberg, T. and Smith, K. (1971) The effect of uncertainty on resource allocation in a general equilibrium model. *Quarterly Journal of Economics*, 85, 440–53.

Samuelson, P. A. (1961) The evaluation of "social income" – capital formation and wealth. In F. Lutz and D. Hague (eds), *The Theory of Capital*. New York: St. Martin's Press.

Samuelson, P. A. (1990) Two conservation laws in theoretical economics. In Sato and Ramachandran (1990, 57–70).

Sato, R. (1990) The invariance principle and income-wealth conservation laws. In Sato and Ramachandran (1990, 71–106).

Sato, R. and Ramachandran, R. V. (eds) (1990) *Conservation Laws and Symmetry-Applications to Economics and Finance*. Boston: Kluwer Academic.

Sefton, J. A. and Weale, M. R. (1996) The net national product and exhaustible resources – the effects of foreign trade. *Journal of Public Economics*, 61(1), 21–47.

Serageldin, I. (1995) Making development sustainable. In I. Serageldin and A. Steer (eds), *Making Development Sustainable – From Concepts to Action.* Washington, DC: The World Bank.

Sidgwick, H. (1907) *Methods of Ethics.* London: Macmillan.

Sinclair, P. (1994) On the optimum trend of fossil fuel taxation. *Oxford Economic Papers,* 46, 869–77.

Slade, M. and Thille, H. (1997) Hotelling confronts CAPM – a test of the theory of exhaustible resources. *Canadian Journal of Economics,* 33(3), 685–708.

Solow, R. M. (1970) *Growth Theory – An Exposition.* New York: Oxford University Press.

Solow, R. M. (1974a) Intergenerational equity and exhaustible resources. *Review of Economic Studies,* 51, 29–45.

Solow, R. M. (1974b) The economics of resources or the resources of economics. *American Economic Review,* 64(2), 1–14.

Solow, R. M. (1986) On the intergenerational allocation of resources. *Scandinavian Journal of Economics,* 88(1), 141–9.

Solow, R. M. (1992) *Sustainability – An Economist's Perspective, The 18th Steward Johnson Lecture, Woods Hole Oceanographic Institution.* Woods Hole: MA.

Solow, R. M. (1994) An almost practical step toward sustainability. In National Research Council, *Assigning Economic Value to Natural Resources.* Washington, DC: National Academy Press.

Solow, R. M. (1996) Comments on net national product. Personal communication to the author.

Stern, P. C., Young, O. R. and Druckman, D. (eds) (1992) *Global Environmental Change – Understanding the Human Dimensions.* Washington, DC: National Academy Press.

Stevens, T. H., Echeverria, J., Glass, R. J., Hager, T., and Moore, T. A. (1991) Measuring the existence value of wildlife – what do CVM estimates really show? *Land Economics,* 67(4).

Strotz, R. H. (1956) Myopia and inconsistency in dynamic utility maximization. *Review of Economic Studies,* 23(3).

Sunstein, C. (1997) *Free Markets and Social Justice.* New York: Oxford University Press.

Thompson, P. B. (1997) Evaluating energy efficiency investments – accounting for risk in the discounting process. *Energy Policy,* 25(12), 989–96.

Toth, F. L. (1995) Discounting in integrated assessments of climate change. *Energy Policy,* 23(4–5), 403–9.

Weitzman, M. L. (1976) On the welfare significance of national product in a dynamic economy. *Quarterly Journal of Economics,* 90, 156–62.

Weitzman, M. L. (1997) Sustainability and technical progress. *Scandinavian Journal of Economics,* 99(1), 1–13.

chapter outline

● CHAPTER 5 ●

Managing the Global Commons

● CHAPTER 5 ●

Managing the Global Commons

God does not play dice with the universe.
Albert Einstein

● 5.1 INTRODUCTION ●

Humans are playing with nature: humans are exerting significant influence on planet Earth, and thus contributing to great uncertainties of vagaries of climate change and its adverse consequences. The largest single common arena of human influence on the planet's climate and development prospects of society is affected via the global commons. These are transboundary environmental resources (in terms of sources and sinks) with free and open access to the ecological space. These are inclusive of both the resources (like water, air, and biodiversity) and environmental facilities (like sink capacities). All these affect the "efficiency" in the provision of nature's services, like carbon recycling and renewal, potential to shield from ultraviolet (UV) radiation, and stability of biogeochemical cycles. The phenomena of sustainable development (SD) tend to be greatly influenced by the dynamics of the stocks and flows of the environmental resources. These affect the sink capacity and induce such effects as that of global warming. This feature, in turn, affects the provision of nature's services, directly influencing environmental and economic sustainability; see chapter 3. The role of the global commons, therefore, is critical in the processes governing SD.

We use the global commons terminology mainly to refer to the open sink characteristics of global environmental problems: the greenhouse gas (GHG) accumulations, the ozone depletion, and the limitations of recycling wastes. The limitations of natural resources like air and water are not minor in their significance for human survival. Nonetheless, the binding constraints over a period of time are more likely to occur as consequences of potential mismanagement of the global commons. At the top of the list of problems stands the impending phenomenon that GHGs lead to global warming, and this phenomenon affects human survival in a variety of ways.

This chapter examines alternative concepts and methods of assessing global warming potential, with particular emphasis on measures to enable policy decision making for stabilizing GHGs. The economics of the greenhouse effect (GE) are examined for an overall macroeconomic perspective. Clearly, the available estimates, from various sources, of costs and benefits are far from comprehensive. Hence, these cannot lead directly to operationally relevant and pragmatic policies. Besides, practical application is hampered so long as disaggregative (or bottom-up) analysis is not fully appreciated. In this context, the relative incidence of costs and benefits needs to be assessed for different economic and social groups with different time horizons of concern. The problem is confounded because of several unknowns and uncertainties in the evolving phenomenon of the GE, some of which are associated with lack of robustness in the predictions of even the best of the climatological models – including a class of global circulation models (GCMs) – and lack of full accounting for all sinks of emitted CO_2.

The concept of global warming potential (GWP) is founded on a number of simple scientific assumptions and on its index form; it does not, however, offer policy guidance or rational decision making at the sectoral or international levels. Accordingly, this definition and alternative formulations are reviewed and potential formulae for adoption in decision making are discussed; these take into account the critical role of the time element in evolving preferences and ranking potential alternatives. Similarly, the economics of the GE are examined with a bearing on the role of the time factor and of changes in technology and preferences. A wide variety of measures to mitigate the GE are examined in this chapter, with a focus on institutional and international ramifications of the global commons problem. Stabilizing GHGs is a definite requirement in the control and mitigation of GHGs and their impacts. A variety of alternative packages seem to merit consideration in this context. It is not possible to suggest that these be ranked only according to least cost criteria, unless the cost function is extremely broadly defined to comprehend all meaningful costs. The critical issue is to seek clarifications: Whose costs? When are these incurred? What are the expected benefits? When and who gets the benefits? Even if all the answers to these questions are not clear, a total evasion of these or simple global aggregativeness is likely to be of very limited use in policy formulation. A few relevant directions of inquiry into detailed assessment of cost incidence or relative roles of different factors like carbon sequestration are examined in a later section. One of the most important elements of fiscal policy involves ecotaxes (green taxes), either directly or indirectly. The feasibility, role, and limitations of this approach is examined.

● 5.2 GLOBAL COMMONS ●

Global commons are defined here as the global environmental resources that cut across national boundaries and that are affected across all regions due to direct and indirect interventions in any one or more regions. The global commons possess varying features over time due to changing human interface with the environment. The main ingredients of concern in the global commons are:

- atmospheric gases that cause the GE and global warming;
- thinning of the ozone layer leading to increased ultraviolet-B (UV-B) radiation;
- transboundary pollution in the air and water; and
- loss of biodiversity.

The roots of anthropogenic contributions in the global commons are largely founded in the open access and free-rider problems of public goods. Thus, the concern created by the emerging problems of the global commons tends to focus on the issues of legitimacy of appropriations of sink capacities without any obligations on the part of the users/polluters. These lead to the legitimacy of any exercise of property rights. Property configurations can be broadly classified in terms of private property, state property, common property, and open access. Various resources like fresh water and biological pools constitute examples of common property, whereas atmospheric concentrations of GHGs and the ozone layer are examples of global commons with open access. We refer to these commons simply as global commons. Unless otherwise stated, these possess open access characteristics.

Lack of any property rights and consequent markets makes this vital segment of the planet a potential threat for the survival of humanity, in as much as it currently is nature's benevolence to provide these avenues as opportunities for survival of all forms of life on Earth. Ironically, even the believers of the universal role of free markets for resource allocation and efficiency (of one type or the other) fell short on the issue of creation of a fair global market for a relatively scarce resource. Emissions trading is a mechanism suggested strongly, but creation of benchmarks for the initial market conditions are far from resolved. It is not the presumption here that the markets are the only suitable forms of global governance for the sustainable management of global commons. A mix of institutional and market factors are required for this purpose. There are hardly any features of property in the open access case unless some restraints like emissions trading and quotas are imposed, institutionally. The relevant ingredients of this framework are given in a later section of this chapter and in chapters 10 and 11.

Tragedy of the Commons?

The phenomenon of the "tragedy of the commons" – Hardin (1968); see also chapter 1 – tends to apply since the sink capacity is tampered with by human contributors without their having to pay for such a destruction of the sink capacity. This problem is also similar to the "free-rider" problem that economists analyze in the economics of public goods but, in those cases, the public goods are paid for by some institutions; in the present case, nature provides it and responds rather belatedly with potentially irreversible adverse consequences.

The problem of the tragedy of the commons arises not in the context of common property, but in the context of no clearly defined property rights, and that the proper terminology is free access resources rather than common property resources. These features are conventionally applied to the problem of governance of commodities or resources arising from one or more common pools of sources, with no cost to the users. Hardin sought to explain the processes of extinction of some of the fish stocks in terms of the "philosophy of the commons." However, the reasoning extends to the problems of governance of sinks (as explained in chapter 2), which is the main concern. In all such cases, the processes underlying the free-rider and open access phenomena need to be addressed. Alternatively, from an equivalent economic pricing perspective, the costs of externalities should be internalized. Users or beneficiaries should be made to pay some kind of "tax" based on their value added "output," loss of sink capacity, and for any losses and damages to the ecosystems or reduction in the ecosystem services.

It is useful to note that any dichotomous treatment of property simply in terms of common (non-private) property and private (exclusive) property is an oversimplification of the issues involved. Another categorization, "anticommons," was suggested in Heller (1998) as an added alternative: anticommons is a property regime in which multiple owners hold effective rights of exclusion to a scarce resource, and the ownership of anticommons property includes the ability by each owner to prevent other owners from obtaining a core bundle of rights in an entity. In this direction of inquiry, non-private property may be analyzed as anticommons property (if the predominant feature is one of rights of exclusion in the use of resources), and commons property (if the exercise of privileges of inclusion remains the dominant feature). Can a tragedy of anticommons occur? Heller suggested that this is possible when too many entities have rights of exclusion in a relatively scarce resource. However, it is the club structure and its features of collusive behavior (or cartelization) that possesses the potential for a kind of tragedy: sub-optimal resource use in a global welfare maximizing sense. Is the real alternative to potential problems in the global commons to be seen in terms of globally representative institutions like those under the UN Framework Convention on Climate Change (UNFCCC)? The answer is obviously in favor of the strengthening of such a forum for effective global environmental management. Some of these issues are discussed later.

The diagnosis of the impediments to sustainability (in biogeophysical and ecological terms) and SD leads to significant concerns about the global climate and contributing global environmental factors. The ramifications cut across national boundaries, but there is no doubt that the global environmental problems have their roots at local, regional and sub-regional levels, and at the levels of individual consumers and producers. Accordingly, the features of the tragedy of the commons apply substantially at all these levels. These problems warrant collective coordinated actions where different societies, countries, and individual entities contribute to alleviate the common current and potential problems. Any

such requirement of coordinated or cooperative effort presumes that all potential contributors to the problems tend to participate and that there are common
perceptions, objectives and comparable means of achieving the objectives among
the participants. These requirements are usually not met in most scenarios; see
also Ostrom (1990). Yet, to the extent that commonalities could be derived, the
approach merits its adoption in terms of devising policies, programs, and actions
for implementation. The analytics of strategic cooperative behavior draw upon
game-theoretic formulations (Mesterton-Gibbons, 1992), and some of these analyses suggest that, in repeat transaction settings with interface between countries
(possibly coordinated under agreements like the Montreal Protocol), there is much
greater scope for cooperative behavior. It was also established that this institutional arrangement is particularly relevant when the valuation of the future is
not heavily discounted.

Since the problem of global warming and climate change is the single most
important problem of sustainability and SD confronting human society at the end
of the twentieth century, we deal primarily with the first aspect in the rest of
this chapter. Other issues are discussed in different sections.

In the assessment of various characteristics of global commons, we need to
focus on several issues:

- The roles of human activities in the observed sink problems.
- Changes over time, historically and trends in the future.
- Geographic differences in the current state and its likely changes.
- Implications of adverse developments on global warming.
- Impact of changes on the well-being and sustainability of human population.
- The roles of anthropogenic factors in the governance of global commons.
- Specific contributions of GHGs in the above.
- Geophysical and economic explanations of changes.
- Institutional aspects of the governance of global commons.
- Scope for devising relevant policies and programs.

The remainder of this chapter is devoted to some of these issues; however,
related issues form recurring themes in several other chapters as well.

Anthropogenic Factors

The role of human factors in the problems of GE and global warming may
be stated here. The combustion of fossil fuels for the consumption and production activities of the human enterprise leads to increases in the concentration
of GHGs in the atmosphere: these are the fundamental factors underlying the
global warming process and are attributable to humans; see also Karl et al. (1997).
These GHGs are primarily CO_2, CH_4, O_3, and N_2O, and halocarbons including
chlorofluorocarbons (CFCs). These gases act asymmetrically with respect to sunlight; they let in the light rays but tend to insulate the planet against the losses

of heat (specifically, they trap infrared radiative energy in the troposphere, the lower atmosphere) – typically the GE. Higher concentration of GHGs does imply much greater possibility of global warming. It was estimated that, since about 1750 (the start of the industrial revolution), humans have altered the natural GE by adding 30 percent more CO_2, 145 percent more CH_4, and a set of other gases (IPCC, 1995a). Most of the GHGs are the toughest to handle because much of these emissions have a longer life span in the atmosphere, about one century. Besides, there are other gases which affect the effectiveness of given levels of the GHGs. These include CO, nitrogen oxides (NO_x), and hydrocarbons. The CO_2 emissions are contributed primarily by fossil fuel combustion and deforestation.

The Ozone Problem

Let us introduce some of the standard terms. In the atmosphere, the tropospheric region is closest to the surface of the Earth, with an altitude less than 15 km from the mean surface level; the stratosphere lies in the range 15–50 km, mesosphere in the range 50–80 km, and the thermosphere/ionosphere at levels exceeding 80 km in altitude. The stratopause lies between stratosphere and mesosphere, and the tropopause lies between troposphere and stratosphere.

The ozone layer is an important ingredient of the atmosphere, shielding the planet's surface from damaging UV radiation from the sun. The ozone is continuously generated by the action of solar radiation on atmospheric oxygen and is amenable to destruction by catalytic processes involving trace amounts of free radical gases like nitrogen oxide. Atmospheric chemists Mario Molina, Sherwood Rowland, and Paul Crutzen won the Nobel Prize for their diagnosis of the role of CFCs in the ozone layer of the stratosphere. It was found that photo decomposition of the CFCs in the stratosphere produces catalysts that cause destruction of ozone; see box 5.1 for details on the ozone loss. The CFCs are very powerful infrared light absorbers; they destroy ozone and tend to contribute very significantly to the GE. The most important CFCs are CFC-11 and CFC-12. The atmospheric residence time of the CFCs is about a century, owing to their very slow diffusion into the stratosphere.

Climate change, to the extent caused by human activities, is fraught with relatively long time horizons like a few decades. Accordingly, any effectiveness of the corrective measures requires substantial gestation lags. The time lags between the causes and effects, as well their interdependence, complicate some of the perceptions of problems and their remedial measures, even when there are no serious problems of noncooperation between various constituents of human society. Effective protection of the climate system requires international cooperation, flexibility, and an appreciation of perspectives for the future. This raises the issues of efficiency and equity in different categories: intra-national, international and intergenerational. Resolving issues in equity remains important for promoting trust, cooperation and effectiveness of policy decisions.

The problems of the global commons cannot be solved by any one set of economic activities or individual or institutional categories for universal application

BOX 5.1   Ozone hole

Whereas ordinary oxygen common in the atmosphere is in the two molecule form O_2, ozone is another form of oxygen: O_3. Whether ozone is useful or harmful to humans and other life forms on this planet depends on its location in the atmosphere. Good ozone and bad ozone differ only in their location in the atmosphere. Named after Gordon Dobson, an Oxford Physicist, it is measured in Dobson units. In the lower troposphere, ozone is an ingredient in the formation of photochemical smog, and causes serious problems in air quality and adverse health effects. The ozone one normally refers to, in the context of the problems of ozone hole and rupture in the ozone shield, is located in the stratosphere and is critically important to shield life forms from UV radiation and its harmful effects. Skin cancer and other health problems are associated strongly with the effects of UV radiation. It is also useful to note that ozone concentration varies with seasons and latitudes around the planet. Roelofs and Lelieveld (1997) observed that the stratospheric O_3 contributes significantly to surface O_3 in winter and spring when the petrochemical lifetime of O_3 is relatively long, and in summer and in the tropics, little O_3 reaches the surface from the stratosphere due to strong petrochemical destruction; surface O_3 is determined largely by petrochemical production. Ozone from the stratosphere accounts for about 75 percent of that consumed in the troposphere each year. Production of O_3 in the troposphere is limited because of less UV light relative to that in the stratosphere.

Chlorine (Cl) is one of the catalysts which turns O_3 into O_2 units, causing destruction of the ozone layer. The role of CFCs in this process was first assessed by Molina and Rowland (1974).

The catalytic action of Cl is given by the reaction

$$Cl + O_3 \rightarrow ClO + O_2$$

Empirical confirmation of the ozone hole was carried out by Farman et al. (1985). CFC-11, until recently used as a refrigerant and propellant, is one of the main CFCs responsible for near half the observed depletion of ozone. The CFCs are mixed gradually in the atmosphere and take decades to reach the stratosphere. Once there, they are decomposed by UV sunlight, releasing the chlorine which begins attacking the ozone. The chemical balancing equation relevant here is:

$$O_3 + UV \text{ radiation} \rightarrow O_2 + O$$

A link between ozone depletion and an increase in the GE was found by Ramanathan (1975): CFCs trap heat the same way that other gases like CO_2 do, and thus are also GHGs.

Sources: Roelofs and Lelieveld (1997); Somerville (1996, pp. 6–23); Schlesinger (1991).

(on planet Earth only!). The poorer regions are contributing to the problems with their continued deforestation and combustion for survival and economic growth, whereas the more developed regions draw upon the fossil fuels for industrial activities to fulfill higher levels of consumption directly and through industrial products for export revenues. The levels of efficiency of resource use and technology adoption for emission control and waste reduction is usually higher in the latter than in the former regions. However, the problems of limited international cooperation, "free riders," and the roles of government regulations and market factors, as well as voluntary compliance and environmental consciousness, require detailed analysis. Some of the issues of interface between trade and environment, debt and environment and of environmental components of international trade are examined in chapter 8. The design of institutional ramifications of the emissions and other global commons problems are discussed in chapter 10.

Global commons need to be evaluated not only for what these features depict in biogeophysical terms but also in terms of the accompanying costs of different levels of these features to the socioeconomic system. A single comprehensive measure of the status of the global commons is difficult to conceptualize for any operationally meaningful purpose. However, some of the components might be amenable for such quantification. The most significant initiative in this direction regards the GHGs and their global warming contribution. The details of these methods are given in the next section.

● 5.3 CLIMATE CHANGE ●

In the history of the evolution of scientific thought, Joseph Fourier (1824) and Savante Arrhenius (1896) were among the pioneers in the study of the effect of increases in the atmospheric concentrations of CO_2 on the temperature of the Earth's surface. However, Arrhenius is credited with being the first to quantify the relationship, which underwent several improvements during the past century. A useful collection of papers was put together in a special issue of the journal *Ambio* in February 1997, detailing historical and contemporary scientific perspectives on the theme of the GE.

If there is one area of concern for unwelcome change, it is climate change. This happens to be rather a consensus view, even if there is not as much agreement on whether anthropogenic factors are the main source of global climate change. The most referred to source of debate on these issues is the 500-strong Intergovernmental Panel on Climate Change (IPCC) constituted by the United Nations (UN) and coordinated under its agencies: World Meteorological Organization (WMO) and United Nations Environment Programme (UNEP). The First Assessment Report of the IPCC was published in 1990. This provided a scientific basis for the UNFCCC which was open for signature at the Earth Summit of 1992 in Rio. The main objective of this Framework Convention was declared in its Article 2:

. . . stabilization of GHG concentrations in the atmosphere at a level that would prevent dangerous anthropogenic interference with the climate system. Such a level should be achieved within a time frame sufficient to allow ecosystems to adapt naturally to climate change, to ensure that food production is not threatened, and to enable economic development to proceed in a sustainable manner.

One of the Synthesis Reports of the IPCC regarding the interpretation of Article 2 of the UNFCCC, based on its Second Assessment Report, stated (para. 1.9): climate change presents the decision maker with a set of formidable complications which include the potential for irreversible damages and unknowns, very long horizons for comprehension and empirical analysis, regional variations in causes and effects, and various levels as well as types of equity in the incidence of costs and benefits of any interventions or lack of actions. According to the report by the IPCC (1995a), "there is a discernible human influence on global climate." This conclusion begs the next pertinent question: How much effect, by what sources and what factors, and what are the likely time-trends in this cause–effect framework? There are not enough convincing answers with any great precision. However, the trends and broad magnitudes of the problem of climate change and its consequences (with and without human intervention) are partly answered in some of the IPCC reports. Besides, many more issues are answered in a series of research studies – contributed by various individuals and institutions worldwide.

The IPCC reports concluded that, in the absence of effective policies and actions to mitigate GHGs, the Earth's temperature could increase between 1–3.5°C (about 2–6.5°F) by 2100. Some of the major consequences include serious health problems, ecological instability, and a rise of the sea level by about 15–95 centimeters (6–38 inches), with potential to inundate several low-lying coastal regions. Climate change is expected to affect human living conditions and health adversely as a consequence of temperature extremes, expanded tropical diseases, floods, storms, dislocation of human habitats, and disturbances of ecological systems (directly and indirectly affecting food security and ecological system services). In financial terms, any estimate of such damages tends to be of the order of dozens of billions of dollars. It was also predicted that a meter rise in the sea level as a result of global warming could lead to loss of coastal land to the extent of 6 percent in the Netherlands, and about 17 percent in Bangladesh, among several other countries and small islands likely to be adversely affected.

The relation between the GE, climate variability in different regions of the planet, and rainfall/precipitation remains a complex one. However, most models predict reduced precipitation in Southern Europe and South Asia, for example, as a result of increased GHGs. In tropical and subtropical regions, rainfall decreased over the past few decades, especially in parts of Sahel and eastward to Indonesia; see, for example, Karl et al. (1997). These are weather externalities caused by spatially distributed sources of anthropogenic GHG emissions, a powerful example of economic and climatological externalities. The relative roles of current and historical emissions of GHGs by each country in this disastrous phenomena are not fully understood. Lack of requisite accountability tends to allow continued exploitation of the ecological space, with features obeying free-rider or open access systems. The economics of climate change warrants proper attention to the complex interdependencies in the physical and economic systems; see Rao (1999) for more details.

The IPCC Reports (Second Assessment) of 1996 confirmed most of the previous IPCC conclusions:

- The climate has changed over the past century, with discernible human influence in this phenomenon.
- GHG concentrations have continued to increase.
- Anthropogenic aerosols, like airborne particles as in coal-burning dust, tend to produce negative radiating forces which could marginally cool down the Earth's temperature.

The role of volcanic eruptions and their contribution to aerosols and cooling of the climate needs to be recognized as well. However, scenarios with high aerosol and GHG emissions contribute to climatic destabilization: with greater uncertainty in mean temperature and a greater likelihood of changes in other climate parameters; see West et al. (1997) for details. The IPCC Summary for Policy Makers did admit the prevalence of uncertainties relating to the parameters of the biogeochemical cycles, climatic feedbacks associated with clouds and vegetation endogenous to the rise in temperatures, and some of the characteristics of global atmospheric circulation models. The single most important message sought to be put out is to reduce the GHG emissions with particular reference to CO_2, given the long atmospheric lifetime of this gas. It is hard to disagree with this imperative, even by the standards of most critics of the science of global warming; see also Kerr (1997). Also, in a recent econometric study, Schmalensee et al. (1998) found that most projections of the carbon emissions in the IPCC reports could be underestimates, which require an upward adjustment.

The GHGs possess lifetimes that are usually sufficiently long enough to allow their mixing well throughout the troposphere and lower stratosphere, so their concentrations vary very little from their corresponding global mean (Mitchell and Johns, 1997). The GE tends to be very partially counteracted by the role of aerosols, the second most influential set of anthropogenic effects on the Earth's radiating budget. The fuel combustion methods generate GHGs as well as aerosols. Whereas the GHGs, especially CO_2, have an atmospheric residency time of about over a century, aerosols have residence times usually less than one week and thus are concentrated at their sources (Karl et al. 1997), whether these are the fuel-burning locations or the volcanic eruption regions. It was established about two decades ago that burning fossil fuels leads to the release of sulfur, which oxidizes and forms hydrated sulfate aerosols. These particles tend to cool the climate because they scatter sunlight. Aerosols produce a global-scale cooling which peaks in northern midlatitudes of the planet (where the aerosol loading or emission is greatest), and also in high altitudes in winter (due to feedbacks between sea-ice and temperature); this latter feature was observed by Mitchell and Johns (1997), who concluded that some of the changes in hydrology predicted to occur with increases in GHGs may be less extreme in the short- and medium-term future (several decades). It was also concluded that the situation may not prevail in the longer term because sulfate concentrations will be maintained only as long as sulfur emissions continue, whereas CO_2 has a lifetime of about a century; this latter feature ensures that the GHG concentrations will remain high for many decades to come.

We now turn to the key ingredient of climate change – global warming – which constitutes the theme for the next section.

● 5.4 GLOBAL WARMING POTENTIAL (GWP) ●

Curtailing GHGs entails costs in some sections and regions. Policy makers attempting to find cost-effective methods of containing global warming or GHGs need to know the relative contributions of each of the main GHGs to target their reduction or stabilization, with regulation, market mechanism and institutional cooperation. The relative unit cost of such reductions can possibly be compared among the constituent GHGs and, if required, some trade-offs can be derived.

There is increasing concern about the definition and role of the conventional measure of GWP due to several difficulties in its ability to guide policy formulation or evaluation. To begin with, let us draw upon the contributions of the IPCC reports to this vital debate. The original aim of the GWP index is to offer a simple characterization of the relative radiative effects of various combinations of gases. It was sought to be created so as to enable policy makers to evaluate options that affect the emissions of various GHGs, by avoiding the need to make complex calculations.

The GWP is a measure of the relative, globally averaged warming effect arising from the emissions of a particular GHG, and defined as the time-integrated change in radiative forcing due to the instantaneous release of one unit weight of a trace gas expressed relative to that from the release of the same unit weight of CO_2 (IPCC, 1990, 1992). The calculation requires a number of important specifications:

- The radiative forcing of the reference gas and of the other species, per unit mass of concentration, change at different levels of operation.
- Atmospheric lifetimes of various gases under consideration and of the reference gas.
- The time horizon over which the radiative forcings have to be integrated.
- The levels of future concentrations of other gases that form the background for interactive effectiveness.
- Global meteorological parameters for the current and future time periods.

A review of the initial formulations and their revisions will be useful in the understanding and refinement of the concept of GWP.

Early Formulae for GWP

The GWP is essentially an assessment of a given GHG's contribution to heat trapping over its lifetime (or, atmospheric residency life interval), and this is normalized for comparison purposes, with respect to a corresponding expression for the reference gas. This reference gas is usually taken as CO_2, given its wider significance in the GE.

The formal definition led to one of the early formulations of the GWP index I (Lashof and Ahuja, 1990; IPCC, 1990):

$$I = \frac{F}{G}$$

with

$$F = \int_0^T f_i(t) C_i(t) \, dt$$

and

$$G = \int_0^T f_c(t) C_c(t) \, dt$$

where T is the time horizon of concern, $C_i(t)$ is the concentration of gas i at time $t = 0$, $f_i(t)$ is the radiating force or heat-trapping ability of the same per unit concentration, $C_c(t)$ and $f_c(t)$ are the corresponding quantities for CO_2. This index depends critically on the specification of T, and decreases with the choice of higher magnitudes of T for the gases having a shorter atmospheric residence than the average for CO_2.

The radiative heating effect per unit mass of various GHGs (given in bracket) relative to CO_2 (taken as one unit) are as follows (Harvey, 1993): CH_4 (72), N_2O (206), CFC-11 (3970), CFC-12 (5750), HCFC-22 (5440).

Some approximations of the GWPs, using the formula given above, are given in table 5.1.

The calculations and data in table 5.1 are provided here to illustrate the role of the time horizon that is taken into account in assessing the GWP of specific GHGs. The input data regarding estimates of atmospheric lifetimes of these gases and their anthropogenic emissions underwent revisions during the mid-1990s; these features will be discussed later in this chapter.

Unless otherwise specified, all GWPs are direct GWPs, i.e. those which ignore any radiative effects due to the products of chemical transformation. Because of lack of information on the latter, indirect GWPs are hard to obtain; even those reported in IPCC (1990) were ignored (IPCC, 1992). For a discussion of a number of limitations of the above definition and operationalization, see IPCC (1992),

Table 5.1   Direct GWP – initial estimates of GHG comparisons

Gas	Atmospheric lifetime (years)	Anthropogenic emissions (megatons/yr)	Proportional GWP	
			20 yrs	100 yrs
CO_2	120	26,000	51	68
CH_4	10	300	37	17
NO_2	150	6	3	5
CFC-11	75	0.3	3	3
CFC-12	110	0.4	6	7

Source: Houghton et al. (1990)

Harvey (1993) and Kandlikar (1996). We propose to deal with these aspects so that alternatives and improvements can be formulated. As pointed out in IPCC (1990), the modeling of radiative transfer within the atmosphere contains uncertainties and also unknowns, and this bears major implications on the assessment and interpretation of the GWP. It was also noted (IPCC, 1992) that "great care must be exercised in applying GWPs in the policy arena." The specific limitations stated in the IPCC (1992) report include the following:

- Since the direct GWP is a measure of the global effect of a given GHG emission, it is appropriate only for well-mixed gases in the troposphere, namely CO_2, CH_4, N_2O, and halocarbons; different gas combinations can yield varying spatial patterns of radiative forcings.
- Since in the assumed scientific model (called the Siegenthaler–Oeschger model underlying the GWP assessments), there is only an ocean CO_2 sink, it is likely to overestimate the concentration changes and lead to an underestimate of both direct and indirect GWPs. The magnitude of this bias depends on the atmospheric lifetime of the gas, and the time horizon.
- Changes in radiative forcing due to CO_2, CH_4 and N_2O changes are nonlinear with respect to these changes. The net effect of these nonlinearities is such that, as CO_2 levels increase from present levels, the GWPs of all non-CO_2 gases would become higher than those evaluated by the present method.
- For gases that are not well-mixed like the tropospheric ozone precursors, the GWP concept may not be relevant.
- The concept does not apply to inhomogenously distributed gases like aerosols, which have a significant interaction in the solar spectrum.

Although these problems, and hence the limitations of the concept and application of the GWP, are significant, a few improvements have been advanced recently. These arise from motivations of practical application. If the economic or the physical project lifetime, like a hydropower plant or coal energy production is limited to a specified number of years, say, about 150 years, the incremental role of this production and its linkage to the radiating budget of the GHGs is what is of concern in the context of the project development or assessment of its environmental contribution.

Improved Formulae

An alternative GWP index is suggested by Harvey (1993). This formulation makes assessment of the relative contribution for the life of the project on a cumulative basis of accounting for the accumulated emissions over the time horizon. Empirical calculations showed that this method leads to a greater role of CO_2 in the global warming phenomenon. This approach does not distinguish the possible economic impact of emissions occurring at different time points in the specified time horizon, i.e. the time-discounting of the cost bases, if any, of alternative emission control policies is irrelevant. Any GHG indices and the GWP measures that do not include economic impact considerations, even approximate ones, are of very little use for any policy analysis. The estimates of the conventional GWPs do not account for the time variation in the economic opportunity costs of incremental values of radiative forcing, and do not recognize the economics of discounting or time value of financial and other resources, as argued by Eckhaus (1992). Thus, the suggested index falls short of possible use in policy analysis based directly on this index. It is possible to provide an additional transformation on Harvey's (1993) formulation by superimposing a dynamic cost or a discounting function. In addition to such attempts, several analytical strengths are added in the contributions of Kandlikar (1995, 1996), and these provide useful approaches to the whole debate. The major features of Kandlikar's contributions are given in box 5.2.

The formulations in box 5.2 reduce to the conventional formula for GWP when a number of drastic simplifications are imposed; these include zero time-discount rate, and constancy of the damage function with any changes in the global mean temperature. The formulation is also shown to be useful in devising cost-effectiveness analysis which is required for most policy analysis. This is carried out by minimizing the total costs subject to a constraint on the global mean temperature of the form

$$T(t) = T^*(t)$$

where $T^*(t)$ is an exogenously specified temperature path. Based on empirical analysis, it was found that the discount rate and the degree of nonlinearity in the damage function continues to be a more critical determinant of the index than the temperature path. The other factors affecting the robustness of the analysis were the uncertainty in methane lifetime, and the costs of abatement of carbon. Kandlikar's (1996) formulations offer a very useful insight into the role and implications of future expectations and discount rates into the impact mechanism of GWPs, converting an otherwise technical and non-economic problem into an economic and strategic decision model; the fact that a discount rate may

BOX 5.2 Global warming potential – formulae

The impact of an incremental emission of the GHG at time $t = 0$ can be described by finding the net present value (NPV) of the damages that arise from the emission of that gas unit. Let NPV(i) denote the corresponding measure and $E(i)$ the incremental rise in the emissions of gas i, with the resulting increase in the global mean temperature $T(i, t)$ leading to climate damage function $D(T(t))$; here D need not be dependent on the specific gas i. Let L denote the time horizon of concern, assume for the moment that this L is easily identified; extensions to the infinite time horizon can be made without major hurdles and these are discussed later. Let a time-dependent discount rate be given by $r(t)$ (a simple generalization of Kandlikar's (1995) constant discounting formulation). Now the NPV(i) is given by:

$$\text{NPV}(i) = \int_0^T \frac{\mathrm{d}D(T(t))}{\mathrm{d}T(t)} \cdot \frac{\mathrm{d}T(t)}{\mathrm{d}e_i(0)} \cdot e^{-r(t)t} \, \mathrm{d}t$$

The above expression was extended to include GHG cycles, radiative forcing and climate system response (Kandlikar, 1995), but the details are not proposed for discussion here.

The expression for the GWP was obtained, using relevant optimization models, and seeking the optimum level defined as equal to the ratio of damages caused per unit emissions of each gas, equated to the ratio of the marginal costs of abatement of a non-CO_2 with that of CO_2, and evaluated at a reference initial time $t = 0$ (Kandlikar, 1996): $I = A/B$, with

$$A = \int_0^{T_h} \frac{\partial D(T(t))}{\partial T(t)} \cdot \left\{ \int_0^t \frac{\partial R(C_i(t))}{\partial C_i(t)} \cdot H(t - J) F_i(J) \, \mathrm{d}J \right\} e^{-rt} \, \mathrm{d}t$$

$$B = \int_{d_0}^{T_h} \frac{\partial D(T(t))}{\partial T(t)} \cdot \left\{ \int_0^t \frac{\partial R(C_c(t))}{\partial C_c(t)} \cdot H(t - J) F_c(J) \, \mathrm{d}J \right\} e^{-rt} \, \mathrm{d}t$$

where r is the constant time discount rate, $F(\cdot)$ is the additional increase in future concentration per unit of the gas released at time $t = 0$, $H(t - J)$ is equal to the change in global temperature at future time t for small change in the radiative forcing at time J, $0 < J < t$; $\partial R(C_i(t))/\partial C_i(t)$ is the instantaneous radiating force of gas i which represents the increase in radiating force due to a unit increase in the atmospheric concentration of the gas; $D(T))/T(t)$ describes changes in damages D due to change in the mean global temperature. The derivation of the above expression for GWP is founded on several steps of technicalities and these are omitted here.

Source: Kandlikar (1995, 1996)

be the key to climate change policy decisions is also reflected in the measures of GWP when properly formulated. This is one of several important reasons for the in-depth analysis of non-constant and endogenous discounting methods offered in chapter 4.

One of the notable empirical studies using variable time discounting is due to Plambeck and Hope (1996), who argued that economic growth will be affected by varying abatement policies and climate change impacts. Based on the projections of global economic growth and using a standard formula for social rate of time preference (see chapter 4), the authors found, based on a pure rate of time preference of 3 percent per year, that the marginal impact of carbon per ton could range from $10 to $48, with an average hovering around $21. These numbers almost double if the pure rate of time preference is brought down to 2 percent, and go up very substantially (about tenfold of the last) if the rate is zero. These demonstrate powerfully the magnitudes of sensitivities involved with respect to the time-discounting factors. The formulations of Kandlikar (1996) can be strengthened to include the possibilities of non-constant time discounting, possibly using an endogenous discount function (see chapter 4), but this may also be seen with an infinite time horizon model rather than arbitrarily finite fixed-time horizon.

Any formulation of GWP needs to incorporate the effects of continued emissions of short-lived aerosols, which tend to provide the cooling effects even in smaller intervals of time. The minimum that can be done to improvise these effects in the framework of Kandlikar is to allow for a series of time-dependent constants to be subtracted from the numerator of the relevant expressions. However, the magnitudes of adjustments involved are likely to be small.

Although the insights into relative roles of different GHGs in the GWP (direct and indirect) are useful in dealing with individual and collective GHG emissions, we need more analysis of the economics of the phenomenon of the GE for an overview of the problem at the global and regional levels. This is addressed next.

● 5.5 ECONOMICS OF THE GREENHOUSE EFFECT (GE) ●

The GE is founded on phenomena that are known with certainty. What is uncertain is the extent of climate change due to anthropogenic influences. In addition, economic processes obey another set of uncertainties. These lead to the reality that the economic estimates tend to be very rough magnitudes of relevant parameters and their effects.

The economics of the GE need to include the costs of avoiding the GE to a desirable extent, and the damages which could accrue if the relevant preventive and corrective measures are not undertaken. There are uncertainties associated with the GE in terms of its likely magnitudes at different time points in the future, and also uncertainties in the type and level of costs for mitigating potential impact. Some of the studies established the possibility that the concentrations of GHGs could lead to the equivalent of double the CO_2 concentrations – under the scenario of "business as usual" (BAU) – by about 2050 relative to the current levels.

This does not provide enough reasoning, although some groups and interests construe that it does, to suggest that we may be incurring certain costs for an uncertain outcome. Gradualistic rather than drastic interventions combined with active information processing, monitoring, and evaluation tend to provide workable approaches. Inaction or allowing BAU in the emissions of the GHGs bear serious irreversible implications for the GE.

The economic impacts of the GE can, in principle, be assessed in terms of both market and nonmarket impacts. The latter include the effect of changes in human morbidity and mortality, damages to the ecological system and related irreversible consequences. The effects which allow market-determined impact include impacts on agricultural production, resource provision costs, productivity losses, costs of adaptation like sea-level rise and flooding, higher energy costs and related effects. Most cost estimates for stabilizing GHGs at the 1990 levels range in the magnitude of $60–240 billion a year (IPCC, 1995b). It would be foolishly simplistic to believe that if somehow this amount of money can be set apart we may not have to worry about the GE. This is because stabilizing at the 1990 levels is not expected to be enough to correct the nature of the problem the planet is faced with, given the atmospheric lifetime of the GHGs that are already in the atmosphere: usually around 110 years. This situation requires continued attention, intervention, and changes in the consumption and production patterns of the human enterprise.

It was argued by Nordhaus (1991) that the economics of the GE is a classic case of a public good, in which the emissions of GHGs involve a significant global externality. It may not be entirely accurate to characterize most features of the global commons in terms of characteristics of public goods. This configuration can make a substantial difference in the recognition of the sink capacity and open access aspects of the GE and the corresponding biogeophysical and socioeconomic impacts of any suggested policies and activities. It was also noted that societies and governments do possess the potential to create economic consequences which could be worse than what can be viewed in terms of typical cost functions surrounding the abatement costs, by an inefficient provision of regulatory regimes (i.e. policies, enforcement, and institutions). The contrary aspect must also be recognized: the roles of social capital and human capital could be extremely cost-effective and the conventional roles of markets and governments could both be strengthened by proper attention to the components of sustainability and SD; barring those cited in chapter 3, these issues are not addressed in the literature so far.

Decomposing the CO_2 Components

For the reason that CO_2 is the single most important source of the GE, it is relevant to look into the economics of the GE partly in terms of the economics of CO_2, its emissions, and also its sequestration via forestry activities. The role and contribution of CO_2 in various consumption and production activities requires a disaggregative analysis. One of the simplest methods to conduct this decomposition is to use the chain rule of calculus. This can be carried out in several alternative expressions, and the formulation is usually guided by the possibility of empirically assessing the ingredients using available data. Illustrative examples are given below; see, for example, Gupta and Hall (1996) for an application of a formulation similar to the first decomposition below using data for India.

Part of the literature – see IPCC (1996a) – refers to the Kaya identity (Kaya, 1989), which applies the chain rule to perform the decomposition:

$$CO_2 = \frac{CO_2}{E} \times \frac{E}{Q} \times \frac{Q}{POP} \times POP$$

where CO_2 is its total emissions, E the total energy use, Q total output, and POP the total population in a region or country.

This same decomposition is expressed in terms of rates of change (as there are no likely discontinuities in the functions or zero levels of their operation – to ensure the existence of relevant derivatives):

$$\frac{d}{dt}(\log CO_2) = \frac{d}{dt}\left(\frac{\log CO_2}{E}\right) + \frac{d}{dt}\left(\log \frac{E}{Q}\right) + \frac{d}{dt}\left(\frac{\log Q}{POP}\right) + \frac{d}{dt}(\log POP)$$

which simply states that, the percentage rate of change in CO_2 emissions equals the sum of the rate of change in CO_2 emissions per unit energy, rate of change requirements per unit output, rate of change in per capita output, and the rate of change in population.

Alternative sets of decomposition can also be contemplated:

$$CO_2 = \frac{CO_2}{CE} \times \frac{CE}{TE} \times \frac{TE}{GDP} \times \frac{GDP}{POP} \times POP$$

$$CO_2 = \frac{CO_2}{TCE} \times \frac{TCE}{FF} \times \frac{FF}{DEF} \times \frac{DEF}{DEBT} \times \frac{DEBT}{GDP} \times \frac{GDP}{POP} \times POP$$

where

> CO_2 = total CO_2 emissions in the economy (millions tons of carbon)
> CE = coal energy (millions tons of oil equivalent)
> TE = total energy usage (millions tons of oil equivalent)
> GDP = gross domestic product at constant prices
> POP = population (millions)
> TCE = total commercial energy (millions tons of oil equivalent)
> FF = fossil fuel usage (millions tons oil equivalent)
> DEF = deforestation (millions tons oil equivalent)
> DEBT = total external debt borrowings outstanding (same units as GDP)

The expressions above, or other variants of these, can be deployed to examine the growth of CO_2 in terms of relevant ingredients contributing to such growth and the latter can be subject to further analysis of costs and benefits of potential alternative changes in their production, consumption, or growth policies.

An empirical study contributed by Han and Chatterjee (1997) used a structural decomposition with a focus on structural changes, as these capture the impacts of development processes on CO_2 emissions. Changes in these emissions are decomposed in terms of changes due to effects of: GDP growth, changes in industrial structure, changes in energy sector composition, interactions in these three elements, changes in levels of final consumption, effects of changes in final consumption, effects of changes in the energy intensities of final consumption activities, and effects of interaction of the preceding three elements. The decomposition formulae were used for a set of countries. The summary of results indicated the significant role of growth of GDP in the CO_2 emissions; the structural shifts from a rural economic base to a manufacturing one resulted in increase of energy demand.

Models and Methods

There are a number of analytical models and their corresponding empirical analyses which try to suggest the magnitudes of costs and benefits or other implications of various actions and inactions in stabilizing GHGs, and the climate in temperature terms. The latter is usually found to be considerably more expensive relative to the focus only on GHGs and hence on the GE. However, these methods are founded on very serious assumptions and tend to magnify uncertainties and unknowns in the scientific, socioeconomic and terrestrial phenomena governing the global commons. Among the best-known contributions in this context are those of Nordhaus (1991, 1992, 1994). Some of the major features of these models are discussed below.

The core model developed by Nordhaus was called the dynamic integrated model of climate and the economy (DICE). The main decision variables were consumption, rate of investment in tangible capital, and the rate of emissions reductions of GHGs. Clearly, this specification of choice variables is rather narrow and geared primarily to developed economies where an economy is almost fully monetized and driven by private capital investments. Besides, the role of human capital, social capital, and institutions is treated as a constant, uniform in the entire global economic system. The objective in the DICE model was to maximize the discounted value of utility of relevant arguments. The formal representations are given below. As Nordhaus (1991) rightly argued, in weighing the global climate change policies, the potential for global warming and the linkage with anthropogenic emissions of GHGs form a key building block. The basic approach of the DICE model is to estimate the "optimal paths" for both capital accumulation and reductions in GHG emissions in the framework of the Ramsey (1928) model of intertemporal choice – the framework that is largely responsible for the foundations of the current neoclassical economic growth models (Solow, 1956; Shell, 1967). In the model, climate change is represented by changes in the global mean surface temperature $T(t)$ at time t.

The structural equations in the DICE model include:

$$T(t) = \alpha[gM(t) - T(t)]$$

and

$$M(t) = \beta E(t) - \delta M(t)$$

where the time derivatives on the left-hand side are those of, respectively, $T(t)$, the increase in global mean surface temperature due to greenhouse warming since the mid-nineteenth century, and $M(t)$, the anthropogenic atmospheric concentration of CO_2 equivalent GHGs (billions of tons CO_2 equivalent). The notation on the right-hand side is as follows: $E(t)$ is the anthropogenic emissions of CO_2 equivalent GHGs (billions of tons of CO_2 equivalent per year), $g[\cdot]$ is the equilibrium increase in global mean temperature in response to increasing CO_2 equivalent concentration, α is the delay parameter of temperature in response to radiative increase per year, β is the fraction of CO_2 equivalent emissions that enter the atmosphere, and δ is the rate of removal of CO_2 equivalent emissions from the atmosphere per year.

The first of these two equations was linearized in Nordhaus (1991) around the mean, for computational convenience. A critical assumption was also made that the economy was in a "resource steady-state," i.e. all physical flows in the global economy are constant although the real value of economic activity may be increasing. Thus, all emissions and concentrations of GHGs are constant per year and "the climatic impacts of industrial activity have been stabilized" in this sense. The DICE model allows for "balanced resource-augmenting technological change," i.e. the useful goods and services produced by the economy are assumed to grow uniformly in each sector although the physical throughputs are constant. These are extremely strong assumptions and tend to undermine the real problems of the human enterprise and the planet simply by assuming there are not several severe impediments to SD. In addition to the above formulation and assumptions, we need to narrate the specifications of the objective function of the model: this is given as the discounted value of streams of consumption.

The optimal programs for allocating resources over time are required to maximize:

$$V = \int_0^\infty u[c(t)] \exp(-\rho t) \, dt$$

where $c(t)$ is the per capita consumption, $u[\cdot]$ is the utility function, and ρ the "pure rate of social time preference," which is a constant discount rate applied for the entire infinite time horizon; see chapter 4 for details.

The empirical analyses of Nordhaus' (1992, 1994) studies, based on the above formulations and related constraints in the optimization model, indicated the role of a carbon tax. This tax represents the shadow price of carbon, estimated at $5 per ton of carbon or its equivalent in other GHGs for the end of the twentieth century, to increase to $10 by 2025 and to $21 by 2095 (at 1990 prices). The above values double if uncertainties are incorporated in the DICE model. Risk-aversion and concave damage functions enhance these values to higher levels (Tol, 1995). The corresponding tax was $100 in the early twenty-first century in the DICE model, if the objective were to stabilize the GHG emissions at the 1990 levels. Fankhouser (1994) derived trajectories for the carbon shadow prices rising from around $20 per tonne by 1991–2000 to $28 by 2021–2030; his sensitivity analysis with discount rate suggested that moving from 3 percent to zero percent discounting could increase marginal costs by a factor of nine.

These conclusions, at their best, are indicative of the relative significance of the GHG emissions in their cost implications. These also bring to light the triviality of the objective function that maximizes discounted per capita consumption based on averaging and ignoring the environment as a factor in the utility function. The DICE models suggested that the net benefit from pursuing the above model-based optimal policy rather than continuing with the BAU approach, i.e. complete inaction and unconcern about the sustainability problems, is about $200 billion for the entire foreseeable time horizon. The greatest fallacy of models like the above is, first they try to replace the unknowns with estimates of approximated parameters and thus treat the unknowns as knowns, and various uncertainties with certainties; and, then they largely ignore the interactive effects and adaptation costs. The models addressed the question of what would be the optimal policy to follow if all the parameters were known with certainty. Since all parameters are not known with certainty, the results of these exercises may yield poor policy advice. Conclusions like stating that the US economy will not be affected by more than about a quarter percentage of GDP if the emissions of CO_2 accumulate to double the 1990 level (Nordhaus, 1991), can be misleading. A program to reduce GHGs would also lead to improvements in the ecological systems, and in sectors like health and agriculture as well. These aspects, as well as a number of non-commercial benefits, are lost in the assessments of Nordhaus. Models which do not incorporate relevant feedback mechanisms, including adaptation responses and endogeneity of social preferences, may not merit recognition beyond being mechanistic.

The primary objective of discussing the above models here is to illustrate the role and limitations of some of the best analytical modeling exercises. These merit their discussion with the hope that further attempts will continue to be made so as to obtain robust and comprehensive models to enable the devising of economic policies for managing the global commons. Without relying on any major optimizing exercises – relying instead on statistical methods – Maddison (1995) examined some of the relevant issues, and also concluded about the policy relevance as quoted above. These are a few of the powerful examples of trying precision when we are not sure of the ground rules: it is prudent to be approximately right rather than being precisely wrong. This requires that the direction of policy is extremely fundamental and the details and mechanics, although very important, should not be allowed to undermine the main focus.

An empirically relevant model was developed by the Organization for Economic Cooperation and Development (OECD) – see Burniaux et al. (1991) – called GREEN (*general equilibrium environmental*). This model focuses on the energy sector, and uses fiscal and carbon tax measures to reduce CO_2 emissions for the time horizon 1985–2020 and, in later versions, to the year 2050. Some of the assumptions of these models include: same magnitudes of inter-energy elasticities of substitution in private and government sectors, and identical forms of production functions in all sectors and regions. A large variety of applied models developed for analyzing various aspects of the economics of the GE were reviewed by Mabey et al. (1997) and a number of limitations of the reviewed models are also indicated. A superior set of models, with capabilities for relatively robust predictions, are still in the development stages with various researchers, given a variety of scientific uncertainties. The problem of mitigating the GE reduces to one of controlling or stabilizing the emissions of the GHGs. These issues form the focus of the next section.

● 5.6 STABILIZATION OF GHGS ●

Most emissions scenarios indicate that, in the absence of mitigation policies, GHG emissions will continue to rise during the next several decades and lead to GHG concentrations that are projected to change global climate by 2100 to such a magnitude that could be double that of the effect since preindustrial times. The IPCC Second Assessment (Working Group I) (1995a) Report stated that if net global anthropogenic emissions (i.e. anthropogenic sources minus anthropogenic sinks) were maintained at current levels (about 7 Gt/yr including emissions from fossil fuel combustion, cement production and land-use change), they would lead to a nearly constant rate of increase in atmospheric concentrations for at least two centuries, reaching about 500 ppmv (approaching twice the preindustrial concentration of 280 ppmv) by the end of the twenty-first century. It was also stated that the importance of the contribution of CO_2 to climate forcing, relative to that of the other GHGs, increases in a number of plausible scenarios for the future, encompassing projections about population, consumption, and other economic factors.

The Energy Origins of Climate Change

A major negative externality of energy generation is the emission of CO_2. Current energy systems are based largely on the combustion of fossil fuels, which accounted for 87 percent of the world's primary commercial energy consumption (EIA, 1994). In large developing economies like China, about 80 percent of GHG emissions were due to the energy production alone. CO_2 is released to the atmosphere as a product of fossil fuel combustion which accounts for the bulk of the annual anthropogenic emissions of CO_2. During the 1980s, fossil fuel combustions contributed an average 5.5 Gt C per year out of the total global CO_2 emission rate of 7.1 Gt C per year, i.e. 77 percent of the total annual emissions.

The energy supply mitigation subgroup of the IPCC's working group developed alternative low CO_2-emitting energy supply systems for the world (LESS models), using alternative combinations of energy supply technologies and strategies using renewable and non-renewable sources of energy. An important feature of the energy-efficient LESS model is that, with the exception of sequestration technologies, all the important technologies that make it possible to achieve low CO_2 emissions (e.g. more energy-efficient conversion and end-use technologies, and renewable energy technologies) would be highly desirable to pursue, even if there were no climate change issues to worry about. The realization of a stabilized CO_2 concentration in the range 400–450 ppmv, as would be achieved in the ecologically driven scenarios and the LESS models, depends on the development of required technologies.

Are there any discernible trends in the decrease of energy intensity in any of the industrial countries? This question was answered by Greening et al. (1998) by decomposing the aggregate carbon intensity for the manufacturing sector. This study was conducted for ten of the OECD countries spanning the period 1971–91, and the findings were as follows: the aggregate carbon intensities declined, the greatest decrease occurred in Sweden (about 73 percent), followed by France, Norway, Japan, and the USA with about 50 percent decreases. Others in this study decreased between 29 and 50 percent: Denmark, Finland, Germany, Italy, and the UK. The primary causes of decline were due to enhanced factor productivity of energy input, or enhanced efficiency of production technologies. Other contributing factors included shifts in the energy consumption sector in favor of electricity use, and energy supply sources shifting in favor of hydropower, nuclear power, and biomass. Greater efficiencies were also observed in response to higher energy prices. This also suggests the potential role of an energy tax as a tool of "green taxes," discussed in the next section. It is also relevant to note here that the OECD countries reduced their energy subsidies by about 20 percent, leading to greater economic incentives for enhanced energy efficiency. The Greening et al. (1998) study observed that economic growth contributed to a decrease in aggregate carbon intensity, since capital formation enabled provision of investment capital for process improvements and equipment replacement. This study seems to lend support to the inverted U-relationship (IUR) discussed in chapter 3. Again, it would be wrong to draw an inference that economic growth, by itself, contributed to the desired declines; very active environmental policies were pursued in each of the countries included in the study. Suffice to say, economic growth remains a necessary, but not sufficient, condition for attaining objectives and goals of economic sustainability or SD.

An important prerequisite for the acceleration of energy-efficient technologies is the resource allocation to research and development (R&D) in these related areas. The private sector alone may not be capable of, or interested in, the optimal deployment of resources. The public sector or government support needs to augment the private sector efforts so as to achieve a socially optimal output in this sector. However, the government support for energy R&D in International Energy Agency member countries fell by about 33 percent in absolute terms and by about 50 percent in proportion to the GDP. More of these details are given in chapter 9.

Relative Roles of GHGs

Over a 100-year period, the GWP – defined and estimated according to the IPCC (1990) – is expected to be increased by the GHGs in the following annual contributions in the early 1990s, globally (ignoring indirect effects) (Rubin et al., 1992; Houghton et al., 1990):

- CO_2 emissions (annual emissions given in million tons per year) – commercial energy (18,800), tropical deforestation (2,600), other (400).
- CH_4 emissions – rice cultivation (110), fuel production (60), tropical deforestation (20), others (130), with total CO_2-equivalent of about 1,050 million tons.
- CFC emissions total 0.6 million tons, with CO_2-equivalent of 1,640 million tons.
- N_2O emissions – fertilizer use (1.5), coal combustion (1), tropical deforestation (0.5), agricultural wastes, fuel and industrial biomass (0.6), land cultivation (0.4), with total CO_2-equivalent contribution of 410 million tons.

The IPCC (1995b) synthesized a number of measures; some of these are summarized here. CO_2, CH_4 and N_2O have natural as well as anthropogenic origins. The anthropogenic emissions of these gases have contributed about 80 percent of the additional climate forcing due to GHGs since preindustrial times, i.e. since about AD 1750. The contribution of CO_2 is about 60 percent of this forcing, about four times that from CH_4. Other GHGs include tropospheric ozone (whose chemical precursors include NO_x, non-methane hydrocarbons and CO), halocarbons – including hydrochlorofluorocarbons (HCFCs) and hydrofluorocarbons (HFCs) – and SF6. Tropospheric aerosols and tropospheric ozone are unevenly distributed in time and space, and their atmospheric lifetimes are short (days to weeks). Sulfate aerosols are amenable to abatement measures, and such measures are presumed in the IPCC scenarios. Most emission scenarios indicate that, in the absence of mitigation policies, GHG emissions will continue to rise during the next century and lead to GHG concentrations that, by the year 2100, are projected to change the climate more than that projected for twice the preindustrial concentrations of CO_2. CO_2 assumes the greatest significance since its atmospheric concentrations have a residence time of more than a century. CH_4 concentrations dissipate over a period of 9–15 years. NO_x has a long lifetime, of about 120 years.

A systems approach that considers interactions and externality costs across the entire fuel cycle, from supply to conversion and end use of, should be used to guide energy supply choices and to guard against unanticipated side-effects. In a pragmatic study, Rubin et al.'s (1992) recommended measures include an expanded R&D program to develop safe, lower-cost non-fossil energy sources, improve the efficiency of existing fossil fuel technology (particularly combined cycle systems using natural gas or coal), and assess the feasibility of CO_2 sequestration and disposal from fossil fuel residues.

The costs of controlling emissions of the GHGs need to be viewed primarily in terms of controlling at the sources of these emissions, and also in terms of offsetting the potential concentrations by adding to the sink capacity or carrying capacity (CC) of the planet; the latter requires carbon sequestration, and is achieved by controlling deforestation and augmenting forest resources. This sequestration approach has several merits; there are additional benefits, like maintaining biodiversity that could accrue as by-products of the forestry approach, besides being cost-effective. The fundamental parameter in this approach is the quantity of carbon contained within a given area of mature forest minus the carbon content of the vegetation. Cline (1992) estimated that the cost of absorbing a ton of carbon is about $5 for tropical regions, and about $20 for temperate zones. These figures suggest magnitudes lower than those in the range of suggested carbon taxes aimed at controlling industrial emissions. However, the major limitations of this direction of actions is the existence of time lags in realizing the anticipated sequestration benefits. Afforestation leads to carbon absorption slowly over a period of about 5–40 years depending on topography, type of vegetation and soils, and other biogeophysical factors. Long-term sequestration requires that forests are periodically harvested for wood products and lumber stocks that are mature and not capable of returning CO_2 to the atmosphere by combustion (Rubin et al., 1992).

Forests constitute one of the important natural resource pools; these also affect the characteristics of the Earth's sink and global commons. As stated by Myers (1996), the environmental services of forests extend far beyond national boundaries by virtue of their watershed functions, atmospheric renewal processes, preservation of biodiversity, and climate systems: "the winds carry no passports." Allowing forests to decline is rational only when we are totally certain that future generations can manage without many, if not most, of the forest benefits we enjoy today. Because of the irreversibility risks associated with deforestation, these issues are of special importance. Some of the economic benefits of forests are not fully integrated into any economic methodology so far: the roles of watershed function, fisheries habitats, genetic resources, effects on climate stabilization, minor forest products, recreation and tourism, in addition to the commercially known timber and wood products. An important ecological function of the forests is their role in the processes of carbon sink renewal. This is achieved with the natural phenomenon of carbon sequestration, discussed below.

Carbon Sequestration

An assessment of potential from carbon sequestration in the tropics is given by Adger and Brown (1994), and is depicted in table 5.2.

A few estimates of the economics of afforestation can be seen in the literature but almost all of them are elementary approximations of the costs based on some

Table 5.2   Carbon sequestration potential

	America	Africa	Asia	Avg carbon increment	Total
		(million ha)		t C / ha	bt C
Plantation					
Forests	33	171	26	61–78	
Woodlands	11	7	3	29–34	
TOTAL	44	178	29		17.8
Protection					
Forests	575	26	336	17–44	
Woodlands	22	0	0	26–30	
Grasslands	37	0	57	5	
TOTAL	634	26	393		28.6
Agroforestry				59–69	
Forests	355	241	194		
Woodlands	142	392	44		
Grasslands	240	256	32		
TOTAL	737	888	270		120.4
Total	1,415	1,093	692		166.8

Source: Adger and Brown (1994); Houghton et al. (1993)

kind of markets and these do not reflect the true socioeconomic evaluations. The following is a sample cost assessment from Dixon et al. (1993), suggesting wide variations in the average costs of sequestration in different countries. It is doubtful if these costs can be really utilized for any operational policy, given the wide variations within each country cited. The indicative averages are given in table 5.3.

The costs reported in table 5.3 are based on costs of establishment (including labor costs, transportation and infrastructure) recurring over a 50-year period, and discounted at 5 percent per annum; these costs do not include land purchase prices or opportunity costs of land. These estimates need to be improved and disaggregated for each region in each country. However, some idea of the costs of sequestration is necessary to compare these costs with any estimates of green taxes proposed to offset GHG emissions, so as to arrive at an integrated assessment of options in controlling CO_2 emissions and absorbing these with sequestration.

A few preliminary estimates of carbon sequestration with afforestation are given by Sedjo and Solomon (1989): about $372 billion (at 1988 prices) for the USA alone, to offset 2.9 bt C. The corresponding estimates for the tropical areas were much lower: $186 billion to offset the same magnitude of carbon. The differences were mainly due to assumptions about the cost of land (taken as zero for the tropical areas). The costs of Moulton and Richards (1990) are much lower because they use land rental costs at $148 per hectare, rather than $400–$1,000

Table 5.3 Costs of carbon sequestration

Country	Sequestration rate (t C per ha)	Average cost of sequestration ($ per t C)
Temperate regions		
Argentina	65.0	25.0
Canada	40.7	11.5
Chile	75.9	2.7
Finland	40.9	27.3
France	115.9	16.6
Germany	56.0	32.4
USA	77.0	5.5
Tropical and sub-tropical		
Australia	107.0	5.9
Brazil	63.5	27.4
China	76.3	5.2
Costa Rica	46.3	31.0
India	78.0	26.8
Mexico	99.0	4.5
Philippines	44.6	2.7

Source: Reprinted from Dixon et al. (1993) with permission from Elsevier Science

used by Sedjo and Solomon (1989). More optimistically, Winjum and Lewis (1993) demonstrated the significance of including the value of the forest stock involved, and found that the net costs are negative: about −$22 to −$48 per ton of carbon, depending on the region and valuation of stocks. A set of estimates regarding the role and costs of carbon sequestration for the Amazon region were given in the World Bank Forest Sector Policy Paper, summarized in box 5.3. One feature is clear: depending on the elements of costs and benefits and their time discounting, the net costs of carbon sequestration vary significantly; a robust estimate of costs will tend to be very low, and could favorably compare with a reasonable proposal for carbon tax per ton. A number of studies cited by the IPCC (1996b) suggest that storage potential for carbon can be tapped at about $10 per ton.

Alternatives for CO_2 Abatement

Some of the operationally relevant CO_2 abatement options include reductions in the atmospheric CO_2 emissions, reducing the existing CO_2 concentrations in the atmosphere, and augmenting the carbon sequestration capacities. The main elements of these include both regulatory and market-based instruments at the national and international levels. Economic instruments like tradable permits and taxes, in conjunction with relevant institutional mechanisms, are the key to the attainment of abatement objectives. Here are some of the specific modes and areas of intervention:

BOX 5.3   Sequestering carbon in the Amazon

Land clearing and burning to create agricultural land and/or cattle grazing pastures peaked at about 80,000 square kilometers in the Brazilian Amazon region during the year 1987. Recent trends suggested an annual depletion of forests at around 20,000 square kilometers. This is equivalent to the release of about 260 million tons of carbon a year as a result of deforestation. Of the total release of carbon, in the early 1990s, of 7.1 billion tons, deforestation accounted for about one-quarter of the total, and Amazonian deforestation about 15 percent of this fraction, i.e. 4 percent of the grand total. If an average hectare of Amazonian forest contains 125 tons of carbon, the sequestered value of carbon in an undisturbed hectare may be in the range $375–$1625, which is at least 18 times larger than the current land prices in the region. Carbon sequestered in new or preserved forests tends to remain an economically meaningful enabling mechanism for reducing total carbon emissions in a cost-effective manner. Opportunities exist between industrial countries and tropical region countries to trade carbon emissions to offset emissions due to industrial activities. This does require an effective global emissions trading mechanism, however.

Source: World Bank's (1991) Forest Sector Policy Paper

- Efficiency improvements, especially power generation and consumption, industry, transportation, and sectors involving all aspects of manufacturing and consumption;
- Curtailments in GHG emissions which positively correlate with CO_2 emissions and with indirect GWP, public consciousness, and voluntary target fixation for reductions in the emissions;
- Energy substitution involving renewable sources of energy and recycling; and
- Carbon sequestration with afforestation, forest preservation, protection and land-use planning.

According to the IPCC (1995b), the global average annual per capita emissions of CO_2 due to the combustion of fossil fuels in 1990 is about 1.1 tonnes as carbon; in addition, a net of about 0.2 tonne per capita are emitted from deforestation and land-use changes. The 1990 estimate of annual average emissions of energy-related CO_2 is about 0.3 tonne per $1,000 output. These average estimates may be relevant as possible references in devising intervention strategies in a cost-effective manner.

The emissions time path may be as important as the concentration level itself in determining the costs of emissions abatement (Richels and Sturm, 1996). Often, cost-effective emissions time paths are those which provide desired flexibility in managing the transition away from fossil fuels. The optimal timing and region-specific policies in this regard are suggested to possess the features of cost-effectiveness in meeting the objectives of mitigating the GHGs to desired levels.

Among the important institutional ramifications leading to the choice of proper policy instruments are the provision of meaningful property rights (PRs). These rights include ownership rights, usage rights, and development rights. As a consequence, the liability for externalities is also devised. The provision of these in a well-defined and enforceable manner is critically dependent on the existence of a legal system with powers to enforce the rules. Many developing countries lag behind in this infrastructure. The characteristics of property rights include: exclusivity of right to use, transferability of the ownership, specifications of duration and quality of rights and duties of ownership, and ease of undertaking of transactions under the property rights regime. Let us note that specifications of property rights with similar sets of characteristics are called PR regimes. The possibility of Pareto-welfare maximizing exists in many such regimes. An application of the Coase theorem (1960) will provide for market solutions to relevant transactions in such settings.

Among the cost-effective instruments for environmental management are one form or other of environmental taxes (green taxes) and market-based, rights-based instruments like the Tradable Emission Permits (TEPs). These are discussed below.

Tradable Emission Permits (TEPs)

Whenever targets of emissions reductions are set or a global cost-effective solutions to the control of GHGs is sought, it makes sense to examine the most efficient methods of achieving the same. TEPs merit consideration in such a context. These are essentially market-based instruments, although their implementation and monitoring by various institutions is required as a complementary task. In the absence of appropriate provision of the latter, the efficient functioning may be infeasible and transaction costs will remain very high. Under TEPs, a given total quantity of specified emission reduction will be allocated initially across different pollution-contributing economic entities. The participating entities have a range of trading options in relation to the pollution emission rights. The least cost menu of options allows choice between options, such as improving technologies and buying TEPs.

External offsets in net GHG concentrations are afforded by investing either in the reductions in emissions (at source or abroad) or in GHG sink enhancements (as in afforestation or other forms of carbon sequestration) at appropriate locations. An international TEPs policy has been suggested by several authors during the 1990s. A study by the UNCTAD (1992) suggested that TEPs are attractive in that they are efficient in GHG emission reductions, effective in appropriate financial and technological resource transfer from industrial countries to developing countries, and they lead to win–win scenarios. In the USA, TEPs proved successful in controlling SO_2 emissions at low cost: a 50 percent reduction relative to the 1980 level is expected to be achieved by the year 2000; see also UN

(1997). The US Environmental Protection Agency (USEPA) is seeking to extend similar schemes to other sectors, including point and non-point sources of water pollution. Some of the fundamental features underlying the market for these permits, both in domestic and in international contexts, include the transaction costs and uncertainties in their implementation (due to legal or other unknowns). High transaction costs alone can reduce the attractiveness and efficiency of the permits auction, trading or exchange; see Stavins (1995) and Montero (1997) for analytical investigations.

The criteria for assessment of global responsibility in the future perspectives of global warming and the role of GHGs remain a major bone of contention between the developed and the developing countries. This is because the former have been largely responsible for the major drag on the global environmental resources and have utilized a major proportion of the sink or CC of the planet as "free riders." However, the magnitude of current emissions and the fact that there are large segment of population living in the developing countries warrants their active role and participation in ensuring environmental protection.

A number of alternative criteria are formulated, some of these are illustrated in table 5.4. These criteria can be interpreted in terms of cumulative emissions, affecting a country's "rights" to emissions; the split between developed and

Table 5.4   Tradable permits entitlements

Criterion	General operating rule	Operational rule for CO_2 entitlements
Horizontal	Equalize net cost of abatement as a proportion of PPP or GDP equal for each country	Allocate entitlements to equalize net cost of abatement as a proportion of PPP or GDP equal for each country
Vertical	Progressively share net cost proportions inversely correlated with per capita PPP or GDP	Progressively distribute entitlements: net cost proportions inversely correlated with per capita PPP or GDP
Egalitarian	Cut back emissions in proportion to the product of population and PPP	Allocate entitlements in proportion to the product of population and PPP
Ability to pay	Equalize abatement costs across countries: gross costs of abatement as proportion of GDP equal for each country	Allocate entitlements to equalize abatement costs: gross cost of abatement as proportion of GDP equal for each country
Polluter pays	Pay for the past and current emissions	Costs shared according to emission levels

Notes: 1. PPP = purchasing power parity income level
     2. Net cost is equal to the sum of mitigation benefits, minus abatement costs, plus permit sales revenues, minus permit purchase costs; gross costs refer to abatement costs only
Source: Adapted from Rose and Tietenberg (1993) and Ringius et al. (1998)

developing countries is estimated as 60 percent for the former and 40 percent for the latter on current emissions basis, and the corresponding numbers for the cumulative basis are about 70 and 30. The contribution of developing countries to CO_2 emissions is expected to rise above 60 percent during the next quarter century.

The importance of maintaining good North–South relations means taking into account the cumulative contributions of industrialized nations to the concentrations of GHGs and the relatively higher future opportunity costs of mitigation with respect to foregone economic growth, i.e. cumulative and future reference bases are likely to receive priority over any current reference base (Rose and Tietenberg, 1993). Transferable entitlement systems could be designed where all trades took place between different economic or other institutional entities. There are three main ingredients of the global division of environmental responsibilities for mitigating the effects of GHGs:

- Fixing reduction targets, time horizons for implementation for each country.
- Devising cost-effective options for effecting the stated goals.
- Providing global and local incentives and disincentives for effecting the operational policies and programmes.

Application of the formal analytical techniques (like goal programming or other multi-objective criteria optimization methods) is relevant for devising broad principles for the management of the global commons; see for example, the analytical methods advocated by Bueler (1997). However, their usefulness is likely to be conditioned by the availability of information, and implementing mechanisms for policies so derived.

The uncertainties associated with various estimates of the past, and projections for the future, continue to haunt various global efforts and sharing responsibilities, compounded by the problems of various fuzzy notions of costs of achieving the targets. If the widely accepted principle of "polluter pays" is extended to the management of global commons, the developed countries will have to shoulder a much greater share of costs and responsibilities than ever in the past and present. Some of the issues are discussed in greater detail in chapter 10.

● 5.7 ECONOMICS OF GREEN TAXES ●

The terms green taxes, environmental taxes, and pollution taxes are interchangeably used here for the present, although they do not precisely mean the same. Although the above categories include carbon taxes, the converse does not hold. Historically, Pigou (1932) is among the economists who advocated pollution taxes: a Pigouvian tax is a tax levied on each unit of pollution output and the tax amount equals the marginal damage the pollution causes to the economic system, at the efficient level of production system or output level. This tax tradition may have some feasibility if the source of pollution and its relative damage are known. Baumol and Oates (1979) classified two alternative bases within the above tradition of taxes:

- Assessment of tax on the basis of optimal production (implying an "optimal tax rate" which may not provide an incentive to the polluting firm to alter the emission pattern of pollution.
- Levy of tax rate iteratively adjusted to relate it to the current magnitudes of marginal damages, which may provide incentives to the polluter to alter the magnitudes of pollutant emissions.

Both these approaches to taxation are built on serious limitations arising out of lack of information and practical implementation problems or enforcement difficulties. These considerations did not bother the economists who carried out some arithmetic to venture an approximation of global average carbon tax estimates on the basis of some notion of global damages due to global warming and divided the cost with current CO_2-equivalent emissions.

Much of the literature on Pigouvian taxes did not address the issue of revenue mobilization or the consequent decisions of levying pollution taxes. Pollution taxes promise the potential to offer a better tax structure for any given economy and also enhance environmental quality, if the tax instruments are properly formulated and implemented: a case of double dividend!

The "principle of polluter pays" (PP) has its application and this was institutionally advocated by the OECD (1975) for adoption in its member countries, which are typically industrial and advanced economies:

- The principle for allocating costs of pollution prevention and control measures to encourage rational use of scarce environmental resources and to avoid distortions in trade and investment is the "Polluter Pays Principle"; the costs of these measures "should be reflected in the costs of goods and services which cause pollution in production and/or consumption."
- When the environmental costs are taken into account, the market fails to reflect these costs in the price system.

Despite these broad principles, the issue of internalizing environmental costs in dealing with international trade in goods and services remains a contentious issue; some of these details are discussed in chapter 9.

In recent years, public policy in the industrial countries favored more of some form of ecotax or green tax or pollution tax, partly to offset personal tax burden and, simultaneously, to achieve some degree of dampening of pollution emissions. An element of revenue-neutrality is also contemplated in these tax shift patterns. Some of the recent examples include: a landfill tax in UK, and carbon taxes in Finland, the Netherlands, and Sweden. The Swedish Tax Reform of 1991 comprised of taxes on both CO_2 and sulfur emissions. The revenues from these new tax instruments were used to reduce relatively heavy income tax and thereby to reduce distortions in work and leisure choices. In a revenue-neutral tax reform, it is possible to increase progressivity elsewhere in the economy or tax system to at least offset the regressivity inherent in the green taxes or carbon taxes; reductions in the lowest tax rates under the income tax system can, for example, address this objective (Oates, 1995).

The phenomena of "dividends" of various types were also touted in support of various types of environmental tax measures.

- *(Single) dividend*: environmental taxation increases total welfare of the society by reducing or eliminating negative environmental externalities.
- *Double dividend*: shifting tax burden from personal taxation to environmental resources reduces the relative cost of labor and augments employment.
- *Triple dividend*: the process leads to a reduction of tax distortions and increases economic output toward more efficient paths – economically and environmentally.

However, in the presence of existing tax distortions, new green taxes can sometimes outweigh the efficiency gains from revenue recycling – no double dividend in such cases! When new taxes are introduced – especially the provision of green taxes – existing twisted tax systems can take advantage in some of the tax regimes and countries, to correct the previous distortions and come on track for a more sensible efficient and equitable system; whether such an approach will, in fact, be adopted is to be answered in terms of political and socioeconomic factors.

In a useful survey, Goulder (1995) examined the theory and empiricism of environmental taxation and various forms of dividend propositions; the rise and fall of the double dividend claims is included. Some of the major conclusions are summarized below. First, define the concept of "gross costs" here: these are the welfare sacrifices associated with environmental tax policies. Under this criterion, the overall efficiency change from a policy initiative is the welfare benefit arising from the change in environmental quality (the gross benefits) minus the gross costs. Three forms of double dividend are distinguished:

1 *Weak form*: this form uses environmental taxes to finance reductions in marginal rates of an existing distortionary tax; cost savings are achieved relative to the case of transfer of tax revenues to the taxpayers in lump-sum fashion.
2 *Intermediate form*: the revenue-neutral substitution of the environmental tax for a distortionary tax is used in such a way that this results in zero or negative gross cost.
3 *Strong form*: the revenue-neutral substitution for the environmental tax for typical or representative distortionary taxes involves a zero or negative gross cost.

Most of the economic models and policies for effecting environmental concerns ignored the interactions of new taxes with the existing tax system. This simplistic approach, including the classic Pigouvian tax method, tends to overestimate the requisite tax for achieving desired ecological goals. The overall effect of the tax consists of:

- the Pigouvian or the partial equilibrium effect;
- the tax interaction effect; and
- the revenue recycling, or more generally, the fiscal effect.

The basic partial equilibrium analysis of optimal environmental tax invokes the Pigouvian method, where the optimal tax rate equals the marginal external costs or marginal environmental damages (MED); this implies the gross marginal cost or marginal abatement cost associated with an environmental tax equals the tax rate. In a more comprehensive general equilibrium analysis, Bovenberg and Goulder (1996) and Bovenberg and de Mooji (1994) established that the presence of prior taxes imposes higher gross costs from the environmental tax, even when revenues are recycled through cuts in the distortionary tax. Parry's (1995, 1997) results support the above conclusions since the tax interaction effect is of greater magnitude than the revenue recycling effect under plausible values of parameters. The optimal environmental tax is about 70 percent of the Pigouvian tax, or of the MED. The Nordhaus (1993) model does not capture the interactive effects of existing taxes. In contrast, the results of Bovenberg and Goulder (1996) suggest that the optimal carbon taxes decline with the level of pre-existing taxes.

The general equilibrium model results of Bovenberg and Goulder (1996) suggest that the tax equals the ratio between marginal environmental damage from the use of this good and the marginal cost of public funds (MCPF). It is useful to note that MCPF depends on the configuration of all taxes.

These results indicate the role of pre-existing taxes whenever ecotaxes or green taxes are considered for their imposition. In general, an optimal green tax induces the level of emissions at which marginal welfare benefits from reducing emissions equals the marginal welfare cost of achieving such reductions. In the absence of pre-existing distortionary taxes, the rule simplifies to that involved in Pigouvian taxes: optimality requires that the green tax be set equal to the marginal benefit from reducing environmental damage. It is seen from the above that the Pigouvian tax rate is optimal if, and only if, the MCPF equals unity. Usually, the MCPF exceeds unity, and this warrants the optimal green tax to be less than its Pigouvian counterpart. It was estimated using empirical models that this ranges from about 57 to 73 percent of the Pigouvian rate. The low percentage corresponds to high value for the intertemporal elasticity of substitution in consumption, and the high percentage to a low value of the corresponding elasticity. Thus, the tax rate is higher when consumption functions depict features of relative inelasticity of substitution.

Reverting to the relevance of environmental taxes, even the studies that cast doubts on the existence of significant double dividends did not have any difficulty in arriving at the conclusion that, so long as the tax yields an environmental benefit, it offers an overall welfare improvement. An evaluation of usefulness of green taxes is linked to environmental benefits assessment. The difficulty of establishing the strong double dividend does not contradict the potential reality that an environmental tax can promote higher national income when revenues are earmarked for capital formation (Goulder, 1995). This conclusion was reached by dropping the stronger requirement of welfare improvement, and replacing it with a milder requirement in terms of income criteria.

A useful general equilibrium analysis methodology, and also a few empirical results are contributed by Bovenberg and Goulder (1996). Optimal environmental taxation criteria with due recognition of existing taxes are furnished. This paper extends previous analyses with the inclusion of pollution taxes like carbon taxes on intermediate inputs of the economy, e.g. fossil fuel inputs and transportation. The empirical results for the US economy suggest that the potential for green taxes is rather subdued when all the tax and revenue recycling effects are taken into account – there exist situations when the tax can be zero or negative. This could occur when the MED of carbon emissions falls below $50 per ton. This is because "the carbon subsidy is an implicit subsidy to labor and capital which helps to offset the distortions to labor and capital markets generated by explicit factor taxes."

To sum up this section, the main findings of recent significant contributions in environmental taxation are as follows:

- There are merits in levying these taxes.
- Because of the tax interaction effect with the prevailing taxes in the economy, the magnitudes of optimal environmental taxes tend to be about 10–30 percent less than those dictated by traditional partial equilibrium analyses.
- Depending on the revenue recycling or other patterns of utilization of these tax revenues, the net effect of the tax levies can be progressive or neutral or regressive for various economic classes.
- The relevance of the tax instruments can be assessed in relation to the changing levels of the marginal environmental damages of one or more pollutants.

● 5.8 CONCLUSIONS ●

The economics and management of global commons, with special reference to GHGs remains the most complex in the set of issues relevant for sustainability and SD. Recent revisions in the methods and assessment of GWP and its implications tend to offer greater policy insight. Global estimates of costs of the GE and of stabilization of concentrations of GHGs offer very limited advice on the possible mitigating strategies, as the aggregates throw no light on the incidence of costs and benefits of mitigating strategies. Thus, a detailed component-based decomposition of relative roles of various factors is necessary for evolving preventive and regulating the effects of GHGs and in the special role of CO_2 as the most important GHG.

By the nature of environmental problems covered in the class of global commons, it is difficult to visualize the role of market factors as alone in achieving desirable objectives of SD in the immediate future. This is not to rule out the role of market institutions or market factors in the governing processes relevant for global commons; these will be derived as products of an overarching policy. For example, the possibility of emissions trading is essentially a market mechanism, but this is to be evolved after assigning the relative roles of various economic and noneconomic factors in the accumulation of GHGs, and after ascertaining the relative apportionment of responsibilities for individual countries. Economics of afforestation and carbon sequestration suggest greater scope for this method of CO_2 stabilization. The costs of natural sequestration are not generally expected to exceed the suggested range of carbon taxes per ton (around $10). More analyses are required to produce realistic comprehensive costs and benefits of such schemes.

Review Exercises

1   What are the limitations of the IPCC (1990) definitions and estimates of global warming potential (GWP)?
2   Examine the sensitivity of the revised formula for GWPs to the choice of
    (a)   the time horizon, and
    (b)   the discount rate?
3   (a)   What relationships exist between tropospheric and stratospheric ozone, chlorine, and ultraviolet (UV) radiation?
    (b)   Examine the relative roles of ozone in the troposphere and stratosphere in terms of human health and effects on other forms of life.
4   Discuss the role and limitations of the DICE model. Indicate the relevant directions for further improvement of this model and summarize the ones which contributed to further development of models, especially the ones allowing for disaggregation of sectors of the economy.
5   Why is the potential for carbon sequestration relatively untapped? Discuss the relative merits and limitations of extensive carbon sequestration with afforestation programs.
6   List various types and degrees of unknowns, uncertainties and unidentified parameters in assessing the costs and benefits of GHG mitigation strategies.
7   Examine the roles of tradable emission permits (TEPs) and carbon taxes in curbing atmospheric GHG concentrations. Can high transaction costs lead to negating the effectiveness (or blunting) of these instruments?
8   What are the public policy imperatives, from a political economy viewpoint, for realizing potential double dividends and triple dividends of green taxes?

References

Adger, W. N. and Brown, K. (1994) *Land Use and the Causes of Global Warming*. Chichester: John Wiley & Sons.

Arrhenius, S. (1896) On the influence of carbonic acid upon the temperature of the ground. *Philosophical Magazine and Journal of Science*, Series 5, 41(251), 237–76.

Baumol, W. J. and Oates, W. E. (1979) *The Theory of Environmental Policy*. Englewood Cliffs, NJ: Prentice-Hall.

Bovenberg, L. and de Mooji, R. A. (1994) Environmental levies and distortionary taxes. *American Economic Review*, 84(4), 1085–9.

Bovenberg, A. L. and Goulder, L. H. (1996) Optimal environmental taxation in the presence of other taxes – general equilibrium analyses. *American Economic Review*, 86, 985–1000.

Bueler, B. (1997) Solving an equilibrium model for trade of CO_2 emission permits. *European Journal of Operational Research*, 102, 393–403.

Burniaux, J.-M., Martin, J. P., Nicoletti, G. and Martins, J. O. (1991) *GREEN – a multi-region dynamic general equilibrium model for quantifying the costs of curbing CO_2 emissions, OECD Working Paper #104.* Paris: OECD.

Cline, W. (1992) *Global Warming – The Economic Stakes.* Washington, DC: Institute for Interational Economics.

Coase, R. (1960) The problem of social cost. *Journal of Law and Economics*, 3, 1–44.

Dixon, R. K., Winjum, J. K. and Schroeder, P. E. (1993) Conservation and sequestration of carbon – the potential of forest and agroforest management practices. *Global Environment Change*, 3, 159–73.

Eckhaus, R. (1992) Comparing the effects of greenhouse gas emissions on global warming. *The Energy Journal*, 13, 25–35.

Energy Information Administration (EIA) (1994) *International Energy Annual 1992*, DOE/EIA-0219(92), US Department of Energy. Washington, DC: US Government Printing Office.

Fankhouser, S. (1994) The social costs of greenhouse gas emissions – an expected value approach. *The Energy Journal*, 2, 157–84.

Farman, J. C., Gardner, B. G. and Shanklin, J. D. (1985) Large losses of total ozone in Antarctica reveal seasonal Cl O_x/NO_x interaction. *Nature*, 315, 207–10.

Fourier, J. (1824) Remarques generales sur les temperatures du globe terrestre et des espaces planetaires. *Annals of Chemical Physics*, 27, 136–67.

Goulder, L. H. (1995) Environmental taxation and the double dividend – a reader's guide. *International Tax and Public Finance*, 2, 157–83.

Greening, L. A., Davis, W. B. and Schipper, L. (1998) Decomposition of aggregate carbon intensity for the manufacturing sector – comparison of declining trends from 10 OECD countries for the period 1971–1991. *Energy Economics*, 20, 43–65.

Gupta, S. and Hall, S. G. (1996) Carbon abatement costs – an integrated approach for India. *Environment and Development Economics*, 1(1), 41–63.

Han, X. and Chatterjee, L. (1997) Impacts of growth and structural change on CO_2 emissions of developing countries. *World Development*, 25(3), 395–407.

Hardin, G. (1968) The tragedy of the commons. *Science*, 162, 1243–8.

Harvey, L. D. (1993) A guide to global warming problems. *Energy Policy*, 21, 24–34.

Heller, M. A. (1998) The tragedy of the anticommons. *Harvard Law Review*, 111(3), 621–88.

Houghton, J. T., Jenkins, G. J. and Ephraums, J. J. (1990) *Climate Change – The IPCC Scientific Assessment.* New York: Cambridge University Press.

Houghton, R. A., Unruh, J. D. and Lefebure, P. A. (1993) Current land cover in the tropics and its potential for sequestering carbon. *Global Biogeochemical Cycles*, 7, 305–20.

IPCC (1990) *Climate Change – The Scientific Assessment.* New York: Cambridge University Press, published for the IPCC.

IPCC (1992): *Global Climate 1992 – A Supplementary Report.* Geneva: IPCC/WMO.

IPCC (1995a) *The Science of Climate Change – Report of the IPCC Working Group I.* Geneva: IPCC/WMO.

IPCC (1995b) *Climate Change 1995 – The IPCC Second Assessment Synthesis of Scientific–Technical Information Relevant to Interpreting Article 2 of the UN Framework Convention on Climate Change.* Geneva: IPCC/WMO.

IPCC (1996a) *Climate Change 1995 – Economic and Social Dimensions of Climate Change*. New York: Cambridge University Press, published for the IPCC.

IPCC (1996b) *Climate Change 1995 – Technical Summary – Impacts, Adaptations, and Mitigation Options*. New York: Cambridge University Press, published for the IPCC.

Kandlikar, M. (1995) The relative roles of trace gas emissions in greenhouse abatement policies. *Energy Policy*, 23, 879–83.

Kandlikar, M. (1996) Indices for comparing greenhouse gas emissions – interpreting science and economics. *Energy Economics*, 18(4), 265–81.

Karl, T., Nichols, N. and Gregory, J. (1997) The coming climate. *Scientific American*, May, 78–83.

Kaya, Y. (1989) Impact of carbon dioxide emission control on GNP growth – Interpretation of proposed scenarios. *IPCC Working Group on Response Strategies*. Quoted in IPCC (1996a).

Kerr, R. A. (1997) Greenhouse forecasting still cloudy. *Science*, 276, 1040–2.

Lashof, D. A. and Ahuja, D. R. (1990) Relative contributions of greenhouse gas emissions to global warming. *Nature*, 344, 529–31.

Mabey, N., Hall, S., Smith, C. and Gupta, S. (1997) *Argument in the Greenhouse*. New York: Routledge.

Maddison, D. (1995) A cost–benefit analysis of slowing climate change. *Energy Policy*, 23, 337–46.

Mesterton-Gibbons, M. (1992) *An Introduction to Game-theoretic Modelling*. Redwood City, CA: Addison-Wesley.

Mitchell, J. F. and Johns, T. C. (1997) On modification of global warning by sulfate aerosols. *Journal of Climate*, 10, 245–67.

Molina, M. J. and Rowland, F. S. (1974) Stratospheric sink for chlorofluoromethanes – chlorine atom catalyzed destruction of ozone. *Nature*, 249, 810–12.

Montero, J. P. (1997) Marketable pollution permits with uncertainty and transaction costs. *Resource and Energy Economics*, 20(1), 27–50.

Moulton, R. J. and Richards, K. R. (1990) *Costs of Sequestering Carbon through Tree Planting and Forest Management in the United States*, General Technical Report WO-58. Washington, DC: USDA Forest Service.

Myers, N. (1996) The world's forests – problems and potentials. *Environmental Conservation*, 23, 156–68.

Nordhaus, W. D. (1991) To slow or not to slow – the economics of the greenhouse effect. *The Economic Journal*, 101, 920–37.

Nordhaus, W. D. (1992) An optimal transition path for controlling greenhouse gases. *Science*, 258, 1315–19.

Nordhaus, W. D. (1993) Rolling the DICE – the optimal transition path for controlling greenhouse gases. *Resource and Energy Economics*, 15, 27–50.

Nordhaus, W. D. (1994) *Managing the Global Commons*. Cambridge, Mass.: MIT Press.

Oates, W. E. (1995) Green taxes, the environment, and the tax system. *Southern Economic Journal*, 61(4), 915–22.

OECD (1975) *The Polluter Pays Principle – Definition, Analysis, Implementation*. Paris: OECD (Organization for Economic Cooperation and Development).

Ostrom, E. (1990) *Governing the Commons*. Cambridge: Cambridge University Press.

Parry, I. (1995) Pollution taxes and revenue recycling. *Journal of Environmental Economics and Management*, 29(3), 564–77.

Parry, I. (1997) Environmental taxes and quotas in the presence of distortionary factor markets. *Resource and Energy Economics*, 19, 203–20.

Pigou, A. C. (1932) *The Economics of Welfare*. London: Macmillan.

Plambeck, E. L. and Hope, C. (1996) PAGE 95 – An updated valuation of the impacts of global warming. *Energy Policy*, 24(9), 783–93.

Ramanathan, V. (1975) Greenhouse effect due to chlorofluorocarbons – climatic implications. *Science*, 190, 50–52.

Ramsey, F. P. (1928) A mathematical theory of savings. *Economic Journal*, 38, 543–59.

Rao, P. K. (1999) *The Economics of Global Climatic Change*. New York: M. E. Sharpe.

Richels, R. and Sturm, P. (1996) The costs of CO_2 emission reductions. *Energy Policy*, 24(10 &11), 875–87.

Ridgley, M. A. (1996) Fair sharing of greenhouse gas burdens. *Energy Policy*, 23, 879–83.

Ringius, L., Torvanger, A. and Holtsmark, B. (1998) Can multi-criteria rules fairly distribute climate burdens? OECD results from three burden sharing rules. *Energy Policy*, 26(10), 777–93.

Roelofs, G.-J. and Lelieveld, J. (1997) Model study of the influence of cross-tropopause O_3 transports on tropospheric O_3 levels. *Tellus*, Series B, 49B(1), 38–55.

Rose, A. and Tietenberg, T. (1993) An international system of tradeable CO_2 entitlements – implications for economic development. *Journal of Environment & Development*, 2(1), 1–36.

Rubin, E. S., Cooper, R. N., Frosch, R. A., Lee, T. H., Marland, G., Rosenfeld, A. H. and Stine, D. D. (1992) Realistic mitigation options for global warming. *Science*, 257, 261–6.

Schlesinger, W. H. (1991) *Biogeochemistry – An Analysis of Global Change*. New York: Academic Press.

Schmalensee, R., Stoker, T. M. and Judson, R. A. (1998) World carbon dioxide emissions 1950–2050. *Review of Economics and Statistics*, 80(1), 15–27.

Sedjo, R. A. and Solomon, A. M. (1989) Climate and forests. In N. J. Rosenberg et al. (eds), *Greenhouse Warming-Abatement and Adaptation*. Washington, DC: Resources for the Future, 105–19.

Shell, K. (ed.) (1967) *Essays on the Theory of Optimal Economic Growth*. Cambridge, Mass.: MIT Press.

Solow, R. M. (1956) A contribution to the theory of economic growth. *Quarterly Journal of Economics*, 70, 65–94.

Somerville, R. (1996) *The Forgiving Air – Understanding Environmental Change*. Berkeley: University of California Press.

Stavins, R. (1995) Transaction costs and tradeable permits. *Journal of Environmental Economics and Management*, 29, 133–48.

Tol, R. J. (1995) The damage costs of climate change – towards more comprehensive calculations. *Environmental and Resource Economics*, 5, 353–74.

UN (United Nations) (1997) *World Economic and Social Survey 1997*. New York: UN.

UNCTAD (1992) *Combating Global Warming – Study on a Global System of Tradeable Carbon Efficiency Entitlements*. New York: UN.

West, J. J., Hope, C. and Lane, S. N. (1997) Climate change and energy policy – the impacts and implications of aerosols. *Energy Policy*, 25(11), 923–39.

Winjum, J. K. and Lewis, D. K. (1993) Forest management and the economics of carbon storage – the nonfinancial component. *Climate Research*, 3, 111–19.

World Bank (1991) *Forest Sector Policy Paper*. Washington, DC: The World Bank.

chapter outline

● CHAPTER 6 ●

Environmental Accounting

Environmental Accounting

For a statesman to try to maximize GNP is about as sensible as for a composer of music to try to maximize the number of notes in a symphony.
Garrett Hardin

● 6.1 INTRODUCTION ●

For about half a century, national income accounting has been a useful tool in understanding national economies, their composition, and growth. Its usefulness apart, the annual changes in natural and environmental resource stocks are usually not reflected in this system. These tend to trickle in to affect the conventional accounts over a period of time (years or decades) when the impact is reflected in the market or related parameters. This may not always be the case even if longer time horizons (but not long enough to enable reflecting the costs of damage) are considered. This is the case, for example, if there is extinction of some biological species. The existence values (EVs) or non-use values of some of the entities may be lost for ever even before the entities are recognized for their value. It becomes too expensive, and too late, to take corrective steps in the public and private arena. This is a serious issue which warrants attention in various kinds of accounting principles and practices. The damages to the planet's resources and ecological capital cannot wait to be attended to till the market forces enter the scene. Even when markets depict some impacts, the market features can be so blurred that it may be impossible to isolate the relative roles of specific items or their "worth." The worth of Central Park in New York City cannot be assessed without proper assessment of its contribution to the psychological well-being of the area residents, among a number of other important benefits. If Central Park were to be dismantled (a terrible premise even for a strictly hypothetical scenario) for building constructions, and health costs soar for the local population after a couple of years, what will the market features do to restore the critical natural facility?

There is no unique approach to accounting for environment and integrating the same with the conventional economic accounting. However, several recent efforts of the 1990s promise revised methods of accounting. One need not be an obsessed environmentalist to appreciate the relevance, role and limitations of integrating environmental accounting with existing national income accounts. With this information base and analysis, policy makers and consumers can formulate their decisions on production, trade, environmental protection, and consumption, as well as taxation and related fiscal policies for sustaining the long-term future of the society. Undoubtedly, the task is not an easy one, especially when some countries are still not good at economic depreciation accounting methods in the current systems dealing with conventional capital goods.

This chapter addresses alternative concepts in the evolution of measures to account for environmental changes. This is expected to be facilitated by properly adjusting or supplementing the existing systems of national accounts. This chapter examines the need for, and implications of, accounting for environmental changes and of expenditures for environmental quality preservation in this adjustment process. Relevant analytical foundations of adjusted national accounting methods are also examined. Some of the important attempts to draw up a list of indicators of sustainability and sustainable development (SD) are summarized. A few of the attempts made in this direction by the World Bank and the UN are also reviewed.

● 6.2 ENVIRONMENTAL DAMAGE AND RESOURCE DEPLETION ●

Global ecological accounting is still in its infancy. Concern for greenhouse gases (GHGs) and carbon accounting (or simply CO_2 emissions, in most cases) is but a manifestation of specific problem-based attention to an aspect of global environmental accounting, motivated by the accelerated greenhouse effect (GE). Similarly, the prohibitions on the manufacture and use of chlorine-derivatives, along with their accounting, arose out of the ozone effects. If humans have to wait for an identified serious problem to account for and intervene in the ecological systems, there is a potential danger of acting too late or being able to do too little at that juncture. Alternatively, this could imply incurring extremely high costs of restoration, or suffering the significant costs of irreversibilities. This does not automatically imply that the current generation or its immediate successor generations should commit excessively burdensome quanta of resources to safeguard against potential loss of resources or their remote adverse impacts. However, a pragmatic strategy (in terms of possible actions, and their entailing costs and benefits) can hardly be expected to arise in the absence of information on the biogeophysical system characteristics. The latter should typically include these factors:

- Data and information on system dynamics and the evolutionary processes.
- Relative roles of anthropogenic and other factors in the evolving dynamics.
- Balance of nature, and fluxes of nature arising out of these.
- Changes in the ecological system resilience.
- Economic forces affecting each of the above.

The concept of ecological carrying capacity (CC), or of the sink capacity of the planet and the changing dynamics of the same are still elusive insofar as the roles of the "missing sinks" for CO_2, or the predictive ability of the global circulation models of the weather patterns are concerned. Any progress in understanding these and related problems is heavily dependent on substantial ecological accounting and the development of a relevant information base.

Even a simplistic assessment of these characteristics warrants massive environmental accounting, usually beyond the scope of any one country or a small group of countries, assessed by current standards of information capabilities. Despite some efforts by institutions such as the United Nations Environment Programme (UNEP), the current level of efforts and allocation of resources for ecological sustainability and SD remain very meager. A number of new initiatives for enhanced information gathering and processing have been introduced since 1996. These attempts are undertaken primarily by a few of the UN institutions as well as international nongovernmental organizations. At least three new global observation systems are noteworthy – collectively, the G3OSs: the Global Climate Observing System (GCOS), the Global Ocean Observing System (GOOS), and the Global Terrestrial Observing System (GTOS). The sponsors for these systems include: the Food and Agriculture Organization (FAO), International Council of Science Unions (ICSU), Intergovernmental Oceanographic Comission (IOC), UNEP, UN Educational Scientific and Cultural Organization (UNESCO), and WMO. An Integrated Global Observing Strategy is proposed, derived from the base information from G3OS. Some of the focus items are well-defined. In the GTOS, five global issues are addressed:

- Changes in land quality.
- Availability of freshwater resources.
- Pollution and toxicity.
- Loss of biodiversity.
- Climate change.

If the proposed "promotion" of integrated analysis of biophysical and socio-economic data does indeed materialize, there is hope for an improved understanding of necessary interlinks. The roles of anthropogenic influences need to be assessed at a fairly detailed and operationally relevant level.

We need to ascertain the changes in the sink capacity in relation to the incidence of possible adverse consequences at regional and global levels. These are applicable specifically for the following, but not limited to them:

- Stabilization of GHGs, ozone, and forest resources.
- Conserving biological resources.
- Regulating local or micro-environmental problems like urban air pollution, solid waste, watersheds and other life-supporting, sanity-retaining services of nature.

All require significant efforts in environmental accounting. In current practices, some of these are sought to be accounted along with the systems of national accounts (as explained below). This forms a very good beginning. However, some of the accounting exercises, when tied strongly to the annual income accounting methods, fail to provide a broader scenario of any impending ecological disaster. Forewarning is not always a priority in routine accounting exercises which tend to provide one type of ex-post assessment. An improved mechanism to account for environmental resources at local, regional, national, and global levels is essential – whether or not these resources are reflected in the market parameters. Such a framework can provide the factual background to enable institutional accountability at different levels for the environment and SD.

Economic growth, as in the oil-exporting economies or major forest resource producer countries, is usually attained at the expense of resource depletion and environmental damage. It is important to keep track of related indicators of progress and entailing costs together. This is not simply an accounting exercise, but is a relevant method to ensure that the future flows of income and nature's services are not allowed to decline, especially in an unprepared manner or with financial and ecological surprises. The latter are usually the results of nonlinear interrelationships between depleted levels of resources and the envo-ecological features (especially when certain threshold levels of stocks in these capital assets are driven down). There are significant problems (technological and otherwise) in measuring the levels of present and future stocks of environmental assets as well as natural resource assets in many cases. In many countries, even the available operational information – for example, the extent of annual resource extraction is not being integrated for the purpose of environmentally responsible policy making. Usually these limitations are attributed to incomplete information, but it is not enough to justify the rationality of decision making on the basis of available information only when addressing the interests of current and future generations. This concern need not be a by-product of an obsession with nature and environment.

As a simple illustration of discrepancies between economic and environmental accounting and their significance, let us consider the problem of soil quality loss. Soil degradation for the current period is reflected at the end of the period in the standard national accounts through diminished yields or through higher costs of production where farmers counteract the degradation, for example, with higher fertilizer applications. The reduction in the stock of this natural capital is not recorded in the conventional system. It represents a depreciation to be reflected in the assessment of so-called genuine savings. From an economic and accounting perspective, the long-term productivity effects resulting from the diminished stock remain very important. The amount of soil eroded, as well as the amount and quality of the residual soil, is important. So are other factors that affect productivity, like the alkaline content. The use of soil quality indicators are being advocated by the FAO, but considerable additional analysis is necessary to integrate the information with the multiple systems of environmental and economic accounts.

Some developed countries have taken the lead in assessing the natural resource and environmental changes, largely in physical terms. Norway and the Netherlands have systematized stock and flow estimates of resources such as oil, forestry, fish, minerals, and energy sources. France has evolved "patrimony natural" accounting, aimed at examining natural resources and environment in terms of economic, ecological and social functions. Continued progress in environmental accounting is being made in the USA. The US Environmental Protection Agency (USEPA) and a number of agencies including the Commerce Department have been involved in some of these efforts. Several studies and country cases of experiences are summarized in box 6.1 on page 221.

At the international level, a number of initiatives have been taken during the 1990s. The Agenda 21 of 1992 sought to "expand existing systems of national accounts in order to integrate environmental and social dimensions in the accounting framework, including at least satellite systems of natural resources in all member States." Some of the features of the UN Statistical Office handbook (1993) are discussed later in this chapter. This approach has been further strengthened and a draft manual issued in 1999 by the UN for its possible practical adoption by the member countries. The World Bank undertook several exercises and case studies for countries such as Mexico and Papua New Guinea; expanded measures of the wealth of nations has been an area of continued effort. Some highlights of these exercises are given later.

Major adjustments to national accounts have been suggested by several authors. Three levels of environmental adjustments can be made (Steer and Lutz, 1994):

1 Physical accounts – based on measures of resource depletion and environmental changes, especially environmental effects of various aspects of national production and income.
2 Nonmonetary impacts–measured in terms of agricultural productivity, morbidity and mortality, soil loss and other features, each of which admit physical impacts in terms of cause–effect relations.
3 Monetary valuation – based on the previous steps, the evaluation can be done (at least in principle) and then appropriate adjustments made to the national accounts.

Two sets of indicators – environmentally adjusted net domestic product (EDP) – were proposed by Steer and Lutz (1994):

$$EDP_1 = NDP - \text{resource depletion costs}$$

$$EDP_2 = EDP_1 - \text{environmental degradation costs}$$

where NDP represents net domestic product, i.e. the capital depreciation-adjusted gross domestic product (GDP).

As an illustration, for Mexico in 1985, assessment of these measures indicated that EDP_1 was 94 percent of the NDP, and EDP_2 was 87 percent of the NDP, suggesting significant differences between conventional national income accounting and the new measures for a national economy – not necessarily atypical of many middle-income and low-income countries.

Prevention and Restoration Activities in Maintenance Costing

Five types of measures for preventing or restoring environmental deterioration by economic activities can be distinguished (UN, 1993; Hueting et al., 1992):

1   Reduction or abstention from economic activities.
2   Substitution of the outcomes of economic activities, i.e. production of other products or modification of household consumption patterns.
3   Substitution of the inputs of economic activities without modifying their outcome (outputs) by applying new technologies.
4   Activities to prevent environmental deterioration without modifying the activities themselves, e.g. by end-of-pipe technologies.
5   Restoration of the environment and measures diminishing the environmental impacts of economic activities.

Finer distinctions between restoration and upkeep tend to make a difference in an assessment of preventive and operational costs. When depletion of biota or freshwater, for example, results in a reduction of economic production, the value added foregone caused by diminished production activities could be taken as the imputed costs at maintenance value. In the case of substitution, additional substitution costs could be used for calculating those costs. If new environment-friendly industries have to be established to avoid a decline in output, the incremental costs could be calculated for estimating depletion costs. In the case of discharging residuals, different types of activities could be carried out to adhere to environmental sustainability standards. These activities are: changes in consumption patterns, technological changes to introduce environment-friendly technologies, as well as choice of appropriate end-of-pipe technologies. The choice of activities for calculating the imputed degradation costs of discharging residuals is expected to depend on relative costs and efficiencies in a fully informed decision-making system; see also UN (1993) and Hueting et al. (1992). Although environmental damage contributed by international free-ride phenomena dominate the global commons of planet Earth (as detailed in chapter 5), actions at the national level are usually more transparent, and accountability is easier to visualize. For this reason, a number of improvements in resource accounting practices at national and local levels are desirable. This is the focus of the next section.

● 6.3 Green National Accounts ●

When Exxon incurred about $3 billion expenditure for the cleanup in Alaska for the oil spill caused in an accident, it adds to the GDP because the conventional income accounting methods are so formulated. The GDP would have been less without the accident, if other effects are not directly and immediately reflected in incomes and expenditures. Here are some of the shortcomings of national accounts with respect to the environment (Bartelmus et al., 1993, p. 108):

- They neglect the scarcities of natural resources that can pose a serious threat to sustained economic productivity and development.
- They pay only limited attention to the effects of the environmental quality on human health and welfare.
- They treat environmental protection and defensive expenditures as increases in national product, which should, instead, be considered as social costs of the preservation or upgradation of environmental quality.

A Review of Concepts

One of the elements of environment–economy accounting relates to the concept of environmentally defensive expenditures (EDEs).

Defensive expenditures comprise those expenditures and activities which are intended to mitigate the adverse (actual or potential) negative effects of the environment. EDEs can arise from a combination of these circumstances:

- The transition from the environment as a free good to the environment as a scarce good.
- The treatment and compensation of damages caused by environment burdens, and other transaction costs.
- Restoration and cleanup activities.
- Avoidance and screening activities.
- Environmental protection, abatement and disposal activities in specific environmental protection facilities.
- Activities for adaptation and changing environmental damaging production and consumption patterns.

A number of corrections and adjustments for the net national product (NNP) concept have been proposed during the past quarter century to account for changes (human-induced or otherwise) in natural resource and environmental stocks. This was considered particularly necessary when part of the manufacturing or economic process is itself directly and significantly contributing to the drawdown of exhaustible resources. A few of these are briefly stated here.

A "measure of economic welfare" (MEW) was proposed by Nordhaus and Tobin (1972):

$$MEW = GNP - DPC + PSA - SDA$$

where PSA is the value of positive social amenities, SDA that of social disamenities – both due to environmental or other resource use – DPC is depreciation of productive capital, and DEC is that of environmental capital. The authors argued that "those social costs of economic activity that are not internalized as private costs should be subtracted in calculating our measures of economic welfare" (p. 49).

Later, Nijkamp (1977) suggested that the ecological imperatives for an unlimited and unbalanced economic growth tend to raise doubts about the validity of GNP as a measure of economic well-being or welfare of the society. It was suggested that it is more relevant to define a measure of net social welfare (NSW) as follows:

$$NSW = GNP - DPC - DEC$$

In one of the early applications of environmental accounting, Zolotas (1981) constructed what was called a measure of economic aspects of welfare, which allowed the deduction of estimated costs of resource depletion and private costs of environmental pollution. Although rather arbitrary, this formed an applied method of adjusting social income to relevant costs of growth simultaneously.

In one of the arguments, the effects of pollution include depreciation of the environmental assets. Thus, GNP declines with environmental effects. The net effect of this could decline marginally or significantly, depending on the efforts countries make to preserve environmental assets and features or quality (Harrison, 1989).

In a relevant analysis, Daly (1996) argued that the present system of national accounts do not reflect the costs of economic growth, and that simple adjustment of depreciation of capital from the GNP estimates do not offer a useful measure of NNP; this NNP cannot be consumed every year because the production of NNP requires supporting activities that are not biogeophysically sustainable. Daly proposed sustainable social NNP (SSNNP) as follows:

$$SSNNP = NNP - EDE - DNC$$

where the EDE is inclusive of costs of environmental protection and upkeep of the quality, pollution control, etc., and DNC represents the depreciation of natural capital.

In a recent and important argument, Solow (1994) suggested that the shadow values of resource depletion should be deducted from the NNP to obtain a "truer NNP that takes account of the depletion of resources." This assertion may be interpreted and a revised NNP (RNNP) may be given by:

RNNP = NNP – value of natural capital depletion – value of environmental capital depletion where the values are separately generated from shadow prices.

It is also important to note that some of the depreciation accounting issues continue to require improvements in their proper valuation methods. In general, it is not enough to invest the "rental" or user cost on the lines of Hotelling rent or Hartwick rule (see chapter 4) for the purpose of sustainability or SD. The depreciation or value of capital depletion for exhaustible resources forms the required magnitude of investment to ensure sustainability; see also Lozada (1995). Viewed in conjunction with environmental asset depreciation, this result has an intuitive appeal because it can be extended to cover all exhaustible assets. The so-called renewable assets cease to be renewable when certain thresholds of the ecology and the environment are crossed, or when the resilience of the system is lost. In all such configurations, it is relevant to pay attention to depreciation aspects – whether or not these parameters can be assessed using market factors. Several alternative methods of "economic depreciation" and improved methods for environmental and resource accounting have been proposed (Lutz, 1993). Most of these tend to proceed under the assumptions of sustained resilience of the systems involved.

Addressing broader issues of socioeconomic well-being and its sustainability, the concept of an index of sustainable economic welfare (ISEW) was developed and revised by Cobb and Cobb (1994). The calculation of the ISEW consists of three steps:

1   The consumption base is calculated by measuring what could be consumed, based on production. Public consumption is taken directly, and private consumption adjusted for durables' lifetime, and unpaid household work valued too.
2   Defensive costs for maintaining the standard of well-being are deducted from the above estimates. These include environmental defensive costs, social defensive costs and any foreseen future welfare reductions.
3   The resulting "raw-ISEW" is converted to ISEW by multiplying it by an index for the inequalities of wages and incomes.

Founded on a complex set of data and valuation requirements, the adoption of ISEW in practical economies is still very limited, although a few case studies in Germany and Austria can be seen; for details, see Stockhammer et al. (1997).

Analytical Bases

Although greening the national accounts sounds fashionable, it is simply a need-based imperative. Nonetheless, its implementation is not always easy. It advocates postulate environmental and economic objectives (both explicit and implicit) and varying perspectives. Some are concerned with preserving the stock of environmental assets intact, in physical or value terms; others are concerned with the effect of environmental change on welfare. The concern here is for the proper measurement of national output and expenditure. The GDP should be adjusted downwards for any resource degradation or capital liquidation. Under conventional accounting, depreciation of produced fixed assets is included in the GDP and magnifies it. Depreciation is deducted for the estimation of the more sustainable NDP and the net profits of an enterprise. In the absence of proper empirical measures for NDP, macroeconomic analyses and policies tend to be based on estimates of the GDP, even though these may not be totally sustainable. Natural asset depletion and environmental deterioration can be large and volatile over time and vary across regions. Accordingly, the significance of the differences between the GDP, and EDP or NDP, and the policy distortions the wrong indicators can cause, varies among countries and regions.

Requirements of SD differ from those of a sustainable natural environment. The former implies a process through time relating to the prosperity of the average individual within a finite natural world, and the natural resource stock per capita therefore becomes relevant; see also El-Serafy (1997). Attempts have been made to extend the objective of sustainability to "human capital" and also to "social capital," the latter consisting of interrelationships believed to sustain communities (Serageldin, 1996). However, for national accounting purposes, the sustainability of environmental capital far outweighs in importance the other forms of "capital."

El-Serafy (1997) suggested that, in regard to "human capital," it would be wrong to treat expenditure on education and training (though in many respects economically justifiable) as investment in human capital since:

(a)   not all education leads to higher productivity – many graduates fail to find productive employment commensurate with their training; and
(b)   improvements in productivity due to education are reflected automatically in the conventional measurements of GDP.

It was also suggested (El-Serafy, 1997) that "human capital deterioration on account of infirmity and death do not threaten the intactness of capital since human knowledge and technology unquestionably raise the stock of such capital all the time, and are bequeathed costlessly to future generations." In the above reasoning, it is doubtful if claim (a) can remain valid; generally, unemployment in life years is either insignificant in some countries or the cohort groups change with time, so a constant magnitude of unemployment (about 7 percent in many countries) needs to be accounted at macro rather than micro levels, since it is not usually the same people who continue to be unemployed forever.

Because national income is recorded in market prices, shadow prices have to be estimated for functions (and their losses) that are directly comparable with prices of manufactured marketed goods. For this purpose, supply and demand curves for functions have to be constructed. In most cases, it is not possible to find complete demand curves. It may be possible to construct supply curves, consisting of the costs of measures eliminating the burden on the environment, arranged by increasing costs per unit burden avoided (Tinbergen and Hueting, 1991). The situation changed after the World Commission on Environment and Development (WCED, 1987) to seeking social acceptance, rather than having to find uniform individual preferences.

One of the procedures for adjusting the GNP was suggested by Hueting (1989), who proposed the following procedure for correcting GNP for environmental losses. First, define physical standards for environmental functions, based on their sustainable use; these standards replace the (unknown) demand curves. Then, formulate measures to meet these standards. Finally, estimate the money involved in implementing the measures. The reduction of national income Y by the amounts found gives a first approximation of the activity level which, in line with the standards applied, is sustainable. Find Y which approximates to Y^*, the sustainable level. The standards can be related to environmental functions. It is possible, for example, to formulate the way in which a forest should be managed to attain a sustainable use of its functions.

One of the arguments suggests that the current value in an aggregative optimal growth problem with heterogeneous capital stocks (including exhaustible, renewable and environmental stocks) is the NNP function (Hartwick, 1990). Hartwick used a constant discount rate over time, without any discussion on this. It was argued that:

$$NNP = C$$

where C is a constant when exhaustible resource rents are the sole source of income for new investment.

The details of analytical explanations given in chapter 4 clarify that this position may hold only in special cases (as in autonomous Hamiltonian systems, which appear when technological or other externalities are ignored).

For a country living entirely on its exhaustible resource capital (and not investing in produced capital), as Dasgupta (1991) pointed out, NNP = 0, since

$$NNP = C + \text{economic depreciation of the exhaustible resource stock} = 0$$

In this approach, the prescription for presenting national accounts is as follows: deduct the rents (evaluated on marginal unit of stock) on the physical amount that the natural resource is "wasted," "run down," or "used up" in the accounting period. This will make the NNP reflect economic depreciation of natural resource capital used in an economic activity.

If real national income is to reflect well-being, accounting prices must be used for the basis. These prices are essentially the difference between market prices and optimum taxes and subsidies or other distortions. Also, the real national income is really the NNP. Thus, NNP is assessed as follows, using consumption as the numeraire (Dasgupta and Maler, 1994):

NNP = consumption + net investment in physical capital
   + the value of the net change in human capital
   + the value of the net change in stock of natural capital
   − the value of the current environmental damages.

The shadow prices or accounting prices are with reference to an optimizing economy, using the consumption numeraire. Both the selection of the numeraire and specification of the optimizing model can make a significant difference to the evaluation measures of the NNP or its variations. Some of the related issues are discussed in chapter 4. Subject to these analytical and empirical considerations, we can still proceed to examine the valuation issues in relation to environmental and ecological capital accounting issues. Investments in these assets deserve to be included in the defensive capital or capital accumulation category in assessing NNP.

It is important to "avoid self inflicted wounds when designing a set of national income and wealth accounts; the most serious of these wounds comes from the failure to link the national accounts to an underlying theoretical model" (Hulten, 1992).

As indicated in several studies – e.g. Dasgupta and Maler (1994) – most of the present practices in the estimation of national income are flawed in favor of underestimating losses and/or depreciation of assets. The NNP estimates are accordingly biased due to a biased set of prices in use. This implies the depreciation of environmental capital as zero. Since these resources are scarce or potentially scarce goods, their shadow prices are positive. The analytical problem in this regard is, again, attributable to the widespread use of autonomous optimization models (some deliberated in chapter 4), usually without even noticing that those are the ones behind much of the narrations and interpretations. Static, or effectively static, formulations of essentially dynamic problems with a critical role for time itself cannot, in general, lead to a positive value for the shadow prices of potentially scarce goods. The extent of the bias, referred to earlier, varies from one country to another. In the case of Costa Rica, Solorzano et al. (1991) estimated that the depreciation of resources of forests, soil and fisheries alone amounted to about 10 percent of GDP in 1989.

Role of Technical Progress

There are a few major considerations in using NNP measures for assessing sustainable consumption patterns, and these arise both in the analytical models and their solutions for interpretation, as well as in the operational accounting aspects of human capital and the dynamics of its externalities. If the role of anticipated technical progress is ignored completely, the NNP could indicate an underestimation of sustainable consumption levels for some periods; the converse could be the case when there is anticipated technical regress (Lofgren, 1992). The extent of this upward or downward bias is the present value of future anticipated marginal technical progress.

Based on a detailed nonautonomous model, Vellinga and Withagen (1996) argued that, if national income (in utility terms) is to reflect welfare, it should include instantaneous utility and should be corrected for the decrease of exhaustible resources, increase in pollution and environmental damages, and also the increase in "national non-resource" stocks based on human capital and technical progress factors. It was also argued that the NNP is a welfare measure when these adjustments (which include externalities of time and technology) are made and if actual prices are not "far off from the optimal prices." As is argued in chapter 4, the NNP measure may not be used as an indicator of sustainability unless all the time influences are accounted for.

If technological change is not attributable to the production factors, it is not generally possible to design a set of social and economic accounts which contain all the relevant information for welfare measurement, based on current entities alone (Aronsson and Lofgren, 1996). The reason behind this assertion was that since technological change affects future consumption possibilities, welfare will depend on time itself. Weitzman (1997) concluded: "sustainability" appears to depend more critically on future projections of exogenous technical change than on the typical corrections now being undertaken in the name of green accounting. NNP – whether conventional or green NNP – is likely to understate an economy's sustainability as long as it ignores the role of technical progress. On another account also, the NNP estimate may be a lower bound: knowledge capital is not bought and sold in markets, not accounted for in conventional national accounts, and does not earn a normal rate of return on investment (Nordhaus, 1997). Hence, the ecological application of Hicksian income seems to force a downward bias in estimating sustainable income because of the exclusion of human and knowledge capital.

In a study by the World Bank (1997) regarding measures of wealth and indicators for environmentally SD, resource depletion was measured as the total rents on resource extraction and harvest. Rents were estimated as the difference between the value of production at world prices and total costs of production, including depreciation of fixed assets and return on capital, for each of the following: bauxite, copper gold, iron ore, lead, nickel, silver, tin, coal, crude, oil, natural gas, and phosphate rock. This measures economic profits on extraction rather than scarcity rents, and gives an upward bias to the value of depletion (and a downward bias to genuine saving). No explicit adjustment was made for resource discoveries, since exploration expenditures are treated as an investment in standard national accounting. Forest resources enter the depletion calculation as the difference between the rental value of roundwood harvest and the corresponding value of natural growth both in forests and plantations. Only where harvest exceeds growth is there a depletion charge made for any given country. This valuation captures the commercial value of forests, but ignores important other services provided by trees, including carbon storage, watershed protection and the supply of non-timber (and nonfuelwood) products. The effects of pollution on output (such as damage to crops, and lost production owing to morbidity) are partly reflected in the standard national accounts, but not explicitly. Yet, some of the long-term effects of slow and sustained pollution on human and plant or other biological species may not be reflected for several years on any market output valuation for standard national accounts. Thus, the standards of these accounts are rather low.

The key pollution adjustment is for welfare effects, valuing the willingness-to-pay (WTP) to avoid excess mortality and the pain and suffering from pollution-linked morbidity. Underlying the treatment of pollution in green national accounting is an extended Hicksian notion of income. It was claimed in the World Bank (1997) study that if societies seek to maximize utility of consumption and environmental quality over long time horizons, then wealth can be conceived as the present value of this stream of welfare at the current time and in the future. However, this assertion merely shifts the focus. It does not absolve the problem of incorporating various ingredients relevant for SD: valuation over time, trade-offs of current and future costs and benefits, and the need to incorporate ecological resilience aspects under different profiles of consumption and production.

Conventionally, "green" NNP is the maximum amount of produced output that can be consumed at a point in time while leaving this measure of wealth constant, and genuine saving is the difference between green NNP and consumption. It was suggested (World Bank, 1997) that for most significant pollutants – such as particulate matter, acid emissions, lead emitted to air, heavy metals and other pollutants in water – the adjustment required to derive green NNP is the deduction of pollution emissions valued at their marginal social costs, as measured by WTP. Some of the green national accounting methods suggest that welfare effects should be deducted from genuine saving if the appropriate marginal WTP measures can be obtained. It is highly doubtful if this can be taken seriously in the applications for developing countries, given the levels of illiteracy and limited understanding of environment–health issues.

As an illustration of the application of genuine savings, the consumption-adjusted green NNP is estimated in a case study for India by Brandon and Hommann (1995), summarized below. The inclusion of pollution damages in genuine savings calculations requires detailed country-specific data and careful consideration of which effects of pollution are properly reflected in a savings measure. In general, the economic cost of pollution damages falls into four categories: the effects on economic assets, the effects on current output, the effects on ecological capital stocks, and the anthropogenic welfare effects associated with excess mortality and morbidity. Brandon and Hommann (1995) valued pollution damages for India, using a macro approach. These indicate the magnitude of damages in a developing country with significant pollution effects, even when only one of the above components is assessed. The study first estimated the loss in disability-adjusted life years (DALYs) associated with the impact of water pollution (largely from sewage) to be of the order of 14.3 million DALYs in 1991. Using India's annual per capita GNP at $330 as the lower bound of WTP to avoid the loss of a DALY, this led to a figure of roughly US$ 4.7 billion as the value of the welfare loss. Since several other effects were not included, the magnitude of damages could only be higher than the estimate.

The summary in box 6.1 provides an illustrative list of sources of some of the national studies and experiences. Based on the need for integration of environmental and economic policies, a number of countries started working on integrated accounting and adopted national environmental action plans (NEAPs) or "green plans."

In addition to some of the conceptual and institutional progress affecting integration of economic and environmental resource accounting, there have also been additional methodologies developed by some of the UN and related organizations. These are discussed in the next section.

BOX 6.1 National level environmental accounting

A few illustrative exercises were undertaken during the 1990s. Some were more focused on the application to sectors like forests, minerals, oils, fish, and soils. The subsoil resource assessment and proper accounting remains a complex task, for the unknowns are significant: the discovered and potential resources, markets and other technical changes.

Austria: a revised index of sustainable economic welfare was seen in the Austrian case, and viewed as a "holistic social reporting system" in the study by Stockhammer et al. (1997). It was found that while GDP continued to rise, this welfare index had stagnated since the middle of the 1980s. The reasons included: increases in income inequalities and reductions in, and stagnation of, unpaid household labor.

Canada: Bom (1992) initiated an exercise in assessing the natural resource accounts. Later, Smith (1994) reported on the work of Statistics Canada to develop accounts for natural resource stocks, pollution emissions, and environmental defense expenditure. These were adjuncts to the conventional national accounts, and there are no plans to produce a green GDP.

Costa Rica: the World Resources Institute undertook a natural resource accounting study (Solorzano et al., 1991). Forest resource depreciation was deducted from gross forestry production, soil depreciation deducted from agricultural value added and fishery depreciation from gross fishery production, generating respective net product components. There remained a puzzle, however: the net forestry product series is negative for most of the years during the period 1978–87.

Mexico: the Van Tongeren et al. (1993) study was conducted by the UN Statistical Office, the World Bank and the National Institute of Statistics, Geography and Informatics of Mexico. The SEEA was constructed and the EDP measures were obtained. These indicated a drop of about 11–15 percent from the NDP when resource depletion and environmental damages were accounted.

The Netherlands: one of the studies of the Statistics Department (Hueting and Bosch, 1994) aimed to measure sustainable national income by valuing environmental losses as the cost of achieving sustainable use of the environment.

Papua New Guinea: some of the most detailed studies on integrated economic and social accounting were conducted by Bartelmus et al. (1993). These formed trend setters for related exercises in a few other countries.

USA: one of the major exercises was undertaken by the Bureau of Economic Analysis (US Department of Commerce, 1994) of the Commerce Department. The Integrated Economic and Environmental Satellite Account (ISEEA) was prepared to examine the effects of changing patterns of demand on natural resource use. Questions relating to economic return to mineral stocks were addressed, along with environmental protection expenditure components.

Sources: Adapted and summarized from Stockhammer et al. (1997), Hamilton and Lutz (1996), and Bartelmus et al. (1994).

● 6.4 INTEGRATED ECONOMIC AND ENVIRONMENTAL ACCOUNTING (IEEA) ●

This methodology owes much to the UN Statistical Office, although many institutions, especially the World Bank, also played significant roles in its development. The objectives of IEEA may be summarized thus (Bartelmus, 1992):

● Segregation and elaboration of all environment-related flows and stocks of traditional accounts
The segregation of all flows and stocks of assets, related to expenditure for the protection or enhancement of different fields of the environment.
This enables identification of that part of the GDP that reflects the costs necessary to compensate for the negative impacts of economic growth, or the environmentally defensive expenditures.
● Linkage of physical resource accounts with monetary environmental accounts and balance sheets
Physical resource accounts cover the total stock or reserves of natural resources and changes therein, even if those resources are not (yet) affected by the economic system.
● Assessment of environmental costs and benefits
The system of integrated environmental and economic accounting (SEEA) seeks to expand and complement the existing system of national accounts (SNA) with regard to costing the use (depletion) of natural resources in production and final demand, and the changes in environmental quality, resulting from pollution and other impacts of production, consumption, and natural events, on the one hand, and environmental protection and enhancement, on the other.
● Accounting for the maintenance of tangible wealth
The concept of capital is to cover not only human-made but also natural capital. Capital formation is changed into a broader concept of capital accumulation allowing for the use/consumption and discovery of environmental assets.
● Elaboration and measurement of indicators of environmentally adjusted product and income
The consideration of the costs of depletion of natural resources and changes in environmental quality permits the calculation of an environmentally adjusted net domestic product (EDP).

The UN handbook on IEEA applies three categories of monetary valuation to environmental assets and their changes:

1   A market valuation approach with rearrangements for environmental changes in asset accounts of the conventional SNA.
2   A maintenance valuation approach which estimates the costs needed to preserve the environmental assets intact during the accounting time interval.

3 An approach which combines the market valuation methods with a contingent valuation approach to make assessment of environmental costs of environmental degradation.

The handbook emphasizes the first two approaches. Reliance on the first approach implies that environmental assets such as air, biodiversity, and watersheds are not included in the SNA economic asset accounts. The second approach caters for some accountability for environmental impacts. The costs caused are interpreted narrowly in relation to the immediate inputs (resource use) into and joint outputs (pollutants emitted) from production and consumption processes. This was supposedly done so as to maintain the closeness of these costs to the economic system, and thus their measurability. "Such valuation introduces a certain amount of inconsistency between market values and (maintenance) costs in the SEEA – an approach that is not totally alien to the SNA" (Bartelmus, 1996, p. 187).

Under the SEEA, the estimation of the stock of natural assets is the main point of departure from which environmental accounting should begin. It was argued by El-Serafy (1997) that, when current prices are used for stock valuation, and changes in stock values are reflected in the flow accounts, "the integrity of the latter is damaged, and very little environmental wisdom will be gained from such a procedure, and even less economic insight." As long as the goal of environmental accounting is to describe the state of the environment, emphasis is required on assessing the environmental stocks, not simply their economic value.

The UN handbook classified and described different types of environmental protection measures to enable defensive expenditure accounting. Although the ingredients are rather comprehensive, the levels of application of the preventive measures or incurring maintenance expenditure in effecting the same remains largely arbitrary. It is also not possible to evolve uniform norms and costs across different regions and countries, given the diversity of the systems. However, a set of marginal and average productivity indicators can be developed, with reference to which evaluation can be made, whether or not relevant optimal expenditures are being incurred, or more generally, whether or not relevant resources are being deployed to ensure preservation of environmental and ecological assets at the desirable levels. A Classification of Environmental Protection Activities (CEPA) given by the UN (1993) led to nine main categories:

1 Protection of ambient air and climate (prevention of air pollution, and treatment of exhaust gases).
2 Protection of ambient water, excluding ground water (prevention of water pollution, industrial pretreatment plants, sewage, and treatment of cooling water).
3 Prevention, collection, transport, treatment and disposal of wastes (collection, transport, treatment of waste, and prevention of waste generation).
4 Recycling of wastes and other residuals.
5 Protection of soil and ground water (decontamination of soil, and cleaning and charging of ground water).

6 Noise abatement (traffic, and industrial process noise).
7 Protection of nature and landscape (protection of species, and habitats; erosion, fire, and avalanche protection).
8 Other environmental protection measures (education, training, and administration).
9 Research and development (R&D).

The discussions thus far tend to bring us closer toward devising a set of meaningful and operationally practical indicators of SD. Some of these attempts are discussed next.

● 6.5 INDICATORS OF SD ●

The debate and application of the processes affecting sustainability and SD have made some noteworthy differences in the way institutions and individuals view the issues and sensitize themselves to the same, although much remains to be done. An important milestone in this context is the wider application of concepts in functional areas. Although marine fisheries is an important sector of the economy in select countries like Norway and Canada, it is negligible in several other countries. In the latter category, it may be adequate to confine to norms of sustainable harvesting and hence sustainability (unless quantum jumps or new initiatives are expected in the development of such sectors, thus affecting large sections of society and significant resources use). However, in the former group additional criteria of SD in relation to this sector are needed. The reason is that when an activity possesses the potential to affect a significant section of humans and resources, including levels of income and economic development, sustainability requirements may be viewed as a corollary to the SD norms.

Like fisheries, timber and forest resources play varying roles in different countries and similar reasoning may be useful in devising policies. At the global level, the International Tropical Timber Organization and the Convention on Security Cooperation in Europe (CSCE) laid down at its Conference in Helsinki 1993, five criteria for sustainable forest policy:

1 Maintaining ecological security.
2 Maintaining the continuity of timber production.
3 Ensuring an acceptable level of environmental impact.
4 Maintaining socioeconomic benefits.
5 Maintaining the contribution of the forest to global ecological cycles.

The UN initiated a number of investigations into the development of various sets of indicators of sustainability and SD (with little distinction maintained on these two categories) following the adoption of Agenda 21 at the Earth Summit in 1992. By the time of the Earth Summit Plus Five (ESPF) in 1997, a set of 134 indicators were proposed for further attention and operational implementation at the national levels; this could also facilitate monitoring progress in the implementation of various elements agreed under Agenda 21. The terminology used, partly in conjunction with the development of environmentally SD indicators at the World Bank (which undertook a broader exercise of Measures of Wealth of Nations), now needs a brief clarification.

The driving-force–state–response (DSR) framework lists the interrelated sets of "driving force," "state," and "response" factors for each indicator in the categories of economic, environmental, and institutional sets. The concept of "pressure" originally sought to be popularized – launched by the Organization for Economic Cooperation and Development (OECD) in some of its studies – was replaced by that of driving force. This set of indicator ingredients indicate human influences and activities that impact on sustainability or SD, depending on the nature of the indicator. State indicators depict the state of sustainability or SD. Finally, the response indicators indicate policy options or other responses to the state factors. Table 6.1 provides an illustrative list of indicators using the DSR framework.

It is not enough to list any economic or related indicator under the classification of indicators of SD. The following list is based on the UN Department for Policy Coordination and Sustainable Development (UNDPCSD) which provided the detailed document online around the time of the ESPF in June 1997. Most of these indicators were known in the literature decades before the debate on SD came to the fore, and it is highly doubtful if these can be genuinely claimed as indicators of SD. Some are neither indicators of sustainability (such as exports and imports) nor of development (such as total Official Development Assistance (ODA) given at country level). However, for further discussions a base list of the proposed indicators may be relevant and is given below.

This list of indicators for economic aspects of SD is provided by the UNDPCSD (1997):

- GDP per capita.
- Net investment share in GDP.
- Sum of exports and imports as a percentage of GDP.
- Environmentally adjusted net domestic product (EDP).
- Share of manufactured goods in total merchandise exports.
- Annual energy consumption.
- Share of natural-resource intensive industries in manufacturing value-added.
- Proven mineral reserves.
- Proven fossil fuel energy reserves.
- Lifetime of proven energy reserves.
- Intensity of material use.
- Share of manufacturing value-added in GDP.
- Share of consumption of renewable energy resources.
- Net resources transfer/GNP.
- Total ODA given or received as a percentage of GNP debt service/export.
- Environmental protection expenditures as a percentage of GDP.
- Amount of new or additional funding for SD.
- Capital goods imports.

Table 6.1 Indicators of environmentally sustainable development

ISSUE	Driving force	State	Response
Economic			
Production	Energy and raw material inputs	NNP	Energy and production efficiency
Public expenditure	Inflation	GNP	Savings/GNP
Per capita income	Population growth	Asset and income inequality	Safety nets
Quality of labor	Wages	Education and human capita	Public and private expertise on skill formation
Urbanization	Rural urban migration	Urban population	Land-use planning; rural development
Housing	Population growth	Quality of housing and homelessness	Public low-cost housing
Public health	Infectious diseases and mortality and morbidity	Life expectancy and DALYs	Provision of public health care
Nutrition	Malnutrition food shortages	Dietary nutrition intake	Food stamps, food subsidies, etc.
Women's status	Maternal mortality rate	Fertility rate and school enrollment	Female education and nutrition
Environmental and ecological			
Water quality	Demands for drinking water and sewerage	Access to water and its quality	Public and private provision of services
Air quality	Transport and energy demand	Particulates, CO, CH_4, SO_2, etc.	Emission control and environmental protection measures
Transport	Urbanization and growth in vehicles	Passengers and freight movements	Public transport and unleaded petrol
Climate change	GHG emissions	GHG concentrations	Sources of energy and energy-use efficiency
Stratospheric ozone	CFC and HCFC consumption	CFC concentrations	Application of Montreal Protocol
Oceans	Discharges	Pollution levels	Dumping prevention laws
Marine resources	Fish harvesting	Stocks of fish	Regulated fishing
Fossil fuels	Extraction rates	Estimated reserves	Energy-use efficiency
Metals and minerals	Extraction policies	Estimated reserves	Recycling
Forest resources	Harvesting and land use	Area and production	Afforestation and harvesting
Land soil	Erosion and land degradation	Area of degraded land	Soil conservation

Source: Adapted and improved from World Bank (1997) and (WBBCSD (1997)

- Foreign direct investments.
- Share of environmentally sound capital goods imports.
- Technical cooperation grants.

Several institutions within and outside the UN system came up with varying lists of indicators, some with greater merit than the above: the United Nations Development Programme's (UNDP) list of a core set of indicators for SD is more useful in their linkup of the DSR mechanisms. Scope for improvement exists, however. For example, the driving force to combat poverty is not simply and only the unemployment rate. Also important are asset and income distribution policies, including labor policies – especially policies that address issues of the minimum wage, unemployment insurance and social safety net components.

Based on the definition of SD in chapter 3, we need to ensure that the ecological system characteristics underlying the uninterrupted provision of nature's services and economic activities are appropriately recognized. Proxies for ensuring the existence and stability of the ecosystem, in terms of resilience features, need to be developed and monitored. Symptoms regarding any loss of ecosystem resilience are not necessarily reflected in the economic factors, as explained in chapters 3 and 4. It is a relatively easier task to identify some of the symptoms of unsustainability or loss of resilience than to draw up a list of indicators which have a direct bearing on the phenomena governing SD. Since non-declining ecological capital is one of the prerequisites of SD, a comprehensive accounting and valuation of ecological capital is relevant in the development of a set of indicators for SD.

These are some of key factors which subsume the specific indicators given in table 6.1:

- An increase in the global warming potential (GWP) (both direct and indirect).
- A net increase in the emissions of the GHGs.
- The extent of deforestation, especially of tropical and rainforests.
- Changes in the stratospheric ozone loss.
- Changes in the rainfall patterns – geographically and seasonally.
- Changes in the public health features like in the incidence of skin cancer, epidemics, and age-structure-adjusted demand for health services for the upkeep of human well-being (physical and mental).
- Extent of the loss of biological species – animal and botanical.
- Changes in the incidence of weather extremities.

These constitute the overarching indicators of SD; these are necessary but not sufficient to ensure SD. When augmented by the list in table 6.1, the list is likely to be comprehensive enough to depict a set of both the necessary as well as the sufficient features governing SD.

None of the above factors are included for "cosmetic reasons"; these are essential foundations for SD. These are also the key ingredients for the continuity of a "rich" and "diverse life" on this planet – as was perhaps the intention of the Higher Authority, i.e. God.

● 6.6 CONCLUSIONS ●

The role and limitations of conventional national income accounting need a review for greater comprehension and integration with development activities, and this integration gives a perspective on current and future development possibilities. Environmental accounting is not necessarily the fancy or wish of environmentalists. This is a fairly normal requirement based on economic reasoning. The stronger stipulations of environmental concern are not entirely connected with this exercise, as those value judgments form a further step wherever found relevant, and are not a prerequisite for the integrated approach. It is also necessary to expand the measures developed so far, to include the contribution of technological and social factors insofar as some of these are not reflected in the production and accounting systems. Considerable additional efforts are needed by nations to meet the new information requirements in attending to the environmental accounting exercises. The role of political and other institutional factors remains relevant in this exercise.

Indicators of SD have been developed in the 1990s. Most of these are centered around traditional economic indicators. Their application, and integration with economic and environmental decision making, has not begun in many countries and international institutions. Refinement of these indicators remains a continuous exercise for further development and sustainability of concepts of SD. One of the broad principles of environmental accounting which is not fully explored in transnational issues relates to the requirement that the social costs of anthropogenic influences be sought to be internalized as private costs at eligible levels of entities. When this is carried out, these entities are also the constellation of institutions which should depict appropriate losses in their measures of economic welfare so as to account for these environmental costs. As an illustration of the relevance of deployment of the broad principle, consider the emissions of GHGs or other pollutants. These continue to remain as externalities. Appropriate accounting of environmental losses at sub-global levels is not yet fully appreciated. Such an environmental accounting would enable assessment of incidence of costs and benefits, as well as devising win–win solutions in a cost-effective manner. A derivative of this could include global emissions trading mechanisms, or other policy strategies.

Review Exercises

1 If environmental externalities need to be internalized for proper cost accounting, how are these reflected in the revised methods for NNP as advanced by the measure in UN SEEA?
2 List the indicators which link the features of the ecosystem resilience, economic growth, and sustainable development.
3 Examine the validity, if any, of this statement: integrated economic and environmental accounting (IEEA) does not recognize the role of social capital and

knowledge and, thus, any calculation of sustainable income on this basis can be an underestimate of the true sustainable income.

4   The following is an extract from the UN Department for Policy Coordination and Sustainable Development online document *Indicators of Sustainable Development* (UNDPCSD, 1997), released around the time of the ESPF (June 97). The document contained several segments, each related to a theme or a chapter of the Agenda 21 of the 1992 Earth Summit; some of the segments are complete and some are incomplete. The specifications contained in the document are rather significant both for what they state and what they do not! Some of the incomplete segments are stated below. Fill in the blanks (shown here as question marks) and also review the contents of the indicators in each segment for possible improvements (surely, there are many!). The chapter numbers given below refer to their original numbers in Agenda 21.

Chapter 3: Combating poverty
Driving force indicators: Unemployment rate
State indicators: Head count index of poverty
                                              Poverty gap index
                                              Squared poverty gap index
                                              Gini index of income inequality
                                              Ratio of average female wage to male wage
Response indicators: ?
Chapter 5: Demographic dynamics and sustainability
Driving forces indicators: Population growth rate
                                              Net migration rate
                                              Total fertility rate
State indicators: Population density
Response indicators: ?
Chapter 16: Environmentally sound management of biotechnology
Driving force indicators: ?
State indicators: ?
Response indicators: R&D expenditure for biotechnology
                                              Existence of national biosafety regulations or
                                              guidelines
Chapter 37: National mechanisms and international cooperation for capacity-building in developing countries
Driving force indicators: ?
State indicators: ?
Response indicators: ?
Chapter 38: International institutional arrangements
Driving force indicators: ?
State indicators: ?
Response indicators: ?
Chapter 39: International legal instruments and mechanisms
Driving force indicators: ?
State indicators: ?
Response indicators: Ratification of global agreements
                                              Implementation of ratified global agreements

Chapter 40: Information for decision making
Driving force indicators: ?
State indicators: Main telephone lines per 100 inhabitants
                              Access to information
Response indicators: Programmes for national environmental statistics

References

Aronsson, T. and Lofgren, K. G. (1996) Social accounting and welfare measurement in a growth model with human capital. *Scandinavian Journal of Economics*, 98(2), 185–201.

Bartelmus, P. (1992) Accounting for sustainable growth and development. *Structural Change and Economic Dynamics*, 3(2), 241–60.

Bartelmus, P. (1996) Green accounting for sustainable development. In P. H. May and R. S. da Motta (eds), *Pricing the Planet – Economic Analysis for Sustainable Development*. New York: Columbia University Press, 180–96.

Bartelmus, P. et al. (1994) Environmental accounting – an operational perspective. In I. Serageldin and A. Steer (eds), *Valuing the Environment*, ESD Proceedings Series #2. Washington, DC: The World Bank, 159–84.

Bartelmus, P., Lutz, E. and Schweinfest, S. (1993) Integrated environmental and economic accounting – a case study for Papua New Guinea. In Lutz (1993, 108–43).

Bom, A. (1992) *Development of Natural Resource Accounts – Physical and Monetary Accounts for Crude Oil and Natural Gas Reserves in Alberta*. Ottawa: Statistics Canada.

Brandon, C. and Hommann, K. (1995) *The Cost of Inaction – Valuing the Economy-wide Cost of Environmental Degradation in India*. Washington, DC: Asia Environment Division, The World Bank.

Cobb, C. and Cobb, J. B. (1994) *The Green National Product – A Proposed Index of Sustainable Economic Welfare*. New York: University Press of America.

Daly, H. (1996) *Beyond Growth – the Economics of Sustainable Development*. Boston: Beacon Press.

Dasgupta, P. (1991) The environment as a commodity. In D. Helm (ed.), *Economic Policy Towards the Environment*. Oxford and Boston: Blackwell.

Dasgupta, P. and Maler, K. G. (1994) *Poverty, Institutions, and the Environmental Resource Base*. Environment Paper #9. Washington, DC: The World Bank.

El-Serafy, S. (1997) Green accounting and economic policy. *Ecological Economics*, 21, 217–29.

Hamilton, K. and Lutz, E. (1996) *Green National Accounts – Policy Uses and Empirical Experience*. Environment Department Paper #39. Washington, DC: The World Bank.

Harrison, A. (1989) Introducing natural captial into the SNA. In Y. A. Ahmed, S. El-Serafy, and E. Lutz (eds), *Environmental Accounting for Sustainable Development*. Washington, DC: The World Bank, 19–25.

Hartwick, J. (1990) Natural resources, national accounting and economic depreciation. *Journal of Public Economics*, 43(3), 291–304.

Hueting, R. (1989) Correcting national income for environmental losses – towards a practical solution. In Y. Ahmad, S. El-Serafy and E. Lutz (eds), *Environmental Accounting for Sustainable Development*. Washington, DC: The World Bank, 32–9.

Hueting, R. and Bosch, P. (1994) *Sustainable National Income in the Netherlands*. Voorburgh: The Netherlands Central Bureau of Statistics.

Hueting, R., Bosch, P. R. and de Boer, B. (1992) *Methodology for the Calculation of Sustainable National Income*. Voorburg: The Netherlands Central Bureau of Statistics.

Hulten, C. R. (1992) Accounting for the wealth of nations – the net versus gross output controversy and its ramifications. *Scandinavian Journal of Economics*, 94, S9–S24.

Lofgren, K. G. (1992) Comment on C. R. Hulten, "Accounting for the wealth of nations." *Scandinavian Journal of Economics*, 94, S25–S28.

Lozada, G. A. (1995) Resource depletion, national income accounting, and the value of optimal dynamic programs. *Resource and Energy Economics*, 17(2), 137–54.

Lutz, E. (ed.) (1993) *Toward Improved Accounting for the Environment*. Washington, DC: The World Bank.

Nijkamp, P. (1977) *Theory and Application of Environmental Economics*. Amsterdam: North-Holland Co.

Nordhaus, W. (1997) *How should we measure Sustainable Income?* Discussion Paper. New Haven: Cowles Foundation/Yale University.

Nordhaus, W. and Tobin, J. (1972) *Economic Growth*. New York: National Bureau of Economic Research.

Rao, P. K. (1998) *Is Net National Product an Indicator of Sustainability?* (in press).

Serageldin, I. (1996) *Sustainability and the Wealth of Nations, ESD Monograph No. 5*. Washington, DC: The World Bank.

Smith, P. (1994) The Canadian National Accounts Environmental Component, Meeting on National Accounts and the Environment, London. Cited in Hamilton and Lutz (1996).

Solorzano, R., de Camino, R., Woodward, R., Tosi, J., Watson, V., Vasquez, A., Villalobos, C., Jimenes, J., Repetto, R. and Cruz, W. (1991) *Accounts Overdue – Natural Resource Depreciation in Costa Rica*. Washington, DC: World Resources Institute.

Solow, R. (1994) An almost practical step toward sustainability. In *Assigning Economic Value to Natural Resources*. Washington, DC: National Research Council, 19–29.

Steer, A. and Lutz, E. (1994) Measuring environmentally sustainable development. In I. Serageldin and A. Steer (eds), *Making Development Sustainable – From Concepts to Action*. Washington, DC: The World Bank (Environmentally Sustainable Division Monograph Series), 17–20.

Stockhammer, E., Hochreiter, H., Obermayr, B. and Steiner, K. (1997) The index of sustainable economic welfare as an alternative to GDP in measuring economic welfare. *Ecological Economics*, 21, 19–34.

Tinbergen, J. and Hueting, R. (1991) GNP and market prices – correction of national income based on sustainable use of environment. In UNESCO *Environmentally Sustainable Economic Development – Building on Brundtland*. Paris: UNESCO, 51–7.

UN (1993) *Integrated Environmental and Economic Accounting*. Annex III. New York: United Nations.

UNDPCSD (UN Department for Policy Coordination and Sustainable Development) (1997) *Indicators for Sustainable Development*. Online document.

US Department of Commerce (Bureau of Economic Analysis) (1994) Accounting for mineral resources; and integrated economic environment analysis. *Survey of Current Business*, 74(4), April, 33–72.

Van Tongeren, J., Schweinfest, S., Lutz, E., Gomez huna, M. and Martin, G. (1993) Integrated Environmental and Economic Accounting – A Case Study for Mexico. In Lutz (1993).

Vellinga, N. and Withagen, C. (1996) On the concept of green national income. *Oxford Economic Papers*, 48, 499–514.

WCED (World Commission on Environment and Development) (1987) *Our Common Future*. New York: Oxford University Press.

Weitzman, M. L. (1997) Sustainability and technical progress. *Scandinavian Journal of Economics*, 99(1), 1–13.

World Bank (1997) *Expanding the Measure of Wealth – Indicators of Environmentally Sustainable Development*. Washington, DC: The World Bank.

Zolotas, X. (1981) *Economic Growth and Declining Social Welfare*. Athens: Bank of Greece.

chapter outline

● CHAPTER 7 ●

Poverty and the Environment

Poverty and the Environment

It would be too bad if sustainability were fashionable not despite its vagueness – but because of its vagueness.
Robert M. Solow

● 7.1 INTRODUCTION ●

The concept of sustainable development (SD) ceases to make a meaningful contribution to the quality of life on the planet if it is devoid of the perspective of the processes leading to poverty and resource deprivation. The evolution of contemporary society has two continuing salient features:

● A highly skewed distribution of assets, resources, and property control;
● Widespread poverty, extensive and severe in most countries.

An examination of the causes of poverty suggests the critical role of certain factors: person-made or manufactured capital, ecological capital, human capital, cultural and social capital. The relative roles of these components of capital vary from one region to another. The persistence and deterioration of the poverty problem is rooted deep in the problems of inequitable initial asset distribution across different sections of the community, and lopsided public policies affecting property rights and property entitlements. Most of these features are distinguishable at the levels of individual countries and communities. However, international transmission of influences also adversely affects the above features. This is effected at the national level via the terms of trade, mechanisms of global financial lending, and a number of geopolitical factors. Various policies of taxation, wage compensation, and other entitlements for labor or other sections of society constitute a dynamic set of influences affecting socioeconomic inequities. These factors need to be juxtaposed on the initial or fixed distribution of assets – like rights to land and other property – if a meaningful and jurisprudential economic approach is to be devised. Poverty is but a byproduct of these configurations, in addition to the effects of the institutional alignments like those of the law and power structure. Thus, the ramifications for the poverty phenomena are to be explored locally, regionally, and internationally. The complex interaction of environment and poverty continues to merit serious attention in this context.

Properly devised policies aimed at helping the poor to accumulate productive assets like schooling, health, and nutrition constitute important bases for the attainment of higher economic growth, as argued by Bruno et al. (1996). The report of the World Commission on Environment and Development (WCED, 1987, p. 8) stated that SD requires meeting people's basic needs and providing the "opportunity to fulfill their aspirations for a better life. A world in which poverty is endemic will always be prone to ecological and other catastrophes." The report emphasized several types of inequities that must be reduced for this purpose. At the international and national levels, there is an urgent need to ensure that the poor do enjoy their fair share of global resources, and equitable costs and benefits of resource use need to be apportioned in regard to the ecological system. Breaking the poverty trap requires much greater provision of resources for the progress and welfare of women and children in most countries, developing as well as developed. This policy would also be effective in curbing the adverse environmental impact of the poverty syndrome.

The causes and ramifications of poverty are to be examined from a number of perspectives, including anthropological, political, and institutional. This chapter is confined to a select few issues within the context of SD. Trends in poverty over the years are assessed in the next section. Subsequently, the processes affecting the cyclical dependency of poverty and environment, and also the links between prosperity and environment, are discussed. Population expansion and high total fertility rates are seen as the byproducts of poverty. Gender discrimination is a root cause of the greater incidence of poverty in women; this aspect exacerbates environmental problems. These aspects are examined later. The links between poverty, the efficiency of rural energy use, and the quality of the environment are explored. The roles of public expenditure policies, and the provision of subsidies for the poor, are examined with a view to assessing their impacts on the phenomena of poverty and environmental deterioration. The politics and economics of micro and macro aspects of poverty alleviation are examined in the last section on political economy.

● 7.2 TRENDS IN POVERTY ●

Some statistical highlights may be relevant to begin this discussion. About 1.3 billion people (constituting about 30 percent of population in developing countries) consumed less than the equivalent of $1 in goods and services a day, and about 3 billion lived on $2 a day in 1993; in the same year about 9 million children under the age of five died of avoidable causes in the developing countries (World Bank, 1998). The total population, which consumed less than $1 a day for the year 1987, was 1.2 billion people. About half a billion people lack access to safe drinking water, and about a billion lack access to sanitation. Infant and child mortality rates in developing countries are five times higher, maternal mortality rate is about 14 times higher.

Some estimates of changes in poverty levels were made by the World Bank (1996). Purchasing power parity (PPP) indices based on consumption were used to convert the $1 per person per day standard into local currency. In the above estimate of a population living below $1 a day, the number does not include the poor in developed countries. About half a billion poor are located in South Asia, with a similar number in the rest of Asia. South Asia led the increase in the number of poor, whereas the rest of Asia contributed to a drop in the numbers during this period. The total number of the poor constituted 30.1 percent of the world's population in 1987, and this number reduced marginally to 29.4 percent in 1993. Sub-Saharan Africa, and Latin America and the Caribbean, showed an increase in the percentages of poor per total population during the same period: from 38.5 to 39.1 percent in the former, and from 22 to 23.5 percent in the latter. Every fourth person, in the regions of East Asia and the Pacific, Latin America and the Caribbean, was qualified for inclusion under the poverty norm. The corresponding figures for South Asia and Sub-Saharan Africa indicated that about 40 percent belonged to this classification.

The UN Development Programme documentation (UNDP, 1996) on global prosperity, and poverty issues and trends, observed that the world has become more polarized, and the gulf between the poor and rich of the world has widened. Of the $23 trillion global gross domestic product (GDP) in 1993, $18 trillion was in the industrial countries; the developing countries, consisting of 80 percent of the total population, claim the other $5 trillion. The poorest 20 percent of the world's people have experienced their share of global income decline from 2.3 percent to 1.4 percent in the past 30 years. Meanwhile, the share of the richest 20 percent rose from 70 to 85 percent of global income. This led to a doubling of the ratio of the shares of the richest and the poorest in their incomes – from 31:1 to 61:1. The assets of the 358 billionaires (in US dollar magnitudes) exceeded the combined annual incomes of countries with 45 percent of the world's people. During the past three decades, the proportion of people enjoying per capita income growth of at least 5 percent a year more than doubled, from 12 percent to 27 percent; while the proportion of those experiencing negative growth went up from 5 percent to 18 percent.

In the context of North–South economic relations and globalization efforts linking economies, the South Commission (1990) put forward the following arguments:

- Severe income inequalities, resulting in particular patterns of demand for industrial goods, contribute to environmental stress in many countries of the South.
- Such income maldistribution is accompanied by the adoption by the rich of the consumption patterns of the North.

- The latter leads to increasing demand for products whose manufacture or use are highly energy-intensive and have impact on the levels of atmospheric pollution.

These identified problems have to be addressed both by domestic authorities as well as global institutions. The respective national governments have the powers and obligation to work toward a just and equitable society. The inequality problem applies within each of the developing countries, and causes economic and environmental externalities. These are in terms of forcing abject poverty on a large segment of society, and rapid depletion of the ecological resources.

These glaring disparities, which negate the survival interests of the poor, do not augur well for a just and equitable society. Such a background will remain a structural impediment to the design and effectiveness of policies and programs aimed at SD.

Rural Poverty

The vast majority of people in the developing world live in rural areas; significant poverty is observed in these regions. Sectoral and geographic decomposition of the incidence of poverty is useful for maintaining proper focus to mitigate the interdependent problems of poverty and environmental degradation. The International Fund for Agriculture and Development projections (IFAD, 1995), based on the assumption of an increase in poverty at the same rate of growth as the expected population growth rate (1.9 percent per annum), indicate that the total number of rural poor in Asia alone will swell to 764 million by the year 2000, and to 922 million by the year 2010. Countries in Asia with more than 50 percent of their rural population in poverty included Afghanistan, Bangladesh, Bhutan, Laos, Nepal, Papua New Guinea, The Philippines, Vietnam, and Western Samoa. Even trends in land ownership and asset holding have undergone change for the worse between the 1960s and the mid-1980s in some of the countries where the landless poor seek hope mainly through land holding. The examples include (Jazairy et al., 1992): Bangladesh, Nepal, and Pakistan.

One of the lessons of the development experience was summarized in the UNDP's Human Development Report (1996, p. 4): "Development that perpetuates today's inequalities is neither sustainable nor worth sustaining." It is important to attend to existing distributions of entitlements – distributions of income and wealth "that are a function not of nature but of law" (Sunstein, 1997). Extreme deprivation denies people the opportunity to form preferences and beliefs that lead to good lives; but this applies if and when such deprivation allows the physical existence of the deprived. Surely, these elements do not contribute to sustainable human development. Hence there is a need for greater efforts at the national and international levels to eradicate poverty while addressing the problems of the environment.

The next section examines the interdependencies of poverty, prosperity, inequality, and the conservation of environmental assets.

● 7.3 POVERTY, PROSPERITY, AND THE ENVIRONMENT ●

Any deterioration in environmental assets affects the poor adversely. Living conditions with much greater exposure to air and water pollution, poor hygiene and sanitation causes undernourishment, which decreases the potential for educational attainment, and hence brings about low human capital, high morbidity, inefficient utilization of time, and low productivity of labor. Such are some of the effects of the environment on the poor. Conversely, poverty affects the environment in several ways, mostly adversely. Behaviorally, the poor tend to visualize relatively constrained time horizons and to deploy heavy discounting of time or future. This is undesirable from the viewpoint of optimal resource management in the long run for the ecosystem, if only the poor could afford to do otherwise. Poor individuals tend to be governed by their essential survival priorities. Their perception of the risk management options tends to exacerbate any potential costs to themselves and to the ecosystem. Hence, the reduction of abject poverty is a collective responsibility at the society level. A just society (which is expressed in contemporary terms and with current concerns) and/or a society with a futuristic outlook can ill-afford continued poverty. Robert Solow's assertion may be stated here: the case for reducing contemporary inequality is as strong as for worrying about the uncertain status of future generations (UNDP, 1996, p. 16).

Poverty and Environmental Feedbacks

Sustained economic growth leads to decreasing incremental per capita emissions of pollution after a certain critical point (under some circumstances and institutional provisions, see chapter 3). This phenomenon varies significantly from one economic system to another. The inverted U-relationship (IUR), as discussed in chapter 3, is neither universal in its applicability to all pollutants and countries. Also, the existence of the critical point is not good enough to avert potential environmental crisis of global proportions. For example, if the "turning point" occurs after about a four-fold increase in greenhouse gas (GHG) emissions and a significant increase in global warming (and all its attendant adverse consequences), what good is it to wait for such a disastrous scenario? In fact, most of the studies on turning points are oblivious to the implications of the consequences whenever the linkages between economic growth and environmental pollution are estimated. We need relevant feedback mechanisms which link economic growth with environmental degradation. This is required not only for specific emissions, but also for their interactive effects with all other environmental features. In such a framework, the estimates of the critical levels are likely to be lower or higher, depending on the changes in production and consumption patterns and in the adoption of technology in the production of goods, services, and environmental products. Such a point of inflection may not even exist. The assertion of Arrow et al. (1995) that the IUR are "less likely to hold whenever the feedback effects of resource stocks are significant" is likely to be an understatement in the larger context of the global ecosystem.

A more useful approach to the analysis of interdependencies, other than a comprehensive economic model using a dynamic general equilibrium analysis, is to hypothesize and estimate the generalized IPAT model on the lines of Dietz and Rosa (1997), as discussed in chapter 3. An alternative model, which reflects the effects of policy changes on poverty and economic inequalities, and their impact on the environment, is suggested at the end of this section.

The relationships between changes in income levels and their environmental impact are fraught with the same limitations as in interpreting the IUR. However, the generalized IPAT model, and the new model below, allow for more parameters. Thus, it is possible to isolate their relative roles, especially the role of changes in the technology factor. These models, formulated mainly for estimation purposes, could illuminate only when based on past experiences. The effects considered in the models do not differentiate changes in institutional and policy factors. These factors are not necessarily endogenous to the other changes considered in the estimation. In other words, policy measures may have to be based on a number of other factors, in addition to these models.

Poverty and Common Property Resources

Environmental damage tends to affect the poor particularly severely; they rely heavily on fragile natural resources for their livelihood, and returns on natural capital are greater than on their human capital. Polluted areas are cheap or free, and the poor reside there. Because of their status as squatters, access to safe drinking water and sanitation is usually denied.

Regarding poverty and deforestation, lessons from Mexico and Indonesia indicate that export-oriented tree crops play an important role in deforestation relative to subsistence-oriented shifting cultivation. The links between undernourishment, destitution, and an erosion of the rural common-property resource base are close and subtle. They have been explored analytically by Dasgupta (1993, ch. 16). A typical case study of state regulated forest policy is given in box 7.1. This provides a few lessons of experience in the forest preservation mechanism and institutional control in Indonesia. Clearly, a program for the control of forest resources cannot be effective unless the forest-dependent local population is provided with alternate means for their survival. The case study is not an isolated one; a number of similar configurations apply in many countries with local populations heavily dependent on forest resources. Poorer sections of society in the developing countries tend to remain extractive users of the common property resources like fuelwood and water; they have a much higher stake in preserving them; see also Parikh (1998). If the conditions governing their choices enable them, they tend to preserve the same so as to extract the resources sustainably. However, this argument presumes the relative fixedness of the location or neighborhood for the habitat and survival of the poor. By the nature of fluctuating demand for labor, many poor are highly mobile; only some farm labor may be stationary in the villages. This feature brings an added dimension to the role of the poor in preserving the common property resources or behaving as effective stakeholders.

BOX 7.1 The poor (people) and the rich (forests)

Forest resources affect both stock and flow externalities in their support for the continuity in the provision of most of the ecosystem services, and in providing a natural sink for CO_2. These externalities are, in effect, subsidies from the forests' host countries to the rest of the world (especially large emitters of GHGs). Often, this is afforded with the cooperation (coerced or willful) of the local communities, especially the rural poor. These poor forego the avenues of income generation, available in principle, from exploiting the forests. Admittedly, the forests are not owned by these poor, but the alignments of institutions and property rights led to a denial of alternate opportunities in the vicinity of their own habitat. The rent seekers who exploit them (usually with the connivance of the state machinery) do not own the forest either. The latter contribute to deforestation, and the former are sometimes the tools in this process.

The prevalence of acute asset holding inequities and poverty causes several problems for social, economic, and ecological sustainability. The effects of the interface between various governing features, unabated rural poverty, and forestry resource preservation was ably documented by Peluso (1992) for a case study in Indonesia. The efficacy of the administrative enforcement of various provisions for preserving forest resources is usually weak in many developing countries. The shadow price of resources to the heavily forest-dependent population remains at very high levels, in the absence of other avenues for income generation. The survival of the population itself would be at stake if they were to obey the semi-feudal laws. In such a context, there is a clear conflict between the needs of the poor and the requirements for sustaining forest resources. This can be alleviated with the provision of public programs which enhance productive employment opportunities, and/or, of innovative rotatory harvesting and replanting methods for gainful tapping of forest resources (without leading to fragmentation of the forest). If such alternatives do not complement state policies for forest preservation, neither poverty is diminished nor are forests preserved, but some undeserving elements usurp the resources. Peluso (1992) concluded that "the state's own control policies have pushed forest villagers away from the state and toward state-defined 'illegal' alternatives for forest land use and forest species disposal . . ." Phenomena like these lead to the result that state policies fail to ameliorate forest degradation and exacerbate poverty among forest-dependent communities.

Common property resources at the local level include such assets as community forests, irrigation tanks, green pastures, rivulets, watersheds, rivers or tank banks and bunds, playground or other recreational facilities, and informal community centers. These assets contribute toward a variety of goods and services for human well-being and sustainability of resources. Examples include: minor forest products and firewood, water, fish, drought period fall back fiber and animal fodder, biomass, and additional crop production possibilities leading to generation of supplemental incomes.

In an empirical study, it was assessed that the extent of household dependence on common property resources in dry regions of India during late 1980s varied from about 17–23 percent of the total income for the poor; the corresponding numbers for the non-poor were much lower: 1–3 percent (Jodha, 1995). Jodha (1986) used data from over 80 villages in 21 dry districts, from seven states in India, to estimate that, among poor families, the proportion of income based directly on common-property resources is for the most part in the range of 15–25 percent; see also Jodha (1990). This constitutes a significant proportion. Moreover, as sources of income, they are often complementary to private-property resources. These are mainly the following: labor, milch and draft animals, cultivation of land and crops, common agricultural tools – e.g. ploughs, harrows, levelers, and hoes – fodder-cutting and rope-making machines, and seeds. Common property resources also provide the rural poor with partial protection in times of unusual economic stress. For the landless people, common property may be the only nonhuman asset at their disposal. A number of resources (such as fuelwood and water for home use, berries and nuts, medicinal herbs, resin and gum) are often the responsibility of women and children (Dasgupta and Maler, 1994). This perpetuates low productivity and poverty, since poor children cannot afford to equip themselves with education and skills.

Poverty and Fertility

In addition to economic underdevelopment in many of the developing countries, a combination of levels of poverty and total fertility rates (number of births per household) are among the most important contributors to environmental and societal underdevelopment. Poverty and high fertility rates have vicious feedback linkages, each feeding into the other. The question why poorer families persist in having more births is addressed by many investigators; see, for example, Dasgupta (1995). Tables 7.1 and 7.2, based on the information from the World Development Report 1997, suggest the influence of high infant mortality rates on high magnitudes of total fertility and population growth rates. The phenomenon of high total fertility rates is analogous to the decision models involving precautionary savings by responsible individuals. Hedged against the expected mortality factor (or an equivalent risk-averse behavior), the resulting expected number of children is usually greater than in societies where the risk perception about infant mortality is not as significant. It is not even illiteracy that seems to be the critical factor leading to fertility decisions, except when it acts via income and private healthcare factors. The data also indicate the following:

- The role of high income levels, which correspond with low infant mortality rates.
- High levels of skill and human capital ingredients, which result in low magnitudes of total fertility rates, and low population growth rates.

Table 7.1 Poverty and total fertility

Country	Per capita GNP $	Infant mortality rate (IMR)	Population growth rate	Total fertility rate (TFR)
Niger	270	320	3.3	7.1
Angola	410	292	3.3	6.7
Sierra Leone	180	284	3	6.1
Mozambique	80	275	2.5	6.1
Guinea-Bissau	250	227	2	5.4
Guinea	550	219	1.4	6.6
Malawi	170	219	2.5	6.7
Liberia	450	216	3.2	6.3
Mali	250	210	3	6.6
Gambia	320	213	2.3	5.2
Somalia	120	211	3.9	7
Zambia	400	203	2.5	5.5
Chad	180	152	2.8	5.5
Ethiopia	100	195	3.2	7
Mauritania	460	195	2.5	5
Bhutan	420	189	2.8	5.9
Nigeria	260	191	2.8	6

Notes: GNP is for the year 1995. Population growth is estimated for the period 1995–2000. IMR is for the year 1995 and TFR is an estimate for the period 1995–2000. Both IMR and TFR were based on the 1996 Revision of data. IMR refers to child mortality under 5 years, per 1,000 live births. TFR indicates the average number of children that would be born if all women (of the specific country) lived through to the end of their childbearing years
Sources: Column 1: World Bank (1997b); Columns 2 and 4: UN Population Division (1999); Column 3: UNICEF (1997)

These aspects should be important enough to influence public policy on poverty reduction and population stabilization in an integrated manner, thus addressing some of the concerns of SD. It makes sense to view poverty as the single most important impediment to attaining the objectives of SD in a cost-effective manner. When population and other ingredients in the IPAT framework are taken together, the costs of intervention tend to be greater in poorer societies than in richer ones. At this point, it may be useful to view the high population growth countries as demographic (and to that extent partly environmental) free-riders affecting the features of SD.

Rural poverty and food insecurity are closely linked. About 800 million people in developing countries face chronic undernutrition, and almost 200 million children suffer from protein or energy deficiencies. By the year 2030, the world's population will have grown by another 3 billion people, thus further stretching the world's food resources. Ensuring adequate and affordable food supplies, through implementation of the commitments of the 1996 World Food

Table 7.2   Prosperity and total fertility

Country	Per capita GNP US $	Population growth rate	Infant mortality rate (IMR)	Total fertility rate (TFR)
Sweden	23,730	0.3	5	1.8
Finland	20,580	0.3	5	1.8
Singapore	26,730	1.5	6	1.8
Japan	39,640	0.2	6	1.5
Denmark	29,890	0.2	7	1.8
Germany	27,510	0.3	7	1.3
Ireland	14,710	0.2	7	1.8
Switzerland	40,630	0.7	7	1.5
UK	18,700	0.1	7	1.7
Austria	26,890	0.6	7	1.4
Canada	19,380	0.9	8	1.6
Norway	31,250	0.4	8	1.9
Netherlands	24,000	0.5	8	1.6
Italy	19,020	0	8	1.2
Australia	18,720	1.1	8	1.9
Korea Republic	9,700	0.9	9	1.8
France	22,490	0.3	9	1.6
USA	26,980	0.8		2

Notes: See table 7.1
Sources: See table 7.1

Summit, will be a major challenge facing developing countries and the international community in the twenty-first century (UN, 1997). These features indicate some of the major issues to be addressed in the context of SD the next few decades.

Next only to the role of domestic government policies, programs and socio-political activities, the role of the international institutions like the World Bank remains very important in affecting poverty and the environment in many developing countries. The 1996 document on poverty reduction (World Bank, 1996) did not depict any recognition of the mutual dependence and the feed-back influences of poverty and the environment. After about half a century of experience, the World Bank (1998) believes that it would "shift from describing poverty to formulating strategies for reducing poverty . . ." and from "counting poverty-focused projects to assessing their impact on the poor." Besides, one of the key lessons which seems to have been recognized is the need to consider all costs in deciding among alternative programs in the areas of social assistance and safety net programs: administrative, transaction, and incentive costs – and to weigh them against potential benefits. Perhaps such an understanding was much overdue. Even this falls short in accounting for relevant ecological costs.

Prosperity and Environmental Feedbacks

Does prosperity cause environmental degradation? If poverty causes environmental degradation, how does prosperity also do the same? Is there some zone between the two that does not cause as much environmental degradation? The relationship between per capita incomes (assuming a somewhat egalitarian distribution of incomes and assets) and changes in the quality of the environment varies proportionately or inversely – depending on the components of the environment. The total fertility rate for high income countries (table 7.2) suggests that the high propensity to consume and contribute to the loss of environmental assets in relation to income levels of more prosperous populations are partly offset by the lower rates of total fertility and population growth. However, it is relevant to assert that developed countries tend to remain as environmental free-riders in the global context. Even though their contribution to the global demographic expansion is minimal, the net effect in terms of consumption and production systems is predominant – whether seen in terms of the volume of the GHGs and other pollution emissions.

In general, the more prosperous countries are contributing more to global environmental problems than others, both in per capita and absolute terms; data in chapter 5 supports this. The prosperity contributes more in the arena of global environmental issues like GHGs, and also in terms of urban air pollution, and other local environmental problems. Consider the following proposition.

Prosperity affects the environment in several ways, including adverse local and global aspects. To the extent that these externalities are captured by market institutions, these are internalized; to the extent that government regulations are effective, the costs of compliance are also internalized; the local environmental problems are covered to a large extent by these regulations; others not covered in the local category tend to be compensated by taxation and other fiscal measures administered by the local government institutions. The rest of the externalities are largely global and may or may not be corrected with compensation mechanisms.

The above proposition also clarifies the limited role of environmental externality-correcting taxes or related measures in affluent societies. Market failures and institutional failures (as understood in the conventional literature), by themselves, could not account for the global environmental problems.

The roles of economic inequalities and size-distribution of severe poverty tend to remain critical factors affecting the dynamics of the environmental features. In general, it appears meaningful to posit the relationship of the environmental impact E in terms of the following: size of the population under poverty S_1, size of the non-poor population S_2, the income inequality index G, level of affluence A, and the technology of production T, in a nonlinear functional form:

$$E = CS_1^a S_2^b G^c A^d T^e$$

or, equivalently, in the log-linear form

$$\log E = a\log S_1 + b\log S_2 + c\log G + d\log A + e\log T + C$$

In the above, C is a proportionality constant obtained via empirical estimation, and a, b, c, d, and e are the nonlinear influences of each of the factors. Evidently, the above specification permits a good degree of flexibility in the precise definition and measurement of the indicators for assessing S_1, G, and T. How is this different from the IPAT model or its improvements as discussed in chapter 3? This model recognizes the explicit roles of the poverty factor and the inequality factor in the determination of environmental quality. It may be hypothesized that an increase in each of these features will contribute to the deterioration in the quality of the environment or loss of the ecological capital.

The crucial role of women in poverty alleviation and environmental conservation is another important issue which has not been addressed in the above formulation and discussions. This is the focus of the next section.

● 7.4 GENDER ASPECTS ●

Poverty has a woman's face: out of the nearly 1.3 billion people living in poverty, 70 percent are women. The problems are rooted in gender disparities prevalent in a wide variety of socioeconomic systems. In Africa and Latin America, only about 10 percent of credit program beneficiaries are women. Women suffer from maternal-related morbidity and mortality. The 1990 estimates – the latest available from the UN (1998) – of maternal mortality indicate that, worldwide, the total number of deaths were about 585,000. The maternal mortality ratio (i.e. maternal deaths per 100,000 live births) varies largely in relation to levels of development: in 1990 in less developed regions, it stood at 480 and for the more developed this was 27. In addition to respiratory diseases caused by the smoke from the cooking processes in developing countries, primary school enrollment is lower and school drop out rates higher than amongst the male children in most of the developing countries.

Wage rates for women are lower, and they work longer hours than men in nearly every country. Although women support 53 percent of the total burden of work in developing countries, about half this work is unpaid household or community work. Trends in women's literacy, life expectancy, and power enhancement indicate very slow improvements. Women's contribution to the household and non-household work outside the market assessments of wages and payments accounts for about half the GDP in most countries, and goes up to two-third in some countries (UN, 1995). The dynamics of change vary with time and influence the country-specific estimates of women's unpaid contributions in terms of variations in the subsidies of the women to society as a whole. These, in turn, are usurped by the rest of the socioeconomic systems and possibly extended globally through subsidized exports to other countries.

The income accounting methods recommended by the UN in its 1990 revised SNA were skewed against proper recognition for women's contribution in nonmarket work. An application of the methods for Bangladesh revealed – see Hamid (1994) for detailed data and analysis – that only about 5 percent of the nonmarket production is recommended for inclusion in the estimates of national income. This did have the implication that 38 percent of men's work will be excluded, but when it comes to women the corresponding percentage jumps to 96 percent. The conventional estimates of GDP indicated that men contributed 75 percent and women contributed 25 percent of the total production of the country. Adjusted for valuations of nonmarket work, these percentages change to 59 and 41, respectively. Considerable wage disparities continue to prevail between male and female workers. These percentages will undergo further revisions only if the labor markets are more equitable.

Ecofeminism offers a critique of the assumptions underlying neoclassical economic theory and its consequences (McMahon, 1997; Shiva, 1992). Ecofeminists see the oppression of women and degradation of nature as theoretically, symbolically, and historically connected (Warren, 1987, 1990). According to the proponents of the theory, one can understand the ecological degradation only by addressing social inequality. Women's historical lack of legal, property and political rights, their continued embeddedness in families and the denial of market value to much of their work, expose the workings of some of the neoclassical economic models. These formulations do not include the following in their stylized facts: there exist invisible subsidies to economic activities – mainly from women and children as well as from the ecosystem.

Women and female children suffer disproportionately from poverty in terms both of over-representation among the impoverished, and of bearing the burdens of household poverty:

- In the rural areas of developing countries, the number of women in poverty has risen by nearly 50 percent in the last two decades.
- Women contributed about $11 trillion output in 1993, but this was not accounted for in the conventionally recorded output (UNDP, 1995).

However, there is still very limited understanding of the gender-related causes and consequences of poverty, or of ways to address these problems. Most poverty surveys are based on household income and do not examine the intra-household distribution of resources. Effective poverty reduction programs therefore require careful examination of the gendered division of labor and decision-making both within and outside the household (UN 1997). This may not be sufficient, however. It is not so much about the limitations on the understanding of the issues of gender inequality, as it is about the lack of coherent and conscious action at most levels within countries as well as globally influential institutions.

Energy in relation to women's work and well-being is evident in women's roles as: users of energy resources for household, subsistence and income-earning activities; producers of traditional biomass fuels and providers of "human energy" services (Cecelski, 1995). Women and children are the primary collectors of fuelwood, other household fuels, and forest products for household consumption and sale to markets. The proportions of rural women affected by fuelwood scarcity are estimated to be 60 percent in Africa, 80 percent in Asia and 40 percent in Latin America (UNDP, 1995). Time spent in fuel collection in fuel-scarce areas can range from 1–5 hrs per day per household. These costs are not reflected in any economic accounting of national income.

Women's contribution to environmental conservation is not uncommon. For recent examples, is it possible to ignore Gro Harlem Brundtland, or Rachel Carson? In an exemplary case in Kenya, the following experience is noteworthy (UN, 1997). In 1977, Kenya's first woman professor, Wangari Maathai, initiated a campaign to combat desertification and launched the Greenbelt Movement. This mobilized large numbers of women in Kenya who devised methods of participatory development to reduce soil erosion, and the conservation of soil and water as well as fuelwood. By the middle of 1990s, the movement consisted of about 50,000 members, largely from poor and illiterate families. The movement has thus far planted over 10 million trees, and owns about 1,500 tree nurseries.

The best examples of success in poverty reduction and also efficient banking involving micro-credit are contributed by women's groups. The Grameen Bank of Bangladesh is illustrative of this. The bank did not initially focus on lending to women when it started functioning on a small scale in 1980, but its experience over the years with credit transactions proved that reliance on women, as borrowers and repayers of loans, was prudent. In the 1990s, about 90 percent of the bank's customers are women. The reduction of poverty was significant: only about 20 percent of members of the Grameen Bank schemes were still considered poor, relative to about 56 percent in comparable non-banking populations. A variety of income-generating activities such as weaving, poultry, and horticulture are undertaken by participating women borrowers to repay loans. Family planning is regularly emphasized. The activities have led to an increased use of contraceptives, and it has also been observed that the credit schemes have an independent effect on the demand for fertility regulation and control (Amin et al., 1994).

Similar to the Grameen Bank, in Malawi the Malawi Muzdi Fund was set up in the early 1990s for lending to small farmers. Just as in the Grameen case, the need for collateral was replaced by social collateral – group guarantees for loan repayment. About 70 percent of the members are women. They are reportedly showing promise for enhanced activities (IFAD, 1995).

There has been no dearth of policy declarations at several global summits in recent years involving the heads of governments. A few recent assertions are briefly recalled below. The UN Conference on Environment and Development (UNCED) in its Rio Declaration Principle 20 stated in 1992: "Women have a vital role in environmental management and development. Their full participation is therefore essential to achieve sustainable development." Women and children have much higher exposure to indoor air pollution which causes respiratory lung disease, amongst other problems. These concerns were reflected in 1995 at the Fourth World Women's Conference in Beijing. These led to the Beijing Platform for Action (ch. c, para. 92 "Women and Health"; ch. k, para. 256 "Women and

Environment") which sought to integrate gender issues in policies and programs for SD. The World Summit for Social Development held in Copenhagen in 1995 focused on poverty and SD. A broad consensus sought to create an economic environment to promote more equitable access to resources and SD. The Copenhagen Declaration (ch. III, para. 50) included suggestions for patterns of growth that maximize employment creation, encouraging the utilization of renewable energy based on local employment-intensive resources, particularly in rural areas. The summit placed energy concerns within the productive realm of sustainable livelihoods, especially for rural development.

The Organization for Economic Cooperation and Development (OECD) Development Assistance Committee (DAC) set forth in 1997 a set of guidelines for its member countries to incorporate policies on gender equality and women empowerment (ge/we), spread across a range of concerns and sectors of activities. Capacity building, participatory development, and institutional development were also addressed.

Gender inequality remains a problem affecting women's socioeconomic status, and a number of rectifying measures and economic incentives are required to address this issue. The subsidies of women continue to add to those of nature without even being acknowledged by many, especially by those who live and swear by the power of market economics. It would be apt to conclude this section with an observation from the UNDP's Human Development Report 1995: "human development, if not engendered, is endangered."

● 7.5 POVERTY REDUCTION AND SUSTAINABILITY ●

The energy sector contributes the most toward emissions of the GHGs as well as affecting their sink capacity. Thus, this sector influences the net concentration of these gases (details as discussed in chapter 5). In this context, the role of rural poverty in the use and efficiency of alternative sources of energy assumes significance. These factors affect the processes of the preservation of the forests, the natural sinks of GHGs. This section examines some of the critical issues from a policy perspective.

Poverty and Energy

People living in poverty tend to use much higher discount rates than do the rich when making decisions about energy carriers in the fixed and variable/recurrent cost components. While low energy consumption is not a cause of poverty, the lack of available energy services correlates closely with many poverty indicators. Energy services for the poor include efficient lighting technology, water pumping technology, efficient cooking stoves and modern energy carriers for cooking. Energy strategies for SD could help to deal with the roots of poverty by promoting employment opportunities. Consequently, cleaner technologies reduce the incidence of environmental decay affecting the poor who at present bear inequitably more of the effect of decay.

The order of fuels on the energy ladders correspond to their efficiency and their "cleanliness," and, hence, moving up the ladder results in declining emissions of CO, SO_2 and particulates. For example, wood, dung, and other biomass represent the lowest rung for cooking; charcoal, coal and kerosene represent the next rungs up; the highest is electricity and LPG (liquefied petroleum gas).

Cross-country data for 114 countries show links between energy consumption and distribution of income. The linkages have implications for devising strategies for alleviating poverty. As an illustration of relevant parameters, the Pakistan Living Standards Measurement Survey (LSMS) (World Bank, 1991) showed that, in the lowest quantile (20 percent of the population), fuel expenditure constituted about 5.4 percent of the total expenditure of the household. The corresponding number for the fifth quantile (the highest) is 22.2 percent.

A number of rural energy sector options are not fully explored in the developing countries. These options create gainful employment opportunities, utilize cleaner technologies, are sufficiently decentralized, do not require huge bureaucratic institutions to manage, and reduce, poverty. As an example, biomass energy offers significant employment opportunities; the program to produce ethanol from sugarcane in Brazil created about 700,000 jobs. More opportunities exist with the development of markets for cane-derived alcohol and electricity, promising enhanced rural prosperity.

Public Expenditure

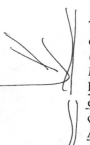

The role of international financial institutions is rather ambivalent in their net contribution toward mitigating poverty. The structural adjustment programs (SAPs) devised in the credit lending processes by the World Bank/International Monetary Fund (IMF) impose a special burden on the poor. "It is children who have paid the heaviest price for the developing world's debts. Fragmentary evidence . . . has shown a picture of rising malnutrition, and in some cases rising child deaths, in some of the most heavily indebted countries of Africa and Latin America" (UNICEF, 1992). By lifting price controls while freezing wages, and by devaluing the local currency, SAPs diminish purchasing power; see also Weston (1997). This reduces the purchasing power of poor families to buy food, health services, and other basic minimum necessities. The social programs designed to protect the most vulnerable groups (such as feeding programs for underweight babies) are usually sharply scaled back precisely when the gap between affordability and demand is the highest.

Discussing lessons for adjustment in the 1990s, the *World Development Report 1990* stated (World Bank, 1990, p. 120):

> In the short run, however, some of the poor may lose out. A combination of effective action on the policy fundamentals (notably changes in relative prices to favor agriculture and efforts to moderate declines in consumption through a pause in investment, for instance) can help many of the poor in most cases. But shifts in the pattern of public spending toward goods and services consumed by poor people and transfers targeted to them will often be necessary as well.

In a case study of the Amazon Basin, Feder (1979) documented the effects of massive private investment on the expansion of cattle production in fragile ecological conditions, supported by domestic government tax concessions and incentives, and also loans from the World Bank. This undertaking resulted in the degradation of large tracts of environmental assets. At best, the result was that it made destitutes of traditional forest dwellers, and at worst it simply eliminated them (Dasgupta and Maler, 1994; Hecht, 1985). Another scenario which deprived the local communities of their source of livelihood or categorized them into perpetrators of "illegal activities" is illustrated in box 7.1; see page 241. Evidently, lack of complementary employment and resource provisions for the local communities remain a major hurdle in the success of forest resource management policies.

Subsidies

The pattern of subsidies for fossil fuels shows that although subsidies are rather small in the OECD countries (constituting about 0.05 percent of GDP in 1995–6), they are widespread among various countries (World Bank, 1997a). Oil-producing countries tended to subsidize petroleum products on an average of about 38 percent (corresponding to global average of 16 percent) for 1995–6. The subsidies ranged from about 12 percent in Mexico to about 77 percent in Iran. When coal and natural gas are also taken into account, the global average of subsidies was estimated at 28 percent of the GDP, constituting about 0.27 percent of the total GDP for the year 1995–6. For oil-producing countries, this amounted to 2.26 percent.

Public expenditure policies in developing countries are, to a substantial degree, affected or even governed by the IMF and the World Bank, to the extent that borrowing countries need to toe the line of the lending institutions for their external borrowings. Although the motives and genuine needs of the borrowing governments and their rulers could be many, the end product in all cases seems to be the same: in their perceived need for controlling deficit financing, overdrafts and inflation, the lenders try to seek creditworthiness and minimization of risks on loan repayments. The so-called austerity measures and the removal of subsidies on some of the basic necessities for needy sections of society are notorious in their inequitous burdening of the poor. Although a human need does not create a right for the needy, the neglect of that need is usually accompanied by serious social, economic, and environmental consequences, for the borrowing countries.

Deforestation and the prevalence of explicit and implicit subsidies for this process are environmentally harmful and unsustainable modes of production. The provision of some of the subsidies was motivated by the need to promote exports (given the debt repayment obligations), and the felt need to convert land for other uses, like habitat and agricultural production. Logging and timber production for exports, besides shifting cultivation practices, are the major driving forces in countries like Indonesia; cattle ranching and habitat settlements are among the motives for deforestation in countries like Brazil. It was observed that, in

Ghana, kerosene subsidy withdrawl accelerated deforestation. In their dominant concern for debt management and loan repayment, the international lending institutions have been stipulating requirements where the negative externalities are ignored. Whenever certain subsidies are removed, the substitutory and compensatory mechanisms must be addressed if one is to achieve specified targets of public expenditure without social and environmental consequences.

Subsidies for renewable energy, protection of soil and water resources, social forestry, waste recycling, enhancement of energy use efficiency, and technical innovations for pollution control and for environmental sustainability, are usually among the obvious examples for illustrating the potentially positive role of subsidies. However, when it comes to basic needs like drinking water, shelter and sanitation, electricity use in low-income households, or some of the elements of a proxy "safety-net" (wherever these are not formally institutionally provided, like unemployment insurance, disability insurance, or social security benefits), it is neither entirely feasible nor desirable to eliminate subsidies for the poor in these specified categories of basic minimum needs for human survival. The above provisions can be tied to work requirements. However, exclusions for those seeking to undergo self-selected voluntary poverty (somewhat like voluntary unemployment) may not be ruled out. This would facilitate integration of the twin objectives of enhancing productivity with individual labor efforts, and raising minimum standards of living. The equivalence of these to the twin objectives of alleviating poverty and controlling degradation of environmental resources can be seen with the following interrelated assumptions. Improved income levels and risk perceptions lead to the following:

- Lower levels of the total fertility rate.
- Reduced population growth.
- Reduced draw down of nature and surroundings for basic survival.
- Enhanced energy use efficiency.
- Improved human capital formation.
- Greater productive roles for women and children.
- Reduced local pollution.
- Enhanced sanitation and public health standards.

To sum up, various policies for reducing public expenditure and subsidies must address the issues of substitution effects and also complementary activity requirements. Only then can such systems minimize the adverse effects on the poor and the environment.

● 7.6 POLICY ALTERNATIVES AND POLITICAL ECONOMY ●

If the governments (elected or other) do not make it a priority to alleviate poverty and enhance environmental quality, they may not find it important to address SD issues, unless there are rewards for the rulers in some way or other.

In other words, there may exist an equilibrium in the policy or resource alloca-tion at the public authority level which tends to match the demand for such provisions with their supply. In developed economies, where the environ-mental problem is due to patterns of high levels of consumption, the poverty reduction and corresponding environmental improvement is of relatively minor significance. This is in contrast with the developing economies where the role of poverty is significant in affecting the environment. In the context of the lat-ter, the role of international institutions is also very significant. This role is both catalytic and direct, depending on the type of external finance, trade, category of projects for funding, and the political set-up of the recipient country. It is, there-fore, important to review the international policies and influences affecting the dynamics of poverty and environment in the developing countries. Interna-tional institutions engaged in the multilateral development finance mechanisms and trade affect the economic and political destiny of many of developing coun-tries. Their role is next only to that of the domestic governments of many devel-oping countries; in some countries, it is even greater.

The World Development Report 1990 of the World Bank focused on poverty. In its section entitled "Lessons for Adjustment in the 1990s," the report (World Bank, 1990, p. 120) stated that "in the short run, however, some of the poor may lose out." This is almost like a death sentence on the poor. When the poor-est are already at the edge of survival, what more can they lose when their sole effort can only be keeping body and soul together? It was stated in a foreword to this report by the Bank's President, Barber Conable, that the most effective way of achieving rapid and politically sustainable improvements in the quality of life for the poor has been through a two-part strategy:

- The pursuit of a pattern of growth that ensures the productive use of the poor's abundant asset – labor.
- Widespread provision to the poor of basic social services, especially primary education, primary health care, and family planning.

It was added that the strategy must be complemented by well-targeted trans-fers, to help those not able to benefit from these policies, and by safety nets, to protect those who are exposed to economic shocks. However, as time and experi-ence showed, the mechanism of complementarity is hardly realized in the borrowing countries. In the client nations, these requirements have been over-ridden by various stipulations on the World Bank loans (or concerted lending involving the Bank, the IMF, and others in the forum of country creditors) regard-ing reductions in public expenditure, ill-conceived structural adjustment specifications, and deletion of safety nets like job security. More details on re-lated issues are given in chapter 10.

International financial institutions like the IMF, the World Bank, and the regional Development Banks can do more to tie in financial lending mechanisms with the attainment of some of the interrelated aspects of the alleviation of poverty and sustainable patterns of development. As long as the cost–benefit calculations and project appraisal methods applied by these institutions do not account for nature's subsidies and those of women and children in their calculations, and as long as the long-term future and the discounting of the future is not judiciously and ethically incorporated in these calculations, it is doubtful if these initiatives can have any positive impact.

In terms of devising new institutional mechanisms to augment the efforts of the non-governmental organizations (NGOs) to promote micro-credit schemes, an international Consultative Group to Assist the Poorest (CGAP) was launched in 1995. Donor members consist of bilateral donors, the European Commission, IFAD, UNDP and its UN Capital Development Fund, the International Labour Office (ILO), the World Bank and the regional development banks like the Asian Development Bank. The efforts are being coordinated by the Vice Presidency for Environmentally Sustainable Development at the World Bank. Although useful in micro-credit mechanisms in most of the poorer regions in the world, the impact can at best be minor since the capital outlay remained extremely meager (as of 1998).

The need to contribute to poverty reduction while applying the UNCED Agenda 21 has been largely ignored during the years that followed the Rio Summit (UNDP, 1997). The UN Commission on Sustainable Development (UNCSD) has been charged with monitoring follow up to both the UNCED Agenda 21 and the World Summit for Social Development, where poverty was the central concern. However, the UNCSD did not view poverty reduction in the context of its relationship to environmental protection and the sustainable use of resources, for about five years since the Rio Summit. Only in 1996 did the UNCSD suggest to its co-ordinating agency, the UN Economic and Social Council, that it would, in its future work, focus attention on the links between poverty and the environment. Also, the Global Environment Facility (GEF), the financing mechanism for meeting the global environmental goals of Agenda 21, does not take account of the poverty–environment relationship in its core activities. It was claimed that poverty reduction remains a focus of work for the United Nations Environment Programme (UNEP) (UN, 1997), including its work within the set of initiatives under the UN System-wide Special Initiative on Africa, namely the links between poverty and environmental degradation and the improvement of access to sustainable water resources and needs of the poor. However, there is no evidence of the impact of the stated activities of the UNEP, nor, anymore, of its sustained focus.

The belated decision of the UNCSD to focus its poverty-related work on links between poverty and the environment was supported by the UN Economic and Social Council. In pursuing this work, the Commission will do well to focus attention on the sustainable management and development of natural resources in fragile environments with abject and persistent poverty. Public works for water conservation, erosion control, afforestation, and other conservation efforts could be used to improve the environment; increased productivity efforts could be used to improve the environment, raise economic productivity and generate incomes for people living in poverty. Community-based and participatory approaches to water management and other SD activities have been successful in some parts of the world – e.g. Thailand and the Philippines – and should be applied more widely. Work on the links between poverty and the environment must also address the problems of low-income urban areas, such as squatter settlements in flood-prone areas, on steep hillsides or riverbanks, in hazardous areas along main roads or railway tracks, or near dangerously polluted industrial areas; see also UN (1997).

In the global commercial sectors, the policies affecting North–South trade were argued (The South Commission, 1990):

- It is in the North's own interest to assist the South in safeguarding the environment.
- A concerted attack on global poverty must be integrated with efforts to protect the environment.

The question is the existence of a forum or an institutional mechanism which recognizes that it is in their own long-term interest for the North to pursue more equitable terms of trade in their import–export activities. As Daily et al. (1995) argued: "trade relations between rich and poor nations also clearly have large (if mostly unanalyzed) impacts on carrying capacity . . . unsustainable exports of timber (at far below social costs) by poor countries to the rich." This descrip-tion is an elucidation of implicit subsidies and the vulnerability of the poor. In a free-trade set-up with market-determined operations in the international trade arena, where is the room for poverty and environment issues? Some relevant details of these issues are discussed in chapter 8.

● 7.7 CONCLUSIONS ●

SD is predicated on intertemporal resource optimization, including efficient man-agement of functions and services of the planet's sources and sinks. Contempor-aneous inequalities and pressing problems of poverty constitute impediments to setting the right "initial conditions" in successive time intervals. Thus, an integral part of the problem of SD is that of poverty and inequality. Glaring eco-nomic and social inequalities are a manifestation of the effects of a set of unfair institutional mechanisms at work, with their deep-rooted foundations. It may not be an easy task to bring about a good degree of egalitarianism, but it is not difficult to perceive the attendent problems in the context of severe economic inequalities. These inequalities compound the problems of the impact of poverty on the environment, and those of excessive consumption on the environment – expressed in terms of both the sources and sinks. In a highly iniquitous world, the poor draw down the supplies from nature's sources rather excessively – whatever comes to hand for basic survival – and the rich contribute to excessive draw down of the sink capacities with their consumption habits and depend-ency on high emissions of GHGs. In other words, poverty, as well as prosperity, adversely affects the environment: the former largely in terms of effects on sources, and the latter in terms of both the sources and sinks. The effects of the former tend to be local, at least initially. The interdependencies between poverty and the environment suggest the need to address both problems in an integrated manner at the national and international levels.

Trends in poverty, especially rural poverty, indicate worsening features in Africa and South Asia. The effects of poverty and a deteriorating environment combined lead to serious multiplier effects and externalities. Poverty leads to continued high levels of total fertility rate. The uncompensated externalities in the global environment are likely to exacerbate unsustainable patterns of consumption and production globally. Greater economic and social equities would lessen the pressures on desperate exploitation of natural resources with possibly extremely high discount rates in some cases.

Gender inequalities add to the problems: the extent of subsidies (offered voluntarily or otherwise) provided by nature and women (and children, because of poverty) are usually appropriated or usurped by domestic and international consumers, and the prevalence of these subsidies tends to give the impression of endless sources of provision of goods and services at very low or zero costs to the users. This impression can hurt societies in a significant manner over a period of time when the relative scarcity of the sources of subsidy constrain prospects of sustainability and SD.

The political economy of poverty suggests that several more concerted efforts are required at local, national, and international levels to restore dignity to human life. Market and non-market, economic and other institutions need to act on these problems. Possibilities for SD are better enhanced in such a constellation.

The world has never been known to be an equitable planet when it comes to prey and predators; there are fundamentals of resource ownership, asset control, power sharing, and income and asset inequalities. This is not to suggest hopelessness. On the contrary, conscious efforts to develop egalitarian socioeconomic patterns – founded on equitable policies governing wages and incomes policies, and fiscal measures – can pave the way for a just society. Problems of SD will also be largely solved in such a system, if and when it happens.

Review Exercises

1 If the poor tend to extract less of the ecological resources (both from sources and sinks) relative to the rich, is there any justification for qualified or conditional subsidies for the basic survival needs of the poor? If the answer is in the affirmative, what could be a set of meaningful conditions enabling prevalence of these subsidies?

2 Examine the effects of gender subsidies on environmental externalities.

3 The lower rungs of the "energy ladder" use energy inefficiently; the highest rung in the ladder uses energy-intensive technologies but relatively energy efficient ones. Is there an optimum in between the two? If so, what are the economic–energy characteristics of this? What role do the renewable energy supplies play in this description?

4 Is there an inverted U-relationship (IUR) between income levels at the household level and the energy consumption efficiency?

5   How does the phenomenon of poverty alleviation affect the trends in
   (a)   the emissions of the concentration of global greenhouse gases (GHGs),
         and
   (b)   the net rise in these concentrations?
6   (a)   Is the problem of persistent abject poverty a manifestation of the prob-
         lem of social indifference, or of resource limitation to meet the demand
         for goods and services?
   (b)   What role, if any, can be played by the international financial institu-
         tions in poverty reduction (recognizing that these institutions also have
         to seek a return on capital, and ensure the debt repaying capacity of the
         borrower countries)?

References

Amin, R., Ahmed, U. A., Choudhury, J. and Ahmed, M. (1994) Poor women's participa-
   tion in income generating projects and their fertility regulation in rural Bangladesh –
   evidence from a recent survey. *World Development,* 22, 555–64.
Arrow, K. J., Bolin, B., Costanza, R., Dasgupta, P., Folke, C., Holling, C. S., Jansson, B.
   O., Levin, S., Maler, K. G., Perrings, C. and Pimental, D. (1995) Economic growth, car-
   rying capacity, and the environment. *Science,* 268, 520–1.
Bruno, M., Ravallion, M. and Squire, L. (1996) *Equity and Growth in Developing Countries
   – Old and New Perspectives on the Policy Issues,* World Bank Working Paper Series # 1563.
   Washington, DC: The World Bank.
Cecelski, E. (1995) From Rio to Beijing – engendering the energy debate. *Energy Policy,*
   23(6).
Daily, G., Ehrlich, A. H. and Ehrlich, P. R. (1995) Socioeconomic equity – a critical ele-
   ment in sustainability. *Ambio,* 24(1), 58–9.
Dasgupta, P. S. (1993) *An Inquiry into Well-Being and Destitution.* Oxford: Clarendon Press.
Dasgupta, P. S. (1995) Population, poverty, and the local environment. *Scientific American,*
   February, 41–5.
Dasgupta, P. S. and Maler, K. G. (1994) *Poverty, Institutions, and the Environmental Resource
   Base.* Environment Paper # 9. Washington, DC: World Bank.
Dietz, T. and Rosa, E. A. (1997) Effects of population and affluence on CO_2 emissions.
   Proc. National Academy of Sciences, 94, 175–9.
Feder, E. (1979) Agricultural resources in underdeveloped countries – competition
   between man and animal. *Economic and Political Weekly,* 14.
Hamid, S. (1994) Non-market work and national income – the case of Bangladesh. *The
   Bangladesh Development Studies,* 22, 1–48.
Hecht, S. (1985) Environment, development and politics – capital accumulation and the
   livestock sector in Eastern Amazonia. *World Development,* 13.
IFAD (1995) *The State of World Rural Poverty – A Profile of Asia.* Rome: IFAD.
Jazairy, I. et al. (1992) *The State of World Rural Poverty – An Inquiry into its Causes and
   Consequences.* Rome: IFAD.
Jodha, N. S. (1986) Common property resources and the rural poor. *Economic and Political
   Weekly,* 21.
Jodha, N. S. (1990) Rural common property resources – contributions and crises.
   Economic and Political Weekly, 25.
Jodha, N. S. (1995) Common property resources and the dynamics of rural poverty in
   India's dry regions. *Unasylva,* 46(180), 22–9.

McMahon, M. (1997) From the ground up – ecofeminism and ecological economics. *Ecological Economics*, 20(2), 163–73.

Parikh, K. (1998) *Poverty and the Environment – Turning the Poor into Agents of Environmental Regeneration*, UNDP Poverty Strategies Initiative Working Paper 1. New York: UNDP.

Peluso, N. L. (1992) *Rich Forests, Poor People*. Berkeley: University of California Press.

Shiva, V. (1992) *Staying Alive – Women, Ecology, and Development*. London: Zed Books.

The South Commission (1990) *The Challenge to the South, Report of the South Commission*. New York: Oxford University Press.

Sunstein, C. (1997) *Free Markets and Social Justice*. New York: Oxford University Press.

UN (1995) *Measurement and Valuation of Unpaid Contributions*. Santa Domingo: INSTRAW.

UN (1997) *Combating Poverty – Overall Progress achieved since the UNCED*. Report of the Secretary General, UNCSD Report E/CN.17/1997/2/Add. New York: UN.

UN (1998) *Report of the Secretary General for the 31st session of the Commission on Population and Development. February 1998*. New York: UN.

UN (1999) *Annual Population 1950–2050*. UN Population Division. Also available on www.un.org.

UNDP (1995) *Human Development Report 1995*. New York: Oxford University Press.

UNDP (1996) *Human Development Report 1996*. New York: Oxford University Press.

UNDP (1997) *Human Development Report 1997*. New York: Oxford University Press.

UNICEF (1992) *State of the World's Children*. New York: Oxford University Press.

UNICEF (1997) *State of the World's Children*. New York: UNICEF.

Warren, K. (1987) Feminism and ecology-making connection. *Environmental Ethics*, 9, 3–20.

Warren, K. (1990) The power and the promise of ecological feminism. *Environmental Ethics*, 12, 121–46.

Weston, J. (1997) Striving for balance – the interrelationship between health, economics, and the natural world. *Ecological Economics Bulletin*, 2(4), 14–17.

World Bank (1990) *World Development Report 1990*. Washington, DC: The World Bank.

World Bank (1991) *Living Standards Measurements Survey – Pakistan*. Washington, DC: The World Bank.

World Bank (1996) *Poverty Reduction and the World Bank – Progress and Challenges in the 1990s*. Washington, DC: The World Bank.

World Bank (1997a) *Expanding the Measures of Wealth*. Washington, DC: The World Bank.

World Bank (1997b) *World Development Indicators (1997)*. Washington, DC: World Bank.

World Bank (1998) *Poverty Reduction and the World Bank – Progress in Fiscal 1996 and 1997*. Website: www.worldbank.org/html/extdr/pov_red/execsum.htm.

World Commission on Environment and Development (WCED) (1987) *Our Common Future*. New York: Oxford University Press.

● CHAPTER 8 ●

Trade, Debt, and the Environment

Trade, Debt, and the Environment

Bureaucratic socialism collapsed because it did
not allow prices to tell the economic truth.
Market economy may ruin the environment and
ultimately itself if prices are not allowed to tell the
ecological truth.

Ernst U. von Weizsacker

● 8.1 INTRODUCTION ●

The interdependencies of global trade, international debt, and the environment
are issues of paramount importance in understanding the underlying dynamics
of sustainable development (SD). These aspects are particularly important for
developing countries, and in the management of the global commons. These are
also relevant for the developed economies' SD, because of environmental and
economic interdependencies. The accelerated trading mechanisms under trade
liberalization practices can lead to greater economic growth, a necessary condition for poverty reduction and development. However, this is not enough for
SD, since the underlying mechanisms supporting the rapid expansion of trade
are currently built on mechanisms involving unsustainable resource exploitation.
In the absence of explicit safeguards to protect ecological resources, trade liberalization remains unsustainable. If resource protection and restoration are not properly addressed, expanded trade promotes depletion of ecological resources and sink
capacities as well. This tends to affect the resilience of the ecosystem and the
efficacy of ecosystem services – the foundations for the existence of viable and
vibrant economic systems. It is not the premise here that null activity, or marginal volumes of international trade or near zero levels of debt, are likely to be
optimal in sustaining the ecological resources eternally. Rather, a careful balancing

of the requirements of economic progress with those of SD must constitute an essential ingredient of the patterns of international trade. The role of debt and its sustainability is critical in the methods of external borrowings for domestic economic growth and repayment obligations. The latter are presently fulfilled with large-scale exports, with ever-worsening terms of trade between primary commodity exporters and industrial countries. Some of these issues are examined in this chapter.

The issues involved are very important for the global economy and its players. Trade and the environment are more linked than usually acknowledged. A "conclusion" to a report of the UN Conference on Trade and Development (UNCTAD, 1997) stated that it may be "necessary to examine the direction of the future trade, environment and development agenda and possible approaches to issues." Clearly, a lot more ground needs to be covered for devising a meaningful strategy. An ecological economics approach would advocate full-cost pricing at all levels and sectors globally, which may avoid some environmental problems caused by unilateral short-run rent-seeking actions. However, more developments in the theory and applications of economics would be required to enable their practical use. Some elements of this chapter are expected to be useful in this effort.

This chapter examines the causal links between trade and environment, debt and trade, and debt and environment. After a brief review of some of the analytical aspects, the next section explores the connections between international trade liberalization and environmental changes. Later sections address the possibilities of reflecting environmental costs in prices of goods traded, changes in debt and its sustainability from a fiscal perspective, and links between international debt and the environment. A number of special aspects of debt management, like the heavily indebted poor countries (HIPC) debt initiative of the World Bank group, the Debt-for-Nature Swaps (DNS) schemes for debt exchanges, and other mechanisms either tried or being implemented, are also deliberated. Also, a set of issues involving the emerging phenomena of internalizing environmental costs, the role of full-cost pricing and operational and institutional issues are examined in various sections.

● 8.2 INTERNATIONAL TRADE AND THE ENVIRONMENT ●

Analytical Aspects

Purely from an environmental resource accounting viewpoint, the export and import activities have differential implications for net national product (NNP). Any of the measures which seek to use NNP as an indicator of sustainability (see chapter 4) need to make adjustments toward an imputed income from the depletion of the stock of resources, based on those exported. In the case of raw exports of non-renewable resources like oil, this can be constructed from an estimate of the total remaining stock of the resource or resources, and an estimate of the present ratio of the domestic to foreign final consumption of the resources; see also Sefton and Weale (1996). The relative accuracy of NNP as a function of this aspect can influence its usability as an indicator of sustainability in economies which significantly export natural and exhaustible resource-based products, and potential changes in the export policies and technology of production with special reference to exports. In a detailed analytical study, Sefton and Weale (1996) established that the implications of international trade are seen as follows. For the resource exporter, the possibility of owning a reserve of exhaustible resources affects the changing rates of prices and extraction with the implication of upward adjustments. The converse holds for the importer, and downward adjustments may be required in national income to compensate for the growing scarcity of the resource. The standard closed-economy results constitute a misapplication of traditional methods. These lead to an under-assessment of the income of the natural resource-exporting countries and an overstatement of the industrial countries.

The international market transmits and enlarges the externalities of the global commons, and policies which ignore these linkages are unlikely to be very useful (Chichilnsky, 1994). Studies which use market analyses to focus on the costs of environmental policies tend to ignore uncorrected and/or uncompensated externalities. Some attempts to model environmental externalities with trade and innovation issues are given by Elbasha and Roe (1996), using rather simplistic formulations. Currently, objective (rather than subjective) studies in real-world scenarios with policy implications are extremely limited. A select few analytical investigations are summarized below.

Smith and Espinosa (1996) clarify how environmental externalities can influence general equilibrium evaluations of trade and how environmental policies emphasize the feedback loop or, more simply, the implications of interactions between agents that arise outside markets due to one or more environmental resources:

- Through non-separabilities, these interactions can play a direct role in the substitutions that influence outcomes within markets.
- To the extent that nonmarketed environmental resources make non-separable contributions to production and preferences, they influence the signals for marketed goods from both sides of market transactions.

These issues are important for the developing economies, where the environmental resources often serve a key role in agriculture or as extractive outputs, but could also contribute (in a preserved status) to watershed protection, micro climatic functions, and natural resource amenities.

Chichilnsky's (1994) analysis used a conventional general equilibrium framework with two countries (designated the North and the South): the North denoting a developed economy with a well-established system of property rights to all resources, and the South designating a developing economy with a different set of conditions describing the availability of factor inputs. Her model relies on the differences in access conditions between private and open-access resources (as factor inputs) to alter the supply function for tradable goods. Because endowments are not fixed and respond to prices, the supply of marketed outputs produced using the environmental resource's services will be greater under open-access conditions. The model allows for the general equilibrium interaction between product and factor market conditions in both economies. Establishing private property rights to the environmental resource (or the global commons) offers the only feasible policy response to the over-exploitation induced by the access conditions to the environmental resources; trade, in its current forms, simply exacerbates the problem.

In another analytical study, Copeland and Taylor (1994) adopted a similar two-country (North/South) setting but introduce externalities, local to each country's decisions. This model adds general equilibrium effects to the social cost issues. The Chichilnsky and the Copeland–Taylor models fail to take into account the substitution effects arising through individual preferences. Pollution itself may alter the composition of goods demanded. For example, because of changing health and productivity implications of pollution legislation.

Barbier and Rauscher (1994) considered a framework that relates more specifically to the problems of developing economies by evaluating the effects of trade on incentives for tropical deforestation. Using an optimal control model, they allow for stock externalities to influence trade policy for economies. As with Chichilnsky and Copeland–Taylor, the model assumes separable preferences, so there are no preference-related substitution effects influencing how the externality in each model influences optimal trade policy (Smith and Espinosa, 1996). Typically, these economic models require treating endogenized preference functions (see chapter 3) which incorporate the effects of pollution externalities on consumption, and trade effects of substitution (and vice versa).

Trade-based economic growth and/or trade liberalization have implications for the environment. The environmental effect is a combined result of three components (Copeland and Taylor, 1994; Beghin et al., 1994):

1   A scale effect that increases pollution.
2   A composition effect that reflects global specialization in industries and their pollution contribution locally.
3   A technical effect that directs substitution-favoring cleaner technologies.

Trade liberalization combined with appropriate internalization of environmental costs promises the potential to augment global welfare in the short run as well as in the long run, and hence may be sustainable. Also, as suggested by Beghin et al. (1994), if pollutants are controlled by marketable permits and quotas, trade liberalization leads to enhanced economic well-being and also restrains environmental degradation within meaningful limits. This assertion might be more relevant if the 1997 Kyoto Protocol and the 1998 Buenos Aires Agreement had led to the widespread application of greenhouse gas (GHG) emission trading mechanisms. However, most local pollution problems are not covered in the Kyoto Protocol. It is doubtful if the problems of local pollution like the quality of water discharges from industrial use can be handled in the same manner, in the absence of relevant market/nonmarket mechanisms to address these issues.

Does trade openness or liberalization enhance environmental quality? There are some answers in rather partial settings. The trade liberalization and consequential environmental effects of the policies of the Uruguay round of trade negotiations were examined by Cole et al. (1998). They considered the implications for five pollutants: NO_2, SO_2, CO_2, CO, and PM (particulate matter). In most of the developing countries, the net increase in each of the pollutants is predicted. In the developed countries, the emissions of CO, SO_2, and PM are expected to fall, but those of the remaining two pollutants continue to rise. The policy implications of this assessment are not clear, however. Trade expansion generally contributes to economic growth as well as environmental pollution. The real questions are about the relative cost-effectiveness of income gains and the enhanced potential as well as the commitment to reduce environmental pollution, both at the source regions, and globally. If the importers use trade liberalization mainly to locate pollution-generating production in the exporter countries, the game is not what was intended under the trade negotiations. Appropriate cognizance needs to be taken in future policy reforms in this direction.

Does the process lead to the location of polluting industries in poor countries? The answers depend on the existence of a judicious mix of domestic environmental policies and the ability of trading partners to internalize the environmental costs of trade. Polluting industries do not find a place in poorer countries, since poor countries are not keen to allow these industries to flourish. Besides, for an industrial enterprise, country risk-assessment is a more important basis on which to decide where to locate, than is finding environmental "safe havens" for dumping pollution. Also, the direct costs of environmental compliance are usually estimated as relatively low: at less than about 3 percent of the total costs of operation (Low, 1993).

In a value-free free-market system, it is possible that trade liberalization will misallocate the planet's resources. Excessive consumerism may not pay attention to any criteria of sustainability, as elucidated by the UN Development Programme (UNDP, 1998). However, these issues deserve a detailed treatment, and are not addressed here.

Deforestation and International Trade

Increased incentives for agricultural production and trade tend to contribute to land conversion and deforestation, if the land-use policies are not properly defined and enforced. The issue is not to find fault with the incentives or trade of agricultural products, but to analyze land and forest conservation policies and their effectiveness. A number of authors – e.g. Anderson and Blackhurst (1992) – argue that the design of domestic policies of incentives and disincentives, including the regulation of environmental degradation, is a better arena for policy interventions (affecting exporters and importers) to address potential adverse environmental consequences of trade. This is an oversimplification of the real problem, and could imply simply shifting the issue to another arena. The processes affecting international trade include the role of environmental subsidies and trade policies. Unilateral country-level actions to protect environmental resources tend to affect the trade and budgets of the poorer and export-dependent economies adversely, as explained later in this chapter. Hence, there is a need for an international policy coordination.

Large-scale exploitation of timber resources poses one of the most significant development-related environmental challenges, but the link between this issue and trade is rather complex. The trade–environment–growth link for tropical forest production seems especially important in countries like Indonesia and Brazil. Although tropical deforestation is alarming in these and other developing economies, commercial logging of tropical wood is not an instrumental contributor to national growth (less than 1 percent of gross domestic product (GDP)) or trade. Often, deforestation is led both by external markets and by land conversion for agriculture; terms of trade, lack of environmental cost inclusion in export pricing, and debt are some of the factors behind the former, whereas these and population pressures are the factors which tend to influence the latter effect. Institutional failures and market imperfections – property right delineation and enforcement, uncertainty and monopolistic practices, and logging contract design and government subsidies – are among the major factors behind the deforestation externalities.

Domestic consumption claims most of the timber production in developing economies. Trade bans and other export restrictions aimed at increasing domestic stock value in wood products have had negative environmental effects. These trade impediments depress domestic prices of logs and increase the log content of domestic products. Some studies estimated that 10 percent of the Indonesian consumption of logs could be saved by removing the export ban. Some proposals of the Organization for Economic Cooperation and Development (OECD) – to fix import quotas of tropical wood and wood products – would have the same qualitative effect and would foster inefficiency in wood-product industries in developing economies. The details of these observations are given by Beghin et al. (1994), Barbier (1994), Gillis (1988), and Braga (1992).

The above discussion suggests, as did some studies earlier – e.g. Sedjo and Wiseman (1983) – that an export ban is a poor policy substitute for judicious resource harvesting and redevelopment in forest resources; and the reasoning can be extended to include the preservation of some of the animal and other biological species. This is not to suggest any lax enforcement of limits to harvesting and redevelopment. The main argument behind allowing exploitation of resources rather than banning them is not to allow artificial depression of domestic prices of commodities or other items covered in the attempted protection. This could lead to a loss of revenues and to possible neglect in the maintenance and preservation of the items sought to be preserved. Besides, the enforcement of a total ban can be much more difficult than that of a regulated harvesting, with the important provision that mandates reforestation.

Trade liberalization is generally popular insofar as its capacity to expand and accelerate transactions of imports and exports of goods and services is concerned. This mechanism of exchange, in a competitive (ideal) world, should promote efficiency of resource utilization. However, the latter can only occur when all the resources are properly accounted for: there are no free goods. The traditional economic view of comparative advantage as the basis for exchange of goods and services is a relevant foundation for international trade or its liberalization, but this criterion does not, in any way, ensure rational and efficient use of ecological resources from the viewpoint of long-term sustainability or SD. When this does not happen, as is the case whenever there are missing markets for some of the goods and services, trade is likely to be a powerful conduit for adverse environmental externalities. These externalities themselves arise from the phenomena of market failure and institutional failure. In its role, accelerated free trade can multiply the environmental problems, which are usually rooted elsewhere: in the problems of production, consumption, economic inequalities, inefficient pricing of traded goods and services, and lack of fair terms of trade. The failure to take into account the environmental costs in marketed commodities leads to a divergence between private costs and social costs. In the absence of appropriate policy interventions, this divergence widens over time and with the scale of operations. International trade can help to correct some of the failures through the provision of incentives for environmental protection and promoting efficient use of resources, but it does the opposite in some cases; for details on these issues, see OECD (1994) pp. 8–12.

The 1992 Rio Summit Declaration (Agenda 21, para 2.14(c)) sought to "reflect efficient and sustainable use of factors of production in the formation of commodity prices, including the reflection of environmental, social and resources costs." The summit itself did not address any specific guidelines or policies in this direction. In addition, an assertion in its Principle 16 was inconsistent with itself: "national authorities should endeavor to promote the internalization of environmental costs and the use of economic instruments, taking into account the approach that the polluter should, in principle, bear the cost of pollution, with due regard to the public interest and without distorting international trade and investment." Some element of distortion of the patterns of international trade is rather essential if the existing distortions are to be corrected. That is the price we may have to pay to correct a wrong. The failure to recognize this imperative is to seek *status quo ante* and still dream about effecting relevant changes. Ineffective changes will, of course, lead to a non-distortive impact on international trade. Disruption of the trading system will be harmful, but the imposition of one distortion (if at all) to correct another existing distortion need not be harmful. No change comes without its costs. The real issue is to find cost-effective methods of effecting meaningful changes, where the concept of cost is the generalized one. It includes (subject to adjustments for overlapping elements) producer and consumer costs, social and private costs, compliance and transaction costs, and environmental costs for the present and future generations.

The post-Rio deliberations at the UN Commission on Sustainable Development (UNCSD) and the UNCTAD did not make any significant progress, however. The United Nations Environment Programme (UNEP) and UNCTAD declared in 1997 that they work together to provide an integration of trade and environment issues, but these are rather powerless players in the international game. The most important was the institution of the General Agreement on Tariffs and

Trade (GATT), which had as its final act the Uruguay round of trade negoti-
ations; these negotiations lasted about seven years and lead to the Marrakesh
Declaration. This ceased to exist at the end of 1994 and was superseded by a
permanent and more comprehensive World Trade Organization (WTO). The WTO
Committee on Trade and Environment (CTE) is currently the focal point for
all the UN institutions for the integration of trade and environmental issues. As
GATT/WTO members noted repeatedly, and as stated in the 1994 Marrakesh
Declaration at the Uruguay round of trade negotiations under GATT, GATT/
WTO had limited competence on trade and environment issues (Prudencio and
Hudson, 1994). Also, in the frenzy to conclude the negotiations after seven long
years of deliberations, GATT ministers left out the long-term mechanisms for the
WTO to integrate trade and environmental issues. The current scenario invol-
ving the role of the multilateral trading system and the WTO is summarized in
box 8.1 below (Rao, 1999).

BOX 8.1 World Trade Organization and the environment

The key entity under the WTO is the Committee on Trade and Environment
(CTE). The WTO CTE was constituted in 1995 to address the following aspects,
among others initially:

- The relationship between the provisions of the multilateral trading system
  and trade measures for environmental purposes, including those pursuant
  to multilateral environmental agreements.
- The relationship between environmental policies relevant to trade and
  environmental measures with significant trade effects and the provisions
  of the multilateral system, including charges and taxes, and requirements
  relating to products, packaging, labeling and recycling for environmental
  purpose.
- The effects of environmental measures on market access, especially for
  developing countries.

Much of the desired work was still in progress as of 1999.

The Marrakesh Declaration called for the CTE to examine the role of the
WTO in relation to the links between environmental measures and new trade
agreements reached in the Uruguay round of negotiations on services and
intellectual property. The WTO would like people to believe that the CTE
has "broken a new ground," on these issues; and this ground consists of two
observations:

- The relevance of any additional measures was not considered necessary
  (other than the existing Article XIV(b)), according to the first report of
  the CTE.

● It was suggested that there is a need to examine further the relationship between the Agreement on Trade-Related Aspects of Intellectual Property Rights (TRIPs) and the Convention on Biological Diversity.

In its first report, submitted at the 1996 WTO Ministerial Conference in Singapore, the CTE feebly expressed the need to integrate the two title words of the committee.

The CTE is reported to take into account a few provisions under Article XX of GATT, and also to assess the interplay of the requirements under various multilateral environmental and trading agreements. The provisions of GATT under Article XX(b) allow a WTO member country to place its public health and safety and national environmental goals ahead of its general obligation not to enhance trade restrictions or utilize discriminatory trade measures. These measures are allowed only to the extent that they are "necessary to protect human, animal or plant life or health." The original Article came into existence in the late 1960s when due recognition of the environmental factors was not a dominant social or economic paradigm. Accordingly, it seems, there was no explicit mention of the word "environment." Relevant modifications in Article XX(b) are essential in light of modern knowledge; see also Rao (1999) and Schoenbaum (1997).

Another important provision is Article XX(g). This allows WTO members to take action to conserve exhaustible natural resources. Based on a tuna/dolphin dispute between Mexico and the USA, it was clarified that the Article does have extra territorial effect but not extra jurisdictional effect. The Tuna/Dolphin II Panel of GATT endorsed national measures designed to protect extra territorial resources; see also Cheyne (1995).

The WTO Committee on Subsidies and Countervailing Measures drafted the Agreement on its title theme in 1998. This specified certain subsidies to meet new environmental requirements and also R&D activities as "non-actionable" or disputable by other WTO members.

Policy developments from the WTO for the integration of environmental and trade factors are essential; those could make a difference between environmentally sustainable trade and unsustainable free trade. The progress in this direction has been tardy during the five years that followed the formation of the WTO. A high-level symposium on trade and environment (followed by another on trade and development) was organized by the WTO in March 1999 in Geneva. A sense of recognition of the issues of SD and the need to integrate trade and environmental considerations emerged. However, the conclusions fell short of specific operational strategies or trading rules. Most of the existing provisions of the Articles of the WTO/GATT framework are obsolete as far as the international law, science, and economics of the environment are concerned. There is cause for concern insofar as the WTO Articles are oblivious to the implications of specific types of trade activities on the global commons and the implied free-rider problems. Even if some trade activities are not the main contributors to the environmental problems, an equitable assignment of the costs of production and trade, inclusive of appropriate environmental costs, is necessary between various members of the WTO. In the absence of such a level playing field and of a concerted action in this regard, individual countries may either attempt to free ride or be unwilling to include such costs for fear of loss of the market share. Alternately, the WTO Articles would bring about an actionable intervention on such members. None of these are conducive for harmonizing trade and the environment. Greater participation of the World Bank and the International Monetary Fund (IMF), to integrate the issues of including debt servicing and environmental issues in assessments, is essential. This integration could be sought in relation to debt and trade as well as trade and environment links. This is particularly relevant if these institutions can appreciate the role of integrating sovereign debt contracts with the compliance mechanisms required of various relevant multilateral environmental agreements (MEAs); see box 8.2. Admittedly, the latter are not the

---

BOX 8.2 Multilateral environmental agreements

This list is expected to include most of the relevant Agreements with implications for international trade. About 17 MEAs were identified by GATT (1992) to contain trade measures, starting in 1933. Each of these have not been ratified by the same set of countries, however.

- International Convention for the Protection of Birds (1950).
- International Plant Protection Agreement (1951).
- Convention on Conservation of North Pacific Fur Seals (1957).
- Agreement Concerning Cooperation in the Quarantine of Plants and their Protection against Pests and Diseases (1959).
- Rio International Convention for the Conservation of Atlantic Tunas (ICCAT) (1966).
- Phyto-sanitary Convention for Africa (1967).
- The African Convention on the Conservation of Nature and Natural Resources (1968).
- The Benelux Convention on the Hunting and Protection of Birds (1970).
- Convention on International Trade in Endangered Species (CITES) of Wild Fauna and Flora (1973).
- Montreal Protocol on Substances that Deplete the Ozone (1987).
- Basel Convention on the Control of Transboundary Movements of Hazardous Wastes and their Disposal (1989).
- Convention for the Prohibition of Fishing with Long Driftnets in the South Pacific (Wellington Convention) (1990).
- Convention on Biological Diversity (1992).

Source: Updated and summarized from GATT (1992)

business of the IMF or World Bank and the former sets of issues do not concern the UN institutions. The lack of proper institutional reform and coordination at the global level entails serious social costs to the world, an avoidable additional burden to society and an impediment to the processes enabling SD. Some of these aspects are explored later in this chapter.

A number of international environmental agreements have been in vogue for at least half a century. Any new measures toward trade liberalization need to take into account these stipulations, and visualize additional requirements for the sustainability of the environment and economy. There are two important aspects of devising international trade policies in consonance with the existing MEAs as listed in box 8.2:

● Reconciliation of the twin objectives of trade liberalization and promoting environmental protection.
● Achieving complementarity with emerging policies toward global commons, especially concentrations of GHGs.

The first aspect is largely in the arena of local pollution problems, while the second is global. Environmental subsidies implicit in some of the exports (especially those of the developing countries) are built on the assumptions of free environmental goods. These affect domestic environmental features of the exporters, and also the transboundary problems of the environment. In other words, cheap imports and their expansion into the industrial countries may not remain as cheap for anyone in the long run.

Developing country exporters are paying for the fall in the quality of public health and productivity of their population (both in the short run and in the long run), and importers are expected to incur other costs due to the effects of the loss of the sink capacity of the planet and deterioration in the global commons. There are three main features of some of these costs:

1   They are not entirely monetary.
2   They are relatively remote in their affliction over time and place.
3   They are diffused and stochastic in their sectoral and spatial incidence.

None of these features justify being ignored as if they do not matter. When the consequences of environmental neglect do materialize, the costs are direct and extremely high; so will be the costs of effecting any corrective measures. A gradual adjustment of relevant ingredients in the trading policies is less disruptive and cost-effective, given the role of the mechanisms of substitution and adaptation. This is feasible when the problems are identified sooner rather than later. Given the current understanding of the issues involved, the WTO/CTE will do well to act toward a meaningful international framework for the integration of trade and environmental protection at local and global levels. It is also important to note that the globally accepted soft international law based on the precautionary principle (PP) – see chapters 3 and 11 – should act as the overarching guiding approach so that any environmental concerns are properly addressed.

Although at least six international commodity agreements – on cocoa, coffee, olive oil and table olives, sugar, tropical timber, and wheat – were renegotiated and have come into force since the 1992 Earth Summit, these do not attempt to improvise features relevant for SD in a significant way (UN, 1997). However, the International Agreement on Jute and Jute Products contains an objective to give due consideration to environmental aspects by creating the awareness of the beneficial effects of the use of jute as a natural product. The International Agreement on Olive Oil and Table Olives also includes a feature requiring consideration of environmental issues at all stages of the production systems. In the International Tropical Timber Agreement, the objectives of sustainable use of resources – the rehabilitation of degraded forest land – are emphasized (UN, 1997).

As an example of national level policy reconciliations, the 1989 Netherlands' Environmental Policy Plan stated that the Dutch government did not see any inherent conflict between an open trading system and sound environmental policy; and that a progressive environmental policy need not be an obstacle to trade if all the countries involved coordinate their environmental aims and instruments. The plan also sought to achieve internationally recognized environmental standards and to ensure the worldwide application of the "polluter pays" (PP) principle. The next section deals with the relevance and implications of internalizing the environmental costs.

● 8.3 REFLECTING ENVIRONMENTAL COSTS IN TRADE ●

Internalization of environmental costs does imply all or some of the following: inclusion of true worth or shadow price of each of the inputs into the production system, post-production costs to consumption stage, and also the costs of disposal at the terminal stage. This inclusion does imply costs which are incurred at different levels of the life cycle. Evidently, in many cases, it is not meaningful to include all costs at a single stage. A multi-stage inclusion of environmental costs is one of the direct methods, but a variety of alternatives can also be contemplated. An alternative perspective suggests the assessment of the opportunity costs of resources being used in the life cycle of the product or service. In an operationally relevant setting, the objective of internalization is to enable various economic entities to adjust prices and markets so as to achieve socially optimal consumption and production patterns. No doubt this is easier stated than accomplished. Any degree of adoption of this approach warrants concerted policy and action at different levels of aggregation of human activities, if any free-rider problems and their corresponding externalities are to be avoided. If a few firms in a few sectors and locations reflect the environmental costs in their prices, the competitors could capture the market share and damage the profitability (and hence the survival) of the adopters of the principle.

In a competitive world, it is well-known that cost-plus methods of pricing might tend to exclude some of the producer markets. This has implications for the uniformity or harmonizing environmental costs by all the players (at least with respect to specific commodities or goods and their substitutes) in the world market: those who seek to free ride on the environment should not have an incentive to do so by their lower pricing of goods and services to clinch the export market. Hence, there is a need for global policy coordination. Instruments for internalization have both income effects and substitution effects at different levels of the market. These effects tend to work in opposite directions; thus, the net effect on exporter income may be positive, negative, or none, as it depends on the specific characteristics of the product and the market under consideration (UNCTAD, 1995a). Internalization acts first on the supply side, and interacts with substitution mechanisms at consumption and production levels.

Is the process of internalization an internationally relevant and significant one, or is it simply a domestic trade policy of a given country? UNCTAD (1995a) observed that internalization of environmental costs and benefits needs to be achieved within the country-specific domestic policies, environmental absorptive capacities, and time preferences involved. This may not be entirely valid, especially when there are unassimilated emissions of pollution, which is more of a global externality: CO_2 remains a good example of this pollutant. Again, this points to the need for an international coordination mechanism, a market-based (like emissions trading) or quota-based or target-based reduction of global environmental pollution. One of the ingredients of internalization of environmental costs is their reflection in the costs of producer prices. Initially, this can create problems in competitiveness, especially in the export markets. When prices of goods transacted in the international market do not properly reflect the social costs of production, they are effectively receiving a subsidy equal to the uncompensated environmental resource use, partly despoiled or lost in the process; see also Porter and Brown (1991). A robust observation is relevant here: export of goods produced under environmentally unsustainable conditions is unsustainable.

In a report, UNCTAD (1997) suggested that full-cost internalization will rarely be optimal and that internalization should only be carried out up to the level where the incremental benefits of avoided environmental damages justify the incremental costs of environmental provisions. This general economic argument could be a step in the right direction, especially when all the costs and benefits are properly taken into account. This approach is not significantly different from the generally accepted (but largely ignored in practice) PP principle, except that internalization of environmental costs method could apply all over the life cycle of the product: polluter-producer, non-polluter consumer, and other intermediaries involved in the sale and distribution. There may be a need for the setting of a floor price specific to some of the commodities in international trade. This might facilitate provision of revenues so generated to augment investments in environmental and ecological conservation; see also Sharma (1994). However, serious administrative enforcement problems could be significant in the application of this principle. A more pragmatic approach was suggested by Elliot (1994): rather than seeking to front-end load all the life-cycle environmental costs on the producer, it is desirable to unbundle part of these costs so that only environmental impacts which can be dealt with at the production stage of a product are internalized at the level of the producer; the costs of environmental impacts incurred at subsequent stages of product life cycle can be apportioned and internalized at the level of those who benefit directly from the consumption of the products under reference. A case study of internalization of costs, reduction in environmental pollution, and implications for competitiveness is given in box 8.3 for palm oil in Malaysia.

BOX 8.3 Palm oil cost internalization – Malaysia

The following is an example of internalizing environmental costs in the international market context. In Malaysia, palm oil cultivation was encouraged in the 1970s and 1980s with the intention of reducing reliance on rubber exports. Although Malaysia supplies about 80 percent of the palm oil that enters the world market, refined palm oil has to compete with 16 other products in the world market of fats and oil (among which soybean oil is the closest substitute). Palm oil output expanded rapidly and accounted for about 40 percent of the increase in agricultural output during the 1980s. In the same period, however, the palm oil processing industry was responsible for more than 60 percent of Malaysia's total water pollution load. The effluent caused a serious depletion of dissolved oxygen and killed fish, prawns and crabs, which are important sources of nutrition and gainful employment.

Effluent abatement regulations were established in 1977 after two years of consultations with the industry. With a command-and-control approach, oil mills were required to reduce the effluent components, using biochemical oxygen demand (BOD) as a parameter. Malaysia's refined palm oil sector lost only 5 percent of the value of output, and the crude palm oil sector lost only about 1 percent of the value of the world oils' market. Internalization did not appear to have affected the palm oil industry. Processors could diversify most of the additional costs on to producers of fresh fruit bunches (FFB), the planters and cultivators of oil palms. FFB producers appear to have borne 84 percent of the total industry losses during the abatement period. Smallholders and plantation owners were compensated to some extent by the provision of inexpensive fertilizers supplied as a by-product of effluent treatment. The palm oil industry was able to promote their by-products: fertilizers, animal feed, and energy generation via methane gases. The effluent standards contained in the environmental regulations were effective in the reduction of discharge. The role of the government in establishing the Palm Oil Research Institute of Malaysia in 1980, and in funding relevant research is noteworthy. These findings demonstrate that internalization need not impair overall competitiveness; changes in the distribution of returns from trade do occur and these call for complementary measures to offset the externalities.

Sources: Vainio (1998), UNCTAD (1995a, 1994), and Khalid and Braden (1993)

Analytically, the problem of inclusion of environmental costs consists of maximizing the total producer surplus and consumer surplus in various stages, with a provision for effecting income redistribution among the classes of economic agents involved in the total system. Such an approach could facilitate distribution of environmental costs in terms of efficiency and equity considerations, rather than simply in terms of stages of processing and their corresponding pollution costs. This is significantly different in its economic considerations compared to the 3Ps. This incorporates social welfare maximization aspects within the context of inclusion of environmental costs for pricing. Operational problems for implementation are likely to be significant, however.

Environmental costs can be minimized with alternate forms of production, but direct costs of production may be higher than usual (possibly due to lower yields). However, in the marketplace, one major difference is that the conventional environment-depleting (or pollution-generating) methods of production allow the option of excluding environmental subsidies and thus passing on the externalities to the rest of the system. In most of the environment-enhancing methods of production, the direct unit cost of production tends to be higher and the producer has little option but to raise the selling price (assuming there are no fiscal incentives). In this case, the ecosystem services are subsidized to a lesser extent, and the costs are internalized to a greater degree than in the conventional production methods. Green preferences represent a new and rapidly growing dimension of trade and environment issues. Such demand-driven forces are not actionable, i.e. disputable by other member countries as non-tariff trade barriers, under the GATT/WTO's Articles. These are influenced by consumer tastes, commercial advertising and other forms of product information dissemination.

When environmental resources are underpriced, the short-term effects of full-cost internalization could include an increase in production costs, and when transmitted into the pricing mechanisms, the higher prices may not help to withstand competitiveness (except in special cases). Internalization could also imply more efficient use of scarce resources, recycling, and the adoption of more efficient methods of production. The adaptation mechanisms on the demand side, as well as on the supply side, might warrant incrementalism in the internalization of environmental costs. Such an approach could be Pareto-welfare improving for the producers and the consumers. The questions of level of aggregation and accounting of costs for this purpose are not yet clear; neither are the methods of deciding marginal unit costs and pricing at the margin or average. Whether sustainability or SD is the implied criterion of environmental protection is another major issue. One of the simpler mechanisms which partially reflects differential environmental costs or inputs is eco-labeling.

Eco-labels and their Trade Impacts

The following illustration is based on Beghin et al. (1994). The Netherlands has a long tradition in horticultural exports such as cut flowers. Dutch dominance on world markets has been eroded recently, however, by the emergence of horticultural production and exports originating in developing economies. The flower industry is chemical-intensive and polluting both in the North and South. Dutch horticulture is also energy-intensive since most production occurs in greenhouses. A proliferation of green labels – e.g. environmental standards defined by flower auction houses – has been occurring in the Dutch horticultural sector, partly to address growing environmental concerns and partly to differentiate their products from those produced by competitors in the South, e.g. Colombia and Morocco. In 1995, the independent environmental foundation, Milieukeur, awarded an independent eco-label for cut flowers considering five production stages and eight environmental dimensions that mimic a cradle-to-grave approach. Importers can apply for the new label, but foreign producers will not be represented on the Milieukeur panels and are not involved in the definition of the label. It is unlikely that the two types of production (natural sunlight versus greenhouse) will be on an equal footing. The emergence of the new ISO standards (see chapter 9) is likely to provide a common level playing field for most producers.

Because of substitution effects, eco-labeling or other forms of credible certification can lead to decreased consumption and price of competition which, by contrast, is presumed environmentally unfriendly. The following is an example of a growing area of differential income potentials for new environmentally conscious consumption markets which bring new avenues for producers, including those in the developing countries. Although the approach may not extend to every commodity or beyond a scale for applicable commodities, it does expand to augment trade and environmental complementarities to some extent with an element of sustainability. This presumes some stability or loyalty or consumer markets which have such tastes (which are often habit-forming). Let us examine an application of trade in coffee.

Coffee and Organic Farming

Coffee is one of the most important organic agricultural exports from the developing countries. Organic standards are increasingly combined with fair trade criteria for coffee imports and exports. The following details are based on UNCTAD (1995a; 1995b). In the case of Max Havelaar coffee, it is estimated that about 30 percent of the price premium is attributable to environmental factors and 70 percent to social advantages. Coffee grown under organic conditions represents only about 0.2 percent of most European markets, but the impact of differentiated products which are environmentally supportive and the consumer level support guarantees higher prices for about 300,000 small coffee producers in 13 countries. Surveys suggest that consumers in North America, Europe, and Japan may generally be prepared to incur a 5–10 percent price premium for the environmentally preferable products.

If a narrow view of environmental pollution is taken – e.g. with the exclusion of GHGs and CO – it may appear that developing countries have a greater absorptive capacity in the financial and environmental regulation sense. The pollution-intensive industries do not necessarily specialize in these countries.

Rather, the industries that exist are allowed to flourish even with severe environmental problems relative to those in the developed countries. However, the externalities are transmitted via the features affecting the global commons, in addition to inflicting local pollution problems. This aspect may be illustrated below in the case of bilateral trade between Indonesia and Japan.

The differences in the pollution intensity of trade between Indonesia and Japan was found in a study by Lee and Roland-Holst (1994). The intensity was measured by a human toxicity index of effluents, of production and trade. If a reference level for normalization is taken as 1 for the aggregative toxicity feature per unit of economic activity in the USA (not because it is the best exemplary system), Japan had an index of 0.86 and Indonesia an index of 2.45, showing the specialization in less clean technologies of production. When it comes to trade, the pollution content of trade from Indonesia to Japan was 10.64 whereas that in the reverse direction was 1.62.

It is not hard to generalize a little on the basis of the above illustration: most of the developing countries are "pollution havens," and various exports in the present form and practice are environmental subsidies of the poor to the rich: a blend of implicit and explicit subsidies of nature, women, and children of the poorer countries to the rich anywhere. Kox (1995) estimated that, in developing countries, costs borne by the society as a result of environmental damage reaches about 17 percent of GDP, and the corresponding estimates for developed countries are much lower. Internalization of environmental costs in exports, which may be more pollution-intensive than other economic activities, generally warrant a 20 percent increase in prices if any rough estimate is taken as an indication of the magnitude of price effects! Selective full-cost pricing is usually worse than a gradual incremental and universal application of principles of internalization of environmental costs, possibly only partially. This is because the life-cycle approach warrants apportioning only part of the costs at the production front-end. Consumers and various intermediaries in the entire chain may be directly identifiable; existing fiscal and other mechanisms can meet the enforcement of the requirements of any environmental or ecotax-like charges. International commodity-related environmental agreements (ICREAs) have been proposed as possible interim solutions to alleviate the international competitive pressures among the primary commodity producers, so as to enable exporting countries to pursue a gradual transition towards ecologically meaningful production methods, with an eventual phasing out (Kox, 1995).

As an illustration of the extent of costs which may need to be reflected in the prices of developing countries' exports, it was estimated that OECD members could have incurred direct pollution control costs of $5.5 billion for their 1980 imports from developing countries if they had been required to meet the environmental standards then prevailing in the US (UNCTAD, 1995a). If the pollution control expenditures associated with the materials that went into the final product had also been counted, the costs would have amounted to $14.2 billion in 1980 (Walter and Loudon, 1986). This should be considered in the light of the fact that industrial countries have generally been more successful than developing ones at including in their export product prices the costs of environmental damage and of controlling that damage (UNCTAD, 1993). Thus, in the case of exports from industrial countries, consumers, including those in developing countries, bear at least part of the burden. However, in the case of exports from developing countries, the consequences of environmental damage are borne overwhelmingly by domestic residents and firms, principally in the form of ill-health, reduced productivity and higher costs. This asymmetry in product-pricing mechanisms is usually founded on the dire need for the developing countries – who are also usually significantly indebted countries – to earn foreign exchange. These motives of export and the implied high discount rate on appropriation of environmental resources (compounded by the myopic high discount rates on time in some ruling regimes) remain a recipe for environmental disaster in some developing countries. In summary, environmental costs which are not internalized, are effectively internationalized with a multiplier effect. Box 8.4 provides a summary of features governing some of the major commodity exporters and their external debt features. Detailed environmental accounting and full-cost pricing in each of these cases might provide an additional insight into the working dynamics of the terms of trade, constrained exports for debt servicing, and environmental implications for long-term sustainability and SD.

If a country believes that it can either substitute or afford to ignore its depletion of natural resources, preservation of the same will not merit any serious attention. However, this is not the same thing as whether the country likes to care for the rest of the environmental resources, because any neglect on this front is founded on serious problems – to the domestic ecosystems as well as the global commons. In other words, attention to the loss of natural capital – see, for example, UNCTAD (1995a) – does not address many of the other environmental resource problems that portend the systems: both their sources and sinks of these resources.

Considering that most of the exporters of non-renewable resources have depicted lower economic growth rates since the 1970s, and that most have rising debt levels (especially during the 1980s and later), any approximate application of sustainability, fiscally and in the natural resource as well as economic sense, suggests negative conclusions. These, among several other countries, need to augment their resource base via diversification of assets and formation of new asset bases to safeguard the future interests of the people. Social forestry, small-scale industries, education and skill formation, judicious management of surface and ground resources, fiscal stability and technological progress are some of the ingredients for a new era which could be environmentally and economically sustainable. A break from debt service obligations for a few years, subject to the borrower countries' acceptance of verifiable performance on adoption of SD criteria, could lead to a win–win solution of debt problems both for the creditor and borrowers. For creditors, an unhealthy borrower economy cannot be more useful than a healthy one.

Since debt management (external debt and domestic debt) and fiscal sustainability issues are fundamental to all economies, and since lack of debt sustainability lays the foundations for potential non-existence of patterns of SD, we address the underlying principles in the next section.

BOX 8.4 Primary commodity exporters and debts

Commodity-specific exporters: Fuel exporter countries are defined as those 15 countries whose total export earnings in 1988–92 exceeded 50 percent: Angola, Algeria, Bahrain, Congo, Gabon, Iran, Iraq, Libya, Nigeria, Oman, Qatar, Saudi Arabia, Trinidad and Tobago, United Arab Emirates, and Venezuela. Similarly defined, there are 14 *mineral exporters*: Bolivia, Botswana, Chile, Guinea, Guyana, Liberia, Mauritania, Namibia, Niger, Peru, Surinam, Togo, Zaire, and Zambia.

Based on data for 1995 (IMF, 1996), the total debt of fuel-exporting countries consists of about one-eighth of the global debt of all developing countries; total exports of goods and services account for a little less than the above share in the corresponding group. However, primary mineral exports tend to have a much lower share (about 2.2 percent) of export value, and a higher share of debt (about 5.1 percent) among developing countries.

If we use the World Bank (1996) classification of economies by major export category and indebtedness, we find the following main categories.

There are no *exporters of manufactures* in low-income countries who are severely indebted; India and Pakistan are moderately indebted. For the middle-income countries Bulgaria is severely indebted: those of the Russian Federation are moderately indebted.

There are no *exporters of fuels (mainly oil)* in low-income countries who are moderately indebted; Congo and Nigeria are severely indebted. For the middle-income countries, Algeria, Angola, Gabon, and Iraq are severely indebted, while Venezuela is moderately indebted.

Many *exporters of nonfuel primary products* in low-income countries are severely indebted: Brazil, Ivory Coast, Ghana, Guinea, Guinea-Bissau, Guyana, Honduras, Liberia, Madagascar, Mali, Mauritania, Myanmar, Nicaragua, Niger, Rwanda, São Tomé and Principe, Somalia, Sudan, Tanzania, Togo, Uganda, Vietnam, Zaire, and Zambia. Albania, Chad, Malawi, and Zimbabwe are moderately indebted.

Of *exporters of nonfuel primary products* in middle-income countries, Bolivia, Cuba, and Peru are severely indebted; and Chile is moderately indebted.

● 8.4 DEBT, GENERATIONAL ACCOUNTING, AND SUSTAINABILITY ●

Debt Sustainability

When the burden of debt on a country is so great that national solvency is threatened, the country's risk rating worsens and so do the terms of borrowing in the international credit markets. Debt "overhang" can seriously constrain a country's ability to use some of the features of the international capital markets for continued development needs. This could only worsen the credit-worthiness of the country and a vicious cycle sets in. The private capital market may fail to maximize the global welfare maximization potential despite the rational behavior of all participants (Krueger and Ruttan, 1989). Debt sustainability analysis is required to examine the future path of the economy and the expected evolution of the country's current obligations to determine any debt service problems. The method typically used involves choosing a time horizon (often 10–20 years) and projecting the change in the main macroeconomic variables to that horizon. These projections, together with estimates of future inflows of private and official capital, are then used to construct the balance of payments accounts and the estimated financing requires much explicit or implicit economic modeling based on assumptions about the indebted country's future economic policy (World Bank, 1997).

For external debt to be judged sustainable, the projected scenario must satisfy two conditions (World Bank, 1997):

1   During the projection period, a balance of payments equilibrium must be achieved without resorting to exceptional financing (such as debt restructuring or emergency borrowing from official sources).
2   Indebtedness at the end of the period must be low enough to make future debt service problems unlikely.

The second condition is typically evaluated by computing indebtedness indicators such as the ratio of debt to GDP or of debt service to exports (possibly on a present value basis) for the last years of the projection period. Empirical analysis of the experience of developing countries and their debt service performance has shown that debt service difficulties become increasingly likely when the ratio of the present value of debt to exports reaches 200–250 percent and the debt service ratio exceeds 20–25 percent (World Bank, 1997). Nevertheless, what constitutes a sustainable debt burden nevertheless varies from one country to another. Countries with fast-growing economies, stable foreign reserves and exchange rates, and exports are likely to be able to sustain higher debt levels than countries with tax and price distortions, and high current expenditure rates.

The positive links between capital-rich countries' public debt levels and global real interest rates are generally well-established (IMF, 1995). Higher interest payments tend to lower living standards, especially with the cumulative effect over a period of time. Mounting real debt and debt-service payments exacerbate the risk premia and cost of capital, thus worsening potential for real development. Persistent budget deficits lead to unsustainable growth paths; debt sustainability depends on the interest rate, the growth rate of the economy, and the ratio of the budget balance excluding interest payments to GDP (IMF, 1996). The role of internal and external debt – the former mainly for the developed countries and the latter for developing countries – makes it imperative that debt sustainability be examined in relation to sustainability of economic growth and development. Rising real debt levels tend to lead to higher discount rates in valuation of the future and thus compromise the long-run sustainability of many ingredients of development, especially those of unmarketed environmental resources. The latter tend to be short-changed in budget deficit systems, where the discount rates are usually higher than in the balanced ones. Thus, any debate on SD needs to examine the mechanisms governing debt burdens, budget deficits, and fiscal policies in general, and their incidence to environmental factors in particular.

Generational Accounting

Generational accounting tends to project the distributional implications of fiscal policies across generations and provides an alternative method for assessing the sustainability of fiscal policies. Some of the ecotax or environmental tax issues discussed in chapter 5 deserve to be integrated in this context, and this remains an area for further work. Given the problems in accounting for budget deficits and debt, and the limitations in economic theory in defining "deficit" or the change in debt in a given period of time, Auerbach et al. (1994) argued that a single measure of the same cannot identify the intergenerational distribution of the burden of government finance at any given time period. Generational accounting was developed by Auerbach, Gokhale and Kotlikoff (1991). These accounts indicate, in present value, what the typical member of each generation can expect to pay now and in the future, in net taxes, i.e. taxes less transfer payments received. The intertemporal budget constraint stipulates that those government bills not paid by current generations must ultimately be paid by future generations: at each date the subsequent net tax payments, in present value, of current and future generations must be sufficient to cover the present value of future government consumption, as well as paying off the government's initial net indebtedness. The requirement is stated as follows (Auerbach et al., 1994):

present value of remaining net tax payments of existing generations
+ present value of net tax payments of future generations
= present value of all future government consumption
− government net wealth

If fiscal policies were to remain unchanged, or changes envisaged with appropriate adjustments like some planned taxes (say, ecotaxes), the requirement is to ensure zero-sum constraint in the present value sense for an intertemporal budget, and to seek an answer to the question of how much each generation would pay in net taxes. The above balancing equation readily suggests that, unless the discount rate is high enough and/or the time horizon of concern is not infinity, the sums involved may not converge to finite values.

These methods in their application rely on several assumptions, one of the most critical one being the rate of discount – which was taken as a constant: the pretax real interest rate. As indicated by the authors, the accounts do not show the full net benefit or burden that any generation receives from government policy as a whole, although the accounts can show a generation's net benefit or burden from a particular alteration of policy affecting taxes and transfer payments.

In the absence of feedback mechanisms relating to secondary effects of tax changes and of changes in the public debt, the accounts provide only a partial set of estimates of cash flows. These accounts are subject to specific assumptions about the patterns of private consumption over time, and their implications vary with the bequest motives or liquidity requirements. Despite these shortcomings, the methods offer approximate scenarios in which to judge the intergenerational fairness of changes in current fiscal policies, especially any proposals on environmental taxes. One of the empirical applications is due to Hagemann and John (1995), who estimated that, in developed countries like the USA, Italy, Norway, and Sweden, present-generation young workers will have to pay $200,000–$300,000 more in taxes over their lifetimes than they receive in benefits, if current benefit levels are kept unchanged, whereas current retirees in these countries may receive about $100,000 or more in benefits than they would have paid in taxes.

There is a link between the degree of cross-generational lack of "fairness" in a country's fiscal policies as quantified by generational accounting and the extent of a country's overall fiscal problems. The variations in the size-distribution of aging populations in different countries possess their own surprises if the fiscal policies are not properly attuned for the future. Generational accounts are likely to be useful mainly as a conceptual tool of policy analysis and as a supplement to standard budget and accounting documents (IMF, 1996). For more details of the role and limitations of generational accounting as a practical technique, see Sturrock (1995), and the Winter 1994 special issue of the *Journal of Economic Perspectives*.

We now return to the issue of servicing external debt and its implications for environmental sustainability. The effects are usually realized through the routes of international trade, and domestic implications are due to debt conditionalities.

● 8.5 INTERNATIONAL DEBT AND THE ENVIRONMENT ●

International debt (comprising external debts of individual countries and other forms of finance for international trade) plays a role in affecting the quality of domestic and global environment as a result of trade-related as well as other effects:

- Enhanced direct effects of consumption and production.
- Changes in the composition and implicit environmental subsidies of export commodities of debtor–exporter countries.
- Possible public expenditure cuts with the result that the impoverished population (usually in the absence of social safety nets) rely on nature-provided services and exploit these at sub-optimal levels.

External Debt

The World Commission on Environment and Development report (WCED, 1987) expressed concern about the adverse effects of unsustainable debt: "Debt that cannot be amortized forces raw material-dependent countries in Africa to deplete their fragile soils, with the result that good land is turned into desert." These observations need not be confined to Africa and desertification. Earning foreign exchange became the first priority in heavily indebted countries like Brazil, where aluminum production for exports has been achieved at significant social and environmental costs and colonization of the Amazon region was allowed to offset potential social unrest; see De Sa (1994) for case studies and related details. Debt repayment obligations forced many countries in Latin America, and elsewhere like Indonesia, to exert greater pressure on forest and land resources and add subsidies of nature, women and children to the export basket so as remain "competitive" and earn foreign exchange.

Several partial causal linkages studies – some cited in Munasinghe and Cruz (1995) – failed to find a statistically valid one-to-one relationship between levels of external debt and environmental degradation. This does not establish the non-existence of the phenomenon. It only reflects on the appropriateness of the estimation models and statistical methods used in the analysis for the diagnosis. The characterization of debt in terms of debt service obligations rather than debt levels is important, and definitions of environmental degradation need to include both the (unsustainable) natural resource depletion features as well as a variety of environmental resources, and the corresponding direct and indirect effects. Relevant time lags in public policy response, its operational effects, and macro debt effects need to be recognized. A high ratio of debt services to exports constitutes a proxy indicator of environmental degradation due to export trade. This is because such a ratio signals the feature that more exports are meeting the debt obligations at an undiminishing pace of implicit subsidies. This leads to losses in the capital of natural resource and environmental sectors. This is an area for continued investigations since the existing studies are insufficient to establish the relevant links empirically.

The nature and extent of external debt stocks and dynamics need some assessment here. The main sources of information are: IMF *World Economic Outlook* reports, OECD reports (available from the OECD Secretariat in Paris) on Geographical Distribution of Financial Flows to Aid Recipient Countries, World Bank's *World Debt Tables* (renamed since 1998 as *Global Development Finance*), and the *World Development Indicators* – issued annually (since 1997). Some of the main observations based on these sources of data are given below.

For the year 1995, the total stock of debt of developing countries rose by 8 percent over the previous year, and stood at $2,068 billion. The corresponding level of debt for 1988 was $1,365 billion. Depreciation of the US dollar penalized the borrowers by increasing the value of debt denominated in other currencies by $13 billion in 1995, and the depreciation trend continued in the subsequent years as well. Also, interest capitalization from debt rescheduling and debt service reduction in some of the countries increased total debt. Debt forgiveness of bilateral official development assistance (ODA) was about $3.3 billion in 1994.

During the 1990s, the external debt of developing countries has been fluctuating in the range of 140–190 percent of the value of exports of goods and services.

Based on data for the year 1995, the World Bank (1997) suggests these countries may have severe debt problems as seen by the percentage (exceeding a rather arbitrary benchmark of 200) of present value of debt to exports of goods and services (the corresponding percentages are given in brackets): Algeria (222), Angola (311), Argentina (296), Bolivia (304), Brazil (257), Bulgaria (279), Burundi (375), Cameroon (355), Central African Republic (254), Congo (374), Ivory Coast (367), Ecuador (237), Ethiopia (302), Ghana (236), Guinea (294), Guinea-Bissau (3252), Haiti (627), Honduras (207), Madagascar (417), Malawi (237), Mali (282), Mauritania (312), Mozambique (904), Myanmar (433), Nicaragua (1123), Niger (312), Pakistan (224), Peru (385), Rwanda (398), Sierra Leone (471), Sudan (2418), Syrian Arab Republic (295), Tanzania (430), and Uganda (291).

Exports of goods and services as a percentage of total debt service exceeded the sustainable benchmark of 20 percent in these countries for the year 1995 (percentages are given in brackets): Algeria (38), Argentina (35), Bolivia (29), Brazil (38), Chile (26), Colombia (25), Ivory Coast (23), Ecuador (27), Guinea (25), Guinea-Bissau (67), Haiti (45), Honduras (31), Hungary (39), India (28), Indonesia (31), Kenya (26), Malawi (26), Mauritania (21), Mexico (24), Morocco (32), Mozambique (35), Nicaragua (39), Pakistan (35), Papua New Guinea (21), Sierra Leone (60), Turkey (28), Uganda (21), Uruguay (24), Venezuela (22), and Zambia (174).

Interest payments as a percentage of exports exceeded 20 in these countries for the period 1992–4: Argentina (34), Ivory Coast (23), Guinea-Bissau (30), Madagascar (21), Mozambique (34), Nicaragua (43), Peru (21), Sao Tome and Principe (35), Sierra Leone (34), Somalia (63), Sudan (63), Tanzania (30), Uganda (24), Zaire (26), and Zambia (21).

A relevant observation in interpreting this information is that most of these features are seen from a one-year or two-year data base; however, it is also the case that most of the ratios are typical of the countries involved, at least in the 1990s. The World Bank's definition of severely indebted countries is: Either the ratio of the present value of debt service to exports of goods and services exceeds 220 percent, or, the ratio of the present value of debt service to gross national product (GNP) exceeds 80 percent. Using these criteria, 48 countries qualified, based on the data for 1994–6. The new members of this club were (World Bank, 1998): Algeria, Burkina Faso, Haiti, and Indonesia.

An interesting feature of the IMF (1996) data is that, among developing countries, the net debtor countries depicted a significantly higher growth rate in the period 1978–97, relative to net creditors. This need not imply relative effectiveness of borrowed capital, however.

The Heavily Indebted Poor Countries (HIPCs) Debt Initiative

The Interim and Development committees of the World Bank–IMF suggested that the World Bank provide some relief to the HIPCs. The Bank established the HIPC Trust Fund in November 1996 and transferred $750 million from its International Bank for Reconstruction and Development (IBRD) surplus as its initial contributions. The IMF established a similar trust for the HIPC debt initiative.

The eligibility criteria for debt relief under this initiative include a "sustained track record of economic reforms" and "[facing] unsustainable debt levels." The target ranges for debt sustainability are usually within the range of 200–250 percent for the ratio of debt (in net present value (NPV) terms) to exports, and 20–25 percent of the ratio of debt service to exports. The criterion using the NPV of debt seems to be founded on fallacious accounting rather than economic reasoning. Had the loan been undertaken in a commercial market, this could make sense. Therefore, what is relevant here is an assessment of the social opportunity cost of the concessional loan. A few methodological improvements which incorporate some of these concerns are advanced by Cosio-Pascal (1997). However, a broader integration of the relevant factors for SD remains distant. In the absence of the latter, it is illogical to presume the prevalence of a sustainable debt management regime.

Uganda (which was spending $3 a person a year on healthcare and $17 a year on servicing its international debt) was the first country to obtain debt relief of about $340 million in NPV terms. The International Development Association (IDA) provided $160 million of the debt relief, which reduced nominal debt service to IDA by about $430 million over time. The Bank and the IMF examined debt sustainability aspects of more countries, and debt relief packages were agreed for the following additional countries in 1997: Bolivia, Burkina Faso and Guyana. The estimated debt relief involved for these three countries was about $815 million. A significant debt relief package was announced for Mozambique in April 1998. Under the new package, Mozambique will be able to reduce its external debt by $1.4 million in 1999; this represents over 70 percent of the country's annual GDP. The commitments of the Paris Club as well as the Russian Federation (Mozambique's single largest creditor) have provided the impetus for the relief package. The debt stock in NPV terms is expected to be reduced to about 200 percent of exports compared to 466 percent without the HIPC initiative. Mali was included for a debt relief of $250 million in September 1998, and its compliance with the reform measures is expected by the end of 1999. The total costs of assistance for eligible countries under the HIPC debt initiative has been estimated (World Bank, 1998) at about $7.4 billion in net present value terms, to be spread over the next few years. The Paris Club, under its Naples Terms (see box 8.5), proposed to offer debt reduction of up to 80 percent for countries qualifying for additional relief under the HIPC initiative.

A rapid solution to the debt problems of the poorest countries may not materialize in spite of the HIPC initiative, given the requirement that the countries establish a performance and policy track record for about three years or more to become eligible for additional relief. This performance is difficult for some of the countries with structural and institutional rigidities, and unresponsive or inefficient administration. However, these constraints on debt relief could also be very significant for any possible progress toward SD. A few criticisms of the HIPC debt initiative from some of the developing countries argue that some of the poorest countries were excluded based on the eligibility criteria. The growth prospects of a country and its attainment of environmental, social, and human development objectives should form the basis of any exercise of assessment of debt sustainability, both short-term and long-term. The role of environmental account-ing (chapter 6) is significant in all such exercises.

BOX 8.5 Paris Club Naples Terms

Paris Club is a body of official creditors that represent the major industrial countries, in addition to the World Bank, IMF, and other multilateral institu-tions and creditors. The Naples Terms were laid out at the end of 1994, repla-cing previous terms of credit (known as Toronto Terms and London Terms) for low-income countries. Some of the salient features of the Naples Terms are summarized below.

- *Eligibility*: decided on a case-by-case basis, mainly using income level criteria.
- *Concessionality*: Most countries obtain a reduction in eligible non-ODA debt of 67 percent in NPV terms; some countries with a per capita income of more than $500 and a debt to exports in present value terms of less than 350 percent receive 50 percent NPV reduction, decided on a case-by-case basis.
- *Choice of options*: Creditors exercise one of two options:
    (a) A debt reduction option involving repayment over 23 years with a 6-year grace period.
    (b) A debt service reduction option in which the NPV reduction is achieved by concessional interest rates, with repayments spread over 33 years, or a moratorium interest option with the same 'old' repay-ment period.
- *Flow reschedulings*: These allow rescheduling of debt service on eligible debts due during the consolidation period (generally in tune with the IMF arrangements of payment periods).

Sources: World Bank (1998) and Boote and Thugge (1997)

Other Mechanisms for Alleviation of Debt Problems

Debt-for-development Swaps

In recent years, interest in debt-for-development swaps has increased, but it is still limited (World Bank, 1996). Rising secondary market prices affect this type of conversion. Some official creditors have implemented programs to convert official debt into local currency funds to support projects.

In a typical debt-for-development swap, an international organization (usually a non-governmental organization (NGO)) purchases sovereign debt in the sec-ondary market at a deep discount. In a few cases, commercial banks donated debt. The NGO then exchanges the debt at par or at a prearranged discount. This redemption price is negotiated before the conclusion of the transaction between the NGO and the central bank of the developing country. "To limit the inflationary impact, local authorities issue a domestic bond (sometimes called an environmental bond) to raise the local currency. Countries without a domestic bond market may use other financial instruments, such as interest-bearing accounts in the central bank. Local currency generated by the exchange is used to finance development projects" (World Bank, 1996).

Debt-for-nature Swaps (DNS)

DNS are perceived for use in reducing a developing country's debt and allocating funds for the protection of nature preserves. The common feature of contracts involving DNS appears to be a "rational vehicle for mitigating the transaction costs inherent in such exchanges" (Deacon and Murphy, 1997). This mechanism was considered an instrument with good potential, but this expectation failed if we consider the minuscule nature of operations, if and when the mechanism is put to use. In general, DNS involves the major steps: the debtor country agencies agree and decide on the conversion quantity and exchange rate in local currency and also conservation strategy; potential swappers then assess the proper mechanisms for debt discounting and the assumption of the responsibility to absolve the debtor of the liability for a specified amount of debt.

DNS have been implemented only in 16 countries since 1987. Bolivia entered into the first DNS with Conservation International, a US-based NGO. Another NGO, the World Wildlife Federation (WWF) entered into an agreement with Ecuador for another DNS, and later participated in a DNS in Costa Rica (along with Nature Conservancy and Conservation International). By 1998, about $153 million has been raised for environmental projects at an initial cost of $46 million (or an average discount of about 70 percent (World Bank, 1998). NGOs were thus able to leverage their funds some 2.3 times, while the external debt stock of participating developing countries was reduced by about $178 million. Latin America has accounted for about 77 percent of all conversion funds in such swaps. In recent years DNS originating with NGOs have slowed to a trickle: only two agreements were carried out in 1997 for about a mere half a million dollars, in Mexico. The following countries have taken advantage of the DNS since 1987: Bolivia, Ecuador, Costa Rica, Madagascar, the Philippines, Zambia, Dominican Republic, Poland, Mexico, Ghana, Nigeria, Jamaica, Guatemala, Brazil, and Panama. Madagascar was perhaps the only country where the DNS enabled its commercial debt to reduce significantly. During the two years 1996 and 1997, Mexico was the only country reportedly involved in DNS, and Conservation International was the only buyer. In these transactions, the amount of face value of debt reduced was only about a quarter of a million dollars in five projects. In the previous transactions for the above countries, the government agencies or NGOs involved in the swap deals included: US Agency for International Aid (USAID), WWF, National Foundation of Costa Rica, the Nature Conservancy, Missouri Botanical Gardens, Rainforest Alliance, Smithsonian Institutions, and Conservation International. The relative significance of the DNS diminished over time with the finding that the effect of the DNS has been "more to reallocate aid than to generate additional resources" (World Bank, 1992, p. 169). Besides, one needs rich and effective NGOs to undertake these transactions, a rare entity in many African and Asian countries.

In general, DNS mechanisms tend to be useful to the debtor countries and the environment if most of the following requirements are met – see also Kraemer and Hartmann (1993):

● Conservation projects constitute net additional (and not substitutory) effort to the host country's efforts.
● Donor funds constitute additional resources complementing other inputs.
● Projects are based on experiences and learning values for increased effectiveness.
● Market discounts are transferred to the benefit of the host country as well.
● The design and implementation of eligible projects forms the joint responsibility of the host government and the intermediary.
● Effective monitoring and evaluation is a part of the contract agreement.
● The scale of the operations are significant to affect economies in the transaction costs of the swaps.

One cannot resist a summary observation on the working of the DNS schemes: it is hard to find many such programmes which are conceptually sound; they promise significant potential contribution, and yet miserably fail in fulfilling the expectations.

Other Debt-for-development Swaps

Three organizations have been the main participants in the debt-for-development swaps: Finance for Development, New York Bay and the United Nations Children Fund (UNICEF). The UNICEF had completed 20 operations in nine countries by 1996: Bolivia, Jamaica, Madagascar, Mexico, Peru, the Philippines, Senegal, Sudan, and Zambia. The program has generated about $53 million in local currency while helping participating countries to reduce their external debt stock by $199 million. These local funds help to finance programs for primary education, women in development, children in especially difficult circumstances, primary health, and water supply and sanitation.

During the period 1991–5, Finance for Development has raised about $69 million in local currency at an initial cost of about $46 million, enabling participating countries to reduce their debt stock by $175 million. Funds went to finance projects in health (24 percent), community development (18 percent), eco-tourism (16 percent), refugee assistance (14 percent), education (13 percent), low-income housing (8 percent), agriculture (6 percent), environment (1 percent), and population (5 percent) (World Bank, 1996).

Since 1993, a debt-for-development swap option has been added to the menu for debt stock operations financed through the IDA Debt Reduction Facility

(IDRF). Under this mechanism, "commercial banks can choose to tender debt to be repurchased by countries financed by grants through the IDRF (debt-buy-back option) or donate or tender debt to be repurchased by NGOs (at the same price as the debt-buy-back option)" (World Bank, 1996). NGOs convert the debt into local currency to finance development projects (debt-for-development option). Two countries have implemented such options: Bolivia in 1993, and Zambia in 1994. The following details of the Zambian case bring to light the proposed operative features of the package.

Zambia's debt-for-development swap is the largest ever concluded with participating NGOs (such as UNICEF, Center for American Relief Everywhere (CARE), World Vision, and a few Zambian organizations). They obtained debt at a price not exceeding the cash buy-back price (11 percent) or through donations. NGOs then exchanged the debt for an amount equal to the cash buy-back price, to be held in an escrow account to support officially approved development projects. "At disbursement, the Zambian government will pay a premium in local currency equal to 50 percent of the amount disbursed from escrow. About $96.5 million in commercial bank debt has been retired at an initial cost of $10.6 million, while generating development funds of $15.9 million (including the 50 percent premium)" (World Bank, 1996). About a third of the commercial banks involved in the debt reduction program chose this option.

Debt-for-development swaps did not progress under the IDRF financing since the mid-1990s. The constraints included: Financial resource limitations on the provision of local funds to the required extent (in terms of matching funds or counterpart funds); magnitudes of discount or premium required by NGOs; and availability of mutually agreed projects between the NGOs and the government.

Debt-for-development Swaps and Bilateral Creditors

Official creditors are more involved in debt-for-development swaps. The Paris Club introduced a new clause making ODA and commercial loans (with an upper limit of 10 percent of claims or $10 million, whichever is the higher) eligible for debt-for-nature or debt-for-aid and debt-equity swaps. First introduced for highly indebted lower-middle-income countries, the program was extended to highly indebted low-income countries and has been included under London terms and more recently, the new Naples terms; details given in box 8.5.

Nine Paris Club creditors or their export credit agencies (Belgium, Canada, France, Germany, Norway, Sweden, Switzerland, UK, and the USA) have implemented conversion programs. By 1996, about $4.5 billion of Paris Club debt has been retired or forgiven, and most counterpart funds have been invested in "environmental projects."

Official creditors outside the Paris Club have also allowed claims to be converted (World Bank, 1996). For example, in February 1993, the first debt-equity swap involving claims of former Soviet states was signed with Tanzania. Argentina has allowed UNICEF to purchase all claims (about $24 million) on Senegal for 25 percent of nominal value. UNICEF exchanged claims for new financial instruments issued by the Republic of Senegal, maturing over three years and with a face value of $11 million. These new financial instruments are hard-currency-denominated, non-interest-bearing, and payable in local currency at the exchange rate prevailing at each payment date.

The Enterprise for the Americas Initiative (EAI) of the US State Department was launched with the involvement of the Inter-American Development Bank in 1992 to promote both trade liberalization and partial debt-reduction in Latin American countries. However, some of the features of the restructuring mechanisms do not reflect an element of relief for the people in the immediate future, since the debt reduction was reduced to an accounting exercise in which the reduction is to the total magnitude of debt and the recipient country is obliged to provide local currency to finance the environmental projects listed under debt conversion at concessional rates (De Bremond, 1993).

The *Global Development Finance 1998* report of the World Bank estimated that during 1989–97, the face value of debt reduced by all instruments (including debt forgiveness and debt swaps and others) was $12.7 billion for all the low-income group countries together; and that for all the countries during the same period, it was $53.2 billion. A number of additional measures like a performance incentive-based debt servicing moratorium to enable some of the deserving borrower countries to adjust better to the requisite perspectives on SD, and devising mechanisms specifically tailored to the institutional and economic factors in each of the target countries will be desirable. The creditor institutions and developed countries could examine these possibilities, rather than attempting to administer straitjacket or one-size-fits-all devices.

● 8.6 CONCLUSIONS ●

In essence, we are only at the initial stages of understanding these issues, and any coordinated action may be years away. Therefore, greater attention is required at the country level. This could, in the short run, cost those economies adopting environmentally sensible trade and pricing policies. Internalization of environmental costs and benefits at a country level is determined by these factors:

- Democratic or other institutional framework of the political institutions.
- The role of market and nonmarket institutions in the price determination for domestic markets and global trade.
- Development priorities.
- Perceptions about global and national problems.
- Assessment of cost sharing in global environmental accords and benefits of participation, renewal and absorption capacities.
- Time preferences affecting consumption and future interests of the society.

National governments tend to view the problems implicitly in terms of their preparedness to forego natural resource base (with or without the assumption that it might be subject to natural renewal) in favor of honoring the export-earning obligations to meet the targets of foreign exchange earnings needed to repay debt or to continue to engage in further activities of imports. In an ever-declining terms of trade or foreign exchange conversion market, many developing countries can ill-afford to take a break from the compulsions of exports at declining real prices and expanding quantities. The question of the erosion of the natural resource base in such a setting is not even secondary; it goes down in the list of priorities. Thus, the multiple adverse effects of the neglect of the local environment manifest themselves locally (in addition to the global effects) over a period of time. Multilateral credit-lending institutions can do better in addressing some of these problems. Many current problems in the loan effectiveness and aid effectiveness in some of the developing countries are being sought to be simplified in their explanation to the role of the host governments. While this remains a primary factor, the role of the international institutions is not insignificant either. Any attempt to implement the principles of SD cannot take short-sighted approaches to current and long-term problems.

Debt and sustainability problems heavily impinge on the potential application of SD principles. Several additional measures are required of the multilateral and bilateral institutions to alleviate the debt burden of the borrower countries, linking their performance in the adoption of SD principles. The primary mineral-exporter countries, among others, seem to depict unsustainable patterns of economic governance. Environmental accounting methods must be used by lending institutions for the appropriate evaluation of projects and pricing of products. Lack of organizations, for example, like certain commodity cartels in exhaustible resources, should not be held against the producers' welfare and future interests.

Generational accounting and environmental accounting could be a complementary exercise to provide relevant directions to SD paths. The data limitations remain a constraint in most countries. New initiatives at the global level might be required in this effort. It seems the sum of component-specific linkage assessments is likely to be an underestimate of the combined effects of the phenomena of trade liberalization, debt overhang, and constrained export strategies without due regard for incorporating environmental costs.

Review Exercises

1 What guidelines may be needed if exhaustible resources, like some minerals in Africa, are to be priced at a producer level with internalization of environmental costs? What constitutes these costs and why?

2 It was suggested by Munasinghe and Cruz (1995) that trade liberalization and the removal of price supports in richer countries would reduce coal output, lead to higher international prices, and consequently decrease coal consumption. Examine the validity, if any, of this observation, taking into account the possible response of "poorer" countries to the policy changes in the richer countries and the global impact.

3 If any two of the following three threshold levels associated with debt are meaningful in assessing the unsustainability of debt in individual countries, list the countries (based on the detailed listings in the text) that depict the potential unsustainability problem:

(a)   Total debt service constitutes over 25 percent of exports.
(b)   Total debt level exceeds 250 percent of exports.
(c)   Interest payments exceed 20 percent of exports.

4   What are the main sets of data required for formulating an intergenerational accounting framework for any specific country? What are the additional information requirements compared to those for environmental accounting (see chapter 6)?

5   If the debt-for-nature schemes (DNS) have relevance, what could possibly "sweeten" these to improve their success?

6   (a)   What are the institutional prerequisites for the workability of commodity-specific rules for internalizing environmental costs?
    (b)   What are the implications for consumption and production changes as a result of such internalization?

7   It was stated in the text that environmental costs which are not internalized are internationalized. Elucidate this assertion and explain its implications for the relative incidence of costs of internationalization on exporters and importers via the effects on the global commons.

References

Anderson, K. and Blackhurst, R. (eds) (1992) *The Greening of World Trade Issues*. New York: Harvester Wheatsheaf.

Auerbach, A. J., Gokhale, J. and Kotlikoff, L. J. (1991) Generational accounting – a meaningful alternative to deficit accounting. In D. Bradford (ed.), *Tax Policy and the Economy*, vol. 5. Cambridge, Mass.: MIT Press, 55–110.

Auerbach, A. J., Gokhale, J. and Kotlikoff, L. J. (1994) Generational accounting – a meaningful way to evaluate fiscal policy. *Journal of Economic Perspectives*, 8(1), 73–94.

Barbier, E. B. (1994) Les effets environnementaux des échanges dans le secteur forestier. In E. B. Barbier (ed.), *Les Effets Environnementaux des Echanges*. Paris: OECD.

Barbier, E. B. and Rauscher, M. (1994) Trade, tropical reforestation and policy interventions. *Environmental and Resource Economics*, 4, 75–90.

Beghin, J., Rolland-Holst, D. and van der Mensbrugge, D. (1994) A survey of the trade and environment nexus – global dimensions. *OECD Economic Studies*, 23, 167–92.

Boote, A. and Thugge, K. (1997) *Debt Relief for Low-income Countries – The HIPC Initiative*. Pamphlet Series # 51. Washington, DC: IMF.

Braga, C. (1992) Tropical forests and trade policy – the case of Indonesia and Brazil. In P. Low (ed.), *International Trade and the Environment*, World Bank Discussion Paper # 159. Washington, DC: The World Bank, 173–95.

Cheyne, I. (1995) Environmental unilateralism and the WTO/GATT system. *Georgia Journal of International and Contemporary Law*, 24, 433–53.

Chichilnsky, G. (1994) North–South trade and the global environment. *American Economic Review*, 84, 851–75.

Cole, M. A., Rayner, A. J. and Bates, J. M. (1998) Trade liberalisation and the environment – the case of the Uruguay round. *The World Economy*, 21(3), 337–47.

Copeland, B. R. and Taylor, M. S. (1994) North–South trade and environment. *Quarterly Journal of Economics*, 109, 755–87.

Cosio-Pascal, E. (1997) *Debt Sustainability and Social and Human Development*. UNCTAD Working Paper # 128. Geneva: UNCTAD.

De Bremond, A. C. (1993) The hidden costs of free trade – environmental and social consequences of economic liberalization in the enterprise for the Americas initiative. *Journal of Environment & Development*, 2(1), 151–80.

De Sa, P. (1994) Brazilian aluminum industry – past choices and present issues. In B. Barham (ed.), *States, Firms, and Raw Materials – the World Economy and Ecology of Aluminum*. Madison: The University of Wisconsin Press, 111–39.

Deacon, R. and Murphy, P. (1997) The structure of an environmental transaction – the debt-for-nature swap. *Land Economics*, 73(1), 1–24.

Elbasha, E. H. and Roe, T. L. (1996) Endogenous growth – the implications of environmental externalities. *Journal of Environmental Economics and Management*, 31, 240–68.

Elliot, G. (1994) *Internalization of Environmental Costs and Implications for the Trading System, GATT Symposium on Trade, Environment and Sustainable Development*. Geneva: GATT.

GATT (1992) *Trade and Environment*. Geneva: GATT.

Gillis, M. (1988) Indonesia – public policies and the tropical forest. In R. Repetto and M. Gillis (eds), *Public Policies and the Misuse of Forest Resources*. Cambridge: Cambridge University Press.

Hagemann, R. P. and John, C. (1995) *The Fiscal Stance in Sweden – A Generational Accounting Perspective*. Working Paper 95/105. Washington, DC: IMF.

IMF (International Monetary Fund) (1995) *Staff Studies for the World Economic Outlook*. September. Washington, DC: IMF.

IMF (1996) *World Economic Outlook 1996*. Washington, DC: IMF.

Khalid, A. R. and Braden, J. B. (1993) Welfare effects of environmental regulation in an open economy – the case of Malaysian palm oil. *Journal of Agricultural Economics*, 44(1), 25–37.

Kox, H. (1995) *LDC Primary Exports and the Polluter-pays-principle: A Case for International Policy Coordination*. UNCTAD Expert Group Meeting on Internalization of Environmental Costs and Resource Values. Geneva: UNCTAD.

Kraemer, M. and Harmann, J. (1993) Policy responses to tropical deforestation – are debt for nature swaps appropriate? *Journal of Environment & Development*, 2(2), 41–65.

Krueger, A. O. and Ruttan, V. (1989) Toward a theory of development assistance. In Krueger. et al. (eds), *Aid and Development*. Baltimore: The Johns Hopkins University Press, 32–52.

Lee, H. and Roland-Holst, D. (1994) International trade and transfer of environmental costs and benefits. In J. Francois and K. Reinert (eds), *Applied Trade Policy Modeling*. Cambridge: Cambridge University Press.

Low, P. (1993) *Trading Free – the GATT and US Trade Policy*. New York: The Twentieth Century Fund.

Munasinghe, M. and Cruz, W. (1995) *Economy-wide Policies and the Environment – Lessons from Experience*. Environment Paper # 10. Washington, DC: The World Bank.

OECD (1994) *The Environmental Effects of Trade*. Paris: OECD.

Porter, G. and Brown, J. W. (1991) *Global Environmental Politics*. Boulder: Westview Press.

Prudencio, R. J. and Hudson, S. J. (1994) *The Road from Marrakesh, Trade and the Environment*. GATT Symposium on Trade, Environment and Sustainable Development. Geneva: GATT.

Rao, P. K. (1999) *World Trade Organization and the Environment*. London: Macmillan.

Schoenbaum, T. J. (1997) International trade and protection of the environment – the continuing search for reconciliation. *American Journal of International Law*, 91(2), 268–313.

Sedjo, R. and Wiseman, C. (1983) The effectiveness of an export restriction on logs. *American Journal of Agricultural Economics*, 65, 113–16.

Sefton, J. A. and Weale, M. R. (1996) The net national product and exhaustible resources – the effects of foreign trade. *Journal of Public Economics*, 61(1), 21–47.

Sharma, R. (1994) *Ownership and Governance, GATT Symposium on Trade, Environment and Sustainable Development*. Geneva: GATT.

Smith, V. K. and Espinosa, J. A. (1996) Environmental and trade policies – some methodological lessons. *Environment and Development Economics*, 1(1), 19–40.

Sturrock, J. (1995) *Who Pays and When? – An Assessment of Generational Accounting*. Washington, DC: US Congressional Budget Office.

UN (1997) *International Cooperation to Accelerate Sustainable Development in Developing Countries and Related Domestic Issues*. UN Document E/CN.17/1997/12/Add.1. New York: UN. Also available on their website: www.un.org/dpcsd

UNCTAD (1993) *Trends in the Field of Trade and Environment in the Framework of International Cooperation*. Report TD/B/40(1)/6. Geneva: UNCTAD.

UNCTAD (1994) *The Internalization of Environmental Costs and Resource Values – A Conceptual Study*, UNCTAD/COM/27. Geneva: UNCTAD.

UNCTAD (1995a) *Sustainable Development and the Possibilities for the Reflection of Environmental Costs in Prices*. Report #TD/B/CN.1/29. Geneva: UNCTAD.

UNCTAD (1995b) *Environmentally Preferable Products as a Trade Opportunity for Developing Countries*. Geneva: UNCTAD. Quoted in UNCTAD (1995a).

UNCTAD (1997) *Trade and Environment – Concrete Progress Achieved and Some Outstanding Issues*. Geneva: UNCTAD.

UNDP (1998) *Human Development Report 1998*. New York: Oxford University Press.

Vainio, M. (1998) *The Effect of Unclear Property Rights on Environmental Degradation and Increase in Poverty*, UNCTAD Discussion Paper # 130. Geneva: UNCTAD.

Walter, I. and Loudon, J. (1986) *Environmental Costs and Patterns of North–South Trade*. Paper prepared for the World Commission on Environment and Development. New York: United Nations.

WCED (1987) *Our Common Future*. New York: Oxford University Press.

World Bank (1992) *World Development Report 1992*. Washington, DC: The World Bank.

World Bank (1996) *World Debt Tables, Vol. I – Analysis and Summary Tables*. Washington, DC: The World Bank.

World Bank (1997) *World Development Indicators 1997*. Washington, DC: The World Bank.

World Bank (1998) *Global Development Finance 1998*. Washington, DC: The World Bank.

chapter outline

● CHAPTER 9 ●

Governance and the Private Sector

● CHAPTER 9 ●

Governance and the Private Sector

An ecological view of life tends toward
putting man at the center stage, as both
protagonist and villain.
Richard A. Falk

● 9.1 INTRODUCTION ●

The role of the private sector remains increasingly important in economic and environmental systems. The roles of the market factors, often complemented by other institutional mechanisms, are critical in cost-effective implementation of several policies and programs. Even where the private sector is largely respons-ible for the environmental ills, there is an important role for market-based in-struments (and hence another segment of the private sector) in correcting the problems. Market solutions to market problems need not be an incongruence. The role of contestable markets (Baumol et al., 1982) is a classic example in this setting. Market solutions for the failure of the nonmarket institutions is rather well known, as is the role of the state in correcting the failures of the market. However, the ultimate social contribution of one or more of these alternatives lies in their relative effectiveness in delivering the goods and services at a rea-sonable transaction cost to the consumer or citizenry. It is not the dichotomy of state versus the market that should be the choice between alternatives; rather, it is the continuum based on a mix of institutions and instruments for the co-ordination of policies and their relative efficacy of implementation that matters in the enhancement of social welfare.

The private sector has assumed a much greater role in recent years than ever before, especially after the collapse of several communist and socialist economies in Europe. Also, the net long-term resource flows to developing countries rose from $98.3 billion in 1990 to $300.3 billion in 1997; of these, the private flows rose from $41.9 billion to $256 billion during the same period (World Bank, 1998). Given the dominating role and significance of the private sector, it is all the more important that the environmental concerns of society are properly reflected by the private industry. Private capital and international capital market mechanisms, or the private sector in general, may not be sufficient to address the sustainable development (SD) needs of developing countries or to ensure that their activities maintain a positive influence on the environment. This does not automatically justify the role of the regulatory wings of the governments as the sole implementing mechanisms. Rather, catalytic interventions from the government and people's institutions can steer the market institutions to achieve desired efficiencies and goals for the environmental upkeep.

Most studies have found that democratic and market institutions are environment enhancing, relative to non-democratic and bureaucratic regimes of control. Democratic institutions and the role of values in the private sector are largely complementary. No doubt, there are social costs of operating a private enterprise; for an early reference, see Kapp (1950). There are also social benefits of the same. One need only review the experiences of working with social enterprises in many systems to appreciate the value of the private enterprise. When productivity and efficiency issues are of little significance in any management regime, the drag of the institutional alignment on the social, ecological, and economic systems remains a significant factor: everyone pays for everyone else's sub-optimal efforts. It is more likely that when environmentally responsible entities – people's institutions, lobby groups, national governments, or international institutions – work closely in cooperation with the private sector, some of the goals of SD can be attained with the minimum amount of adaptation costs or transaction costs.

Private sector industry is powerful enough to foster the changes needed to ensure ecological sustainability, but this does require that the agents in this decision process are sufficiently motivated with the combined effects of profit motives, foresight and environmental concern, institutional stipulations, and requirements of competitive advantage. In general, self-enforcing business conduct enables environmental protection when sustainable business leads to an element of competitive advantage, both in the short run and in the long run. In short, this is a question of incentive-compatibility.

This chapter examines the role of the characteristics and emerging features of the environmental markets and the environment industry in the processes to support SD. Both the employment potential and revenue potential in the environment industry depict increasing trends for the past two decades. The elements of corporate environmentalism and illustrative examples of corporate dynamism in environmental leadership, and the role of the financial institutions in affecting environmental enhancement are examined. The role of the government sector in encouraging R&D, and thus contributing to technical progress is an essential component for sustainability and SD. Various trends in this direction do not indicate any enhancement of the efforts, especially in the government sector. This remains a cause for concern in the context of SD. The scope for the adoption of standardization methods like appropriate certification and adoption of the recent ISO 14000 code for environmentally sound management principles and practices, application of life-cycle analysis and related issues are examined in the last part of this chapter.

● 9.2 ENVIRONMENTAL MARKETS
AND THE ENVIRONMENT INDUSTRY ●

Much of the basis for economic analysis of the market transactions tends to utilize one or other of the ingredients of the Coase (1960) result which states that when property rights are well-defined and transaction costs are insignificant, economic entities tend to negotiate and obtain a solution that mimics that of an efficient market, even without the intervention of the government or regulatory authority. This Coasean set-up assumes the existence of a rather static state of the economic system in competitive equilibrium. Given the almost instantaneous destabilizing influence of information and technical change, it is difficult to perceive the practical application of some of the implications of the result in a world of changing preferences and flexible decision making with little commitment (or value-free utility maximization).

Traditionally, the origin of the environmental problems has been viewed in terms of the market failure features, specifically those related to uncompensated externalities. Several forms of government interventions led to the wide usage of the regimes of bureaucratic regulation and enforcement. Whereas the legal provisions for environmental protection are essential, the bureaucratic implementation methods have not been cost-effective in most countries. The failure of these institutional forms brings us back to the possibility of improving the functioning of market institutions in conjunction with a meaningful role of the government regulatory and policy framework. The scope for incorporating environmental elements in the market systems can be examined with an improvisation of new instruments of policy (including support or subsidy for enhanced R&D), and development of new market areas. These direct and catalytic interventions affect the demand for, and supply of, environmental goods and services. The key is in finding a balance without obstructing the efficient design and functioning of market institutions. Often, the key to correct market failures is to create another set of newer markets, or a set of contestable markets which have the effect of actually competing markets. Ironically, an institutional economic approach would attest to the phenomena that public enforcement mechanisms lead to private markets (and externalities) in a different sense: enhanced lobbying and intermediation, bribery to avoid compliance, rent-seeking and extortion in tyrannical regimes.

Environmental markets are those affecting the demand for, and supply of, goods and services which are environmentally significant. These markets can be seen as derivatives of public policy as well individual preferences of humans. These markets are products of the following:

- Regulatory policies devised at the national, local, and international levels.
- Environmental concerns at the entity level.
- Influences due to public awareness and environmental demands from influential groups.
- By-products of changing technologies and government policies with linkages to the environment.
- Changing preferences of consumers.
- Economic activities and anthropogenic influences on the environment, in general.

The main factors affecting demand for environmental goods and services are changes in regulations and their enforcement, provision of incentives for good performance or exceeding compliance targets; public awareness and consumer preferences; and public policies affecting its expenditures and technological progress.

The shift from regulations in implementing environmental policy in favor of environment-enhancing market-based strategies will support the environmental markets and environmental industry. Fiscal and market instruments can be used as complementary economic instruments. In many countries public expenditures for pollution abatement and control equipment, and activities of the industry such as water supply, drainage and treatment affect the above. Although still an expanding area and not yet common in most developing countries, the emission permits trading program merits a discussion because of its future potential for wider applications. This constitutes an example of an environmental market.

Tradable Emission Permits (TEPs)

Among the important potentially effective market-based instruments of environmental management are the TEPs. They are but an illustration of marketable permits which tend to allow for three ingredients: potential cost savings – across firms, over time, and averaging between different emission sources of a given firm. The relative reduction in the uncertainty of the goal achievement in the TEP, compared to a conventional regulatory mechanism is one of the several merits of the market-based mechanism. The relative costs of enforcement and the role of transaction costs in the TEP compared to effluent fees is an added feature; see also Baumol and Oates (1988). Several analytical models have been developed in recent years which seek to copy the structure of the TEPs. An illustration of the application of optimization methods for the CO_2 emission permits is given by Bueler (1997).

Under the conventional regulatory regimes, a bureaucratic agency could fix a target emission reduction level and/or specify the types of control devices to be used – even where to buy these, in some countries. This approach can be arbitrary, inefficient in its effectiveness – in some cases, this could be due to leakages and corruption in the enforcement systems – and costs of compliance tend to be very high. The fact that the cost function at the firm level is not uniform for all producers – even in the same industry or under a single enterprise at its multiple units – suggests that the firms should be allowed to optimize in terms of resource costs and ingredients of various inputs so as to achieve the desired emission goals in a least-cost manner. A TEP scheme places a sectoral or an aggregated limit on total emissions from all firms in a given category, and provides an initial allocation of entitlements for each firm based on objective criteria, such as historical emissions or industry norms. Firms are free to buy and sell within that system. Any firm that can reduce its emissions for costs less than the market price of a permit under the trading mechanism could do so and sell its unused permits to others who find it cheaper to buy them at the prevailing price and/or who find it more expensive to effect reductions in the emissions. Either way, the desired emission reduction is realized at lower costs than under traditional regulation. Box 9.1 provides an illustration: an experience of air quality in California.

The emissions trading approach is, in principle, extendible to a number of pollution-reducing mechanisms. An example of an extension came from Panayotou (1995): it was suggested that corporations in developed countries could be given credit for buying into tradable right, for example, through relaxation of

---

BOX 9.1 Pollution trading example – California

Based on several years of deliberations, the USEPA (US Environmental Protection Agency) issued a Final Emissions Trading Policy Statement on December 4, 1986. In late 1991, the EPA issued a rule that apportioned about 600 million kg of the baseline CFC allowances. Similarly, a number of state and local authorities devised and implemented a few emission control methods with their reliance on market mechanisms. An example from California is summarized below; see also Anderson et al. (1997) and Tietenberg (1998).

The origins of emissions trading date back to 1975 when the USEPA initiated trials of such schemes, to save on the costs of regulation enforcement and information management. South California's Air Quality Management District (SCAQMD) began in October 1990 its new emissions trading regime, which was called the Regional Clean Air Incentives Market (RECLAIM). It took more than three years to elicit public opinion, deliberate and devise rules for implementation. The RECLAIM program became operational from January 1, 1994. It involved 390 major sources of nitrogen oxide emissions, including 41 of these for SO_2 emissions. The production units in the program can choose from: purchasing traded emissions and devising methods of pollution prevention and treatment. It was estimated that, in 1997, the tradable permit program reduced the private sector compliance costs to $636 million, from the estimate of $930 million in the absence of the RECLAIM program. When carried out properly, mechanisms like RECLAIM can effectively replace regulatory regimes.

domestic regulatory obligations. Such a proposition may not recognize the adverse contributions to local pollution caused by the involved companies, if the reliance is simply in terms of offsetting emissions of some of the major green-house gases (GHGs). Possibilities of extending market-based instruments for environmental markets are given in the US President's Economic Report (USA, 1998); see also chapter 11.

Environment Industry

One of the operational definitions used as a starting point for the concept of environment industry was due to the European Commission (EC, 1994). Building on its earlier work, the Organization for Economic Cooperation and Development (OECD), in 1995, drafted a definition stating that the environmental industry (activities or businesses) is defined as "producing goods and services used for measuring, preventing, limiting or correcting environmental damage to water, air and soil as well as problems related to waste, noise and ecosystems." The environmental industry was also defined as including some proportion of the industries that produce clean technologies, processes and products (hardware, software, systems and services) which reduce environmental risk and minimize pollution and material use. In broader terms, it is meaningful to include the private sector activities in TEP and other market-based instruments of pollution control in the category of environment industry. Clearly, these might be classified as environment markets but this has little meaning without any reference to the industry itself.

Cleaner technologies are difficult to measure because improvements which are less polluting cannot be separated from general improvements which are more efficient. Hence, the share of costs related to environmental improvement cannot easily be separated from those of general improvements, or production-efficiency improvements. One way of describing the industry is to include goods and services which provide environmental protection in different domains; these are not necessarily mutually exclusive, however. The resulting classification was suggested by the OECD (1996). The main elements are given in three segments:

1 *Environmental equipment*: waste-water treatment equipment; waste management and recycling equipment; air pollution control equipment; noise reduction equipment; monitoring instruments; research and laboratory equipment; natural resource conservation/protection; and urban amenities.
2 *Environmental services*: waste-water processing and reuse operations; waste handling and facility operations; air pollution control operations; noise reduction operations; analytical, monitoring and related conservation and protection services; technical and engineering services; environmental R&D; environmental training and education; accounting and legal services; consulting services; other environmental business services such as software development for improved environmental planning and management; and others like eco-tourism.

3   *Integrated environmental technologies in industrial processes and cleaner products*: cleaner production equipment; efficient energy generation and conservation equipment; and ecological quality-enhancing products.

The business sector has been incurring increasing expenditures for environment goods and services for several reasons:

- To comply with environmental regulations;
- To capture economic benefits from reducing the consumption of raw materials and energy;
- To minimize waste and pollution.

More enterprises are recognizing that the environmental inputs and outputs are scarce resources, and are investing in environmental management.

The economic importance, in addition to its environmental significance, of the environment industry has been increasing over time. Market trends for the global environmental industry projected an annual growth rate of about 5.5 percent (OECD, 1996). Pollution abatement expenditures were estimated around 3 percent or more for the USA, Japan, and Germany; the corresponding estimates for other countries were lower. Estimates of employment in the environment industry in the USA depict an increasing trend: the rise has been from about half a million in 1980 to about 1.3 million in 1996. The estimates of the environment industry revenues (at 1995–6 prices) went up from $52 billion to $184 billion during the same period.

Estimates of the size of the global market indicate that, by the year 2000, the global market – due to regulatory effects alone – will be of the order of $500 billion per annum, or around 2 percent of the entire world gross domestic product (GDP) at that time. The International Finance Corporation (IFC), using a broader definition for the industry, estimated it will be about $600 billion by 2000 (IFC, 1992). The OECD countries account for about two-thirds of the current global market; the share of the Asia and Pacific region is expected to more than double by the year 2000. Latin America's share of the market is estimated to increase from 2 percent to around 3 percent in 2010.

Despite the drop in input by government in R&D contributions (as explained in section 9.3), the role of the respective governments in positively affecting the environmental industries is not insignificant in some developed countries. Here are some recent examples of government programs to support environment technology development (OECD, 1996):

- *France*: The EUREKA program led to commercially oriented R&D projects in areas including waste treatment.
- *Germany*: Development of environmental technologies is largely supported. Programs are promoting focused environmental R&D: environmental and climate research, biotechnology and new materials research and research for renewable energy. There are also programs to support implementation of environmental technologies in the industrial sector: financial support to

promote investment to control pollution, and grants for innovative measures to improve the environment which go beyond statutory requirements.

- *Japan*: Funding collaborative R&D (firms with national laboratories and universities) on environment-related industrial technologies, managed by the Research Institute of Innovative Technology for the Earth. Seven international environment-related projects were being carried out in 1993 in Japanese and foreign laboratories. Japan also has tax incentives to develop environment-friendly technologies.
- *Netherlands*: Stimulation of technological innovation is a major part of industry policy with a special focus on the environment. Specific incentives are available for environmental technology R&D (reuse and recycling and energy technology R&D as well as general R&D), personnel tax advantages, and technology development credits. Moreover, cooperation among government, industry, technological institutes, and universities has been successful in developing environmental technologies.
- *Norway*: Environmental technologies have been supported by research programs on environmental technology for export. There are sustainable process industries (with 50 percent co-financing), and a cleaner technology program to develop, demonstrate, and transfer cleaner technologies (with 50 percent co-financing).
- *Sweden*: There are programs to support development of cleaner technologies and products, particularly in the energy sector (energy-saving and alternative sources).
- *UK*: The UK is promoting collaborative research, for example, on engine emissions, and is supporting some R&D linked with the wider diffusion of best practice environmental technology.
- *USA*: A wide range of programs support the development of environmental technologies. The inter-agency environmental technology initiative, coordinated by the USEPA, partly supports the private sector to promote technology development. The Department of Energy has programs related to energy efficiency and renewable energy. The Department of Defense has a funding program to support R&D in environmental compliance and environmental R&D in general. The Department of Commerce, NASA and the Bureau of Mines all fund R&D for environmental technologies. The general approach has been to support not only R&D for new solutions favorable to the environment but also commercial applications.

Environmental investment takes place primarily in the following categories of firms (see also Gentry, 1995):

- Environmental industry companies – offering any of the broad range of environmental goods and services described above.
- Environmental projects – mostly involving infrastructure and projects providing environmental goods or services, such as urban water supply systems or waste treatment facilities (and usually controlled directly or indirectly by government institutions); investments designed to improve the environmental

effects of existing projects or activities such as a production process (as would be the case if TEP makes an impact) or reforestry, and also covering new investments possibly involving financial institutions.

- Environmentally efficient companies – companies which are not primarily in the business of providing environmental goods or services, but which efficiently manage the environmental opportunities facing their entire range of enterprise activities, beyond regulatory compliance; these could include the effects of participating in a TEP.

There may be several limitations in the ever-expanding role of environmental business and private sector seeking to appropriate profits. One such area is in the control, exploitation, and conservation of biological resources. This is illustrated below.

Bioprospecting: Limits for the Private Sector?

One of the complex areas of private business in biological resources is in the area of bioprospecting. Bioprospecting involves the use of biological materials for the development of pharmaceuticals or genetic strains of crops. Given the potential to benefit humanity in a significant way, especially in enhanced medical treatment possibilities through the discovery of new medicines, bioprospecting seems very relevant. Global revenue from bioprospecting might well run into a few billions of dollars. Usually, a bioprospecting project involves a multinational enterprise from an industrial country and the biological resources to be exploited for commercial use tend to be located in one of the developing countries; this need not be the case in every project, but the biospecies geography could require such an arrangement. Thus, it involves a host government and a set of cooperating institutions from the latter, an international contract agreement and compensation mechanisms. Apart from the magnitudes of cash flows which these business activities generate, the complex interactions of the following factors determine the success and its maintainability of most bioprospecting proposals: intellectual property rights (IPR), undocumented but conventional rights of indigenous populations, equity and provision of incentives for conservation, and ensuring cooperation of explicitly participating and implicitly non-participating interests in an international bioprospecting agreement, its legal contract design and enforcement. Shiva (1997) argued that several of the bioprospecting methods combined with the market monopolization potential and using the regimes of IPR led to "biopiracy." This was facilitated to a greater extent when the traditional or indigenous knowledge is exploited, considering the fact that the former never subscribed to the emerging new international IPR regimes. The new instruments seeking to control the old knowledge are considered a discriminatory approach to the issue of IPR.

Most of the world's biodiversity is located in the tropics: about 50–80 percent of the world's species live in tropical forests. This suggests that, in principle, the developing world can expect to secure most of this market. Countries like Brazil and Indonesia would enjoy the lion's share. Some of the studies produce very low values for pharmaceuticals; the value of undiscovered tropical forest drugs to the pharmaceutical companies is $2.8–4 billion. It is unrealistic to derive even a rough estimate, but considering that each of the "successful" drugs in the late 1990s are fetching a revenue of no less than a billion dollars, the above range could be an extraordinarily low estimate.

Considering the geographic distribution or concentration of biological species in tropical forests and coral reefs, the role of distribution of gains of commercial exploitation remains an important one if any equity dimension is to be invoked. Indigenous people who have been custodians of these resources in some of the tropics must be given due attention and are entitled to share the income from the benefits of bioprospecting; see also Reid (1995). The potential for over-exploitation and destruction of resources cannot be entirely ruled out in the existing mechanisms of bioprospecting. It could lead to a net gain or Pareto-welfare improving scenario mainly in some of the regions where gross neglect is the norm of the local authorities. Even in such cases, a monopolistic approach in the bioprospecting methods can be disastrous to the ecosystem and the host country. If bioprospecting is to serve the objectives of sustainable use and conservation of biodiversity, these aspects must form part of a verifiable and enforceable contract – see also Hunter (1997) – for example, how the goals will be accomplished and in what time schedules. Conservation is assumed to occur, or expected to take shape out of the revenues realized in bioprospecting and to be shared with the host authority, according to most of the existing contracts.

Discussed above is a complex area where the big businesses seeking to expand into new desirable businesses must ensure that profit is one of several criteria to be fulfilled so as to ensure sustainable business development. This warrants a great deal of vision and corporate leadership, beyond possibly complying with the regulatory and legal requirements.

● 9.3 COMPLIANCE AND BEYOND ●

One of the earliest legal acts in the western world was in 1821. The British Parliament passed a law which enabled individuals to take legal action against owners whose furnaces were emitting significant pollution, mainly particulate matter. Then, in 1863, a pollution standard called the Alkali Act required the manufacturers of alkali to remove 95 percent of the hydrochloric acid. An Alkali Inspectorate was created as the first pollution control agency. Several legislative and administrative provisions have been made in most countries during the twentieth century, and, more importantly, since the 1970s. Depending on the enforcement mechanisms, prevailing norms and relative costs of compliance or otherwise at the business entity level, the environmental stipulations are applied with varying degrees of sincerity. However, a few corporate and other economic entities have been taking exemplary initiatives which go beyond the requirements of the law. These have found such measures compatible with long-run economy in the costs of their operations and environment enhancing in the activities. Two examples are narrated below.

Environmental Compliance and Beyond

Box 9.2 gives two illustrations of enterprise initiatives which go beyond simply seeking to ensure regulatory compliance. One of the major enterprises taking initiatives on their own to implement measures and policies which are both environmentally supportive and enhance economic efficiency at the corporate level is 3M in the USA. Many cost elements and environmental impacts described in this case resemble those at several production units in the industrial sector. It is yet to be seen how many more could emulate these examples and improve upon them. The next case study is an illustration of approaches to planning and the implementation of energy-efficiency improvement.

BOX 9.2 Corporate initiatives

3M Case Study

Pollution prevention became an area of concern at 3M in 1975 when the company initiated its pollution prevention pays (3P) program; this was the first time a major company made pollution prevention an integral and permanent element of all of its operations. 3M's 3P program is directed at improving management of air, water, and land resources. A pollution prevention project must meet established criteria to be recognized as an approved 3P project: it must, through process change, product reformulation, or other preventive means, eliminate or reduce a pollution and produce an environmental benefit through reduction in energy consumption, more efficient use of raw materials, or improvement in the use of other natural resources. It should involve an innovative approach, or unique design. It must have some monetary benefit for 3M through reduced pollution control or manufacturing costs, or increased sales.

Since 3P started in 1975, more than 4,200 approved projects worldwide were estimated to have resulted in the prevention of more than 650,000 tons of pollutants. Energy consumption per manufactured unit has been reduced by 60 percent during the mid-1970s to mid-1990s period. Air emissions were reduced by about 70 percent during the period 1989–93.

Savings from all of the 3P projects since 1975 were estimated to add up to about $800 million by 1998. Based on the success of the 3P, 3M decided in 1989 to expand its voluntary commitment to improve environmental quality: the 3P+ program was established, setting specific waste reduction goals for the year 2000. The Environmental Management System focuses on two key elements: life cycle management techniques, and challenging environmental goals for the year 2000. 3M spends about $150 million a year on ecological R&D, and about $200 million a year on special environmental programs all over the world. It received the US Presidential Award for Sustainable Development in 1996.

Sources: Smart (1992) and MMM Environmental (1998).

Ontario Hydro's Sustainable Energy Development

Ontario Hydro is one of the world's largest utilities. Until recently, it was characterized by poor environmental performance, high rates, and lack of accountability to stakeholders. However, in 1994, this public utility's stated mission was to become "a leader in energy efficiency and sustainable development, and to provide customers with safe and reliable energy services at competitive prices" (Ontario Hydro, 1994). Under the utility's new Sustainable Energy Development Strategy, principles and practices in support of SD include practicing eco-efficiency, taking a precautionary approach to human health risks and environmental damage, integrating environmental and social factors into decision making, participating in the development of public policies promoting SD, encouraging employees to conduct activities sustainably, and monitoring progress toward SD.

Investment decision criteria developed in 1994 require the following to be considered (Ontario Hydro, 1994):

● Full life-cycle costs, from design to decommissioning and disposal.
● Expected damage to ecosystems, communities, and human health.
● Potential environmental impacts of alternatives.
● Quantification and monetization of potential environmental impacts.
● The trade-offs made in selecting the preferred alternative.

An internal assessment of this new strategy during the first year of implementation concluded that significant progress had been made, particularly in programs relating to ozone-depleting substances, renewable energy, GHGs, in-house energy efficiency, criteria for decision making, and tracking personnel performance through indicators. Progress had been slow in internal motivation and education, funding for initiatives, moving from environmental compliance to leadership, customer energy-efficiency programs, reforming R&D programs, and introducing full-cost accounting.

Sources: Ontario Hydro (1994) and Dower et al. (1997).

R&D and the Related Role of the Government Sector

In general, public policies have two kinds of impacts on the supply industry:

● Indirect impacts operate on the demand side through environmental regulations and standards, economic instruments and incentives, and government–industry agreements.
● Direct impacts by promotion of the industry through support for environmental R&D, general incentives for all industry, or specific incentives for the environment industry.

The private sector decision to invest in environmental R&D is influenced by three factors common to all R&D decisions (Grilliches, 1984; Rao and Pray, 1997):

- The appropriability – the ability of the firm to benefit from R&D resource deployments.
- Technological opportunity – the likely productivity of R&D in producing new products and processes.
- Expected demand, including implications for competitive advantage.

It is also generally established that the private sector concentrates its efforts at the applied end of the R&D process, rather than at the fundamental and analytical segment. The existence of exogenous and endogenous uncertainties governing the R&D output generate risk-averse behavior at the firm level. This situation requires the provision of risk-reducing mechanisms. One of these pertains to regulatory uncertainty. A continuing complementary input by the government sector is a prerequisite to realize the full potential of technical progress, the key to SD. The environment industry also has some features which have a particular bearing on R&D decisions. Development of new environment goods and services can be encouraged by reducing regulatory uncertainty and the timing of regulatory measures; see also Gentry (1995).

The R&D budgets of the private sector must keep pace and offset the effects of reductions from the complementary R&D budgets of the government sector. This situation is a little more demanding than it should have been, if the principles of public economics have any role here. It is well known that social returns to R&D are usually greater than that for the private sector in R&D in sectors like the environment, which possess many of the features of public goods. The private sector may not have enough incentives to undertake socially optimal levels of research, given the added uncertainties of the science of global climatic phenomena and the longer than normal gestation lags in product marketability. Issues like the effective management of the global commons require the development of products within the arena of the private sector. However, given the nature of indivisibilities in the costs and benefits of globally beneficial programs, several additional initiatives have to be undertaken by governments and international institutions.

In most countries, the government budget appropriations for environmental R&D have not shown any significant increase as a percentage share of the GDP during the past 15 years. UNDP (1997) reported – quoting sources IEA (1995) and OECD (1994) – that the total R&D budgets in the government sector for the energy sector declined in member countries to almost half in terms of their percentage to GDP; the decline was from 0.12 percent in 1983 to about 0.06 percent in 1992, and the trend seems to have continued thereafter. In absolute magnitudes of total expenditures (at constant 1994 dollars), this amounted to $12.4 billion in 1983, and $8.72 billion in 1994. The decline in fossil energy R&D was from $1.7 billion to $0.98 billion in 1994, and, in the case of renewable energy, it was from $1.05 billion to $0.7 billion during the same period.

A closer look at some of the related features in the US economy are revealing and supportive of the same trends as in the larger scenario. R&D expenditures are reported as part of data on pollution abatement and control expenditures in the *Statistical Abstract* of the US (USA, 1997). Using constant 1987 dollar terms, the total R&D expenditures have come down, in a rather systematic trend, from $2.33 billion in 1973 to $1.43 billion in 1993. However, the total expenditures on pollution control and abatement (excluding R&D expenditures) have gone up significantly: from $47.35 billion in 1973 to $90.4 billion in 1993. The private sector pollution abatement expenditure during the same period moved up from $32 billion to $59 billion.

The trends depicted above do not lend support to a desirable pattern of complementarity of private sector and government sector R&D efforts, the key requirement for sustained technical progress, which is a prerequisite for SD. It is very likely that the trends in all categories of R&D expenditures are not fully captured in the above estimates, but the observations are unlikely to be different even after any such adjustments in the data. There appears to be a definite need for the government sector to augment the efforts of the private sector in the R&D resources. A few private enterprises do initiate and succeed in their innovations and corporate environment leadership, but this set must expand if sustainability of business and of the environment is to be secured. As discussed in chapter 8, subsidies and related incentives for environmental quality purposes are unlikely to attract provisions under the "disputable actions" provisions of the GATT/WTO, given the exemptions for subsidies under Article XX of the GATT (General Agreement on Tariffs and Trade).

Corporate Environmentalism

Green Concerns

The report of the World Commission on Environment and Development (WCED, 1987) suggested that private industry "has the power to enhance or degrade the environment – it invariably does both." Concerns for environmentalism or green issues was not new to some companies, even decades ago. However, a bundle of incentives and resources, disincentives and penalties, and environmental enforcement mechanisms were required to ensure that some enterprises comply with their obligations in the short run and in the long run. The compliance mechanisms dictated by government regulations is only one aspect of greening at the firm level; greening or environmental concern remains a continuous process and needs to be reflected in almost all the activities and operations of corporate sector.

A large variety of alternative approaches to defining and operationalizing environmental concerns at the corporate level may be seen in the debate on these issues. Approaches suggested by a sample of four institutions are summarized below from a list of 20 "multistakeholder" approaches; for details, see Miller and Szekely (1995). Most of these do maintain a comparable content even when the objectives and means of attaining the same are usually specified as if these are interchangeable. These are the criteria used in each institution:

- *UN Environment Programme (UNEP) Industry and Environment Office*: corporate environmental management based on responsibility, accountability, and sustainability; voluntary endorsement of environmental conduct codes.
- *European Commission DGX1*: efficient use of raw materials resources; prevention, reduction, and elimination of pollution at source; reduction of environmental impact across the entire life cycle.
- *International Chamber of Commerce*: having management practices in place to effect environmental improvement, according to 16 principles under the Business Council for Sustainable Development (BCSD).
- *CERES Coalition*: voluntary adoption of CERES' (Center for Environmentally Responsible Economics) ten-point environmental ethic, pledging to go beyond legal compliance; engagement in a process of continuous environmental improvement.

Several unorganized civic communities tend to use their own traditional criteria of respect for nature, but the conflict of interests of requirements of resilience of nature with the current needs of humans do not necessarily ensure environmental sustainability. Businesses located in such areas can possibly promote stewardship on a voluntary basis. Why should companies invest resources in "green" elements? Consumer markets cannot absorb the greater costs of adopting full-cost prices which internalize environmental costs and/or environmentally supportive practices. Becoming green enables companies to become sustainable, and to incorporate the standards of compliance, leading to savings on the costs of compliance and the potential costs of non-compliance. If the green concept is appropriately applied, companies derive many types of benefits (Miller and Szekely, 1995): they become sustainable, avert risks and damages, improve business efficiency, enhance customer focus, become more competitive, and respond to society's environmental needs in an ethical and equitable manner.

The BCSD (with its affiliation under the International Chamber of Commerce) sought business growth to remain "eco-efficient," defined as a process of adding ever more value while steadily decreasing resource use, waste, and pollution (Schmidheiny and BCSD, 1992). This is a requirement similar to the statement of the Brundtland Report (WCED, 1987), which asserted that SD "is not a fixed state of harmony, but rather a process of change in which the exploitation of resources, the direction of investments, the orientation of technological development, and institutional change are made consistent with future as well as present needs."

The 1992 Declaration of the BCSD sought to encourage open and competitive markets, and to foster innovation and efficiency, and stated two important requirements:

- The markets must give the right signals.
- The prices of goods and services must increasingly recognize and reflect the environmental costs of their production, use, recycling, and disposal.

The BCSD sought to internalize environmental costs and related externalities through a series of measures geared to achieve this feature using gradual, harmonized, predictable and transparent use of market-based instruments. Many of the above stipulations require improved methods of calibration of process and product standards, the concern of the next section.

● 9.4 STANDARDS AND CERTIFICATION ●

An environmental management system (EMS) is typically composed of an entity's operations and overall management functions reflecting the entity level recognition of the environmental policy. Usually, an EMS which is simply compliance-based to satisfy existing environmental regulations may not be sufficient not only from the environmental viewpoint but also in seeking continuous efficiency improvements and raising productivity levels. A well-developed EMS may be devised taking – in addition to creation of a positive image – the following potential benefits into account – see also Welch (1998):

● Economy in the costs of continued compliance and operating costs;
● Prevention of pollution and waste;
● Reduction of potential legal liabilities; and
● Improvement of competitive edge and market access.

As an example, the USEPA's Code of Environmental Principles (CEMP) calls for the following provisions in the EMS: management commitment, compliance assurance and pollution prevention, enabling systems and human capacity building, performance accountability, measurement and improvement. In the UK, the British Standards Institute (BSI) developed an EMS called BS 7750 in 1992. This served as a model for the new ISO 14000 series discussed below. The EU adopted the Eco-Management and Audit Scheme (EMAS) as a relevant framework for the EMS in respect of companies undertaking business in the EU.

The growing use of international standards and certification programs is sometimes suggested as evidence of product quality and compliance with environmental standards. Much of this work has been led by the International Standards Organization (ISO), which has national organizations in 111 countries. The ISO has been at the forefront of developing international standards and methods for certifying the quality of production systems. The most popular of these are the ISO 9000 series of product quality standards. Increasingly, certification of a production line or facility as in compliance with ISO 9000 has been a valuable commercial asset, particularly in export markets. About 70,000 companies participate in the certification process.

ISO 14000

Moving beyond the compliance mechanisms into a proactive era, the new standards of ISO 14000 focus on the process rather than performance of products, and prevention of an environmental ill. The ISO 14000 series pertains to the environmental area. The ISO developed these series, which include the ISO 14001 standard for environmental management, in 1996. The standards cover the following areas, among others:

- Specifications for pollution prevention and environmental management systems.
- Environmental auditing.
- Environmental performance evaluation.
- Life-cycle assessment.
- The environmental aspects of product standards.
- Environmental labeling.

An important distinguishing feature of the new standards is that these enable process rather than conventionally understood quality standards. Thus, the means of achieving certain quality standards is seen here as an important ingredient of product development and of its final quality. One may have the finest quality fur to wear, but how good is it in terms of loss of biological species, or methods of animal slaughter, or disposal of the corresponding residuals? Hence there is a need for process as well as quality standards for a meaningful consumption pattern for the humans, assuming anthropogenic superiority as legitimate.

The financial stakes of enterprises are being increasingly linked to environmental considerations and potential liabilities. This trend indicates that, at some time in the near future, the commercial lenders could seek environmental certification of the ISO 14000 standards. The ISO 14000 series standard is based on the fundamental concepts of quality assurance (QA) and total quality management (TQM) developed over the years and summarized in the 9,000 series. The main objective of the standard is to support environmental protection and to use the best available technology where appropriate and economically viable. The standard is not intended to address aspects of occupational health and safety management, and does not state specific environmental performance criteria; see also Lamprecht (1997). SD is mentioned in the Introduction in a relatively feeble manner, but most steps suggested in the standards are expected to contribute toward implementation in the right direction.

ISO 14001 requires an organization or enterprise to perform the following tasks, among others:

- Define its environmental policy in relation to its products, activities, and services.
- Identify environmental aspects of its activities.
- Ensure that environmental impacts of these activities are considered in setting the objectives of the organization.
- Keep information up-to-date.
- Consider legal and other requirements when reviewing objectives of the organization.
- Provide resources essential to the implementation and control of the environmental management system.

- Require all personnel to be sufficiently trained.
- Consider processes for external communication on its significant environmental aspects and record its decision.
- Review and revise emergency preparedness and response procedures.
- Evaluate compliance with relevant environmental legislation and standards, and the management review the environmental system to ensure that it is effective.
- Address possible need for change in policy or objectives and related aspects.

ISO 14000 may not be within the feasibility for implementation in most of the small and medium companies (constituting the bulk of production in the world, especially in the developing countries). Care must be exercised to see that this may not automatically be interpreted as non-compliance or non-adoption of the standards by any other criterion. The danger in such misinterpretations can lead to one form of discrimination against such entities; see also Roberts (1998). Many small sector and developing country industries expressed the possibility of potential non-competitiveness if the ISO 14000 is sought to be viewed as the norm for international trade. It may be relevant – in the interests of pursuit of fairness – to devise decentralized or sub-sectoral characteristics for their possible adoption in such cases. However, in the larger enterprise levels, the implementation of these standards and systems may, in the future, be seen as a basis for assessing a company's environmental rating, insurance premium rates, access to capital markets and financial institutions, and cost of capital borrowings, stockholder participation or stock appreciation, in addition to public appreciation and corporate image.

Since most financial institutions function as private sector businesses, it is relevant to examine some of the links between these and environmental factors. The next section deals with these aspects.

● 9.5 FINANCIAL INSTITUTIONS AND THE ENVIRONMENT ●

The activities of the financial institutions are usually highly regulated by the government or central bank (in the case of banking institutions). However, a significant degree of leverage in their policies rests with their respective management bodies. Like the non-financial institutions, constraints toward environmentally enhancing activities are usually based on profitability criteria. The interface between environmental problems and their negative effects is more directly felt by the insurance industry. Some of the measures proposed by this industry are described later in this section.

A useful focus on the environmental improvements can arise from a wide range of investments, both general economic activities and those of the "environmental industry." Some illustrations of the role of financial institutions, given below, may be relevant; see also Gentry (1997).

The US Export–Import Bank offers increased support for exports of environmental goods and services. It offers special enhanced support for environmentally beneficial projects and products in its loan, guarantee and insurance programs, and resources to projects that provide renewable energy, improve energy efficiency result in the reduction of GHGs, assist in environmental clean-up efforts, or have other beneficial affects on the environment. A new Environmental Directorate has been established at this bank to assist the US businesses with loans for environmental projects overseas. The funding for environmental projects at the Export–Import Bank exceeds $1 billion.

Examples of commercial banks funding environmental projects in emerging markets include two by Chase Manhattan Bank in Mexico and Argentina. International commercial bank supported projects are frequently catalytic or direct influences of local and international environmental requirements. Projects involving commercial banks require a high degree of cooperation between the public and private sectors as, for example, in the infrastructure projects. Finding ways to increase the effectiveness of cooperation between public institutions and the private sector, and to extend it to smaller scale projects is critical to expanding the role of private finance in environmental investment. In a multilevel financing mechanism, the latter can be handled by the local financial institutions. The provision to the financial sector of more sophisticated analyses of companies' environmental performance as part of their investment ratings will be an additional support for environmentally sustainable financing.

Banks' Collective Declaration

By 1997, more than 90 banks from 26 countries (most of these with global operations) signed the "Statements by Banks on the Environment and Sustainable Development" which was originally prepared just before the 1992 Earth Summit. The Statement contained some pledges including the following – see also UNEP (1996):

> We will endeavor to ensure that our policies and business actions promote sustainable development . . . a fundamental aspect of sound business management . . . ; we are moving towards the integration of environmental considerations into banking operations and business decisions in a manner which enhances sustainable development . . . ; we recommend that banks develop and publish a statement of their environmental policy and periodically report on its implementation.

The statement also included an assertion that they subscribe to the precautionary approach to environmental management, which strives to anticipate and prevent potential environmental degradation.

The processes of private ratings of enterprises for their environmental performance, risk exposure or other role in potentially enhancing or affecting developing countries are also assessed. Box 9.3 contains a few illustrative examples of environmental rating companies undertaking these activities.

Environmental risk exposure is required to be disclosed by companies covered under the US Securities and Exchange Commission for trading operations in debt and equity instruments. Besides, the legal requirements under "due diligence

BOX 9.3   Environmental rating companies

This illustrative summary – based on Gentry (1995) – is by no means an exhaustive list of environmental rating companies. The purpose is to highlight the emerging trends that affect corporate rating with increasing awareness and requirement of environmental contribution of businesses; these ratings could possibly complement the adoption of the Codes of the ISO 14000 for a similar objective.

● *Eco-Rating International*, a Zurich-based firm, provides ratings in the form of a numerical score for a company as a whole, or for specific products and processes. The majority of their clients use the ratings as management tools and as information for potential investors.

● The *Investor Responsibility Research Center (IRRC)* provides information about US companies' environmental liabilities and performance to institutional investors, corporations and other entities. Company profiles contain information obtained from regulatory agencies on environmental compliance, enforcement actions and penalties, annual toxic pollutant releases, and waste clean-up responsibilities. IRRC has rated all the companies in Standard and Poor's 500 index.

● The London-based *Center for the Study of Financial Innovation (CSFI)* produces a bond-style rating taking into account both a company's financial strength and environmental performance. Environmental risk is interpreted to include both the usual measures of liabilities from pollution, and also risk-mitigators like management capability and the financial, as well as the regulatory fiscal and political, context of relevant consequences.

Source: based on Gentry (1995).

and lender liability" in countries like the USA require the banking and other lending institutions to ensure compliance with existing environmental regulations and anticipation of environmental risks. However, in the non-banking industry sectors, a Price Waterhouse survey of 1994–5 (Schmidheiny and Zorraquin, 1996) covering 1,100 US companies found that 62 percent of respondents made no mention of their environmental exposures, suggesting possibly that the companies might privately admit their environmental costs but may not go public on the matter by strategic choice of information revelation or because of ignorance, or a combination of both.

Risk Underwriting

Risk underwriting has come to stay as an insurance mechanism to promote private investments in rather risky projects. The Multilateral Investment Guarantee Agency

(MIGA) is an affiliate of the World Bank, and sells political risk-underwriting insurance in eligible cases. In addition, investors in some developed countries have access to risk-underwriting institutions that are private or government-sponsored institutions. The Overseas Private Investment Corporation (OPIC) in the US, and EID/MITI in Japan are such institutions. Others include, at the multilateral level, the Inter-American Development Bank (which started this activity only in April 1997), the Asian Development Bank (which started these operations in 1988, but carried out business only to the magnitude of $252 million by 1998), the European Bank for Reconstruction and Development (which was insuring about $500 million by 1997), the West African Development Bank, and the East African Development Bank.

The issue that requires further attention is how far such institutions offer "leverage" or additional risk-bearing mechanisms for environment-enhancing investments. Additional investigations could shed new light on the provision of greater incentives for private investment and risk management in promoting sustainable environmental development, building on initiatives already under way in the Global Environmental Facility (GEF).

The UNEP Insurance Initiative

The UNEP Insurance Initiative led to a position paper and participation of several insurance companies, in the knowledge that the insurance industry in the financial sector is the one most likely to be hit by global climate change (which include more of the extreme events: coastal flooding, etc.), with the possibility that property and casualty insurance aspects, as well as life assurance and pension fund investment portfolios are likely to be adversely affected.

Potential changes in human morbidity (because of adverse effects in the spread of diseases due to global warming) and mortality also have implications for the health and life insurance industries. Regional variations in these and related effects could be significant, however. The Insurance Initiative sought to advocate the application of the Precautionary Principle (PP) as a guiding approach in the UN Framework Convention on Climate Change (UNFCCC) negotiations and control of global pollution emissions. This is a desirable situation where the insurance industry – as in its normal business – suggests what constitutes an insurable risk (except that the industry may not derive an immediate dividend or premium in this case). Also, this explains a rare situation where a non-polluter (at least directly) is concerned with sustainability issues as a matter of business. Besides, as an investor group, the insurance industry has a responsibility to manage long-term savings; the mutual interest of the insurers and the insured tend to coincide, and this happens in respect of some of the key ingredients of SD processes. In the long run, security and return on investment are also influenced by the attitude taken by creditors towards the environment (UNEP, 1996). The insurance industry seems to have recognized that "prevention is better than cure." Given the resources at its command, the industry can play a more active role by supporting major initiatives in the information systems and analysis areas of global warming, SD, and identification of several more win–win solutions.

● 9.6 CONCLUSIONS ●

The role of the private sector continues to grow in every aspect of life, and so does its responsibility toward the environment and its sustainability. Private industry has the most significant potential to contribute its might to the processes, principles, and practices relevant for SD. This is feasible even without cumbersome compliance procedures and bureaucratic controls, provided the vision of a typical industry firm includes attention to the needs of environmental sustainability, in addition to profitability. If the world is to be governed only by regulations enforced by the government bureaucracies, it will be a sad state of affairs for a wide variety of reasons. Private industry needs to go beyond compliance requirements, and when more than a critical size of industries and businesses participate in environmental and ecological resource-augmenting activities, the competitive advantage principle in business does not impose an additional burden nor does it hinder business efficiency principles (as the 3M case, for example, amplifies).

The voluntary adoption of the ISO 14000 code and investor consciousness in using some of the environmental ratings will pave the way for greater motivation and adherence to ecological principles in addition to conventional business methods. Financial institutions can do much in this regard by requiring the credit borrowers of large size businesses to produce their ISO 14000 certification and, in subsequent stages, the appropriate environmental ratings.

The complementarity of the government sector and private sector is a phenomenon which leads to cost-effective policies and programs for the larger social benefit. Due attention to these features lowers the transaction costs and adaptation costs of desirable changes for SD processes. New markets and incentives, and market-based instruments for improving environmental implications of economic activities, are examples of direct intervention by government which can effectively facilitate socially-beneficial outcomes. Another important area with implications for the basic requirement of SD is technical innovations and the role of the government. The government sector in many industrial countries has shown over the past two decades a trend of declining investments in the R&D efforts for environmental development. This is hardly a satisfactory state of affairs, considering that certain basic research is unlikely to take place at the private industry level and the social returns to such research activities are usually higher than private returns to research – and the latter may not be attractive enough for investments among the alternatives by the private sector.

Review Exercises

1   Can the "Environment Industry" itself cause environmental problems like contributing to pollution? If so, what measures might be expected to be undertaken to mitigate the damages?

2   (a)   Discuss the information requirements for the implementation of the Tradable Missions Permit program.

    (b)   How is this a cost-effective method for environmental compliance?

3 If the 3M case is applicable in many similar enterprises, what are the likely factors behind their non-adoption of similar initiatives? What incentives from the government might be relevant in this context?

4 If the multilateral institutions like MIGA (the Multilateral Investment Guarantee Agency) can play a greater role in risk-underwriting, what other risks limit the potential investments in the global environmental industry?

5 What constitute the determinants of the demand for, and supply of, environment/ecology-enhancing industrial goods and services?

6 Examine the complementary role of the government sector in promoting the private sector environmental industry.

7 In the methods of standards and certification, examine the significance and limitations of ISO 14000 in attaining environmental objectives of:
   (a) developing countries;
   (b) industrial countries.

References

Anderson, R. C., McGartland, A. M. and Weinberger, J. B. (1997) Cost savings from the use of market incentives for pollution control. In R. F. Kosobud and J. M. Zimmerman (eds), *Market Based Approaches to Environmental Policy*. New York: Van Nostrand Reinhold.

Baumol, W. J. and Oates, W. (1988) *The Theory of Environmental Policy*. New York: Cambridge University Press.

Baumol, W. J., Panzar, J. and Willig, R. (1982) *Contestable Markets and the Theory of Industry Structure*. New York: Harcourt Brace Jovanovich.

Bueler, B. (1997) Solving an equilibrium model for trade of CO_2 emission permits. *European Journal of Operations Research*, 102, 393–403.

Coase, R. (1960) The problem of social cost. *Journal of Law & Economics*, 3, 1–44.

Dower, R. D., Ditz, P., Faeth, N., Johnson, N. and Mackenzie, J. (1997) *Frontiers of Sustainability*. Washington, DC: Island Press/World Resources Institute.

EC (1994) *Eco-industries in the EC, in Panorama of EU Industry 94*. Brussels: European Commission.

Gentry, B. (1995) *Making Private Investment Work for the Environment, UNEP Round Table on Investing in the Environment, October 95*. London: EBRD/UNEP.

Gentry, B. (1997) *Making Private Investment Work for the Environment, UNDP/ODS Discussion Paper*. New York: UNDP/ODS.

Grilliches, Z. (ed.) (1984) *R&D, Patents and Productivity*. Chicago: The University of Chicago Press.

Hunter, C. J. (1997) Sustainable bioprospecting. *Boston College Environmental Affairs Law Review*, 25(1), 129–74.

IEA (International Energy Agency) (1995) *Energy Policies of IEA Countries*. Paris: IEA/OECD.

IFC (International Finance Corporation) (1992) *Investing in Environment – Business Opportunities in Developing Countries*. Washington, DC: IFC.

Kapp, W. (1950) *The Social Costs of Private Enterprise*. Cambridge, Mass.: Harvard University Press.

Lamprecht, J. L. (1997) *ISO 14000 – Issues & Implementation Guidelines for Responsible Environmental Management*. New York: Amacom–American Management Association.

Miller, J. and Szekely, F. (1995) What is Green? *Environmental Impact Assessment Review*, 15(5), 401–20.

MMM Environmental (1998) Information from 3M web site: www.mmm.com.

OECD (Organization for Economic Cooperation and Development) (1994) *National Income Accounts 1960–1992*. Paris: OECD.

OECD (1996) *The Global Environmental Goods and Services Industry*. Geneva: OECD.

Ontario Hydro (1994) *Ontario Hydro Annual Report*. Ontario, Canada: Ontario Hydro, April.

Panayotou, T. (1995) Conservation of biodiversity and economic development – the concept of transferable development rights. In C. Perrings, K. G. Maler, and C. Folke (eds), *Biodiversity Conservation – Policy Issues and Options*, Amsterdam: Kluwer Academic Press, 301–18.

Rao, P. K. and Pray, C. (1997) *Economics of Technical Change, R&D, Innovations, and Market Structures*. In press.

Reid, W. V. (1995) Biodiversity and health – prescription for progress. *Environment*, July, 1.

Roberts, J. T. (1998) Emerging global environmental standards. *Journal of Developing Societies*, 14(1), 144–63.

Schmidheiny, S. and the Business Council for Sustainable Development (BCSD) (1992) *Changing Course – A Global Business Perspective on Development and the Environment*. Cambridge, Mass.: MIT Press.

Schmidheiny, S. and Zorraquin, F. (1996) *Financing Change – The Financial Community, Eco-efficiency, and Sustainable Development*. Cambridge, Mass.: MIT Press.

Shiva, V. (1997) *Biopiracy – The Plunder of Nature and Knowledge*. Boston: South End Press.

Smart, B (1992) *Beyond Compliance – A New Industry View of the Environment*. Washington, DC: World Resources Institute.

Tietenberg, T. (1998) Ethical influences on the evolution of the US tradeable permit approach to pollution control. *Ecological Economics*, 24(2), 241–57.

UNDP (1997) *Energy After Rio – Prospects and Challenges*. New York: UNDP.

UNEP (1996) *UNEP Insurance Initiative Position Paper on Climate Change*. Geneva: UNEP Environment and Trade Unit.

USA (1997) *Statistical Abstract 1997*. Washington, DC: US Commerce Department.

USA (1998) *Economic Report of the President 1998*. Washington, DC: USGPO.

WCED (World Commission on Environment and Development) (1987) *Our Common Future*. New York: Oxford University Press.

Welch, T. E. (1998) *Moving Beyond Environmental Compliance – A Handbook for Integrating Pollution Prevention with ISO 14000*. Boca Raton, Fl: Lewis Publishers/CRC Press LLC.

World Bank (1998) *Global Development Finance 1998*. Washington, DC: World Bank.

chapter outline

● CHAPTER 10 ●

International Institutions

International Institutions

One touch of nature makes the whole world kin.
William Shakespeare

● 10.1 INTRODUCTION ●

The role of the international institutions, financial or other, remains very important in shaping the policies and programs of economic development in most countries. This is particularly relevant in many of the developing countries. Despite the rise of private capitalism, multilateral institutions tend to affect the direction of policies, especially in areas like the environment where "bottom line" or pure profits may not be the sole relevant driving force of future progress. Besides, even the knowledge sector in this area is perhaps unlikely to be supported at socially optimal levels by the private sector, since the potential gains are more likely in the public arena. The social benefits or return on investment are usually much greater than what the private sector could appropriate in profits. This warrants attention by the government and international institutions to provide the required levels of information and related inputs for sustainable development (SD).

Institutions affecting the process of SD include both the formal and the informal institutions. The former include international institutions of global governance like those under the UN system, international and multilateral financial institutions like the World Bank and the International Monetary Fund (IMF), and multinational banks and other financial intermediaries. Institutions created for the working arrangements of global transactions like the international commodity and trade agreements or the UN Framework Convention on Climate Change (UNFCCC) also fit into this category. Basically, these are the institutional arrangements which have a formal role in credit mechanisms and environmental policies, including devising, monitoring, and enforcing policies and compliance. The informal institutions include non-governmental organizations (NGOs), networks of environmental or other lobby groups – however, most of these are formally organized institutions – and opinion and information disseminating groups in a decentralized and unconnected spatial framework. These also include people and entities which could positively or negatively affect the process in an active or passive sense. The role of indigenous people, for example, is in the latter category; their interface with the globalization of their local knowledge in the form of patenting by multinational enterprises is one area that brings to surface the international institutional nature of issues like biodiversity and local people.

This chapter examines the role of the international financial institutions like the World Bank, the role of international agreements, and that of globalization of indigenous knowledge and effects of development projects on the life of the indigenous peoples. The environmental implications of some of the practices of the World Bank and the IMF, like "structural adjustment" and "stabilization" are examined. It is seen that several additional reforms are required at the level of these institutions to ensure environmentally responsible conduct of their operations. These aspects are briefly explored. Alternative methods of international debt management needed to incorporate environmental implications are examined. Specific issues in water resource management and international fisheries are explored in case analyses.

● 10.2 INTERNATIONAL FINANCIAL INSTITUTIONS ●

The role of the financial institutions is usually proportional to the decline in other forms of official development assistance (ODA). The ODA was lower in the years that followed the 1992 Earth Summit (perhaps not because of it, but in spite of it): about 0.3 percent of the developed donor country's gross national product (GNP). Only Denmark, the Netherlands, Norway, and Sweden achieved the UN Conference on Environment and Development's (UNCED) suggested level of 0.7 percent. The average ODA for the least developed countries dropped to less than 0.1 percent during the 1990s, worsening the plight of the poorer countries. The main reasons for the low levels of ODA in the early 1990s include budgetary austerity in donor countries, poor utilization in recipient countries, aid fatigue, and the general feeling that private sector and private sector capital flows could perform the miracle of addressing dire human needs. Given the critical role that financial institutions play in this setting, it is important to examine the crucial implications of their policies and operations on sustainability and SD.

The World Bank

Starting from a relatively minor portfolio of about a billion dollars before the 1992 Earth Summit, the World Bank increased its lending portfolio for the environment and related sectors to about $15 billion by 1999. This amount was spread around 62 countries. The bank's awakening on environmental issues in the 1990s is primarily due to the directives of the US Government in connection with a fresh replenishment of capital funding for the bank's operations. The bank launched green accounting of the past projects starting in 1993, involving an outlay of about $87 billion. It started active participation in the guidance and management of the Global Environmental Facility (GEF), and the Montreal Protocol Multilateral Fund.

During the two decades preceding the mid-1990s, the bank financed activities involving colonization of rain forests in parts of Brazil and Indonesia, excessive grazing operations in Latin America and Africa (Porter and Brown, 1991) and encouragement of exports of products which have been environmentally subsidized and unsustainable. Even tobacco production was very much encouraged – a cash crop after all, why not? An Evaluation Study of the World Bank reviewed 335 projects funded in the pre-1990s in agriculture and forestry sectors and found that severe environmental damage accrued with a gestation lag. These effects started when the projects neared completion or after their completion (Rao, 1997; Tietenberg, 1996). Some projects adversely affect the environment and the borrower debt, and the new projects propose to effect the opposite – both at the expense of the borrower. As an illustration, the experience in Nepal may be relevant: the Nepal Settlement Project sought to convert about 43,000 acres of tropical forest in the Terai region in 1974, followed by another loan transaction to launch the Terai Forestry Project in 1983. A detailed narration of critical reviews of the major international institutions depicting their relative ineffectiveness was given by Hancock (1989), and by Rich (1994) specifically for the World Bank. Considering several incomplete assessments which led to avoidable adverse consequences in the borrower countries, it appears important that there was a provision of lender liability in the debt contracts with the World Bank and the IMF.

Several irrigation projects during this period were funded without adequate provision for drainage and conjunctive use of ground and surface waters, leading to environmental problems like water logging and salination – some of these problems are very severe and irreversible. Even after considerable debate on the environment dimension at the World Bank, its 1993 Water Sector Policy did not recognize the need to incorporate guidelines for water pricing to include environmental costs; see box 10.1. The Bretton Woods Committee (1994) asserted that the Bank was "justly criticized for being environmentally insensitive in the past," and it seemed to believe that, in recent years, it has reformed its ways significantly. This belief is only partially sustainable. Chapter 7 gives details of the lack of interlinks between poverty reduction attempts and the environment. The case analysis in box 10.1 establishes an inconsistency between stated objectives of environmental sustainability and sectoral and broader policies. A number of similar incongruences are seen between policy declarations and their implementation. The significant role of the international institutions in affecting SD requires further analysis.

BOX 10.1   Water (resources) and the (World) Bank

The World Bank financed projects amounting to several billion dollars in dozens of countries. It has a major influence on resource use efficiency and agricultural income generation: the main source of livelihood for the vast majority of the populations in developing countries. The Bank's policy document was issued in September 1993 as a framework and a set of guidelines for adoption by the borrower institutions. The document vows to contribute to "reduce poverty by supporting the efforts of countries to promote equitable, efficient, and sustainable development . . . the new approach is designed to help countries achieve these objectives more effectively while sustaining water environment . . ." In terms of institutional reforms, the policy document was sensible to seek an active role for the stakeholders (especially water users) in various projects financed by the bank. This is a desirable contrast with its own irrational policies of the past. Those policies were enforced by the World Bank through its borrower country authorities on such items as farm crop restrictions under an unrealistic "design cropping pattern;" water allocation was based on that pattern, with no guarantee that the crops thus produced would be marketable or generate income. Many of the adverse implications included resource-use externalities, exacerbated water shortages, and corrupt practices in the enforcement. However, this was not recognized in the policy document which sought to bring in an element of "authority" and "enforcement" in compliance with its policies.

The policy document advocated water pricing on the basis of: (a) the need to make the water supply management undertaking financially viable; and then (b) eventually to a proposed opportunity cost pricing, based on scarcity value of water in alternative uses. This remains an ill-conceived prescription since it ignores environmental considerations altogether – see also Rao (1994) – with no assessment of consumptive and depletive withdrawals of water, its return flows and their quality characteristics, or various externalities of water use (especially those arising from varying combinations of ground and surface waters). Many of these extern-alities have surfaced in several of the bank-supported projects during the past two decades, but that experience was perhaps redundant when it came to devising pricing mechanisms. Part (a) suggests pricing water based on arbit-rary cost and inefficiency factors when the cost factors of bureaucratically administered water supply entities are proposed to be passed on to the water users. Part (b) of the proposal is also irrelevant since water does not belong to a perfectly competitive market. In fact, there are hardly any water markets in most developing countries, and the allocation of a resource on the basis of non-existent or highly imperfect markets is founded on the principles of ecological and economic disasters. Besides, the Agenda 21 (Chapter 18) of the 1992 Earth Summit rightly suggested that "in developing and using water resources, priority has to be given to the satisfaction of basic needs and the safeguarding of ecosystems." Opportunity cost pricing may eventually be relevant only after these fundamental considerations are accounted for.

The World Bank's New Initiatives

Since the mid-1990s, the World Bank has been paying much more attention to environmental issues. Not only is the lending portfolio much more full of environment-dominating projects, even the environmental accounting methods are applied to most of the projects in operation. The World Bank President, James Wolfensohn, stated at the 1997 Earth Plus Five Summit in New York:

> As an institution dedicated to reducing poverty, we at the Bank are more aware than ever of the continuing link between the degrading environment and the poverty still afflicting so many of the world's people. Less than a quarter of the world's people consume three-quarters of its raw materials, while three billion people still live on less than $2 a day. At the global level, we have not achieved our objectives.

The Bank President "wholeheartedly committed the Bank to do all it can to forge a global partnership to promote equitable approaches to global environmental issues," and proposed five new initiatives where the Bank seeks cooperation from the governments (mainly the Third World borrowers), environmental NGOs and the private sector:

1 *Climate change*: The Bank proposed a "carbon offset fund" if the signatories of the UNFCCC were interested, and asserted that the Bank would routinely assess the potential impact of its energy projects on climate change and possibly assist the borrower countries to finance more climate-friendly options.
2 *Protection of biodiversity*: The Bank and the World Wildlife Fund (WWF) were to join efforts to conserve and sustainably manage millions of hectares of tropical, temperate, and northern forests to help control the rapid depletion of global forestry.
3 *Ozone depletion*: New funds are proposed to control the production of Chlorofluovocarbons (CFCs) in Russia and their black market smuggling activities.
4 *Desertification*: As the world's largest financier of projects which try to curb the spread of new desert lands, the Bank suggests the terms of the Desertification Convention be implemented by the ratifying countries, and claimed that it stands ready to do its part in supporting better agricultural and land management practices.
5 *Water*: About 20–40 countries are expected to suffer serious problems of water shortages during the next few years, and most countries require substantial investments to meet the demands for water and to maintain its quality. The Bank expects to lend about $35 billion during the next two decades as a priority.

The World Bank found a new market and took initiatives to play an early mover role: the Global Carbon Initiative (GCI) was launched soon after the December 1997 Kyoto Protocol. This initiative explores market-based instruments for greenhouse gas (GHG) emission reductions, and develops four new financial products: Carbon Investment Funds, Carbon Neutral Products, Specific Purpose Funds, and Specific Services. Most of these new businesses opportunities have been planned based on the demand expected to be created by the compelling needs of the Organization for Economic Cooperation and Development (OECD) countries; these are expected to meet their emission targets with a global emissions trading offsets program. The carbon investment fund was expected to form a vehicle for companies to reach the "green consumer" with a preference for carbon-free products.

MIGA (Multilateral Investment Guarantee Agency) and the Environment

In fiscal 1997, MIGA increased its guarantees business, issuing 70 guarantee contracts for $613.8 million in coverage; it expanded its membership to 141 countries. In 1998, MIGA issued guarantees for about $830 million in 26 countries (World Bank, 1997a; 1998a). The International Finance Corporation (IFC) has served as MIGA's environmental advisor on all environmental matters. MIGA has made a special effort to assist those private sector investments deemed environmentally beneficial, supporting investments in natural habitat conservation, natural resource management, pollution control, recycling, and renewable energy sources:

- MIGA has supported a unique ecotourism and research facility in Costa Rica.
- The Rain Forest Aerial Tram has demonstrated the feasibility of an "unusual environmentally sustainable investment by preserving the rain forest and yielding an acceptable financial return."
- MIGA extended its guarantee insurance to Purolite International for its investment in two ion exchange resin manufacturing plants in China. (Ion exchange resins are used in water purification processes.)

Global Environmental Facility (GEF)

In October 1991, the tripartite agreement "Operational Cooperation under the GEF" was signed. This agreement formally established the GEF and specified the responsibilities of each of the three implementing agencies – UN Environment Programme (UNEP), the UN Development Programme (UNDP), and the World Bank – and chairmanship of the GEF was entrusted to the World Bank.

The GEF was foreseen initially as a three-year pilot initiative (July 1991 to June 1994), funded at one billion Special Drawing Rights (roughly US$1.2 billion). It was to focus on the protection of biodiversity, reduction of global warming, protection of international waters, and reduction of the substances that contribute to the depletion of the stratospheric ozone layer. The funds would be additional to regular development assistance and provided as untied grants or on highly concessional terms to countries with a per capita gross national product under US$4,000 in 1989, on condition that they have a UNDP program. Project funding has been limited to financing the incremental costs required to achieve global benefits. By 1998, the GEF allocation resources reached about $2 billion in grants and concessional loans since 1991 for over 500 projects in more than 119 countries. The GEF second replenishment was agreed in March 1998; this enables an additional $2.75 billion for eligible projects during the subsequent three years. The allocation of GEF resources by focal area of the pilot phase are, in a hierarchy of resources used: biodiversity (about half the total); global warming; international water; and ozone depletion (less than 5 percent of resources). Also, the GEF has supported a few conservation trust funds as a mechanism of providing long-term funding for the conservation of biodiversity.

The Global Environmental Facility and the Montreal Protocol

The World Bank shares responsibility for implementing GEF activities with the UNEP and the UNDP. The Bank is currently responsible for a GEF work program of about $1 billion, covering four focal areas: biodiversity, global warming, ozone-depleting substances phase out, and international waters. At the end of fiscal 1997, World Bank management had approved 69 projects in over 50 countries, totaling GEF grant commitments of $675 million and leveraging an additional $2.848 billion (World Bank, 1997b). The second GEF replenishment of funds were allotted in 1998.

The World Bank, which remains the implementing agency for the GEF, has also the same role for the Multilateral Fund for the Montreal Protocol (MFMP). In the latter, it coordinates with the UN Industrial Development Organization (UNIDO). By the end of June 1998, 379 projects were initiated under the MFMP with a total funding of $270 million. It was estimated that the effect will be to phase out the consumption of 30,000 tons of ozone-depleting substances (World Bank, 1998a).

The role of interventionist policies of creditors like the World Bank and the IMF remains very significant in most of the developing countries. These policies and programs include the widely known stipulations of structural adjustment reforms in the borrower country economies. These have been manifesting wide-ranging implications. Some of these aspects are discussed in the next section.

● 10.3 STRUCTURAL ADJUSTMENT AND THE ENVIRONMENT ●

Social and political upheavals in several countries – and hence the social destabilization and economic costs thereof – are very significant in many of the countries which were administered the "shock therapy" treatments in the name of adjustments. The approaches of the IMF/World Bank start with a calibrated structural adjustment lending (SAL) method of credit lending. These tend to assume that the "one-size-fits-all" approach makes real sense in the development context of several diverse socioeconomic systems. It is naive to expect that the so-called general equilibrium models are capable of catering for diverse socio-economic systems and institutional ramifications.

In a case study relating to the African and Latin American regions, Stewart (1995) found that per capita expenditure on the social sectors fell significantly among the "adjusting countries" by about 30 percent and about 17 percent in Latin America. It was also observed that cuts in food subsidies were part of the programs of adjustment; any replacements with target subsidies were inadequate because they rarely maintained the purchasing power and a larger proportion of people were left out. It was also observed that, within the low-income and sub-Saharan groups of countries, the growth and performance of non-adjusting countries was superior to that of the countries which received adjustment loans from the World Bank and IMF; see also Mosley (1994) and Stewart (1991). Several studies documented the relevance of a significant drop in education and public health services for the poor in most of the countries in Africa; see, for example, Ruderman (1990).

Regarding the effects of structural adjustment programs in Africa, a World Bank study (1994, p. 171) stated that there were cuts in social services, and that "poverty reduction was not an explicit central objective of early adjustment programs." It was also claimed in this study that little attention was given to the quantum and composition of social expenditures, and that this feature was being corrected.

There is very little evidence that any of the IMF policies recognized the problems of poverty and environment (and their synergistic interactions), even when they occasionally mention some of the poverty issues to modernize the debate. Stewart (1995) argued that the strongest verifiable criticism against the Bank and the IMF is that adverse effects on poverty and the environment occurred when the borrower countries undertook adjustment policies at the instance and insistence of these global institutions, and many of the problems were foreseeable and avoidable; yet these institutions did not share any responsibility for these adverse consequences. This is a form of exercise of lender power, and an illustration of possible misuse of lack of lender liability clauses in the debt contract agreements.

Unsustainable exploitation of natural resources, increased income inequalities, and social disruption have been noted as some of the consequences of the IMF loan mechanisms; see also Chatterjee and Finger (1994). FAO of the UN (UNFAO, 1989, p. 12) argued:

> . . . the adjustment process . . . often results in a sharp fall in real purchasing power of some of the poor and limits their ability to purchase food and other essential items. At the same time, the expected growth has not so far materialized in many countries. . . . Negative effects on the poor are often certain and immediate, whereas positive effects are uncertain and have long gestation periods.

The environmental repercussions of so-called stabilization problems are environment destabilizing, and the usual methods of the one-size-fits-all approach are founded on fallacious assumptions. These include norms like "getting the prices right" even before a definition of markets and prices, or getting institutional structures right, which are founded on limited understanding of the issues involved. These must be understood by the credit-lending and development-role-assuming institutions as an essential prerequisite for any policy and program oriented toward SD. As stated by Opschoor and Jongma (1996), the environmental repercussions are basically indirect (like degradation and poverty link up), unpredictable in direction and depend on the period during which the programs are carried out.

The prescriptions from the IMF and the World Bank have tended to confuse the real issues – see also Chaibva (1996) – with improperly understood solutions to wrongly diagnosed problems, and human misery tends to be aggravated as a consequence. This is not to state that almost every measure these institutions propose is fraught with such disaster. Nonetheless, the fact there are so many disasters at the expense of the borrower countries and taxpayers of the developed countries contributing to the capital funds for lending is itself a feature spreading externalities.

Let us recall one of the main Articles of Agreement of 1945 for the formation of the IMF.

> To give confidence to members by making the general resources of the fund temporarily available to them under adequate safeguards, thus providing them with opportunities to correct maladjustments in their balance of payments without resorting to measures destructive of national or international prosperity.

However, in practice, the maladjustment is often either misdiagnosed or a strict short-term view of "balance of payments" (BoP) is taken into account. Destruction of potential prosperity is not independent of measures taken to correct the BOP. The role of environmental accounting is still in its infancy; the computation of the BoP remains a financial accounting assessment, rather than an economic assessment. Rationally, the latter should guide the former, but the practice of maintaining focus on the BoP does the converse. As a result, medium- and long-term costs, as well as unquantified nonfinancial costs incurred by some major segments of society have been systematically ignored. In the context of social capital and human capital, when disturbances occur – as in the case of imposition of terms of "structural adjustment" – the arguments of Putnam (1993) remain relevant here: lack of measurement or recognition of collective costs in the current account schemes does not mean that they do not matter; "shred enough of the social fabric and we all pay." Similarly, the failure to take into account the implications of the terms of "adjustments" (and of lending) imposed on the environmental costs can only haunt the economic infrastructure and the BoP in the later time intervals. The potential to cross thresholds of the environmental resources or loss of resilience of the systems should be a matter of concern in any financial reform mechanism.

An apparent realization seems to have dawned on most international financial bodies:

- Policy reforms take a long time to design, implement and deliver results in the developing countries.
- The institutions should take a relatively long-term view in dealing with structural problems.

However, such a consensus is not always reflected in the way the structural adjustment programs are formulated and implemented; see also the UN (1997) report. The structural adjustment facilities deal with very short time horizons of 1–3 years, with assessments every six months. These tend to force the borrower country policy makers to seek quick and politically expeditious decisions rather than to consider policies that yield results on a sustainable basis. The UN report also pointed to the usual problem of inadequate financing in the face of external shocks, forcing countries to make a swift adjustment in their balance of payments and leading to accelerated export earnings (usually priced by an exchange rate deflation, implying more volume of exports required to earn the same fixed level of foreign exchange). This carries substantial environmental costs, and is detrimental to the sustainability of the credit worthiness of the borrowers.

> Such distress exports were particularly notable among the middle income debtors in the 1980s, when most of them were forced to accommodate not only sharp declines in commodity prices but also cutbacks in lending and mounting debt-service obligations. In some cases, efforts to obtain a swift payments adjustment were an important reason for further downward pressure on commodity prices through the fallacy of composition effect. Similar conditions still prevail today among the HIPCs (Heavily Indebted Poor Countries). (UN, 1997)

Institutional Coordination and Oversight

Ineffectiveness in environmental aid is substantially increased by agency maximands and organizational internalities (see chapter 1), in addition to interagency coordination failures and organizational inertia. In other words, the transaction costs of a unit of net benefit delivery is extremely high in the current institutional alignments. When international institutions confronting new environmental problems proceed with the bureaucratic style of "business as usual," their unwillingness or inability to dovetail policy interventions to suit the new and potential problems leads to negative effects. Resource allocative mechanisms that do not always fit the problems and the recipients' environmental priorities are not assessed from the viewpoint of the requirements of local people, and the applicable ecosystem and its resilience features. In eastern Europe, for example, donor institutions' reliance on their favorite solutions and a pre-existing stock of financial mechanisms has contributed to widespread neglect of local air pollution problems, the most important priority in the region from the standpoint of human health (Connolly and Keohane, 1996).

Lack of transparency remains a major problem at some of the institutions like the World Bank, despite the fact that several major reforms have been initiated in its disclosure and inspection policies during the most recent years. Shultz and Dam (1997) questioned the relevance of some of the IMF operations as these tend to remain out of tune with the original spirit of its formation. As long as the international institutions fail to become trendsetters in their accountability and in the transparency of their operations, it is futile to issue sermons to their clientele on these aspects; see also Shultz and Dam (1997). Any compromise on hard facts so as to continue to loan out more money – the loan pusher phenomena – can only lead to major disasters for the borrower groups, as exemplified in the case of Indonesia in 1998; a detailed investigation is given in July 14, 1998 issue of *The Wall Street Journal*. There are two keys to institutional reforms:

1   Full transparency, including disclosure of reward and punishment systems for the functionaries of the institutions in directing a particular volume of business or its content.
2   Institutional oversight mechanisms, not just within individual agencies but also in collaborative forms with people's institutions to monitor the aggregate aid process.

This could reduce transaction costs, enhance resource-use efficiency and environmental sustainability.

In another case of failure of coordinative efforts, GEF's operations during its pilot phase provide an example of how not to accomplish effective institutional oversight, as explained by Connolly and Keohane (1996). Because the UNEP and the UNDP refused to acknowledge the weak authority of the GEF chairman, a World Bank official originally designated to oversee project implementation and mediate inter-agency disputes, a "turf war broke out." The three implementing agencies failed to coordinate projects, approaches, or evaluation procedures during the pilot phase. However, subsequent negotiations about GEF's restructuring addressed the need to overcome such organizational inertia and conflict.

The variant of institutional oversight mechanisms embodied in the MFMP has been most effective. The fund's executive committee and strong independent secretariat impose discipline on implementing agencies by insisting on coordinated work programs and sectoral approaches to organizing projects. As a result, recipients and implementing agencies have been forced to alter their practices to produce quality projects designed to phase out ozone-depleting substances. The implementing agencies, including the World Bank and the UNDP, have been willing to submit to such oversight; there are two possible reasons for this:

1   The criticisms of the World Bank from several developing countries.
2   The success of their efforts during the Montreal Protocol negotiations to secure greater representation and strong oversight within the executive committee.

There have been increasing demands on the institutions for better accountability and coordination. Reforms are also being initiated internally within the organizations, but substantial additional effort is required before these institutions can fulfill their stated goals.

The methods of coordination and effecting compliance with international agreements, mainly of debts and of the environmental aspects are examined in the next section.

● 10.4 INTERNATIONAL AGREEMENTS AND COMPLIANCE ●

In most cases, international agreements are coordinated by one or more of the UN institutions. A list of the UN bodies with environmental responsibilities includes UNEP, UNIDO, UNDP, Food and Agricultural Organization (FAO), UN Children's Fund (UNICEF), World Food Program (WFP), World Health Organization (WHO), UN Fund for Population Activities (UNFPA), UN Conference on Trade and Development (UNCTAD), World Trade Organization (WTO), International Maritime Organization (IMO), World Meteorological Organization (WMO), and *ad hoc* bodies like the Intergovernmental Panel on Climate Change (IPCC). In addition, at the UN headquarters, the Commission on Sustainable Development (UNCSD) plays a key role in coordinating a few policy issues with the apex body the UN Economic and Social Council.

It is useful to note that there are multiple organizations on each of the major issues involving focus on the environment, as each issue admits multiple programs for effecting desired results.

● In the areas of environment and poverty, the main UN organizations with their discernible influence are UNDP, UNICEF, International Fund for Agriculture and Development (IFAD), WFP, UNEP, and International Labour Office (ILO).
● The areas of environment and development are addressed by UNDP, UNFPA, WHO, IFAD, FAO, ILO, and UNESCO.
● The interface between trade and environment is the concern of the WTO and the UNCTAD.

There are a few Agreements which are reasonably effective, but most others do not merit such a distinction. In the former category, one would consider the Montreal Protocol on Substances that Deplete the Ozone Layer of 1987. This is an historic agreement and a good model for the following reasons: it was the first international agreement to set a time-bound reduction of pollution emissions with roles assigned to the developed and other countries. Even the modifications over the subsequent years were more enthusiastic in the implementation than in the original as they tried to accelerate the implementation schedules. The agreement was also the first to apply the precautionary principle (PP) to international policy application. Also, the noncompliance provisions were deliberated in the agreement.

The tradition and respect for the rule of law, the public support based on informed opinion, and the level of socioeconomic development are among those domestic factors which affect compliance regarding international agreements, in the absence of explicit and consequential incentives for compliance, or enforceable disincentives for noncompliance. Also, the effectiveness of mechanisms for monitoring and evaluation of compliance regimes and verifiability are significant – the provisions can be generally characterized as self-interest sustaining and self-enforcement inducing.

Institutionalized compliance regulation and control can be classified by a variety of criteria (Lang, 1995):

- Composition and size of the control body;
- Regulatory and control powers of the body;
- Investigation triggering origins of control activities;
- Procedural duties of the (potentially) noncompliant state;
- Causes of noncompliance;
- Consequences of noncompliance.

Three elements related to compliance, essentially the forward and backward linkages in connection with features of compliance itself, may be distinguished – see also Weiss (1995): implementation, regular compliance, and effectiveness. The first refers to the legislation, the regulations, and other aspects required to implement the agreement. Regular compliance refers not only to whether countries adhere to the provisions of the agreement and implementing measures, but whether the fixation of the goals and targets induced any undesirable changes in their behavior. Compliance may also be distinguished in terms of procedural compliance and substantive compliance, and it is the latter that could lead to the effectiveness of the spirit of the agreement. An agreement may be declared as complied with but the objectives may not be attained – a case of ineffectiveness. For example, a treaty that prohibits ivory trade can lead to the neglect or near extinction of the animal species when their market worth is reduced to zero because of the export prohibition. We now explore the provisions and emerging scenarios in the area of international fisheries.

International Fisheries

Harvesting and conservation of international fisheries is influenced by a number of market and institutional factors. The latter include the role of international agreements and provisions of the law governing territorial waters and rights of resource exploitation. The First UN Conference on the Law of the Sea in 1958 failed to arrive at an agreement on the concept of exclusive fishery zones, and the extent of territorial fishing rights. This vagueness left some coastal states to try new methods and this led to international disputes. Box 10.2 provides an historical summary of the Iceland Fisheries Dispute with West Germany in the 1970s. Later developments are noteworthy. The UN Convention on the Law of the Sea was drafted in 1982, and entered into force in 1994. This establishes fishing and water rights within the exclusive zone of 12 miles from the coast for the adjacent sovereign states, and binding procedures for the settlement of disputes over sea resources outside the 12-mile zone. This agreement provides property rights with little obligation for the conservation of the corresponding resources. The UN Conference on Straddling Stocks and Highly Migratory Fish Stocks Agreement was formally adopted in December 1995. This seeks an application of the PP to monitor stocks and conserve fishery resources in the sovereign and international waters.

> ## BOX 10.2   International fisheries disputes
>
> In the late 1950s, Iceland unilaterally issued a regulation establishing an exclus-
> ive fisheries zone extending up to 12 miles around its coasts. After diplomatic
> initiatives, England and West Germany concluded provisional agreements with
> Iceland; in these agreements, the preferential rights of Iceland were recognized
> in the exclusive zone. Later, Iceland took another unilateral action in 1971 to
> extend its exclusive fishery zone to 50 miles, declaring bilateral agreements
> with England and West Germany null and void. The affected two countries took
> up the issue with the International Court of Justice (ICJ). The court delivered
> its verdict (*United Kingdom* v. *Iceland*) on July 25, 1974: Iceland had no right to
> unilaterally exclude the affected countries from the zone of 12 miles to 50 miles.
> It was observed (ICJ, 1974): "It is one of the advances in maritime international
> law, resulting from the intensification of fishing, that the former *laissez-faire*
> treatment of the living resources of the sea in the high seas had been replaced
> by a recognition of a duty to have due regard to the rights of other States and
> the needs of conservation for the benefit of all." The ICJ determined that the
> law pertaining to fisheries must accept the primacy of the requirement of con-
> servation based on scientific data, said a former Chief Justice of the ICJ (Singh,
> 1988). A property rights-based approach to the resolution of the disputes was
> adopted in this case, and the Court acted as a steward for the environment in
> its inclusion of conservation as a requirement for fisheries management in inter-
> national waters (Konisky, 1998). Some of these guidelines were found useful
> in the international agreements of the 1980s and 1990s.

Although the enabling clause of compliance control was discussed in 1987, it
was three years later that the second meeting of the parties (London Amendments) adopted a rather full-fledged but interim noncompliance procedure. A
system of "legal innovation" in the Protocol implementation was instituted with
three main features (Lang, 1995):

- The compliance investigation procedure may be triggered by parties suspi-
  cious of their fellow member's performance, by the Secretariat and by a party
  that considers itself unable to comply fully with its mandated obligations.
- The Implementation Committee may obtain and act upon information,
  including on-the-spot investigations if the suspected party agrees, or seek
  amicable solutions at the Committee level.
- At the Meeting of the Parties, the options for "drawing consequences" are
  available: issuance of cautions, suspension of rights and privileges under the
  Protocol such as trade, or financial assistance.

An important aspect of reforms needed in the substantive contents of the
international agreements is to pay attention to the ecosystem view rather than a
compartmental or regimented view of the issues involved. The latter is generally

seen in many of the existing agreements with the consequences that the spill-over effects are ignored, thus leading to potential conflicts between some of the agreements. Simultaneously, the provisions of the international law must keep pace with scientific developments regarding ecosystem interdependencies and the need to recognize such phenomena in an integrated manner whenever one or more components are addressed. This is a minimal requirement that needs to be fulfilled before additional considerations of ensuring system resilience and sustainability are incorporated in conjunction with the PP. Internationalization of resource management issues is not the first step in devising responsible policies – rather, recognition of the common concern and incorporating relevant provisions in the operating rules is more pragmatic; see also Brunnee and Toope (1997).

"Joint implementation" is another formal institutional arrangement proposed as a pilot phase at the 1995 Berlin Conference of Parties under the UNFCCC: an industrial country can barter with another in financial or other terms, with the objective of reducing emissions of CO_2 to desired or target levels. Mexico and Poland undertook projects under this experimental scheme, which is expected to be reviewed by the end of the twentieth century. The need for setting up a new International Bank for Environmental Settlements was argued by Chichilnsky (1995), with the background that a market for emissions trading must be complemented by other institutional arrangements to reach efficient solutions. This is because, of all possible ways of allocating a given total emission rights across countries, only a small number of allocations may qualify for "efficient" or "optimal" patterns of resource allocation to lead to any form of Pareto-welfare improvement.

International Debt Contracts

There are a number of significant environmental implications of international debts; see chapter 8. Here, we turn our attention to two potentially innovative features:

1 The design of sovereign debt contracts and incentives in coordination with environmental performance features.
2 The provision of new articles of agreement to allow more flexible debt restructuring.

Inflation control, reduction in public expenditure, privatization of public enterprises, and fiscal balancing with taxation are some of the conventional features the international financial institutions have been emphasizing in their country credit worthiness and debt-rating evaluations. While most of these are desirable, the costs at which these are being achieved has remained an irrelevant issue for these institutions. Some of the major costs include deprivation of basic survival rights of the poor, adverse environmental externalities, for example, the reduction of subsidies on kerosene – which is used for cooking in some countries – leads to significant deforestation, and neglect of the essential needs of children and women. These negative effects are usually exacerbated over time when the loan repayment phases set in: the borrowers become more desperate to fulfill loan repayment schedules because the default costs are very high. Some of these adverse impacts can be minimized if the lender institutions recognize the composition of the environmental wealth of the borrower, and seek to preserve and upgrade the same, in complementarity with other financial and economic criteria. A potential trade-off in the achievement targets of all the features involving environmental and some of the conventional criteria enables a balanced development approach. A cross-default provision in the debt contract agreement could serve this purpose; see also Mohr and Thomas (1998) for some of the analytical investigations.

Potentially, an internationalized version of the US Insolvency Chapter 9 (usually applied in relevant municipal institutions in the US) could be useful to address international debt contract enforcement issues; see Raffer (1990) for a detailed proposal. This provision could enable a public hearing of the involved parties and lead to environmentally benign policies in the borrower countries as it diminishes pressures of constrained and ecologically destructive exports for meeting debt obligations. In short, another form of debt restructuring with soft landing and transparency can be effected by this legal provision. More alternative mechanisms of debt management can also be considered, possibly provided in the *ab initio* loan contract. These alternatives in the menu are expected to enhance compliance of the borrowers to the terms of the debt contracts, minimize disequilibrating effects of the entire loan processes, and enhance environmental sustainability and SD. A useful analysis of the "menu approach" to debt relief and rescheduling is given by Franke (1991); this can be extended to include explicit provisions of environmental dimensions, environmental markets, and global emissions trading and their financial integration with debt instruments.

● 10.5 INDIGENOUS PEOPLE, KNOWLEDGE, AND GLOBALIZATION ●

Granting intellectual property rights (IPR) to innovations and knowledge products is a conventional method of converting public goods into private goods (Demsetz, 1967). However, patenting and commercializing is far from conventional in many societies, especially in respect of indigenous knowledge like the pharmacological prescriptions of tribal communities. The system information remains in the informal sector, and is usually uncodified and unwritten knowledge. In the absence of external disequilibrating forces like multinational pharmaceutical companies, the knowledge base is preserved and localized for the benefit of local people. Potentially, efforts to commercialize and globalize can benefit vast multitudes of people all over the planet and deserve support. The path from wild or exotic biota to their medicinal or other commercial production can be significantly shortened in some cases by using the knowledge of the indigenous people. Of the 119 known pure chemical compounds being used in the world, 88 were discovered through leads from traditional and alternative medicinal knowledge (Wilson, 1992). However, the crucial issues of equity and justice as well as rights of indigenous people cannot be ignored for ethical or efficiency reasons if the methods are to be generally acceptable and expandable without a sinful discredit!

Some of the "development projects" tend to dislocate the life and livelihood of the indigenous people, without any consent of the latter in the process. The role of multilateral lending institutions like the World Bank remains significant in these activities. The Bank has issued its own directives and guidelines relatively recently. However, the significance attached to the issues remains feeble. For example, Operational Directive 4.01 on Environmental Assessment states: "Issues related to indigenous peoples are commonly identified through the environmental assessment or social impact assessment, and appropriate measures should be taken under environmental mitigation actions." The problem lies in the compliance of the directive, and in presuming that there exist mitigation actions to offset irreversible problems of uprooting and exploiting the indigenous peoples. The Bank maintains that its policy is based on the strategy of "informed participation of the indigenous people" and that a "full range of positive actions by the borrower must ensure that indigenous people benefit from development investments" (World Bank, 1998b, OD 4.20).

The UN Convention on Biological Diversity (UNCBD) did have some of the significant provisions:

- The requirement that all countries adopt regulations to conserve their biological resources.
- The transfer of technology to developing countries on preferential and concessional terms, where such transfer does not prejudice IPRs or patents.
- Participation in biotech research by countries providing genetic resources.
- Fair access to benefits of genetic research by countries providing genetic resources.
- Funding to assist the developing countries in implementing the Convention's provisions.
- Compensation to developing countries for extraction of their genetic materials.

However, as noted by Raustiala and Victor (1996), the UNCBD has serious problems at both the grand level of principles and the operational guidelines, largely because of its vagueness and ambiguity; some of the provisions of the UNCBD intersect the national laws on wildlife, ecosystems, and plant protection varieties.

Aside from benefit sharing in biological resource development or bioprospecting, a number of unresolved issues surround the subject of intellectual property rights versus indigenous people and their knowledge. The Group of Indigenous Peoples called for a moratorium on bioprospecting because of the group's opposition to the commercialization and exploitation of the knowledge base of the indigenous peoples in different parts of the world. The controversy over the patenting of life forms is not confined to indigenous people, however. The Agreement on Trade-Related Intellectual Property Rights (TRIPS) of the WTO allows national governments to devise legislative measures to offer plant protection; countries have the right and opportunity to enact laws to safeguard commercial plant varieties while protecting the interests of indigenous people and local farmers.

The major utilitarian argument for creating IPRs for biological resources is suggested to be the resource conservation aspect (Sedjo, 1992). While this conservation aspect may be relevant, a win–win scenario of exploitation of resources and knowledge rests heavily on the relative distribution of gains of exploitation and, more importantly, the recognition of the eligible parties and people in this mechanism.

The UN Convention on Biodiversity entered into force on December 29, 1993. By the end of 1996, the number of countries which signed the treaty reached 165. One of the three objectives of the Convention on Biodiversity is "the fair and equitable sharing of the benefits arising out of the utilization of genetic resources." The Convention uses the term "genetic resources" to refer to the genetic material found in biodiversity that has value, for instance, as a source of crop varieties or biotechnological products; see also Grifo and Downes (1996). Countries are obligated to make efforts to give other parties access to their genetic resources for "environmentally sound uses," but they have the right to define the terms of access through domestic legislation. Also relevant is Article 8(j) of the convention, which requires parties to protect the interests of local and indigenous communities: "respect, preserve and maintain knowledge, innovations and practices of indigenous and local communities embodying traditional lifestyles relevant for conservation and sustainable use of biological diversity."

The International Cooperative Biodiversity Groups (ICBG) Program

The US National Institutes of Health (NIH), the US National Science Foundation (NSF), and the US Agency for International Development (USAID) launched the program in 1992 with three linked goals:

1   to develop and implement innovative strategies for the conservation and sustainable management of biological diversity, through
2   screening of organisms for discovery of compounds active against both developing and developed country diseases, as well as agricultural and veterinary purposes, so as to lead on to
3   sustainable economic activity in the form of sharing of the benefits.

There may be no identity of purpose between national agencies and indigenous people in many countries. This implies several ethical issues of imposition of the will of one set of people against another. The role of the international institutions – especially that of the financial institutions – is thus more delicate.

The disjointedness of ruling regimes and the indigenous societies implies the following, as argued by Dove (1996):

● Compensation for IPR is likely to go to the bureaucratic set-up rather than the indigenous people.

- The desired end products may not result. Even the model Merck–INBio agreement specifies that only one-half of the compensation will be used for conservation efforts, and there is no guarantee that any of it will serve local communities.
- Proposed use of IPR may wind up contributing not to the support but rather to the degradation of biodiversity, and the rights of local communities to develop and conserve.

A number of agreements sought to integrate the rights of affected people with mechanisms of resource exploration. A select few are summarized in table 10.1. Only a few of these are effectively enforced or even widely recognized. National governments and international institutions need to encourage greater participation

Table 10.1 Key agreements for traditional resource rights

Right	Legally binding agreements	Non-legally binding agreements
Self-determination	ICESCR and ICCPR	DDRIP and VDPA
Collective rights	ILO169, ICESCR, and ICCPR	DDRIP and VDPA
Land and territorial rights	ILO169	DDRIP
Right to development	ICESCR, ICCPR, and ILO169	DDRIP, DHRD, VDPA
Prior informed consent	CBD, NLs	DDRIP
Environmental integrity	CBD	RD
IPRs	WIPO, GATT, UPOV, NLs, CBD	
Recognition of customary law and practice	ILO169, NLs	DDRIP
Farmers' rights		FAO-IUPGR

Notes:

- GATT = the final Marrakesh Agreement of the Uruguay Round of Trade Negotiations under the General Agreement of Tariffs and Trade
- ICESR = the UN International Covenant on Economic, Social, and Cultural Rights
- ILO169 = the International Labor Organization Convention 169
- NLs = National laws
- ICCPR = the UN International Covenant on Civil and Political Rights
- UPOV = the International Union for the Protection of New Varieties of Plants
- WIPO = the World Intellectual Property Organization
- DDRIP = UN Draft Declaration on the Rights of Indigenous People
- DHRD = the UN Declaration on the Human Right to Development
- FAO-IUPGR = the FAO International Undertaking on Plant Genetic Resources
- RD = the 1992 Rio Summit Declaration.
- UDHR = the Universal Declaration of Human Rights
- VDPA = the UN Vienna Declaration and Programme of Action

Source: Adapted from Posey (1996, p. 39)

by the indigenous communities in enhancing their opportunities, with or without large-scale commercialization of their knowledge or other resources.

● 10.6 CONCLUSIONS ●

Today, institutions are evolving, both formally and informally, in response to the dynamics of policy change at the global level; such evolution is, in effect, a continuous measure of (lagged) responses to unfolding information about Earth matters. Of particular significance are issues regarding climate change and the role of transboundary pollution emissions: their interaction is an indication of the existence of global and national responses to potential adversities caused by human activity. The willingness of the global community is not usually consensual when it comes to relative accountability and the sharing of costs and benefits, economic or other. The role of informal institutions, especially the NGOs in various countries, both developing and developed, tends to be increasing with time and over different regions of the world. The experiences in the UK and elsewhere, for example, of the Carbon Storage Trust, Future Forests, and the International Federation for Carbon Sequestration aiming to offset carbon emissions with extensive forestation – see Henderson (1997, p. 17) for more details – and the proposal of the World Bank to launch millions of acres of forest conservation jointly with the WWF are recent examples of the trend.

The international financial institutions as well as development organizations need to address the issues of SD much more consistently. For example, the World Bank cannot preach poverty eradication, but simply devise new "financial products" to maximize the stock value in the bank assets. Similarly, the IMF should ensure that it does not marginalize sections of the society with their austerity drive and public expenditure control, leading to impoverishment and environmental degradation, thus negating any positive contributions of other organizations. Working at cross purposes is a net burden to the developing world; it does not serve the interests of the developed world either.

Review Exercises

1   In the World Bank Water Sector Policy case, what improvements in the pricing mechanism are possible, considering the pricing mechanism in terms of a configuration of price determination process and ingredients of the pricing formulae, collection of water rates, and their enforcement?
2   Why are "structural adjustments" environmentally damaging?
3   (a)   If risk-sharing is a desirable concept for international project lending, is it addressed with provisions of lender liability, and why?
    (b)   Alternatively, is it more meaningful to devise a formula for debt repayment with contingent claims (resulting from varying states of the financial, economic, and environmental results of projects supported by the lenders) imposing conditions for the project formulation, implementation and operations?

4 Examine the role and limitations of the carbon offset fund and carbon trade mechanisms devised by the World Bank.
5 Why is the role of equitable compensation for the indigenous populations a relevant feature for the conservation of biological resources? Examine alternative incentives in resource conservation efforts in this context.

References

Bretton Woods Committee (1994) *Bretton Woods – Looking to the Future*. Washington, DC: The Bretton Woods Commission.

Brunnee, J. and Toope, S. J. (1997) Environmental security and freshwater resources – ecosystem regime building. *The American Journal of International Law*, 91(1), 26–59.

Chaibva, S. (1996) Drought, famine, and environmental degradation in Africa. *Ambio*, 25(3), 212–13.

Chatterjee, P. and Finger, M. (1994) *The Earth Brokers – Power, Politics, and World Development*. London: Routledge.

Chichilnsky, G. (1995) *Global Environmental Markets – the case for an International Bank for Environmental Settlements, Third Annual World Bank Conference on Effective Financing of Environmentally Sustainable Development*. Washington, DC: The World Bank.

Connolly, B. and Keohane, R. O. (1996) Institutions for environmental aid – politics, lessons and opportunities. *Environment*, 38(5), 41.

Demsetz, H. (1967) Toward a theory of property rights. *American Economic Review*, 57, 347–59.

Dove, M. R. (1996) Center, periphery, and biodiversity. In Brush and Stabinsky (1996, 41–67).

Franke, G. (1991) Avenues for the reduction of LDC debt – An institutional analysis. *Journal of Institutional and Theoretical Economics*, 147(2), 274–95.

Grifo, F. T. and Downes, D. R. (1996) Agreements to collect biodiversity for pharmaceutical research – major issues and proposed principles. In Brush and Stabinsky (1996, 281–304).

Hancock, G. (1989) *Lords of Poverty – The Power, Prestige, and Corruption of the International Aid Business*. New York: The Atlantic Monthly Press.

Henderson, C. (1997) Right climate for change. *Financial Times*, August 6.

ICJ (International Court of Justice) (1974) *1974 Report*. New York: UN.

Konisky, D. M. (1998) The UN dispute settlement system and international environmental disputes. *Journal of Public and International Affairs*, 9, 1–24.

Lang, W. (1995) Compliance-control in respect of the Montreal Protocol. In *American Society of International Law Proceedings of the 89th Annual Meeting "Structures of World Order."* New York.

Mohr, E. and Thomas, J. P. (1998) Pooling sovereign risks – the case of environmental treaties and international debt. *Journal of Development Economics*, 55, 173–90.

Mosley, P. (1994) Decomposing the effects of structural adjustment – the case of sub-Saharan Africa. In R. Van der Hoeven and F. Van der Kraaji (eds), *Structural Adjustment and Beyond in sub-Saharan Africa*. London: James Currey.

Opschoor, J. B. and Jongma, S. M. (1996) Structural adjustment policies and sustainability. *Environment and Development Economics*, 1, 1–21.

Porter, G. and Brown, J. W. (1991) *Global Environmental Politics*. Boulder: Westview Press.

Posey, D. A. (1996) Protecting indigenous peoples' rights to biodiversity. *Environment*, 38(8), 38–9.

Putnam, R. D. (1993) The prosperous community – social capital and public life. *The American Prospect*, 13, 35–42.

Raffer, K. (1990) Applying chapter 9 insolvency to international debts – an economically efficient solution with a human face. *World Development*, 18(2), 301–11.

Rao, P. K. (1994) Learning by doing – a review of the World Bank's water sector policy paper. *UN Natural Resources Forum*, May.

Rao, P. K. (1997) The critical role of the World Bank in economic growth. *The Earth Times*, September 9.

Raustiala, K. and Victor, D. G. (1996) Biodiversity since Rio – the future of the convention on biological diversity. *Environment*, 38(4), 43.

Rich, B. (1994) *Mortgaging the Earth – The World Bank, Environmental Impoverishment, and the Crisis of Development*. Boston: Beacon Press.

Ruderman, A. P. (1990) Economic adjustment and the future of health services in the Third World. *Journal of Public Health Policy*, Winter, 481–9.

Sedjo, R. A. (1992) Property rights, genetic resources, and biotechnological change. *Journal of Law and Economics*, 35, 199–213.

Shultz, G. P. and Dam, K. W. (1997) *Economic Policy Beyond the Headlines*. Chicago: University of Chicago Press.

Singh, N. (1988) The UN and the development of international law. In A. Roberts and B. Kingsbury (eds), *UN – Divided World*. Oxford: Clarendon Press, 183.

Stewart, F. (1991) The many faces of adjustment. *World Development*, 19, 12–25.

Stewart, F. (1995) *Adjustment and Poverty – Options and Choices*. New York: Routledge.

Tietenberg, T. H. (1996) Managing the transition to sustainable development – the role of economic incentives. In P. H. May and R. S. da Motta (eds), *Pricing the Planet*. New York: Columbia University Press, 123–38.

UN (1997) *International Cooperation to Accelerate Sustainable Development in Developing Countries and Related Domestic Policies*. New York: UN Document E/CN.17/1997/12/Add.1, made available from the UN Web site.

UNFAO (United Nations Food and Agriculture Organization) (1989) *Aspects of Stabilization and Structural Adjustment Programmes on Food Security*. Rome: FAO Economic and Social Development Paper 89.

Weiss, E. B. (1995) Remarks on compliance-control in respect of the Montreal Protocol. *American Society of International Law Proceedings of the 89th Annual Meeting on "Structures of World Order."* New York.

Wilson, E. (1992) *The Diversity of Life*. Cambridge, Mass.: Belknap/Harvard University Press.

World Bank (1994) *Adjustment in Africa – Reforms, Results, and the Road Ahead*. New York: Oxford University Press.

World Bank (1997a) *Environment Matters at the World Bank Annual Review 1997*. Washington, DC: The World Bank.

World Bank (1997b) *World Bank Annual Report 1997*. Washington, DC: The World Bank.

World Bank (1998a) *World Bank Annual Report 1998*. Washington, DC: The World Bank.

World Bank (1998b) *Operational Manual of the World Bank*. Washington, DC: World Bank.

chapter outline

● CHAPTER 11 ●

Policy Framework

● CHAPTER 11 ●

Policy Framework

*We have always held to the hope, the belief, the
conviction that there is a better life, a better
world, beyond the horizon.*
Franklin Delano Roosevelt

● 11.1 INTRODUCTION ●

A pragmatic policy framework is usually founded on the appreciation of concerns for sustainability as well as sustainable development (SD), from a scientific perspective. Here, the role of economic factors – largely introduced via the anthropogenic influences on the ecosystem services – becomes important. This chapter does not attempt to synthesize the elements and ideas discussed so far in the previous chapters. Instead, this aims to supplement a few features, leading to a broad policy framework governing SD at different levels.

Let us recall the main ingredients in the description of the planet Earth, as suggested by the mineralogist Vladimir Vernadsky (1929) in his book *La Biosphere*: geosphere, biosphere, and noosphere. The noosphere was defined as the mind-intellect role in the geophysical world. Clearly, any amount of careful preservation of environmental assets will resemble the existence of potential energy without ever being converted to kinetic energy (to borrow the terminology of physics), if we cannot utilize mind power judiciously and efficiently with a vision for the present and the future. Preservation of everything for preservation's sake is neither desirable nor sustainable. Let us note that in human history, the vulnerability of populations to the vagaries of the ecosystem was much more significant until the early part of this century. This was during a period when the societies were anthropogenically much less burdensome to the environmental sources and sinks. However, that did not save them from disastrous crop failures and famine, nor from major epidemics; a significant percentage of populations perished as a result.

A set of major issues addressed in the next section tries to incorporate the role of environmental factors in the economic functions of different systems. A cross-sectoral and multilevel approach is usually relevant in the combining of the entire spectrum of potential areas of intervention. These aspects are deliberated later. A few illustrations of analytical aspects of cooperation and its stability are proposed in terms of a strategy-formulating perspective. Relevant crucial factors are listed. Priorities for SD, and the need to integrate SD in terms of social, environmental, and economic priorities are furnished. Constant vigilance remains a fundamental eternal requirement for ensuring SD.

● 11.2 SUSTAINABLE ECONOMY AND GREEN POLICIES ●

In this section, we consider: the precautionary principle (PP); the ecology, economy, and macroeconomics; fiscal policies; markets and market-based instruments; and institutional reforms.

The Precautionary Principle (PP)

The PP (see chapter 3) led to the process of creating institutionalized caution, as it formed the basis of substantive international law. It helps to formulate policies or decision-making strategies for the purpose of protecting the environment, based on rather incomplete information generated by the knowledge of science, economics and technological management. This approach is explicitly and implicitly based on the assumed vulnerability of the environment, the limitations of science to predict threats to the environment with great accuracy or certainty, risk-averse rather than risk-seeking behavior, and the existence of other options to address the issues; see also Hey (1992).

The PP needs to be widely adopted in national, regional, and local levels. Most countries still lag behind in this direction of required progress. However, a number of applications of the PP can be seen in the international environmental agreements; see McIntyre and Mosedale (1997) for a detailed description of several applications. For example, the 1995 Agreement Relating to the Conservation and Management of Straddling Fish Stocks and Highly Migratory Fish Stocks stipulates that parties – and over a hundred countries have adopted this Agreement – are required, under Article 5(c) of the Agreement, to apply the PP. A wide usage of the PP is likely to raise public awareness and effective participation as well. This is because any environmentally sensitive decision by a policy maker is expected to be scrutinized in terms of the recognition of potential consequences and proceeding to take a conscious decision. An assessment of an admissible level of environmental risk or change "necessary" for the activity becomes a regular feature. A meaningful application of the PP does require that governments and other institutions develop a comprehensive and operationally meaningful system of information for effective decision making at different levels of the economic and other systems.

Ecology, Economy, and Macroeconomics

Most conventional economic analyses, and the content of the policies based on such analyses, are usually centered around traditional economic reasoning, rather than an attempt to integrate ecology and economics. In fact, this may not be allowed in the standard procedures under many government rules. This has to change drastically. Every activity need not be refereed by the department of environment. It should form a part of routine analysis and information-reporting. This calls for several changes in the legal provisions and specifications in the administrative manuals of various authorities and administrative units. Unless and until this is systematically attended to, there will be either reluctance to incorporate the essential elements or a great degree of arbitrariness in their application, if not both. Hence, there is a need for an updating of legal and administrative provisions for the effective implementation of requisite integration of environmental aspects with conventional economic and financial considerations. This is rather farfetched, considering that much of the so-called economic analysis in administrative settings is a rudimentary financial cash-flow assessment, and there may be very little economic aspect in the analysis. In addition, if ecological and environmental aspects are to be incorporated, it may seem to require a complex analysis. To avoid some of these problems, an appropriate manual incorporating environmental accounting and assessment needs to accompany any stipulation of integration of the various dimensions. Adoption of the ISO 14000 standards will be a good start, but several additional steps are required: dovetailing these standards at local and small enterprise levels, adoption of the PP at these levels, and institutionalization of these features.

Fiscal Policies

The usefulness of ecotaxes or green taxes is not fully examined in most countries. Revenue recycling, tax interaction, and substitution effects of green taxes are examined in chapter 5. In general, the double dividend effect requires tapping: correcting market failures, and reducing welfare costs of the tax system when revenues are used to reduce other taxes. One limitation must be noted, however: it ignores loss of efficiency due to tax interaction effects. Parry (1997) suggests that revenue-raising may be a necessary condition for environmental policy to be welfare-improving. Taxation may be unpopular in many societies, but tax redistribution or adjustment that serves the needs of the economy and the environment need not be. This is particularly meaningful when the redistributive effort leads, at the aggregate level of the economy, to a revenue-neutral situation.

Just as the tax interaction effects lead to lowering the estimates of the impact of green tax provisions, the converse is also valid: the reduction of some of the subsidies will also lead to subdued impact compared to the estimates of any simplistic partial equilibrium analysis. For these and related reasons, the advocacy of the institutions like the International Monetary Fund (IMF) or World Bank to phase out most subsidies is founded on the fallacy of assuming the interaction effects. A simple example may be cited: withdrawal of kerosene subsidies (with little provision for reasonable substitutes) led to large-scale deforestation in Ghana.

Also, at the global level, the Tobin tax proposal – for conceptual and operational details, see Haq et al. (1996) – could earn no less than $150 billion a year, and this could be used for the protection of environmental assets, global and regional. This proposal made by James Tobin in 1972 calls for a tax on the foreign exchange transactions worldwide. In 1995, these were estimated at $1,300 billion a day, leading to $312 trillion in the year (with 240 business days). A small tax at 0.005 percent could generate $312 billion. The original idea was to impose a transaction cost tax so as to enhance the efficacy of macroeconomic policy.

Markets and Market-based Instruments

Environmental markets, in addition to other markets, can be made to function more efficiently with the provision of new incentives and instruments. Tradable emissions permits (TEPs) are an example of market-based instruments, and environmental cost internalization is a catalytic intervention relevant for all players in the international and regional trade business. The major role of the private sector in effecting necessary environmental reforms includes greater life-cycle analysis and accountability to internalize environmental costs.

Transaction cost minimization is the task of both the government institutions and the market institutions. A well-conceived concept like the TEPs can run into serious implementation problems if insufficient preparatory work in placing the informational and institutional framework is carried out at any of the stages of implementation. Since the measurement and monitoring of pollution emissions in respect of every pollutant is prohibitively costly, some regulation of the corresponding inputs leading to these outputs may be relevant. As pointed out in the US President's Economic Report 1998, high transaction costs could discourage emissions trading, thus eroding the potential gains from such market-based instruments (US President, 1998).

In addition to the TEPs, another mechanism has been proposed. Clean development methods (CDM) are new proposals originated in the US proposal and adopted at the Kyoto Protocol as new offset mechanisms for the industrial countries and their private enterprises who can contribute to activities like afforestation in a developing country at a relatively lesser cost than effecting reductions through alternate methods in their home country. Since greenhouse gases (GHGs) are not only globally affecting, but also locally affecting on the environmental quality, there are obvious limits to this approach if the domestic concerns are to be addressed properly. However, within certain thresholds, it is expected to be a win–win scenario for the industrial and the developing country.

Institutional Reforms

Although not all declared democracies are alike nor possibly will they ever be alike, the democratic content of the decision-making process at the government and corporate levels, and even at the household levels – for example, whether women are allowed to have a say in family management and budget or expenditure aspects – are usually functions of tradition and culture, in addition to religion and legal institutions. Thus, any desirable changes in the human enterprise, viewed from a disaggregated or micro level is expected to be slow and sluggish when it comes to the underpinnings of the principles, policies, and practices of SD.

Vonkeman and Maxson (1995) argued that the lack of democratic institutions and "democracy content" of some of the so-called democratic institutions in many domestic and international settings continues to pose one of the most significant obstacles to possible SD initiatives. It was also stated: ". . . in the domain of international decision-making on sustainability, we still lack almost everything: accepted fundamental philosophies, principles and quantifiable targets, adequate institutions, legislation and instruments."

At the government level, the least that a governing set-up can do is to visualize the sustainability of resource use – resources considered here include all inputs, monetized or other, material or other. The simple realization of the nature of boundedness of most of the elements involved in sustaining the pace of one or more of the system components should signal the limitations of some of the approaches. The least an entity can do to assess the situation is to undertake, for example, environmental accounting, as a start. The key impediment to some of the requisite considerations of SD is usually the assumed myopic time horizon of some of the key decision makers in systems where the legality or constitutionality of decisions is not subject to any reasonable scrutiny. This horizon is much smaller than what they usually claim, indicating also an implicitly high rate of time discounting. This is somewhat analogous to the high rate of time discounting on the part of the desperately poor, but greed is usually the factor that governs the behavior of the former whereas sheer survival (physical) drives the latter to the same attitude toward economic decision making; environment becomes a casualty in the process in both of the two situations.

Douglass North (1995b) asserted: "Effective institutions and organizations can reduce the transactions . . . so as to realize more of the potential gains of human interaction." It was also stated that there will never be "true" models about the environment, technical progress, or a number of other issues. Human-induced limitations to SD are also expressible in terms of economic institutions, among others (Gowdy, 1994): the limitations arise through stifling human ingenuity by imposing artificial restrictions on free markets, by institutional barriers to technological change, or by the social relations of production. When we extend the arguments beyond the confines of economics, we realize that, in reality, it is a combination of all three factors which affect the optimal production possibility frontiers. In addition, organizations generate their own agency internalities and maximands which are usually sub-optimal for efficient economic progress. This is not to suggest that organizational forms are undesirable; but to indicate the nature of human-induced inefficiencies which must be addressed. The design of incentives and disincentives – as well as information systems to bring about least asymmetry at different levels of decision making – remains an important requirement.

While market forces convey the opportunities for economic gain, economic and individual freedom enables individuals to undertake these opportunities to improve their ability to meet their demands. As stated by Peacock (1989), economic freedom is compatible with human dignity, and is a necessary prerequisite for the economic growth and its adaptability to changes in preferences with market factors. Freedom is viewed as a cause and an effect of economic growth; freedom enables economic growth, which in turn delivers individuals from the predicament of need and thereby enlarges human freedom (Verburg and Wiegel, 1997). Finally, let us recall an observation of North (1995a, p. 16) that "institutions are not necessarily created to be socially efficient; rather they are created to serve the interests of those with the bargaining power to devise new rules."

Among other issues of green development are the mechanisms of evolution of relevant policies, based on the perceptions about the environment. One view of the environmental phases comprises recognition of the following in an almost sequential hierarchy (DCLTEP, 1995): environmental pollution as a side effect; environmental pollution as a cost factor; the environment as a boundary condition; the environment as a policy-determining input; and the environment as an objective.

Can some countries afford to adopt green advice? The answer depends mainly on the content of the "green advice" rather on the country itself. In general, a more relevant question is: Can an economy survive *without* green policies? The recent problems of environmental health contributed by pollution alone accounts for about 2–3 percent of gross domestic product (GDP) in some countries like China, Indonesia and Pakistan; see the *Human Development Report 1998* (UNDP, 1998). Clearly, local and regional environmental problems seem to affect the individual country economies. In general, any single measure of green policy is likely to be operationally significant if it cannot take into account the factors: socioeconomic, ecological, institutional features like tradition and democratic representation of people's voices, and the role of consumers in influencing the market and non-market institutions play a critical role.

Well-defined resource and property rights regimes, in addition to environmental responsibilities, are expected to be useful in minimizing the discrepancies between observed behavior and desirable behavior. Green development is not a prejudiced or partial attitude toward the economic development process. Instead, as long as it remains pragmatic, it only seeks to maintain a complementarity of environmental and economic resources. In such a framework, it could be possible to correct a lopsided economic approach to its better comprehension so as to realize the scarce nature or finiteness of what have conventionally been taken for granted as infinite resources and their capacities in the supply of economic goods. Various political and economic institutions will do well to accept the relevant approaches adopted to fit the local situational variations, while some of the fundamentals remain largely relevant in most countries and regions.

● 11.3 INTERNATIONAL SHARING OF RESPONSIBILITIES ●

Benefit sharing is characterized by free rider and nonrival public goods features. Costs are inflicted by contributors with these features:

- Relative anonymity of damage-causing agents;
- Uncertainty in their magnitudes;
- Probability of incidence in a given sector or region and time.

This makes the problem of accountability and fixing responsibility more difficult.

Global environmental problems need to be solved with a collective responsibility approach from various countries, the polluters of different potential environmental contributions, and various institutions which affect the environment directly and indirectly, positively or negatively. The common problem is that of fixing responsibilities for global emissions of pollution (especially GHGs) as well as trading in environmentally harmful goods and services when there is no compensation in terms of environmental costs. Cost sharing, on the basis of agreed shares of responsibility by each of the countries, is one of several features of cooperation required if the global environmental issues are to be meaningfully and objectively addressed. The evolution of cooperation is affected by several institutional and behavioral factors; only some of these seem to admit some degree of analytical characterization at this stage.

A few analytical aspects, based on simple game theory methods, may be stated. These two propositions, due to Axelrod (1984), are useful:

1 If the discount factor is sufficiently high, there is no best strategy independent of the strategy of the other player/participant (p. 15).
2 Any strategy which may be the first to cooperate can be collectively stable only when the discount factor is sufficiently large (p. 61).

Also, in the "iterated or repeat prisoner's dilemma," the potential for cooperation is enhanced when there is high probability of future interaction between parties (Mesterton-Gibbons, 1992); the Prisoner's Dilemma is explained in box 11.1.

This suggests that when countries and institutions perceive their continued interaction and potential gain by acting credibly, genuine cooperation is more likely. Also, if the effects, especially benefits of cooperation are likely to occur, cooperation is more likely.

The traditional contributions of global commons – see, for example, Ostrom (1990) – describe countries' environmental interaction as a rather non-repetitive Prisoner's Dilemma where the free-riding nature of resource exploitation leads to the "tragedy of the commons." A few authors like Barrett (1992) discuss the

BOX 11.1   The Prisoner's Dilemma

Game theory was developed about half a century ago as a strategic approach to decision making. A simple static one-period description of a noncooperative two-player game with two alternatives at each player's command is described in terms of a Prisoner's Dilemma, illustrated here. Two suspects are questioned separately. If both confess to an offense, the punishment is, say, 10 units of penalty for each; if both cooperate and hold out, the punishment is 2 units for each player. However, if player X confesses, while player Y does not, X is relieved of any punishment but Y gets 15 units of penalty, and the roles of X and Y are symmetric. In a typical Prisoner's Dilemma with no additional features of communication, cooperation and commitment, a noncooperative game is at work. A cooperative game is a game in which the players can make binding commitments, but they cannot do so in a noncooperative game.

In a multi-period or repeat game, the role of time discounting enters the calculus of each player's valuation of the outcomes at different stages and future time instants. In such a game, the discount rate and discount factor (see chapter 3) play a critical role, and some of these implications are seen in the propositions stated above.

phenomenon that, in a repeat Prisoners' Dilemma situation, the set of possible equilibrium outcomes is much larger and the possible set of cooperative outcomes relevant for international environmental agreement or consensus is greater in such a description of the global scenarios. Carraro and Siniscalo (1993) examined the strategic behavioral models relevant for some of the international environmental protection agreements and suggested that it may not be very pragmatic to study the optimality of agreements if these are intrinsically unstable institutional arrangements.

Criteria for Cost Sharing

According to World Bank/Global Environmental Facility (GEF) estimates (Sharma, 1994), if carbon emission rights were sold at $25 per ton of carbon, the industrialized world would have to pay developing countries about $70 billion to afford one year's emissions at the 1988 level. Are there identifiable factors to share responsibility or costs of environmental protection? Income and economic affluence adds more than population growth to the consumption influence on environmental problems like GHG emissions; this is because the average per capita elasticity of CO_2 emissions with respect to GDP per capita is about 1.2, with the implication that each doubling of income could add more than each doubling of population (Parikh and Painuly, 1994). However, this may require modification to include the role of the high total fertility factor rather than (net) population growth to assess the doubling effect, for example.

A number of alternative criteria, not necessarily mutually exclusive, can be posited: culpability (those who cause the environmental problems should bear the associated burdens, whether historical for a chosen or varying time periods, and also current period), culpability with rights, ability to pay, per capita or other standards of emissions assessment, size of population, per capita income in nominal terms or purchasing power parity terms. Choice of a judicious mix of these and any additional factors is by no means simply a technical exercise. A numerical simulation exercise was conducted by Ridgley (1996) to examine the relative burden-sharing implications for various regions of the world using 11 different criteria; as expected, the assessed shares vary widely with changing criteria. Some countries have demanded an amnesty for their historical role in the environmental problems, by simply denying any burden sharing on such a basis. If the current period parameters are the only ones that need to be considered, the following approach may be useful, although it is not a policy accepted by any of the developed countries.

Chichilnsky and Heal (1994) established a proposition:

> At a Pareto-efficient allocation, the fraction of income which each country allocates to carbon emission abatement must be proportional to that country's income level, and the constant of proportionality increases with the efficiency of the country's abatement technology.

It is not clear if the purchasing power parity criterion of income assessment should form the basis of cost sharing if this assertion is adopted, but this does suggest the critical role of income.

North–South Issues

Since raising the basic standards of living remains the major concern of the developing countries, and since this cannot be attained without the use of additional energy sources including fossil fuels (the main sources of emission of CO_2), it is extremely unrealistic to expect that the developing countries can stabilize their contributions to the GHG emissions anytime soon. However, their increasing rate of contribution can possibly be controlled with new methods of mitigating these emissions. Energy-efficient technologies are of foremost importance in the control of GHG emissions; this requires a lot more R&D of relevant technologies and techniques of production. Herein arises the role of international financial institutions and of the developed countries in facilitating adoption of pollution controlling and energy-efficient technology in the developing countries. This arena of industrial activity could generate global export markets for the developed countries and lead to win–win solutions to the environmental and economic aspects of all countries. An earlier estimate of the World Bank suggests an investment of the magnitude of $30 billion would meet the infrastructural and adaptation costs of the developing countries for controlling acid deposition and particulate matter emissions from coal-fired power generation, and for reducing industrial emissions and waste treatment. If the above estimate is somewhat realistic, it should be feasible for a consortium of industries in the developed countries or the Organization for Economic Cooperation and Development (OECD) or other institutional arrangements, to implement a meaningful soft-loan based development financing to facilitate the transfer of technology. Some elements require simply resources for afforestation and the control of deforestation.

This approach may prove to be a cost-effective method of reducing global GHGs and potential global warming. The global concentration or budgeting of the GHGs is the real concern for the international community and thus the cost-effectiveness should apply at that level, as long as these do not warrant stunted growth for the developing world. Country-specific targets in the reduction of GHG emissions become rather superfluous if an economic approach to the overall problem is adopted and fair sharing of the overall costs by individual countries can be assessed. The crucial issue that still needs to be resolved in this transformation from physical targets to economic cost sharing, in relation to the global magnitudes of reductions of GHGs, is the basis or criteria for cost sharing. The underlying mechanism becomes operationally pragmatic if it can be linked to market-based factors and institutions, and made flexible in the magnitudes and timing. The flexibility should be interpreted in terms of adoption of strategies that seek to reduce the net balance of GHGs, both stocks in their atmospheric concentration and their additional emissions. The market should apply to both these aspects.

Afforestation and consequential carbon sequestration mechanism work to offset part of the GHG concentration of the stocks in the atmosphere; advanced technologies for energy conservation, cleaner methods of industrial production, pollution control and recycling activities – in addition to possible substitution of sources of energy away from fossil fuels – would significantly contribute to the control of continued flows of the GHGs. None of these are confined in their scientific applicability only to the developed or the developing countries. However, the applicable resource options and the cost aspects do vary across various countries very significantly and, in some cases, seek greater sacrifices in living standards than in others. As argued in a fairly robust empirical and policy study contributed by Rubin et al. (1992), it is desirable that the developed countries prefer to underwrite efforts to contain the GHG stocks and flows in the developing countries before undertaking more expensive options, some of which could disrupt their domestic economies or their competitiveness. This is not to imply that there is little else the USA or other developed countries could do. In fact, any such euphoria could hamper any progress toward the development of new technologies for energy efficiency and pollution control. The targeted concessional development financing for the developing countries in the context of offsetting GHG balance, more specifically that of CO_2, could be among the least cost options to mitigate the greenhouse effects (GEs). Also, the economics of comparative advantage suggest that the developed countries take major initiatives in the development of marketable technologies to mitigate the emissions of GHGs and to contain the demand for those underlying factors of production. This is not a moral prescription, but a business proposition with some incentives from the domestic governments of the developed countries or their consortium in the initial development stage. The role of the government cannot be divorced from this setting, although the market forces can eventually determine the scope and implementation of such strategies.

The elements in the global policy for controlling GHGs and global warming are not necessarily confined to the developed countries of the North. If the South with its current levels of development is to participate in target fixation for mitigating GHG emissions, any realistic approach that takes into account the collective economic interests of both the North and the South will have to allow for growing emissions of these gases, but the growth rate needs to be limited. This is feasible with the collective participation of all the countries, possibly with a framework which allows for carbon budgeting: the monitoring and control of GHG stocks and flows attributable to different countries and sources. In this context, the recent proposal of the World Bank President James Wilfensohn at the global Earth Summit merits serious consideration. In addition to large-scale afforestation and protection of forests in various parts of the globe, the proposal calls for mechanisms for carbon offsets and budgeting accountability on the part of individual countries and economic entities including industries. This approach, including the proposal for the creation of the Carbon Offset Fund, can lead to effective emissions control, their trading permits and efficient market exchanges, possibly under the purview of the World Bank and also other institutions.

The approach suggested above seeks to convert any targets of GHG reduction into their corresponding economic equivalents by finding globally cost-effective methods of these reductions, rather than individual country-specific targets; the latter are reflected in their cost-sharing elements in the global containment approach. The latter also recognizes the distinction of stocks and current flows of the gases, and the historic responsibility of the developed countries for the accumulation of the GHG concentrations as one of the main reasons for greater sharing of the costs of global reduction of these gases. Besides, these arguments also augur well with the economics of comparative advantage and win–win solutions.

The December 1997 Kyoto Protocol is an important step in the progress toward containing GHGs and in relative sharing of responsibilities and costs. The Agreement, subject to ratification by member countries, seeks to place binding commitments for Annex I countries (mostly industrial nations) in respect of the GHGs: CO_2, CH_4, N_2O, sulfur hexafluoride, Perfluorocarbons (PFCs), and hydrochlorofluorocarbons (HCFCs). Each industrial country's baseline is based on its 1990 emissions of CO_2, CH_4, and N_2O, and its choice of 1990 or 1995 levels of the other three gases. The target levels vary from one industrial country to another: USA agreed to a target of 7 percent below 1990 levels to be achieved during 2008–12. The target for the EU is 8 percent, and for Japan 6 percent below the 1990 levels. At an aggregate level, all industrial countries are to reduce by about 5 percent relative to their 1990 levels. The specification of the reduction requirements for each country is governed by QELROs (quantified carbon emission limitation and reduction commitments). The Buenos Aires Plan of Action of November 1998, with the participation of 170 countries, specifies more measures aimed at effective implementation of the Kyoto Protocol. However, even after the ratification of the Protocol by about 60 countries including the USA, several impediments remain. The USA needs ratification by the Senate, and many details of the implementation mechanisms are still left vague. More details are proposed to be spelled out in the year 2000.

An important scientific underpinning that needs to be incorporated in all these formulations relates to the revised concepts of global warming potential (GWP); see chapter 5. Alternative premises of assessment of direct and indirect contributions of the GHGs to the global warming process, the time horizon of concern, and the time-discounting factors carry varying implications for policy and target fixation for GHG reductions. These factors may have to be based on a global consensus, rather than left to the discretion of the individual countries, but a recognition of the ingredients of the global warming process could enable consideration of an enhanced basket of choices of combinations of GHGs to meet a target in a cost-effective manner specific to each country.

Also, a mechanism of trading emissions with offshore regions – i.e. those countries which do not meet their own emission targets could work out an economic arrangement with other nations that do better than required, to buy their excess "quota" level – possesses the potential to lead to cost-effective methods of effecting global reduction of GHGs. The next section examines alternative methods of intervention for SD at different levels of economic and other systems.

● 11.4 MULTILEVEL FRAMEWORK ●

A multilevel approach to the understanding, action planning, and implementation of relevant policies, programs, and activities enables a more effective coordination of desired influences to effect SD. Although this classification enables a systematic process of analysis, there are dangers of excessive compartmentalization if the non-exclusive nature of these categories and their interdependencies (especially feedback mechanisms) are not fully recognized.

Preventive and mitigation options of anthropogenic influences on the systems and phenomena governing environmental sustainability and SD are better addressed with a comprehensive simultaneous combining approach. This is like a combat operation where no escape routes are allowed. If there must be scope for some flexibility, it is provided only with a conscious decision to do so, and not inadvertently. Here is a broad classification of different levels, and the critical elements of analysis or information content to be ascertained at each of these levels:

● *Ecosystem*: application of the PP; assessment of implications on transitory and permanent equilibria, threshold effects, resilience features under plausible scenarios; effects on the sources and sink capacities of the planet; implications for the economic systems; and assessment of biogeophysical externalities.

● *Macroeconomic systems*: integration of economic and environmental policies; integration of domestic and international policies in respect of trade, debt, export obligations; internalization of environmental costs; implementation of various provisions of international environmental and multilateral trade agreements; application of the PP; providing guidance to regional and local institutions regarding various policies for SD; institutionalizing green taxes or equivalent effective fiscal policies for environmental protection; reforming institutions for enhanced equity and productivity of resources; reduction of poverty and fulfillment of basic minimum needs; support of R&D and technical innovations; integration of social, environmental, and economic objectives of development; and internalization of costs of economic and environmental externalities.

- *Sectoral*: devising policies and operational programs conducive to sustainability and SD; recognition of inter-sectoral linkages and internalization of externalities; assessment of income distributional implications of policies and programs; provision of pricing systems and pricing policies to ensure internalization of environmental costs and of other externalities; control and mitigation of local pollution and of features affecting the global commons; enhancing innovative management practices and utilizing people's participation.

- *Territorial*: integration of national, international, regional, and local systems to move in harmony; interregional and inter-sectoral consistency of policies and programs; mechanisms to control and mitigate any spillovers; recognition of the role of "bottom up" methods of information generation and actions to control environmental deterioration; utilization of indigenous resources to arrive at win–win solutions.

- *Socioeconomic*: ensuring gender inequality; according priority to the needs of women and children; recognition of poverty eradication and its complementarity with environmental development; investing in people and human capital formation; economic growth to be attained without ignoring the requirements of social justice or improved income distribution policies; upliftment of the "weaker" sections of the society.

- *Institutions*: support of democratization and democracy content of institutions, rule of law, strengthening market institutions and the private sector, public or government sector to effect catalytic support and provide a complementary rather than substitutory role; encouraging people's institutions and genuine non-governmental organizations (NGOs) at different levels of the governance of social, political, and economic areas; bureaucracies to develop management systems with improved integrative effects which recognize cross-departmental linkages and reduce transaction costs; performance accountability at various levels of the government bureaucracy to ensure management by objectives.

A number of formal and informal entities come to interact, in the concordance or otherwise, of environmental management. Combined with this institutional aspect, the features of the environment itself might require attention in terms of local (e.g. point-source and non-point source water pollution), regional (e.g. transboundary pollution emissions between Mexico and USA), and global (e.g. the

GHGs). It is useful to adopt a multilevel approach to various environmental and economic development issues, even if the levels are not necessarily coterminus with powers of decision making or geographic or such similar well-defined boundaries. The purpose is to deal with each package of sets of internally consistent policies and programs, to be integrated with similar frameworks from the rest of the components or subsystems of the global system.

A number of principles can be drawn from a regional or local ecological systems perspective for building system resilience. Such approaches combine the social factors, indigenous know-how and know-why, and develop an information base in a more organized way than is currently available in most of the diffused systems. This effort itself can be a destabilizing factor for the harmony of the system if proper steps to contain intrusion are not undertaken.

A number of National Environmental Action Plans (NEAPs) were initiated in the developing borrower countries of the World Bank following its support and requirements starting July 1992 (World Bank's Operational Directive 4.02 – Environmental Action Plans). A review of 33 of such plans in a 1995 publication of the World Bank (Lampietti and Subramanian, 1995) led to the following observations:

- A major shortcoming of the NEAPs is the lack of a realistic appraisal of the array of costs associated with alternative institutional arrangements; for example, basic flaws in legal systems often aggravate environmental problems.
- If delays in the enforcement of a law go on for too long, in itself this may be an incentive to ignore the law completely.
- Providing incentives to both public and private institutions is often one of the cheapest and most effective methods of altering behavior, but the NEAPs did not reflect this recognition.
- The inflexibility of bureaucratic regimentation prevents the necessary inter-sectoral policy making, integration, and coordination required to deal with environmental problems and is reflected in vague recommendations like "improve capacity," or "strengthen institutions."

Every country would do well to undertake a comprehensive assessment of its status and perspectives on SD. The result can at least form a good step in the right direction. For illustrative purposes, stated below are some of the suggestions of a multi-institutional inter-sectoral Commission in the USA – some of the policy recommendations (adding to a few dozens) of the US President's Council on Sustainable Development (1996):

1   The federal government should cooperate in key international agreements – from ratifying the UNCBD to taking the lead in achieving full implementation of specific commitments made in international agreements to which the USA is a party.
2   The federal government should ensure open access for, and participation of, NGOs and private industry in international agreements and decision-making processes.

3 The public and private sectors should enhance efforts to provide educational, economic, and social opportunities for women, particularly those in their teens.

4 The federal government should provide incentive grants to landowners who act to protect and manage the habitat for native species.

5 Federal, state, and local tax laws, including estate and inheritance tax laws, should encourage private landowners to protect biodiversity by managing lands for conservation, improving degraded habitat, or donating land into protected status.

6 Nonformal educators should encourage learning about sustainability through adult education programs, including those under 4-H clubs.

7 Schools, colleges, and universities should promote curriculum and community awareness about SD and follow sustainable practices on campus; degree courses in accounting and business administration can offer courses on environmental accounting.

8 Individual, government, and business purchasers should ask suppliers to provide information on environmental characteristics of products and should take these considerations into their purchasing decisions.

Sectoral Focus

Sectoral focus helps to identify the relevant measures aimed at sustainability of the functions of the sector, and its interlinks with other sectors, especially the larger ecosystem and its resilience. As the energy sector is the most significant contributor of GHGs, additional efforts to control net emissions and net concentrations will be fruitful. The mitigation strategies which rely on carbon sequestration via forestry preservation and expansion are also rather constrained, and thus the need to limit the emissions in the first place is very great. Reforestation does provide a method of offsetting CO_2 emissions. Carbon is captured and stored during the growth period of the thick plantations and would need to be preserved, or optimally rotated for harvesting without vitiating the carbon balances. The estimated costs vary from \$4 to \$30, depending on the cost of land and other inputs. To illustrate the size of the forestry required to offset the emissions of a 500 MW coal-fired power plant (emitting about 0.8 Mt of carbon per year), a forestry development of the size of 1700 square kilometers is needed (Watson et al., 1996). This was assessed on the assumptions of the sequestration of 2–4 tons per hectare per year during 50 years of forest growth, and a storage of 100–200 tons of carbon per hectare in a mature forest. Slowing deforestation can be a lower-cost mechanism of offsetting carbon emissions.

Given below is an illustrative case of the identification of policies and actions in a single sector in the USA. Here are some of the recommendations for sustainable US Agriculture (Dower et al., 1997):

1 The industrial countries should eliminate agricultural trade barriers.

2 The government agencies should support institutions which protect agriculturally important germ plasm, seed banks, and related preservation activities.

3   All federal and state agencies should phase out irrigation subsidies.
4   Agricultural production should be subject to minimum environmental standards.
5   States should tax fertilizer and pesticide pollution to encourage efficient use of fertilizers and agrochemicals.
6   States and municipalities should devise tradable nutrient emissions schemes to improve water quality.

Sub-sectoral Issues

A number of economic inputs and outputs tend to escape attention if we adopt only a sectoral approach without proper disaggregation of its constituents. For example, in the agriculture sector, the importance of pesticides is such that a sub-sectoral focus is warranted. An analysis of the environmental dimension in this focus is given in box 11.2.

Research and Development (R&D)

Broader aspects of SD hinge heavily on the knowledge sector, with its engine: R&D. The interactions of science and policy in atmospheric sciences is advancing at an unprecedented rate in the last decade of the twentieth century, and there are sufficient reasons to believe that this process will continue for the next few years in search of more definitive answers with scientific diagnosis and mitigation strategies. One area for greater global support is meteorology. As Zillman (1997), President of the World Meteorological Organization (WMO), stated: the essential basic meteorological infrastructure of individual countries needs to be strengthened and maintained; the regime of international cooperation under the WMO needs to be reinforced, and the convention of free and unrestricted exchange of basic meteorological and related environmental data and products need to be preserved; and a coordinated international framework is required for implementing and operating an integrated global observing system built on the World Weather Watch and the Global Climate, Ocean and Terrestrial Observing Systems developed by the WMO and other institutions.

Reverting to the priority problem of achieving a goal of stable emissions, an empirical exercise using the improved versions of the IPAT models (Dietz and Rosa, 1997) suggested that carbon use efficiency must improve at least 1.8 percent a year till 2025 if the GHGs are to stabilize at 1991 levels, considering plausible growth in population and the economic growth rates. This appears feasible but substantial efforts are required to achieve the goals. However, the trends in the share of government expenditure for environmental R&D in the total expenditure (measured in "purchasing power parity" dollars for various OECD countries) for the period 1981–92 seem to suggest that there are a few countries like USA, Greece, Belgium, Norway, which have declined in the share during this period (OECD, 1996). This could be a source for concern, although the private sector

BOX 11.2 Sub-sectoral focus: Pesticides

Pesticides continue to play a contributory role in augmenting agricultural production, but these are also a major health risk factor. Consumption of these continues to be subsidized (a powerful example of environmentally hazardous subsidies) and encouraged in most countries. Some varieties, which are banned in industrial countries like the USA, continue to be in use in many developing countries. Their supply is both domestic production-based as well as imported from some of the countries where their domestic use is banned. In an empirical study, Pimental et al. (1993) estimated that pesticides provide about $16 billion a year in saved US crops, and the environmental and social costs (like adverse public health effects and contamination of groundwater) add to about $8 billion, in addition to the loss of life of thousands of people due to pesticide-induced illnesses. Using alternate methods of agriculture and organic farming – see also NAS (1989) – at least half the use of pesticides could be reduced at a cost of about $820 million, with an implication of increase in produce prices at less than 1 percent level (Pimental et al., 1991). The environmental and economic externalities of pesticide use are significant: most off-site costs are borne by people other than the chemical producers and farm producers. Based on the analysis in chapter 8, it is clear that an appropriate pricing of pesticides using a life-cycle analysis (LCA) is pertinent here. A definition closer to its possible use in this specific commodity is elucidated below. Let us also note that the export of domestically banned chemicals does very little good to the importer and even the exporter country: the agricultural products utilizing the banned inputs are partly exported back to the pesticide-exporting country. This is an additional case of the spread of externalities, and the failure of mechanisms to include environmental costs in the prices of goods thus traded. The role of the neem tree (*Azadirachta indica*) as a natural pesticide was recognized by the NRC (1992), based on some of the major scientific properties. However, the progress in adoption is slow, because of a number of international patenting and commercialization problems.

In this context, it is relevant to note that the LCA is defined by the Society for Environmental Toxicology and Chemistry (SETAC, 1993, p. 5) as: the process to evaluate the environmental burdens associated with a product, process, or activity by identifying and quantifying energy and materials used and wastes released to the environment; to assess the impact of these uses and releases to the environment; and to examine the options to effect environmental improvements. It was also noted that the assessment includes the entire life cycle of the product, process, or activity, encompassing raw material extraction and processing, manufacturing, transport and distribution, recycling and final disposal.

is expected to invest substantial resources in this sector during the next few years. Government support is justified on the grounds that there is under-investment in environmental R&D by firms due to these factors (OECD, 1996):

● Externalities associated with environmental research, where individual firms are unable to capture sufficient benefits from R&D to justify their expend-iture but social returns on investment are high.
● Possibly larger than normal business uncertainties about the existing mar-kets and future markets for new products.
● Uncertainties in local and international regulations and environmental laws affecting products and processes in demand from time to time.

In addition to the need for enhanced and accelerated investments in relevant R&D support from the government sector, a number of other technical and man-agerial innovations need to be supported and implemented. These include vari-ous types of eco-efficiency measures, design for environment (DFE) approaches in structures and systems of technologies and industrial ecology. DFE is defined as the systematic consideration of design performance with respect to environ-mental, health, and safety objectives over the full product and process life cycle; see, for example, Fiksel (1996).

The tools of greening include: design for eco-efficiency, environmental ac-counting, LCA, full-cost pricing to include environmental costs, recognition of the industrial and human ecology of the environment, and scientific informa-tion gathering and analysis of environmental parameters (local and global). Tools of greening tend to contribute to development in the right direction, but fail to inform decision makers about the discrepancy relative to the potential or target regions of sustainability; see also Gladwin et al. (1995).

Consumer Level

Moderation in consumerism is not likely to be a social welfare reducing activity. On the other hand, it could enhance environmental sustainability. For example, in the area of food consumption, the role of vegetarianism is significant: it takes about 100 pounds of plant protein to produce less than five pounds of edible meat protein. If more vegetable protein were consumed by people, instead of being fed to livestock, the demand for consumptive use of water, and for irriga-tion would come down rather significantly (National Water Commission, 1973, pp. 15 and 138). Reduction in the energy usage from fossil fuels may be desir-able if the adverse role of GHG emissions is to be mitigated. In general, one needs to view the entire system in terms of the influences on the demand and on the supply of consumption of resources, affecting both the sources and sinks of the planet.

Box 11.3 provides an illustrative list of relevant priorities by major categories, and the effective instruments for addressing the priorities.

BOX 11.3 SD: Priorities and effective instruments

Social priorities
  Enhancement of the status of women and attention to health upgradation
  Focus on youth programs and child development
  Eradication of illiteracy and poverty
Environmental priorities
  Maintaining ecosystem resilience
  Reduction and stabilization of the GHGs and ozone depletion
  Improvement of environmental public health
  Control of point and non-point sources of pollution
  Preservation of biodiversity
Economic priorities
  Fulfillment of basic minimum needs of population
  Debt reduction to sustainable levels
  Poverty reduction and economic growth
  Improvement of productivity and equity of resource utilization
  Integration of economic and environmental policies
Main instruments
  Adoption of PP
  Adoption of PPP
  Adoption of environmental accounting
  Adoption of market-based or market-supportive instruments for practical
    policy
  Environmental taxation or other effective instruments for fiscal policy
  Investing in human capital
  Promotion of technical progress
  Afforestation and control of deforestation
  Enhancement of energy efficiency and use of renewable sources of energy
  Improving provision of public health inputs
  Adoption of appropriate alternate methods of agriculture and natural
    pesticides
  Slowing population growth
  LCA as a basis of recycling, and pricing of goods and services
  Internalization of environmental costs
  Environmental literacy campaigns
  Involvement of people's institutions and NGOs
  Urban air pollution control and recycling solid wastes

● 11.5 CONCLUDING OBSERVATIONS ●

Sustainability is a necessary but not sufficient condition for SD. The latter warrants a delicate balance of policies and priorities that are aimed at social, environmental, and economic development. In all these, ensuring the resilience of the ecosystem remains a fundamental requirement. Resilience is not described by a one-to-one relationship, nor by linear mechanics of the structures. A number of biogeophysical phenomena are built on nonlinear interrelationships, and feedback mechanisms. Threshold effects and discontinuities are significant too. Neglect of any of these essential features can lead to irreversible impacts.

Global warming leads to a number of additional enhanced effects because of the feedback phenomena. For example, the role of global warming in enhancing the albedo factor, and the interactive effects of global warming and the albedo factor can be very significant. Similarly, in deforestation, it is not only the extent of deforestation which is relevant, but also the type of deforestation which is important. Genus is greatly disturbed in rainforest area with greater implications for biodiversity and the flux of nature, than in the case of loss of forest in a regular forest region. Most economic studies do not recognize the implications of some of these scientific processes. As such, those studies depict under-assessments of the real impacts of environmental deterioration.

One of the fundamental issues in the focus on SD is to ensure the uninterrupted supply of environmental goods and services, in the contemporaneous and futuristic time frames. Public institutions have a responsibility to plan and act so that there is no undersupply of these public goods and resources. Environmental protection is an economic as well as ethical issue. Requiring polluting entities to bear the full environmental costs of their activities constitutes only a fair arrangement. If the existing markets did not have the capability to incorporate factors based on environmental knowledge and feedbacks, but would rather wait for the ecological feedbacks to surface in economic terms, it may be too late or too expensive to correct the damage done by then. In other words, the current structure of markets is not fully capable of responding to environmental issues with any foresight. The lagged adjustment is socially sub-optimal for resource management. Let us also recall Amartya Sen's (1985) observation that goods and commodities are important for enriching human lives, but their effectiveness in welfare enhancement depends on the traits of the society and its institutions. Thus, the focus extends to the fulfillment of human capability to cope with changes.

In terms of the current trends, the 1997 Earth Summit Plus Five (ESPF) Special Session of the UN General Assembly lamented that after five years of the Rio Earth Summit, "the overall trends for sustainable development are worse today than they were in 1992" (UN, 1997), and proposed to ensure that there will be significant progress by 2002, the next comprehensive review stage. However, the subsequent Kyoto Protocol of December 1997 is an important milestone in the global and national involvement in containing the GHGs and their effects.

The Agreement needs to be ratified by the participating country governments, however.

Among the countries, the eight environmental heavyweights (E8) consist of: USA, Russia, Japan, Germany, China, India, Indonesia, and Brazil; see Flavin (1997) for details. These constitute about 54–60 percent of the global totals in each of the following features: population, gross world product, world carbon emissions, world forest area, and plant species. These countries have the largest influence in directing the world environment and sustainability of future generations.

Greening development can be seen as a misnomer, since there is hardly a reasonable and meaningful way of defining development without recognizing the role of the environment and ecology. Whenever "greening" is suggested, it is often misunderstood in different sections of the society (except possibly environmentalists of one variety or the other) as a biased view which affects the conduct of various functions and business transactions adversely. One need not be an environmentalist to recognize the implications of callous behavior toward the ecological aspects of consumption and production, to appreciate the relevance of environmental and green dimensions in the life activities on this planet. Do poor people care about the environment? Environmental considerations are not for the rich only; see chapter 7 and also other sections of this book. A Gallup poll in 24 diverse countries found that people expressed strong support for environmental protection (Dunlap et al., 1993).

Multinational enterprises operating in countries with less rigorous standards than in their home base countries should not seek to exploit the situation to the fullest advantage at the expense of the well-being of the local population and local as well as global environment. This may not sound good economics of profit maximization, but is better economics of profit maximization for futuristic businesses with a relatively longer time horizon and lower rate of time-discounting. International measures of trade, such as the adoption of ISO 14000 and eco-labeling, are likely to prove good business and better environmental ethics. The fact that Wall Street does not generally reward greater equity prices for businesses with environmental liability is only one of several factors which could act as a pointer to the direction of further development. Those companies which undertake business in more than one country should be required by the World Trade Organization (WTO) to file a ISO 14001 certificate every year for public scrutiny. Countries should reflect on the patterns of international trade which permit export of domestically banned items such as low-grade pesticides to other countries, thus discounting the value of the life of others.

A number of win–win solutions can be considered, although their implementation is not always an easy task in most countries. If, for example, enhancing women's status and eradication of poverty are agreeable priorities, and if environmental literacy is also an important vehicle of desirable change and development, how about devising policies and programs that involve poor women for environmental literacy and its campaign as one of the topmost priorities? The real difficulty may not be in identifying mechanisms that possess the potential to meet more than one objective simultaneously, and thus become priorities and very cost-effective approaches to multiple problems in a single scheme of win–win solutions; there are several institutional constraints – inertia, hindrances based on habits and so on – but the operational problems could be in terms of financing these otherwise meritorious interventions in the development processes: these may not generate internal revenues or finances of their own in the short run and/or in the private returns sense. Public funds may be scarce in most countries. It may be desirable to seek some form of green tax or ecotax to finance these activities. The private sector must assume a greater role in these efforts.

A basic right of human life, which cannot be enforced by international agreements, is the right to live under a democratic polity and to enjoy individual freedom. "Democracy, respect for all human rights and fundamental freedoms, including the right to development, transparent and accountable governance in all sectors of society, as well as effective participation by civil society, are also an essential part of the necessary foundations for the realization of social and people-centered sustainable development" (UN, 1997).

Finally, but most importantly, the following may constitute a set of fundamental underlying principles of SD: humane values, democratic institutions, economic growth with social justice, uninterrupted processes of innovations, nature conservancy, modest consumption habits, reformed international financial and development institutions for improved effectiveness, enhanced role of people's institutions, environmental literacy, and respect for all forms of life.

Review Exercises

1 What makes environmental factors and economic factors (a) complements, and alternately, (b) substitutes?
2 Examine the economic effects of the loss of ecosystem resilience.
3 When planet Earth's albedo increases because of global warming, examine the feedback effects and the nature of magnitude of cost increases for mitigation strategies.
4 Examine the role of the Precautionary Principle (PP) in the energy sector management.
5 Examine the role of R&D and technical progress critical for sustainable development.
6 If adaptation costs of changes in consumption are high, is it feasible that they can only be higher later, in the absence of requisite adaptation for environmental sustainability? Also, explain the assumptions made in reaching the conclusions.
7 Using the life-cycle analysis (LCA) approach, if the environmental costs are required to be internalized, examine the pricing implications for the fossil fuel coal.
8 Examine the implications of low time-discount rate on repeat transactions of international environmental and debt agreements, in the framework of iterated/repeat Prisoner's Dilemma.

9 Elucidate a set of win–win policies for sustainable development from each of these perspectives:
   (a) North–South countries;
   (b) Poor and non-poor in any country;
   (c) Public sector and private sector;
   (d) Importers and exporters;
   (e) Social systems and ecosystems;
   (f) Economic systems and ecosystems.

References

Axelrod, R. (1984) *The Evolution of Cooperation*. New York: Basic Books, Inc.

Barrett, S. (1992) International environmental agreements as games, In R. Pethig (ed.), *Conflicts and Cooperation in Managing Environmental Resources*. Berlin: Springer-Verlag, 18–33.

Carraro, C. and Siniscalo, D. (1993) Strategies for international protection of the environment. *Journal of Public Economics*, 52, 309–28.

Chichilnsky, G. and Heal, G. (1994) Who should abate carbon emissions? An international perspective. *Economics Letters*, 44, 443–9.

DCLTEP (Dutch Committee for Long-term Environmental Policy) (1995) *The Environment – Towards a Sustainable Future*. Boston: Kluwer Academic Publishers.

Dietz, T. and Rosa, E. A. (1997) Effects of population and effluence on CO_2 emissions. *Proceedings of the National Academy of Sciences*, 94, 175–9.

Dower, R., Ditz, D., Faeth, P., Johnson, N. and Mackenzie, J. (1997) *The Frontiers of Sustainability*. Washington, DC: World Resources Institute/Island Press.

Dunlap, R. E., Gallup, Jr., G. H. and Gallup, A. M. (1993) *Health of the Planet*. Princeton, NJ: Gallup International Institute.

Fiksel, J. (ed.) (1996) *Design for Environment – Creating Eco-efficient Products and Processes*. New York: McGraw-Hill.

Flavin, C. (1997) The legacy of Rio. In Worldwatch Institute, *State of the World 1997*. New York: W.W. Norton, ch. 1.

Gladwin, T., Kennelly, J. and Krause, T. (1995) Shifting paradigms for sustainable development – implications for management theory and research. *Academy of Management Review*, 20(4), 874–907.

Gowdy, J. M. (1994) Progress and environmental sustainability. *Environmental Ethics*, 16, 49.

Haq, M., Kaul, I. and Grunberg, I. (eds) (1996) *The Tobin Tax*. New York: Oxford University Press.

Hey, E. (1992) The precautionary concept in environmental policy and law – institutionalizing caution. *Georgetown International Environmental Law Review*, 4, 303–18.

Lampietti, J. A. and Subramanian, U. (1995) *Taking Stock of National Environmental Strategies, Environmental Management Series Paper # 10*. Washington, DC: The World Bank.

McIntyre, O. and Mosedale, T. (1997) The precautionary principle as a norm of customary international law. *Journal of Environmental Law*, 9(2), 221–41.

Mesterton-Gibbons, M. (1992) On the iterated Prisoner's Dilemma in a finite population. *Bulletin of Mathematical Biology*, 54(2–3), 423–43.

NAS (National Academy of Sciences) (1989) *Alternative Agriculture*. Washington, DC: NAS.

National Water Commission (1973) *National Water Policies for the Future – Final Report of the Commission*. Port Washington, NY: Water Information Center Inc.

North, D. (1995a) *Institutions, Institutional Change and Economic Performance*. New York: Cambridge University Press.

North, D. (1995b) Constraints on institutional innovation – transaction costs, incentive compatibility, and historical considerations. In V. Ruttan (ed.), *Agriculture, Environment and Health – Sustainable Development in the 21st Century*. Minneapolis: University of Minnesota Press, 48–70.

NRC (National Research Council) (1992) *Neem – A Tree for Solving Global Problems, Report of an Ad Hoc Panel of the Board on Science and Technology for International Development*. Washington, DC: National Academy Press. Edited by N. D. Vietmeyer.

OECD (1996) *The Global Environmental Goods and Services Industry*. Paris: OECD.

Ostrom, E. (1990) *Governing the Commons*. Cambridge: Cambridge University Press.

Parikh, J. K. and Painuly, J. P. (1994) Population, consumption patterns and climate change – a socioeconomic perspective from the South. *Ambio*, 23(7), 434–7.

Parry, I. (1997) Environmental taxes and quotas in the presence of distortionary factor markets. *Resource and Energy Economics*, 19, 203–20.

Peacock, A. (1989) Economic freedom. In J. Eatwell, M. Milgate and P. Newman (eds), *The New Palgrave – The Invisible Hand*. New York: W. W. Norton, 90.

Pimental, D. et al. (1991) Environmental and economic impacts of reducing US agricultural pesticide use. In D. Pimental (ed.), *Handbook on Pest Management in Agriculture*. Boca Raton, FL: CRC Press, 679–718.

Pimental, D. et al. (1993) Assessment of environmental and economic impacts of pesticide use. In D. Pimental and H. Lehman (eds), *The Pesticide Question – Environment, Economics, and Ethics*. New York: Chapman & Hall, 47–84.

Ridgley, M. A. (1996) Fair sharing of greenhouse gas burdens. *Energy Policy*, 24, 517–29.

Rubin, R., Cooper, R. N., Frosch, R. A., Lee, T. H., Marland, G., Rosenfeld, A. H. and Stine, D. D. (1992) Realistic mitigation options for global warming. *Science*, 257, 148–9; 261–6.

Sen, A. K. (1985) *Commodities and Capabilities*. Amsterdam: North-Holland.

SETAC (Society for Environmental Toxicology) (1993) *Guidelines for Life Cycle Assessment – A "Code of Practice."* Pensacola, FL: SETAC.

Sharma, R. (1994) *Ownership and Governance, Symposium on Trade, Environment and Sustainable Development*. Geneva: GATT Secretariat.

UN (1997) *Programme for the Further Implementation of Agenda 21, Adopted by the Special Session of the General Assembly, June 23–27, 1997*. Available through the UN web site.

UNDP (1998) *Human Development Report 1998*. New York: Oxford University Press.

US President (1998) *President's Economic Report 1998*. Washington, DC: US Government Printing Office.

US President's Council on Sustainable Development (1996) *Sustainable America – A New Consensus*. Washington, DC: US Government Printing Office.

Verburg, R. M. and Wiegel, V. (1997) On the compatibility of sustainability and economic growth. *Environmental Ethics*, 19(3), 247–66.

Vernadsky, V. (1929) *La Biosphere*. Paris: Felix Alcan.

Vonkeman, G. H. and Maxson, P. (1995) *International Views on Long-term Environmental Policy*. In DCLTEP (1995, 219–45).

Watson, R. T., Zinyowera, M. C. and Moss, R. H. (eds) (1996) *Climate Change 1995 – Impacts*. Berlin: IPCC; New York: Cambridge University Press.

Zillman, J. W. (1997) Atmospheric science and public policy. *Science*, 276, May 16, 1084–6.

Web Site Addresses

Given below is a sample of the web sites; many others can be found on the links provided on several of the major sites. All these addresses are under hypertext transfer protocol; in simple terms this means they all start with the initial part of the web site address as http://. Many important NGOs have not been listed here, but they can be found on links like that of the UNDP or IISD. It is also possible that some of the listed web sites undergo transformations from time to time, including possible extinction in a very few cases. However, most sites listed here tend to remain relatively robust (their survival capabilities are great).

● IMPORTANT INTERNATIONAL SITES ●

United Nations	www.un.org	This has several links to the UN organizations involved in development and environment issues. However, a few direct links may also be useful. These are listed below.
United Nations Development Programme (UNDP)	www.undp.org	This site will also provide greater details on poverty-related issues.
United Nations Environment Programme (UNEP)	www.unep.ch	This does provide a few additional clues to the information bases, as well as a few modeling exercises where the UNEP coordinates some efforts.

UN Department of Policy Coordination and Sustainable Development	www.un.org/dpcsd	This site of the UN secretariat office gives a few details of its coordinating activities, especially those of the UN Commission on Sustainable Development, and of a few Conventions and Conferences.
UN Population Information Network	www.undp.org/popin/popin.htm	Emerging trends and issues of population can be seen in this site.
World Health Organization (WHO)	www.who.org	A number of significant changes took place recently at the WHO, including an active Sustainable Development Division. This site provides details on these activities and public health issues in connection with global climate changes and the role of poverty.
UN Framework Convention on Climate Change	www.unfccc.de	This coordinating secretariat's site includes details of policies, mainly those on GHGs and conclusions of the Conference of Parties (COP), including the Kyoto Protocol and other agreements preceding and succeeding this Protocol.
World Trade Organization	www.wto.ch	This site provides details of global trade and its liberalization, with a rather limited discussion of environmental issues.
World Bank	www.worldbank.org	This site includes several important features on development focus, poverty, and environmental issues.
	www.esd.worldbank.org	This important site of the Environmentally Sustainable Development (ESD) Vice Presidency of the World Bank provides more details of the environmental features and operations of the World Bank.
	www.worldbank.org/nipr	This is another site within the World Bank system which deals with industrial pollution policy and regulation aspects.

| OECD | www.oecd.org | The OECD secretariat at Paris undertook several significant studies, and several details can be seen on this site. |

● IMPORTANT SITES IN THE USA ●

USEPA	www.epa.gov	This site is useful to gauge the operational activities as well as new proposals such as market-based instruments for pollution control, and environmental management.
	www.epa.gov/ globalwarming/ index.text.html	At this site, the USEPA devotes links to global warming issues.
US Geological Survey (USGS) Global Information Database (GRID)	grid2.cr.usgs.gov/grid/grid.html	
US Senate Committee on Environment and Public Works	www.senate.gov/committee/ environment.html	
National Climatic Data Center	www.ncdc.noaa.gov	
US Census Bureau International Program Center	www.census.gov/ipc/www	

● RESEARCH / INSTITUTIONAL / MEDIA SITES ●

| Association of University Leaders for a Sustainable Future | www.ulsf.org | This site offers information about environmental literacy and educational facilities. |
| The Beijer Institute of the Royal Swedish Academy of Sciences | www.beijer.kva.se | An international institute of ecological economics; lists a few research programs and documents. |

CIESIN Information	www.ciesin.org/kiosk/ subindex.html	Provides a wide array of sources of information and links on papers and documents on environmental themes.
CNN Earth Main Page	cnn.com/EARTH	Provides current information on several environmental features.
International Environment Resources	www.contact.org/ environs.htm	This is useful for various links to other relevant sites on environmental issues.
Second Nature	www.2nature.org	This site provides links to several useful sites, including the following one.
	www.2nature.org/program/ starfish/sfhome.nsf	This site provides details of interdisciplinary relevant educational materials.
International Institute of Sustainable Development (IISD)	www.iisd.ca/linkages	
World Resources Institute	www.wri.org	
Carnegie–Mellon University	www.ce.cmu.edu:8000/GDI	
University of Oregon	gladstne.uoregon.edu/eaglej	This site provides a detailed introduction to the mechanics of global warming and link pages.
Center for Environmentally Responsible Economics (CERES)	www.cerc.wvu.edu/ ceres/ceres_index.html	This includes the CERES Global Knowledge Network information.
The Worldwatch Institute	www.worldwatch.org	Known for a few important publications including the annual State of the World Report; undertakes research work.
Resources for the Future	www.rff.org	
Oak Ridge National Laboratories (ORNL) Environmental Science Division	www.eso.ornl.gov	

Econet	www.econet.apc.org/econet	This site provides comprehensive information on several environmental upkeep measures and links to several sites of interest.
World Conservation Union/International Union for the Conservation of Nature (IUCN)	www.iucn.ch	This is a vast network of governmental, multilateral, and NGOs with considerable influence on global policies and their implementation.
Stockholm Environmental Institute	www.tellus.com	This Institute has four locations and a few interesting study programs and publications.
EnviroLink Network	www.envirolink.org	This is a significant database regarding institutions, products and links.
International Institute for Sustainable Development (IISD)	iisd1.iisd.ca	This site has much useful information and excellent links to other sites.
International Development Research Centre (IDRC)	www.idrc.ca	
International Institute of Applied Systems Analysis	www.iiasa.ac.at	

● SITES WITH FUNCTIONAL APPLICATIONS ●

Pollution Prevention

The USEPA Office of Pollution Prevention Program	www.epa.gov/docs/ GCDOAR/OAR-APPD.html
Los Alamos National Laboratory for Pollution Prevention	perseus.lanl.gov
American Institute for Pollution Prevention	es.inel.gov/aipp

Recycling

	www.grn.com/grn	This site is maintained by the Global Recycling Network.
	www.epa.gov/epaoswer/wastewise.html	This is a USEPA web site dealing with waste management.

Ozone

USEPA	www.epa.gov/ozone	This site is part of the USEPA information and links regarding the ozone layer.

Software

	www.greenware.ca/software/iso14000.htm	This is a software based on the ISO14000 standards, managed by the Greenware Environmental Systems Inc.

Design and manufacturing

	www.me.berkeley.edu/green/cgdm.html	This is a University of California Center for Green Design and Manufacturing web site. The information on the Green Design Initiative at Carnegie–Mellon University is also located at the site for the university listed earlier.

Environmental Law

	www.asil.org	This is the site for the American Society of International Law, but provides other links as well.
	www.law.indiana.edu/law/intenvlaw.html	This is located on the Indiana University site dealing with international environmental law.
Standards (ISO14000)	www.ISO14000.com	

● ENVIRONMENTAL GROUPS AND NGOS ●

The Earth Pledge Foundation	www.earthpledge.org	Founded to promote the UN Pledge at the Earth Summit; provides references to literature and select activities.
Environmental Defense Fund	www.edf.org	
Natural Resources Defense Council (NRDC)	www.nrdc.org	
World Conservation Monitoring Centre	www.wcmc.org.uk	
Friends of the Earth International	www.foe.co.uk	
Greenpeace International	www.greenpeace.org	
World Wildlife Fund (World Wide Fund for Nature International)	www.panda.org	

Glossary

Sources: Definitions adapted from those developed by UNEP, USEPA, and a number of other sources.

absorption of radiation: the uptake of a solid body, liquid or gas
   The absorbed energy may be transferred or remitted. It also includes the process of conversion into heat of a part of the radiation an object is exposed to.

acid rain: also known as acid deposition
   This is the combination of dry deposition of acidic substances and precipitation. The acidic conversion is usually the result of fossil-fuel burning which releases sulfur dioxide and nitrogen oxide into the atmosphere. Acidic aerosols in the atmosphere are deposited via rain, snow, fog (wet deposition) or dry particles (dry deposition). The aerosols are present in the atmosphere primarily due to discharges of gaseous sulfur oxides and nitrogen oxides either from anthropogenic sources or natural sources. In the atmosphere, these gases combine with water to form acids.

activated carbon: carbon which has been treated to remove hydrocarbons, thus enhancing its absorption; widely used for odor control and in air-freshening types of applications

adiabatic: change or exchange occurring without the exchange of heat
   It is a change in the volume and pressure of a gas, for example, without an exchange of heat or change in temperature.

aerosols: extremely small particles of fine liquid or dust as gaseous suspensions in the atmosphere
   Aerosols are classified as smoke, fumes, mist, and dust. Burning coal, for example, releases sulfur dioxide which, in the atmosphere, is transformed into sulfate aerosols.

afforestation: establishing new forests and trees on unforested land
   Afforrestation of large areas of land can grow trees which will absorb and store carbon from the atmosphere and could slow CO_2 buildup.

Agenda 21: developed at the United Nations Conference on Environment and Development (UNCED) at Rio de Janeiro in Brazil in June 1992

airshed: an area within which pollutants or specified gas contents interact – and possibly concentrate – unless chemically diffused

albedo: the total fraction of light striking a surface (expressed as a percentage) that is reflected by that surface
The Earth's average albedo is about 50 percent; an albedo of 100 percent implies complete reflection.

aldehydes: a class of chemical compounds which are intermediate between acids and alcohols; used in a variety of applications like production of vitamins, polymer compounds, perfume ingredients, and in the production of other compounds

Amazon rainforest: a wide tropical rainforest covering the watersheds and drainage basins of the Amazon river and its tributaries in Brazil covering about an area of 7 million square kilometers; it is the largest such basin in the world

amortization: the periodic repayment of principal and interest over a prescribed time span

annuity: a constant sum for each period over a number of periods
If the payments are made over an infinite horizon, the annuity is called a perpetuity and has a present value s/r, s being the sum in each period, r the discount rate.

Antarctic Treaty: signed by 25 nations in 1959, this enables the conducting of scientific research around the arctic without interference from national sovereignties
Several international agreements arose out of this Treaty, like the Antarctic Protocol on Environmental Protection, the Convention on the Conservation of the Antarctic Marine Resources, and the ban on mining exploration in the region.

anthropocentric: the viewpoint that humans are the central feature of planet Earth, and that environment and ecology should be valued in terms of their utility or lack of it for humans

anthropogenic: caused or created by human beings

anthropogenic climate change: changes in the world's climate system that are a result of human actions and inactions

aridity: a general term used to describe areas suffering from lack of rain or drought; more specifically, a condition in which evaporation exceeds precipitation

atmosphere: a mix of gases surrounding the Earth
The Earth's atmosphere consists of 79.1 percent nitrogen (by volume), 20.9 percent oxygen, 0.03 percent CO_2 and trace amounts of other gases. It can be divided into a number of layers according to thermal properties (temperature). The layer nearest the earth is called the troposphere (up to about 10–15 km above the surface 0; next is the stratosphere (up to about 50 km), followed by the mesosphere (up to 80 km) and finally the thermosphere or ionosphere which extends into space. There is little mixing of gases between layers.

backstop technology: a substitute technology, which becomes economically feasible when the price of a non-renewable natural resource has risen to a level (resulting from continued extraction)

Beaver Report: the report by Sir Hugh Beaver in the UK on Air Pollution in 1954; this report led to the Clean Air Act of 1956 in Britain

benzene: a highly toxic liquid hydrocarbon derived from coal and petroleum, used in the manufacture of plastics

Berlin Mandate: the decision by a 1995 UN climate conference in Berlin to seek commitments beyond the 1992 Rio agreement, under which developed nations volunteered to limit greenhouse emissions; precursor to the 1997 Kyoto talks on these reductions

biochemical oxidation: the process of transforming organic pollutants into settleable organic substances or inert mineral materials

biochemical oxygen demand (BOD): considered usually as an indicator of water pollution; represents – subject to appropriate accounting of relevant chemical effects within the compounds involved – the extent of biochemically degradable substances in water

biodiversity: the number of different kinds of plant and animal species that live in a region

Biodiversity includes (a) genetic variability, and (b) the number of species. On land, tropical rain forests have the highest biodiversity.

biogenic: the effect of the activities of living organisms

biomass: the amount of living matter or life forms in a particular region, usually expressed as weight (mass) per unit area (e.g. tons per acre)

biomass energy: energy produced by combusting biomass materials such as wood
The CO_2 from burning biomass will not increase the total atmosphere CO_2 if this consumption is done on a sustainable basis (i.e. if in a given period of time, regrowth of biomass takes up as much CO_2 as is released from combustion). Biomass energy is often suggested as a replacement for fossil fuel combustion which has large GHG emissions.

biome: a characterization of the ecosystem in terms of the nature and composition of its vegetation; a community of plants and animals in a specified region

biosphere: the segments of the Earth and its atmospheric surroundings that can support life; in principle, the region on land, in the oceans, and in the atmosphere inhabited by living organisms

biota: the collection of all living things, including plants and animals

biotic element: any member of the organisms which form the populations and communities in an ecosystem

British Antarctic Survey (BAS): a scientific body engaged in all aspect of research on the continent of Antarctica

British Standard 7750: aimed at environmental audit and accountability, this was devised to enable independent certifiers to assess individual companies and organizations regarding their compliance with the set standards

capital consumption allowance (CCA): the investment allowance for replacing used capital is called depreciation allowance or CCA

capitalized value: the capital value of an asset or liability, valued at current market terms

carbon budget: the amount of carbon released into the atmosphere by net sources, whether natural factors, like dying plants, or human activities, like burning fossil fuel, minus the amount of carbon absorbed by the ocean, growing green plants and other carbon "sinks"

carbon cycle: the process by which carbon is cycled through the environment
Carbon, in the form of CO_2, is absorbed from the atmosphere and used by plants in the process of photosynthesis to store energy. Plants and animals then return CO_2 to the atmosphere through respiration when they consume this energy. A quarter of the total atmospheric CO_2 is cycled each year, approximately half of which is exchanged with the land biota.

carbon dioxide (CO_2): a molecule formed from one atom of carbon and two of oxygen
Carbon dioxide is a GHG of major concern in the study of global warming. It is estimated that the amount in the air is increasing by 0.25–0.5 percent annually. Anthropogenic carbon dioxide is emitted mainly through the burning of fossil fuels and deforestation.

carbon equivalent (CE): a metric measure used to gauge the emissions of the different GHGs based on their global warming potential (GWP)
GHG emissions in the USA are most commonly expressed as "million metric tons of carbon equivalents" (MMTCE). Warming potentials are used to convert GHG CO_2 equivalents. Carbon dioxide equivalent can then be converted to carbon equivalents by multiplying CO_2 equivalents by 12/44 (the ratio of the weight of carbon to CO_2). Thus, the formula derived for carbon equivalents is:

$$MMTCE = \text{million metric tons of a gas} \times (\text{GWP of the gas}) \times \frac{12}{44}$$

carbon sequestration: the uptake and storage of carbon in natural systems
Trees, plants and bioresources of oceans are among the most significant sinks of carbon dioxide. These tend to offset concentrations of carbon dioxide. Forest expansions serve as an important mechanism for carbon sequestration.

catalytic converter: a device fitted to car exhausts which removes harmful emissions of air pollutants such as hydrocarbons

chlorinated hydrocarbons: these are also known as organochlorines, and include pesticides such as DDT, aldrin, endrin, and PCBs
These compounds are highly toxic, and are not biodegradable.

chlorofluorocarbons (CFCs): a set of synthetic compounds belonging to the family of GHGs used in air conditioning, as industrial solvents and in other commercial applications
CFCs destroy ozone in the stratosphere (see *ozone*), and are being eliminated under an international agreement negotiated in Montreal in 1987.

climate: the prevalent long-term weather conditions in a particular area
Climatic elements include precipitation, temperature, humidity, sunshine and wind velocity and phenomena such as fog, frost, and hail storms. Climate deals not only with the atmosphere but also its variations.

climate feedback: a secondary process resulting from primary climate change which may increase (positive feedback) or diminish (negative feedback) the magnitude of climate change

Club of Rome: a voluntary association formed by a group of professionals from ten countries in 1968

The Club of Rome brought out the influential publication *Limits to Growth* in 1972, followed by later reports on similar issues.

Coase's Theorem: if there are property rights, and no transaction costs, efficient bargaining leads to Pareto optimality in the presence of externality without government intervention

Ronald Coase (1960) The problem of social cost. *Journal of Law and Economics*, 3.

Codex (Codex Alimentarius Committee): a committee set up by the UN Food and Agriculture Organization (FAO) and the World Health Organization (WHO) to devise standards for foods so as to provide health safety protection to consumers Codex publishes the Codex Maximum Residue Limits (MRL); these are the maximum permissible limits of undesirable substances in foods for humans or animals, and in pesticide residues. The Codex standards have become norms as per the 1993 GATT directives. It remains an ironic enforcement mechanism of standards in countries which seek to stay below the MRL, which are then deemed as non-tariff barriers to trade, and not supported under international trade agreements.

cogeneration: combined heat and power generation method

compensated demand curve: a demand curve in which the income effect of price change is excluded so that, along the demand curve, real income is held constant

The demand curve exhibits only the substitution effect. In the Marshallian demand curve, both the income and substitution effects are allowed.

composite commodity theorem (J. R. Hicks, 1939, Value and Capital. Oxford University Press): this states that a set of goods, whose relative prices do not change over an entire time horizon of concern, can be treated as if they were one commodity-composite single commodity

contestable market: the market characterized by free entry and exit for potential entrants using the same technologies as in the case of the incumbent firms or economic entities, and having access to the demand and market functions as in the case of the incumbents

Convention on the Control of Transboundary Movement of Hazardous Wastes and Their Disposal (the Basel Convention): an international convention of 1992 which was held against the background of the dumping of hazardous wastes by industrial countries in developing countries – with a nominal compensation; complete phasing out of such activities by the end of 1997 was planned as per a follow-up resolution of the convention in 1994

Copenhagen Amendment: a second amendment to the Montreal Protocol to speed up the phase out of chemicals that deplete the ozone layer

cryosphere: that part of the Earth's surface consisting of ice masses and snow deposits

This includes continental ice sheets, mountain glaciers, sea ice, surface snow cover, lake and river ice, and Siberia and the Arctic Ocean.

DDT (dichlorodiphenyltrichloroethane): a chlorinated hydrocarbon insecticide with extremely toxic features, supposedly banned worldwide

dioxins: a class of dangerous chlorinated organic compounds arising from the manufacture of herbicides, bleaches and a few similar products

disembodied technical progress: this is technical progress which appears costless, and independent of other economic variables

Dobson unit (DU): a unit measuring the total amount of ozone in a vertical column above the Earth's surface in the stratosphere

Ozone varies with latitude and season, and ranges typically from 250 to 450 DU. A value of less than 200 DU is associated with the presence of an ozone hole.

ecology: the study of the interactions of organisms with their physical environment and with the other organisms associated with it

ecosystem: a system of interdependent forms of life and their physical environment; could be described at local, regional or other demarcations of levels

El Niño: a climate phenomenon occurring at irregular time-intervals for every 2–7 years during Christmas (El Niño means Christ child) in the surface oceans of the Southeast Pacific

The phenomenon involves seasonal changes in the direction of Pacific winds and abnormally warm surface ocean temperatures. The changes normally only affect the Pacific region, but major events and global weather patterns are still matters of continued investigations.

El-Serafy formula: the El-Serafy formula defines "user costs" or economic depreciation as

$$R - X = R(1 + r)^{-n+1}$$

where R is current profit, X the Hicksian income, n the number of time units, and r the interest rate

embodied technical progress: technical progress which cannot take place unless it is embodied in new capital

endemic: a species native to a specific location, occurring naturally in a specific region or a characterization of biogeophysical features; a species or a race native to a particular location

enhanced greenhouse effect: the natural greenhouse effect (GE) has been enhanced by anthropogenic emission of GHGs. Increased concentrations of carbomethane, and nitrous oxide, CFCs, HFCs, PFCs, SF6, and other photochemically important gases caused by activities such as fossil fuel consumption and adding to waste landfills, trap more infrared radiation, thereby exerting warming influence on the climate

environment: the surroundings of an organism or a species; the physical, chemical, and biological traits of the ecosystem in which it lives

ethnocentrism: the valuation of things and activities in terms of the cultural beliefs of a population or race

European Economic Community (EEC): established on March 25, 1957 by the treaty of Rome by the governments of Belgium, France, the Federal Republic of Germany, Italy, Luxembourg, and the Netherlands

The treaty provided for the removal of trade and capital barriers in the member countries. In 1962, a common agricultural policy (CAP) was formed. Denmark, Ireland, and UK joined the community in 1973, and were followed by Greece in 1982, and Portugal and Spain in 1986.

European Union (EU): the member countries are Austria, Belgium, Denmark, Finland, France, Germany, Greece, Ireland, Italy, Luxembourg, the Netherlands, Portugal, Spain, Sweden, and the UK
  Current initiatives include entry to another three East European countries, with a possible further expansion soon.

existence value: the utility derived by the notion of the existence of a desirable entity

exothermic: a reaction that takes place with the release of heat

externality: uncompensated effect of economic or physical activity
  An externality arises when production or consumption or other activities of an entity provides: (a) utility to the latter without paying for costs imposed on other entities, or (b) receives no compensation commensurate with the benefits provided to others.

Exxon Valdez disaster: the disaster involving the oil tanker Exxon Valdez in 1989 in Prince William Sound, Alaska
  One-quarter million barrels of oil leaked into the sea; billion dollar damages were incurred.

factor augmenting technical progress: technical progress which raises the level of output even when the stocks of capital and labor remain fixed

fauna: animal life, usually specific to a region or time

feedback: a sequence of interactions in which the final interaction leads to influence the initial one
  A positive feedback is one that amplifies the changes mechanism, and a negative feedback contributes toward retardation or dampening of the change.

feedback mechanisms: a mechanism that connects one aspect of a system to another
  The connection can be amplifying (positive feedback) or moderating (negative feedback).

fiscal drag: the effect of inflation on tax rates

flora: plant life, usually specific to a region or time interval

fluorocarbons (FCs): organic compounds similar to hydrocarbons in which one or more hydrogen atoms are replaced by fluorine
  FCs containing chlorine are CFCs.

free rider: deriving benefits without having to pay any costs

General Agreement on Tariffs and Trade (GATT): a multilateral trade agreement signed in 1947 and effective since January 1948
  Barring customs unions and free trade areas, all contracting parties are bound by the most favored nation (MFN) clause: prohibiting import quotas and other restrictive trade practices. Several major trade negotiations were held in different rounds under GATT, the last one being the Uruguay Round which ended in 1994. At this point, GATT dissolved and transformed into the new World Trade Organization (WTO).

general equilibrium (economy): all markets in an economy are simultaneously in equilibrium
  With balanced demand and supply, prices do not vary.

genus: a group of species with similar characteristics

geosphere: the soils, sediments, and rock layers of the Earth's crust, both continental and beneath the oceans; the mineral abiotic portion of the Earth

Global Environment Monitoring System (GEMS): administered by the UNEP as a monitoring system on several aspects of the global environment like the atmosphere and airborne pollutants, with its units in about 48 countries

Golden rule of accumulation: the path of balanced growth where each generation saves for successive generations that constant fraction which was saved for it by the previous generation

halocarbons: chemicals consisting of carbon, sometimes hydrogen, and one or more of the halogens: chlorine, fluorine, bromine or iodhalons

halogen: any of the five highly reactive elements: chlorine, flourine, bromine and iodhalons, and a specific (in group ViiB of the periodic table) astatine

halons: organic compounds containing chlorine/bromine
These constitute a class of stratospheric ozone-depleting compounds, and have long atmospheric lifetimes.

Helsinki Agreement: the 1989 agreement by 80 countries to cease production of all CFCs by the end of the twentieth century, to protect the ozone layer

Hicks neutral technical progress: a classification of disembodied technical progress which compares growth processes, holding capital–labor ratio constant

Hotelling rent: defined as profits on the last ton mined; computed as price minus marginal cost on the last ton mined
Hotelling rent is different from the usual meaning of rent (see *rent* below).

Hotelling rule: for the time path of extraction to be optimal, the net profit (selling price – extraction cost) of a unit of reserve resource in the ground must rise at a rate equal to the interest rate; this rule is suggested for perfectly competitive markets

hydrocarbons: substances containing only hydrogen and carbon
Fossil fuels are made up of hydrocarbons. Hydrocarbon compounds are major air pollutants.

hydrofluorocarbons (HFCS): these were introduced as alternatives to depleting substances in serving many industrial, commercial, and personal needs
HFCs are emitted as by-products from industrial processes and are also used in manufacturing. They do not significantly deplete the stratospheric ozone layer. They are powerful GHGs with GWPs ranging from 140 (HFC-152a) to 12,100.

hydrosphere: that part of the earth composed of water including oceans, seas, ice caps, glaciers, lakes, rivers and underground water supplies

infrared radiation: electromagnetic radiation of lower frequencies and longer wavelengths than visible light
Solar ultra-violet (UV) radiation is absorbed by the Earth's surface and remitted as infrared radiation.

International Development Association (IDA): an affiliate of the World Bank, set up in 1960 to provide capital for project development in member countries with percapita income of $480 (in 1987 prices), at more favorable terms than in the rest of capital markets

invisible hand: the effect of free market economic forces in the socioeconomic milieu; a term originally used by Adam Smith (1723–90)

The responsiveness of forces affecting the demand for and supply of goods and services is presumed to take care of necessary correction in the market system.

ionosphere: also known as the thermosphere, a layer in the atmosphere above the mesosphere extending from about 80 km above the Earth's surface

It can be considered a distinct layer due to a rise in air temperature with increasing height. Atmospheric densities here are very low.

lifetime (atmospheric): also known as residence time. The approximate amount of time a pollutant will spend in the atmosphere before either being converted to another chemical compound or being taken out of the atmosphere via a sink. This time depends on the pollutant's sources and sinks as well as its reactivity. Lifetime affects the mixing of pollutants in the atmosphere; a long lifetime will allow the pollutant to mix well in the atmosphere. Average lifetimes can vary from one day (nitrogen dioxide) to 5,000 years (oxygen) and beyond.

lithosphere: the crust enclosing the kernel of the Earth, extending up to about 80 km from the planet's surface

London Amendment: a first amendment to the Montreal Protocol to speed up the phase out of chemicals that deplete the ozone layer

Malthusian Theory: based on Thomas Malthus's 1798 book *An Essay on the Principle of Population*; predicts the phenomena of geometric progression of human population with resources and food lagging behind and possibly leading to major shortages and disasters

marginal physical product: the addition to total output with the deployment of an additional unit of labor holding other factors constant

marginal product: the additional output attributable to additional use of a given factor of production

market failure: usually a reference to the feature that, in competitive market situations, the market price of an item differs from its social cost (defined as the private cost plus environmental or other external costs or benefits)

When the markets are imperfect or non-competitive, the feature is automatically assumed to prevail.

mesosphere: the region of the upper atmosphere between about 50 and 80 km above the surface of the Earth

Montreal Protocol: an international treaty signed in 1987 that limits production of chlorofluorocarbons

The discovery of an ozone hole over Antarctica prompted action to control the use of gases which have a destructive effect on the ozone layer. From this concern emerged the Montreal Protocol on substances that deplete the ozone layer, signed by 24 countries in 1987. It came into force in 1989 and has since been ratified by 120 countries. The original agreement was to control and phase out the production and supply of ozone-depleting chemicals, specifically CFCs and derivatives. A meeting in 1992 was held in Copenhagen to revise the protocol. This meeting agreed to bring forward the phasing out of halons to 1994, and other halocarbons to 1996. At present these targets have been, or are being, met.

Multilateral Investment Guarantee Agency (MIGA): created as an affiliate of the World Bank in 1988, it provides, at a cost, to its member country transactions, the investment insurance (covering political risks), and marketing services for private or other foreign direct investment

OECD (Organization for Economic Cooperation and Development): this organization, with its head office in Paris, is an economic club (in an economic sense) of relatively developed countries

The original member countries were Austria, Belgium, Canada, Denmark, France, Germany, Greece, Iceland, Italy, Luxembourg, Netherlands, Norway, Portugal, Spain, Sweden, Switzerland, Turkey, UK, and the USA. Later they were joined by (the year of joining given in brackets): Japan (1964), Finland (1969), Australia (1971), New Zealand (1973), Mexico (1994), and the Czech Republic (1995).

OECD objectives: formulate, coordinate and promote policies for economic growth and stability, expand multilateral trade on a non-discriminatory basis, and co-ordinate Third World aid

open access resource: a material resource with no property right held by any individual or entity

ozone: an unstable gas in which three molecules of oxygen occur together (O_3)

Ozone is a GHG. In the atmosphere, ozone occurs at two different altitudes. Low-altitude tropospheric ozone is a form of air pollution (part of smog) produced by the emissions from cars and trucks. High in the atmosphere, a thin layer of stratospheric ozone is naturally created by sunlight. This ozone layer shields the earth from dangerous (cancer-causing) UV radiation from the sun. Chlorine gas from CFCs speeds the breakdown of ozone in the ozone layer.

ozone depletion: the loss or destruction of the stratospheric ozone layer

This is usually effected by the catalytic actions of compounds containing chlorine, fluorine, and/or bromine.

ozone hole: the Antarctic ozone hole; first detected in 1985 and measured by a vertical column of ozone in the atmosphere in Dobson units

The hole appears every Southern Hemisphere spring (August to October) before disappearing during the summer months (December/January). This fall in total ozone concentration in the atmosphere leads to a consequent rise in the penetration of UV radiation which, among other effects, could cause an increase in skin cancer. It was realized that this hole was being created by man-made substances such as CFCs. This led to a rapid response in the form of the Montreal Protocol. However, due to the long lifetimes of CFCs the ozone layer is not expected to fully recover for at least half a century.

ozone layer: the ozone in the stratosphere

This layer is very diffuse, occupying a region many kilometers in thickness, but is conventionally described as a layer to aid understanding.

Pareto improvement: a reallocation of resources which leads to improving the welfare of some without worsening the welfare of others; named after Vilfredo Pareto (1848–1923)

Pareto optimum: claimed to have been attained by an economy when resources and output cannot be reallocated in a Pareto improvement sense

Paris Club: the forum, mostly comprising of some of the OECD member countries, where creditor countries negotiate with borrower countries over debt levels and rescheduling aspects

perfluorocarbons (PFCs): a group of human-made chorines composed of carbon and fluorine only: CF_4 and C_2F_6

Chemicals, specifically C_2F_6 (along with hydrofluorocarbons), were introduced as alternatives to ozone-depleting substances. In addition, they are emitted as by-products of industrial processes and are also used in manufacturing. PFCs do not harm the stratospheric ozone layer, but they are powerful GHGs: a global warming potential (GWP) of 6,300 and C_2F_6 GWP of 12,500.

phenology: the branch of science dealing with the relationship between climate and periodic biological phenomena related to or affected by climatic factors, like bird migration or plant flowering

Pigouvian taxes: named after the author Arthur C. Pigou of the 1930s; refers to taxes or equivalent penalties and charges assessed as required to correct for externalities caused by economic agents or producer-polluters

polluter pays principle (PPP): first officialized by the OECD in 1975; represents an allocation of property rights on the environmental assets to consumers making producer-polluters pay the difference between the social costs and private costs of provision goods and services

polychlorinated biphenyls (PCBs): the compounds resulting from the reaction of chlorine with biphenyl

These are generally used as lubricants, paints and packaging materials, and have been toxic to marine life – particularly fish.

Prisoner's Dilemma: arises out of lack of cooperation or coordination in the confession strategies of two co-partner offenders

If both deny, they could be better off. If any one denies but the other confesses both receive a different punishment; but if both confess, they are much worse off.

public goods: the goods that exhibit both consumption indivisibilities and non-excludability, and combine the features respectively: once the resource is provided, even those who do not pay for it cannot be excluded from the benefits they confer; and one person's consumption of the good does not diminish the amount available for others

rent: used by classical economists to describe the value added, or true income, from land

We do not use this term, except in "Hotelling rent" which means something else.

rental: used to describe per period profits earned by an asset; used interchangeably with "(net) receipts"; see also *Hotelling rent*

sequester: to remove or segregate

Activities, such as planting trees, remove CO_2 from the atmosphere, and thus sequester CO_2.

sink: a reservoir of any medium which assimilates or absorbs pollutants, and thus uptakes a pollutant from a part of the atmospheric cycle

Soil and trees tend to act as natural sinks. For example, the oceans absorb about 50 percent of the CO_2 released into the atmosphere. Oceans and forests function as CO_2 sinks.

stratosphere: the upper part of the Earth's atmosphere, above about 7 miles

transaction costs: the totality of costs (not including market prices of sale/purchase) of exchanging and enforcing property rights or of undertaking market/non-market transactions

troposphere: the lowest layer of the atmosphere, extending up to about 7 miles from the Earth's surface

Tropopause is the interface between the troposphere and stratosphere.

tropospheric ozone (O_3): ozone that is located in the troposphere and plays a significant role in the GE and urban smog

tropospheric ozone precursor: gases that influence the levels of tropospheric ozone; these include: carbon monoxide (CO), nitrogen oxide (NO_x), and nonmethane volatile organic compounds (NMVOC)

ultra-violet radiation (UV): electromagnetic radiation of higher frequencies and shorter wavelength than visible light

It is divided into three regions based on wavelength: UV-A, B, and C. With the discovery of the ozone hole, it was realized that there would be an increase in the penetration of UV-B radiation with possible adverse effects being an increase in skin cancer or related health problems.

Index

Related Economics titles from Blackwell Publishers

Global Environmental Economics
Equity and the Limits to Markets
Edited by Mohammed H. I. Dore and Timothy D. Mount
1999   355 pages   paperback   0–631–21030–X

Growth and Development from an Evolutionary Perspective
John Fei and Gustav Ranis
1997   340 pages   hardcover   1–55786–079–3

The Economics of Gender
Second Edition
Joyce P. Jacobsen
1998   550 pages   paperback   0–631–20727–9

The Handbook of Environmental Economics
Edited by Daniel W. Bromley
1995   368 pages   paperback   1–55786–641–4

To order call:

1–800–216–2522 (North American orders only) or
24-hour freephone on 0500 008205 (UK orders only)

Visit us on the web: *http://www.blackwellpublishers.co.uk*

NEW PERSPECTIVES

Microsoft® Office 365™ & Word 2016

INTERMEDIATE

Ann Shaffer
Katherine T. Pinard

CENGAGE
Learning®

Australia • Brazil • Mexico • Singapore • United Kingdom • United States

CENGAGE
Learning®

**New Perspectives Microsoft® Office 365™ &
Word 2016, Intermediate**
Ann Shaffer, Katherine T. Pinard

SVP, GM Skills & Global Product Management:
  Dawn Gerrain

Product Director: Kathleen McMahon

Senior Product Team Manager: Lauren Murphy

Product Team Manager: Andrea Topping

Associate Product Manager: Melissa Stehler

Senior Director, Development: Marah Bellegarde

Product Development Manager: Leigh Hefferon

Senior Content Developers: Kathy Finnegan,
  Marjorie Hunt

Developmental Editor: Mary Pat Shaffer

Product Assistant: Erica Chapman

Marketing Director: Michele McTighe

Marketing Manager: Stephanie Albracht

Senior Production Director: Wendy Troeger

Production Director: Patty Stephan

Senior Content Project Manager: Jennifer Goguen
  McGrail

Art Director: Diana Graham

Text Designer: Althea Chen

Composition: GEX Publishing Services

Cover Template Designer: Wing-Ip Ngan,
  Ink Design, Inc.

Cover image(s): BEPictured/Shutterstock.com

For product information and technology assistance, contact us at
Cengage Learning Customer & Sales Support, 1-800-354-9706

For permission to use material from this text or product, submit all
requests online at **www.cengage.com/permissions**.
Further permissions questions can be e-mailed to
permissionrequest@cengage.com

Mac users: If you're working through this product using a Mac, some of the steps may
vary. Additional information for Mac users is included with the Data Files for this
product.

Some of the product names and company names used in this book have been used for
identification purposes only and may be trademarks or registered trademarks of their
respective manufacturers and sellers.

Windows® is a registered trademark of Microsoft Corporation. © 2012 Microsoft.
Microsoft and the Office logo are either registered trademarks or trademarks of
Microsoft Corporation in the United States and/or other countries. Cengage Learning is
an independent entity from Microsoft Corporation and not affiliated with Microsoft in
any manner.

Disclaimer: Any fictional data related to persons or companies or URLs used throughout
this text is intended for instructional purposes only. At the time this text was published,
any such data was fictional and not belonging to any real persons or companies.

Disclaimer: The material in this text was written using Microsoft Office 365 ProPlus and
Microsoft Word 2016 running on Microsoft Windows 10 Professional and was Quality
Assurance tested before the publication date. As Microsoft continually updates the
Microsoft Office suite and the Windows 10 operating system, your software experience may
vary slightly from what is presented in the printed text.

Library of Congress Control Number: 2016937098
ISBN: 978-1-305-88096-2

Cengage Learning
20 Channel Center Street
Boston, MA 02210
USA

Cengage Learning is a leading provider of customized learning solutions
with employees residing in nearly 40 different countries and sales in more
than 125 countries around the world. Find your local representative at
www.cengage.com.

Cengage Learning products are represented in Canada by
Nelson Education, Ltd.

To learn more about Cengage Learning, visit **www.cengage.com**

Purchase any of our products at your local college store or at our
preferred online store **www.cengagebrain.com**

Printed in the United States of America
Print Number: 01   Print Year: 2016

BRIEF CONTENTS

TABLE OF CONTENTS

WORD MODULES

Module 2 Navigating and Formatting a Document
*Editing an Academic Document According to
MLA Style* . . . . **WD 61**

Module 3 Creating Tables and a Multipage Report
Writing a Recommendation . . . . **WD 119**

Productivity Apps for School and Work

Corinne Hoisington

© Rawpixel/Shutterstock.com

Lochlan keeps track of his class notes, football plays, and internship meetings with OneNote.

Zoe is using the annotation features of Microsoft Edge to take and save web notes for her research paper.

Nori is creating a Sway site to highlight this year's activities for the Student Government Association.

Hunter is adding interactive videos and screen recordings to his PowerPoint resume.

Being computer literate no longer means mastery of only Word, Excel, PowerPoint, Outlook, and Access. To become technology power users, Hunter, Nori, Zoe, and Lochlan are exploring Microsoft OneNote, Sway, Mix, and Edge in Office 2016 and Windows 10.

In this Module

Learn to use productivity apps!
Links to companion **Sways**, featuring **videos** with hands-on instructions, are located on www.cengagebrain.com.

Introduction to OneNote 2016

notebook | section tab | To Do tag | screen clipping | note | template | Microsoft OneNote Mobile app | sync | drawing canvas | inked handwriting | Ink to Text

Bottom Line

- OneNote is a note-taking app for your academic and professional life.
- Use OneNote to get organized by gathering your ideas, sketches, webpages, photos, videos, and notes in one place.

As you glance around any classroom, you invariably see paper notebooks and notepads on each desk. Because deciphering and sharing handwritten notes can be a challenge, Microsoft OneNote 2016 replaces physical notebooks, binders, and paper notes with a searchable, digital notebook. OneNote captures your ideas and schoolwork on any device so you can stay organized, share notes, and work with others on projects. Whether you are a student taking class notes as shown in **Figure 1** or an employee taking notes in company meetings, OneNote is the one place to keep notes for all of your projects.

Figure 1: OneNote 2016 notebook

Each **notebook** is divided into sections, also called **section tabs**, by subject or topic.

Use **To Do tags**, icons that help you keep track of your assignments and other tasks.

Type on a page to add a **note**, a small window that contains text or other types of information.

Personalize a page with a **template**, or stationery.

Write or draw directly on the page using drawing tools.

Pages can include pictures such as **screen clippings**, images from any part of a computer screen.

Attach files and enter equations so you have everything you need in one place.

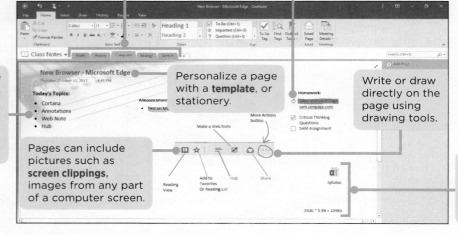

Creating a OneNote Notebook

OneNote is divided into sections similar to those in a spiral-bound notebook. Each OneNote notebook contains sections, pages, and other notebooks. You can use OneNote for school, business, and personal projects. Store information for each type of project in different notebooks to keep your tasks separate, or use any other organization that suits you. OneNote is flexible enough to adapt to the way you want to work.

When you create a notebook, it contains a blank page with a plain white background by default, though you can use templates, or stationery, to apply designs in categories such as Academic, Business, Decorative, and Planners. Start typing or use the buttons on the Insert tab to insert notes, which are small resizable windows that can contain text, equations, tables, on-screen writing, images, audio and video recordings, to-do lists, file attachments, and file printouts. Add as many notes as you need to each page.

Learn to use OneNote!

Links to companion **Sways**, featuring **videos** with hands-on instructions, are located on www.cengagebrain.com.

Syncing a Notebook to the Cloud

OneNote saves your notes every time you make a change in a notebook. To make sure you can access your notebooks with a laptop, tablet, or smartphone wherever you are, OneNote uses cloud-based storage, such as OneDrive or SharePoint. **Microsoft OneNote Mobile app**, a lightweight version of OneNote 2016 shown in **Figure 2**, is available for free in the Windows Store, Google Play for Android devices, and the AppStore for iOS devices.

If you have a Microsoft account, OneNote saves your notes on OneDrive automatically for all your mobile devices and computers, which is called **syncing**. For example, you can use OneNote to take notes on your laptop during class, and then open OneNote on your phone to study later. To use a notebook stored on your computer with your OneNote Mobile app, move the notebook to OneDrive. You can quickly share notebook content with other people using OneDrive.

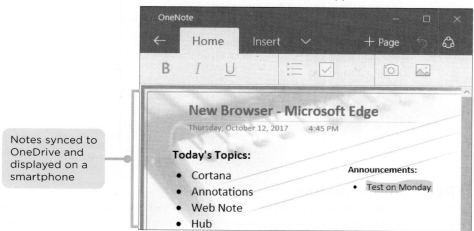

Figure 2: Microsoft OneNote Mobile app

Notes synced to OneDrive and displayed on a smartphone

Taking Notes

Use OneNote pages to organize your notes by class and topic or lecture. Beyond simple typed notes, OneNote stores drawings, converts handwriting to searchable text and mathematical sketches to equations, and records audio and video.

OneNote includes drawing tools that let you sketch freehand drawings such as biological cell diagrams and financial supply-and-demand charts. As shown in **Figure 3**, the Draw tab on the ribbon provides these drawing tools along with shapes so you can insert diagrams and other illustrations to represent your ideas. When you draw on a page, OneNote creates a **drawing canvas**, which is a container for shapes and lines.

On the Job Now

OneNote is ideal for taking notes during meetings, whether you are recording minutes, documenting a discussion, sketching product diagrams, or listing follow-up items. Use a meeting template to add pages with content appropriate for meetings.

Figure 3: Tools on the Draw tab

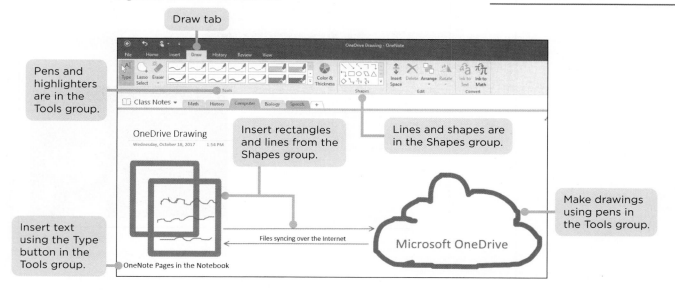

Draw tab

Pens and highlighters are in the Tools group.

Insert rectangles and lines from the Shapes group.

Lines and shapes are in the Shapes group.

Insert text using the Type button in the Tools group.

Make drawings using pens in the Tools group.

Converting Handwriting to Text

When you use a pen tool to write on a notebook page, the text you enter is called **inked handwriting**. OneNote can convert inked handwriting to typed text when you use the **Ink to Text** button in the Convert group on the Draw tab, as shown in **Figure 4**. After OneNote converts the handwriting to text, you can use the Search box to find terms in the converted text or any other note in your notebooks.

Figure 4: Converting handwriting to text

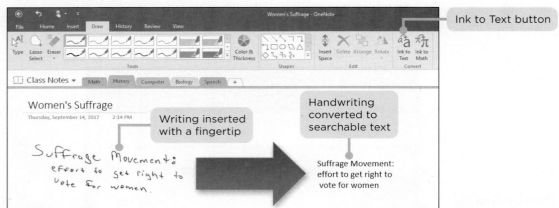

Recording a Lecture

If your computer or mobile device has a microphone or camera, OneNote can record the audio or video from a lecture or business meeting as shown in **Figure 5**. When you record a lecture (with your instructor's permission), you can follow along, take regular notes at your own pace, and review the video recording later. You can control the start, pause, and stop motions of the recording when you play back the recording of your notes.

Figure 5: Video inserted in a notebook

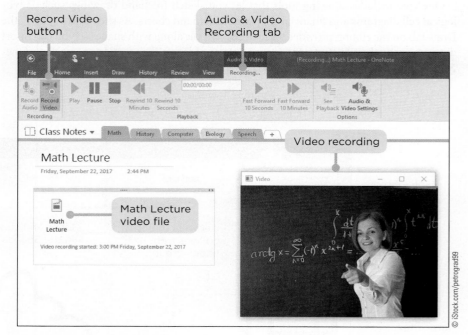

© iStock.com/petrograd99

Try This Now

Learn to use OneNote!
Links to companion **Sways**, featuring **videos** with hands-on instructions, are located on www.cengagebrain.com.

1: Taking Notes for a Week

As a student, you can get organized by using OneNote to take detailed notes in your classes. Perform the following tasks:

a. Create a new OneNote notebook on your Microsoft OneDrive account (the default location for new notebooks). Name the notebook with your first name followed by "Notes," as in **Caleb Notes**.

b. Create four section tabs, each with a different class name.

c. Take detailed notes in those classes for one week. Be sure to include notes, drawings, and other types of content.

d. Sync your notes with your OneDrive. Submit your assignment in the format specified by your instructor.

2: Using OneNote to Organize a Research Paper

You have a research paper due on the topic of three habits of successful students. Use OneNote to organize your research. Perform the following tasks:

a. Create a new OneNote notebook on your Microsoft OneDrive account. Name the notebook **Success Research**.

b. Create three section tabs with the following names:

- **Take Detailed Notes**
- **Be Respectful in Class**
- **Come to Class Prepared**

c. On the web, research the topics and find three sources for each section. Copy a sentence from each source and paste the sentence into the appropriate section. When you paste the sentence, OneNote inserts it in a note with a link to the source.

d. Sync your notes with your OneDrive. Submit your assignment in the format specified by your instructor.

3: Planning Your Career

Note: This activity requires a webcam or built-in video camera on any type of device.

Consider an occupation that interests you. Using OneNote, examine the responsibilities, education requirements, potential salary, and employment outlook of a specific career. Perform the following tasks:

a. Create a new OneNote notebook on your Microsoft OneDrive account. Name the notebook with your first name followed by a career title, such as **Kara - App Developer**.

b. Create four section tabs with the names **Responsibilities, Education Requirements, Median Salary**, and **Employment Outlook**.

c. Research the responsibilities of your career path. Using OneNote, record a short video (approximately 30 seconds) of yourself explaining the responsibilities of your career path. Place the video in the Responsibilities section.

d. On the web, research the educational requirements for your career path and find two appropriate sources. Copy a paragraph from each source and paste them into the appropriate section. When you paste a paragraph, OneNote inserts it in a note with a link to the source.

e. Research the median salary for a single year for this career. Create a mathematical equation in the Median Salary section that multiplies the amount of the median salary times 20 years to calculate how much you will possibly earn.

f. For the Employment Outlook section, research the outlook for your career path. Take at least four notes about what you find when researching the topic.

g. Sync your notes with your OneDrive. Submit your assignment in the format specified by your instructor.

Introduction to Sway

Sway site | responsive design | Storyline | card | Creative Commons license | animation emphasis effects | Docs.com

Bottom Line

- Drag photos, videos, and files from your computer and content from Facebook and Twitter directly to your Sway presentation.
- Run Sway in a web browser or as an app on your smartphone, and save presentations as webpages.

Expressing your ideas in a presentation typically means creating PowerPoint slides or a Word document. Microsoft Sway gives you another way to engage an audience. Sway is a free Microsoft tool available at Sway.com or as an app in Office 365. Using Sway, you can combine text, images, videos, and social media in a website called a **Sway site** that you can share and display on any device. To get started, you create a digital story on a web-based canvas without borders, slides, cells, or page breaks. A Sway site organizes the text, images, and video into a **responsive design**, which means your content adapts perfectly to any screen size as shown in **Figure 6**. You store a Sway site in the cloud on OneDrive using a free Microsoft account.

Figure 6: Sway site with responsive design

You can display a Sway presentation in a web browser.

Sway uses responsive design to make sure pages fit perfectly on any device.

Learn to use Sway!

Links to companion **Sways**, featuring **videos** with hands-on instructions, are located on www.cengagebrain.com.

Creating a Sway Presentation

You can use Sway to build a digital flyer, a club newsletter, a vacation blog, an informational site, a digital art portfolio, or a new product rollout. After you select your topic and sign into Sway with your Microsoft account, a **Storyline** opens, providing tools and a work area for composing your digital story. See **Figure 7**. Each story can include text, images, and videos. You create a Sway by adding text and media content into a Storyline section, or **card**. To add pictures, videos, or documents, select a card in the left pane and then select the Insert Content button. The first card in a Sway presentation contains a title and background image.

Figure 7: Creating a Sway site

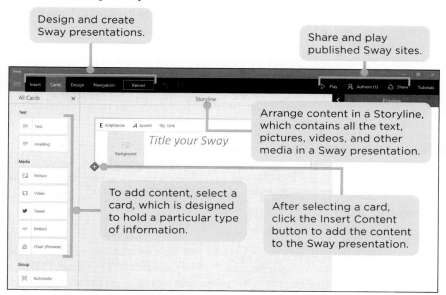

Design and create Sway presentations.

Share and play published Sway sites.

Arrange content in a Storyline, which contains all the text, pictures, videos, and other media in a Sway presentation.

To add content, select a card, which is designed to hold a particular type of information.

After selecting a card, click the Insert Content button to add the content to the Sway presentation.

Adding Content to Build a Story

As you work, Sway searches the Internet to help you find relevant images, videos, tweets, and other content from online sources such as Bing, YouTube, Twitter, and Facebook. You can drag content from the search results right into the Storyline. In addition, you can upload your own images and videos directly in the presentation. For example, if you are creating a Sway presentation about the market for commercial drones, Sway suggests content to incorporate into the presentation by displaying it in the left pane as search results. The search results include drone images tagged with a **Creative Commons license** at online sources as shown in **Figure 8**. A Creative Commons license is a public copyright license that allows the free distribution of an otherwise copyrighted work. In addition, you can specify the source of the media. For example, you can add your own Facebook or OneNote pictures and videos in Sway without leaving the app.

On the Job Now

If you have a Microsoft Word document containing an outline of your business content, drag the outline into Sway to create a card for each topic.

Figure 8: Images in Sway search results

Select the source of media objects

Information about Creative Commons licenses

Storyline title

The Market for Commercial Drones

Drag an image to the picture placeholder box

Suggested images in the search results

Designing a Sway

Sway professionally designs your Storyline content by resizing background images and fonts to fit your display, and by floating text, animating media, embedding video, and removing images as a page scrolls out of view. Sway also evaluates the images in your Storyline and suggests a color palette based on colors that appear in your photos. Use the Design button to display tools including color palettes, font choices, **animation emphasis effects**, and style templates to provide a personality for a Sway presentation. Instead of creating your own design, you can click the Remix button, which randomly selects unique designs for your Sway site.

Publishing a Sway

Use the Play button to display your finished Sway presentation as a website. The Address bar includes a unique web address where others can view your Sway site. As the author, you can edit a published Sway site by clicking the Edit button (pencil icon) on the Sway toolbar.

Sharing a Sway

When you are ready to share your Sway website, you have several options as shown in **Figure 9**. Use the Share slider button to share the Sway site publically or keep it private. If you add the Sway site to the Microsoft **Docs.com** public gallery, anyone worldwide can use Bing, Google, or other search engines to find, view, and share your Sway site. You can also share your Sway site using Facebook, Twitter, Google+, Yammer, and other social media sites. Link your presentation to any webpage or email the link to your audience. Sway can also generate a code for embedding the link within another webpage.

Figure 9: Sharing a Sway site

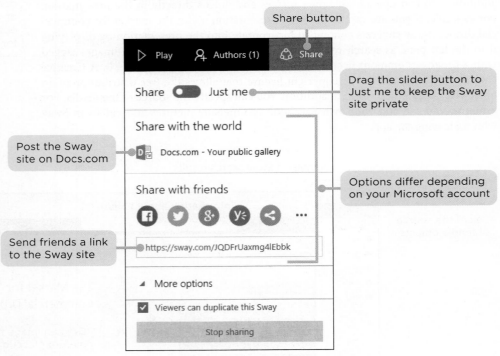

Try This Now

Learn to use Sway! Links to companion **Sways**, featuring **videos** with hands-on instructions, are located on www.cengagebrain.com.

1: Creating a Sway Resume

Sway is a digital storytelling app. Create a Sway resume to share the skills, job experiences, and achievements you have that match the requirements of a future job interest. Perform the following tasks:

    a. Create a new presentation in Sway to use as a digital resume. Title the Sway Storyline with your full name and then select a background image.

    b. Create three separate sections titled **Academic Background, Work Experience**, and **Skills**, and insert text, a picture, and a paragraph or bulleted points in each section. Be sure to include your own picture.

    c. Add a fourth section that includes a video about your school that you find online.

    d. Customize the design of your presentation.

    e. Submit your assignment link in the format specified by your instructor.

2: Creating an Online Sway Newsletter

Newsletters are designed to capture the attention of their target audience. Using Sway, create a newsletter for a club, organization, or your favorite music group. Perform the following tasks:

    a. Create a new presentation in Sway to use as a digital newsletter for a club, organization, or your favorite music group. Provide a title for the Sway Storyline and select an appropriate background image.

    b. Select three separate sections with appropriate titles, such as Upcoming Events. In each section, insert text, a picture, and a paragraph or bulleted points.

    c. Add a fourth section that includes a video about your selected topic.

    d. Customize the design of your presentation.

    e. Submit your assignment link in the format specified by your instructor.

3: Creating and Sharing a Technology Presentation

To place a Sway presentation in the hands of your entire audience, you can share a link to the Sway presentation. Create a Sway presentation on a new technology and share it with your class. Perform the following tasks:

    a. Create a new presentation in Sway about a cutting-edge technology topic. Provide a title for the Sway Storyline and select a background image.

    b. Create four separate sections about your topic, and include text, a picture, and a paragraph in each section.

    c. Add a fifth section that includes a video about your topic.

    d. Customize the design of your presentation.

    e. Share the link to your Sway with your classmates and submit your assignment link in the format specified by your instructor.

Introduction to Office Mix

add-in | clip | slide recording | Slide Notes | screen recording | free-response quiz

To enliven business meetings and lectures, Microsoft adds a new dimension to presentations with a powerful toolset called Office Mix, a free add-in for PowerPoint. (An **add-in** is software that works with an installed app to extend its features.) Using Office Mix, you can record yourself on video, capture still and moving images on your desktop, and insert interactive elements such as quizzes and live webpages directly into PowerPoint slides. When you post the finished presentation to OneDrive, Office Mix provides a link you can share with friends and colleagues. Anyone with an Internet connection and a web browser can watch a published Office Mix presentation, such as the one in **Figure 10**, on a computer or mobile device.

Figure 10: Office Mix presentation

Adding Office Mix to PowerPoint

To get started, you create an Office Mix account at the website mix.office.com using an email address or a Facebook or Google account. Next, you download and install the Office Mix add-in (see **Figure 11**). Office Mix appears as a new tab named Mix on the PowerPoint ribbon in versions of Office 2013 and Office 2016 running on personal computers (PCs).

Figure 11: Getting started with Office Mix

Capturing Video Clips

A **clip** is a short segment of audio, such as music, or video. After finishing the content on a PowerPoint slide, you can use Office Mix to add a video clip to animate or illustrate the content. Office Mix creates video clips in two ways: by recording live action on a webcam and by capturing screen images and movements. If your computer has a webcam, you can record yourself and annotate the slide to create a **slide recording** as shown in **Figure 12**.

On the Job Now

Companies are using Office Mix to train employees about new products, to explain benefit packages to new workers, and to educate interns about office procedures.

Figure 12: Making a slide recording

Record your voice; also record video if your computer has a camera.

Use the Slide Notes button to display notes for your narration.

For best results, look directly at your webcam while recording video.

Choose a video and audio device to record images and sound.

Use inking tools to write and draw on the slide as you record.

When you are making a slide recording, you can record your spoken narration at the same time. The **Slide Notes** feature works like a teleprompter to help you focus on your presentation content instead of memorizing your narration. Use the Inking tools to make annotations or add highlighting using different pen types and colors. After finishing a recording, edit the video in PowerPoint to trim the length or set playback options.

The second way to create a video is to capture on-screen images and actions with or without a voiceover. This method is ideal if you want to show how to use your favorite website or demonstrate an app such as OneNote. To share your screen with an audience, select the part of the screen you want to show in the video. Office Mix captures everything that happens in that area to create a **screen recording**, as shown in **Figure 13**. Office Mix inserts the screen recording as a video in the slide.

On the Job Now

To make your video recordings accessible to people with hearing impairments, use the Office Mix closed-captioning tools. You can also use closed captions to supplement audio that is difficult to understand and to provide an aid for those learning to read.

Figure 13: Making a screen recording

Record the action on the screen within the red dashed outline.

Select Area button

Record audio while capturing your on-screen actions.

Inserting Quizzes, Live Webpages, and Apps

To enhance and assess audience understanding, make your slides interactive by adding quizzes, live webpages, and apps. Quizzes give immediate feedback to the user as shown in **Figure 14**. Office Mix supports several quiz formats, including a **free-response quiz** similar to a short answer quiz, and true/false, multiple-choice, and multiple-response formats.

Figure 14: Creating an interactive quiz

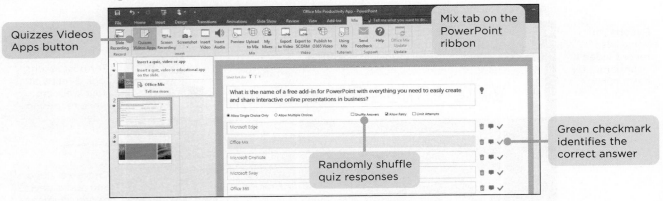

Sharing an Office Mix Presentation

When you complete your work with Office Mix, upload the presentation to your personal Office Mix dashboard as shown in **Figure 15**. Users of PCs, Macs, iOS devices, and Android devices can access and play Office Mix presentations. The Office Mix dashboard displays built-in analytics that include the quiz results and how much time viewers spent on each slide. You can play completed Office Mix presentations online or download them as movies.

Figure 15: Sharing an Office Mix presentation

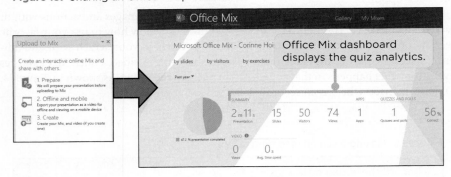

Try This Now

1: Creating an Office Mix Tutorial for OneNote

Note: This activity requires a microphone on your computer.

Office Mix makes it easy to record screens and their contents. Create PowerPoint slides with an Office Mix screen recording to show OneNote 2016 features. Perform the following tasks:

a. Create a PowerPoint presentation with the Ion Boardroom template. Create an opening slide with the title **My Favorite OneNote Features** and enter your name in the subtitle.
b. Create three additional slides, each titled with a new feature of OneNote. Open OneNote and use the Mix tab in PowerPoint to capture three separate screen recordings that teach your favorite features.
c. Add a fifth slide that quizzes the user with a multiple-choice question about OneNote and includes four responses. Be sure to insert a checkmark indicating the correct response.
d. Upload the completed presentation to your Office Mix dashboard and share the link with your instructor.
e. Submit your assignment link in the format specified by your instructor.

2: Teaching Augmented Reality with Office Mix

Note: This activity requires a webcam or built-in video camera on your computer.

A local elementary school has asked you to teach augmented reality to its students using Office Mix. Perform the following tasks:

a. Research augmented reality using your favorite online search tools.
b. Create a PowerPoint presentation with the Frame template. Create an opening slide with the title **Augmented Reality** and enter your name in the subtitle.
c. Create a slide with four bullets summarizing your research of augmented reality. Create a 20-second slide recording of yourself providing a quick overview of augmented reality.
d. Create another slide with a 30-second screen recording of a video about augmented reality from a site such as YouTube or another video-sharing site.
e. Add a final slide that quizzes the user with a true/false question about augmented reality. Be sure to insert a checkmark indicating the correct response.
f. Upload the completed presentation to your Office Mix dashboard and share the link with your instructor.
g. Submit your assignment link in the format specified by your instructor.

3: Marketing a Travel Destination with Office Mix

Note: This activity requires a webcam or built-in video camera on your computer.

To convince your audience to travel to a particular city, create a slide presentation marketing any city in the world using a slide recording, screen recording, and a quiz. Perform the following tasks:

a. Create a PowerPoint presentation with any template. Create an opening slide with the title of the city you are marketing as a travel destination and your name in the subtitle.
b. Create a slide with four bullets about the featured city. Create a 30-second slide recording of yourself explaining why this city is the perfect vacation destination.
c. Create another slide with a 20-second screen recording of a travel video about the city from a site such as YouTube or another video-sharing site.
d. Add a final slide that quizzes the user with a multiple-choice question about the featured city with five responses. Be sure to include a checkmark indicating the correct response.
e. Upload the completed presentation to your Office Mix dashboard and share your link with your instructor.
f. Submit your assignment link in the format specified by your instructor.

Introduction to Microsoft Edge

Reading view | Hub | Cortana | Web Note | Inking | sandbox

Microsoft Edge is the default web browser developed for the Windows 10 operating system as a replacement for Internet Explorer. Unlike its predecessor, Edge lets you write on webpages, read webpages without advertisements and other distractions, and search for information using a virtual personal assistant. The Edge interface is clean and basic, as shown in **Figure 16**, meaning you can pay more attention to the webpage content.

Figure 16: Microsoft Edge tools

Forward button | New tab button | Web address in the Address bar | Add to favorites or reading list button

Back button | Reading view button | More button

Refresh (F5) button | Hub (Favorites, reading list, history, and downloads) button | Share Web Note button | Make a Web Note button

Browsing the Web with Microsoft Edge

One of the fastest browsers available, Edge allows you to type search text directly in the Address bar. As you view the resulting webpage, you can switch to **Reading view**, which is available for most news and research sites, to eliminate distracting advertisements. For example, if you are catching up on technology news online, the webpage might be difficult to read due to a busy layout cluttered with ads. Switch to Reading view to refresh the page and remove the original page formatting, ads, and menu sidebars to read the article distraction-free.

Consider the **Hub** in Microsoft Edge as providing one-stop access to all the things you collect on the web, such as your favorite websites, reading list, surfing history, and downloaded files.

Locating Information with Cortana

Cortana, the Windows 10 virtual assistant, plays an important role in Microsoft Edge. After you turn on Cortana, it appears as an animated circle in the Address bar when you might need assistance, as shown in the restaurant website in **Figure 17**. When you click the Cortana icon, a pane slides in from the right of the browser window to display detailed information about the restaurant, including maps and reviews. Cortana can also assist you in defining words, finding the weather, suggesting coupons for shopping, updating stock market information, and calculating math.

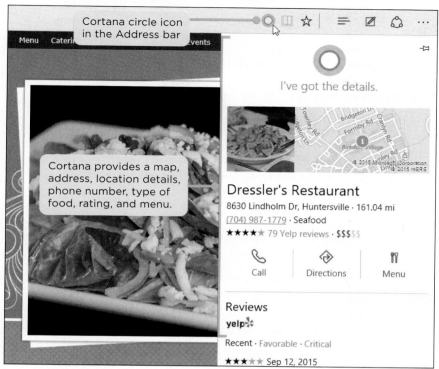

Cortana circle icon in the Address bar

Cortana provides a map, address, location details, phone number, type of food, rating, and menu.

I've got the details.

Dressler's Restaurant
8630 Lindholm Dr, Huntersville · 161.04 mi
(704) 987-1779 · Seafood
★★★★★ 79 Yelp reviews · $$$$$

📞 Call | ◈ Directions | 🍴 Menu

Reviews
yelp

Recent · Favorable · Critical
★★★★★ Sep 12, 2015

Annotating Webpages

One of the most impressive Microsoft Edge features are the **Web Note** tools, which you use to write on a webpage or to highlight text. When you click the Make a Web Note button, an **Inking** toolbar appears, as shown in **Figure 18**, that provides writing and drawing tools. These tools include an eraser, a pen, and a highlighter with different colors. You can also insert a typed note and copy a screen image (called a screen clipping). You can draw with a pointing device, fingertip, or stylus using different pen colors. Whether you add notes to a recipe, annotate sources for a research paper, or select a product while shopping online, the Web Note tools can enhance your productivity. After you complete your notes, click the Save button to save the annotations to OneNote, your Favorites list, or your Reading list. You can share the inked page with others using the Share Web Note button.

On the Job Now

To enhance security, Microsoft Edge runs in a partial sandbox, an arrangement that prevents attackers from gaining control of your computer. Browsing within the **sandbox** protects computer resources and information from hackers.

Figure 18: Web Note tools in Microsoft Edge

Inking toolbar with Web Note tools for making annotations

Writing and drawing created with the Pen tool

Highlighted text

Work anywhere

The integrated Kickstand features multiple positions so you can work comfortably whether you're on a plane, at your desk, or in front of the television.

I am considering purchasing the new Surface Pro for school

Save a copy of the webpage with annotations

Typed note

Try This Now

1: Using Cortana in Microsoft Edge

Note: This activity requires using Microsoft Edge on a Windows 10 computer.

Cortana can assist you in finding information on a webpage in Microsoft Edge. Perform the following tasks:

a. Create a Word document using the Word Screen Clipping tool to capture the following screenshots.

- Screenshot A—Using Microsoft Edge, open a webpage with a technology news article. Right-click a term in the article and ask Cortana to define it.
- Screenshot B—Using Microsoft Edge, open the website of a fancy restaurant in a city near you. Make sure the Cortana circle icon is displayed in the Address bar. (If it's not displayed, find a different restaurant website.) Click the Cortana circle icon to display a pane with information about the restaurant.
- Screenshot C—Using Microsoft Edge, type **10 USD to Euros** in the Address bar without pressing the Enter key. Cortana converts the U.S. dollars to Euros.
- Screenshot D—Using Microsoft Edge, type **Apple stock** in the Address bar without pressing the Enter key. Cortana displays the current stock quote.

b. Submit your assignment in the format specified by your instructor.

2: Viewing Online News with Reading View

Note: This activity requires using Microsoft Edge on a Windows 10 computer.

Reading view in Microsoft Edge can make a webpage less cluttered with ads and other distractions. Perform the following tasks:

a. Create a Word document using the Word Screen Clipping tool to capture the following screenshots.

- Screenshot A—Using Microsoft Edge, open the website **mashable.com**. Open a technology article. Click the Reading view button to display an ad-free page that uses only basic text formatting.
- Screenshot B—Using Microsoft Edge, open the website **bbc.com**. Open any news article. Click the Reading view button to display an ad-free page that uses only basic text formatting.
- Screenshot C—Make three types of annotations (Pen, Highlighter, and Add a typed note) on the BBC article page displayed in Reading view.

b. Submit your assignment in the format specified by your instructor.

3: Inking with Microsoft Edge

Note: This activity requires using Microsoft Edge on a Windows 10 computer.

Microsoft Edge provides many annotation options to record your ideas. Perform the following tasks:

a. Open the website **wolframalpha.com** in the Microsoft Edge browser. Wolfram Alpha is a well-respected academic search engine. Type **US$100 1965 dollars in 2015** in the Wolfram Alpha search text box and press the Enter key.

b. Click the Make a Web Note button to display the Web Note tools. Using the Pen tool, draw a circle around the result on the webpage. Save the page to OneNote.

c. In the Wolfram Alpha search text box, type the name of the city closest to where you live and press the Enter key. Using the Highlighter tool, highlight at least three interesting results. Add a note and then type a sentence about what you learned about this city. Save the page to OneNote. Share your OneNote notebook with your instructor.

d. Submit your assignment link in the format specified by your instructor.

WORD

OBJECTIVES

Session 1.1
- Create and save a document
- Enter text and correct errors as you type
- Use AutoComplete and AutoCorrect
- Select text and move the insertion point
- Undo and redo actions
- Adjust paragraph spacing, line spacing, and margins
- Preview and print a document
- Create an envelope

Session 1.2
- Open an existing document
- Use the Spelling and Grammar task panes
- Change page orientation, font, font color, and font size
- Apply text effects and align text
- Copy formatting with the Format Painter
- Insert a paragraph border and shading
- Delete, insert, and edit a photo
- Use Word Help

Creating and Editing a Document

Writing a Business Letter and Formatting a Flyer

Case | *Sandy Hill Portrait Studio*

Sandy Hill Portrait Studio in Baltimore, Maryland, specializes in wedding photography and family portraits. It also offers weekend and evening classes for new and experienced photographers. The sales manager, Tim Bartolutti, has asked you to create a cover letter to accompany a set of prints that he needs to send to a client, and an envelope for sending a class schedule to another client. He also wants your help creating a flyer announcing a class that focuses on photographing pets.

You will create the letter and flyer using **Microsoft Office Word 2013** (or simply **Word**), a word-processing program. You'll start by opening Word and saving a new document. Then you'll type the text of the cover letter and print it. In the process of entering the text, you'll learn several ways to correct typing errors and how to adjust paragraph and line spacing. When you create the envelope, you'll learn how to save it as part of a document for later use. As you work on the flyer, you will learn how to open an existing document, change the way text is laid out on the page, format text, and insert and resize a photo. Finally, you'll learn how to use Word's Help system.

STARTING DATA FILES

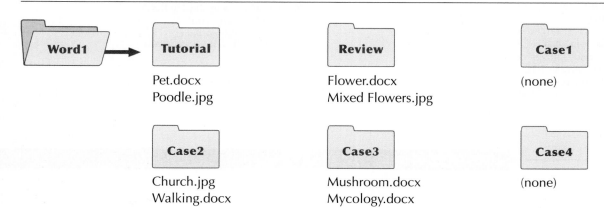

Word1 → Tutorial	Review	Case1
Pet.docx Poodle.jpg	Flower.docx Mixed Flowers.jpg	(none)

Case2	Case3	Case4
Church.jpg Walking.docx	Mushroom.docx Mycology.docx	(none)

Session 1.1 Visual Overview:

The **Quick Access Toolbar** is a collection of buttons that provides one-click access to commonly used commands, such as Save, Undo, and Repeat.

Each **tab** includes commands related to particular activities or tasks. The HOME tab includes options for formatting and editing text.

The **title bar** displays the name of the open file and the program.

The **ribbon** is the main set of buttons and other tools you can use to complete tasks. It is organized into tabs and groups.

The dark gray areas on the ruler represent the document's margins. **Margins** are the blank spaces around the edges of a document's content.

The **insertion point** shows where characters will appear when you start typing.

The **paragraph mark** indicates the end of a paragraph. It is only visible if nonprinting characters are turned on. **Nonprinting characters** appear on the screen but not on the printed page.

Buttons for related commands are organized on a tab in **groups**. The buttons in this group can be used to change the appearance of a paragraph.

The **status bar** provides information about the current document, such as the current page and number of words in the document; it also contains buttons and other controls for working with the document.

You can choose to display the rulers, which help you position elements in a document.

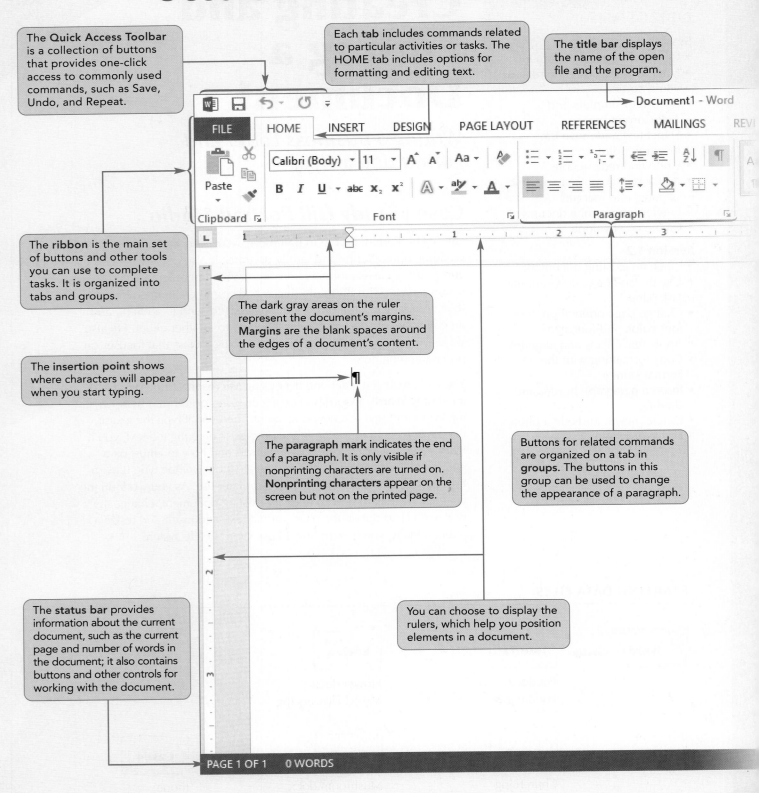

The Word Window

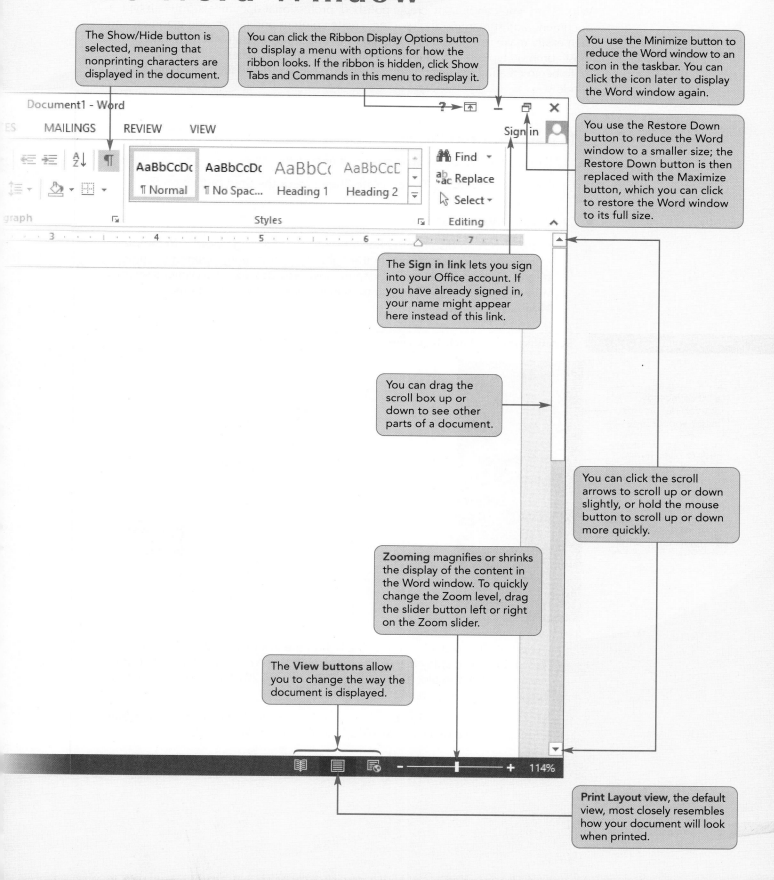

The Show/Hide button is selected, meaning that nonprinting characters are displayed in the document.

You can click the Ribbon Display Options button to display a menu with options for how the ribbon looks. If the ribbon is hidden, click Show Tabs and Commands in this menu to redisplay it.

You use the Minimize button to reduce the Word window to an icon in the taskbar. You can click the icon later to display the Word window again.

You use the Restore Down button to reduce the Word window to a smaller size; the Restore Down button is then replaced with the Maximize button, which you can click to restore the Word window to its full size.

The **Sign in link** lets you sign into your Office account. If you have already signed in, your name might appear here instead of this link.

You can drag the scroll box up or down to see other parts of a document.

You can click the scroll arrows to scroll up or down slightly, or hold the mouse button to scroll up or down more quickly.

Zooming magnifies or shrinks the display of the content in the Word window. To quickly change the Zoom level, drag the slider button left or right on the Zoom slider.

The **View buttons** allow you to change the way the document is displayed.

Print Layout view, the default view, most closely resembles how your document will look when printed.

Starting Word

With Word, you can quickly create polished, professional documents. You can type a document, adjust margins and spacing, create columns and tables, add graphics, and then easily make revisions and corrections. In this session, you will create one of the most common types of documents—a block style business letter.

To begin creating the letter, you first need to start Word and then set up the Word window.

To start Microsoft Word:

▶ **1.** Display the Windows Start screen, if necessary.

Using Windows 7? To complete Step 1, click the Start button on the taskbar.

▶ **2.** Click the **Word 2013** tile.

Word starts and displays the Recent screen in Backstage view, with template options for new documents on the right. A list of recently opened documents might appear on the left. **Backstage view** provides access to various screens with commands that allow you to manage files and Word options. See Figure 1-1.

Figure 1-1	Recent screen in Backstage view

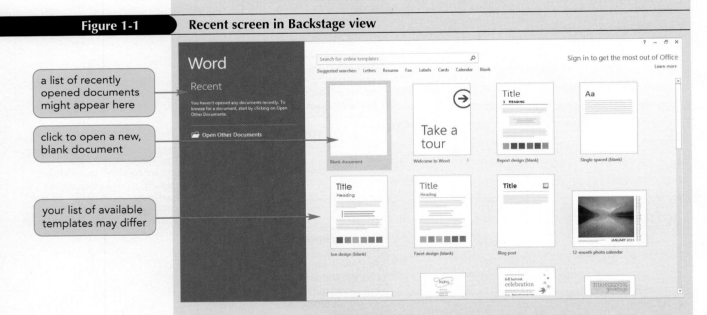

a list of recently opened documents might appear here

click to open a new, blank document

your list of available templates may differ

Trouble? If you don't see Word 2013 on the Windows Start screen, type Word 2013 to display the Apps screen with the Word 2013 tile highlighted, and then click the tile. If you still can't find Word 2013, ask your instructor or technical support person for help.

Using Windows 7? To complete Step 2, point to All Programs on the Start menu, click Microsoft Office 2013, and then click Word 2013.

▶ **3.** Click **Blank document**. The Word window opens, with the ribbon displayed.

   Trouble? If you don't see the ribbon, click the Ribbon Display Options button 🔼, as shown in the Session 1.1 Visual Overview, and then click Show Tabs and Commands.

   Don't be concerned if your Word window doesn't match the Session 1.1 Visual Overview exactly. You'll have a chance to adjust its appearance shortly.

Working in Touch Mode

You can interact with the Word screen using a mouse, or, if you have a touch screen, you can work in Touch Mode, using a finger instead of the mouse pointer. In **Touch Mode**, extra space around the buttons on the ribbon allows your finger to tap the specific button you need. The figures in this text show the screen with Mouse Mode on, but it's helpful to learn how to switch back and forth between Touch Mode and Mouse Mode.

Note: The following steps assume that you are using a mouse. If you are instead using a touch device, please read these steps but don't complete them so that you remain working in Touch Mode.

To switch between Touch and Mouse Mode:

▶ **1.** On the Quick Access Toolbar, click the **Customize Quick Access Toolbar** button ▾ to open the menu. The Touch/Mouse Mode command near the bottom of the menu does not have a checkmark next to it, indicating that it is currently not selected.

   Trouble? If the Touch/Mouse Mode command has a checkmark next to it, press the Esc key to close the menu, and then skip to Step 3.

▶ **2.** On the menu, click **Touch/Mouse Mode**. The menu closes, and the Touch/Mouse Mode button 👆 appears on the Quick Access Toolbar.

▶ **3.** On the Quick Access Toolbar, click the **Touch/Mouse Mode** button 👆. A menu opens with two options—Mouse and Touch. The icon next to Mouse is shaded blue to indicate it is selected.

   Trouble? If the icon next to Touch is shaded blue, press the Esc key to close the menu and skip to Step 5.

▶ **4.** On the menu, click **Touch**. The menu closes, and the ribbon increases in height so that there is more space around each button on the ribbon. See Figure 1-2.

Figure 1-2   **Word window in Touch Mode**

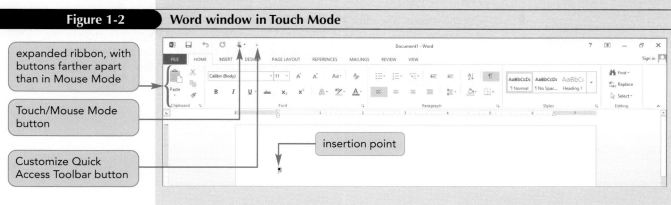

expanded ribbon, with buttons farther apart than in Mouse Mode

Touch/Mouse Mode button

Customize Quick Access Toolbar button

insertion point

Trouble? If you are working with a touch screen and want to use Touch Mode, skip Steps 5 and 6.

▶ **5.** On the Quick Access Toolbar, click the **Touch/Mouse Mode** button 👆, and then click **Mouse**. The ribbon changes back to its Mouse Mode appearance, as shown in the Session 1-1 Visual Overview.

▶ **6.** On the Quick Access Toolbar, click the **Customize Quick Access Toolbar** button ⤓, and then click **Touch/Mouse Mode** to deselect it. The Touch/Mouse Mode button is removed from the Quick Access Toolbar.

Setting Up the Word Window

Before you start using Word, you should make sure you can locate and identify the different elements of the Word window, as shown in the Session 1.1 Visual Overview. In the following steps, you'll make sure your screen matches the Visual Overview.

To set up your Word window to match the figures in this book:

▶ **1.** If the Word window does not fill the entire screen, click the **Maximize** button ☐ in the upper-right corner of the Word window.

The insertion point on your computer should be positioned about an inch from the top of the document, as shown in Figure 1-2, with the top margin visible.

Trouble? If the insertion point appears at the top of the document, with no white space above it, position the mouse pointer between the top of the document and the horizontal ruler, until it changes to ÷, double-click, and then scroll up to top of the document.

▶ **2.** On the ribbon, click the **VIEW** tab. The ribbon changes to display options for changing the appearance of the Word window.

▶ **3.** In the Show group, click the **Ruler** check box to insert a checkmark, if necessary. If the rulers were not displayed, they are displayed now.

Next, you'll change the Zoom level to a setting that ensures that your Word window will match the figures in this book. To increase or decrease the screen's magnification, you could drag the slider button on the Zoom slider in the lower-right corner of the Word window. But to choose a specific Zoom level, it's easier to use the Zoom dialog box.

TIP

Changing the Zoom level affects only the way the document is displayed on the screen; it does not affect the document itself.

▶ **4.** In the Zoom group, click the **Zoom** button to open the Zoom dialog box. Double-click the **Percent** box to select the current zoom percentage, type **120**, and then click the **OK** button to close the Zoom dialog box.

▶ **5.** On the status bar, click the **Print Layout** button 🔲 to select it, if necessary. As shown in the Session 1.1 Visual Overview, the Print Layout button is the middle of the three View buttons located on the right side of the status bar. The Print Layout button in the Views group on the View tab is also now selected.

Before typing a document, you should make sure nonprinting characters are displayed. Nonprinting characters provide a visual representation of details you might otherwise miss. For example, the (¶) character marks the end of a paragraph, and the (•) character marks the space between words.

To verify that nonprinting characters are displayed:

▶ **1.** On the ribbon, click the **HOME** tab.

▶ **2.** In the blank Word document, look for the paragraph mark (¶) in the first line of the document, just to the right of the blinking insertion point.

   Trouble? If you don't see the paragraph mark, click the Show/Hide ¶ button ¶ in the Paragraph group.

   In the Paragraph group, the Show/Hide ¶ button should be highlighted in blue, indicating that it is selected, and the paragraph mark (¶) should appear in the first line of the document, just to the right of the insertion point.

Saving a Document

Before you begin working on a document, you should save it with a new name. When you use the Save button on the Quick Access Toolbar to save a document for the first time, Word displays the Save As screen in Backstage view. In the Save As screen, you can select the location where you want to store your document. After that, when you click the Save button, Word saves your document to the same location you specified earlier, and with the same name.

To save the document:

▶ **1.** On the Quick Access Toolbar, click the **Save** button 🖫. Word switches to the Save As screen in Backstage view, as shown in Figure 1-3.

Figure 1-3	Save As screen in Backstage view

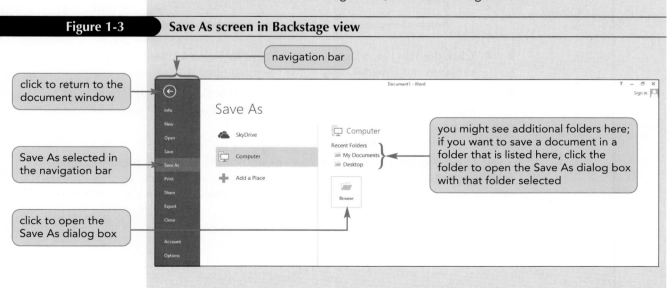

navigation bar

click to return to the document window

Save As selected in the navigation bar

click to open the Save As dialog box

Document1 - Word

Save As

SkyDrive

Computer

Recent Folders
My Documents
Desktop

Browse

Add a Place

you might see additional folders here; if you want to save a document in a folder that is listed here, click the folder to open the Save As dialog box with that folder selected

Because a document is now open, more commands are available in Backstage view than when you started Word. The **navigation bar** on the left contains commands for working with the open document and for changing settings that control how Word works.

2. Click **Computer**, if necessary, and then click the **Browse** button. The Save As dialog box opens.

   Trouble? If your instructor wants you to save your files to your SkyDrive account, click SkyDrive, log in to your account, if necessary, and then click the Browse button.

3. Navigate to the location specified by your instructor. The default filename, "Doc1," appears in the File name box. You will change that to something more descriptive. See Figure 1-4.

Figure 1-4 **Save As dialog box**

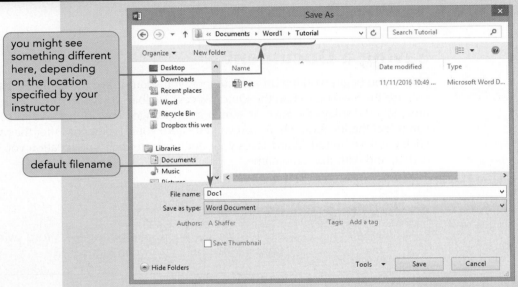

you might see something different here, depending on the location specified by your instructor

default filename

---

4. Click the File name box, and then type **Robbins Letter**. The text you type replaces the selected text in the File name box.

5. Click the **Save** button. The file is saved, the dialog box and Backstage view close, and the document window appears again, with the new filename in the title bar.

Now that you have saved the document, you can begin typing the letter. Tim has asked you to type a block style letter to accompany a set of family portraits that will be sent to Sonia Robbins, a regular client. Figure 1-5 shows the block style letter you will create in this tutorial.

Figure 1-5 **Completed block style letter**

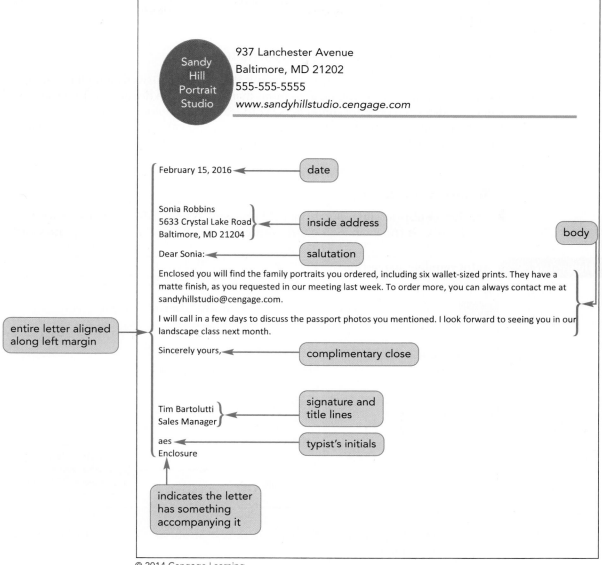

© 2014 Cengage Learning

Written Communication: Creating a Business Letter

Several styles are considered acceptable for business letters. The main differences among the styles have to do with how parts of the letter are indented from the left margin. In the block style, which you will use in this tutorial, each line of text starts at the left margin. In other words, nothing is indented. Another style is to indent the first line of each paragraph. The choice of style is largely a matter of personal preference, or it can be determined by the standards used in a particular business or organization. To further enhance your skills in writing business correspondence, you should consult an authoritative book on business writing that provides guidelines for creating a variety of business documents, such as *Business Communication: Process & Product,* by Mary Ellen Guffey.

PROSKILLS

Entering Text

The letters you type in a Word document appear at the current location of the blinking insertion point.

Inserting a Date with AutoComplete

The first item in a block style business letter is the date. Tim plans to send the letter to Sonia on February 15, so you need to insert that date into the document. To do so, you can take advantage of **AutoComplete**, a Word feature that automatically inserts dates and other regularly used items for you. In this case, you can type the first few characters of the month and let Word insert the rest.

To insert the date:

▶ **1.** Type **Febr** (the first four letters of February). A ScreenTip appears above the letters, as shown in Figure 1-6, suggesting "February" as the complete word.

Figure 1-6   **AutoComplete suggestion**

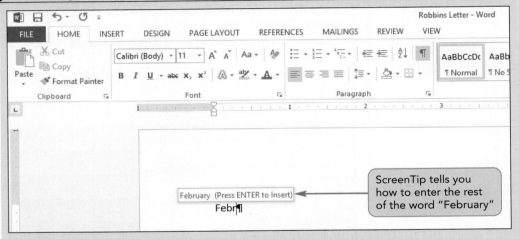

ScreenTip tells you how to enter the rest of the word "February"

A **ScreenTip** is a box with descriptive text about an object or button you are pointing to.

If you wanted to type something other than "February," you could continue typing to complete the word. You want to accept the AutoComplete suggestion.

▶ **2.** Press the **Enter** key. The rest of the word "February" is inserted in the document. Note that AutoComplete works for long month names like February but not shorter ones like May, because "Ma" could be the beginning of many words besides "May."

▶ **3.** Press the **spacebar**, type **15, 2016** and then press the **Enter** key twice, leaving a blank paragraph between the date and the line where you will begin typing the inside address, which contains the recipient's name and address. Notice the nonprinting character (•) after the word "February" and before the number "15," which indicates a space. Word inserts this nonprinting character every time you press the spacebar.

> **Trouble?** If February happens to be the current month, you will see a second AutoComplete suggestion displaying the current date after you press the spacebar. To ignore that AutoComplete suggestion, continue typing the rest of the date as instructed in Step 3.

Continuing to Type the Block Style Letter

In a block style business letter, the inside address appears below the date, with one blank paragraph in between. Some style guides recommend including even more space between the date and the inside address. But in the short letter you are typing, more space would make the document look out of balance.

To insert the inside address:

1. Type the following information, pressing the **Enter** key after each item:

   Sonia Robbins

   5633 Crystal Lake Road

   Baltimore, MD 21204

   Remember to press the Enter key after you type the zip code. Your screen should look like Figure 1-7. Don't be concerned if the lines of the inside address seem too far apart. You'll use the default spacing for now, and then adjust it after you finish typing the letter.

| Figure 1-7 | Letter with inside address |

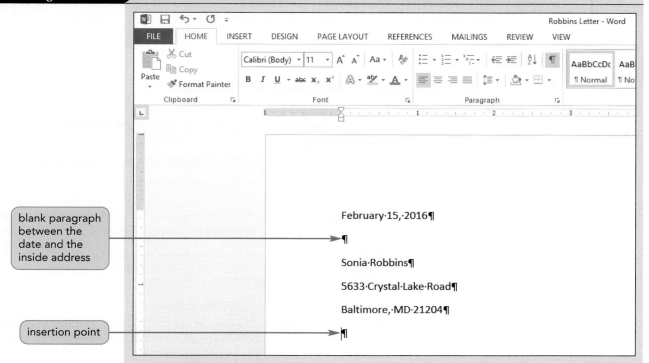

blank paragraph between the date and the inside address

insertion point

> **Trouble?** If you make a mistake while typing, press the Backspace key to delete the incorrect character, and then type the correct character.

Now you can move on to the salutation and the body of the letter. As you type the body of the letter, notice that Word automatically moves the insertion point to a new line when the current line is full.

To type the salutation and the body of the letter:

1. Type **Dear Sonia:** and then press the **Enter** key to start a new paragraph for the body of the letter.

2. Type the following sentence, including the period: **Enclosed you will find the family portraits you ordered, including six wallet-sized prints.**

3. Press the **spacebar**. Note that you should only include one space between sentences.

4. Type the following sentence, including the period: **They have a matte finish, as you requested in our conversation last week.**

5. On the Quick Access Toolbar, click the **Save** button 🔲. Word saves the document as Robbins Letter to the same location you specified earlier.

TIP

The obsolete practice of pressing the spacebar twice at the end of a sentence dates back to the age of typewriters, when the extra space made it easier to see where one sentence ended and another began.

The next sentence you need to type includes Tim's email address.

Typing a Hyperlink

When you type an email address and then press the spacebar or the Enter key, Word converts it to a hyperlink, with blue font and an underline. A **hyperlink** is text or a graphic you can click to jump to another file or to somewhere else in the same file. The two most common types of hyperlinks are: 1) an email hyperlink, which you can click to open an email message to the recipient specified by the hyperlink; and 2) a web hyperlink, which opens a webpage in a browser. Hyperlinks are useful in documents that you plan to distribute via email. In printed documents, where blue font and underlines can be distracting, you'll usually want to convert a hyperlink back to regular text.

To add a sentence containing an email address:

1. Press the **spacebar**, and then type the following sentence, including the period: **To order more, you can always contact me at sandyhillstudio@cengage.com.**

2. Press the **Enter** key. Word converts the email address to a hyperlink, with blue font and an underline.

3. Position the mouse pointer over the hyperlink. A ScreenTip appears, indicating that you could press and hold the Ctrl key and then click the link to follow it—that is, to open an email message addressed to Sandy Hill Portrait Studio.

4. With the mouse pointer positioned over the hyperlink, right-click—that is, press the right mouse button. A shortcut menu opens with commands related to working with hyperlinks.

You can right-click many items in the Word window to display a **shortcut menu** with commands related to the item you right-clicked. The **Mini toolbar** also appears when you right-click or select text, giving you easy access to the buttons and settings most often used when formatting text. See Figure 1-8.

Figure 1-8	Shortcut menu

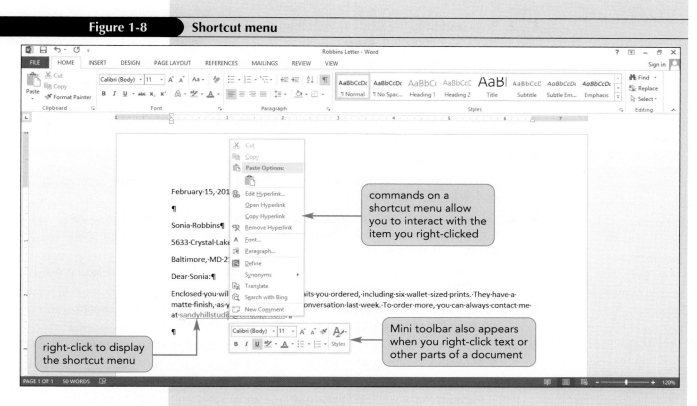

5. Click **Remove Hyperlink** in the shortcut menu. The shortcut menu and the Mini toolbar are no longer visible. The email address is now formatted in black, like the rest of the document text.

6. On the Quick Access Toolbar, click the **Save** button 🔲.

Using the Undo and Redo Buttons

To undo (or reverse) the last thing you did in a document, click the Undo button on the Quick Access Toolbar. To restore your original change, click the Redo button, which reverses the action of the Undo button (or redoes the undo). To undo more than your last action, you can continue to click the Undo button, or you can click the Undo button arrow on the Quick Access Toolbar to open a list of your most recent actions. When you click an action in the list, Word undoes every action in the list up to and including the action you clicked.

Tim asks you to change the word "conversation" to "meeting" in the second-to-last sentence you typed. You'll make the change now. If Tim decides he doesn't like it after all, you can always undo it. To delete a character, space, or blank paragraph to the right of the insertion point, you use the Delete key; or to delete an entire word, you can use the Ctrl+Delete key combination. To delete a character, space, or blank paragraph to the left of the insertion point, you use the Backspace key; or to delete an entire word, you can use the Ctrl+Backspace key combination.

To change the word "conversation":

1. Press the ↑ key once and then press the → key as necessary to move the insertion point to the left of the "c" in the word "conversation."

▶ 2. Press and hold the **Ctrl** key, and then press the **Delete** key to delete the word "conversation."

▶ 3. Type **meeting** as a replacement, and then press the **spacebar**.

  After reviewing the sentence, Tim decides he prefers the original wording, so you'll undo the change.

▶ 4. On the Quick Access Toolbar, click the **Undo** button ↶. The word "meeting" is removed from the sentence.

▶ 5. Click the **Undo** button ↶ again to restore the word "conversation."

  Tim decides that he does want to use "meeting" after all. Instead of retyping it, you'll redo the undo.

▶ 6. On the Quick Access Toolbar, click the **Redo** button ↷ twice. The word "meeting" replaces "conversation" in the document, so that the phrase reads "...in our meeting last week."

  You can also press the Ctrl+Z keys to execute the Undo command, and press the Ctrl+Y keys to execute the Redo command.

▶ 7. Press and hold the **Ctrl** key, and then press the **End** key to move the insertion point to the blank paragraph at the end of the document.

▶ 8. On the Quick Access Toolbar, click the **Save** button 🖫. Word saves your letter with the same name and to the same location you specified earlier.

In the previous steps, you used the arrow keys and a key combination to move the insertion point to specific locations in the document. For your reference, Figure 1-9 summarizes the most common keystrokes for moving the insertion point in a document.

Figure 1-9   **Keystrokes for moving the insertion point**

To Move the Insertion Point	Press
Left or right one character at a time	← or →
Up or down one line at a time	↑ or ↓
Left or right one word at a time	Ctrl+← or Ctrl+→
Up or down one paragraph at a time	Ctrl+↑ or Ctrl+↓
To the beginning or to the end of the current line	Home or End
To the beginning or to the end of the document	Ctrl+Home or Ctrl+End
To the previous screen or to the next screen	Page Up or Page Down
To the top or to the bottom of the document window	Alt+Ctrl+Page Up or Alt+Ctrl+Page Down

© 2014 Cengage Learning

Correcting Errors as You Type

As you have seen, you can use the Backspace or Delete keys to remove an error, and then you can type a correction. In many cases, however, Word's AutoCorrect feature will do the work for you. Among other things, **AutoCorrect** automatically corrects common typing errors, such as typing "adn" instead of "and." For example, you might have noticed AutoCorrect at work if you forgot to capitalize the first letter in a sentence as you typed the letter. After you type this kind of error, AutoCorrect automatically corrects it when you press the spacebar, the Tab key, or the Enter key.

Word draws your attention to other potential errors by marking them with wavy underlines. If you type a word that doesn't match the correct spelling in Word's dictionary, or if a word is not in the dictionary at all, a wavy red line appears beneath it. A wavy red underline also appears if you mistakenly type the same word twice in a row. Misused words (for example, "your" instead of "you're") are underlined with a wavy blue line. Likewise, punctuation errors, problems with possessives and plurals, and grammatical errors are marked with a wavy blue underline.

You'll see how this works as you continue typing the letter and make some intentional typing errors.

To learn more about correcting errors as you type:

▶ **1.** Type the following sentence, including the errors shown here: **i will call in a few few days to disuss teh pasport photos you mentioned.**

As you type, AutoCorrect changes the lowercase "i" at the beginning of the sentence to uppercase. It also changes "teh" to "the" and "pasport" to "passport." The spelling error "disuss" and the second "few" are marked with wavy red underlines. You will correct these errors after you finish typing the rest of the paragraph.

▶ **2.** Press the **spacebar**, and then type the following sentence, including the extra period and the other errors: **I look forward too seeing you in our landscape class next month..** The word "too" is underlined with a wavy blue line, indicating a misused word. The sentence also contains a punctuation error, but Word won't identify it until you start a new sentence or press the Enter key to begin a new paragraph.

▶ **3.** Press the **Enter** key to begin a new paragraph. As shown in Figure 1-10, the two periods at the end of the sentence are now underlined in blue.

Figure 1-10	Errors marked in the document

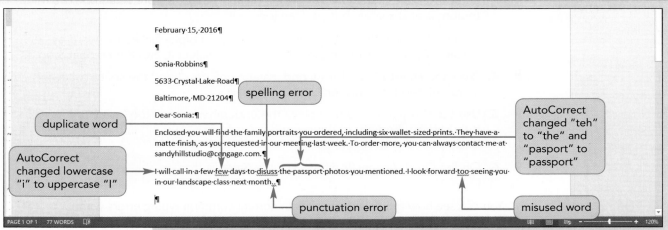

To correct an error marked with a wavy underline, you can right-click the error, and then click a replacement in the shortcut menu. If you don't see the correct word in the shortcut menu, click anywhere in the document to close the menu, and then type the correction yourself. You can also bypass the shortcut menu entirely, and simply delete the error and type a correction.

To correct the spelling and grammar errors:

▸ **1.** Right-click **disuss** to display the shortcut menu shown in Figure 1-11.

Figure 1-11	**Shortcut menu with suggested spellings**

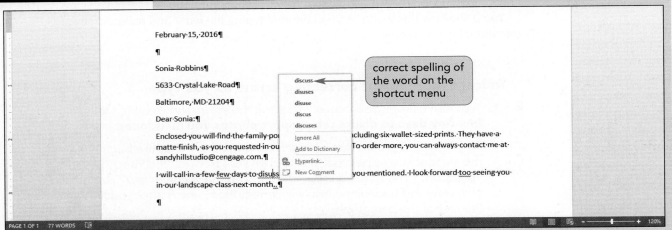

Trouble? If you see a shortcut menu other than the one shown in Figure 1-11, you didn't right-click exactly on the word "disuss." Press the Esc key to close the menu, and then repeat Step 1.

▸ **2.** On the shortcut menu, click **discuss**. The correct word is inserted into the sentence, and the shortcut menu closes. You could use a shortcut menu to remove the second instance of "few," but in the next step you'll try a different method—selecting the word and deleting it.

▸ **3.** Double-click anywhere in the underlined word **few**. The word and the space following it are highlighted in gray, indicating that they are selected. The Mini toolbar is also visible, but you can ignore it.

Trouble? If the entire paragraph is selected, you triple-clicked the word by mistake. Click anywhere in the document to deselect it, and then repeat Step 3.

▸ **4.** Press the **Delete** key. The second instance of "few" and the space following it are deleted from the sentence.

▸ **5.** Use the shortcut menu to replace the underlined word "too" with "to," and then click to the right of the second period after "month" and press the **Backspace** key to delete it.

▸ **6.** On the Quick Access Toolbar, click the **Save** button 🖫.

You can see how quick and easy it is to correct common typing errors with AutoCorrect and the wavy red and blue underlines, especially in a short document that you are typing yourself. If you are working on a longer document or a document typed by someone else, you'll also want to have Word check the entire document for errors. You'll learn how to do this in Session 1.2.

Next, you'll finish typing the letter.

To finish typing the letter:

1. Press the **Ctrl+End** keys. The insertion point moves to the end of the document.

2. Type **Sincerely yours,** (including the comma).

3. Press the **Enter** key three times to leave space for the signature.

4. Type **Tim Bartolutti** and then press the **Enter** key. Because Tim's last name is not in Word's dictionary, a wavy red line appears below it. You can ignore this for now.

5. Type your first, middle, and last initials in lowercase, and then press the **Enter** key. AutoCorrect wrongly assumes your first initial is the first letter of a new sentence, and changes it to uppercase.

6. On the Quick Access Toolbar, click the **Undo** button. Word reverses the change, replacing the uppercase initial with a lowercase one.

7. Type **Enclosure**. At this point, your screen should look similar to Figure 1-12. Notice that as you continue to add lines to the letter, the top part of the letter scrolls off the screen. For example, in Figure 1-12, you can no longer see the date.

TIP

You only need to include your initials in a letter if you are typing it for someone else.

Figure 1-12	Robbins Letter

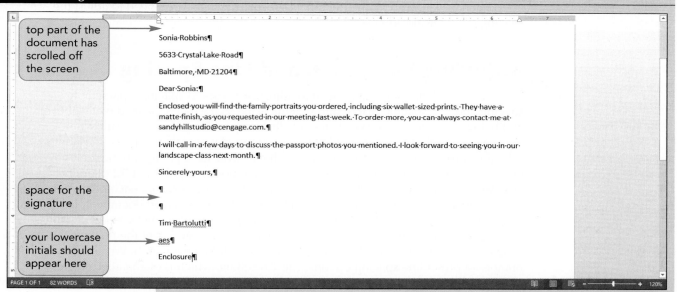

8. Save the document.

Now that you have finished typing the letter, you need to proofread it.

Proofreading a Document

After you finish typing a document, you need to proofread it carefully from start to finish. Part of proofreading a document in Word is removing all wavy underlines, either by correcting the text or by telling Word to ignore the underlined text because it isn't really an error. For example, Tim's last name is marked as an error, when in fact it is spelled correctly. You need to tell Word to ignore "Bartolutti" wherever it occurs in the letter. You need to do the same for your initials.

To proofread and correct the remaining marked errors in the letter:

▶ **1.** Right-click **Bartolutti**. A shortcut menu opens.

▶ **2.** On the shortcut menu, click **Ignore All** to indicate that Word should ignore the word "Bartolutti" each time it occurs in this document. (The Ignore All option can be particularly helpful in a longer document.) The wavy red underline disappears from below Tim's last name. If your initials do not form a word, a red wavy underline appears beneath them; otherwise, a blue wavy underline appears there.

▶ **3.** If you see a wavy red underline below your initials, right-click your initials. On the shortcut menu, click **Ignore All** to remove the red wavy underline. If you didn't see a wavy blue underline below your initials before, you should see one now.

▶ **4.** Right-click your initials again. On the shortcut menu, click **Ignore Once** to remove the blue underline.

▶ **5.** Read the entire letter to proofread it for typing errors. Correct any errors using the techniques you have just learned.

▶ **6.** Save the document.

The text of the letter is finished. Now you need to think about how it looks—that is, you need to think about the document's **formatting**. First, you need to adjust the spacing in the inside address.

Adjusting Paragraph and Line Spacing

When typing a letter, you might need to adjust two types of spacing—paragraph spacing and line spacing. **Paragraph spacing** is the space that appears directly above and below a paragraph. In Word, any text that ends with a paragraph mark symbol (¶) is a paragraph. So, a **paragraph** can be a group of words that is many lines long, a single word, or even a blank line, in which case you see a paragraph mark alone on a single line. Paragraph spacing is measured in points; a **point** is 1/72 of an inch. The default setting for paragraph spacing in Word is 0 points before each paragraph and 8 points after each paragraph. When laying out a complicated document, resist the temptation to simply press the Enter key to insert extra space between paragraphs. Changing the paragraph spacing gives you much more control over the final result.

Line spacing is the space between lines of text within a paragraph. Word offers a number of preset line spacing options. The 1.0 setting, which is often called **single-spacing**, allows the least amount of space between lines. All other line spacing options are measured as multiples of 1.0 spacing. For example, 2.0 spacing (sometimes called **double-spacing**) allows for twice the space of single-spacing. The default line spacing setting is 1.08, which allows a little more space between lines than 1.0 spacing.

Now consider the line and paragraph spacing in the Robbins letter. The three lines of the inside address are too far apart. That's because each line of the inside address is actually a separate paragraph. Word inserted the default 8 points of paragraph spacing after each of these separate paragraphs. See Figure 1-13.

Figure 1-13	Line and paragraph spacing in the letter to Sonia Robbins

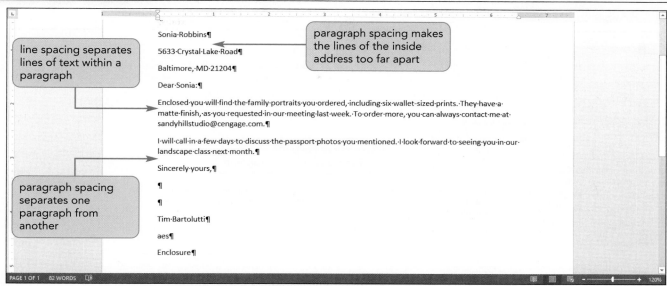

line spacing separates lines of text within a paragraph

paragraph spacing makes the lines of the inside address too far apart

Sonia·Robbins¶

5633·Crystal·Lake·Road¶

Baltimore,·MD·21204¶

Dear·Sonia:¶

Enclosed·you·will·find·the·family·portraits·you·ordered,·including·six·wallet-sized·prints.·They·have·a·matte·finish,·as·you·requested·in·our·meeting·last·week.·To·order·more,·you·can·always·contact·me·at·sandyhillstudio@cengage.com.¶

I·will·call·in·a·few·days·to·discuss·the·passport·photos·you·mentioned.·I·look·forward·to·seeing·you·in·our·landscape·class·next·month.¶

Sincerely·yours,¶

¶

¶

Tim·Bartolutti¶

aes¶

Enclosure¶

paragraph spacing separates one paragraph from another

To follow the conventions of a block style business letter, the three paragraphs that make up the inside address should have the same spacing as the lines of text within a single paragraph—that is, they need to be closer together. You can accomplish this by removing the 8 points of paragraph spacing after the first two paragraphs in the inside address. To conform to the block style business letter format, you also need to close up the spacing between your initials and the word "Enclosure" at the end of the letter.

To adjust paragraph and line spacing in Word, you use the Line and Paragraph Spacing button in the Paragraph group on the HOME tab. Clicking this button displays a menu of preset line spacing options (1.0, 1.15, 2.0, and so on). The menu also includes two paragraph spacing options, which allow you to add 12 points before a paragraph or remove the default 8 points of space after a paragraph.

Next you'll adjust the paragraph spacing in the inside address and after your initials. In the process, you'll also learn some techniques for selecting text in a document.

To adjust the paragraph spacing in the inside address and after your initials:

1. Move the pointer to the white space just to the left of "Sonia Robbins" until it changes to a right-facing arrow.

2. Click the mouse button. The entire name, including the paragraph symbol after it, is selected.

3. Press and hold the mouse button, drag the pointer down to select the next paragraph of the inside address as well, and then release the mouse button.

   The name and street address are selected as well as the paragraph marks at the end of each paragraph. You did not select the paragraph containing the city, state, and zip code because you do not need to change its paragraph spacing. See Figure 1-14.

TIP

The white space in the left margin is sometimes referred to as the selection bar because you click it to select text.

| Figure 1-14 | Inside address selected |

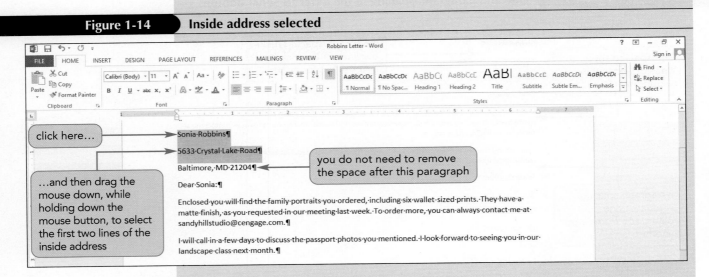

4. Make sure the HOME tab is selected on the ribbon.

5. In the Paragraph group on the HOME tab, click the **Line and Paragraph Spacing** button. A menu of line spacing options appears, with two paragraph spacing options at the bottom. See Figure 1-15. At the moment, you are only interested in the paragraph spacing options. Your goal is to remove the default 8 points of space after the first two paragraphs in the inside address.

| Figure 1-15 | Line and paragraph spacing options |

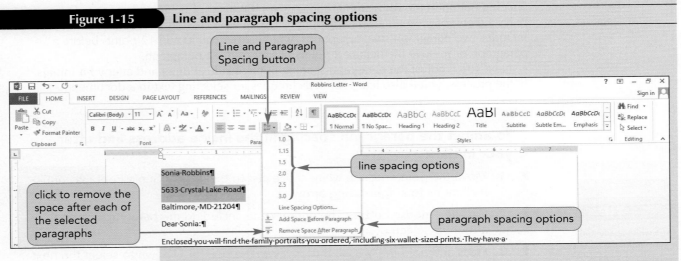

6. Click **Remove Space After Paragraph**. The menu closes, and the paragraphs are now closer together.

7. Double-click your initials to select them and the paragraph symbol after them.

8. In the Paragraph group, click the **Line and Paragraph Spacing** button, click **Remove Space After Paragraph**, and then click anywhere in the document to deselect your initials.

Another way to compress lines of text is to press the Shift+Enter keys at the end of a line. This inserts a **manual line break**, also called a **soft return**, which moves the insertion point to a new line without starting a new paragraph. You will use this technique now as you add Tim's title below his name in the signature line.

To use a manual line break to move the insertion point to a new line without starting a new paragraph:

▶ **1.** Click to the right of the "i" in "Bartolutti."

▶ **2.** Press the **Shift+Enter** keys. Word inserts a small arrow symbol ↵ , indicating a manual line break, and the insertion point moves to the line below Tim's name.

▶ **3.** Type **Sales Manager**. Tim's title now appears directly below his name with no intervening paragraph spacing, just like the lines of the inside address.

▶ **4.** Save the document.

INSIGHT

Understanding Spacing Between Paragraphs

When discussing the correct format for letters, many business style guides talk about single-spacing and double-spacing between paragraphs. In these style guides, to single-space between paragraphs means to press the Enter key once after each paragraph. Likewise, to double-space between paragraphs means to press the Enter key twice after each paragraph. With the default paragraph spacing in Word 2013, however, you only need to press the Enter key once after a paragraph. The space Word adds after a paragraph is not quite the equivalent of double-spacing, but it is enough to make it easy to see where one paragraph ends and another begins. Keep this in mind if you're accustomed to pressing the Enter key twice; otherwise, you could end up with more space than you want between paragraphs.

As you corrected line and paragraph spacing in the previous set of steps, you used the mouse to select text. Word provides multiple ways to select, or highlight, text as you work. Figure 1-16 summarizes these methods and explains when to use them most effectively.

Figure 1-16	Methods for selecting text		

To Select	Mouse	Keyboard	Mouse and Keyboard
A word	Double-click the word	Move the insertion point to the beginning of the word, press and hold Ctrl+Shift, and then press →	
A line	Click in the white space to the left of the line	Move the insertion point to the beginning of the line, press and hold Shift, and then press ↓	
A sentence	Click at the beginning of the sentence, then drag the pointer until the sentence is selected		Press and hold Ctrl, then click any location within the sentence
Multiple lines	Click and drag in the white space to the left of the lines	Move the insertion point to the beginning of the first line, press and hold Shift, and then press ↓ until all the lines are selected	
A paragraph	Double-click in the white space to the left of the paragraph, or triple-click at any location within the paragraph	Move the insertion point to the beginning of the paragraph, press and hold Ctrl+Shift, and then press ↓	
Multiple paragraphs	Click in the white space to the left of the first paragraph you want to select, and then drag to select the remaining paragraphs	Move the insertion point to the beginning of the first paragraph, press and hold Ctrl+Shift, and then press ↓ until all the paragraphs are selected	
An entire document	Triple-click in the white space to the left of the document text	Press Ctrl+A	Press and hold Ctrl, and click in the white space to the left of the document text
A block of text	Click at the beginning of the block, then drag the pointer until the entire block is selected		Click at the beginning of the block, press and hold Shift, and then click at the end of the block
Nonadjacent blocks of text			Press and hold Ctrl, then drag the mouse pointer to select multiple blocks of nonadjacent text

© 2014 Cengage Learning

Adjusting the Margins

Another important aspect of document formatting is the amount of margin space between the document text and the edge of the page. You can check the document's margins by changing the Zoom level to display the entire page.

To change the Zoom level to display the entire page:

▶ **1.** On the ribbon, click the **VIEW** tab.

▶ **2.** In the Zoom group, click the **One Page** button. The entire document is now visible in the Word window. See Figure 1-17.

Figure 1-17 **Document zoomed to show entire page**

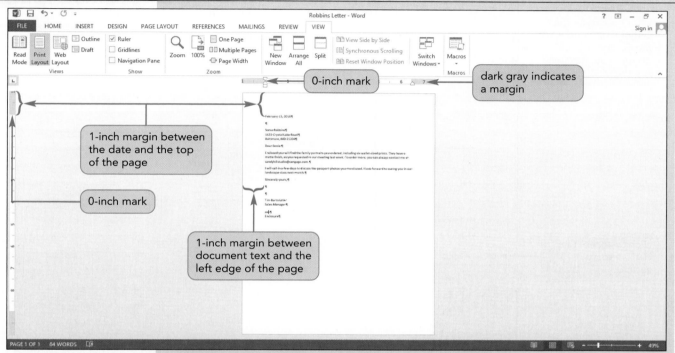

Trouble? If the wavy blue underline reappears under your initials, you can ignore it.

On the rulers, the margins appear dark gray. By default, Word documents include 1-inch margins on all sides of the document. By looking at the vertical ruler, you can see that the date in the letter, the first line in the document, is located 1 inch from the top of the page. Likewise, the horizontal ruler indicates the document text begins 1 inch from the left edge of the page.

Reading the measurements on the rulers can be tricky at first. On the horizontal ruler, the 0-inch mark is like the origin on a number line. You measure from the 0-inch mark to the left or to the right. On the vertical ruler, you measure up or down from the 0-inch mark.

Tim plans to print the letter on Sandy Hill Portrait Studio letterhead, which includes a graphic and the company's address. To allow more blank space for the letterhead, and to move the text down so it doesn't look so crowded at the top of the page, you need to increase the top margin. The settings for changing the page margins are located on the PAGE LAYOUT tab on the ribbon.

To change the page margins:

▶ **1.** On the ribbon, click the **PAGE LAYOUT** tab. The PAGE LAYOUT tab displays options for adjusting the layout of your document.

> **2.** In the Page Setup group, click the **Margins** button. The Margins gallery opens, as shown in Figure 1-18.

| Figure 1-18 | Margins gallery |

most recent margin settings selected via the Custom Margins option; you may not see this

predefined, commonly used margin settings

click to access the custom margin settings

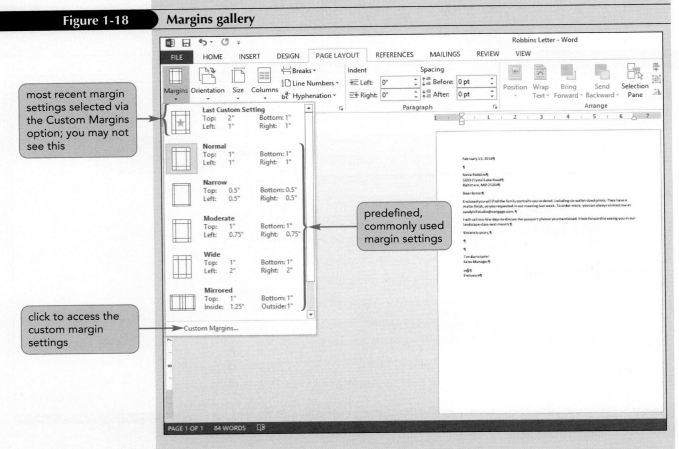

In the Margins gallery, you can choose from a number of predefined margin options, or you can click the Custom Margins command to select your own settings. After you create custom margin settings, the most recent set appears as an option at the top of the menu. For the Robbins letter, you will create custom margins.

> **3.** Click **Custom Margins**. The Page Setup dialog box opens with the Margins tab displayed. The default margin settings are displayed in the boxes at the top of the Margins tab. The top margin of 1" is already selected, ready for you to type a new margin setting.

> **4.** In the Top box in the Margins section, type **2.5**. You do not need to type an inch mark ("). See Figure 1-19.

| **Figure 1-19** | **Creating custom margins in the Page Setup dialog box** |

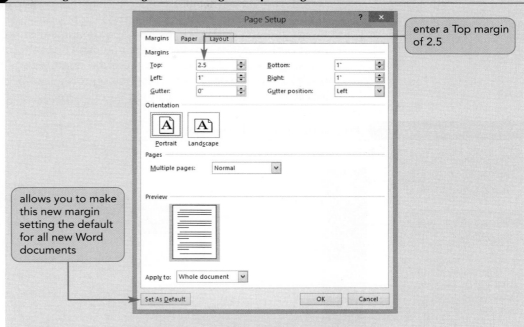

enter a Top margin of 2.5

allows you to make this new margin setting the default for all new Word documents

▶ **5.** Click the **OK** button. The text of the letter is now lower on the page. The page looks less crowded, with room for the company's letterhead.

▶ **6.** Change the Zoom level back to **120%**, and then save the document.

For most documents, the Word default of 1-inch margins is fine. In some professional settings, however, you might need to use a particular custom margin setting for all your documents. In that case, define the custom margins using the Margins tab in the Page Setup dialog box, and then click the Set As Default button to make your settings the default for all new documents. Keep in mind that most printers can't print to the edge of the page; if you select custom margins that are too narrow for your printer's specifications, Word alerts you to change your margin settings.

Previewing and Printing a Document

To make sure the document is ready to print, and to avoid wasting paper and time, you should first review it in Backstage view to make sure it will look right when printed. Like the One Page zoom setting you used earlier, the Print option in Backstage view displays a full-page preview of the document, allowing you to see how it will fit on the printed page. However, you cannot actually edit this preview. It simply provides one last opportunity to look at the document before printing.

To preview the document:

▶ **1.** Proofread the document one last time and correct any remaining errors.

▶ **2.** Click the **FILE** tab to display Backstage view.

▶ **3.** In the navigation bar, click **Print**.

The Print screen displays a full-page version of your document, showing how the letter will fit on the printed page. The Print settings to the left of the preview allow you to control a variety of print options. For example, you can change the number of copies from the default setting of "1." The 1 Page Per Sheet button opens a menu where you can choose to print multiple pages on a single sheet of paper, or to scale the printed page to a particular paper size. You can also use the navigation controls at the bottom of the screen to display other pages in a document. See Figure 1-20.

Figure 1-20	Print settings in Backstage view

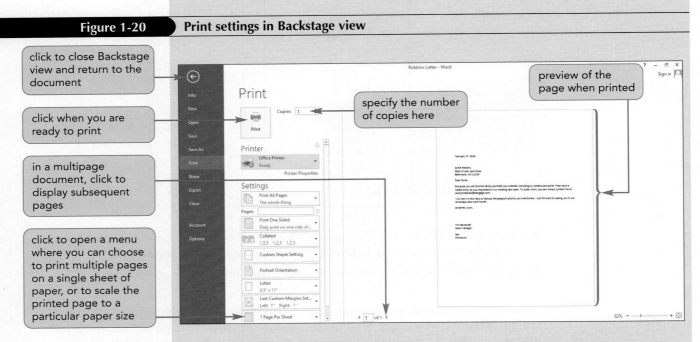

click to close Backstage view and return to the document

click when you are ready to print

in a multipage document, click to display subsequent pages

click to open a menu where you can choose to print multiple pages on a single sheet of paper, or to scale the printed page to a particular paper size

specify the number of copies here

preview of the page when printed

4. Review your document and make sure its overall layout matches that of the document in Figure 1-20. If you notice a problem with paragraph breaks or spacing, click the **Back** button at the top of the navigation bar to return to the document, make any necessary changes, and then start again at Step 2.

At this point, you can print the document or you can leave Backstage view and return to the document in Print Layout view. In the following steps, you should only print the document if your instructor asks you to. If you will be printing the document, make sure your printer is turned on and contains paper.

To leave Backstage view or to print the document:

1. Click the **Back** button at the top of the navigation bar to leave Backstage view and return to the document in Print Layout view, or click the **Print** button. Backstage view closes, and the letter prints if you clicked the Print button.

2. Click the **FILE** tab, and then click **Close** in the navigation bar to close the document without closing Word.

Next, Tim asks you to create an envelope he can use to send a class schedule to another client.

Creating an Envelope

Before you can create the envelope, you need to open a new, blank document. To create a new document, you can start with a blank document—as you did with the letter to Sonia Robbins—or you can start with one that already contains formatting and generic text commonly used in a variety of professional documents, such as a fax cover sheet or a memo. These preformatted files are called **templates**. You could use a template to create a formatted envelope, but first you'll learn how to create one on your own in a new, blank document. You'll have a chance to try out a template in the Case Problems at the end of this tutorial.

To create a new document for the envelope:

1. Click the **FILE** tab, and then click **New** in the navigation bar. The New screen is similar to the one you saw when you first started Word, with a blank document in the upper-left corner, along with a variety of templates. See Figure 1-21.

| Figure 1-21 | New options in Backstage view |

use this search box to find even more templates online

click to open a document that describes Word's features

click to create a blank document

document templates; your list of available templates may differ

scroll down to see more templates

2. Click **Blank document**. A new document named Document2 opens in the document window, with the HOME tab selected on the ribbon.

3. If necessary, change the Zoom level to **120%**, and display nonprinting characters and the rulers.

4. Save the new document as **Keating Envelope** in the location specified by your instructor.

To create the envelope:

▶ **1.** On the ribbon, click the **MAILINGS** tab. The ribbon changes to display the various Mailings options.

▶ **2.** In the Create group, click the **Envelopes** button. The Envelopes and Labels dialog box opens, with the Envelopes tab displayed. The insertion point appears in the Delivery address box, ready for you to type the recipient's address. Depending on how your computer is set up, and whether you are working on your own computer or a school computer, you might see an address in the Return address box.

▶ **3.** In the Delivery address box, type the following address, pressing the Enter key to start each new line:

Lakeisha Keating

2245 Farley Lane

Baltimore, MD 21206

Because Tim will be using the studio's printed envelopes, you don't need to print a return address on this envelope.

▶ **4.** Click the **Omit** check box to insert a checkmark, if necessary.

At this point, if you had a printer stocked with envelopes, you could click the Print button to print the envelope. To save an envelope for printing later, you need to add it to the document. Your Envelopes and Labels dialog box should match the one in Figure 1-22.

Figure 1-22   **Envelopes and Labels dialog box**

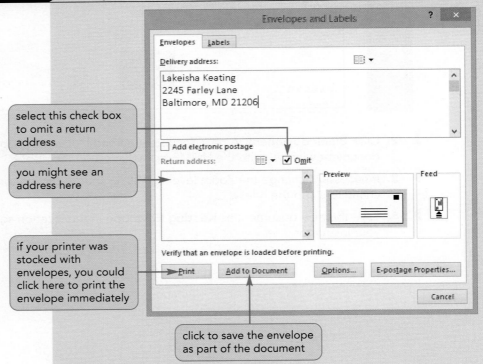

5. Click the **Add to Document** button. The dialog box closes, and you return to the document window. The envelope is inserted at the top of your document, with 1.0 line spacing. The double line with the words "Section Break (Next Page)" is related to how the envelope is formatted, and will not be visible when you print the envelope. The envelope will print in the standard business envelope format.

6. Save the document. Tim will print the envelope later, so you can close the document now.

7. Click the **FILE** tab and then click **Close** in the navigation bar. The document closes, but Word remains open.

INSIGHT

Creating Documents with Templates

Microsoft offers predesigned templates for all kinds of documents, including calendars, reports, and thank you cards. You can use the scroll bar on the right of the New screen (shown earlier in Figure 1-21) to scroll down to see more templates, or you can use the Search for online templates box in the New screen to search among hundreds of other options available at Office.com. When you open a template, you actually open a new document containing the formatting and text stored in the template, leaving the original template untouched. A typical template includes placeholder text that you replace with your own information.

Templates allow you to create stylish, professional-looking documents quickly and easily. To use them effectively, however, you need to be knowledgeable about Word and its many options for manipulating text, graphics, and page layouts. Otherwise, the complicated formatting of some Word templates can be more frustrating than helpful. As you become a more experienced Word user, you'll learn how to create your own templates.

You're finished creating the cover letter and the envelope. In the next session, you will modify a flyer that announces an upcoming class by formatting the text and adding a photo.

REVIEW

Session 1.1 Quick Check

1. In a block style letter, does each line of text start at the left or right margin?

2. What do you call the recipient's address, which appears below the date in a block style letter?

3. Explain how to use a hyperlink in a Word document to open a new email message.

4. Explain how to display nonprinting characters.

5. Define the term "paragraph spacing."

6. How does Word indicate a potential spelling error?

Session 1.2 Visual Overview:

Alignment buttons control the text's **alignment**—that is, the way it lines up between the left and right margins. Here, the Center button is selected because the text containing the insertion point is center-aligned.

You can click the Clear All Formatting button to restore selected text to the default font, font size, and color.

Clicking the Format Painter button displays the Format Painter pointer, which you can use to copy formatting from the selected text to other text in the document.

The Font group on the HOME tab includes the Font box and the Font size box for setting the text's font and the font size, respectively. A **font** is a set of characters that uses the same typeface.

This document has a landscape orientation, meaning it is wider than it is tall.

You can insert a photo or another type of picture in a document by using the **Pictures button** located on the INSERT tab of the ribbon. After you insert a photo or another picture, you can format it with a style that adds a border or a shadow, or changes its shape.

You click the Shading button arrow to apply a colored background to a selected paragraph.

The boldface and blue font color applied to this text are examples of formatting that you would use sparingly to draw attention to a specific part of a document.

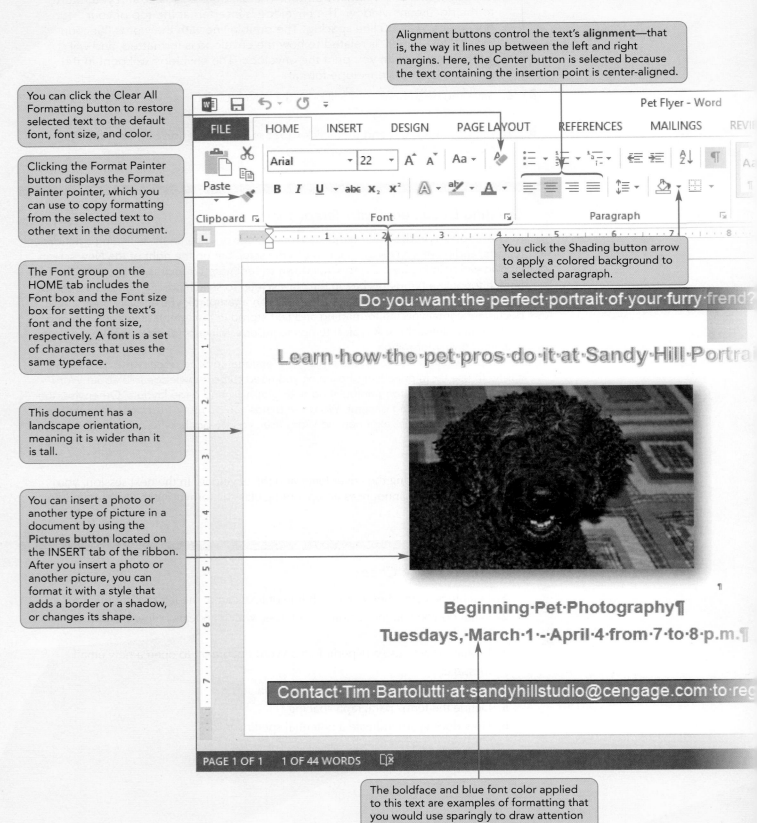

Formatting a Document

The black border and dark orange shading around this paragraph are examples of **paragraph formatting** because they affect the entire paragraph.

The Microsoft Word Help button opens the **Word Help** window, where you can find information about Word commands and features, as well as instructions for using them.

You use the Borders button arrow to apply an outline to the selected paragraph. The image on the Borders button reflects the most recently used Border option.

The misspelled word is highlighted in the document. A suggested correction is highlighted in the Spelling task pane.

The blue font color and white outline used for this paragraph are examples of **text effects**, special visual enhancements such as outlines, shading, shadows, and reflections, that you add to the text's font.

A **task pane** is a window that helps you navigate through a complex task or feature. This one, the **Spelling task pane**, opens when you click the Spelling & Grammar button in the Proofing group on the HOME tab. You can use it to correct spelling errors. Similarly, you can use the **Grammar task pane** to correct grammar errors.

The white font color used on this text is an example of **character formatting** because it affects individual characters.

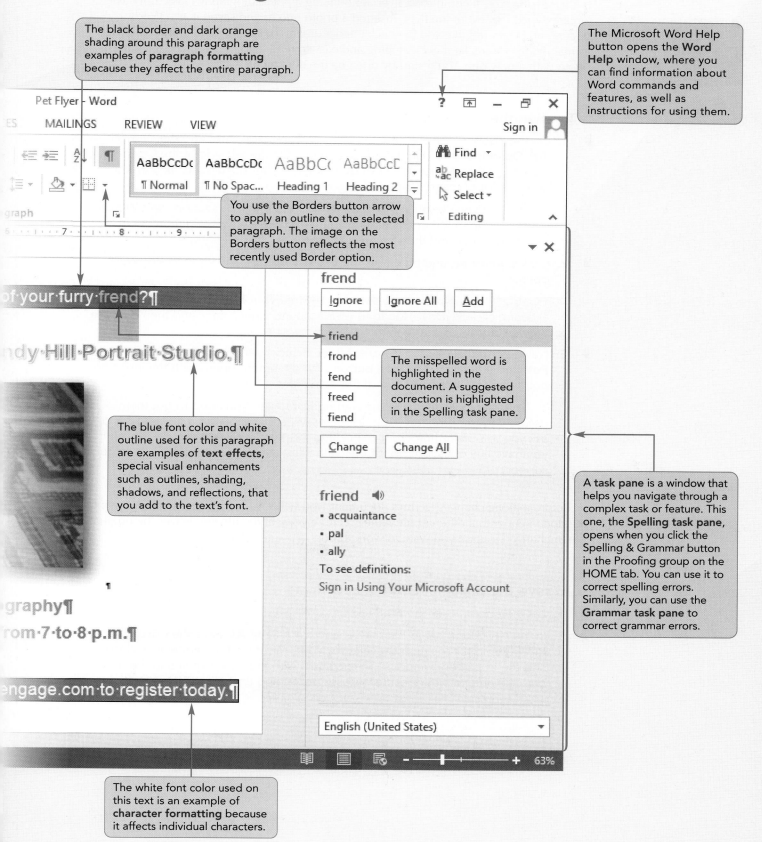

Opening an Existing Document

In this session, you'll complete a flyer announcing a pet photography class. Tim has already typed the text of the flyer, inserted a photo into it, and saved it as a Word document. He would like you to check the document for spelling and grammar errors, format the flyer to make it eye-catching and easy to read, and then replace the current photo with a new one. You'll start by opening the document.

To open the flyer document:

1. On the ribbon, click the **FILE** tab to open Backstage view, and then verify that **Open** is selected in the navigation bar. On the left side of the Open screen is a list of places you can go to locate other documents, and on the right is a list of recently opened documents.

   Trouble? If you closed Word at the end of the previous session, start Word now, click Open Other Documents at the bottom of the navigation bar in Backstage view, and then begin with Step 2.

2. Click **Computer**, and then click the **Browse** button. The Open dialog box opens.

   Trouble? If your instructor asked you to store your files to your SkyDrive account, click SkyDrive, log in to your account, if necessary, and then click the Browse button.

3. Navigate to the Word1 ▶ Tutorial folder included with your Data Files, click **Pet**, and then click the **Open** button. The document opens with the insertion point blinking in the first line of the document.

   Trouble? If you don't have the starting Data Files, you need to get them before you can proceed. Your instructor will either give you the Data Files or ask you to obtain them from a specified location (such as a network drive). If you have any questions about the Data Files, see your instructor or technical support person for assistance.

Before making changes to Tim's document, you will save it with a new name. Saving the document with a different filename creates a copy of the file and leaves the original file unchanged in case you want to work through the tutorial again.

To save the document with a new name:

1. On the ribbon, click the **FILE** tab.

2. In the navigation bar in Backstage view, click **Save As**. Save the document as **Pet Flyer** in the location specified by your instructor. Backstage view closes, and the document window appears again with the new filename in the title bar. The original Pet document closes, remaining unchanged.

PROSKILLS

Decision Making: Creating Effective Documents

Before you create a new document or revise an existing document, take a moment to think about your audience. Ask yourself these questions:

- Who is your audience?
- What do they know?
- What do they need to know?
- How can the document you are creating change your audience's behavior or opinions?

Every decision you make about your document should be based on your answers to these questions. To take a simple example, if you are creating a flyer to announce an upcoming seminar on college financial aid, your audience would be students and their parents. They probably all know what the term "financial aid" means, so you don't need to explain that in your flyer. Instead, you can focus on telling them what they need to know—the date, time, and location of the seminar. The behavior you want to affect, in this case, is whether or not your audience will show up for the seminar. By making the flyer professional looking and easy to read, you increase the chance that they will.

You might find it more challenging to answer these questions about your audience when creating more complicated documents, such as corporate reports. But the focus remains the same—connecting with the audience. As you are deciding what information to include in your document, remember that the goal of a professional document is to convey the information as effectively as possible to your target audience.

Before revising a document for someone else, it's a good idea to familiarize yourself with its overall structure.

To review the document:

1. Verify that the document is displayed in Print Layout view and that nonprinting characters are displayed. For now, you can ignore the wavy underlines that appear in the document.

2. Change the Zoom level to **120%**, if necessary.

   At this point, the document is very simple. By the time you are finished, it will look like the document shown in the Session 1.2 Visual Overview, with the spelling and grammar errors corrected. Figure 1-23 summarizes the tasks you will perform.

Figure 1-23   **Formatting changes requested by Tim**

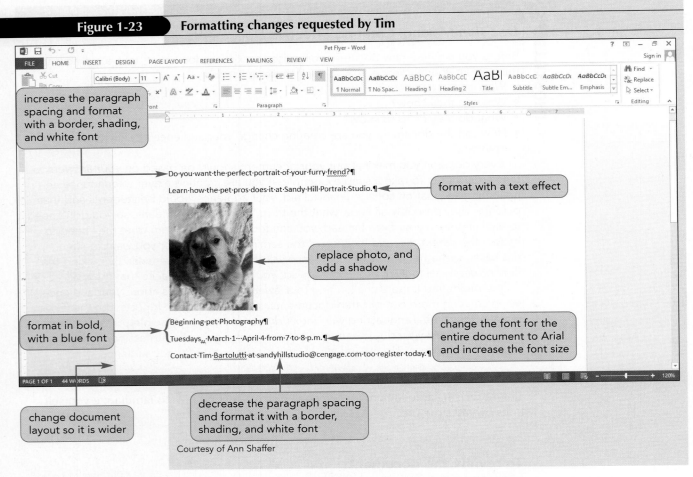

increase the paragraph spacing and format with a border, shading, and white font

Do·you·want·the·perfect·portrait·of·your·furry·frend?¶

Learn·how·the·pet·pros·does·it·at·Sandy·Hill·Portrait·Studio.¶

format with a text effect

replace photo, and add a shadow

format in bold, with a blue font

Beginning·pet·Photography¶

Tuesdays,·March·1---April·4·from·7·to·8·p.m.¶

change the font for the entire document to Arial and increase the font size

Contact·Tim·Bartolutti·at·sandyhillstudio@cengage.com·too·register·today.¶

PAGE 1 OF 1   44 WORDS

change document layout so it is wider

decrease the paragraph spacing and format it with a border, shading, and white font

Courtesy of Ann Shaffer

You will start by correcting the spelling and grammar errors.

Using the Spelling and Grammar Task Panes

As you learned in Tutorial 1, Word marks possible spelling and grammatical errors with wavy underlines as you type so you can quickly go back and correct those errors. A more thorough way of checking the spelling in a document is to use the Spelling and Grammar task panes to check a document word by word for a variety of errors. You can customize the spelling and grammar settings to add or ignore certain types of errors.

Tim asks you to use the Spelling and Grammar task panes to check the flyer for mistakes. Before you do, you'll configure the grammar settings to look for subject/verb agreement, in addition to other types of errors.

To customize the grammar settings:

1. On the ribbon, click the **FILE** tab, and then click **Options** in the navigation bar. The Word Options dialog box opens. You can use this dialog box to change a variety of settings related to how Word looks and works.

2. In the left pane, click **Proofing**, and then, in the "When correcting spelling and grammar in Word" section, click the **Settings** button. The Grammar Settings dialog box opens.

3. If necessary, scroll down in the Grammar Settings dialog box to display all the check boxes under "Grammar," and then click the **Subject-verb agreement** check box to insert a checkmark. See Figure 1-24.

Figure 1-24	Grammar Settings dialog box

click to display settings related to proofing a document

click to insert a checkmark

click to recheck words that you chose to ignore in Session 1.1

click to display the Grammar Settings dialog box

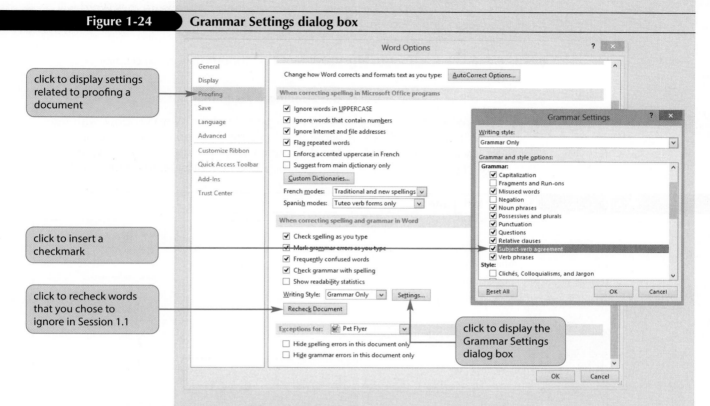

4. Click the **OK** button to close the Grammar Settings dialog box and return to the Word Options dialog box.

To ensure that Word checks the entire Pet Flyer document, and doesn't skip any words that you chose to ignore when you checked the Robbins Letter in Session 1.1, you can click the Recheck Document button.

5. Click the **Recheck Document** button, and then click **Yes** in the warning dialog box.

6. In the Word Options dialog box, click the **OK** button to close the dialog box.

You return to the Pet Flyer document, where three errors are now marked with wavy blue underlines. The two new errors are related to subject-verb agreement. You should also see two words marked with wavy red underlines, including Tim's last name in the final paragraph.

Now you are ready to check the document's spelling and grammar. All errors marked with red underlines are considered spelling errors, while all errors marked with blue underlines are considered grammatical errors.

To check the Pet Flyer document for spelling and grammatical errors:

▶ **1.** Press the **Ctrl+Home** keys, if necessary, to move the insertion point to the beginning of the document, to the left of the "D" in "Do." By placing the insertion point at the beginning of the document, you ensure that Word will check the entire document from start to finish without having to go back and check an earlier part.

▶ **2.** On the ribbon, click the **REVIEW** tab. The ribbon changes to display reviewing options.

▶ **3.** In the Proofing group, click the **Spelling & Grammar** button.

The Spelling task pane opens on the right side of the Word window, with the word "frend" listed as a possible spelling error. The same word is highlighted in gray in the document. In the task pane's list of possible corrections, the correctly spelled word "friend" is highlighted in light blue. See Figure 1-25.

Figure 1-25   Spelling task pane

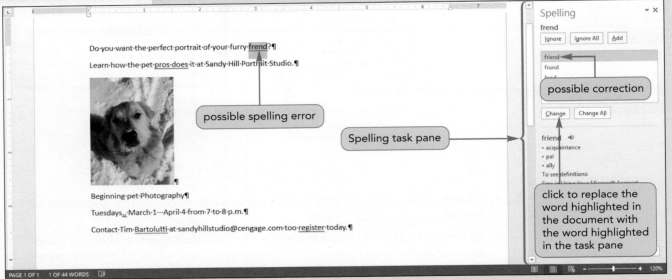

Courtesy of Ann Shaffer

▶ **4.** In the task pane, click the **Change** button. The misspelled word "frend" is replaced with "friend."

Next, Word highlights the entire second sentence, indicating another possible error. The Spelling task pane changes to the Grammar task pane, and the information at the bottom of the task pane explains that the error is related to subject-verb agreement.

▶ **5.** Verify that "pros do" is selected in the Grammar task pane, and then click the **Change** button. The second to last paragraph of text is now highlighted in the document. The explanation at the bottom of the task pane indicates that the error is related to punctuation.

▶ **6.** Verify that the comma is selected in the Grammar task pane, and then click the **Change** button.

Tim's last name is now highlighted in the document, and the Grammar task pane changes to the Spelling task pane. Although the Spelling task pane doesn't recognize "Bartolutti" as a word, it is spelled correctly, so you can ignore it.

7. Click the **Ignore** button in the Spelling task pane.

The last paragraph in the document is highlighted, and the Grammar task pane indicates a possible subject-verb agreement problem related to the word "register." However, the real problem is the word "too," just before "register." It should be replaced with "to." You can fix this problem by typing directly in the document.

8. In the document, click to the right of the word "too," delete the second letter "o," and then click the **Resume** button in the task pane. The task pane closes and a dialog box opens indicating that the spelling and grammar check is complete.

9. Click the **OK** button to close the dialog box.

Finally, you'll restore the grammar settings to their original configuration.

10. Click the **FILE** tab, and then click **Options**.

11. In the Word Options dialog box, click **Proofing**, and then click the **Settings** button.

12. Scroll down, and then click the **Subject-verb agreement** check box to remove the checkmark.

13. Click the **OK** button to close the Grammar Settings dialog box, and then click the **OK** button to close the Word Options dialog box.

PROSKILLS

Written Communication: Proofreading Your Document

Although the Spelling and Grammar task panes are useful tools, they won't always catch every error in a document, and they sometimes flag "errors" that are actually correct. This means there is no substitute for careful proofreading. Always take the time to read through your document to check for errors the Spelling and Grammar task panes might have missed. Keep in mind that the Spelling and Grammar task panes cannot pinpoint inaccurate phrases or poorly chosen words. You'll have to find those yourself. To produce a professional document, you must read it carefully several times. It's a good idea to ask one or two other people to read your documents as well; they might catch something you missed.

You still need to proofread the Pet Flyer document. You'll do that next.

To proofread the Pet Flyer document:

1. Review the document text for any remaining errors. In the third paragraph of text, change the lowercase "p" in "pet" to an uppercase "P."

2. In the last line of text, replace "Tim Bartolutti" with your first and last name, and then save the document. Including your name in the document will make it easier for you to find your copy later if you print it on a shared printer.

Now you're ready to begin formatting the document. You will start by turning the page so it is wider than it is tall. In other words, you will change the document's **orientation**.

Changing Page Orientation

Portrait orientation, with the page taller than it is wide, is the default page orientation for Word documents because it is the orientation most commonly used for letters, reports, and other formal documents. However, Tim wants you to format the pet flyer in **landscape orientation**—that is, with the page turned so it is wider than it is tall to better accommodate the photo. You can accomplish this task by using the Orientation button located on the PAGE LAYOUT tab on the ribbon. After you change the page orientation, you will select narrower margins so you can maximize the amount of color on the page.

To change the page orientation:

▶ 1. Change the document zoom setting to **One Page** so that you can see the entire document.

▶ 2. On the ribbon, click the **PAGE LAYOUT** tab. The ribbon changes to display options for formatting the overall layout of text and images in the document.

▶ 3. In the Page Setup group, click the **Orientation** button, and then click **Landscape** on the menu. The document changes to landscape orientation.

▶ 4. In the Page Setup group, click the **Margins** button, and then click the **Narrow** option on the menu. The margins shrink from 1 inch to .5 inch on all four sides. See Figure 1-26.

| Figure 1-26 | Document in landscape orientation with narrow margins |

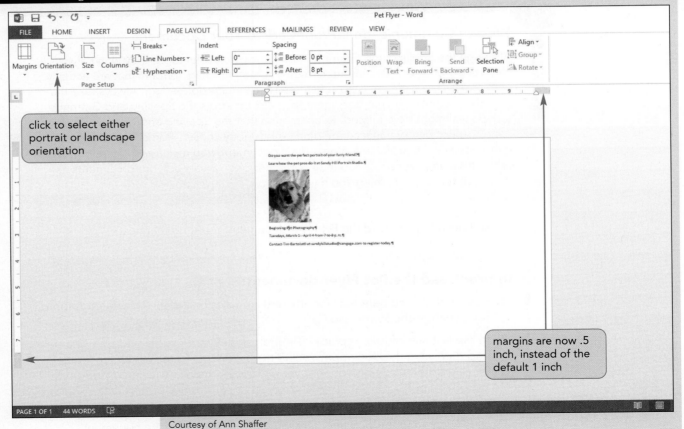

click to select either portrait or landscape orientation

margins are now .5 inch, instead of the default 1 inch

Courtesy of Ann Shaffer

Changing the Font and Font Size

Tim typed the document in the default font size, 11 point, and the default font, Calibri, but he would like to switch to the Arial font instead. Also, he wants to increase the size of all five paragraphs of the document text. To apply these changes, you start by selecting the text you want to format. Then you select the options you want in the Font group on the HOME tab.

To change the font and font size:

1. On the ribbon, click the HOME tab.

2. Change the document Zoom level to **120%**.

3. To verify that the insertion point is located at the beginning of the document, press the **Ctrl+HOME** keys.

4. Press and hold the **Shift** key, and then click to the right of the second paragraph marker, at the end of the second paragraph of text. The first two paragraphs of text are selected, as shown in Figure 1-27.

Figure 1-27 Selected text, with default font displayed in Font box

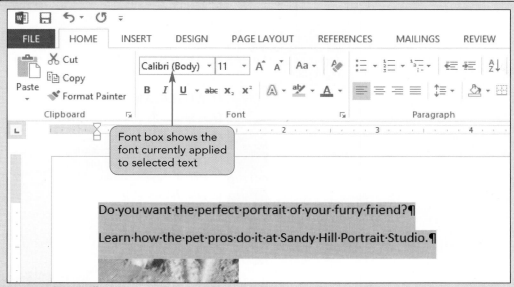

Courtesy of Ann Shaffer

The Font box in the Font group displays the name of the font applied to the selected text, which in this case is Calibri. The word "Body" next to the font name indicates that the Calibri font is intended for formatting body text. **Body text** is ordinary text, as opposed to titles or headings.

5. In the Font group on the HOME tab, click the **Font** arrow. A list of available fonts appears, with Calibri Light and Calibri at the top of the list. Calibri is highlighted in blue, indicating that this font is currently applied to the selected text. The word "Headings" next to the font name "Calibri Light" indicates that Calibri Light is intended for formatting headings.

Below Calibri Light and Calibri, you might see a list of fonts that have been used recently on your computer, followed by a complete alphabetical list of all available fonts. (You won't see the list of recently used fonts if you just installed Word.) You need to scroll the list to see all the available fonts. Each name in the list is formatted with the relevant font. For example, the name "Arial" appears in the Arial font. See Figure 1-28.

Figure 1-28 **Font list**

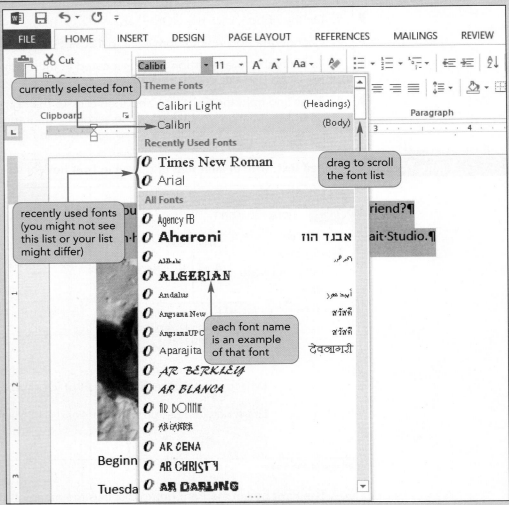

Courtesy of Ann Shaffer

▶ **6.** Without clicking, move the pointer over a dramatic-looking font in the font list, such as Algerian or Arial Black, and then move the pointer over another font.

The selected text in the document changes to show a Live Preview of the font the pointer is resting on. **Live Preview** shows the results that would occur in your document if you clicked the option you are pointing to.

▶ **7.** When you are finished reviewing the Font list, click **Arial**. The Font menu closes, and the selected text is formatted in Arial.

Next, you will make the text more eye-catching by increasing the font size. The Font Size box currently displays the number "11," indicating that the selected text is formatted in 11-point font.

8. Verify that the two paragraphs are still selected, and then click the **Font Size** arrow in the Font group to display a menu of font sizes. As with the Font menu, you can move the pointer over options in the Font Size menu to see a Live Preview of that option.

9. On the Font Size menu, click **22**. The selected text increases significantly in size and the Font Size menu closes.

10. Select the three paragraphs of text below the photo, format them in the Arial font, and then increase the paragraphs' font size to 22 points.

11. Click a blank area of the document to deselect the text, and then save the document.

Tim examines the flyer and decides he would like to apply more character formatting, which affects the appearance of individual characters, in the middle three paragraphs. After that, you can turn your attention to paragraph formatting, which affects the appearance of the entire paragraph.

Applying Text Effects, Font Colors, and Font Styles

To really make text stand out, you can use text effects. You access these options by clicking the Text Effects button in the Font group on the HOME tab. Keep in mind that text effects can be very dramatic. For formal, professional documents, you probably only need to use **bold** or *italic* to make a word or paragraph stand out.

Tim suggests applying text effects to the second paragraph.

To apply text effects to the second paragraph:

1. Scroll up, if necessary, to display the beginning of the document, and then click in the selection bar to the left of the second paragraph. The entire second paragraph is selected.

2. In the Font group on the HOME tab, click the **Text Effects and Typography** button A ▾.

   A gallery of text effects appears. Options that allow you to fine-tune a particular text effect, perhaps by changing the color or adding an even more pronounced shadow, are listed below the gallery. A **gallery** is a menu or grid that shows a visual representation of the options available when you click a button.

3. In the middle of the bottom row of the gallery, place the pointer over the blue letter "A." This displays a ScreenTip with the text effect's full name, which is "Fill - Blue, Accent 1, Outline - Background 1, Hard Shadow - Accent 1." A Live Preview of the effect appears in the document. See Figure 1-29.

Figure 1-29	Live Preview of a text effect

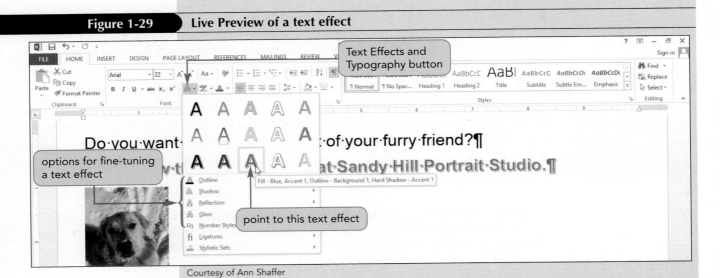

Courtesy of Ann Shaffer

4. In the bottom row of the gallery, click the blue letter "A." The text effect is applied to the selected paragraph and the Text Effects gallery closes. The second paragraph is formatted in blue, as shown in the Session 1.2 Visual Overview. The Bold button in the Font group is now highlighted because bold formatting is part of this text effect.

Next, to make the text stand out a bit more, you'll increase the font size. This time, instead of using the Font Size button, you'll use a different method.

5. In the Font group, click the **Increase Font Size** button. The font size increases from 22 points to 24 points.

6. Click the **Increase Font Size** button again. The font size increases to 26 points. If you need to decrease the font size of selected text, you can use the Decrease Font Size button.

Tim asks you to emphasize the third and fourth paragraphs by adding bold and a blue font color.

To apply a font color and bold:

1. Select the third and fourth paragraphs of text, which contain the class name as well as the dates and times.

2. In the Font group on the Home tab, click the **Font Color button arrow**. A gallery of font colors appears. Black is the default font color and appears at the top of the Font Color gallery, with the word "Automatic" next to it.

The options in the Theme Colors section of the menu are complementary colors that work well when used together in a document. The options in the Standard Colors section are more limited. For more advanced color options, you could use the More Colors or Gradient options. Tim prefers a simple blue.

Trouble? If the class name turned red, you clicked the Font Color button instead of the arrow next to it. On the Quick Access Toolbar, click the Undo button, and then repeat Step 2.

3. In the Theme Colors section, place the mouse pointer over the square that's second from the right in the top row. A ScreenTip with the color's name, "Blue, Accent 5," appears. A Live Preview of the color appears in the document, where the text you selected in Step 1 now appears formatted in blue. See Figure 1-30.

Figure 1-30 **Font Color gallery showing a Live Preview**

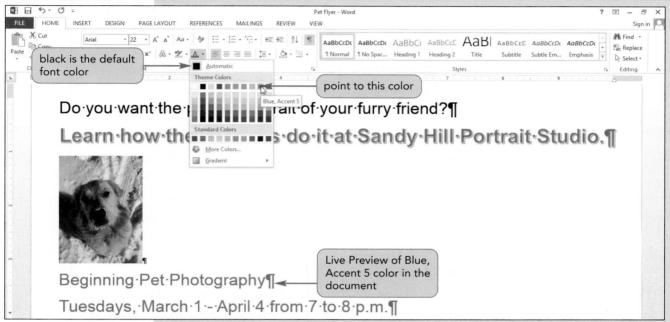

Courtesy of Ann Shaffer

4. Click the **Blue, Accent 5** square. The Font color gallery closes, and the selected text is formatted in blue. On the Font Color button, the bar below the letter "A" is now blue, indicating that if you select text and click the Font Color button, the text will automatically change to blue.

5. In the Font group, click the **Bold** button B. The selected text is now formatted in bold, with thicker, darker lettering.

TIP

You can use other buttons in the Font group on the HOME tab to apply other character attributes, such as underline, italic, or superscript.

Next, you will complete some paragraph formatting, starting with paragraph alignment.

Aligning Text

Alignment refers to how text and graphics line up between the page margins. By default, Word aligns text along the left margin, with the text along the right margin **ragged**, or uneven. This is called **left alignment**. With **right alignment**, the text is aligned along the right margin and is ragged along the left margin. With **center alignment**, text is centered between the left and right margins and is ragged along both the left and right margins. With **justified alignment**, full lines of text are spaced between both the left and the right margins, and no text is ragged. Text in newspaper columns is often justified. See Figure 1-31.

| Figure 1-31 | Varieties of text alignment |

left alignment

The term "alignment" refers to the way a paragraph lines up between the margins. The term "alignment" refers to the way a paragraph lines up between the margins.

right alignment

The term "alignment" refers to the way a paragraph lines up between the margins. The term "alignment" refers to the way a paragraph lines up between the margins.

center alignment

The term "alignment" refers to the way a paragraph lines up between the margins.

justified alignment

The term "alignment" refers to the way a paragraph lines up between the margins. The term "alignment" refers to the way a paragraph lines up between the margins.

© 2014 Cengage Learning

The Paragraph group on the HOME tab includes a button for each of the four major types of alignment described in Figure 1-31: the Align Left button, the Center button, the Align Right button, and the Justify button. To align a single paragraph, click anywhere in that paragraph, and then click the appropriate alignment button. To align multiple paragraphs, select the paragraphs first, and then click an alignment button.

You need to center all the text in the flyer now. You can center the photo at the same time.

To center-align the text:

Use the Ctrl+A keys to select the entire document, instead of dragging the mouse pointer. It's easy to miss part of the document when you drag the mouse pointer.

1. Press the **Ctrl+A** keys to select the entire document, and make sure the HOME tab is still selected.

2. In the Paragraph group, click the **Center** button ☰, and then click a blank area of the document to deselect the selected paragraphs. The text and photo are now centered on the page, similar to the centered text shown earlier in the Session 1.2 Visual Overview.

3. Save the document.

Adding a Paragraph Border and Shading

A **paragraph border** is an outline that appears around one or more paragraphs in a document. You can choose to apply only a partial border—for example, a bottom border that appears as an underline under the last line of text in the paragraph—or an entire box around a paragraph. You can select different colors and line weights for the border as well, making it more prominent or less prominent as needed. You apply paragraph borders using the Borders button in the Paragraph group on the HOME tab. **Shading** is background color that you can apply to one or more paragraphs and can be used in conjunction with a border for a more defined effect. You apply shading using the Shading button in the Paragraph group on the HOME tab.

Now you will apply a border and shading to the first paragraph, as shown earlier in the Session 1.2 Visual Overview. Then you will use the Format Painter to copy this formatting to the last paragraph in the document.

To add shading and a paragraph border:

1. Select the first paragraph. Be sure to select the paragraph mark at the end of the paragraph.

2. On the HOME tab, in the Paragraph group, click the **Borders button arrow**. A gallery of border options appears, as shown in Figure 1-32. To apply a complete outline around the selected text, you use the Outside Borders option.

Figure 1-32   **Border gallery**

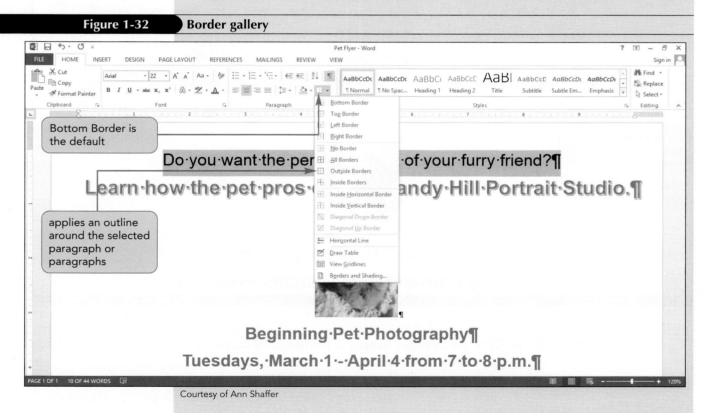

Courtesy of Ann Shaffer

Trouble? If the gallery does not open, and instead the paragraph becomes underlined with a single underline, you clicked the Borders button instead of the arrow next to it. On the Quick Access Toolbar, click the Undo button, and then repeat Step 2.

3. In the Border gallery, click **Outside Borders**. The menu closes and a black border appears around the selected paragraph, spanning the width of the page. In the Paragraph group, the Borders button ⊞ changes to show the Outside Borders option.

   Trouble? If the border around the first paragraph doesn't extend all the way to the left and right margins, and instead only encloses the text, you didn't select the paragraph mark as directed in Step 1. Click the Undo button ↺ repeatedly to remove the border, and begin again with Step 1.

4. In the Paragraph group, click the **Shading button arrow** 🖾▾. A gallery of shading options opens, divided into Theme Colors and Standard Colors. You will use a shade of orange in the sixth column from the left.

5. In the second row from the bottom in the Theme Colors section, move the pointer over the square in the sixth column from the left to display a ScreenTip that reads "Orange, Accent 2, Darker 25%." A Live Preview of the color appears in the document. See Figure 1-33.

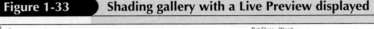

Figure 1-33   **Shading gallery with a Live Preview displayed**

Courtesy of Ann Shaffer

6. Click the **Orange, Accent 2, Darker 25%** square to apply the shading to the selected text.

   On a dark background like the one you just applied, a white font creates a striking effect. Tim asks you to change the font color for this paragraph to white.

7. Make sure the HOME tab is still selected.

8. In the Font group, click the **Font Color button arrow** 🗛▾ to open the Font Color gallery, and then click the **white** square in the top row of the Theme Colors. The Font Color gallery closes and the paragraph is now formatted with white font.

9. Click a blank area of the document to deselect the text, review the change, and then save the document. See Figure 1-34.

Figure 1-34   **Paragraph formatted with dark orange shading, a black border, and white font**

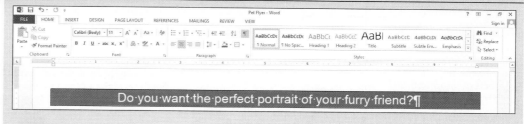

To add balance to the flyer, Tim suggests formatting the last paragraph in the document with the same shading, border, and font color as the first paragraph. You'll do that next.

Copying Formatting with the Format Painter

You could select the last paragraph and then apply the border, shading, and font color one step at a time. But it's easier to copy all the formatting from the first paragraph to the last paragraph using the Format Painter button in the Clipboard group on the HOME tab.

REFERENCE

Using the Format Painter

- Select the text whose formatting you want to copy.
- On the HOME tab, in the Clipboard group, click the Format Painter button; or to copy formatting to multiple sections of nonadjacent text, double-click the Format Painter button.
- The mouse pointer changes to the Format Painter pointer, the I-beam pointer with a paintbrush.
- Click the words you want to format, or drag to select and format entire paragraphs.
- When you are finished formatting the text, click the Format Painter button again to turn off the Format Painter.

You'll use the Format Painter now.

To use the Format Painter:

1. Change the document Zoom level to **One Page** so you can easily see both the first and last paragraphs.

2. Select the first paragraph, which is formatted with the dark orange shading, the border, and the white font color.

3. On the ribbon, click the HOME tab.

4. In the Clipboard group, click the **Format Painter** button to activate, or turn on, the Format Painter.

5. Move the pointer over the document. The pointer changes to the Format Painter pointer ![icon] when you move the mouse pointer near an item that can be formatted. See Figure 1-35.

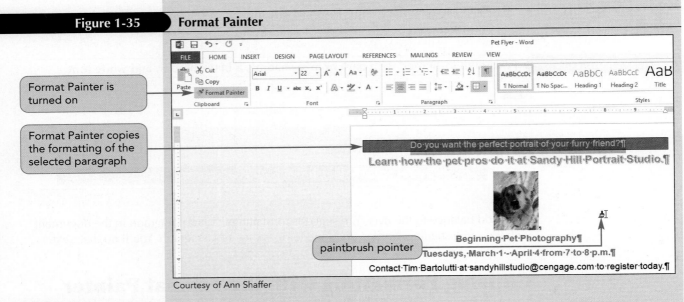

Format Painter is turned on

Format Painter copies the formatting of the selected paragraph

paintbrush pointer

Courtesy of Ann Shaffer

6. Click and drag the Format Painter pointer 📌𝕀 to select the last paragraph in the document. The paragraph is now formatted with dark orange shading, a black border, and white font. The mouse pointer returns to its original I-beam shape 𝕀.

Trouble? If the text in the newly formatted paragraph wrapped to a second line, replace your full name with your first name, or, if necessary, use only your initials so the paragraph is only one line long.

7. Click anywhere in the document to deselect the text, review the change, and then save the document.

You're almost finished working on the document's paragraph formatting. Your last step is to increase the paragraph spacing below the first paragraph and above the last paragraph. This will give the shaded text even more weight on the page. To complete this task, you will use the settings on the PAGE LAYOUT tab, which offer more options than the Line and Paragraph Spacing button on the HOME tab.

To increase the paragraph spacing below the first paragraph and above the last paragraph:

1. Click anywhere in the first paragraph, and then click the **PAGE LAYOUT** tab. On this tab, the Paragraph group contains settings that control paragraph spacing. Currently, the paragraph spacing for the first paragraph is set to the default 0 points before the paragraph and 8 points after.

2. In the Paragraph group, click the **After** box to select the current setting, type **42**, and then press the **Enter** key. The added space causes the second paragraph to move down 42 points.

3. Click anywhere in the last paragraph.

4. On the PAGE LAYOUT tab, in the Paragraph group, click the **Before** box to select the current setting, type **42**, and then press the **Enter** key. The added space causes the last paragraph to move down 42 points.

INSIGHT

Formatting Professional Documents

In more formal documents, use color and special effects sparingly. The goal of letters, reports, and many other types of documents is to convey important information, not to dazzle the reader with fancy fonts and colors. Such elements only serve to distract the reader from your main point. In formal documents, it's a good idea to limit the number of colors to two and to stick with left alignment for text. In a document like the flyer you're currently working on, you have a little more leeway because the goal of the document is to attract attention. However, you still want it to look professional.

Finally, Tim wants you to replace the photo of the golden retriever with one that will look better in the document's new landscape orientation. You'll replace the photo, and then you'll resize it so the flyer fills the entire page.

Working with Pictures

A **picture** is a photo or another type of image that you insert into a document. To work with a picture, you first need to select it. Once a picture is selected, a contextual tab—the PICTURE TOOLS FORMAT tab—appears on the ribbon, with options for editing the picture and adding effects such as a border, a shadow, a reflection, or a new shape. A **contextual tab** appears on the ribbon only when an object is selected. It contains commands related to the selected object so you can manipulate, edit, and format the selected object. You can also use the mouse to resize or move a selected picture. To insert a new picture, you use the Pictures button in the Illustrations group on the INSERT tab.

To delete the current photo and insert a new one:

▶ **1.** Click the photo to select it.

The squares, called **handles**, around the edge of the photo indicate the photo is selected. The Layout Options button, to the right of the photo, gives you access to options that control how the document text flows around the photo. You don't need to worry about these options now. Finally, note that the PICTURE TOOLS FORMAT tab appeared on the ribbon when you selected the photo. See Figure 1-36.

Figure 1-36	Selected photo

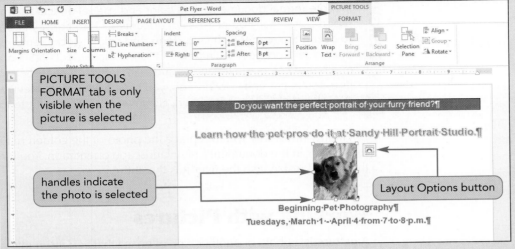

Courtesy of Ann Shaffer

▶ **2.** Press the **Delete** key. The photo is deleted from the document. The insertion point blinks next to the paragraph symbol. You will insert the new photo in that paragraph.

▶ **3.** On the ribbon, click the **INSERT** tab. The ribbon changes to display the Insert options.

▶ **4.** In the Illustrations group, click the **Pictures** button. The Insert Picture dialog box opens.

▶ **5.** Navigate to the Word1 ▶ Tutorial folder included with your Data Files, and then click **Poodle** to select the file. The name of the selected file appears in the File name box.

▶ **6.** Click the **Insert** button to close the Insert Picture dialog box and insert the photo. An image of a black poodle appears in the document, below the text. The photo is selected, as indicated by the handles that appear on its border.

Now you need to enlarge the photo to fit the available space on the page. You could do so by clicking one of the picture's corner handles, holding down the mouse button, and then dragging the handle to resize the picture. But using the Shape Height and Shape Width boxes on the PICTURE TOOLS FORMAT tab gives you more precise results.

To resize the photo:

▶ **1.** Make sure the PICTURE TOOLS FORMAT tab is still selected on the ribbon.

▶ **2.** In the Size group on the far right edge of the ribbon, locate the Shape Height box, which tells you that the height of the selected picture is currently 2.46". The Shape Width box tells you that the width of the picture is 3.69". As you'll see in the next step, when you change one of these measurements, the other changes accordingly, keeping the overall shape of the picture the same. See Figure 1-37.

Figure 1-37 | **Shape Height and Shape Width boxes**

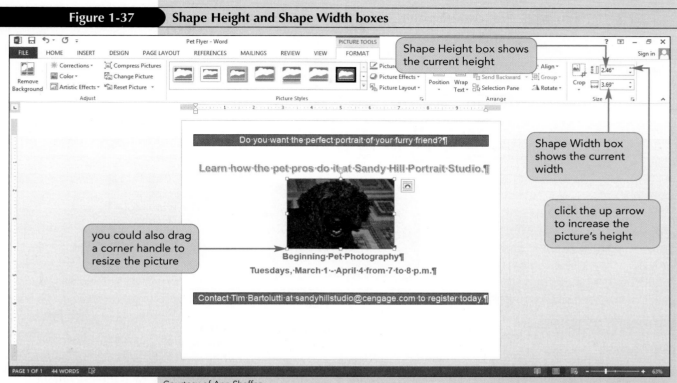

Courtesy of Ann Shaffer

> **3.** Click the **up arrow** in the Shape Height box in the Size group. The photo increases in size slightly. The measurement in the Shape Height box increases to 2.5" and the measurement in the Shape Width box increases to 3.75".

> **4.** Click the **up arrow** in the Shape Height box repeatedly until the picture is 3.3" tall and 4.95" wide.

Finally, to make the photo more noticeable, you can add a **picture style**, which is a collection of formatting options, such as a frame, a rounded shape, and a shadow. You can apply a picture style to a selected picture by clicking the style you want in the Picture Styles gallery on the PICTURE TOOLS FORMAT tab. In the following steps, you'll start by displaying the gallery.

To add a style to the photo:

> **1.** Make sure the PICTURE TOOLS FORMAT tab is still selected on the ribbon.

> **2.** In the Picture Styles group, click the **More** button to the right of the Picture Styles gallery to open the gallery and display more picture styles. Some of the picture styles simply add a border, while others change the picture's shape. Other styles combine these options with effects such as a shadow or a reflection.

> **3.** Place the mouse pointer over various styles to observe the Live Previews in the document, and then place the mouse pointer over the Drop Shadow Rectangle style, which is the middle style in the top row. See Figure 1-38.

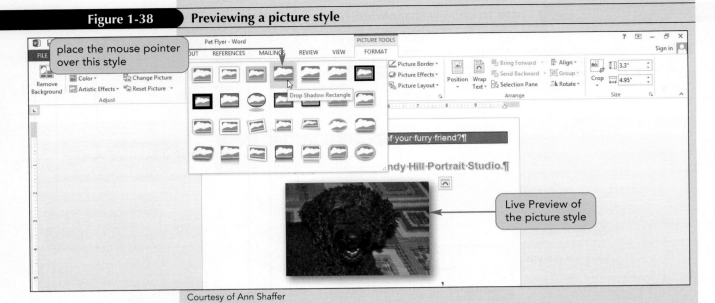

Figure 1-38   Previewing a picture style

Courtesy of Ann Shaffer

4. In the gallery, click the **Drop Shadow Rectangle** style to apply it to the photo and close the gallery. The photo is formatted with a shadow on the bottom and right sides, as shown earlier in the Session 1.2 Visual Overview.

5. Click anywhere outside the photo to deselect it, and then, save the document.

6. Click the **FILE** tab, and then click **Close** in the navigation bar to close the document without closing Word.

INSIGHT

Working with Inline Pictures

By default, when you insert a picture in a document, it is treated as an inline object, which means its position changes in the document as you add or delete text. Also, because it is an inline object, you can align the picture just as you would align text, using the alignment buttons in the Paragraph group on the HOME tab. Essentially, you can treat an inline picture as just another paragraph.

When you become a more advanced Word user, you'll learn how to wrap text around a picture so that the text flows around the picture—with the picture maintaining its position on the page no matter how much text you add to or delete from the document. The alignment buttons don't work on pictures that have text wrapped around them. Instead, you can drag the picture to the desired position on the page.

The flyer is complete and ready for Tim to print later. Because Tim is considering creating a promotional brochure that would include numerous photographs, he asks you to look up information about other ways to format a picture. You can do that using Word's Help system.

Getting Help

To get the most out of Help, your computer must be connected to the Internet so it can access the reference information stored at Office.com.

To look up information in Help:

TIP

You can also open the Word Help window by pressing the F1 key.

1. Verify that your computer is connected to the Internet, and then, on the title bar, click the **Microsoft Word Help** button ?. The Word Help window opens, with its Home page displayed. You might see the topics shown in Figure 1-39, or you might see other topics. You can click the various options in the Word Help window to browse among topics, or you can use the Search online help box to look up information on a particular topic.

Figure 1-39   **Word Help window**

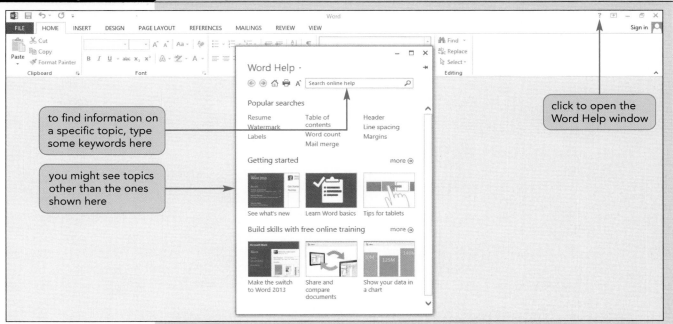

to find information on a specific topic, type some keywords here

you might see topics other than the ones shown here

click to open the Word Help window

2. Click in the **Search online help** box, type **format picture**, and then press the **Enter** key. The Word Help window displays a list of articles related to inserting pictures in a document.

3. Click the first topic listed, and then read the article to see if it contains any information about formatting pictures that might be useful to Tim. Note that to print information about a topic, you can click the Print button near the top of the Word Help window.

4. When are you finished reading the article, click the **Back** button ⊖ near the top of the Word Help window to return to the previous list of topics.

5. Click the **Home** button ⌂ to return to the Home page.

6. Click the **Close** button ✗ in the upper-right corner to close the Word Help window.

Word Help is a great way to learn more about Word's many features. Articles on basic skills provide step-by-step guides for completing tasks, while more elaborate, online tutorials walk you through more complicated tasks. Be sure to take some time on your own to explore Word Help so you can find the information you want when you need it.

REVIEW

Session 1.2 Quick Check

1. Explain how to open the Spelling and Grammar task panes.
2. What is the default page orientation for Word documents?
3. What is the default font size?
4. Explain how to use the Format Painter button.
5. What button do you use to insert a photo in a document?
6. Explain how to open the Help window.

SAM Projects

Put your skills into practice with SAM Projects! SAM Projects for this tutorial can be found online. If you have a SAM account, go to www.cengage.com/sam2013 to download the most recent Project Instructions and Start Files.

Review Assignments

Data Files needed for the Review Assignments: Flower.docx, Mixed Flowers.jpg

Tim asks you to write a cover letter to accompany a wedding photography contract. After that, he wants you to create an envelope for the letter, and to format a flyer announcing a class about photographing flowers. Change the Zoom level as necessary while you are working. Complete the following steps:

1. Open a new, blank document and then save the document as **Sommer Letter** in the location specified by your instructor.

2. Type the date **February 16, 2016** using AutoComplete for "February."

3. Press the Enter key twice, and then type the following inside address, using the default paragraph spacing and pressing the Enter key once after each line:

    Kiley Sommer

    2355 Greenwillow Drive

    Baltimore, MD 21204

4. Type **Dear Ms. Sommer:** as the salutation, press the Enter key, and then type the following as the body of the letter:

    Enclosed you will find the contract summarizing our plans for your wedding. Please return your signed copy to me by next Monday, along with the down payment specified in the contract.

    As you'll see, the second page of the contract lists the specific shots we've already agreed on. For more ideas about possible group shots, please see our website at www.sandyhillstudio. cengage.com. Of course, the photographer will be taking candid shots throughout the day.

5. Press the Enter key, type **Sincerely yours,** as the complimentary closing, press the Enter key three times, type **Tim Bartolutti** as the signature line, insert a manual line break, and type **Sales Manager** as his title.

6. Press the Enter key, type your initials, insert a manual line break, and then use the Undo button to make your initials all lowercase, if necessary.

7. Type **Enclosure** and save the document.

8. Scroll to the beginning of the document and proofread your work. Remove any wavy underlines by using a shortcut menu or by typing a correction yourself. Remove the hyperlink formatting from the web address.

9. Remove the paragraph spacing from the first two lines of the inside address.

10. Change the top margin to 2.75 inches. Leave the other margins at their default settings.

11. Save your changes to the letter, preview it, print it if your instructor asks you to, and then close it.

12. Create a new, blank document, and then create an envelope. Use Kiley Sommer's address (from Step 3) as the delivery address. Use your school's name and address for the return address. Add the envelope to the document. If you are asked if you want to save the return address as the new return address, click No.

13. Save the document as **Sommer Envelope** in the location specified by your instructor, and then close the document.

14. Open the file **Flower**, located in the Word1 ► Review folder included with your Data Files, and then check your screen to make sure your settings match those in the tutorial.

15. Save the document as **Flower Flyer** in the location specified by your instructor.

16. Configure the grammar settings to check for subject-verb agreement errors, and then use the Spelling and Grammar task panes to correct any errors marked with wavy underlines. When you are finished, return the grammar settings to their original configuration.

17. Proofread the document and correct any other errors. Be sure to change "gardens" to "garden's" in the first paragraph.

18. Change the page orientation to Landscape and the margins to Narrow.

19. Format the document text in 22-point Times New Roman font.

20. Center the text and the photo.

21. Format the first paragraph with an outside border, and then add green shading, using the Green, Accent 6, Darker 25% color in the Theme Colors section of the Shading gallery. Format the paragraph text in white.

22. Format the last paragraph in the document using the same formatting you applied to the first paragraph.

23. Increase the paragraph spacing after the first paragraph to 42 points. Increase the paragraph spacing before the last paragraph in the document to 42 points.

24. Format the second paragraph with the Fill - Orange, Accent 2, Outline - Accent 2 text effect. Increase the paragraph's font size to 26 points.

25. Format the third and fourth paragraphs (containing the class name, date, and time) in green, using the Green, Accent 6, Darker 50% font color, and then add bold and italic.

26. Delete the photo and replace it with the **Mixed Flowers.jpg** photo, located in the Word1 ► Review folder included with your Data Files.

27. Resize the new photo so that it is 3.8" tall, and then add the Soft Edge Rectangle style in the Pictures Styles gallery.

28. Save your changes to the flyer, preview it, and then close it.

29. Start Word Help and look up the topic "work with pictures." Read the article, return to the Help home page, and then close Help.

Case Problem 1

APPLY

There are no Data Files needed for this Case Problem.

Prairie Public Health Consultants   You are a program administrator at Prairie Public Health Consultants. Over the past few months, you have collected handwritten surveys from high school students about their exercise habits. Now you need to send the surveys to the researcher in charge of compiling the data. Create a cover letter to accompany the surveys by completing the following steps. Because your office is currently out of letterhead, you'll start the letter by typing a return address. As you type the letter, remember to include the appropriate number of blank paragraphs between the various parts of the letter. Complete the following steps:

1. Open a new, blank document, and then save the document as **Prairie Letter** in the location specified by your instructor. If necessary, change the Zoom level to 120%.

2. Type the following return address, using the default paragraph spacing, and replacing [Your Name] with your first and last names:

[Your Name]

Prairie Public Health Consultants

6833 Erickson Lane

Des Moines, IA 50301

3. Type **November 7, 2016** as the date, leaving a blank paragraph between the last line of the return address and the date.

4. Type the following inside address, using the default paragraph spacing and leaving the appropriate number of blank paragraphs after the date:

Dr. Anna Witinski

4643 University Circle

Ames, IA 50010

5. Type **Dear Dr. Witinski:** as the salutation.

6. To begin the body of the letter, type the following paragraph:

Enclosed please find the surveys I have collected so far. I hope to have another 200 for you in a week, but I thought you would like to get started on these now. After you've had a chance to review the surveys, please call or email me with your answers to these questions:

7. Add the following questions as separate paragraphs, using the default paragraph spacing:

Do you need help tabulating the survey responses?

Should we consider expanding the survey to additional schools?

Should we rephrase any of the survey questions?

8. Insert a new paragraph before the second question, and then add the following as the new second question in the list:

Have you hired a student to help you with your analysis?

9. Insert a new paragraph after the last question, and then type the complimentary closing **Sincerely,** (including the comma).

10. Leave the appropriate amount of space for your signature, type your full name, insert a manual line break, and then type **Program Administrator**.

11. Type **Enclosure** in the appropriate place.

12. Use the Spelling and Grammar task panes to correct any errors. Instruct the Spelling task pane to ignore the recipient's name.

13. Italicize the four paragraphs containing the questions.

14. Remove the paragraph spacing from the first three lines of the return address. Do the same for the first two paragraphs of the inside address.

15. Center the four paragraphs containing the return address, format them in 16-point font, and then add the Fill - Black, Text 1, Shadow text effect.

16. Save the document, preview it, and then close it.

17. Create a new, blank document, and create an envelope. Use Dr. Witinski's address (from Step 4) as the delivery address. Use the return address shown in Step 2. Add the envelope to the document. If you are asked if you want to save the return address as the new return address, click No.

18. Save the document as **Witinski Envelope** in the location specified by your instructor, and then close the document.

Case Problem 2

Data Files needed for this Case Problem: Church.jpg, Walking.docx

Walking Tours of Old San Juan You work as the guest services coordinator at Hotel Azul, a luxury resort hotel in San Juan, Puerto Rico. You need to create a flyer promoting a daily walking tour of Old San Juan, the historic Colonial section of Puerto Rico's capital city. Complete the following steps:

1. Open the file **Walking** located in the Word1 ▶ Case2 folder included with your Data Files, and then save the document as **Walking Tour Flyer** in the location specified by your instructor.

2. In the document, replace "Student Name" with your first and last names.

3. Use the Spelling and Grammar task panes to correct any errors, including problems with subject-verb agreement. Instruct the Spelling task pane to ignore the Spanish church names, as well as your name if Word marks it with a wavy underline.

4. Change the page margins to Narrow.

5. Complete the flyer as shown in Figure 1-40. Use the file **Church.jpg** located in the Word1 ▶ Case2 folder included with your Data Files. Use the default line spacing and paragraph spacing unless otherwise specified in Figure 1-40.

Figure 1-40 **Formatted Walking Tour flyer**

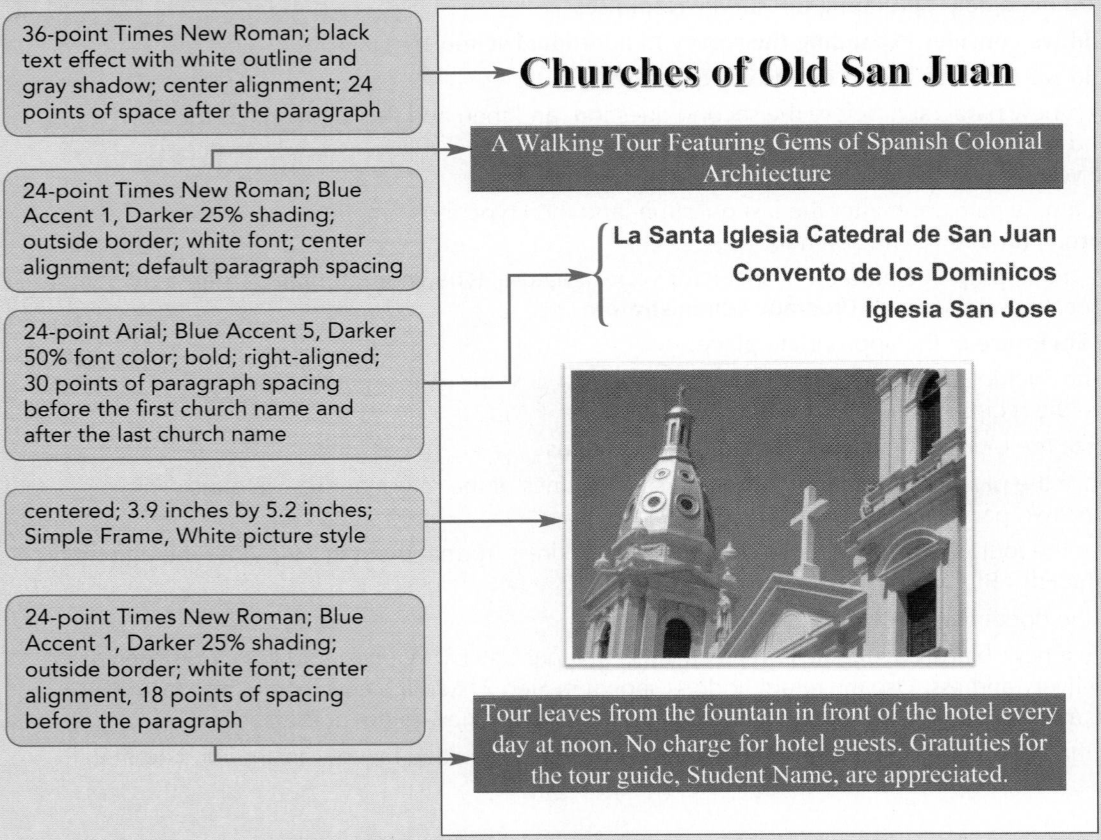

36-point Times New Roman; black text effect with white outline and gray shadow; center alignment; 24 points of space after the paragraph

24-point Times New Roman; Blue Accent 1, Darker 25% shading; outside border; white font; center alignment; default paragraph spacing

24-point Arial; Blue Accent 5, Darker 50% font color; bold; right-aligned; 30 points of paragraph spacing before the first church name and after the last church name

centered; 3.9 inches by 5.2 inches; Simple Frame, White picture style

24-point Times New Roman; Blue Accent 1, Darker 25% shading; outside border; white font; center alignment, 18 points of spacing before the paragraph

Churches of Old San Juan

A Walking Tour Featuring Gems of Spanish Colonial Architecture

La Santa Iglesia Catedral de San Juan

Convento de los Dominicos

Iglesia San Jose

Tour leaves from the fountain in front of the hotel every day at noon. No charge for hotel guests. Gratuities for the tour guide, Student Name, are appreciated.

Courtesy of Ann Shaffer

6. Save the document, preview it, and then close it.

TROUBLESHOOT

Case Problem 3

Data Files needed for this Case Problem: Mushroom.docx, Mycology.docx

Green Valley Arborists You work as the office manager for Green Valley Arborists, a tree care service in Billings, Montana. One of the company's arborists noticed a bright orange fungus growing on a tree stump in a client's backyard. She has started writing a letter to a mycologist at the local community college to ask if he can identify the fungus. The letter is almost finished, but the arborist needs help correcting errors and formatting the text to match the block style. The photo itself is stored in a separate document. The arborist mistakenly applied a picture style to the photo that is inappropriate for professional correspondence. She asks you to remove the picture style and then format the page. Complete the following steps:

1. Open the file **Mycology** located in the Word1 ▶ Case3 folder included with your Data Files, and then save the document as **Mycology Letter** in the location specified by your instructor.

2. Use the Spelling and Grammar task panes to correct any errors, including subject-verb errors. When you are finished, return the Grammar settings to their original configuration.

⚙ **Troubleshoot** 3. Make any necessary changes to ensure that the letter matches the formatting of a block style business letter, including the appropriate paragraph spacing. Keep in mind that the letter will include an enclosure. Include your initials where appropriate.

⚙ **Troubleshoot** 4. The letterhead for Green Valley Arborists requires a top margin of 2.5 inches. Determine if the layout of the letter will work with the letterhead, make any necessary changes, and then save the letter.

5. Save the document and preview it.

6. With the letter still open, create an envelope. Use the delivery address taken from the letter, but edit the delivery address. Click the Omit check box to deselect it (if necessary), and then, for the return address, type your school's name and address. Add the envelope to the document. If you are asked if you want to save the return address as the new default return address, answer No.

7. Save the document, preview it, and then close it.

8. Open the file **Mushroom** located in the Word1 ▶ Case3 folder included with your Data Files, and then save the document as **Mushroom Photo** in the location specified by your instructor.

⚙ **Troubleshoot** 9. Reset the picture to its original appearance, before the arborist mistakenly added the style with the reflection.

⚙ **Troubleshoot** 10. Modify the page layout and adjust the size of the photo so the photo fills as much of the page as possible without overlapping the page margins.

11. Save the document, preview it, and then close it.

CHALLENGE

Case Problem 4

There are no Data Files needed for this Case Problem.

Hapsburg Interior Design   As a design assistant at Hapsburg Interior Design, you are responsible for distributing manufacturer samples throughout the office so the firm's designers can stay up to date on newly available paint colors, wallpaper patterns, and fabrics. Along with each sample, you need to include an explanatory memo. Complete the following steps:

✛ **Explore** 1. Open a new document—but instead of selecting the Blank document option, search for a memo template online. In the list of search results, click the Memo (Simple design) template, and then click the Create button. A memo template opens in the Word window. Above the memo template is the Document Properties panel, where you could enter information about the document that might be useful later. You don't need the panel for this project, so you can ignore it, as well as any entries in the text boxes in the panel.

2. Save the document as **Samples Memo** in the location specified by your instructor. If you see a dialog box indicating that the document will be upgraded to the newest file format, click the OK button. Note that of the hundreds of templates available online, only a small portion have been created in the most recent version of Word, so you will often see this dialog box when working with templates.

✛ **Explore** 3. In the document, click the text "[Company name]." The placeholder text appears in a box with gray highlighting. The box containing the highlighted text (with the small rectangle attached) is called a document control. You can enter text in a document control just as you enter text in a dialog box. Type **Hapsburg Interior Design**, and then press the Tab key. The "[Recipient names]" placeholder text now appears in a document control next to the word "To." (*Hint*: As you work on the memo in the following steps, keep in mind that if you accidentally double-click the word "memo" at the top of the document, you will access the header portion of the document, which is normally closed to editing. In that case, press the Esc key to return to the main document.)

4. Type **All Designers** and then press the Tab key twice. A document control is now visible to the right of the word "From." Depending on how your computer is set up, you might see your name or another name here, or the document control might be empty. Delete the name, if necessary, and then type your first and last names.

✛ **Explore** 5. Continue using the Tab key to edit the remaining document controls as indicated below. If you press the Tab key too many times and accidentally skip a document control, you can click the document control to select it.

   - In the CC: document control, delete the placeholder text.
   - In the Date document control, click the down arrow, and then click the current date in the calendar.
   - In the Re: document control, type **Rowley Fabrics**.
   - In the Comments document control, type **Here are the latest offerings from Rowley Fabrics. After you have reviewed the collection, please write your initials at the bottom of this memo and pass the collection on to another designer. If you are the last of the group to review the samples, please return them to my desk. Thank you.**

6. Use the Spelling and Grammar task panes to correct any underlined errors, and then proofread the document to look for any additional errors.

7. Save the document, preview it, and then close it.

Navigating and Formatting a Document

Editing an Academic Document According to MLA Style

OBJECTIVES

Session 2.1
- Read, reply to, delete, and add comments
- Create bulleted and numbered lists
- Move text using drag and drop
- Cut and paste text
- Copy and paste text
- Navigate through a document using the Navigation pane
- Find and replace text
- Format text with styles
- Apply a theme to a document

Session 2.2
- Review the MLA style for research papers
- Indent paragraphs
- Insert and modify page numbers
- Create citations
- Create and update a bibliography
- Modify a source

Case | *Rivas-Garcia College*

Kaya Cho, a student at Rivas-Garcia College, works part-time in the college's Media Studies department. She has written a handout describing the requirements for a Media Studies major, and asks you to help her finish it. The text of the handout needs some reorganization and other editing. It also needs formatting so the finished document looks professional and is easy to read.

Kaya is also taking a Media Studies class this semester, and is writing a research paper on the history of newspapers. To complete the paper, she needs to follow a set of very specific formatting and style guidelines for academic documents.

Kaya has asked you to help her edit these two very different documents. In Session 2.1, you will review and respond to some comments in the handout, and then revise and format that document. In Session 2.2, you will review the MLA style for research papers, and then format Kaya's research paper to match the MLA specifications.

STARTING DATA FILES

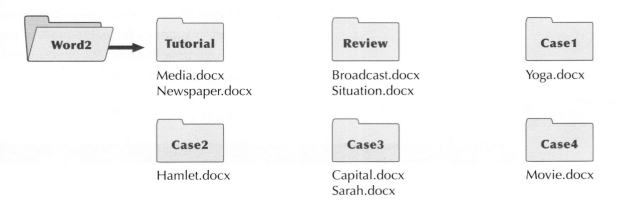

Word2 → Tutorial
Media.docx
Newspaper.docx

Review
Broadcast.docx
Situation.docx

Case1
Yoga.docx

Case2
Hamlet.docx

Case3
Capital.docx
Sarah.docx

Case4
Movie.docx

Session 2.1 Visual Overview:

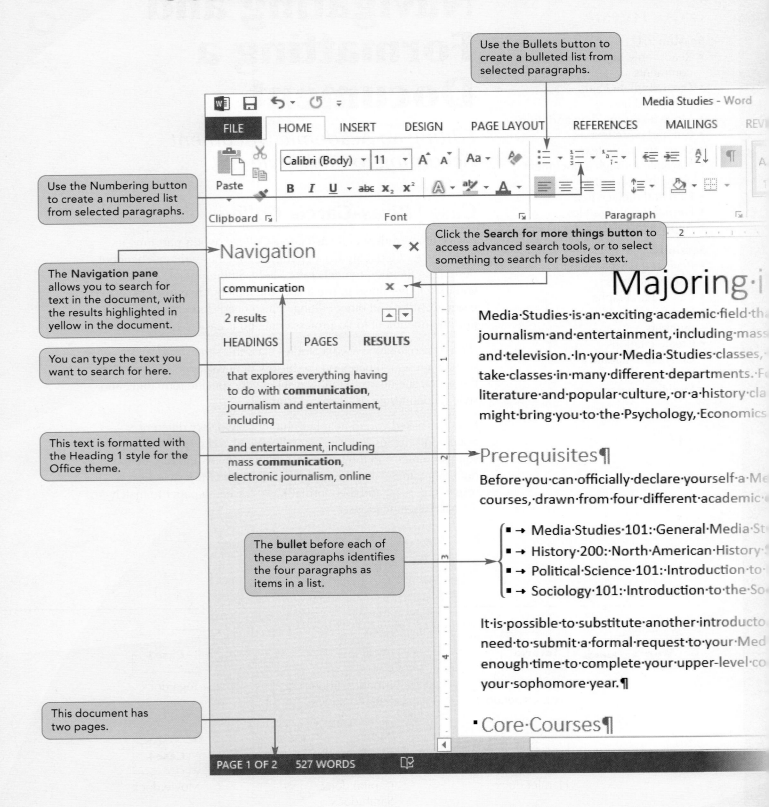

Use the Bullets button to create a bulleted list from selected paragraphs.

Use the Numbering button to create a numbered list from selected paragraphs.

Click the **Search for more things button** to access advanced search tools, or to select something to search for besides text.

The **Navigation pane** allows you to search for text in the document, with the results highlighted in yellow in the document.

You can type the text you want to search for here.

This text is formatted with the Heading 1 style for the Office theme.

The **bullet** before each of these paragraphs identifies the four paragraphs as items in a list.

This document has two pages.

Media Studies - Word

FILE   HOME   INSERT   DESIGN   PAGE LAYOUT   REFERENCES   MAILINGS   REVI

Calibri (Body)   11

Paste

Clipboard   Font   Paragraph

Navigation

communication   X

2 results

HEADINGS   PAGES   **RESULTS**

that explores everything having to do with **communication**, journalism and entertainment, including

and entertainment, including mass **communication**, electronic journalism, online

Majoring i

Media·Studies·is·an·exciting·academic·field·tha
journalism·and·entertainment,·including·mass
and·television.·In·your·Media·Studies·classes,·
take·classes·in·many·different·departments.·Fe
literature·and·popular·culture,·or·a·history·cla
might·bring·you·to·the·Psychology,·Economics

Prerequisites¶

Before·you·can·officially·declare·yourself·a·Me
courses,·drawn·from·four·different·academic·

■ → Media·Studies·101:·General·Media·St
■ → History·200:·North·American·History·
■ → Political·Science·101:·Introduction·to·
■ → Sociology·101:·Introduction·to·the·So

It·is·possible·to·substitute·another·introducto
need·to·submit·a·formal·request·to·your·Med
enough·time·to·complete·your·upper-level·co
your·sophomore·year.¶

Core·Courses¶

PAGE 1 OF 2   527 WORDS

Working with Lists and Styles

Styles allow you to apply a set of formatting options with one click in the Style gallery.

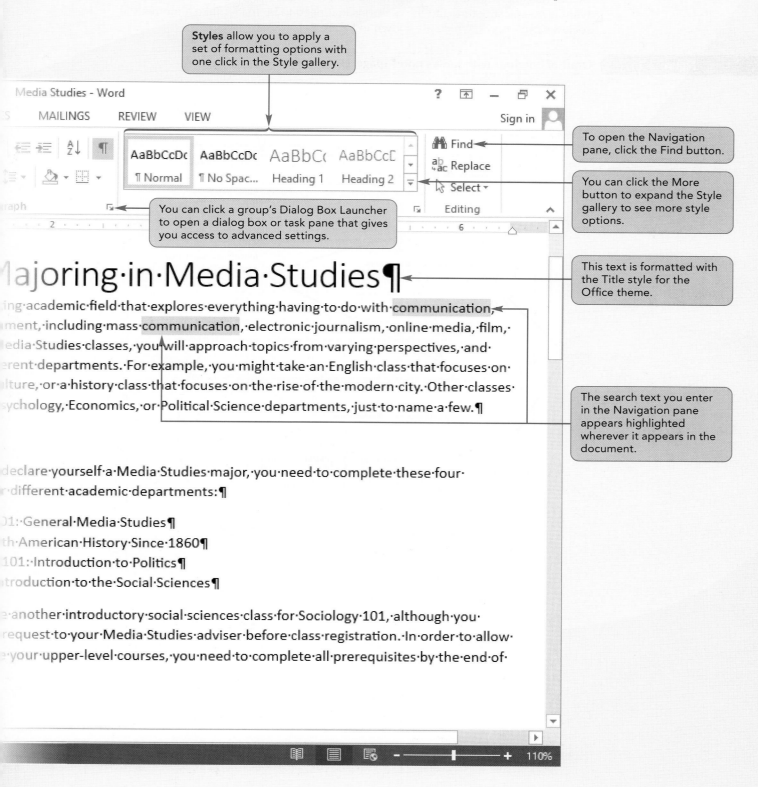

To open the Navigation pane, click the Find button.

You can click the More button to expand the Style gallery to see more style options.

You can click a group's Dialog Box Launcher to open a dialog box or task pane that gives you access to advanced settings.

This text is formatted with the Title style for the Office theme.

The search text you enter in the Navigation pane appears highlighted wherever it appears in the document.

Reviewing the Document

Before revising a document for someone else, it's a good idea to familiarize yourself with its overall structure and the revisions that need to be made. Take a moment to review Kaya's notes, which are shown in Figure 2-1.

Figure 2-1   Draft of handout with Kaya's notes (page 1)

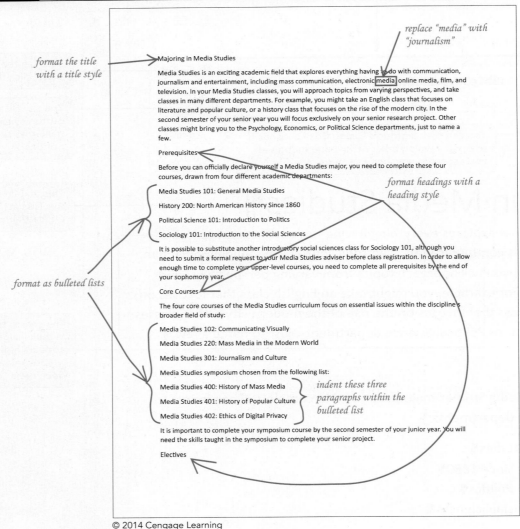

© 2014 Cengage Learning

Figure 2-1   **Draft of handout with Kaya's notes (page 2)**

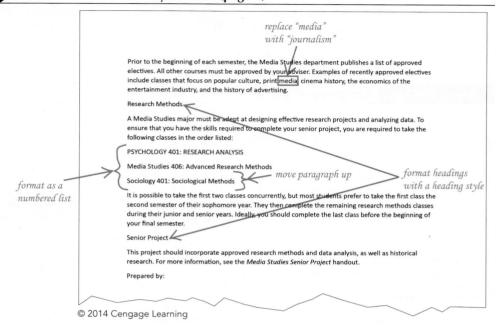

© 2014 Cengage Learning

Kaya also included additional guidance in some comments she added to the document file. A **comment** is like an electronic sticky note attached to a word, phrase, or paragraph in a document. Comments appear in the margin, along with the name of the person who added them. Within a single document, you can add new comments, reply to existing comments, and delete comments.

You will open the document now, save it with a new name, and then review Kaya's comments in Word.

To open and rename the document:

1. Open the document named **Media** located in the Word2 ▶ Tutorial folder included with your Data Files.

2. Save the document as **Media Studies** in the location specified by your instructor.

3. Verify that the document is displayed in Print Layout view, that the zoom is set to **120%**, and that the rulers and nonprinting characters are displayed.

4. On the ribbon, click the **REVIEW** tab to display the tools used for working with comments. Comments can be displayed in several different ways, so your first step is to make sure the comments in the Media Studies document are displayed to match the figures in this book—using Simple Markup view.

5. In the Tracking group, click the **Display for Review** arrow, and then click **Simple Markup** to select it, if necessary. At this point, you might see comment icons to the right of the document text, or you might see the full text of each comment.

6. In the Comments group, click the **Show Comments** button several times to practice displaying and hiding the comments, and then, when you are finished, make sure the Show Comments button is selected so the full text of each comment is displayed.

▶ **7.** At the bottom of the Word window, drag the horizontal scroll bar all the way to the right so you can read the full text of each comment. See Figure 2-2. Note that the comments on your screen might be a different color than the ones shown in the figure.

Figure 2-2   Comments displayed in the document

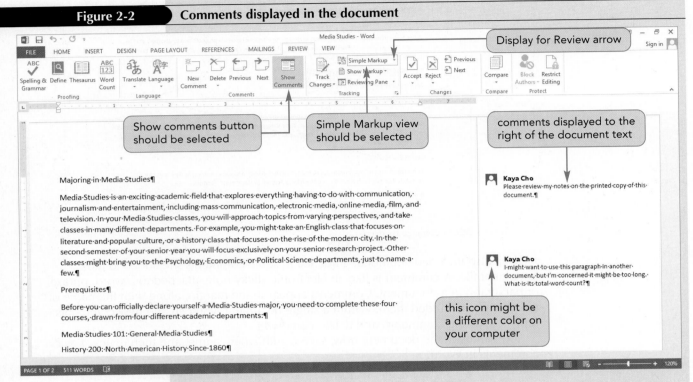

Note that when working on a small monitor, it can be helpful to switch the document Zoom level to Page Width, in which case Word automatically reduces the width of the document to accommodate the comments on the right.

▶ **8.** Read the document, including the comments. The handout includes the title "Majoring in Media Studies" at the top, as well as headings (such as "Prerequisites" and "Core Courses") that divide the document into parts. Right now the headings are hard to spot because they don't look different from the surrounding text. Kaya used the default font size, 11-point, and the default font, Calibri (Body), for all the text in the document. Note, too, that the document includes some short paragraphs that would work better as bulleted or numbered lists.

▶ **9.** Scroll down until you can see the first line on page 2, which begins "Prior to the beginning of each semester…." and then click anywhere in that sentence. The message "PAGE 2 OF 2" in the status bar, in the lower-left corner of the Word window, tells you that the insertion point is currently located on page 2 of the two-page document. The shaded space between the first and second pages of the document indicates a page break. To hide the top and bottom margins in a document, as well as the space between pages, you can double-click the shaded space between any two pages.

▶ **10.** Position the mouse pointer over the shaded space between page 1 and page 2 until the pointer changes to ⬌, and then double-click. The shaded space disappears. Instead, the two pages are now separated by a gray, horizontal line.

Trouble? If the HEADER & FOOTER TOOLS DESIGN tab appears on the ribbon, you double-clicked the top or bottom of one of the pages, instead of in the space between them. Click the Close Header and Footer button on the DESIGN tab, and then repeat Step 10.

▶ **11.** Use the ╬ pointer to double-click the gray horizontal line between pages 1 and 2. The shaded space between the two pages is redisplayed.

Working with Comments

Now that you are familiar with the Media Studies document, you can review and respond to Kaya's comments. The Comment group on the REVIEW tab includes helpful tools for working with comments.

REFERENCE

Working with Comments

- On the ribbon, click the REVIEW tab.
- To display comments in an easy-to-read view, in the Tracking group, click the Display for Review button, and then click Simple Markup.
- To see the text of each comment in Simple Markup view, click the Show Comments button in the Comments group.
- To move the insertion point to the next or previous comment in the document, click the Next button or the Previous button in the Comments group.
- To delete a comment, click anywhere in the comment, and then click the Delete button in the Comments group.
- To delete all the comments in a document, click the Delete button arrow in the Comments group, and then click Delete All Comments in Document.
- To add a new comment, select the document text you want to comment on, click the New Comment button in the Comments group, and then type the comment text.
- To reply to a comment, click the Reply button to the right of the comment, and then type your reply.
- To indicate that a comment or an individual reply to a comment is no longer a concern, right-click the comment or reply, and then click Mark Comment Done in the shortcut menu. To mark a comment and all of the replies attached to it as done, right-click the original comment and then click Mark Comment Done.

To review and respond to the comments in the document:

▶ **1.** Press the **Ctrl+Home** keys to move the insertion point to the beginning of the document.

▶ **2.** On the REVIEW tab, in the Comments group, click the **Next** button. The first comment now has an outline, indicating that it is selected. See Figure 2-3.

In the document, the word "Majoring" is highlighted. A line connects the comment to the word "Majoring," indicating that the comment is attached to that word. Because Kaya created the comment, her name appears at the beginning of the comment, followed by the date on which she created it. The insertion point blinks at the beginning of the comment, and is ready for you to edit the comment if you want.

| Figure 2-3 | Comment attached to document text |

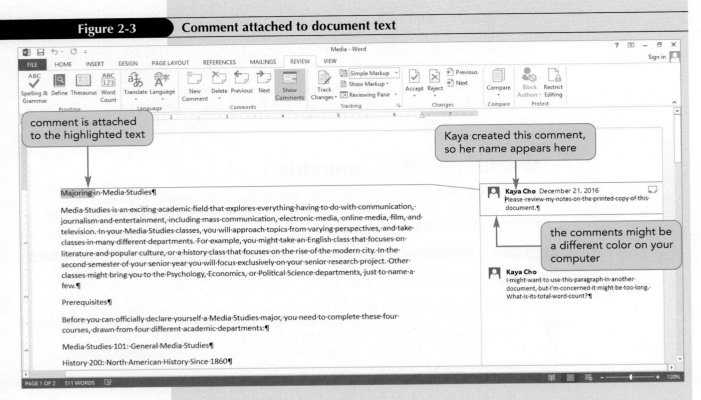

3. Read the comment, and then in the Comments group, click the **Next** button to select the next comment. According to this comment, Kaya wants to know the total word count of the paragraph the comment is attached to. You can get this information by selecting the entire paragraph and locating the word count in the status bar.

4. Triple-click anywhere in the second paragraph of the document (which begins "Media studies is an exciting academic field…") to select the paragraph. In the status bar, the message "110 of 511" tells you that 110 of the document's 511 words are currently selected. So the answer to Kaya's question is 110.

5. Point to the second comment to select it again, click the **Reply** button 🗨️, and then type **110**. Your reply appears below Kaya's original comment.

Trouble? If you do not see the Reply button in the comment box, drag the horizontal scroll bar at the bottom of the Word window to the right until you can see it.

The name that appears in your reply comment is taken from the User name box in the General tab of the Word Options dialog box. If your name is the username for your computer, your name appears attached to the comment. If you are working on a shared computer at school, or on a computer owned by someone else, another name will appear in the comment.

You can quickly open the General tab of the Word Options dialog box by clicking the Dialog Box Launcher in the Tracking group on the REVIEW tab, and then clicking Change User Name. From there, you can change the username and the initials associated with your copy of Word. However, there is no need to change these settings for this tutorial, and you should never change them on a shared computer at school unless specifically instructed to do so by your instructor.

6. In the Comments group, click the **Next** button to move the insertion point to the next comment, which asks you to insert your name after "Prepared by:" at the end of the document.

7. Click after the colon in "Prepared by:", press the **spacebar**, and then type your first and last name. To indicate that you have complied with Kaya's request by adding your name, you could right-click the comment, and then click Mark Comment Done. However, in this case, you'll simply delete the comment. Kaya also asks you to delete the first comment in the document.

8. Click anywhere in the final comment, and then in the Comments group, click the **Delete** button.

9. In the Comments group, click the **Previous** button three times to select the comment at the beginning of the document, and then click the **Delete** button to delete the comment.

As you reviewed the document, you might have noticed that, on page 2, one of the class names in the Research Methods section appears in all uppercase letters. This is probably just a typing mistake. You can correct it, and then add a comment that points out the change to Kaya.

To correct the mistake and add a comment:

1. Scroll down to page 2, and then select the fourth paragraph on the page, which contains the text "PSYCHOLOGY 401: RESEARCH ANALYSIS."

2. On the ribbon, click the **HOME** tab.

3. In the Font group, click the **Change Case** button Aa ▾, and then click **Capitalize Each Word**. The text changes to read "Psychology 401: Research Analysis."

4. Verify that the paragraph is still selected, and then click the **REVIEW** tab on the ribbon.

5. In the Comments group, click the **New Comment** button. A new comment appears, with the insertion point ready for you to begin typing.

6. In the new comment, type **I assumed you didn't want this all uppercase, so I changed it.** and then save the document.

   You can now hide the text of the comments because you are finished working with them.

7. In the Comments group, click the **Show Comments** button. You now see a comment icon in the document margin rather than on the right side of the Word screen. A comment icon alerts you to the presence of a comment without taking up all the space required to display the comment text. You can click a comment icon to read a particular comment without displaying the text of all the comments.

8. Click the comment icon ⌨. The comment icon is highlighted, and the full comment is displayed, as shown in Figure 2-4.

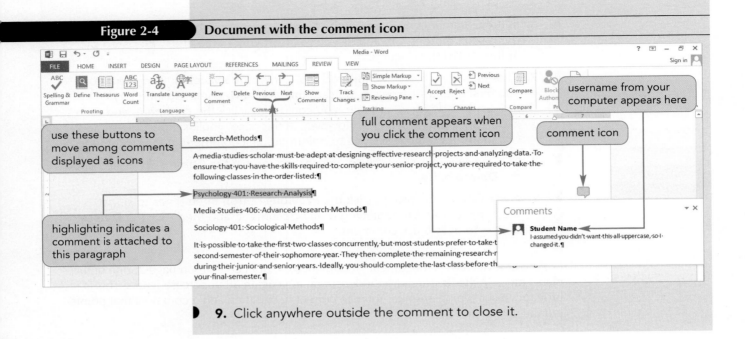

Figure 2-4　　**Document with the comment icon**

9. Click anywhere outside the comment to close it.

Creating Bulleted and Numbered Lists

A **bulleted list** is a group of related paragraphs with a black circle or other character to the left of each paragraph. For a group of related paragraphs that have a particular order (such as steps in a procedure), you can use consecutive numbers instead of bullets to create a **numbered list**. If you insert a new paragraph, delete a paragraph, or reorder the paragraphs in a numbered list, Word adjusts the numbers to make sure they remain consecutive.

PROSKILLS

Written Communication: Organizing Information in Lists

Bulleted and numbered lists are both great ways to draw the reader's attention to information. But it's important to know how to use them. Use numbers when your list contains items that are arranged by priority in a specific order. For example, in a document reviewing the procedure for performing CPR, it makes sense to use numbers for the sequential steps. Use bullets when the items in the list are of equal importance, or when they can be accomplished in any order. For example, in a resume, you could use bullets for a list of professional certifications.

To add bullets to a series of paragraphs, you use the Bullets button in the Paragraph group on the HOME tab. To create a numbered list, you use the Numbering button in the Paragraph group instead. Both the Bullets button and the Numbering button have arrows you can click to open a gallery of bullet or numbering styles.

Kaya asks you to format the list of prerequisites on page 1 as a bulleted list. She also asks you to format the list of core courses on page 1 as a separate bulleted list. Finally, you need to format the list of research methods classes on page 2 as a numbered list.

To apply bullets to paragraphs:

1. Scroll up until you see the paragraphs containing the list of prerequisites, which begins with "Media Studies 101: General Media Studies," and then select this paragraph and the three that follow it.

2. On the ribbon, click the **HOME** tab.

3. In the Paragraph group, click the **Bullets** button. Black circles appear as bullets before each item in the list. Also, the bulleted list is indented and the paragraph spacing between the items is reduced.

After reviewing the default, round bullet in the document, Kaya decides she would prefer square bullets.

4. In the Paragraph group, click the **Bullets button arrow**. A gallery of bullet styles opens. See Figure 2-5.

Figure 2-5 | **Bullets gallery**

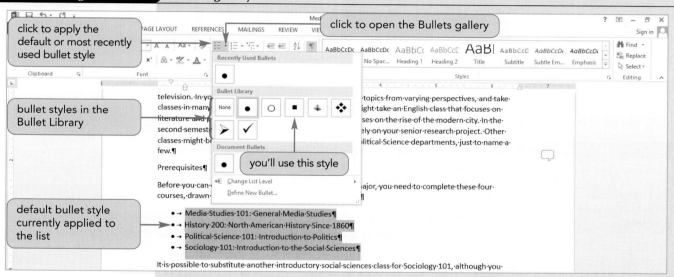

- click to apply the default or most recently used bullet style
- click to open the Bullets gallery
- bullet styles in the Bullet Library
- you'll use this style
- default bullet style currently applied to the list

The Recently Used Bullets section appears at the top of the gallery of bullet styles; it displays the bullet styles that have been used since you started Word, which, in this case, is just the round black bullet style that was applied by default when you clicked the Bullets button. The **Bullet Library**, which offers a variety of bullet styles, is shown below the Recently Used Bullets. To create your own bullets from a picture file or from a set of predesigned symbols including diamonds, hearts, or Greek letters, click Define New Bullet, and then click the Symbol button or the Picture button in the Define New Bullet dialog box.

5. Move the mouse pointer over the bullet styles in the Bullet Library to see a Live Preview of the bullet styles in the document. Kaya prefers the black square style.

6. In the Bullet Library, click the **black square**. The round bullets are replaced with square bullets.

Next, you need to format the list of core courses on page 1 with square bullets. When you first start Word, the Bullets button applies the default, round bullets you saw earlier. But after you select a new bullet style, the Bullets button applies the last bullet style you used. So, to add square bullets to the decorating styles list, you just have to select the list and click the Bullets button.

To add bullets to the list of core courses:

▶ 1. Scroll down in the document and select the paragraphs listing the core courses, starting with "Media Studies 102: Communicating Visually" and ending with "Media Studies 402: Ethics of Digital Privacy."

▶ 2. In the Paragraph group, click the **Bullets** button ⊞. The list is now formatted with square black bullets.

The list is finished except for one issue. A Media Studies major only needs to take one of the last three classes in the list, but that's not clear because of the way the list is currently formatted. To clarify this information, you can use the Increase Indent button in the Paragraph group to indent the last three bullets. When you do this, Word inserts a different style bullet to make the indented paragraphs visually subordinate to the bulleted paragraphs above.

To indent the last three bullets:

▶ 1. In the list of core courses, select the last three paragraphs.

▶ 2. In the Paragraph group, click the **Increase Indent** button ⊞. The three paragraphs move to the right, and the black square bullets are replaced with open circle bullets.

TIP

To remove the indent from selected text, click the Decrease Indent button in the Paragraph group.

Next, you will format the list of research methods classes on page 2. Kaya wants you to format this information as a numbered list because the classes must be taken in a specific order.

To apply numbers to the list of research methods classes:

▶ 1. Scroll down to page 2 until you see the "Psychology 401: Research Analysis" paragraph. You added a comment to this paragraph earlier, but that will have no effect on the process of creating the numbered list.

▶ 2. Select the three paragraphs containing the list of research methods classes, starting with "Psychology 401: Research Analysis" and ending with "Sociology 401: Sociological Methods."

▶ 3. In the Paragraph group, click the **Numbering** button ⊞. Consecutive numbers appear in front of each item in the list. See Figure 2-6.

| Figure 2-6 | Numbered list |

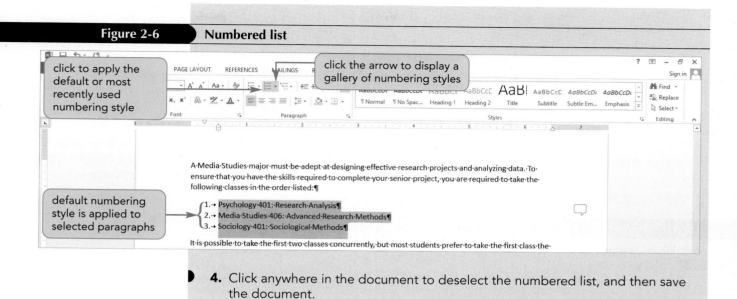

click to apply the default or most recently used numbering style

click the arrow to display a gallery of numbering styles

default numbering style is applied to selected paragraphs

A·Media·Studies·major·must·be·adept·at·designing·effective·research·projects·and·analyzing·data.·To·ensure·that·you·have·the·skills·required·to·complete·your·senior·project,·you·are·required·to·take·the·following·classes·in·the·order·listed:¶

1.→ Psychology·401:·Research·Analysis¶
2.→ Media·Studies·406:·Advanced·Research·Methods¶
3.→ Sociology·401:·Sociological·Methods¶

It·is·possible·to·take·the·first·two·classes·concurrently,·but·most·students·prefer·to·take·the·first·class·the·

4. Click anywhere in the document to deselect the numbered list, and then save the document.

TIP

The Numbering button is a toggle button, which means you can click it to add or remove numbering from selected text.

As with the Bullets button arrow, you can click the Numbering button arrow and then select from a library of numbering styles. You can also indent paragraphs in a numbered list to create an outline, in which case the indented paragraphs will be preceded by lowercase letters instead of numbers. To apply a different list style to the outline (for example, with Roman numerals and uppercase letters), select the list, click the Multilevel List button in the Paragraph group, and then click a multilevel list style.

Moving Text in a Document

One of the most useful features of a word-processing program is the ability to move text easily. For example, Kaya wants to reorder the information in the numbered list. You could do this by deleting a paragraph and then retyping it at a new location. However, it's easier to select and then move the text. Word provides several ways to move text—drag and drop, cut and paste, and copy and paste.

Dragging and Dropping Text

To move text with **drag and drop**, you select the text you want to move, press and hold the mouse button while you drag the selected text to a new location, and then release the mouse button.

In the numbered list you just created, Kaya wants you to move the paragraph that reads "Sociology 401 Sociological Methods" up so it is the first item in the list.

To move text using drag and drop:

1. Select the third paragraph in the numbered list, "Sociology 401: Sociological Methods," being sure to include the paragraph marker at the end. The number 3 remains unselected because it's not actually part of the paragraph text.

2. Position the pointer over the selected text. The pointer changes to a left-facing arrow.

3. Press and hold the mouse button until the drag-and-drop pointer appears. A dark black insertion point appears within the selected text.

4. Without releasing the mouse button, drag the pointer to the beginning of the list until the insertion point is positioned to the left of the "P" in "Psychology 401: Research Analysis." Use the insertion point, rather than the mouse pointer, to guide the text to its new location. See Figure 2-7.

Trouble? If the numbers in the numbered list appear highlighted in gray, you moved the mouse pointer too close to the numbers. Ignore the highlighting and position the insertion point just to the left of the "P" in "Psychology 401: Research Analysis."

Figure 2-7	**Moving text with the drag-and-drop pointer**

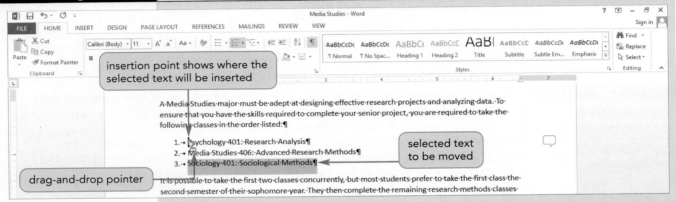

5. Release the mouse button, and then click a blank area of the document to deselect the text. The text "Sociology 401: Sociological Methods" is now the first item in the list, and the remaining paragraphs have been renumbered as paragraphs 2 and 3. See Figure 2-8.

Figure 2-8	**Text in new location**

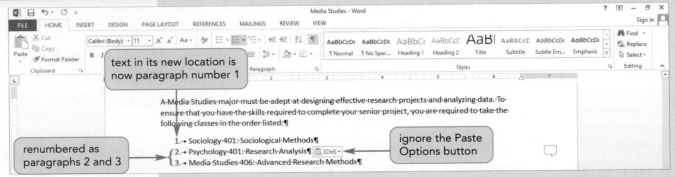

The Paste Options button appears near the newly inserted text, providing access to more advanced options related to pasting text. You don't need to use the Paste Options button right now; it will disappear when you start performing another task.

Trouble? If the selected text moves to the wrong location, click the Undo button 🔄 on the Quick Access Toolbar, and then repeat Steps 2 through 5.

▶ **6.** Save the document.

Dragging and dropping works well when you are moving text a short distance. When you are moving text from one page to another, it's easier to cut, copy, and paste text using the Clipboard.

Cutting or Copying and Pasting Text Using the Clipboard

The **Office Clipboard** is a temporary storage area on your computer that holds objects such as text or graphics until you need them. To **cut** means to remove text or another item from a document and place it on the Clipboard. Once you've cut something, you can paste it somewhere else. To **copy** means to copy a selected item to the Clipboard, leaving the item in its original location. To **paste** means to insert a copy of whatever is on the Clipboard into the document, at the insertion point. When you paste an item from the Clipboard into a document, the item remains on the Clipboard so you can paste it again somewhere else if you want. The buttons for cutting, copying, and pasting are located in the Clipboard group on the HOME tab.

By default, Word pastes text in a new location in a document with the same formatting it had in its old location. To select other ways to paste text, you can use the Paste Options button, which appears next to newly pasted text, or the Paste button arrow in the Clipboard group. Both buttons display a menu of paste options. Two particularly useful paste options are Merge Formatting, which combines the formatting of the copied text with the formatting of the text in the new location, and Keep Text Only, which inserts the text using the formatting of the surrounding text in the new location.

When you need to keep track of multiple pieces of cut or copied text, it's helpful to open the **Clipboard task pane**, which displays the contents of the Clipboard. You open the Clipboard task pane by clicking the Dialog Box Launcher in the Clipboard group on the HOME tab. When the Clipboard task pane is displayed, the Clipboard can store up to 24 text items. When the Clipboard task pane is *not* displayed, the Clipboard can hold only the most recently copied item.

Kaya would like to move the second-to-last sentence under the heading "Majoring in Media Studies" on page 1. You'll use cut and paste to move this sentence to a new location.

To move text using cut and paste:

▶ **1.** Make sure the HOME tab is selected on the ribbon.

▶ **2.** Scroll up until you can see the second paragraph in the document, just below the heading "Majoring in Media Studies."

▶ **3.** Press and hold the **Ctrl** key, and then click anywhere in the sentence near the end of the second paragraph, which begins "In the second semester of your senior year...." The entire sentence and the space following it are selected.

TIP

You can also press the Ctrl+X keys to cut selected text. Press the Ctrl+V keys to paste the most recently copied item.

4. In the Clipboard group, click the **Cut** button. The selected text is removed from the document and copied to the Clipboard.

5. Scroll down to page 2, and then click at the beginning of the second-to-last paragraph in the document, just to the left of the "T" in "This project should...."

6. In the Clipboard group, click the **Paste** button. The sentence and the space following it are displayed in the new location. The Paste Options button appears near the newly inserted sentence.

> **Trouble?** If a menu opens below the Paste button, you clicked the Paste button arrow instead of the Paste button. Press the Esc key to close the menu, and then repeat Step 6, taking care not to click the arrow below the Paste button.

7. Save the document.

Kaya explains that she'll be using some text from the Media Studies document as the basis for another department handout. She asks you to copy that information and paste it into a new document. You can do this using the Clipboard task pane.

To copy text to paste into a new document:

1. In the Clipboard group, click the **Dialog Box Launcher**. The Clipboard task pane opens on the left side of the document window, as shown in Figure 2-9.

Figure 2-9   **Clipboard task pane**

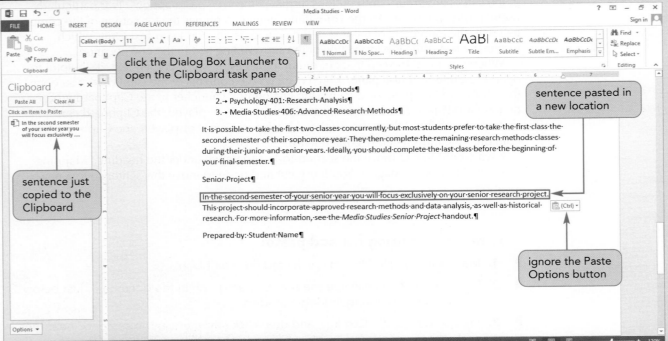

Notice the Clipboard contains the sentence you copied in the last set of steps, although you can only see the first part of the sentence. You'll copy the last two sentences in the current paragraph for use in Kaya's other document.

2. Select the text **This project should incorporate approved research methods and data analysis, as well as historical research. For more information, see the *Media Studies Senior Project* handout.** Do not select the paragraph mark.

TIP

You can also copy selected text by pressing the Ctrl+C keys.

3. In the Clipboard group, click the **Copy** button. The first few words of the text appear at the top of the Clipboard task pane, but in fact the entire two sentences are now stored on the Clipboard.

4. Click anywhere in the document to deselect the text, scroll up, if necessary, and then locate the first sentence on page 2.

5. Press and hold the **Ctrl** key, and then click anywhere in the first sentence on page 2, which begins "A Media Studies major must be adept...." The sentence and the space following it are selected.

6. In the Clipboard group, click the **Copy** button. The first part of the sentence appears at the top of the Clipboard task pane, as shown in Figure 2-10.

Figure 2-10	Items in the Clipboard task pane

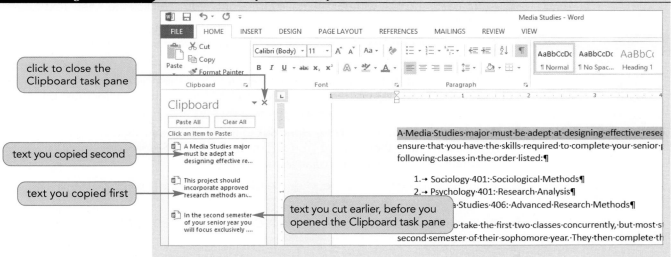

Now you can use the Clipboard task pane to insert the copied text into a new document.

To insert the copied text into a new document:

1. Open a new, blank document. If necessary, open the Clipboard task pane.

2. In the Clipboard task pane, click the second item in the list of copied items, which begins "This project should incorporate...." The text is inserted in the document and the "*Media Studies Senior Project*" title retains its italic formatting.

Kaya doesn't want to keep the italic formatting in the newly pasted text. You can remove this formatting by using the Paste Options button, which is visible just below the pasted text.

3. Click the **Paste Options** button [(Ctrl) ▾ in the document. The Paste Options menu opens, as shown in Figure 2-11.

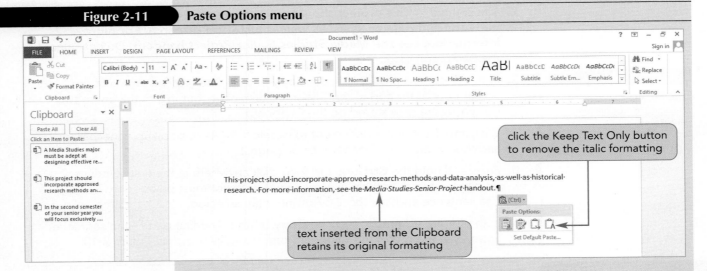

Figure 2-11 Paste Options menu

To paste the text without the italic formatting, you can click the Keep Text Only button.

4. Click the **Keep Text Only** button 📋. Word removes the italic formatting from "Media Studies Senior Project."

TIP
To select a paste option before pasting an item, click the Paste button arrow in the Clipboard group, and then click the paste option you want.

5. Press the **Enter** key to start a new paragraph, and then click the first item in the Clipboard task pane, which begins "A Media Studies major must be adept...." The text is inserted as the second paragraph in the document.

6. Save the document as **New Handout** in the location specified by your instructor, and then close it. You return to the Media Studies document, where the Clipboard task pane is still open.

7. In the Clipboard task pane, click the **Clear All** button. The copied items are removed from the Clipboard.

8. In the Clipboard task pane, click the **Close** button ✖. The Clipboard task pane closes.

9. Click anywhere in the document to deselect the paragraph, and then save the document.

Using the Navigation Pane

The Navigation pane simplifies the process of moving through a document page by page. You can also use the Navigation pane to locate a particular word or phrase. You start by typing the text you're searching for—the **search text**—in the Search box at the top of the Navigation pane. As shown in the Session 2.1 Visual Overview, Word highlights every instance of the search text in the document. At the same time, a list of the **search results** appears in the Navigation pane. You can click a search result to go immediately to that location in the document.

To become familiar with the Navigation pane, you'll use it to navigate through the Media Studies document page by page. You'll start by moving the insertion point to the beginning of the document.

To navigate through the document page by page:

▶ **1.** Press the **Ctrl+Home** keys to move the insertion point to the beginning of the document, making sure the HOME tab is still selected on the ribbon.

▶ **2.** In the Editing group, click the **Find** button. The Navigation pane opens on the left side of the Word window.

In the Search document box at the top, you can type the text you want to find. The three links below the Search document box—HEADINGS, PAGES, and RESULTS—allow you to navigate through the document in different ways. As you become a more experienced Word user, you'll learn how to use the HEADINGS link; for now, you'll ignore it. To move quickly among the pages of a document, you can use the PAGES link.

▶ **3.** In the Navigation pane, click the **PAGES** link. The Navigation pane displays thumbnail icons of the document's two pages, as shown in Figure 2-12. You can click a page in the Navigation pane to display that page in the document window.

| Figure 2-12 | Document pages displayed in the Navigation pane |

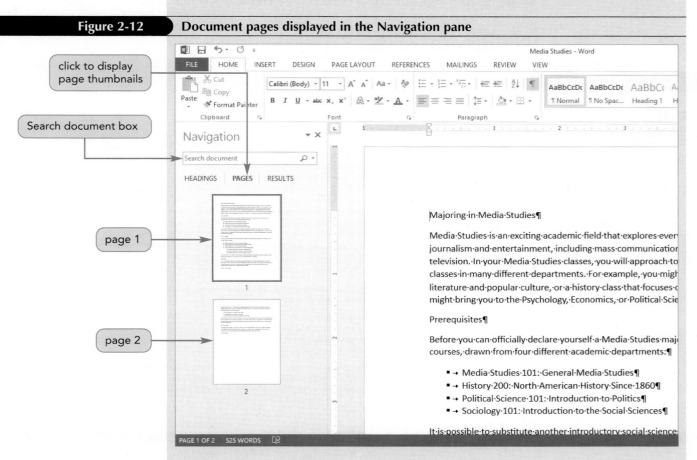

▶ **4.** In the Navigation pane, click the **page 2** thumbnail. Page 2 is displayed in the document window, with the insertion point blinking at the beginning of the page.

▶ **5.** In the Navigation pane, click the **page 1** thumbnail to move the insertion point back to the beginning of the document.

Kaya thinks she might have mistakenly used the word "media" when she actually meant to use "journalism" in certain parts of the document. She asks you to use the Navigation pane to find all instances of "media."

To search for the word "media" in the document:

1. In the Navigation pane, click the **RESULTS** link, click the **Search document** box, and then type **media**. You do not have to press the Enter key.

Every instance of the word "media" is highlighted in yellow in the document. The yellow highlight is only temporary; it will disappear as soon as you begin to perform any other task in the document. A full list of the 24 search results is displayed in the Navigation pane. Some of the search results contain the word "Media" (with an uppercase "M") while others contain the word "media" (with a lowercase "m"). To narrow the search results, you need to tell Word to match the case of the search text.

2. In the Navigation pane, click the **Search for more things** button ▼. This displays a two-part menu. In the bottom part, you can select other items to search for, such as graphics or tables. The top part provides more advanced search tools. See Figure 2-13.

Figure 2-13 **Navigation pane with Search for more things menu**

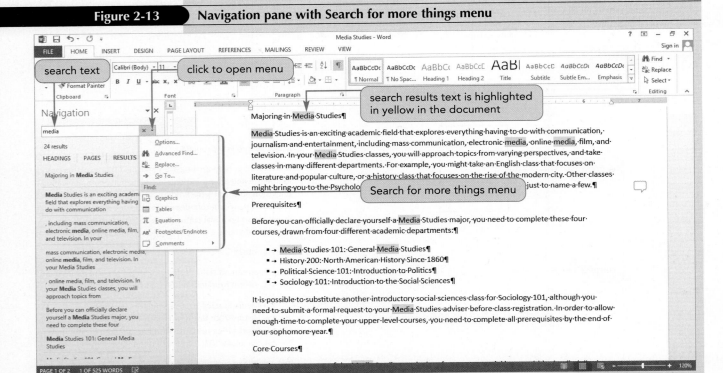

3. At the top of the Search for more things menu, click **Options** to open the Find Options dialog box.

The check boxes in this dialog box allow you to fine-tune your search. For example, to ensure that Word finds the search text only when it appears as a separate word, and not when it appears as part of another word, you could select the Find whole words only check box. Right now, you are only concerned with making sure the search results have the same case as the search text.

▶ **4.** Click the **Match case** check box to select it, and then click the **OK** button to close the Find Options dialog box. Now you can search the document again.

▶ **5.** Press the **Ctrl+Home** keys to move the insertion point to the beginning of the document, click the **Search document** box in the Navigation pane, and then type **media**. This time, there are only three search results in the Navigation pane, and they all start with a lowercase "m."

To move among the search results, you can use the up and down arrows in the Navigation pane.

▶ **6.** In the Navigation pane, click the **down arrow** button ▾. Word selects the first instance of "media" in the Navigation pane, as indicated by a blue outline. Also, in the document, the first instance has a gray selection highlight over the yellow highlight. See Figure 2-14.

Figure 2-14	Navigation pane with the first search result selected

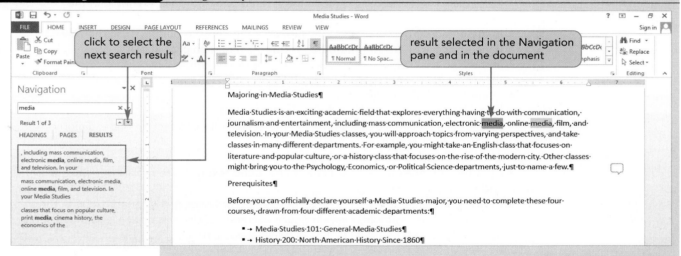

Trouble? If the second instance of "media" is selected in the Navigation pane, then you pressed the Enter key after typing "media" in Step 5. Click the up arrow button ▴ to select the first instance.

▶ **7.** In the Navigation pane, click the **down arrow** button ▾. Word selects the second instance of "media" in the document and in the Navigation pane.

▶ **8.** Click the **down arrow** button ▾ again to select the third search result, in the paragraph after "Electives," and then click the **up arrow** button ▴ to select the second search result again.

You can also select a search result in the document by clicking a search result in the Navigation pane.

▶ **9.** In the Navigation pane, click the third search result, which begins "classes that focus on popular culture…." The third search result is selected in the document and in the Navigation pane.

After reviewing the search results, Kaya decides she would like to replace two of the three instances of "media" with the word "journalism." You can do that by using the Find and Replace dialog box.

Finding and Replacing Text

To open the Find and Replace dialog box from the Navigation pane, click the Find more things button, and then click Replace. This opens the **Find and Replace dialog box**, with the Replace tab displayed by default. The Replace tab provides options for finding a specific word or phrase in the document and replacing it with another word or phrase. To use the Replace tab, type the search text in the Find what box, and then type the text you want to substitute in the Replace with box. You can also click the More button on the Replace tab to display the Search Options section, which includes the same options you saw earlier in the Find Options dialog box, including the Find whole words only check box and the Match case check box.

After you have typed the search text and selected any search options, you can click the Find Next button to select the first occurrence of the search text; you can then decide whether or not to substitute the search text with the replacement text.

REFERENCE

Finding and Replacing Text

- Press the Ctrl+Home keys to move the insertion point to the beginning of the document.
- In the Editing group on the HOME tab, click the Replace button; or, in the Navigation pane, click the Search for more things button, and then click Replace.
- In the Find and Replace dialog box, click the More button, if necessary, to expand the dialog box and display the Search Options section of the Replace tab.
- In the Find what box, type the search text.
- In the Replace with box, type the replacement text.
- Select the appropriate check boxes in the Search Options section of the dialog box to narrow your search.
- Click the Find Next button.
- Click the Replace button to substitute the found text with the replacement text and find the next occurrence.
- Click the Replace All button to substitute all occurrences of the found text with the replacement text without reviewing each occurrence. Use this option only if you are absolutely certain that the results will be what you expect.

You'll use the Find and Replace dialog box now to replace two instances of "media" with "journalism."

To replace two instances of "media" with "journalism":

1. Press the **Ctrl+Home** keys to move the insertion point to the beginning of the document.

2. In the Navigation pane, click the **Search for more things** button ▼ to open the menu, and then click **Replace**. The Find and Replace dialog box opens with the Replace tab on top.

   The search text you entered earlier in the Navigation pane, "media," appears in the Find what box. If you hadn't already conducted a search, you would need to type your search text now. Because you selected the Match case check box earlier in the Find Options dialog box, "Match Case" appears below the Find what box.

3. In the lower-left corner of the dialog box, click the **More** button to display the search options. Because you selected the Match case check box earlier in the Find Options dialog box, it is selected here.

   Trouble? If you see the Less button instead of the More button, the search options are already displayed.

4. Click the **Replace with** box, and then type **journalism**.

5. Click the **Find Next** button. Word highlights the first instance of "media" in the document. See Figure 2-15.

Figure 2-15 **Find and Replace dialog box**

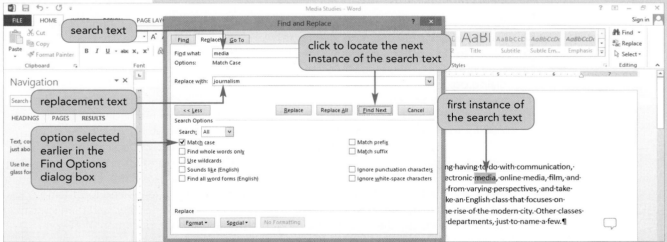

6. Click the **Replace** button. Word replaces "media" with "journalism," so the text reads "electronic journalism." Then, Word selects the next instance of "media," which happens to be in the same sentence. Kaya does not want to replace this instance, so you can find the next one.

7. Click the **Find Next** button. Word selects the last instance of "media," located in the sentence just before the "Research Methods" heading.

> **8.** Click the **Replace** button. Word makes the substitution, so the text reads "print journalism," and then displays a message box telling you that Word has finished searching the document.
>
> **9.** Click the **OK** button to close the message box, and then in the Find and Replace dialog box, click the **Close** button.

You are finished with the Navigation pane, so you can close it. But first you need to restore the search options to their original settings. It's a good practice to restore the original search settings so that future searches are not affected by any settings that might not apply.

To restore the search options to their original settings:

> **1.** In the Navigation pane, open the Find Options dialog box, deselect the Match case check box, and then click the **OK** button to close the Find Options dialog box.
>
> **2.** Click the **Close** button ⊠ in the upper-right corner of the Navigation pane.
>
> **3.** Save the document.

Searching for Formatting

You can search for formatting just as you can search for text. For example, you might want to check a document to look for text formatted in bold and the Arial font. To search for formatting from within the Navigation pane, click the Search for more things button to display the menu, and then click Advanced Find. The Find and Replace dialog box opens with the Find tab displayed. Click the More button, if necessary, to display the Search Options section of the Find tab. Click the Format button at the bottom of the Search Options section, click the category of formatting you want to look for (such as Font or Paragraph), and then select the formatting you want to find.

You can look for formatting that occurs only on specific text, or you can look for formatting that occurs anywhere in a document. If you're looking for text formatted in a certain way (such as all instances of "Media Studies" that are bold), enter the text in the Find what box and then specify the formatting you're looking for. To find formatting on any text in a document, leave the Find what box empty, and then specify the formatting. Use the Find Next button to move through the document, from one instance of the specified formatting to another.

You can follow the same basic steps on the Replace tab to replace one type of formatting with another. First, click the Find what box and select the desired formatting. Then click the Replace with box and select the desired formatting. If you want, type search text and replacement text in the appropriate boxes. Then proceed as with any Find and Replace operation.

Now that the text in the Media Studies document is final, you will turn your attention to styles and themes, which affect the look of the entire document.

Working with Styles

A style is a set of formatting options that you can apply by clicking an icon in the Style gallery on the HOME tab. Each style is designed for a particular use. For example, the Title style is intended for formatting the title at the beginning of a document.

All the text you type into a document has a style applied to it. By default, text is formatted in the Normal style, which applies 11-point Calibri font, left alignment, 1.08 line spacing, and a small amount of extra space between paragraphs. In other words, the Normal style applies the default formatting you learned about when you first began typing a Word document.

Note that some styles apply **paragraph-level formatting**—that is, they are set up to format an entire paragraph, including the paragraph and line spacing. The Normal, Heading, and Title styles all apply paragraph-level formatting. Other styles apply **character-level formatting**—that is, they are set up to format only individual characters or words (for example, emphasizing a phrase by adding italic formatting and changing the font color).

One row of the Style gallery is always visible on the HOME tab. To display the entire Style gallery, click the More button in the Styles group. After you begin applying styles in a document, the visible row of the Style gallery changes to show the most recently used styles.

You are ready to use the Style gallery to format the document title.

To display the entire Style gallery and then format the document title with a style:

1. Press the **Ctrl+Home** keys to move the insertion point to the beginning of the document, if necessary.

2. Make sure the HOME tab is still selected and locate the More button in the Styles group, as shown earlier in the Session 2.1 Visual Overview.

3. In the Styles group, click the **More** button. The Style gallery opens, displaying a total of 16 styles arranged in two rows, as shown in Figure 2-16. If your screen is set at a lower resolution than the screenshots in this book, the Style gallery on your screen might contain more than two rows.

Figure 2-16 Displaying the Style gallery

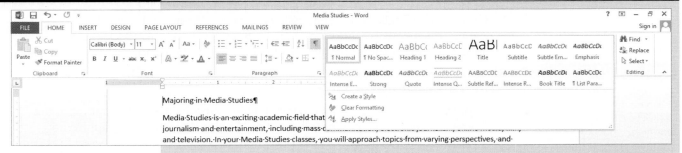

You don't actually need any of the styles in the bottom row now, so you can close the Style gallery.

4. Press the **Esc** key to close the Style gallery.

5. Click anywhere in the first paragraph, "Majoring in Media Studies," and then point to (but don't click) the **Title** style, which is the fifth style from the left in the top row of the gallery. The ScreenTip "Title" is displayed, and a Live Preview of the style appears in the paragraph containing the insertion point, as shown in Figure 2-17. The Title style changes the font to 28-point Calibri Light.

Figure 2-17 **Title style in the Style gallery**

6. Click the **Title** style. The style is applied to the paragraph. To finish the title, you need to center it.

7. In the Paragraph group, click the **Center** button ▤. The title is centered in the document.

Next, you will format the document headings using the heading styles, which have different levels. The highest level, Heading 1, is used for the major headings in a document, and it applies the most noticeable formatting with a larger font than the other heading styles. (In heading styles, the highest, or most important, level has the lowest number.) The Heading 2 style is used for headings that are subordinate to the highest level headings; it applies slightly less dramatic formatting than the Heading 1 style.

The Media Studies handout only has one level of headings, so you will only apply the Heading 1 style.

To format text with the Heading 1 style:

1. Click anywhere in the "Prerequisites" paragraph.

2. On the HOME tab, in the Style gallery, click the **Heading 1** style. The paragraph is now formatted in blue, 16-point Calibri Light. The Heading 1 style also inserts some paragraph space above the heading.

3. Scroll down, click anywhere in the "Core Courses" paragraph, and then click the **Heading 1** style in the Style gallery.

4. Repeat Step 3 to apply the Heading 1 style to the "Electives" paragraph, the "Research Methods" paragraph and the "Senior Project" paragraph. When you are finished, scroll up to the beginning of the document to review the new formatting. See Figure 2-18.

Figure 2-18   **Document with Title and Heading 1 styles**

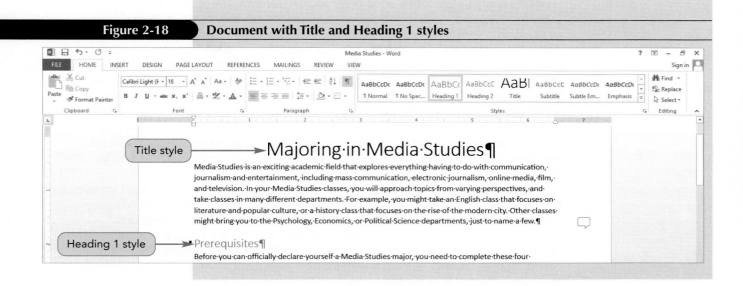

Understanding the Benefits of Heading Styles

By default, the Style gallery offers 16 styles, each designed for a specific purpose. As you gain more experience with Word, you will learn how to use a wider array of styles. You'll also learn how to create your own styles. Styles allow you to change a document's formatting in an instant. But the benefits of heading styles go far beyond attractive formatting. Heading styles allow you to reorganize a document or generate a table of contents with a click of the mouse. Also, the heading styles are set up to keep a heading and the body text that follows it together, so a heading is never separated from its body text by a page break. Each Word document includes nine levels of heading styles, although only the Heading 1 and Heading 2 styles are available by default in the Style gallery. Whenever you use the lowest heading style in the Style gallery, the next-lowest level is added to the Style gallery. For example, after you use the Heading 2 style, the Heading 3 style appears in the Styles group in the Style gallery.

After you format a document with a variety of styles, you can alter the look of the document by changing the document's theme.

Working with Themes

A **theme** is a coordinated collection of fonts, colors, and other visual effects designed to give a document a cohesive, polished look. A variety of themes are installed with Word, with more available online at Office.com. When you open a new blank document in Word, the Office theme is applied by default. To change a document's theme, you click the Themes button, which is located in the Document Formatting group on the DESIGN tab, and then click the theme you want. Pointing to the Themes button displays a ScreenTip that tells you what theme is currently applied to the document.

When applying color to a document, you usually have the option of selecting a color from a palette of colors designed to match the current theme, or from a palette of standard colors. For instance, recall that the colors in the Font Color gallery are divided into Theme Colors and Standard Colors. When you select a Standard Color, such as Dark Red, that color remains the same no matter which theme you apply to the document. But when you click one of the Theme Colors, you are essentially telling Word to use the color located in that particular spot on the Theme Colors palette. Then, if you change the document's theme later, Word substitutes a color from the same location on the Theme Colors palette. This ensures that all the colors in a document are drawn from a group of colors coordinated to look good together. So as a rule, if you are going to use multiple colors in a document (perhaps for paragraph shading and font color), it's a good idea to stick with the Theme Colors.

A similar substitution takes place with fonts when you change the theme. However, to understand how this works, you need to understand the difference between headings and body text. Kaya's document includes the headings "Prerequisites," "Core Courses," "Electives," "Research Methods," and "Senior Project"—all of which you have formatted with the Heading1 style. The title of the document, "Majoring in Media Studies," is now formatted with the Title style, which is also a type of heading style. Everything else in the Media Studies document is body text.

To ensure that your documents have a harmonious look, each theme assigns a font for headings and a font for body text. Typically, in a given theme, the same font is used for both headings and body text, but not always. In the Office theme, for instance, they are slightly different; the heading font is Calibri Light, and the body font is Calibri. These two fonts appear at the top of the Font list as "Calibri Light (Headings)" and "Calibri (Body)" when you click the Font box arrow in the Font group on the HOME tab. When you begin typing text in a new document with the Office theme, the text is formatted as body text with the Calibri font by default.

When applying a font to selected text, you can choose one of the two theme fonts at the top of the Font list, or you can choose one of the other fonts in the Font list. If you choose one of the other fonts and then change the document theme, that font remains the same. But if you use one of the theme fonts and then change the document theme, Word substitutes the appropriate font from the new theme. When you paste text into a document that has a different theme, Word applies the theme fonts and colors of the new document. To retain the original formatting, use the Keep Source Formatting option in the Paste Options menu.

Figure 2-19 compares elements of the default Office theme with the Integral theme. The Integral theme was chosen for this example because, like the Office theme, its heading and body fonts are different.

| Figure 2-19 | Comparing the Office theme to the Integral theme |

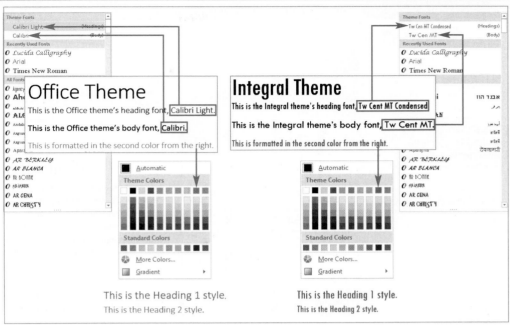

© 2014 Cengage Learning

Each document theme is designed to convey a specific look and feel. The Office theme is designed to be appropriate for standard business documents. Other themes are designed to give documents a flashier look. Because Kaya has not yet selected a new theme, the Office theme is currently applied to the Media Studies document. However, she thinks the Facet theme might be more appropriate for the Media Studies document. She asks you to apply it now.

To change the document's theme:

1. If necessary, press the **Ctrl+Home** keys to move the insertion point to the beginning of the document. With the title and first heading visible, you will more easily see what happens when you change the document's theme.

2. On the ribbon, click the **DESIGN** tab.

3. In the Document Formatting group, point to the **Themes** button. A ScreenTip appears containing the text "Current: Office Theme" as well as general information about themes.

4. In the Document Formatting group, click the **Themes** button. The Themes gallery opens. See Figure 2-20.

Figure 2-20	Themes gallery displayed

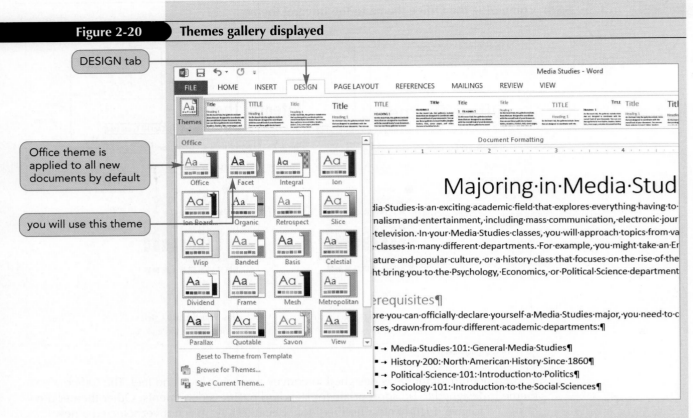

DESIGN tab

Office theme is applied to all new documents by default

you will use this theme

5. Move the mouse pointer (without clicking it) over the various themes in the gallery to see a Live Preview of each theme in the document. The heading and body fonts as well as the heading colors change to reflect the fonts associated with the various themes.

6. In the Themes gallery, click the **Facet** theme. The text in the Media Studies document changes to the body and heading fonts of the Facet theme, with the headings formatted in green. To see exactly what the Facet theme fonts are, you can point to the Fonts button in the Document Formatting group.

7. In the Document Formatting group, point to the **Fonts** button. A ScreenTip appears, listing the currently selected theme (Facet), the heading font (Trebuchet MS), and the body font (Trebuchet MS). See Figure 2-21.

| **Figure 2-21** | **Fonts for the Facet theme** |

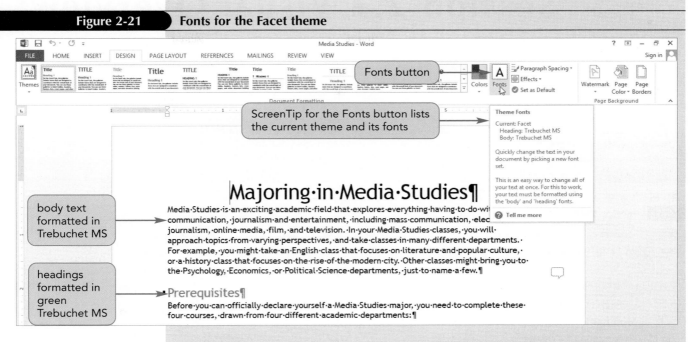

Trouble? If a menu appears, you clicked the Fonts button instead of pointing to it. Press the Esc key, and then repeat Step 7.

8. Save your changes and then close the document.

Kaya's Media Studies document is ready to be handed in to her supervisor. The use of styles, bulleted and numbered lists, and a new theme gives the document a professional look appropriate for use in a department handout.

Session 2.1 Quick Check

REVIEW

1. Explain how to display comments to the right of the document text in Simple Markup view.
2. What term refers to the process of using the mouse to drag text to a new location?
3. How can you ensure that the Navigation pane will find "ZIP code" instead of "zip code"?
4. What is a style?
5. What style is applied to all text in a new document by default?
6. Explain the relationship between a document's theme and styles.

Session 2.2 Visual Overview:

Use an easy-to-read font, such as the default Calibri, set to 12 point.

An MLA-style research paper does not require a separate title page; instead, type your name, your instructor's name, the course number, and the date in the upper-left corner of the first page.

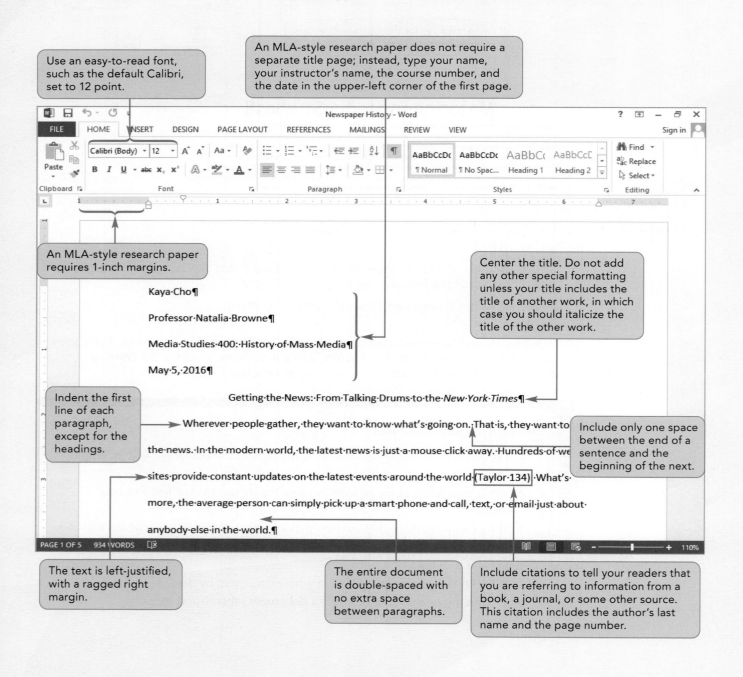

An MLA-style research paper requires 1-inch margins.

Center the title. Do not add any other special formatting unless your title includes the title of another work, in which case you should italicize the title of the other work.

Kaya·Cho¶

Professor·Natalia·Browne¶

Media·Studies·400:·History·of·Mass·Media¶

May·5,·2016¶

Getting·the·News:·From·Talking·Drums·to·the·*New·York·Times*¶

Indent the first line of each paragraph, except for the headings.

Wherever·people·gather,·they·want·to·know·what's·going·on.·That·is,·they·want·to

the·news.·In·the·modern·world,·the·latest·news·is·just·a·mouse·click·away.·Hundreds·of·we

sites·provide·constant·updates·on·the·latest·events·around·the·world·(Taylor·134).·What's·

more,·the·average·person·can·simply·pick·up·a·smart·phone·and·call,·text,·or·email·just·about·

anybody·else·in·the·world.¶

Include only one space between the end of a sentence and the beginning of the next.

PAGE 1 OF 5   934 WORDS   110%

The text is left-justified, with a ragged right margin.

The entire document is double-spaced with no extra space between paragraphs.

Include citations to tell your readers that you are referring to information from a book, a journal, or some other source. This citation includes the author's last name and the page number.

MLA Formatting Guidelines

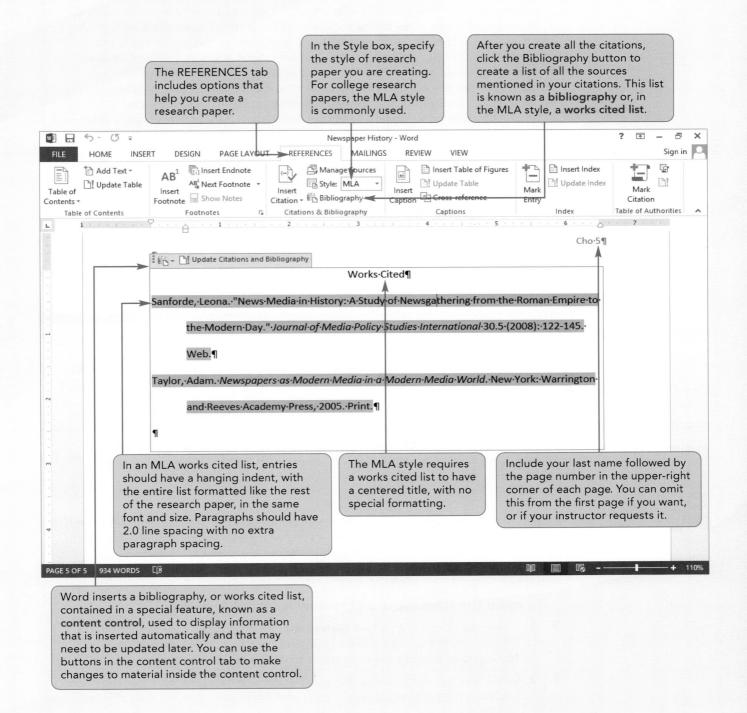

The REFERENCES tab includes options that help you create a research paper.

In the Style box, specify the style of research paper you are creating. For college research papers, the MLA style is commonly used.

After you create all the citations, click the Bibliography button to create a list of all the sources mentioned in your citations. This list is known as a **bibliography** or, in the MLA style, a **works cited list**.

In an MLA works cited list, entries should have a hanging indent, with the entire list formatted like the rest of the research paper, in the same font and size. Paragraphs should have 2.0 line spacing with no extra paragraph spacing.

The MLA style requires a works cited list to have a centered title, with no special formatting.

Include your last name followed by the page number in the upper-right corner of each page. You can omit this from the first page if you want, or if your instructor requests it.

Word inserts a bibliography, or works cited list, contained in a special feature, known as a **content control**, used to display information that is inserted automatically and that may need to be updated later. You can use the buttons in the content control tab to make changes to material inside the content control.

Reviewing the MLA Style

A **style guide** is a set of rules that describe the preferred format and style for a certain type of writing. People in different fields use different style guides, with each style guide designed to suit the needs of a specific discipline. For example, journalists commonly use the *Associated Press Stylebook*, which focuses on the concise writing style common in magazines and newspapers. In the world of academics, style guides emphasize the proper way to create **citations**, which are formal references to the work of others. Researchers in the social and behavioral sciences use the **American Psychological Association (APA) style**, which is designed to help readers scan an article quickly for key points and emphasizes the date of publication in citations. Other scientific and technical fields have their own specialized style guides.

In the humanities, the **Modern Language Association (MLA) style** is widely used. This is the style Kaya has used for her research paper. She followed the guidelines specified in the *MLA Handbook for Writers of Research Papers*, published by the Modern Language Association of America. These guidelines focus on specifications for formatting a research document and citing the sources used in research conducted for a paper. The major formatting features of an MLA-style research paper are illustrated in the Session 2.2 Visual Overview. Compared to style guides for technical fields, the MLA style is very flexible, making it easy to include citations without disrupting the natural flow of the writing. MLA-style citations of other writers' works take the form of a brief parenthetical entry, with a complete reference to each item included in the alphabetized bibliography, also known as the works cited list, at the end of the research paper.

INSIGHT

Formatting an MLA-Style Research Paper

The MLA guidelines were developed, in part, to simplify the process of transforming a manuscript into a journal article or a chapter of a book. The style calls for minimal formatting; the simpler the formatting in a manuscript, the easier it is to turn the text into a published document. The MLA guidelines were also designed to ensure consistency in documents, so that all research papers look alike. Therefore, you should apply no special formatting to the text in an MLA-style research paper. Headings should be formatted like the other text in the document, with no bold or heading styles.

Kaya has started writing a research paper on the history of newspapers for her Media Studies class. You'll open the draft of Kaya's research paper and determine what needs to be done to make it meet the MLA style guidelines for a research paper.

To open the document and review it for MLA style:

▶ **1.** Open the document named **Newspaper** located in the Word2 ▶ Tutorial folder included with your Data Files, and then save the document as **Newspaper History** in the location specified by your instructor.

▶ **2.** Verify that the document is displayed in Print Layout view, and that the rulers and nonprinting characters are displayed. Make sure the Zoom level is set to **120%**.

> **3.** Review the document to familiarize yourself with its structure. First, notice the parts of the document that already match the MLA style. Kaya included a block of information in the upper-left corner of the first page, giving her name, her instructor's name, the course name, and the date. The title at the top of the first page also meets the MLA guidelines in that it is centered and does not have any special formatting except for "*New York Times*," which is italicized because it is the name of a newspaper. The headings ("Early News Media," "Merchant Newsletters," "Modern American Newspapers," and "Looking to the Future") have no special formatting; but unlike the title, they are left-aligned. Finally, the body text is left-aligned with a ragged right margin, and the entire document is formatted in the same font, Calibri, which is easy to read.

What needs to be changed in order to make Kaya's paper consistent with the MLA style? Currently, the entire document is formatted using the default settings, which are the Normal style for the Office theme. To transform the document into an MLA-style research paper, you need to complete the checklist shown in Figure 2-22.

Figure 2-22   Checklist for formatting a default Word document to match the MLA style

> ✓ Double-space the entire document.
>
> ✓ Remove paragraph spacing from the entire document.
>
> ✓ Increase the font size for the entire document to 12 points.
>
> ✓ Indent the first line of each body paragraph .5 inch from the left margin.
>
> ✓ Add the page number (preceded by your last name) in the upper-right corner of each page. If you prefer, you can omit this from the first page.

© 2014 Cengage Learning

You'll take care of the first three items in the checklist now.

To begin applying MLA formatting to the document:

> **1.** Press the **Ctrl+A** keys to select the entire document.

> **2.** Make sure the HOME tab is selected on the ribbon.

> **3.** In the Paragraph group, click the **Line and Paragraph Spacing** button ⏸▾, and then click **2.0**.

> **4.** Click the **Line and Spacing** button ⏸▾ again, and then click **Remove Space After Paragraph**. The entire document is now double-spaced, with no paragraph spacing, and the entire document is still selected.

> **5.** In the Font group, click the **Font Size** arrow, and then click **12**. The entire document is formatted in 12-point font.

> **6.** Click anywhere in the document to deselect the text.

> **7.** In the first paragraph of the document, replace Kaya's name with your first and last name, and then save the document.

Now you need to indent the first line of each body paragraph.

Indenting a Paragraph

Word offers a number of options for indenting a paragraph. You can move an entire paragraph to the right, or you can create specialized indents, such as a **hanging indent**, where all lines except the first line of the paragraph are indented from the left margin. As you saw in the Session 2.2 Visual Overview, all the body paragraphs (that is, all the paragraphs except the information in the upper-left corner of the first page, the title, and the headings) have a first-line indent in MLA research papers. Figure 2-23 shows some examples of other common paragraph indents.

Figure 2-23 **Common paragraph indents**

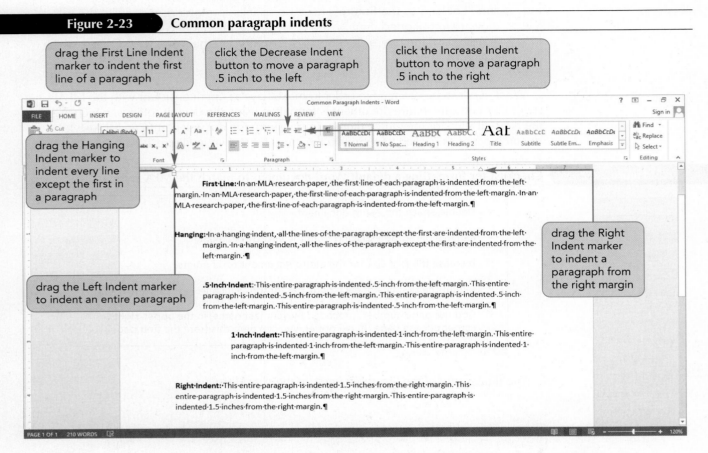

To quickly indent an entire paragraph .5 inch from the left, position the insertion point in the paragraph you want to indent and then click the Increase Indent button in the Paragraph group on the HOME tab. You can continue to indent the paragraph in increments of .5 inch by repeatedly clicking the Increase Indent button. To move an indented paragraph back to the left .5 inch, click the Decrease Indent button.

To create first line, hanging, or right indents, you can use the indent markers on the ruler. First, click in the paragraph you want to indent, or select multiple paragraphs. Then drag the appropriate indent marker to the left or right on the horizontal ruler. The indent markers are small and can be hard to see. As shown in Figure 2-23, the **First Line Indent marker** looks like the top half of an hourglass; the **Hanging Indent marker** looks like the bottom half. The rectangle below the Hanging Indent marker is the **Left Indent marker**. The **Right Indent Marker** looks just like the Hanging Indent marker except that it is located on the far-right side of the horizontal ruler.

Note that when you indent an entire paragraph using the Increase Indent button, the three indent markers, shown stacked on top of one another in Figure 2-23, move as a unit along with the paragraphs you are indenting.

In Kaya's paper, you will indent the first lines of the body paragraphs .5 inch from the left margin, as specified by the MLA style.

To indent the first line of each paragraph:

1. On the first page of the document, just below the title, click anywhere in the first main paragraph, which begins "Wherever people gather...."

2. On the horizontal ruler, position the mouse pointer over the First Line Indent marker ▽. When you see the ScreenTip that reads "First Line Indent," you know the mouse is positioned correctly.

3. Press and hold the mouse button as you drag the **First Line Indent** marker ▽ to the right, to the .5-inch mark on the horizontal ruler. As you drag, a vertical guide line appears over the document, and the first line of the paragraph moves right. See Figure 2-24.

| Figure 2-24 | Dragging the First Line Indent marker |

First Line Indent marker

.5-inch mark

as you drag the indent marker, a guide line appears and the first line of the paragraph moves right

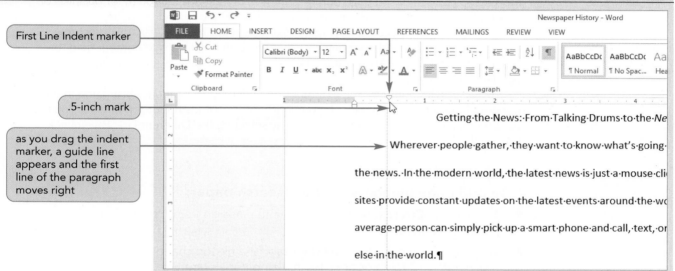

TIP

You can also click in the paragraph you want to indent, or select multiple paragraphs. Click the Dialog Box Launcher in the Paragraph group, and then adjust the Indentation settings.

4. When the First Line Indent marker ▽ is positioned at the .5-inch mark on the ruler, release the mouse button. The first line of the paragraph containing the insertion point indents .5 inch and the vertical guide line disappears.

5. Scroll down, if necessary, click anywhere in the next paragraph in the document, which begins "These days, it's not hard to know...," and then drag the **First Line Indent** marker ▽ to the right, to the .5-inch mark on the horizontal ruler. As you move the indent marker, you can use the vertical guide line to ensure that you match the first line indent of the preceding paragraph.

   You could continue to drag the indent marker to indent the first line of the remaining body paragraphs, but it's faster to use the Repeat button on the Quick Access Toolbar.

6. Scroll down and click in the paragraph below the heading "Early News Media," and then on the Quick Access Toolbar, click the **Repeat** button ↻.

7. Click in the next paragraph, at the top of page 2, which begins "Early news media took many forms," and then click the **Repeat** button ↻.

8. Continue using the **Repeat** button ↻ to indent the first line of all of the remaining body paragraphs. Take care not to indent the headings, which in this document are formatted just like the body text.

9. Scroll to the top of the document, verify that you have correctly indented the first line of each body paragraph, and then save the document.

Next, you need to insert page numbers.

Inserting and Modifying Page Numbers

When you insert page numbers in a document, you don't have to type a page number on each page. Instead, you insert a **page number field**, which is an instruction that tells Word to insert a page number on each page, no matter how many pages you eventually add to the document. Word inserts page number fields above the top margin, in the blank area known as the **header**, or below the bottom margin, in the area known as the **footer**. You can also insert page numbers in the side margins, although for business or academic documents, it's customary to place them in the header or footer.

After you insert a page number field, Word switches to Header and Footer view. In this view, you can add your name or other text next to the page number field, or use the HEADER & FOOTER TOOLS DESIGN tab to change various settings related to headers and footers.

The MLA style requires a page number preceded by the student's last name in the upper-right corner of each page. If you prefer (or if your instructor requests it), you can omit the page number from the first page by selecting the Different First Page check box on the DESIGN tab.

To add page numbers to the research paper:

1. Press the **Ctrl+Home** keys to move the insertion point to the beginning of the document.

2. On the ribbon, click the **INSERT** tab. The ribbon changes to display the Insert options, including options for inserting page numbers.

3. In the Header & Footer group, click the **Page Number** button to open the Page Number menu. Here you can choose where you want to position the page numbers in your document—at the top of the page, at the bottom of the page, in the side margins, or at the current location of the insertion point.

4. Point to **Top of Page**. A gallery of page number styles opens. You can scroll the list to review the many styles of page numbers. Because the MLA style calls for a simple page number in the upper-right corner, you will use the Plain Number 3 style. See Figure 2-25.

TIP

To remove page numbers from a document, click the Remove Page Numbers command on the Page Number menu.

Figure 2-25   Gallery of page number styles

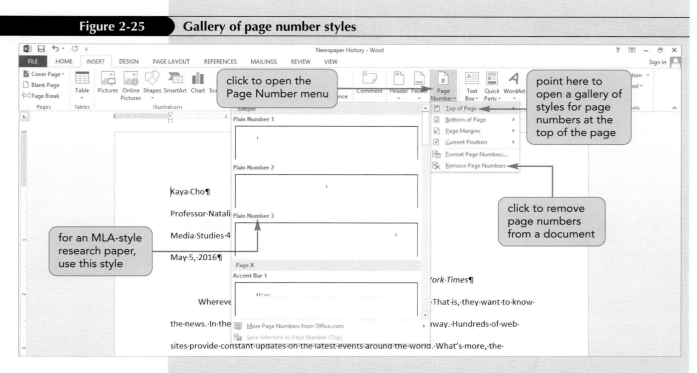

5. In the gallery, click the **Plain Number 3** style. The Word window switches to Header and Footer view, with the page number for the first page in the upper-right corner. The page number has a gray background, indicating that it is actually a page number field and not simply a number that you typed.

The HEADER & FOOTER TOOLS DESIGN tab is displayed on the ribbon, giving you access to a variety of formatting options. The insertion point blinks to the left of the page number field, ready for you to add text to the header if you wish. Note that in Header and Footer view, you can only type in the header or footer areas. The text in the main document area is a lighter shade of gray, indicating that it cannot be edited in this view.

6. Type your last name, and then press the **spacebar**. If you see a wavy red line below your last name, right-click your name, and then click **Ignore** on the Shortcut menu. See Figure 2-26.

Figure 2-26 **Last name inserted next to the page number field**

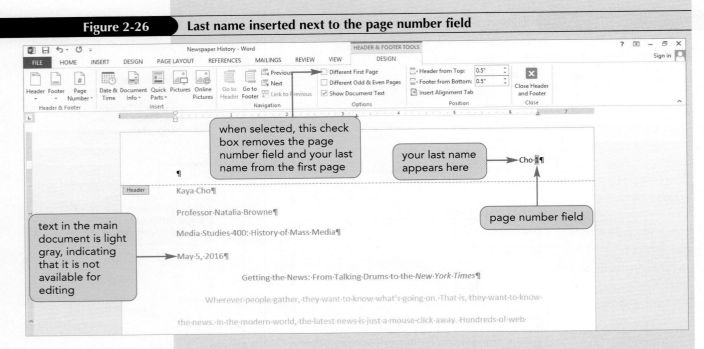

> **7.** Scroll down and observe the page number (with your last name) at the top of pages 2, 3, and 4. As you can see, whatever you insert in the header on one page appears on every page of the document by default.

> **8.** Press the **Ctrl+Home** keys to return to the header on the first page.

> **9.** On the HEADER & FOOTER TOOLS DESIGN tab, in the Options group, click the **Different First Page** check box to insert a check. The page number field and your last name are removed from the first page header. The insertion point blinks at the header's left margin in case you want to insert something else for the first page header. In this case, you don't.

> **10.** In the Close group, click the **Close Header and Footer** button. You return to Print Layout view, and the HEADER & FOOTER TOOLS DESIGN tab is no longer displayed on the ribbon.

> **11.** Scroll down to review your last name and the page number in the headers for pages 2, 3, and 4. In Print Layout view, the text in the header is light gray, indicating that it is not currently available for editing.

TIP

After you insert page numbers, you can reopen Header and Footer view by double-clicking a page number in Print Layout view.

You have finished all the tasks related to formatting the MLA-style research paper. Now Kaya wants your help with creating the essential parts of any research paper—the citations and the bibliography.

Creating Citations and a Bibliography

A bibliography (or, as it is called in the MLA style, the works cited list) is an alphabetical list of all the books, magazine articles, websites, movies, and other works referred to in a research paper. The items listed in a bibliography are known as **sources**. The entry for each source includes information such as the author, the title of the work, the publication date, and the publisher.

Within the research paper itself, you include a parenthetical reference, or citation, every time you quote or refer to a source. Every source included in your citations then has a corresponding entry in the works cited list. A citation should include enough information to identify the quote or referenced material so the reader can easily locate the source in the accompanying works cited list. The exact form for a citation varies depending on the style guide you are using and the type of material you are referencing.

Some style guides are very rigid about the form and location of citations, but the MLA style offers quite a bit of flexibility. Typically, though, you insert an MLA citation at the end of a sentence in which you quote or refer to material from a source. For books or journals, the citation itself usually includes the author's last name and a page number. However, if the sentence containing the citation already includes the author's name, you only need to include the page number in the citation. Figure 2-27 provides some sample MLA citations for books and journals. For detailed guidelines, you can consult the *MLA Handbook for Writers of Research Papers, Seventh Edition,* which includes many examples.

Figure 2-27   **MLA guidelines for citing a book or journal**

Citation Rule	Example
If the sentence includes the author's name, the citation should only include the page number.	Peterson compares the opening scene of the movie to a scene from Shakespeare (188).
If the sentence does not include the author's name, the citation should include the author's name and the page number.	The opening scene of the movie has been compared to a scene from Shakespeare (Peterson 188).

© 2014 Cengage Learning

Word greatly simplifies the process of creating citations and a bibliography. You specify the style you want to use, and then Word takes care of setting up the citation and the works cited list appropriately. Every time you create a citation for a new source, Word prompts you to enter the information needed to create the corresponding entry in the works cited list. If you don't have all of your source information available, Word also allows you to insert a temporary, placeholder citation, which you can replace later with a complete citation. When you are finished creating your citations, Word generates the bibliography automatically. Note that placeholder citations are not included in the bibliography.

Written Communication: Acknowledging Your Sources

A research paper is a means for you to explore the available information about a subject and then present this information, along with your own understanding of the subject, in an organized and interesting way. Acknowledging all the sources of the information presented in your research paper is essential. If you fail to do this, you might be subject to charges of plagiarism, or trying to pass off someone else's thoughts as your own. Plagiarism is an extremely serious accusation for which you could suffer academic consequences ranging from failing an assignment to being expelled from school.

To ensure that you don't forget to cite a source, you should be careful about creating citations in your document as you type. It's very easy to forget to go back and cite all your sources correctly after you've finished typing a research paper. Failing to cite a source could lead to accusations of plagiarism and all the consequences that entails. If you don't have the complete information about a source, you should at least insert a placeholder citation. But take care to go back later and substitute complete citations for any placeholders.

Creating Citations

Before you create citations, you need to select the style you want to use, which in the case of Kaya's paper is the MLA style. Then, to insert a citation, you click the Insert Citation button in the Citations & Bibliography group on the REFERENCES tab. If you are citing a source for the first time, Word prompts you to enter all the information required for the source's entry in the bibliography or works cited list. If you are citing an existing source, you simply select the source from the Insert Citation menu.

By default, an MLA citation includes only the author's name in parentheses. However, you can use the Edit Citation dialog box to add a page number. You can also use the Edit Citation dialog box to remove, or suppress, the author's name, so only the page number appears in the citation. However, in an MLA citation, Word will replace the suppressed author name with the title of the source, so you need to suppress the title as well, by selecting the Title check box in the Edit Citation dialog box.

REFERENCE

Creating Citations

- On the ribbon, click the REFERENCES tab. In the Citations & Bibliography group, click the Style button arrow, and then select the style you want.
- Click in the document where you want to insert the citation. Typically, a citation goes at the end of a sentence, before the ending punctuation.
- To add a citation for a new source, click the Insert Citation button in the Citations & Bibliography group, click Add New Source, enter information in the Create Source dialog box, and then click the OK button.
- To add a citation for an existing source, click the Insert Citation button, and then click the source.
- To add a placeholder citation, click the Insert Citation button, click Add New Placeholder, and then, in the content control, type placeholder text, such as the author's last name, that will serve as a reminder about which source you need to cite. Note that a placeholder citation cannot contain any spaces.
- To add a page number to a citation, click the citation in the document, click the Citation Options button, click Edit Citation, type the page number, and then click the OK button.
- To display only the page number in a citation, click the citation in the document, click the Citation Options button, and then click Edit Citation. In the Edit Citation dialog box, select the Author and Title check boxes to suppress this information, and then click the OK button.

So far, Kaya has referenced information from two different sources in her research paper. You'll select a style and then begin adding the appropriate citations.

To select a style for the citation and bibliography:

1. On the ribbon, click the **REFERENCES** tab. The ribbon changes to display references options.

2. In the Citations & Bibliography group, click the **Style button arrow**, and then click **MLA Seventh Edition** if it is not already selected.

3. Press the **Ctrl+F** keys to open the Navigation pane.

4. Use the Navigation pane to find the phrase "As at least one historian has observed," which appears on page 1, and then click in the document at the end of that sentence (between the end of the word "medium" and the closing period).

5. Close the Navigation pane, and then click the **REFERENCES** tab on the ribbon, if necessary. You need to add a citation that informs the reader that historian Adam Taylor made the observation described in the sentence. See Figure 2-28.

Figure 2-28 | **MLA style selected and insertion point positioned for new citation**

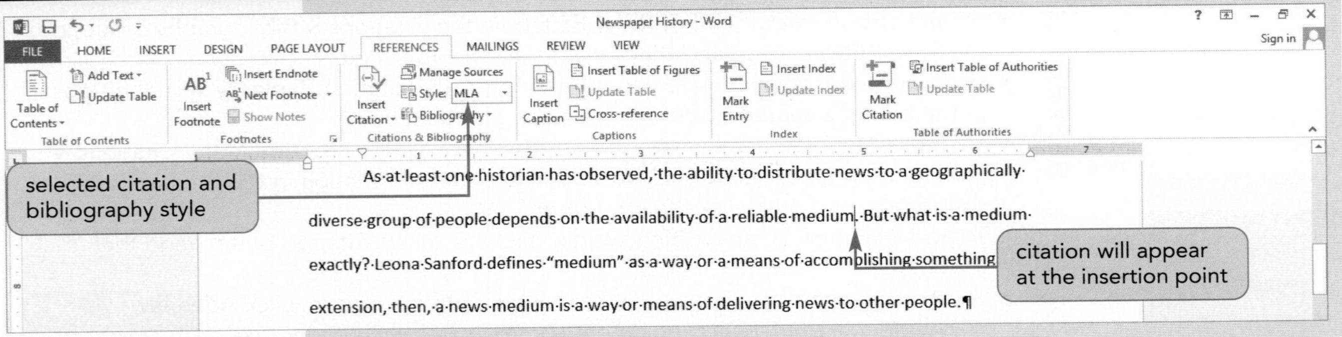

selected citation and bibliography style

As·at·least·one·historian·has·observed,·the·ability·to·distribute·news·to·a·geographically·

diverse·group·of·people·depends·on·the·availability·of·a·reliable·medium.·But·what·is·a·medium·

exactly?·Leona·Sanford·defines·"medium"·as·a·way·or·a·means·of·accomplishing·something·

citation will appear at the insertion point

extension,·then,·a·news·medium·is·a·way·or·means·of·delivering·news·to·other·people.¶

▶ **6.** In the Citations & Bibliography group, click the **Insert Citation** button to open the menu. At this point, you could click Add New Placeholder on the menu to insert a temporary, placeholder citation. However, because you have all the necessary source information, you can go ahead and create a complete citation.

▶ **7.** On the menu, click **Add New Source**. The Create Source dialog box opens, ready for you to add the information required to create a bibliography entry for Adam Taylor's book.

▶ **8.** If necessary, click the **Type of Source** arrow, scroll up or down in the list, and then click **Book**.

TIP

When entering information in a dialog box, you can press the Tab key to move the insertion point from one box to another.

▶ **9.** In the Author box, type **Adam Taylor**.

▶ **10.** Click in the **Title** box, and then type **Newspapers as Modern Media in a Modern Media World**.

▶ **11.** Click in the **Year** box, and then type **2005**. This is the year the book was published. Next, you need to enter the name and location of the publisher.

▶ **12.** Click the **City** box, type **New York**, click the **Publisher** box, and then type **Warrington and Reeves Academy Press**.

Finally, you need to indicate the medium used to publish the book. In this case, Kaya used a printed copy, so the medium is "Print." For books or journals published online, the correct medium would be "Web."

▶ **13.** Click the **Medium** box, and then type **Print**. See Figure 2-29.

Figure 2-29 | **Create Source dialog box with information for the first source**

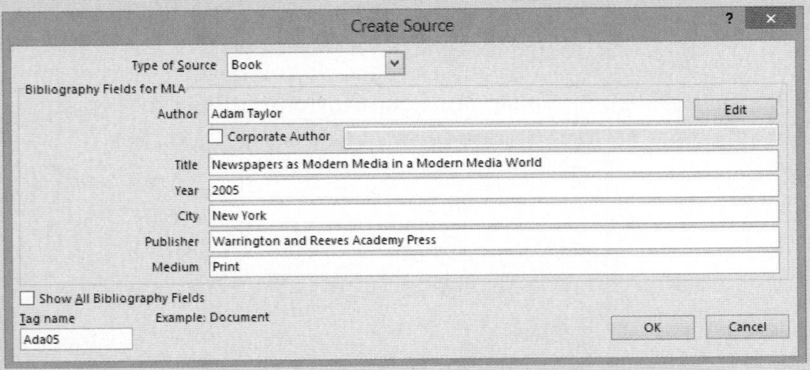

14. Click the **OK** button. Word inserts the parenthetical "(Taylor)" at the end of the sentence in the document.

Although the citation looks like ordinary text, it is actually contained inside a content control, a special feature used to display information that is inserted automatically and that may need to be updated later. You can only see the content control itself when it is selected. When it is unselected, you simply see the citation. In the next set of steps, you will select the content control, and then edit the citation to add a page number.

To edit the citation:

TIP

To delete a citation, click the citation to display the content control, click the tab on the left side of the content control, and then press the Delete key.

1. In the document, click the citation **(Taylor)**. The citation appears in a content control, which is a box with a tab on the left and an arrow button on the right. The arrow button is called the Citation Options button.

2. Click the **Citation Options** button ⬚. A menu of options related to editing a citation opens, as shown in Figure 2-30. To edit the information about the source, you click Edit Source. To change the information that is displayed in the citation itself, you use the Edit Citation option.

Figure 2-30 **Citation Options menu**

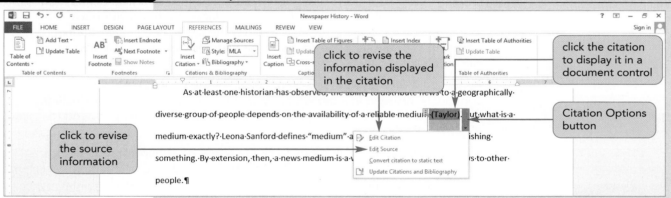

3. On the Citation Options menu, click **Edit Citation**. The Edit Citation dialog box opens, as shown in Figure 2-31.

Figure 2-31 **Edit Citation dialog box**

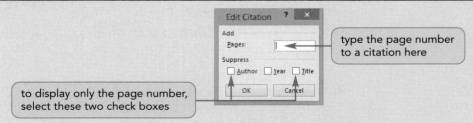

To add a page number for the citation, you type the page number in the Pages box. If you want to display only the page number in the citation (which would be necessary if you already mentioned the author's name in the same sentence in the text), then you would also select the Author and Title check boxes in this dialog box to suppress this information.

4. Type **45** to insert the page number in the Pages box, click the **OK** button to close the dialog box, and then click anywhere in the document outside the citation content control. The revised citation now reads "(Taylor 45)."

Next, you will add two more citations, both for the same journal article.

To insert two more citations:

1. Click at the end of the second-to-last sentence of the current paragraph (which begins "Leona Sanford defines…"), between the word "something" and the period. This sentence mentions historian Leona Sanford; you need to add a citation to one of her journal articles.

2. In the Citations & Bibliography group, click the **Insert Citation** button to open the Insert Citation menu. Notice that Adam Taylor's book is now listed as a source on this menu. You could click Taylor's book on the menu to add a citation to it, but right now you need to add a new source.

3. Click **Add New Source** to open the Create Source dialog box, click the **Type of Source** arrow, and then click **Journal Article**.

   The Create Source dialog box displays the boxes, or fields, appropriate for a journal article. The information required to cite a journal article differs from the information you entered earlier for the citation for the Taylor book. For journal articles, you are prompted to enter the page numbers for the entire article. If you want to display a particular page number in the citation, you can add it later.

   By default, Word displays boxes, or fields, for the information most commonly included in a bibliography. In this case, you also want to include the volume and issue numbers for Leona Sanford's article, so you need to display more fields.

4. In the Create Source dialog box, click the **Show All Bibliography Fields** check box to select this option. The Create Source dialog box expands to allow you to enter more detailed information. Red asterisks highlight the fields that are recommended, but these recommended fields don't necessarily apply to every source.

5. Enter the following information, scrolling down to display the necessary boxes:

   Author: **Leona Sanford**

   Title: **News Media in History: A Study of Newsgathering from the Roman Empire to the Modern Day**

   Journal Name: **Journal of Media Policy Studies International**

   Year: **2008**

   Pages: **122–145**

   Volume: **30**

   Issue: **5**

   Medium: **Web**

   When you are finished, your Create Source dialog box should look like the one shown in Figure 2-32.

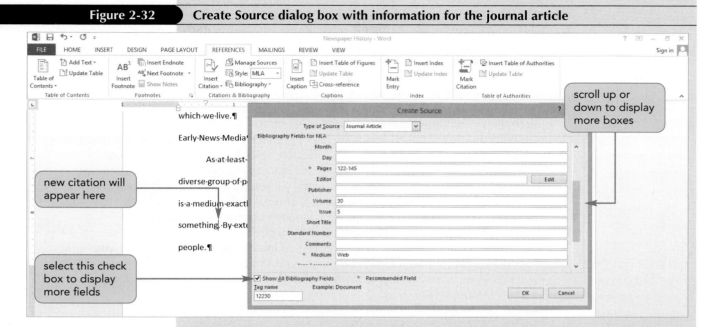

Figure 2-32   **Create Source dialog box with information for the journal article**

new citation will appear here

scroll up or down to display more boxes

select this check box to display more fields

6. Click the **OK** button. The Create Source dialog box closes, and the citation "(Sanford)" is inserted in the text. Because the sentence containing the citation already includes the author's name, you will edit the citation to include the page number and suppress the author's name.

7. Click the **(Sanford)** citation to display the content control, click the **Citation Options** button ▯, and then click **Edit Citation** to open the Edit Citation dialog box.

8. In the Pages box, type **142**, and then click the **Author** and **Title** check boxes to select them. You need to suppress both the author's name and the title because otherwise Word will replace the suppressed author name with the title. When using the MLA style, you don't ever have to suppress the year because the year is never included as part of an MLA citation. When working in other styles, however, you might need to suppress the year.

9. Click the **OK** button to close the Edit Citation dialog box, and then click anywhere outside the content control to deselect it. The end of the sentence now reads "…accomplishing something (142)."

10. Use the Navigation pane to find the sentence that begins "Throughout history…" on the second page. Click at the end of the sentence, to the left of the period after "news," and then close the Navigation pane.

11. On the REFERENCES tab, in the Citations & Bibliography group, click the **Insert Citation** button, and then click the **Sanford, Leona** source at the top of the menu. You want the citation to refer to the entire article instead of just one page, so you will not edit the citation to add a specific page number.

12. Save the document.

You have entered the source information for two sources.

Generating a Bibliography

Once you have created a citation for a source in a document, you can generate a bibliography. When you do, Word scans all the citations in the document, collecting the source information for each citation, and then it creates a list of information for each unique source. The format of the entries in the bibliography will reflect the style you specified when you created your first citation, which in this case is the MLA style. The bibliography itself is a **field**, similar to the page number field you inserted earlier in this session. In other words, it is really an instruction that tells Word to display the source information for all the citations in the document. Because it is a field and not actual text, you can update the bibliography later to reflect any new citations you might add.

You can choose to insert a bibliography as a field directly in the document, or you can insert a bibliography enclosed within a content control that also includes the heading "Bibliography" or "Works Cited." Inserting a bibliography enclosed in a content control is best because the content control includes a useful button that you can use to update your bibliography if you make changes to the sources.

In the MLA style, the bibliography (or works cited list) starts on a new page. So your first step is to insert a manual page break. A **manual page break** is one you insert at a specific location; it doesn't matter if the previous page is full or not. To insert a manual page break, use the Page Break button in the Pages group on the INSERT tab.

To insert a manual page break:

1. Press the **Ctrl+End** keys to move the insertion point to the end of the document.

2. On the ribbon, click the **INSERT** tab.

3. In the Pages group, click the **Page Break** button. Word inserts a new, blank page at the end of the document, with the insertion point blinking at the top. Note that you could also use the Ctrl+Enter keyboard shortcut to insert a manual page break.

4. Scroll up to see the dotted line with the words "Page Break" at the bottom of the text on page 4. See Figure 2-33.

TIP

Use the Blank Page button to insert a new, blank page in the middle of a document.

Figure 2-33 Manual page break inserted into the document

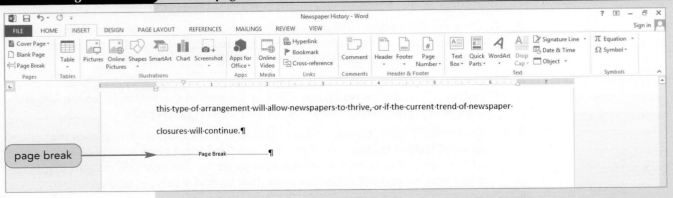

Now you can insert the bibliography on the new page 5.

To insert the bibliography:

1. Scroll down so you can see the insertion point at the top of page 5.

2. On the ribbon, click the **REFERENCES** tab.

3. In the Citations & Bibliography group, click the **Bibliography** button. The Bibliography menu opens, displaying three styles with preformatted headings—"Bibliography," "References," and "Works Cited." The Insert Bibliography command at the bottom inserts a bibliography without a preformatted heading. See Figure 2-34.

Figure 2-34   **Bibliography menu**

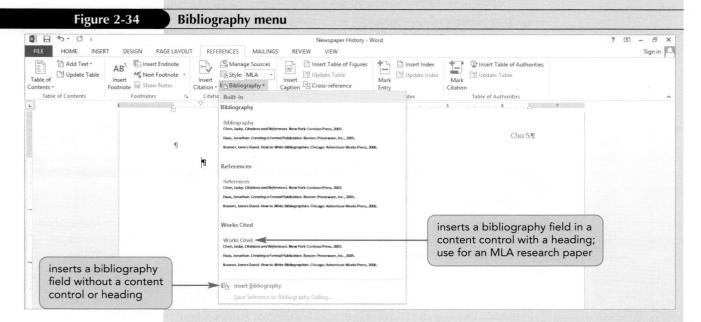

inserts a bibliography field in a content control with a heading; use for an MLA research paper

inserts a bibliography field without a content control or heading

---

4. Click **Works Cited**. Word inserts the bibliography, with two entries, below the "Works Cited" heading.

   The bibliography text is formatted in Calibri, the default font for the Office theme. The "Works Cited" heading is formatted with the Heading 1 style. To see the content control that contains the bibliography, you need to select it.

5. Click anywhere in the bibliography. Inside the content control, the bibliography is highlighted in gray, indicating that it is a field and not regular text. The content control containing the bibliography is also now visible in the form of a rectangular border and a tab with two buttons. See Figure 2-35.

| Figure 2-35 | Bibliography displayed in a content control |

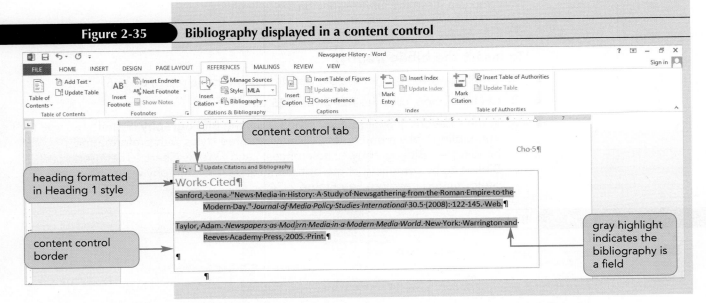

As Kaya looks over the works cited list, she realizes that she misspelled the last name of one of the authors. You'll correct the error now, and then update the bibliography.

INSIGHT

Managing Sources

When you create a source, Word adds it to a Master List of sources, which is available to any document created using the same user account on that computer. Word also adds each new source to the Current List of sources for that document. Both the Master List and the Current List are accessible via the Source Manager dialog box, which you open by clicking the Manage Sources button in the Citations & Bibliography group on the REFERENCES tab. Using this dialog box, you can copy sources from the Master List into the Current List, and vice versa. As you begin to focus on a particular academic field and turn repeatedly to important works in your chosen field, you'll find this ability to reuse sources very helpful.

Modifying an Existing Source

To modify information about a source, you click a citation to that source in the document, click the Citation Options button on the content control, and then click Edit Source. After you are finished editing the source, Word prompts you to update the master list and the source information in the current document. In almost all cases, you should click Yes to ensure that the source information is correct in all the places it is stored on your computer.

To edit a source in the research paper:

▶ **1.** Click in the blank paragraph below the bibliography content control to deselect the bibliography.

▶ **2.** Scroll up to display the last paragraph on page 2, and then click the **(Sanford)** citation you entered earlier in the first line of the paragraph. The content control appears around the citation.

> **3.** Click the **Citation Options** button ⧉, and then click **Edit Source**. The Edit Source dialog box opens. Note that Word displays the author's last name first in the Author box, just as it would appear in a bibliography.

> **4.** Click the **Author** box, and then add an "e" to the last name "Sanford" to change it to "Sanforde."

> **5.** Click the **OK** button. A message dialog box opens, asking if you want to update the master source list and the current document.

> **6.** Click the **Yes** button, and then click anywhere on the second page to deselect the citation content control. The revised author name in the citation now reads "Sanforde."

> **7.** Scroll up to the last paragraph on page 1, locate "Sanford" in the last paragraph on the page, and then change "Sanford" to "Sanforde."

> **8.** Save the document.

You've edited the document text and the citation to include the correct spelling of "Sanforde," but now you need to update the bibliography to correct the spelling.

Updating and Finalizing a Bibliography

The bibliography does not automatically change to reflect edits you make to existing citations or to show new citations. To incorporate the latest information stored in the citations, you need to update the bibliography. To update a bibliography in a content control, click the bibliography, and then, in the content control tab, click Update Citations and Bibliography. To update a bibliography field that is not contained in a content control, right-click the bibliography, and then click Update Field on the shortcut menu.

To update the bibliography:

> **1.** Scroll down to page 5 and click anywhere in the works cited list to display the content control.

> **2.** In the content control tab, click **Update Citations and Bibliography**. The works cited list is updated, with "Sanford" changed to "Sanforde" in the first entry.

Kaya still has a fair amount of work to do on her research paper. After she finishes writing it and adding all the citations, she will update the bibliography again to include all her cited sources. At that point, you might think the bibliography would be finished. However, a few steps remain to ensure that the works cited list matches the MLA style. To finalize Kaya's works cited list to match the MLA style, you need to make the changes shown in Figure 2-36.

Figure 2-36   **Steps for finalizing a bibliography to match MLA guidelines for a Works Cited list**

1. Format the "Works Cited" heading to match the formatting of the rest of the text in the document.

2. Center the "Works Cited" heading.

3. Double-space the entire works cited list, including the heading, and remove extra space after the paragraphs.

4. Change the font size for the entire works cited list to 12 points.

To format the bibliography as an MLA style works cited list:

1. Click in the **Works Cited** heading, and then click the **HOME** tab on the ribbon.

2. In the Styles group, click the **Normal** style. The "Works Cited" heading is now formatted in Calibri body font like the rest of the document. The MLA style for a works cited list requires this heading to be centered.

3. In the Paragraph group, click the **Center** button ▤.

4. Select the entire works cited list, including the heading. Change the font size to **12** points, change the line spacing to **2.0**, and then remove the paragraph spacing after each paragraph.

5. Click below the content control to deselect the works cited list, and then review your work. See Figure 2-37.

Figure 2-37	MLA-style Works Cited list

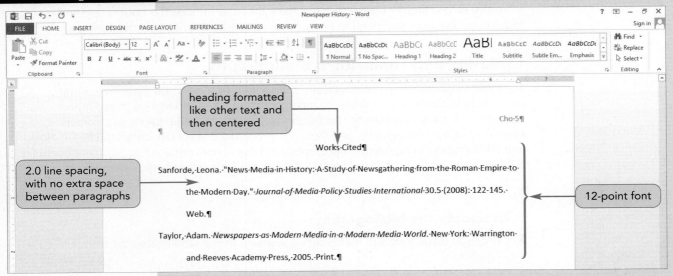

6. Save the document and close it.

Kaya's research paper now meets the MLA style guidelines.

Session 2.2 Quick Check

REVIEW

1. List the five tasks you need to perform to make a default Word document match the MLA style.

2. How do you indent a paragraph one inch from the left margin using an option on the ribbon?

3. Explain how to remove a page number from the first page of a document.

4. What is a bibliography called according to the MLA style?

5. Explain how to create a citation for a new source.

6. Explain how to edit a citation to display only the page number.

SAM Projects

Put your skills into practice with SAM Projects! SAM Projects for this tutorial can be found online. If you have a SAM account, go to www.cengage.com/sam2013 to download the most recent Project Instructions and Start Files.

Review Assignments

Data Files needed for the Review Assignments: Broadcast.docx, Situation.docx

Because the Media Studies document turned out so well, Kaya has been asked to help a student assistant in the Journalism department create a handout describing the classes required for a major in Broadcast Journalism. Kaya asks you to help her revise and format the document. She also asks you to create a document listing the prerequisites and core courses. Finally, as part of her Media Studies class, Kaya is working on a research paper on the history of situation comedy. She asks you to help her format the paper according to the MLA style, and to create some citations and a bibliography. She has inserted the uppercase word "CITATION" wherever she needs to insert a citation. Complete the following steps:

1. Open the file **Broadcast** located in the Word2 ▸ Review folder included with your Data Files, and then save the document as **Broadcast Journalism** in the location specified by your instructor.

2. Read the first comment, which provides an overview of the changes you will be making to the document in the following steps. Perform the task described in the second comment, and then delete both comments.

3. On page 2, in the second paragraph, revise the name of the first public speaking class so that only the first letter of each word is capitalized. Attach a comment to this paragraph that explains the change.

4. On page 2, move the "Senior Project" heading up to position it before the paragraph that begins "This project should incorporate...."

5. Replace the first instance of "journalism" with "media," being sure to match the case.

6. On page 1, format the list of four prerequisite classes as a bulleted list with square bullets. Do the same for the list of core courses, and then indent the three symposium names so they are formatted with an open circle bullet.

7. At the top of page 2, format the list of three public speaking classes as a numbered list, using the "1), 2), 3)" numbering style.

8. In the numbered list, move paragraph 3 ("Broadcast Journalism 220: Video Reporting") up to make it paragraph 2.

9. Format the title "Majoring in Broadcast Journalism" using the Title style. Format the following headings with the Heading 1 style: "Prerequisites," "Core Courses," "Electives," "Public Speaking," and "Senior Project."

10. Change the document theme to the Integral theme.

11. Display the Clipboard task pane. Copy the bulleted list of prerequisites to the Clipboard, and then copy the heading "Prerequisites" to the Clipboard. To ensure that you copy the heading formatting, be sure to select the paragraph mark after "Prerequisites" before you click the Copy button.

12. Open a new, blank document, and then save the document as **Prerequisite List** in the location specified by your instructor.

13. At the beginning of the document, paste the heading "Prerequisites," and then, from the Paste Options menu, apply the Keep Source Formatting option. Below the heading, paste the list of prerequisites, which begins with the text "Journalism 101...."

14. At the end of the document, insert a new paragraph, and then type **Prepared by:** followed by your first and last names.

15. Save the Prerequisite List document and close it.

16. In the Broadcast Journalism document, clear the contents of the Clipboard task pane, close the Clipboard task pane, save the document, and then close it.

17. Open the file **Situation** located in the Word2 ▸ Review folder included with your Data Files.

18. Save the document as **Situation Comedy** in the location specified by your instructor.

19. In the first paragraph, replace Kaya's name with your own.

20. Adjust the font size, line spacing, paragraph spacing, and paragraph indents to match the MLA style.

21. Insert your last name and a page number on every page except the first.

22. If necessary, select MLA Seventh Edition as the citations and bibliography style.

23. Use the Navigation pane to highlight all instances of the uppercase word "CITATION." Keep the Navigation pane open so you can continue to use it to find the locations where you need to insert citations in Steps 24–28.

24. Delete the first instance of "CITATION" and the space before it, and then create a new source with the following information:

    Type of Source: **Book**
    Author: **Cecile Webster**
    Title: **The Comedy of Situations: A History in Words and Pictures**
    Year: **2008**
    City: **Boston**
    Publisher: **Boston Valley Press**
    Medium: **Print**

25. Edit the citation to add **203** as the page number. Display only the page number in the citation.

26. Delete the second instance of "CITATION" and the space before it, and then create a new source with the following information:

    Type of Source: **Journal Article**
    Author: **Oliver Bernault**
    Title: **How Slapstick Conquered the World**
    Journal Name: **Pacific Film Quarterly: Criticism and Comment**
    Year: **2011**
    Pages: **68–91**
    Volume: **11**
    Issue: **2**
    Medium: **Web**

27. Edit the citation to add "80" as the page number.

28. Delete the third instance of "CITATION" and the space before it, and then insert a citation for the book by Cecile Webster.

29. At the end of the document, start a new page and insert a bibliography in a content control with the heading "Works Cited."

30. In the second source you created, add an "e" to change the last name "Bernault" to "Bernaulte," and then update the bibliography.

31. Finalize the bibliography to create an MLA-style Works Cited list.

32. Save the **Situation Comedy** document and close it.

33. Close any other open documents.

Case Problem 1

APPLY

Data File needed for this Case Problem: Yoga.docx

Green Willow Yoga Studio and Spa   Karl Boccio, the manager of Green Willow Yoga Studio and Spa, created a flyer to inform clients of the studio's move to a new location. The flyer also lists classes for the summer session and explains the registration process. It's your job to format the flyer to make it look professional and easy to read. Karl included comments in the document explaining what he wants you to do. Complete the following steps:

1. Open the file **Yoga** located in the Word2 ▸ Case1 folder included with your Data Files, and then save the file as **Yoga Flyer** in the location specified by your instructor.
2. Format the document as directed in the comments. After you complete a task, delete the relevant comment. Respond "Yes" to the comment asking if twenty is the correct number of years. When you are finished with the formatting, the comment with the question and the comment with your reply should be the only remaining comments.
3. Move the third bulleted item (which begins "Yoga for Relaxation...") up to make it the first bulleted item in the list.
4. Change the theme to the Ion theme, and then attach a comment to the title listing the heading and body fonts applied by the Ion theme.
5. Save the document and then close it.

Case Problem 2

APPLY

Data File needed for this Case Problem: Hamlet.docx

South Valley Community College   Jaleel Reynolds is a student at South Valley Community College. He's working on a research paper about Shakespeare's tragic masterpiece, *Hamlet*. The research paper is only partly finished, with notes in brackets indicating the material Jaleel still plans to write. He also inserted the uppercase word "CITATION" wherever he needs to insert a citation. Jaleel asks you to help him format this early draft to match the MLA style. He also asks you to help him create some citations and a first attempt at a bibliography. He will update the bibliography later, after he finishes writing the research paper. Complete the following steps:

1. Open the file **Hamlet** located in the Word2 ▸ Case2 folder included with your Data Files, and then save the document as **Hamlet Paper** in the location specified by your instructor.
2. In the first paragraph, replace "Jaleel Reynolds" with your name, and then adjust the font size, line spacing, paragraph spacing, and paragraph indents to match the MLA style.
3. Insert your last name and a page number in the upper-right corner of every page except the first page in the document.
4. If necessary, select MLA Seventh Edition as the citations and bibliography style.
5. Use the Navigation pane to find three instances of the uppercase word "CITATION."
6. Delete the first instance of "CITATION" and the space before it, and then create a new source with the following information:
   Type of Source: **Book**
   Author: **Andre Kahn**
   Title: **Tragic Drama in a Tragic Age**
   Year: **2000**
   City: **Chicago**
   Publisher: **Houghton University Press**
   Medium: **Print**
7. Edit the citation to add **127** as the page number.

8. Delete the second instance of "CITATION" and the space before it, and then create a new source with the following information:

Type of Source: **Sound Recording**

Performer: **Avery Pohlman**

Title: **Live From New York's Golden Arch Theater**

Production Company: **Prescott**

Year: **1995**

Medium: **CD**

City: **New York**

9. Edit the citation to suppress the Author and the Year, so that it displays only the title.

10. Delete the third instance of "CITATION" and the space before it, and then insert a second reference to the book by Andre Kahn.

11. Edit the citation to add **35** as the page number.

12. At the end of the document, start a new page, and then insert a bibliography with the preformatted heading "Works Cited."

13. Edit the first source you created, changing the last name from "Kahn" to **Klann.**

14. Update the bibliography so it shows the revised name "Klann."

15. Finalize the bibliography so that it matches the MLA style.

16. Save the Hamlet Paper document and close it.

Case Problem 3

CREATE

Data Files needed for this Case Problem: Capital.docx, Sarah.docx

Sports Training   Sarah Vang has more than a decade of experience as an athletic trainer in several different settings. After moving to a new city, she is looking for a job as a trainer in a hospital. She has asked you to edit and format her resume. As part of the application process, she will have to upload her resume to the hospitals' employee recruitment websites. Because these sites typically request a simple page design, Sarah plans to rely primarily on heading styles and bullets to organize her information. When the resume is complete, she wants you to remove any color applied by the heading styles. She also needs help formatting a document she created for a public health organization for which she volunteers. Complete the following steps:

1. Open the file **Sarah** located in the Word2 ► Case3 folder included with your Data Files, and then save the file as **Sarah Resume** in the location specified by your instructor.

2. Read the comment included in the document, and then perform the task it specifies.

3. Respond to the comment with the response **I think that's a good choice for the theme.**, and then mark Sarah's comment as done.

4. Replace all occurrences of "Mesacrest" with **Mesa Crest**.

5. Format the resume as shown in Figure 2-38. To ensure that the resume fits on one page, pay special attention to the paragraph spacing settings specified in Figure 2-38.

Figure 2-38   **Formatting for Sarah Vang's resume**

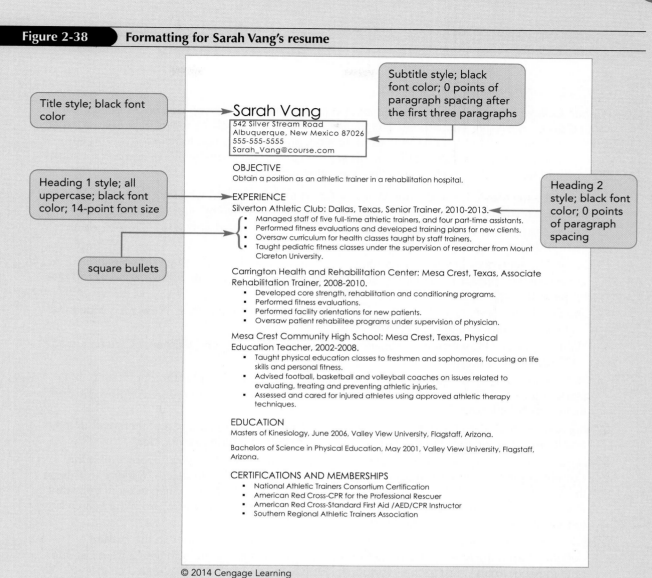

Title style; black font color

Subtitle style; black font color; 0 points of paragraph spacing after the first three paragraphs

Heading 1 style; all uppercase; black font color; 14-point font size

Heading 2 style; black font color; 0 points of paragraph spacing

square bullets

Sarah Vang

542 Silver Stream Road
Albuquerque, New Mexico 87026
555-555-5555
Sarah_Vang@course.com

OBJECTIVE
Obtain a position as an athletic trainer in a rehabilitation hospital.

EXPERIENCE
Silverton Athletic Club: Dallas, Texas, Senior Trainer, 2010-2013.
- Managed staff of five full-time athletic trainers, and four part-time assistants.
- Performed fitness evaluations and developed training plans for new clients.
- Oversaw curriculum for health classes taught by staff trainers.
- Taught pediatric fitness classes under the supervision of researcher from Mount Clareton University.

Carrington Health and Rehabilitation Center: Mesa Crest, Texas, Associate Rehabilitation Trainer, 2008-2010.
- Developed core strength, rehabilitation and conditioning programs.
- Performed fitness evaluations.
- Performed facility orientations for new patients.
- Oversaw patient rehabilitee programs under supervision of physician.

Mesa Crest Community High School: Mesa Crest, Texas, Physical Education Teacher, 2002-2008.
- Taught physical education classes to freshmen and sophomores, focusing on life skills and personal fitness.
- Advised football, basketball and volleyball coaches on issues related to evaluating, treating and preventing athletic injuries.
- Assessed and cared for injured athletes using approved athletic therapy techniques.

EDUCATION
Masters of Kinesiology, June 2006, Valley View University, Flagstaff, Arizona.

Bachelors of Science in Physical Education, May 2001, Valley View University, Flagstaff, Arizona.

CERTIFICATIONS AND MEMBERSHIPS
- National Athletic Trainers Consortium Certification
- American Red Cross-CPR for the Professional Rescuer
- American Red Cross-Standard First Aid /AED/CPR Instructor
- Southern Regional Athletic Trainers Association

© 2014 Cengage Learning

6. In the email address, replace "Sarah_Vang" with your first and last names, separated by an underscore, and then save the document and close it.

7. Open the file **Capital** located in the Word2 ▶ Case4 folder included with your Data Files, and then save the file as **Capital Campaign** in the location specified by your instructor. Search for the text "Your Name", and then replace it with your first and last names.

8. Select the three paragraphs below your name, and then decrease the indent for the selected paragraphs so that they align at the left margin. Create a .5-inch hanging indent for the selected paragraphs instead.

9. Change the document theme to Ion, and then add a comment to the first word in the document that reads "I changed the theme to Ion."

10. Use the Advanced Find dialog box to search for bold formatting. Remove the bold formatting from the fourth bold element in the document, and then add a comment to that element that reads "I assumed bold here was a mistake, so I removed it."

11. Save and close the document.

CHALLENGE

Case Problem 4

Data File needed for this Case Problem: Movie.docx

Winona College Tristan Giroux is a student at Winona College. She's working on a research paper about disaster movies for Film Studies 105, taught by Professor Douglas Fischer. The research paper is only partly finished, but before she does more work on it, she asks you to help format this early draft to match the MLA style. She also asks you to help her create some citations, add a placeholder citation, and manage her sources. Complete the following steps:

1. Open the file **Movie** located in the Word2 ► Case4 folder included with your Data Files, and then save the document as **Movie Paper** in the location specified by your instructor.

2. Revise the paper to match the MLA style, seventh edition. Instead of Tristan's name, use your own. Also, use the current date.

3. Locate the sentences in which the authors Dana Someya and Peter Williams are mentioned. At the end of the appropriate sentence, add a citation for page 135 in the following book and one for page 152 in the following journal article:

   Someya, Dana. *Society and Disaster in the Silent Era: A Modern Analysis.* New York: Movie House Academy Press, 1997. Print.

   Williams, Peter. "Romance in the Shadow of Disaster." *New England Journal of Cinema Studies* (2012): 133–155. Web.

4. At the end of the second-to-last sentence in the document, insert a placeholder citation that reads "Candela." At the end of the last sentence in the document, insert a placeholder citation that reads "Goldman."

⊕ **Explore** 5. Use Word Help to look up the topic "Create a bibliography," and then, within that article, read the sections titled "Find a source" and "Edit a citation placeholder."

⊕ **Explore** 6. Open the Source Manager, and search for the name "Someya." From within the Current List in the Source Manager, edit the Dana Someya citation to delete "Society and" from the title, so that the title begins "Disaster in the Silent Era…." Click Yes when asked if you want to update the source in both lists. When you are finished, delete "Someya" from the Search box to redisplay all the sources in both lists.

⊕ **Explore** 7. From within the Source Manager, copy a source not included in the current document from the Master List to the Current List. Examine the sources in the Current List and note the checkmarks next to the two sources for which you have already created citations, and the question marks next to the placeholder sources. Sources in the Current list that are not actually cited in the text have no symbol next to them in the Current List. For example, if you copied a source from the Master List into your Current List, that source has no symbol next to it in the Current List.

8. Close the Source Manager, create a bibliography in the MLA style, and note which works appear in it.

⊕ **Explore** 9. Open the Source Manager, and then edit the Goldman placeholder source to include the following information about a journal article:

   Goldman, Simon. "Attack of the Killer Disaster Movie." *Cinema International Journal* (2009): 72–89. Web.

10. Update the bibliography.

⊕ **Explore** 11. Open Internet Explorer and use the Web to research the difference between a works cited list and a works consulted list. If necessary, open the Source Manager, and then delete any uncited sources from the Current List to ensure that your document contains a true works cited list, as specified by the MLA style, and not a works consulted list. (Tristan will create a full citation for the "Candela" placeholder later.)

12. Update the bibliography, finalize it so it matches the MLA style, save the document and close it.

OBJECTIVES

Session 3.1
- Review document headings in the Navigation pane
- Reorganize document text using the Navigation pane
- Collapse and expand body text in a document
- Create and edit a table
- Sort rows in a table
- Modify a table's structure
- Format a table

Session 3.2
- Set tab stops
- Turn on automatic hyphenation
- Create footnotes and endnotes
- Divide a document into sections
- Create a SmartArt graphic
- Create headers and footers
- Insert a cover page
- Change the document's theme
- Review a document in Read Mode

Creating Tables and a Multipage Report

Writing a Recommendation

Case | *Orchard Street Art Center*

Katherine Hua is the facilities director for Orchard Street Art Center, a nonprofit organization that provides performance, rehearsal, and classroom space for arts organizations in St. Louis, Missouri. The center's facilities include a 300-seat indoor theater, a 200-seat outdoor theater, public terraces and lobbies, five classrooms, 20 rehearsal rooms, and several offices. Katherine hopes to improve the wireless network that serves the center's staff and patrons through a process known as a wireless site survey. She has written a multiple-page report for the center's board of directors summarizing basic information about wireless site surveys. She has asked you to finish formatting the report. Katherine also needs your help with adding a table and a diagram to the end of the report.

In this tutorial, you'll use the Navigation pane to review the document headings and reorganize the document. You will also insert a table, modify it by changing the structure and formatting, set tab stops, create footnotes and endnotes, hyphenate the document, and insert a section break. In addition, you'll create a SmartArt graphic and add headers and footers. Finally, you will insert a cover page and review the document in Read Mode.

WORD

STARTING DATA FILES

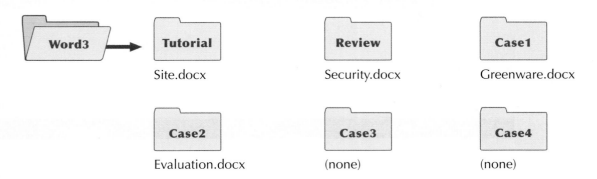

Word3 → Tutorial
Site.docx

Review
Security.docx

Case1
Greenware.docx

Case2
Evaluation.docx

Case3
(none)

Case4
(none)

Session 3.1 Visual Overview:

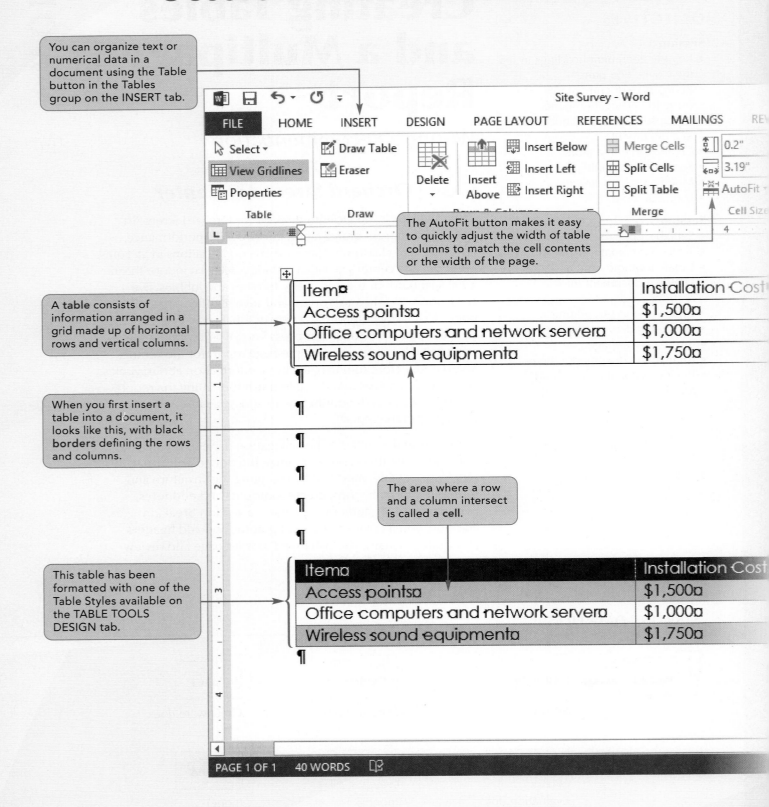

You can organize text or numerical data in a document using the Table button in the Tables group on the INSERT tab.

The AutoFit button makes it easy to quickly adjust the width of table columns to match the cell contents or the width of the page.

A table consists of information arranged in a grid made up of horizontal rows and vertical columns.

When you first insert a table into a document, it looks like this, with black borders defining the rows and columns.

The area where a row and a column intersect is called a cell.

This table has been formatted with one of the Table Styles available on the TABLE TOOLS DESIGN tab.

Organizing Information in Tables

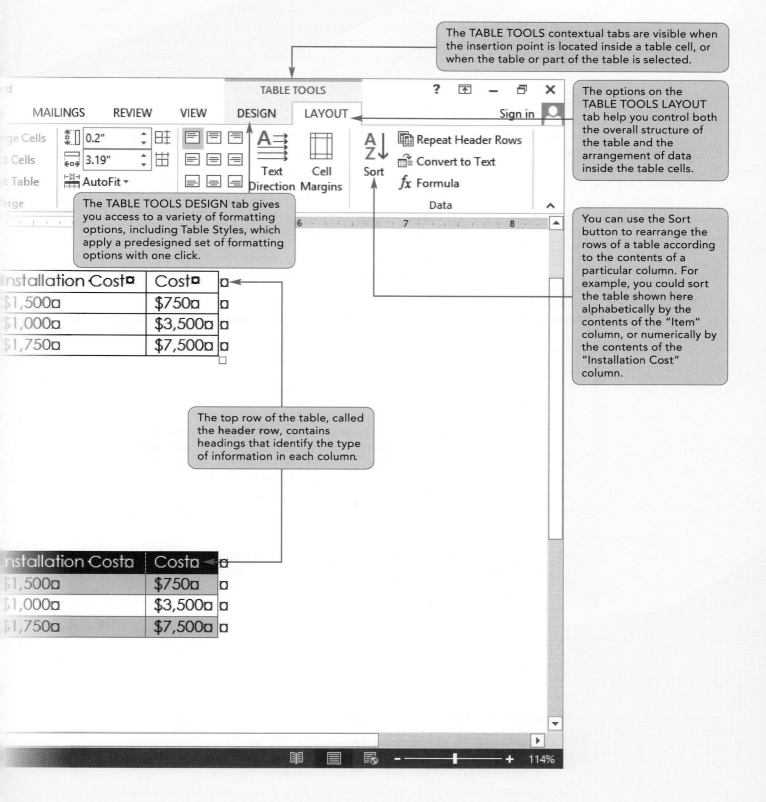

The TABLE TOOLS contextual tabs are visible when the insertion point is located inside a table cell, or when the table or part of the table is selected.

The options on the TABLE TOOLS LAYOUT tab help you control both the overall structure of the table and the arrangement of data inside the table cells.

The TABLE TOOLS DESIGN tab gives you access to a variety of formatting options, including Table Styles, which apply a predesigned set of formatting options with one click.

You can use the Sort button to rearrange the rows of a table according to the contents of a particular column. For example, you could sort the table shown here alphabetically by the contents of the "Item" column, or numerically by the contents of the "Installation Cost" column.

The top row of the table, called the **header row**, contains headings that identify the type of information in each column.

Working with Headings in the Navigation Pane

When used in combination with the Navigation pane, Word's heading styles make it easier to navigate through a long document and to reorganize a document. You start by formatting the document headings with heading styles, displaying the Navigation pane, and then clicking the Headings link. This displays a hierarchy of all the headings in the document, allowing you to see, at a glance, an outline of the document headings.

Paragraphs formatted with the Heading 1 style are considered the highest level headings and are aligned at the left margin of the Navigation pane. Paragraphs formatted with the Heading 2 style are considered **subordinate** to Heading 1 paragraphs, and are indented slightly to the right below the Heading 1 paragraphs. Subordinate headings are often referred to as **subheadings**. Each successive level of heading styles (Heading 3, Heading 4, and so on) is indented farther to the right. To simplify your view of the document outline in the Navigation pane, you can choose to hide lower-level headings from view, leaving only the major headings visible.

From within the Navigation pane, you can **promote** a subordinate heading to the next level up in the heading hierarchy. For example, you can promote a Heading 2 paragraph to a Heading 1 paragraph. You can also do the opposite—that is, you can **demote** a heading to a subordinate level. You can also click and drag a heading in the Navigation pane to a new location in the document's outline. When you do so, any subheadings—along with their subordinate body text—move to the new location in the document.

REFERENCE

Working with Headings in the Navigation Pane

- Format the document headings using Word's heading styles.
- On the ribbon, click the HOME tab.
- In the Editing group, click the Find button, or press the Ctrl+F keys, to display the Navigation pane.
- In the Navigation pane, click the HEADINGS link to display a list of the document headings, and then click a heading to display that heading in the document window.
- In the Navigation pane, click a heading, and then drag it up or down in the list of headings to move that heading and the body text below it to a new location in the document.
- In the Navigation pane, right-click a heading, and then click Promote to promote the heading to the next-highest level. To demote a heading, right-click it, and then click Demote.
- To hide subheadings in the Navigation pane, click the Collapse arrow next to the higher level heading above them. To redisplay the subheadings, click the Expand arrow next to the higher level heading.

Katherine saved the draft of her report as a Word document named Site. You will use the Navigation pane to review the outline of Katherine's report and make some changes to its organization.

To review the document headings in the Navigation pane:

▶ **1.** Open the document named **Site** located in the Word3 ▶ Tutorial folder included with your Data Files, and then save the file with the name **Site Survey Report** in the location specified by your instructor.

▶ **2.** Verify that the document is displayed in Print Layout view, and that the rulers and nonprinting characters are displayed.

3. Make sure the Zoom level is set to **120%**, and that the HOME tab is selected on the ribbon.

4. Press the **Ctrl+F** keys. The Navigation pane opens to the left of the document.

5. In the Navigation pane, click the **HEADINGS** link. The document headings are displayed in the Navigation pane, as shown in Figure 3-1. The blue highlighted heading ("Summary") indicates which part of the document currently contains the insertion point.

Figure 3-1 **Headings displayed in the Navigation pane**

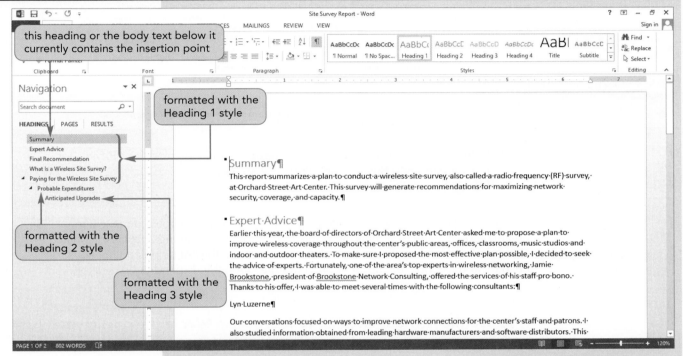

6. In the Navigation pane, click the **What Is a Wireless Site Survey?** heading. Word displays the heading in the document window, with the insertion point at the beginning of the heading. "The What Is a Wireless Site Survey?" heading is highlighted in blue in the Navigation pane.

7. In the Navigation pane, click the **Paying for the Wireless Site Survey** heading. Word displays the heading in the document window. In the Navigation pane, you can see that there are subheadings below this heading.

8. In the Navigation pane, click the **Collapse** arrow ◢ next to the "Paying for the Wireless Site Survey" heading. The subheadings below this heading are no longer visible in the Navigation pane. This has no effect on the text in the actual document. See Figure 3-2.

Figure 3-2	Heading 2 and Heading 3 text hidden in Navigation pane

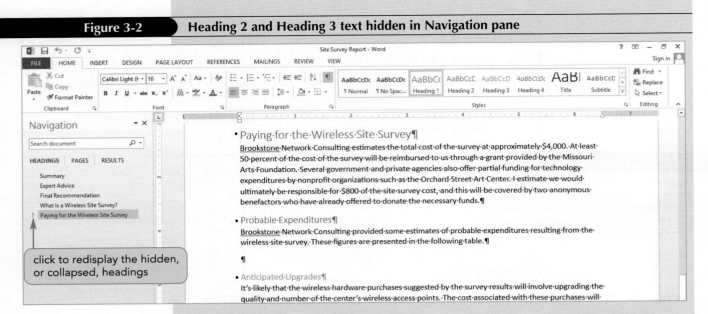

▶ **9.** In the Navigation pane, click the **Expand** arrow ▷ next to the "Paying for the Wireless Site Survey" heading. The subheadings are again visible in the Navigation pane.

Now that you have had a chance to review the report, you need to make a few organizational changes. Katherine wants to promote the Heading 3 text "Anticipated Upgrades" to Heading 2 text. Then she wants to move the "Anticipated Upgrades" heading and its body text up, so it precedes the "Probable Expenditures" section.

To use the Navigation pane to reorganize text in the document:

▶ **1.** In the Navigation pane, right-click the **Anticipated Upgrades** heading to display the shortcut menu.

▶ **2.** Click **Promote**. The heading moves to the left in the Navigation pane, aligning below the "Probable Expenditures" heading. In the document window, the text is now formatted with the Heading 2 style, with its slightly larger font.

▶ **3.** In the Navigation pane, click and drag the **Anticipated Upgrades** heading up. As you drag the heading, the pointer changes to ▷, and a blue guideline is displayed. You can use the guideline to position the heading in its new location.

▶ **4.** Position the guideline directly below the "Paying for the Wireless Site Survey" heading, as shown in Figure 3-3.

Figure 3-3   **Moving a heading in the Navigation pane**

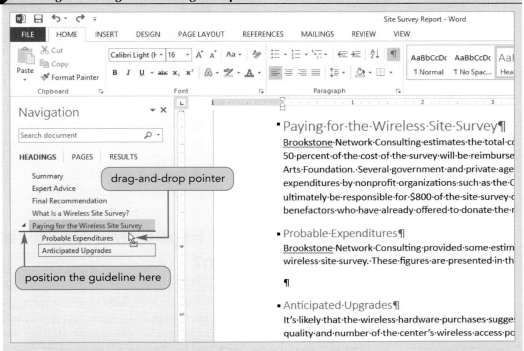

5. Release the mouse button. The "Anticipated Upgrades" heading is displayed in its new position in the Navigation pane, as the second-to-last heading in the outline. The heading and its body text are displayed in their new location in the document, before the "Probable Expenditures" heading. See Figure 3-4.

Figure 3-4   **Heading and body text in new location**

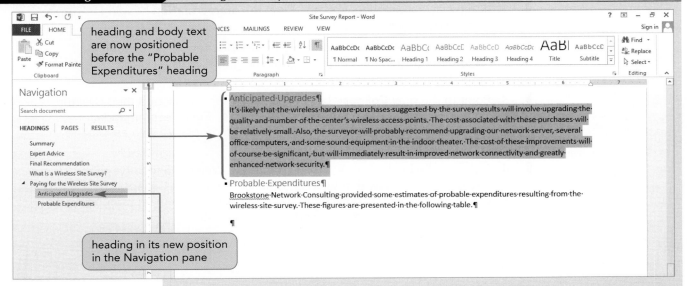

6. Click anywhere in the document to deselect the text, and then save the document.

Katherine also wants you to move the "Final Recommendation" heading and its accompanying body text. You'll do that in the next section, using a different method.

Promoting and Demoting Headings

When you promote or demote a heading, Word applies the next higher or lower level heading style to the heading paragraph. You could accomplish the same thing by using the Style gallery to apply the next higher or lower level heading style, but it's easy to lose track of the overall organization of the document that way. By promoting and demoting headings from within the Navigation pane, you ensure that the overall document outline is right in front of you as you work.

You can also use Outline view to display, promote, and demote headings, and to reorganize a document. Turn on Outline view by clicking the VIEW tab, and then clicking the Outline button in the Views group to display the OUTLINING tab on the ribbon. To hide the OUTLINING tab and return to Print Layout view, click the Close Outline View button on the ribbon or the Print Layout button in the status bar.

Collapsing and Expanding Body Text in the Document

The Navigation pane gives you an overview of the entire document, and dragging headings within the Navigation pane is the best way to reorganize a document. However, you can also hide, or collapse, the body text below a heading in a document. You do this from within the document window, without using the Navigation pane. After you collapse the body text below a heading, you can drag the heading to a new location in the document. When you do, the body text moves along with the heading, just as if you had dragged the heading in the Navigation pane. You'll use this technique now to move the "Final Recommendation" heading and its body text.

To collapse and move a heading in the document:

1. In the Navigation pane, click the **Final Recommendation** heading to display it in the document window.

2. In the document window, place the mouse pointer over the **Final Recommendation** heading to display the gray Collapse button ◢ to the left of the heading.

3. Point to the gray **Collapse** button ◢ until it turns blue, and then click the **Collapse** button ◢. The body text below the "Final Recommendation" heading is now hidden. The Collapse button is replaced with an Expand button.

4. Collapse the body text below the "What Is a Wireless Site Survey?" heading. The body text below that heading is no longer visible. Collapsing body text can be helpful when you want to hide details in a document temporarily, so you can focus on a particular part. See Figure 3-5.

Figure 3-5   **Body text collapsed in the document**

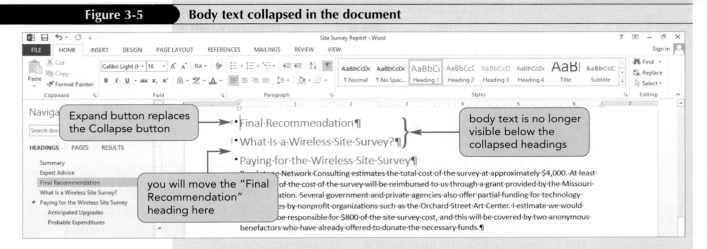

> **5.** Select the **Final Recommendation** heading.

> **6.** Click and drag the heading down. As you drag, a dark black insertion point moves along with the mouse pointer.

> **7.** Position the dark black insertion point to the left of the "P" in the "Paying for the Wireless Site Survey" heading, and then release the mouse button. The "Final Recommendation" heading and its body text move to the new location, before the "Paying for the Wireless Site Survey" heading.

> Finally, you need to expand the body text below the two collapsed headings.

> **8.** Click anywhere in the document to deselect the text.

> **9.** Point to the **Expand** button ▷ to the left of the "Final Recommendation" heading until it turns blue, and then click the **Expand** button ▶ to redisplay the body text below the heading.

> **10.** Point to the **Expand** button ▷ to the left of the "What Is a Wireless Site Survey?" heading until it turns blue, and then click the **Expand** button ▶ to redisplay the body text below the heading.

> **11.** Save the document.

The document is now organized the way Katherine wants it. Next, you need to create a table summarizing her data on probable expenditures.

Inserting a Blank Table

A table is a useful way to present information that is organized into categories, or **fields**. For example, you could use a table to organize contact information for a list of clients. For each client, you could include information in the following fields: first name, last name, street address, city, state, and zip code. The complete set of information about a particular client is called a **record**. In a typical table, each column is a separate field, and each row is a record. A header row at the top contains the names of each field.

The sketch in Figure 3-6 shows what Katherine wants the table in her report to look like.

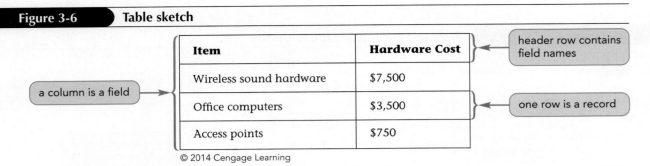

© 2014 Cengage Learning

Katherine's table includes two columns, or fields—"Item" and "Hardware Cost." The header row contains the names of these two fields. The three rows below contain the records.

Creating a table in Word is a three-step process. First, you use the Table button on the INSERT tab to insert a blank table structure. Then you enter information into the table. Finally, you format the table to make it easy to read.

Before you begin creating the table, you'll insert a page break before the "Probable Expenditures" heading. This will move the heading and its body text to a new page, with plenty of room below for the new table. As a general rule, you should not use page breaks to position a particular part of a document at the top of a page. If you add or remove text from the document later, you might forget that you inserted a manual page break, and you might end up with a document layout you didn't expect. By default, Word heading styles are set up to ensure that a heading always appears on the same page as the body text paragraph below it, so you'll never need to insert a page break just to move a heading to the same page as its body text. However, in this case, a page break is appropriate because you need the "Probable Expenditures" heading to appear at the top of a page with room for the table below.

To insert a page break and insert a blank table:

1. In the Navigation pane, click **Probable Expenditures** to display the heading in the document, with the insertion point to the left of the "P" in "Probable."

2. Close the Navigation pane, and then press the **Ctrl+Enter** keys to insert a page break. The "Probable Expenditures" heading and the body text following it move to a new, third page.

3. Scroll to position the "Probable Expenditures" heading at the top of the Word window, and then press the **Ctrl+End** keys to move the insertion point to the blank paragraph at the end of the document.

4. On the ribbon, click the **INSERT** tab.

5. In the Tables group, click the **Table** button. A table grid opens, with a menu at the bottom.

6. Use the mouse pointer to point to the upper-left cell of the grid, and then move the mouse pointer down and across the grid to highlight **two columns** and **four rows**. (The outline of a cell turns orange when it is highlighted.) As you move the pointer across the grid, Word indicates the size of the table (columns by rows) at the top of the grid. A Live Preview of the table structure is displayed in the document. See Figure 3-7.

Figure 3-7   Inserting a blank table

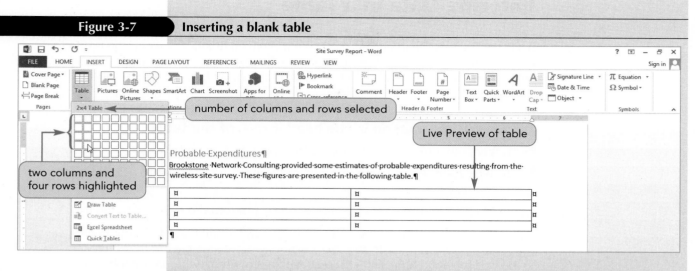

7. When the table size is 2×4, click the lower-right cell in the block of selected cells. An empty table consisting of two columns and four rows is inserted in the document, with the insertion point in the upper-left cell. See Figure 3-8.

Figure 3-8   Blank table inserted in document

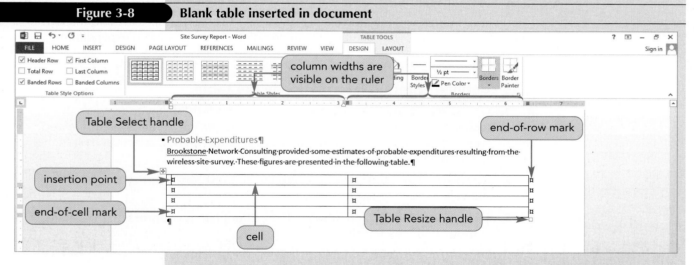

The two columns are of equal width. Because nonprinting characters are displayed in the document, each cell contains an end-of-cell mark, and each row contains an end-of-row mark, which are important for selecting parts of a table. The Table Select handle is displayed at the table's upper-left corner. You can click the Table Select handle to select the entire table, or you can drag it to move the table. You can drag the Table Resize handle, which is displayed at the lower-right corner, to change the size of the table. The TABLE TOOLS DESIGN and LAYOUT contextual tabs appear on the ribbon.

Trouble? If you inserted a table with the wrong number of rows or columns, click the Undo button on the Quick Access Toolbar to remove the table, and then repeat Steps 4 through 7.

The blank table is ready for you to begin entering information.

Entering Data in a Table

You can enter data in a table by moving the insertion point to a cell and typing. If the data takes up more than one line in the cell, Word automatically wraps the text to the next line and increases the height of that row. To move the insertion point to another cell in the table, you can click in that cell, use the arrow keys, or use the Tab key.

To enter information in the header row of the table:

▶ **1.** Verify that the insertion point is located in the upper-left cell.

▶ **2.** Type **Item**. As you type, the end-of-cell mark moves right to accommodate the text.

▶ **3.** Press the **Tab** key to move the insertion point to the next cell to the right.

   Trouble? If Word created a new paragraph in the first cell rather than moving the insertion point to the second cell, you pressed the Enter key instead of the Tab key. Press the Backspace key to remove the paragraph mark, and then press the Tab key to move to the second cell in the first row.

▶ **4.** Type **Hardware Cost** and then press the **Tab** key to move to the first cell in the second row.

You have finished entering the header row—the row that identifies the information in each column. Now you can enter the information about the various expenditures.

To continue entering information in the table:

▶ **1.** Type **wireless sound hardware** and then press the **Tab** key to move to the second cell in the second row. Notice that the "w" in "wireless" is capitalized, even though you typed it in lowercase. By default, AutoCorrect capitalizes the first letter in a cell entry.

▶ **2.** Type **$7,500** and then press the **Tab** key to move the insertion point to the first cell in the third row.

▶ **3.** Enter the following information in the bottom two rows, pressing the **Tab** key to move from cell to cell:

   Office computers; **$3,500**

   Access points; **$750**

At this point, the table consists of a header row and three records. Katherine realizes that she needs to add one more row to the table. You can add a new row to the bottom of a table by pressing the Tab key when the insertion point is in the rightmost cell in the bottom row.

To add a row to the table:

▶ **1.** Verify that the insertion point is in the lower-right cell (which contains the value "$750") and then press the **Tab** key. A new, blank row is added to the bottom of the table.

▶ **2.** Type **Network server**, press the **Tab** key, and then type **$2,200**. When you are finished, your table should look like the one shown in Figure 3-9.

Figure 3-9   **Table with all data entered**

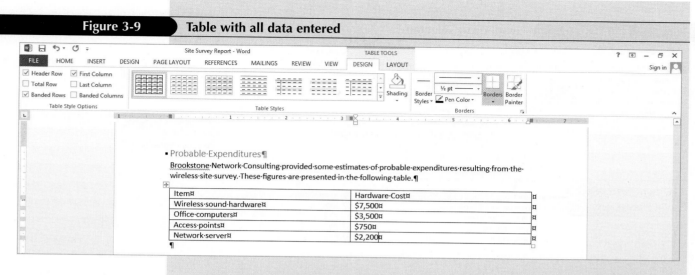

> **Trouble?** If a new row is added to the bottom of your table, you pressed the Tab key after entering "$2,200". Click the Undo button 🔄 on the Quick Access Toolbar to remove the extra row from the table.

The table you've just created presents information about expenditures in an easy-to-read format. To make it even easier to read, you can format the header row in bold so it stands out from the rest of the table. To do that, you need to first select the header row.

Selecting Part of a Table

TIP

To merge multiple cells into one cell, select the cells you want to merge, and then click the Merge Cells button in the Merge group on the TABLE TOOLS LAYOUT tab.

When selecting part of a table, you need to make sure you select the end-of-cell mark in a cell or the end-of-row mark at the end of a row. If you don't, the formatting changes you make next might not have the effect you expect. The foolproof way to select part of a table is to click in the cell, row, or column you want to select; click the Select button on the TABLE TOOLS LAYOUT contextual tab; and then click the appropriate command—Select Cell, Select Column, or Select Row. (You can also click Select Table to select the entire table.) To select a row, you can also click in the left margin next to the row. Similarly, you can click just above a column to select it. After you've selected an entire row, column, or cell, you can drag the mouse to select adjacent rows, columns, or cells.

Note that in the following steps, you'll position the mouse pointer until it takes on a particular shape so that you can then perform the task associated with that type of pointer. Pointer shapes are especially important when working with tables and graphics; in many cases, you can't perform a task until the pointer is the right shape. It takes some patience to get accustomed to positioning the pointer until it takes on the correct shape, but with practice you'll grow to rely on the pointer shapes as a quick visual cue to the options currently available to you.

To select and format the header row:

1. Position the mouse pointer in the selection bar, to the left of the header row. The pointer changes to a right-facing arrow ⤢.

2. Click the mouse button. The entire header row, including the end-of-cell mark in each cell and the end-of-row mark, is selected. See Figure 3-10.

Figure 3-10 Header row selected

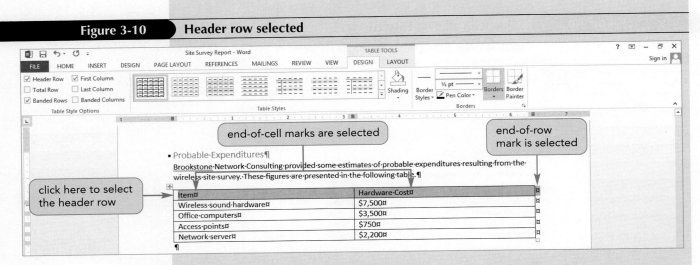

3. Press the **Ctrl+B** keys to apply bold to the text in the header row. You can also use the formatting options on the HOME tab to format selected text in a table, including adding italics, changing the font, aligning text within cells, or applying a style.

4. Click anywhere in the table to deselect the header row, and then save the document.

INSIGHT

Formatting a Multipage Table

In some documents, you might have a long table that extends across multiple pages. To make a multipage table easier to read, you can format the table header row to appear at the top of every page. To do so, click in the header row, click the TABLE TOOLS LAYOUT tab, and then click the Properties button in the Table group. In the Table Properties dialog box, click the Row tab, and then select the "Repeat as header row at the top of each page" check box.

Now that you have created a very basic table, you can sort the information in it and improve its appearance.

Sorting Rows in a Table

The term **sort** refers to the process of rearranging information in alphabetical, numerical, or chronological order. You can sort a series of paragraphs, including the contents of a bulleted list, or you can sort the rows of a table.

When you sort a table, you arrange the rows based on the contents of one of the columns. For example, you could sort the table you just created based on the contents of the "Item" column—either in ascending alphabetical order (from *A* to *Z*) or in descending alphabetical order (from *Z* to *A*). Alternatively, you could sort the table based on the contents of the "Hardware Cost" column—either in ascending numerical order (lowest to highest) or in descending numerical order (highest to lowest).

Clicking the Sort button in the Data group on the TABLE TOOLS LAYOUT tab opens the Sort dialog box, which provides a number of options for fine-tuning the sort, including options for sorting a table by the contents of more than one column. This is useful if, for example, you want to organize the table rows by last name, and then by first name within each last name. By default, Word assumes your table includes a header row that should remain at the top of the table—excluded from the sort.

REFERENCE

Sorting the Rows of a Table

- Click anywhere within the table.
- On the ribbon, click the TABLE TOOLS LAYOUT tab.
- In the Data group, click the Sort button.
- In the Sort dialog box, click the Sort by arrow, and then select the header for the column you want to sort by.
- In the Type box located to the right of the Sort by box, select the type of information stored in the column you want to sort by; you can choose Text, Number, or Date.
- To sort in alphabetical, chronological, or numerical order, verify that the Ascending option button is selected. To sort in reverse order, click the Descending option button.
- To sort by a second column, click the Then by arrow, and then click a column header. If necessary, specify the type of information stored in the Then by column, and the sort order.
- At the bottom of the Sort dialog box, make sure the Header row option button is selected. This indicates that the table includes a header row that should not be included in the sort.
- Click the OK button.

Katherine would like you to sort the contents of the table in ascending numerical order based on the contents of the "Hardware Cost" column.

To sort the information in the table:

1. Make sure the insertion point is located somewhere in the table.

2. On the ribbon, click the **TABLE TOOLS LAYOUT** tab.

3. In the Data group, click the **Sort** button. The Sort dialog box opens. Take a moment to review its default settings. The leftmost column in the table, the "Item" column, is selected in the Sort by box, indicating the sort will be based on the contents in this column. Because the "Item" column contains text, "Text" is selected in the Type box. The Ascending option button is selected by default, indicating that Word will sort the contents of the "Item" column from A to Z. The Header row option button is selected in the lower-left corner of the dialog box, ensuring the header row will not be included in the sort. You want to sort the column by the contents of the "Hardware Cost" column, so you need to change the Sort by setting.

4. Click the **Sort by** button arrow, and then click **Hardware Cost**. Because the "Hardware Cost" column contains numbers, the Type box now displays "Number". The Ascending button is still selected, indicating that Word will sort the numbers in the "Hardware Cost" column from lowest to highest. See Figure 3-11.

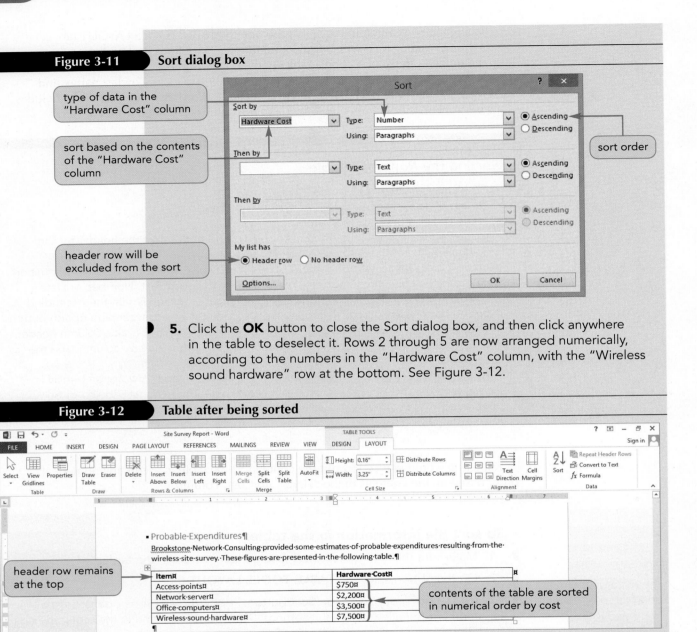

Figure 3-11 | **Sort dialog box**

type of data in the "Hardware Cost" column

sort based on the contents of the "Hardware Cost" column

header row will be excluded from the sort

sort order

▶ **5.** Click the **OK** button to close the Sort dialog box, and then click anywhere in the table to deselect it. Rows 2 through 5 are now arranged numerically, according to the numbers in the "Hardware Cost" column, with the "Wireless sound hardware" row at the bottom. See Figure 3-12.

Figure 3-12 | **Table after being sorted**

header row remains at the top

- Probable·Expenditures¶
Brookstone·Network·Consulting·provided·some·estimates·of·probable·expenditures·resulting·from·the· wireless·site·survey.··These·figures·are·presented·in·the·following·table.¶

Item¤	Hardware·Cost¤
Access·points¤	$750¤
Network·server¤	$2,200¤
Office·computers¤	$3,500¤
Wireless·sound·hardware¤	$7,500¤

contents of the table are sorted in numerical order by cost

▶ **6.** Save the document.

Katherine decides that the table should also include the installation cost for each item. She asks you to insert an "Installation Cost" column.

Inserting Rows and Columns in a Table

To add a column to a table, you can use the tools in the Rows & Columns group on the TABLE TOOLS LAYOUT tab, or you can use the Add Column button in the document window. To use the Add Column button, make sure the insertion point is located somewhere within the table. When you position the mouse pointer at the top of the table, pointing to the border between two columns, the Add Column button appears. When you click that button, a new column is inserted between the two existing columns.

To insert a column in the table:

▶ **1.** Verify that the insertion point is located anywhere in the table.

▶ **2.** Position the mouse pointer at the top of the table, so that it points to the border between the two columns. The Add Column button ⊕ appears at the top of the border. A blue guideline shows where the new column will be inserted. See Figure 3-13.

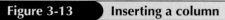
Figure 3-13   Inserting a column

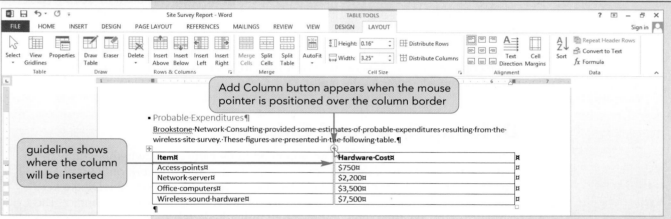

TIP

You can also use the buttons in the Rows & Columns group on the TABLE TOOLS LAYOUT tab to insert a column or row.

▶ **3.** Click the **Add Column** button ⊕. A new, blank column is inserted between the "Item" and "Hardware Cost" columns. The three columns in the table are narrower than the original two columns, but the overall width of the table remains the same.

▶ **4.** Click in the top cell of the new column, and then enter the following header and data. Use the ↓ key to move the insertion point down through the column.

Installation Cost

$1,500

$850

$1,000

$1,750

Your table should now look like the one in Figure 3-14.

Figure 3-14   **New "Installation Cost" column**

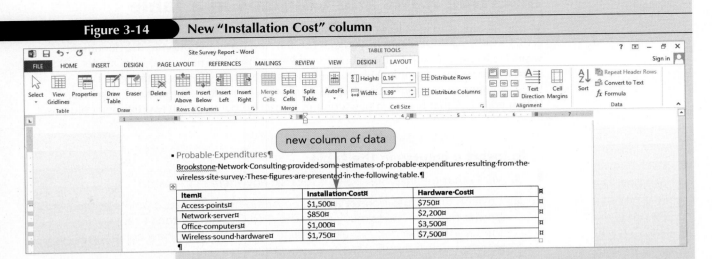

Because you selected the entire header row when you formatted the original headers in bold, the newly inserted header, "Installation Cost," is also formatted in bold.

Katherine just learned that the costs listed for office computers actually cover both office computers and the network server. Therefore, she would like you to delete the "Network server" row from the table.

Deleting Rows and Columns

When you consider deleting a row, you need to be clear about whether you want to delete the *contents* of the row, or the contents and the *structure* of the row. You can delete the contents of a row by selecting the row and pressing the Delete key. This removes the information from the row but leaves the row structure intact. The same is true for deleting the contents of an individual cell, a column, or the entire table. To delete the structure of a row, a column, or the entire table—including its contents—you select the row (or column or the entire table) and then use the Delete button in the Rows & Columns group, or on the Mini toolbar. To delete multiple rows or columns, start by selecting all the rows or columns you want to delete.

Before you delete the Network server row, you need to edit the contents in the last cell in the first column to indicate that the items in that row are for office computers and a server.

To delete the Network server row:

1. In the cell containing the text "Office computers," click to the right of the "s," press the **spacebar**, and then type **and network server**. The cell now reads "Office computers and network server." Part of the text wraps to a second line within the cell. Next, you can delete the Network server row, which is no longer necessary.

2. Click in the selection bar to the left of the **Network server** row. The row is selected, with the Mini toolbar displayed on top of the selected row.

> **3.** On the Mini toolbar, click the **Delete** button. The Delete menu opens, displaying options for deleting cells, columns, rows, or the entire table. See Figure 3-15.

Figure 3-15   Deleting a row

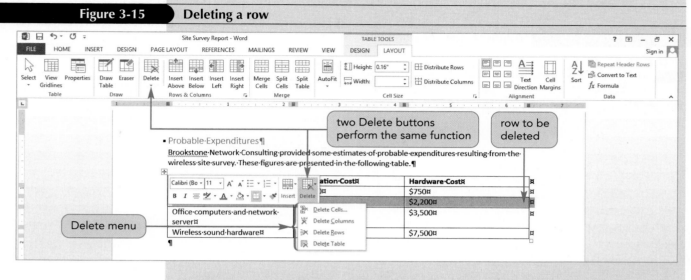

> **4.** Click **Delete Rows**. The "Network server" row is removed from the table, and the Mini toolbar disappears.

> **5.** Save your work.

The table now contains all the information Katherine wants to include. Next, you'll adjust the widths of the three columns.

Changing Column Widths

Columns that are too wide for the material they contain can make a table hard to read. You can change a column's width by dragging the column's right border to a new position. Or, if you prefer, you can double-click a column border to make the column width adjust automatically to accommodate the widest entry in the column. To adjust the width of all the columns to match their widest entries, click anywhere in the table, click the AutoFit button in the Cell Size group on the TABLE TOOLS LAYOUT tab, and then click AutoFit Contents. To adjust the width of the entire table to span the width of the page, click the AutoFit Contents button and then click AutoFit Window.

You'll adjust the columns in Katherine's table by double-clicking the right column border. You need to start by making sure that no part of the table is selected. Otherwise, when you double-click the border, only the width of the selected part of the table will change.

When resizing a column, be sure that no part of the table is selected. Otherwise, you'll resize just the selected part.

To change the width of the columns in the table:

▶ **1.** Verify that no part of the table is selected, and then position the mouse pointer over the right border of the "Installation Cost" column until the pointer changes to ◀‖▶. See Figure 3-16.

Figure 3-16 **Adjusting the column width**

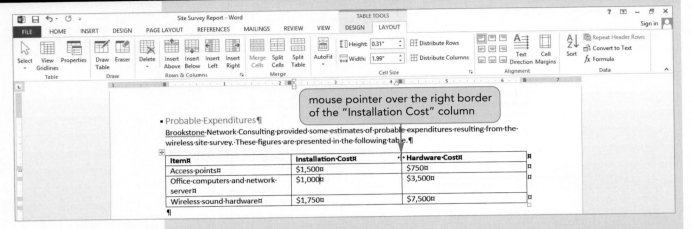

mouse pointer over the right border of the "Installation Cost" column

> • Probable·Expenditures¶
> Brookstone·Network·Consulting·provided·some·estimates·of·probable·expenditures·resulting·from·the· wireless·site·survey.·These·figures·are·presented·in·the·following·table.¶

Item¤	Installation·Cost¤	Hardware·Cost¤	¤
Access·points¤	$1,500¤	$750¤	¤
Office·computers·and·network·server¤	$1,000¤	$3,500¤	¤
Wireless·sound·hardware¤	$1,750¤	$7,500¤	¤

¶

TIP

To change the height of a row, position the mouse pointer over the bottom row border and drag the border up or down.

▶ **2.** Double-click the mouse button. The right column border moves left so that the "Installation Cost" column is just wide enough to accommodate the widest entry in the column.

▶ **3.** Verify that no part of the table is selected, and that the insertion point is located in any cell in the table.

▶ **4.** Make sure the TABLE TOOLS LAYOUT tab is selected on the ribbon.

▶ **5.** In the Cell Size group, click the **AutoFit** button, and then click **AutoFit Contents**. All of the table columns adjust so that each is just wide enough to accommodate its widest entry. The text "Office computers and network server" in the lower-left cell no longer wraps to a second line.

To finish the table, you will add some formatting to improve the table's appearance.

Formatting Tables with Styles

To adjust a table's appearance, you can use any of the formatting options available on the HOME tab. To change a table's appearance more dramatically, you can use table styles, which allow you to apply a collection of formatting options, including shading, color, borders, and other design elements, with a single click.

By default, a table is formatted with the Table Grid style, which includes only black borders between the rows and columns, no paragraph spacing, no shading, and the default black font color. You can select a more colorful table style from the Table Styles group on the TABLE TOOLS DESIGN tab. Whatever table style you choose, you'll give your document a more polished look if you use the same style consistently in all the tables in a single document.

Some table styles format rows in alternating colors, called **banded rows**, while others format the columns in alternating colors, called **banded columns**. You can choose a style that includes different formatting for the header row than for the rest of the table. Or, if the first column in your table is a header column—that is, if it contains headers identifying the type of information in each row—you can choose a style that instead applies different formatting to the first column.

REFERENCE

Formatting a Table with a Table Style

- Click in the table you want to format.
- On the ribbon, click the TABLE TOOLS DESIGN tab.
- In the Table Styles group, click the More button to display the Table Styles gallery.
- Position the mouse pointer over a style in the Table Styles gallery to see a Live Preview of the table style in the document.
- In the Table Styles gallery, click the style you want.
- To apply or remove style elements (such as special formatting for the header row, banded rows, or banded columns), select or deselect check boxes as necessary in the Table Style Options group.

Katherine wants to use a table style that emphasizes the header row with special formatting, does not include column borders, and uses color to separate the rows.

To apply a table style to the Probable Expenditures table:

1. Click anywhere in the table, and then scroll to position the table at the very bottom of the Word window. This will make it easier to see the Live Preview in the next few steps.

2. On the ribbon, click the **TABLE TOOLS DESIGN** tab. In the Table Styles group, the plain Table Grid style is highlighted, indicating that it is the table's current style.

3. In the Table Styles group, click the **More** button. The Table Styles gallery opens. The default Table Grid style now appears under the heading "Plain Tables." The more elaborate styles appear below, in the "Grid Tables" section of the gallery.

4. Use the gallery's vertical scroll bar to view the complete collection of table styles. When you are finished, scroll up until you can see the "Grid Tables" heading again.

5. Move the mouse pointer over the style located in the fourth row of the Grid Tables section, second column from the right. See Figure 3-17.

Figure 3-17 Table Styles gallery

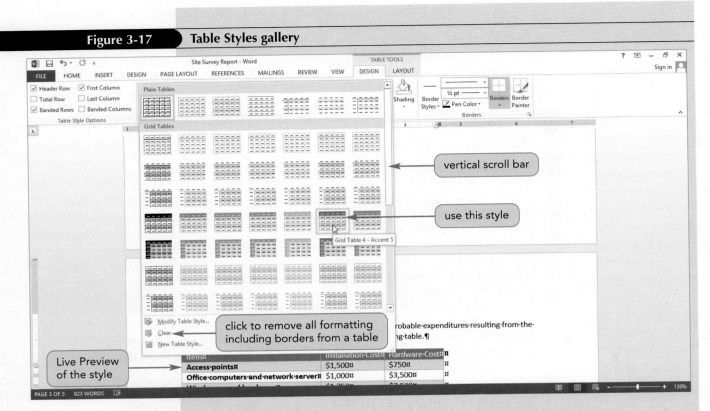

A ScreenTip displays the style's name, "Grid Table 4 - Accent 5." The style consists of a dark blue heading row, with alternating rows of light blue and white below. A Live Preview of the style is visible in the document.

▶ **6.** Click the **Grid Table 4 - Accent 5** style. The Table Styles gallery closes.

▶ **7.** Scroll to position the table at the top of the Word window, so you can review it more easily. The table's header row is formatted with dark blue shading and white text. The rows below appear in alternating colors of light blue and white.

The only problem with the newly formatted table is that the text in the first column is formatted in bold. In tables where the first column contains headers, bold would be appropriate—but this isn't the case with Katherine's table. You'll fix this by deselecting the First Column check box in the Table Style Options group.

To remove the bold formatting from the first column:

▶ **1.** In the Table Style Options group, click the **First Column** check box to deselect this option. The bold formatting is removed from the entries in the Item column. Note that the Header Row check box is selected. This indicates that the table's header row is emphasized with special formatting (dark blue shading with white text). The Banded Rows check box is also selected because the table is formatted with banded rows of blue and white. Figure 3-18 shows the finished table.

Figure 3-18 ▸ **Completed table**

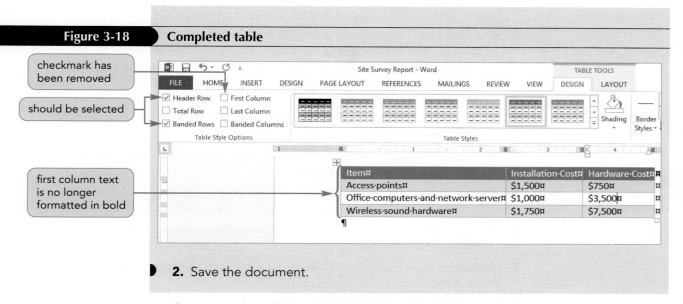

checkmark has been removed

should be selected

first column text is no longer formatted in bold

▸ **2.** Save the document.

After you apply a table style, it's helpful to know how to remove it in case you want to start over from scratch. The Clear option on the menu below the Table styles gallery removes the current style from a table, including the borders between cells. When a table has no borders, the rows and columns are defined by **gridlines**, which are useful as guidelines but do not appear when you print the table.

In the following steps, you'll experiment with clearing the table's style, displaying and hiding the gridlines, and removing the table's borders.

To experiment with table styles, gridlines, and borders:

▸ **1.** In the Table Styles group, click the **More** button, and then click **Clear** in the menu below the gallery. Next, you need to make sure the table gridlines are displayed.

▸ **2.** On the ribbon, click the **TABLE TOOLS LAYOUT** tab.

▸ **3.** In the View group, click the **View Gridlines** button, if necessary, to select it. The table now looks much simpler, with no shading or font colors. Instead of the table borders, dotted gridlines separate the rows and columns. The text in the table is spaced farther apart because removing the table style restored the default paragraph and line spacing of the Normal style. The bold formatting that you applied earlier, which is not part of a table style, is visible again.

It is helpful to clear a table's style and view only the gridlines if you want to use a table to lay out text and graphics on a page, but you want no visible indication of the table itself. You'll have a chance to try this technique in the Case Problems at the end of this tutorial.

Another option is to remove only the table borders, leaving the rest of the table style applied to the table. To do this, you have to select the entire table. But first you need to undo the style change.

▸ **4.** On the Quick Access Toolbar, click the **Undo** button 🔄 to restore the Grid Table 4 - Accent 5 style, so that your table looks like the one in Figure 3-18.

▸ **5.** In the upper-left corner of the table, click the **Table Select** handle ⊞ to select the entire table, and then click the **TABLE TOOLS DESIGN** tab.

6. In the Borders group, click the **Borders button arrow** to open the Borders gallery, click **No Borders**, and then click anywhere in the table to deselect it. The borders are removed from the table, leaving only the nonprinting gridlines to separate the rows and columns. To add borders of any color to specific parts of a table, you can use the Border Painter.

7. In the Borders group, click the **Border Painter** button, and then click the **Pen Color** button to open the Pen Color gallery.

8. In the Pen Color gallery, click the **Orange, Accent 2** square in the sixth column of the first row of the gallery.

9. Use the Border Painter pointer ✐ to click any gridline in the table. An orange border is added to the cell where you clicked.

10. Continue experimenting with the Border Painter pointer, and then press the **Esc** key to turn off the Border Painter pointer when you are finished.

11. Reapply the Grid Table 4 - Accent 5 table style to make your table match the one shown earlier in Figure 3-18.

12. Save the document and then close it.

PROSKILLS

Problem Solving: Fine-Tuning Table Styles

After you apply a table style to a table, you might like the look of the table but find that it no longer effectively conveys your information or is not quite as easy to read. To solve this problem, you might be inclined to go back to the Table Styles gallery to find another style that might work better. Another method to correct problems with a table style is to identify the table elements with problematic formatting, and then manually make formatting adjustments to only those elements using the options on the TABLE TOOLS DESIGN tab. For example, you can change the thickness and color of the table borders using the options in the Borders group, and you can add shading using the Shading button in the Table Styles group. Also, if you don't like the appearance of table styles in your document, consider changing the document's theme and previewing the table styles again. The table styles have a different appearance in each theme. When applying table styles, remember there are many options for attractively formatting the table without compromising the information being conveyed.

In the next session, you'll complete the rest of the report by organizing information using tab stops, creating footnotes and endnotes, dividing the document into sections, inserting headers and footers, and finally inserting a cover page.

REVIEW

Session 3.1 Quick Check

1. What must you do before you can display document headings in the Navigation pane?
2. Explain how to insert a table in a document.
3. After you enter data in the last cell in the last row in a table, how can you insert a new row?
4. Explain how to insert a new column in a table.
5. What button do you use to sort a table?
6. To adjust the width of a table's column to fit its widest entry, would you use the AutoFit Contents option or the AutoFit Window option?
7. How can you adjust a table style so that the first column in the table is formatted like all the others?

Session 3.2 Visual Overview:

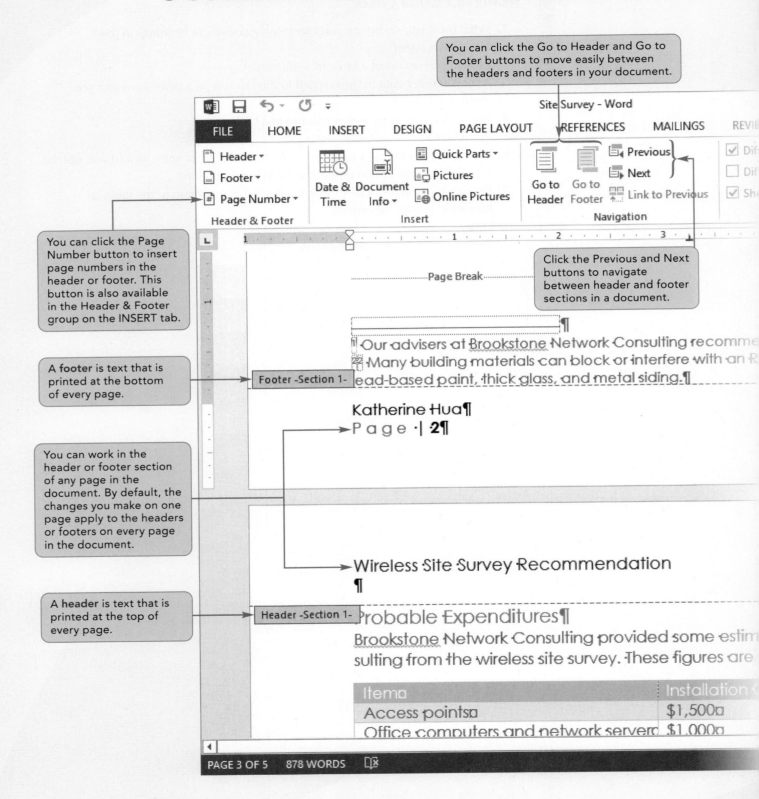

You can click the Go to Header and Go to Footer buttons to move easily between the headers and footers in your document.

You can click the Page Number button to insert page numbers in the header or footer. This button is also available in the Header & Footer group on the INSERT tab.

Click the Previous and Next buttons to navigate between header and footer sections in a document.

A **footer** is text that is printed at the bottom of every page.

You can work in the header or footer section of any page in the document. By default, the changes you make on one page apply to the headers or footers on every page in the document.

A **header** is text that is printed at the top of every page.

Site Survey - Word

FILE   HOME   INSERT   DESIGN   PAGE LAYOUT   REFERENCES   MAILINGS   REVIE

Header ▾   Footer ▾   Page Number ▾   Date & Time   Document Info ▾   Quick Parts ▾   Pictures   Online Pictures   Go to Header   Go to Footer   Previous   Next   Link to Previous

Header & Footer   Insert   Navigation

----Page Break----

¶

¶ Our advisers at Brookstone Network Consulting recomme

¶ Many building materials can block or interfere with an R

Footer -Section 1-   ead-based paint, thick glass, and metal siding.¶

Katherine Hua¶

P a g e ·| 2¶

Wireless Site Survey Recommendation

¶

Header -Section 1-   Probable Expenditures¶

Brookstone Network Consulting provided some estim

sulting from the wireless site survey. These figures are

Item□	Installation □
Access points□	$1,500□
Office computers and network server□	$1,000□

PAGE 3 OF 5   878 WORDS

Working with Headers and Footers

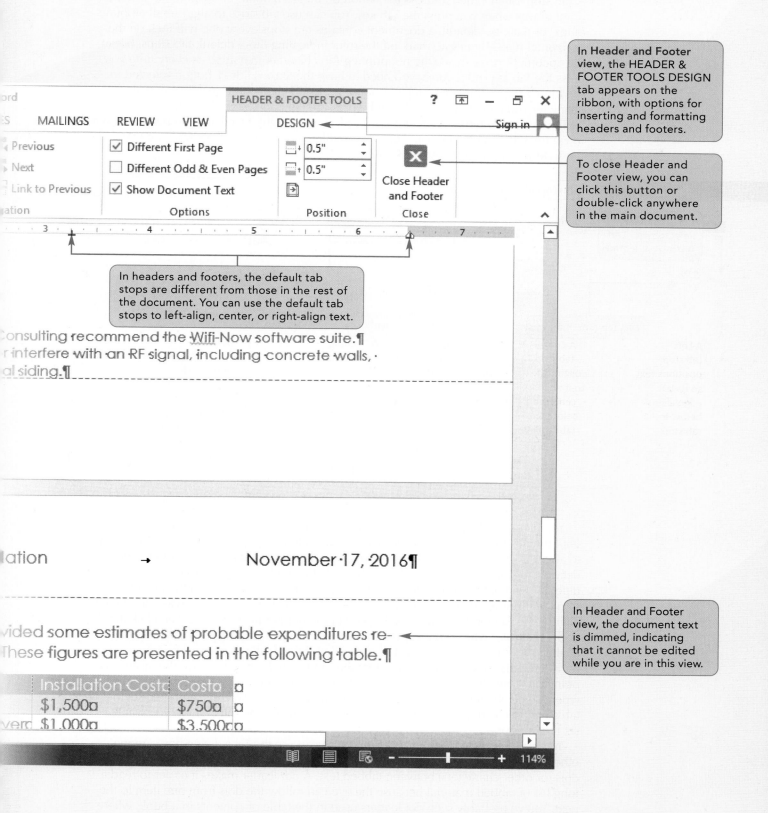

In **Header and Footer view**, the HEADER & FOOTER TOOLS DESIGN tab appears on the ribbon, with options for inserting and formatting headers and footers.

To close Header and Footer view, you can click this button or double-click anywhere in the main document.

In headers and footers, the default tab stops are different from those in the rest of the document. You can use the default tab stops to left-align, center, or right-align text.

In **Header and Footer** view, the document text is dimmed, indicating that it cannot be edited while you are in this view.

HEADER & FOOTER TOOLS

MAILINGS   REVIEW   VIEW   DESIGN   Sign in

Previous   ☑ Different First Page   0.5"
Next   ☐ Different Odd & Even Pages   0.5"   Close Header
Link to Previous ☑ Show Document Text   and Footer
ation   Options   Position   Close

...onsulting recommend the Wifi-Now software suite.¶
...r interfere with an RF signal, including concrete walls, ·
...al siding.¶

...lation   →   November·17, 2016¶

...vided some estimates of probable expenditures re-
...These figures are presented in the following table.¶

Installation Costs	Costs
$1,500	$750
...vers $1,000	$3,500

114%

Setting Tab Stops

A **tab stop** (often called a **tab**) is a location on the horizontal ruler where the insertion point moves when you press the Tab key. You can use tab stops to align small amounts of text or data. By default, a document contains tab stops every one-half inch on the horizontal ruler. There's no mark on the ruler indicating these default tab stops, but in the document you can see the nonprinting Tab character that appears every time you press the Tab key. (Of course, you need to have the Show/Hide ¶ button selected to see these nonprinting characters.) A nonprinting tab character is just like any other character you type; you can delete it by pressing the Backspace key or the Delete key.

The five major types of tab stops are Left, Center, Right, Decimal, and Bar, as shown in Figure 3-19. The default tab stops on the ruler are all left tab stops because that is the tab style you'll probably use most often.

Figure 3-19	Tab stop alignment styles

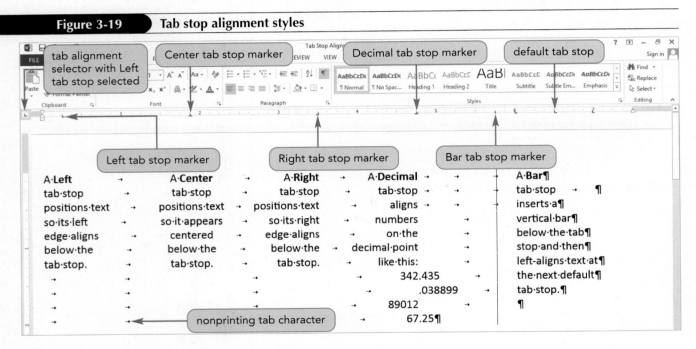

You can use tab stops a few different ways. The simplest is to press the Tab key until the insertion point is aligned where you want it, and then type the text you want to align. Each time you press the Tab key, the insertion point moves right to the next default tab stop, with the left edge of the text aligning below the tab stop. To use a different type of tab stop, or to use a tab stop at a location other than the default tab stop locations (every half-inch on the ruler), first select an alignment style from the tab alignment selector, located at the left end of the horizontal ruler, and then click the horizontal ruler where you want to insert the tab stop. This process is called setting a tab stop. When you set a new tab stop, all of the default tab stops to its left are removed. This means you have to press the Tab key only once to move the insertion point to the newly created tab stop. To set a new tab stop in text you have already typed, select the text including the nonprinting tab stop characters, and then set the tab stop by selecting an alignment style and clicking on the ruler where you want to set the tab stop.

To create more complicated tab stops, you can use the Tabs dialog box. Among other things, the Tabs dialog box allows you to insert a **dot leader**, which is a row of dots (or other characters) between tabbed text. A dot leader makes it easier to read a long list of tabbed material because the eye can follow the dots from one item to the next. You've probably seen dot leaders used in the table of contents in a book, where the dots separate the chapter titles from the page numbers.

To create a left tab stop with a dot leader, click the Dialog Box Launcher in the Paragraph group on the HOME tab, click the Indents and Spacing tab, if necessary, and then click the Tabs button at the bottom of the dialog box. In the Tab stop position box in the Tabs dialog box, type the location on the ruler where you want to insert the tab. For example, to insert a tab stop at the 4-inch mark, type 4. Verify that the Left option button is selected in the Alignment section, and then, in the Leader section, click the option button for the type of leader you want. Click the Set button and then click the OK button.

Setting, Moving, and Clearing Tab Stops

- To set a tab stop, click the tab alignment selector on the horizontal ruler until the appropriate tab stop alignment style is displayed, and then click the horizontal ruler where you want to position the tab stop.
- To move a tab stop, drag it to a new location on the ruler. If you have already typed text that is aligned by the tab stop, select the text before dragging the tab stop to a new location.
- To clear a tab stop, drag it off the ruler.

In the Site Survey Report document you have been working on, you need to type the list of consultants and their titles. You can use tab stops to quickly format this small amount of information in two columns. As you type, you'll discover whether Word's default tab stops are appropriate for this document or whether you need to set a new tab stop. Before you get started working with tabs, you'll take a moment to explore Word's Resume Reading feature.

To enter the list of consultants using tabs:

▶ 1. Open the **Site Survey Report** document. The document opens with the "Summary" heading at the top of the Word window. In the lower-right corner, a "Welcome back!" message is displayed briefly, and is then replaced with the Resume Reading button ⧉.

▶ 2. Point to the **Resume Reading** button ⧉ to expand its "Welcome back!" message. See Figure 3-20.

Figure 3-20	"Welcome back!" message displayed in reopened document

indoor·and·outdoor·theaters.·To·make·sure·I·proposed·the·most·effective·plan·possible,·I·decided·to·seek·
the·advice·of·experts.·Fortunately,·one·of·the·area's·top·experts·in·wireless·networking,·Jamie·
Brookstone,·president·of·Brookstone·Network·Consulting,·offered·the·services·of·his·staff·pro·bono.·
Thanks·to·his·offer,·I·was·able·to·meet·several·times·with·the·foll[...]

Lyn·Luzerne¶

Our·conversations·focused·on·ways·to·improve·network·connect[...]
also·studied·information·obtained·from·leading·hardware·manufacturers·and·software·distributors.·This·

click to display the part of the document you were working on before

Welcome back!
Pick up where you left off:

Probable Expenditures
8 minutes ago

▶ 3. Click the **Welcome back!** message. The document window scrolls down to display the table, which you were working on just before you closed the document.

▶ 4. Scroll up to display the "Expert Advice" heading on page 1.

▶ 5. Confirm that the ruler and nonprinting characters are displayed, and that the document is displayed in Print Layout view, zoomed to 120%.

▶ 6. Click to the right of the last "e" in "Lyn Luzerne."

7. Press the **Tab** key. An arrow-shaped tab character appears, and the insertion point moves to the first tab stop after the last "e" in "Luzerne." This tab stop is the default tab located at the 1-inch mark on the horizontal ruler. See Figure 3-21.

Figure 3-21   **Tab character**

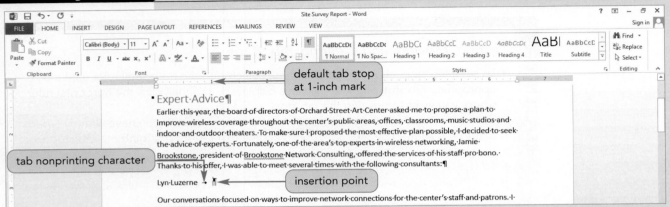

8. Type **Associate Engineer**, and then press the **Enter** key to move the insertion point to the next line.

9. Type **Dean Armstrong**, and then press the **Tab** key. The insertion point moves to the next available tab stop, this time located at the 1.5-inch mark on the rule.

10. Type **Senior Engineer**, and then press the **Enter** key to move to the next line. Notice that Dean Armstrong's title does not align with Lyn Luzerne's title on the line above it. You'll fix this after you type the last name in the list.

11. Type **Suzanne J. Sheffield-Harper**, press the **Tab** key, and then type **Project Manager**. See Figure 3-22.

Figure 3-22   **List of consultants**

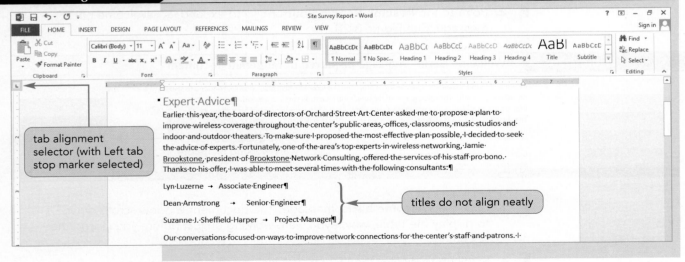

The list of names and titles is not aligned properly. You can fix this by inserting a new tab stop.

To add a new tab stop to the horizontal ruler:

1. Make sure the HOME tab is displayed on the ribbon, and then select the list of consultants and their titles.

2. On the horizontal ruler, click at the 2.5-inch mark. Because the current tab stop alignment style is Left tab, Word inserts a left tab stop at that location. Remember that when you set a new tab stop, all the default tab stops to its left are removed. The column of titles shifts to the new tab stop. See Figure 3-23.

Figure 3-23   **Titles aligned at new tab stop**

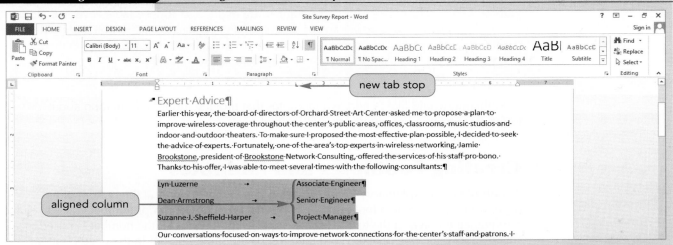

To complete the list, you need to remove the paragraph spacing after the first two paragraphs in the list, so the list looks like it's all one paragraph. You can quickly reduce paragraph and line spacing to 0 points by clicking the No Spacing style in the Styles group. In this case, you want to reduce only the paragraph spacing to 0 points, so you'll use the Line and Paragraph Spacing button instead.

3. Select the first two paragraphs in the list, which contain the names and titles for Lyn and Dean.

4. In the Paragraph group, click the **Line and Paragraph Spacing** button, and then click **Remove Space After Paragraph**.

5. Click anywhere in the document to deselect the list, and then save your work.

Decision Making: Choosing Between Tabs and Tables

When you have information that you want to align in columns in your document, you need to decide whether to use tabs or tables. Whatever you do, don't try to align columns of data by adding extra spaces with the spacebar. Although the text might seem precisely aligned on the screen, it probably won't be aligned when you print the document. Furthermore, if you edit the text, the spaces you inserted to align your columns will be affected by your edits; they get moved just like regular text, ruining your alignment.

So what is the most efficient way to align text in columns? It depends. Inserting tabs works well for aligning small amounts of information in just a few columns and rows, such as two columns with three rows, but tabs become cumbersome when you need to organize a lot of data over multiple columns and rows. In this case, using a table to organize columns of information is better. Unlike with tabbed columns of data, it's easy to add data to tables by inserting columns. You might also choose tables over tab stops when you want to take advantage of the formatting options available with table styles. As mentioned earlier, if you don't want the table structure itself to be visible in the document, you can clear its table style and then hide its gridlines.

Katherine would like to add two footnotes that provide further information about topics discussed in her report. You will do that next.

Creating Footnotes and Endnotes

A **footnote** is an explanatory comment or reference that appears at the bottom of a page. When you create a footnote, Word inserts a small, superscript number (called a **reference marker**) in the text. The term **superscript** means that the number is raised slightly above the line of text. Word then inserts the same number in the page's bottom margin and positions the insertion point next to it so you can type the text of the footnote. **Endnotes** are similar, except that the text of an endnote appears at the end of a section or, in the case of a document without sections, at the end of the document. (You'll learn about dividing a document into sections later in this tutorial.) By default, the reference marker for an endnote is a lowercase Roman numeral.

Word automatically manages the reference markers for you, keeping them sequential from the beginning of the document to the end, no matter how many times you add, delete, or move footnotes or endnotes. For example, if you move a paragraph containing footnote 4 so that it falls before the paragraph containing footnote 1, Word renumbers all the footnotes in the document to keep them sequential.

Inserting a Footnote or an Endnote

- Click the location in the document where you want to insert a footnote or an endnote.
- On the ribbon, click the REFERENCES tab.
- In the Footnotes group, click the Insert Footnote button or the Insert Endnote button.
- Type the text of the footnote in the bottom margin of the page, or type the text of the endnote at the end of the document.
- When you are finished typing the text of a footnote or an endnote, click in the body of the document to continue working on the document.

Katherine asks you to insert a footnote that explains the phrase "barriers to RF signal propagation."

To add a footnote to the report:

▶ 1. Use the Navigation pane to find the phrase "barriers to RF signal propagation" near the bottom of page 1, and then click to the right of the period after "propagation."

▶ 2. Close the Navigation pane.

▶ 3. On the ribbon, click the **REFERENCES** tab.

▶ 4. In the Footnotes group, click the **Insert Footnote** button. A superscript "1" is inserted to the right of the period after "propagation." Word also inserts the number "1" in the bottom margin below a separator line. The insertion point is now located next to the number in the bottom margin, ready for you to type the text of the footnote.

▶ 5. Type **Many building materials can block or interfere with an RF signal, including concrete walls, lead-based paint, thick glass, and metal siding.** See Figure 3-24.

Figure 3-24	Inserting a footnote

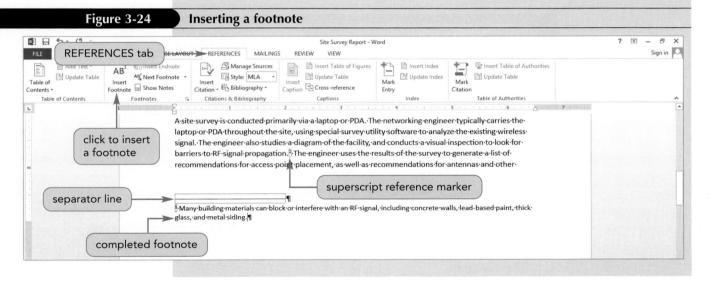

Now, Katherine would like you to insert a second footnote.

To insert a second footnote:

▶ 1. In the third line of the same paragraph, click at the end of the second sentence to position the insertion point to the right of the period after "signal."

▶ 2. In the Footnotes group, click the **Insert Footnote** button, and then type **Our advisers at Brookstone Network Consulting recommend the Wifi-Now software suite.** Because this footnote is placed earlier in the document than the one you just created, Word inserts a superscript "1" for this footnote, and then renumbers the other footnote as "2." See Figure 3-25.

Figure 3-25	Inserting a second footnote

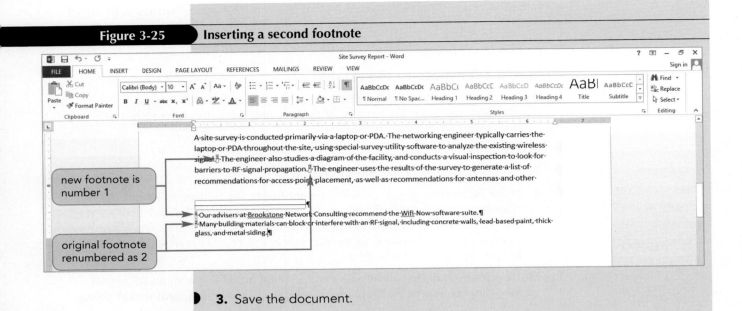

3. Save the document.

Understanding Endnotes, Footnotes, and Citations

It's easy to confuse footnotes with endnotes, and endnotes with citations. Remember, a footnote appears at the bottom, or foot, of a page, and always on the same page as its reference marker. You might have one footnote at the bottom of page 3, three footnotes at the bottom of page 5, and one at the bottom of page 6. By contrast, an endnote appears at the end of the document or section, with all the endnotes compiled into a single list. Both endnotes and footnotes can contain any kind of information you think might be useful to your readers. Citations, however, are only used to list specific information about a book or other source you refer to or quote from in the document. A citation typically appears in parentheses at the end of the sentence containing information from the source you are citing, and the sources for all of the document's citations are listed in a bibliography, or a list of works cited, at the end of the document.

Now you're ready to address some other issues with the document. First, Katherine has noticed that the right edges of most of the paragraphs in the document are uneven, and she'd like you to try to smooth them out. You'll correct this problem in the next section.

Hyphenating a Document

By default, hyphenation is turned off in Word documents. That means if you are in the middle of typing a word and you reach the end of a line, Word moves the entire word to the next line instead of inserting a hyphen and breaking the word into two parts. This can result in ragged text on the right margin. To ensure a smoother right margin, you can turn on automatic hyphenation—in which case, any word that ends within the last .25 inch of a line will be hyphenated.

To turn on automatic hyphenation in the document:

▶ **1.** Review the paragraph above the footnotes on page 1. The text on the right side of this paragraph is uneven. Keeping an eye on this paragraph will help you see the benefits of hyphenation.

▶ **2.** On the ribbon, click the **PAGE LAYOUT** tab.

▶ **3.** In the Page Setup group, click the **Hyphenation** button to open the Hyphenation menu, and then click **Automatic**. The Hyphenation menu closes. Throughout the document, the text layout shifts to account for the insertion of hyphens in words that break near the end of a line. For example, in the last paragraph on page 1, the word "recommendations" is now hyphenated. See Figure 3-26.

Figure 3-26	Hyphenated document

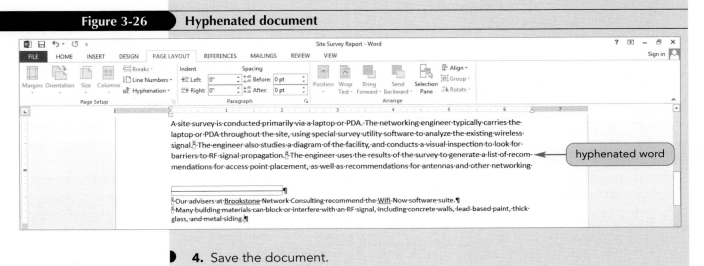

▶ **4.** Save the document.

Katherine plans to post a handout on the bulletin board at the art center to help inform the staff about the upcoming site survey, and she wants to include a sample handout in the report. Before you can add the sample of the handout, you need to divide the document into sections.

Formatting a Document into Sections

A **section** is a part of a document that can have its own page orientation, margins, headers, footers, and so on. In other words, each section is like a document within a document. To divide a document into sections, you insert a **section break**. You can select from a few different kinds of section breaks. One of the most useful is a Next page section break, which inserts a page break and starts the new section on the next page. Another commonly used kind of section break, a Continuous section break, starts the section at the location of the insertion point without changing the page flow. To insert a section break, you click the Breaks button in the Page Setup group on the PAGE LAYOUT tab and then select the type of section break you want to insert.

Katherine wants to format the handout in landscape orientation, but the report is currently formatted in portrait orientation. To format part of a document in an orientation different from the rest of the document, you need to divide the document into sections.

To insert a section break below the table:

▌ 1. Press the **Ctrl+End** keys to move the insertion point to the end of the document, just below the table.

▌ 2. In the Page Setup group, click the **Breaks** button. The Breaks gallery opens, as shown in Figure 3-27.

Figure 3-27 **Breaks gallery**

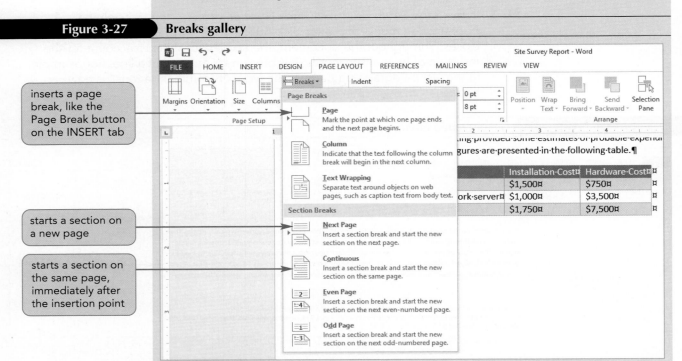

inserts a page break, like the Page Break button on the INSERT tab

starts a section on a new page

starts a section on the same page, immediately after the insertion point

The Page Breaks section of the gallery includes options for controlling how the text flows from page to page. The first option, Page, inserts a page break. It has the same effect as pressing the Page Break button on the INSERT tab or pressing the Ctrl+Enter keys. The Section Breaks section of the gallery includes four types of section breaks. The two you'll use most often are Next Page and Continuous.

▌ 3. Under "Section Breaks," click **Next Page**. A section break is inserted, and the insertion point moves to the top of the new page 4.

▌ 4. Scroll up until you can see the double-dotted line and the words "Section Break (Next Page)" below the table on page 3. This line indicates that a new section begins on the next page.

▌ 5. Save the document.

TIP

To delete a section break, click to the left of the line representing the break, and then press the Delete key.

You've created a new page that is a separate section from the rest of the report. The sections are numbered consecutively. The first part of the document is section 1, and the new page is section 2. Now you can format section 2 in landscape orientation without affecting the rest of the document.

To format section 2 in landscape orientation:

▶ **1.** Scroll down and verify that the insertion point is positioned at the top of the new page 4.

▶ **2.** Change the Zoom level to **30%** so you can see all four pages of the document displayed side-by-side.

▶ **3.** On the ribbon, click the **PAGE LAYOUT** tab.

▶ **4.** In the Page Setup group, click the **Orientation** button, and then click **Landscape**. Section 2, which consists solely of page 4, changes to landscape orientation, as shown in Figure 3-28. Section 1, which consists of pages 1–3, remains in portrait orientation.

Figure 3-28	Page 4 formatted in landscape orientation

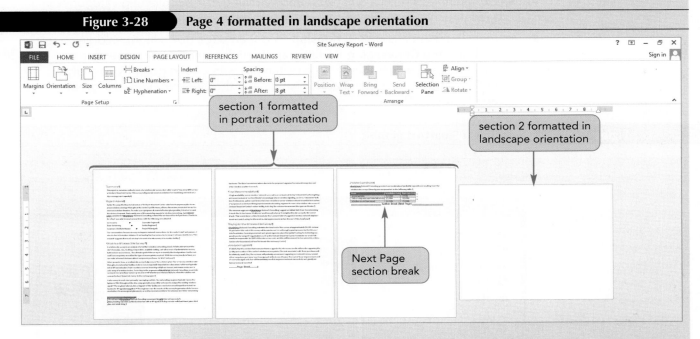

▶ **5.** Change the Zoom level back to **120%**, and then save the document.

Page 4 is now formatted in landscape orientation, ready for you to create Katherine's handout, which will consist of a graphic that shows the benefits of a site survey. You'll use Word's SmartArt feature to create the graphic.

Creating SmartArt

A **SmartArt** graphic is a diagram of shapes, such as circles, squares, or arrows. A well-designed SmartArt graphic can illustrate concepts that might otherwise require several paragraphs of explanation. To create a SmartArt graphic, you switch to the INSERT tab and then, in the Illustrations group, click the SmartArt button. This opens the Choose a SmartArt Graphic dialog box, where you can select from eight categories of graphics, including graphics designed to illustrate relationships, processes, and hierarchies. Within each category, you can choose from numerous designs. Once inserted into your document, a SmartArt graphic contains placeholder text that you replace with your own text. When a SmartArt graphic is selected, the SMARTART TOOLS DESIGN AND FORMAT tabs appear on the ribbon.

To create a SmartArt graphic:

▶ **1.** Verify that the insertion point is located at the top of page 4, which is blank.

▶ **2.** On the ribbon, click the **INSERT** tab.

▶ **3.** In the Illustrations group, click the **SmartArt** button. The Choose a SmartArt Graphic dialog box opens, with categories of SmartArt graphics in the left panel. The middle panel displays the graphics associated with the category currently selected in the left panel. The right panel displays a larger image of the graphic that is currently selected in the middle panel, along with an explanation of the graphic's purpose. By default, All is selected in the left panel.

▶ **4.** Explore the Choose a SmartArt Graphic dialog box by selecting categories in the left panel and viewing the graphics displayed in the middle panel.

▶ **5.** In the left panel, click **Relationship**, and then scroll down in the middle panel and click the **Converging Radial** graphic (in the first column, seventh row from the top), which shows three rectangles with arrows pointing to a circle. In the right panel, you see an explanation of the Converging Radial graphic. See Figure 3-29.

Figure 3-29 ▶ **Selecting a SmartArt graphic**

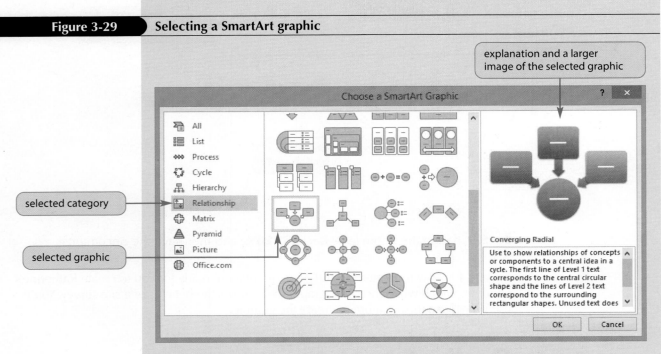

▶ **6.** Click the **OK** button. The Converging Radial graphic, with placeholder text, is inserted at the top of page 4. The graphic is surrounded by a rectangular border, indicating that it is selected. The SMARTART TOOLS contextual tabs appear on the ribbon. To the left or right of the graphic, you also see the Text pane, a small window with a title bar that contains the text "Type your text here." See Figure 3-30.

Figure 3-30   **SmartArt graphic with Text pane displayed**

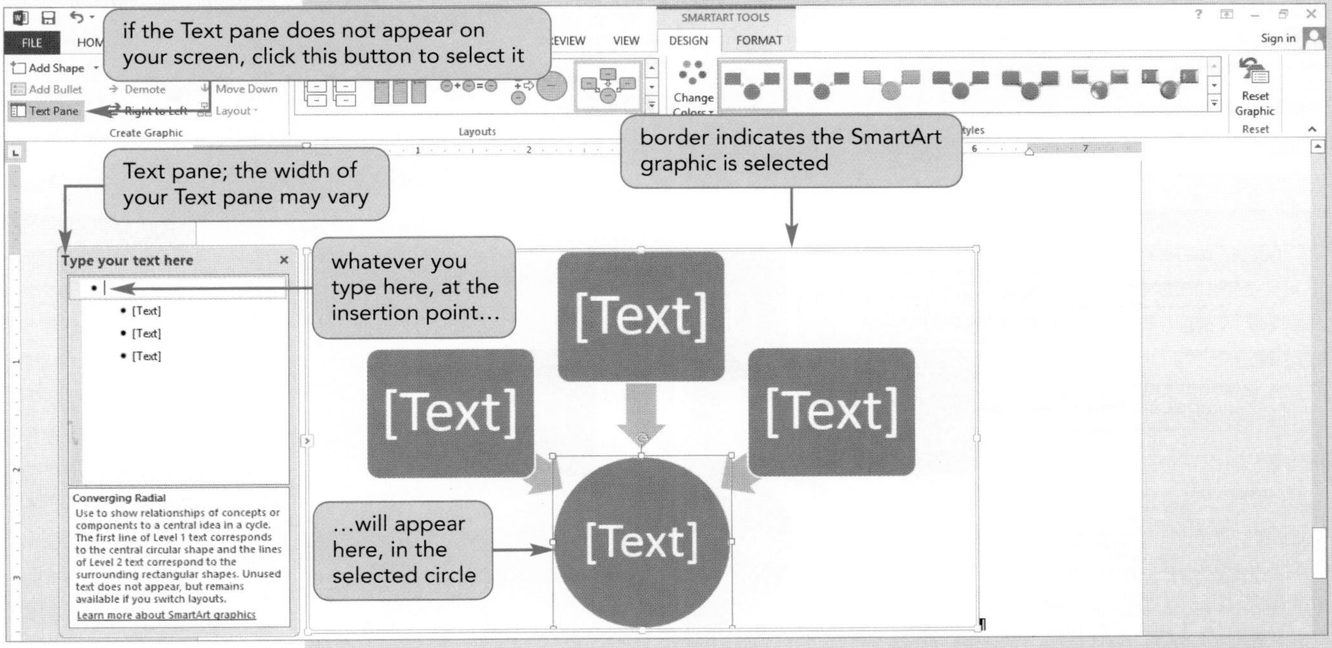

if the Text pane does not appear on your screen, click this button to select it

border indicates the SmartArt graphic is selected

Text pane; the width of your Text pane may vary

whatever you type here, at the insertion point…

…will appear here, in the selected circle

Converging Radial
Use to show relationships of concepts or components to a central idea in a cycle. The first line of Level 1 text corresponds to the central circular shape and the lines of Level 2 text correspond to the surrounding rectangular shapes. Unused text does not appear, but remains available if you switch layouts.
Learn more about SmartArt graphics

Trouble? If you do *not* see the Text pane, click the Text Pane button in the Create Graphic group on the SMARTART TOOLS DESIGN tab to select it.

The insertion point is blinking next to the first bullet in the Text pane, which is selected with an orange rectangle. The circle at the bottom of the SmartArt graphic is also selected, as indicated by the border with handles. At this point, anything you type next to the selected bullet in the Text pane will also appear in the selected circle in the SmartArt graphic.

Trouble? If you see the Text pane but the first bullet is not selected as shown in Figure 3-30, click next to the first bullet in the Text pane to select it.

Now you are ready to add text to the graphic.

To add text to the SmartArt graphic:

1. Type **Better Wireless Network**. The new text is displayed in the Text pane and in the circle in the SmartArt graphic. Now you need to insert text in the three rectangles.

2. Press the ↓ key to move the insertion point down to the next placeholder bullet in the Text pane, and then type **Site Survey**. The new text is displayed in the Text pane and in the blue rectangle on the left. See Figure 3-31.

Figure 3-31 New text in Text pane and in SmartArt graphic

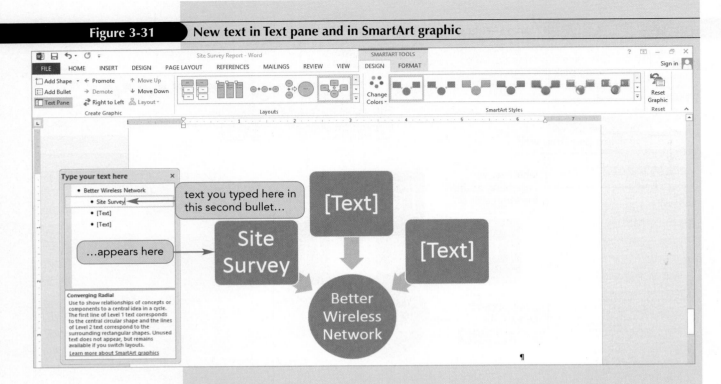

3. Press the ↓ key to move the insertion point down to the next placeholder bullet in the Text pane, and then type **Network Upgrades**. The new text appears in the middle rectangle and in the Text pane. You don't need the third rectangle, so you'll delete it.

4. Press the ↓ key to move the insertion point down to the next placeholder bullet in the Text pane, and then press the **Backspace** key. The rectangle on the right is deleted from the SmartArt graphic. The two remaining rectangles and the circle enlarge and shift position.

5. Make sure the SMARTART TOOLS DESIGN tab is still selected on the ribbon.

6. In the Create Graphic group, click the **Text Pane** button to deselect it. The Text pane closes.

7. Click in the white area inside the SmartArt border.

Next, you need to resize the SmartArt graphic so it fills the page.

TIP

To add a shape to a SmartArt graphic, click a shape in the SmartArt graphic, click the Add Shape arrow in the Create Graphic group on the DESIGN tab, and then click a placement option.

To adjust the size of the SmartArt graphic:

1. Zoom out so you can see the entire page. As you can see on the ruler, the SmartArt is currently six inches wide. You could drag the SmartArt border to resize it, just as you can with any graphic, but you will get more precise results using the Size button on the SMARTART TOOLS FORMAT tab.

2. On the ribbon, click the **SMARTART TOOLS FORMAT** tab.

3. On the right side of the SMARTART TOOLS FORMAT tab, click the **Size** button to display the Height and Width boxes.

4. Click the **Height** box, type **6.5**, click the **Width** box, type **9**, and then press the **Enter** key. The SmartArt graphic resizes, so that it is now 9 inches wide and 6.5 inches high, taking up most of the page. See Figure 3-32.

Figure 3-32	Resized SmartArt

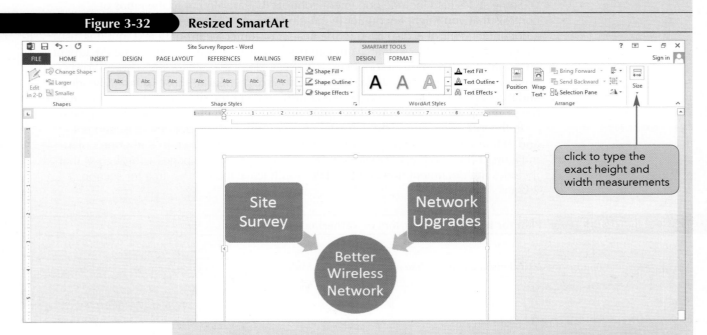

click to type the exact height and width measurements

Trouble? If one of the shapes in the SmartArt graphic was resized, rather than the entire SmartArt graphic, the insertion point was located within the shape rather than in the white space. On the Quick Access Toolbar, click the Undo button, click in the white area inside the SmartArt border, and then repeat Steps 3 and 4.

5. Click outside the SmartArt border to deselect it, and then review the graphic centered on the page.

Next, you need to insert a header at the top of each page in the report and a footer at the bottom of each page in the report.

Adding Headers and Footers

The first step to working with headers and footers is to open Header and Footer view. You can do that in three ways: (1) insert a page number using the Page Number button in the Header & Footer group on the INSERT tab; (2) double-click in the header area (in a page's top margin) or in the footer area (in a page's bottom margin); or (3) click the Header button or the Footer button on the INSERT tab.

By default, Word assumes that when you add something to the header or footer on any page of a document, you want the same text to appear on every page of the document. To create a different header or footer for the first page, you select the Different First Page check box in the Options group on the HEADER & FOOTER TOOLS DESIGN tab. When a document is divided into sections, like the Site Survey Report document, you can create a different header or footer for each section.

For a simple header or footer, double-click the header or footer area, and then type the text you want directly in the header or footer area, formatting the text as you would any other text in a document. To choose from a selection of predesigned header or footer styles, use the Header and Footer buttons on the HEADER & FOOTER TOOLS DESIGN tab (or on the INSERT tab). These buttons open galleries that you can use to select from a number of header and footer styles, some of which include page numbers and graphic elements such as horizontal lines or shaded boxes.

Some styles also include document controls that are similar to the kinds of controls that you might encounter in a dialog box. Any information that you enter in a document control is displayed in the header or footer as ordinary text, but it is also stored in the Word file so that Word can easily reuse it in other parts of the document. For example, later in this tutorial you will create a cover page for the report. Word's predefined cover pages include document controls similar to those found in headers and footers. So if you use a document control to enter the document title in the header, the same document title will show up on the cover page; there's no need to retype it.

In the following steps, you'll create a footer for the whole document (sections 1 and 2) that includes the page number and your name. As shown in Katherine's plan in Figure 3-33, you'll also create a header for section 1 only (pages 1 through 3) that includes the document title and the date. You'll leave the header area for section 2 blank.

Figure 3-33 **Plan for headers and footers in Katherine's report**

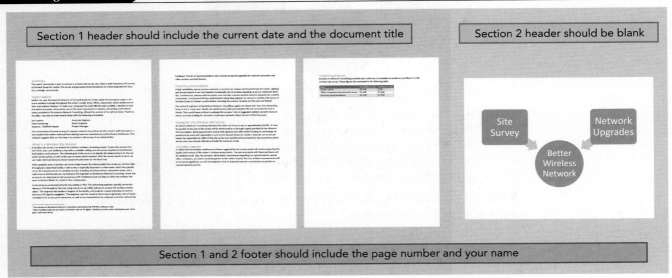

© 2014 Cengage Learning

First you will create the footer on page 1, so you can see how the footer fits below the footnotes at the bottom of the page.

To create a footer for the entire document:

1. Change the Zoom level to **120%**, and then scroll up until you can see the bottom of page 1 and the top of page 2.

2. Double-click in the white space below the footnotes on page 1. The document switches to Header and Footer view. The HEADER & FOOTER TOOLS DESIGN tab is displayed on the ribbon. The insertion point is positioned on the left side of the footer area, ready for you to begin typing. The label "Footer -Section 1-" tells you that the insertion point is located in the footer for section 1. The document text (including the footnotes) is gray,

indicating that you cannot edit it in Header and Footer view. The header area for section 1 is also visible on top of page 2. The default footer tab stops (which are different from the default tab stops in the main document) are visible on the ruler. See Figure 3-34.

Figure 3-34	Creating a footer

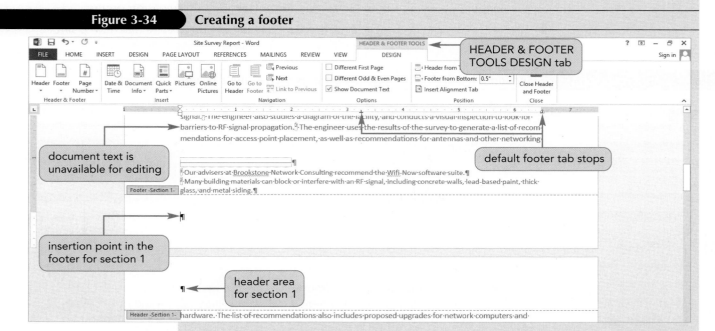

3. Type your first and last name, and then press the **Enter** key. The insertion point moves to the second line in the footer, aligned along the left margin. This is where you will insert the page number.

4. In the Header & Footer group, click the **Page Number** button. The Page Number menu opens. Because the insertion point is already located where you want to insert the page number, you'll use the Current Position option.

5. Point to **Current Position**. A gallery of page number styles opens. Katherine wants to use the Accent Bar 2 style.

6. Click the **Accent Bar 2** style (the third style from the top). The word "Page," a vertical bar, and the page number are inserted in the footer.

Next, you'll check to make sure that the footer you just created for section 1 also appears in section 2. To move between headers or footers in separate sections, you can use the buttons in the Navigation group on the HEADER & FOOTER TOOLS DESIGN tab.

7. In the Navigation group, click the **Next** button. Word displays the footer for the next section in the document—that is, the footer for section 2, which appears at the bottom of page 4. The label at the top of the footer area reads "Footer -Section 2-" and it contains the same text (your name and the page number) in this footer as in section 1. Word assumes, by default, that when you type text in one footer, you want it to appear in all the footers in the document.

Now you need to create a header for section 1. Katherine does not want to include a header in section 2 because it would distract attention from the SmartArt graphic. So you will first separate the header for section 1 from the header for section 2.

To separate the headers for section 1 and section 2:

1. Verify that the insertion point is located in the section 2 footer area at the bottom of page 4, and that the HEADER & FOOTER TOOLS DESIGN tab is selected on the ribbon. To switch from the footer to the header in the current section, you can use the Go to Header button in the Navigation group.

2. In the Navigation group, click the **Go to Header** button. The insertion point moves to the section 2 header at the top of page 4. See Figure 3-35.

Figure 3-35 Section 2 header is currently the same as the previous header, in section 1

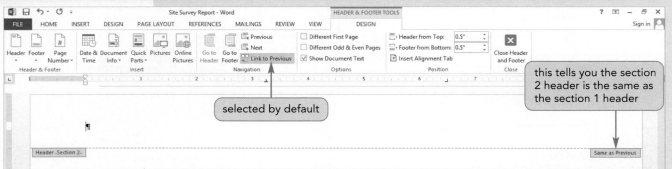

Notice that in the Navigation group, the Link to Previous button is selected. In the header area in the document window, the gray tab on the right side of the header border contains the message "Same as Previous," indicating that the section 2 header is set up to display the same text as the header in the previous section, which is section 1. To make the section 2 header a separate entity, you need to break the link between the section 1 and section 2 headers.

3. In the Navigation group, click the **Link to Previous** button to deselect it. The Same as Previous tab is removed from the right side of the section 2 header border.

4. In the Navigation group, click the **Previous** button. The insertion point moves up to the nearest header in the previous section, which is the section 1 header at the top of page 3. The label "Header -Section 1-" identifies this as a section 1 header.

5. In the Header & Footer group, click the **Header** button. A gallery of header styles opens.

6. Scroll down and review the various header styles, and then click the **Grid** style (eighth style from the top). The placeholder text "[Document title]" is aligned at the left margin. The placeholder text "[Date]" is aligned at the right margin.

7. Click the **[Document title]** placeholder text. The placeholder text is now selected within a document control. See Figure 3-36.

TIP

When you create a header for a section, it doesn't matter what page you're working on as long as the insertion point is located in a header in that section.

Figure 3-36   Adding a header to section 1

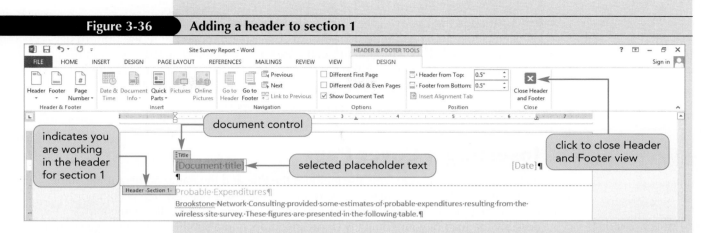

8. Type **Wireless Site Survey Recommendation**. The text you just typed is displayed in the document control instead of the placeholder text. Next, you need to add the date. The header style you selected includes a date picker document control, which allows you to select the date from a calendar.

9. Click the **[Date]** placeholder text to display an arrow in the document control, and then click the arrow. A calendar for the current month appears, as shown in Figure 3-37. In the calendar, the current date is outlined in dark blue.

Figure 3-37   Adding a date to the section 1 header

10. Click the current date. The current date, including the year, is inserted in the document control.

11. Scroll up slightly and click anywhere in the Section 1 footer (on the preceding page) to deselect the date document control. You are finished creating the header and footer for Katherine's report, so you can close Header and Footer view and return to Print Layout view.

12. In the Close group, click the **Close Header and Footer** button, or double-click anywhere in the main document, and then save your work.

▶ **13.** Change the Zoom level to **30%** so you can see all four pages of the document, including the header at the top of pages 1–3 and the footer at the bottom of pages 1–4. Take a moment to compare your completed headers and footers with Katherine's plan for the headers and footers shown earlier in Figure 3-33.

Finally, you need to insert a cover page for the report.

Inserting a Cover Page

A document's cover page typically includes the title and the name of the author. Some people also include a summary of the report on the cover page, which is commonly referred to as an abstract. In addition, you might include the date, the name and possibly the logo of your company or organization, and a subtitle. A cover page should not include the document header or footer.

To insert a preformatted cover page at the beginning of the document, you use the Cover Page button on the INSERT tab. You can choose from a variety of cover page styles, all of which include document controls in which you can enter the document title, the document's author, the date, and so on. These document controls are linked to any other document controls in the document. For example, you already entered "Wireless Site Survey Recommendation" into a document control in the header of Katherine's report. So if you use a cover page that contains a similar document control, "Wireless Site Survey Recommendation" will be displayed on the cover page automatically. Note that document controls sometimes display information entered when either Word or Windows was originally installed on your computer. If your computer has multiple user accounts, the information displayed in some document controls might reflect the information for the current user. In any case, you can easily edit the contents of a document control.

To insert a cover page at the beginning of the report:

▶ **1.** Verify that the document is still zoomed so that you can see all four pages, and then press the **Ctrl+Home** keys. The insertion point moves to the beginning of the document.

▶ **2.** On the ribbon, click the **INSERT** tab.

▶ **3.** In the Pages group, click the **Cover Page** button. A gallery of cover page styles opens.

Notice that the names of the cover page styles match the names of the preformatted header styles you saw earlier. For example, the list includes a Grid cover page, which is designed to match the Grid header used in this document. To give a document a uniform look, it's helpful to use elements with the same style throughout.

▶ **4.** Scroll down the gallery to see the cover page styles, and then locate the Grid cover page style.

▶ **5.** Click the **Grid** cover page style. The new cover page is inserted at the beginning of the document.

▶ **6.** Change the Zoom level to **120%**, and then scroll down to display the report title in the middle of the cover page. The only difference between the title "Wireless Site Survey Recommendation" here and the title you entered in the document header is that here the title is displayed in all uppercase. The cover page also includes document controls for a subtitle and an abstract. See Figure 3-38.

TIP

To delete a cover page that you inserted from the Cover Page gallery, click the Cover Page button in the Pages group, and then click Remove Current Cover Page.

| Figure 3-38 | Newly inserted cover page |

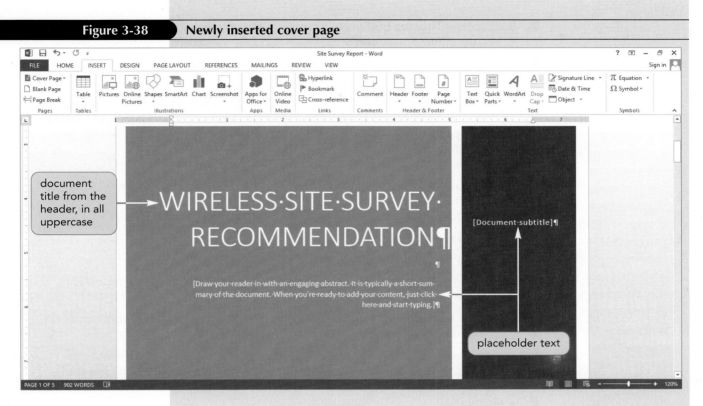

You need to type a subtitle in the subtitle document control on the right side of the page.

▶ **7.** Click the **[Document subtitle]** placeholder text, and then type **Orchard Street Art Center**. Next, you will remove the abstract document control because you do not need an abstract for this report.

▶ **8.** Below the document title, right-click the placeholder text that begins **[Draw your reader in...** to display the shortcut menu, and then click **Remove Content Control**. The content control is removed from the cover page.

▶ **9.** Save the document.

Changing the Theme

The report now contains several formatting elements that are controlled by the document's theme, so changing the theme will affect the document's overall appearance. Katherine suggests that you apply a different theme to the document.

To change the document's theme:

▶ **1.** Change the Zoom level to **40%** so you can see the first four pages side-by-side, with part of the fifth page visible on the bottom.

▶ **2.** On the ribbon, click the **DESIGN** tab.

▶ **3.** Click the **Themes** button, select any theme you want, and then review the results in the document.

▶ **4.** Apply three or four more different themes of your choice and review the results of each in the document.

▶ **5.** Click the **Retrospect** theme, and then save the document. The cover page is now orange and olive green, the headings as well as the header and footer text are orange, and the table is formatted with an olive green header row and gray shading.

Your work on the report is finished. You should preview the report before closing it.

To preview the report:

▶ **1.** On the ribbon, click the **FILE** tab.

▶ **2.** In the navigation bar, click the **Print** tab. The cover page of the report is displayed in the document preview in the right pane.

▶ **3.** Examine the document preview, using the arrow buttons at the bottom of the pane to display each page.

▶ **4.** If you need to make any changes to the report, return to Print Layout view, edit the document, preview the document again, and then save the document.

▶ **5.** Display the document in Print Layout view.

▶ **6.** Change the Zoom level back to **120%**, and then press the **Ctrl+Home** keys to make sure the insertion point is located on the first page.

Reviewing a Document in Read Mode

The members of the board of directors might choose to print the report, but some might prefer to read it on their computers instead. In that case, they can take advantage of **Read Mode**, a document view designed to make reading on a screen as easy as possible. Unlike Print Layout view, which mimics the look of the printed page with its margins and page breaks, Read Mode focuses on the document's content. Read Mode displays as much content as possible on the screen at a time, with buttons that allow you to display more. Note that you can't edit text in Read Mode. To do that, you need to switch back to Page Layout view.

To display the Site Survey document in Read Mode:

▶ **1.** In the status bar, click the **Read Mode** button 📖. The document switches to Read Mode, with a reduced version of the cover page on the left and the first part of the document text on the right. On the left edge of the status bar, the message "SCREENS 1-2 OF 8" explains that you are currently viewing the first two screens out of a total of 8.

Trouble? If your status bar indicates that you have a different number of screens, change the Zoom level as needed so that the document is split into 8 screens.

The title page on the left is screen 1. The text on the right is screen 2. To display more of the document, you can click the arrow button on the right. See Figure 3-39.

Figure 3-39   Document displayed in Read Mode

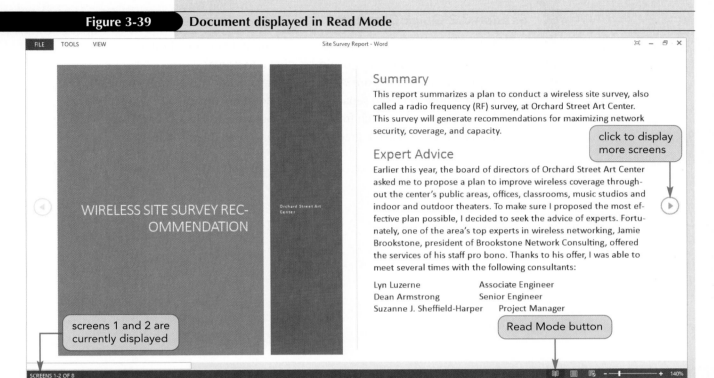

2. Click the **right arrow** button ⊙ on the right to display screens 3 and 4. A left arrow button now appears on the left side of the screen. You could click it to move back to the previous screens.

3. Click the **right arrow** button ⊙ to display screens 5 and 6, and then click the **right arrow** button ⊙ again to display the final two screens. To zoom in on the SmartArt graphic, you can double-click it.

4. Double-click the SmartArt graphic. An object zoom window opens, with the SmartArt graphic displayed. You can display an object zoom window like this for any graphic.

5. In the upper-right corner of the object zoom window, click the **magnifying glass** button Ⓠ to zoom in on the SmartArt graphic even more.

6. Click the **magnifying glass** button Ⓠ to return to the previous zoom level.

7. Click anywhere outside the object zoom window to return to screens 7 and 8 in Read Mode.

8. Click the **left arrow** button ⊙ on the left as necessary to return to screens 1 and 2, and then click the **Print Layout** button ▤ in the status bar to return to Page Layout view.

9. Close the document.

You now have a draft of the Site Survey Report document, including a cover page, the report text, a nicely formatted table, and the SmartArt graphic (in landscape orientation).

REVIEW

Session 3.2 Quick Check

1. Where are the default tab stops located on the horizontal ruler?
2. What tab do you click to begin creating a footnote?
3. Explain how to configure Word to hyphenate a document automatically.
4. Explain how to create separate headers for a document with two sections.
5. List three ways to switch from Page Layout view to Header and Footer view.
6. Explain how to make a graphic easier to view in Read Mode.

ASSESS

SAM Projects

Put your skills into practice with SAM Projects! SAM Projects for this tutorial can be found online. If you have a SAM account, go to www.cengage.com/sam2013 to download the most recent Project Instructions and Start Files.

PRACTICE

Review Assignments

Data File needed for the Review Assignments: Security.docx

The wireless site survey has been completed, and the Orchard Street Art Center has upgraded its network. Now, Katherine Hua is organizing a series of network security training classes for the art center staff. She has begun working on a report for the board that outlines basic information about the training. You need to format the report, add a table at the end containing a preliminary schedule, and create a sample graphic that Katherine could use in a handout announcing the training. Complete the following steps:

1. Open the file **Security** located in the Word3 ▸ Review folder included with your Data Files, and then save it as **Security Training Report** in the location specified by your instructor.

2. Promote the "Training Schedule" and "Level 1 Equipment Needs" headings from Heading 2 text to Heading 1 text, and then move the "Level 1 Equipment Needs" heading and its body text up above the "Training Schedule" heading.

3. Insert a page break before the "Training Schedule" heading. Insert a blank paragraph at the end of the new page 2, and then insert a table using the information shown in Figure 3-40. Format the header row in bold.

Figure 3-40	Information for training schedule table

Date	Topic
April 21	Applications
March 16	User account permissions
April 28	Firewall procedures
April 6	Wireless devices
March 3	Password security

© 2014 Cengage Learning

4. Sort the table by the contents of the "Date" column in ascending order.
5. In the appropriate location in the table, insert a new row for a **User privacy** class on **March 23**.
6. Delete the "Applications" row from the table.
7. Modify the widths of both columns to accommodate the widest entry in each.
8. Apply the Grid Table 4 - Accent 2 style to the table.
9. On page 1, replace the text "[instructor names]" with a tabbed list of instructors and their specialties, using the following information: **Jackie Fuhrman-Dunaway, Wireless security; Marcolo Jimenez, Multimedia wireless security; Surila Jin, Web privacy; Elizabeth Lawson, User support**. Insert a tab after each name, and don't include any punctuation in the list.
10. Use a left tab stop to align the instructors' specialities 2.5 inches from the left margin, and then adjust the list's paragraph spacing so it appears to be a single paragraph.

11. Locate the first sentence below the "Level 1 Equipment Needs" heading. At the end of that sentence, insert a footnote that reads **Some board members mentioned the possibility of holding classes in the concert hall, but the instructors prefer the smaller lecture hall, where microphones are unnecessary**.

12. Hyphenate the document using the default settings.

13. After the training schedule table on page 2, insert a section break that starts a new, third page, and then format the new page in landscape orientation. Insert a SmartArt graphic that illustrates the advantages of computer classes. Use the Equation graphic from the Process category, and, from left to right, include the following text in the SmartArt diagram: **User Education**, **Good Network Management**, and **Secure Wireless Network**. Do not include any punctuation in the SmartArt. Size the SmartArt graphic to fill the page.

14. Create a footer for sections 1 and 2 that aligns your first and last names at the left margin. Insert the page number, without any design elements and without the word "Page," below your name.

15. Separate the section 1 header from the section 2 header, and then create a header for section 1 using the Retrospect header style. Enter **SECURITY TRAINING** as the document title, and select the current date. Note that the document title will be displayed in all uppercase no matter how you type it.

16. Insert a cover page using the Retrospect style. If you typed the document title in all uppercase in the header, it will be displayed in all uppercase here. If you used a mix of uppercase and lowercase in the header, you'll see a mix here. Revise the document title as necessary to make it all uppercase, and then add the following subtitle: **A REPORT FOR THE ORCHARD STREET ART CENTER BOARD OF DIRECTORS**. Enter your name in the Author document control (you might have to replace a default name inserted by Word), and then delete the Company Name and Company Address document controls.

17. Change the document theme to Integral, save and preview the report, and then close it.

Case Problem 1

APPLY

Data File needed for this Case Problem: Greenware.docx

Greenware Consortium   You are the assistant business manager of Greenware Consortium, a professional organization for LEED contractors in Seattle, Washington and the surrounding area. LEED, which is short for Leadership in Energy and Environmental Design, is a certification system designed to encourage environmentally friendly building construction and maintenance. Contractors join the Greenware Consortium to make professional contacts with like-minded vendors and customers. You have been asked to help prepare an annual report for the board of directors. The current draft is not complete, but it contains enough for you to get started. Complete the following steps:

1. Open the file **Greenware** located in the Word3 ► Case1 folder included with your Data Files, and then save it as **Greenware Report** in the location specified by your instructor.

2. Adjust the heading levels so that the "Greenware Faire" and "Green Tech Fest" headings are formatted with the Heading 2 style.

3. Move the "Membership Forecast" heading and its body text down to the end of the report.

4. Format the Board of Directors list using a left tab stop with a dot leader at the 2.2-inch mark. (*Hint*: Use the Dialog Box Launcher in the Paragraph group on the PAGE LAYOUT tab to open the Paragraph dialog box, and then click the Tabs button at the bottom of the Indents and Spacing tab to open the Tabs dialog box.)

5. At the end of the first paragraph below the "Going Green Walking Tours" heading, insert the following footnote: **The Going Green walking tours are sponsored by the Seattle Public Works Department in association with the Seattle Green for Life Foundation**.

6. Locate the "Purpose" heading on page 1. At the end of the body text below that heading, insert the following footnote: **We recently signed a ten-year contract renewal with our website host, NetMind Solutions**.

7. Insert a page break that moves the "Membership Forecast" heading to the top of a new page, and then, below the body text on the new page, insert a table consisting of three columns and four rows.

8. In the table, enter the information shown in Figure 3-41. Format the column headings in bold.

Figure 3-41   **Information for membership forecast table**

Membership Type	2016	Projected 2017
Contractor	260	285
Vendor	543	670
Building Owner/Operator	350	400

© 2014 Cengage Learning

9. Sort the table in ascending order by membership type.

10. In the appropriate location in the table, insert a row for a **Student/Apprentice** membership type, with **250** members in 2016, and **300** projected members in 2017.

11. Adjust the column widths so each column accommodates the widest entry.

12. Format the table using the Grid Table 4 - Accent 1 table style without banded rows or a first column.

13. Hyphenate the document using the default settings.

14. Insert a Blank footer, and then type your name to replace the selected placeholder text in the footer's left margin. In the right margin, insert a page number using the Accent Bar 3 style. (*Hint:* Press the Tab key twice to move the insertion point to the right margin before inserting the page number, and then insert the page number at the current location.)

15. Insert a cover page using the Sideline style. Enter the company name, **Greenware Consortium**, and the title, **Annual Report**, in the appropriate document controls. In the subtitle document control, enter **Prepared by [Your Name]** (but replace "[Your Name]" with your first and last names). Delete the Author document control, which might contain a default name inserted by Word, and then insert the current date in the Date document control.

16. Change the document theme to Ion.

17. Save, preview, and then close the document.

TROUBLESHOOT

Case Problem 2

Data File needed for this Case Problem: Evaluation.docx

Customer Evaluation Report   Academy Art Tours specializes in European tours emphasizing art and architecture. After managing this year's Masters of Architecture tour, Lisa Marisca has begun writing a report summarizing the customer evaluation forms. She asks you to review her incomplete draft and fix some problems. Complete the following steps:

1. Open the file named **Evaluation** located in the Word3 ▸ Case2 folder included with your Data Files, and then save it as **Evaluation Report** in the location specified by your instructor.

⚙ Troubleshoot 2. Adjust the document so that the following are true:

- The heading "Problems Acquiring Updated Passports," its body text, and the SmartArt graphic appear on the last page in landscape orientation, with the rest of the report in portrait orientation.

- In section 1, the heading "Summary" is displayed at the top of page 2.

- The document header contains your first and last names but not a content control for the document title.

- Neither the header nor the footer is displayed on page 1.

- The footer is not displayed on the last page of the document. (*Hint:* After you break the link between sections, you'll need to delete the contents of the footer in one section.)

⚙ Troubleshoot 3. On pages 2 and 3, promote headings as necessary so all the headings are on the same level.

4. Increase the paragraph spacing before the first paragraph, "Masters of Architecture," on page 1 as much as necessary so that the paragraph is located at about the 2-inch mark on the vertical ruler. When you're finished, the text should be centered vertically on the page, so it looks like a cover page.

⚙ **Troubleshoot** 5. On page 2, remove any extra rows and columns in the table, and sort the information in a logical way. When you are finished, format it with a style that applies green (Accent 6) shading to the header row, with banded rows below, and remove any bold formatting as necessary.

6. Add a fourth shape to the SmartArt Graphic with the text **Submit completed form, photo, and fee to post office clerk**. Resize the graphic to fill the white space below the document text.

7. Save the document, review it in Read Mode, preview it, and then close it.

Case Problem 3

CREATE

There are no Data Files needed for this Case Problem.

"Aiden Eats" Blog and Newsletter   Aiden Malloy publishes his reviews of Minneapolis restaurants both in his blog, Aiden Eats, and in a printed newsletter of the same name. These publications have become so popular that Aiden has decided to try selling advertising space in both venues to local businesses. A colleague has just emailed him a list of potential advertisers. Aiden asks you to create and format a table containing the list of advertisers. When you're finished with that project, you'll create a table detailing some of his recent expenses. Complete the following steps:

1. Open a new, blank document, and then save it as **Advertiser Table** in the location specified by your instructor.

2. Create the table shown in Figure 3-42.

Figure 3-42	Advertiser table

Business	Contact	Phone
Allenton Knife Sharpening	Peter Allenton	555-5555
Bizmark Restaurant Supply	Nolan Everdeen	555-5555
Spices Boutique	Sigrid Larson	555-5555
WestMark Kitchen Design	Sheryl Wu	555-5555

© 2014 Cengage Learning

For the table style, start with the Grid Table 4 - Accent 1 table style, and then make any necessary changes. Use the Blue, Accent 1 color for the borders. The final table should be about 6.5 inches wide and 2.5 inches tall, as measured on the horizontal and vertical rulers. (*Hint:* Remember that you can drag the Table Resize handle to increase the table's overall size.)

3. Replace "Peter Allenton" with your first and last names.

4. Save, preview, and then close the Advertiser Table document.

5. Open a new, blank document, and then save it as **Expense Table** in the location specified by your instructor.

6. Create the table shown in Figure 3-43.

Figure 3-43   **Expense table**

Restaurant	Date	Expense
Beverly Coffee and Bake Shoppe	2/3/16	$13.50
Vietnam Noodle House	2/10/16	$23.00
The Everett Club	2/23/16	$45.50
	Total	$82.00

© 2014 Cengage Learning

For the table style, start with the Grid Table 4 - Accent 1 table style, and then make any necessary changes. Use the Blue, Accent 1 color for the borders. Note that in the bottom row, you'll need to merge two cells and right-align text within the new, merged cell.

7. For the total, use a formula instead of simply typing the amount. (*Hint:* Click in the cell where you want to insert a formula to sum the values, click the TABLE TOOLS LAYOUT tab, and then click the Formula button in the Data group to open the Formula dialog box, and then click the OK button.)

8. Save, preview, and then close the Expense Table document.

Case Problem 4

There are no Data Files needed for this Case Problem.

Friends of Triangle Beach   Kate Chomsky coordinates volunteers who monitor and protect native plant species on Triangle Beach, a nature preserve on the eastern coast of Florida. She needs a flyer to hand out at an upcoming neighborhood festival, where she hopes to recruit more volunteers. You can use Word's table features to lay out the flyer as shown in Kate's sketch in Figure 3-44. At the very end, you'll remove the table borders.

Figure 3-44   **Sketch for Triangle Beach flyer**

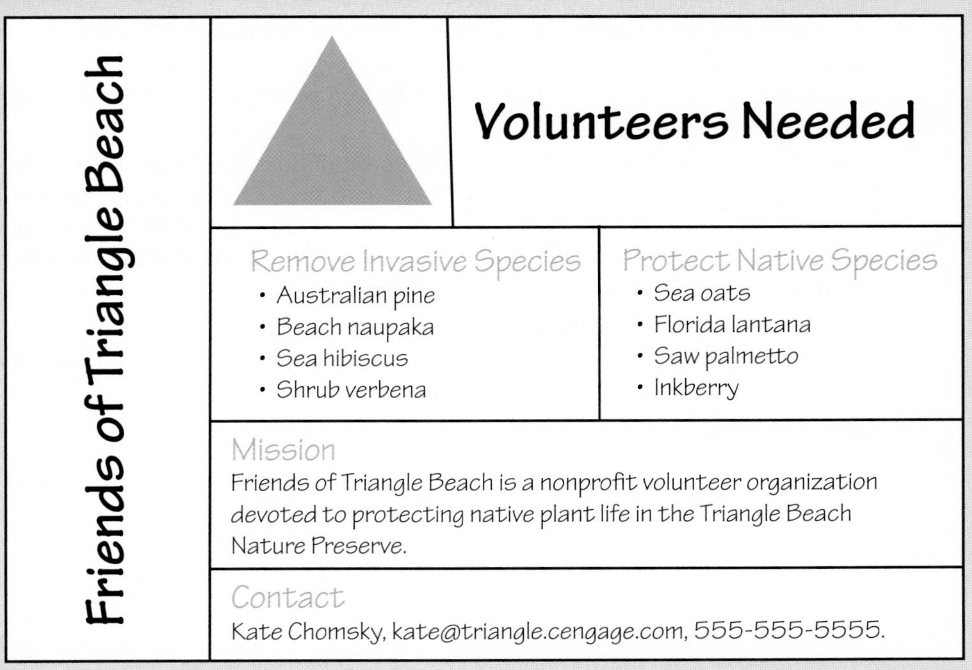

© 2014 Cengage Learning

Complete the following steps:

1. Open a new, blank document, and then save it as **Triangle Beach** in the location specified by your instructor.

2. Change the document's orientation to landscape.

✛ **Explore** 3. Use the Table button on the INSERT tab, to access the Insert Table menu, and then click Draw Table at the bottom of the menu to activate the Draw Table pointer (which looks like a pencil). Click in the upper-left corner of the document (near the paragraph mark), and, using the rulers as guides, drag down and to the right to draw a rectangle that is 9 inches wide and 6 inches high. After you draw the rectangle, you can adjust its height and width using the Height and Width boxes in the Cell Size group on the TABLE TOOLS LAYOUT tab, if necessary. (*Hint*: If the Draw Table pointer disappears after you change the table's height and width, you can turn it back on by clicking the Draw Table button in the Draw group on the TABLE TOOLS LAYOUT tab.)

✛ **Explore** 4. Use the Draw Table pointer to draw the columns and rows shown in Figure 3-44. For example, to draw the column border for the "Friends of Triangle Beach" column, click the top of the rectangle at the point where you want the right column border to be located, and then drag down to the bottom of the rectangle. Use the same technique to draw rows. (*Hint:* To delete a border, click the Eraser button in the Draw group on the TABLE TOOLS LAYOUT tab, click anywhere on the border you want to erase, and then click the Eraser button again to turn it off.)

5. When you are finished drawing the table, press the Esc key to turn off the Draw Table pointer.

✛ **Explore** 6. In the left column, type the text **Friends of Triangle Beach**. With the pointer still in that cell, click the TABLE TOOLS LAYOUT tab, and then in the Alignment group, click the Text Direction button twice to position the text vertically so that it reads from bottom to top. Using the formatting options on the HOME tab, format the text in 36-point font. Use the Align Center button in the Alignment group to center the text in the cell. (*Hint:* You will probably have to adjust and readjust the row and column borders throughout these steps until all the elements of the table are positioned properly.)

7. Type the remaining text as shown in Figure 3-44. Replace "Kate Chomsky" with your own name, remove the hyperlink formatting from the email address, and format it in bold. Change the font size for "Volunteers Needed" to 36 points, and center align the text in that cell. Use the Heading 1 style for the following text—"Remove Invasive Species," "Protect Native Species," "Mission," and "Contact." Change the font size for this text to 20 points. For the remaining text, use the Normal style, and then change the font size to 16 points. If the table expands to two pages, drag a row border up slightly to reduce the row's height. Repeat as necessary until the table fits on one page.

✛ **Explore** 8. On the INSERT tab, use the Shapes button in the Illustrations group to draw the Isosceles Triangle shape, similar to the way you drew the table rectangle, by dragging the pointer. Draw the triangle in the blank cell in the top row. If the triangle isn't centered neatly in the cell, click the Undo button and try again until you draw a triangle that has the same proportions as the one in Figure 3-44. Until you change the theme in the next step, the triangle will be blue.

9. Change the document theme to Facet.

10. Remove the table borders. When you are finished, your flyer should match the table shown in Figure 3-44, but without the table borders.

11. Save your work, preview the document, and then close it.

OBJECTIVES

Session 4.1
- Use continuous section break for page layout
- Format text in columns
- Insert symbols and special characters
- Distinguish between inline and floating objects
- Wrap text around an object
- Insert and format text boxes
- Insert drop caps

Session 4.2
- Create and modify WordArt
- Insert and crop a picture
- Add clip art to a document
- Rotate and adjust a picture
- Remove a photo's background
- Balance columns
- Add a page border
- Save a document as a PDF
- Open a PDF in Word

Enhancing Page Layout and Design

Creating a Newsletter

Case | *Williamson Health Care*

Estefan Silva is a public outreach specialist at Williamson Health Care, a health maintenance organization located in Carson City, Nevada. He has written the text of a newsletter describing an upcoming series of wellness classes. Now he needs you to transform the text into an eye-catching publication with a headline, photos, drop caps, and other desktop publishing elements. Estefan's budget doesn't allow him to hire a professional graphic designer to create the document using desktop publishing software. But there's no need for that because you can do the work for him using Word's formatting, graphics, and page layout tools. After you finish the newsletter, Estefan wants you to save the newsletter as a PDF so he can email it to the printing company. You also need to make some edits to a document that is currently available only as a PDF.

STARTING DATA FILES

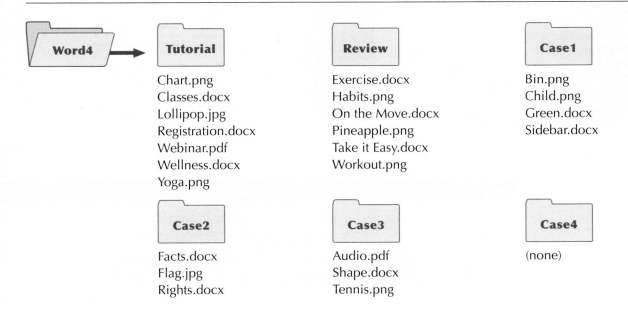

Word4 → **Tutorial**

Chart.png
Classes.docx
Lollipop.jpg
Registration.docx
Webinar.pdf
Wellness.docx
Yoga.png

Review

Exercise.docx
Habits.png
On the Move.docx
Pineapple.png
Take it Easy.docx
Workout.png

Case1

Bin.png
Child.png
Green.docx
Sidebar.docx

Case2

Facts.docx
Flag.jpg
Rights.docx

Case3

Audio.pdf
Shape.docx
Tennis.png

Case4

(none)

Session 4.1 Visual Overview:

Desktop publishing is the process of preparing commercial-quality printed material, such as the newsletter shown here, using a personal computer. Using Word, you can create documents that have elements of desktop publishing, such as special font treatments, graphics, and page layout options, as well as design elements such as page borders.

This specially formatted text is an example of WordArt, which is created using the WordArt button in the Text group on the INSERT tab.

These are examples of text boxes, which are like mini documents within a document.

This photo and the drawing of the woman in a yoga pose under a tree (on the next page) are examples of clip art. Clip art consists of premade electronic illustrations, photographs, and other graphics. Audio and video clip art are also available.

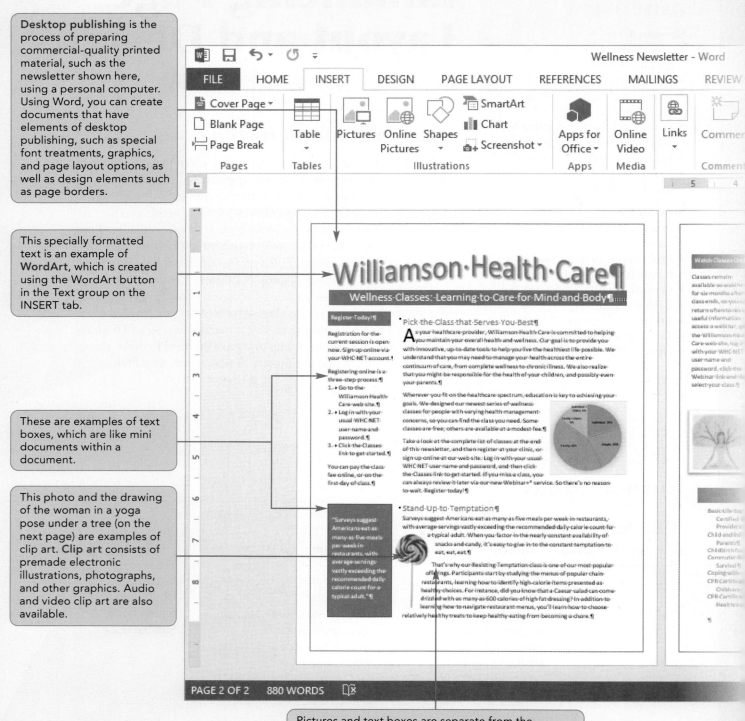

Pictures and text boxes are separate from the document text; you need to adjust the way text flows, or wraps, around them. Here, the Tight text wrap option is used to make text flow as closely as possible around the shape of the lollipop.

Elements of Desktop Publishing

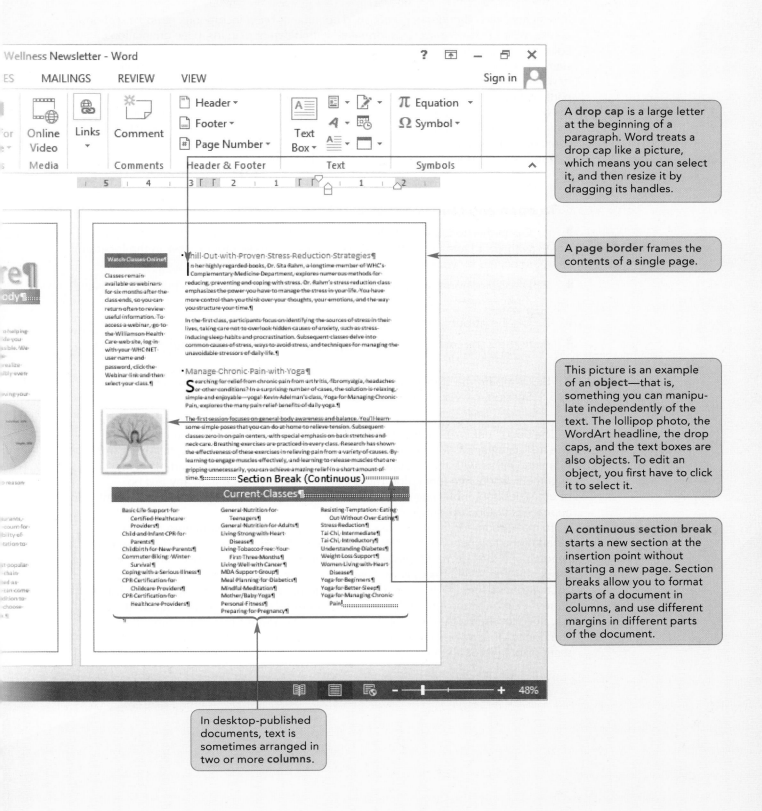

A **drop cap** is a large letter at the beginning of a paragraph. Word treats a drop cap like a picture, which means you can select it, and then resize it by dragging its handles.

A **page border** frames the contents of a single page.

This picture is an example of an **object**—that is, something you can manipulate independently of the text. The lollipop photo, the WordArt headline, the drop caps, and the text boxes are also objects. To edit an object, you first have to click it to select it.

A **continuous section break** starts a new section at the insertion point without starting a new page. Section breaks allow you to format parts of a document in columns, and use different margins in different parts of the document.

In desktop-published documents, text is sometimes arranged in two or more **columns**.

Using Continuous Section Breaks to Enhance Page Layout

Newsletters and other desktop-published documents often incorporate multiple section breaks, with the various sections formatted with different margins, page orientations, column settings, and other page layout options. Continuous section breaks, which start a new section without starting a new page, are especially useful when creating a newsletter because they allow you to apply different page layout settings to different parts of a single page. To create the newsletter shown in the Session 4.1 Visual Overview, the first step is to insert a series of section breaks that will allow you to use different margins for different parts of the document. Section breaks will also allow you to format some of the text in multiple columns.

You'll start by opening and reviewing the document.

To open and review the document:

▶ **1.** Open the document **Wellness** from the Word4 ▶ Tutorial folder included with your Data Files, and then save it as **Wellness Newsletter** in the location specified by your instructor.

▶ **2.** Display nonprinting characters and the rulers, and switch to Print Layout view, if necessary.

▶ **3.** On the ribbon, click the **VIEW** tab.

▶ **4.** In the Zoom group, click **Multiple Pages** so you can see both pages of the document side-by-side.

▶ **5.** Compare the document to the completed newsletter shown in the Session 4.1 Visual Overview.

The document is formatted with the Office theme, using the default margins. The first paragraph is formatted with the Title style, and the remaining headings are formatted either with the Heading 1 style, or with blue paragraph shading, center alignment, and white font color. The document doesn't yet contain any text boxes or other desktop publishing elements. The list of classes at the end of the document appears as a standard, single column of text.

To make room for the text boxes, you need to change the left margin to 2.5 inches for all of the text between the "Wellness Classes: Learning to Care for Mind and Body" heading and the "Current Classes" heading. To accomplish this, you'll insert a section break after the "Wellness Classes: Learning to Care for Mind and Body" heading and another one before the "Current Classes" heading. You'll eventually format the list of current classes, at the end of the document, in three columns. To accomplish that, you need to insert a third section break after the "Current Classes" heading. Because you don't want any of the section breaks to start new pages, you will use continuous sections breaks for all three. See Figure 4-1.

| Figure 4-1 | Wellness Newsletter document before adding section breaks |

To insert continuous section breaks in the document:

1. Change the Zoom level to **120%**.

2. In the document, click at the beginning of the third paragraph, which contains the heading "Pick the Class that Serves You Best."

3. On the ribbon, click the **PAGE LAYOUT** tab.

4. In the Page Setup group, click the **Breaks** button, and then click **Continuous**. A short dotted line, indicating a continuous section break, appears in the blue shading at the end of the preceding paragraph. If the paragraph text were shorter, you would see a longer line with the words "Section Break (Continuous)." You'll be able to see the section break text more clearly when you insert the next one.

5. Scroll down to page 2, click at the beginning of the shaded paragraph "Current Classes," and then insert a continuous section break. A dotted line with the words "Section Break (Continuous)" appears at the end of the preceding paragraph.

6. Click at the beginning of the next paragraph, which contains the first class title "Basic Life Support for Certified Healthcare Providers," and then insert a continuous section break. A dotted line with the words "Section Break (Continuous)" appears in the blue shading at the end of the preceding paragraph.

Now that you have created sections within the Wellness Newsletter document, you can format the individual sections as if they were separate documents. In the following steps, you'll format the first and third sections by changing their left and right margins to .75 inch. Then, you'll format the second section by changing its left margin to 2.5 inches.

To set custom margins for sections 1, 2, and 3:

1. Press the **Ctrl+Home** keys to position the insertion point in section 1.

2. In the Page Setup group, click the **Margins** button, and then click **Custom Margins** to open the Page Setup dialog box.

3. Change the Left and Right margin settings to **.75** inch, and then click the **OK** button. The blue shading expands slightly on both sides of the paragraph.

4. On page 1, click anywhere in the heading "Pick the Class that Serves You Best" to position the insertion point in section 2.

5. In the Page Setup group, click the **Margins** button, and then click **Custom Margins** to open the Page Setup dialog box.

6. Change the Left margin setting to **2.5** inches, and then click the **OK** button. The text in section 2 shifts to the right, and the document text flows to a third page. Throughout this tutorial, as you add and resize various elements, the text will occasionally expand from two pages to three or four. But by the time you are finished, the newsletter will consist of only two pages.

7. Scroll down to page 2, click in the shaded heading "Current Classes" to position the insertion point in section 3, and then change the Left and Right margin settings to **.75** inch.

8. On the ribbon, click the **VIEW** tab.

9. In the Zoom group, click **Multiple Pages** so you can see all three pages of the document side-by-side. See Figure 4-2.

Figure 4-2 | **Sections 1, 2, and 3 with new margins**

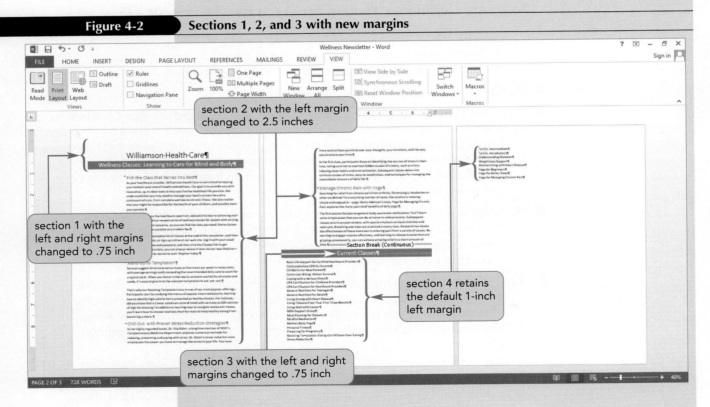

10. Save the document.

In addition to allowing you to format parts of a document with different margins, section breaks allow you to format part of a document in columns. You'll add some columns to section 4 next.

Formatting Text in Columns

Text meant for quick reading is often laid out in columns, with text flowing down one column, continuing at the top of the next column, flowing down that column, and so forth. To get started, click the Columns button in the Page Setup group on the PAGE LAYOUT tab, and then click the number of columns you want in the Columns gallery. For more advanced column options, you can use the More Columns command to open the Columns dialog box. In this dialog box, you can adjust the column widths and the space between columns, and choose to format either the entire document in columns or just the section that contains the insertion point.

As shown in the Session 4.1 Visual Overview, Estefan wants section 4 of the newsletter document, which consists of the class list, to be formatted in three columns.

To format section 4 in three columns:

1. Click anywhere in the list of classes at the end of the document to position the insertion point in section 4.

2. On the ribbon, click the **PAGE LAYOUT** tab.

3. In the Page Setup group, click the **Columns** button to display the Columns gallery. At this point, you could simply click Three to format section 4 in three columns of equal width. However, it's helpful to take a look at the columns dialog box so you can get familiar with some more advanced column options.

4. Click **More Columns** to open the Columns dialog box, and then in the Presets section, click **Three**. See Figure 4-3.

Figure 4-3   Columns dialog box

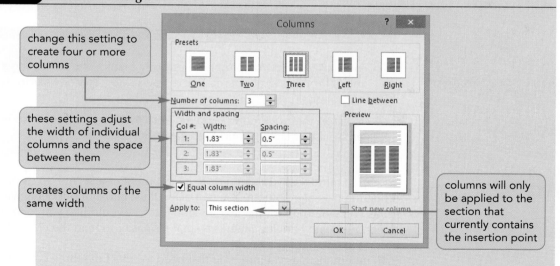

change this setting to create four or more columns

these settings adjust the width of individual columns and the space between them

creates columns of the same width

columns will only be applied to the section that currently contains the insertion point

To format text in four or more columns, you can change the setting in the Number of columns box instead of selecting an option in the Presets section. By default, the Apply to box, in the lower-left corner, displays "This section," indicating that the three-column format will be applied only to the current section. To apply columns to the entire document, you could click the Apply to arrow and then click Whole document. To change the width of the individual columns or the spacing between the columns, you can use the settings in the Width and spacing section of the Columns dialog box.

▶ **5.** Click the **OK** button. Section 4 is now formatted in three columns of the default width. See Figure 4-4.

Figure 4-4 **Section 4 formatted in three columns**

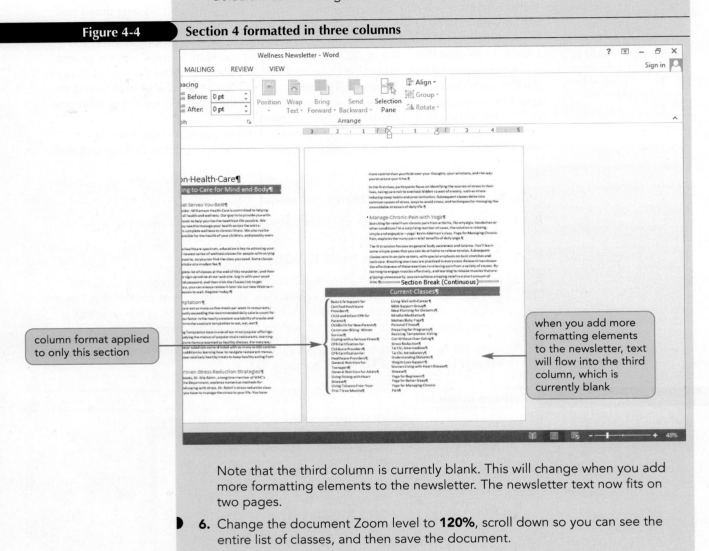

column format applied to only this section

when you add more formatting elements to the newsletter, text will flow into the third column, which is currently blank

Note that the third column is currently blank. This will change when you add more formatting elements to the newsletter. The newsletter text now fits on two pages.

▶ **6.** Change the document Zoom level to **120%**, scroll down so you can see the entire list of classes, and then save the document.

Keep in mind that you can restore a document or a section to its original format by formatting it as one column. You can also adjust paragraph indents within columns, just as you would in normal text. In fact, Estefan would like you to format the columns in section 4 with hanging indents so that it's easier to read the class titles that take up more than one line.

To indent the class names, you first need to select the three columns of text. Selecting columns of text by dragging the mouse can be tricky. It's easier to use the Shift+click method instead.

To format the columns in section 4 with hanging indents:

1. Make sure the **PAGE LAYOUT** tab is selected on the ribbon.

2. Click at the beginning of the first class name ("Basic Life Support for Certified Healthcare Providers"), press and hold the **Shift** key, and then click at the end of the last class name ("Yoga for Managing Chronic Pain"). The entire list of classes is selected.

3. In the Paragraph group, click the **Dialog Box Launcher** to open the Paragraph dialog box with the Indents and Spacing tab displayed.

4. In the Indentation section, click the **Special** arrow, click **Hanging**, and then change the By setting to **0.2"**.

5. Click the **OK** button to close the Paragraph dialog box, and then click anywhere in the list to deselect it. The class list is now formatted with a hanging indent, so the second line of each paragraph is indented .2 inches. See Figure 4-5.

| Figure 4-5 | **Text formatted in columns with hanging indent** |

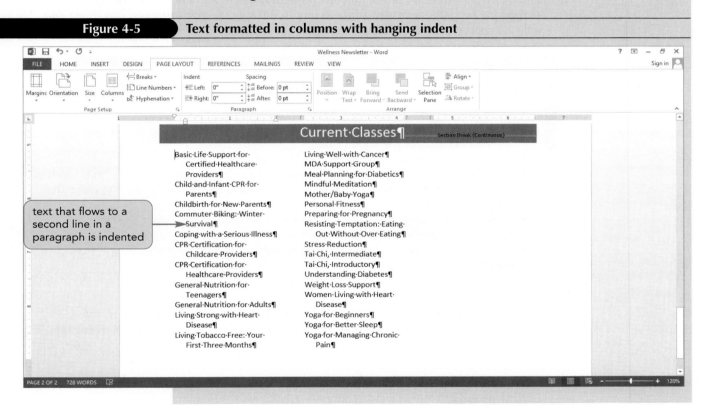

Inserting Symbols and Special Characters

When creating documents in Word, you can change some of the characters available on the standard keyboard into special characters or symbols called **typographic characters**. Word's AutoCorrect feature automatically converts some standard characters into typographic characters as you type. In some cases, you need to press the spacebar and type more characters before Word inserts the appropriate typographic character. If Word inserts a typographic character that you don't want, you can click the Undo button to revert to the characters you originally typed. See Figure 4-6.

Figure 4-6   Common typographic characters

To insert this symbol or character	Type	Word converts to
Em dash	word--word	word—word
Smiley face	:)	☺
Copyright symbol	(c)	©
Trademark symbol	(tm)	™
Registered trademark symbol	(r)	®
Fractions	1/2, 1/4	½, ¼
Arrows	<-- or -->	← or →

© 2014 Cengage Learning

Most of the typographic characters in Figure 4-6 can also be inserted using the Symbol button on the INSERT tab, which opens a gallery of commonly used symbols, and the More Symbols command, which opens the Symbol dialog box. The Symbol dialog box provides access to all the symbols and special characters you can insert into a Word document.

REFERENCE

Inserting Symbols and Special Characters from the Symbol Dialog Box

- Move the insertion point to the location in the document where you want to insert a particular symbol or special character.
- On the ribbon, click the INSERT tab.
- In the Symbols group, click the Symbol button.
- If you see the symbol or character you want in the Symbol gallery, click it to insert it in the document. For a more extensive set of choices, click More Symbols to open the Symbol dialog box.
- In the Symbol dialog box, locate the symbol or character you want on either the Symbols tab or the Special Characters tab.
- Click the symbol or special character you want, click the Insert button, and then click the Close button.

Estefan forgot to include a registered trademark symbol (®) after "Webinar+" on page 1. He asks you to add one now. After you do, you'll explore the Symbol dialog box.

To insert the registered trademark symbol and explore the Symbol dialog box:

1. Use the Navigation pane to find the term **Webinar+** in the document, and then close the Navigation pane.

2. Click to the right of the plus sign to position the insertion point between the plus sign and the space that follows it.

3. Type **(r)**. AutoCorrect converts the "r" in parentheses into the superscript ® symbol.

   If you don't know which characters to type to insert a symbol or special character, you can review the AutoCorrect replacements in the AutoCorrect: English (United States) dialog box.

4. On the ribbon, click the **FILE** tab.

5. In the navigation bar, click **Options** to open the Word Options dialog box.

6. In the left pane, click **Proofing**, and then click the **AutoCorrect Options** button. The AutoCorrect: English (United States) dialog box opens, with the AutoCorrect tab displayed.

7. Review the table at the bottom of the AutoCorrect tab. The column on the left shows the characters you can type, and the column on the right shows what AutoCorrect inserts as a replacement. See Figure 4-7.

Figure 4-7   **AutoCorrect: English (United States) dialog box**

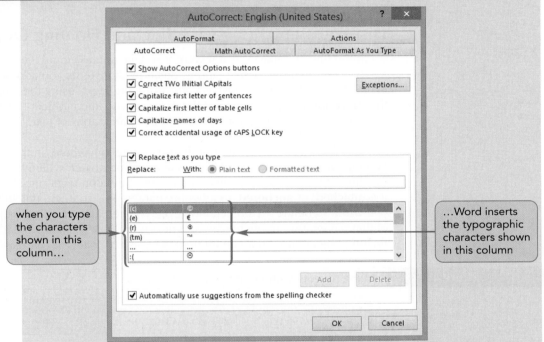

when you type the characters shown in this column…

…Word inserts the typographic characters shown in this column

---

8. Scroll down to review the AutoCorrect replacements, click the **Cancel** button to close the AutoCorrect: English (United States) dialog box, and then click the **Cancel** button to close the Word Options dialog box.

Now you can explore the Symbol dialog box, which offers another way to insert symbols and special characters.

9. On the ribbon, click the **INSERT** tab.

10. In the Symbols group, click the **Symbol** button, and then click **More Symbols**. The Symbol dialog box opens with the Symbols tab displayed.

11. Scroll down the gallery of symbols on the Symbols tab to review the many symbols you can insert into a document. To insert one, you would click it, and then click the Insert button.

12. Click the **Special Characters** tab. The characters available on this tab are often used in desktop publishing. Notice the shortcut keys that you can use to insert many of the special characters.

13. Click the **Cancel** button to close the Symbol dialog box.

Introduction to Working with Objects

An object is something that you can manipulate independently of the document text. In desktop publishing, you use objects to illustrate the document or to enhance the page layout. To complete the newsletter for Estefan, you'll need to add some text boxes, drop caps, and pictures. These are all examples of objects in Word.

Inserting Graphic Objects

Objects used for illustration purposes or to enhance the page layout are sometimes called **graphic objects**, or simply **graphics**. The INSERT tab is the starting point for adding graphics to a document. After you insert a graphic object, you typically need to adjust its position on the page. Your ability to control the position of an object depends on whether it is an inline object or a floating object.

Distinguishing Between Inline and Floating Objects

An **inline object** behaves as if it were text. Like an individual letter, it has a specific location within a line of text, and its position changes as you add or delete text. You can align an inline object just as you would align text, using the alignment buttons in the Paragraph group on the HOME tab. However, inline objects are difficult to work with because every time you add or remove paragraphs of text, the object moves to a new position.

In contrast, you can position a **floating object** anywhere on the page, with the text flowing, or wrapping, around it. Unlike an inline object, which has a specific position in a line of text, a floating object has a more fluid connection to the document text. It is attached, or **anchored**, to an entire paragraph—so if you delete that paragraph, you will also delete the object. However, you can also move the object independently of that paragraph. An anchor symbol next to an object tells you that the object is a floating object rather than an inline object, as illustrated in Figure 4-8.

| Figure 4-8 | Inline objects compared to floating objects |

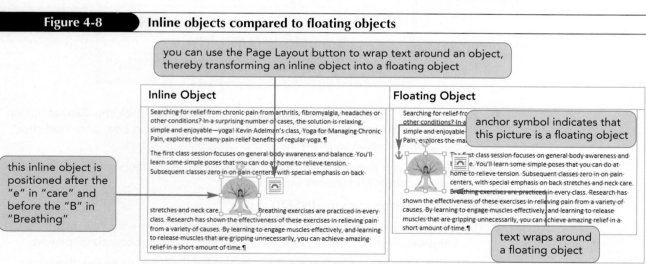

Image used with permission of Microsoft Corporation

You'll typically want to transform all inline objects into floating objects because floating objects are far more flexible.

Wrapping Text Around an Object

To transform an inline object into a floating object, you apply a **text wrapping setting** to it. First, click the object to select it, click the Layout Options button next to the object, and then click an option in the Layout Options gallery. For example, you can select Square text wrapping to make the text follow a square outline as it flows around the object, or you can select Tight text wrapping to make the text follow the shape of the object more exactly. Figure 4-9 describes the different types of wrapping.

Figure 4-9   **Text wrapping options in the Layout Options gallery**

Menu Icon	Type of Wrapping	Description
	Square	Text flows in a square outline around the object, regardless of the shape of the object; by default, Square text wrapping is applied to preformatted text boxes inserted via the Text Box button on the INSERT tab.
	Tight	Text follows the exact outline of the object; if you want the text to flow around an object, this is usually the best option.
	Through	Text flows through the object, filling up any open areas; this type is similar to Tight text wrapping.
	Top and Bottom	Text stops above the object and then starts again below the object.
	Behind Text	The object is layered behind the text, with the text flowing over it.
	In Front of Text	The object is layered in front of the text, with the text flowing behind it; if you want to position an object in white space next to the text, this option gives you the greatest control over its exact position. By default, In Front of Text wrapping is applied to any shapes inserted via the Shapes button in the Illustrations group on the INSERT tab.

© 2014 Cengage Learning

Most graphic objects, including photos and SmartArt, are inline by default. All text boxes and shapes are floating by default. Objects that are inserted as floating objects by default have a specific text wrapping setting assigned to them, but you can change the default setting to any text wrapping setting you want.

INSIGHT

Displaying Gridlines

When formatting a complicated document like a newsletter, you'll often have to adjust the position of objects on the page until everything looks the way you want. To make it easier to see the relative position of objects, you can display the document's gridlines. These vertical and horizontal lines are not actually part of the document. They are simply guidelines you can use when positioning text and objects on the page. By default, when gridlines are displayed, objects align with, or **snap to**, the nearest intersection of a horizontal and vertical line. The figures in this tutorial do not show gridlines because they would make the figures difficult to read. However, you will have a chance to experiment with gridlines in the Case Problems at the end of this tutorial. To display gridlines, click the VIEW tab on the ribbon, and then click the Gridlines check box to insert a check.

Inserting Text Boxes

You can choose to add a preformatted text box to a document, or you can create your own text box from scratch and adjust its appearance. To insert a preformatted text box, you use the Text Box button in the Text group. Text boxes inserted this way include placeholder text that you can replace with your own text. Preformatted text boxes come with preset font and paragraph options that are designed to match the text box's overall look. However, you can change the appearance of the text in the text box by using the options on the HOME tab, just as you would for ordinary text. The text box, as a whole, is designed to match the document's current theme. You could alter its appearance by using the Shape Styles options on the DRAWING TOOLS FORMAT tab, but there's typically no reason to do so.

Because the preformatted text boxes are so professional looking, they are usually a better choice than creating your own. However, if you want a very simple text box, you can use the Shapes button in the Illustrations group to draw a text box. After you draw the text box, you can adjust its appearance by using the Shape Styles options on the DRAWING TOOLS FORMAT tab. You can type any text you want inside the text box at the insertion point. When you are finished, you can format the text using the options on the HOME tab.

REFERENCE

Inserting a Text Box

- To insert a preformatted, rectangular text box, click in the document where you want to insert the text box.
- On the ribbon, click the INSERT tab.
- In the Text group, click the Text Box button to open the Text Box gallery, and then click a text box style to select it.
- In the text box in the document, delete the placeholder text, type the text you want to include, and then format the text using the options on the HOME tab.

or

- To insert and format your own rectangular text box, click the INSERT tab on the ribbon.
- In the Text group, click the Shapes button to open the Shapes gallery, and then click Text Box.
- In the document, position the pointer where you want to insert the text box, press and hold the mouse button, and then drag the pointer to draw the text box.
- In the text box, type the text you want to include, and then format the text using the options on the HOME tab.
- Format the text box using the options in the Shape Styles group on the DRAWING TOOLS FORMAT tab.

Inserting a Preformatted Text Box

Estefan's newsletter requires three text boxes. You need to insert the first text box on page 1, to the left of the "Pick the Class that Serves You Best" heading. For this text box, you'll insert one that is preformatted to work as a sidebar. A **sidebar** is a text box designed to look good positioned to the side of the main document text. A sidebar is typically used to draw attention to important information.

To insert a preformatted text box in the document:

1. Scroll up to the top of page 1, and then click anywhere in the "Pick the Class that Serves You Best" heading.

2. Change the Zoom level to **Multiple Pages** so you can see both pages of the document.

3. On the ribbon, click the **INSERT** tab.

4. In the Text group, click the **Text Box** button to display the Text Box gallery, and then use the scroll bar to scroll down the gallery to locate the Ion Sidebar 1 text box.

5. Click **Ion Sidebar 1**. The text box is inserted in the left margin of page 1. See Figure 4-10.

Figure 4-10 **Text box inserted on page 1**

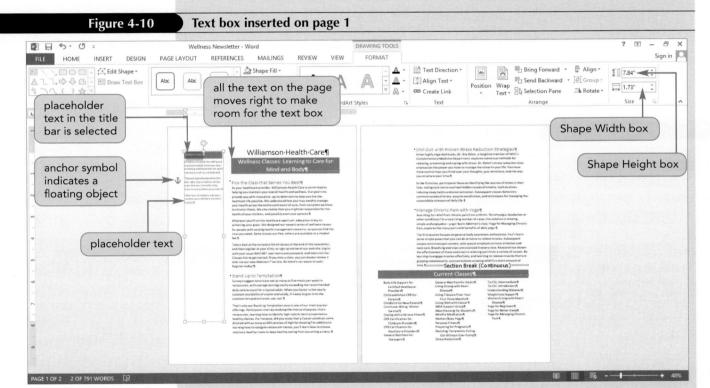

All the text on page 1 moves right to make room for the text box. Later, after you resize and move the text box, the first two paragraphs will resume their original positions, centered at the top of the page. The anchor symbol next to the text box tells you it is a floating object.

The text box consists of a blue title bar at the top that contains placeholder text, with additional placeholder text below the title bar. The dotted outline with handles indicates the borders of the text box. When you first insert a text box, the placeholder text in the title bar is selected, ready for you to type your own title. In this case, however, before you add any text, you'll resize and reposition the text box.

6. On the ribbon, click the **DRAWING TOOLS FORMAT** tab, if necessary.

7. In the Size group, click the **Shape Height** box, type **4.3**, click the **Shape Width** box, type **1.5**, and then press the **Enter** key. The text box is now shorter and narrower.

8. Change the Zoom level to **120%**.

   Next, you need to drag the text box down below the first two paragraphs. Currently, only the placeholder text in the text box title bar is selected. Before you can move it, you need to select the entire text box.

9. Position the pointer somewhere over the text box border until the pointer changes to ⤡.

10. Click the text box border to select the entire text box. The text box border changes from dotted to solid, and the Layout Options button appears to the right of the text box.

11. Position the pointer ⤡ over the text box's title bar, press and hold the mouse button, and then drag the text box down so that the top of the text box aligns with the first line of text below the "Pick the Class that Serves You Best" heading. The left edge of the text box should align with the left edge of the blue shaded heading "Wellness Classes: Learning to Care for Mind and Body." The anchor symbol remains in its original position, next to the shaded paragraph.

12. When you are sure the text box is positioned correctly, release the mouse button. See Figure 4-11.

Figure 4-11 | **Resized and repositioned text box**

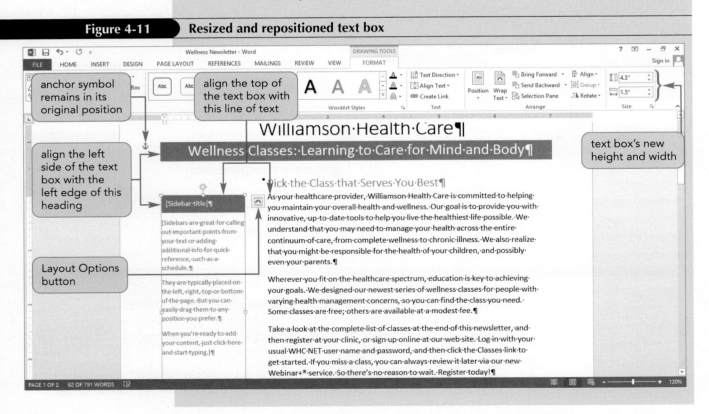

After you insert a text box or other object, you usually need to adjust its relationship to the surrounding text; that is, you need to adjust its text wrapping setting.

Changing the Text Wrapping Setting for the Text Box

A preformatted text box inserted via the Text box button on the INSERT tab is, by default, a floating object formatted with Square text wrapping. You will verify whether this is true when you open the Layout Options gallery in the following steps. Then you'll select the In Front of Text option instead to gain more control over the exact position of the text box on the page.

To open the Layout Options gallery and change the wrapping option:

1. Change the Zoom level to **One Page** so you can see the text box's position relative to the text on page 1.

2. Click the **Layout Options** button. The Layout Options gallery opens with the Square option selected. See Figure 4-12.

Figure 4-12	Square text wrapping currently applied to text box

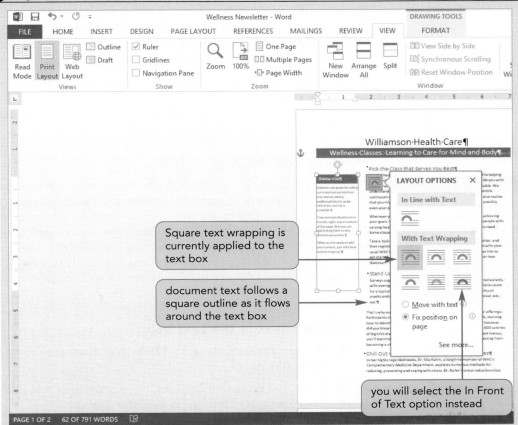

Square text wrapping is currently applied to the text box

document text follows a square outline as it flows around the text box

you will select the In Front of Text option instead

Square text wrapping is currently applied to the text box. You can see evidence of Square text wrapping where the document text flows around the lower-right corner of the text box. You'll have a chance to see some more dramatic examples of text wrapping later in this tutorial, but it's important to be able to identify subtle examples of it.

Trouble? If the Layout Options button is not visible, click the text box border to select the entire text box and display the Layout Options button.

▶ **3.** Click any of the other options in the Layout Options gallery and observe how the document text and the text box shift position. Continue exploring the Layout Options gallery, trying out several of the options.

▶ **4.** Click the **In Front of Text** option ▣ and then click the **Close** button ✖ in the upper-right corner of the Layout Options gallery to close the gallery. The document text shifts so that it now flows directly down the left margin, without wrapping around the text box.

Your next formatting task is to make sure the text box is assigned a fixed position on the page. You could check this setting on the Layout Options button, but you'll use the Wrap Text button in the Arrange group instead.

▶ **5.** On the ribbon, click the **DRAWING TOOLS FORMAT** tab.

▶ **6.** In the Arrange group, click the **Wrap Text** button. The Wrap Text menu gives you access to all the options in the Layout Options gallery, plus some more advanced settings.

▶ **7.** Verify that Fix Position on Page has a checkmark next to it. To avoid having graphic objects move around unexpectedly on the page as you add or delete other elements, it's a good idea to check this setting either in the Wrap Text menu or in the Layout Options menu for every graphic object.

▶ **8.** Click anywhere in the document to close the gallery, and then save the document.

Adding Text to a Text Box

Now that the text box is positioned where you want it, with the correct text wrapping, you can add text to it. In some documents, text boxes are used to present new information, while others highlight a quote from the main document. A direct quote from a document formatted in a text box is known as a **pull quote**. To create a pull quote text box, you can copy the text from the main document, and then paste it into the text box. You can also simply type text in a text box. Finally, you can insert text from another Word document by using the Object button arrow on the INSERT tab.

To insert text in the text box:

▶ **1.** Change the Zoom level to **120%**, and then scroll as necessary so you can see the entire text box.

▶ **2.** In the text box's title bar, click the placeholder text **[Sidebar title]** to select it, if necessary, and then type **Register Today!**

▶ **3.** Click the placeholder text below the title bar to select it. See Figure 4-13.

Figure 4-13   Text box with placeholder text selected

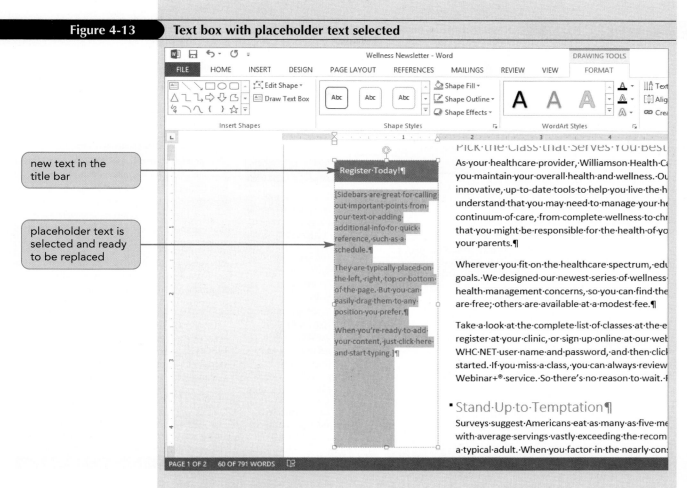

new text in the title bar

placeholder text is selected and ready to be replaced

4. Press the **Delete** key to delete the placeholder text. Now you can insert new text from another Word document.

5. On the ribbon, click the **INSERT** tab.

6. In the Text group, click the **Object button arrow** to open the Object menu, and then click **Text from File**. The Insert File dialog box opens. Selecting a Word document to insert is just like selecting a document in the Open dialog box.

7. Navigate to the Word4 ▶ Tutorial folder included with your Data Files, click **Registration** to select the file, and then click the **Insert** button. The registration information contained in the Registration document is inserted directly into the text box. The inserted text was formatted in 9-point Calibri in the Registration document, and it retains that formatting when you paste it into the Wellness Newsletter document. To make the text easier to read, you'll increase the font size to 11 points.

8. With the insertion point located in the last paragraph in the text box (which is blank), press the **Backspace** key to delete the blank paragraph, and then click and drag the mouse pointer to select all the text in the text box, including the title in the shaded title box.

9. On the ribbon, click the **HOME** tab.

10. In the Font group, click the **Font Size** arrow, and then click **11**. The size of the text in the text box increases to 11 points. See Figure 4-14.

| Figure 4-14 | Registration information inserted in text box |

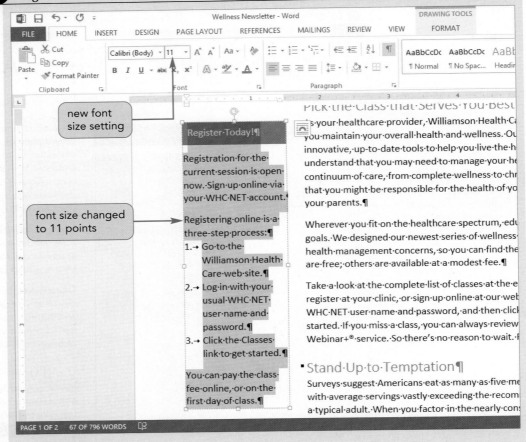

Trouble? Don't be concerned if the text in your text box wraps slightly differently from the text shown in Figure 4-14. The same fonts can vary slightly from one computer to another, causing slight differences in the way text wraps within and around text boxes.

▶ **11.** Click anywhere outside the text box to deselect it, and then save the document.

The first text box is complete. Now you need to add one more on page 1, and another on page 2. Estefan wants the second text box on page 1 to have a different look from the first one, so he asks you to use the Shapes button to draw a text box.

Drawing and Formatting a Text Box Using the Shapes Menu

A text box is considered a shape, just like the other shapes you can insert via the Shapes button on the INSERT tab. This is true whether you insert a text box via the Text Box button or via the Shapes button. While text boxes are typically rectangular, you can actually turn any shape into a text box. Start by using the Shapes button to draw a shape of your choice, and then, with the shape selected, type any text you want. You won't see an insertion point inside the shape, but you can still type text inside it and then format it. You can format the shape itself by using the Shape Styles options on the DRAWING TOOLS FORMAT tab.

To draw and format a text box:

▶ **1.** Scroll down to display the bottom half of page 1.

▶ **2.** On the ribbon, click the **INSERT** tab.

▶ **3.** In the Illustrations group, click the **Shapes** button to display the Shapes gallery. See Figure 4-15.

Figure 4-15   Shapes gallery

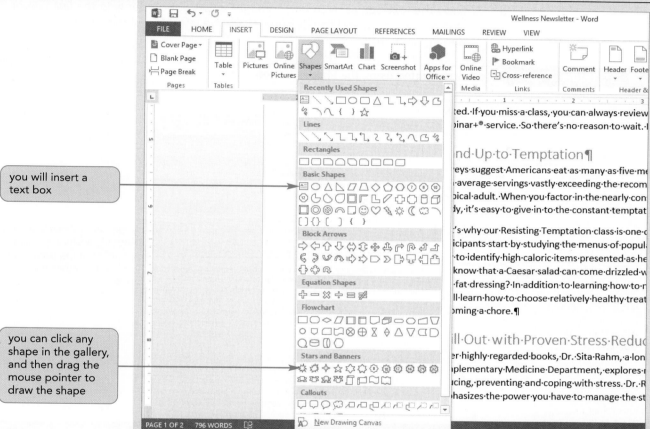

you will insert a text box

you can click any shape in the gallery, and then drag the mouse pointer to draw the shape

At this point, you could click any shape in the gallery, and then drag the pointer in the document to draw that shape. Then, after you finish drawing the shape, you could start typing in the selected shape to insert text.

▶ **4.** In the Basic Shapes section of the Shapes gallery, click the **Text Box** icon ▣. The gallery closes and the mouse pointer turns to a black cross ✚.

▶ **5.** Position the pointer in the blank area in the left margin at about the 6-inch mark (according to the vertical ruler), and then click and drag down and to the right to draw a text box approximately **1.5** inches wide and **2.5** inches tall. When you are satisfied with the text box, release the mouse button.

Don't be concerned about the text box's exact dimensions or position on the page. For now, just make sure it fits in the blank space to the left of the last two paragraphs on the page.

The new text box is selected, with handles on its border and the insertion point blinking inside. The Layout Options button is visible and the text box's anchor symbol is positioned to the left of the paragraph below the heading "Stand Up to Temptation." By default, a shape is always anchored to the nearest paragraph that begins above the shape's top border. It doesn't matter where the insertion point is located.

6. Use the Shape Height and Shape Width boxes on the DRAWING TOOLS FORMAT tab to set the height to **2.7** inches and the width to **1.5** inches.

7. Drag the text box as necessary to align its bottom border with the last line of text on the page, and its left border with the left edge of the text box above. See Figure 4-16.

Figure 4-16 **Text box created using the Shapes button**

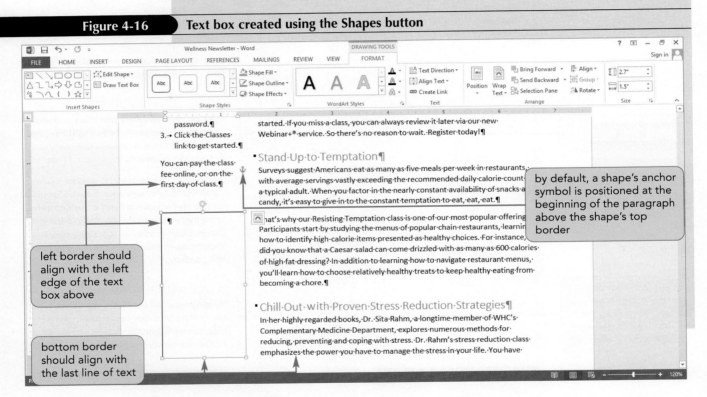

Now you need to add some text to the blank text box. Instead of inserting text from another Word document, you will copy a sentence from the newsletter and paste it into the text box to create a pull quote. After you add the text, you'll format the text box to make it match the one shown earlier in the Session 4.1 Visual Overview.

To copy text from the newsletter and paste it into the text box:

1. Select the first sentence after the heading "Stand Up to Temptation," which begins "Surveys suggest...," and then press the **Ctrl+C** keys to copy it to the Office Clipboard.

2. Click in the blank text box, and then press the **Ctrl+V** keys to paste the copied sentence into the text box. The newly inserted sentence is formatted in 11-point Calibri, just as it was in the main document.

3. Add quotation marks at the beginning and end of the sentence, so it's clear the text box is a pull quote. Your next task is to center the sentence between the top and bottom borders of the text box. Then you'll add some color.

4. On the ribbon, click the **DRAWING TOOLS FORMAT** tab, if necessary.

5. In the Text group, click the **Align Text** button to display the Align text menu, and then click **Middle**. The text is now centered between the top and bottom borders of the text box. Next, you'll change the text's font color and add a background color.

6. In the Shape Styles group, click the **More** button to display the Shape Styles gallery. Like the text styles you have used to format text, shape styles allow you to apply a collection of formatting options, including font color and shading, with one click.

7. Move the mouse pointer over the various options in the Shape Styles gallery and observe the Live Previews in the document. When you are finished, position the mouse pointer over the Colored Fill - Blue, Accent 5, style, which is a dark blue box, the second from the right in the second row. See Figure 4-17.

> **TIP**
>
> You can use the Text Direction button in the Text group to rotate text within a text box.

| Figure 4-17 | Shape Styles gallery |

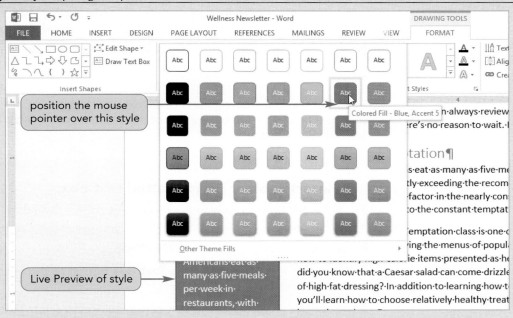

8. In the Shape Styles gallery, click the **Colored Fill - Blue, Accent 5** style. The style is applied to the text box, and the Shape Styles gallery closes.

> **Trouble?** Don't be concerned if the text in your text box wraps slightly differently from the text shown in Figure 4-17. The same fonts can vary slightly from one computer to another, causing slight differences in the way text wraps within and around text boxes.

Now, you need to make sure the text box is located in a fixed position on the page. In the following steps, you'll also experiment with making some changes involving the text box's anchor symbol. It's important to understand the role the anchor symbol plays in the document's overall layout.

To fix the text box's position on the page and experiment with the anchor symbol:

▶ 1. Verify that the text box is still selected, with the DRAWING TOOLS FORMAT tab displayed on the ribbon.

▶ 2. In the Arrange group, click the **Wrap Text** button. A checkmark appears next to Move with Text because that is the default setting for shapes.

▶ 3. Click **Fix Position on Page** to add a checkmark and close the Wrap Text menu. This setting helps ensure that the text box will remain in its position on page 1, even if you add text above the paragraph it is anchored to. However, if you add so much text that the paragraph moves to page 2, then the text box will also move to page 2, but it will be positioned in the same location on the page that it occupied on page 1—that is, in the bottom, lower-left corner.

   If you select the entire paragraph to which the text box is anchored, you will also select the text box, as you'll see in the next step.

▶ 4. Triple-click the paragraph below the "Stand Up to Temptation" heading. The entire paragraph and the text box are selected. If you pressed the Delete key at this point, you would delete the paragraph of text and the text box. If you ever need to delete a paragraph but not the graphic object that is anchored to it, you should first drag the anchor to a different paragraph.

▶ 5. Click anywhere in the document to deselect the text and the text box, and then save the document.

You've finished creating the second text box on page 1. Estefan wants you to add a third text box at the top of page 2. For this text box, you'll again use the preformatted Ion Side Bar 1 text box.

To insert another preformatted text box:

▶ 1. Scroll down to display the top half of page 2, and then click in the first line on page 2.

▶ 2. On the ribbon, click the **INSERT** tab.

▶ 3. In the Text group, click the **Text Box** button to display the menu, scroll down, and then click **Ion Sidebar 1**.

▶ 4. Click the border of the text box to select the entire text box and display the Layout Options button.

▶ 5. Click the **Layout Options** button 🖼, click the **In Front of Text** 🖼 option, verify that the Fix position on page button is selected, and then close the Layout Options gallery.

▶ 6. Drag the text box left to center it in the blank space to the left of the document text, with the top of the text box aligned with the first line of text on page 2.

▶ 7. Change the text box's height to **3.5** inches and the width to **1.5** inches.

▶ 8. In the title bar, replace the placeholder text with **Watch Classes Online**.

▶ 9. In the main text box, click the placeholder text to select it, and then press the **Delete** key.

10. On the ribbon, click the **INSERT** tab.

11. In the Text group, click the **Object button arrow**, and then click **Text from File**.

12. Navigate to the Word4 ▶ Tutorial folder, if necessary, and then insert the document named **Classes**.

13. Delete the extra paragraph at the end of the text box, increase the font size for the text to **11** points, and then make sure your text box is positioned like the one shown in Figure 4-18.

| Figure 4-18 | Completed text box on page 2 |

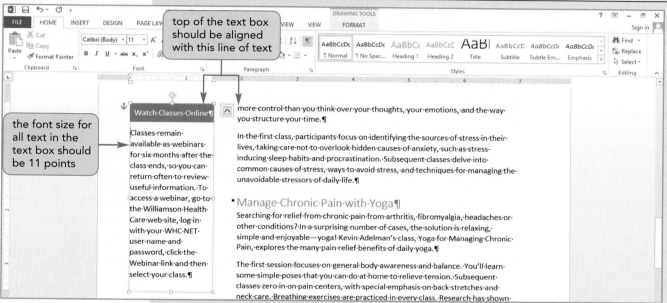

14. Click anywhere in the document to deselect the text box, and then save the document.

INSIGHT

Linking Text Boxes

If you have a large amount of text that you want to place in different locations in a document, with the text continuing from one text box to another, you can use linked text boxes. For example, in a newsletter, you might have an article that starts in a text box on page 3 of the newsletter and continues in a text box on page 4. To flow the text automatically from one text box to a second, blank text box, click the first text box to select it (this text box should already contain some text). Next, on the ribbon, click the DRAWING TOOLS FORMAT tab, click the Create Link button in the Text group, and then click the empty text box. The text boxes are now linked. You can resize the first text box without worrying about how much text fits in the box. The text that no longer fits in the first text box is moved to the second text box. Note that you'll find it easier to link text boxes if you use simple text boxes without title bars.

To make the main document text look more polished, you will add some drop caps.

Inserting Drop Caps

As you saw in the Session 4.1 Visual Overview, a drop cap is a graphic that replaces the first letter of a paragraph. Drop caps are commonly used in newspapers, magazines, and newsletters to draw the reader's attention to the beginning of an article. You can place a drop cap in the margin or next to the paragraph, or you can have the text of the paragraph wrap around the drop cap. By default, a drop cap extends down three lines, but you can change that setting in the Drop Cap dialog box.

Estefan asks you to create a drop cap for some of the paragraphs that follow the headings. He wants the drop cap to extend two lines into the paragraph, with the text wrapping around it.

To insert drop caps in the newsletter:

1. Scroll up to page 1, and then click anywhere in the paragraph below the "Pick the Class that Serves You Best" heading.

2. On the ribbon, click the **INSERT** tab.

3. In the Text group, click the **Drop Cap** button. The Drop Cap gallery opens.

4. Move the mouse pointer over the **Dropped** option and then the **In margin** option, and observe the Live Preview of the two types of drop caps in the document. The default settings applied by these two options are fine for most documents. Clicking Drop Cap Options, at the bottom of the menu, allows you to select more detailed settings. In this case, Estefan wants to make the drop cap smaller than the default. Instead of extending down through three lines of text, he wants the drop cap to extend only two lines.

5. Click **Drop Cap Options**. The Drop Cap dialog box opens.

6. Click the **Dropped** icon, click the **Lines to drop** box, and then change the setting to **2**. See Figure 4-19.

Figure 4-19 **Drop Cap dialog box**

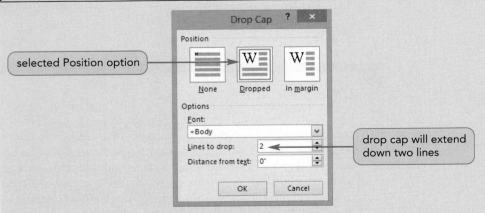

7. Click the **OK** button. Word formats the first character of the paragraph as a drop cap "A," as shown in the Session 4.1 Visual Overview. The dotted box with selection handles around the drop cap indicates it is selected.

TIP

To delete a drop cap, click the paragraph that contains it, open the Drop Cap dialog box and then click None.

8. Near the bottom of page 1, insert a similar drop cap in the paragraph following the "Chill Out with Proven Stress Reduction Strategies" heading. You skipped the paragraph following the "Stand Up to Temptation" heading because you'll eventually insert a graphic there. Including a drop cap there would make the paragraph look too cluttered.

9. On page 2, insert a similar drop cap in the paragraph following the "Manage Chronic Pain with Yoga" heading.

10. Click anywhere in the text to deselect the drop cap, and then save your work.

PROSKILLS

Written Communication: Writing for a Newsletter

Clip art, WordArt, and other design elements can make a newsletter very appealing to readers. They can also be a lot of fun to create and edit. But don't let the design elements in your desktop-published documents distract you from the most important aspect of any document—clear, effective writing. Because the newsletter format feels less formal than a report or letter, some writers are tempted to use a casual, familiar tone. If you are creating a newsletter for friends or family, that's fine. But in most other settings—especially in a business or academic setting—you should strive for a professional tone, similar to what you find in a typical newspaper. Avoid jokes; you can never be certain that what amuses you will also amuse all your readers. Worse, you risk unintentionally offending your readers. Also, space is typically at a premium in any printed document, so you don't want to waste space on anything unessential. Finally, keep in mind that the best writing in the world will be wasted in a newsletter that is overburdened with too many design elements. You don't have to use every element covered in this tutorial in a single document. Instead, use just enough to attract the reader's attention to the page, and then let the text speak for itself.

REVIEW

Session 4.1 Quick Check

1. Explain how to format a document in two columns of the default width.
2. Explain how to insert the ® symbol in a document.
3. What symbol tells you that an object is a floating object?
4. How do you convert an inline object to a floating object?
5. Which text wrapping option gives you the greatest control over an object's exact position, and is also the default text wrapping applied to shapes inserted via the Shapes button?
6. Explain how to insert a preformatted text box designed to match the current theme.

Session 4.2 Visual Overview:

You can only use the Remove Background button for photos. For all other pictures, you need to crop instead.

You can click the Crop button arrow to access more advanced cropping options, including cropping to a shape such as an oval or an arrow.

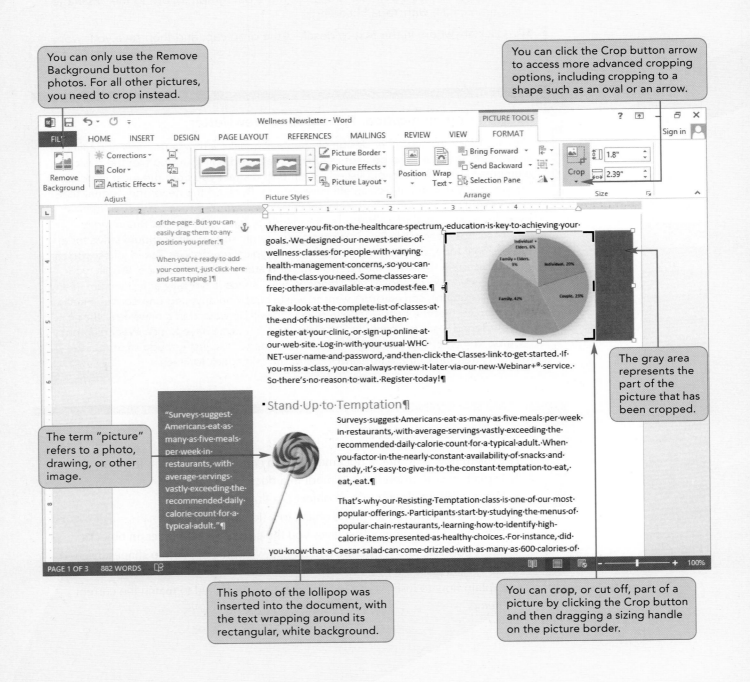

The gray area represents the part of the picture that has been cropped.

The term "picture" refers to a photo, drawing, or other image.

This photo of the lollipop was inserted into the document, with the text wrapping around its rectangular, white background.

You can **crop**, or cut off, part of a picture by clicking the Crop button and then dragging a sizing handle on the picture border.

Editing Pictures

Clicking the Remove Background button in the Adjust group on the PICTURE TOOLS FORMAT tab displays the BACKGROUND REMOVAL tab, with tools for removing a photo's background.

The photo of the lollipop is displayed here with its background removed, which allows the text to wrap around the shape of the lollipop itself.

You can use these buttons to mark areas in the photo that you want to keep, and to mark areas that you want to remove along with the rest of the photo background.

The pink area is the part of the photo that Word considers to be the background.

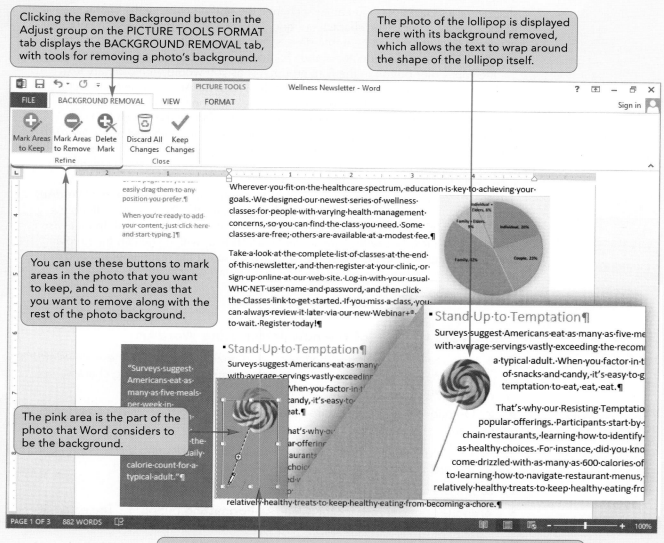

This border helps Word distinguish between the background and the parts of the image you want to keep. Any area of the image outside the border will be automatically excluded. In this case, part of the lollipop spiral lies outside the border, so Word considers it part of the background. To fix that, you can drag one of the border handles to expand the border until the entire lollipop spiral is inside the border.

Formatting Text with WordArt

To create special text elements such as a newspaper headline, you can use decorative text known as WordArt. Essentially, WordArt is text in a text box that is formatted with a text effect. Before you move on to learning about WordArt, it's helpful to review the formatting options available with text effects.

To begin applying a text effect, you select the text you want to format. Then you can choose from several preformatted text effects via the Text Effects and Typography button in the Font group on the HOME tab. You can also modify a text effect by choosing from the options on the Text Effects and Typography menu. For example, you can add a shadow or a glow effect. You can also change the **outline color** of the characters—that is, the exterior color of the characters—and you can change the style of the outline by making it thicker or breaking it into dashes, for example. To change the character's **fill color**—that is, the interior color of the characters—you just select a different font color via the Font Color button in the Font group, just as you would with ordinary text.

All of these text effect options are available with WordArt. However, the fact that WordArt is in a text box allows you to add some additional effects. You can add rounded, or **beveled**, edges to the letters in WordArt, format the text in 3-D, and transform the text into waves, circles, and other shapes. You can also rotate WordArt text so it stretches vertically on the page. In addition, because WordArt is in a text box, you can use page layout and text wrap settings to place it anywhere you want on a page, with text wrapped around it.

To start creating WordArt, you can select text you want to transform into WordArt, and then click the WordArt button in the Text group on the INSERT tab. Alternatively, you can start by clicking the WordArt button without selecting text first. In that case, Word inserts a text box with placeholder WordArt text, which you can then replace with something new. In the following steps, you'll select the first paragraph and format it as WordArt to create the newsletter title that Estefan wants.

To create the title of the newsletter using WordArt:

1. If you took a break after the last session, make sure the Wellness Newsletter is open and zoomed to 120%, with the rulers and nonprinting characters displayed.

2. On page 1, select the entire paragraph containing the "Williamson Health Care" heading, including the paragraph mark.

   To avoid unexpected results, you should start by clearing any formatting from the text you want to format as WordArt, so you'll do that next.

Be sure to select the paragraph mark so the page layout in your newsletter matches the figures.

3. On the ribbon, click the **HOME** tab.

4. In the Font group, click the **Clear All Formatting** button 🌢. The paragraph reverts to the Normal style. Now you can convert the text to WordArt.

5. On the ribbon, click the **INSERT** tab.

6. In the Text group, click the **WordArt** button. The WordArt gallery opens.

7. Position the mouse pointer over the WordArt style that is second from the left in the top row. A ScreenTip describes some elements of this WordArt style—"Fill - Blue, Accent 1, Shadow." See Figure 4-20.

Figure 4-20   **WordArt gallery**

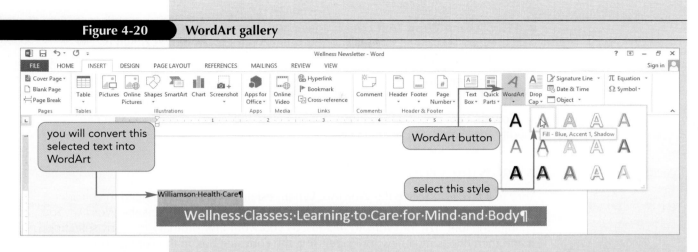

- you will convert this selected text into WordArt
- WordArt button
- select this style
- Williamson·Health·Care¶
- Wellness·Classes:·Learning·to·Care·for·Mind·and·Body¶

> **8.** Click the WordArt style **Fill - Blue, Accent 1, Shadow**. The gallery closes, and a text box containing the formatted text is displayed in the document. See Figure 4-21.

Figure 4-21   **WordArt text box inserted in document**

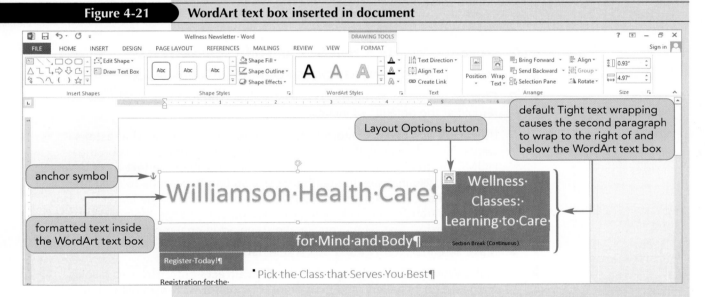

- Layout Options button
- default Tight text wrapping causes the second paragraph to wrap to the right of and below the WordArt text box
- anchor symbol
- Williamson·Health·Care¶
- Wellness· Classes:· Learning·to·Care· for·Mind·and·Body¶
- formatted text inside the WordArt text box
- Section Break (Continuous)
- Register·Today!¶
- Pick·the·Class·that·Serves·You·Best¶
- Registration·for·the·

Because the WordArt text box is formatted with Tight text wrapping by default, the shaded paragraph "Wellness Classes: Learning to Care for Mind and Body" wraps to the right of and below the WordArt text box. The DRAWING TOOLS FORMAT tab appears as the active tab on the ribbon, displaying a variety of tools that you can use to edit the WordArt. Before you change the look of the WordArt, you need to fix its position on the page and change its text wrap setting.

> **9.** Make sure the **DRAWING TOOLS FORMAT** tab is selected on the ribbon.

> **10.** In the Arrange group, click the **Wrap Text** button to open the Wrap Text menu, click **Fix Position on Page** to insert a checkmark, and then close the Wrap Text menu.

▶ **11.** Click the **Wrap Text** button again, and then click **Top and Bottom**. The Wrap Text menu closes, and the shaded paragraph moves down below the WordArt text box.

▶ **12.** Save the document.

Now that the document text is wrapped below the WordArt text box, you can modify the WordArt in several ways.

Modifying WordArt

Your first task is to resize the WordArt. When resizing WordArt, you need to consider both the font size of the text and the size of the text box that contains the WordArt. You change the font size for WordArt text just as you would for ordinary text—by selecting it and then choosing a new font size using the Font size box in the Font group on the HOME tab. If you choose a large font for a headline, you might also need to resize the text box to ensure that the resized text appears on a single line. Estefan is happy with the font size of the new WordArt headline, so you only need to adjust the size of the text box so it spans the width of the page. The larger text box will then make it possible for you to add some more effects.

To resize the WordArt text box and add some effects:

▶ **1.** Make sure the **DRAWING TOOLS FORMAT** tab is selected on the ribbon.

▶ **2.** Change the width of the text box to **7** inches. The text box height should remain at the default .93 inches.

By default, the text is centered within the text box, which is what Estefan wants. Note, however, that you could use the alignment buttons on the HOME tab to align the text any way you wanted within the text box borders. You could also increase the text's font size so that it expands to span the full width of the text box. Instead, you will take advantage of the larger text box to apply a transform effect, which will expand and change the overall shape of the WordArt text. Then you'll make some additional modifications.

▶ **3.** Make sure the WordArt text box is selected.

▶ **4.** In the WordArt Styles group, click the **Text Effects** button [A ▾] to display the Text Effects gallery, and then point to **Transform**. The Transform menu displays options for changing the WordArt's shape.

▶ **5.** Move the mouse pointer over the options in the Transform menu and observe the Live Previews in the WordArt text box. Note that you can always remove a transform effect that has been previously applied by clicking the option in the No Transform section, at the top of the gallery. When you are finished, position the mouse pointer over the Chevron Up effect. See Figure 4-22.

Figure 4-22 Applying a Transform text effect

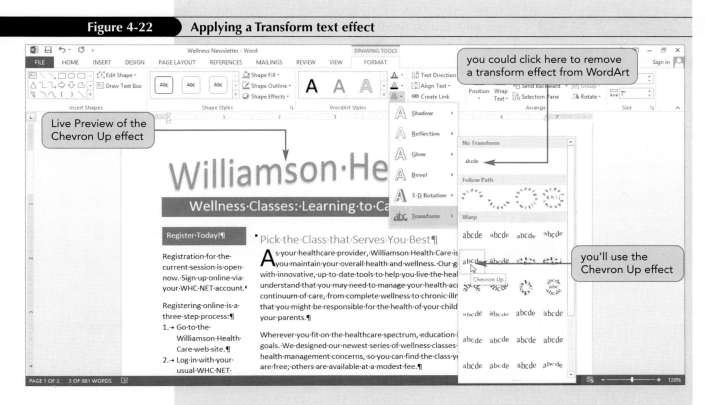

Trouble? If you don't see the Live Preview of the transform effect, that's okay. Continue with these steps.

 6. Click the **Chevron Up** effect. The Transform menu closes, and the effect is applied to the WordArt. Now you will make some additional changes using the options in the WordArt Styles group. You'll start by changing the fill color.

 7. In the WordArt Styles group, click the **Text Fill button arrow** [A] to display the Text Fill color gallery.

 8. In the Theme Colors section of the gallery, click the square that is second from the right in the top row to select the **Blue, Accent 5** color. The Text Fill gallery closes, and the WordArt is formatted in a shade of blue that matches the shading in the paragraph below. Next, you'll add a shadow to make the headline more dramatic.

 9. In the WordArt Styles group, click the **Text Effects** button [A] to display the Text Effects menu, and then point to **Shadow** to display the Shadow gallery. This menu is divided into several sections.

 10. In the Outer section, point to the top-left option to display a ScreenTip that reads "Offset Diagonal Bottom Right."

 11. Click the **Offset Diagonal Bottom Right** shadow style. A shadow is added to the WordArt text. See Figure 4-23.

Figure 4-23	Completed WordArt headline

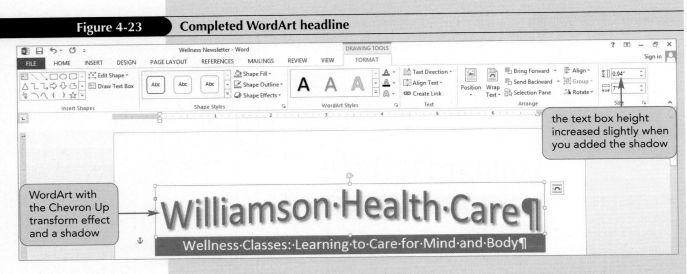

Note that the height of the text box that contains the WordArt increased slightly, to 0.94 inches.

▶ **12.** Click a blank area of the document to deselect the WordArt, and then save the document.

The WordArt headline is complete. Your next job is to add some pictures to the newsletter.

Working with Pictures

In Word, a picture is a photo, drawing, or other image. Although you can copy and paste pictures into a document from other documents, you'll typically insert pictures via either the Pictures button or the Online Pictures button, both of which are located in the Illustrations group on the INSERT tab. You use the Pictures button to insert a picture from a file stored on your computer. You use the Online Pictures button to insert images, including clip art, that you find using the Bing search engine. As you saw in the Session 4.1 Visual Overview, the final version of the Wellness Newsletter document will contain two pieces of clip art—a photograph of a lollipop and a drawing of a woman doing yoga. The newsletter will also contain a picture of a chart, which Estefan's coworker created earlier and saved as a separate file.

After you insert a picture into a document, it functions as an object that you can move, resize, wrap text around, and edit in other ways using the appropriate contextual tab on the ribbon. In general, the skills you used when modifying text boxes apply to pictures as well.

Written Communication: Understanding Copyright Laws

The ownership of all forms of media, including text, line drawings, photographs, and video, is governed by copyright laws. You should assume that anything you find on the web is owned by someone who has a right to control its use. It's your responsibility to make sure you understand copyright laws and to abide by them. The U.S. Copyright Office maintains a Frequently Asked Questions page that should answer any questions you might have: www.copyright.gov/help/faq.

Generally, copyright laws allow a student to reuse a photo, drawing, or other item for educational purposes, on a one-time basis, without getting permission from the owner. However, to avoid charges of plagiarism, you need to acknowledge the source of the item in your work. You don't ever want to be accused of presenting someone else's work as your own. Businesses face much more stringent copyright restrictions. To reuse any material, you must request permission from the owner, and you will often need to pay a fee.

When you use Bing Image Search in the Insert Pictures window, all of the images that initially appear as a result of your search will be licensed under a Creative Commons license. There are several types of Creative Commons licenses. One type allows you to use an image for any reason, including commercial use, and to modify the image, as long as the photographer is credited, or attributed, (similar to the credits under the photos in some figures in this book). Another type allows you to use an image with an attribution as long as it is not for commercial purposes and as long as you do not modify the image. Even if an image has a Creative Commons license, you must still review the exact license on the Web site on which the image is stored. When you click an image, its Web site appears as a link at the bottom of the Insert Pictures window.

Inserting and Cropping a Picture

You can use the Chart button in the Illustrations group on the INSERT tab to enter data into a data sheet and then create a chart that illustrates the data. However, the chart Estefan wants to insert in the newsletter was created by a coworker using a different program, and then saved as a PNG file named Chart.png. That means you can insert the chart as a picture using the Pictures button in the Illustrations group.

Estefan asks you to insert the chart picture on page 1.

To insert the chart picture on page 1:

▶ **1.** On page 1, click at the end of the first paragraph below the "Pick the Class that Serves You Best" heading to position the insertion point between "…your parents." and the paragraph mark. Normally, there's no need to be so precise about where you click before inserting a picture, but doing so here will ensure that your results match the results described in these steps exactly.

▶ **2.** On the ribbon, click the **INSERT** tab.

▶ **3.** In the Illustrations group, click the **Pictures** button to open the Insert Pictures dialog box.

▶ **4.** Navigate to the Word4 ▶ Tutorial folder included with your Data Files, and then insert the picture file named **Chart.png**. The chart picture is inserted in the document as an inline object. It is selected, and the PICTURE TOOLS FORMAT tab is displayed on the ribbon.

▶ **5.** Scroll down if necessary so you can see the entire chart.

The chart is wider than it needs to be and would look better as a square. So you'll need to cut off, or crop, part of it. In addition to the ability to crop part of a picture, Word offers several more advanced cropping options. The one you'll probably use most often is cropping to a shape, which means trimming the edges of a picture so it fits into a star, an oval, an arrow, or another shape. You can also crop to a specific ratio of height to width.

Whatever method you use, once you crop a picture, the part you cropped is hidden from view. However, it remains a part of the picture in case you change your mind and want to restore the cropped picture to its original form.

Before you crop off the sides of the chart, you'll try cropping it to a specific shape.

To crop the chart picture:

▶ **1.** In the Size group, click the **Crop button arrow** to display the Crop menu, and then click **Crop to Shape**. A gallery of shapes is displayed, similar to the gallery you saw in Figure 4-15.

▶ **2.** In the Basic Shapes section of the gallery, click the **Lightning Bolt** shape 🗲 (third row down, sixth from the right). The chart picture takes on the shape of a lightning bolt, with everything outside the lightning bolt shape cropped off.

Obviously, this isn't a useful option for the chart, but cropping to shapes can be very effective with photos in informal documents such as party invitations or posters, especially if you then use the Behind Text wrapping option, so that the document text flows over the photo.

▶ **3.** Press the **Ctrl+Z** keys to undo the cropping.

▶ **4.** In the Size group, click the **Crop** button (not the Crop button arrow). Dark black sizing handles appear around the picture borders.

▶ **5.** Position the pointer directly over the middle sizing handle on the right border. The pointer changes to ⊢.

▶ **6.** Press and hold down the mouse button. The pointer changes to ✛.

▶ **7.** Drag the pointer toward the left until the chart border aligns with the 3.75-inch mark on the horizontal ruler, as shown in Figure 4-24.

Figure 4-24   Cropping a picture

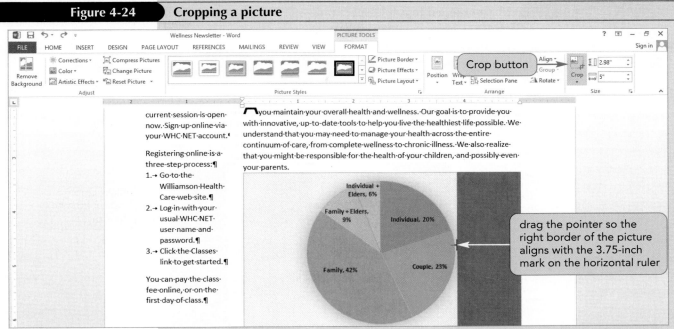

© 2014 Cengage Learning

8. When the chart looks like the one shown in Figure 4-24, release the mouse button. The right portion of the chart picture is no longer visible. The original border remains, indicating that the cropped portion is still saved as part of the picture in case you want to undo the cropping.

9. Drag the middle handle on the left border to the right until the left border aligns with the 2-inch mark on the horizontal ruler.

   The chart now takes up much less space, but it's not exactly a square. To ensure a specific ratio, you can crop the picture by changing its **aspect ratio**—that is, the ratio of width to height. You'll try that next. But first, you'll restore the picture to its original state.

TIP

If you aren't sure what formatting has been applied to a picture, and you want to start over, use the Reset Picture button.

10. In the Adjust group, click the **Reset Picture button arrow** to display the Reset Picture menu, and then click **Reset Picture & Size**. The chart picture returns to its original state.

11. In the Size group, click the **Crop button arrow**, and then point to **Aspect Ratio** to display the Aspect Ratio menu, which lists various ratios of width to height. A square has a 1-to-1 ratio of width to height.

12. Under "Square," click **1:1**. The chart is cropped to a square shape. See Figure 4-25.

Figure 4-25 **Chart cropped to a 1:1 aspect ratio**

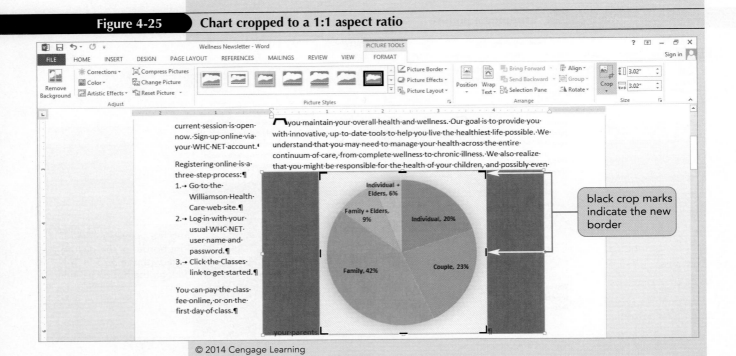

© 2014 Cengage Learning

13. Click anywhere outside the chart to deselect it and complete the cropping procedure.

Next, you need to change the chart from an inline object to a floating object by wrapping text around it. You also need to position it on the page. You can complete both of these tasks at the same time by using the Position button in the Arrange group.

To change the chart's position and wrapping:

1. Change the Zoom level to **One Page**, and then click the chart to select it.

2. On the ribbon, click the **PICTURE TOOLS FORMAT** tab.

3. In the Arrange group, click the **Position** button to display the Position gallery. You can click an icon in the "With Text Wrapping" section to move the selected picture to one of nine preset positions on the page. As with any gallery, you can see a Live Preview of the options before you actually select one.

4. Move the mouse pointer over the various icons and observe the changing Live Preview in the document, with the chart picture moving to different locations on the page and the text wrapping around it.

5. Point to the icon in the middle row on the far right side to display a ScreenTip that reads "Position in Middle Right with Square Text Wrapping," and then click the **Position in Middle Right with Square Text Wrapping** icon. The chart picture moves to the middle of the page along the right margin. By default, it is formatted with Tight text wrapping, so the text wraps to its left, following its square outline.

Your final step is to resize the chart picture to make it a bit smaller.

▶ **6.** In the Size group, click the **Shape Height** box, type **1.8**, and then press the **Enter** key. The settings in both the Shape Height and Shape Width boxes change to 1.8 inches. For most types of graphics, the aspect ratio is locked, meaning that when you change one dimension, the other changes to match. In this case, because the aspect ratio of the chart is 1:1, when you changed the height to 1.8 inches, the width also changed to 1.8 inches, ensuring that the chart retained its square shape.

▶ **7.** Click anywhere outside the chart picture to deselect it, and then save the document.

INSIGHT

Aligning Graphic Objects and Using the Selection Task Pane

The steps in this tutorial provide precise directions about where to position graphic objects in the document. However, when you are creating a document on your own, you might find it helpful to use the Align button in the Arrange group on the PICTURE TOOLS FORMAT tab to align objects relative to the margin or the edge of the page. Aligning a graphic relative to the margin, rather than the edge of the page, is usually the best choice because it ensures that you don't accidentally position a graphic outside the page margins, causing the graphic to get cut off when the page is printed.

After you choose whether to align to the page or margin, you can open the Align menu again and choose an alignment option. For example, you can align the top of an object at the top of the page, or align the bottom of an object at the bottom of the page. You can also choose to have Word distribute multiple objects evenly on the page. To do this, it's helpful to open the Selection task pane first by clicking the PAGE LAYOUT tab and then clicking Selection Pane. Press and hold the Ctrl key, and then in the Selection task pane, click the objects you want to select. After the objects are selected, there's no need to switch back to the PICTURE TOOLS FORMAT tab. Instead, you can take advantage of the Align button in the Arrange group on the PAGE LAYOUT tab to open the Align menu, where you can then click Distribute Horizontally or Distribute Vertically.

The chart picture is finished. Next, Estefan asks you to insert the lollipop clip art near the bottom of page 1.

Searching for and Inserting Clip Art

The first step in using clip art is finding the clip art you want. Most clip art websites include a search box where you can type some descriptive keywords to help you narrow the selection down to a smaller range.

If you were going to use the Online Pictures command to search for an image using Bing Image Search, you would click the Online Pictures button in the Illustrations group on the INSERT tab. Doing so opens the Insert Pictures window, as shown in Figure 4-26. You would type keywords, such as "striped lollipop," in the Bing Image Search box, and then click the Search button. Images that have the keywords "striped lollipop" and that are licensed under Creative Commons would appear below the Search box. To insert one of those images, you would click it, and then click the Insert button.

Figure 4-26 Insert Pictures window

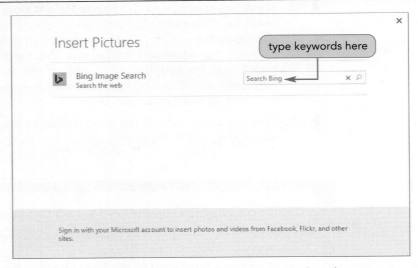

Because results from an online search can change, to complete these steps, you will insert an image included with your Data Files.

To insert a clip art file in the Wellness Newsletter document:

1. Zoom in so you can read the document text at the bottom of page 1, and then click at the end of the first paragraph below the "Stand Up to Temptation" heading to position the insertion point between "…eat, eat." and the paragraph mark.

2. Change the Zoom level to **Multiple Pages** so you can see the entire document.

3. On the ribbon, click the **INSERT** tab.

4. In the Illustrations group, click the **Pictures** button to display the Insert Picture dialog box, and then navigate to the **Word4 ▸ Tutorial** folder included with your Data Files. See Figure 4-27.

Figure 4-27 Insert Picture dialog box

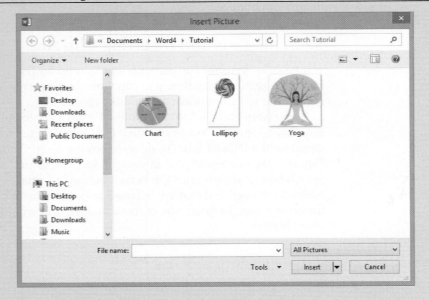

5. Click **Lollipop**, and then click the **Insert** button. The dialog box closes, and the photo of a striped lollipop is inserted as an inline object at the current location of the insertion point. See Figure 4-28.

| Figure 4-28 | Clip art photo inserted as inline object |

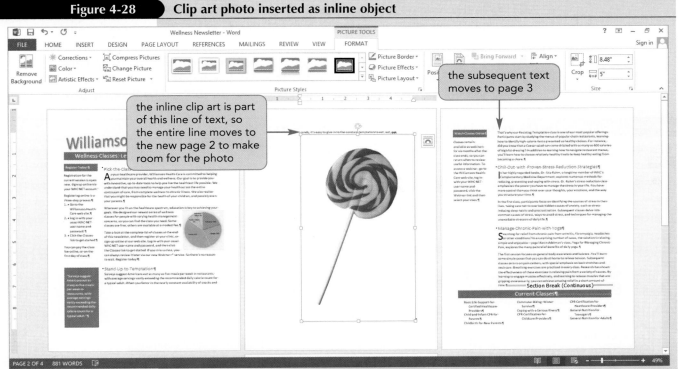

the inline clip art is part of this line of text, so the entire line moves to the new page 2 to make room for the photo

the subsequent text moves to page 3

© 2014 Cengage Learning; Image used with permission of Microsoft Corporation

Because the photo is too large to fit on page 1, the line of text that contains the insertion point jumps to page 2, with the photo displayed below the text. The rest of the document text starts on page 3 and flows to page 4. The clip art photo is selected, as indicated by its border with handles. The PICTURE TOOLS FORMAT tab is displayed on the ribbon. Now you can reduce the photo's size, wrap text around it, and position it on the page.

6. In the Size group, click the **Shape Height** box, type **2**, and then press the **Enter** key. To maintain the photo's preset aspect ratio, Word changes the photo's width to 1.18 inches. Some of the text from page 3 moves up to fill the space below the smaller photo on page 2.

7. In the Arrange group, click the **Wrap Text** button, and then click **Tight**. The photo, which is now a floating object, moves to the top of page 1, with text wrapping to its right.

8. Drag the photo down to position it so the first line of the paragraph under "Stand Up to Temptation" wraps above it. See Figure 4-29. The anchor symbol for the photo is not visible because it's covered by the blue text box.

Figure 4-29 **Resized clip art photo as a floating object**

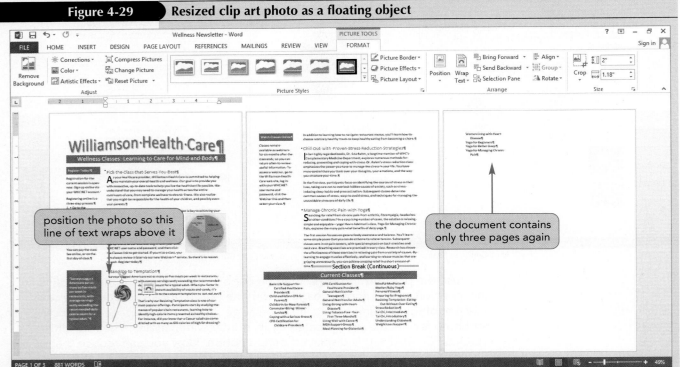

© 2014 Cengage Learning; Image used with permission of Microsoft Corporation

Trouble? Don't be concerned if you can't get the text to wrap around the lollipop photo exactly as shown in Figure 4-29.

9. Click the **Layout Options** button, click **Fix position on page**, and then close the Layout Options menu.

Estefan likes the photo, but he asks you to make a few changes. First, he wants you to rotate the lollipop to the left to position it vertically on the page. Also, Estefan wants the text to wrap around the curved shape of the lollipop itself, instead of around its rectangular outline. To accomplish that, you need to remove the photo's background.

Rotating a Picture

You can quickly rotate a picture by dragging the Rotation handle that appears on the photo's border when the photo is selected. To access some preset rotation options, you can click the Rotate button in the Arrange group to open the Rotate menu. To quickly rotate a picture 90 degrees, click Rotate Right 90° or Rotate Left 90° in the Rotate menu. You can also flip a picture, as if the picture were printed on both sides of a card and you wanted to turn the card over. To do this, click Flip Vertical or Flip Horizontal in the Rotate menu.

Estefan only wants to rotate the lollipop picture slightly. You can do that by dragging the Rotation handle.

To rotate the clip art photo:

1. Change the document Zoom level to **120%**, and then scroll down so you can see the bottom half of page 1.

2. Click the lollipop picture, if necessary, to select it, and then position the mouse pointer over the circular rotation handle above the middle of the photo's top border. The mouse pointer changes to ⟳.

3. Drag the mouse pointer down and to the left, until the lollipop rotates to a vertical position. See Figure 4-30.

| Figure 4-30 | **Dragging the Rotation handle** |

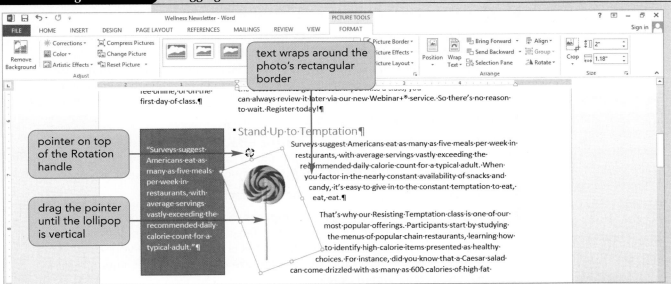

Image used with permission of Microsoft Corporation

Don't be concerned if the text wrapping around your rotated picture looks different from the text wrapping in Figure 4-30.

4. Release the mouse button. The lollipop is displayed in the new, rotated position, with the text wrapped around the photo's tilted, rectangular border.

5. Save the document.

You're almost finished editing the lollipop photo. Your last task is to remove its background so the text wraps around the shape of the lollipop itself. But before you remove the background from the lollipop photo, you'll explore the options in the Adjust group.

Adjusting a Picture

The Adjust group on the PICTURE TOOLS FORMAT tab provides several tools for adjusting a picture's overall look. Some, such as the Remove Background button, only work for photos. Others, such as the Color button, provide some options that work only for photos and some that work for both photos and line drawings. You'll explore some of these options in the following steps.

To try out some options in the Adjust group:

▶ **1.** Make sure that the lollipop photo is still selected, and that the **PICTURE TOOLS FORMAT** tab is selected on the ribbon.

▶ **2.** In the Adjust group, click the **Corrections** button, and then move the mouse pointer over the various options in the Corrections gallery and observe the Live Preview in the document. You can use the Corrections gallery to sharpen or soften a photo's focus, or to adjust the brightness of a photo or line drawing.

▶ **3.** Press the **Esc** key to close the Corrections gallery.

▶ **4.** In the Adjust group, click the **Color** button, and then move the mouse pointer over the options in the Color gallery and observe the Live Preview in the document. For photos, you can adjust the color saturation and tone. For photos and line drawings, you can use the Recolor options to completely change the picture's colors.

▶ **5.** Press the **Esc** key to close the Color gallery.

▶ **6.** In the Adjust group, click the **Artistic Effects** button, and then move the mouse pointer over the options in the Artistic Effects gallery and observe the Live Preview in the document. Artistic Effects can only be used on photos.

▶ **7.** Press the **Esc** key to close the Artistic Effects gallery.

▶ **8.** In the Adjust group, click the **Compress Pictures** button to open the Compress Pictures dialog box. In the Target output portion of the dialog box, you can select the option that reflects the purpose of your document. Compressing pictures reduces the file size of the Word document, but can result in some loss of detail.

▶ **9.** Click the **Cancel** button to close the Compress Pictures dialog box.

Now you are ready to remove the white background from the lollipop photo.

Removing a Photo's Background

Removing a photo's background can be tricky, especially if you are working on a photo with a background that is not clearly differentiated from the foreground image. For example, you might find it difficult to remove a white, snowy background from a photo of an equally white snowman. You start by clicking the Remove Background button in the Adjust group, and then making changes to help Word distinguish between the background that you want to exclude and the image you want to keep.

Removing a Photo's Background

- Select the photo, and then on the PICTURE TOOLS FORMAT tab, in the Adjust group, click the Remove Background button.
- Drag the handles on the border as necessary to include any parts of the photo that have been incorrectly marked for removal.
- To mark areas to keep, click the Mark Areas to Keep button in the Refine group on the BACKGROUND REMOVAL tab, and then use the drawing pointer to select areas of the photo to keep.
- To mark areas to remove, click the Mark Areas to Remove button in the Refine group on the BACKGROUND REMOVAL tab, and then use the drawing pointer to select areas of the photo to remove.
- Click the Keep Changes button in the Close group.

You'll start by zooming in so you can clearly see the photo as you edit it.

To remove the white background from the lollipop photo:

1. On the Zoom slider, drag the **slider button** to change the Zoom level to **180%**, and then scroll as necessary to display the selected lollipop photo.

2. In the Adjust group, click the **Remove Background** button. See Figure 4-31.

Figure 4-31	Removing the background of a photo

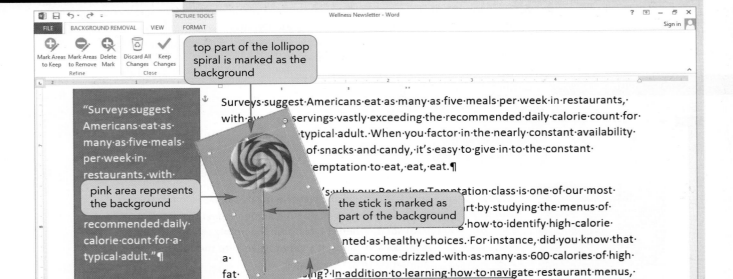

Image used with permission of Microsoft Corporation

The part of the photo that Word considers to be the background turns pink, and the BACKGROUND REMOVAL tab appears on the ribbon. A blue border with white handles surrounds the lollipop. The blue border helps Word narrow the area of focus as it tries to distinguish between the background and the parts of the image you want to keep. Word will automatically remove any part of the image outside the blue border when you click the Keep Changes button.

Trouble? If you don't see the blue border with the white handles, click the Mark Areas to Remove button in the Refine group on the BACKGROUND REMOVAL tab, and then click in the pink background, in the upper-right corner of the picture. This will insert a small white circle with a negative sign inside it, which you can ignore. The blue border with the white handles should now be displayed.

Notice that the lollipop stick is pink, indicating that Word considers it to be part of the background. The same might also be true for a small section at the top of the lollipop spiral, although this can vary from one computer to another. To ensure that Word keeps the entire lollipop spiral, you need to expand the blue border with the white handles. Then you can make additional adjustments using the tools on the BACKGROUND REMOVAL tab.

3. If necessary, drag the square handle in the upper-right corner of the blue border up slightly until the border contains the entire red and white lollipop spiral. The entire red and white spiral should now be visible in its original colors, with no pink shading, indicating that Word no longer considers any part of the spiral to be part of the background. The only problem is that Word still considers the lollipop stick part of the background. You can fix that problem by marking the stick as an area to keep.

4. On the BACKGROUND REMOVAL tab, click the **Mark Areas to Keep** button in the Refine group, and then move the drawing pointer ✐ over the lollipop. You can use this pointer to draw a line on the lollipop stick.

5. Position the mouse pointer at the top of the stick, and then press and hold the mouse button down as you drag the pointer down to the bottom of the stick. The pointer changes to a white arrow, and a dotted line appears as you drag the pointer. See Figure 4-32.

Figure 4-32	Marking an area to keep

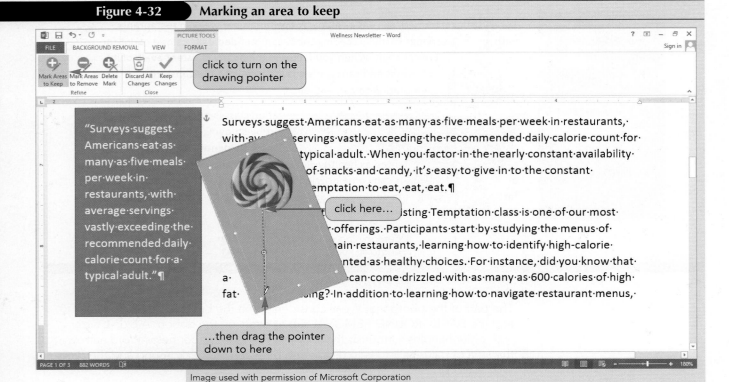

Image used with permission of Microsoft Corporation

6. Release the mouse button. A plus sign in a white circle appears on the dotted line, indicating that you have marked that part of the photo as an area to keep. The stick now appears in its original color, without pink shading. Now you will accept the changes you made to the photo.

   Trouble? If Word uncovers a line of white from the background rather than the lollipop stick, you didn't draw the line precisely down the middle of the stick. Use the Undo button to reverse the change, and then begin again with Step 4.

7. In the Close group, click the **Keep Changes** button. The background is removed from the photo, leaving only the image of the lollipop. Now the text wrapping follows the curved shape of the lollipop, just as Estefan requested. Depending on exactly where you positioned the lollipop, some of the text might now wrap to the left of the lollipop stick.

8. Change the Zoom level to **100%** so that you can see the entire lollipop, as well as the top of page 2, and then drag the lollipop as necessary so the text wraps similarly to the text shown in Figure 4-33.

Figure 4-33   **Lollipop with background removed**

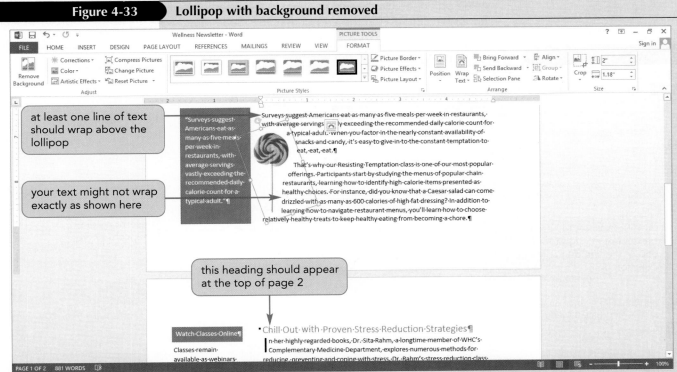

Image used with permission of Microsoft Corporation

Don't be concerned if you can't get the text wrapping to match exactly. The most important thing is that when you are finished, the "Chill Out with Proven Stress Reduction Strategies" heading should be positioned at the top of page 2. Also, at least one line of text should wrap above the lollipop.

9. Click outside the picture to deselect it, and then save the document.

You're finished with your work on the lollipop photo. Now Estefan asks you to add one more piece of clip art—the yoga drawing on page 3.

Inserting and Editing a Clip Art Drawing

You search for a clip art drawing the same way you would search for a clip art photo—by clicking the Online Pictures button in the Illustrations group on the INSERT tab and then typing some keywords. In the following steps, you will insert a clip art drawing from a file. Then, you'll add a picture style to it from the Picture Styles gallery.

To insert and add a style to the yoga clip art drawing:

▶ **1.** Change the Zoom level to **120%**, and then scroll to display the middle of page 2. You'll insert the yoga drawing in the blank space below the text box.

▶ **2.** Click at the end of the paragraph below the "Manage Chronic Pain with Yoga" heading to position the insertion point between "…daily yoga." and the paragraph mark.

▶ **3.** On the ribbon, click the **INSERT** tab.

▶ **4.** In the Illustrations group, click the **Pictures** button, navigate to the **Word4 ▸ Tutorial** folder included with your Data Files, click **Yoga**, and then click the **Insert** button. The drawing of the woman in a yoga pose is inserted as an inline object below the line containing the insertion point because there is not enough room for it at the end of that line. See Figure 4-34.

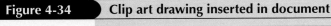

Figure 4-34   **Clip art drawing inserted in document**

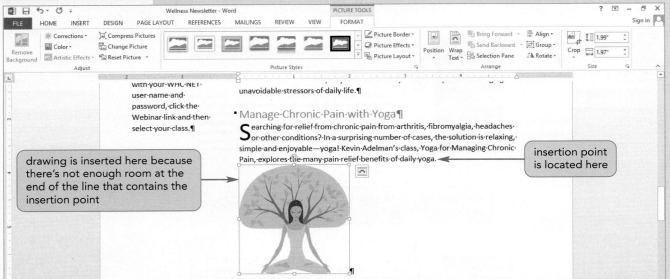

Image used with permission of Microsoft Corporation

Next, you need to resize the drawing, apply a picture style, wrap text around it, and then position it on the page.

5. In the Size group, click the **Shape Height** box, type **1.4**, and then press the **Enter** key. To maintain the picture's preset aspect ratio, the width automatically adjusts to 1.39 inches. The picture moves up to the preceding line because it's now small enough to fit.

6. In the Arrange group, click the **Wrap Text** button to open the Wrap Text menu. The In line with Text option is selected. Because the picture is still an inline picture, the Move with Text and Fix Position on Page options are grayed out, indicating that they are not available.

7. Click **In Front of Text** to select it and close the Wrap Text menu.

8. Click the **Wrap Text** button again, and then click **Fix Position on Page**. The yoga picture appears layered on top of the document text. Keep in mind that even though you selected Fix Position on Page, the picture is not stuck in one place. You can drag it anywhere you want. The point of the Fix Position on Page setting is that it prevents the picture from moving unexpectedly as you make changes to other parts of the document.

TIP

To add a simple border without adding a style, click the Picture Border button, and then click a color in the color gallery.

9. In the Picture Styles group, click the **Simple Frame, White** style, which is the first style in the visible row of the Picture Styles gallery. A frame and a shadow are applied to the yoga drawing.

10. Drag the picture to center it in the white space below the text box in the margin, deselect it, and then save the document. See Figure 4-35.

Figure 4-35   Resized yoga picture with picture style

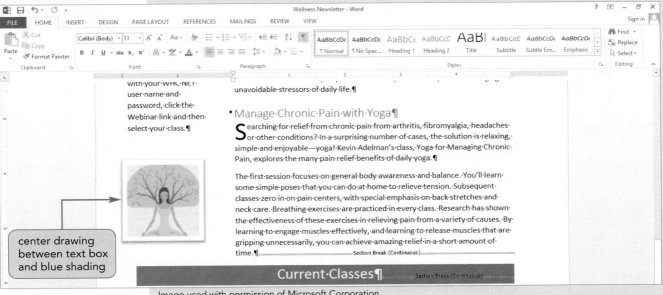

Image used with permission of Microsoft Corporation

INSIGHT

Working with Digital Picture Files

Digital picture files come in two main types—vector graphics and raster graphics. A vector graphics file stores an image as a mathematical formula, which means you can increase or decrease the size of the image as much as you want without affecting its overall quality. Vector graphics are often used for line drawings and, because they tend to be small, are widely used on the web. File types for vector graphics are often proprietary, which means they only work in specific graphics programs. In Word, you will sometimes encounter files with the .wmf file extension, which is short for Windows Metafiles. A .wmf file is a type of vector graphics file created specifically for Windows.

In most cases, though, you'll work with raster graphics, also known as bitmap graphics. A **bitmap** is a grid of square colored dots, called **pixels**, that form a picture. A bitmap graphic, then, is essentially a collection of pixels. The most common types of bitmap files are:

- BMP—These files, which have the .bmp file extension, tend to be very large, so it's best to resave them in a different format before using them in a Word document.
- GIF—These files are suitable for most types of simple line art, without complicated colors. A GIF file is compressed, so it doesn't take up much room on your computer. A GIF file has the file extension .gif.
- JPEG—These files are suitable for photographs and drawings. Files stored using the JPEG format are even more compressed than GIF files. A JPEG file has the file extension .jpg. If conserving file storage space is a priority, use JPEG graphics for your document.
- PNG—These files are similar to GIF files, but suitable for art containing a wider array of colors.
- TIFF—These files are commonly used for photographs or scanned images. TIFF files are usually much larger than GIF or JPEG files, but smaller than BMP files. A TIFF file has the file extension .tif.

Now that you are finished arranging the graphics in the newsletter, you need to make sure the columns are more or less the same length.

Balancing Columns

To **balance** columns on a page—that is, to make them equal length—you insert a continuous section break at the end of the last column. Word then adjusts the flow of content between the columns so they are of equal or near-equal length. The columns remain balanced no matter how much material you remove from any of the columns later. The columns also remain balanced if you add material that causes the columns to flow to a new page; the overflow will also be formatted in balanced columns.

To balance the columns:

▶ **1.** Press the **Ctrl+End** keys to move the insertion point to the end of the document, if necessary.

▶ **2.** Insert a continuous section break. See Figure 4-36.

Figure 4-36   **Newsletter with balanced columns**

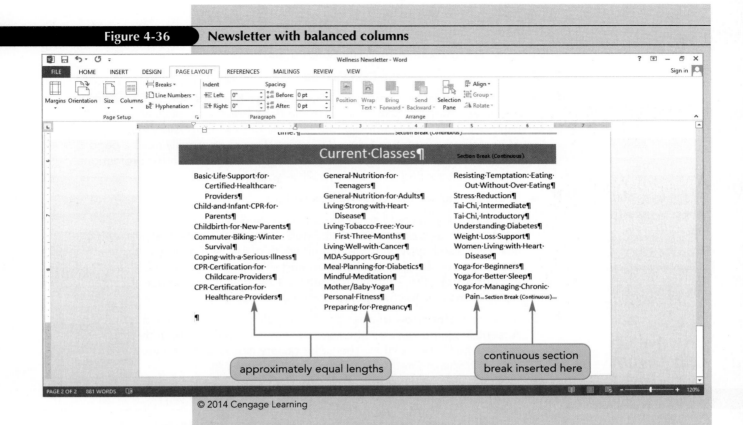

© 2014 Cengage Learning

Word balances the text between the three columns, moving some text from the bottom of the left column to the middle column, and from the middle column to the right column, so the three columns are approximately the same length.

Note that you can also adjust the length of a column by inserting a column break using the Breaks button in the Page Setup group on the PAGE LAYOUT tab. A column break moves all the text and graphics following it to the next column. Column breaks are useful when you have a multipage document formatted in three or more columns, with only enough text on the last page to fill some of the columns. In that case, balancing columns on the last page won't work. Instead, you can use a column break to distribute an equal amount of text over all the columns on the page. However, as with page breaks, you need to be careful with column breaks because it's easy to forget that you inserted them. Then, if you add or remove text from the document, or change it in some other significant way, you might end up with a page layout you didn't expect.

Inserting a Border Around a Page

The newsletter is almost finished. Your last task is to add a border around both pages. The default style for a page border is a simple black line that forms a box around each page in the document. However, you can choose more elaborate options, including a dotted line, double lines, and, for informal documents, a border of graphical elements such as stars or trees. In this case, Estefan prefers the default line style, but he wants it to be blue.

To insert a border around both pages of the newsletter:

1. Change the Zoom level to **Multiple Pages**.

2. On the ribbon, click the **DESIGN** tab.

3. In the Page Background group, click the **Page Borders** button. The Borders and Shading dialog box opens with the Page Border tab displayed. You can use the Setting options on the left side of this tab to specify the type of border you want. Because a document does not normally have a page border, the default setting is None. The Box setting is the most professional and least distracting choice, so you'll select that next.

> Be sure to select the Box setting before you select other options for the border. Otherwise, when you click OK, your document won't have a page border, and you'll have to start over.

4. In the Setting section, click the **Box** setting.

   At this point, you could scroll the Style box and select a line style for the border, such as a dotted line, but Estefan prefers the default style—a simple line. He's also happy with the default width of 1/2 pt. For very informal documents, you could click the Art arrow and select a predesigned border consisting of stars or other graphical elements. However, the only change Estefan wants to make is to change the border color to blue.

5. Click the **Color** arrow to open the Color gallery, and then click the **Blue, Accent 5** square, which is the second square from the right in the top row of the Theme Colors section. The Color gallery closes and the Blue, Accent 5 color is displayed in the Color box. See Figure 4-37.

Figure 4-37 | Adding a border to the newsletter

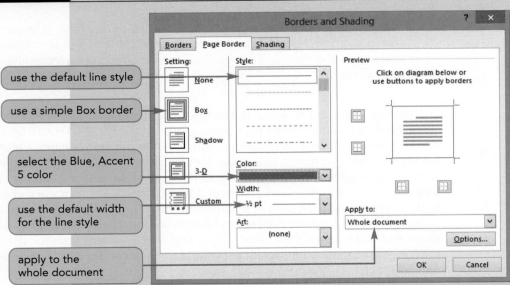

6. In the lower-right corner of the Borders and Shading dialog box, click the **Options** button. The Border and Shading Options dialog box opens.

   By default, the border is positioned 24 points from the edges of the page. If you plan to print your document on an older printer, it is sometimes necessary to change the Measure from setting to Text, so that the border is positioned relative to the outside edge of the text rather than the edge of the page. Alternatively, you can increase the settings in the Top, Bottom, Left, and Right boxes to move the border closer to the text. For most modern printers, however, the default settings are fine.

▶ **7.** In the Border and Shading Options dialog box, click the **Cancel** button, and then click the **OK** button in the Borders and Shading dialog box. The newsletter now has a simple, blue border, as shown earlier in the Session 4.1 Visual Overview.

▶ **8.** Save the document. Finally, to get a better sense of how the document will look when printed, it's a good idea to review it with nonprinting characters turned off.

▶ **9.** On the ribbon, click the **HOME** tab.

▶ **10.** In the Paragraph group, click the **Show/Hide** button to turn off nonprinting characters. Notice that the WordArt headline increases slightly in size to take up the space formerly occupied by the nonprinting paragraph mark.

▶ **11.** Change the Zoom level to **120%**, and then scroll to display page 2.

▶ **12.** On page 2, in the first line below the heading, replace "Dr. Sita Rahm" with your first and last name, and then save the document.

Estefan plans to have the newsletter printed by a local printing company. Betsy, his contact at the printing company, has asked him to email her the newsletter as a PDF.

Saving a Document as a PDF

A **PDF**, or **Portable Document Format file**, contains an image showing exactly how a document will look when printed. Because a PDF can be opened on any computer, saving a document as a PDF is a good way to ensure that it can be read by anyone. This is especially useful when you need to email a document to people who might not have Word installed on their computers. All PDFs have a file extension of .pdf. By default, PDFs open in Adobe Acrobat Reader, a free program installed on most computers for reading PDFs, or in Adobe Acrobat, a PDF-editing program available for purchase from Adobe.

TIP

To save a document as a PDF and attach it to an email message in Outlook, click the FILE tab, click Share in the navigation bar, click Email, and then click Send as PDF.

To save the Wellness Newsletter document as a PDF:

▶ **1.** On the ribbon, click the **FILE** tab to display Backstage view.

▶ **2.** In the navigation bar, click **Export** to display the Export screen with Create PDF/XPS Document selected.

▶ **3.** Click the **Create PDF/XPS Document** button. The Publish as PDF or XPS dialog box opens.

▶ **4.** If necessary, navigate to the location specified by your instructor for saving your files, and then verify that "Wellness Newsletter" appears in the File name box. Below the Save as type box, the "Open file after publishing" check box is selected. By default, the "Standard (publishing online and printing)" button is selected. This generates a PDF suitable for printing. If you plan to distribute a PDF only via email or over the web, you should select the "Minimum size (publishing online)" button instead. See Figure 4-38.

Figure 4-38   Publish as PDF or XPS dialog box

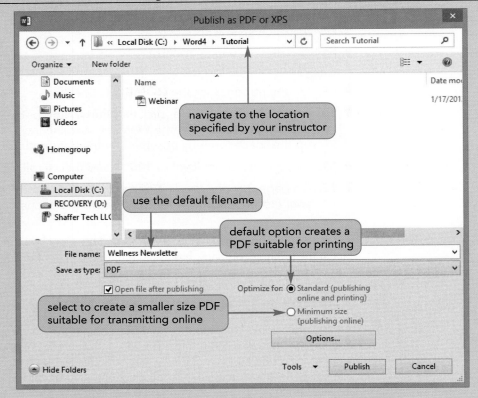

5. Click the **Publish** button. The Publish as PDF or XPS dialog box closes, and, after a pause, either Adobe Acrobat Reader or Adobe Acrobat opens with the Wellness Newsletter PDF displayed.

Trouble? If the Wellness Newsletter PDF does not open, your computer might not have Acrobat Reader or Acrobat installed. In that case, skip Step 6.

6. Scroll down and review the PDF, and then close Adobe Acrobat Reader or Adobe Acrobat.

7. In Word, close the Wellness Newsletter document, but keep Word running.

In addition to saving a Word document as a PDF, you can convert a PDF to a Word document.

Converting a PDF to a Word Document

TIP

If the PDF's creator restricted the file's security using settings available in Adobe Acrobat, you will not be able to copy text from the PDF or convert it to a Word document.

You may sometimes need to use text from a PDF in your own Word documents. Before you can do this, of course, you need to make sure you have permission to do so. Assuming you do, you can open the PDF in Acrobat or Acrobat Reader, drag the mouse pointer to select the text you want to copy, press the Ctrl+C keys, return to your Word document, and then press the Ctrl+V keys to paste the text into your document. If you need to reuse or edit the entire contents of a PDF, it's easier to convert it to a Word document. This is a very useful option with PDFs that consist mostly of text. For more complicated PDFs, such as the Wellness Newsletter.pdf file you just created, the results are less predictable.

Estefan has a PDF containing some text about the Webinar+ service. He asks you to open it in Word and make some minor edits before converting it back to a PDF.

To open the Webinar PDF in Word:

▶ **1.** On the ribbon, click the **FILE** tab to display Backstage view.

▶ **2.** In the navigation bar, click **Open**, if necessary, to display the Open screen, and then navigate to the Word4 ▸ Tutorial folder included with your Data Files.

▶ **3.** If necessary, click the arrow to the right of the File name box, and then click **All Files**.

▶ **4.** In the file list, click **Webinar**, click the **Open** button, and then, if you see a dialog box explaining that Word is about to convert a PDF to a Word document, click the **OK** button. The PDF opens as a Word document, with the name "Webinar" in the title bar. At this point, the Webinar.docx file is a temporary file stored in the temporary folder on your computer. If you want to retain a copy of the document, you need to save it.

▶ **5.** Save the document as **Webinar Revised** in the location specified by your instructor.

▶ **6.** Turn on nonprinting characters, set the Zoom level to **120%**, and then review the document, which consists of a WordArt headline and two paragraphs formatted in italic. If you see some extra spaces at the end of the paragraphs, they were added during the conversion from a PDF to a Word document. In a more complicated document, you might see graphics overlaid on top of text, or columns broken across multiple pages.

▶ **7.** Delete any extra spaces, remove the italic formatting from both paragraphs, and then save the document. You are finished editing the document, so now you can convert it back to a PDF.

▶ **8.** On the ribbon, click the **FILE** tab to display Backstage view.

▶ **9.** In the navigation bar, click **Export**.

▶ **10.** Click the **Create PDF/XPS Document** button.

▶ **11.** If necessary, navigate to the location specified by your instructor for saving your files, verify that "Webinar Revised" appears in the File name box, and then click the **Publish** button.

▶ **12.** Review the PDF in Acrobat or Acrobat Reader, close Acrobat or Acrobat Reader, and then close the Webinar Revised document in Word.

REVIEW

Session 4.2 Quick Check

1. What is WordArt?
2. Name five types of bitmap files.
3. Can you assume that any clip art you find online is available for commercial use?
4. When cropping a picture, how can you maintain a specific ratio of width to height?
5. How do you rotate a picture?
6. Explain how to balance columns in a document.
7. What is a PDF?

SAM Projects

Put your skills into practice with SAM Projects! SAM Projects for this tutorial can be found online. If you have a SAM account, go to www.cengage.com/sam2013 to download the most recent Project Instructions and Start Files.

Review Assignments

Data Files needed for the Review Assignments: Exercise.docx, Habits.png, On the Move.docx, Pineapple.png, Take it Easy.docx, Workout.png

Estefan is working on another newsletter. This one provides information about the benefits of exercise and good nutrition, and includes a list of exercise and nutrition classes. He has already written the text, and he asks you to transform it into a professional-looking newsletter. He also asks you to save the newsletter as a PDF so he can email it to the printer, and to edit some text currently available only as a PDF. The finished newsletter should match the one shown in Figure 4-39.

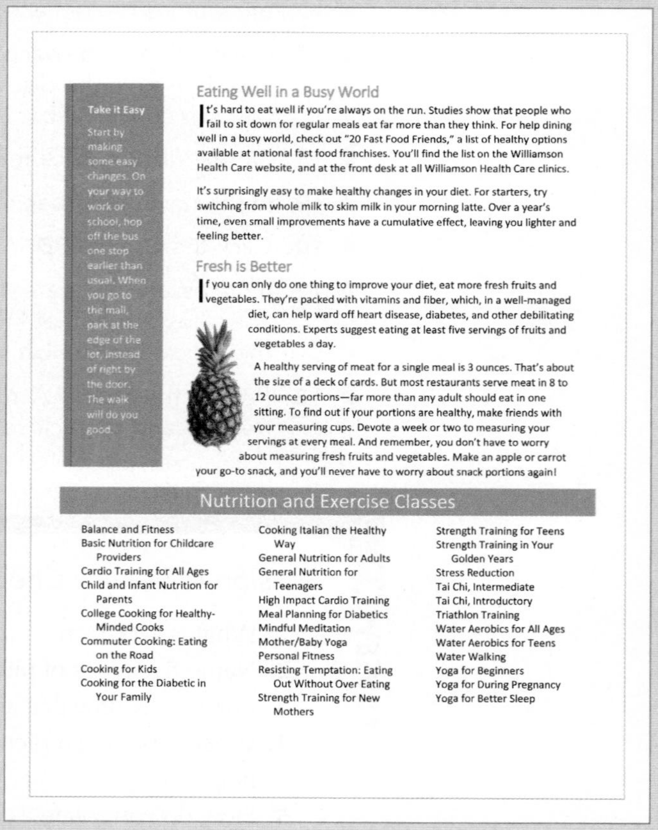

Figure 4-39 Completed Exercise Newsletter document

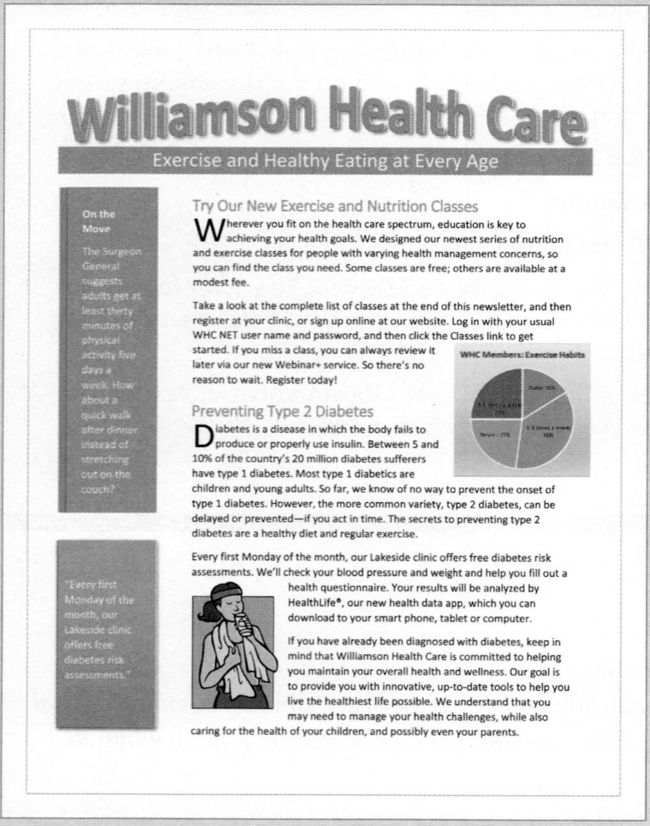

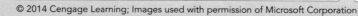

© 2014 Cengage Learning; Images used with permission of Microsoft Corporation

Complete the following steps:

1. Open the file **Exercise** from the Word4 ▸ Review folder included with your Data Files, and then save the document as **Exercise Newsletter** in the location specified by your instructor.

2. Insert continuous section breaks in the following locations:

    • On page 1, at the beginning of the "Try Our New Exercise and Nutrition Classes" heading, to the left of the "T" in "Try"

    • On page 2, at the beginning of the shaded heading "Nutrition and Exercise Classes," to the left of the "N" in "Nutrition"

    • On page 2, at the beginning of the first class name, to the left of the "B" in "Balance"

3. In sections 1 and 3, change the left and right margins to .75 inches. In section 2, change the left margin to 2.5 inches.

4. Format section 4 in three columns of equal width, and then format the entire list of class names with a 0.2-inch hanging indent.

5. Search for the term **HealthLife**, and then add the ® symbol to the right of the final "e."

6. On page 1, click anywhere in the "Try Our New Exercise and Nutrition Classes" heading, and then insert a preformatted text box using the Retrospect Sidebar option.

7. Change the text wrapping setting for the text box to In Front of Text. Change the height of the text box to 4.4 inches and its width to 1.2 inches, and then drag it left to position it in the white space in the left margin, with its top edge aligned with the first line of text below the "Try Our New Exercise and Nutrition Classes" heading. The left border of the text box should align with the left edge of the shaded paragraph above. Verify that the text box's position is fixed on the page, but note that its placement will shift slightly as you add other elements to the newsletter.

8. Delete all the placeholder text in the text box, and then insert the text of the Word document **On the Move**, which is located in the Word4 ▸ Review folder included with your Data Files. Delete any extra paragraph marks at the end of the text, if necessary.

9. On the INSERT tab, use the Shapes button to draw a rectangular text box that roughly fills the blank space in the lower-left margin of page 1. When you are finished, adjust the height and width as necessary to make the text box 2.5 inches tall and 1.3 inches wide.

10. Make sure the text wrap setting for the text box is set to In Front of Text, and that the text box has a fixed position on the page. Drag the text box's anchor up next to the "Preventing Type-2 Diabetes" heading to keep the text box from moving to page 2 later, when you add a graphic to page 1.

11. On page 1, in the second paragraph below the "Preventing Type 2 Diabetes" heading, select the first sentence (which begins "Every first Monday…"), and then copy it to the Office Clipboard.

12. Paste the copied sentence into the text box at the bottom of page 1, and then add quotation marks at the beginning and end.

13. Use the Align Text button to align the text in the middle of the text box, and then apply the Intense Effect - Orange, Accent 2 shape style (the orange style option in the bottom row of the Shape Styles gallery).

14. On page 2, click in the first paragraph, and then insert a preformatted text box using the Retrospect Sidebar option.

15. Change the text wrapping setting for the text box to In Front of Text. Change the height of the text box to 5.2 inches and its width to 1.2 inches, and then drag it left to position it in the white space in the left margin, with its top edge aligned with the first line of text. Verify that its position is fixed on the page. Don't be concerned that it overlaps the shaded paragraph below. This will change as you add more elements to the newsletter.

16. Delete all the placeholder text in the text box, and then insert the text of the Word document **Take it Easy**, which is located in the Word4 ▸ Review folder included with your Data Files. Delete any extra paragraph marks at the end of the text, if necessary.

17. After each of the four headings formatted with orange font, insert a drop cap that drops two lines.

18. On page 1, select the entire first paragraph, "Williamson Health Care," including the paragraph mark. Clear the formatting from the paragraph, and then format the text as WordArt, using the Fill - Orange, Accent 2, Outline - Accent 2 style.

19. Use the Position button to place the WordArt in the top center of the document, with square text wrapping, and make sure the WordArt has a fixed position on the page.

20. Change the text box width to 7 inches and retain the default height of .87 inches.

21. Apply the Chevron Up transform text effect, change the text fill to Orange, Accent 2 (the orange square in the top row of the Theme Colors section), and then add a shadow using the Offset Diagonal Bottom Right style (the first option in the top row of the Outer section).

22. Click at the end of the paragraph below the "Try Our New Exercise and Nutrition Classes" heading, and then insert the picture file named **Habits.png** from the Word4 ▶ Review folder included with your Data Files.

23. Practice cropping the chart to a shape, and then try cropping it by dragging the cropping handles. Use the Reset Picture button as necessary to restore the picture to its original appearance. When you are finished, crop the picture using a square aspect ratio, and then change its height and width to 1.8 inches. Use the Position button to place the chart picture in the middle of the right side of page 1 with square text wrapping.

24. On page 1, click at the end of the second paragraph below the "Preventing Type 2 Diabetes" heading, and then insert the clip art drawing **Workout.png** from the Word4 ▶ Review folder included with your Data Files.

25. Apply Square text wrapping, change the picture's height to 1.7 inches, change the width to 1.13 inches, and position the picture as shown in Figure 4-39. When the picture is properly positioned, the heading "Eating Well in a Busy World" should be positioned at the top of page 2, as shown in Figure 4-39.

26. On page 2, click at the end of the first paragraph below the "Fresh is Better" heading, and then insert the clip art photo **Pineapple.png** from the Word4 ▶ Review folder included with your Data Files.

27. Change the photo's width to 2 inches and retain the default height of 1.34 inches. Apply Tight text wrapping, fix its position on the page, and then remove the photo's background.

28. Rotate the photo so the pineapple is positioned vertically, with the leaves on top, and then drag the photo to position it as shown in Figure 4-39.

29. Balance the columns at the bottom of page 2.

30. Insert a simple box outline of the default style and width for the entire document. For the border color, use Blue, Accent 1 (the fifth square from the left in the top row of the Theme Colors).

31. In the top text box on page 1, replace "The surgeon general" with your first and last name. If you can't fit your entire name on the first two lines of the text box, use your first initial and your last name. Make any additional adjustments necessary to ensure that your newsletter matches the one shown in Figure 4-39.

32. Save the document, and then save it again as a PDF named **Exercise Newsletter.pdf** in the location specified by your instructor. Wait for the PDF to open, review it, and then close the program in which it opened. Close the **Exercise Newsletter.docx** document, but leave Word open.

33. In Word, open the **Exercise Newsletter.pdf** file, save it as a Word document named **Exercise Newsletter from PDF.docx**, review its appearance, note the problems with the formatting that you would have to correct if you actually wanted to use this new DOCX file, and then close it.

Case Problem 1

Data Files needed for this Case Problem: Bin.png, Child.png, Green.docx, Sidebar.docx

Green Commission, Morelos, Arizona   Clarice Stephan is the coordinator for the Green Commission in Morelos, Arizona, a citizen committee charged with encouraging environmentally friendly practices such as recycling, LEED construction, and water conservation. She has written the text of the commission's bimonthly newsletter. Now she needs your help to finish it. The newsletter must fit on one page so the commission's recycling guidelines can be printed on the other side. The finished newsletter should match the one shown in Figure 4-40.

Figure 4-40   **Completed Green Newsletter document**

Recycle, Reuse, Renew
Green Commission Updates

Recycling Review

Each household is entitled to one recycling bin. You can recycle an unlimited amount of materials, with no extra fee for materials that exceed the limit of your household's recycling bin. Please place extra materials in a clean box that is clearly labeled "Recycling," and place it next to your bin.

See the complete recycling guidelines on the other side of this newsletter.

Morelos Receives $5000 Recycling Grant

We're extremely happy to announce that the Morelos Green Commission has been awarded a $5000 Change It Up grant from the Arizona Department of Public Works. The money will pay for new recycling bins at all city parks. Many thanks go to Suzette Orleans, who spent many hours completing the grant application, along with James Suarez and Leah Chang.

The recycling bins will be installed at the end of the summer. The Department of Sanitation will be responsible for emptying them twice a week during the summer, and once a week the rest of the year. The Morelos High School Honor Society has offered to clean the bins once a month as part of their student volunteer program.

Hazardous Waste Collection

The next city-wide hazardous waste collection is scheduled for the week of July 15. Sanitation workers will retrieve the items from the curb next to your trash bins on your usual trash pickup day. Please keep all hazardous waste items indoors until the morning of your scheduled trash pickup. For a list of all accepted items, go to the City of Morelos web site, and click Hazardous Waste Pickup.

Many household hazardous wastes can be recycled cleanly and effectively by recycling professionals. Aren't sure what's considered hazardous waste? The labels of most products will provide helpful clues. Look for the following words: caution, warning, toxic, pesticide, keep away from children, flammable, and warning. Acceptable materials include antifreeze, brake fluid, kerosene, oil-based paint, furniture polish, pesticides, herbicides, household batteries, pool chemicals and fertilizers.

Winners of the Citizen Green Award

Kendra Ann Ramirez-Beech	Aralee Erbe	Marcos Jeschke	Harriet Soles
Michael Paul Bernault	Henry Douglas	Jaques Lambeau	Micah Schwerz
Beatrice Cai	Jose Caruccio	Maria Morelo-Jimenez	Alyssa Tonette
Emma Comerez	Sophie Carrucio	Elizabeth Juarez	Pamela Twist-Chamberlain
Jonathan Carnala	Krista Dennis	Mario Mondre	Roberto Oriel
Laydra Carole	Seamus Van Buren	Helena Pentakota Roys	
Samuel Butler	Jacqueline Fey-Esperanza	Maximillian Del Rio	
	Haiyan Jiang		

Complete the following steps:

1. Open the file **Green** located in the Word4 ▸ Case1 folder included with your Data Files, and then save it as **Green Newsletter** in the location specified by your instructor.

2. Change the document margins to Narrow, and then, where indicated in the document, insert continuous section breaks. Remember to delete each instance of the highlighted text "[INSERT SECTION BREAK]" before you insert a section break.

3. In section 2, change the left margin to 3 inches, and then format section 4 in four columns, with a 0.3-inch hanging indent.

4. Format the second paragraph in the document ("Green Commission Updates") as WordArt, using the Gradient Fill - Dark Green, Accent 1, Reflection style (second from the left in the middle row of the WordArt gallery). Change the text box height to 0.7 inches and the width to 7 inches. If necessary, drag the WordArt text box to center it between the left and right margins.

5. Insert drop caps that drop two lines in the first paragraph after the "Morelos Receives $5000 Recycling Grant" heading, and in the first paragraph after the "Hazardous Waste Collection" heading.

6. Click in the fourth paragraph in the document (the one with the drop cap "W"), and then insert a preformatted text box using the Ion Sidebar 1 option. Change the text wrapping setting for the text box to In Front of Text, and then change its height to 3 inches and its width to 2 inches.

7. Drag the text box down, and then align its top border with the "Morelos Receives $5000 Recycling Grant" heading.

8. Delete the title placeholder text in the text box, and type **Recycling Review**. In the main text box, delete the placeholder text and insert the text of the Word document **Sidebar** from the Word4 ▸ Case1 folder included with your Data Files. Change the font size for all the text in the text box, including the title, to 11 points.

9. In the blank space below the "Recycling Review" text box, draw a rectangular text box. When you are finished, adjust the height and width to make the text box 1.3 inches tall and 2 inches wide. Apply the Moderate Effect - Blue, Accent 2 shape style (third from the left in the second row from the bottom), and then position the text box as shown in Figure 4-40, leaving room for the recycling bin graphic you will add later.

10. In the text box, type **See the complete recycling guidelines on the other side of this newsletter**. Align the text in the middle of the text box, and then use the Center button to center the text between the text box's left and right borders.

11. At the end of the fifth paragraph (which begins "The recycling bins will be…"), insert the clip art drawing **Child.png** from the Word4 ▸ Case1 folder included with your Data Files. Crop the picture to an oval shape, apply Tight text wrapping, fix its position on the page, and then change its height to 1 inch. Drag the picture to position it so the first line in the fifth paragraph wraps above it, as shown in Figure 4-40.

12. At the end of the first paragraph below the "Hazardous Waste Collection" heading, insert the clip art drawing **Bin.png** from the Word4 ▸ Case1 folder included with your Data Files. Change the picture's height to 1.3 inches, apply In Front of Text text wrapping, add the Center Shadow Rectangle picture style (second from right in the second row of the Picture Styles gallery), and then position the picture in the left margin, centered between the two text boxes, with a fixed position on the page, as shown in Figure 4-40.

13. Add a box page border using a line style with a thick exterior line and a thinner interior line, in the default width, and in the same color as the font for the "Morelos Receives $5000 Recycling Grant" heading.

14. In the last paragraph, replace "Roberto Oriel" with your first and last names.

15. Make any adjustments necessary so that your newsletter matches the one shown in Figure 4-40, and then save the document.

16. Save the document as a PDF named **Green Newsletter** in the location specified by your instructor. Review the PDF and then close the program in which it opened.

17. In Word, open the PDF named **Green Newsletter.pdf**, save it as **Green Newsletter from PDF.docx**, review its contents, note the corrections you would have to make if you actually wanted to use this document, and then close it.

Case Problem 2

Data Files needed for this Case Problem: Facts.docx, Flag.jpg, Rights.jpg

Alexander Hamilton High School   Paula McQuiddy teaches American history at Alexander Hamilton High School in Ruby Falls, Wisconsin. She has decided to create a series of handouts about important historical documents. Each handout will contain the text of the historical document, with red and blue accent colors, along with a picture of the American flag and a text box with essential facts about the document. Paula has asked you to help her complete her first handout, which is about the Bill of Rights. You will create the handout shown in Figure 4-41.

Figure 4-41	Completed Bill of Rights handout

© 2014 Cengage Learning; Image used with permission of Microsoft Corporation

Complete the following steps:

1. Open the file **Rights** located in the Word4 ▸ Case2 folder included with your Data Files, and then save it as **Bill of Rights** in the location specified by your instructor.

2. Display the document gridlines.

3. Change the document margins to Narrow, change the theme to Facet, and format all the heading text using the Dark Blue font color in the Standard Colors section of the Font Color gallery.

4. At the top of the document, add the text **The Bill of Rights** as a new paragraph, and then format it as WordArt, using the Gradient Fill - Red, Accent 1, Reflection style (the second from the left in the middle row). Add Top and Bottom text wrapping, and then fix the text box's position on the page. If the position of the WordArt shifts, drag it back up to the top of the page. Change its height to 1.3 inches and its width to 7 inches. Apply the Square transform text effect (the first effect in the top row of the Warp section). Remove the reflection effect. Drag the WordArt as necessary to center it at the top of the page. The top edge of the text box should align with the top gridline.

5. At the end of the paragraph below the WordArt, insert the clip art photo **Flag.jpg** from the Word4 ► Case2 folder included with your Data Files.

6. Apply Tight text wrapping to the photo, change the height to 2 inches, remove the photo's background, and then position it along the left margin, so the first two lines of regular text wrap above it, as shown in Figure 4-41.

7. Format the list of amendments in two columns. Use column breaks to format the amendments as shown in Figure 4-41, with Amendment IV at the top of the second column on page 1, and Amendment VIII at the top of the second column on page 2.

8. At the end of the last paragraph on page 2, insert a preformatted text box using the Grid Sidebar style. Apply In Front of Text text wrapping, and then change the height to 5.3 inches and the width to 7 inches. Position the text box at the bottom of page 2, centered in the white space, with a fixed position on the page.

9. Delete the placeholder text in the text box, and then insert the text of the Word document named **Facts** from the Word4 ► Case2 folder included with your Data Files. If necessary, delete any extra paragraph marks.

10. Add a box page border, using the default style, in the default width, and in the same color as the headings with the amendment numbers.

11. Make any adjustments necessary so that your newsletter matches the one shown in Figure 4-41, and then hide the gridlines.

12. At the end of the text box on page 2, insert a new, bulleted paragraph, remove the bullet formatting, right-align the paragraph, and then insert the text **Prepared by Student Name**, with your first and last names replacing the text "Student Name." Save the document.

13. Save the document as a PDF named **Bill of Rights.pdf** in the location specified by your instructor. Review the PDF in Acrobat or Acrobat Reader.

14. From within Acrobat or Acrobat Reader, use the appropriate keyboard shortcut to copy the bulleted paragraphs in the blue text box, open a new, blank Word document, and then paste the copied text into it. In a new bulleted list at the end of the document, list three differences between the formatting of the bulleted list in the current document and in the Bill of Rights.pdf file. Format the new paragraphs in red so they are easy to spot.

15. Save the Word document as **Facts from PDF** in the location specified by your instructor and then close it. Close Acrobat or Acrobat Reader.

Case Problem 3

Data Files needed for this Case Problem: Audio.pdf, Shape.docx, Tennis.png

Shape Crafter 3D Printing   You have recently been hired as an assistant in the Human Resources department at Shape Crafter 3D Printing in Indianapolis, Indiana. Your supervisor explains that while working on the company's monthly newsletter, he left his laptop briefly unattended. His young daughter took advantage of the opportunity to make some unwelcome changes to his Word document. You've offered to troubleshoot the document and format the newsletter to look like the one shown in Figure 4-42. Your second task is to open a PDF containing a newsletter announcing a new program for employees, and edit the text to remove any irregularities that occurred in the conversion from a PDF to a Word document.

Figure 4-42 Completed Shape Crafter newsletter

change the left margin to 1.75 inches

change the WordArt text direction setting to Rotate all text 270°; change its height to 9.94 inches and its width to 1.3 inches; and then change the font size to 72 points

for the border, use the Dark Red, Accent 1 color and the default line style and width

insert the file Tennis.png from the Word4 ▶ Case3 folder

square text box shape with 1.5-inch sides; use the Light 1 Outline, Colored Fill - Dark Red, Accent 1 shape style

use the Blue - Gray, Accent color 5 Dark option in the Recolor section of the Color gallery

for the headings' shading, use the Dark Red, Accent 1 color; switch to white font

text is hyphenated

change spacing between columns to 0.2"

square text box shape with 1.25-inch sides

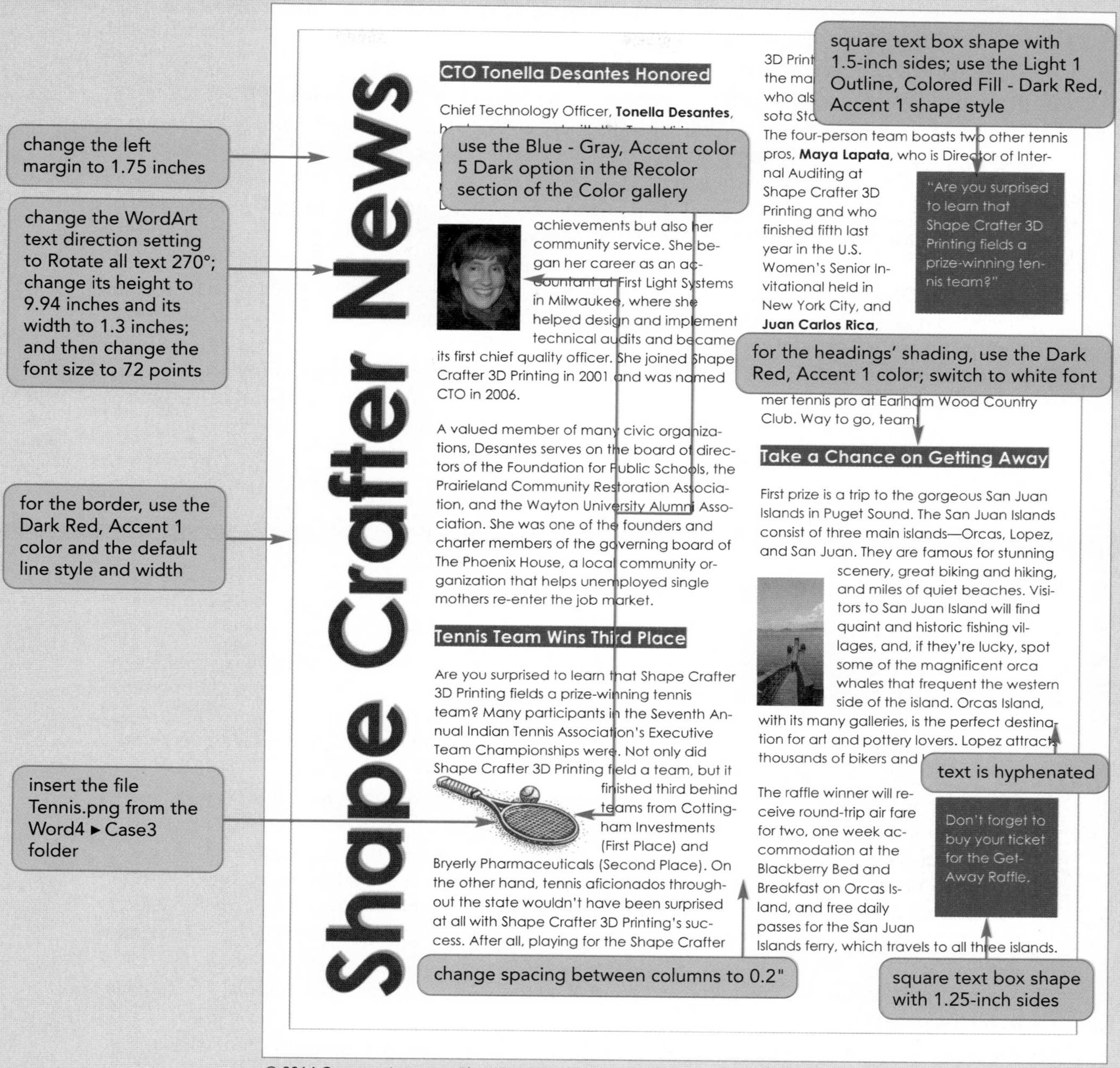

© 2014 Cengage Learning; Photos courtesy of Ann Shaffer

Complete the following steps:

1. Open the file **Shape** located in the Word4 ▶ Case3 folder included with your Data Files, and then save it as **Shape Crafter Newsletter** in the location specified by your instructor.

⚙ **Troubleshoot** 2. Revise the document to match the newsletter shown in Figure 4-42. Start by fixing the border, changing the left margin, and resetting the pictures. Keep in mind that you can use the Selection Task Pane to select a picture, and remember to crop the photos so they match the ones shown in Figure 4-42. Also, you'll need to flip two of the pictures horizontally. You should be able to size the pictures appropriately by looking at their sizes relative to the text in Figure 4-42.

⚙ **Troubleshoot** 3. In the Arrange group, use the Selection task pane and the Align Objects button to align the photo of Tonella Desantes and the tennis racquet with the left margin. Also, align the two text boxes with the right margin.

4. Replace the double hyphens with an em dash.

5. In the middle of the second column, replace "Juan Carlos Rica" with your first and last names.

⚙ **Troubleshoot** 6. Make any adjustments necessary so that your newsletter matches the one shown in Figure 4-42. You might need to drag the WordArt text box left slightly to keep all the text on one page. Save the document.

7. Save the document as a PDF named **Shape Crafter Newsletter.pdf** in the location specified by your instructor. Review the PDF in Acrobat or Acrobat Reader, and then close Acrobat or Acrobat Reader.

8. Open the PDF **Audio.pdf** located in the Word4 ▸ Case3 folder included with your Data Files, and then save it as a Word document named **Audio Download Program** in the location specified by your instructor.

⚙ **Troubleshoot** 9. Edit the text to remove the picture, the WordArt, and the shaded text. Format the blue headings using the Heading 1 style, and then remove any extra spaces and paragraph breaks. Make any other edits necessary so that the text is formatted with consistent paragraph and line spacing throughout.

10. Save the document, and then close it. Close any other open documents.

Case Problem 4

CREATE

There are no Data Files needed for this Case Problem.

Glenfield Graphic Design   You are an intern at Glenfield Graphic Design, a firm that specializes in designing fund-raising materials, including newsletters, for nonprofit organizations. As part of your training, your supervisor asks you to review examples of newsletter designs on the web, and then re-create the design of one of those newsletters in a Word document. Instead of writing the complete text of a newsletter, you can use placeholder text. Complete the following steps:

1. Open a new, blank document, and then save it as **Newsletter Design** in the location specified by your instructor.

2. Open your browser and search online for images of sample newsletters by searching for the keywords **newsletter image**. Review at least a dozen images of newsletters before picking a style that you want to re-create in a Word document. The style you choose should contain at least two pictures. Keep the image of the newsletter you select visible in your browser so you can return to it for reference as you work.

3. In your Word document, create the first page of the newsletter. To generate text that you can use to fill the page, type **=lorem()** and then press the Enter key.

4. Add at least two pictures to the newsletter, using clip art that you find online. Rotate or flip pictures and remove the background from photos as necessary to make them work in the newsletter layout.

5. Make any other changes necessary so that the layout and style of your document match the newsletter example that you found online.

6. Somewhere in the document, attach a comment that reads **I used the following webpage as a model for this newsletter design:**, and then include the URL for the newsletter image you used as a model. To copy a URL from a browser window, click the URL in the browser's Address box, and then press the Ctrl+C keys.

7. Save the document, close it, and then close your browser.

Written Communication

Writing Clear and Effective Business Documents

Whether it's a simple email message sent to a group, a memo to provide information on an upcoming event, or a press release introducing a new product to the market, the quality of your written communication tells the world how prepared, informed, and detail-oriented you are. When searching for a job, the ability to write clearly and effectively is essential. After all, your first contact with a company is often a cover letter and resume. For a prospective employer, these documents provide the first indicators of the kind of employee you might be. To make the best possible impression, follow these important rules in all types of business communication.

Rule One: Identify Your Audience

Who will read your document? What do they already know about your subject? For starters, you can assume your audience is made up of busy people who will only take the time to read what is important and relevant to them. They don't want to be entertained. They just want to read the information as quickly as possible. In the case of a resume and cover letter, your audience is typically one or more professional people who don't know you. Therefore, the goal of your resume and cover letter should be to introduce yourself quickly and efficiently.

Rule Two: Do Your Research

Provide all the information the reader will need to make a decision or take action. Be absolutely certain that the facts you present are correct. Don't assume that something is true just because a friend told you it was, or because you read it online. Verify all your facts using reputable sources. Remember, your goal as a writer is to make the reader trust you. Nothing alienates a reader faster than errors or misleading statements. When applying for a job, make sure you are knowledgeable about the company so that you can mention relevant and accurate details in your cover letter.

Rule Three: State Your Purpose

At the beginning of the document, explain why you are writing. The reader shouldn't have to wonder. Are you writing to inform, or do you want action to be taken? Do you hope to change a belief or simply state your position? In a cover letter accompanying your resume, state clearly that you are writing to apply for a job, and then explain exactly what job you are applying for. That might sound obvious, but many job applicants forget about directness in their efforts to come across as clever or interesting. This only hurts their chances because prospective employers typically have many cover letters to read, with no time to spare for sorting through irrelevant information.

Rule Four: Write Succinctly

Use as few words as possible. Don't indulge in long, complicated words and sentences because you think they make you sound smart. The most intelligent writing is usually short and to the point. Keep in mind that hiring a new employee is a very time-consuming process. In small companies, people in charge of hiring often have to do it while performing their regular duties. Thus, the more succinct your resume and cover letter, the greater the chances that a potential employer will actually read both documents.

Rule Five: Use the Right Tone

Be professional and courteous. In the case of writing to a prospective employer, don't make the mistake of being overly friendly because it might indicate to the reader that you are not taking the job application process seriously.

Rule Six: Revise, Revise, Revise

After you finish a document, set it aside for a while, and then proofread it when it's no longer fresh in your mind. Even a small grammar or punctuation error can cause a potential employer to set aside your resume in favor of a more polished one with no errors. Remember, the best writers in the world seek out readers who can provide constructive suggestions, so consider having a friend or colleague read it and provide feedback. If someone points out an unclear passage, make every attempt to improve it.

Following these basic rules will help to ensure that you develop strong, professional written communication skills.

Create a Resume and Cover Letter

You've seen how Microsoft Word 2013 allows you to create polished, professional-looking documents in a variety of business settings. The word-processing skills you've learned will be useful to you in many areas of your life. For example, you could create a Word table to keep track of a guest list for a wedding, or you could use Word's desktop publishing features to create a flyer promoting a garage sale or a concert for a friend's band. In the following exercise, you'll create a table summarizing information about prospective employers, and then you'll use that information to create a resume and a cover letter.

Note: Please be sure *not* to include any personal information of a sensitive nature in the documents you create to be submitted to your instructor for this exercise. Later on, you can update the documents with such information for your own personal use.

1. Pick a career field that interests you, and then go online and look up information about four companies or organizations in that field for which you would like to work.

2. Create a table that summarizes your research. Your table should include one column with information about how to apply for a job. Does the company require you to email your resume and cover letter as PDFs, to submit them as Word documents via a website, to paste them into a form on a website, or to mail printed copies? The process of applying for a job can vary widely from one company to another—and from one industry to another—so make sure you clearly explain the process for each company in your table and include any relevant website addresses. Include three columns in your table with general information that would be useful for you in a job interview. For example, you might include a "Most Important Product" column and a "Facts About Company Founder" column. Create a complete record for each company, and then sort the table alphabetically by company name.

3. Create a resume that you could use to apply for jobs at the four companies you researched. To ensure that your resume is suitable for your chosen field, search the web for sample resumes in your field. Find a resume design that you like, and then adapt the design for your resume. Your goal should be to create the most elegant, professional-looking resume you can, using advanced page layout options as necessary. For example, you could use a table to organize the page layout.

4. After creating your resume, proofread it for any errors, and then revise it for proper tone and clear and succinct content. If possible, ask a classmate or a family member to read it and provide constructive feedback.

5. Create a copy of your resume, and then revise this new version to use the simplest possible formatting. This time, your goal should be to create a resume that you could easily paste into a form on a website.

6. Create a cover letter to accompany your resume. Make sure that your letter clearly states your purpose, and that the letter is formatted correctly and written succinctly. When reviewing your cover letter and revising it, make sure your writing is professional and uses an appropriate tone.

7. Review all your documents carefully in Print Preview, make any necessary changes, and then save the documents.

8. Save your two resumes and your cover letter as PDFs.

MODULE 5

OBJECTIVES

Session 5.1
- Create a new document from a template
- Move through a document using Go To
- Use the thesaurus to find synonyms
- Customize a document theme
- Save a custom theme
- Select a style set
- Customize a style
- Change character spacing

Session 5.2
- Create a new style
- Inspect styles
- Reveal and compare text formatting details
- Review line and page break settings
- Generate and update a table of contents
- Create and use a template
- Create a Quick Part

Working with Templates, Themes, and Styles

Creating a Summary Report

Case | *Dakota Tech Incubator*

The Sioux Falls Center for Business and Technology, in Sioux Falls, South Dakota, is spearheading construction of the Dakota Tech Incubator. The facility will house new, technically oriented companies (known as startups) that require the specialized kind of support needed in the fast-moving technology world. Benjamin Witinski, a project manager at the Sioux Falls Center for Business and Technology, is responsible for creating a report designed to help generate interest in the Dakota Tech Incubator. Benjamin has asked you to help him prepare the report. He's also interested in learning more about Word templates, so he'd like you to do some research by opening a few templates and examining the styles they offer. Next, he wants you to modify the formatting currently applied to his report document, including modifying the theme and one of the styles, creating a new style, and adding a table of contents. Then he wants you to create a template that can be used for all reports produced by his organization, as well as a reusable text box containing the current mailing address and phone number for the Sioux Falls Center for Business and Technology, which his coworkers can insert into any Word document via the Quick Parts gallery.

STARTING DATA FILES

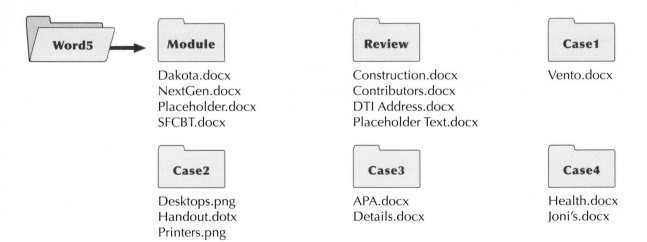

Word5 → **Module**

Dakota.docx
NextGen.docx
Placeholder.docx
SFCBT.docx

Review

Construction.docx
Contributors.docx
DTI Address.docx
Placeholder Text.docx

Case1

Vento.docx

Case2

Desktops.png
Handout.dotx
Printers.png

Case3

APA.docx
Details.docx

Case4

Health.docx
Joni's.docx

Session 5.1 Visual Overview:

The **theme colors** are the colors you see in the Theme Colors section of any color gallery, such as the Font Color gallery. Theme colors are used in the document's styles to format headings, body text, and other elements.

Every document has two **theme fonts**, which are used in the document's styles. The theme fonts appear at the top of the font list when you click the Font arrow in the Font group on the Home tab.

Collectively, all the styles available in a document are called a **style set**. This style set, named Word, is applied to all new documents by default.

Theme effects, such as reflections or shadows, can be used to modify shapes.

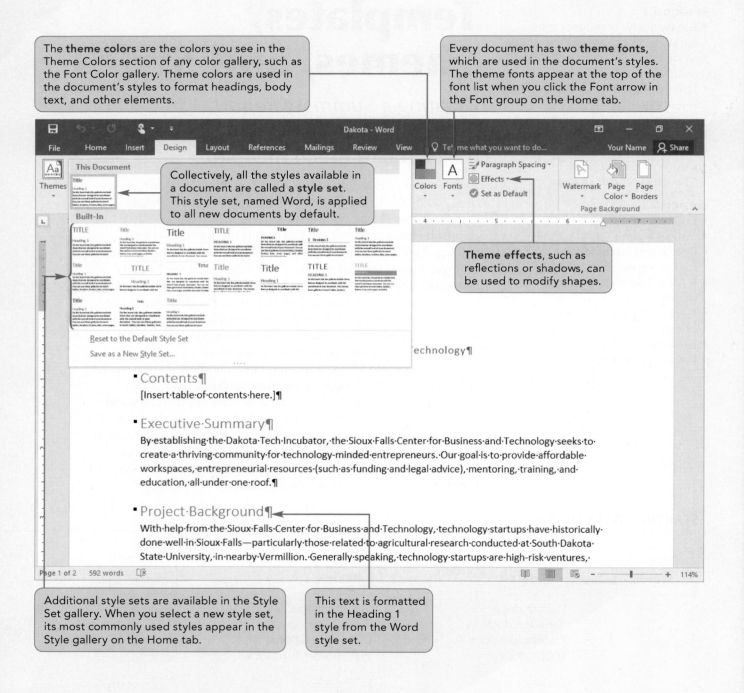

Additional style sets are available in the Style Set gallery. When you select a new style set, its most commonly used styles appear in the Style gallery on the Home tab.

This text is formatted in the Heading 1 style from the Word style set.

Custom Themes and Style Sets

This style set, named Shaded, is applied to the Dakota document, shown below. In the Shaded style set, the Heading 1 style formats text with blue paragraph shading and a white font color.

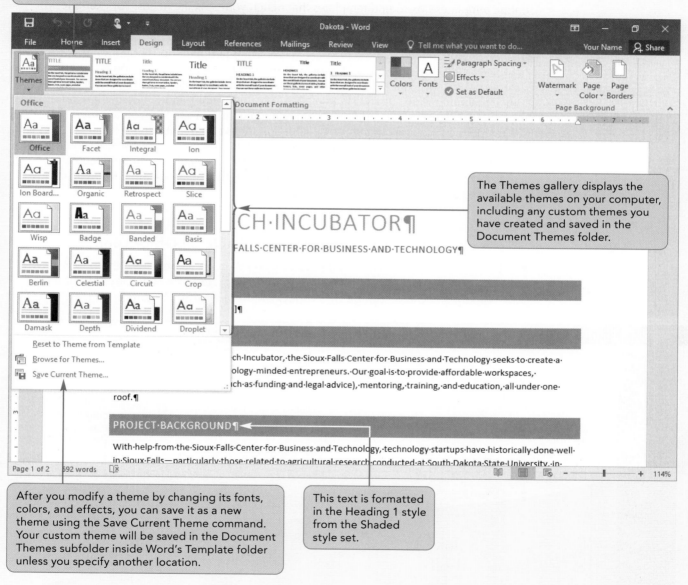

The Themes gallery displays the available themes on your computer, including any custom themes you have created and saved in the Document Themes folder.

After you modify a theme by changing its fonts, colors, and effects, you can save it as a new theme using the Save Current Theme command. Your custom theme will be saved in the Document Themes subfolder inside Word's Template folder unless you specify another location.

This text is formatted in the Heading 1 style from the Shaded style set.

Creating a New Document from a Template

A template is a file that you use as a starting point for a series of similar documents so that you don't have to re-create formatting and text for each new document. A template can contain customized styles, text, graphics, or any other element that you want to repeat from one document to another. In this module, you'll customize the styles and themes in a Word document and then save the document as a template to use for future documents. Before you do that, however, you will investigate some of the ready-made templates available at Office.com.

When you first start Word, the Recent screen in Backstage view displays a variety of templates available from Office.com. You can also enter keywords in the Search for online templates box to find templates that match your specific needs. For example, you could search for a calendar template, a birthday card template, or a report template.

Every new, blank document that you open in Word is a copy of the Normal template. Unlike other Word templates, the **Normal template** does not have any text or graphics, but it does include all the default settings that you are accustomed to using in Word. For example, the default theme in the Normal template is the Office theme. The Office theme, in turn, supplies the default body font (Calibri) and the default heading font (Calibri Light). The default line spacing and paragraph spacing you are used to seeing in a new document are also specified in the Normal template.

Benjamin would like you to review some templates designed for reports. As you'll see in the following steps, when you open a template, Word actually creates a document that is an exact copy of the template. The template itself remains unaltered, so you can continue to use it as the basis for other documents.

To review some report templates available on Office.com:

1. On the ribbon, click the **File** tab to open Backstage view, and then click **New** in the navigation bar. The New screen in Backstage view displays thumbnail images of the first page of a variety of templates. See Figure 5-1.

Figure 5-1 Featured templates on the New screen in Backstage view

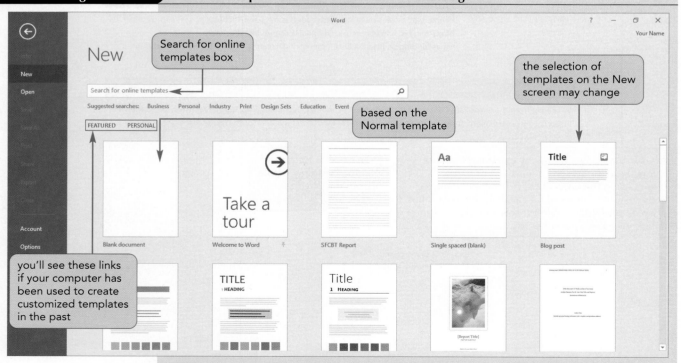

Trouble? If you just started Word, you'll see the list of templates on the Recent screen. You'll be able to complete the next step using the Search for online templates box on the Recent screen.

Below the Search for online templates box are template options available from Office.com. You've already used the Blank document template to open a new, blank document that is based on the Normal template. The list of templates changes as new templates become available, so your screen probably won't match Figure 5-1 exactly.

If your computer has been used to create customized templates, two additional links are displayed below the Search for online templates box—FEATURED and PERSONAL. You can ignore those links for now. In this case, you want to open a document based on a template designed specifically for reports.

▶ **2.** Click the **Search for online templates** box, type **report** and then press the **Enter** key. The New screen displays thumbnail images for a variety of report templates. If you scroll down to the bottom, you'll see options for searching for templates to use in other Office applications. The Category pane on the right displays a list of report categories. You could click any category to display only the templates in that category.

▶ **3.** Click the first template in the top row. A window opens with a preview of the template. Note that the template indicates it is provided by Microsoft Corporation. Figure 5-2 shows the Student report with cover photo template. The template that opens on your computer might be different.

Figure 5-2	Previewing a template

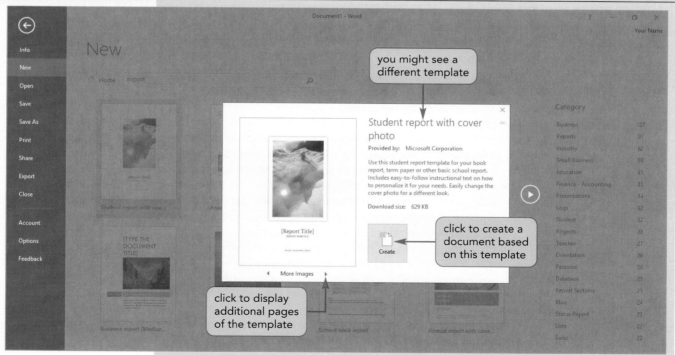

You could click the Close button to close the preview window and browse other report templates, but Benjamin asks you to continue investigating the current template.

4. Click the **Create** button. A new document based on the Student report with cover photo template opens. It begins with a cover page and contains a number of content controls designed specifically for the template, similar to the content controls you've seen in other documents. It also contains some placeholder text, a footer, and graphics.

At this point, you could save the document with a new name and then begin revising it to create an actual report. But since your goal now is to review various templates, you'll close the document.

5. Close the document without saving any changes.

6. On the ribbon, click the **File** tab, and then click **New** in the navigation bar.

7. Search online for newsletter templates, open a document based on one of the templates, and then review the document, making note of the various elements it includes.

8. Close the newsletter document without saving it.

9. Return to the New screen, and search for templates for flyers. Open a new document based on one of the templates, review the document, and then close it without saving it.

PROSKILLS

Decision Making: Using Templates from Other Sources

The Office.com website offers a wide variety of templates that are free to Microsoft Office users. Countless other websites offer templates for free, for individual sale, as part of a subscription service, or a combination of all three. However, you need to be wary when searching for templates online. Keep in mind the following when deciding which sites to use:

- Files downloaded from the Internet can infect your computer with viruses and spyware, so make sure your computer has up-to-date antivirus and anti-malware software before downloading any templates.
- Evaluate a site carefully to verify that it is a reputable source of virus-free templates. Verifying the site's legitimacy is especially important if you intend to pay for a template with a credit card. Search for the website's name and URL using different search engines (such as Bing and Google) to see what other people say about it.
- Some websites claim to offer templates for free, when in fact the offer is primarily a lure to draw visitors to sites that are really just online billboards, with ads for any number of businesses completely unrelated to templates or Word documents. Avoid downloading templates from these websites.
- Many templates available online were created for earlier versions of Word that did not include themes or many other Word 2016 design features. Make sure you know what you're getting before you pay for an out-of-date template.

Now that you are finished reviewing report templates, you will open the document containing the report about the Dakota Tech Incubator.

To open Benjamin's report document:

 1. Open the document **Dakota** from the Word5 > Module folder, and then save it as **Dakota Report** in the location specified by your instructor.

 2. Display nonprinting characters and the rulers, switch to Print Layout view if necessary, and then change the Zoom level to **120%**, if necessary. See Figure 5-3.

Figure 5-3   **Dakota Report document**

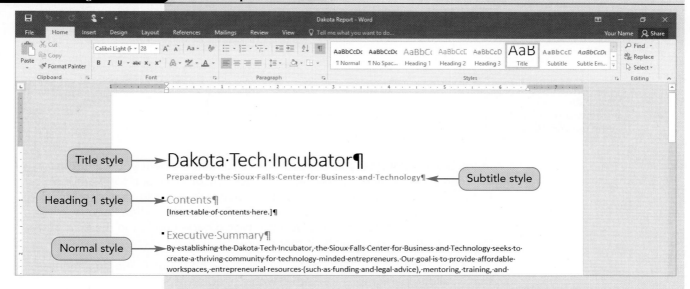

The report is formatted using the default settings of the Normal template, which means its current theme is the Office theme. Text in the report is formatted using the Title, Subtitle, Heading 1, Heading 2, and Normal styles. The document includes a footer containing "Dakota Tech Incubator" and a page number field.

Before you begin revising the document, you should review its contents. To get a quick overview of a document, it's helpful to use the Go To feature.

Using Go To

The Go To tab in the Find and Replace dialog box allows you to move quickly among elements in a document. For example, you can use it to move from heading to heading, from graphic to graphic, or from table to table. In a long document, this is an efficient way to review your work. Although the Dakota Report document is not very long, you can still review its contents using Go To.

To use the Go To feature to review the Dakota Report document:

 1. If necessary, press the **Ctrl+Home** keys to move the insertion point to the beginning of the document.

 2. On the ribbon, make sure the Home tab is displayed.

3. In the Editing group, click the **Find button arrow** to display the Find menu, and then click **Go To**. The Find and Replace dialog box opens, with the Go To tab displayed. See Figure 5-4.

Figure 5-4   **Go To tab in the Find and Replace dialog box**

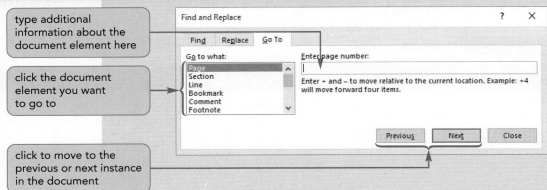

type additional information about the document element here

click the document element you want to go to

click to move to the previous or next instance in the document

In the Go to what box, you can click the document element you want to go to. Then click the Next or Previous buttons to move back and forth among instances of the selected element in the document. You can also enter more specific information in the box on the right. For instance, when Page is selected in the Go to what box, you can type a page number in the box, and then click Next to go directly to that page.

Right now, Benjamin would like to review all the headings in the document—that is, all the paragraphs formatted with a heading style.

4. Scroll down to the bottom of the Go to what box, click **Heading**, and then click the **Next** button. The document scrolls down to position the first document heading, "Contents," at the top of the document window.

5. Click the **Next** button again. The document scrolls down to display the "Executive Summary" heading at the top of the document window.

6. Click the **Next** button five more times to display the last heading in the document, "Accelerate Investments," at the top of the document window.

7. Click the **Previous** button to display the "Coleman 3D Printing" heading at the top of the document window, and then close the Find and Replace dialog box.

INSIGHT

Choosing Between Go To and the Navigation Pane

Both the Go To tab in the Find and Replace dialog box and the Navigation pane allow you to move through a document heading by heading. Although you used Go To in the preceding steps, the Navigation pane is usually the better choice for working with headings; it displays a complete list of the headings, which helps you keep an eye on the document's overall organization. However, the Go To tab is more useful when you want to move through a document one graphic at a time, or one table at a time. In a document that contains a lot of graphics or tables, it's a good idea to use the Go To feature to make sure you've formatted all the graphics or tables similarly.

Next, before you begin formatting the document, Benjamin asks you to help him find a synonym for a word in the text.

Using the Thesaurus to Find Synonyms

In any kind of writing, choosing the right words to convey your meaning is important. If you need help, you can use Word's thesaurus to look up a list of synonyms, or possible replacements, for a specific word. You can right-click a word to display a shortcut menu with a short list of synonyms or open the Thesaurus task pane for a more complete list.

Benjamin is not happy with the word "innovators" in the paragraph about Coleman 3D Printing because he thinks it is overused in writing about technical entrepreneurs. He asks you to find a synonym.

To look up a synonym in the thesaurus:

1. In the last line one page 1, right-click the word **innovators**. A shortcut menu opens.

2. Point to **Synonyms**. A menu with a list of synonyms for "innovators" is displayed, as shown in Figure 5-5.

Figure 5-5   **Shortcut menu with list of synonyms**

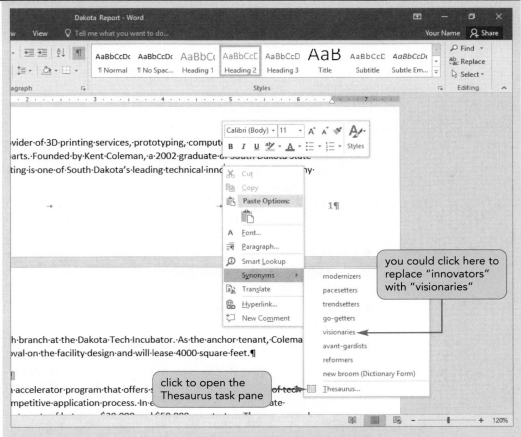

Benjamin thinks one word in the list, "visionaries," is a good replacement for "innovators." You could click "visionaries" to insert it in the document in place of "innovators," but Benjamin asks you to check the Thesaurus task pane to see if it suggests a better option.

3. At the bottom of the shortcut menu, click **Thesaurus**. The Thesaurus task pane opens on the right side of the document window, with the word "innovators" at the top and a more extensive list of synonyms below. The word "innovators" is also selected in the document, ready to be replaced. See Figure 5-6.

Figure 5-6 **Thesaurus task pane**

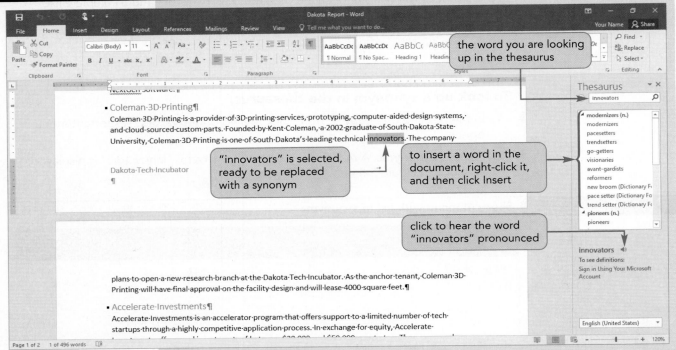

The synonym list in the task pane is organized by different shades of meaning, with words related to the idea of "modernizers" at the top of the list. You can scroll down the list to see other groups of synonyms. Below the list of synonyms, the word "innovators" appears in blue, with a speaker icon next to it. If your computer has a speaker, you can click the speaker icon to hear the word "innovators" pronounced correctly.

4. In the Thesaurus task pane, move the mouse pointer over the list of synonyms to display the scroll bar, scroll down to display other synonyms, and then scroll back up to the top of the list.

5. Point to **visionaries**. The word is highlighted in blue, and a down arrow appears to the right.

6. Click the **down arrow**. A menu opens.

   Trouble? If the Thesaurus task pane changes to display a set of synonyms for the word "visionaries," you clicked the word "visionaries" instead of just pointing at it. Click the Back button ⊙ to redisplay the synonyms for "innovators," and then begin again with Step 5.

7. Click **Insert** to replace "innovators" with "visionaries" in the document, and then close the Thesaurus task pane.

8. Save the document.

Looking Up Information in the Insight Pane

Word's Smart Lookup feature makes it easy to search the web for information about a topic in your document. To get started, select a word or phrase in your document, click the Review tab, and then click the Smart Lookup button in the Insights group. This opens the Insights task pane, with links to various sources related to your selected topic. Depending on the topic, the task pane might also display thumbnails of relevant images. Click any link or picture to display its complete web page in your browser. When you're finished, return to Word, and close the Insights task pane.

Now that the document text is finished, you can get to work on the formatting. You'll start by customizing the document theme.

Customizing the Document Theme

A document theme consists of three main components—theme colors, theme fonts, and theme effects. A specific set of colors, fonts, and effects is associated with each theme, but you can mix and match them to create a customized theme for your document. The theme fonts are the fonts used in a document's styles. You see them at the top of the font list when you click the Font arrow in the Font group on the Home tab. The theme colors are displayed in the Theme Colors section of any color gallery. The colors used to format headings, body text, and other elements are all drawn from the document's theme colors. Theme effects alter the appearance of shapes. Because they are generally very subtle, theme effects are not a theme element you will typically be concerned with.

When you change the theme colors, fonts, or effects for a document, the changes affect only that document. However, you can also save the changes you make to create a new, custom theme, which you can then use for future documents.

The Dakota Report document, which was based on the Normal template, is formatted with the Office theme—which applies a blue font color to the headings by default and formats the headings in the Calibri Light font. Benjamin wants to select different theme colors and theme fonts. He doesn't plan to include any graphics, so there's no need to customize the theme effects. You'll start with the theme colors.

Changing the Theme Colors

The theme colors, which are designed to coordinate well with each other, are used in the various document styles, including the text styles available on the Home tab. They are also used in shape styles, WordArt styles, and picture styles. So when you want to change the colors in a document, it's always better to change the theme colors rather than selecting individual elements and applying a new color to each element from a color gallery. That way you can be sure colors will be applied consistently throughout the document—for example, the headings will all be shades of the same color.

Reports created by the Sioux Falls Center for Business and Technology are typically emailed to many recipients, some of whom might choose to print the reports. To keep printing costs as low as possible for all potential readers of his report, Benjamin wants to format his document in black and white. He asks you to apply a set of theme colors consisting of black and shades of gray.

To change the theme colors in the document:

▶ **1.** Press the **Ctrl+Home** keys to display the beginning of the document.

▶ **2.** On the ribbon, click the **Design** tab.

3. In the Document Formatting group, move the mouse pointer over the **Colors** button. A ScreenTip is displayed, indicating that the current theme colors are the Office theme colors.

4. Click the **Colors** button. A gallery of theme colors opens, with the Office theme colors selected at the top of the gallery. See Figure 5-7.

Figure 5-7	Theme Colors gallery

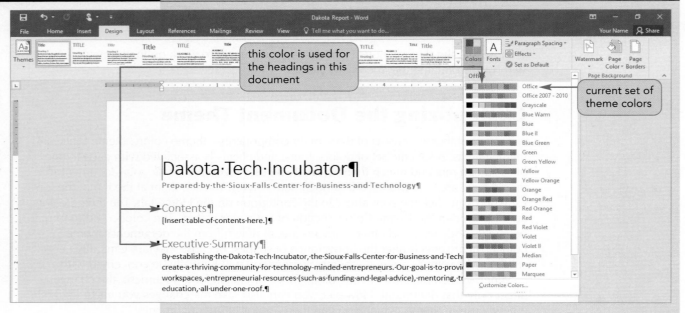

Each set of colors contains eight colors, with each assigned to specific elements. For example, the third color from the left is the color used for headings. The remaining colors are used for other types of elements, such as hyperlinks, page borders, shading, and so on.

Trouble? If you see additional theme colors at the top of the gallery under the "Custom" heading, then custom theme colors have been created and stored on your computer.

5. Move the mouse pointer over the options in the gallery to observe the Live Preview of the colors in the document.

6. Near the top of the gallery, click the **Grayscale** color set, which is the third from the top. The document headings are now formatted in gray.

7. Save the document.

The new colors you selected affect only the Dakota Report document. Your changes do not affect the Office theme that was installed with Word. Next, Benjamin asks you to customize the document theme further by changing the theme fonts.

Changing the Theme Fonts

As with theme colors, you can change the theme fonts in a document to suit your needs. Each theme uses two coordinating fonts—one for the headings and one for the body text. In some themes, the same font is used for the headings and the body text. When changing the theme fonts, you can select from all the font combinations available in any of the themes installed with Word.

To select a different set of theme fonts for the document:

1. In the Document Formatting group, move the mouse pointer over the **Fonts** button. A ScreenTip is displayed, indicating that the current fonts are Calibri Light for headings and Calibri for body text.

2. Click the **Fonts** button. The Theme Fonts gallery opens, displaying the heading and body font combinations for each theme.

3. Scroll down to review the fonts. Benjamin prefers the Franklin Gothic set of theme fonts, which includes Franklin Gothic Medium for headings and Franklin Gothic Book for the body text.

4. In the Theme Fonts gallery, point to **Franklin Gothic** to display a Live Preview in the document. See Figure 5-8.

Figure 5-8	Theme Fonts gallery

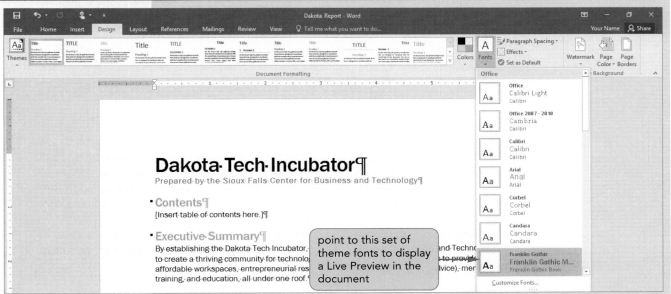

point to this set of theme fonts to display a Live Preview in the document

5. Click **Franklin Gothic**. The Theme Fonts gallery closes, and the new fonts are applied to the document.

6. Save the document.

The changes you have made to the theme fonts for the Dakota Report document do not affect the original Office theme that was installed with Word and that is available to all documents. To make your new combination of theme fonts and theme colors available to other documents, you can save it as a new, custom theme.

Creating Custom Combinations of Theme Colors and Fonts

The theme color and font combinations installed with Word were created by Microsoft designers who are experts in creating harmonious-looking documents. It's usually best to stick with these preset combinations rather than trying to create your own set. However, in some situations you might need to create a customized combination of theme colors or fonts. When you do so, that set is saved as part of Word so that you can use it in other documents.

To create a custom set of theme colors, you click the Colors button in the Document Formatting group on the Design tab and then click Customize Colors to open the Create New Theme Colors dialog box, in which you can select colors for different theme elements and enter a descriptive name for the new set of theme colors. The custom set of theme colors will be displayed as an option in the Theme Colors gallery. To delete a custom set of colors from the Theme Colors gallery, right-click the custom color set in the gallery, click Delete, and then click Yes.

To create a custom set of heading and body fonts, you click the Fonts button in the Document Formatting group on the Design tab, click Customize Fonts, select the heading and body fonts, and then enter a name for the new set of fonts in the Name box. The custom set of theme fonts is displayed as an option in the Theme Fonts gallery. To delete a custom set of fonts from the Theme Fonts gallery, right-click the custom font set in the gallery, click Delete, and then click Yes.

Saving a Custom Theme

You can save a custom theme to any folder, but when you save a custom theme to the default location—the Document Themes subfolder inside the Templates folder—it is displayed as an option in the Themes gallery. To delete a custom theme saved in the Document Themes folder, click the Themes button on the Design tab, right-click the theme, click Delete, and then click Yes.

Benjamin asks you to save his combination of theme fonts and theme colors as a new custom theme, using "SFCBT," the acronym for "Sioux Falls Center for Business and Technology," as part of the filename.

To save the new custom theme:

▶ **1.** In the Document Formatting group, click the **Themes** button, and then click **Save Current Theme**. The Save Current Theme dialog box opens. See Figure 5-9.

Figure 5-9 **Save Current Theme dialog box**

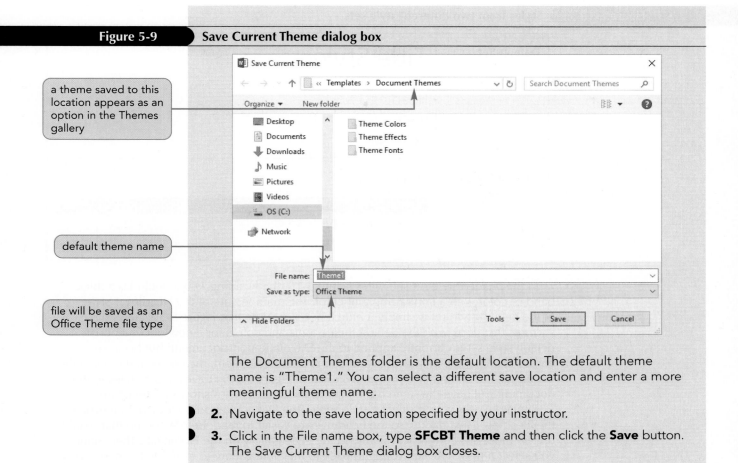

a theme saved to this location appears as an option in the Themes gallery

default theme name

file will be saved as an Office Theme file type

The Document Themes folder is the default location. The default theme name is "Theme1." You can select a different save location and enter a more meaningful theme name.

2. Navigate to the save location specified by your instructor.

3. Click in the File name box, type **SFCBT Theme** and then click the **Save** button. The Save Current Theme dialog box closes.

Benjamin plans to use the new theme to help standardize the look of all documents created in his department. When he is ready to apply it to a document, he can click the Themes button in the Document Formatting group on the Design tab, click Browse for Themes, navigate to the folder containing the custom theme, and then select the theme. If he wants to be able to access his theme from the Themes gallery instead, he will need to save it to the Document Themes folder first.

Benjamin likes the document's new look, but he wants to make some additional changes. First, he wants to select a different style set.

Selecting a Style Set

Recall that a style is a set of formatting options that you can apply to a specific text element in a document, such as a document's title, heading, or body text. So far, you have used only the default set of styles available in the Style gallery on the Home tab. You can access 16 additional style sets, or groups of styles, in the Style Set gallery, which is located in the Document Formatting group on the Design tab.

Each style set has a Normal style, a Heading 1 style, a Heading 2 style, and so on, but the formatting settings associated with each style vary from one style set to another. See Figure 5-10.

Figure 5-10	**Styles from two different style sets**

Default Set	# Title Style
	Heading 1 style
	Heading 2 style
	Normal style
Shaded Style Set	TITLE STYLE
	HEADING 1 STYLE
	HEADING 2 STYLE
	Normal style

In the Shaded style set shown in Figure 5-10, the Heading 1 style includes a thick band of color with a contrasting font color. The main feature of the Heading 1 style of the default style set is simply a blue font color. Note that Figure 5-10 shows the styles as they look with the default theme fonts and colors for a new document. The default style set is currently applied to the Dakota Report document; but because you've changed the theme fonts and colors in the document, the colors and fonts in the document are different from what is shown in Figure 5-10. However, the styles in the document still have the same basic look as the default styles shown in the figure.

Benjamin asks you to select a style set for the Dakota Report document that makes the Heading 1 text darker, so the headings are easier to read. Before you do that, you'll review the styles currently available in the Style gallery on the Home tab. Then, after you select a new style set, you'll go back to the Style gallery to examine the new styles.

To review the styles in the Style gallery and select a new style set for the document:

▶ **1.** On the ribbon, click the **Home** tab.

▶ **2.** In the Styles group, click the **More** button, and then review the set of styles currently available in the Style gallery. Note that the icon for the Heading 1 style indicates that it applies a light gray font color.

▶ **3.** On the ribbon, click the **Design** tab.

▶ **4.** In the Document Formatting group, click the **More** button to open the Style Set gallery. Move the mouse pointer across the icons in the gallery to display their ScreenTips and to observe the Live Previews in the document.

▶ **5.** Point to the **Lines (Stylish)** style set, which is on the far-right side of the top row. In the Lines (Stylish) style set, the Heading 1 style applies a black font color, with a light gray line that spans the width of the document. See Figure 5-11.

| Figure 5-11 | Live Preview of the Lines (Stylish) style set |

Notice that the theme fonts you specified earlier—Franklin Gothic Medium for headings and Franklin Gothic Book for body text—are still applied, as are the Grayscale theme colors.

6. Click the **Lines (Stylish)** style set. The styles in the document change to reflect the styles in the Lines (Stylish) style set. You can verify this by looking at the Style gallery on the Home tab.

7. On the ribbon, click the **Home** tab.

8. In the Styles group, click the **More** button to review the styles available in the Style gallery. The icon for the Heading 1 style indicates that it now applies a black font color. The style also applies a light gray underline, although that is not visible in the Style gallery icon.

9. Click anywhere in the document to close the Style gallery, and then save the document.

INSIGHT

The Set as Default Button: A Note of Caution

The Set as Default button in the Document Formatting group on the Design tab saves the document's current formatting settings as the default for any new blank documents you create in Word. In other words, it saves the current formatting settings to the Normal template. You might find this a tempting option, but, as you will learn in Session 5.2, when working with styles, modifying the Normal template is almost never a good idea. Instead, a better option is to save a document with the formatting you like as a new template, which you can then use as the basis for future documents. Exercise similar caution with the Set as Default button in the Font dialog box, which allows you to change the default font for the Normal template.

Customizing Styles

The ability to select a new style set gives you a lot of flexibility when formatting a document. However, sometimes you will want to customize an individual style to better suit your needs. To do so, you can modify the style or you can update it. When you modify a style, you open the Modify Style dialog box, where you select formatting attributes to add to the style. When you update a style, you select text in the document that is already formatted with the style, apply new formatting to the text, and then update the style to incorporate the new formatting. Updating a style is usually the better choice because it allows you to see the results of your formatting choices in the document, before you change the style itself.

Benjamin asks you to update the Heading 1 style for the report by expanding the character spacing and applying italic formatting. You will begin by applying these changes to a paragraph that is currently formatted with the Heading 1 style. Then you can update the Heading 1 style to match the new formatting. As a result, all the paragraphs formatted with the Heading 1 style will be updated to incorporate expanded character spacing and italic formatting.

Changing Character Spacing

The term **character spacing** refers to the space between individual characters. To add emphasis to text, you can expand or contract the spacing between characters. As with line and paragraph spacing, space between characters is measured in points, with one point equal to 1/72 of an inch. To adjust character spacing for selected text, click the Dialog Box Launcher in the Font group on the Home tab, and then click the Advanced tab in the Font dialog box. Of the numerous settings available on this tab, you'll find two especially useful.

First, the Spacing box allows you to choose Normal spacing (which is the default character spacing for the Normal style), Expanded spacing (with the characters farther apart than with the Normal setting), and Condensed spacing (with the characters closer together than with the Normal setting). With both Expanded and Condensed spacing, you can specify the number of points between characters.

Second, the Kerning for fonts check box allows you to adjust the spacing between characters to make them look like they are spaced evenly. Kerning is helpful when you are working with large font sizes, which can sometimes cause evenly spaced characters to appear unevenly spaced. Selecting the Kerning for fonts check box ensures that the spacing is adjusted automatically.

To add expanded character spacing and italic formatting to a paragraph formatted with the Heading 1 style:

1. In the document, scroll down if necessary, and select the **Executive Summary** heading, which is formatted with the Heading 1 style.

2. Make sure the Home tab is selected on the ribbon.

3. In the Font group, click the **Dialog Box Launcher**. The Font dialog box opens.

4. Click the **Advanced** tab. The Character Spacing settings at the top of this tab reflect the style settings for the currently selected text. The Spacing box is set to Normal. The more advanced options, located in the OpenType Features section, allow you to fine-tune the appearance of characters.

5. Click the **Spacing** arrow, and then click **Expanded**. See Figure 5-12.

Figure 5-12   **Changing character spacing in the Font dialog box**

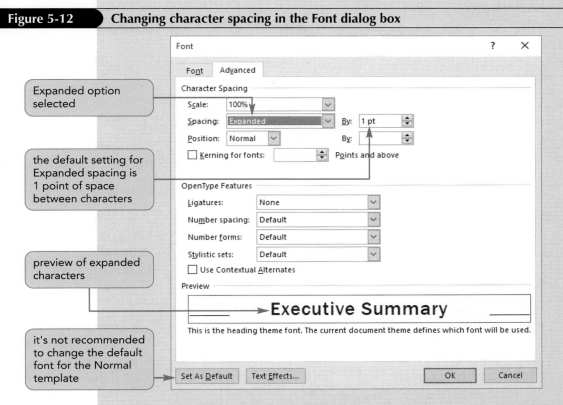

Expanded option selected

the default setting for Expanded spacing is 1 point of space between characters

preview of expanded characters

it's not recommended to change the default font for the Normal template

The By box next to the Spacing box indicates that each character is separated from the other by 1 point of space. You could increase the point setting; but in the current document, 1 point is fine. The Preview section shows a sample of the expanded character spacing.

Next, you need to apply italic formatting, which you could do from the Font group on the Home tab. But since you have the Font dialog box open, you'll do it from the Font tab in the Font dialog box instead.

6. In the Font dialog box, click the **Font** tab.

Here you can apply most of the settings available in the Font group on the Home tab and a few that are not available in the Font group—such as colored underlines and **small caps** (smaller versions of uppercase letters). You can also hide text from view by selecting the Hidden check box.

7. In the Font style box, click **Italic**. The Preview section of the Font tab shows a preview of the italic formatting applied to the "Executive Summary" heading. See Figure 5-13.

TIP

Text formatted as hidden is visible only when nonprinting characters are displayed.

Figure 5-13   **Applying italic formatting to text using the Font dialog box**

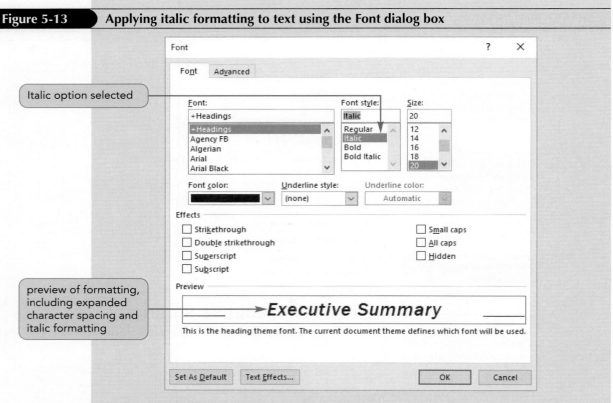

Italic option selected

preview of formatting, including expanded character spacing and italic formatting

The other font attributes associated with the Heading 1 style are also visible on the Font tab.

8. Click the **OK** button to close the Font dialog box. The selected heading is now italicized, with the individual characters spread slightly farther apart.

9. Click anywhere in the "Executive Summary" heading to deselect the text, and then save the document.

Now that the selected heading is formatted the way you want, you can update the Heading 1 style to match it. When working with styles, it's helpful to open the Styles pane to see more information about the styles in the current style set, so you'll do that next.

Displaying the Styles Pane

The Styles pane shows you more styles than are displayed in the Style gallery. You can click a style in the Styles pane to apply it to selected text, just as you would click a style in the Style gallery.

The Styles pane provides detailed information about each style. In particular, it differentiates between character styles, paragraph styles, and linked styles. A **character style** contains formatting options that affect the appearance of individual characters, such as font style, font color, font size, bold, italic, and underline. When you click a character style, it formats the word that contains the insertion point or, if text is selected in the document, any selected characters.

A **paragraph style** contains all the character formatting options as well as formatting options that affect the paragraph's appearance—including line spacing, text alignment, tab stops, and borders. When you click a paragraph style, it formats the entire paragraph that contains the insertion point, or, if text is selected in the document, it formats all selected paragraphs (even paragraphs in which just one character is selected).

A **linked style** contains both character and paragraph formatting options. If you click in a paragraph or select a paragraph and then apply a linked style, both the paragraph styles and character styles are applied to the entire paragraph. If you apply a linked style to a selected word or group of words rather than to an entire paragraph, only the character styles for that linked style are applied to the selected text; the paragraph styles are not applied to the paragraph itself. All of the heading styles in Word are linked styles.

To open the Styles pane to review information about the styles in the current style set:

1. Make sure the Home tab is selected on the ribbon.

2. In the Styles group, click the **Dialog Box Launcher**. The Styles pane opens on the right side of the document window. See Figure 5-14.

Figure 5-14	Styles pane

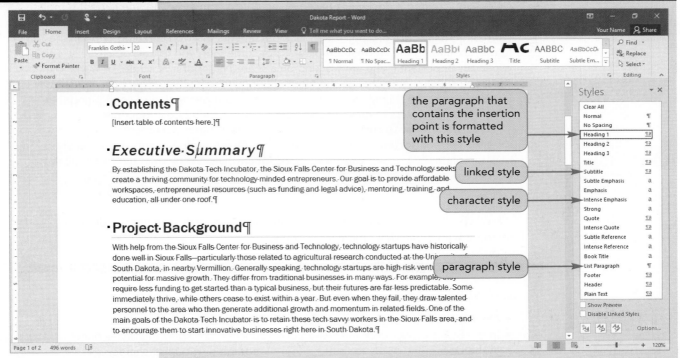

The outline around the Heading 1 style indicates that the insertion point is currently located in a paragraph formatted with that style. A paragraph symbol to the right of a style name indicates a paragraph style, a lowercase letter "a" indicates a character style, and a combination of both indicates a linked style. You can display even more information about a style by moving the mouse pointer over the style name in the Styles pane.

3. In the Styles pane, move the mouse pointer over **Heading 1**. An arrow is displayed to the right of the Heading 1 style name, and a ScreenTip with detailed information about the Heading 1 style opens below the style name.

The information in the ScreenTip relates only to the formatting applied by default with the Heading 1 style; it makes no mention of italic formatting or expanded character spacing. Although you applied these formatting changes to the "Executive Summary" heading, they are not yet part of the Heading 1 style.

TIP

If the Styles pane is floating over the top of the document window, you can double-click the pane's title bar to dock it on the right side of the document window.

You'll incorporate the new formatting into the Heading 1 style in the next section, when you update the style.

Updating a Style

Word is set up to save all customized styles to the current document by default. In fact, when you update a style, you don't even have a choice about where to save it—the updated style is automatically saved to the current document, rather than to the current template. If for some reason you needed to save a customized style to the current template instead, you would need to modify the style using the Modify Style dialog box, where you could then select the New documents based on this template button to save the modified style to the current template.

Preserving the Normal Template

Unless you created a document based on an <u>Office.com</u> template, the current template for any document is probably the Normal template. Any changes you make to the Normal template will affect all new, blank documents that you create in Word in the future, so altering the Normal template is not something you should do casually. This is especially important if you are working on a shared computer at school or work. In that case, you should never change the Normal template unless you have been specifically instructed to do so. Many organizations even take the precaution of configuring their networked computers to make changing the Normal template impossible.

If you want to make customized styles available in other documents, you can always save the current document as a new template. All future documents based on your new template will contain your new styles. Meanwhile, the Normal template will remain unaffected by the new styles.

Next, you'll use the Styles pane to update the Heading 1 style to include italic formatting with expanded character spacing.

Updating a Style

- On the ribbon, click the Home tab.
- In the Styles group, click the Dialog Box Launcher to display the Styles pane.
- In the document, apply formatting to a paragraph or group of characters.
- Click in the formatted paragraph (if you are updating a paragraph or linked style) or in the formatted group of characters (if you are updating a character style).
- In the Styles pane, right-click the style you want to update to display a shortcut menu.
- Click Update Style to Match Selection (where Style is the name of the style you want to update).

To update the Heading 1 style:

The insertion point must be located in the "Executive Summary" heading to ensure that you update the Heading 1 style with the correct formatting.

1. In the document, make sure the insertion point is located in the paragraph containing the "Executive Summary" heading, which is formatted with the Heading 1 style.

2. In the Styles pane, right-click **Heading 1**. A menu opens with options related to working with the Heading 1 style. See Figure 5-15.

Figure 5-15   Heading 1 style menu

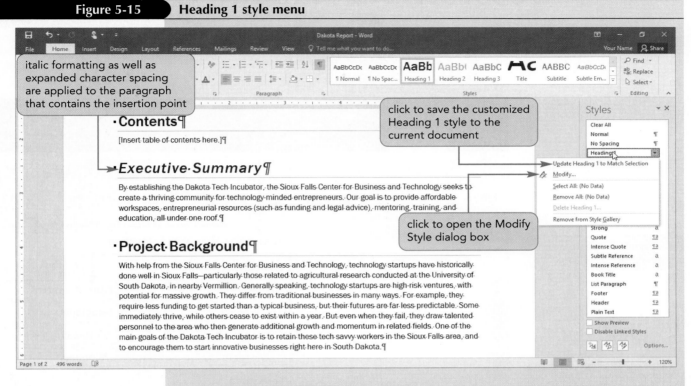

3. Click **Update Heading 1 to Match Selection**. The Heading 1 style is updated to reflect the changes you made to the "Executive Summary" heading. As a result, all the headings in the document formatted in the Heading 1 style now have italic formatting with expanded character spacing.

4. Save the document. The updated Heading 1 style is saved along with the document. No other documents are affected by this change to the Heading 1 style.

You can also use the Styles pane to create a new style for a document. You will do that in the next session.

Session 5.1 Quick Check

REVIEW

1. What is a template?

2. Suppose you want to move through a document one graphic at a time. Should you use the Navigation pane or the Go To tab in the Find and Replace dialog box?

3. Explain how to change a document's theme colors.

4. Explain how to select a new style set.

5. Suppose you create a new, blank document by clicking Blank document on the New screen in Backstage view. What is the name of the document's template?

6. What is the difference between a character style and a paragraph style?

Session 5.2 Visual Overview:

You use the options in the Create New Style from Formatting dialog box to create a new style based on the formatting applied to selected text.

By default, each new style is based on the style originally applied to the selected text.

You should give your new style a descriptive name.

You can use these options to add additional formatting to the new style.

The new style will consist of all the formatting applied to the selected text, such as an orange font color and italic formatting.

Clicking the Format button gives you access to more formatting options, including paragraph spacing and border options.

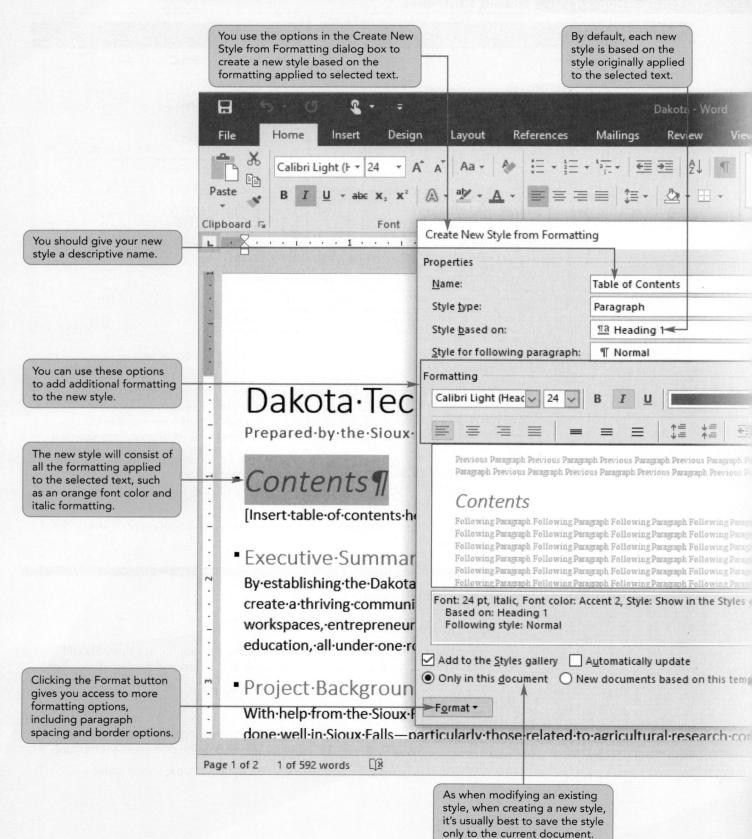

As when modifying an existing style, when creating a new style, it's usually best to save the style only to the current document.

Creating a New Style

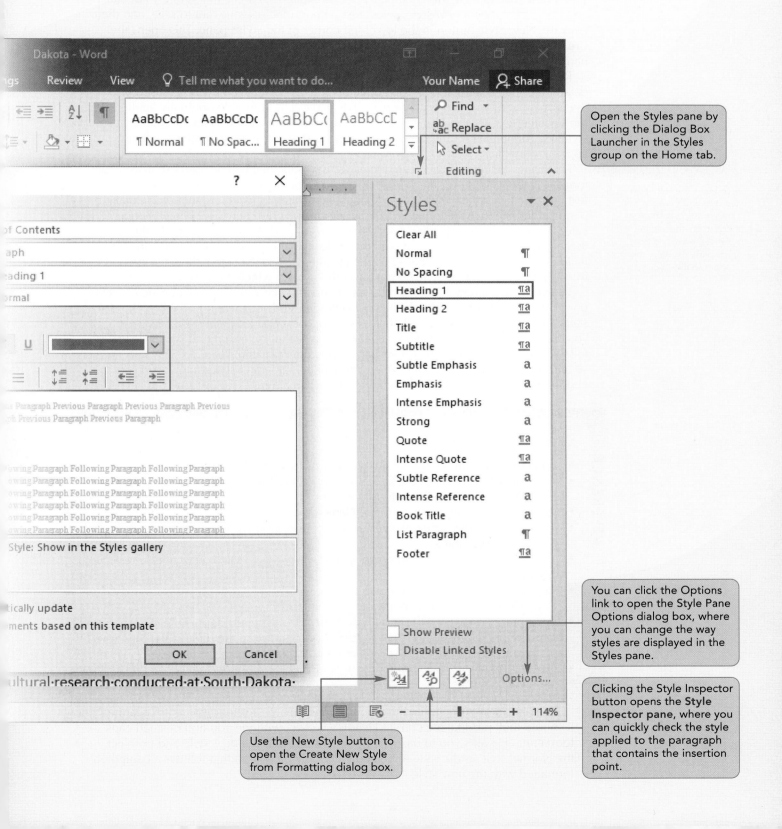

Open the Styles pane by clicking the Dialog Box Launcher in the Styles group on the Home tab.

You can click the Options link to open the Style Pane Options dialog box, where you can change the way styles are displayed in the Styles pane.

Clicking the Style Inspector button opens the **Style Inspector** pane, where you can quickly check the style applied to the paragraph that contains the insertion point.

Use the New Style button to open the Create New Style from Formatting dialog box.

Creating a New Style

Creating a new style is similar to updating a style, except that instead of updating an existing style to match the formatting of selected text, you save the text's formatting as a new style. By default a new style is saved to the current document. You can choose to save a new style to the current template, but, as explained earlier, that is rarely advisable.

To begin creating a new style, select text with formatting you want to save, and then click the New Style button in the lower-left corner of the Styles pane. This opens the Create New Style from Formatting dialog box, where you can assign the new style a name and adjust other settings.

Remember that all text in your document has a style applied to it, whether it is the default Normal style or a style you applied. When you create a new style based on the formatting of selected text, the new style is based on the style originally applied to the selected text. That means the new style retains a connection to the original style, so that if you make modifications to the original style, these modifications will also be applied to the new style.

For example, suppose you need to create a new style that will be used exclusively for formatting the heading "Budget" in all upcoming reports. You could start by selecting text formatted with the Heading 1 style, then change the font color of the selected text to purple, and then save the formatting of the selected text as a new style named "Budget." Later, if you update the Heading 1 style—perhaps by adding italic formatting—the text in the document that is formatted with the Budget style will also be updated to include italic formatting because it is based on the Heading 1 style. Note that the opposite is not true—changes to the new style do not affect the style on which it is based.

When creating a new style, you must also consider what will happen when the insertion point is in a paragraph formatted with your new style, and you then press the Enter key to start a new paragraph. Typically, that new paragraph is formatted in the Normal style, but you can choose a different style if you prefer. You make this selection using the Style for following paragraph box in the Create New Style from Formatting dialog box.

In most cases, any new styles you create will be paragraph styles. However, you can choose to make your new style a linked style or a character style instead.

REFERENCE

Creating a New Style

- Select the text with the formatting you want to save as a new style.
- In the lower-left corner of the Styles pane, click the New Style button to open the Create New Style from Formatting dialog box.
- Type a name for the new style in the Name box.
- Make sure the Style type box contains the correct style type. In most cases, Paragraph style is the best choice.
- Verify that the Style based on box displays the style on which you want to base your new style.
- Click the Style for following paragraph arrow, and then click the style you want to use. Normal is usually the best choice.
- To save the new style to the current document, verify that the Only in this document option button is selected; or to save the style to the current template, click the New documents based on this template option button.
- Click the OK button.

Benjamin wants you to create a new paragraph style for the "Contents" heading. It should look just like the current Heading 1 style, with the addition of small caps formatting. He asks you to base the new style on the Heading 1 style and to select the Normal style as the style to be applied to any paragraph that follows a paragraph formatted with the new style.

To format the "Contents" heading in small caps:

1. If you took a break after the last session, make sure the Dakota Report document is open in Print Layout view with the nonprinting characters and the ruler displayed. Confirm that the document Zoom level is set at 120% and that the Styles pane is docked on the right side of the document window.

2. Make sure the Home tab is selected on the ribbon.

3. In the document, select the **Contents** heading.

4. In the Font group, click the **Dialog Box Launcher**, and then, in the Font dialog box, click the **Font** tab, if necessary.

5. In the Effects section, click the **Small caps** check box to select it. See Figure 5-16.

Figure 5-16	Formatting the "Contents" heading

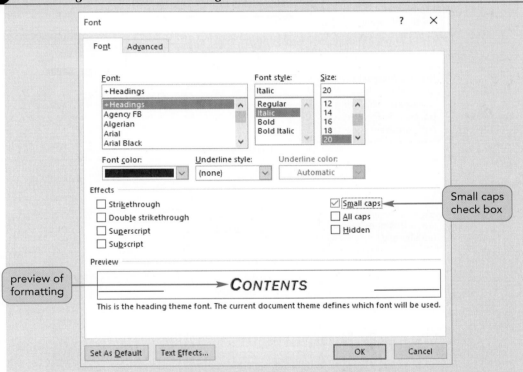

6. Click the **OK** button. The Font dialog box closes, and the "Contents" heading is formatted in small caps.

Now that the text is formatted the way you want, you can save its formatting as a new style.

To save the formatting of the "Contents" heading as a new style:

1. Verify that the "Contents" heading is still selected.

2. In the lower-left corner of the Styles pane, click the **New Style** button . The Create New Style from Formatting dialog box opens. A default name for the new style, "Style1," is selected in the Name box. The name "Style1" is also displayed in the Style for following paragraph box.

3. Type **Contents** to replace the default style name with the new one. The Style type box contains Paragraph by default, which is the type of style you want to create. The Style based on box indicates that the new Contents style is based on the Heading 1 style, which is also what you want. Notice that the Style for following paragraph box is now blank. You need to select the Normal style.

4. Click the **Style for following paragraph** arrow, and then click **Normal**. See Figure 5-17.

Figure 5-17   **Creating a new style**

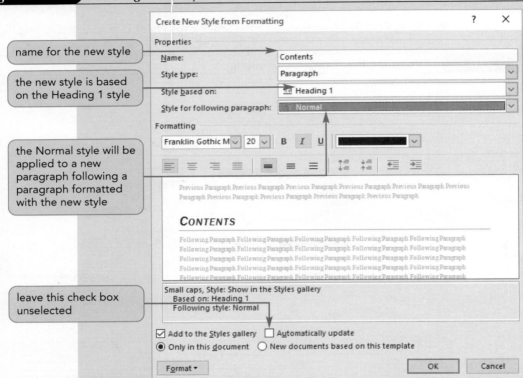

name for the new style

the new style is based on the Heading 1 style

the Normal style will be applied to a new paragraph following a paragraph formatted with the new style

leave this check box unselected

5. In the lower-left corner of the dialog box, verify that the Only in this document button is selected.

   Note that, by default, the Automatically update check box is not selected. As a general rule, you should not select this check box because it can produce unpredictable results in future documents based on the same template.

   If you plan to use a new style frequently, it's helpful to assign a keyboard shortcut to it. Then you can apply the style to selected text simply by pressing the keyboard shortcut.

TIP

To assign a keyboard shortcut to an existing style, right-click the style in the Styles pane, click Modify, click the Format button, and then click Shortcut key.

6. In the lower-left corner of the Create New Style from Formatting dialog box, click the **Format** button, and then click **Shortcut key** to open the Customize Keyboard dialog box. If you wanted to assign a keyboard shortcut to the Contents style, you would click in the Press new shortcut key box, press a combination of keys not assigned to any other function, and then click the Assign button. For now, you can close the Customize Keyboard dialog box without making any changes.

7. Click the **Close** button. You return to the Create New Style from Formatting dialog box.

8. Click the **OK** button. The Create New Style from Formatting dialog box closes. The new Contents style is added to the Style gallery and to the Styles pane. See Figure 5-18.

Figure 5-18   Contents style added to Style gallery and Styles pane

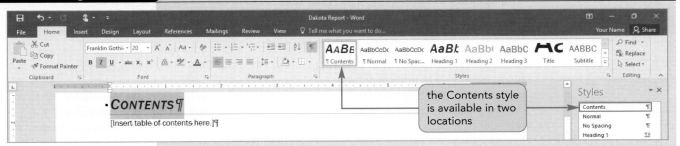

After you update a style or create a new one, you can create a custom style set that contains the new or updated style.

9. On the ribbon, click the **Design** tab.

10. In the Document Formatting group, click the **More** button, and then click **Save as a New Style Set**. The Save as a New Style Set dialog box opens, with the QuickStyles folder selected as the save location by default. Only style sets saved to the QuickStyles folder will appear in the Style Set gallery.

In this case, you don't actually want to create a new style set, so you can close the Save as a New Style Set dialog box.

11. Click the **Cancel** button, and then save the document.

INSIGHT

Managing Your Styles

If you create a lot of styles, the Style gallery can quickly become overcrowded. To remove a style from the Style gallery without deleting the style itself, right-click the style in the Style gallery, and then click Remove from Style Gallery.

To delete a style entirely, open the Styles pane, and then right-click the style. What happens next depends on the type of style you are trying to delete. If the style was based on the Normal style, you can click Delete *Style* (where *Style* is the name of the style you want to delete), and then click Yes. If the style was based on any other style, you can click Revert to *Style* (where *Style* is the style that the style you want to delete was based on), and then click Yes.

If you create a new style and then paste text formatted with your style in a different document, your new style will be displayed in that document's Style gallery and Styles pane. This means that a document containing text imported from multiple documents can end up with a lot of different styles. In that case, you'll probably reformat the document to use only a few styles of your choosing. But what do you do about the remaining, unused styles? You could delete them, but that can be time-consuming. It's sometimes easier to hide the styles that are not currently in use in the document. At the bottom of the Styles pane, click the Options link to open the Style Pane Options dialog box, click the Select styles to show arrow, and then click In current document.

The styles used in the Dakota Report document are relatively simple. However, in a long document with many styles, it's easy to lose track of the style applied to each paragraph and the formatting associated with each style. In that case, it's important to know how to display additional information about the document's formatting.

Displaying Information About Styles and Formatting

When you need to learn more about a document's formatting—perhaps because you're revising a document created by someone else—you should start by opening the Styles pane. To quickly determine which style is applied to a paragraph, you can click a paragraph (or select it) and then look to see which style is selected in the Styles pane. To display a brief description of the formatting associated with that style, you can point to the selected style in the Styles pane. However, if you need to check numerous paragraphs in a long document, it's easier to use the Style Inspector pane, which remains open while you scroll through the document and displays only the style for the paragraph that currently contains the insertion point. To see a complete list of all the formatting applied to a paragraph, you can use the **Reveal Formatting pane**. Within the Reveal Formatting pane, you can also choose to compare the formatting applied to two different paragraphs.

Inspecting Styles

You can use the Style Inspector to examine the styles attached to each of the paragraphs in a document. When you are using the Style Inspector, it's also helpful to display the Home tab on the ribbon so the Style gallery is visible.

To use the Style Inspector pane to examine the styles in the document:

1. On the ribbon, click the **Home** tab.

2. On page 1, click anywhere in the **[Insert table of contents here.]** paragraph. The Normal style is selected in both the Style gallery and the Styles pane, indicating that the paragraph is formatted with the Normal style.

3. At the bottom of the Styles pane, click the **Style Inspector** button. The Style Inspector pane opens and is positioned next to the Styles pane. See Figure 5-19.

Figure 5-19   Style Inspector pane

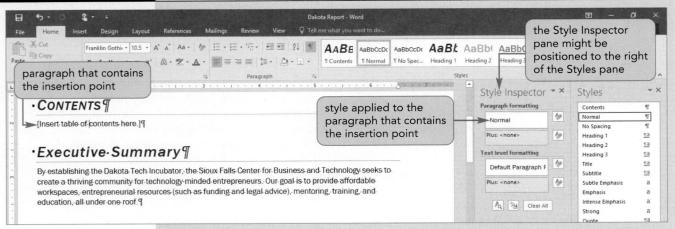

> **Trouble?** If the Style Inspector pane on your computer is floating over the top of the document window, drag it to position it the left of the Styles pane, and then double-click the pane's title bar to dock the Style Inspector pane next to the Styles pane.

In the Style Inspector pane, the top box under "Paragraph formatting" displays the name of the style applied to the paragraph that currently contains the insertion point.

▶ 4. Press the **Ctrl+↓** keys. The insertion point moves down to the next paragraph, which contains the "Executive Summary" heading. The Style Inspector pane tells you that this paragraph is formatted with the Heading 1 style.

▶ 5. Press the **Ctrl+↓** keys as necessary to move the insertion point down through the paragraphs of the document, observing the style names displayed in the Style Inspector pane as well as the styles selected in the Styles pane. Note that the bulleted paragraphs below the "Dakota Tech Incubator Board of Directors" heading are formatted with the List Paragraph style. This style is applied automatically when you format paragraphs using the Bullets button in the Paragraph group on the Home tab.

▶ 6. Scroll up, and select the paragraph **[Insert table of contents here.]**.

INSIGHT

Finding Styles

Suppose you want to find all the paragraphs in a document formatted with a specific style. One option is to right-click the style in the Styles pane, and then click Select All *Number* Instances, where *Number* is the number of paragraphs in the document formatted with the style.

Another way to find paragraphs formatted with a particular style is by using the Find tab in the Find and Replace dialog box. If necessary, click the More button to display the Format button in the lower-left corner of the Find tab. Click the Format button, click Style, select the style you want in the Find Style dialog box, and then click the OK button. If you want to find specific text formatted with the style you selected, you can type the text in the Find what box on the Find tab, and then click Find Next to find the first instance. If, instead, you want to find any paragraph formatted with the style, leave the Find what box blank.

You can also use the Find and Replace dialog box to find paragraphs formatted with one style and then apply a different style to those paragraphs. On the Replace tab, click in the Find what box and use the Format button to select the style you want to find. Then, click in the Replace with box and use the Format button to select the style you want to use as a replacement. Click Find Next to find the first instance of the style, and then click Replace to apply the replacement style. As you've probably guessed, you can also type text in the Find what and Replace with boxes to find text formatted with a specific style and replace it with text formatted in a different style.

Next, Benjamin wants you to use the Reveal Formatting panes to learn more about the formatting applied by the Normal and Heading 2 styles.

Examining and Comparing Formatting in the Reveal Formatting Pane

You access the Reveal Formatting pane by clicking a button in the Style Inspector pane. Because the Reveal Formatting pane describes only formatting details without mentioning styles, it's helpful to keep the Style Inspector pane open while you use the Reveal Formatting pane.

To examine formatting details using the Reveal Formatting pane:

1. At the bottom of the Style Inspector pane, click the **Reveal Formatting** button. The Reveal Formatting pane opens, displaying detailed information about the formatting applied to the selected paragraph. It is positioned to the right of the Styles pane in Figure 5-20, but on your computer it might be to the left of the Styles pane or to the left of the Style Inspector.

Figure 5-20   **Displaying formatting details in the Reveal Formatting pane**

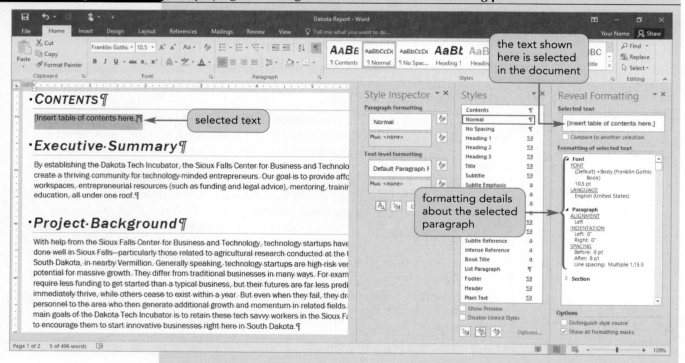

Trouble? If the Reveal Formatting pane on your computer is floating over the top of the document window, double-click the pane's title bar to dock the Reveal Formatting pane next to the other two task panes.

The Formatting of selected text box displays information about the formatting applied to the paragraph that contains the insertion point. Note that this information includes no mention of the style used to apply this formatting, but you can still see the style's name, Normal, displayed in the Style Inspector pane.

Now that you have the Reveal Formatting pane open, you can use it to compare one paragraph's formatting to another's. Benjamin asks you to compare text formatted with the Normal style to text formatted with the Heading 2 style.

To compare the formatting of one paragraph to another:

1. In the Reveal Formatting pane, click the **Compare to another selection** check box to select it. The options in the Reveal Formatting pane change to allow you to compare the formatting of one paragraph to that of another. Under Selected text, both text boxes display the selected text, "[Insert table of contents here.]" This tells you that, currently, the formatting applied to the selected text is being compared to itself.

   Now you'll compare this paragraph to one formatted with the Heading 2 style.

2. In the document, scroll down to page 2 and select the heading text **Coleman 3D Printing**, which is formatted with the Heading 2 style. The text "Coleman 3D Printing" is displayed in the Reveal Formatting pane, in the text box below "[Insert table of contents here.]" The Formatting differences section displays information about the formatting applied to the two different paragraphs. See Figure 5-21.

Figure 5-21	Comparing one paragraph's formatting with another's

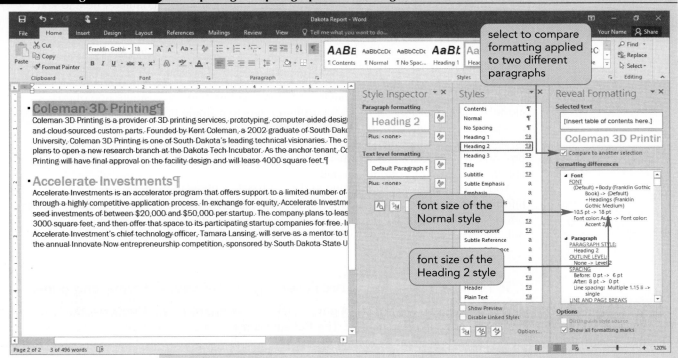

TIP

Text formatted in a white font is not visible in the text boxes at the top of the Reveal Formatting pane. To use the Reveal Formatting pane with white text, temporarily format it in black.

The information in the Reveal Formatting pane is very detailed. But, generally, if you see two settings separated by a hyphen and a greater than symbol, the item on the right relates to the text in the bottom box. For example, in the Font section, you see "10.5 pt -> 18 pt." This tells you that the text in the top text box, "[Insert table of contents here.]," is formatted in a 10.5-point font, whereas the text in the bottom text box, "Coleman 3D Printing," is formatted in an 18-point font.

The Paragraph section of the Reveal Formatting pane provides some information about two important default settings included with all of Word's heading styles—line and page break settings.

Reviewing Line and Page Break Settings

By default, all of Word's heading styles are set up to ensure that a heading is never separated from the paragraph that follows it. For example, suppose you have a one-page document that includes a heading with a single paragraph of body text after it. Then suppose you add text before the heading that causes the heading and its paragraph of body text to flow down the page so that, ultimately, the entire paragraph of body text moves to page 2. Even if there is room for the heading at the bottom of page 1, it will move to page 2, along with its paragraph of body text. The setting that controls this is the **Keep with next** check box on the Line and Page Breaks tab in the Paragraph dialog box. By default, the Keep with next check box is selected for all headings.

A related setting on the same tab is the **Keep lines together** check box, which is also selected by default for all headings. This setting ensures that if a paragraph consists of more than one line of text, the lines of the paragraph will never be separated by a page break. This means that if one line of a paragraph moves from page 1 to page 2, all lines of the paragraph will move to page 2.

A nonprinting character in the shape of a small black square is displayed next to any paragraph for which either the Keep lines together setting or the Keep with next setting is selected. Because both settings are selected by default for all the heading styles (Heading 1 through Heading 9), you always see this nonprinting character next to text formatted with a heading style. By default, the Keep lines together setting and the Keep with next setting are deselected for all other styles. However, if you have a paragraph of body text that you want to prevent from breaking across two pages, you could apply the Keep lines together setting to that paragraph.

One helpful setting related to line and page breaks—Widow/Orphan control—is selected by default for all Word styles. The term **widow** refers to a single line of text alone at the top of a page. The term **orphan** refers to a single line of text at the bottom of a page. When selected, the **Widow/Orphan control** check box, which is also found on the Line and Page Breaks tab of the Paragraph dialog box, ensures that widows and orphans never occur in a document. Instead, at least two lines of a paragraph will appear at the top or bottom of a page.

You can see evidence of the line and page break settings in the formatting information displayed in the Reveal Formatting pane. Benjamin asks you to check these settings for the Dakota Report document. You'll start by displaying information about only the paragraph formatted with the Heading 2 style.

To review line and page break settings in the Reveal Formatting pane:

▶ **1.** In the Reveal Formatting pane, click the **Compare to another selection** check box to deselect it. The Reveal Formatting pane changes to display information only about the formatting applied to the text "Coleman 3D Printing," which is currently selected in the document.

The Style Inspector pane tells you that "Coleman 3D Printing" is formatted with the Heading 2 style, so all the information in the Reveal Formatting pane describes the Heading 2 style.

▶ **2.** In the Formatting of selected text box, scroll down to display the entire Paragraph section.

▶ **3.** Review the information below the blue heading "LINE AND PAGE BREAKS." The text "Keep with next" and "Keep lines together" tells you that these two settings are active for the selected text. The blue headings in the Reveal Formatting pane are actually links that open a dialog box with the relevant formatting settings.

4. In the Formatting of selected text box, click **LINE AND PAGE BREAKS**. The Paragraph dialog box opens, with the Line and Page Breaks tab displayed. See Figure 5-22.

Figure 5-22 **Line and Page Breaks tab in the Paragraph dialog box**

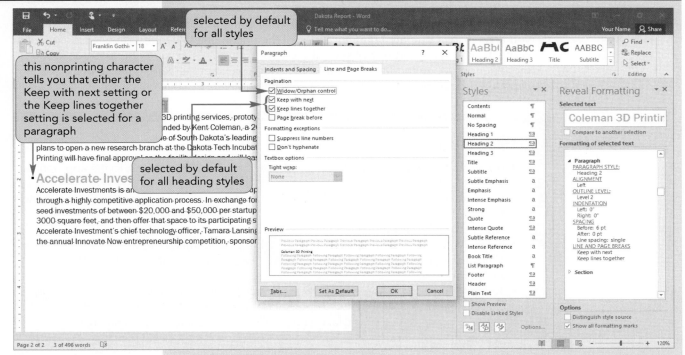

The settings on the tab are the settings for the selected paragraph, which is formatted with the Heading 2 style. The Widow/Orphan control, Keep with next, and Keep lines together check boxes are all selected, as you would expect for a heading style.

You are finished reviewing formatting information, so you can close the Paragraph dialog box and the Reveal Formatting pane.

5. In the Paragraph dialog box, click the **Cancel** button; and then, in the Reveal Formatting pane, click the **Close** button ☒.

6. In the Style Inspector pane, click the **Close** button ☒; and then, in the Styles pane, click the **Close** button ☒.

7. Click anywhere in the document to deselect the "Colman 3D Printing" heading.

You are almost finished working on the Dakota Report document. Your next task is to add a table of contents.

Generating a Table of Contents

TIP

To delete a table of contents, click the Table of Contents button, and then click Remove Table of Contents.

You can use the Table of Contents button in the Table of Contents group on the References tab to generate a table of contents that includes any text to which you have applied heading styles. A **table of contents** is essentially an outline of the document. By default, in a table of contents, Heading 1 text is aligned on the left, Heading 2 text is indented slightly to the right below the Heading 1 text, Heading 3 text is indented slightly to the right below the Heading 2 text, and so on.

The page numbers and headings in a table of contents in Word are hyperlinks that you can click to jump to a particular part of the document. When inserting a table of contents, you can insert one of several predesigned formats. If you prefer to select from more options, open the Table of Contents dialog box where, among other settings, you can adjust the level assigned to each style within the table of contents.

REFERENCE

Generating a Table of Contents

- Apply heading styles, such as Heading 1, Heading 2, and Heading 3, to the appropriate text in the document.
- Move the insertion point to the location in the document where you want to insert the table of contents.
- On the ribbon, click the References tab.
- In the Table of Contents group, click the Table of Contents button.
- To insert a predesigned table of contents, click one of the Built-In styles in the Table of Contents menu.
- To open a dialog box where you can choose from a variety of table of contents settings, click Custom Table of Contents to open the Table of Contents dialog box. Click the Formats arrow and select a style, change the Show levels setting to the number of heading levels you want to include in the table of contents, verify that the Show page numbers check box is selected, and then click the OK button.

The current draft of Benjamin's report is fairly short, but the final document will be much longer. He asks you to create a table of contents for the report now, just after the "Contents" heading. Then, as Benjamin adds sections to the report, he can update the table of contents.

To insert a table of contents into the document:

1. Scroll up to display the "Contents" heading on page 1.

2. Below the heading, delete the placeholder text **[Insert table of contents here.]**. Do not delete the paragraph mark after the placeholder text. Your insertion point should now be located in the blank paragraph between the "Contents" heading and the "Executive Summary" heading.

3. On the ribbon, click the **References** tab.

4. In the Table of Contents group, click the **Table of Contents** button. The Table of Contents menu opens, displaying a gallery of table of contents formats. See Figure 5-23.

Figure 5-23   Table of Contents menu

options for generating a table of contents made up of the document headings

option for generating a table of contents with placeholder text

click to open a dialog box where you can adjust the table of contents settings

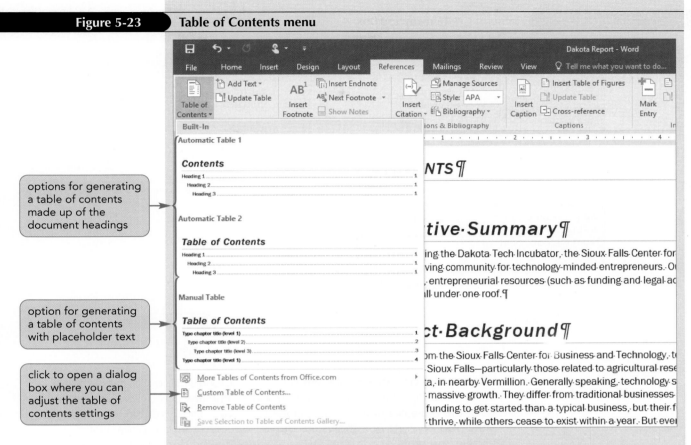

The Automatic Table 1 and Automatic Table 2 options each insert a table of contents made up of the first three levels of document headings in a predefined format. Each of the Automatic options also includes a heading for the table of contents. Because Benjamin's document already contains the heading "Contents," you do not want to use either of these options.

The Manual option is useful only in specialized situations, when you need to type the table of contents yourself—for example, when creating a book manuscript for an academic publisher that requires a specialized format.

You'll use the Custom Table of Contents command to open the Table of Contents dialog box.

5. Below the Table of Contents gallery, click **Custom Table of Contents**. The Table of Contents dialog box opens, with the Table of Contents tab displayed. See Figure 5-24.

Figure 5-24 Table of Contents dialog box

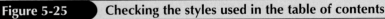

The Print Preview box on the left shows the appearance of the table of contents in Print Layout view, while the Web Preview box on the right shows what the table of contents would look like if you displayed it in Web Layout view. The Formats box shows the default option, From template, which applies the table of contents styles provided by the document's template.

In the Print Preview section, notice that the Contents heading style, which you created in Session 5.1, appears in the table of contents at the same level as the Heading 1 style.

▶ **6.** In the lower-right corner of the Table of Contents dialog box, click the **Options** button. The Table of Contents Options dialog box opens. The Styles check box is selected, indicating that Word will compile the table of contents based on the styles applied to the document headings.

▶ **7.** In the TOC level list, review the priority level assigned to the document's styles, using the vertical scroll bar, if necessary. See Figure 5-25.

Figure 5-25 Checking the styles used in the table of contents

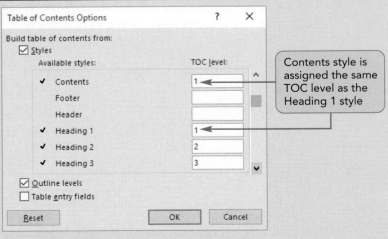

If the box next to a style name is blank, then text formatted with that style does not appear in the table of contents. The numbers next to the Contents, Heading 1, Heading 2, and Heading 3 styles tell you that any text formatted with these styles appears in the table of contents. Heading 1 is assigned to level 1, and Heading 2 is assigned to level 2.

Like Heading 1, the Contents style is assigned to level 1; however, you don't want to include the "Contents" heading in the table of contents itself. To remove any text formatted with the Contents style from the table of contents, you need to delete the Contents style level number.

8. Delete the **1** from the TOC level box for the Contents style, and then click the **OK** button. "Contents" is no longer displayed in the sample table of contents in the Print Preview and Web Preview sections of the Table of Contents dialog box.

9. Click the **OK** button to accept the remaining default settings in the Table of Contents dialog box. Word searches for text formatted with the Heading 1, Heading 2, and Heading 3 styles, and then places those headings and their corresponding page numbers in a table of contents. The table of contents is inserted at the insertion point, below the "Contents" heading. See Figure 5-26.

Figure 5-26   Table of contents inserted into document

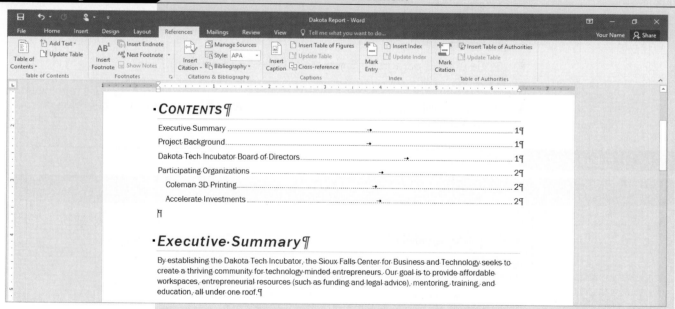

The text in the table of contents is formatted with the TOC styles for the current template. Depending on how your computer is set up, the table of contents might appear on a light gray background.

You can check the hyperlink formatting to make sure the headings really do function as links.

10. Press and hold the **Ctrl** key while you click **Coleman 3D Printing** in the table of contents. The insertion point moves to the beginning of the "Coleman 3D Printing" heading near the bottom of page 2.

11. Save the document.

Updating a Table of Contents

If you add or delete a heading in the document or add body text that causes one or more headings to move to a new page, you can quickly update the table of contents by clicking the Update Table button in the Table of Contents group on the References tab. To add text that is not formatted as a heading to the table of contents, you can select the text, format it as a heading, and then update the table of contents. However, if you already have the References tab displayed, it's more efficient to select the text in the document, use the Add Text button in the Table of Contents group to add a Heading style to the selected text, and then update the table of contents.

Benjamin has information on a third participating organization saved as a separate Word file, which he asks you to insert at the end of the Dakota Report document. You will do this next and then add the new heading to the table of contents.

To add a section to the Dakota Report document and update the table of contents:

1. Press the **Ctrl+End** keys to move the insertion point to the end of the document, and then press the **Enter** key.

2. On the ribbon, click the **Insert** tab.

3. In the Text group, click the **Object button arrow**, and then click **Text from File**.

4. Navigate to the **Word5 > Module** folder, click **NextGen**, and then click the **Insert** button.

5. Select the paragraph **Sioux Falls NextGen Software**.

6. On the ribbon, click the **References** tab.

7. In the Table of Contents group, click the **Add Text** button. The Add Text menu opens. See Figure 5-27.

Figure 5-27   Add Text menu

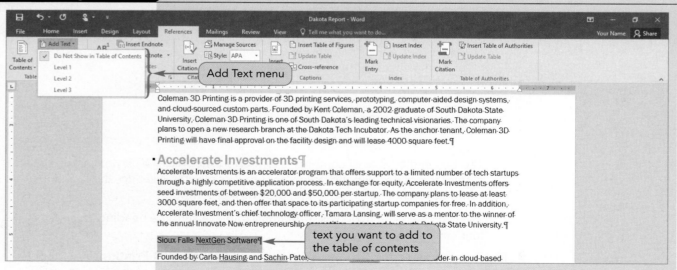

8. Click **Level 2**. The text is formatted with the Heading 2 style to match the headings for the sections about the other participating organizations. Now that the text is formatted with a heading style, you can update the table of contents.

9. Scroll up so you can see the table of contents, and then, in the Table of Contents group, click the **Update Table** button. The Update Table of Contents dialog box opens.

You can use the Update page numbers only option button if you don't want to update the headings in the table of contents. This option is useful if you add additional content that causes existing headings to move from one page to another. In this case, you want to update the entire table of contents.

10. Click the **Update entire table** option button to select it, and then click the **OK** button. The table of contents is updated to include the "Sioux Falls NextGen Software" heading. See Figure 5-28.

| Figure 5-28 | Updated table of contents |

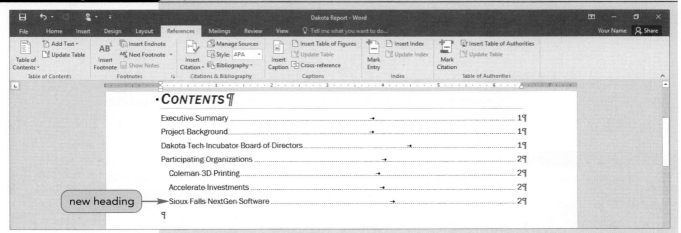

11. In the document, scroll down below the "Dakota Tech Incubator Board of Directors" heading on page 1, and replace "Lana Rivers" with your first and last names.

12. Press the **Ctrl+End** keys to move the insertion point to the last paragraph in the document, which is blank, and then press the **Delete** key to delete the blank paragraph.

13. Save the document.

Now that you are finished working on the Dakota Report document, Benjamin asks you to use the document to create a template that can be used for all reports issued by the Sioux Falls Center for Business and Technology.

Saving a Document as a Template

If you frequently need to create a particular type of document, it's a good idea to create your own template for that type of document. Organizations often use templates to ensure that all employees use the same basic format for essential documents. When creating a template, you can save it to any folder on your computer. After you save it, you can open the template to revise it just as you would open any other document. You can also use the Save As option in Backstage view to create a new document based on the template, in which case Word Document will be selected as the file type in the Save As dialog box. If you want to be able to open a new document based on the template from the New screen, you need to save your template to the Custom Office Templates folder that is installed with Word.

Saving a Document as a Template

- On the ribbon, click the File tab, and then click Export in the navigation bar.
- Click Change File Type, click Template, and then click the Save As button to open the Save As dialog box with Word Template selected in the Save as type box.
- Navigate to the folder in which you want to save the template. To save the template to the Custom Office Templates folder that is installed with Word, click the Documents folder in the navigation pane of the Save As dialog box, and then click Custom Office Templates.
- In the File name box, type a name for the template.
- Click the Save button.

You will save the new Sioux Falls Center for Business and Technology template in the location specified by your instructor; however, you'll also save it to the Custom Office Templates folder so you can practice opening a new document based on your template from the New screen in Backstage view.

To save the Dakota Report document as a new template:

1. Save the **Dakota Report** document to ensure that you have saved your most recent work.

TIP

You can also click the File tab, click Save As, and then select Template as the file type.

2. On the ribbon, click the **File** tab, and then click **Export** in the navigation bar. On the Export screen, you could click Create PDF/XPS to save the document as a PDF. However, the Change File Type option gives you additional file type possibilities, which you will review next.

3. Click **Change File Type**. The Export screen displays options for various file types you can use when saving a file. For example, you could save a Word document as a Plain Text file that contains only text, without any formatting or graphics. See Figure 5-29.

Figure 5-29 Export screen with Change File Type options in Backstage view

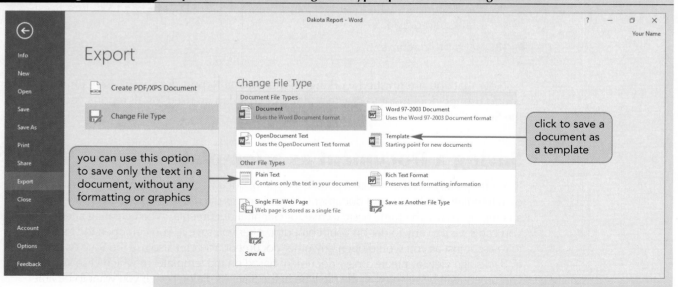

4. Under Change File Type, click **Template**, and then click the **Save As** button. The Save As dialog box opens with Word Template selected in the Save as type box.

5. If necessary, navigate to the location specified by your instructor. Next, you'll replace the selected, default filename with a new one that includes the acronym for the Sioux Falls Center for Business and Technology.

6. In the File name box, type **SFCBT Report**. See Figure 5-30.

Figure 5-30	Saving a document as a template

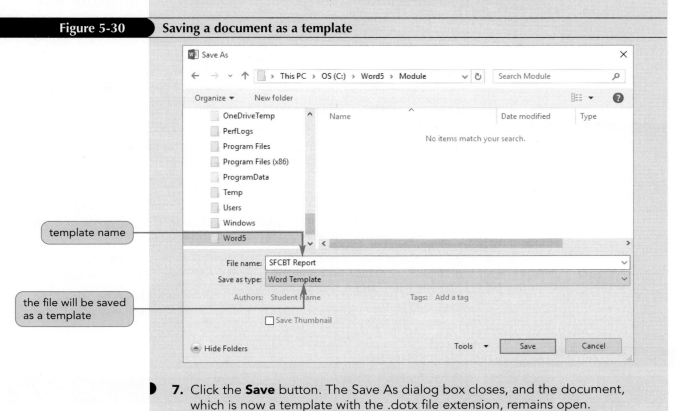

template name

the file will be saved as a template

7. Click the **Save** button. The Save As dialog box closes, and the document, which is now a template with the .dotx file extension, remains open.

PROSKILLS

Written Communication: Standardizing the Look of Your Documents

Large companies often ask their employees to use a predesigned template for all corporate documents. If you work for an organization that does not require you to use a specific template, consider using one anyway in order to create a standard look for all of your documents. A consistent appearance is especially important if you are responsible for written communication for an entire department because it ensures that colleagues and clients will immediately recognize documents from your department.

Be sure to use a professional-looking template. If you decide to create your own, use document styles that make text easy to read, with colors that are considered appropriate in your workplace. Don't try to dazzle your readers with design elements. In nearly all professional settings, a simple, elegant look is ideal.

To make the new SFCBT Report template really useful to Benjamin's colleagues, you need to delete the specific information related to the Dakota Tech Incubator and replace it with placeholder text explaining the type of information required in each section. In the following steps, you will delete the body of the report and replace it with some placeholder text. Benjamin wants to use the current subtitle, "Prepared by the Sioux Falls Center for Business and Technology," as the subtitle in all reports, so there's no need to change it. However, the title will vary from one report to the next, so you need to replace it with a suitable placeholder. You'll retain the table of contents. When Benjamin's colleagues use the template to create future reports, they can update the table of contents to include any headings they add to their new documents.

To replace the information about the Dakota Tech Incubator with placeholder text:

1. Scroll up to the top of the document, and then replace the report title "Dakota Tech Incubator" with the text **[Insert title here.]**. Be sure to include the brackets so the text will be readily recognizable as placeholder text. To ensure that Benjamin's colleagues don't overlook this placeholder, you can also highlight it.

2. On the ribbon, click the **Home** tab, if necessary.

3. In the Font group, click the **Text Highlight Color** button, and then click and drag the highlight pointer over the text **[Insert title here.]**. The text is highlighted in yellow, which is the default highlight color.

4. Press the **Esc** key to turn off the highlight pointer.

5. Scroll down below the table of contents, and then delete everything in the document after the "Executive Summary" heading so all that remains is the "Executive Summary" heading.

6. Press the **Enter** key to insert a blank paragraph below the heading. Now you can insert a file containing placeholder text for the body of the template.

7. In the blank paragraph under the "Executive Summary" heading, insert the **Placeholder** file from the Word5 > Module folder included with your Data Files. See Figure 5-31.

> **TIP**
>
> To remove highlighting from selected text, click the Text Highlight Color button arrow, and then click No Color.

Figure 5-31   **Template with placeholder text**

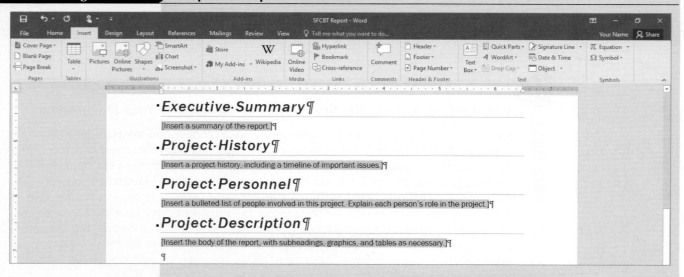

Scroll up to review the document, and notice that the inserted placeholder text is highlighted and the headings are all correctly formatted with the Heading 1 style. When Benjamin created the Placeholder document, he formatted the text in the default Heading 1 style provided by the Office theme. But when you inserted the file into the template, Word automatically applied your updated Heading 1 style. Now you can update the table of contents.

> **8.** On the ribbon, click the **References** tab.

> **9.** In the Table of Contents group, click the **Update Table** button. The table of contents is updated to include the new headings.

> **10.** On the Quick Access Toolbar, click the **Save** button 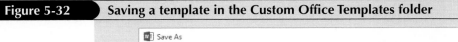 to save your changes to the template just as you would save a document.

At this point, you have a copy of the template stored in the location specified by your instructor. If you closed the template, clicked the File tab, and then opened the template again from the same folder, you would be opening the template itself and not a new document based on the template. If you want to be able to open a new document based on the template from the New screen, you have to save the template to the Custom Office Templates folder. You'll do that next. You can also open a new document based on a template by double-clicking the template file from within File Explorer. You'll have a chance to try that in the Case Problems at the end of this module.

To save the template to the Custom Office Templates folder:

> **1.** On the ribbon, click the **File** tab, and then click **Save As** in the navigation bar.

> **2.** Click **Computer** if necessary, and then click the **Browse** button to open the Save As dialog box.

> **3.** In the navigation pane of the Save As dialog box, click the **Documents** folder, and then, in the folder list on the right, double-click **Custom Office Templates**. See Figure 5-32.

Figure 5-32	Saving a template in the Custom Office Templates folder

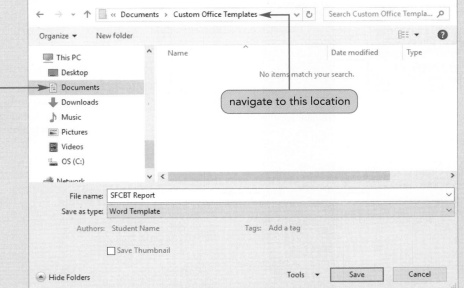

the Custom Office Templates folder is a subfolder of the Documents folder

navigate to this location

> **4.** Click the **Save** button to save the template to the Custom Office Templates folder and close the Save As dialog box.

> **5.** On the ribbon, click the **File** tab, and then click **Close** in the navigation bar to close the template, just as you would close a document.

The template you just created will simplify the process of creating new reports in Benjamin's department.

Opening a New Document Based on Your Template

Documents created using a template contain all the text and formatting included in the template. Changes you make to this new document will not affect the template file, which remains unchanged in the Custom Office Templates folder.

Benjamin would like you to use the SFCBT Report template to begin a report on SFCBT's annual coding academy.

To open a new document based on the SFCBT Report template:

▶ **1.** On the ribbon, click the **File** tab, and then click **New** in the navigation bar.

Because you have created and saved a template, the New screen in Backstage view now includes two links—FEATURED and PERSONAL. The FEATURED link is selected by default, indicating that the templates currently featured by Office.com are displayed. To open the template you just saved to the Custom Office Templates folder, you need to display the personal templates instead.

▶ **2.** Click **PERSONAL**. The SFCBT Report template is displayed as an option on the New screen. See Figure 5-33.

Figure 5-33	Opening a document based on the SFCBT Report template

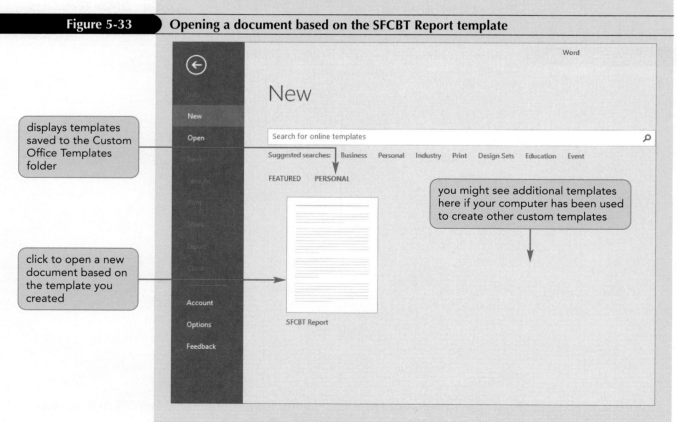

displays templates saved to the Custom Office Templates folder

you might see additional templates here if your computer has been used to create other custom templates

click to open a new document based on the template you created

SFCBT Report

▶ **3.** Click **SFCBT Report**. A new document opens, containing the text and formatting from the SFCBT Report template.

▶ **4.** Delete the placeholder **[Insert title here.]**, and type **Annual Coding Academy** in its place.

Benjamin and his colleagues will add new material to this report later. For now, you can close it.

▶ **5.** Save the document as **Coding Academy** in the location specified by your instructor, and then close the document.

Next, to ensure that you can repeat the steps in this module if you choose to, you will delete the SFCBT Report template from the Custom Office Templates folder. You can delete it from within the Open dialog box.

▶ **6.** On the ribbon, click the **File** tab, and then click **Open** in the navigation bar.

▶ **7.** Click the **Browse** button.

▶ **8.** In the navigation pane of the Open dialog box, click the **Documents** folder, and then double-click **Custom Office Templates**. The SFCBT Report template is displayed in the file list.

▶ **9.** Right-click **SFCBT Report** to display a shortcut menu, and then click **Delete**. The template file is removed from the file list.

Trouble? If you see a message box asking you to confirm that you want to move the file to the Recycle Bin, click Yes.

▶ **10.** Click the **Cancel** button to close the Open dialog box, and then close Backstage view.

Creating a template makes it easy to create a series of similar documents. But what if you want to insert specific text such as an address or email address or a graphic such as a logo in many different documents? In that case, you can save the item as a Quick Part.

Creating a New Quick Part

A **Quick Part** is reusable content that you create and that you can then insert into any document later with a single click in the Quick Parts gallery. For example, you might create a letterhead with your company's address and logo. To save the letterhead as a Quick Part, you select it and then save it to the Quick Parts gallery. Later, you can insert the letterhead into a document by clicking it in the Quick Parts gallery.

By default, a new Quick Part appears as an option in the Quick Parts gallery. However, you can assign a Quick Part to any gallery you want. For example, you could assign a text box Quick Part to the Text Box gallery so that every time you click the Text Box button on the Insert tab, you see your text box as one of the options in the Text Box gallery.

Quick Parts are just one type of a larger category of reusable content known as **building blocks**. All of the ready-made items that you can insert into a document via a gallery are considered building blocks. For example, preformatted headers, preformatted text boxes, and cover pages are all examples of building blocks. Some reference sources use the terms "building block" and "Quick Part" as if they were synonyms, but in fact a Quick Part is a building block that you create.

When you save a Quick Part, you always save it to a template; you can't save a Quick Part to an individual document. Which template you save it to depends on what you want to do with the Quick Part. If you want the template to be available to all new documents created on your computer, you should save it to the Building Blocks template. The **Building Blocks template** is a special template that contains all the building blocks installed with Word on your computer, as well as any Quick Parts you save to it. If you want to restrict the Quick Part to only documents based on the current template, or if you want to be able to share the Quick Part with someone else, you should save it to the current template. To share the Quick Part, you simply distribute the template to anyone who wants to use the Quick Part.

Creating and Using Quick Parts

- Select the text, text box, header, footer, table, graphic, or other item you want to save as a Quick Part.
- On the ribbon, click the Insert tab.
- In the Text group, click the Quick Parts button, and then click Save Selection to Quick Parts Gallery.
- In the Create New Building Block dialog box, replace the text in the Name box with a descriptive name for the Quick Part.
- Click the Gallery arrow, and then choose the gallery to which you want to save the Quick Part.
- To make the Quick Part available to all documents on your computer, select Building Blocks in the Save in box. To restrict the Quick Part to the current template, select the name of the template on which the current document is based.
- Click the OK button.

Benjamin has created a text box containing the address and phone number for the Sioux Falls Center for Business and Technology. He asks you to show him how to save the text box as a Quick Part. He wants the Quick Part to be available to all new documents created on his computer, so you'll need to save it to the Building Blocks template.

To save a text box as a Quick Part:

1. Open the document **SFCBT** from the Word5 > Module folder, and then save it as **SFCBT Address** in the location specified by your instructor.

2. Display nonprinting characters and the rulers, switch to Print Layout view, and then change the Zoom level to **120%**, if necessary.

3. Click the **text box** to select it, taking care to select the entire text box and not the text inside it. When the text box is selected, you'll see the anchor symbol in the left margin.

4. On the ribbon, click the **Insert** tab.

5. In the Text group, click the **Quick Parts** button. If any Quick Parts have been created on your computer, they will be displayed in the gallery at the top of the menu. Otherwise, you will see only the menu shown in Figure 5-34.

Figure 5-34 **Quick Parts menu, with no Quick Parts visible**

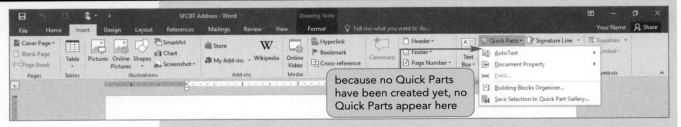

because no Quick Parts have been created yet, no Quick Parts appear here

---

6. At the bottom of the menu, click **Save Selection to Quick Part Gallery**. The Create New Building Block dialog box opens. The name of this dialog box is appropriate because a Quick Part is a type of building block. See Figure 5-35.

Figure 5-35   **Create New Building Block dialog box**

the first two words in the text box are used as the name of the new building block by default

the new building block will be saved in the Quick Parts gallery by default

the new building block will be saved to the Building Blocks template by default

Create New Building Block   ?   ×

Name: Sioux Falls
Gallery: Quick Parts
Category: General
Description:
Save in: Building Blocks
Options: Insert content only

OK   Cancel

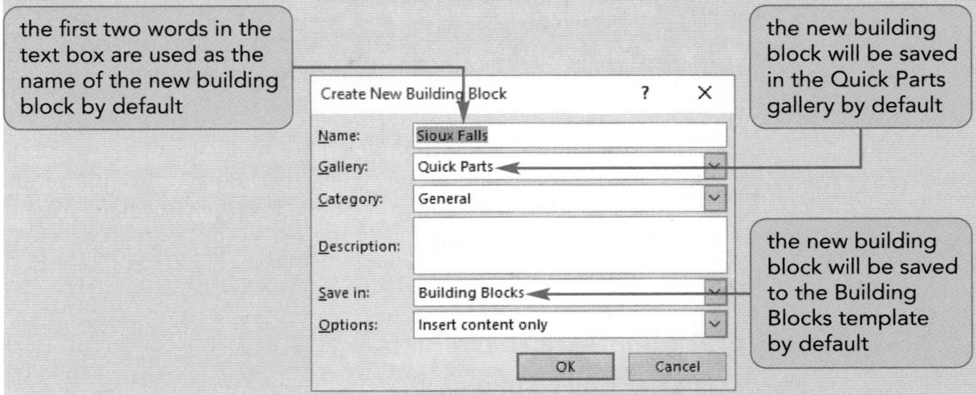

By default, the first two words in the text box, "Sioux Falls," are used as the default name for the new building block. You could type a new name, but Benjamin is happy with the default. Also, the default setting in the Gallery box tells you that the new building block will be saved in the Quick Parts gallery. You could change this by selecting a different gallery name. The Save in box indicates that the Quick Part will be saved to the Building Blocks template, which means it will be available to all documents on your computer.

Benjamin asks you to accept the default settings.

7. Click the **OK** button to accept your changes and close the Create New Building Block dialog box.

You've finished creating the new Quick Part. Now you can try inserting it in the current document.

To insert the new Quick Part into the current document:

1. Press the **Ctrl+End** keys to move the insertion point to the end of the document.

2. In the Text group, click the **Quick Parts** button. This time, the Quick Parts gallery is displayed at the top of the menu. See Figure 5-36.

Figure 5-36   **New Quick Part in the Quick Parts gallery**

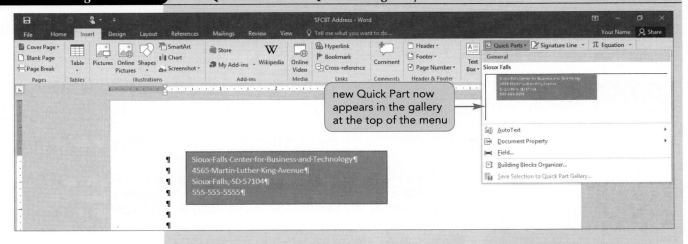

new Quick Part now appears in the gallery at the top of the menu

> **3.** Click the **Sioux Falls** Quick Part. A copy of the green text box is inserted at the end of the document, at the insertion point.
>
> **4.** In the newly inserted text box, replace the phone number with your first and last names, and then save the document.

The new Quick Part is stored in the Quick Parts gallery, ready to be inserted into any document. However, after reviewing the Quick Part, Benjamin has decided he wants to reformat the address text box and save it as a new Quick Part later. So you'll delete the Quick Part you just created.

To delete a Quick Part:

> **1.** In the Text group, click the **Quick Parts** button, and then click **Building Blocks Organizer** to open the Building Blocks Organizer dialog box. Here you see a list of all the building blocks available in your copy of Word, including Quick Parts. See Figure 5-37.

Figure 5-37 ▶ **Building Blocks Organizer dialog box**

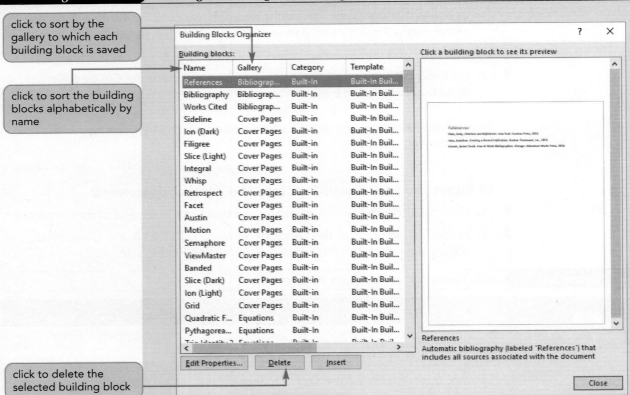

click to sort by the gallery to which each building block is saved

click to sort the building blocks alphabetically by name

click to delete the selected building block

The list on your computer will be somewhat different from the list shown in Figure 5-37.

You can click a building block in the list and then click the Edit Properties button to open a dialog box where you can rename the building block and make other changes. You can also use the Building Blocks Organizer to delete a building block.

▶ 2. Click the **Name** column header to sort the building blocks alphabetically by name, scroll down and click **Sioux Falls**, click the **Delete** button, and then click the **Yes** button in the warning dialog box. The Department Quick Part is deleted from the list in the Building Blocks Organizer.

▶ 3. Click the **Close** button.

▶ 4. In the Text group, click the **Quick Parts** button, and verify that the Sioux Falls Quick Part is no longer displayed in the Quick Parts gallery.

Finally, to completely delete the Quick Part from the Building Blocks template, you need to save the current document. In the process of saving the document, Word will save your changes to the Building Blocks template, which controls all the building blocks available in your copy of Word. If you don't save the document now, you'll see a warning dialog box later, when you attempt to close the document. It's easy to get confused by the wording of this warning dialog box, and you might end up restoring your Quick Part rather than deleting it. To avoid seeing this warning dialog box entirely, remember to save the current document after you delete a Quick Part.

▶ 5. Save the **SFCBT Address** document, and then close it.

Benjamin is happy to know how to save Quick Parts to the Building Blocks template. He'll create a new Quick Part later and save it to a custom template so that he can make it available to everyone at the Sioux Falls Center for Business and Technology.

REVIEW

Session 5.2 Quick Check

1. By default, is a new style saved to the current document or to the current template?

2. Explain how to create a new style.

3. What pane displays information about the style applied to the paragraph that currently contains the insertion point?

4. Which setting on the Line and Page Breaks tab of the Paragraph dialog box ensures that if a paragraph consists of more than one line of text, the lines of the paragraph will never be separated by a page break?

5. What must you do to your document before you can create a table of contents for it?

6. Where should you save a custom template if you want to be able to access it from the New screen in Backstage view?

7. What is a Quick Part?

Review Assignments

Data Files needed for the Review Assignments: Construction.docx, Contributors.docx, DTI Address.docx, Placeholder Text.docx

Benjamin's SFCBT Report template is now used for all reports created by employees of the Sioux Falls Center for Business and Technology. Inspired by Benjamin's success with the template, a project manager for the Dakota Tech Incubator Planning Commission, Layla Farhad, wants you to help with a report on construction plans for the new facility. After you format the report, she'd like you to save the document as a new template and then create a Quick Part. Complete the following steps:

1. Create a new document based on the Report (Essential design) template from Office.com. (If you can't find that template, choose another.) Replace the first placeholder in the document with your name, and then save the document as **Document from Office.com Template** in the location specified by your instructor. If you see a dialog box explaining that the document is being upgraded to the newest file format, click the OK button.

2. Close the document.

3. Open the document **Construction** from the Word5 > Review folder included with your Data Files, and then save it as **Construction Report** in the location specified by your instructor.

4. Use the Go To feature to review all the headings in the document.

5. In the fourth line of the "Project Background" section, use the Thesaurus task pane to replace "ancillary" with a synonym. Use the fourth synonym in the list of words related to "auxiliary."

6. Change the theme colors to Grayscale, and then change the theme's fonts to the Georgia fonts.

7. Save the new colors and fonts as a theme named **DTI Theme** in the location specified by your instructor.

8. Change the style set to Minimalist.

9. Change the formatting of the "Project Background" heading by adding italic formatting and by changing the character spacing so that it is expanded by 1 point between characters.

10. Update the Heading 1 style to match the newly formatted "Project Background" heading.

11. Revise the "Likely Challenges" heading by changing the font size to 16 points, and then update the Heading 2 style to match the newly formatted "Likely Challenges" heading.

12. Create a new paragraph style for the "Contents" heading that is based on the Heading 1 style but that also includes Gray-50%, Accent 3 paragraph shading, and the White, Background 1 font color. Name the new style **Contents**, select Normal as the style for the following paragraph, and then save the new style to the current document.

13. Open the Style Inspector pane, and check the style applied to each paragraph in the document. Then use the Reveal Formatting pane to compare the formatting applied to the "Contents" heading with the formatting applied to the "Project Background" heading.

14. Delete the placeholder text below the "Contents" heading, and then insert a custom table of contents that does not include the Contents style. Except for excluding the Contents style, use the default settings in the Table of Contents dialog box.

15. Insert a blank paragraph at the end of the document, and then insert the **Contributors** file from the Word5 > Review folder. Add the text **Contributing Staff Members** to the table of contents as a Level 1 heading, and then delete the blank paragraph at the end of the document.

16. At the end of the report, replace "Student Name" with your first and last names.

17. Save your changes to the Construction Report document.

18. Save the Construction Report document as a Word Template named **DTI Report** in the location specified by your instructor.

19. On page 1, replace the title "CONSTRUCTING THE DAKOTA TECH INCUBATOR" with the placeholder text **[INSERT TITLE HERE.]**, and then highlight the placeholder in the default yellow color.

20. Delete everything in the report after the blank paragraph after the table of contents.

21. In the blank paragraph below the table of contents, insert the **Placeholder Text** file from the Word5 > Review folder.

22. In the Business Community Personnel section, replace "Student Name" with your first and last names, and then update the table of contents.

23. Save the template, save it again to the Custom Office Templates folder, and then close it.

24. Open a new document based on the DTI Report template, enter **PROJECTIONS FOR GROWTH** as the document title, save the new document as **Projections** in the location specified by your instructor, and then close it.

25. Delete the DTI Report template from the Custom Office Templates folder.

26. Open the document **DTI Address** from the Word5 > Review folder, and then save it as a Word Template named **DTI Address Box** in the location specified by your instructor.

27. Save the green text box as a Quick Part named **Address**. Save it to the DTI Address Box template, not to the Building Blocks template.

28. Save the template and close it.

Case Problem 1

Data File needed for this Case Problem: Vento.docx

Vento Energy Experts   Haley Porter is a consultant for Vento Energy Experts, a firm that helps clients lower their energy bills by replacing outdated heating and cooling systems with more efficient options. For each client, Haley needs to prepare an "Energy Efficiency Report for Existing and Proposed Systems." These reports can be quite long, so it's necessary to include a table of contents on the first page. Your job is to create a template that Haley and her fellow consultants can use when compiling their reports. Complete the following steps:

1. Open the document **Vento** from the Word5 > Case1 folder included with your Data Files, and then save it as **Vento Report** in the location specified by your instructor.

2. Use Go To to review all the tables in the document.

3. Change the document's theme to the Facet theme, and then change the theme colors to Blue Green. Change the style set to Basic (Stylish).

4. Highlight in yellow the three instances of placeholder text below the company name and above the "Contents" heading.

5. Format the "Contents" heading by changing the character spacing to Expanded, with the default amount of space between the expanded characters. Increase the font size to 22 points, add italic formatting, and then change the font color to one shade darker, using the Blue, Accent 6, Darker 50% font color. Update the Heading 1 style for the current document to match the newly formatted heading.

6. Create a new paragraph style for the company name at the top of the document that is based on the Heading 1 style but that also includes Blue, Accent 6, Darker 50% paragraph shading; White, Background 1 font color; 36-point font size; and center alignment. Reduce the points of paragraph spacing before the paragraph to 0, and increase the points after the paragraph to 36. Name the new style **Company**. Select the Normal style as the style for the following paragraph, and save the style to the current document.

7. Remove the Company style from the Style gallery.

8. Below the "Contents" heading, replace the placeholder text with a custom table of contents that does not include the Company style.

9. In the document, delete the paragraph containing the "Contents" heading, and then update the table of contents to remove "Contents" from it.

10. Click in the paragraph before the table of contents, and increase the spacing after it to 24 points.

11. Add the "General Recommendations" heading, in the second to last paragraph of the document, to the table of contents at the same level as the "Project Summary" heading.

12. In the document's last paragraph, replace "improving" with a synonym. In the Thesaurus task pane, use the second synonym in the list of words related to "bettering."

13. Save your changes to the Vento Report document, and then save the Vento Report document as a template named **Vento Template** in the location specified by your instructor.

14. On page 4, save the complete "Analysis, Proposed System X" section (including the heading, the placeholder text, the table, and the blank paragraph below the table) as a Quick Part named **Additional Analysis**. Save the Quick Part to the Vento Template template.

15. Delete the complete "Analysis, Proposed System X" section from the body of the template, including the heading, the placeholder text, the table, and the blank paragraph after the table.

16. Update the table of contents to remove the "Analysis, Proposed System X" heading.

17. Save the template to its current location, and then save the template again to the Custom Office Templates folder. Close the template.

18. Open a document based on your new template, and then save the new document as **Bachman Report** in the location specified by your instructor.

19. Replace the first placeholder with the current date, replace the second placeholder with **Robert Bachman**, and then replace the third placeholder with your first and last names.

20. To the left of the "G" in the "General Recommendations" heading, insert the Additional Analysis Quick Part.

21. Replace the "X" in the new heading with the number "2" so that the heading reads "Analysis, Proposed System 2."

22. Update the table of contents to include the new heading.

23. Save and close the document, and then delete the Vento Template template from the Custom Office Templates folder.

Case Problem 2

Data Files needed for this Case Problem: Desktops.png, Handout.dotx, Printers.png

Turnaround Solutions   Isaiah Chandler is the founder of Turnaround Solutions, a volunteer organization that accepts outdated electronics from local businesses, refurbishes them, and then donates them to schools and social service agencies. Isaiah's organization hosts recycling fairs several times a year, with each fair focusing on a different type of electronic device, such as printers or desktop computers. He has created a template that he hopes will simplify the task of creating handouts announcing these recycling fairs, but it's not quite finished. He asks you to finish the template by adding two graphics as Quick Parts: one graphic for desktop recycling fairs, and one for printer recycling fairs. Then he would like you to use the new template to create a handout for an upcoming printer recycling fair. Your completed handout should look like the one shown in Figure 5-38.

CREATE

Figure 5-38   **Flyer for Turnaround Solutions**

Complete the following steps:

1. Open the template **Handout** from the Word5 > Case2 folder included with your Data Files, then save it as a template named **Turnaround Handout** in the location specified by your instructor. Notice that the parts of the template are laid out using a table structure. If necessary, display the table gridlines so you can see the template's structure.

2. Replace the [Insert Graphic 1 here.] placeholder with the picture in the file **Desktops.png** located in the Word5 > Case2 folder, and then change the picture's height to 4".

3. Save the picture as a Quick Part named **Handout Graphic, Desktops** to the Turnaround Handout template.

4. Delete the picture and, in its place, insert the file **Printers.png** from the Word5 > Case2 folder. Change the picture's height to 4".

5. Save the picture as a Quick Part named **Handout Graphic, Printers** to the Turnaround Handout template.

6. Delete the picture, and insert the placeholder text **[From the Quick Parts menu, insert the graphic for the type of device that will be collected at the recycling fair.]**.

7. Save the Turnaround Handout template in its current location, and then save it again to the Custom Office Templates folder. Close the template.

8. Open a document based on the **Turnaround Handout** template, and then save the new document as **Printer Fair Handout** in the location specified by your instructor.

9. Replace the placeholder that begins "[From the Quick Parts menu..." with the Quick Part named Handout Graphic, Printers.

10. Replace the [DATE] placeholder with the text **JUNE 24, 2017**.

11. Replace the [Time] placeholder with the text **Noon to 4:30 p.m.**

12. Replace the [EVENT TITLE] placeholder with the text **PRINTER RECYCLING FAIR**.

13. Replace the [Location] placeholder with the text **Wilson Avenue Community Center.**

14. Replace the remaining placeholder text as follows:
    - [Insert first point here.]: **Color printers urgently needed for local schools this year.**
    - [Insert second point here.]: **We are currently accepting used toner cartridges, which we can refurbish and refill.**
    - [Insert third point here.]: **Unfortunately, we can no longer accept dot matrix printers.**
    - [Insert fourth point here.]: **Please provide the original packaging for your printer, if possible.**

15. In the lower-right corner of the document, in the blank paragraph below the web address, insert your name. If it doesn't fit on one line, abbreviate it, perhaps by using only your first initial and your last name, so that it fits on one line.

16. Hide gridlines and nonprinting characters, and review the handout.

17. Open the Styles pane and review the list of styles. Attach a comment to the word "JUNE" that reads: **The Styles pane for this document contains *number* paragraph styles, number linked styles, and number character styles.** For each type of style, replace *number* with the correct number.

18. Save and close the document.

19. Delete the Turnaround Handout template from the Custom Office Templates folder.

Case Problem 3

Data Files needed for this Case Problem: APA.docx, Details.docx

APA-Style Research Paper Template   You are the lab manager for Dr. Leah Krishna, a professor of social psychology at Holbrook State University. Each year, Dr. Krishna's graduate students write several research papers, using the style specified by the American Psychological Association (APA). To make it easier for her students to focus on writing about their research, rather than the formatting details of the APA style, Dr. Krishna wants to provide them with a Word template for an APA-style research paper. She asks you to create the template for her. You'll start by doing some research on specifications for the APA style, and, in the process, you will create a custom theme that Dr. Krishna can use for other lab documents. Complete the following steps:

1. Open the document **Details** from the Word5 > Case3 folder included with your Data Files, and then save it as **APA Details** in the location specified by your instructor.

2. In the second paragraph, insert your name where indicated.

3. Change the document's theme to the Office theme, and then change the theme colors to Red. Change the style set to Centered.

4. Save the customized theme as **KrishnaLab.thmx** in the location specified by your instructor.

5. Using a source on the web or an up-to-date print publication, research the characteristics of an APA-style research paper.

6. In the APA Details document, fill in the table with the necessary information about APA-style research papers.

7. Save the APA Details document, and then use it for reference as you complete the remaining steps in this Case Problem.

8. Open the document **APA** from the Word5 > Case3 folder, and then save it as a Word template named **APA Paper** in the location specified by your instructor.

9. Review the template, which contains all the necessary headings and placeholder text, along with paragraphs that Dr. Krishna generated by typing =lorem() and pressing the Enter key. You can use this text as body text to separate placeholder headings in the template.

10. Change the margins as necessary to match the APA style, and add page breaks where necessary.

11. Format the entire document using the appropriate font, font size, line spacing, and character spacing.

12. Edit the comment to insert the appropriate examples after each colon, and then add your name where indicated. In the comment, format the citation examples and your name with yellow highlighting.

13. Add an APA-style document header. Use the placeholder text **"[INSERT TITLE.]"** where appropriate. Remember to create a different header for the title page, as specified by the APA style.

14. Format the text on the first two pages appropriately.

15. In the main body of the paper, format the title placeholder, the headings placeholders, and the sample body text appropriately.

16. Format the "References" title appropriately.

17. Save the APA Paper template, and then close it.

Case Problem 4

CHALLENGE

Data File needed for this Case Problem: Health.docx, Joni's.docx

Health Time Software   You are the assistant to Joni Duboff, a technical writer at Health Time Software, a medical software company in Paterson, New Jersey. Joni often uses Word styles in the reports and other publications she creates for the company, and she wants to learn more about managing styles. In particular, she wants to learn how to copy styles from one document to another. She's asked you to help her explore the Style Pane Options, Manage Styles, and Organizer dialog boxes. She would also like your help creating a Quick Part for a memo header. Complete the following steps:

1. Open the document **Health** from the Word5 > Case4 folder included with your Data Files, and then save it as **Health Time Memo** in the location specified by your instructor. This document contains the text you will eventually save as a Quick Part. It contains all the default styles available in any new Word document, as well as one style, named "Memorandum," which Joni created earlier. In the following steps, you will copy styles from another document to this document. For now, you can close it.

2. Close the Health Time Memo document.

3. Open the document **Joni's** from the Word5 > Case4 folder, and then save it as **Joni's Styles** in the location specified by your instructor. This document contains styles created by Joni, which you will copy to the Health Time Memo document. It also includes sample paragraphs formatted with Joni's styles, and one paragraph that you will format with a style later in this Case Problem.

⊕ **Explore** 4. Open the Style Pane Options dialog box, and then change the settings so the Styles pane displays only the styles in the current document, in alphabetical order. Before closing this dialog box, verify that these settings will be applied only to the current document rather than to new documents based on this template.

⊕ **Explore** 5. Open a new, blank document, and then use the Screenshot button in the Illustrations group on the Insert tab to create a screenshot of the Joni's Styles document.

6. Copy the screenshot to the Clipboard, and then paste it in the blank paragraph at the end of the Joni's Styles document, just as you would paste text that you had previously copied to the Clipboard. Close the document in which you created the screenshot without saving it.

✛ **Explore** 7. At the bottom of the Styles pane, click the Manage Styles button, and then click the Import/Export button to open the Organizer dialog box. Close the Normal template, and open the Health Time Memo document instead. (*Hint*: On the right, under the In Normal.dotm box, click the Close File button, and then click the Open File button. In the Open dialog box, you'll need to display all files.)

✛ **Explore** 8. Copy the following styles from the Joni's Styles document to the Health Time Memo document: Company Name, Department, Documentation Heading, and Product Description. Then copy the Memorandum style from the Health Time Memo document to the Joni's Styles document.

9. Close the Organizer dialog box, and then save your changes to the Health Time Memo document.

10. In the Joni's Styles document, apply the Memorandum style to the text "Sample of Memorandum style," in the document's third to last paragraph.

11. Save the Joni's Styles document, and then close it.

12. Open the **Health Time Memo** document, and then review the list of styles in the Styles pane to locate the styles you just copied to this document from the Joni's Styles document.

13. Apply the Company Name style to "Health Time Software" in the second paragraph.

14. Save the Health Time Memo document, and then save it again as a template named **Health Time Memo Template** in the location specified by your instructor.

15. Select all of the text in the document, and then save it as a Quick Part named **Gray Memo**. Save the Quick Part to the current template, not to the Building Blocks template.

16. Change the Paragraph shading for the first paragraph to gold, using the Gold, Accent 4, Darker 25% color, and then save the document text as a new Quick Part named **Gold Memo**. Again, save the Quick Part to the current template.

17. Delete all the text from the document, save the Health Time Memo Template file, and then close it.

✛ **Explore** 18. Open a File Explorer window, and then navigate to the location where you saved the Health Time Memo Template file. Open a new document based on the template by double-clicking the template's filename in File Explorer.

19. Save the new document as **Sample Health Time Memo** in the location specified by your instructor, insert the Gold Memo Quick Part in the document, and then save and close the document.

Using Mail Merge

Creating a Form Letter, Mailing Labels, and a Telephone Directory

Case | *Tupelo Family Farm*

Chris Tupelo owns and manages Tupelo Family Farm, a peach orchard and packing facility in Fort Valley, Georgia. The company has just opened its newly expanded farm market store. To generate business, Chris plans to send a form letter to regular customers announcing the new market store and offering a dozen free peaches to customers who bring their copies of the letter to the store.

The form letter will also contain specific details for individual customers, such as name, address, and favorite variety of peach. Chris has already written the text of the form letter. She plans to use the mail merge process to add the personal information for each customer to the form letter. She asks you to revise the form letter by inserting a Date field in the document that will display the current date. Then she wants you to use the Mail Merge feature in Word to create customized letters for her customers. After you create the merged letters, Chris would like you to create mailing labels for the envelopes and a directory of employee phone numbers. Finally, you'll convert some text to a table so that it can be used in a mail merge.

STARTING DATA FILES

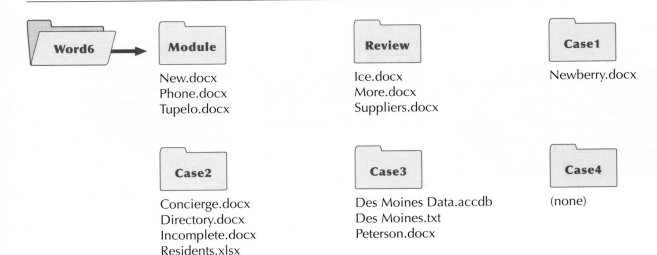

Word6 →	Module	Review	Case1
	New.docx	Ice.docx	Newberry.docx
	Phone.docx	More.docx	
	Tupelo.docx	Suppliers.docx	

Case2	Case3	Case4
Concierge.docx	Des Moines Data.accdb	(none)
Directory.docx	Des Moines.txt	
Incomplete.docx	Peterson.docx	
Residents.xlsx		

Session 6.1 Visual Overview:

Use the Start Mail Merge button to select the type of main document you are creating. Possible types include letters, envelopes, emails, labels, and directories.

The Select Recipients button allows you to select an existing data source or create a new one in the New Address List dialog box.

The Mailings tab contains four groups of options that, working left to right, walk you through the process of creating a mail merge.

To complete the mail merge, you click the Finish & Merge button. This creates a new document, the **merged document**, which contains a separate copy of the main document for each record in the data source.

The Edit Recipient List button allows you to make changes to a data source.

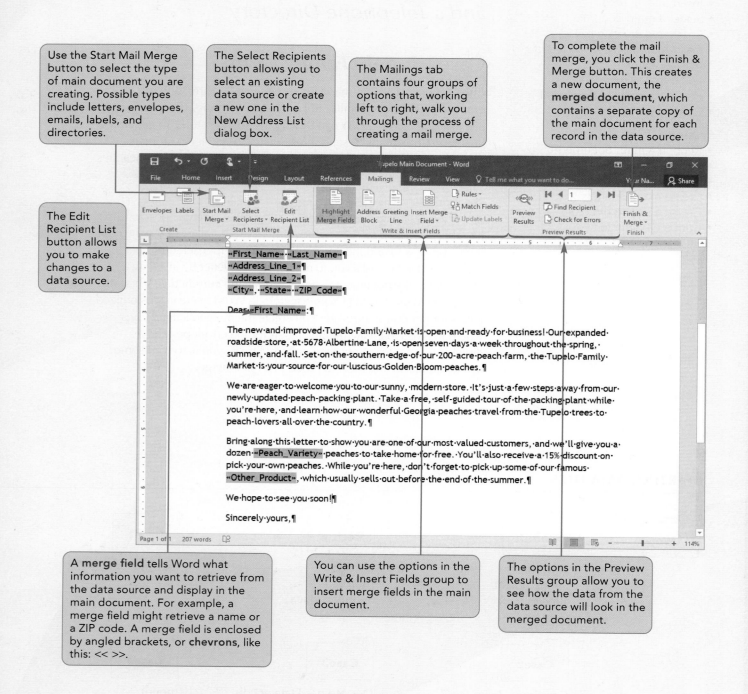

A **merge field** tells Word what information you want to retrieve from the data source and display in the main document. For example, a merge field might retrieve a name or a ZIP code. A merge field is enclosed by angled brackets, or **chevrons**, like this: << >>.

You can use the options in the Write & Insert Fields group to insert merge fields in the main document.

The options in the Preview Results group allow you to see how the data from the data source will look in the merged document.

Mail Merge

A **data source** is a file that contains information, such as names and addresses, that is organized into fields and records; the merge fields cause the information in the data source to be displayed in the main document. You can use a Word table, an Excel spreadsheet, or other types of files as data sources, or you can create a new data source using the New Address List dialog box.

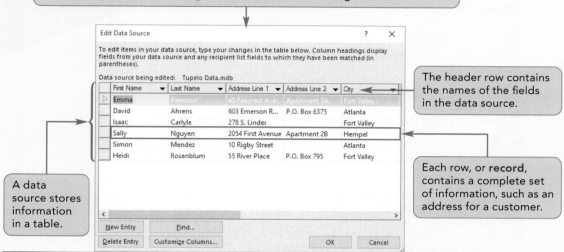

Edit Data Source   ? ✕

To edit items in your data source, type your changes in the table below. Column headings display fields from your data source and any recipient list fields to which they have been matched (in parentheses).

Data source being edited: Tupelo Data.mdb

First Name ▾	Last Name ▾	Address Line 1 ▾	Address Line 2 ▾	City ▾
Emma	Peterson	45 Faircrest Ave...	Apartment 5A	Fort Valley
David	Ahrens	603 Emerson R...	P.O. Box 6375	Atlanta
Isaac	Carlyle	278 S. Linder		Fort Valley
Sally	Nguyen	2054 First Avenue	Apartment 2B	Hempel
Simon	Mendez	10 Rigby Street		Atlanta
Heidi	Rosenblum	55 River Place	P.O. Box 795	Fort Valley

New Entry   Find...

Delete Entry   Customize Columns...   OK   Cancel

The header row contains the names of the fields in the data source.

A data source stores information in a table.

Each row, or **record**, contains a complete set of information, such as an address for a customer.

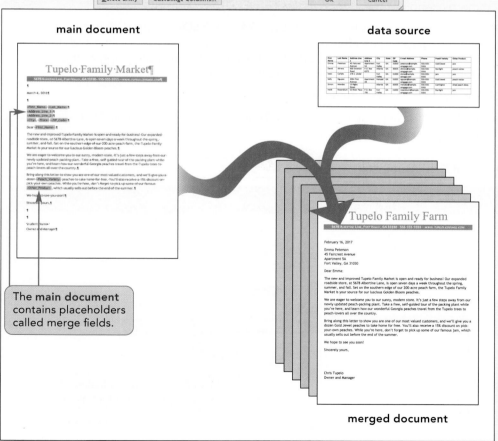

main document

Tupelo·Family·Market¶

data source

The **main document** contains placeholders called merge fields.

Tupelo Family Farm

merged document

Inserting a Date Field

A **Date field** is an instruction that tells Word to display the current date in a document. Although a Date field is not a merge field, it's common to use Date fields in mail merge documents to ensure that the main document always includes the current date. Every time you open a document containing a Date field, it updates to display the current date. To insert a Date field, you use the Date and Time dialog box to select from a variety of date formats. In addition to displaying the date with the current day, month, and year, you can include the current time and the day of the week. Word inserts a Date field inside a content control; unless the content control is selected, the field looks like ordinary text.

Chris asks you to insert a Date field in her document before beginning the mail merge process.

To open Chris's document and insert a Date field:

▶ 1. Open the document **Tupelo** from the Word6 > Module folder included with your Data Files, and then save it as **Tupelo Main Document** in the location specified by your instructor.

▶ 2. Display nonprinting characters, switch to Print Layout view, display the rulers, and then set the Zoom level to **120%**.

▶ 3. Review the contents of the letter. Notice that the fourth paragraph includes the placeholder text "[INSERT DATE FIELD]."

▶ 4. Delete the placeholder text **[INSERT DATE FIELD]**, taking care not to delete the paragraph mark after the placeholder text. When you are finished, the insertion point should be located in the second blank paragraph of the document, with two blank paragraphs below it.

▶ 5. On the ribbon, click the **Insert** tab.

▶ 6. In the Text group, click the **Date & Time** button. The Date and Time dialog box opens. See Figure 6-1.

Figure 6-1   Date and Time dialog box

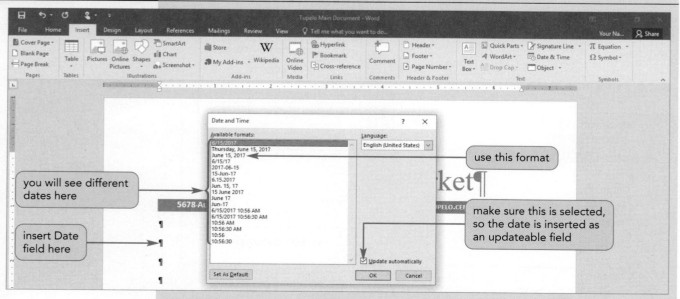

The Available formats list provides options for inserting the current date and time. In this case, you want to insert the date as a content control in a format that includes the complete name of the month, the date, and the year (for example, March 11, 2017).

▶ **7.** In the Available formats list, click the third format from the top, which is the month, date, and year format.

▶ **8.** Make sure the **Update automatically** check box is selected so the date is inserted as a content control that updates every time you open the document.

▶ **9.** Click the **OK** button. The current date is inserted in the document. At this point, it looks like ordinary text. To see the content control, you have to click the date.

▶ **10.** Click the date to display the content control. If you closed the document and then opened it a day later, the content control would automatically display the new date. See Figure 6-2.

Figure 6-2 **Date field inside content control**

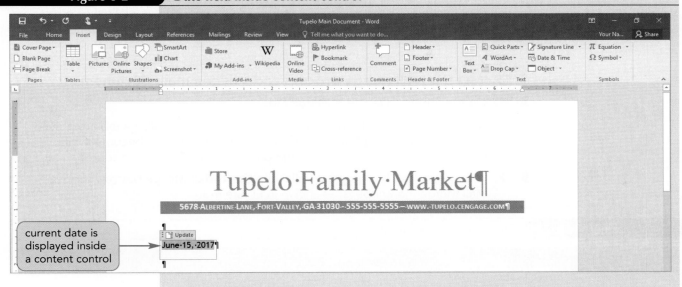

current date is displayed inside a content control

▶ **11.** Scroll down to display the letter's closing, change "Chris Tupelo" to your first and last names, and then scroll back up to the beginning of the letter.

▶ **12.** Save the document.

Now that the document contains the current date, you can begin the mail merge process.

Performing a Mail Merge

When you perform a mail merge, you insert individualized information from a data source into a main document. A main document can be a letter or any other kind of document containing merge fields that tell Word where to insert names, addresses, and other variable information from the data source. When you **merge** the main document with information from the data source, you produce a new document called a merged document. The Session 6.1 Visual Overview summarizes mail merge concepts.

Chris's main document is the letter shown in the Session 6.1 Visual Overview. In this session, you will insert the merge fields shown in this letter. You'll also create Chris's data source, which will include the name and address of each customer. The data source will also include information about each customer's favorite items at the store.

You can perform a mail merge by using the Mail Merge task pane, which walks you through the steps of performing a mail merge. You access the Mail Merge task pane by clicking the Start Mail Merge button in the Start Mail Merge group on the Mailings tab and then clicking the Step-by-Step Mail Merge Wizard command on the menu. You can also use the options on the Mailings tab, which streamlines the process and offers more tools. In this module, you'll work with the Mailings tab to complete the mail merge for Chris. The Mailings tab organizes the steps in the mail merge process so that you can move from left to right across the ribbon using the buttons to complete the merge.

Starting the Mail Merge and Selecting a Main Document

The first step in the mail merge process is selecting the type of main document. Your choice of main document type affects the commands that are available to you later as you continue through the mail merge process, so it's important to make the correct selection at the beginning. In this case, you will use a letter as the main document.

To start the mail merge process and select a main document:

▶ **1.** On the ribbon, click the **Mailings** tab.

Notice that most of the buttons in the groups on the Mailings tab are grayed out, indicating the options are unavailable. These options become available only after you begin the mail merge process and select a data source.

▶ **2.** In the Start Mail Merge group, click the **Start Mail Merge** button. The Start Mail Merge menu opens, as shown in Figure 6-3.

| Figure 6-3 | Start Mail Merge menu |

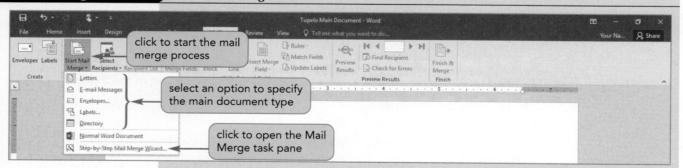

The first five options on the menu allow you to specify the type of main document you will create. Most of the options involve print items, such as labels and letters, but you can also select an email message as the type of main document. In this case, you'll create a letter.

▶ **3.** Click **Letters**. The Start Mail Merge menu closes.

Next, you need to select the list of recipients for Chris's letter; that is, you need to select the data source.

4. In the Start Mail Merge group, click the **Select Recipients** button. The Select Recipients menu allows you to create a new recipient list, use an existing list, or select from Outlook Contacts (the address book in Outlook).

Because Chris hasn't had a chance to create a data source yet, she asks you to create one.

5. Click **Type a New List**. The New Address List dialog box opens, as shown in Figure 6-4.

Figure 6-4	New Address List dialog box

fields included in the new data source by default

The default fields for a data source are displayed in this dialog box. Before you begin creating the data source, you need to identify the fields and records Chris wants you to include.

Creating a Data Source

As described in the Session 6.1 Visual Overview, a data source is a file that contains information organized into fields and records. Typically, the data source for a mail merge contains a list of names and addresses, but it can also contain email addresses, telephone numbers, and other data. Various kinds of files can be used as the data source, including an Excel workbook or an Access database. You can also use a file from another kind of database, such as one created by a company to store its sales information. For a simple mail merge project, such as a telephone directory, you can use a table stored in a Word document.

When performing a mail merge, you'll usually select an existing data source file—created in another application—that already contains the necessary information. However, in this module, you'll create a new data source in Word and then enter the data into it so you can familiarize yourself with the basic structure of a data source. After creating the new data source, you'll save the file in its default format as an Access database file, with an .mdb file extension. Microsoft Outlook also uses MDB files to store contact information—in which case they are referred to as Microsoft Office Address Lists files.

When you create a new data source, Word provides a number of default fields, such as First Name, Last Name, and Company. You can customize the data source by adding new fields and removing the default fields that you don't plan to use. When creating a data source, keep in mind that each field name must be unique; you can't have two fields with the same name.

The Microsoft Office Address Lists file you will create in this session will contain information about Chris's customers, including each customer's name, address, preferred variety of peach, and another favorite product. Chris collected all the necessary information by asking customers to sign up for the farm's mailing list. Figure 6-5 shows one of the forms she used to collect the information.

Figure 6-5 **Customer comment card**

Tupelo Family Market

Sign up for our mailing list to receive special offers and information about our latest products.

First Name_____ Last Name _____

Street Address _____ Apartment _____

City _____ Zip Code _____

Email Address _____

Home delivery customers, please include a phone number (home or cell) _____

Which variety of peach do you like best?   _____

Which of our other peach products do you like best?   _____

The information on each form will make up one record in the data source. Each blank on the form translates into one field in the data source as shown in Figure 6-6.

Figure 6-6 **Fields to include in the data source**

Field Names	Description
First Name	Customer's first name
Last Name	Customer's last name
Address Line 1	Customer's street address
Address Line 2	Additional address information, such as an apartment number
City	City
State	State
ZIP Code	ZIP code
E-mail Address	Customer's email address
Phone	Customer's home or cell phone number
Peach Variety	Customer's favorite peach variety
Other Product	Customer's favorite other peach product

Even though you won't need the customers' email addresses or phone numbers to complete the mail merge, you can still include them in the data source. That way, Chris can reuse the data source in future mail merges to send emails to her customers or when creating a directory of phone numbers for home delivery customers.

REFERENCE

Creating a Data Source for a Mail Merge

- On the ribbon, click the Mailings tab.
- In the Start Mail Merge group, click the Select Recipients button, and then click Type a New List to open the New Address List dialog box.
- To select the fields for your data source, click the Customize Columns button to open the Customize Address List dialog box.
- To delete an unnecessary field, select it, click the Delete button, and then click the Yes button.
- To add a new field, click the Add button, type the name of the field in the Add Field dialog box, and then click the OK button.
- To rearrange the order of the field names, click a field name, and then click the Move Up button or the Move Down button.
- To rename a field, click a field name, click the Rename button to open the Rename Field dialog box, type a new field name, and then click the OK button to close the Rename Field dialog box.
- Click the OK button to close the Customize Address List dialog box.
- In the New Address List dialog box, enter information for the first record, click the New Entry button, and then enter the information for the next record. Continue until you are finished entering all the information for the data source, and then click the OK button to open the Save Address List dialog box.
- Type a name for the data source in the File name box. By default, Word will save the file to the My Data Sources folder unless you specify another save location. Click the Save button. The file is saved with the .mdb file extension.

You're ready to create the data source for the form letter using information Chris has given you for three of her customers. However, before you begin entering information, you need to customize the list of fields to include only the fields Chris requires.

To customize the list of fields before creating the data source:

1. In the New Address List dialog box, click the **Customize Columns** button. The Customize Address List dialog box opens. Here you can delete the fields you don't need, add new ones, and arrange the fields in the order you want. You'll start by deleting some fields.

2. In the Field Names box, verify that **Title** is selected, and then click the **Delete** button. A message is displayed, asking you to confirm the deletion.

3. Click the **Yes** button. The Title field is deleted from the list of field names.

4. Continue using the Delete button to delete the following fields: **Company Name**, **Country or Region**, and **Work Phone**.

   Next, you need to add some new fields. When you add a new field, it is inserted below the selected field, so you'll start by selecting the last field in the list.

5. In the Field Names box, click **E-mail Address**, and then click the **Add** button. The Add Field dialog box opens, asking you to type a name for your field. See Figure 6-7.

Figure 6-7 Add Field dialog box

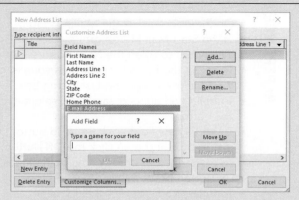

▶ **6.** Type **Peach Variety** and then click the **OK** button. The field "Peach Variety" is added to the Field Names list.

▶ **7.** Use the Add button to add the **Other Product** field below the Peach Variety field.

Next, you need to move the E-mail Address field up above the Home Phone field, so that the fields are in the same order as they appear on the form shown in Figure 6-5.

▶ **8.** Click **E-mail Address**, and then click the **Move Up** button. The E-mail Address field moves up, so it is now displayed just before the Home Phone field.

Finally, because Chris's form asks customers to fill in a home or cell phone number, you need to change "Home Phone" to simply "Phone."

▶ **9.** Click **Home Phone**, and then click the **Rename** button to open the Rename Field dialog box.

▶ **10.** In the To box, replace "Home Phone" with **Phone** and then click the **OK** button to close the Rename Field dialog box and return to the Customize Address List dialog box. See Figure 6-8.

Figure 6-8 Customized list of field names

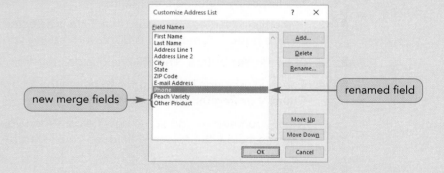

11. Click the **OK** button in the Customize Address List dialog box to close it and return to the New Address List dialog box. This dialog box reflects the changes you just made. For instance, it no longer includes the Title field. The fields are listed in the same order as they appeared in the Customize Address List dialog box.

12. Use the horizontal scroll bar near the bottom of the New Address List dialog box to scroll to the right to display the Peach Variety and Other Product fields. See Figure 6-9.

| Figure 6-9 | Changes made to New Address List dialog box |

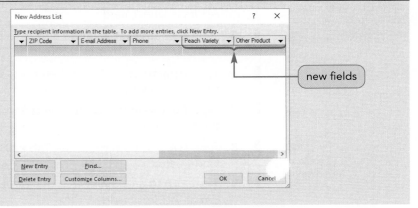

new fields

Organizing Field Names

INSIGHT

Although the order of field names in the data source doesn't affect their placement in the main document, it's helpful to arrange field names logically in the data source so you can enter information quickly and efficiently. For example, you'll probably want the First Name field next to the Last Name field. To make it easier to transfer information from a paper form to a data source, it's a good idea to arrange the fields in the same order as on the form, just like you did in the preceding steps. Also, note that if you include spaces in your field names, Word will replace the spaces with underscores when you insert the fields into the main document. For example, Word transforms the field name "First Name" into "First_Name."

Now that you have specified the fields you want to use, you are ready to enter the customer information into the data source.

Entering Data into a Data Source

Chris has given you three completed customer information forms and has asked you to enter the information from the forms into the data source. You'll use the New Address List dialog box to enter the information. As you press the Tab key to move right from one field to the next, the dialog box will scroll to display fields that are not currently visible.

To enter data into a record using the New Address List dialog box:

1. In the New Address List dialog box, scroll to the left to display the First Name field.

2. Click in the **First Name** field, if necessary, and then type **Emma** to enter the first name of the first customer.

   Do not press the spacebar after you finish typing an entry in the New Address List dialog box.

3. Press the **Tab** key to move the insertion point to the Last Name field.

4. Type **Peterson** and then press the **Tab** key to move the insertion point to the Address Line 1 field.

5. Type **45 Faircrest Avenue** and then press the **Tab** key to move the insertion point to the Address Line 2 field.

6. Type **Apartment 5A** and then press the **Tab** key to move the insertion point to the City field.

7. Type **Fort Valley** and then press the **Tab** key to move the insertion point to the State field.

8. Type **GA** and then press the **Tab** key to move the insertion point to the ZIP Code field.

9. Type **31030** and then press the **Tab** key to move the insertion point to the E-mail Address field.

10. Type **peterson@sample.cengage.com** and then press the **Tab** key to move the insertion point to the Phone field.

11. Type **555-555-5555** and then press the **Tab** key to move the insertion point to the Peach Variety field.

12. Type **Gold Jewel** and then press the **Tab** key. The insertion point is now in the Other Product field, which is the last field in the data source.

13. Type **jam** and then stop. Do not press the Tab key.

14. Use the horizontal scroll bar to scroll to the left, and then review the data in the record. See Figure 6-10.

> **TIP**
>
> You can press the Shift+Tab keys to move the insertion point to the previous field.

Figure 6-10   Completed record

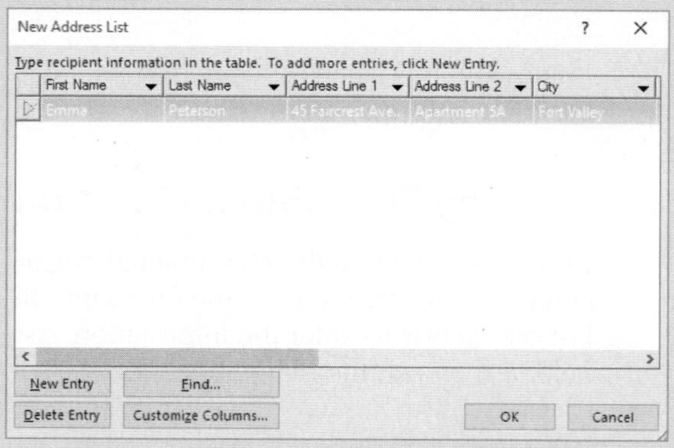

You have finished entering the information for the first record of the data source. Now you're ready to enter information for the next two records. You can create a new record by clicking the New Entry button, or by pressing the Tab key after you have finished entering information into the last field for a record. Note that within a record, you can leave some fields blank. For example, only two of Chris's three customers included information for the Address Line 2 field.

To add additional records to the data source:

1. In the New Address List dialog box, click the **New Entry** button. A new, blank record is created.

2. Enter the information shown in Figure 6-11 for the next two records. To start the Isaac Carlyle record, press the **Tab** key after entering the Other Product field for the David Ahrens record.

Figure 6-11	Information for records 2 and 3

First Name	Last Name	Address Line 1	Address Line 2	City	State	ZIP Code	E-mail Address	Phone	Peach Variety	Other Product
David	Ahrens	603 Emerson Road	P.O. Box 6375	Atlanta	GA	30305	ahrens@sample.cengage.com	555-555-5555	Starlight	peach nectar
Isaac	Carlyle	278 S. Linder		Fort Valley	GA	31030	carlyle@sample.cengage.com	555-555-5555	Starlight	jam

Note that the Address Line 2 field should be blank in the Isaac Carlyle record.

Trouble? If you start a fourth record by mistake, click the Delete Entry button to remove the blank fourth record.

You have entered the records for three customers. Chris's data source eventually will contain hundreds of records for Tupelo Family Farm customers. The current data source, however, contains the records Chris wants to work with now. Next, you need to save the data source.

Saving a Data Source

TIP

In File Explorer, the file type for a Microsoft Office Address Lists file is "Microsoft Access Database."

After you finish entering data for your new data source, you can close the New Address List dialog box. When you do so, the Save Address List dialog box opens, where you can save the data source using the default file type, Microsoft Office Address Lists.

To save the data source:

1. In the New Address List dialog box, click the **OK** button. The New Address List dialog box closes, and the Save Address List dialog box opens, as shown in Figure 6-12.

Figure 6-12   Saving the data source

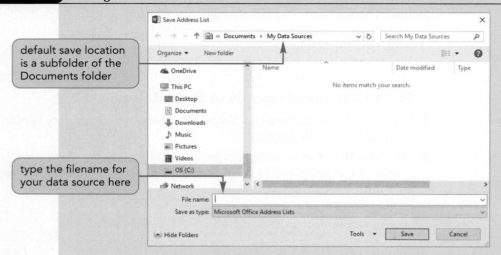

default save location is a subfolder of the Documents folder

type the filename for your data source here

The Save as type box indicates that the data source will be saved as a Microsoft Office Address Lists file. The File name box is empty; you need to name the file before saving it.

2. Click the **File name** box, if necessary, and then type **Tupelo Data**.

   Unless you specify another save location, Word will save the file to the My Data Sources folder, which is a subfolder of the Documents folder.

   In this case, you'll save the data source in the same location in which you saved the main document.

3. Navigate to the location in which you saved the main document, and then click the **Save** button. The Save Address List dialog box closes, and you return to the main document.

The next step in the mail merge process is to add the necessary merge fields to the main document. For Chris's letter, you need to add merge fields for the inside address, for the salutation, and for each customer's favorite variety of peach and other product.

PROSKILLS

Decision Making: Planning Your Data Source

When creating a data source, think beyond the current mail merge task to possible future uses for your data source. For example, Chris's data source includes both an E-mail Address field and a Phone field—not because she wants to use that information in the current mail merge project, but because she can foresee needing these pieces of information at a later date to communicate with her customers. Having all relevant customer information in one data source will make it easier to retrieve and use the information effectively.

In some cases, you'll also want to include information that might seem obvious. For example, Chris's data source includes a State field even though all of her current customers live in or around Fort Valley, Georgia. However, she included a State field because she knows that her pool of addresses could expand sometime in the future to include residents of other states.

Finally, think about the structure of your data source before you create it. Try to break information down into as many fields as seems reasonable. For example, it's always better to include a First Name field and a Last Name field, rather than simply a Name field, because including two separate fields makes it possible to alphabetize the information in the data source by last name. If you entered first and last names in a single Name field, you could alphabetize only by first name.

If you're working with a very small data source, breaking information down into as many fields as possible is less important. However, it's very common to start with a small data source and then, as time goes on, find that you need to continually add information to the data source, until you have a large file. If you failed to plan the data source adequately at the beginning, the expanded data source could become difficult to manage.

Another important issue is what type of file you use to store your data source. In this session, you created a data source from within Word and saved it as a Microsoft Office Address Lists file. However, in most situations, you should save your data source in a spreadsheet or database file so that you can utilize the data manipulation options a spreadsheet program or database program provides.

Inserting Merge Fields

When inserting merge fields into the main document, you must include proper spacing around the fields so that the information in the merged document will be formatted correctly. To insert a merge field, you move the insertion point to the location where you want to insert the merge field, and then click the Insert Merge Field button arrow in the Write & Insert Fields group.

For Chris's letter, you will build an inside address by inserting individual merge fields for the address elements. The letter is a standard business letter, so you'll place merge fields for the customer's name and address below the date.

To insert a merge field in the main document:

 1. Click in the second blank paragraph below the date.

 2. In the Write & Insert Fields group, click the **Insert Merge Field button arrow**. A menu opens with the names of all the merge fields in the data source. Note that the spaces in the merge field names have been replaced with underscores. See Figure 6-13.

Figure 6-13 Insert Merge Field menu

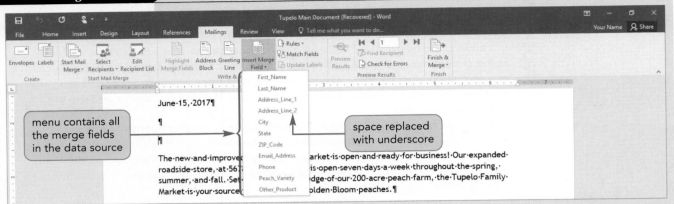

Trouble? If the Insert Merge Field dialog box opens, you clicked the Insert Merge Field button instead of the Insert Merge Field button arrow. Close the dialog box and repeat Step 2.

3. Click **First_Name**. The Insert Merge Field menu closes, and the merge field is inserted into the document.

   The merge field consists of the field name surrounded by double angled brackets << >>, also called chevrons.

   Trouble? If you make a mistake and insert the wrong merge field, click to the left of the merge field, press the Delete key to select the field, and then press the Delete key again to delete it.

4. In the Write & Insert Fields group, click the **Highlight Merge Fields** button. The First_Name merge field is displayed on a gray background, making it easier to see in the document. See Figure 6-14.

TIP

You can only insert merge fields into a main document using the tools on the Mailings tab or in the Mail Merge task pane. You cannot type merge fields into the main document—even if you type the angled brackets.

Figure 6-14 First_Name merge field highlighted in main document

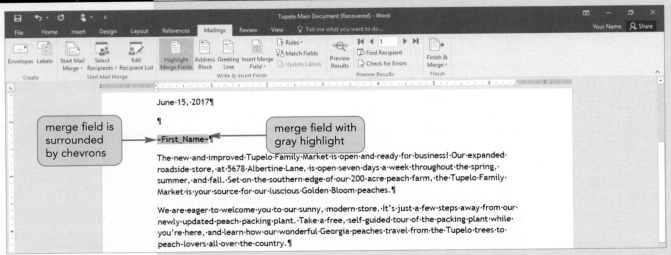

Later, when you merge the main document with the data source, Word will replace the First_Name merge field with information from the First Name field in the data source.

Now, you're ready to insert the merge fields for the rest of the inside address. You'll add the necessary spacing and punctuation between the merge fields as well. You might be accustomed to pressing the Shift+Enter keys to start a new line in an inside address without inserting paragraph spacing. However, because your data source includes a record in which one of the fields (the Address Line 2 field) is blank, you need to press the Enter key to start each new line. As you will see later in this Module, this ensures that Word hides the Address Line 2 field in the final merged document whenever that field is blank. To maintain the proper spacing in the main document, you'll adjust the paragraph spacing after you insert all the fields.

To insert the remaining merge fields for the inside address:

1. Press the **spacebar** to insert a space after the First_Name merge field, click the **Insert Merge Field button arrow**, and then click **Last_Name**.

2. Press the **Enter** key to start a new paragraph, click the **Insert Merge Field button arrow**, and then click **Address_Line_1**. Word inserts the Address_Line_1 merge field into the form letter.

3. Press the **Enter** key, click the **Insert Merge Field button arrow**, and then click **Address_Line_2**. Word inserts the Address_Line_2 merge field into the form letter.

4. Press the **Enter** key, insert the **City** merge field, type **,** (a comma), press the **spacebar** to insert a space after the comma, and then insert the **State** merge field.

5. Press the **spacebar**, and then insert the **ZIP_Code** merge field. The inside address now contains all the necessary merge fields. See Figure 6-15.

Figure 6-15	Main document with merge fields for inside address

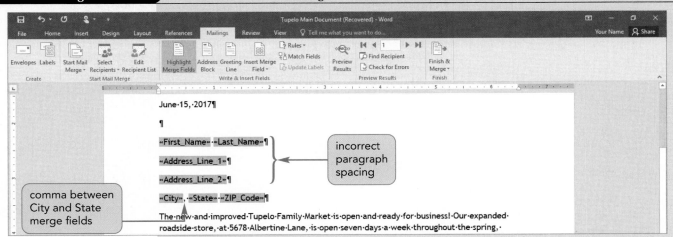

Next, you will adjust the paragraph spacing for the inside address.

6. Select the first three paragraphs of the inside address.

7. On the ribbon, click the **Home** tab.

8. In the Paragraph group, click the **Line and Paragraph Spacing** button , and then click **Remove Space After Paragraph**. The paragraph spacing is removed, so that the paragraphs of the inside address are now correctly spaced.

You can now add the salutation of the letter, which will contain each customer's first name.

To insert the merge field for the salutation:

▶ **1.** Insert a new paragraph after the ZIP_Code field, type **Dear** and then press the **spacebar**.

▶ **2.** On the ribbon, click the **Mailings** tab.

▶ **3.** In the Write & Insert Fields group, click the **Insert Merge Field button arrow**, click **First_Name** to insert this field into the document, and then type **:** (a colon).

▶ **4.** Save the document.

You'll further personalize Chris's letter by including merge fields that will allow you to reference each customer's favorite variety of peach and favorite other product.

To add merge fields for each customer's favorite items:

▶ **1.** If necessary, scroll down to display the complete third paragraph in the body of the letter, which begins "Bring along this letter...."

▶ **2.** In the third paragraph in the body of the letter, select the placeholder text **[PEACH VARIETY]**, including the brackets. You'll replace this phrase with a merge field. Don't be concerned if you also select the space following the closing bracket.

▶ **3.** Insert the **Peach_Variety** merge field. Word replaces the selected text with the Peach_Variety merge field.

▶ **4.** Verify that the field has a single space before it and after it. Add a space on either side if necessary.

▶ **5.** Replace the placeholder text "[OTHER PRODUCT]" in the third paragraph in the body of the letter with the **Other_Product** merge field, and adjust the spacing as necessary. See Figure 6-16.

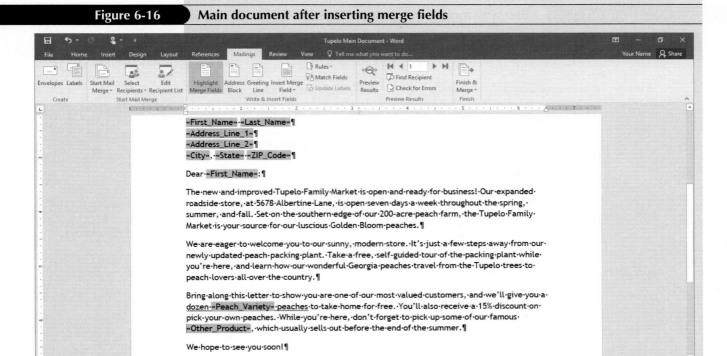

Figure 6-16   Main document after inserting merge fields

Trouble? The text before and after the inserted merge fields might be marked with a wavy blue underline because Word mistakenly identifies the text as a grammatical error. You can ignore the wavy underlines.

6. Save the document.

The main document now contains all the necessary merge fields.

Previewing the Merged Document

Your next step is to preview the merged document to see how the letter will look after Word inserts the information for each customer. When you preview the merged document, you can check one last time for any missing spaces between the merge fields and the surrounding text. You can also look for any other formatting problems, and, if necessary, make final changes to the data source.

To preview the merged document:

1. In the Preview Results group, click the **Preview Results** button, and then scroll up to display the inside address. The data for the first record (Emma Peterson) replaces the merge fields in the form letter. On the ribbon, the Go to Record box in the Preview Results group shows which record is currently displayed in the document. See Figure 6-17.

Figure 6-17 Letter with merged data for first record

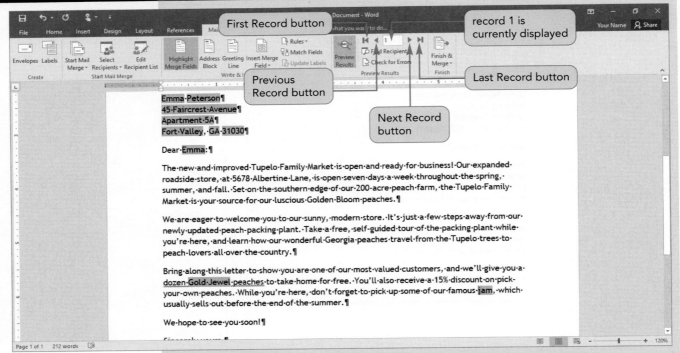

Note that the inside address, which includes information from the Address Line 2 field, contains a total of four lines.

2. Carefully check the Emma Peterson letter to make sure the text and formatting are correct, and make any necessary corrections. In particular, make sure that the spacing before and after the merged data is correct; it is easy to accidentally omit spaces or add extra spaces around merge fields.

3. In the Preview Results group, click the **Next Record** button. The data for David Ahrens is displayed in the letter. As with the preceding record, the inside address for this record includes four lines of information.

4. Click the **Next Record** button again to display the data for Isaac Carlyle in the letter. In this case, the inside address includes only three lines of information. See Figure 6-18.

Figure 6-18 Address for third record

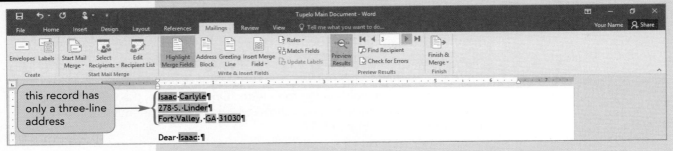

5. In the Preview Results group, click the **First Record** button to redisplay the first record in the letter (with data for Emma Peterson).

The main document of the mail merge is complete. Now that you have previewed the merged documents, you can finish the merge.

Merging the Main Document and the Data Source

When you finish a merge, you can choose to merge directly to the printer. In other words, you can choose to have Word print the merged document immediately without saving it as a separate file. Alternatively, you can merge to a new document, which you can save using a new filename. If your data source includes an E-mail Address field, you can also create a mail merge in email format, generating one email for every email address in the data source.

Chris wants to save an electronic copy of the merged document for her records, so you'll merge the data source and main document into a new document.

To complete the mail merge:

1. In the Finish group, click the **Finish & Merge** button. The Finish & Merge menu displays the three merge options. See Figure 6-19.

Figure 6-19 | **Finishing the merge**

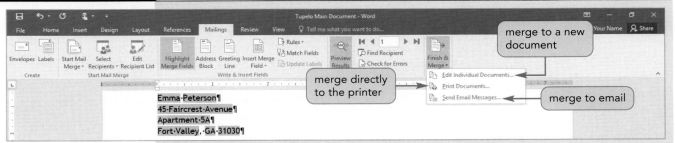

2. In the Finish & Merge menu, click **Edit Individual Documents**. The Merge to New Document dialog box opens. Here, you need to specify which records to include in the merge. You want to include all three records from the data source.

3. Verify that the **All** option button is selected, and then click the **OK** button. Word creates a new document named Letters1, which contains three pages—one for each record in the data source. See Figure 6-20.

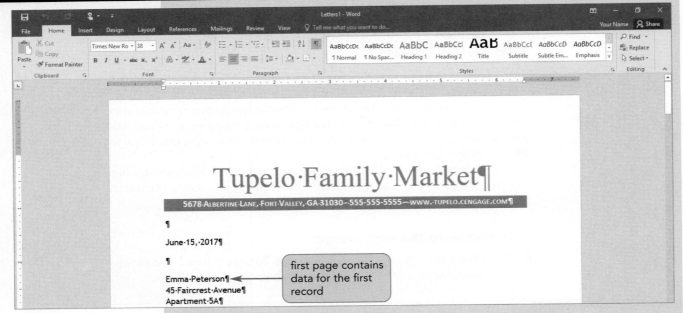

Figure 6-20 Merged document

In this new document, the merge fields have been replaced by the specific names, addresses, and so on from the data source.

▶ 4. Scroll down and review the contents of the document. Note that each letter is addressed to a different customer, and that the favorite peach variety and other product vary from one letter to the next.

▶ 5. Scroll back to the first page of the document, and as you scroll, notice that the letters are separated by Next Page section breaks.

▶ 6. Save the merged document in the location specified by your instructor, using the filename **Tupelo Merged Letters 1**.

▶ 7. Close the **Tupelo Merged Letters 1** document. The document named "Tupelo Main Document" is now the active document.

After completing a merge, you need to save the main document. That ensures that any changes you might have made to the data source during the course of the mail merge are saved along with the main document.

▶ 8. Save and close the **Tupelo Main Document** file.

Note that if you need to take a break while working on a mail merge, you can save the main document and close it. The data source and field information are saved along with the document. When you're ready to work on the merge again, you can open the main document and update the connection to the data source. You'll see how this works at the beginning of the next session, when you will learn how to use additional mail merge features.

REVIEW

Session 6.1 Quick Check

1. Explain how to insert a Date field that updates automatically every time the document is opened.

2. Define the following:
   a. merge field
   b. record
   c. main document
   d. data source

3. List at least three types of files that you can use as data sources in a mail merge.

4. What is the first step in performing a mail merge?

5. Explain how to use the options on the Mailings tab to insert a merge field into a main document.

6. What are the last two steps in the mail merge process?

Session 6.2 Visual Overview:

The Edit Recipient List button opens the Mail Merge Recipients dialog box.

In the Mail Merge Recipients dialog box, you can make changes that affect individual records or the structure and organization of the data source itself.

To sort a data source according to the contents of a particular field, click that field's column header. To sort in ascending order, click the field header once. To sort in descending order, click it twice.

A checkmark indicates that a record will be included in the merge. By default, all records are checked. To omit a record from the merge, click its check box to delete the checkmark.

To make changes to the contents of individual records, select the data source in the Data Source box, and then click the Edit button to open the Edit Data Source dialog box.

To sort by more than one field, click the Sort command.

You can click the Filter command to further customize a data source. When you **filter** data, you temporarily display only records that contain a particular value in a particular field.

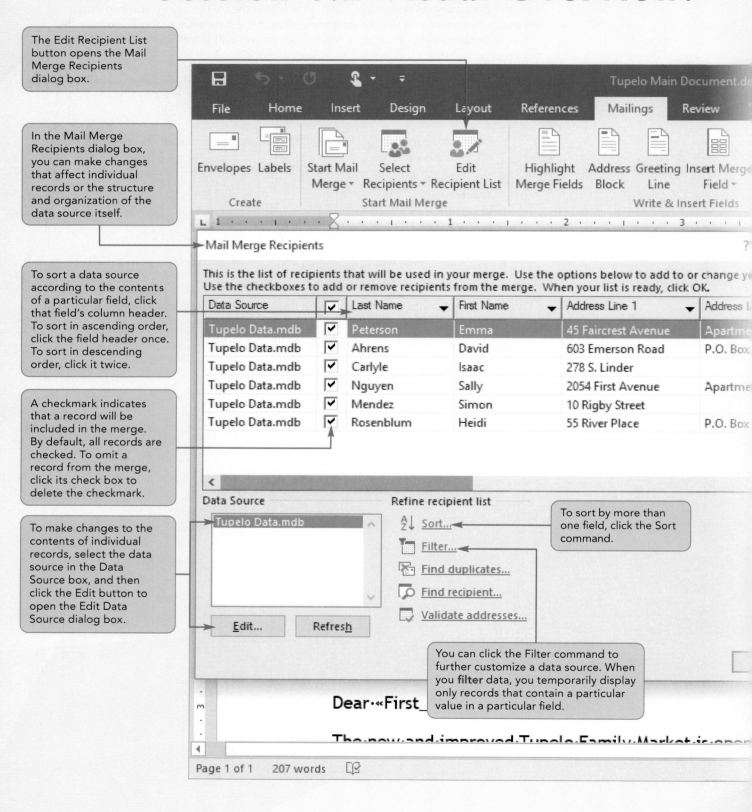

Editing a Data Source

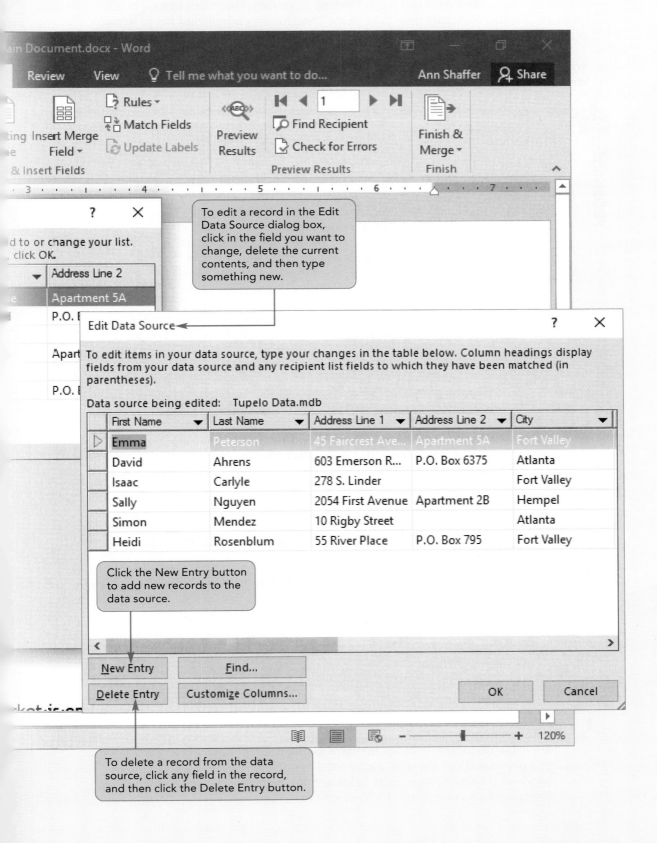

ain Document.docx - Word

Review   View   Tell me what you want to do...   Ann Shaffer   Share

Rules
Match Fields
ting Insert Merge   Update Labels   Preview   Find Recipient   Finish &
Field   Results   Check for Errors   Merge

& Insert Fields   Preview Results   Finish

To edit a record in the Edit Data Source dialog box, click in the field you want to change, delete the current contents, and then type something new.

d to or change your list. click OK.

Address Line 2

Apartment 5A

P.O.

Apart

P.O.

Edit Data Source   ?   ✕

To edit items in your data source, type your changes in the table below. Column headings display fields from your data source and any recipient list fields to which they have been matched (in parentheses).

Data source being edited: Tupelo Data.mdb

First Name ▼	Last Name ▼	Address Line 1 ▼	Address Line 2 ▼	City ▼
Emma	Peterson	45 Faircrest Ave...	Apartment 5A	Fort Valley
David	Ahrens	603 Emerson R...	P.O. Box 6375	Atlanta
Isaac	Carlyle	278 S. Linder		Fort Valley
Sally	Nguyen	2054 First Avenue	Apartment 2B	Hempel
Simon	Mendez	10 Rigby Street		Atlanta
Heidi	Rosenblum	55 River Place	P.O. Box 795	Fort Valley

Click the New Entry button to add new records to the data source.

New Entry   Find...

Delete Entry   Customize Columns...   OK   Cancel

120%

To delete a record from the data source, click any field in the record, and then click the Delete Entry button.

Reopening a Main Document

Performing a mail merge creates a connection between the main document file and the data source file. This connection persists even after you close the main document and exit Word. The connection is maintained as long as you keep both files in their original locations. The two files don't have to be in the same folder; each file just has to remain in the folder it was in when you first performed the mail merge.

When you reopen a main document, you see a warning dialog box explaining that data from a database (that is, the data source) will be placed in the document you are about to open. You can click Yes to open the document with its connection to the data source intact.

PROSKILLS

Teamwork: Sharing Main Documents and Data Sources

In professional settings, a mail merge project often involves files originating from multiple people. The best way to manage these files depends on your particular situation. For instance, at a small office supply company, the marketing manager might supply the text of a main document introducing monthly sales on printer supplies, while the sales manager might supply an updated list of names and addresses of potential customers every month. Suppose that you are the person responsible for performing the mail merge on the first of every month. You'll be able to work more efficiently if you, the marketing manager, and the sales manager agree ahead of time on one storage location for the project. For example, you might set up a special folder on the company network for storing these files.

In large companies that maintain massive databases of customer information, a data source is typically stored at a fixed network location. In those situations, you'll probably need to work with the technical staff who manage the databases to gain access to the data sources you need for your mail merge projects. Maintaining the security of such data sources is extremely important, and you usually can't access them without a password and the appropriate encryption software.

Chris has new customer information she wants you to add to the data source that you used in the previous mail merge, and she wants to perform another merge with the new data. To add the new customer information, you will start by opening the Tupelo Main Document, which is linked to the data source.

To reopen the main document with its connection to the data source intact:

▶ **1.** Open the document **Tupelo Main Document** from the location in which you stored it in Session 6.1.

Word displays a warning message indicating that opening the document will run a SQL command. SQL (usually pronounced *sequel*) is the database programming language that controls the connection between the main document and the data source.

▶ **2.** Click the **Yes** button to open the main document with its link to the data source intact.

▶ **3.** On the ribbon, click the **Mailings** tab.

The main document displays the data for the last record you examined when you previewed the merged document (Emma Peterson). You can alternate between displaying the merge fields and the customer data by toggling the Preview Results button on the Mailings tab.

Trouble? If you see the merge fields instead of the data for one of the customers, skip to Step 5.

▶ **4.** In the Preview Results group, click the **Preview Results** button to deselect it. The merge fields are displayed in the main document. At the beginning of the letter, the Date field, which is not a merge field, continues to display the current date.

▶ **5.** If necessary, highlight the merge fields by clicking the **Highlight Merge Fields** button in the Write & Insert Fields group.

INSIGHT

Maintaining, Breaking, and Reestablishing the Connection to a Data Source

As you have seen, when you reopen a main document, Word displays a warning dialog box, where you can click Yes to open the document with its connection to the data source intact. But what if you want to break the connection between the main document and the data source? One option is to click No in the warning dialog box. In that case, the main document opens with no connection to the data source. If the main document is currently open and already connected to the data source, you can break the connection by clicking Normal Word Document on the Start Mail Merge menu. You can reestablish the connection at any time by starting the mail merge over again and using the Select Recipients button to select the data source.

Keep in mind that you could also break the connection between a main document and its data source if you move one or both of the files to a different folder. Exactly what happens in this case depends on how your computer is set up and where you move the files. In the case of a broken connection, when you open the main document, you'll see a series of message boxes informing you that the connection to the data source has been broken. Eventually, you will see a Microsoft Word dialog box with a button labeled Find Data Source, which you can click, and then use the Select Data Source dialog box to locate and select your data source.

If you are creating mail merges for personal use, it's a good idea to either store the data source in the default My Data Sources folder and keep it there, or store the data source and the main document in the same folder (a folder other than the My Data Sources folder). The latter option is best if you think you might need to move the files to a different computer. That way, if you do need to move them, you can move the entire folder.

Editing a Data Source

After you complete a mail merge, you might need to make some changes to the data source and redo the merge. You can edit a data source in two ways—from within the program used to create the data source, or via the Mail Merge Recipients dialog box in Word. If you are familiar with the program used to create the data source, the simplest approach is to edit the file from within that program. For example, if you were using an Excel worksheet as your data source, you could open the file in Excel, edit it (perhaps by adding new records), save it, and then reselect the file as your data source. To edit the Microsoft Office Address Lists file that you created as a data source for this project, you can use the Mail Merge Recipients dialog box.

REFERENCE

Editing a Microsoft Office Address Lists Data Source in Word

- Open the main document for the data source you want to edit.
- On the ribbon, click the Mailings tab.
- In the Start Mail Merge group, click the Edit Recipient List button.
- In the Data Source box in the Mail Merge Recipients dialog box, select the data source you want to edit, and then click the Edit button.
- To add a record, click the New Entry button, and then enter the data for the new record.
- To delete a record, click any field in the record, and then click the Delete Entry button.
- To add or remove fields from the data source, click the Customize Columns button, click Yes in the warning dialog box, make any changes, and then click the OK button. Remember that if you remove a field, you will delete any data entered into that field for all records in the data source.
- Click the OK button in the Edit Data Source dialog box, click the Yes button in the Microsoft Office Word dialog box, and then click the OK button in the Mail Merge Recipients dialog box.

Chris would like you to add information for three new customers to the data source.

To edit the data source by adding records:

1. In the Start Mail Merge group, click the **Edit Recipient List** button. The Mail Merge Recipients dialog box opens, displaying the contents of the data source that is currently connected to the main document—the Tupelo Data file.

   This dialog box is designed to let you edit any data source, not just the one currently connected to the main document. To edit the Tupelo Data file, you first need to select it in the Data Source box in the lower-left corner. If you had multiple data sources stored in the same folder as the Tupelo Data file, you would see them all in this list box.

2. In the Data Source box, click **Tupelo Data.mdb**. The filename is selected.

   Note that the file has the extension .mdb, which is the file extension for an Access database file—the default format for a data source created in Word. See Figure 6-21.

| Figure 6-21 | Tupelo Data.mdb file selected in the Data Source box of the Mail Merge Recipients dialog box |

data source is an Access database file with an .mdb file extension

click to select the data source

Edit button

3. Click the **Edit** button. The Edit Data Source dialog box opens.

4. Click the **New Entry** button, and then enter the information for the three new records shown in Figure 6-22.

| Figure 6-22 | New Customer data |

First Name	Last Name	Address Line 1	Address Line 2	City	State	ZIP Code	E-Mail Address	Phone	Peach Variety	Other Product
Sally	Nguyen	2054 First Avenue	Apartment 2B	Hempel	GA	31035	nguyen@ sample. cengage.com	555-555-5555	Gold Jewel	peach nectar
Simon	Mendez	10 Rigby Street		Atlanta	GA	30305	mendez@ sample. cengage.com	555-555-5555	Carrington	dried peach slices
Heidi	Rosenblum	55 River Place	P.O. Box 795	Fort Valley	GA	31030	rosenblum@ sample. cengage.com	555-555-5555	Starlight	jam

When you are finished, you will have a total of six records in the data source. Notice that the record for Simon Mendez contains no data in the Address Line 2 field.

5. Click the **OK** button, and then click the **Yes** button in the message box that asks if you want to update the Tupelo Data.mdb file. You return to the Mail Merge Recipients dialog box, as shown in Figure 6-23.

Figure 6-23 New records added to data source

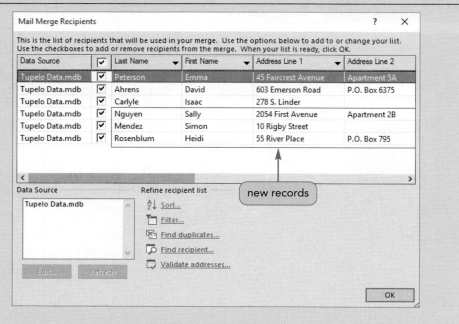

Trouble? If your records look different from those in Figure 6-23, select the data source, click the Edit button, edit the data source, and then click the OK button.

You'll leave the Mail Merge Recipients dialog box open so you can use it to make other changes to the data source.

Sorting Records

You can sort, or rearrange, information in a data source table just as you can sort information in any other table. To quickly sort information in ascending order (*A* to *Z*, lowest to highest, or earliest to latest) or in descending order (*Z* to *A*, highest to lowest, or latest to earliest), click a field's heading in the Mail Merge Recipients dialog box. The first time you click the heading, the records are sorted in ascending order. If you click it a second time, the records are sorted in descending order.

To perform a more complicated sort, you can click the Sort command in the Mail Merge Recipients dialog box to open the Filter and Sort dialog box, where you can choose to sort by more than one field. For example, you could sort records in ascending order by last name, and then in ascending order by first name. In that case, the records would be organized alphabetically by last name, and then, in cases where multiple records contained the same last name, those records would be sorted by first name.

REFERENCE

Sorting a Data Source by Multiple Fields

- On the ribbon, click the Mailings tab.
- In the Start Mail Merge group, click the Edit Recipient List button to open the Mail Merge Recipients dialog box.
- Click Sort to open the Sort Records tab in the Filter and Sort dialog box.
- Click the Sort by arrow, select the first field you want to sort by, and then select either the Ascending option button or the Descending option button.
- Click the Then by arrow, select the second field you want to sort by, and then select either the Ascending option button or the Descending option button.
- If necessary, click the Then by arrow, select the third field you want to sort by, and then select either the Ascending option button or the Descending option button.
- Click the OK button to close the Filter and Sort dialog box.
- Click the OK button to close the Mail Merge Recipients dialog box.

As Chris looks through the letters to her customers in the merged document, she notices one problem—the letters are not grouped by ZIP codes. Currently, the letters are in the order in which customers were added to the data source file. Chris plans to use business mail (also known as bulk mail) to send her letters, and the U.S. Postal Service offers lower rates for mailings that are separated into groups according to ZIP code. She asks you to sort the data file by ZIP code and then by last name, and then merge the main document with the sorted data source.

To sort the data source by ZIP code:

1. In the Mail Merge Recipients dialog box, click **Sort**. The Filter and Sort dialog box opens, with the Sort Records tab displayed.

2. Click the **Sort by** arrow to display a menu, scroll down in the menu, and then click **ZIP Code**. The Ascending button is selected by default, which is what you want.

3. In the Then by box, directly below the Sort by box, click the **Then by** arrow, and then click **Last Name**. See Figure 6-24.

Figure 6-24 Sorting by ZIP code and by last name

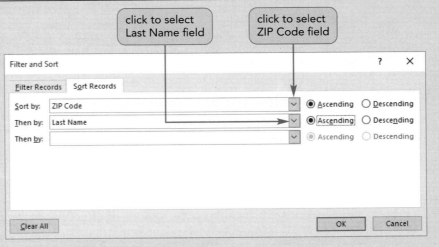

4. Click the **OK** button. Word sorts the records from lowest ZIP code number to highest; and then, within each ZIP code, it sorts the records by last name.

   In the Mail Merge Recipients dialog box, the record for David Ahrens, with ZIP code 30305, is now at the top of the data source list. The record for Simon Mendez, which also has a ZIP code of 30305, comes second. The remaining records are sorted similarly, with the record for Sally Nguyen the last in the list. When you merge the data source with the form letter, the letters will appear in the merged document in this order.

5. Click the **OK** button. The Mail Merge Recipients dialog box closes.

6. On the Mailings tab, in the Preview Results group, click the **Preview Results** button. The data for David Ahrens is displayed in the main document.

7. In the Finish group, click the **Finish & Merge** button, and then click **Edit Individual Documents**.

8. In the Merge to New Document dialog box, verify that the **All** option button is selected, and then click the **OK** button. Word generates the new merged document with six letters—one letter per page as before, but this time the first letter is addressed to David Ahrens.

9. Scroll down and verify that the letters in the newly merged document are arranged in ascending order by ZIP code and then in ascending order by last name.

10. Save the new merged document in the location specified by your instructor, using the filename **Tupelo Merged Letters 2**, and then close it. You return to the Tupelo Main Document.

11. Save the **Tupelo Main Document** file, and keep it open for the next set of steps.

Next, Chris would like you to create a set of letters to send to customers who listed "Starlight" as their favorite peach variety.

Filtering Records

TIP

To omit an individual record from a merge, you can deselect the corresponding check box in the Mail Merge Recipients dialog box rather than using a filter.

Chris wants to inform customers that Starlight peaches are now available fresh or frozen. She asks you to modify the form letter and then merge it with the records of customers who have indicated that Starlight is their favorite variety. To select specific records in a data source, you filter the data source to temporarily display only the records containing a particular value in a particular field.

To filter the data source to select specific records for the merge:

1. In the Preview Results group, click the **Preview Results** button to deselect it and display the merge fields in the Tupelo Main Document file instead of the data from the data source.

2. Save the Tupelo Main Document with the new name **Starlight Main Document** in the location specified by your instructor.

3. In the document, scroll down to the third paragraph in the body of the letter, and then, in the second line of that paragraph, click to the right of the word "peaches."

4. Insert a space, type **(now available fresh or frozen)** and then verify that the sentence reads "...and we'll give you a dozen <<Peach_Variety>> peaches (now available fresh or frozen) to take home for free."

5. In the Start Mail Merge group, click the **Edit Recipient List** button to open the Mail Merge Recipients dialog box, and then scroll to the right so you can see the Peach Variety field.

6. In the header row, click the **Peach Variety** arrow. A menu opens, listing all the entries in the Peach Variety field, as well as a few other options. See Figure 6-25.

Figure 6-25	Filtering records in a data source

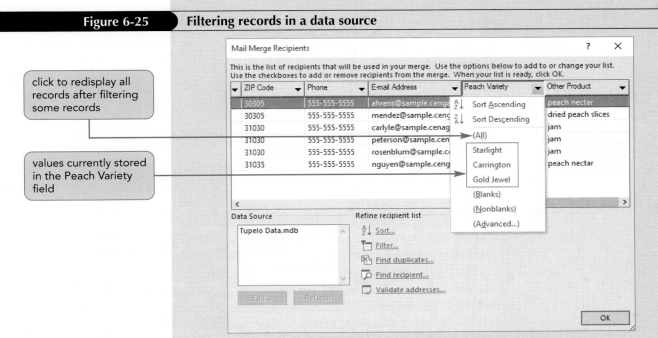

click to redisplay all records after filtering some records

values currently stored in the Peach Variety field

Trouble? If the records sort by Peach Variety, with the record for Carrington peaches at the top, you clicked the Peach Variety column header instead of the arrow. That's not a problem; you don't need to undo the sort. Repeat Step 6, taking care to click the arrow.

You can use the "(All)" option to redisplay all records after previously filtering a data source. The "(Advanced)" option takes you to the Filter Records tab in the Filter and Sort dialog box, where you can perform complex filter operations that involve comparing the contents of one or more fields to a particular value to determine whether a record should be displayed. In this case, however, you can use an option in this menu.

7. Click **Starlight**. Word temporarily hides all the records in the data source except those that contain "Starlight" in the Peach Variety field. See Figure 6-26.

Figure 6-26 **Filtered data source**

only records with "Starlight" in the Peach Variety field are visible

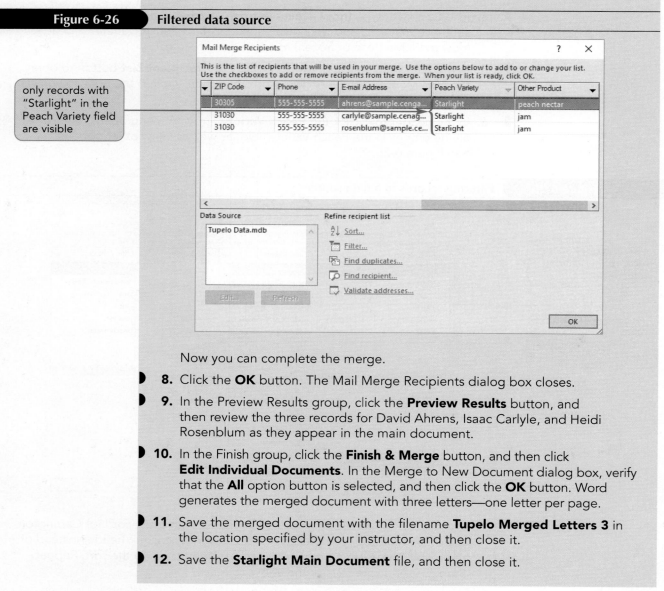

Now you can complete the merge.

8. Click the **OK** button. The Mail Merge Recipients dialog box closes.

9. In the Preview Results group, click the **Preview Results** button, and then review the three records for David Ahrens, Isaac Carlyle, and Heidi Rosenblum as they appear in the main document.

10. In the Finish group, click the **Finish & Merge** button, and then click **Edit Individual Documents**. In the Merge to New Document dialog box, verify that the **All** option button is selected, and then click the **OK** button. Word generates the merged document with three letters—one letter per page.

11. Save the merged document with the filename **Tupelo Merged Letters 3** in the location specified by your instructor, and then close it.

12. Save the **Starlight Main Document** file, and then close it.

Next, you'll create and print mailing labels for the form letters.

Creating Mailing Labels

Chris could print the names and addresses for the letters directly on envelopes, or she could perform a mail merge to create mailing labels. The latter method is easier because she can print 14 labels at once rather than printing one envelope at a time.

Chris has purchased Avery® Laser Printer labels, which are available in most office-supply stores. Word supports most of the Avery label formats, allowing you to choose the layout that works best for you. Chris purchased labels in 8 1/2 × 11-inch sheets that are designed to feed through a printer. Each label measures 4 × 1.33 inches. Each sheet contains seven rows of labels, with two labels in each row, for a total of 14 labels. See Figure 6-27.

TIP

It is a good idea to print one page of a label document on regular paper so you can check your work before printing on the more expensive sheets of adhesive labels.

Figure 6-27   Layout of a sheet of Avery® labels

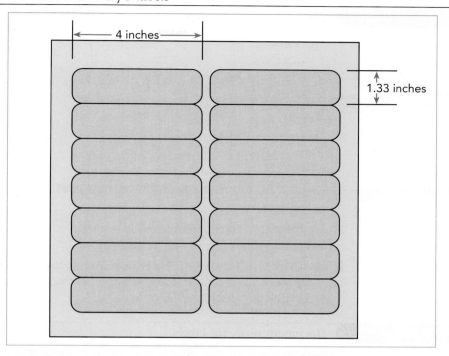

Performing a mail merge to create mailing labels is similar to performing a mail merge to create a form letter. You begin by selecting Labels as the type of main document and then you specify the brand and product number for the labels you are using. You will also need to specify a data source file. In this case, you'll use the Microsoft Office Address Lists data source file, Tupelo Data.mdb, which you created and used in the form letter mail merges.

To specify the main document for creating mailing labels:

▶ **1.** Open a new, blank document, and then save the document as **Tupelo Labels Main Document** in the location specified by your instructor.

▶ **2.** Make sure nonprinting characters are displayed, and zoom out so you can see the whole page.

▶ **3.** On the ribbon, click the **Mailings** tab.

▶ **4.** In the Start Mail Merge group, click the **Start Mail Merge** button.

At this point, if you wanted to merge to envelopes instead of labels, you could click Envelopes to open the Envelope Options dialog box, where you could select the envelope size you wanted to use. In this case, however, you want to merge to labels.

▶ **5.** Click **Labels**. The Label Options dialog box opens.

▶ **6.** Click the **Label vendors** arrow to display a list of vendors, scroll down, and then click **Avery US Letter**.

▶ **7.** Scroll down the Product number box, and then click **5162 Easy Peel Address Labels**. See Figure 6-28.

Figure 6-28   **Label Options dialog box**

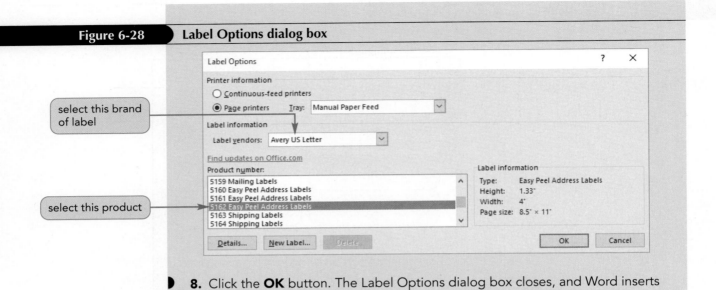

select this brand of label

select this product

8. Click the **OK** button. The Label Options dialog box closes, and Word inserts a table structure into the document, with one cell for each of the 14 labels on the page, as shown in Figure 6-29.

Figure 6-29   **Document ready for labels**

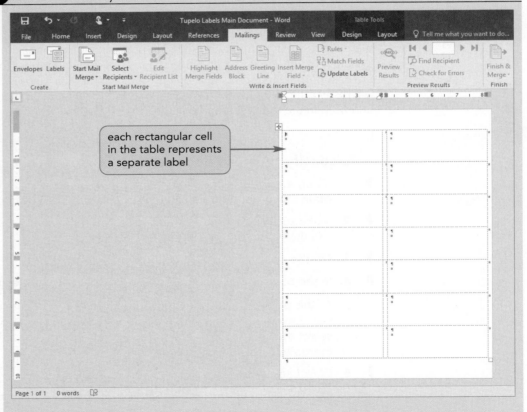

each rectangular cell in the table represents a separate label

As with all table gridlines, these gridlines are visible only on the screen; they will not be visible on the printed labels.

Trouble? If you don't see the table gridlines, click the Table Tools Layout tab, and then, in the Table group, click the View Gridlines button to select it.

You have finished setting up the document. Next, you need to select the data source you created earlier. Note that the changes you made to the data source as a whole earlier in this session (sorting the records and selecting only some records) have no effect on the data source in this new mail merge. However, the changes you made to individual records (such as editing individual records or adding new records) are retained.

To continue the mail merge for the labels:

1. In the Start Mail Merge group, click the **Select Recipients** button, and then click **Use an Existing List**. The Select Data Source dialog box opens.

2. Navigate to the location where you stored the Tupelo Data file, select the **Tupelo Data** file, and then click the **Open** button. The Select Data Source dialog box closes, and you return to the main document.

3. Change the Zoom level to **120%** so you can read the document.

   In each label except the first one, the code <<Next Record>> is displayed. This code tells Word to retrieve the next record from the data source for each label.

4. Verify that the insertion point is located in the upper-left label, and make sure the Mailings tab is still selected on the ribbon.

5. In the Write & Insert Fields group, click the **Address Block** button. The Insert Address Block dialog box opens. The left pane displays possible formats for the name in the address block. The default format, "Joshua Randall Jr.," simply inserts the first and last names, which is what Chris wants. The Preview pane on the right currently shows the first address in the data source, which is the address for Emma Peterson.

6. In the Preview section of the Insert Address Field dialog box, click the **Next** button ▷. The record for David Ahrens is displayed in the Preview pane, as shown in Figure 6-30.

Figure 6-30   **Previewing addresses in the Insert Address Block dialog box**

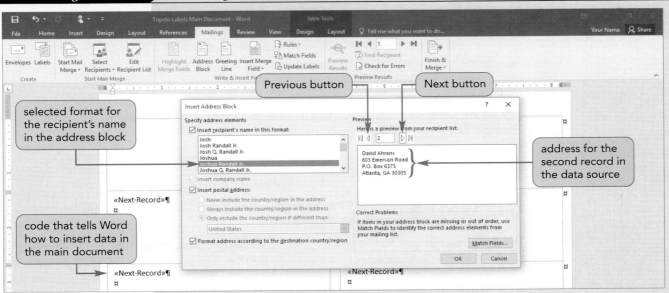

7. Click the **OK** button. The Insert Address Block dialog box closes, and an AddressBlock merge field is displayed in the upper-left label on the page. Next, you need to update the remaining labels to match the one containing the AddressBlock merge field.

8. In the Write & Insert Fields group, click the **Update Labels** button. The AddressBlock merge field is inserted into all the labels in the document, as shown in Figure 6-31.

Figure 6-31 **Field codes inserted into document**

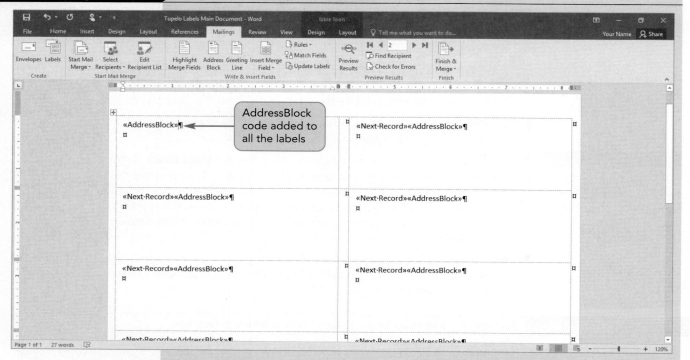

In all except the upper-left label, the Next Record code is displayed to the left of the AddressBlock merge field.

You are ready to preview the labels and complete the merge. To ensure that you see all the labels in the preview, you need to make sure the Go to Record box in the Preview Results group displays the number "1".

To preview the labels and complete the merge:

1. If necessary, click the **First Record** button in the Preview Results group to display "1" in the Go to Record box.

2. In the Preview Results group, click the **Preview Results** button. The addresses for Chris's six customers are displayed in the main document. See Figure 6-32.

Figure 6-32   Previewing addresses in labels

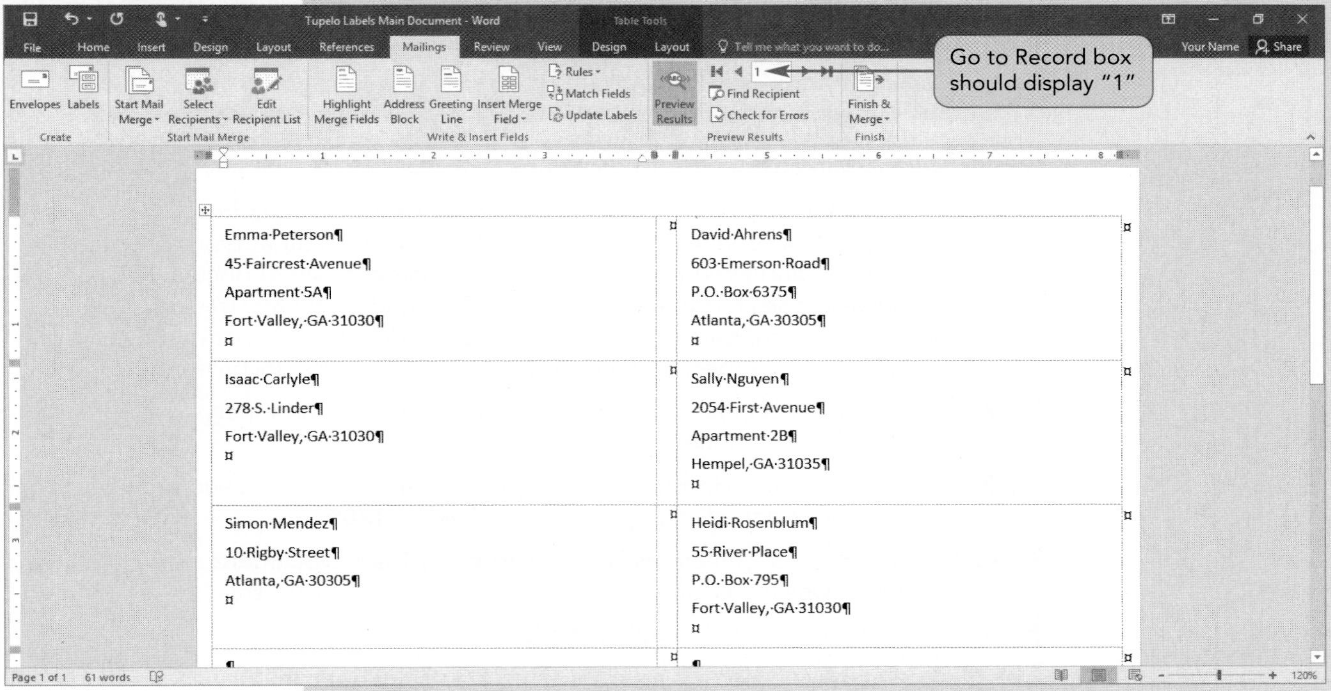

Go to Record box should display "1"

3. In the Finish group, click the **Finish & Merge** button, and then click **Edit Individual Documents**.

4. In the Merge to New Document dialog box, verify that the **All** option button is selected, and then click the **OK** button. The finished labels are inserted into a new document named Labels1.

5. Scroll through the document. The document contains space for 14 labels; but because the data source contains only six records, the new document only contains addresses for six labels.

6. In the upper-left label, change "Emma Peterson" to your first and last names, and then save the merged document as **Tupelo Merged Labels** in the location specified by your instructor.

7. Close the **Tupelo Merged Labels** document, then save and close the **Tupelo Labels Main Document** file.

Creating a Telephone Directory

Next, Chris wants you to create a telephone directory for all store employees. She has already created a Word document containing the phone numbers; you will use that document as the data source for the merge. You'll set up a mail merge as before, except this time you will select Directory as the main document type. Keep in mind that you should use a Word document as a data source only for a simple project like a directory. For letters, it's better to use an Access database, an Excel workbook, or a Microsoft Office Address Lists file. You'll start by examining the Word document that Chris wants you to use as the data source, and then you'll create the main document.

To review the data source and create the main document for the directory:

▶ **1.** Open the document **Phone** from the Word6 > Module folder, and then save it as **Tupelo Phone Data** in the location specified by your instructor. The information in this document is arranged in a table with three column headings—"First Name," "Last Name," and "Phone." The information in the table has already been sorted in alphabetical order by last name.

The Mail Merge Recipients dialog box does not display data from a Word document data source in the same way that it displays other types of data. Also, sorting and filtering does not work the same for Word document data sources as it does for other types of files. To avoid problems, it's easier to edit a Word document data source by opening the document separately, making any necessary changes, and then saving and closing the document.

▶ **2.** Replace "Kiley Bradoff" with your first and last names, and then save and close the Tupelo Phone Data document.

▶ **3.** Open a new, blank document, display nonprinting characters and the rulers, if necessary, and then change the Zoom level to **120%**.

▶ **4.** Save the main document as **Tupelo Directory Main Document** in the location in which you saved the Tupelo Phone Data document.

▶ **5.** On the ribbon, click the **Mailings** tab.

▶ **6.** In the Start Mail Merge group, click the **Start Mail Merge** button, and then click **Directory**.

▶ **7.** In the Start Mail Merge group, click the **Select Recipients** button, and then click **Use an Existing List** to open the Select Data Source dialog box.

▶ **8.** Navigate to and select the Word document named **Tupelo Phone Data**, and then click the **Open** button.

You're ready to insert the fields in the main document. Chris wants the directory to include the names at the left margin of the page and the phone numbers at the right margin, with a dot leader in between. Recall that a dot leader is a dotted line that extends from the last letter of text on the left margin to the beginning of the nearest text aligned at a tab stop.

To set up the directory main document with dot leaders:

▶ **1.** With the insertion point in the first line of the document, insert the **First_Name** merge field, insert a **space**, and then insert the **Last_Name** merge field.

▶ **2.** In the Write & Insert Fields group, click the **Highlight Merge Fields** button. The First_Name and Last_Name merge fields are displayed on a gray background. Now you'll set a tab stop at the right margin (at the 5.5-inch mark on the horizontal ruler) with a dot leader.

▶ **3.** On the ribbon, click the **Home** tab.

TIP

You can click the Clear All button in the Tabs dialog box to delete all the tab stops in the document.

▶ **4.** In the Paragraph group, click the **Dialog Box Launcher** to open the Paragraph dialog box, and then in the lower-left corner of the Indents and Spacing tab, click the **Tabs** button. The Tabs dialog box opens.

▶ **5.** In the Tab stop position box, type **5.5** and then click the **Right** option button in the Alignment section.

▶ **6.** Click the **2 ....** option button in the Leader section. See Figure 6-33.

Figure 6-33   Creating a tab with a dot leader

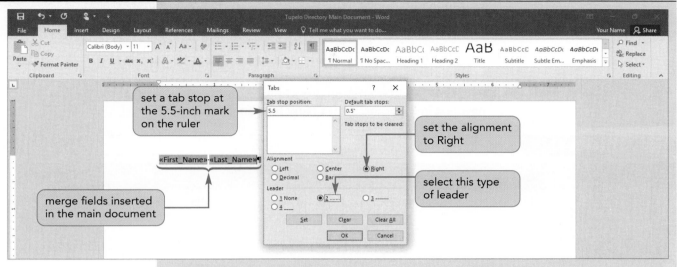

7. Click the **OK** button. Word clears the current tab stops and inserts a right-aligned tab stop at the 5.5-inch mark on the horizontal ruler.

8. Press the **Tab** key to move the insertion point to the new tab stop. A dotted line stretches from the Last_Name merge field to the right side of the page.

9. On the ribbon, click the **Mailings** tab.

Be sure to press the Enter key here to ensure that each name and telephone number is displayed on a separate line.

10. Insert the **Phone** merge field at the insertion point. The dot leader shortens to accommodate the inserted merge fields.

11. Press the **Enter** key. The completed main document should look like the one shown in Figure 6-34.

Figure 6-34   Completed main document for the telephone directory

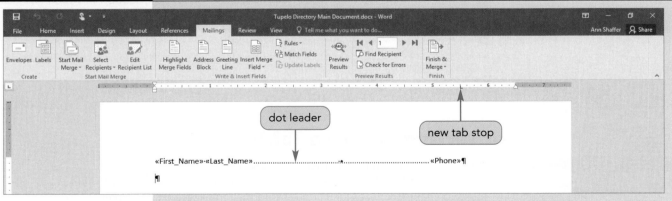

You are now ready to merge this file with the data source.

To finish the merge for the telephone directory:

1. In the Preview Results group, click the **Preview Results** button, and then review the data for the first record in the document.

> **2.** In the Finish group, click the **Finish & Merge** button, and then click **Edit Individual Documents**. In the Merge to New Document dialog box, verify that the **All** option button is selected, and then click the **OK** button. Word creates a new document that contains the completed telephone list.

> **3.** Press the **Enter** key to insert a new paragraph at the beginning of the document.

> **4.** Click in the new paragraph, type **Employee Directory** and then format the new text in **22-point, Times New Roman**. See Figure 6-35.

Figure 6-35 Completed telephone directory

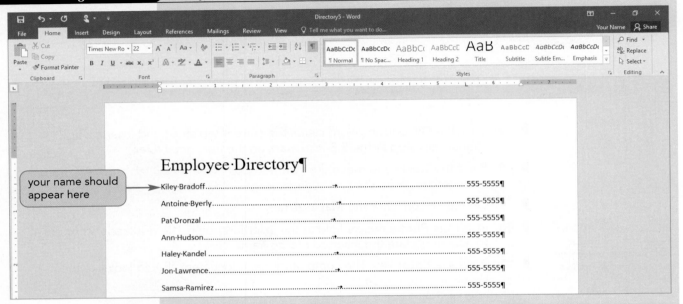

your name should appear here

> **5.** Save the document as **Tupelo Merged Directory** in the location in which you saved the main document, and then close it.

> **6.** Save and close the **Tupelo Directory Main Document** file.

Chris needs your help with one other task related to managing information about the store's customers and employees.

Converting Text to a Table

To be completely proficient in mail merges, you should be able to take information from a variety of sources and set it up for use as a data source. In particular, it's helpful to be able to convert text to a table. For example, address information exported from email and contact management programs often takes the form of a **CSV (comma-separated value) file**, a text file in which each paragraph contains one record, with the fields separated by commas. CSV files can have a .txt or .csv file extension. The commas in a CSV file are known as **separator characters**, or sometimes **delimiters**.

You can use the Convert Text to Table command on the Table menu to transform text from a Word document or a CSV file into a table. But first you need to make sure the text is set up correctly; that is, you need to make sure that separator characters are used consistently to divide the text into individual fields. In a CSV file, commas are used as separator characters, but you might encounter a Word document that uses tab characters, or other characters, as separator characters. After you verify that separator characters are used consistently within a document, you need to make sure each paragraph in the document contains the same number of fields.

Upon conversion, each field is formatted as a separate cell in a column, and each paragraph mark starts a new row, or record. Sometimes a conversion might not turn out the way you expect. In that case, undo it, and then review the text to make sure each paragraph contains the same number of data items, with the items divided by the same separator character.

Chris's assistant, who isn't familiar with Word tables, typed some information about new customers as text in a Word document. He forgot to include an email address and phone number for each customer. Chris wants to convert the text to a table and then add columns for the missing information. The next time the customers visit the store, one of the store clerks can ask for the missing information and then add it to the table.

To convert text into a table:

1. Open the document named **New** from the Word6 > Module folder, and then save it as **New Customers Table** in the location specified by your instructor.

2. Display nonprinting characters, if necessary, and then change the Zoom level to **120%**. See Figure 6-36.

Figure 6-36   **Text with inconsistent separator characters**

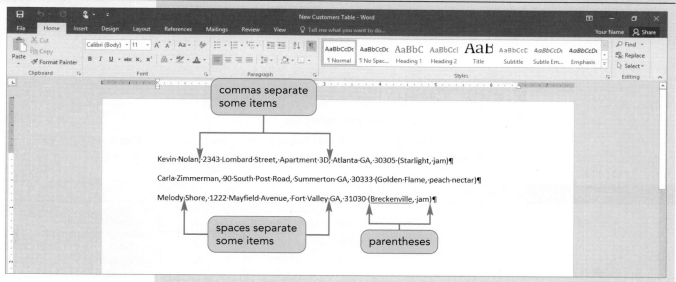

The document consists of three paragraphs, each of which contains a customer's name, address, city, state, ZIP code, favorite peach variety, and favorite other product. Some of the fields are separated by commas and spaces (for example, the address and the city), but some are separated only by spaces, with no punctuation character (for example, the first and last names). Also, the favorite peach variety and other product are enclosed in parentheses. You need to edit this information so that fields are separated by commas, with no parentheses enclosing the last two items.

3. Edit the document to insert a comma after each first name, city, and ZIP code, and then delete the parentheses in each paragraph.

Before you can convert the text into a table, you also need to make sure each paragraph includes the same fields. Currently, the first paragraph includes two pieces of address information—a street address and an apartment number, which is equivalent to an Address Line 1 field and an Address Line 2 field. However, the other paragraphs only include an Address Line 1 field.

▶ **4.** In the second paragraph, click to the right of the comma after "Road," press the **spacebar**, and then type **,** (a comma).

▶ **5.** In the third paragraph, click to the right of the comma after "Avenue," press the **spacebar**, and then type **,** (a comma). Now the second and third paragraphs each contain a blank field. See Figure 6-37.

Figure 6-37   **Text set up for conversion to a table**

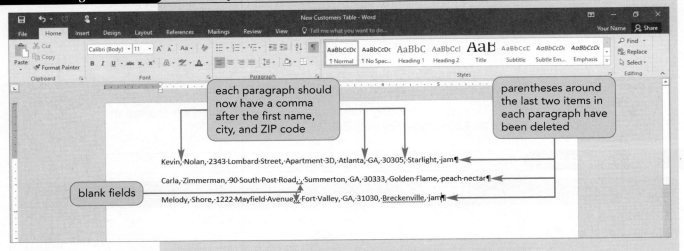

▶ **6.** Press the **Ctrl+A** keys to select the entire document.

▶ **7.** On the ribbon, click the **Insert** tab.

▶ **8.** In the Tables group, click the **Table** button, and then click **Convert Text to Table**. The Convert Text to Table dialog box opens. See Figure 6-38.

Figure 6-38   **Converting text to a table**

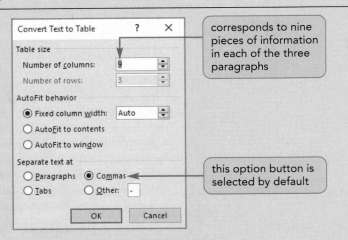

Note that the Number of columns setting is 9, and the Number of rows setting is 3. This corresponds to the nine fields in each of the three paragraphs.

In the Separate text at section of the dialog box, you can choose from three possible separator characters—paragraphs, commas, and tabs. If the text in your document was separated by a character other than paragraphs, commas, or tabs, you could type the character in the box to the right of the Other button. In this case, though, the default option, Commas, is the correct choice because the information in each paragraph is separated by commas.

▶ 9. Click the **OK** button. The Convert Text to Table dialog box closes, and the text in the document is converted into a table consisting of nine columns and three rows.

▶ 10. Save the document.

Now that you have converted the text to a table, you need to finish the table by adding the columns for the phone numbers and email addresses and adding a header row to identify the field names.

To finish the table by adding columns and a header row:

▶ 1. Switch to Landscape orientation, and then select the column containing the ZIP codes.

▶ 2. On the ribbon, click the **Table Tools Layout** tab.

▶ 3. In the Rows & Columns group, click the **Insert Right** button twice to add two blank columns to the right of the column containing ZIP codes.

▶ 4. Select the table's top row, and then in the Rows & Columns group, click the **Insert Above** button.

▶ 5. Enter the column headings shown in Figure 6-39, and format the column headings in bold.

Figure 6-39   **Table with new columns and column headings**

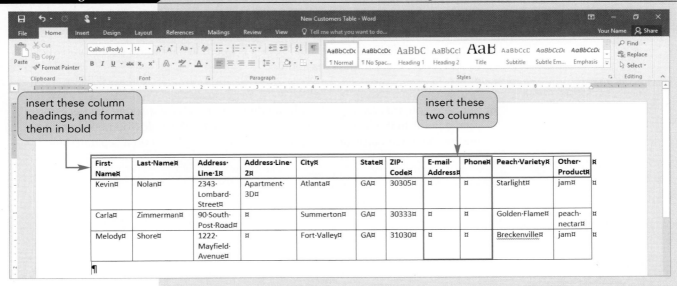

First Name	Last Name	Address Line 1	Address Line 2	City	State	ZIP Code	E-mail Address	Phone	Peach Variety	Other Product
Kevin	Nolan	2343 Lombard Street	Apartment 3D	Atlanta	GA	30305			Starlight	jam
Carla	Zimmerman	90 South Post Road		Summerton	GA	30333			Golden Flame	peach nectar
Melody	Shore	1222 Mayfield Avenue		Fort Valley	GA	31030			Breckenville	jam

insert these column headings, and format them in bold

insert these two columns

▶ 6. Save the **New Customers Table** document, and then close it.

You have finished converting text into a table. Chris can use the table later as the data source for another mail merge. As her business expands, she plans to continue to use Word's mail merge feature to inform her customers about new products and specials.

Combining Data with a Microsoft Office Address Lists File

If you have data in a Word file that you want to combine with data in a Microsoft Office Address Lists file, or any other Microsoft Access file, start by setting up the Word document as a table. That way, you can be sure that each record includes the same fields. You can also review the table quickly to confirm that you have entered data in the various fields in a consistent format. Once you are confident that you have set up the table correctly, you can begin the process of combining it with the Microsoft Office Address Lists file.

First, delete the heading row, and then convert the table back to text by clicking the Table Tools Layout tab, clicking Convert to Text in the Data group, clicking the Commas button, and then clicking OK. Next, save the Word file as a Plain Text file with the .txt file extension. Finally, open the Microsoft Office Address Lists file in Access, click the External Data tab, and then click the Text File button in the Import & Link group to begin importing the text file into the Microsoft Office Address Lists file. In the Get External Data - Text File dialog box, click the Append a copy of the records to the table button, and then click the Browse button to select the plain text file.

Session 6.2 Quick Check

1. Does the connection between a main document and its data source persist after you close the main document, if you keep both files in their original locations?

2. What are two ways to edit a data source?

3. Suppose you want to edit a Microsoft Office Address Lists data source named Employees, and the Mail Merge Recipients dialog box is open. What must you do to begin editing the data source?

4. Suppose the Edit Data Source dialog box is open. What button should you click to add a new entry to the data source?

5. Explain how to filter a data source.

6. Suppose you are creating a telephone directory and have inserted the necessary merge fields in the first paragraph of the document. What do you need to do to ensure that each name and telephone number is displayed on a separate line?

Review Assignments

PRACTICE

Data Files needed for the Review Assignments: Ice.docx, More.docx, Suppliers.docx

The expanded Tupelo Family Market is a big hit. Chris has greatly expanded her customer base, and now she is adding a home delivery service. Customers who sign up for monthly peach deliveries also receive a free quart of homemade ice cream. On the home delivery sign-up form, customers can choose between vanilla peach or cinnamon peach ice cream. Now she wants to send a letter inviting weekly home delivery customers to reserve their free ice cream three days before they want it delivered. She also needs to create an email directory of suppliers she deals with regularly. Finally, she needs to convert some additional customer information into a table that she can use as a data source. Complete the following steps:

1. Open the document **Ice** from the Word6 > Review folder included with your Data Files, and then save the document as **Ice Cream Main Document** in the location specified by your instructor.
2. In the first paragraph, replace the placeholder text "[INSERT DATE FIELD]" with a Date field that displays the current month, day, and year—in the format March 11, 2017.
3. Begin the mail merge by selecting Letters as the type of main document.
4. Create a data source with the following fields in the following order: First Name, Last Name, Address Line 1, Address Line 2, City, State, ZIP Code, E-mail Address, Phone, and Ice Cream Type. Remove any extra fields, and rename fields as necessary.
5. Create four records using the information shown in Figure 6-40.

Figure 6-40   **Information for new data source**

First Name	Last Name	Address Line 1	Address Line 2	City	State	ZIP Code	E-mail Address	Phone	Ice Cream Type
Lara	Pushkin	821 Ruby Lane		Robbins	GA	31035	lara@sample.cengage.com	555-555-5555	cinnamon peach
Marcus	Hesse	933 Nakoma Way		Marigold	GA	31028	marcus@sample.cengage.com	555-555-5555	cinnamon peach
Derrick	Greely	52 Red Earth Road	P.O. Box 2233	Fort Valley	GA	31030	derrick@sample.cengage.com	555-555-5555	vanilla peach
Calista	Cutler	299 Eton Avenue	Apartment 4A	Fort Valley	GA	31030	calista@sample.cengage.com	555-555-5555	vanilla peach

6. Save the data source as **Ice Cream Data** in the location in which you saved the main document.
7. Edit the data source to replace "Marcus Hesse" with your first and last names.
8. Sort the data source in ascending order by ZIP code and then by last name.
9. Replace the placeholder text "[INSERT INSIDE ADDRESS]" with an inside address consisting of the necessary separate merge fields. Adjust the paragraph spacing in the inside address as necessary.
10. In the salutation, replace the placeholder text "[INSERT FIRST NAME]" with the First_Name merge field.
11. In the body of the letter, replace the placeholder text "[INSERT ICE CREAM TYPE]" with the Ice_Cream_Type merge field.
12. Save your changes to the main document, and then preview the merged document. Correct any formatting or spacing problems.
13. Merge to a new document, save the merged document as **Merged Free Ice Cream Letters** in the location in which you saved the main document, and then close the file.

14. Filter the data source to display only records for customers who requested a free cinnamon peach ice cream, and then complete a second merge. Save the new merged document as **Merged Cinnamon Peach Letters** in the location in which you saved the main document. Close all documents, saving all changes.

15. Open a new, blank document, and create a set of mailing labels using the vendor Avery US Letters and product number 5162. Save the main document as **Ice Cream Labels Main Document** in the location in which you saved the Ice Cream Data file.

16. Select the Ice Cream Data file you created earlier in this assignment as the data source.

17. Insert an AddressBlock merge field in the "Joshua Randall Jr." format, and then update the labels.

18. Preview the merged labels, merge to a new document, and then save the new document as **Merged Ice Cream Labels** in the location in which you saved the main document. Save and close all open documents.

19. Open the document **Suppliers** from the Word6 > Review folder, and then save it as **Suppliers Data** in the location specified by your instructor. Change "Carl Siska" to your first and last names, save the document, and close it.

20. Open a new, blank document, and then save it as **Suppliers Directory Main Document** in the location in which you saved the Suppliers Data file. Create a directory main document. Select the Suppliers Data file as the data source.

21. Set a right tab at 6 inches with a dot leader, and insert the necessary merge fields so that the directory shows a contact followed by a comma, followed by the contact's company name, and, on the right side of the page, the email address for each company. Merge to a new document, and then, at the top of the merged document, insert the heading **Supplier Contacts** formatted in 22-point, Times New Roman, with the Green, Accent 6 font color. Save the merged document as **Merged Suppliers Directory** in the location in which you saved the main document. Save and close all open documents.

22. Open the document **More** from the Word6 > Review folder, and then save it as **More Customer Data** in the location specified by your instructor. Convert the data in the document to a table with eight columns. Insert a header row with the following column headers formatted in bold—**First Name**, **Last Name**, **Address Line 1**, **Address Line 2**, **City**, **State**, **ZIP Code**, and **Ice Cream Type**. Replace "Jo Essenberg" with your first and last names. Save and close the document.

Case Problem 1

APPLY

Data File needed for this Case Problem: Newberry.docx

Newberry Glen School   Yolanda Baird is the executive director of Newberry Glen School, an institution in Las Vegas, Nevada, devoted to helping adults earn high school degrees. As part of a new fund-raising campaign for the school, Yolanda plans to send out customized letters to last year's donors, asking them to consider donating the same amount or more this year. She asks you to help her create the letters and the envelopes for the campaign. Complete the following steps:

1. Open the document **Newberry** from the Word6 > Case1 folder, and then save it as **Newberry Glen Main Document** in the location specified by your instructor. In the closing, replace "Yolanda Baird" with your first and last names.

2. In the first paragraph, replace the placeholder text "[INSERT DATE FIELD]" with a Date field that displays the current month, day, and year—in the format March 11, 2017.

3. Begin the mail merge by selecting Letters as the type of main document.

4. Create a data source with the following field names, in the following order—**Title**, **First Name**, **Last Name**, **Address Line 1**, **Address Line 2**, **City**, **State**, **ZIP Code**, **E-mail Address**, and **Donation Amount**.

5. Enter the four records shown in Figure 6-41.

Figure 6-41   **Four records for new data source**

Title	First Name	Last Name	Address Line 1	Address Line 2	City	State	ZIP Code	E-mail Address	Donation Amount
Mr.	Tenzen	Sung	844 Sumerdale Way	Unit 6	Las Vegas	NV	89101	sung@sample.cengage.com	$2,000
Mr.	Jerome	Fuhrman	1577 Shanley Boulevard	Apartment 4C	Las Vegas	NV	89105	fuhrman@sample.cengage.com	$600
Ms.	Susannah	Royal	4424 Gatehouse Lane		New Mesa	NV	89099	royal@sample.cengage.com	$150
Mr.	Adriano	Borrego	633 Desert View		Las Vegas	NV	89105	borrego@sample.cengage.com	$325

6. Save the data source as **Newberry Glen Data** in the location in which you saved the main document.

7. Edit the data source to replace "Tenzen Sung" with your first and last names. Change the title to **Ms.** if necessary.

8. Sort the data source alphabetically by last name.

9. Build an inside address using separate merge fields. Adjust paragraph spacing as necessary.

10. Add a salutation using the Title and Last_Name merge fields, as indicated in the document. Verify that you deleted all placeholder text in the date paragraph, inside address, and the salutation.

11. In the paragraph that begins "In order to continue…," insert the Donation_Amount merge field where indicated. Delete the placeholder text.

12. Save your changes to the Newberry Glen Main Document file. Preview the merged document, and then merge to a new document.

13. Save the merged letters document as **Merged Newberry Glen Letters** in the location in which you saved the main document, and then close it.

14. Save the Newberry Glen Main Document file, and then close it.

15. Open a new, blank document, and then save it as **Newberry Glen Envelopes Main Document** in the location in which you saved the Newberry Glen Data file. The school has envelopes with a preprinted return address, so you don't need to type a return address. Begin the mail merge by selecting Envelopes as the type of main document, and then select Size 10 (4 1/8 × 9 1/2 in) as the envelope size in the Envelope Options dialog box.

16. Use the Newberry Glen Data file you created earlier as the data source. In the recipient address area of the envelope, insert an AddressBlock merge field in the format "Mr. Joshua Randall Jr.".

17. Filter the records in the Newberry Glen Data file so that only records with Las Vegas addresses are included in the merge.

18. Merge to a new document.

19. Save the merged document as **Merged Envelopes** in the location in which you saved the main document, and then close it. Save the main document, and close it.

Case Problem 2

Data Files needed for this Case Problem: Concierge.docx, Directory.docx, Incomplete.docx, Residents.xlsx

Willow Bay Village Luxury Condominiums You are the director of concierge services at Willow Bay Village, a luxury condominium community in Gulf Shores, Alabama. You need to send letters to people around the country who have recently purchased newly built condominiums as winter getaway homes. Your data for the mail merge is saved as an Excel file. The data file includes names and addresses. It also includes the concierge service that most interests each new resident, as well as the name of the concierge at Willow Bay Village responsible for that service. To ensure that you can maintain the connection between the data source and the main document files, you will first start Excel and then save the data source file to the location specified by your instructor. Complete the following steps:

1. Start Excel, and on the Recent screen, click Open Other Workbooks. Navigate to the Word6 > Case2 folder included with your Data Files, and then open the Excel workbook **Residents**.
2. Click the File tab, click Save As, save the Excel workbook as **Residents Data** in the location specified by your instructor, and then close Excel.
3. Open the document **Concierge** from the Word6 > Case2 folder.
4. Save the Word document as **Concierge Services Main Document** in the location in which you saved the Client Data file.
5. In the letter's closing, replace "Student Name" with your first and last names.
6. Replace the field that displays the date and time with a Date field that displays the current month, day, and year—in the format March 11, 2017.
7. Begin the mail merge by selecting Letters as the type of main document.
8. For the data source, select the Excel workbook Residents Data that you just saved. Click the OK button in the Select Table dialog box.
9. From within Word, edit the data source to replace "StudentFirstName" and "StudentLastName" with your first and last names.
10. Delete the placeholder text for the inside address, and then insert an AddressBlock merge field for the inside address in the format "Joshua Randall Jr.".
11. In the salutation, insert the First_Name merge field where indicated.
12. In the body of the letter, replace the placeholders "[INSERT CONCIERGE SERVICE]" and "[INSERT CONCIERGE NAME]" with the appropriate merge fields.
13. Sort the records in the data source in ascending order by Concierge Service.
14. ⚙ **Troubleshoot** Preview the merged document, and note that the lines of the inside address (inserted by the AddressBlock merge field) are spaced too far apart. Make any changes necessary so the inside address and the salutation include the appropriate amount of paragraph and line spacing.
15. Preview all the records in the document.
16. Merge to a new document. Save the merged document as **Merged Concierge Services Letters** in the location in which you saved the main document.
17. Close all open documents, saving all changes.
18. ⚙ **Troubleshoot** Open the document **Incomplete** from the Word6 > Case2 folder, and save it as **Incomplete Labels** in the location specified by your instructor. Attach a comment to the ZIP code in the first label that explains what error in the main document would result in a set of labels that includes information for only one record. Save and close the document.
19. Create a main document for generating mailing labels on sheets of Avery US Letter Address labels, product number 5162, using the Residents Data file as your data source. Use the AddressBlock merge field in the format "Joshua Randall Jr.". Save the main document as **New Residents Labels Main Document** in the location in which you saved the Residents Data file.

20. Preview the merged document, merge to a new document, and then save the merged document as **Merged New Residents Labels** in the location in which you saved the main document. Close all open documents, saving any changes.

21. Re-open the **Concierge Services Main Document**, maintaining the connection to its data source, and then save it as **Concierge Services Main Document, Filtered** in the same folder. Filter out all records in the data source except records for clients interested in valet services, and then, if necessary, sort the filtered records so the one containing your name is displayed first.

22. Complete the merge to a new document. Save the merged document as **Merged Valet Letters** in the location in which you saved the main document.

23. Close all open documents, saving any changes.

⚙ **Troubleshoot** 24. Open the document **Directory** from the Word6 > Case2 folder, and save it as **Incomplete Directory** in the location specified by your instructor. This directory is supposed to list each resident, along with the concierge service that most interests that resident. Attach a comment to the first name in the directory that explains what error in the main document would result in a directory formatted like the one in the Problem Directory file.

25. Save and close the document.

Case Problem 3

CHALLENGE

Data Files needed for this Case Problem: Des Moines Data.accdb, Des Moines.txt, Peterson.docx

Peterson Dental Health   Meghan Dougherty is the patient services manager for Peterson Dental Health, a chain of dental clinics in Des Moines, Iowa. Meghan's company has just bought out a competitor, Des Moines Dentistry. Meghan needs to send a letter to patients of Des Moines Dentistry explaining that their records will be transferred to Peterson Dental Health. In the letter, she also wants to remind Des Moines Dentistry patients of the date of their next appointment. The patient data has been saved in a text file, with the data fields separated by commas. Meghan needs your help to convert the text file to a Word table. She will then ask one of her colleagues to import the Word table into an Access database, so that you can use it in the mail merge. Note that it is possible to import a simple text file into an Access database, but it's hard to tell if the data is set up properly. By converting the text file to a table in a Word document first, you can verify that the records all contain the same fields. Complete the following steps:

1. In Word, open the text file **Des Moines.txt** from the Word6 > Case3 folder included with your Data Files. (*Hint*: If the file is not listed in the Open dialog box, make sure All Files is selected in the box to the right of the File name box.)

2. Save the Des Moines.txt file as a Word document named **Des Moines Table** in the location specified by your instructor. (*Hint*: In the Save As dialog box, remember to select Word Document as the file type.)

3. Format the document text using the Normal style, and then switch to Landscape orientation.

4. Convert the text to a table with eight columns. Insert a header row with the following column headers formatted in bold—**First Name**, **Last Name**, **Address Line 1**, **Address Line 2**, **City**, **State**, **ZIP Code**, and **Appointment Date**. Save and close the document.

5. Open the document **Peterson** from the Word6 > Case3 folder, and then save it as **Peterson Main Document** in the location specified by your instructor.

6. In the first paragraph, replace the placeholder text "[INSERT DATE FIELD]" with a Date field that displays the current month, day, and year—in the format 3/11/17.

7. Start the mail merge by selecting Letters as the type of main document.

8. Select the Des Moines Data.accdb file as the data source. This Access database file contains all the data from the Des Moines Table document.

9. Replace the placeholder text "[INSERT INSIDE ADDRESS]" with an AddressBlock merge field in the format "Joshua Randall Jr.". Format the paragraph containing the AddressBlock merge field using the No Spacing style.

⊕ **Explore** 10. Delete the placeholder text "[INSERT SALUTATION]." Insert a salutation using the Greeting Line button in the Write & Insert Fields group on the Mailings tab. In the Insert Greeting Line dialog box, create a salutation that includes "Dear" and the customer's first name followed by a colon. For invalid recipient names (that is, recipients for which the First Name field in the data source is blank), select the "(none)" option. Add 12 points of paragraph spacing before the salutation paragraph.

11. In the body of the letter, replace the placeholder text "[INSERT APPOINTMENT DATE]" with the Appointment_Date merge field.

⊕ **Explore** 12. Use the Rules button in the Write & Insert Fields group on the Mailings tab to replace the placeholder text "[NEW CLINIC]" with a merge field that displays the message **We will soon complete construction on our new Pilot Plaza clinic, conveniently located near you.** if the value in the ZIP Code field is equal to 50305; otherwise, the field should display **We will soon complete construction on several new clinics.** (*Hint*: In the Rules menu, click If…Then…Else…, select ZIP_Code as the Field name, select Equal to as the Comparison, and type 50305 in the Compare to box. Insert the appropriate text in the Insert this text box and in the Otherwise insert this text box.)

⊕ **Explore** 13. In the Mail Merge Recipients dialog box, use the Filter command to display only the records that include either 5/1/2017 or 6/1/2017 in the Appointment Date field. (*Hint*: On the Filter Records tab of the Filter and Sort dialog box, you need to fill in two rows. Select Appointment Date in the Field box in both rows; in the first list box on the far left, select Or instead of And; select Equal to in the Comparison box for both rows; and type the correct dates in the Compare to boxes.)

14. In the Mail Merge Recipients dialog box, sort the displayed records in ascending order by ZIP code.

15. Preview the merged documents, adjust spacing around the merge fields as necessary, and then merge to a new document. Save the merged document as **Merged Peterson Letters** in the location in which you saved the main document.

16. Close all open documents, saving any changes.

Case Problem 4

RESEARCH

There are no Data Files needed for this Case Problem.

Population Research Associates Quinn Erickson is a senior scholar at Population Research Associates, a multidisciplinary center that conducts research in the field of human population growth. He is beginning research for an article on world population, but before he can get started, Quinn needs to organize a great deal of printed information into file folders. As his student intern, it's your job to create labels for the file folders, with one label for the top ten most populous countries in the world. You will retrieve a list of countries and their populations from the web, and then use it as the data source for a mail merge. Complete the following steps:

1. Open a new, blank document, and then save it as **Population Data** in the location specified by your instructor.

2. Open a browser, go to bing.com, and search for **population by country**. Explore the search results, looking for information arranged in a simple table format.

3. Click and drag the mouse to select information for the top ten most populous countries, and then copy it to the Clipboard.

4. Paste the information into the Population Data document, and then edit it as necessary to create a simple table with two columns, with the headings **Country** and **Population**. You might need to delete graphics, extra spaces, extra rows or columns, hyperlinks, or other elements. Format the text in the Normal style. If you can't remove special formatting from some of the text, try using the Format Painter to copy the Normal style where necessary. Remove any fill color. When you are finished, you should have a simple table with two columns, and the header row formatted in bold.

5. Save and close the Population Data file.

6. Open a new, blank document, and then save it as **Population Labels Main Document** in the location in which you saved the Population Data file.

7. Select Labels as the type of main document, using the Avery product 5966 Filing Labels.

8. Select the Population Data file as your data source.

9. In the first label, insert the Country merge field, type **,** (a comma), insert a space, and then insert the Population merge field.

10. Format the Country merge field in bold.

11. Update the labels, and preview the merge results.

12. In the "United States" label, type **,** (a comma) after the population, and then type your first and last names.

13. Merge to a new document, and then save the new document as **Merged Population Labels** in the location in which you saved the main document.

14. Close the Merged Population Labels document and any other open documents, saving any changes.

MODULE 7

OBJECTIVES

Session 7.1
- Track changes in a document
- Compare and combine documents
- Accept and reject tracked changes
- Embed an Excel worksheet
- Modify an embedded Excel worksheet

Session 7.2
- Link an Excel chart
- Modify and update a linked Excel chart
- Create bookmarks
- Insert and edit hyperlinks
- Optimize a document for online viewing
- Create and publish a blog post

Collaborating with Others and Integrating Data

Preparing an Information Sheet

Case | *Film Buff Trivia*

Rima Khouri is the marketing director for DBQ Games. The company is currently developing a new board game called Film Buff Trivia. Like many game companies, DBQ Games plans to use a crowdfunding website to raise the money required to finish developing and marketing its latest product. As part of her marketing effort, Rima also plans to email an information sheet about the fund-raising campaign to interested gamers she met at a recent gaming convention. Rima has asked James Benner, the company's development manager, to review a draft of the information sheet. While James is revising the document, Rima has asked you to work on another copy, making additional changes. When you are finished with your review, Rima wants you to merge James's edited version of the document with your most recent draft.

After you create a new version of the document for Rima, she wants you to add some fund-raising data from an Excel workbook. She also needs you to add a pie chart James created and optimize the information sheet for online viewing. Finally, Rima wants you to help her create a blog post in Word discussing the crowdfunding campaign.

STARTING DATA FILES

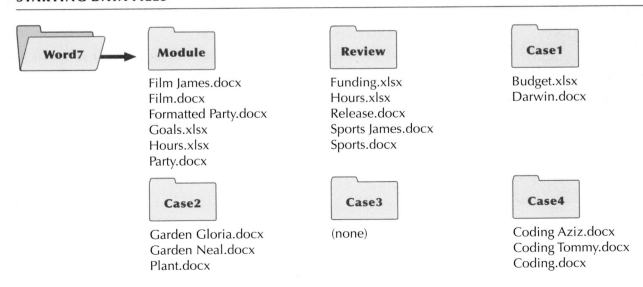

Word7 → **Module**

Film James.docx
Film.docx
Formatted Party.docx
Goals.xlsx
Hours.xlsx
Party.docx

Review

Funding.xlsx
Hours.xlsx
Release.docx
Sports James.docx
Sports.docx

Case1

Budget.xlsx
Darwin.docx

Case2

Garden Gloria.docx
Garden Neal.docx
Plant.docx

Case3

(none)

Case4

Coding Aziz.docx
Coding Tommy.docx
Coding.docx

Session 7.1 Visual Overview:

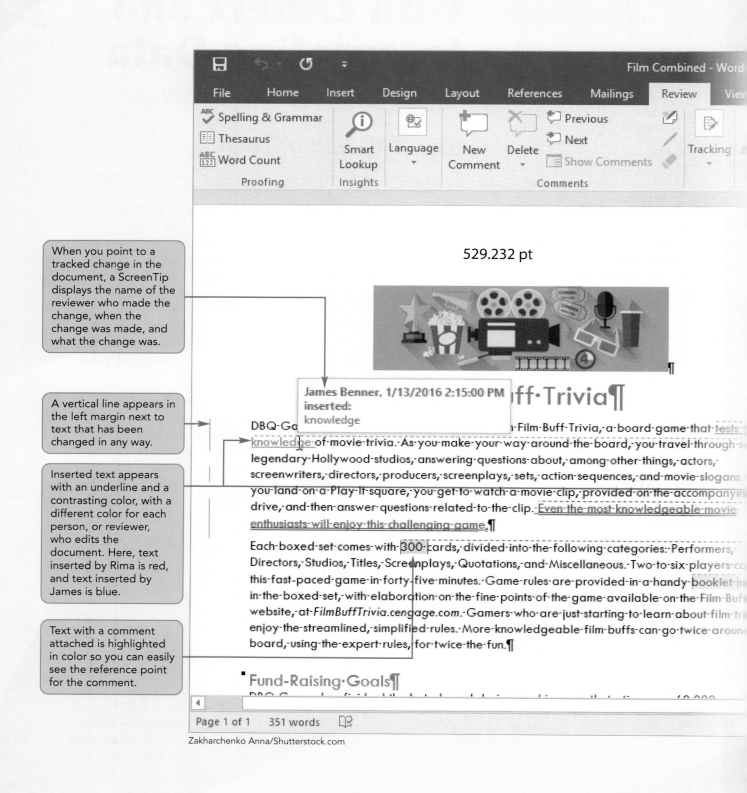

When you point to a tracked change in the document, a ScreenTip displays the name of the reviewer who made the change, when the change was made, and what the change was.

A vertical line appears in the left margin next to text that has been changed in any way.

Inserted text appears with an underline and a contrasting color, with a different color for each person, or reviewer, who edits the document. Here, text inserted by Rima is red, and text inserted by James is blue.

Text with a comment attached is highlighted in color so you can easily see the reference point for the comment.

529.232 pt

James Benner, 1/13/2016 2:15:00 PM
inserted:
knowledge

...uff·Trivia¶

DBQ·Ga...   ...n·Film·Buff·Trivia,·a·board·game·that·tests·
knowledge·of·movie·trivia.·As·you·make·your·way·around·the·board,·you·travel·through·s...
legendary·Hollywood·studios,·answering·questions·about,·among·other·things,·actors,·
screenwriters,·directors,·producers,·screenplays,·sets,·action·sequences,·and·movie·slogans...
you·land·on·a·Play·It·square,·you·get·to·watch·a·movie·clip,·provided·on·the·accompanyin...
drive,·and·then·answer·questions·related·to·the·clip.·Even·the·most·knowledgeable·movie·
enthusiasts·will·enjoy·this·challenging·game.¶

Each·boxed·set·comes·with·300·cards,·divided·into·the·following·categories:·Performers,
Directors,·Studios,·Titles,·Screenplays,·Quotations,·and·Miscellaneous.·Two·to·six·players·ca...
this·fast-paced·game·in·forty-five·minutes.·Game·rules·are·provided·in·a·handy·booklet·in...
in·the·boxed·set,·with·elaboration·on·the·fine·points·of·the·game·available·on·the·Film·Buf...
website,·at·*FilmBuffTrivia*.cengage.com.·Gamers·who·are·just·starting·to·learn·about·film·tri...
enjoy·the·streamlined,·simplified·rules.·More·knowledgeable·film·buffs·can·go·twice·aroun...
board,·using·the·expert·rules,·for·twice·the·fun.¶

Fund-Raising·Goals¶

Page 1 of 1   351 words

Zakharchenko Anna/Shutterstock.com

Tracking Changes

The Review tab contains all the options you need for editing a document using tracked changes and comments.

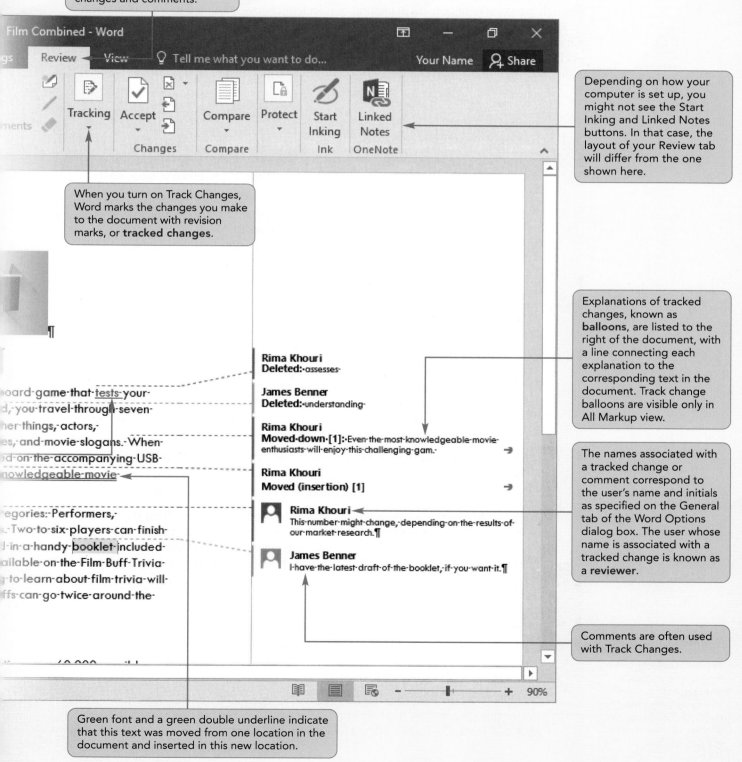

Depending on how your computer is set up, you might not see the Start Inking and Linked Notes buttons. In that case, the layout of your Review tab will differ from the one shown here.

When you turn on Track Changes, Word marks the changes you make to the document with revision marks, or **tracked changes**.

Explanations of tracked changes, known as **balloons**, are listed to the right of the document, with a line connecting each explanation to the corresponding text in the document. Track change balloons are visible only in All Markup view.

The names associated with a tracked change or comment correspond to the user's name and initials as specified on the General tab of the Word Options dialog box. The user whose name is associated with a tracked change is known as a **reviewer**.

Comments are often used with Track Changes.

Green font and a green double underline indicate that this text was moved from one location in the document and inserted in this new location.

Editing a Document with Tracked Changes

The Track Changes feature in Word simulates the process of marking up a hard copy of a document with a colored pen, but offers many more advantages. Word keeps track of who makes each change, assigning a different color to each reviewer and providing ScreenTips indicating details of the change, such as the reviewer's name and the date and time the change was made. Using the buttons on the Review tab, you can move through the document quickly, accepting or rejecting changes with a click of the mouse.

Rima is ready to revise her first draft of the document. She asks you to turn on Track Changes before you make the edits for her. To ensure that her name is displayed for each tracked change, and that your screens match the figures in this module, you will temporarily change the username on the General tab of the Word Options dialog box to "Rima Khouri." You'll also change the user initials to "RK."

To change the username and turn on Track Changes:

1. Open the document **Film** located in the Word7 > Module folder included with your Data Files, and then save it as **Film Rima** in the location specified by your instructor.

2. Switch to Print Layout view if necessary, display the rulers and nonprinting characters, and change the document Zoom level to **110%**. You'll use this Zoom setting for the first part of this module to ensure that you can see all the tracked changes in the document.

3. On the ribbon, click the **Review** tab.

4. In the Tracking group, click the **Dialog Box Launcher** to open the Track Changes Options dialog box, and then click **Change User Name**. The Word Options dialog box opens, with the General tab displayed.

5. On a piece of paper, write down the current username and initials, if they are not your own, so you can refer to it when you need to restore the original username and initials later in this module. Although the user initials do not appear on the Word screen, in a printed document, the username is replaced with the user initials to save space. Therefore, you should always change the user initials whenever you change the username.

6. Click in the **User name** box, delete the current username, and then type **Rima Khouri**.

7. Click in the Initials box, delete the current initials, and then type **RK**.

8. Click the **Always use these values regardless of sign in to Office** checkbox to insert a check, if necessary. If you don't check this box, the name of the person currently signed into Office.com will appear in the document's tracked changes, no matter what user name is entered in the User name box.

9. Click the **OK** button. The Word Options dialog box closes, and you return to the Track Changes Options dialog box.

10. Click the **OK** button to close the Track Changes Options dialog box.

11. In the Tracking group, click the **Track Changes** button. The gray highlighting on the Track Changes button tells you that it is selected, indicating that the Track Changes feature is turned on.

   Trouble? If you see a menu, you clicked the Track Changes button arrow rather than the button itself. Press the Esc key to close the menu, and then click the Track Changes button to turn on Track Changes.

TIP

To prevent collaborators from turning off Track Changes, click the Track Changes button arrow, click Lock Tracking, create a password if you want to use one, and then click the OK button.

12. In the Tracking group, verify that the Display for Review box displays "All Markup." This setting ensures that tracked changes are displayed in the document as you edit it.

   Trouble? If the Display for Review box does not display "All Markup," click the Display for Review arrow, and then click All Markup.

13. In the Tracking group, click the **Show Markup** button, and then point to **Balloons**. See Figure 7-1.

Figure 7-1	Track Changes turned on

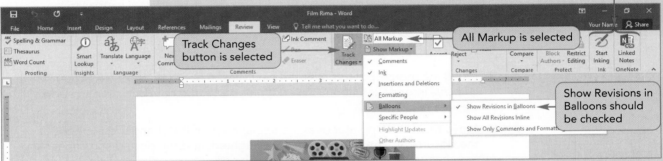

Zakharchenko Anna/Shutterstock.com

14. If you do not see a checkmark next to Show Revisions in Balloons, click **Show Revisions in Balloons** now to select it and close the menu. Otherwise, click anywhere in the document to close the menu.

Now that Track Changes is turned on, you can begin editing Rima's document. First, Rima needs to change the word "assesses" in the first sentence to "tests."

To edit Rima's document and view the tracked changes:

1. In the line below the "Film Buff Trivia" heading, select the word **assesses** and then type **tests**. The new word, "tests," is displayed in color, with an underline. A vertical line is displayed in the left margin, drawing attention to the change. To the right of the document, the username associated with the change (Rima Khouri) is displayed, along with an explanation of the change. See Figure 7-2.

Figure 7-2 **Edit marked as tracked change**

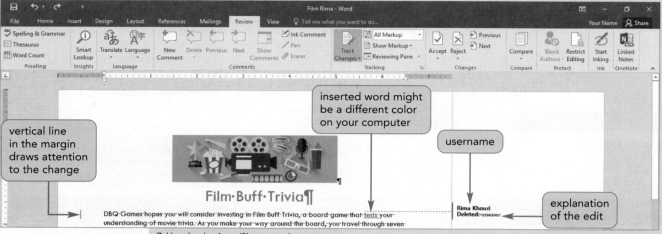

Zakharchenko Anna/Shutterstock.com

▶ **2.** Move the mouse pointer over the newly inserted word "tests." A ScreenTip displays information about the edit, along with the date and time the edit was made.

▶ **3.** Move the mouse pointer over the explanation of the change to the right of the document. The explanation is highlighted, and the dotted line connecting the change in the document to the explanation turns solid. In a document with many tracked changes, this makes it easier to see which explanation is associated with which tracked change.

Next, Rima wants you to move the second-to-last sentence in this paragraph to the end of the paragraph.

▶ **4.** Press the **Ctrl** key, and then click in the sentence that begins "Even the most knowledgeable…." The entire sentence is selected. Don't be concerned that the word "game," at the end of the sentence is misspelled. You'll correct that error shortly.

▶ **5.** Drag the sentence to insert it at the end of the paragraph, and then click anywhere in the document to deselect it. See Figure 7-3.

| Figure 7-3 | Tracked changes showing text moved to a new location |

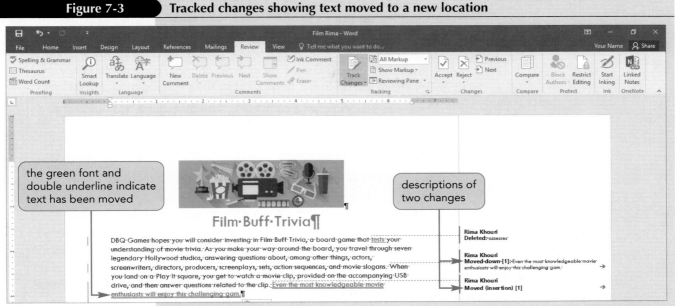

the green font and double underline indicate text has been moved

descriptions of two changes

Zakharchenko Anna/Shutterstock.com

The sentence is inserted with a double underline in green, which is the color Word uses to denote moved text. Word also inserts a space before the inserted sentence and marks the nonprinting space character as a tracked change. A vertical bar in the left margin draws attention to the moved text.

To the right of the document, descriptions of two new changes are displayed. The "Moved down [1]" change shows the text of the sentence that was moved. The "Moved (insertion) [1]" change draws attention to the sentence in its new location at the end of the paragraph.

A blue, right-facing arrow next to a tracked change explanation indicates that the change is related to another change. You can click the arrow to select the related change.

6. Next to the "Moved (insertion) [1]" change, click the blue, right-facing arrow ➡ to select the moved sentence in the "Moved down [1]" balloon. See Figure 7-4.

| Figure 7-4 | Selecting a related change |

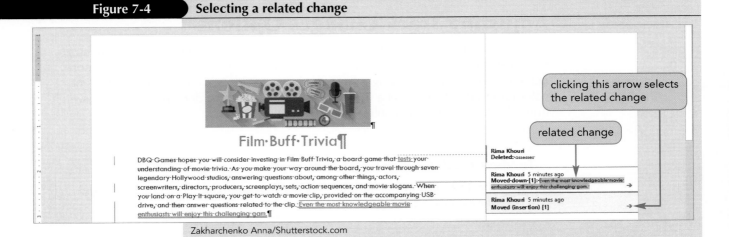

clicking this arrow selects the related change

related change

Zakharchenko Anna/Shutterstock.com

After reviewing the sentence in its new location at the end of the paragraph, Rima notices that she needs to add an "e" to the last word in the sentence so that it reads "...this challenging game."

7. In the sentence you moved in Step 5, click to the right of the "m" in "gam," and then type the letter **e**. The newly inserted letter is displayed in the same color as the word "tests" at the beginning of the paragraph.

Finally, Rima asks you to insert a comment reminding her that the number of cards in each boxed set might change. Comments are commonly used with tracked changes. In All Markup view, they are displayed, along with other edits, to the right of the document.

8. In the first line of the second main paragraph (which begins "Each boxed set comes with 300..."), select the number **300**.

9. In the Comments group, click the **New Comment** button. The number "300" is highlighted in the same color used for the word "tests," and the insertion point moves to the right of the document, ready for you to type the comment text.

10. Type **This number might change, depending on the results of our market research.** See Figure 7-5.

Figure 7-5 | **Comment added to document**

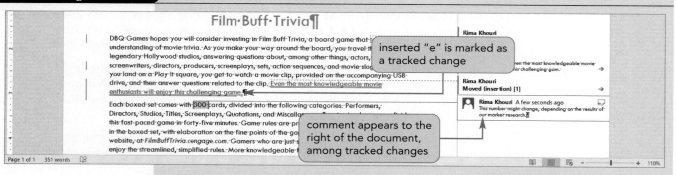

11. Save your document.

Adjusting Track Changes Options

The default settings for Track Changes worked well as you edited Rima's document. However, you can change these settings if you prefer. For instance, you could choose not to display formatting changes as tracked changes, or you could select a different color for inserted text. To get a more streamlined view of the document, you can switch from All Markup view to Simple Markup view.

To view Track Changes options:

1. In the Tracking group, click the **Dialog Box Launcher**. The Track Changes Options dialog box opens. See Figure 7-6.

Figure 7-6 Track Changes Options dialog box

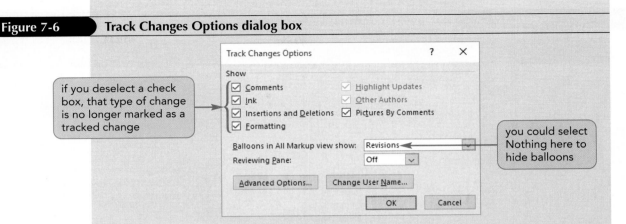

if you deselect a check box, that type of change is no longer marked as a tracked change

you could select Nothing here to hide balloons

The check boxes in the Show section control which types of edits are marked as tracked changes. For example, the Formatting check box is currently selected. If you didn't want formatting changes to be marked as tracked changes, you could deselect the Formatting check box. Note that Revisions is currently selected in the "Balloons in All Markup view show" box. To turn off the balloon feature, so that no track changes or comment balloons are displayed to the right of the document in All Markup view, you could select Nothing instead.

2. Click **Advanced Options**. The Advanced Track Changes Options dialog box opens.

The options in this dialog box allow you to select the colors you want to use for various types of edits. For example, you can use the Color box next to the Insertions box to select a color to use for inserted text. Note that the default setting for Insertions, Deletions, Comments, and Formatting is By author. This means that Word assigns one color to each person who edits the document. When you are working with multiple reviewers, you should always retain the By author settings to ensure that you can easily distinguish the edits made by each reviewer.

3. Click the **Cancel** button to close the Advanced Track Changes Options dialog box, and then click the **Cancel** button to close the Track Changes Options dialog box.

After reviewing the tracked changes with you, Rima decides the number of details shown in All Markup view makes the document too difficult to read. She wants you to switch to Simple Markup view instead.

To switch to Simple Markup view:

1. In the Tracking group, click the **Display for Review** arrow, and then click **Simple Markup**. See Figure 7-7.

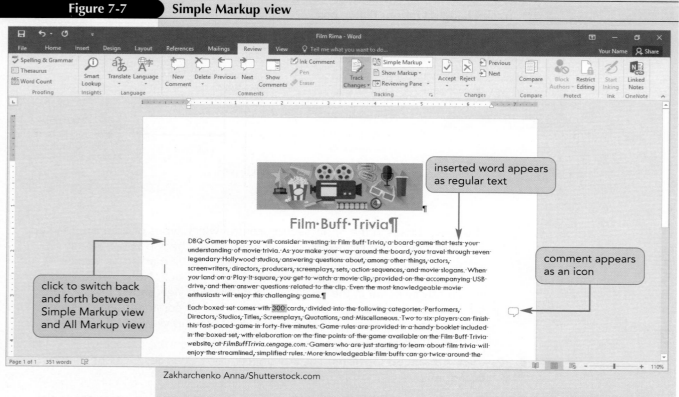

Zakharchenko Anna/Shutterstock.com

Trouble? If the comment balloon is still visible on your screen, click the Show Comments button in the Comments group on the Review tab to deselect it.

All of the tracked changes in the document are now hidden, and the comment balloon is replaced with an icon in the right margin. The inserted word "tests" is in black font, like the surrounding text, as is the sentence you moved to the end of the paragraph. The only signs that the document contains tracked changes is the red vertical bar in the left margin. You can click a vertical bar to switch back and forth between Simple Markup view and All Markup view.

2. Click the red vertical bar to the left of the paragraph that begins "DBQ Games hopes...." The document switches to All Markup view, with all the tracked changes and the comment visible. The vertical bar in the left margin changes from red to gray.

3. Click the gray vertical bar to the left of the paragraph that begins "DBQ Games hopes...." The document switches back to Simple Markup view.

Rima has received James's edited copy of the first draft via email, and now she'd like your help in combining her edited copy of the Film Rima document with James's copy.

Comparing and Combining Documents

When you work in a collaborative environment with multiple people contributing to the same document, Word's Compare and Combine features are essential tools. They allow you to see the difference between multiple versions of a document, with tracked changes highlighting the differences. The Compare and Combine features are similar, but they have different purposes.

The **Compare** feature, which is designed to help you quickly spot the differences between two copies of a document, is intended for documents that do not contain tracked changes. In a compared document, differences between the revised document and the original document are marked with tracked changes, with all the tracked changes assigned to the username associated with the revised document.

The **Combine** feature, which is designed for documents that do contain tracked changes, allows you to see which reviewers made which changes. In a combined document, each reviewer's tracked changes are displayed, with each tracked change assigned to the reviewer who made that change. The Combine feature works well when you want to combine, or **merge**, two documents to create a third, combined document, with which you can then combine additional documents, until you have incorporated all the tracked changes from all your reviewers. Because the Combine feature allows you to incorporate more than two documents into one, it's the option you'll use most when collaborating with a group.

When you compare or combine documents, you select one document as the original and one as the revised document. Together, these two documents are known as the **source documents**. By default, Word then creates a new, third document, which consists of the original document's text edited with tracked changes to show how the revised document differs. The source documents themselves are left unchanged. If Word detects a formatting conflict—that is, if identical text is formatted differently in the source documents—Word displays a dialog box allowing you to choose which formatting you want to keep. You can choose to keep the formatting of the original document or the revised document, but not both. Occasionally, Word will display this formatting conflict dialog box even if both source documents are formatted exactly the same. If so, keep the formatting for the original document, and continue with the process of combining the documents.

REFERENCE

Comparing and Combining Documents

- On the ribbon, click the Review tab.
- In the Compare group, click the Compare button.
- Click Compare to open the Compare Documents dialog box, or click Combine to open the Combine Documents dialog box.
- Next to the Original document box, click the Browse button, navigate to the location of the document, select the document, and then click the Open button.
- Next to the Revised document box, click the Browse button, navigate to the location of the document, select the document, and then click the Open button.
- Click the More button, if necessary, to display options that allow you to select which items you want marked with tracked changes, and then make any necessary changes.
- Click the OK button.

When you start combining or comparing documents, it's not necessary to have either the original document or the revised document open. In this case, however, the Film Rima document, which you will use as the original document, is open. You'll combine this document with James's edited copy.

To combine Rima's document with James's document:

1. Make sure you have saved your changes to the Film Rima document.

2. In the Compare group, click the **Compare** button. A menu opens with options for comparing or combining two versions of a document.

3. Click **Combine**. The Combine Documents dialog box opens.

4. Click the **More** button. The dialog box expands to display check boxes, which you can use to specify the items you want marked with tracked changes.

> **Trouble?** If the dialog box has a Less button instead of a More button, the dialog box is already expanded to show the check boxes for selecting additional options. In this case, skip Step 4.

In the Show changes section at the bottom of the dialog box, the New document option button is selected by default, indicating that Word will create a new, combined document rather than importing the tracked changes from the original document into the revised document, or vice versa.

Now you need to specify the Film Rima document as the original document. Even though this document is currently open, you still need to select it.

5. Next to the Original document box, click the **Browse** button 🗀 to open the Open dialog box.

6. If necessary, navigate to the location where you saved the Film Rima document, click **Film Rima** in the file list, and then click the **Open** button. You return to the Combine Documents dialog box, where the filename "Film Rima" is displayed in the Original document box.

Next, you need to select the document you want to use as the revised document.

7. Next to the Revised document box, click the **Browse** button 🗀, navigate to the Word7 > Module folder included with your Data Files if necessary, select the document **Film James**, and then click the **Open** button. The filename "Film James" is displayed in the Revised document box. See Figure 7-8.

Figure 7-8	Selecting the original and revised documents

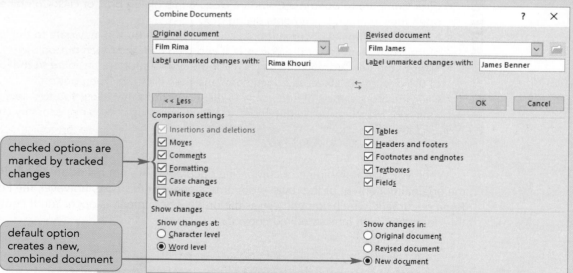

checked options are marked by tracked changes

default option creates a new, combined document

8. Click the **OK** button. The Combine Documents dialog box closes.

A new document opens. It contains the tracked changes from both the original document and the revised document.

At this point, depending on the previous settings on your computer, you might see only the new, combined document, or you might also see the original and revised documents open in separate windows. You might also see the Reviewing pane, which includes a summary of the number of revisions in the combined document along with a list of all the changes, as shown in Figure 7-9.

Figure 7-9   **Two documents combined**

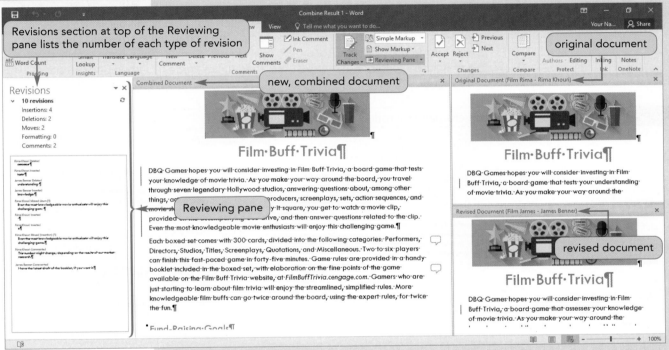

Zakharchenko Anna/Shutterstock.com

Note that your combined document might have a different name than shown in Figure 7-9. For instance, it might be named "Document 1," instead of "Combine Result 1."

9. In the Compare group, click the **Compare** button, and then point to **Show Source Documents.**

10. If a checkmark appears next to Show Both, press the **Esc** key twice to close both menus; otherwise, click **Show Both.** Your screen should now match Figure 7-9.

Trouble? If the Reviewing pane is still not displayed, click the Reviewing Pane button in the Tracking group to display the Reviewing pane.

Trouble? If your Reviewing pane is displayed horizontally rather than vertically, as shown in Figure 7-9, click the Reviewing Pane button arrow in the Tracking group, and then click Reviewing Pane Vertical.

Note that the combined document and the two source documents are all displayed in Simple Markup. Also, instead of Print Layout view, which you typically use when working on documents, the three documents are displayed in Web Layout view. You'll learn more about Web Layout view later in this module. For now, all you need to know is that in Web Layout view, the line breaks change to suit the size of the document window, making it easier to read text in the small windows.

It's helpful to have the source documents displayed when you want to quickly compare the two documents. For example, right now Rima wants to scroll down the documents to see how they differ. When you scroll up or down in the Revised Document pane, the other documents scroll as well.

To scroll the document panes simultaneously:

▶ **1.** Move the mouse pointer over the Revised Document (Film James - James Benner) pane to display its scroll bar, and then drag the scroll bar down to display the "Fund-Raising Goals" heading. The text in the Combined Document pane and in the Original Document (Film Rima - Rima Khouri) pane scrolls down to match the text in the Revised Document (Film James - James Benner) pane. See Figure 7-10.

Figure 7-10 | **Document panes scrolled to compare versions**

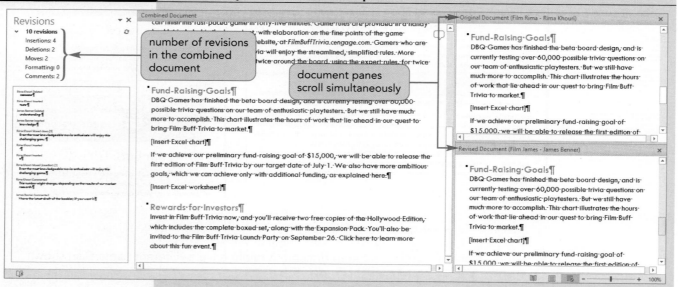

Now that you've reviewed both documents, you can hide the source documents to make the combined document easier to read. After you hide the source documents, you can review the edits in the Reviewing pane.

To hide the source documents and review the edits in the Reviewing pane:

▶ **1.** In the Compare group, click the **Compare** button, point to the **Show Source Documents** button, and then click **Hide Source Documents**. The panes displaying the original and revised documents close, and the combined document window switches to Print Layout view. Next, you will change the Zoom setting in the Reviewing pane to make its contents easier to read.

> **Trouble?** If the combined window does not switch to Print Layout view, click the Print Layout view button 📄 on the status bar.

2. Click anywhere in the list of edits in the Reviewing pane, and then change the Zoom setting in the status bar to **100%**, if necessary.

3. Move the mouse pointer over the list of edits in the Reviewing pane to display the vertical scroll bar, and then scroll down and review the list of edits. Notice that the document contains the edits you made earlier (under Rima's name) as well as edits made by James Benner.

Rima prefers to review changes using All Markup view instead of the Reviewing pane.

4. In the Tracking group, click the **Reviewing Pane** button to deselect it. The Reviewing pane closes.

5. In the Tracking group, click the **Display for Review** arrow, and then click **All Markup**.

6. In the Tracking group, click the **Show Markup** arrow, point to Balloons, and then make sure **Show Revisions in Balloons** is selected.

7. Save the document as **Film Combined** in the location specified by your instructor.

8. In the Tracking group, click the **Track Changes** button to turn off Track Changes. This ensures that you won't accidentally add any additional edit marks as you review the document.

9. Change the Zoom level to **120%**.

INSIGHT

Using Real-Time Co-Authoring to Collaborate with Others

Combining documents is a powerful way to incorporate the work of multiple people in one document. The only drawback to combining documents is that, typically, one person is charged with combining the documents, reviewing the tracked changes, and then making decisions about what to keep and what to delete. In some situations, it's more effective to give all team members the freedom to edit a document at the same time, with every person's changes showing up on everyone else's screen. You can accomplish this by saving a document to OneDrive and then sharing it using Word's co-authoring feature.

To get started, click Share in the upper-right corner of the Word window to open the Share pane, click Save to Cloud, and then save the document to OneDrive. Next, use the options in the Share pane to either: 1) share the document with specific people, in which case Microsoft will send an email to the people you specified, inviting them to work on the document; or 2) create a sharing link, which you can then email to your collaborators, and which they can then click to open the document in Office 365, the online version of Microsoft Office. After a delay of a few minutes or less, you and all of your collaborators can begin editing the document, while being able to see everyone else's changes to the document in real time.

Next, you will review the edits in the Film Combined document to accept and reject the changes as appropriate.

Accepting and Rejecting Changes

The document you just created contains all the edits from two different reviewers—Rima's changes made in the original document, and James's changes as they appeared in the revised document. In the combined document, each reviewer's edits are displayed in a different color, making it easy to see which reviewer made each change.

When you review tracked changes in a document, the best approach is to move the insertion point to the beginning of the document, and then navigate through the document one change at a time using the Next and Previous buttons in the Changes group on the Review tab. This ensures you won't miss any edits. As you review a tracked change, you can either accept the change or reject it.

REFERENCE

Accepting and Rejecting Changes

- Move the insertion point to the beginning of the document.
- On the ribbon, click the Review tab.
- In the Changes group, click the Next button to select the first edit or comment in the document.
- To accept a selected change, click the Accept button in the Changes group.
- To reject a selected change, click the Reject button in the Changes group.
- To accept all the changes in the document, click the Accept button arrow, and then click Accept All Changes.
- To reject all the changes in the document, click the Reject button arrow, and then click Reject All Changes.

To accept and reject changes in the Film Combined document:

1. Press the **Ctrl+Home** keys to move the insertion point to the beginning of the document.

2. In the Changes group, click the **Next** button. To the right of the document, in a tracked change balloon, the deleted word "assesses" is selected, as shown in Figure 7-11.

Figure 7-11 First change in document selected

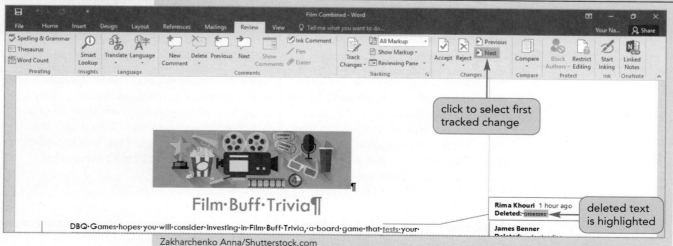

click to select first tracked change

deleted text is highlighted

Rima Khouri 1 hour ago
Deleted: assesses

James Benner

Film·Buff·Trivia¶

DBQ·Games·hopes·you·will·consider·investing·in·Film·Buff·Trivia,·a·board·game·that·tests·your·

Zakharchenko Anna/Shutterstock.com

Trouble? If the insertion point moves to Rima's comment, you clicked the Next button in the Comments group instead of the Next button in the Changes group. Repeat Steps 1 and 2.

3. In the Changes group, click the **Accept** button. The tracked change balloon is no longer displayed, indicating that the change has been accepted. The inserted word "tests" is now selected in the document.

Trouble? If you see a menu below the Accept button, you clicked the Accept button arrow by mistake. Press the Esc key to close the menu, and then click the Accept button.

4. Click the **Accept** button. In a tracked change balloon to the right of the document, James's deletion of the word "understanding" is selected. See Figure 7-12.

Figure 7-12   **Reviewing James's changes**

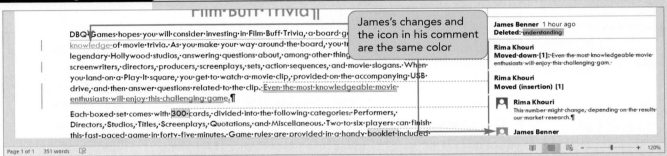

James deleted the word "understanding" and replaced it with the word "knowledge," which is displayed in the document as a tracked change. The inserted word, the tracked change balloon for the deleted word, and the icon in James's comment are all the same color.

Because the word "knowledgeable" is used later in this same paragraph, Rima prefers to keep the original word, "understanding," so you need to reject James's change.

5. In the Changes group, click the **Reject** button to reject the deletion of the word "understanding." The tracked change balloon is no longer displayed, and the word "understanding" is restored in the document, to the left of the inserted word "knowledge," which is now selected. See Figure 7-13.

Figure 7-13   **Document after rejecting change**

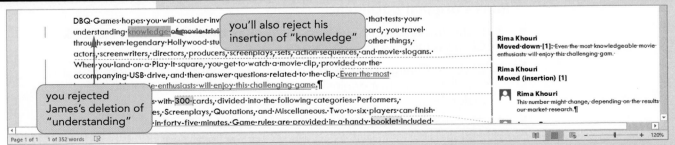

Next, you need to reject the insertion of the word "knowledge."

6. Click the **Reject** button. The inserted word "knowledge" is removed from the document. To the right of the document, in a tracked change balloon, the sentence that you moved is now selected.

7. Click the **Accept** button. The tracked change balloon containing the moved sentence and the related "Moved (insertion) [1]" tracked change balloon are no longer displayed. In the document, the sentence itself is displayed in black, like the surrounding text, indicating that the change has been accepted. Now the space before the moved sentence, which Word automatically inserted when you moved the sentence, is selected.

8. Click the **Accept** button to accept the insertion of the space, and then click the **Accept** button again to accept the insertion of the letter "e" at the end of "gam."

The insertion point moves to the beginning of Rima's comment. Rima has received final confirmation that 300 is indeed the correct number of cards, so you can delete the comment.

9. In the Comments group, click the **Delete** button to delete the comment.

10. In the Changes group, click the **Next** button. (You could also click the Next button in the Comments group since the next item is a comment.)

The insertion point moves to the beginning of James's comment. Rima has already seen a draft of the rules booklet, so you can delete the comment.

11. In the Comments group, click the **Delete** button to delete the comment.

12. In the Changes group, click the **Next** button. A Microsoft Word dialog box opens with a message indicating that there are no more comments or tracked changes in the document.

13. Click the **OK** button to close the dialog box.

14. At the end of the last paragraph in the document, click to the left of the period, and type **, or contact *your name***, where *your name* is your first and last name. When you are finished, the text should read "about this fun event, or contact *your name*."

Now that you have finished editing and reviewing the document with tracked changes, you need to restore the original username and initials settings. Then you can close Rima's original document, which you no longer need.

To restore the original username and initials settings and close Rima's original document:

1. In the Tracking group, click the **Dialog Box Launcher** to open the Track Changes Options dialog box.

2. Click the **Change User Name** button, and then change the username and initials back to their original settings on the General tab of the Word Options dialog box.

3. Click the **OK** button to close the Word Options dialog box, and then click the **OK** button again to close the Track Changes Options dialog box.

4. On the taskbar, click the **Word** button, and then click the **Film Rima - Word** thumbnail to display the document.

5. Close the **Film Rima** document.

> **6.** Save the **Film Combined** document, and then display the rulers.

> **7.** On the ribbon, click the **Home** tab.

INSIGHT

Checking for Tracked Changes

Once a document is finished, you should make sure it does not contain any tracked changes or comments. This is especially important in situations where comments or tracked changes might reveal sensitive information that could jeopardize your privacy or the privacy of the organization you work for.

You can't always tell if a document contains comments or tracked changes just by looking at it because the comments or changes for some or all of the reviewers might be hidden. Also, the Display for Review box in the Tracking group on the Review tab might be set to No Markup, in which case all tracked changes would be hidden. To determine whether a document contains any tracked changes or comments, open the Reviewing pane and verify that the number of revisions for each type is 0. You can also use the Document Inspector to check for a variety of issues, including leftover comments and tracked changes. To use the Document Inspector, click the File tab, click Info, click Check for Issues, click Inspect Document, and then click the Inspect button.

Now that you have combined James's edits with Rima's, you are ready to add the Excel worksheet data and the pie chart to the document.

Embedding and Linking Objects from Other Programs

The programs in Office 2016 are designed to accomplish specific tasks. As you've seen with Word, you can use a word-processing program to create, edit, and format documents such as letters, reports, newsletters, and proposals. On the other hand, Microsoft Excel, a **spreadsheet program**, allows you to organize, calculate, and analyze numerical data in a grid of rows and columns and to illustrate data in the form of charts. A spreadsheet created in Microsoft Excel is known as a **worksheet**. Each Excel file—called a **workbook**—can contain multiple worksheets. Throughout this module, a portion of an Excel worksheet is referred to as a **worksheet object**, and a chart is referred to as a **chart object**.

Sometimes it is useful to combine information created in the different Office programs into one file. For her document, Rima wants to use fund-raising goals from an Excel worksheet. She also wants to include an Excel chart that shows the hours of work remaining on the project. You can incorporate the Excel data and chart into Rima's Word document by taking advantage of **object linking and embedding**, or **OLE**, a technology that allows you to share information among the Office programs. This process is commonly referred to as **integration**.

Before you start using OLE, you need to understand some important terms. Recall that in Word, an object is anything that can be selected and modified as a whole, such as a table, picture, or block of text. Another important term, **source program**, refers to the program used to create the original version of an object. The program into which the object is integrated is called the **destination program**. Similarly, the original file that contains the object you are integrating is called the **source file**, and the file into which you integrate the object is called the **destination file**.

You can integrate objects by either embedding or linking. **Embedding** is a technique that allows you to insert a copy of an object into a destination document. You can double-click an embedded object in the destination document to access the tools of the source program, allowing you to edit the object within the destination document using the source program's tools. Because the embedded object is a copy, any changes you make to it are not reflected in the original source file and vice versa. For instance, you could embed data from a worksheet named Itemized Expenses into a Word document named Travel Report. Later, if you change the Itemized Expenses file, those revisions would not be reflected in the Travel Report document. The opposite is also true; if you edit the embedded object from within the Travel Report file, those changes will not be reflected in the source file Itemized Expenses. The embedded object retains no connection to the source file.

Figure 7-14 illustrates the relationship between an embedded Excel worksheet object in Rima's Word document and the source file.

Figure 7-14	Embedding an Excel worksheet object in a Word document

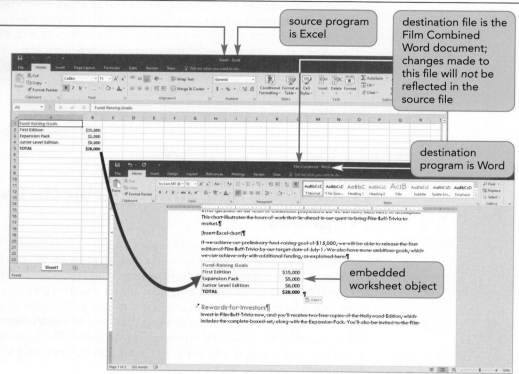

Linking is similar to embedding, except that the object inserted into the destination file maintains a connection to the source file. Just as with an embedded object, you can double-click a linked object to access the tools of the source program. However, unlike with an embedded object, changes to a linked object show up in both the destination file and the source file. The linked object in the destination document is not a copy; it is a shortcut to the original object in the source file.

Figure 7-15 illustrates the relationship between the data in James's Excel chart and the linked object in Rima's Word document.

| Figure 7-15 | Linking an Excel chart object to a Word document |

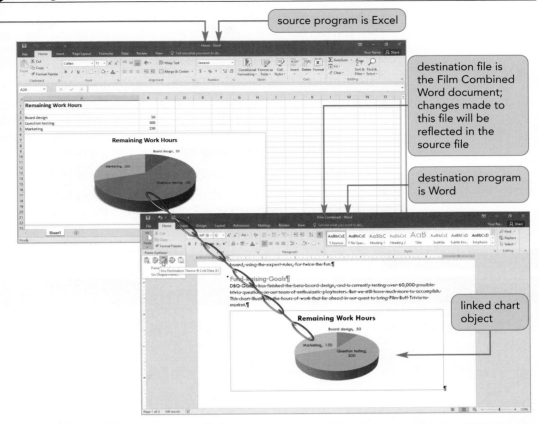

source file is an Excel workbook named Hours; changes made to this file will be reflected in the destination file

source program is Excel

destination file is the Film Combined Word document; changes made to this file will be reflected in the source file

destination program is Word

linked chart object

Decision Making: Choosing Between Embedding and Linking

Embedding and linking are both useful when you know you'll want to edit an object after inserting it into Word. But how do you decide whether to embed or link the object? Create an embedded object if you won't have access to the original source file in the future, or if you don't need (or want) to maintain the connection between the source file and the document containing the linked object. Two advantages of embedding are that the source file is unaffected by any editing in the destination document, and the two files can be stored separately. You could even delete the source file from your disk without affecting the copy embedded in your Word document. A disadvantage is that the file size of a Word document containing an embedded object will be larger than the file size of a document containing a linked object.

Create a linked object whenever you have data that is likely to change over time and when you want to keep the object in your document up to date. In addition to the advantage of a smaller destination file size, both the source file and the destination file can reflect recent revisions when the files are linked. A disadvantage to linking is that you have to keep track of two files (the source file and the destination file) rather than just one.

Embedding an Excel Worksheet Object

To embed an object from an Excel worksheet into a Word document, you start by opening the Excel worksheet (the source file) and copying the Excel object to the Office Clipboard. Then, in the Word document (the destination file), you open the Paste Special dialog box. In this dialog box, you can choose to paste the copied Excel object in a number of different forms. To embed it, you select Microsoft Office Excel Worksheet Object.

Rima wants to include the company's fund-raising goals in her document. If she needs to adjust numbers in the fund-raising goals later, she will need access to the Excel tools for recalculating the data. Therefore, you'll embed the Excel object in the Word document. Then you can use Excel commands to modify the embedded object from within Word.

To embed the Excel data in the Word document:

1. Scroll down to the paragraph above the "Rewards for Investors" heading, and then delete the placeholder text [**Insert Excel worksheet**], taking care not to delete the paragraph mark after it. The insertion point should now be located in a blank paragraph above the "Rewards for Investors" heading.

   Now you need to open James's Excel file and copy the fund-raising data.

2. Start Microsoft Excel 2016, open the file **Goals** located in the Word7 > Module folder included with your Data Files, and then maximize the Excel program window if necessary. See Figure 7-16.

Figure 7-16 Goals file open in Excel

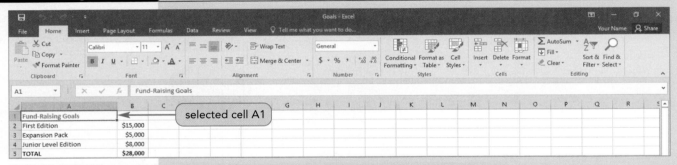

An Excel worksheet is arranged in rows and columns, just like a Word table. The intersection between a row and a column is called a **cell**; an individual cell takes its name from its column letter and row number. For example, the intersection of column A and row 1 in the upper-left corner of the worksheet is referred to as cell A1. Currently, cell A1 is selected, as indicated by its dark outline.

To copy the fund-raising data to the Office Clipboard, you need to select the entire block of cells containing the fund-raising data.

3. Click cell **A1** (the cell containing the text "Fund-Raising Goals"), if necessary, press and hold the **Shift** key, and then click cell **B5** (the cell containing "$28,000"). See Figure 7-17.

Figure 7-17 Fund-raising data selected in worksheet

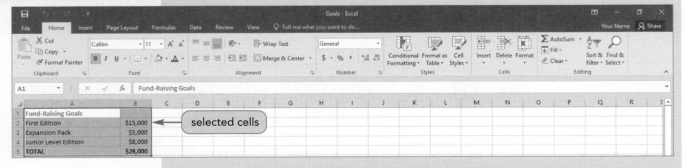

Now that the data is selected, you can copy it to the Office Clipboard.

Be sure to keep Excel open; otherwise, you won't have access to the commands for embedding the data in Word.

4. Press the **Ctrl+C** keys. The border around the selected cells is now flashing, indicating that you have copied the data in these cells to the Office Clipboard. Next, you will switch to Word without closing Excel.

5. On the taskbar, click the **Word** button ◻ to return to the Film Combined document. The insertion point is still located in the blank paragraph above the "Rewards for Investors" heading.

6. On the ribbon, click the **Home** tab, if necessary.

7. In the Clipboard group, click the **Paste button arrow**, and then click **Paste Special** to open the Paste Special dialog box.

8. In the As list, click **Microsoft Excel Worksheet Object**. See Figure 7-18.

Figure 7-18	Paste Special dialog box

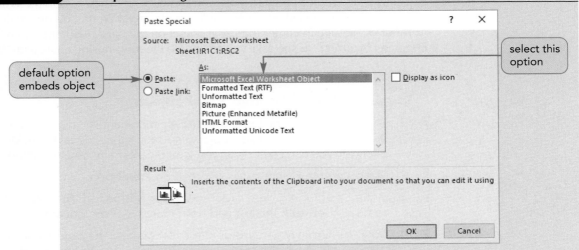

Next, you can choose to embed the Excel object or link it, depending on whether you select the Paste button (for embedding) or the Paste link button (for linking). The Paste button is selected by default, which is what you want in this case.

9. Click the **OK** button. The Excel worksheet object is inserted in the Word document, as shown in Figure 7-19.

Figure 7-19	Excel worksheet object embedded in Word document

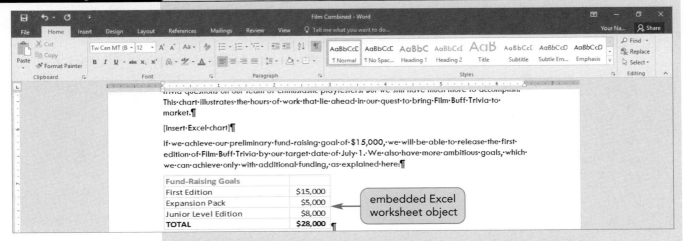

Trouble? If you don't see the top or bottom horizontal gridline in the embedded Excel object, don't be concerned. It won't affect the rest of the steps.

At this point, the Excel data looks like an ordinary table. But because you embedded it as an Excel worksheet object, you can modify it from within Word, using Excel tools and commands.

Modifying an Embedded Worksheet Object

After you embed an object in Word, you can modify it in two different ways. First, you can click the object to select it, and then move or resize it just as you would a graphic object. Second, you can double-click the object to display the tools of the source program on the Word ribbon and then edit the contents of the object. After you modify the embedded object using the source program tools, you can click anywhere else in the Word document to deselect the embedded object and redisplay the usual Word tools on the ribbon.

Rima would like to center the Excel object on the page. Also, the value for the First Edition is incorrect, so she asks you to update the fund-raising goals with the new data.

To modify the embedded Excel object:

1. Click anywhere in the Excel object. Selection handles and a dotted outline are displayed around the Excel object, indicating that it is selected. With the object selected, you can center it as you would center any other selected item.

2. Make sure the **Home** tab is selected on the ribbon.

3. In the Paragraph group, click the **Center** button ▤. The Excel object is centered between the left and right margins of the document.

4. Double-click anywhere inside the Excel object. The object's border changes to resemble the borders of an Excel worksheet, with horizontal and vertical scroll bars, row numbers, and column letters. The Word tabs on the ribbon are replaced with Excel tabs.

   Trouble? If you don't see the Excel borders around the worksheet object, click outside the worksheet object to deselect it, and then repeat Step 4. If you still don't see the Excel borders, save the document, close it, reopen it, and then repeat Step 4.

   You need to change the value for the First Edition from $15,000 to $20,000. Although you can't see it, a formula automatically calculates and displays the total in cell B5. After you increase the value for the First Edition, the formula will increase the total in cell B5 by $5,000.

5. Click cell **B2**, which contains the value $15,000, and then type **20,000**.

6. Press the **Enter** key. The new value "$20,000" is displayed in cell B2. The total in cell B5 increases from $28,000 to $33,000. See Figure 7-20.

Figure 7-20   **Revised data in embedded Excel object**

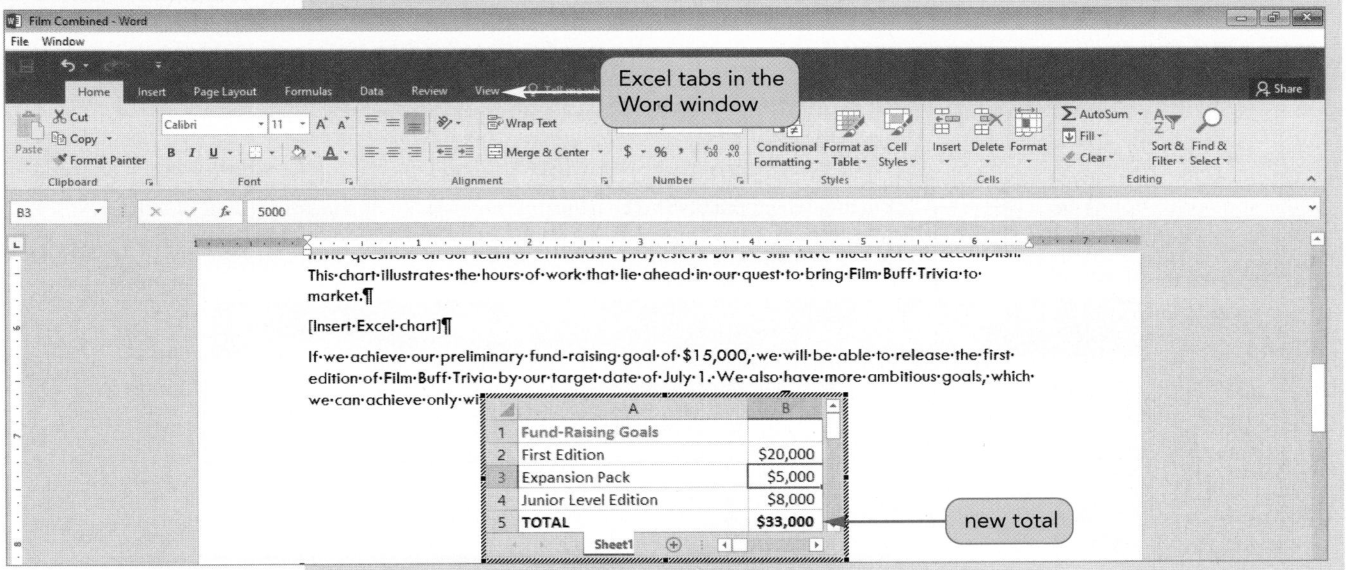

> **7.** In the document, click outside the borders of the Excel object to deselect it. The Word tabs are now visible on the ribbon again.

> **8.** On the taskbar, click the **Microsoft Excel** button ▣ to display the Excel window.
>
> Because you embedded the Excel object rather than linking it, the First Edition value of $15,000 and the Total of $28,000 remain unchanged.

> **9.** On the ribbon, click the **File** tab, and then click **Close** in the navigation bar. The Goals workbook closes, but Excel remains open.

In this session, you worked with tracked changes in a document. You learned how to combine and compare documents, and you accepted and rejected tracked changes in a combined document. You also embedded an Excel Worksheet object in a Word document and modified the embedded worksheet object from within Word. In the next session, you'll learn how to link an object instead of embedding it. You'll also create bookmarks, insert and edit hyperlinks in a document, and optimize the document for online viewing. Finally, you'll learn how to create and publish a blog post.

Session 7.1 Quick Check

REVIEW

1. How can you ensure that your name is displayed for each tracked change?

2. Explain how to turn on Track Changes.

3. Which provides a more streamlined view of a document's tracked changes, All Markup view or Simple Markup view?

4. What should you do before using the Next and Previous buttons to review the tracked changes in a document?

5. Explain the difference between a linked object and an embedded object.

6. How do you start editing an embedded Excel object in Word?

Session 7.2 Visual Overview:

To link an Excel chart object to a Word document, you first need to open the Excel workbook that contains the chart.

The two paste buttons with chain links on them allow you to paste the chart as a linked object. Here, the mouse is pointing to the Use Destination Theme & Link Data button, which pastes the chart using the green theme colors of the Word document, which is the destination file.

The Keep Source Formatting & Link Data button pastes the chart using the blue theme colors of the Excel workbook, which is the source file.

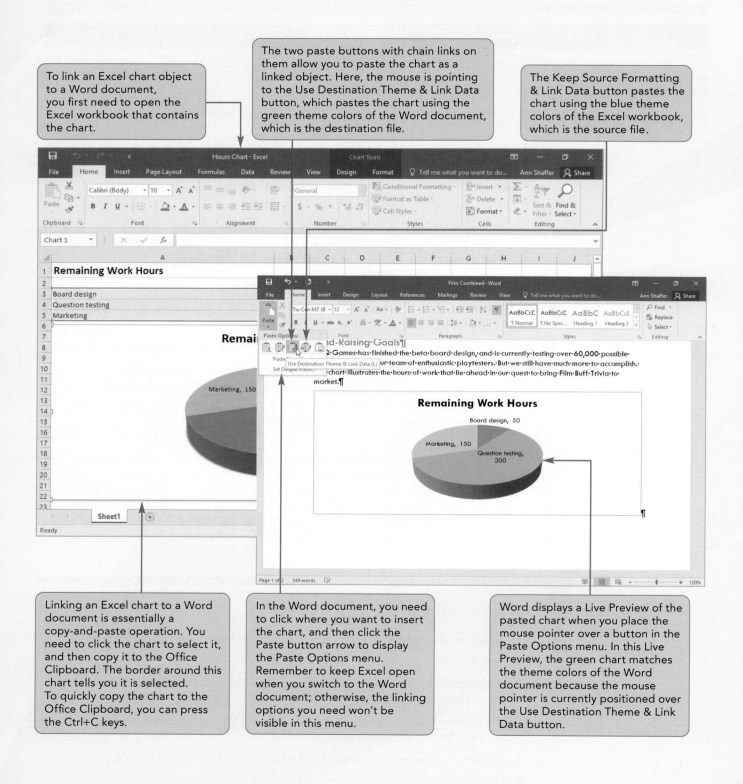

Linking an Excel chart to a Word document is essentially a copy-and-paste operation. You need to click the chart to select it, and then copy it to the Office Clipboard. The border around this chart tells you it is selected. To quickly copy the chart to the Office Clipboard, you can press the Ctrl+C keys.

In the Word document, you need to click where you want to insert the chart, and then click the Paste button arrow to display the Paste Options menu. Remember to keep Excel open when you switch to the Word document; otherwise, the linking options you need won't be visible in this menu.

Word displays a Live Preview of the pasted chart when you place the mouse pointer over a button in the Paste Options menu. In this Live Preview, the green chart matches the theme colors of the Word document because the mouse pointer is currently positioned over the Use Destination Theme & Link Data button.

Linking an Excel Chart Object

You can edit a linked chart object from within the Word document.

After you select the chart in the Word document, you click the Edit Data button on the Chart Tools Design tab. This opens a spreadsheet window with the Excel source file displayed.

If the chart in the Word window does not change to reflect changes made to data in the spreadsheet window, you can click the Refresh Data button to update the chart in the Word window.

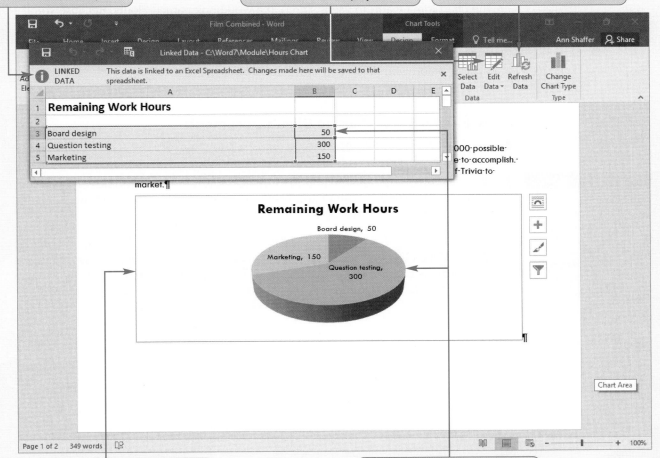

The first step in editing a linked chart object is clicking the chart in the Word document to select it. The border around this chart tells you it is selected.

Any change you make to the data in this spreadsheet window will show up in the linked chart in the Word document.

Linking an Excel Chart Object

When you link an object to a Word document, you start by selecting the object in the source program and copying it to the Office Clipboard. Then you return to Word and select one of the linking options from the Paste Options menu. The Paste Options menu displays different options depending on what you have copied to the Office Clipboard, with specific options related to tables, pictures, and other elements.

Rima wants you to insert James's Excel chart, which illustrates the remaining hours of work on the project, into her Word document. Because James will be sending Rima updated figures for the chart soon, she decides to link the chart rather than embed it. That way, once the chart is updated in the source file, the new data will be displayed in Rima's Word document as well.

The chart Rima wants to use is stored in a workbook named Hours. Because you'll make changes to the chart after you link it, you will save the workbook with a new name before you link it. This leaves the original workbook file unchanged in case you want to repeat the module steps later. Normally, you don't need to save a file with a new name before you link it to a Word document.

TIP

To link a Word file to the current document: on the Insert tab, click the Object button, click the Create from File tab, select the Link to file checkbox, click the Browse button, and select the file.

To link the Excel chart to Rima's document:

1. If you took a break after the previous session, make sure the **Film Combined** document is open in Print Layout view and that Excel is open.

2. In Excel, open the file named **Hours** from the Word7 > Module folder included with your Data Files, and then save it with the name **Hours Chart** in the location specified by your instructor.

   The worksheet includes data and a pie chart illustrating the data.

3. Click the chart border. Do not click any part of the chart itself. A selection border is displayed around the chart. The worksheet data used to create the chart is also highlighted in purple and blue. See Figure 7-21.

Figure 7-21	**Pie chart selected in worksheet**

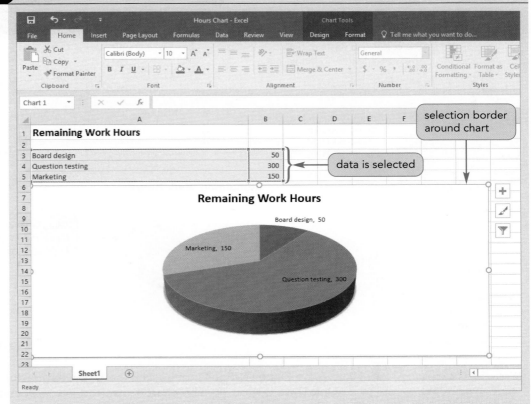

Trouble? If you see borders or handles around individual elements of the pie chart, you clicked the chart itself rather than the border. Click in the worksheet outside the chart border, and then repeat Step 3.

4. Press the **Ctrl+C** keys to copy the pie chart to the Office Clipboard.

5. On the taskbar, click the **Word button** to display the Word window with the Film Combined document.

6. On the ribbon, make sure the Home tab is selected.

7. In the second paragraph after the "Fund-Raising Goals" heading, delete the placeholder text **[Insert Excel chart]** but not the paragraph symbol after it, and then verify that the insertion point is located in a blank paragraph between two paragraphs of text.

8. In the Clipboard group, click the **Paste button arrow** to display the Paste Options menu.

9. Move the mouse pointer over the icons on the Paste Options menu, and notice the changing appearance of the chart's Live Preview, depending on which Paste Option you are previewing.

For linking, you can choose between the Use Destination Theme & Link Data option, which formats the chart with the font and green colors of the Word document's current theme, and the Keep Source Formatting & Link Data option, which retains the font and blue colors of the Excel workbook. See Figure 7-22.

Figure 7-22   Linking options on the Paste Options menu

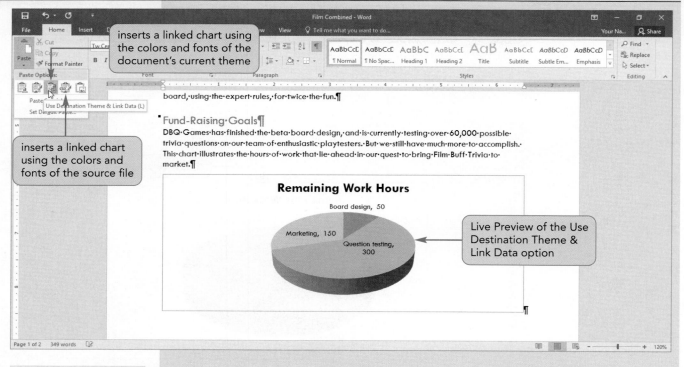

10. On the Paste Options menu, click the **Use Destination Theme & Link Data** button. The chart is inserted in the document. It is formatted with the green colors and font of the Circuit theme used in the Word document.

Use the button's ScreenTip to verify you are about to click the Use Destination Theme & Link Data button. It's easy to click the wrong button on the Paste Options menu.

INSIGHT

Storing Linked Files

When linking objects, it is important to keep the source and destination files in their original storage locations. If you move the files or the folders in which they are stored, you will disrupt the connection between the source file and the document containing the linked object because the shortcut in the destination file will no longer have a valid path to the source file.

For example, suppose you insert a linked Excel file into a Word document, and then later a colleague moves the Excel file to a different folder. The next time you open the Word document and try to update the linked object, you will see a dialog box explaining that the linked file is not available. At that point, you can make the link functional again by updating the path to the linked objects. To do so, click the File tab on the ribbon, and then click Info in the navigation bar, if necessary. On the Info screen, click Edit Links to Files. In the Links dialog box, click the link whose location has changed, click the Change Source button, and then navigate to the new location of the source file.

Modifying the Linked Chart Object

The advantage of linking compared to embedding is that you can change the data in the source file, and those changes will automatically be reflected in the destination file as well.

Rima has received James's updated data about the total hours remaining on the project, and she wants the chart in her document to reflect this new information. You will update the data in the source file. You'll start by closing Excel so you can clearly see the advantages of working with a linked object.

To modify the chart in the source file:

▶ **1.** On the taskbar, click the **Microsoft Excel** button ◻ to display the Excel window, and then close Excel.

▶ **2.** On the taskbar, click the **Word** button ◻, if necessary, to display the Word window.

▶ **3.** Click anywhere in the white area inside the chart border. The selection border is displayed around the chart, and the two Chart Tools contextual tabs are displayed on the ribbon.

   Trouble? If you see a selection border around the pie chart itself, in addition to the selection border around the chart and the title, you can ignore it.

▶ **4.** On the ribbon, click the **Chart Tools Design** tab. See Figure 7-23.

| **Figure 7-23** | **Chart selected in Word** |

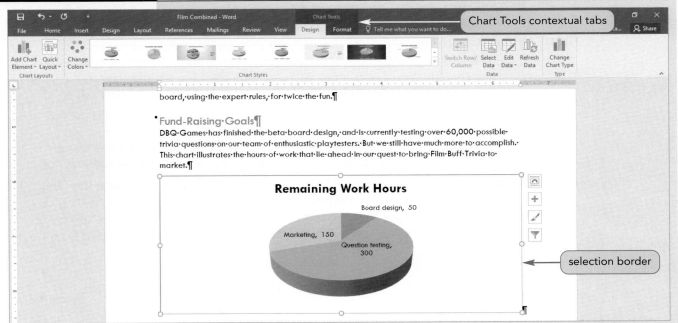

TIP

To edit the source file directly in Excel, click the Edit Data button arrow to display a menu, and then click Edit Data in Excel.

▶ **5.** In the Data group, click the **Edit Data** button. A spreadsheet that contains the chart data opens on top of the Word document. Your spreadsheet might be larger or smaller than the one shown in Figure 7-24.

Figure 7-24 Spreadsheet window with chart data

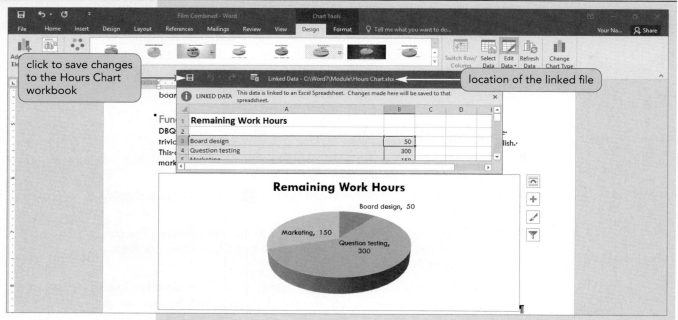

The file path at the top of the spreadsheet window shows the location of the linked file you are about to edit.

6. In the Excel window, click cell **B3**, which contains the value "50," and then type **100**.

7. Press the **Enter** key. The new value is entered in cell B3, and the label in the "Board Design" section of the pie chart changes from 50 to 100 in the linked chart in the Word document. Although you can't see the pie chart in the Excel spreadsheet window, it has also been updated to display the new value.

   Trouble? If the chart in the Word document does not change to show the new value, click anywhere in the white area inside the chart border, and then click the Refresh Data button in the Data group on the Chart Tools Design tab in the Word window. Then, click cell B4 in the spreadsheet window.

8. In the Excel window, type **350** in cell B4, and then press the **Enter** key. The new number is entered in cell B4, and the value in the "Question testing" section of the pie charts in both the Excel and Word windows changes to match. See Figure 7-25.

Figure 7-25   Modifying the linked chart data

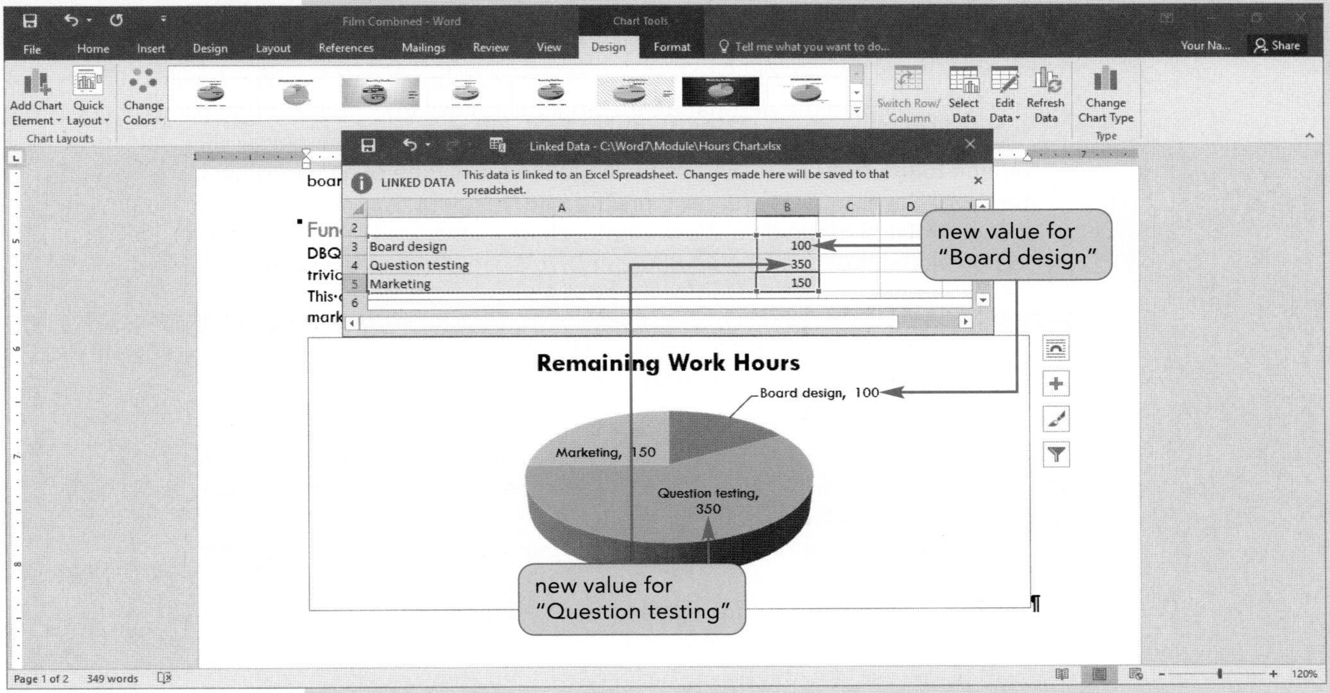

> **9.** At the top of the spreadsheet window, click the **Save** button 🖫, and then click the **Close** button ✕ to close the spreadsheet window.

> **10.** In the Word document, click anywhere outside the chart to deselect it, and then save the Film Combined document.

When you edited the data in the spreadsheet window, you were actually editing the Hours Chart workbook. If you wanted, you could start Excel and open the Hours Chart workbook to verify that it contains the new values.

INSIGHT

Editing a Linked Worksheet Object

The steps for editing a linked worksheet object are slightly different from the steps for editing a linked chart object. Instead of editing a linked worksheet object from within Word, you need to start Excel, open the workbook, and then edit the worksheet in Excel. You can quickly open the workbook in Excel by right-clicking the linked worksheet object in Word, pointing to Linked Worksheet Object on the shortcut menu, and then clicking Edit Link. This opens the workbook in Excel, where you can edit the data and save your changes. When you are finished, close the workbook, and then return to the Word document. Finally, to update the data within the Word document, right-click the linked worksheet object in the Word document to open a shortcut menu, and then click Update Link. When you open a Word document containing a linked worksheet object, you might see a dialog box asking if you want to update the document with the data from the linked files. Click Yes to continue.

Rima is finished with her work on the chart. She does not expect the data in it to change, so she wants to break the link between the Excel workbook and the Word document.

Breaking Links

If you no longer need a link between files, you can break it. When you break a link, the source file and the destination file no longer have any connection to each other, and changes made in the source file do not affect the destination file. After breaking the link to the source file, you can change the formatting of a chart object from within the Word document, using the Chart Tools contextual tabs, but you can't make any changes related to the data shown in the chart. In the case of an Excel worksheet, after you break the link to the source file, the worksheet turns into a Word table.

REFERENCE

Breaking a Link to a Source File

- On the ribbon, click the File tab.
- On the Info screen, click Edit Links to Files to open the Links dialog box.
- In the list of links in the document, click the link that you want to break.
- Click the Break Link button.
- Click the Yes button in the dialog box that opens, asking you to confirm that you want to break the link.
- Click the OK button to close the Links dialog box.

Now, you will break the link between Rima's document and the Hours Chart workbook.

To break the link between the Word document and the Excel workbook:

1. On the ribbon, click the **File** tab. Backstage view opens with the Info screen displayed.

2. In the lower-right corner of the Info screen, click **Edit Links to Files**. The Links dialog box opens with the only link in the document (the link to the Hours Chart workbook) selected. See Figure 7-26.

Figure 7-26	The Links dialog box

3. In the Links dialog box, click the **Break Link** button, and then click **Yes** in the dialog box that opens, asking if you are sure you want to break the link. The list in the Links dialog box now indicates there is no source file for the chart in the document.

4. Click the **OK** button to close the dialog box. You return to the Info screen in Backstage view.

   With the link broken, you can no longer edit the Excel data from within Word. You can verify this by looking at the Chart Tools Design tab.

5. At the top of the navigation bar, click the **Back** button 🔙 to close Backstage view and return to the document.

6. Click anywhere inside the chart border to select the chart.

7. On the ribbon, click the **Chart Tools Design** tab, if necessary. Notice that the Edit Data button in the Data group is grayed out, indicating this option is no longer available.

8. Click anywhere outside the chart border to deselect it, and then save the document.

Next, Rima asks you to turn your attention to adding hyperlinks to her document. Although hyperlinks are widely used in webpages, you can also use them in ordinary Word documents.

Using Hyperlinks in Word

A hyperlink is a word, phrase, or graphic that you can click to jump to another part of the same document, to a separate Word document, to a file created in another program, or to a webpage. When used thoughtfully, hyperlinks make it possible to navigate a complicated document or a set of files quickly and easily. And as you know, you can also include email links in documents, which you can click to create email messages.

Rima wants you to add two hyperlinks to the document—one that jumps to a location within the document, and one that opens a different document.

Inserting a Hyperlink to a Bookmark in the Same Document

Creating a hyperlink within a document is actually a two-part process. First, you need to mark the text you want the link to jump to—either by formatting the text with a heading style or by inserting a bookmark. A **bookmark** is an electronic marker that refers to specific text, a picture, or another object in a document. Second, you need to select the text that you want users to click, format it as a hyperlink, and specify the bookmark or heading as the target of the hyperlink. The **target** is the place in the document to which the link connects. In this case, Rima wants to create a hyperlink at the beginning of the document that targets the embedded Fund-Raising Goals Excel worksheet object near the end of the document. Figure 7-27 illustrates this process.

| Figure 7-27 | Hyperlink that targets a bookmark |

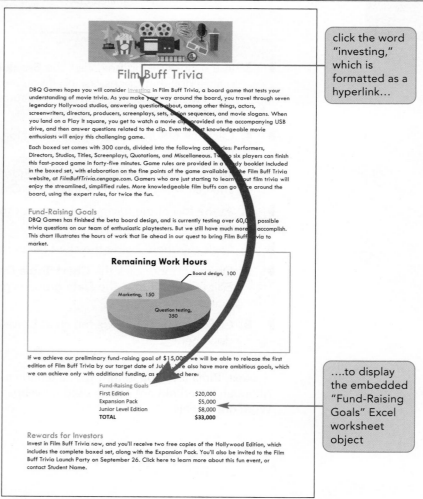

Zakharchenko Anna/Shutterstock.com

To create a hyperlink in Rima's document, you'll first need to designate the worksheet object as a bookmark.

To insert a bookmark:

1. Scroll down and click the "Fund-Raising Goals" worksheet object, on page 2. A dotted outline and handles are displayed around the worksheet object, indicating that it is selected.

2. On the ribbon, click the **Insert** tab.

3. In the Links group, click the **Bookmark** button. The Bookmark dialog box opens. You can now type the bookmark name, which cannot contain spaces.

4. In the Bookmark name box, type **Goals**. See Figure 7-28.

Figure 7-28   Creating a bookmark

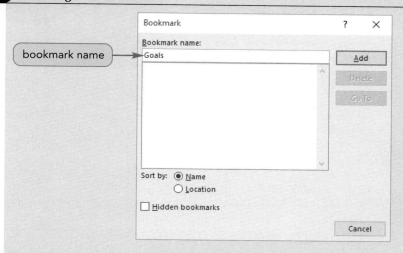

TIP

To delete a bookmark, click it in the Bookmark dialog box, and then click the Delete button.

5. Click the **Add** button. The Bookmark dialog box closes. Although you can't see any change in the document, the "Fund-Raising Goals" worksheet object has been designated as a bookmark.

The bookmark you just created will be the target of a hyperlink, which you will create next.

REFERENCE

Creating a Hyperlink to a Location in the Same Document

- Select the text, graphic, or other object that you want to format as a hyperlink.
- On the ribbon, click the Insert tab.
- In the Links group, click the Hyperlink button to open the Insert Hyperlink dialog box.
- In the Link to pane, click Place in This Document.
- In the Select a place in this document list, click the bookmark or heading you want to link to, and then click the OK button.

Rima wants you to format the word "investing" at the beginning of the document as a hyperlink that will target the bookmark you just created.

To create and test a hyperlink to the bookmark:

1. Scroll up to page 1, and then, in the first line under the "Film Buff Trivia" heading, select the word **investing**.

2. In the Links group, click the **Hyperlink** button. The Insert Hyperlink dialog box opens.

3. In the Link to pane, click **Place in This Document** to select it, if necessary. The "Select a place in this document" list shows the headings and bookmarks in the document. Here you can click the bookmark or heading you want as the target for the hyperlink.

4. Under Bookmarks, click **Goals**. See Figure 7-29.

Figure 7-29   Inserting a hyperlink to a location in the same document

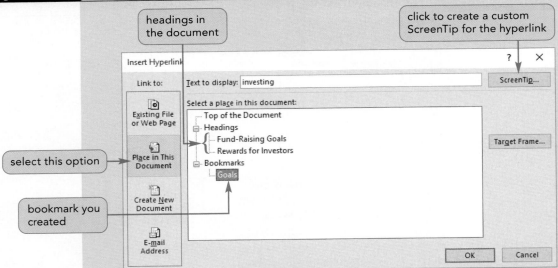

You can click the ScreenTip button to open the Set Hyperlink ScreenTip dialog box and type custom text for the hyperlink's ScreenTip, which appears when you place the mouse pointer over the hyperlink in the document. In this case, however, Rima prefers to use the default ScreenTip.

5. Click the **OK** button. The word "investing" is now formatted in the hyperlink style for the Circuit theme, which applies a green font color with an underline. The hyperlink targets the Goals bookmark that you created in the last set of steps. You can verify this by clicking the hyperlink.

6. Move the mouse pointer over the hyperlink **investing**. The default ScreenTip displays the name of the bookmark and instructions for following the link. See Figure 7-30.

TIP

To change a hyperlink's font color, open the Styles pane and modify the Hyperlink style.

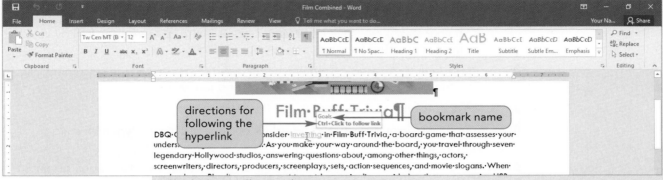

Figure 7-30   **Displaying the ScreenTip for a hyperlink**

Zakharchenko Anna/Shutterstock.com

▶ **7.** Press and hold the **Ctrl** key, and then click the **investing** hyperlink. The insertion point jumps to the "Fund-Raising Goals" worksheet object on page 2.

▶ **8.** Scroll up to review the "investing" hyperlink. It is now turquoise, which is the color for clicked links in the Circuit theme.

▶ **9.** Save your document.

Next, you will create a hyperlink that jumps to a different document.

Creating Hyperlinks to Other Documents

When you create a hyperlink to another document, you need to specify the document's filename and storage location as the hyperlink's target. The document can be stored on your computer or on a network; it can even be a webpage stored somewhere on the web. In that case, you need to specify the webpage's URL (web address) as the target. When you click a hyperlink to another document, the document opens on your computer, with the beginning of the document displayed. Keep in mind that if you move the document containing the hyperlink, or if you move the target document, the hyperlink will no longer work. However, if you create a hyperlink to a webpage on the Internet, the link will continue to work no matter where you store the document containing the hyperlink.

REFERENCE

Creating a Hyperlink to Another Document

- Select the text, graphic, or other object you want to format as a hyperlink.
- On the ribbon, click the Insert tab.
- In the Links group, click the Hyperlink button to open the Insert Hyperlink dialog box.
- In the Link to pane, click Existing File or Web Page.
- To target a specific file on your computer or network, click the Look in arrow, navigate to the folder containing the file, and then click the file in the file list.
- To target a webpage, type its URL in the Address box.
- Click the OK button.

Rima wants to insert a hyperlink that, when clicked, will open a Word document containing details about the Film Buff Trivia Launch Party. You'll start by opening the document containing the party details and saving it with a new name.

To create a hyperlink to a document with details about the Film Buff Trivia Launch Party:

▶ **1.** Open the document **Party** located in the Word7 > Module folder included with your Data Files, save it as **Party Details** in the location specified by your instructor, and then close it.

▶ **2.** In the Film Combined document, scroll down to the end of the document, and then select the word **here** in the second to last line.

▶ **3.** On the ribbon, click the **Insert** tab, if necessary.

▶ **4.** In the Links group, click the **Hyperlink** button. The Insert Hyperlink dialog box opens.

▶ **5.** In the Link to pane, click **Existing File or Web Page**. The dialog box displays options related to selecting a file or a webpage.

▶ **6.** Click the **Look in** arrow, navigate to the location where you stored the Party Details file, if necessary, and then click **Party Details** in the file list. See Figure 7-31.

Figure 7-31   **Inserting a hyperlink to a different document**

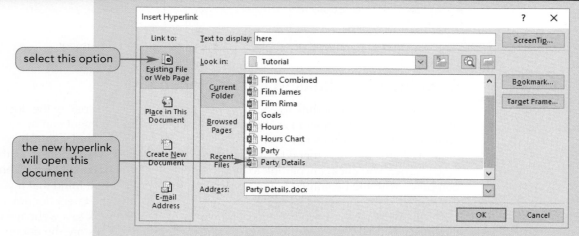

▶ **7.** Click the **OK** button. The new "here" hyperlink is formatted in green with an underline. Now, you will test the hyperlink.

▶ **8.** Press and hold the **Ctrl** key, and then click the **here** hyperlink. The Party Details document opens. See Figure 7-32.

Figure 7-32   Party Details document

Film·Buff·Trivia·
Launch·Party¶
Saturday·September·26·at·8·p.m.¶

Page 1 of 1   52 words   120%

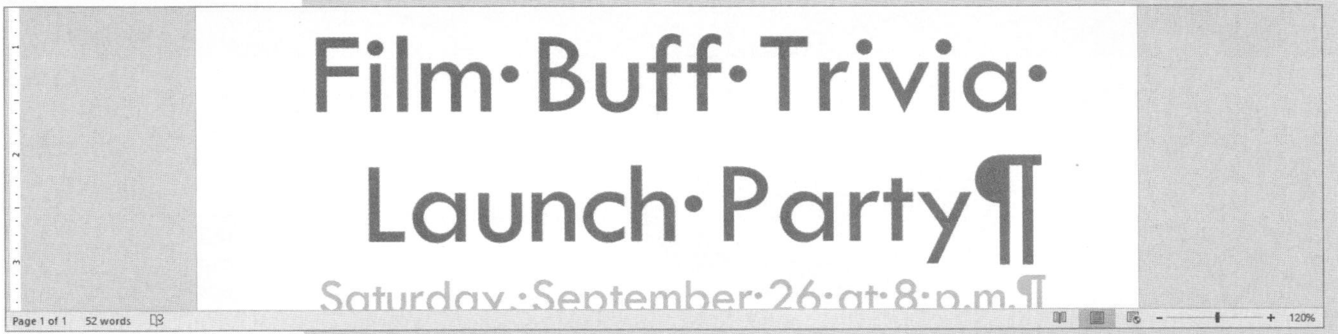

▶ **9.** Close the Party Details document, and then return to the Film Combined document. The link is now turquoise because you clicked it.

▶ **10.** Save your document.

Now that you have finalized the document and added the necessary hyperlinks, you will optimize the document for online viewing by switching to Web Layout view and adding some formatting that is useful for documents that will be viewed online.

Optimize a Document for Online Viewing

When preparing a document intended solely for online distribution, you can focus on how the page will look on the screen, without having to consider how it will look when printed. This means you can take advantage of some formatting options that are visible only on the screen, such as a background page color or a background fill effect. You can also switch to **Web Layout view**, which displays a document as it would look in a web browser.

In Web Layout view, the text spans the width of the screen, with no page breaks and without any margins or headers and footers. The advantage of Web Layout view is that it allows you to zoom in on the document text as close as you want, with the text rewrapping to accommodate the new Zoom setting. By contrast, in Print Layout view, if you increase the Zoom setting too far, you end up having to scroll from side-to-side to read an entire line of text. The only downside to Web Layout view is that graphics may shift position as the text wrapping changes. However, these changes are only visible in Web Layout view. When you switch back to Print Layout view, you will see the original page layout.

Rima wants to switch to Web Layout view before she continues formatting the document.

TIP

Zooming in on text in Web Layout View is helpful when you have multiple panes open; the text wraps for easy reading.

To switch to Web Layout view:

▶ **1.** On the status bar, click the **Web Layout** button 🖳. The document text expands to span the entire Word screen.

▶ **2.** Use the Zoom slider on the status bar to increase the Zoom setting to **160%**. The text rewraps to accommodate the new setting.

▶ **3.** Scroll down and review the entire document, which no longer has any page breaks. See Figure 7-33.

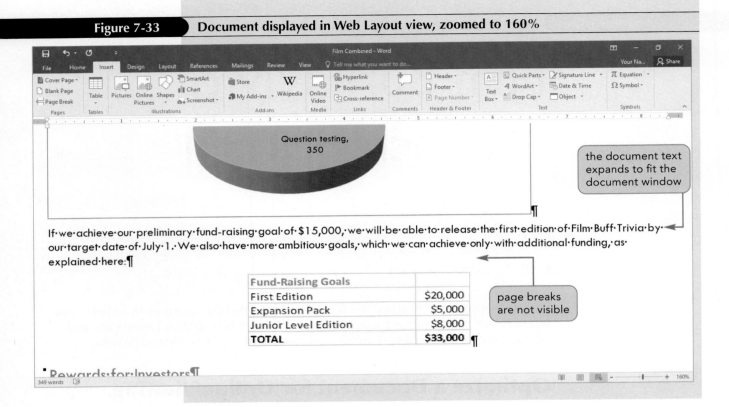

Figure 7-33   Document displayed in Web Layout view, zoomed to 160%

Applying a Background Fill Effect

To make the document more eye-catching when it's displayed on a screen, Rima wants to add a background fill effect. A **background fill effect** is a repeating graphic element, such as a texture, a photo, or a color gradient, that is visible only when a document is displayed online. It's essential to use fill effects judiciously. In the hands of a trained graphic designer, they can be striking; if used carelessly, they can be garish and distracting. As a general rule, you should avoid using photos and textures and instead stick with simple colors or color gradients.

Rima decides to use a gradient background in shades of blue.

To apply a background fill effect to the document:

1. On the ribbon, click the **Design** tab.

2. In the Page Background group, click the **Page Color** button. The Page Color gallery opens, with a menu at the bottom. You could click a color in the gallery to select it as a background color for the page. To select another type of background effect, you need to click Fill Effects.

3. Click **Fill Effects** to open the Fill Effects dialog box, and then click the **Gradient** tab, if necessary. Note that you could use other tabs in this dialog box to add a textured, patterned, or picture background.

4. In the Colors section, click the **Two colors** button. The Color 1 and Color 2 boxes and arrows are displayed.

5. Click the **Color 1** arrow, and then click **Blue, Accent 5**, the ninth color from the left in the first row of the Theme Colors section.

6. Click the **Color 2** arrow, and then click **Sky Blue, Background 2, Lighter 60%**, the third color from the left in the third row of the Theme Colors section.

7. In the Shading styles section, click the **Vertical** option button to change the gradient pattern so it stretches vertically up and down the page. Compare your dialog box to Figure 7-34.

Figure 7-34   **Selecting a gradient background**

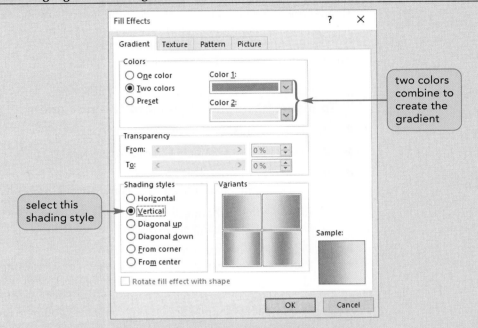

8. Click the **OK** button. The document's background is now a gradient that varies between light and dark blue.

9. Scroll down, if necessary, so you can see the Fund-Raising Goals worksheet object.

The gradient background is light enough to make the document text easy to read. However, it's now hard to see the gridlines of the worksheet object. You can fix that by changing the object's background color.

To change the background for the Fund-Raising Goals worksheet object:

1. Right-click the worksheet object to display a shortcut menu, and then click **Picture**. The Format Object dialog box opens, with the Picture tab displayed.

2. Click the **Colors and Lines** tab to display settings related to the colors used in the worksheet object. In the Fill section, the Color box currently displays "No Color," indicating that the object's background is the same as the document's background.

3. In the Fill section, click the **Color** arrow, and then click **White, Background 1**, the first square in the top row of the Theme Colors section.

4. Click the **OK** button to close the Format Object dialog box. The worksheet object now has a white background, which makes the gridlines easier to see.

> **5.** Click outside the worksheet object to deselect it, and then save the document.

Next, you will add horizontal lines to separate the various sections of the document.

Inserting Horizontal Lines

Horizontal lines allow you to see at a glance where one part of a document ends and another begins. Unlike background colors and fill effects, horizontal lines do appear in printed documents, along with the document text. However, they are commonly used in documents that are meant to be viewed only online.

Rima wants you to add a horizontal line before the "Fund-Raising Goals" heading and before the "Rewards for Investors" heading.

To insert horizontal lines into the document:

> **1.** Scroll up and click at the beginning of the "Fund-Raising Goals" heading.

> **2.** On the ribbon, click the **Home** tab.

> **3.** In the Paragraph group, click the **Borders button arrow** to open the Borders gallery, and then click **Horizontal Line** to insert a default gray line.

> Rima wants to change the line's color. She also wants to make the line shorter, so it doesn't span the full page.

> **4.** Right-click the horizontal line to display a shortcut menu, and then click **Picture**. The Format Horizontal Line dialog box opens, with settings for changing the line's width, height, color, and alignment. The current Width setting is 100%, meaning that the line spans the entire page from left to right. To leave a little space on each side, you need to lower the percentage.

> **5.** Triple-click the **Width** box, and then type **75**. Because the Center alignment option at the bottom of the dialog box is selected by default, the shorter line will be centered on the page, with space to its left and its right.

> **6.** Click the **Color** arrow, and then click **Blue, Accent 5, Darker 50%**, the ninth square from the left in the sixth row of the Theme Colors section. The Color gallery closes, and the Use solid color (no shade) check box is now selected. See Figure 7-35.

Figure 7-35 **Format Horizontal Line dialog box**

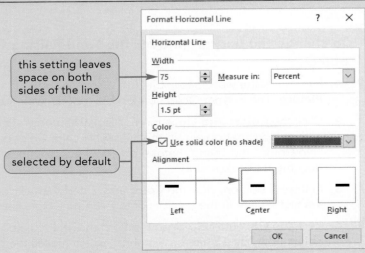

7. Click the **OK** button, and then click anywhere in the document to deselect the horizontal line. Your document should look similar to Figure 7-36.

Figure 7-36 **Newly inserted horizontal line**

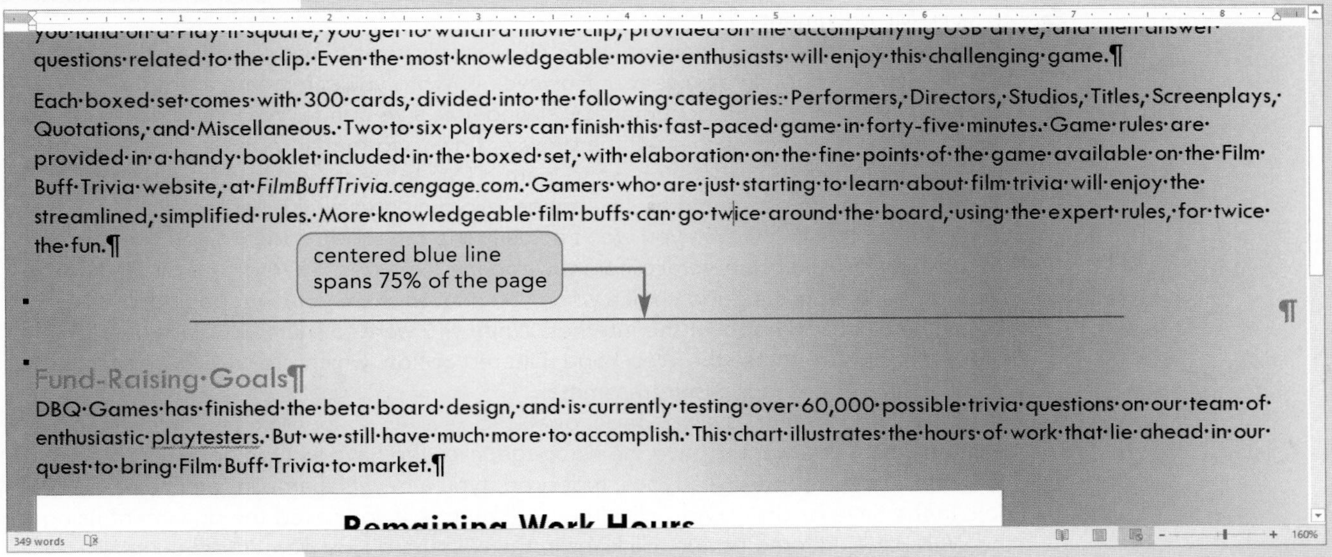

you·land·on·a·Play·It·square,·you·get·to·watch·a·movie·clip,·provided·on·the·accompanying·USB·drive,·and·then·answer· questions·related·to·the·clip.·Even·the·most·knowledgeable·movie·enthusiasts·will·enjoy·this·challenging·game.¶

Each·boxed·set·comes·with·300·cards,·divided·into·the·following·categories:·Performers,·Directors,·Studios,·Titles,·Screenplays,· Quotations,·and·Miscellaneous.·Two·to·six·players·can·finish·this·fast-paced·game·in·forty-five·minutes.·Game·rules·are· provided·in·a·handy·booklet·included·in·the·boxed·set,·with·elaboration·on·the·fine·points·of·the·game·available·on·the·Film· Buff·Trivia·website,·at·*FilmBuffTrivia.cengage.com*.·Gamers·who·are·just·starting·to·learn·about·film·trivia·will·enjoy·the· streamlined,·simplified·rules.·More·knowledgeable·film·buffs·can·go·twice·around·the·board,·using·the·expert·rules,·for·twice· the·fun.¶

centered blue line
spans 75% of the page

Fund-Raising·Goals¶
DBQ·Games·has·finished·the·beta·board·design,·and·is·currently·testing·over·60,000·possible·trivia·questions·on·our·team·of· enthusiastic·playtesters.·But·we·still·have·much·more·to·accomplish.·This·chart·illustrates·the·hours·of·work·that·lie·ahead·in·our· quest·to·bring·Film·Buff·Trivia·to·market.¶

Remaining Work Hours

349 words   160%

Now, you can copy the line, and then insert it before the other heading.

8. Click the horizontal line to select it, and then press the **Ctrl+C** keys to copy it to the Clipboard.

9. Scroll down, click to the left of the "R" in the "Rewards for Investors" heading, and then press the **Ctrl+V** keys to insert the horizontal line before the heading.

10. Save the document.

TIP

To remove a horizontal line, click the line to select it, and then press the Delete key.

You've finished formatting the Film Combined document. Next, Rima needs to edit the hyperlink that opens the document with information about the launch party.

Saving a Word Document as a Webpage

Webpages are special documents designed to be viewed in a program called a **browser**. The browser included in Windows 10 is Microsoft Edge. Because webpages include code written in Hypertext Markup Language, or **HTML**, they are often referred to as HTML documents.

To create sophisticated webpages, you'll probably want to use a dedicated HTML editor, such as Adobe Dreamweaver. However, in Word you can create a simple webpage from an existing document by saving it as a webpage. When you do so, Word inserts HTML codes that tell the browser how to format and display the text and graphics. Fortunately, you don't have to learn HTML to create webpages with Word. When you save the document as a webpage, Word creates all the necessary HTML codes (called tags); however, you won't actually see the HTML codes in your webpage.

You can choose from several different webpage file types in Word. The Single File Web Page file type is a good choice when you plan to share your webpage only over a small network and not over the Internet. When you want to share your files over the Internet, it's better to use the Web Page, Filtered option, which breaks a webpage into multiple smaller files, for easier transmittal.

To save a document as a webpage, open the Save As dialog box, navigate to the location where you want to save the webpage, click the Save as type arrow, and then click one of the webpage file types. If desired, type a new filename in the File name box. In the Save As dialog box, click the Save button. If you saved the document using the Web Page, Filtered option, click Yes in the warning dialog box. After you save a document as a webpage, Word displays it in Web Layout view.

Editing Hyperlinks

Rima's document contains two hyperlinks—the "investing" link, which jumps to the Fund-Raising Goals worksheet object, and the "here" link, which jumps to the Party Details document. To give all the Film Buff Trivia documents a coherent look, Rima formatted the Party Details document with a fill effect. She saved the newly formatted document as file named "Formatted Party." Now she wants you to edit the "here" hyperlink, so it opens this new version of the document. To make it possible to repeat these steps later if you want, you'll start by saving the Formatted Party document with a new name.

To edit the "here" hyperlink:

1. Open the document **Formatted Party** located in the Word7 > Module folder included with your Data Files, and then switch to Web Layout view, if necessary, so you can see the two-color gradient background.

2. Save the document as **Formatted Party Details** in the location specified by your instructor, and then close it.

3. In the Film Combined document, scroll down to the end of the document, and then position the pointer over the **here** hyperlink near the end of the document to display a ScreenTip, which indicates that the link will jump to a document named Party Details.docx.

   Trouble? If you also see a ScreenTip that reads "Chart Area" you can ignore it.

4. Right-click the **here** hyperlink to open a shortcut menu, and then click **Edit Hyperlink**. The Edit Hyperlink dialog box opens. It looks just like the Insert Hyperlink dialog box, which you have already used. To edit the hyperlink, you simply select a different target file.

5. In the Link to pane, verify that the Existing File or Web Page option is selected.

6. Navigate to the location where you saved the Formatted Party Details document, if necessary, and then click **Formatted Party Details** in the file list.

7. Click the **OK** button. You return to the Film Combined document.

8. Place the mouse pointer over the list hyperlink to display a ScreenTip, which indicates that the link will now jump to a document named Formatted Party Details.docx.

9. Press and hold the **Ctrl** key, and then click the **here** hyperlink. The Formatted Party Details document opens.

10. Close the Formatted Party Details document, and then save and close the Film Combined document.

PROSKILLS

Teamwork: Emailing Word Documents

After you optimize a document for online viewing, you can share it with colleagues via email. To get started emailing a document, first make sure you have set up Microsoft Outlook as your email program. Then, in Word, open the document you want to email. On the ribbon, click the File tab, and then click Share in the navigation bar. On the Share screen, click Email, and then select the email option you want. When you email documents, keep in mind the following:

- Many email services have difficulty handling attachments larger than 4 MB. Consider storing large files in a compressed (or zipped) folder to reduce their size before emailing them.
- Other word-processing programs and early versions of Word might not be able to open files created in Word 2016. To avoid problems with conflicting versions, you have two options. You can save the Word document as a rich text file (using the Rich Text File document type in the Save As dialog box) before emailing it; all versions of Word can open rich text files. Another option is to save the document as a PDF.
- If you plan to email a document that contains links to other files, remember to email all the linked files.
- Attachments, including Word documents, are sometimes used maliciously to spread computer viruses. Remember to include an explanatory note with any email attachment so that the recipient can be certain the attachment is legitimate. Also, it's important to have a reliable virus checker program installed if you plan to receive and open email attachments.

The new documents are just one way to share information about Film Buff Trivia. Rima also wants to write a blog post discussing the game's development. She asks you to help her create a blog post in Word.

Creating and Publishing a Blog Post

Creating a blog post in Word is similar to creating a new Word document except that instead of clicking Blank document on the New screen in Backstage view, you click Blog post. Note that before you can publish your blog post using Word, you need to register a blog account with an Internet blog provider that is compatible with Microsoft Word 2016.

Rima asks you to help her create a blog post about the development of the Film Buff Trivia game.

To create and publish a blog post:

▶ 1. On the ribbon, click the **File** tab, and then click **New** in the navigation bar to display the icons for the various document templates.

▶ 2. Scroll down if necessary, and then click **Blog post**.

▶ 3. In the Blog post window, click the **Create** button. A blank blog post opens. Assuming you have not previously registered for a blog account, you also see the Register a Blog Account dialog box.

To register a blog account, you could click the Register Now button to open the New Blog Account dialog box. From there, you could follow the prompts to register your blog account. Rima will register her blog account later, so you can skip the registration step for now.

▶ 4. Click the **Register Later** button to close the dialog box.

▶ 5. At the top of the blog post, click the **[Enter Post Title Here]** placeholder, and then type **Film Buff Trivia**.

▶ 6. Click in the blank paragraph below the blog title, and then type **Film Buff Trivia is a board game that tests your knowledge of film trivia.** See Figure 7-37.

Figure 7-37	Blog post

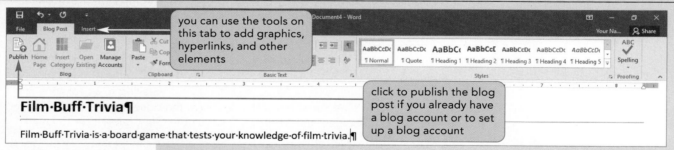

At this point, you could use the tools on the Insert tab to add hyperlinks, graphics, and other items to your blog post. Rima plans to add more text and some graphics to her blog post later. For now, you can save the post, and then explore options for publishing it.

▶ 7. Save the blog post as **Film Buff Trivia Blog Post** in the location specified by your instructor. Note that a blog post is a regular Word document file, with a .docx extension.

▶ 8. On the Blog Post tab, in the Blog group, click the **Publish** button.

Assuming you have not previously registered for a blog account, you see the Register a Blog Account dialog box again. At this point, you could click the Register an Account button and then follow the on-screen instructions to register a blog account and publish your blog. Because Rima plans to do that later, you can close the blog post for now.

Trouble? If you see a menu below the Publish button, you clicked the Publish button arrow instead of the Publish button. Press the Esc key, and then click the Publish button.

TIP

To add, remove, or change blog accounts, click the Manage Accounts button in the Blog group on the Blog Post tab.

▶ **9.** Click the **Cancel** button to close the Register a Blog Account dialog box, and then click the **OK** button in the Microsoft Word dialog box.

▶ **10.** Close the blog post.

Rima plans to write weekly blog posts describing the company's progress with the new game. Combined with the fact sheet, they will help generate interest in the company's crowd-sourcing effort.

INSIGHT

Working with Saved and Unsaved Document Versions

As you work on a document, versions of it are automatically saved every ten minutes. (To change how often a version is saved, click the File tab, click Options in the navigation bar, click Save in the navigation bar in the Word Options dialog box, and then change the number of minutes in the Save AutoRecover information every box.) If you want to open a version of a document that was autosaved, open the document, and click the File tab to display the Info screen. If autosaved versions of the document are available, they are listed in the Manage Document section, along with the date and time each version was saved. Click a version to open it in Read Mode as a read-only document with the AutoSaved Version bar below the title bar. To restore the version that you opened, click the Restore button in the AutoSaved Version bar. To compare the version you opened with the current version of the document before deciding whether to restore it, click the Compare button in the AutoSaved Version bar. When you do this, a Compare Result document opens, similar to the Compare Result document that opens when you use the Compare or Combine command. If you want to delete a saved version of a document, right-click the version in the Manage Document section of the Info screen, and then click Delete This Version.

If your computer is shut down unexpectedly while a document is open, the next time you start Word, the left pane of the Recent screen includes a Recovered section. To recover an unsaved version of a document, click Show Recovered Files in the Recovered section to create a new, blank document with the Document Recovery pane open. In the pane, click the unsaved version of the document that you want to open. You can also click the Manage Document button on the Info Screen, and then click Recover Unsaved Documents to display the Open dialog box to the folder that contains unsaved versions of files. If you want to delete all unsaved versions of all files, click Delete All Unsaved Documents on the Manage Document menu.

REVIEW

Session 7.2 Quick Check

1. Describe two options on the Paste Options menu that allow you to control the formatting applied to a linked Excel chart.

2. What is the first step in creating a hyperlink to a location in the same document?

3. Are horizontal lines displayed on a printed page?

4. What is the difference between the way text is displayed in Web Layout view and the way it is displayed in Print Layout view?

5. Explain how to edit a hyperlink.

6. What do you need to do before you can publish a blog post?

PRACTICE

Review Assignments

Data Files needed for the Review Assignments: Funding.xlsx, Hours.xlsx, Release.docx, Sports James.docx, Sports.docx

Rima is working on a document about a new game. She has written a draft of the document and has emailed it to James. While he reviews it, Rima asks you to turn on Track Changes and continue working on the document. Then, she can combine her edited version of the document with James's, accepting or rejecting changes as necessary. She also needs you to insert some data from an Excel worksheet as an embedded object and insert an Excel chart as a linked object. She then wants you to create a version of the document with hyperlinks, optimize the document for online viewing, and create a blog post. Complete the following steps:

1. Open the document **Sports** located in the Word7 > Review folder included with your Data Files. Save the file as **Sports Rima** in the location specified by your instructor.

2. Change the username to **Rima Khouri** and the user initials to **RK**, and then turn on Track Changes.

3. In the second paragraph, move the sentence that begins "When you land on a Ref It square…" to the end of the paragraph, and then add an **s** to the word "drive" in that sentence so the text reads "…USB drives…."

4. In the third paragraph, in the first line, attach a comment to the number "300" that reads **Should this be 325?**

5. Just before the period at the end of the document, add **or contact *your name*** (replacing *your name* with your first and last name) so that the sentence reads "Click here to learn more about this fun event, or contact *your name*."

6. Save your changes to the Sports Rima document.

7. Combine the Sports Rima document with James's edited version, which is named **Sports James**. Use the Sports Rima document as the original document.

8. Save the combined document as **Sports Combined** in the location specified by your instructor.

9. Turn off Track Changes, and then reject James's deletion of "chart" and his insertion of "graph." Accept all the other changes in the document. Delete all comments.

10. Change the username and initials back to their original settings, and then save the Sports Combined document. Close the Sports Rima document, saving changes if you didn't save them earlier.

11. In the Sports Combined document, replace the placeholder "[Insert Excel worksheet]" with the funding goals in the **Funding.xlsx file**. Include everything from cell A1 through cell B5. Insert the worksheet as an embedded object, and then close the Funding.xlsx file.

12. Center the embedded object, and then change the "Complete and Release Expansion Pack" value in the embedded worksheet object from $6,000 to **$7,000**.

13. Open the workbook **Hours.xlsx**, and then save it as **Hours Chart.xlsx** in the location specified by your instructor. Copy the pie chart to the Office Clipboard.

14. Return to the Sports Combined document, and then replace the placeholder "[Insert Excel chart]" with a linked copy of the chart using the destination theme. Save the Sports Combined document, and then close it.

15. Return to the Hours Chart workbook in Excel. Edit the data in the workbook by changing the hours for online test marketing to **100**, and the hours for trivia question development to **325**. Save the workbook, and then close Excel.

16. Open the **Sports Combined** document and review the chart. If it doesn't contain the new numbers, click the chart, and use the Refresh Data button to update the chart.

17. Save the Sports Combined document, and then save the document with the new name **Sports No Links** in the location specified by your instructor.

18. Break the link to the Excel workbook, and then save the document.

19. Format the Excel worksheet object as a bookmark named **Funding**. In the first line of the third paragraph below the page title, format the phrase "Sports Fan Trivia Expansion Pack" as a hyperlink that targets the "Funding" bookmark. Test the hyperlink to make sure it works. Save the document.

20. Open the document **Release** from the Word7 > Review folder included with your Data Files, and then save the file as **Release Party** in the location specified by your instructor. Close the Release Party document, and return to the Sports No Links document.

21. In the last paragraph of the document, format the word "here" as a hyperlink that targets the Release Party document. Test the hyperlink to make sure it works, and then close the Release Party document. Save the Sports No Links document.

22. Switch to Web Layout view, and add a two-color gradient page color using Dark Blue, Text 2, Lighter 80% as Color 1 and White, Background 1 as Color 2—with the shading style set to Diagonal up.

23. Change the background color for the worksheet object to white, and center the chart.

24. Insert a horizontal line before the "Our Goals" heading. Keep the default color, but change the width to 75%. Insert an identical horizontal line before the "Your Reward for Investing" heading.

25. Save and close the Sports No Links document.

26. Create a new blog post without attempting to register a blog account. Save the blog post as **Sports Blog Post** in the location specified by your instructor. Insert **Future Game Development** as the post title, and then type the following as the text of the blog post: **DBQ games has many exciting new sports games in development**.

27. Save and close the Sports Blog Post file.

Case Problem 1

Data Files needed for this Case Problem: Budget.xlsx, Darwin.docx

Silver Day Wedding Planners   You recently started working as a wedding planner at Silver Day Wedding Planners, in Raleigh, North Carolina. A client just called and asked you to send a copy of the wedding budget you discussed with her recently. The budget information is stored in an Excel workbook. You need to respond with a letter that contains the budget embedded as an Excel worksheet object. After you embed the worksheet object, you need to make some edits to the document using Track Changes. Finally, the company owner is considering using Word to create posts for the company's new wedding-planning blog, so she asks you to create a sample blog post. Complete the following steps:

1. Open the document **Darwin** from the Word7 > Case1 folder included with your Data Files. Save the file as **Darwin Letter** in the location specified by your instructor.

2. In the signature line, replace "Student Name" with your name.

3. Delete the placeholder "[Insert Excel worksheet]."

4. Start Excel, open the workbook **Budget** from the Word7 > Case1 folder included with your Data Files, and then save it as **Darwin Budget** in the location specified by your instructor.

APPLY

5. Select the two-column list of items and amounts, from cell A6 through cell B10, and then copy the selection to the Clipboard.

6. Insert the worksheet data into the Word document in the blank paragraph that previously contained the placeholder text. Insert the data as a linked object that uses the destination styles.

7. Save the Word document, and then return to the Darwin Budget workbook and close Excel.

8. Starting from within the Word window, edit the linked worksheet object to change the amount for flowers to **700.00**. (*Hint*: Remember that the steps for editing a linked worksheet object are different from the steps for editing a linked chart. Also, note that you don't need to type the dollar sign. Excel adds that automatically.) Save the workbook, close Excel, and then update the link in Word.

9. Save the Darwin Letter document, and then save it again as **Darwin Letter No Links** in the location specified by your instructor.

10. Break the link in the Darwin Letter No Links document.

11. If necessary, change the username to your first and last names, change the initials to your initials, and then turn on Track Changes.

12. At the beginning of the letter, delete the date, and then type the current date using the format 1/1/17.

13. In the inside address, change "Road" to **Lane**.

14. At the end of the paragraph that reads "Please call if you have any questions." add the sentence **I will contact you next week to provide the username and password for your online account**.

15. Open the Reviewing pane and note the total number of revisions, the number of insertions, and the number of deletions in the document. Attach a comment to the word "Planners" in the first paragraph that reads **This document contains *x* insertions and *x* deletions. It contains a total of *x* revisions**. Replace the three instances of *x* with the correct numbers. (*Hint:* The total number of revisions will change when you insert the comment. The number that you type in the comment should reflect this updated total.)

16. Close the Reviewing pane, save your changes to the Darwin Letter No Links document, and then save it with the new name **Darwin Letter Changes Accepted** in the location specified by your instructor.

17. Turn off Track Changes, delete the comment, and then reject the replacement of "Lane" for "Road." Accept all the other changes in the document.

18. Return the username and initials to their original settings.

19. Save the Darwin Letter Changes Accepted document, and then close it.

20. Create a new blog post without attempting to register a blog account. Save the blog post as **Wedding Blog Post** in the location specified by your instructor. Insert **News from Silver Day Wedding Planners** as the post title, and then type the following as the text of the blog post: **We will be hosting a weekend wedding-planning seminar later this spring.**

21. Save and close the blog post.

Case Problem 2

Data Files needed for this Case Problem: Garden Gloria.docx, Garden Neal.docx, Plant.docx

Bennington Park and Botanical Gardens   You are an office assistant at Bennington Park and Botanical Gardens, located in Bennington, Oklahoma. Your supervisor, Neal Caves, is working on a set of documents about rain gardens, a type of garden designed to take advantage of rainwater runoff. He's already edited the main document using Track Changes. Now, he asks for your help in combining his copy of the edited file with a copy edited by his colleague, Gloria. Complete the following steps:

1. Open the document **Garden Gloria** from the Word7 > Case2 folder included with your Data Files, review its contents, and then close it.

2. Open the document **Garden Neal** from the Word7 > Case2 folder included with your Data Files, and then review its contents.

3. Combine the Garden Neal and Garden Gloria documents, using the Garden Neal file as the original document. Save the resulting new document as **Garden Combined** in the location specified by your instructor. Close the Garden Neal document.

4. In the Garden Combined document, review the tracked changes. Reject Gloria's deletion of "colorful." Accept the rest of the changes in the document, and then delete the comment.

5. Change the username and initials to yours, and then turn on Track Changes, if necessary.

6. Edit the title at the beginning of the document so it reads **Creating a Rain Garden**. Delete the extra space at the end of the second paragraph (after the phrase "and streams."), and then, in the last line of the document, replace "Neal Caves" with your first and last name.

7. Save the Garden Combined document, and then save it again as **Rain Garden Information** in the location specified by your instructor.

8. Accept all changes in the Rain Garden Information document, turn off Track Changes, and then change the username and initials back to their original settings.

9. Open the document **Plant** from the Word7 > Case2 folder included with your Data Files, and then save it as **Plant Information** in the location specified by your instructor.

⚙ **Troubleshoot** 10. Because the Rain Garden Information and Plant Information documents will be emailed together, the overall look of the documents should match. Make any necessary changes to the page background, theme, and the style set in the Plant Information document to match the settings in the Rain Garden Information document.

⚙ **Troubleshoot** 11. The Plant Information document contains an erroneous hyperlink that jumps to an unrelated external website. Remove that hyperlink from the document. Check the remaining hyperlink to make sure it jumps to the appropriate target in the current document. Make any necessary edits to the hyperlink to correct any errors.

12. In the last paragraph of the Plant Information document, format the word "here" as a hyperlink that jumps to the Rain Garden Information document.

13. In the last sentence of the Rain Garden Information document, format the word "list" as a hyperlink that jumps to the Plant Information document.

14. Test the links, save both documents, and then close them.

Case Problem 3

There are no Data Files needed for this Case Problem.

J. Q. Whittier Foundation You have just started an internship in the communications department at the J. Q. Whittier Foundation, an organization that makes large donations to nonprofits around the country. As part of your job, you will eventually learn how to use a full-blown web design program. But first, your supervisor asks you to demonstrate your understanding of hyperlinks by creating a set of linked pages using Microsoft Word. The pages should focus on charitable organizations that you would like the foundation to consider funding. The charitable organizations you choose should all operate in a similar field—for example, you might choose healthcare charities that combat various diseases. On each page, include multiple graphics and links to live webpages accessible via the Internet. Your supervisor asks you to use all your formatting skills to create an attractive set of pages. Complete the following steps:

1. Select a field that interests you, such as health care, education, or the environment. Because you are creating sample pages for your work supervisor, choose a topic that is appropriate for a professional setting.

2. Open a new, blank Word document, and save it as **Main Page** in the location specified by your instructor.

3. Create two more new, blank documents named **Linked Page 1** and **Linked Page 2**, saving them in the location specified by your instructor.

4. In the Main Page file, add text and at least three pictures that introduce the reader to your chosen charitable field. The page should explain why the J.Q. Whittier Foundation should donate to charities in your chosen field. Use your own pictures or search for pictures online. Include at least three headings.

5. In the Linked Page 1 document, add text that provides details about a related nonprofit organization. For example, if your Main Page document discusses healthcare charities, then your Linked Page 1 document might contain information about the American Cancer Society. The text should mention one external webpage available via the Internet. Include at least one picture and at least one heading at the beginning of the page. Do the same in the Linked Page 2 document.

6. In the Linked Page 1 document, format the text that refers to an external webpage as a hyperlink that jumps to that page. Do the same in the Linked Page 2 file. (*Hint:* Use your browser to display the external webpage, right-click the URL in the box at the top of the browser window, and then click Copy. In the Insert Hyperlink dialog box, use the appropriate keyboard shortcut to paste the URL into the Address box.)

7. In the Main Page file, add hyperlinks that jump to the Linked Page 1 file and to the Linked Page 2 file.

8. In the Linked Page 1 and Linked Page 2 files, add hyperlinks that jump back to the Main Page file.

9. Format the three pages identically, using a theme, heading styles, and a style set of your choice. Use horizontal lines to separate the different sections on each page, and add a two-color gradient page background to all three documents.

10. Test the hyperlinks, and then close any open Word documents.

Case Problem 4

Data Files needed for this Case Problem: Coding Aziz.docx, Coding Tommy.docx, Coding.docx

123 Coding Academy Kendall Aihara is the marketing manager for 123 Coding Academy, a computer programming school that specializes in weekend coding camps and week-long classes on specific topics. She is creating a series of fact sheets that she can email to potential students. The fact sheets will summarize course offerings at the school. Each fact sheet will also include a link to an Internet video about learning to code. Kendall has already emailed a draft of her first fact sheet to her two colleagues, Aziz and Tommy, and she now needs to combine their versions with hers to create a final draft. However, because Aziz forgot to turn on Track Changes before he edited the document, Kendall will need to compare her draft with his so that she can see his changes marked as tracked changes.

After she finishes accepting and rejecting changes, Kendall wants you to show her how to add a video to the document. A video production company is preparing a series of videos that she will eventually incorporate into her fact sheets before distributing them; but for now, she asks you to show her how to insert any video from the Internet. Finally, after the fact sheet is finished, Kendall would like you to help her create a chart that illustrates the average distance each client travels to 123 Coding Academy. Complete the following steps:

1. Open the document **Coding** from the Word7 > Case4 folder included with your Data Files, save it as **Coding Kendall** in the location specified by your instructor, review the document to familiarize yourself with its contents, and then close it.

2. Open the document **Coding Aziz** from the Word7 > Case4 folder, review its contents, and then close it.

⊕ **Explore** 3. Compare the Coding Kendall document with the Coding Aziz document, using Coding Kendall as the original document, and show the changes in a new document.

4. Review the new document to verify that Aziz's changes to Kendall's draft are now displayed as tracked changes, and then save the document as **Coding Aziz Tracked Changes** in the location specified by your instructor.

5. Combine the Coding Tommy document with the Coding Aziz Tracked Changes document, using the Coding Tommy file as the original document.

6. Save the new document as **Coding Academy Fact Sheet** in the location specified by your instructor.

7. Accept all changes in the document, turn off Track Changes, if necessary, and then use the Spelling and Grammar checker to correct any errors caused by missing spaces.

⊕ **Explore** 8. Use Word Help to learn how to insert an Internet video in a document. In the blank paragraph at the end of the document, insert a video of a coding tutorial. Take care to choose a video that is appropriate for a professional setting. After you insert the video in the document, click the Play button on the video image to test it. Press the Esc button to close the video window when you are finished watching it.

⊕ **Explore** 9. In the Word document, size the video image just as you would an ordinary picture so that it fits on the first page.

10. Save the Coding Academy Fact Sheet document, and close it and any other open documents.

11. Open a new, blank document, and then save it as **Student Travel Time Chart** in the location specified by your instructor.

⊕ **Explore** 12. Use Word Help to learn how to create a chart using Word's Chart tool. Create a bar chart using the 3-D Stacked Bar type. For the chart title, use **Miles Driven by Students for Weekend, Week-Long, and Month-Long Classes**. Use the Chart Elements button (which appears next to the chart when it is selected) to include the following elements: axes, chart title, gridlines, and legend. Include the data shown in Figure 7-38.

Figure 7-38   **Data for bar chart**

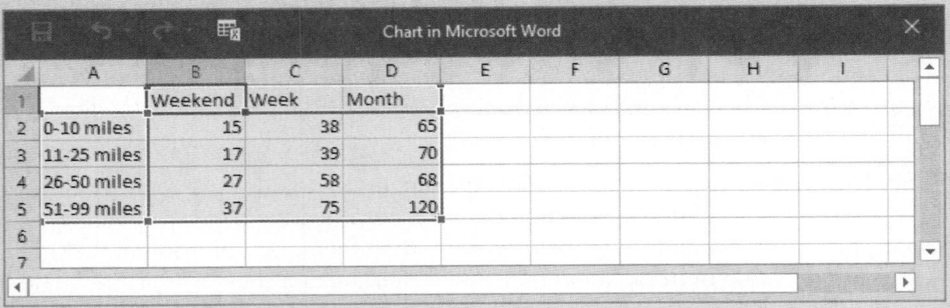

	A	B	C	D
1		Weekend	Week	Month
2	0-10 miles	15	38	65
3	11-25 miles	17	39	70
4	26-50 miles	27	58	68
5	51-99 miles	37	75	120
6				
7				

Chart in Microsoft Word

⊕ **Explore** 13. Format the chart with the Style 2 chart style.

14. Change the document's theme to Facet.

15. Save and close all documents.

INDEX